050

D0475918

30

PERIODICAL TITLE ABBREVIATIONS

SECOND EDITION

Covering Periodical Title Abbreviations in Science,
the Social Sciences, the Humanities, Law, Medicine,
Religion, Library Science, Engineering, Education,
Business, Art, and Many Other Fields

compiled and edited by
LELAND G. ALKIRE, JR.
Humanities Reference Librarian
Eastern Washington State College

Editorial Assistant
MARGARET E. SCHULTZ

Gale Research Company • Book Tower • Detroit, Michigan 48226

Copyright © 1977 by Leland G. Alkire, Jr.

Library of Congress Cataloging in Publication Data

Alkire, Leland G
    Periodical title abbreviations.

    First ed. by C. E. Wall.
    Includes index.
    1. Periodicals--Abbreviations of titles.
I. Wall, C. Edward. Periodical title abbreviations.
II. Title.
Z6945.A2W34   1977   050'.1'48   76-52617
ISBN 0-8103-0336-1

CONTENTS

INTRODUCTION

Purpose and Scope

This edition of *Periodical Title Abbreviations*, like the first edition, translates magazine, journal and newspaper title abbreviations into full titles. It does so in response to what has generally been recognized as a major bibliographic obstacle. In spite of attempts by organizations and individuals to prescribe standard periodical abbreviations or rules for constructing periodical abbreviations, the uniform citation has remained an admirable but elusive ideal. In actual practice, such rules are, more often than not, completely disregarded. *Periodical Title Abbreviations*, as a consequence, is not intended to be used as an authority file or standard for periodical abbreviations, but merely as a record of the myriad ways in which commonly used indexing and abstracting services abbreviate periodical titles. While it may be vexing that the same title is abbreviated several different ways by a single indexing service, and disconcerting that a single abbreviation can stand for more than one title, *Periodical Title Abbreviations* is intended only as a translation device. In those occasional instances where the same abbreviation is used for two or more periodical titles, the user should consult such standard serial records as the *Union List of Serials, New Serial Titles, Ulrich's International Periodicals Directory*, or *The British Union Catalogue of Periodicals*, for the publishing history of the periodical one suspects the abbreviation represents. Normally, when this information is compared with the year and volume number of the citation in question, a satisfactory identification is possible.

For a discussion of the full range of difficulties associated with periodical abbreviations, the reader is directed to Mary R. Kinney's *The Abbreviated Citation — A Bibliographical Problem*, Association of College and Research Libraries Monographs, Number 28, Chicago, American Library Association, 1967.

Periodical Title Abbreviations is intended to be used by reference, periodical and inter-library loan librarians in a wide range of public, academic and special libraries. In addition, the researcher who is frequently baffled by the cryptic, short-form citation should also find this work valuable.

With this edition, the content of *Periodical Title Abbreviations* has been doubled to nearly 20,000 entries. The following list of major sources reveals the inclusion of abbreviations from a number of standard indexing and abstracting services and may be considered a response to those users of the first edition who expressed the need for increased coverage. Ideally, every abbreviated title, wherever and whenever used, should appear in this dictionary. Unfortunately, if this were the case, the work would run to many volumes, be prohibitive in price and defeat its original purpose as a generally applicable tool. While many scientific title abbreviations appear here, the user is cautioned that the many thousands of periodical abbreviations used by *Biological Abstracts* and *Chemical Abstracts* have not been included due to the sheer number and complexity of such abbreviations. Happily, both abstracting services provide abbreviation keys, and this dictionary is intended to be used in conjunction with them.

Arrangement, Format and Other Editorial Policies

The complex and sometimes challenging filing system of the first edition has been dropped in favor of arranging the abbreviations by strict letter-by-letter sequence, regardless of spacing, punctuation or capitalization. Arabic and Roman numerals are read as if written out, and ampersands are read as *and*. Because of font limitations, many diacritical marks have been eliminated or altered according to accepted standards. Thus, the German word Für becomes fuer. In all decisions, the principle of simplicity of use has been kept foremost. In certain indexing services, periodical abbreviations were found to change from one year to the next. While this accounts for the seemingly elegant variation of some abbreviations found in this dictionary, the user should also be aware that several thousand nearly repetitive entries have been eliminated after having been judged to add nothing to the identification process. With this exception, and with minor alterations for uniform format and corrections of typographical errors found in the source materials, the abbreviations and periodical titles reproduced in this dictionary conform to the information found in the source materials.

vi

Like sailors long at sea, who derive great satisfaction from a curious cloud formation or the sight of a bird, those who labor over abbreviations dictionaries look for and celebrate anything which seems to break the monotony. In this work the typographical error provided occasional diversions, some repeatable and several not. My lightest moment came with the permutation of the *Yen Ching Journal* into the *Wenching Journal*. Many errors have been eliminated but, no doubt, some will remain. Though no work of this sort is ever completely error-proof, those which remain must be laid at my door. I ask only the user's understanding of the difficulties involved in dealing with a dozen or more languages simultaneously, and the problems posed by the error-sprinkled source materials.

ACKNOWLEDGEMENTS

To C. Edward Wall, editor of the first edition, my thanks for beginning the task. I wish also to express my gratitude to Eastern Washington State College for the opportunity to complete this work and to the many individuals attached to that institution for their aid and encouragement in the production of the manuscript and final copy. Among these are:
Dr. Charles Baumann, College Librarian
Denise Brown, Periodicals Department
Don Lake, Reference Librarian
Nancy Larkin, Cataloger (formerly)
Marilyn Lewis, Music Library
Cathy McAlister, Circulation Department
Elizabeth A. Nelson, Assistant College Editor
Harriet O'Swald, Modern Languages Department
Brenton Stark, College Editor
Joan Tracy, Assistant Librarian for Technical Services
A final salute must go to my fellow crew members of the good ship Safari, who have only just recently forgiven me for having brought page-proofs along during a sailing cruise of the San Juan Islands.

MAJOR SOURCES OF ABBREVIATIONS
Contained in Periodical Title Abbreviations

Abridged Index Medicus
American-German Review
American Literature Abstracts
Annee-Philologique
Annual Bibliography of English Language and Literature
Applied Science and Technology Index
Art Index
Bibliographic Index
Biography Index
Biological and Agricultural Index
Book Review Digest
Book Review Index
British Education Index
British Technology Index
Business Education Index
Business Periodicals Index
Canadian Periodical Index
Classified Shakespeare Bibliography
Education Index
Engineering Index
English Language Notes
English Literary History (ELH)
Germanic Review
Harvard Guide to American History
Humanities Index
Index to Economic Articles
Index to Legal Periodicals
Index to Little Magazines
Index to Religious Periodical Literature
Index to Science Fiction Magazines
Industrial Arts Index

Journal of Aesthetics and Art Criticism
Journal of American Folklore
Journal of English and Germainic Philology
Keats-Shelley Journal
Library Literature
Modern Humanities Research Association: Annual Bibliography of
    English Language and Literature
Modern Language Quarterly
Modern Philology
Music Index
Nineteenth Century Reader's Guide
Philological Quarterly
Philosopher's Index
PMLA Bibliography
Poole's Index to Periodical Literature
Popular Periodicals Index
Progress of Medieval and Renaissance Studies in the United States
    and Canada
Quarterly Journal of Speech
Readers' Guide to Periodical Literature
Revue d'Histoire Ecclesiastique
Romanic Review
Scandinavian Studies
Science Citation Index
Science Fiction Book Review Index
Selective Bibliography of Shakespeare (McManaway and Roberts)
Shakespeare Quarterly
Social Sciences Index
Social Science Citation Index
Southern Folklore Quarterly
Speech Monographs
Studies in Philology
Topicator
Victorian Studies
Writings on American History
Yearbook of Comparative and General Literature
Year's Work in English Studies
Year's Work in Modern Language Studies

A

A . . . . AMERICA
A . . . . ARCHIV FUER DAS STUDIUM DER NEUEREN SPRACHEN
A . . . . ARTHURIANA
A . . . . AUFBAU
AA . . . . ADVERTISING AGE
AA . . . . AMAZING STORIES ANNUAL
AA . . . . AMERICAN ANTHROPOLOGIST
AA . . . . AMERICAN ARCHIVIST
AA . . . . ANTWERPSCH ARCHIEVENBLAD
AA . . . . ARCHAEOLOGISCHER ANZEIGER
AA . . . . ART AND ARCHITECTURE
AA . . . . ASIAN AFFAIRS
AA . . . . AUT AUT
AAA . . . . ACTA ACADEMIAE ABOENSIS, HUMANIORA
AAA . . . . ANNALS OF THE AMERICAN ACADEMY OF POLITICAL AND SOCIAL SCIENCE
AAA . . . . ARCHIVIO PER L'ALTO ADIGE
AAAB . . . . ANNALES DE L'ACADEMIE ROYALE D'ARCHEOLOGIE DE BELGIQUE
AAAd . . . . ARCHIVIO PER L' ALTO ADIGE
AAAH . . . . ACTA ACADEMIAE ABOENSIS, HUMANIORA
AAA Hum . . . . ACTA ACADEMIAE ABOENSIS, HUMANIORA
AAAPSS . . . . ANNALS OF THE AMERICAN ACADEMY OF POLITICAL AND SOCIAL SCIENCES
AAAr . . . . ATTI DELL'ACCADEMIA DEGLI ARCADI
AAASH . . . . ACTA ANTIQUA ACADEMIAE SCIENTIARUM HUNGARICAE
AABAn . . . . ANNALES DE L'ACADEMIE ROYALE D'ARCHEOLOGIE DE BELIGIQUE
AACE Bull . . . . AMERICAN ASSOCIATION OF COST ENGINEERS. BULLETIN
AACMP . . . . ANALES DE LA ACADEMIA DE CIENCIAS MORALES Y POLITICAS
AAEPC . . . . ANALES DE LA ASOCIACION ESPANOLA PARA EL PROGRESO DE LAS CIENCIAS
AAF . . . . ATTI DELL'ACCADEMIA FIORENTINA
AAFV . . . . ANUARIO DE LA ASOCIACION FRANCISCO DE VITORIA
AAG . . . . ANNALS OF AMERICAN GEOGRAPHERS
AAg . . . . ARCHIVO AGUSTINIANO
AAHG . . . . ANZEIGER FUER DIE ALTERTUMSWISSENSCHAFT. HERAUSGEGEBEN VON DER OESTERREICHISCHEN
HUMANISTISCHEN GESELLSCHAFT
AAL . . . . ANNALS OF ARCHAEOLOGY OF THE UNIVERSITY OF LIVERPOOL
AAL . . . . ATTI DELL ACCADEMIA DEI LINCEI
AALIAM . . . . ARCADIA, ACCADEMIA LETTERARIA ITALIANA. ATTI E MEMORIE
AALS News . . . . ASSOCIATION OF AMERICAN LIBRARY SCHOOLS. NEWSLETTER
AALS Proc . . . . ASSOCIATION OF AMERICAN LAW SCHOOLS. PROCEEDINGS
AAM . . . . ARTE ANTICA E MODERNA
AAM . . . . ATTI E MEMORIE DELL'ACCADEMIA DI SCIENZE, LETTERE, ED ARTE DI MODENA
AAM . . . . ATTI E MEMORIE DELLA REALE ACCADEMIA VIRGILIANA DI SCIENZE, LETTERE ED ARTI DI
MONTOVA
AAMod . . . . ATTI E MEMORIE DELL'ACCADEMIA DI SCIENZE, LETTERE ED ARTI DI MODENA
AAn . . . . AMERICAN ANTHROPOLOGIST
AAn . . . . ARCHIV FUER ANTHROPOLOGIE
AAN . . . . ATTI DELLA REALE ACCADEMIA DI ARCHEOLOGIA, LETTERE E BELLE ARTI DI NAPOLI
A&A . . . . ANTIKE UND ABENDLAND
A&A . . . . ART AND ARCHAEOLOGY

A&A . . . . ARTS AND ARCHITECTURE
A&A . . . . ARTA SI ARHEOLOGIA
A&CS . . . . AREA AND CULTURE STUDIES (TOKYO)
A&M . . . . ARCHIVES AND MANUSCRIPTS
A&R . . . . ATENE E ROMA
A&S . . . . ARTS AND SCIENCES
A & SP . . . . ADVERTISING AND SALES PROMOTION
AANL . . . . ATTI DELL'ACCADEMIA NAZIONALE DEI LINCEI
AANLR . . . . ATTI DELL'ACCADEMIA NAZIONALE DEI LINCEI. RENDICONTI DELLA CLASSE DI SCIENZE
              MORALI, STORICHE E FILOLOGISCHE
AaNo . . . . AARBOGER FOER NORDISK OLDKYNDIGHED OG HISTORIE
AAnt . . . . ACTA ANTIQUA ACADEMIAE SCIENTIARUM HUNGARICAE
A ANTH . . . . AMERICAN ANTHROPOLOGIST
AAnthr . . . . AMERICAN ANTHROPOLOGIST
AAntHung . . . . ACTA ANTIQUA ACADEMIAE SCIENTIARUM HUNGARICAE
AAP . . . . ATTI DELL'ACCADEMIA DI PALERMO
AAP . . . . ATTI E MEMORIE DELL'ACCADEMIA DI PADOVA
AAP . . . . ATTI E MEMORIE DELLA R. ACADEMIA DI SCIENZE, LETTERE ED ARTI IN PADOVA
AAPad . . . . ATTI E MEMORIE DELL'ACCADEMIA DI PADOVA
AAPal . . . . ATTI DELL'ACCADEMIA DI PALERMO
AAPF . . . . ARCTOS: ACTA PHILOLOGICA FENNICA
AAPG BULL . . . . . . AAPG (AMERICAN ASSOCIATION OF PETROLEUM GEOLOGISTS) BULLETIN
AAPJ . . . . ACTA ACADEMIAE PAEDAGOGICAE JYVASKYLAENSIS
AAPN . . . . ATTI DELL'ACCADEMIA PONTANIANA (NAPLES)
AAPont . . . . ATTI DELL'ACCADEMIA PONTANIANA (NAPLES)
AAPS . . . . ANNALS OF THE AMERICAN ACADEMY OF POLITICAL AND SOCIAL SCIENCE
AAPSS MG . . . . AMERICAN ACADEMY OF POLITICAL AND SOCIAL SCIENCE. MONOGRAPHS
AAR . . . . AMERICAN ANTHROPOLOGIST
AAR . . . . ANNALES DE L'ACADEMIE DES SCIENCES DE RUSSIE
AAR . . . . ATTI DELLA R. ACCADEMIA D'ITALIA. ROMA. MEMORIE DELLA CLASSE DI SCIENZE MORALI E
              STORICHE
AARA . . . . ATTI DELL'ACCADEMIA ROVERETANA DEGLI AGIATI
AARAB . . . . ANNALES DE L'ACADEMIE ROYALE D'ARCHEOLOGIE DE BELGIQUE
AARB . . . . ANNUAIRE DE L' ACADEMIE ROYALE DE BELGIQUE
AArch . . . . ACTA ARCHAEOLOGICA
A ARCH . . . . AMERICAN ARCHIVIST
AArchHung . . . . ACTA ARCHAEOLOGICA ACADEMIAE SCIENTIARUM HUNGARICAE
AArchSlov . . . . ACTA ARCHAEOLOGICA. ARHEOLOSKI VESTNIK. LJUBLJANA, ACADEMIE SLOVENE
AArchSyr . . . . ANNALES ARCHEOLOGIQUES DE SYRIE
AArt . . . . AMERICAN ARTIST
AAS . . . . AMERICAN ANTIQUARIAN SOCIETY. PROCEEDINGS
AAS . . . . ASIAN AND AFRICAN STUDIES
AASB . . . . ATTI DELL ACCADEMIA DELLE SCIENZE DELL ISTITUTO DI BOLOGNA
AASF . . . . ANNALES ACADEMIAE SCIENTIARUM FENNICAE
AASN . . . . ATTI DELL'ACCADEMIA DI SCIENZE MORALI E POLITICHE DI NAPOLI
AASO . . . . ANNUAL OF THE AMERICAN SCHOOLS OF ORIENTAL RESEARCH
AASOR . . . . ANNUAL OF THE AMERICAN SCHOOLS OF ORIENTAL RESEARCH
AASPS . . . . ANNALS OF THE AMERICAN ACADEMY OF SOCIAL AND POLITICAL SCIENCE
AAST . . . . ATTI DELLA R. ACCADEMIA DELLE SCIENZE DI TORINO. CLASSE DI SCIENZE MORALI, STORICHE
              E FILOLOGICHE
AAT . . . . ATTI DELL'ACCADEMIA DELLE SCIENZE DI TORINO

AATB . . . . AFRO-ASIAN THEATRE BULLETIN
Aatseel . . . . AMERICAN ASSOCIATION OF TEACHERS OF SLAVIC AND EAST EUROPEAN LANGUAGES. BULLETIN
Aatseel Bull . . . . . . AMERICAN ASSOCIATION OF TEACHERS OF SLAVIC AND EAST EUROPEAN LANGUAGES. BULLETIN
Aatseel Jour . . . . . . AMERICAN ASSOCIATION OF TEACHERS OF SLAVIC AND EAST EUROPEAN LANGUAGES. JOURNAL
AAU . . . . ATTI DELL'ACCADEMIA DI SCIENZE, LETTERE E ARTI DI UDINE
AAUg . . . . ANALECTA AUGUSTINIANA
AAUPB . . . . AMERICAN ASSOCIATION OF UNIVERSITY PROFESSORS. BULLETIN
AAUP Bul . . . . AAUP (AMERICAN ASSOCIATION OF UNIVERSITY PROFESSORS) BULLETIN
AAV . . . . ACTA ACADEMIAE VELEHRADENSIS
AAV . . . . ATTI DELL'ACCADEMIA DI AGRICOLTURA, SCIENZE E LETTERE DI VERONA
AAV . . . . AUS AACHENS VORZEIT
AAVPC . . . . ANNUARIUM VAN DE APOLOGETISCHE VEREENIGING (PETRUS CANISIUS)
AAW . . . . AFRO-ASIAN WRITINGS
AAW . . . . ANNALES DU CERCLE ARCHEOLOGIQUE DU PAYS DE WAES
AAWG . . . . ABHANDLUNGEN DER AKADEMIE DER WISSENSCHAFTEN, GOETTINGEN
AAWL . . . . ABHANDLUNGEN DER AKADEMIE DER WISSENSCHAFTEN UND DER LITERATUR IN MAINZ, GEISTES-UND SOZIALWISSENSCHAFTLICHE KLASSE
AAWW . . . . ANZEIGER DER AKADEMIE DER WISSENSCHAFTEN IN WIEN
AB . . . . AB BOOKMAN'S WEEKLY
Ab . . . . ABRUZZO
AB . . . . ACTA BALTICA
AB . . . . AMERICAN ASSOCIATION OF TEACHERS OF SLAVIC AND EAST EUROPEAN LANGUAGES. BULLETIN
AB . . . . (AMERICAN) BOOKMAN
AB . . . . ANALECTA BOLLANDIANA
AB . . . . ART BULLETIN
AB . . . . AUGUSTANA BULLETIN
Aba . . . . ABACO
ABa . . . . ANNEE BALZACIENNE
ABA ANTITRUST L J . . AMERICAN BAR ASSOCIATION ANTITRUST LAW, JOURNAL
ABaG . . . . AMSTERDAMER BEITRAEGE ZUR AELTEREN GERMANISTIK
ABA J . . . . AMERICAN BAR ASSOCIATION. JOURNAL
AbAn . . . . ABSTRACTS IN ANTHROPOLOGY
ABAP . . . . ANAIS DAS BIBLIOTECAS E ARQUIVOS DE PORTUGAL
ABA Sect Antitrust L . . AMERICAN BAR ASSOCIATION. SECTION OF ANTITRUST LAW
ABA Sect Crim L . . . AMERICAN BAR ASSOCIATION. SECTION OF CRIMINAL LAW
ABA SECT INS N & CL . . AMERICAN BAR ASSOCIATION. SECTION OF INSURANCE, NEGLIGENCE, & COMPENSATION LAW
ABA Sect Int & Comp L . . AMERICAN BAR ASSOCIATION. SECTION OF INTERNATIONAL & COMPARATIVE LAW
ABA Sect Int & Comp L Bull . . AMERICAN BAR ASSOCIATION. SECTION OF INTERNATIONAL & COMPARATIVE LAW BULLETIN
ABA Sect Lab Rel L . . AMERICAN BAR ASSOCIATION. SECTION OF LABOR RELATIONS LAW
ABA Sect M& NRL . . AMERICAN BAR ASSOCIATION. SECTION OF MINERAL & NATURAL RESOURCES LAW
ABA Sect Real Prop L . . AMERICAN BAR ASSOCIATION. SECTION OF REAL PROPERTY, PROBATE & TRUST LAW PROCEEDINGS
ABAW . . . . ABHANDLUNGEN DER BAYERISCHEN AKADEMIE DER WISSENSCHAFTEN, PHILOSOPHISCH-HISTORISCHE KLASSE
ABB . . . . ARCHIVES ET BIBLIOTHEQUES DE BELGIQUE

AB Bkman's W . . . . . AB BOOKMAN'S WEEKLY
ABC . . . . AMERICAN BOOK COLLECTOR
ABCA Bul . . . . ABCA (AMERICAN BUSINESS COMMUNICATIONS ASSOCIATION) BULLETIN
ABCD . . . . ARCHIVES, BIBLIOTHEQUES, COLLECTIONS, DOCUMENTATION
ABelges . . . . ARCHIVES BELGES
AbEnSt . . . . ABSTRACTS OF ENGLISH STUDIES
AbFolkSt . . . . ABSTRACTS OF FOLKLORE STUDIES
AbFS . . . . ABSTRACTS OF FOLKLORE STUDIES
ABG . . . . ARCHIV FUER BEGRIFFSGESCHICHTE
Abh Deut Akad Wiss Berlin, KI Math . . ABHANDLUNGEN DER DEUTSCHEN AKADEMIE DER WISSENSCHAFTEN ZU
BERLIN, KLASSE FUER MATHEMATIK, PHYSIK UND TECHNIK
Abh Inst Hochspannungs-technik Elektr Anlagen . . ABHANDLUNGEN DES INSTITUTS FUER HOCHSPANNUNGSTECHNIK
UND ELEKTRISCHE ANLAGEN
ABI . . . . ACCADEMIE E BIBLIOTECHE D'ITALIA
ABK . . . . AJIA BUNKA (ASIAN CULTURE)
ABMB . . . . ARCHIVES, BIBLIOTHEQUES ET MUSEES DE BELGIQUE
AbMilt . . . . ABSTRACTS OF MILITARY BIBLIOGRAPHY
ABMK . . . . ARCHIWA, BIBLIOTEKI I MUZEA KOSCIELNE
ABN . . . . ANIAS DA BIBLIOTECA NACIONAL, RIO DE JANEIRO
ABNG . . . . AMSTERDAMER BEITRAEGE ZUR NEUEREN GERMANISTIK
ABOD . . . . ARBEITEN ZUR BAYERISCH-OESTERREICHISCHEN DIALEKTGEOGRAFIE
ABORI . . . . ANNALS OF THE BHANDARKAR ORIENTAL RESEARCH INSTITUTE
ABourg . . . . ANNALES DE BOURGOGNE
ABP . . . . ARQUIVO DE BIBLIOGRAFIA PORTUGUESA
AbPhoto . . . . ABSTRACTS OF PHOTOGRAPHIC SCIENCE AND ENGINEERING LITERATURE
ABR . . . . AMERICAN BENEDICTINE REVIEW
ABr . . . . ANNALES DE BRETAGNE ET DES PAYS DE L'OUEST
ABRASIV ENG . . . . . ABRASIVE ENGINEERING
ABret . . . . ANNALES DE BRETAGNE
AbrIMed . . . . ABRIDGED INDEX MEDICUS
AbrRG . . . . ABRIDGED READERS' GUIDE
ABs . . . . ABSIDE
ABS . . . . ACTA BALTICO-SLAVICA
ABS . . . . AMERICAN BEHAVIORAL SCIENTIST
ABSA . . . . ANNUAL OF THE BRITISH SCHOOL AT ATHENS
ABSHF . . . . ANNUAIRE-BULLETIN DE LA SOCIETE DE L'HISTOIRE DE FRANCE
AbSocWk . . . . ABSTRACTS FOR SOCIAL WORKERS
ABS PAP ACS . . . . . ABSTRACTS OF PAPERS AMERICAN CHEMICAL SOCIETY
ABUC . . . . ARCHIVIO BIBLIOGRAPHICO DA BIBLIOTHECA DA UNIVERSIDADE DE COIMBRA
ABul . . . . ART BULLETIN
ABull . . . . ART BULLETIN
AbVoc . . . . ABSTRACTS OF RESEARCH AND RELATED MATERIALS IN VOCATIONAL AND TECHNICAL
EDUCATION
AC . . . . ALBIA CHRISTIANA
AC . . . . AMERICAN CITY
AC . . . . ANALECTA CISTERCIENSA
AC . . . . ANALES CERVANTINOS
AC . . . . ANALES-CONFERENCIA
AC . . . . ANTIQUITE CLASSIQUE
AC . . . . ARCHAEOLOGIA CAMBRENSIS
AC . . . . ARCHAEOLOGIA CLASSICA

AC............ ARCHIVOS DEL FOLKLORE CHILENO
ACA........... AMERICAN COMPOSERS ALLIANCE BULLETIN
ACACS.......... ANNALES DU CERCLE ARCHEOLOGIQUE DU CANTON DE SOIGNIES
Acad Ag France Comptes Rendus.. ACADEMIE D'AGRICULTURE DE FRANCE. COMPTES RENDUS DES SEANCES
Acad Ag France Compt Rend.. ACADEMIE D'AGRICULTURE DE FRANCE. COMPTES RENDUS DES SEANCES
Acad d Inscrip Memoires.. ACADEMIE DES INSCRIPTIONS ET BELLES-LETTRES. MEMOIRES
Acad d Inscr Mon et Mem.. ACADEMIE DES INSCRIPTIONS ET BELLES-LETTRES. MONUMENTS ET MEMOIRES
Acad d Inscr Paris Mem.. ACADEMIE DES INSCRIPTIONS ET BELLES-LETTRES. MEMOIRES. PARIS
Acad d Inscr Paris Mon et Mem.. ACADEMIE DES INSCRIPTIONS ET BELLES-LETTRES. MONUMENTS ET MEMOIRES.
        PARIS
Acad d Sci d Belgique Mem 8 Cl d Beaux-arts.. ACADEMIE ROYALE DE BELGIQUE CLASSE DES BEAUX-ARTS.
        MEMOIRES. COLLECTION IN-8
Acad d Sci d Belgique Mem 8 Cl d Lett.. ACADEMIE ROYALE DES SCIENCES, DES LETTRES ET DES BEAUX-ARTS DE
        BELGIQUE. MEMOIRES 8. CLASSE DES LETTRES
Acad d Sci d Belgique Mem 8 Cl d Sci.. ACADEMIE ROYALE DES SCIENCES, DES LETTRES, ET DES BEAUX-ARTS DE
        BELGIQUE. MEMOIRES 8. CLASSE DES SCIENCES
Acad d Sci d Belgique Mem 4 Cl d Lett.. ACADEMIE ROYALE DES SCIENCES DES LETTRES ET DES BEAUX-ARTS DE
        BELGIQUE. MEMOIRES 4. CLASSE DES LETTRES
Acad d Sci d Belgique Mem 4 Cl d Sci.. ACADEMIE ROYALE DES SCIENCES, DES LETTRES, ET DES BEAUX-ARTS DE
        BELGIQUE. MEMOIRES 4. CLASSE DES SCIENCES
Acad d Sci Mor et Pol Paris Mem.. ACADEMIE DES SCIENCES MORALES ET POLITIQUES MEMOIRES (PARIS)
Acad d Sci Paris Mem.. ACADEMIE DES SCIENCES. MEMOIRES (PARIS)
Acad d Sci Paris Mem Div Savants.. ACADEMIE DES SCIENCES. MEMOIRES PRESENTES PAR DIVERS SAVANTS (PARIS)
Acad Esp Bol...... REAL ACADEMIA ESPANOLA. BOLETIN
Acad Inscr Paris Mem Div Savants.. ACADEMIE DES INSCRIPTIONS ET BELLES LETTRES. PARIS. MEMOIRES PRESENTES
        PAR DIVERS SAVANTS
Acad Inscr Paris Mon et Mem.. INSTITUT DE FRANCE. PARIS. ACADEMIE DES INSCRIPTIONS ET BELLES-LETTRES.
        MONUMENTS ET MEMOIRES
Acad Mgt J....... ACADEMY OF MANAGEMENT. JOURNAL
Acad Natur Sci Phila Proc.. ACADEMY OF NATURAL SCIENCES OF PHILADELPHIA. PROCEEDINGS
Acad of Nat Sci Jour.. JOURNAL OF THE ACADEMY OF NATURAL SCIENCES
Acad of Sci of St Louis Trans.. ACADEMY OF SCIENCE OF ST. LOUIS. TRANSACTIONS
Acad Pol Sci Proc... ACADEMY OF POLITICAL SCIENCE. PROCEEDINGS
Acad Roy Sci Outre-Mer Bul Seances.. ACADEMIE ROYALE DES SCIENCES D'OUTRE-MER. BULLETIN DES SEANCES
Acad Sci Belg Bul Cl Beaux-Arts.. ACADEMIE ROYALE DE BELGIQUE. CLASSE DES BEAUX-ARTS. BULLETIN
Acad Sci Belg Bul Cl Lett.. ACADEMIE ROYALE DE BELGIQUE. CLASSE DES LETTRES ET DES SCIENCES MORALES ET
        POLITIQUES. BULLETIN
Acad Sci Belg Bul Cl Sci.. ACADEMIE ROYALE DE BELGIQUE. CLASSE DES SCIENCES. BULLETIN
Acad Sci Belg Mem 8 Cl Lett.. ACADEMIE ROYALE DE BELGIQUE. CLASSE DES LETTRES ET DES SCIENCES MORALES ET
        POLITIQUES. MEMOIRES. COLLECTION IN-8
Acad Sci Belg Mem 8 Cl Sci.. ACADEMIE ROYALE DE BELGIQUE. CLASSE DES SCIENCES. MEMOIRES. COLLECTION IN-8
Acad Sci Belg Mem 4 Cl Sci.. ACADEMIE ROYALE DE BELGIQUE. CLASSE DES SCIENCES. MEMOIRES. COLLECTION IN-4
Acad Sci Paris Mem.. ACADEMIE DES SCIENCES. PARIS. MEMOIRES
Acad Sci St Louis Trans.. ACADEMY OF SCIENCE OF ST LOUIS. TRANSACTIONS
Acad (Syr)........ ACADEMY (SYRACUSE)
ACAD THER....... ACADEMIC THERAPY
ACAE.......... ACTES DU CONGRES INTERNATIONAL DES SCIENCES ANTHROPOLOGIQUES, ET ETHNOLOGIQUES
ACAE.......... ANNALES DU CERCLE ARCHEOLOGIQUE D'ENGHIEN
ACAM.......... ANNALES DU CERCLE ARCHEOLOGIQUE DE MONS
ACAPW......... ANNALES DU CERCLE ARCHEOLOGIQUE DU PAYS DE WAES

PERIODICAL TITLE ABBREVIATIONS

ACBLF BUL . . . . ASSOCIATION CANADIENNE DES BIBLIOTHECAIRES DE LANGUE FRANCAISE. BULLETIN
Acc . . . . ACCENT
Accad e Bibl Italia . . ACCADEMIE E BIBLIOTECHE D'ITALIA
ACC CHEM RE . . . . . ACCOUNTS OF CHEMICAL RESEARCH
Accident Anal Prev . . ACCIDENT ANALYSIS AND PREVENTION
Accounting R . . . . . . ACCOUNTING REVIEW
ACC REVIEW . . . . . . ACCOUNTING REVIEW
Acctg Rev . . . . ACCOUNTING REVIEW
ACCV . . . . ANALES DEL CENTRO DE CULTURA VALENCIANA
ACE . . . . ANNALS OF PUBLIC AND CO-OPERATIVE ECONOMY
ACEC . . . . ACTES DU CONTRES DE LA FEDERATION INTERNATIONAL DES ASSOCIATIONS D'ETUDES
                  CLASSIQUES
ACELB . . . . ACTAS DEL COLOQUIO INTERNACIONAL DE ESTUDOS LUSO-BRASILEIROS
ACer . . . . ANALES CERVANTINOS
ACF . . . . ANNALI DI CA' FOSCARI
ACFF . . . . ANNALES DU COMITE FLAMAND DE FRANCE
ACGKH . . . . AICHI GAKUGEI DAIGAKU KENKYU HOKOKU (BULLETIN OF THE AICHI GAKUGEI UNIVERSITY:
                  CULTURAL SCIENCES)
ACHR . . . . AMERICAN CATHOLIC HISTORICAL RESEARCHES
ACHS . . . . AMERICAN CATHOLIC HISTORICAL SOCIETY, RECORDS
ACHSB . . . . ANNALES DU CERCLE HUTOIS DES SCIENCES ET BEAUX-ARTS
ACIAm . . . . ACTAS DEL CONGRESSO INTERNACIONAL DE AMERICANISTAS
ACILR . . . . ACTES CONGRESSO INTERNATIONAL DE LINGUISTIQUE ROMANICO
ACIS Newsletter . . . AMERICAN COMMITTEE FOR IRISH STUDIES. NEWSLETTER
ACISR . . . . ATTI DELLA CONGRESSO INTERNAZIONALE DI STUDI ROMANZI
ACist . . . . ANALECTA CISTERCIENSIS
AcL . . . . ACTA LINGUISTICA
AClass . . . . ACTA CLASSICA. VERHANDELINGE VAN DIE KLASSIEKE VERENIGING VAN SUID-AFRIKA
AcLLB . . . . ACADEMIE ROYALE DE LANGUE ET DE LITTERATURE FRANCAISE DE BELGIQUE. BULLETIN
ACLSN . . . . AMERICAN COUNCIL OF LEARNED SOCIETIES. NEWSLETTER
ACM . . . . ANUARUL COMISIUNII MONUMENTELOR ISTORICE, SECTIA PENTRU TRANSILVANIA
Acme . . . . ANNALE DELLA FACOLTA DI FILOSOFIA E LETTERE DELL'UNIVERSITA STATALE DI MILANO
ACo . . . . ACTA COMENIANA
ACO . . . . ACTES DU CONGRES INTERNATIONAL DES ORIENTALISTES
ACom . . . . ACTA COMENIANA
Acor . . . . ACOREANA
AcOr . . . . ACTA ORIENTALIA
Acoust Soc Am J . . . ACOUSTICAL SOCIETY OF AMERICA. JOURNAL
ACPFM . . . . AMITIE CHARLES PEGUY. FEUILLETS MENSUELS
ACQR . . . . AMERICAN CATHOLIC QUARTERLY REVIEW
Acr . . . . ACROPOLE. REVUE DU MONDE HELLENIQUE
ACS SYMP S . . . . . . ACS SYMPOSIUM SERIES
ACSU . . . . ATTI DEL COLLOQUIO SLAVISTICO DI UPPSALA
ActaA . . . . ACTA ASIATICA
Acta Am . . . . ACTA AMERICANA
Acta Electron . . . . . ACTA ELECTRONICA
ActaG . . . . ACTA GERMANICA (CAPETOWN)
ACT AGRON H . . . . ACTA AGRONOMICA ACADEMIAE SCIENTIARUM HUNGARICAE
Acta Hist Art . . . . . MAGYAR TUDOMANYOS AKADEMIA. ACTA HISTORIAE ARTIUM
ACTA HISTOCHEM . . ACTA HISTOCHEMICA
Acta Inf . . . . ACTA INFORMATICA

6

ActaL . . . . ACTA LATGALICA
Acta Linguist Hung . . ACTA LINGUISTICA ACADEMIAE SCIENTIARUM HUNGARIAE
Acta Lit Hung . . . . . ACTA LITTERARIA ACADEMIAE SCIENTIARUM HUNGARIAE
ACT ALLERG . . . . . . ACTA ALLERGOLOGICA
Acta Mech . . . . ACTA MECHANICA
Acta Mech Sinica . . . ACTA MECHANICA SINICA
Acta Med Scand . . . . ACTA MEDICA SCANDINAVICA
Acta Metall . . . . ACTA METALLURGICA
ACTA MUS . . . . ACTA MUSICOLOGICA
ACT ANAE SC . . . . . . ACTA ANAESTHESIOLOGICA SCANDINAVICA
ACT ANATOM . . . . . ACTA ANATOMICA
Acta Philol Scand . . . ACTA PHILOLOGICA SCANDINAVICA
Acta Polytech Scand Civ Eng Build Constru Ser . . ACTA POLYTECHNICA SCANDINAVICA. CIVIL ENGINEERING AND
    BUILDING CONSTRUCTION SERIES
Acta Polytech Scand Elec Eng Ser . . ACTA POLYTECHNICA SCANDINAVICA. ELECTRICAL ENGINEERING SERIES
Acta Polytech Scand Electr Ser . . ACTA POLYTECHNICA SCANDINAVICA. ELECTRICAL SERIES
Acta Polytech Scand Math Comput Mach Ser . . ACTA POLYTECHNICA SCANDINAVICA. MATHEMATICS AND
    COMPUTING MACHINERY SERIES
Acta Polytech Scand Mech Eng Ser . . ACTA POLYTECHNICA SCANDINAVICA. MECHANICAL ENGINEERING SERIES
Acta Polytech Scand Phys Incl Nucl Ser . . ACTA POLYTECHNICA SCANDINAVICA. PHYSICS INCLUDING NUCLEONICS
    SERIES
Acta Protozool . . . . ACTA PROTOZOOLOGICA
ACT ARCHAEO . . . . . ACTA ARCHAEOLOGICA
ACTA SAG . . . . ACTA SAGITTARIANA
Acta Sociol . . . . ACTA SOCIOLOGICA
ACT ASTRON . . . . . . ACTA ASTRONAUTICA
Acta Tech (Budap) . . ACTA TECHNICA (BUDAPEST)
Acta Tech CSAV . . . . ACTA TECHNICA CSAV (CESKOSLOVENSKA AKADEMIE VED)
ACT BIO C B . . . . . . ACTA BIOLOGICA CRACOVIENSIA. SERIES BOTANICA
ACT BIOCH H . . . . . . ACTA BIOCHIMICA AND BIOPHYSICA ACADEMIAE SCIENTIARUM HUNGARICAE
ACT BIOCH P . . . . . . ACTA BIOCHIMICA POLONICA
ACT BIO C Z . . . . . . ACTA BIOLOGICA CRACOVIENSIA SERIES ZOOLOGIA
ACT BIO IRA . . . . . . ACTA BIOCHIMICA IRANICA
ACT BIOL H . . . . ACTA BIOLOGICA ACADEMIAE SCIENTIARUM HUNGARICAE
ACT BIO MED . . . . . ACTA BIOLOGICA ET MEDICA GERMANICA
ACT BOT NEE . . . . . ACTA BOTANICA NEERLANDICA
ACT CARDIOL . . . . . ACTA CARDIOLOGICA
ACT CHEM A . . . . . . ACTA CHEMICA SCANDINAVICA. SERIES A
ACT CHEM B . . . . . . ACTA CHEMICA SCANDINAVICA. SERIES B
ACT CHIM H . . . . . . ACTA CHIMICA ACADEMIAE SCIENTIARUM HUNGARICAE
ACT CHIR B . . . . ACTA CHIRURGICA BELGICA
ACT CHIR H . . . . ACTA CHIRURGICA ACADEMIAE SCIENTIARUM HUNGARICAE
ACT CHIR SC . . . . . . ACTA CHIRURGICA SCANDINAVICA
ACT CIENT V . . . . . . ACTA CIENTIFICA VENEZOLANA
ACT CLIN B . . . . ACTA CLINICA BELGICA
ACT CRYST A . . . . . . ACTA CRYSTALLOGRAPHICA. SECTION A
ACT CRYST B . . . . . . ACTA CRYSTALLOGRAPHICA. SECTION B
ACT CYTOL . . . . ACTA CYTOLOGICA
ACT DER-VEN . . . . . ACTA DERMATO VENEREOLOGICA
ACT DIABET . . . . . . ACTA DIABETOLOGICA LATINA
ACT EC . . . . L'ACTUALITE ECONOMIQUE

ACT ENDOCR . . . . . . ACTA ENDOCRINOLOGICA
ACT ENT BOH . . . . . ACTA ENTOMOLOGICA BOHEMOSLOVACA
ACT ENTHNOGR . . . . ACTA ETHNOGRAPHICA
ACT GASTR B . . . . . . ACTA GASTRO-ENTEROLOGICA BELGICA
ACT GENET M . . . . . ACTA GENETICAE MEDICAE ET GEMELLOLOGIAE
ACT GEOGR . . . . ACTA GEOGRAPHICA (FRANCE)
ACT HAEMAT . . . . . ACTA HAEMATOLOGICA
ACT HEP-GAS . . . . . ACTA HEPATO-GASTROENTEROLOGICA
ACT HIST CY . . . . . . ACTA HISTOCHEMICA ET CYTOCHEMICA
ACT HISTOCH . . . . . ACTA HISTOCHEMICA
ACTIV NERV . . . . . . ACTIVITAS NERVOSA SUPERIOR
ActLingH . . . . ACTA LINGUISTICA ACADEMIAE SCIENTIARUM HUNGARICAE
ActLitH . . . . ACTA LITTERARIA ACADEMIAE SCIENTIARUM HUNGARICAE
ACT MATH . . . . ACTA MATHEMATICA
ACT MATH H . . . . . . ACTA MATHEMATICA ACADEMIAE SCIENTIARUM HUNGARICAE
ACT MECHAN . . . . . ACTA MECHANICA
ACT MED H . . . . ACTA MEDICA ACADEMIAE SCIENTIARUM HUNGARICAE
ACT MED OKA . . . . . ACTA MEDICINAE OKAYAMA
ACT MED SC . . . . . . ACTA MEDICA SCANDINAVICA
ACT METALL . . . . . . ACTA METALLURGICA
ACT MIC P A . . . . . . ACTA MICROBIOLOGICA POLONICA. SERIES A
ACT MIC P B . . . . . . ACTA MICROBIOLOGICA POLONICA. SERIES B
ACT MICRO H . . . . . ACTA MICROBIOLOGICA ACADEMIAE SCIENTIARUM HUNGARICAE
ACT MORPH H . . . . . ACTA MORPHOLOGICA ACADEMIAE SCIENTIARUM HUNGARICAE
ACT MORPH N . . . . . ACTA MORPHOLOGICA NEERLANDO-SCANDINAVICA
ActN . . . . L'ACTION NATIONALE
ACT NAT . . . . L'ACTION NATIONALE
ACT NEUROB . . . . . . ACTA NEUROBIOLOGIAE EXPERIMENTALIS
ACT NEUROCH . . . . . ACTA NEUROCHIRURGICA
ACT NEUROP . . . . . . ACTA NEUROPATHOLOGICA
ACT NEUR SC . . . . . . ACTA NEUROLOGICA SCANDINAVICA
ACT OBST SC . . . . . . ACTA OBSTETRICIA ET GYNECOLOGICA SCANDINAVICA
ACT ODON SC . . . . . ACTA ODONTOLOGICA SCANDINAVICA
ACT OECON . . . . ACTA OECONOMICA
ACT OPHTH K . . . . . ACTA OPHTHALMOLOGICA. KOBENHAVN
ACT ORTH SC . . . . . . ACTA ORTHOPAEDICA SCANDINAVICA
ACT OTO-LAR . . . . . ACTA OTO-LARYNGOLOGICA
ACT PAED H . . . . . . ACTA PAEDIATRICA ACADEMIAE SCIENTIARUM HUNGARICAE
ACT PAEDOPS . . . . . ACTA PAEDOPSYCHIATRICA
ACT PAED SC . . . . . . ACTA PAEDIATRICA SCANDINAVICA
ACT PAT JAP . . . . . . ACTA PATHOLOGICA JAPONICA
ACT PAT S A . . . . . . ACTA PATHOLOGICA ET MICROBIOLOGICA SCANDINAVICA. SECTION A PATHOLOGY
ACT PAT S B . . . . . . ACTA PATHOLOGICA ET MICROBIOLOGICA SCANDINAVICA. SECTION B MICROBIOLOGY
ACT PAT S C . . . . . . ACTA PATHOLOGICA ET MICROBIOLOGICA SCANDINAVICA. SECTION C IMMUNOLOGY
ACT PHARM S . . . . . ACTA PHARMACEUTICA SUECICA
ACT PHARM T . . . . . ACTA PHARMACOLOGICA ET TOXICOLOGICA
ACT PHY P A . . . . . . ACTA PHYSICA POLONICA A
ACT PHY P B . . . . . . ACTA PHYSICA POLONICA B
ACT PHYS AU . . . . . ACTA PHYSICA AUSTRIACA
ACT PHYS CH . . . . . ACTA PHYSICA ET CHEMICA
ACT PHYS H . . . . . . ACTA PHYSICA ACADEMIAE SCIENTIARUM HUNGARICAE

ACT PHYSL H . . . . . . ACTA PHYSIOLOGICA ACADEMIAE SCIENTIARUM HUNGARICAE
ACT PHYSL L . . . . . . ACTA PHYSIOLOGICA LATINO-AMERICANA
ACT PHYSL P . . . . . . ACTA PHYSIOLOGICA POLONICA
ACT PHYSL S . . . . . . ACTA PHYSIOLOGICA SCANDINAVICA
ACT POL PH . . . . . . ACTA POLONIAE PHARMACEUTICA
ACT POLY CH . . . . . ACTA POLYTECHNICA SCANDINAVICA. CHEMISTRY
ACT POLY CI . . . . . . ACTA POLYTECHNICA SCANDINAVICA. CIVIL ENGINEERING AND BUILDING CONSTRUCTION
                       SERIES
ACT POLY EL . . . . . . ACTA POLYTECHNICA SCANDINAVICA. ELECTRICAL ENGINEERING SERIES
ACT POLY MA . . . . . ACTA POLYTECHNICA SCANDINAVICA. MATHEMATICS AND COMPUTING MACHINERY SERIES
ACT POLY ME . . . . . ACTA POLYTECHNICA SCANDINAVICA. MECHANICAL ENGINEERING SERIES
ACT POLY PH . . . . . ACTA POLYTECHNICA SCANDINAVICA. PHYSICS INCLUDING NUCLEONICS SERIES
ACT PSIQ PS . . . . . . ACTA PSIQUIATRICA Y PSICOLOGICA DE AMERICA LATINA
ACT PSYC SC . . . . . . ACTA PSYCHIATRICA SCANDINAVICA
ACT PSYCHOL . . . . . ACTA PSYCHOLOGICA
ACT PSYCH T . . . . . . ACTA PSYCHOLOGICA TAIWANICA
ACT RAD DGN . . . . . ACTA RADIOLOGICA DIAGNOSIS
ACT RAD TPB . . . . . ACTA RADIOLOGICA. THERAPY, PHYSICS, BIOLOGY
ACT RES REP . . . . . . AMERICAN COLLEGE TESTING RESEARCH REPORTS
ACT SCI MAT . . . . . . ACTA SCIENTIARUM MATHEMATICARUM
ACT SOCIOL . . . . . . ACTA SOCIOLOGICA
ACT TECHN H . . . . . ACTA TECHNICA ACADEMIAE SCIENTIARUM HUNGARICAE
ACTUAL Specif Eng . . ACTUAL SPECIFYING ENGINEER
ACTU ECON . . . . ACTUALITE ECONOMIQUE
ACT VET H . . . . ACTA VETERINARIA ACADEMIAE SCIENTIARUM HUNGARICAE
ACT VET SC . . . . ACTA VETERINARIA SCANDINAVICA
ACT VIROLOG . . . . . ACTA VIROLOGICA (ENGLISH EDITION)
ACT VIT ENZ . . . . . . ACTA VITAMINOLOGICA ET ENZYMOLOGICA
ACT ZOOL H . . . . . . ACTA ZOOLOGICA ACADEMIAE SCIENTIARUM HUNGARICAE
ACUM . . . . ANNALES DU CENTRE UNIVERSITAIRE MEDITERRANEEN DE NICE
ACUN . . . . ANNALES DU CENTRE UNIVERSITAIRE DE NICE
Ad . . . . ADELPHI
AD . . . . AMAZING DETECTIVE TALES
AD . . . . AMERICAN DOCUMENTATION
AD . . . . ARCHITECTURAL DESIGN
AD . . . . ARCHIV FUER DIPLOMATIK
AD . . . . ART DIGEST
ADA . . . . ANZEIGER FUER DEUTSCHES ALTERTUM UND DEUTSCHE LITERATUR
ADA . . . . ARQUIVO DO DISTRITO DE AVEIRO
ADAM INT R . . . . . . ADAM (ARTS, DRAMA, ARCHITECTURE, MUSIC) INTERNATIONAL REVIEW
ADAW . . . . ABHANDLUNGEN DER DEUTSCHEN AKADEMIE DER WISSENSCHAFTEN ZU BERLIN, KLASSE FUER
                       SPRACHEN, LITERATUR UND KUNST
ADE . . . . ARCHIVIO DI DIRITTO ECCLESIASTICO
ADEB . . . . ASSOCIATION OF DEPARTMENTS OF ENGLISH. BULLETIN
Adel . . . . ADELPHI
Adel . . . . NEW ADELPHI
ADELAIDE L REV . . . ADELAIDE LAW REVIEW
ADGB . . . . ARCHIV FUER GESCHICHTE DES BUCHWESENS
Adhes Age . . . . ADHESIVES AGE
AdL . . . . AMOR DI LIBRO
AdL . . . . ANUARIO DE LETRAS

AD LAW REV . . . . . . ADMINISTRATIVE LAW REVIEW
AdLB . . . . ADYAR LIBRARY BULLETIN
ADML . . . . AUTOMATIC DOCUMENTATION AND MATHEMATICAL LINGUISTICS
Adm Law R . . . . ADMINISTRATIVE LAW REVIEW
ADM MENT HE . . . . . ADMINISTRATION IN MENTAL HEALTH
Adm Mgt . . . . ADMINISTRATIVE MANAGEMENT
Adm Sci . . . . ADMINISTRATIVE SCIENCE QUARTERLY
ADM SCI QUA . . . . . ADMINISTRATIVE SCIENCE QUARTERLY
ADM SOCIE . . . . . . ADMINISTRATION AND SOCIETY
ADP . . . . ARCHIVO DE DERECHO PUBLICO
ADPh . . . . ARBEITEN ZUR DEUTSCHEN PHILOLOGIE
ADRS . . . . ARCHIVIO DELLA R. DEPUTAZIONE ROMANA DI STORIA PATRIA
ADRSP . . . . ARCHIVIO DELLA R. DEPUTAZIONE ROMANA DI STORIA PATRIA
ADSPM . . . . ATTI E MEMORIE DELLA DEPUTAZIONE DI STORIA PATRIA PER LE ANTICHE PROVINCE MODENESI
ADSPR . . . . ATTI E MEMORIE DELLA DEPUTAZIONE DI STORIA PATRIA PER LE PROVINCE DI ROMAGNA
ADT . . . . AMAZING DETECTIVE TALES
AdTb . . . . ALTDEUTSCHE TEXTBIBLIOTHEK
Adult Ed . . . . ADULT EDUCATION
Adult Ed and Lib . . . . ADULT EDUCATION AND THE LIBRARY
Adult Ed Bul . . . . . . ADULT EDUCATION BULLETIN
Adult Ed J . . . . ADULT EDUCATION JOURNAL
ADULT ED-W . . . . . . ADULT EDUCATION-WASHINGTON
Adult Lead . . . . ADULT LEADERSHIP
Adv Age . . . . ADVERTISING AGE
Adv Agency Mag . . . ADVERTISING AGENCY MAGAZINE
Advan Appl Mech . . ADVANCES IN APPLIED MECHANICS
Advan Appl Probab . . ADVANCES IN APPLIED PROBABILITY
Advan Astronaut Sci . . ADVANCES IN THE ASTRONAUTICAL SCIENCES
Advanced Mgt . . . . . ADVANCED MANAGEMENT
Advanced Mgt J . . . ADVANCED MANAGEMENT JOURNAL
Advanced Mgt Office Exec . . ADVANCED MANAGEMENT-OFFICE EXECUTIVE
Advancement Sci . . . ADVANCEMENT OF SCIENCE
Advan Chem Eng . . . ADVANCES IN CHEMICAL ENGINEERING
Advan Chem Ser . . . ADVANCES IN CHEMISTRY SERIES
Advan Cryog Eng . . . ADVANCES IN CRYOGENIC ENGINEERING
Adv & Sell . . . . ADVERTISING AND SELLING
Advan Electron and Electron Phys . . ADVANCES IN ELECTRONICS AND ELECTRON PHYSICS
Advan Geophys . . . . ADVANCES IN GEOPHYSICS
Advan Manage J . . . ADVANCED MANAGEMENT JOURNAL
Advan Mol Relaxation Processes . . ADVANCES IN MOLECULAR RELAXATION PROCESSES
Advan Phys . . . . ADVANCES IN PHYSICS
Advan Polymer Sci Fortschr Hochpolym-Forsch . . ADVANCES IN POLYMER SCIENCE FORTSCHRITTE DER HOCHPOLY-MEREN-FORSCHUNG
ADV APPL P . . . . . . ADVANCES IN APPLIED PROBABILITY
Adv Astronaut Sci . . ADVANCES IN THE ASTRONAUTICAL SCIENCES
ADV CHEM SE . . . . . ADVANCES IN CHEMISTRY SERIES
ADV COLL IN . . . . . . ADVANCES IN COLLOID AND INTERFACE SCIENCE
Adv Electron Electron Phys . . ADVANCES IN ELECTRONICS AND ELECTRON PHYSICS
ADV ENZYM . . . . . . ADVANCES IN ENZYMOLOGY
ADV GENETIC . . . . . ADVANCES IN GENETICS

PERIODICAL TITLE ABBREVIATIONS

Adv Heat Transfer . . ADVANCES IN HEAT TRANSFER
ADV HUM GEN . . . . ADVANCES IN HUMAN GENETICS
ADV MAR BIO . . . . . ADVANCES IN MARINE BIOLOGY
ADV MATH . . . . ADVANCES IN MATHEMATICS
ADV MOL REL . . . . . ADVANCES IN MOLECULAR RELAXATION PROCESSES
Advmt Sci . . . . ADVANCEMENT OF SCIENCE
ADV OBSTET . . . . . . ADVANCES IN OBSTETRICS AND GYNECOLOGY
Adv of Science . . . . . ADVANCEMENT OF SCIENCE
ADV OPHTHAL . . . . ADVANCES IN OPHTHALMOLOGY
Adv Phys . . . . ADVANCES IN PHYSICS
ADV PHYSICS . . . . . ADVANCES IN PHYSICS
ADV PSY MED . . . . . ADVANCES IN PSYCHOSOMATIC MEDICINE
ADV R PHYSL . . . . . ADVANCES IN REPRODUCTIVE PHYSIOLOGY
ADV SPA SCI . . . . . . ADVANCES IN SPACE SCIENCE AND TECHNOLOGY
ADz . . . . AKADEMISKA DZIVE (INDIANAPOLIS)
AE . . . . ACTA ETHNOGRAPHICA
AE . . . . ADULT EDUCATION
AE . . . . AESTHETICS
Ae . . . . AEVUM
AE . . . . ANNALES DE L'EST
AE . . . . ARHEOLOGIJA UN ETNOGRAFIJA
AEA . . . . AMERICA, REVISTA DE LA ASOCIACION DE ESCRITORES Y ARTISTAS AMERICANOS
AEA . . . . ANUARIO DE ESTUDIOS ATLANTICOS
AEA . . . . ARCHIVO ESPANOL DE ARQUEOLOGIA
AEA . . . . ARCHIVO ESPANOL DE ARTE
AEAA . . . . ARCHIVO ESPANOL DE ARTE Y ARQUEOLOGIA
AEAls . . . . ARCHIVES DE L'EGLISE D'ALSACE
AEArq . . . . ARCHIVO ESPANOL DE ARQUEOLOGIA
AEASH . . . . ACTA ETHNOGRAPHICA ACADEMIAE SCIENTIARUM HUNGARICAE
Aeb . . . . ARCHIVES ET BIBLIOTHEQUES
AECO . . . . ARCHIVUM EUROPAE CENTRO-ORIENTALIS
AEF . . . . ANEJOS DE ESTUDIOS FILOLOGICOS
Aeg . . . . AEGYPTUS, RIVISTA ITALIANA DI EGITTOLOGIA E DI PAPIROLOGIA
AEG-Telefunken Progr . . AEG (ALLGEMEINE ELEKTRICITAETS-GESELLSCHAFT)- TELEFUNKEN PROGRESS
AEH . . . . ACTA ETHNOGRAPHICA ACADEMIAE SCIENTIARUM HUNGARICAE
AEHEG . . . . ANNALES DE L'ECOLE DES HAUTES-ETUDES DE GAND
AEHR . . . . AUSTRALIAN ECONOMIC HISTORY REVIEW
AEJ . . . . ADULT EDUCATION JOURNAL
AEKG . . . . ARCHIV FUER ELSAESSISCHE KIRCHENGESCHICHTE
AEM . . . . ANUARIO DE ESTUDIOS MEDIEVALES
AEM . . . . ARCHEION EUBOIKON MELETON
AEN . . . . ANNALES DE L'EST ET DU NORD
AeP . . . . ANIMA E PENSIERO
AEP . . . . AUSTRALIAN ECONOMIC PAPERS
AER . . . . AMERICAN ECCLESIATICAL REVIEW
AER . . . . AUSTRALIAN ECONOMIC REVIEW
Aero Eng R . . . . AERONAUTICAL ENGINEERING REVIEW
Aero J . . . . AERONAUTICAL JOURNAL
Aeronaut J . . . . AERONAUTICAL JOURNAL
Aeronaut Q . . . . AERONAUTICAL QUARTERLY
Aeron J . . . . AERONAUTICAL JOURNAL

Aeron Q......... AERONAUTICAL QUARTERLY
Aerosol Rep...... AEROSOL REPORT
Aero/Space Eng.... AERO/SPACE ENGINEERING
Aerospace Tech.... AEROSPACE TECHNOLOGY
AErt........... ARCHAEOLOGIAI ERTESITO
AERTJ.......... ASSOCIATION OF EDUCATION BY RADIO-TELEVISION JOURNAL
AESC........... ANNALES: ECONOMIES, SOCIETES, CIVILISATIONS
AEU-ARCH EL...... AEU-ARCHIV FUER ELEKTRONIK UND UEBERTRAGUNGSTECHNIK
Aev........... AEVUM
AF............ AMERICAN FORESTS
AF............ AMERIQUE FRANCAISE
AF............ ANGLISTISCHE FORSCHUNGEN
AF............ ARCHITECTURAL FORUM
AF............ ARCHIVIO DI FILOSOFIA
AF............ ARTE FIGURATIVA
AFA........... ARCHIVO DE FILOLOGIA ARAGONESA
AFA........... ASOCIACION FOLKLORICA ARGENTINA, ANALES
AfB........... AFRICANA BULLETIN (WARSAW)
AFC........... ANALES DE FILOLOGIA CLASICA
AFCU.......... ARCHIVOS DEL FOLKLORE CHILENO UNIVERSIDAD DE CHILE
AfD........... ARCHIV FUER DIPLOMATIK
AFF........... ANALI FILOLOSKOG FAKULTETA, BELGRADE
AFGK.......... ARCHIV FUER FRANKFURTS GESCHICHTE UND KUNST
AFH........... ARCHIVUM FRANCISCANUM HISTORICUM (FIRENZE)
AFHL.......... ANNUAIRE DE LA FEDERATION HISTORIQUE DE LORRAINE
AFig.......... ARTI FIGURATIVE; RIVISTA D'ARTE ANTICA E MODERNA
AFilos......... ARCHIVIO DI FILOSOFIA
AFIPS Conf Proc Fall Jt Comput Conf..AMERICAN FEDERATION OF INFORMATION PROCESSING SOCIETIES
            CONFERENCE PROCEEDINGS FALL JOINT COMPUTER CONFERENCE
AFIPS Conf Proc Fall Spring Jt Comput Conf..AMERICAN FEDERATION OF INFORMATION PROCESSING SOCIETIES
            CONFERENCE PROCEEDINGS. FALL AND SPRING JOINT COMPUTER CONFERENCES
AFIPS Conf Proc Spring Jt Comput Conf..AMERICAN FEDERATION OF INFORMATION PROCESSING SOCIETIES
            CONFERENCE PROCEEDINGS. SPRING JOINT COMPUTER CONFERENCE
AFIPS Natl Comput Conf Expo Conf Proc..AMERICAN FEDERATION OF INFORMATION PROCESSING SOCIETIES
            NATIONAL COMPUTER CONFERENCE AND EXPOSITION. CONFERENCE PROCEEDINGS
AF JAG L REV..... AIR FORCE JAG LAW REVIEW
AFLA........... ANNALES DE LA FACULTE DES LETTRES D'AIX
AFLC........... ANNALI DELLA FACOLTA DI LETTERE, FILOSOFIA E MAGISTERO DELLA UNIVERSITA DI CAGLIARI
AFLFB.......... ANNALI DELLA FACOLTA DI LETTERE E FILOSOFIA DELL'UNIVERSITA DI BARI
AFLFP.......... ANNALI DELLA FACOLTA DI LETTERE E FILOSOFIA DELL' UNIVERSITA DI PERUGIA
AFLFUM......... ANNALI DELLA FACOLTA DI LETTERE FILOSOFIA DELL'UNIVERSITA DI MACERATA
AFLN........... ANNALI DELLA FACOLTA DI LETTERE E FILOSOFIA DELL'UNIVERSITA DI NAPOLI
AFLQ........... ARCHIVES DE FOLKLORE. UNIVERSITE LAVAL (QUEBEC)
AF L R.......... AIR FORCE LAW REVIEW
AFLT........... AFRICAN LITERATURE TODAY
AFLT........... ANNALES PUBLIEES PAR LA FACULTE DES LETTRES DE TOULOUSE
AFLToul......... ANNALES PUBLIEES PAR LA FACULTE DES LETTRES ET SCIENCES HUMAINES DE TOULOUSE (VIA
            DOMITIA)
AFM........... ANNALES FONDS MAETERLINCK
AfM........... ARCHIV FUER MUSIKWISSENSCHAFT
AFMag......... ANNALI DELLA FACOLTA DI MAGISTERO (UNIVERSITY OF PALERMO)
AFMUB......... ANNALI DELLA FACOLTA DI MAGISTERO DELL'UNIVERSITA DI BARI

AF MUS. . . . . AFRICAN MUSIC
AFO. . . . . ARCHIV FUER ORIENTFORSCHUNG (GRAZ)
AForum. . . . . AFRICAN FORUM: A QUARTERLY JOURNAL OF CONTEMPORARY AFFAIRS
AFP. . . . . ARCHIVUM FRATRUM PRAEDICATORUM (ROMA)
AFQ. . . . . ALBERTA FOLKLORE QUARTERLY
AFR. . . . . AFRICA; REVISTA ESPANOLA DE COLONIZACION
AFR. . . . . ANGLO-FRENCH REVIEW
AFR. . . . . ARCHIV FUER REFORMATIONSGFSCHICHTE. TEXTE UND UNTERSUCHUNGEN
AFR. . . . . ARCHIVUM FRATRUM PRAEDICATORUM
AFR. . . . . AVON FANTASY READER
AfrA. . . . . AFRICAN ARTS/ARTS D'AFRIQUE
AfrAb. . . . . AFRICAN ABSTRACTS
AfrAf. . . . . AFRICAN AFFAIRS
AFR AFFAIRS. . . . . . AFRICAN AFFAIRS
AfrAms. . . . . AFRO-AMERICAN STUDIES: AN INTERDISCIPLINARY JOURNAL
AFR-AM STUD. . . . . AFRO-AMERICAN STUDIES
Afric Affairs. . . . . . AFRICAN AFFAIRS
AfricaL. . . . . AFRICA (LONDON)
Africana J. . . . . AFRICANA JOURNAL
Africana Lib J. . . . . AFRICANA LIBRARY JOURNAL
African J Ednl Research. . AFRICAN JOURNAL OF EDUCATIONAL RESEARCH
African Stud. . . . . . AFRICAN STUDIES
African Stud Bul. . . AFRICAN STUDIES BULLETIN
African Stud R. . . . . AFRICAN STUDIES REVIEW
Africa Rep. . . . . . . AFRICA REPORT
Afric Lit Today. . . . AFRICAN LITERATURE TODAY
Afric Stud. . . . . . . AFRICAN STUDIES
Afric Stud R. . . . . . AFRICAN STUDIES REVIEW
AfrL. . . . . AFRICANA LINGUISTICA (TERVUREN)
AfrLJ. . . . . AFRICANA LIBRARY JOURNAL
AfrLRev. . . . . AFRICAN LANGUAGE REVIEW
AfrLS. . . . . AFRICAN LANGUAGE STUDIES
AfrM. . . . . AFRICANA MARBURGENSIA
AfrN. . . . . AFRICAN NOTES (IBADAN)
AFrP. . . . . ATHLONE FRENCH POETS
AfrS. . . . . AFRICAN STUDIES (JOHANNESBURG)
AfrSch. . . . . AFRICAN SCHOLAR
AFR SOC RES. . . . . . AFRICAN SOCIAL RESEARCH
AfrSR. . . . . AFRICAN STUDIES REVIEW
AFR STUD. . . . . . . AFRICAN STUDIES
AFR TODAY. . . . . . AFRICA TODAY
Afr WS. . . . . AFRICAN WRITERS SERIES
AFS. . . . . ASIAN FOLKLORE STUDIES
AFS Cast Met Res J. . AFS (AMERICAN FOUNDRYMEN'S SOCIETY) CAST METALS RESEARCH JOURNAL
AFTU. . . . . ARCHIV FUER REFORMATIONSGESCHICHTE. TEXTE UND UNTERSUCHUNGEN
AG. . . . . ADVANCE GUARD
AG. . . . . ANALES GALDOSIANOS
AG. . . . . ANGLICA GERMANICA
AG. . . . . ARCHIVO GIURIDICO
AG. . . . . AUGUST
Ag Am. . . . . AGRICULTURE IN THE AMERICAS

Ag & Livestock India.. AGRICULTURE AND LIVESTOCK IN INDIA
AGARD Adv Rep... AGARD ADVISORY REPORT
AGARD Conf Proc.. AGARD CONFERENCE PROCEEDINGS
AGARD Lect Ser.... AGARD LECTURE SERIES
AGARD Rep....... AGARD REPORT
AGAU........... ARCHIEF VOOR DE GESCHIEDENIS VAN HET AARTSBISDOM UTRECHT
AGB............ ANHALTISCHE GESCHICHTSBLAETTER
AGB............ ARCHIV FUER GESCHICHTE DES BUCHWESENS
AGB............ ASSOCIATION GUILLAUME BUDE, BULLETIN
AG CHEM........ AG CHEM AND COMMERCIAL FERTILIZER
Ag Chem......... AGRICULTURAL CHEMICALS
Ag Chemicals..... AGRICULTURAL CHEMICALS
Ag Digest........ AGRICULTURAL DIGEST
Ag Econ Res...... AGRICULTURAL ECONOMICS RESEARCH
Ag Ed........... AGRICULTURAL EDUCATION
Ag Eng.......... AGRICULTURAL ENGINEERING
AGENT ACTIO..... AGENTS AND ACTIONS
Ag Gaz of Canada.. AGRICULTURAL GAZETTE OF CANADA
Ag Gaz of New South Wales.. AGRICULTURAL GAZETTE OF NEW SOUTH WALES
AGHA........... ARCHIV FUER GESCHICHTE DES HOCHSTIFTS AUGSBURG
Ag Hist.......... AGRICULTURAL HISTORY
Ag Hist R........ AGRICULTURAL HISTORY REVIEW
AGI............. ARCHIVIO GLOTTOLOGICO ITALIANO (TORINO)
Ag Inst R........ AGRICULTURE INSTITUTE REVIEW
Ag J of British Columbia.. AGRICULTURAL JOURNAL OF BRITISH COLUMBIA
Ag J of Egypt...... AGRICULTURAL JOURNAL OF EGYPT
Ag J of India...... AGRICULTURAL JOURNAL OF INDIA
AGKKN......... ARCHIEF VOOR DE GESCHIEDENIS VAN DE KATHOLIEKE KERK IN NEDERLAND
AglGr........... ANGLO-GERMAN REVIEW
AGM............ SUDHOFFS ARCHIV FUER GESCHICHTE DER MEDIZIN UND DER NATURWISSENSCHAFTEN.
AGN............ ANZEIGER DES GERMANISCHEN NATIONALMUSEUMS
AgN............ L'AGE NOUVEAU. IDEES, LETTRES, ARTS
Ag N L.......... AGRICULTURAL NEWS LETTER
AGNM.......... ANZEIGER DES GERMANISCHEN NATIONALMUSEUMS
AGO............ AMERICAN GUILD OF ORGANISTS QUARTERLY
AGP............ ARCHIV FUER GESCHICHTE DER PHILOSOPHIE
AGPh........... ARCHIV FUER GESCHICHTE DER PHILOSOPHIE
Ag R............ AGRICULTURAL REVIEW
AGR............ AMERICAN-GERMAN REVIEW
A GRAEFES A...... ALBRECHT VON GRAEFES ARCHIV FUER KLINISCHE UND EXPERIMENTELLE OPHTHALMOLOGIE
AGR BIOL CH...... AGRICULTURAL AND BIOLOGICAL CHEMISTRY
AGR ECON RE..... AGRICULTURAL ECONOMICS RESEARCH
AGR EDUC MA..... AGRICULTURAL EDUCATION MAGAZINE
AGR ENG......... AGRICULTURAL ENGINEERING
Ag Res.......... AGRICULTURAL RESEARCH
AGRESSOLOG...... AGRESSOLOGIE
AGR HOR GEN..... AGRI HORTIQUE GENETICA
Agric & Biol Chem.. AGRICULTURAL & BIOLOGICAL CHEMISTRY
Agric Econ Res.... AGRICULTURAL ECONOMICS RESEARCH
AGRIC EDUC MAG.. THE AGRICULTURAL EDUCATION MAGAZINE
Agric Engin....... AGRICULTURAL ENGINEERING

PERIODICAL TITLE ABBREVIATIONS

Agric Eng (St. Joseph, Mich).. AGRICULTURAL ENGINEERING (ST. JOSEPH, MICH)
Agric Hist........ AGRICULTURAL HISTORY
Agric Mach J...... AGRICULTURAL MACHINERY JOURNAL
Agric Sci R........AGRICULTURAL SCIENCE REVIEW
AGR METEOR...... AGRICULTURAL METEOROLOGY
AGRON J.........AGRONOMY JOURNAL
AGR RES......... AGRICULTURAL RESEARCH
Ag Sci J..........AGRICULTURAL SCIENCE JOURNAI
Ag Sci R......... AGRICULTURAL SCIENCE REVIEW
AGSD........... ACTA GERMANICA ZUR SPRACHE UND DICHTUNG DEUTSCHLANDS
Ag Situation...... AGRICULTURAL SITUATION
AGWG..........ABHANDLUNGEN DER GESELLSCHAFT DER WISSENSCHAFT ZU GOTTINGEN
AH............. AGRICULTURAL HISTORY
AH............. AMERICAN HERITAGE
AH............. ANJOU HISTORIQUE
AH............. ARCHIVIUM HIBERNICUM
AH............. ARCHIVO HISPALENSE
AHA........... HITOTSUBASHI ACADEMY. ANNALS
AHAG........... ANNALES DE LA SOCIETE D'HISTOIRE ET D'ARCHEOLOGIE DE GAND
AHA Newsletter... AMERICAN HISTORICAL ASSOCIATION. NEWSLETTER
AHAW..........ABHANDLUNGEN DER HEIDELBERGER AKADEMIE DER WISSENSCHAFT
AHCE.......... ASOCIACION PARA LA HISTORIA DE LA CIENCIA ESPANOLA
AHCP.......... ARQUIVOS DE HISTORIA DE CULTURA PORTUGUESA
AHD........... ARCHIVES D'HISTOIRE DOMINICAINE
AHDE.......... ANUARIO DE LA HISTORIA DEL DERECHO ESPANOL
AHDLMA........ ARCHIVES D'HISTOIRE DOCTRINALE ET LITTERAIRE DU MOYEN AGE
AHDO.......... ARCHIVES D'HISTOIRE DU DROIT ORIENTAL
AHE........... ANNALES D'HISTOIRE ECONOMIQUE
AHEB.......... ANALECTES POUR SERVIR A L'HISTOIRE ECCLESIASTIQUE DE LA BELGIQUE
AHES...........ANNALES D'HISTOIRE ECONOMIQUE ET SOCIALE
AHF........... ARCHIVUM HISTORII FILOZOFII I MYSLI SPOLECZNEJ
AHG........... ARCHIVES HISTORIQUE DE LA GIRONDE
AHGAK......... ARCHIV FUER HESSISCHE GESCHICHTE UND ALTERTUMSKUNDE
AHIL Q........ ASSOCIATION OF HOSPITAL AND INSTITUTION LIBRARIES QUARTERLY
A HistHung....... ACTA HISTORICA ACADEMIAE SCIENTIARUM HUNGARICAE
AHL........... ANNUAIRE D'HISTOIRE LIEGEOISE
AHMA..........ARCHIVES D'HISTOIRE DOCTRINALE ET LITTERAIRE DU MOYEN-AGE
AHN........... ATTI E MEMORIE DELL'ISTITUTO ITALIANO DI NUMISMATICA
AHNRH......... ANNALEN DES HISTORISCHEN VEREINS FUER DEN NIERDERRHEIN
AHP........... ARCHIVUM HISTORIAE PONTIFICIAE
AHQ........... ARKANSAS HISTORICAL QUARTERLY
AHR........... AMERICAN HISTORICAL REVIEW
AHRF.......... ANNALES HISTORIQUES DE LA REVOLUTION FRANCAISE
AHS........... ANNALES D'HISTOIRE SOCIALE
AHS........... ARCHIVES HERALDIQUES SUISSE
AHSJ...........ARCHIVUM HISTORICUM SOCIETATIS JESU
AHSoc......... ANNALES D'HISTOIRE SOCIALE
AHVMF......... ARCHIV DES HISTORISCHEN VEREINS VON MAINFRANKEN
AHVNR......... ANNALEN DES HISTORISCHEN VEREINS FUER DEN NIEDERRHEIN
AHVNRh........ ANNALEN DES HISTORISCHEN VEREINS FUER DEN NIEDERRHEIN
AHVsLund....... KUNGL. HUMANISTISKA VETENSKAPSSAMFUNDET I LUND. ARSBERATTELSE

AHVsUppsala . . . . . KUNGL. HUMANISTISKA VETENSKAPSSAMFUNDET I UPPSALA. ARSBOK
AHVUA . . . . ARCHIV DES HISTORISCHEN VEREINS VON UNTERFRANKEN UND ASCHAFFENBURG
AI . . . . AFRICA ITALIANA
AI . . . . AMERICAN IMAGO
AI . . . . AMERICA INDIGENA. ORGANO OFICIAL DEL INSTITUTO INDIGENISTA INTERAMERICANO
AI . . . . ANNALS OF IOWA
AI . . . . ARS ISLAMICA
AI . . . . ART INTERNATIONAL
AIa . . . . ANNALS OF IOWA
AIA . . . . ARCHIVO IBERO-AMERICANO
AIAA . . . . ARCHIVO ESPANOL DE ARTE Y ARQUEOLOGIA
AIAA J . . . . AIAA (AMERICAN INSTITUTE OF AERONAUTICS AND ASTRONAUTICS) JOURNAL
AIAA Stud J . . . . . . AIAA (AMERICAN INSTITUTE OF AERONAUTICS AND ASTRONAUTICS) STUDENT JOURNAL
AIA J . . . . AIA (AMERICAN INSTITUTE OF ARCHITECTS) JOURNAL
AIAK . . . . AKTEN DES INTERNATIONALEN AMERIKANISTEN KONGRESSES
AIAL . . . . ANNALES DE L'INSTITUT ARCHEOLOGIQUE DU LUXEMBOURG
AIB . . . . AUGUSTANA INSTITUTE BULLETIN
AIBL . . . . ACADEMIE DES INSCRIPTIONS ET BELLES-LETTRES COMPTES RENDUS DES SEANCES
AIBLCr . . . . ACADEMIE DES INSCRIPTIONS ET BELLES-LETTRES COMPTES RENDUS DES SEANCES
AIChEJ . . . . AMERICAN INSTITUTE OF CHEMICAL ENGINEERS JOURNAL
AIChE Pap . . . . AMERICAN INSTITUTE OF CHEMICAL ENGINEERS. PAPERS
AIChE Symp Ser . . . . AICHE (AMERICAN INSTITUTE OF CHEMICAL ENGINEERS) SYMPOSIUM SERIES
AICS . . . . ANUARUL INSTITUTUL DE STUDII CLASICE
AIEA . . . . ARCHIVOS DEL INSTITUTO DE ESTUDIOS AFRICANOS
AIEC . . . . ANALES DEL INSTITUTO DE ETNOGRAFIA AMERICANA DE LA UNIVERSIDAD NACIONAL DE CUYO
AIEC . . . . ANUARI DE L'INSTITUT DE'ESTUDIOS CATALANS
AIEG . . . . ANALES DEL INSTITUTO DE ESTUDIOS GERUNDENSES
AIEM . . . . ANALES DEL INSTITUTO DE ESTUDIOS MADRILENOS
AIEN . . . . ANALES DEL INSTITUTO ETNICO NACIONAL. ARGENTINA
AIEO . . . . ANNALES DE L'INSTITUT D'ETUDES OCCITANES
AIF . . . . ANZEIGER FUER INDOGERMANISCHE SPRACH- UND ALTERTUMSKUNDE
AIF . . . . ANNALES DE L'INSTITUT FRANCAIS DE ZAGREB
AIHI . . . . ARCHIVES INTERNATIONALES D'HISTOIRE DES IDEES
AIHM . . . . ARCHIVOS IBEROAMERICANOS DE HISTORIA DE LA MEDICINA
AIHS . . . . ARCHIVES INTERNATIONALES D'HISTOIRE DES SCIENCES
AIIE . . . . ANALES DEL INSTITUTO DE INVESTIGACIONES ESTETICAS
AIIE Trans . . . . AIIE (AMERICAN INSTITUTE OF INDUSTRIAL ENGINEERS) TRANSACTIONS
AIIN . . . . ATTI E MEMORIE DELL'ISTITUTO ITALIANO DI NUMISMATICA
AIL . . . . ANALES DEL INSTITUTO DE LINGUISTICA (CUYO)
AILC . . . . ANALES DEL INSTITUTO DE LINGUISTICA DE LA UNIVERSIDAD NACIONAL DE CUYO
AILC . . . . ANALES DEL INSTITUTO DE LITERATURAS CLASICAS
AILM . . . . ANALES DELL'ISTITUTO DI LINGUISTICA DE MENDOZA
AIM . . . . ANNALI DELL'ISTURZIONE MEDIA
AIMAV . . . . ASSOCIATION INTERNATIONALE POUR LA RECHERCHE ET LA DIFFUSION DES METHODES AUDIO-
                          VISUELLES ET STRUCTUROGLOBALES
AIN . . . . ATTI E MEMORIE DELL'ISTITUTO ITALIANO DI NUMISMATICA
AINAH . . . . ANALES DEL INST. NACIONAL DE ANTHROPOLOGIA E HISTORIA
AInd . . . . ART INDEX
AInst . . . . ANNALES INSTITUTORUM QUAE IN URBE ERECTA SUNT
AiolikaG . . . . AIOLIKA GRAMMATA
AION . . . . ANNALI. ISTITUTO UNIVERSITARIO ORIENTALE. SEZIONE GERMANICA
AION-G . . . . ANNALI. ISTITUTO UNIVERSITARIO ORIENTALE. SEZIONE GERMANICA

Aion-L . . . . ANNALI. ISTITUTO UNIVERSITARIO ORIENTALE. SEZIONE LINGUISTICA
AION-O . . . . ANNALI. ISTITUTO UNIVERSITARIO ORIENTALE. SEZIONE ORIENTALE
AION-R . . . . ANNALI. ISTITUTO UNIVERSITARIO ORIENTALE. SEZIONE ROMANZA
AION-S . . . . ANNALI. ISTITUTO UNIVERSITARIO ORIENTALE. SEZIONE SLAVA
AION-SG . . . . ANNALI. ISTITUTO UNIVERSITARIO ORIENTALE. SEZIONE GERMANICA
AION-SL . . . . ANNALI. ISTITUTO UNIVERSITARIO ORIENTALE. SEZIONE LINGUISTICA
AION-SO . . . . ANNALI. ISTITUTO UNIVERSITARIO ORIENTALE. SEZIONE ORIENTALE
AION-SR . . . . ANNALI. ISTITUTO UNIVERSITARIO ORIENTALE. SEZIONE ROMANZA
AION-SS . . . . ANNALI. ISTITUTO UNIVERSITARIO ORIENTALE. SEZIONE SLAVA
AIPhO . . . . ANNUAIRE DE L'INSTITUT DE PHILOLOGIE ET D'HISTOIRE ORIENTALES (BRUXELLES)
AIPhOS . . . . ANNUAIRE DE L'INSTITUT DE PHILOLOGIE ET D'HISTOIRE ORIENTALES ET SLAVES (BRUXELLES)
AIPS . . . . ANNUAIRE DE L'INSTITUT DE PHILOLOGIE ET D'HISTOIRE ORIENTALES ET SLAVES (BRUXELLES)
AIR . . . . ADAM INTERNATIONAL REVIEW
Airc Engng . . . . AIRCRAFT ENGINEERING
Air Commerce Bul . . AIR COMMERCE BULLETIN
Air Cond & Refrig N . . AIR CONDITIONING AND REFRIGERATION NEWS
Air Cond Heat & Ven . . AIR CONDITIONING HEATING AND VENTILATING
AIRCR ENG . . . . . . AIRCRAFT ENGINEERING
AirPolAb . . . . AIR POLLUTION ABSTRACTS
Air Poll Cont Assn J . . AIR POLLUTION CONTROL ASSOCIATION. JOURNAL
Air Pollut . . . . AIR POLLUTION
Air Univ Rev . . . . . . AIR UNIVERSITY REVIEW
AirUnLibI . . . . AIR UNIVERSITY LIBRARY INDEX TO MILITARY PERIODICALS
AISD . . . . ANNALI DELL'ISTITUTO DI STUDI DANTESCHI
AISI Steel Prod Man . . AMERICAN IRON AND STEEL INSTITUTE STEEL PRODUCTS MANUAL
AISLN . . . . ANNALI DELL'ISTITUTO SUPERIORE DI SCIENZE E LETTERE DI SANTA CHIERA (NAPOLI)
AISP . . . . ANNALES DE L'INSTITUT SUPERIEUR DE PHILOSOPHIE
AIUN . . . . ANNALI. ISTITUTO UNIVERSITARIO ORIENTALE. SEZIONE GERMANICA
AIUO . . . . ANNALI. ISTITUTO UNIVERSITARIO ORIENTALE, SEZIONE GERMANICA
AIV . . . . ATTI DEL R. INSTITUTO VENETO DI SCIENZE. LETTERE ED ARTI. CLASSE DI SCIENZE MORALI E
               LETTERE
AIVSML . . . . ATTI DEL R. ISTITUTO VENETO DI SCIENZE. LETTERE ED ARTI. CLASSE DI SCIENZE MORALI E
               LETTERE
AJ . . . . ALLIANCE JOURNAL
AJ . . . . ARCHAEOLOGICAL JOURNAL
AJ . . . . ART JOURNAL
AJA . . . . AMERICAN JEWISH ARCHIVES
AJA . . . . AMERICAN JOURNAL OF ARCHAEOLOGY
AJAE . . . . AMERICAN JOURNAL OF AGRICULTURAL ECONOMICS
AJAr . . . . AMERICAN JOURNAL OF ARCHAEOLOGY
AJES . . . . AMERICAN JOURNAL OF ECONOMICS AND SOCIOLOGY
AJFS . . . . AUSTRALIAN JOURNAL OF FRENCH STUDIES
AJHQ . . . . AMERICAN JEWISH HISTORICAL QUARTERLY
AJHS . . . . AMERICAN JEWISH HISTORICAL SOCIETY. PUBLICATIONS
AJIA KEIZAI . . . . . . AJIA KEIZAI. JOURNAL OF THE INSTITUTE OF DEVELOPING ECONOMICS
AJJR . . . . ANNALES DE LA SOCIETE JEAN-JACQUES ROUSSEAU
AJM . . . . ARCHIVO JOSE MARTI (CUBA)
AJN . . . . AMERICAN JOURNAL OF NUMISMATICS
AJOPs . . . . AMERICAN JOURNAL OF ORTHOPSYCHIATRY

AJP . . . . AMERICAN JOURNAL OF PHILOLOGY
AJP . . . . AMERICAN JOURNAL OF PSYCHOANALYSIS
AJPh . . . . AMERICAN JOURNAL OF PHILOLOGY
AJPhil . . . . AMERICAN JOURNAL OF PHILOLOGY
AJPs . . . . AMERICAN JOURNAL OF PSYCHOLOGY
AJPsy . . . . AMERICAN JOURNAL OF PSYCHIATRY
AJPst . . . . AMERICAN JOURNAL OF PSYCHOTHERAPY
AJPsych . . . . AMERICAN JOURNAL OF PSYCHOLOGY
AJS . . . . AMERICAN JOURNAL OF SOCIOLOGY
AJSL . . . . AMERICAN JOURNAL OF SEMITIC LANGUAGES AND LITERATURES
AJT . . . . AMERICAN JOURNAL OF THEOLOGY
AJTh . . . . AMERICAN JOURNAL OF THEOLOGY
AK . . . . ANTIKE KUNST
AK . . . . ATENEUM KAPLANSKIE
Akad d Wiss Denksch Philos-Hist KL . . AKADEMIE DER WISSENSCHAFTEN IN WIEN. PHILOSOPHISCH-HISTORISCHE
          KLASSE. DENKSCHRIFTEN.
Akad d Wiss Sitzungsb Philos-Hist Kl . . AKADEMIE DER WISSENSCHAFTEN IN WIEN. PHILOSOPHISCH-HISTORISCHE
          KLASSE. SITZUNGSBERICHTE
AKAW . . . . ANZEIGER DER KAISERLICH AKADEMIE DER WISSENSCHAFTEN IN WIEN
AKG . . . . ARCHIV FUER KULTURGESCHICHTE
AKK . . . . ARCHIV FUER KATHOLISCHES KIRCHENRECHT
AKKR . . . . ARCHIV FUER KATHOLISCHES KIRCHENRECHT
AKML . . . . ABHANDLUNGEN ZUR KUNST MUSIK UND LITERATURWISSENSCHAFT
AKRON L REV . . . . . AKRON LAW REVIEW
Akust Zh . . . . AKUSTICHESKII ZHURNAL
Akz . . . . AKZENTE
AL . . . . ACTA LINGUISTICA
AL . . . . ALIGHIERI
AL . . . . AMERICAN LITERATURE
AL . . . . ANNALI LATERANENSI
ALA . . . . ANNALES DE LA FACULTE DE LETTRES D'AIX-EN-PROVINCE
ALA . . . . L'AFRIQUE LITTERAIRE ET ARTISTIQUE
Ala Ag Exp . . . . ALABAMA AGRICULTURAL EXPERIMENT STATION. PUBLICATIONS
ALA Bul . . . . AMERICAN LIBRARY ASSOCIATION. BULLETIN
Ala Geol Surv Bull . . ALABAMA GEOLOGICAL SURVEY. BULLETIN
Ala Geol Surv Circ . . ALABAMA GEOLOGICAL SURVEY. CIRCULAR
ALA Hosp Bk Guide . . AMERICAN LIBRARY ASSOCIATION. ASSOCIATION OF HOSPITAL AND INSTITUTION LIBRARIES.
          BOOK GUIDE.
AlaHQ . . . . ALABAMA HISTORICAL QUARTERLY
ALA Intellectual Freedom Newsl . . AMERICAN LIBRARY ASSOCIATION. INTELLECTUAL FREEDOM COMMITTEE
          NEWSLETTER
ALA LAW . . . . ALABAMA LAWYER
Ala Libn . . . . ALABAMA LIBRARIAN
ALA Lib Period Round Table Newsl . . AMERICAN LIBRARY ASSOCIATION. LIBRARY PERIODICALS ROUND TABLE.
          NEWSLETTER
ALA Lib Serv to Labor News . . AMERICAN LIBRARY ASSOCIATION. ADULT SERVICES DIVISION. JOINT COMMITTEE
          ON LIBRARY SERVICE TO LABOR GROUPS. LIBRARY SERVICE TO LABOR NEWSLETTER
Ala L Rev . . . . ALABAMA LAW REVIEW
Al-An . . . . AL-ANDALUS
Ala R . . . . ALABAMA REVIEW
ALA Ref Serv Div . . . AMERICAN LIBRARY ASSOCIATION. REFERENCE SERVICES DIVISION. RQ

Ala Rev . . . . ALABAMA REVIEW
ALASH . . . . ACTA LINGUISTICA ACADEMIAE SCIENTIARUM HUNGARICAE
Alaska Ag Exp . . . . . ALASKA AGRICULTURAL EXPERIMENT STATION. PUBLICATIONS
Alaska Univ Anthrop Pa . . ALASKA. UNIVERSITY. ANTHROPOLOGICAL PAPERS
ALA Wash Newsl . . . AMERICAN LIBRARY ASSOCIATION. WASHINGTON NEWSLETTER
ALAZ . . . . ALA ZURNALS
ALB . . . . ADYAR LIBRARY BULLETIN
Alb . . . . ALBANIA
ALB . . . . ALLGEMEINES LITERATURBLATT
ALB . . . . ALMANACCO LETTERARIO BOMPIANI
ALB . . . . ANNALES DE LA FACULTE DE LETTRES DE BESANCON
ALBANY L R . . . . . . ALBANY LAW REVIEW
ALBER J EDU . . . . . . ALBERTA JOURNAL OF EDUCATIONAL RESEARCH
Alberta J Educ Res . . ALBERTA JOURNAL OF EDUCATIONAL RESEARCH
Alberta L R . . . . . . ALBERTA LAW REVIEW
ALBr . . . . ANUARIO DA LITERATURA BRASILEIRA
Alb Stud . . . . ALBERTINA STUDIEN
Alc . . . . ALCANTARA
ALCGP . . . . ANNALI DEL LICEO CLASSICO GARIBALDI DI PALERMO
A LEAD . . . . ADULT LEADERSHIP
ALet . . . . ARMAS Y LETRAS
ALet . . . . ASPETTI LETTERARI
Alfold . . . . ALFOELD: IRODALMI ES MUVELODESI FOLYOIRAT
Alfred Univ NY State Coll Ceram Mon Rep . . ALFRED UNIVERSITY. NEW YORK STATE. COLLEGE OF CERAMICS, MONTHLY REPORT
ALG . . . . ALGOL
ALGGM . . . . ANNUARIO DEL LICEO GINNASIO G. MAMELI
Alg Log . . . . ALGEBRA AND LOGIC
ALGP . . . . ANNUARIO DEL LICEO GINNASIO STATALE G. PALMIERI
ALH . . . . ACTA LINGUISTICA ACADEMIAE SCIENTIARUM HUNGARICAE
ALH . . . . ACTA LINGUISTICA HAFNIENSIA
ALHa . . . . ACTA LINGUISTICA HAFNIENSIA
ALi . . . . AMOR DI LIBRO
A Lib . . . . AMERICAN LIBRARIES
Alighieri . . . . L'ALIGHIERI
ALIL . . . . ANUAR DE LINGVISTICA SI ISTORIE LITERARA
ALing . . . . ARCHIVUM LINGUISTICUM
ALingHung . . . . . . ACTA LINGUISTICA ACADEMIAE SCIENTIARUM HUNGARICAE
ALitASH . . . . ACTA LITTERARIA ACADEMIAE SCIENTIARUM HUNGARICAE
ALitH . . . . ACTA LITTERARIA ACADEMIAE SCIENTIARUM HUNGARICAE
ALJ . . . . ALEMANNISCHES JAHRBUCH
ALJ . . . . AUSTRALIAN LIBRARY JOURNAL
ALKM . . . . ARCHIV FUER LITERATUR UND KIRCHENGESCHICHTE DES MITTELALTERS
AIL . . . . ALMANACH DES LETTRES
AllaB . . . . ALLA BOTTEGA
ALLCB . . . . ASSOCIATION FOR LITERARY AND LINGUISTIC COMPUTING BULLETIN
ALLEY MUS . . . . . . ALLEY MUSIC
ALLG . . . . ARCHIV FUER LATEINISCHE LEXIKOGRAPHIE UND GRAMMATIK
All the Year . . . . . . ALL THE YEAR ROUND
Allum Nuova Met . . . ALLUMINIO E NUOVA METALLURGIA
ALM . . . . ARCHIVES DES LETTRES MODERNES

ALMA . . . . ARCHIVUM LATINITATIS MEDII AEVI
AlmOAW . . . . ALMANACH DER OESTERREICHISCHEN AKADEMIE DER WISSENSCHAFTEN
ALOS . . . . ANNUAL OF LEEDS UNIVERSITY ORIENTAL SOCIETY
ALPS . . . . ALABAMA LINGUISTIC AND PHILOLOGICAL SERIES
ALQ . . . . ABRAHAM LINCOLN QUARTERLY
ALR . . . . AMERICAN LITERARY REALISM, 1870-1910
ALS . . . . AUSTRALIAN LITERARY STUDIES
ALT . . . . AFRICAN LITERATURE TODAY
ALT . . . . ANNALES DE LA FACULTE DES LETTRES DE TOULOUSE
Alta Freq . . . . ALTA FREQUENZA
ALTA HIST R . . . . . . ALBERTA HISTORICAL REVIEW
ALTAPro . . . . AMERICAN THEOLOGICAL LIBRARY ASSOCIATION. PROCEEDINGS
Alumin Cour . . . . . . ALUMINIUM COURIER
ALUOS . . . . LEEDS UNIVERSITY ORIENTAL SOCIETY. ANNUAL
ALV . . . . ARCHIV FUER LITERATUR UND VOLKSDICHTUNG
ALW . . . . ARCHIV FUER LITURGIEWISSENSCHAFT
AM . . . . ACTA MUSICOLOGICA
AM . . . . ALANTIC MONTHLY
AM . . . . ALMA MATER
AM . . . . AMERICA
AM . . . . AMERICAN MERCURY
AM . . . . AMERICAS
AM . . . . ANNALES DU MIDI
AM . . . . ANNALI MANZONIANI
AM . . . . ARCHIVIO MURATORIANO
AM . . . . ASIA MAJOR
AMA . . . . AMAZING STORIES ANNUAL
AmA . . . . AMERICAN ANNUAL
AmA . . . . AMERICAN ANTHROPOLOGIST
AMA . . . . ATTI E MEMORIE DELL'ARCADIA
Am Acad Arts & Sci Mem . . AMERICAN ACADEMY OF ARTS AND SCIENCES. MEMOIRS
Am Acad Arts & Sci Proc . . AMERICAN ACADEMY OF ARTS AND SCIENCES. PROCEEDINGS
Am Acad Pol & Soc Sci Ann . . AMERICAN ACADEMY OF POLITICAL AND SOCIAL SCIENCE. ANNALS
Am Acad Relig J . . . AMERICAN ACADEMY OF RELIGION. JOURNAL
Am Acad Rome Mem . . AMERICAN ACADEMY IN ROME. MEMOIRS
Am Alma . . . . AMERICAN ALMANAC
AMAM . . . . ATTI E MEMORIE DELL'ACCADEMIA DI SCIENZE, LETTERE ED ARTI DI MODENA
AMan . . . . ACCADEMIA DI MANTOVA, ATTIE E MEMORIE
Am Ann . . . . AMERICANA ANNUAL
Am Ann Deaf . . . . . . AMERICAN ANNALS OF THE DEAF
AM ANTHROP . . . . . AMERICAN ANTHROPOLOGIST
Am Antiq . . . . AMERICAN ANTIQUARIAN
Am Antiq . . . . AMERICAN ANTIQUITY
Am Antiq Soc Proc . . AMERICAN ANTIQUARIAN SOCIETY. PROCEEDINGS
AM ANTIQUIT . . . . . AMERICAN ANTIQUITY
AMAP . . . . ATTI E MEMORIE DELL'ACCADEMIA PATAVINA DI SCIENZE, LETTERE ED ARTI
AMAPe . . . . ATTI E MEMORIE DELL'ACCADEMIA PETRARCA
Am Arch . . . . AMERICAN ARCHITECT
Am Archiv . . . . AMERICAN ARCHIVIST
AM ARCHIVIS . . . . . AMERICAN ARCHIVIST
Am Artist . . . . AMERICAN ARTIST

Am Art J . . . . AMERICAN ART JOURNAL
Am Assn Coll Reg J . . AMERICAN ASSOCIATION OF COLLEGIATE REGISTRARS. JOURNAL
Am Assn Col Teach Educ Yrbk . . AMERICAN ASSOCIATION OF COLLEGES FOR TEACHER EDUCATION. YEARBOOK
Am Assn Pet Geol Bul . . AMERICAN ASSOCIATION OF PETROLEUM GEOLOGISTS. BULLETIN
Am Assn Sch Adm Off Rep . . AMERICAN ASSOCIATION OF SCHOOL ADMINISTRATORS. OFFICIAL REPORT
Am Assn Univ Prof B . . AMERICAN ASSOCIATION OF UNIVERSITY PROFESSORS. BULLETIN
Am Assn Univ Women J . . AMERICAN ASSOCIATION OF UNIVERSITY WOMEN. JOURNAL
American Assoc Arch Blb . . AMERICAN ASSOCIATION OF ARCHITECTURAL BIBLIOGRAPHERS. PAPERS
Am Assoc Pet Geol Bull . . AMERICAN ASSOCIATION OF PETROLEUM GEOLOGISTS. BULLETIN
Am Assoc State Local Hist Bull . . AMERICAN ASSOCIATION FOR STATE AND LOCAL HISTORY. BULLETIN
AMAT . . . . ATTI E MEMORIE DELL'ACCADEMIA TOSCANA, LA COLOMBARIA
Am Aviation . . . . . . AMERICAN AVIATION
Am Bankr L J . . . . . . AMERICAN BANKRUPTCY LAW JOURNAL
AM BANKRUPT . . . . AMERICAN BANKRUPTCY LAW JOURNAL
AM BAR A J . . . . . . AMERICAN BAR ASSOCIATION. JOURNAL
Am Bar Assn J . . . . . AMERICAN BAR ASSOCIATION. JOURNAL
Am Bee J . . . . AMERICAN BEE JOURNAL
Am Behav Sci . . . . AMERICAN BEHAVIORAL SCIENTIST
Am Bibliop . . . . AMERICAN BIBLIOPOLIST
Am Bib Repos . . . . . AMERICAN BIBLICAL REPOSITORY
AM BIOL TEA . . . . . AMERICAN BIOLOGY TEACHER
Am Bk Collec . . . . . . AMERICAN BOOK COLLECTOR
Am Bld . . . . AMERICAN BUILDER
Am Bsns . . . . AMERICAN BUSINESS
Am Bsns Ed . . . . . . AMERICAN BUSINESS EDUCATION
Am Bsns Ed Yrbk . . . AMERICAN BUSINESS EDUCATION YEARBOOK
Am Business . . . . . . AMERICAN BUSINESS
AM BUS LAW . . . . . AMERICAN BUSINESS LAW JOURNAL
AM BUS L J . . . . AMERICAN BUSINESS LAW JOURNAL
Am Butter R . . . . . . AMERICAN BUTTER & CHEESE REVIEW
AmCathHS . . . . AMERICAN CATHOLIC HISTORICAL SOCIETY. RECORDS
Am Cath Q . . . . AMERICAN CATHOLIC QUARTERLY REVIEW
Am Cattle Prod . . . . AMERICAN CATTLE PRODUCER
AM CERAM S . . . . . . AMERICAN CERAMIC SOCIETY. BULLETIN
Am Cer Soc Bul . . . . AMERICAN CERAMIC SOCIETY. BULLETIN
Am Cer Soc J . . . . . . AMERICAN CERAMIC SOCIETY. JOURNAL
Am Chem Soc J . . . . AMERICAN CHEMICAL SOCIETY. JOURNAL
Am Child . . . . AMERICAN CHILD
Am Childh . . . . AMERICAN CHILDHOOD
AM CHORAL R . . . . . AMERICAN CHORAL REVIEW
Am Church Mo . . . . AMERICAN CHURCH MONTHLY
Am Church R . . . . . AMERICAN CHURCH REVIEW
AMCILR . . . . ACTAS Y MEMORIAS DEL CONGRESO INTERNATIONAL DE LINGUISTICA ROMANICA, ACTAS Y
                       MEMORIAS
AMCIM . . . . ACTES ET MEMOIRES DU CONGRES INTERNATIONAL DE LANGUE ET LITTERATURE DU MIDI DE
                       LA FRANCE
AMCISO . . . . ACTES ET MEMOIRES DU CONGRES INTERNATIONAL DES SCIENCES ONOMASTIQUES
AMCIT . . . . ACTES ET MEMOIRES DU CONGRES INTERNATIONAL DE TOPONYMIE
Am City . . . . AMERICAN CITY
Am City (C ed) . . . . AMERICAN CITY (CITY EDITION)
Am City (T & C ed) . . AMERICAN CITY (TOWN AND COUNTRY EDITION)
Am Coll . . . . AMERICAN COLLECTOR

Am Concrete Inst J. AMERICAN CONCRETE INSTITUTE. JOURNAL
Am Concr Inst. Monogr. . AMERICAN CONCRETE INSTITUTE. MONOGRAPH
Am Coop J. . . . . . . AMERICAN CO-OPERATIVE JOURNAL
Am Creamery. . . . . AMERICAN CREAMERY AND POULTRY PRODUCE REVIEW
AM CRIM LAW. . . . . AMERICAN CRIMINAL LAW REVIEW
Am Crim L Q. . . . . . AMERICAN CRIMINAL LAW QUARTERLY
AM CRIM L REV. . . . AMERICAN CRIMINAL LAW REVIEW
AmD. . . . . AMERICAN DIALOG
Am Dairy Prod R. . . AMERICAN DAIRY PRODUCTS REVIEW
AM DAIRY R. . . . . . AMERICAN DAIRY REVIEW
Amdel Bul. . . . . AMDEL (AUSTRALIAN MINERAL DEVELOPMENT LABORATORIES) BULLETIN
Am Dietet Assn J. . . AMERICAN DIETETIC ASSOCIATION. JOURNAL
AMDM. . . . . ATTI E MEMORIE DELLA DEPUTAZIONE DI STORIA PATRIA PER LE ANTICHE PROVINCIE DI MODENA
Am Doc. . . . . AMERICAN DOCUMENTATION
Am Druggist. . . . . . AMERICAN DRUGGIST
Am Druggist Merch. . AMERICAN DRUGGIST MERCHANDISING
AMDSPAM. . . . . . . ATTI E MEMORIE DELLA DEPUTAZIONE DI STORIA PATRIA PER LE ANTICHE PROVINCE MODENESI
AMDSPPM. . . . . . . ATTI E MEMORIE DELLA DEPUTAZIONE DI STORIA PATRIA PER LE PROVINCIE DELLE MARCHE
AM DYE REP. . . . . . AMERICAN DYESTUFF REPORTER
Am Eccles Rev. . . . . AMERICAN ECCLESIASTICAL REVIEW
Am Ecl. . . . . AMERICAN ECLECTIC
Am Econ. . . . . AMERICAN ECONOMIST
Am Econ Assn Bul. . AMERICAN ECONOMIC ASSOCIATION. BULLETIN
Am Econ Assoc Publ. . AMERICAN ECONOMIC ASSOCIATION. PUBLICATIONS
Am Economist. . . . . AMERICAN ECONOMIST
Am Econ Rev. . . . . . AMERICAN ECONOMIC REVIEW
Am Econ R Pa & Proc. . AMERICAN ECONOMIC REVIEW. PAPERS AND PROCEEDINGS
Am Ec Rev. . . . . . . AMERICAN ECONOMIC REVIEW
Am Ed. . . . . AMERICAN EDUCATION
Am Ed Res J. . . . . . AMERICAN EDUCATIONAL RESEARCH JOURNAL
AM EDUC RES. . . . . AMERICAN EDUCATIONAL RESEARCH JOURNAL
Am Egg & Poultry R. . AMERICAN EGG AND POULTRY REVIEW
Am Electrochem Soc Trans. . AMERICAN ELECTRO-CHEMICAL SOCIETY. TRANSACTIONS
Amer. . . . . AMERICAN
Amer Acad Arts & Sci Mem. . AMERICAN ACADEMY OF ARTS AND SCIENCES. MEMOIRS
Amer Acad of Arts and Sciences Proc. . AMERICAN ACADEMY OF ARTS AND SCIENCES. PROCEEDINGS
Amer Anthropol. . . . AMERICAN ANTHROPOLOGIST
Amer Antiq Soc Proc. . AMERICAN ANTIQUARIAN SOCIETY. PROCEEDINGS
Amer Assoc Pet Geol Bull. . AMERICAN ASSOCIATION OF PETROLEUM GEOLOGISTS. BULLETIN
Amer Bookman. . . . BOOKMAN (PUBLISHED IN U.S.A.)
Amer Ceram Soc Bull. . AMERICAN CERAMIC SOCIETY. BULLETIN
Amer Chem Soc Div Fuel Chem Prepr. . AMERICAN CHEMICAL SOCIETY. DIVISION OF FUEL CHEMISTRY. PREPRINTS
Amer Chem Soc Div Org Coatings Plast Chem Prepr. . AMERICAN CHEMICAL SOCIETY. DIVISION OF ORGANIC COATINGS AND PLASTICS CHEMISTRY. PREPRINTS
Amer Chem Soc Div Petrol/Chem Prepr. . AMERICAN CHEMICAL SOCIETY. DIVISION OF PETROLEUM CHEMISTRY. PREPRINTS
Amer Chem Soc Div Polym Chem Prepr. . AMERICAN CHEMICAL SOCIETY. DIVISION OF POLYMER CHEMISTRY. PREPRINTS
Amer Chem Soc Div Water Air Waste Chem Gen Pap. . AMERICAN CHEMICAL SOCIETY. DIVISION OF WATER, AIR AND WASTE CHEMISTRY. GENERAL PAPERS

Amer City . . . . AMERICAN CITY
Amer Concr Inst Monogr . . AMERICAN CONCRETE INSTITUTE. MONOGRAPH
Amer Concr Inst Stand . . AMERICAN CONCRETE INSTITUTE. STANDARDS
Amer Doc . . . . AMERICAN DOCUMENTATION
Amer Dyestuff Rep . . AMERICAN DYESTUFF REPORTER
Amer Eng . . . . AMERICAN ENGINEER
Amer Gas Ass Mon . . AMERICAN GAS ASSOCIATION MONTHLY
Amer Gas Ass Oper Sect Proc . . AMERICAN GAS ASSOCIATION. OPERATING SECTION PROCEEDINGS
Amer Gas J . . . . AMERICAN GAS JOURNAL
Amer Gear Mfr Ass Stand . . AMERICAN GEAR MANUFACTURERS ASSOCIATION. STANDARDS
AmerH . . . . AMERICA: HISTORY AND LIFE
Amer Highways . . . . AMERICAN HIGHWAYS
American Church R . . AMERICAN CHURCH REVIEW
Amer Iron Steel Inst Contrib Met Steel . . AMERICAN IRON AND STEEL INSTITUTE. CONTRIBUTIONS TO THE METALLURGY OF STEEL
Amer Iron Steel Inst Reg Tech Meetings Addresses . . AMERICAN IRON AND STEEL INSTITUTE. REGIONAL TECHNICAL MEETINGS. ADDRESSES
Amer Iron Steel Inst Steel Prod Manual . . AMERICAN IRON AND STEEL INSTITUTE. STEEL PRODUCTS MANUAL
Amer Iron Steel Steel Res Constr Bull . . AMERICAN IRON AND STEEL INSTITUTE. STEEL RESEARCH FOR CONSTRUCTION. BULLETIN
Amer Jour Psych . . . AMERICAN JOURNAL OF PSYCHOLOGY
Amer J Philo . . . . . . AMERICAN JOURNAL OF PHILOLOGY
Amer J Phys . . . . . . AMERICAN JOURNAL OF PHYSICS
Amer J Sci . . . . AMERICAN JOURNAL OF SCIENCE
AmerLitAb . . . . AMERICAN LITERATURE ABSTRACTS
Amer Mach . . . . AMERICAN MACHINIST
Amer Manage Ass Res Stud . . AMERICAN MANAGEMENT ASSOCIATION. RESEARCH STUDY
Amer Mineral . . . . . AMERICAN MINERALOGIST
Amer Oriental Soc Jour . . AMERICAN ORIENTAL SOCIETY. JOURNAL
Amer Pap Ind . . . . . AMERICAN PAPER INDUSTRY
Amer Petrol Inst Div Prod Drilling Prod Pract Pap . . AMERICAN PETROLEUM INSTITUTE. DIVISION OF PRODUCTION, DRILLING AND PRODUCTION PRACTICE. PAPERS
Amer Petrol Inst Stand . . AMERICAN PETROLEUM INSTITUTE. STANDARDS
Amer Phil Quart . . . AMERICAN PHILOSOPHICAL QUARTERLY
Amer Philos Soc Proc . . AMERICAN PHILOSOPHICAL SOCIETY. PROCEEDINGS
Amer Philos Soc Trans . . AMERICAN PHILOSOPHICAL SOCIETY. TRANSACTIONS
AmerS . . . . AMERICAN STUDIES
Amer Sci . . . . AMERICAN SCIENTIST
Amer Soc Abrasive Method Nat Tech Conf Proc . . AMERICAN SOCIETY FOR ABBRASIVE METHODS. NATIONAL TECHNICAL CONFERENCE. PROCEEDINGS
Amer Soc Quality Contr Annu Aircraft Missile Conf Nat Conf Trans . . AMERICAN SOCIETY FOR QUALITY CONTROL. ANNUAL AIRCRAFT AND MISSILE CONFERENCE. NATIONAL CONFERENCE TRANSACTIONS
Amer Soc Quality Contr Tech Conf Trans . . AMERICAN SOCIETY FOR QUALITY CONTROL. ANNUAL TECHNICAL CONFERENCE TRANSACTIONS
Amer Sp . . . . AMERICAN SPEECH
Amer Welding Soc Stand . . AMERICAN WELDING SOCIETY. STANDARDS
Amer Zool . . . . AMERICAN ZOOLOGIST
Am Exporter . . . . . . AMERICAN EXPORTER
AMF . . . . A. MERRITT'S FANTASY MAGAZINE
AmF . . . . THE AMERICAS (ACADEMY OF AMERICAN FRANCISCAN HISTORY)
Am Fabrics . . . . AMERICAN FABRICS

AM FAM PHYS..... AMERICAN FAMILY PHYSICIAN
Am Fam Physician.. AMERICAN FAMILY PHYSICIAN
Am Farm Bur N L... AMERICAN FARM BUREAU FEDERATION. WEEKLY NEWS LETTER
Am Fed.......... AMERICAN FEDERATIONIST
Am Fert......... AMERICAN FERTILIZER AND ALLIED CHEMICALS
Am Flor.......... AMERICAN FLORIST
Am For.......... AMERICAN FORESTS
Am For Serv Jour... AMERICAN FOREIGN SERVICE JOURNAL
Am Fruit Grower... AMERICAN FRUIT GROWER
AM GAS AS M..... AMERICAN GAS ASSOCIATION MONTHLY
Am Gas J........ AMERICAN GAS JOURNAL
Am Geneal....... AMERICAN GENEALOGIST
Am Geog Soc Bul... AMERICAN GEOGRAPHICAL SOCIETY. BULLETIN
Am Geog Soc Jour.. AMERICAN GEOGRAPHICAL SOCIETY. JOURNAL
Am Geophys Union Trans.. AMERICAN GEOPHYSICAL UNION. TRANSACTIONS
AM HARP J....... AMERICAN HARP JOURNAL
AM HEART J...... AMERICAN HEART JOURNAL
Am Heritage...... AMERICAN HERITAGE
Am Highw........ AMERICAN HIGHWAYS
Am Hist Assn Rept.. AMERICAN HISTORICAL ASSOCIATION. REPORTS
Am Hist R........ AMERICAN HISTORICAL REVIEW
Am Hist Rec...... AMERICAN HISTORICAL RECORD
Am Hist Reg...... AMERICAN HISTORICAL REGISTER
Am Hist Rev..... AMERICAN HISTORICAL REVIEW
Am Home........ AMERICAN HOME
Am Homes....... AMERICAN HOMES AND GARDENS
Am Hort......... AMERICAN HORTICULTURIST
Am Hort Mag..... AMERICAN HORTICULTURAL MAGAZINE
AMHR........... ANNUAIRE DU MUSEE D'HISTOIRE DE LA RELIGION ET DE L'ATHEISME
AMid.......... ANNALES DU MIDI
Am Ill.......... AMERICANA ILLUSTRATED
Am Imago....... AMERICAN IMAGO
Am Ind......... AMERICAN INDUSTRIES
AM IND HYG..... AMERICAN INDUSTRIAL HYGIENE ASSOCIATION. JOURNAL
Am Inst Arch J.... AMERICAN INSTITUTE OF ARCHITECTS. JOURNAL
Am Inst Bank Bul... AMERICAN INSTITUTE OF BANKING. BULLETIN
Am Instit Crim Law and Criminol Jour.. AMERICAN INSTITUTE OF CRIMINAL LAW AND CRIMINOLOGY. JOURNAL
Am inst of Instruc.. AMERICAN INSTITUTE OF INSTRUCTION
Am Inst Plan J..... AMERICAN INSTITUTE OF PLANNERS. JOURNAL
Am J Ag Econ..... AMERICAN JOURNAL OF AGRICULTURAL ECONOMICS
AM J AGR EC...... AMERICAN JOURNAL OF AGRICULTURAL ECONOMICS
AM J ANAT....... AMERICAN JOURNAL OF ANATOMY
AM J ARCHAE..... AMERICAN JOURNAL OF ARCHAEOLOGY
AM J ART TH...... AMERICAN JOURNAL OF ART THERAPY
Am J Bot......... AMERICAN JOURNAL OF BOTANY
AM J Card........ AMERICAN JOURNAL OF CARDIOLOGY
Am J Cardiol...... AMERICAN JOURNAL OF CARDIOLOGY
Am J Clin Hypnosis.. AMERICAN JOURNAL OF CLINICAL HYPNOSIS
AM J CLIN N...... AMERICAN JOURNAL OF CLINICAL NUTRITION
Am J Clin Nutr..... AMERICAN JOURNAL OF CLINICAL NUTRITION
Am J Clin Nutrition.. AMERICAN JOURNAL OF CLINICAL NUTRITION

AM J CLIN P . . . . . . AMERICAN JOURNAL OF CLINICAL PATHOLOGY
Am J Clin Pathol . . . AMERICAN JOURNAL OF CLINICAL PATHOLOGY
AM J COMP L . . . . . AMERICAN JOURNAL OF COMPARATIVE LAW
Am J Correction . . . AMERICAN JOURNAL OF CORRECTION
AM J CRIM L . . . . . . AMERICAN JOURNAL OF CRIMINAL LAW
AM J DIG DI . . . . . . AMERICAN JOURNAL OF DIGESTIVE DISEASES
Am J Dig Dis . . . . . . AMERICAN JOURNAL OF DIGESTIVE DISEASES
AM J DIS CH . . . . . . AMERICAN JOURNAL OF DISEASES OF CHILDREN
Am J Dis Child . . . . . AMERICAN JOURNAL OF DISEASES OF CHILDREN
Am J Econ . . . . AMERICAN JOURNAL OF ECONOMICS AND SOCIOLOGY
AM J ECON S . . . . . . AMERICAN JOURNAL OF ECONOMICS AND SOCIOLOGY
Am J Educ . . . . AMERICAN JOURNAL OF EDUCATION
AM J ENOL V . . . . . . AMERICAN JOURNAL OF ENOLOGY AND VITICULTURE
AM J EPIDEM . . . . . AMERICAN JOURNAL OF EPIDEMIOLOGY
Am Jew Arch . . . . . . AMERICAN JEWISH ARCHIVES
Am Jew Hist Q . . . . . AMERICAN JEWISH HISTORICAL QUARTERLY
Am Jew Hist Soc Publ . . AMERICAN JEWISH HISTORICAL SOCIETY. PUBLICATIONS
AM JEWISH H . . . . . AMERICAN JEWISH HISTORICAL QUARTERLY
Am Jew Yr Bk . . . . . AMERICAN JEWISH YEARBOOK
AM J GASTRO . . . . . AMERICAN JOURNAL OF GASTROENTEROLOGY
AM J HOSP P . . . . . . AMERICAN JOURNAL OF HOSPITAL PHARMACY
AM J HU GEN . . . . . AMERICAN JOURNAL OF HUMAN GENETICS
Am J Human Genet . . AMERICAN JOURNAL OF HUMAN GENETICS
Am J Hum Genet . . . AMERICAN JOURNAL OF HUMAN GENETICS
Am J Int Law . . . . . . AMERICAN JOURNAL OF INTERNATIONAL LAW
Am J Int Law Proc . . AMERICAN JOURNAL OF INTERNATIONAL LAW. PROCEEDINGS
AM J JURIS . . . . AMERICAN JOURNAL OF JURISPRUDENCE
AM J LEGAL HIST . . . AMERICAN JOURNAL OF LEGAL HISTORY
Am J Math . . . . AMERICAN JOURNAL OF MATHEMATICS
AM J MED . . . . AMERICAN JOURNAL OF MEDICINE
AM J MED SC . . . . . . AMERICAN JOURNAL OF THE MEDICAL SCIENCES
Am J Med Sci . . . . . . AMERICAN JOURNAL OF THE MEDICAL SCIENCES
AM J MED TE . . . . . . AMERICAN JOURNAL OF MEDICAL TECHNOLOGY
AM J MENT D . . . . . AMERICAN JOURNAL OF MENTAL DEFICIENCY
Am Jnl Archae . . . . . AMERICAN JOURNAL OF ARCHAEOLOGY
Am Jnl Econ & Soc . . AMERICAN JOURNAL OF ECONOMICS AND SOCIOLOGY
Am Jnl Philol . . . . . . AMERICAN JOURNAL OF PHILOLOGY
Am Jnl Soc . . . . AMERICAN JOURNAL OF SOCIOLOGY
Am J Nurs . . . . AMERICAN JOURNAL OF NURSING
Am J Obstet Gynecol . . AMERICAN JOURNAL OF OBSTETRICS AND GYNECOLOGY
AM J OBST G . . . . . . AMERICAN JOURNAL OF OBSTETRICS AND GYNECOLOGY
AM J OCCU T . . . . . . AMERICAN JOURNAL OF OCCUPATIONAL THERAPY
AM J OPHTH . . . . . . AMERICAN JOURNAL OF OPHTHALMOLOGY
Am J Ophthalmol . . . AMERICAN JOURNAL OF OPHTHALMOLOGY
AM J OPTOM . . . . . . AMERICAN JOURNAL OF OPTOMETRY AND PHYSIOLOGICAL OPTICS
AM J ORTHOD . . . . . AMERICAN JOURNAL OF ORTHODONTICS
AM J ORTHOP . . . . . AMERICAN JOURNAL OF ORTHOPSYCHIATRY
AM J ORTHOPSYCH . . AMERICAN JOURNAL OF ORTHOPSYCHIATRY
Am Jour Econ Sociol . . AMERICAN JOURNAL OF ECONOMICS AND SOCIOLOGY
Am Jour Internatl Law . . AMERICAN JOURNAL OF INTERNATIONAL LAW
Am Jour Legal Hist . . AMERICAN JOURNAL OF LEGAL HISTORY

Am Jour Phys Anthropol. . AMERICAN JOURNAL OF PHYSICAL ANTHROPOLOGY
Am Jour Psychiatry. . AMERICAN JOURNAL OF PSYCHIATRY
Am Jour Sociol. . . . . AMERICAN JOURNAL OF SOCIOLOGY
AM J P ANTH. . . . . AMERICAN JOURNAL OF PHYSICAL ANTHROPOLOGY
AM J PATH. . . . . . . AMERICAN JOURNAL OF PATHOLOGY
Am J Pathol. . . . . . AMERICAN JOURNAL OF PATHOLOGY
AM J PHAR E. . . . . . AMERICAN JOURNAL OF PHARMACEUTICAL EDUCATION
AM J PHARM. . . . . AMERICAN JOURNAL OF PHARMACY
Am J Phil. . . . . AMERICAN JOURNAL OF PHILOLOGY
Am J Philol. . . . . . . AMERICAN JOURNAL OF PHILOLOGY
AM J PHYS. . . . . . . AMERICAN JOURNAL OF PHYSICS
Am J Phys Anthrop. . AMERICAN JOURNAL OF PHYSICAL ANTHROPOLOGY
Am J Phys Anthrop ns. . AMERICAN JOURNAL OF PHYSICAL ANTHROPOLOGY. NEW SERIES
Am J Physics. . . . . AMERICAN JOURNAL OF PHYSICS
Am J Physiol. . . . . AMERICAN JOURNAL OF PHYSIOLOGY
AM J PHYSL. . . . . . AMERICAN JOURNAL OF PHYSIOLOGY
AM J PHYS M. . . . . AMERICAN JOURNAL OF PHYSICAL MEDICINE
Am J Phys Med. . . . AMERICAN JOURNAL OF PHYSICAL MEDICINE
Am J Pol. . . . . AMERICAN JOURNAL OF POLITICS
AM J POL SC. . . . . AMERICAN JOURNAL OF POLITICAL SCIENCE
Am J Psych. . . . . . AMERICAN JOURNAL OF PSYCHIATRY
AM J PSYCHA. . . . . AMERICAN JOURNAL OF PSYCHOANALYSIS
AM J PSYCHI. . . . . . AMERICAN JOURNAL OF PSYCHIATRY
Am J Psychiatry. . . AMERICAN JOURNAL OF PSYCHIATRY
AM J PSYCHO. . . . . AMERICAN JOURNAL OF PSYCHOLOGY
Am J Psychoanal. . . AMERICAN JOURNAL OF PSYCHOANALYSIS
Am J Psychol. . . . . AMERICAN JOURNAL OF PSYCHOLOGY
Am J Psychother. . . AMERICAN JOURNAL OF PSYCHOTHERAPY
AM J PSYCHT. . . . . AMERICAN JOURNAL OF PSYCHOTHERAPY
AM J PUB HE. . . . . . AMERICAN JOURNAL OF PUBLIC HEALTH
Am J Public Health. . AMERICAN JOURNAL OF PUBLIC HEALTH
AM J ROENTG. . . . . AMERICAN JOURNAL OF ROENTGENOLOGY
Am J Roentgenol Radium Ther Nucl Med. . AMERICAN JOURNAL OF ROENTGENOLOGY, RADIUM THERAPY AND NUCLEAR MEDICINE
Am J School Hygiene. . AMERICAN JOURNAL OF SCHOOL HYGIENE
Am J Sci. . . . . AMERICAN JOURNAL OF SCIENCE
Am J Sem Lang. . . . AMERICAN JOURNAL OF SEMITIC LANGUAGES AND LITERATURES
Am J Soc. . . . . AMERICAN JOURNAL OF SOCIOLOGY
Am J Soc Sci. . . . . . AMERICAN JOURNAL OF SOCIAL SCIENCE
AM J SURG. . . . . . AMERICAN JOURNAL OF SURGERY
Am J Theol. . . . . . . AMERICAN JOURNAL OF THEOLOGY
AM J TROP M. . . . . AMERICAN JOURNAL OF TROPICAL MEDICINE AND HYGIENE
Am J Trop Med Hyg. . AMERICAN JOURNAL OF TROPICAL MEDICINE AND HYGIENE
AM J VET RE. . . . . . AMERICAN JOURNAL OF VETERINARY RESEARCH
AmL. . . . . AMOR DI LIBRO
Am Labor Leg R. . . . AMERICAN LABOR LEGISLATION REVIEW
Am Law R. . . . . . . AMERICAN LAW REVIEW
Am Lib. . . . . AMERICAN LIBRARIES
Am Lib Assn Bul. . . . AMERICAN LIBRARY ASSOCIATION. BULLETIN
AmLit. . . . . AMERICAN LITERATURE
Am Lit M. . . . . AMERICAN LITERARY MAGAZINE

Am Lit Realism. . . . AMERICAN LITERARY REALISM 1870-1910
Am Livestock J. . . . AMERICAN LIVESTOCK JOURNAL
Am M. . . . . AMERICAN MAGAZINE
AmM. . . . . AMERICAN MERCURY
Am Mach. . . . . . . AMERICAN MACHINIST
Am Mag. . . . . AMERICAN MAGAZINE
Am Mag Art. . . . . . AMERICAN MAGAZINE OF ART
Am Management R. . AMERICAN MANAGEMENT REVIEW
Am M Art. . . . . AMERICAN MAGAZINE OF ART
Am Math Mo. . . . . . AMERICAN MATHEMATICAL MONTHLY
Am Math Soc Bul. . . AMERICAN MATHEMATICAL SOCIETY. BULLETIN
Am Math Soc Memoirs. . AMERICAN MATHEMATICAL SOCIETY. MEMOIRS
Am M Civics. . . . . . AMERICAN MAGAZINE OF CIVICS
Am Med Assn J. . . . AMERICAN MEDICAL ASSOCIATION. JOURNAL
AmMerc. . . . . AMERICAN MERCURY
Am Mercury. . . . . . AMERICAN MERCURY
Am Meth M. . . . . . . AMERICAN METHODIST MAGAZINE
Am Micros Soc Trans. . AMERICAN MICROSCOPICAL SOCIETY. TRANSACTIONS
Am Midl Nat. . . . . . AMERICAN MIDLAND NATURALIST
Am Milk R. . . . . AMERICAN MILK REVIEW
Am Min. . . . . AMERICAN MINERALOGIST
AM MINERAL. . . . . . AMERICAN MINERALOGIST
Am Mo M. . . . . AMERICAN MONTHLY MAGAZINE
Am Mo R. . . . . AMERICAN MONTHLY REVIEW
Am Mus Dgt. . . . . . AMERICAN MUSICAL DIGEST
Am Musicol Soc J. . . AMERICAN MUSICOLOGICAL SOCIETY. JOURNAL
AM MUS TCR. . . . . . AMERICAN MUSIC TEACHER
AM MUS TEACH. . . . THE AMERICAN MUSIC TEACHER
AMN. . . . . AMAZING STORIES SCIENCE FICTION NOVELS
AMN. . . . . ANALECTA MEDIAEVALIA NAMURCENSIA
Am N & Q. . . . . . . AMERICAN NOTES AND QUERIES
Am Nat. . . . . AMERICAN NATURALIST
Am Natural. . . . . . AMERICAN NATURALIST
Am Neptune. . . . . . AMERICAN NEPTUNE
Am Notes & Queries. . AMERICAN NOTES AND QUERIES
AMNP. . . . . ANNUAIRE DU MUSEE NATIONAL ARCHEOLOGIQUE DE PLOVDIV
Am Num Soc Mus Notes. . AMERICAN NUMISMATIC SOCIETY. MUSEUM NOTES
Am Nut J. . . . . AMERICAN NUT JOURNAL
AMo. . . . . ATLANTIC MONTHLY
Am Oil Chem Soc J. . AMERICAN OIL CHEMISTS' SOCIETY JOURNAL
AMon. . . . . ANALECTA MONASTICA
AMontserr. . . . . . . ANALECTA MONTSERRATENSIA
Am Opinion. . . . . . AMERICAN OPINION
Am Org. . . . . AMERICAN ORGANIST
Am Orient Soc J. . . . AMERICAN ORIENTAL SOCIETY. JOURNAL
AmOx. . . . . AMERICAN OXONIAN
Amp. . . . . AMPURIAS
Am P Advocate. . . . AMERICAN POULTRY ADVOCATE
Am Pap Ind. . . . . . AMERICAN PAPER INDUSTRY
Am Perfumer. . . . . AMERICAN PERFUMER AND COSMETICS
Am Perfumer & Aromatics. . AMERICAN PERFUMER AND AROMATICS

Am Pet Inst Bul.... AMERICAN PETROLEUM INSTITUTE. BULLETIN
Am Pet Inst Proc... AMERICAN PETROLEUM INSTITUTE. PROCEEDINGS
Am Philos Q...... AMERICAN PHILOSOPHICAL QUARTERLY
Am Philos Soc Lib Bull.. AMERICAN PHILOSOPHICAL SOCIETY. LIBRARY BULLETIN
Am Philos Soc Proc.. AMERICAN PHILOSOPHICAL SOCIETY. PROCEEDINGS
Am Philos Soc Trans.. AMERICAN PHILOSOPHICAL SOCIETY. TRANSACTIONS
Am Philos Soc Yearbook.. AMERICAN PHILOSOPHICAL SOCIETY. YEARBOOK
Am Phot......... AMERICAN PHOTOGRAPHY
Am Phys Ed Assn Res Q.. AMERICAN PHYSICAL EDUCATION ASSOCIATION. RESEARCH QUARTERLY
Am Phys Educ R.... AMERICAN PHYSICAL EDUCATION REVIEW
Am P J.......... AMERICAN POULTRY JOURNAL
AM POLI SCI...... AMERICAN POLITICAL SCIENCE REVIEW
AM POLIT Q...... AMERICAN POLITICS QUARTERLY
Am Pol Sci R...... AMERICAN POLITICAL SCIENCE REVIEW
Am Pom Soc Pro... AMERICAN POMOLOGICAL SOCIETY. PROCEEDINGS
Am Potato J...... AMERICAN POTATO JOURNAL
Am Poultry J..... AMERICAN POULTRY JOURNAL
Am Prefs........ AMERICAN PREFACES
Am Presb R....... AMERICAN PRESBYTERIAN REVIEW
Am Prod R....... AMERICAN PRODUCE REVIEW
AM-Ps.......... ANNALES MEDICO-PSYCHOLOGIQUES
Am Psychoanal Assn J.. AMERICAN PSYCHOANALYTIC ASSOCIATION. JOURNAL
Am Psychol....... AMERICAN PSYCHOLOGIST
AMQ........... AMAZING STORIES QUARTERLY
Am Q........... AMERICAN QUARTERLY
Am Q........... AMERICAN QUARTERLY REVIEW(1827-1837)
Am Q Obs....... AMERICAN QUARTERLY OBSERVER
Am Q Reg....... AMERICAN QUARTERLY REGISTER
Am Quar........ AMERICAN QUARTERLY
AMR........... AMAZING STORIES QUARTERLY REISSUE
Am R.......... AMERICAN REVIEW
AMRAC......... ANNALES DU MUSEE ROYAL DE L'AFRIQUE CENTRALE
Am Railw Eng Assoc Bull.. AMERICAN RAILWAY ENGINEERING ASSOCIATION. BULLETIN
AM REC G....... AMERICAN RECORD GUIDE
Am Rec Guide..... AMERICAN RECORD GUIDE
AM RECORDER..... AMERICAN RECORDER
Am Record Gd..... AMERICAN RECORD GUIDE
Am Rev......... AMERICAN REVIEW
Am Rev Resp Dis... AMERICAN REVIEW OF RESPIRATORY DISEASE
AMrhKG......... ARCHIV FUER MITTELRHEINISCHE KIRCHENGESCHICHTE
AM R RESP D...... AMERICAN REVIEW OF RESPIRATORY DISEASES
AmS............ AMERICAN SPEECH
AmS............ AMERICAN STUDIES
AMS............ AMERICAS: A QUARTERLY REVIEW OF INTER-AMERICAN CULTURAL HISTORY
AMS............ AMERICAN MUSICOLOGICAL SOCIETY. JOURNAL
AMS............ JOSEPH QUINCY ADAMS MEMORIAL STUDIES
AMSAC......... AMSAC (AMERICAN SOCIETY FOR AFRICAN CULTURE) NEWSLETTER
AMSAPM........ ATTI E MEMORIE DELLA DEPUTAZIONE DI STORIA PATRIA PER LE ANTICHE PROVINCIE MODENESI
Am Scand R....... AMERICAN-SCANDINAVIAN REVIEW
Am Sch & Univ..... AMERICAN SCHOOL AND UNIVERSITY

Am Sch Bd J...... AMERICAN SCHOOL BOARD JOURNAL
Am Scholar....... AMERICAN SCHOLAR
Am Sch Orient Res Bul.. AMERICAN SCHOOLS OF ORIENTAL RESEARCH. BULLETIN
AM SCIENT....... AMERICAN SCIENTIST
AMSDSP......... ATTI E MEMORIE DELLA SOCIETA DALMATA DI STORIA
AMSER.......... ATTI E MEMORIE DELLA R. DEPUTAZIONE DI STORIA PATRIA PER L'EMILIA ET LA ROMAGNA
Am Sheep B & W... AMERICAN SHEEP BREEDER AND WOOL GROWER
AMSI.......... ATTI E MEMORIE DELLA SOCIETA ISTRIANA DI ARCHEOLOGIA E STORIA PATRIA
AMSIstriana...... ATTI E MEMORIE DELLA SOCIETA ISTRIANA DI ARCHEOLOGIA E STORIA PATRIA
AMS JL......... AMERICAN MUSICOLOGICAL SOCIETY. JOURNAL
Am Slavic R...... AMERICAN SLAVIC AND EAST EUROPEAN REVIEW
AMSM.......... ATTI ET MEMORIE DELLA R. DEPUTAZIONE DI STORIA PATRIA PER' LE MARCHE
Am Soc Abrasive Methods Natl Tech Conf Proc.. AMERICAN SOCIETY FOR ABRASIVE METHODS, NATIONAL TECHNICAL CONFERENCE. PROCEEDINGS
Am Soc Ag Eng..... AMERICAN SOCIETY OF AGRICULTURAL ENGINEERS. TRANSACTIONS
Am Soc Agron J.... AMERICAN SOCIETY OF AGRONOMY. JOURNAL
Am Soc C E Proc.... AMERICAN SOCIETY OF CIVIL ENGINEERS. PROCEEDINGS
Am Soc Church Hist Papers.. AMERICAN SOCIETY OF CHURCH HISTORY. PAPERS
Am Soc Civil Engineers Trans.. AMERICAN SOCIETY OF CIVIL ENGINEERS. TRANSACTIONS
Am Soc Civil Eng Proc.. AMERICAN SOCIETY OF CIVIL ENGINEERS. PROCEEDINGS
Am Soc Eng Educ COED Trans.. AMERICAN SOCIETY FOR ENGINEERING EDUCATION, COMPUTERS IN EDUCATION DIVISION. TRANSACTIONS
Am Soc Hort Sci J... AMERICAN SOCIETY FOR HORTICULTURAL SCIENCE. JOURNAL
Am Soc Inf Sci J.... AMERICAN SOCIETY OF INFORMATION SCIENCE. JOURNAL
Am Soc Int Law Proc.. AMERICAN SOCIETY OF INTERNATIONAL LAW. PROCEEDINGS
Am Soc Int L Proc.. AMERICAN SOCIETY OF INTERNATIONAL LAW. PROCEEDINGS
AM SOCIOL....... AMERICAN SOCIOLOGIST
Am Sociol R...... AMERICAN SOCIOLOGICAL REVIEW
Am Soc Naval Eng J.. AMERICAN SOCIETY OF NAVAL ENGINEERS. JOURNAL
Am Soc Psychical Res J.. AMERICAN SOCIETY FOR PHYSICAL RESEARCH. JOURNAL
Am Soc R......... AMERICAN SOCIOLOGICAL REVIEW
Am Soc Safety Eng J.. AMERICAN SOCIETY OF SAFETY ENGINEERS. JOURNAL
Am Soc Sci J...... AMERICAN JOURNAL OF SOCIAL SCIENCE
Am Sp.......... AMERICAN SPEECH
AMSPR.......... ATTI E MEMORIE DELLA DEPUTAZIONE DI STORIA PATRIA PER LE PROVINCIE DI ROMAGNA
Am Stat Assn J.... AMERICAN STATISTICAL ASSOCIATION. JOURNAL
Am Stat Assoc Quar Publ.. AMERICAN STATISTICAL ASSOCIATION. QUARTERLY PUBLICATIONS
Am Statis Assn.... AMERICAN STATISTICAL ASSOCIATION. QUARTERLY PUBLICATIONS
AM STATISTN..... AMERICAN STATISTICIAN
Amstel.......... AMSTELODAMUM
Am Stud......... AMERICAN STUDIES
AMt............ ANALECTA MONTSERRATENSIA
Am Teach........ AMERICAN TEACHER
Am Theol Lib Assn Newsl.. AMERICAN THEOLOGICAL LIBRARY ASSOCIATION. NEWSLETTER
Am Thresherman... AMERICAN THRESHERMAN
Am Trial Lawyers Assn J.. AMERICAN TRIAL LAWYERS ASSOCIATION. JOURNAL
AMu............ ANNALES MUSICOLOGIQUES
AMUCS......... ANNALES UNIVERSITATIS MARIAE CURIE-SKLODOWSKA. SECTIO F, NAUKI FILOZOFICZNE I HUMANISTYCZNE
Am U L Rev....... AMERICAN UNIVERSITY LAW REVIEW
AMur.......... ARCHIVIO MURATORIANO

AMus . . . . ASIAN MUSIC
Am Veg Grower . . . . AMERICAN VEGETABLE GROWER
Am Vet Med Assn J . . AMERICAN VETERINARY MEDICAL ASSOCIATION. JOURNAL
Am Vet Med Assn Proc . . AMERICAN VETERINARY MEDICAL ASSOCIATION. PROCEEDINGS
Am Voc J . . . . AMERICAN VOCATIONAL JOURNAL
Am Water Works Assn J . . AMERICAN WATER WORKS ASSOCIATION. JOURNAL
Am West . . . . AMERICAN WEST
Am Whig R . . . . . . AMERICAN WHIG REVIEW
AMZ . . . . AMAZING STORIES
Am Zool . . . . AMERICAN ZOOLOGIST
AM ZOOLOG . . . . . . AMERICAN ZOOLOGIST
AN . . . . ACTA NEOPHILOLOGICA
AN . . . . AGE NOUVEAU
AN . . . . AMERICANA NORVEGICA
AN . . . . ART NEWS
AnAB . . . . ANNALES DE LA SOCIETE D'ARCHEOLOGIE DE BRUXELLES
ANABA . . . . ASOCIACION NACIONAL DE BIBLIOTECARIOS, ARQUIVEROS Y ARQUEOLOGOS (MADRID)
AN AC BRASI . . . . . ANAIS DA ACADEMIA BRASILEIRA DE CIENCIAS
Anal Chem . . . . . . ANALYTICAL CHEMISTRY
AnaliFF . . . . ANALI FILOLOSKOG FAKULTETA BEOGGRADSKOG UNIVERZITETA
ANAL LETTER . . . . . . ANALYTICAL LETTERS
Anal M . . . . ANALECTIC MAGAZINE
ANAL PREVIS . . . . . ANALYSE ET PREVISION
Analysts J . . . . ANALYSTS JOURNAL
ANALYT BIOC . . . . . ANALYTICAL BIOCHEMISTRY
ANALYT BIOCHEM . . ANALYTICAL BIOCHEMISTRY
ANALYT CHEM . . . . . ANALYTICAL CHEMISTRY
ANALYT CHIM . . . . . ANALYTICA CHIMICA ACTA
AN ANAT . . . . ANALES DE ANATOMIA
AN&Q . . . . AMERICAN NOTES AND QUERIES
AnAr . . . . ANADOLU ARASTIRMALARI
AN AS QUIM . . . . . . ANALES DE LA ASOCIACION QUIMICA ARGENTINA
ANAT EMBRYO . . . . ANATOMY AND EMBRYOLOGY
ANAT HIS EM . . . . . . ANATOMIA HISTOLOGIA EMBRYOLOGIA/ZENTRALBLATT FUER VETERINARMEDIZIN, REIHE C
ANAT REC . . . . ANATOMICAL RECORD
AnatS . . . . ANATOLIAN STUDIES
AnB . . . . ANIMAL BEHAVIOUR
AnB . . . . ANNALES DE BOURGOGNE
AnBol . . . . ANALECTA BOLLANDIANA
AnBr . . . . ANNALES DE BRETAGNE
AnBret . . . . ANNALES DE BRETAGNE
An Cated Suarez . . . ANALES DE LA CATEDRA FRANCISCO SUAREZ
Anchor Rev . . . . . . ANCHOR REVIEW
And . . . . ANDERSENIANA
AndNewQ . . . . THE ANDOVER NEWTON QUARTERLY
And R . . . . ANDOVER REVIEW
AnE . . . . ANNALES DE L'EST ET DU NORD
AnEN . . . . ANNALES DE L'EST ET DU NORD
ANESTH ANAL . . . . ANESTHESIA AND ANALGESIA
ANESTH AN R . . . . . ANESTHESIE ANALGESIE, REANIMATION
ANESTHESIOL . . . . . . ANESTHESIOLOGY

ANF . . . . ARKIV FOER NORDISK FILOLOGI
AN FISICA . . . . ANALES DE FISICA
AnFP . . . . ANALECTA SACRI ORDINIS FRATRUM PRAEDICATORUM
Ang . . . . ANGLIA
Ang Bbl . . . . ANGLIA BEIBLATT
Angew Bot . . . . ANGEWANDTE BOTANIK
Angew Chem . . . . . . ANGEWANDTE CHEMIE
Angew Inf Appl Inf . . ANGEWANDTE INFORMATIK APPLIED INFORMATICS
ANGEW INFOR . . . . . ANGEWANDTE INFORMATIK
ANGEW MAKRO . . . . ANGEWANDTE MAKROMOLEKULARE CHEMIE
AnglB . . . . ANGLIA BEIBLATT
Angl Bei . . . . ANGLIA BEIBLATT
ANGL ORTHOD . . . . ANGLE ORTHODONTIST
Angl Th R . . . . ANGLICAN THEOLOGICAL REVIEW
Animal Behav . . . . . ANIMAL BEHAVIOUR
Animal Prod . . . . . . ANIMAL PRODUCTION
ANIM LEAR B . . . . . . ANIMAL LEARNING AND BEHAVIOR
ANIM PRODUC . . . . ANIMAL PRODUCTION
AnINA . . . . ANALES DEL INSTITUTO NACIONAL DE ANTROPOLOGIA E HISTORIA. MEXICO
AnIowa . . . . ANNALS OF IOWA
AnkUDerg . . . . ANKARA UNIVERSITESI. DIL VE TARIH COGRAFYA FAKULTESI DERGISI
AnL . . . . ANTHROPOLOGICAL LINGUISTICS
ANLMSF . . . . ACCADEMIA NAZIONALE DEI LINCEI. RENDICONTI DELLA CLASSE DI SCIENZE MORALI,
STORICHE E FILOLOGICHE
AnM . . . . ANNALES DU MIDI
AnM . . . . ANNUALE MEDIAEVALE
AnN . . . . ANNALES DE LA NORMANDIE
AnnAB . . . . ANNUAIRE DE L'ACADEMIE ROYALE DE BELGIQUE
ANN AGRON . . . . . . ANNALES AGRONOMIQUES
ANN ALLERGY . . . . . ANNALS OF ALLERGY
ANNALES-ESC . . . . . ANNALES-ECONOMIES SOCIETES CIVILISATIONS
Annals Am Acad . . . ANNALS OF THE AMERICAN ACADEMY OF POLITICAL AND SOCIAL SCIENCE
Annals Lib Sci . . . . . ANNALS OF LIBRARY SCIENCE
Annals Math Log . . . ANNALS OF MATHEMATICAL LOGIC
Ann Am Acad . . . . . ANNALS OF THE AMERICAN ACADEMY OF POLITICAL AND SOCIAL SCIENCE
ANN AM POLI . . . . . ANNALS OF THE AMERICAN ACADEMY OF POLITICAL AND SOCIAL SCIENCE
ANN ANIM PS . . . . . ANNUAL OF ANIMAL PSYCHOLOGY
Ann Ap Biol . . . . . . ANNALS OF APPLIED BIOLOGY
ANN A PLANT . . . . . ANNALES DE L'AMELIORATION DES PLANTES
ANN AS AM G . . . . . ANNALS OF THE ASSOCIATION OF AMERICAN GEOGRAPHERS
Ann Ass Int Calcul Analogique . . ANNALES DE L'ASSOCIATION INTERNATIONALE POUR LE CALCUL ANALOGIQUE
AnnBhl . . . . ANNALS OF THE BHANDARKAR ORIENTAL RESEARCH INSTITUTE
ANN BIOL AN . . . . . ANNALES DE BIOLOGIE ANIMALE BIOCHIMIE ET BIOPHYSIQUE
ANN BIOL CL . . . . . . ANNALES DE BIOLOGIE CLINIQUE
ANN BIOMED . . . . . ANNALS OF BIOMEDICAL ENGINEERING
Ann Biomed Eng . . . ANNALS OF BIOMEDICAL ENGINEERING
Ann Bot . . . . ANNALS OF BOTANY
AnnBourg . . . . ANNALES DE BOURGOGNE
AnnBret . . . . ANNALES DE BRETAGNE
ANN BRUX I . . . . . . ANNALES DE LE SOCIETE SCIENTIFIQUE DE BRUXELLES. SERIE I
ANN CARD AN . . . . . ANNALES DE CARDIOLOGIE ET D'ANGEIOLOGIE

ANN CHEM . . . . . . ANNALEN DER CHEMIE, JUSTUS LIEBIG
ANN CHIM . . . . . . ANNALI DI CHIMICA
ANN CHIM FR . . . . . ANNALES DE CHIMIE (PARIS, FRANCE)
Ann Chim (Paris) . . . ANNALES DE CHIMIE (PARIS, FRANCE)
ANN CHIR . . . . ANNALES DE CHIRURGIE
ANN CHIR GY . . . . . ANNALES CHIRURGIAE ET GYNAECOLOGIAE FENNIAE
ANN CHIR IN . . . . . . ANNALES DE CHIRURGIE INFANTILE
ANN CHIR PL . . . . . . ANNALES DE CHIRURGIE PLASTIQUE
Ann CIRP . . . . ANNALS OF THE CIRP
ANN CLIN R . . . . . . ANNALS OF CLINICAL RESEARCH
Ann de Bret . . . . . . ANNALES DE BRETAGNE
Ann Dem Hist . . . . . ANNALES DE DEMOGRAPHIE HISTORIQUE
ANN DER SYP . . . . . ANNALES DE DERMATOLOGIE ET DE SYPHLIGRAPHIE
ANN ECON SM . . . . . ANNALS OF ECONOMIC AND SOCIAL MEASUREMENT
ANN ECON SO . . . . . ANNALES D'ECONOMIE ET DE SOCIOLOGIE RURALES
Annee Psychol . . . . . ANNEE PSYCHOLOGIQUE
ANN ENDOCR . . . . . ANNALES D' ENDOCRINOLOGIE
Ann Entom Soc Am . . ANNALS OF THE ENTOMOLOGICAL SOCIETY OF AMERICA
ANN ENT S A . . . . . . ANNALS OF THE ENTOMOLOGICAL SOCIETY OF AMERICA
Ann Est . . . . ANNALES DE L'EST
Ann Esth . . . . ANNALES D'ESTHETIQUE
AnnEth . . . . ANNALES D'ETHIOPIE
Ann Fac Lett Filosof . . ANNALI DELLA FACOLTA DI LETTERE E FILOSOFIA
ANN GASTRO . . . . . . ANNALES DE GASTROENTEROLOGIE ET D' HEPATOLOGIE
ANN GENET . . . . . . ANNALES DE GENETIQUE
ANN GEOFIS . . . . . . ANNALI DI GEOFISICA
Ann Geog . . . . ANNALES DE GEOGRAPHIE
ANN GEOGR . . . . . . ANNALES DE GEOGRAPHIE
ANN GEOPHYS . . . . . ANNALES DE GEOPHYSIQUE
ANN HISTOCH . . . . . ANNALES D' HISTOCHIMIE
AnnHL . . . . ANNUAIRE D'HISTOIRE LIEGEOISE
ANN HUM BIO . . . . . ANNALS OF HUMAN BIOLOGY
ANN HUM GEN . . . . ANNALS OF HUMAN GENETICS
ANN HYDROB . . . . . ANNALES D'HYDROBIOLOGIE
AnnIEO . . . . ANNALES DE L'INSTITUT D'ETUDES ORIENTALES DE LA FACULTE DES LETTRES D'ALGER
AnnIEOc . . . . ANNALES DE L'INSTITUT D'ETUDES OCCIDENTES
ANN I FOUR . . . . ANNALES DE L' INSTITUT FOURIER
ANN I HEN A . . . . . . ANNALES DE L' INSTITUT HENRI POINCARE SECTION A
ANN I HEN B . . . . . . ANNALES DE L' INSTITUT HENRI POINCARE SECTION B
ANN IMMUNOL . . . . ANNALES D' IMMUNOLOGIE
Ann Inst Tech Batim Trav Publics . . ANNALES DE L'INSTITUT TECHNIQUE DU BATIMENT ET DES TRAVAUX PUBLICS
Ann Intern Med . . . . ANNALS OF INTERNAL MEDICINE
ANN INT MED . . . . . ANNALS OF INTERNAL MEDICINE
ANN I OCEAN . . . . . ANNALES DE L' INSTITUT OCEANOGRAPHIQUE
AnnION . . . . ANNALI. ISTITUTO UNIVERSITARIO ORIENTALE (NAPOLI)
Ann Iowa . . . . ANNALS OF IOWA
AnnIPhO . . . . ANNUAIRE DE L'INSTITUT DE PHILOLOGIE ET D'HISTOIRE ORIENTALES ET SLAVES
ANN I STAT . . . . ANNALS OF THE INSTITUTE OF STATISTICAL MATHEMATICS
AnnLat . . . . ANNALI LATERANENSI
AnnMAfrC . . . . ANNALES. MUSEE ROYAL DE L'AFRIQUE CENTRALE
ANN MATH . . . . ANNALS OF MATHEMATICS

AnnMCB-L........ ANNALES DU MUSEE ROYAL DU CONGO BELGE. LINGUISTIQUE
Ann Med......... ANNUALE MEDIAEVALE
Ann Med Hist..... ANNALS OF MEDICAL HISTORY
ANN MED IN...... ANNALES DE MEDECINE INTERNE
ANN MED PSY..... ANNALES MEDICO-PSYCHOLOGIQUES
ANN MICROB..... ANNALES DE MICROBIOLOGIE-INSTITUT PASTEUR
Ann Midi......... ANNALES DU MIDI
Ann Mines .... ANNALES DES MINES
Ann Mines Belg.... ANNALES DES MINES DE BELGIQUE
ANN MO BOT...... ANNALS OF THE MISSOURI BOTANICAL GARDEN
AnnNorm........ ANNALES DE NORMANDIE
Ann Normandie.... ANNALES DE NORMANDIE
ANN NUC ENG..... ANNALS OF NUCLEAR ENERGY
Ann Nucl Sci Engng.. ANNALS OF NUCLEAR SCIENCE ENGINEERING
ANN NUTR AL..... ANNALES DE LA NUTRITION ET DE L' ALIMENTATION
ANN NY ACAD..... ANNALS OF THE NEW YORK ACADEMY OF SCIENCES
Ann NY Acad Sci... ANNALS OF THE NEW YORK ACADEMY OF SCIENCES
ANN OCULIST..... ANNALES D'OCULISTIQUE
Ann Or Napoli..... ANNALI. ISTITUTO UNIVERSITARIO ORIENTALE (NAPOLI)
ANN OTO-LAR..... ANNALES D'OTO-LARYNGOLOGIE ET DE CHIRURGIE CERVICO-FACIALE
ANN OTOL RH..... ANNALS OF OTOLOGY RHINOLOGY AND LARYNGOLOGY
Ann Oto Rhinol Laryngol.. ANNALS OF OTOLOGY, RHINOLOGY AND LARYNGOLOGY
ANN PHARM F..... ANNALES PHARMACEUTIQUES FRANCAISES
ANN PHYS BI...... ANNALES DE PHYSIQUE BIOLOGIQUE ET MEDICALE
ANN PHYSICS..... ANNALS OF PHYSICS
ANN PHYSIK...... ANNALEN DER PHYSIK
ANN PHYSIQ...... ANNALES DE PHYSIQUE
Ann Phys (Leipzig).. ANNALEN DER PHYSIK (LEIPZIG)
Ann Phys (New York).. ANNALS OF PHYSICS (NEW YORK)
Ann Phys (Paris)... ANNALES DE PHYSIQUE (PARIS)
Ann Pol et Litt..... ANNALES POLITIQUES ET LITTERAIRES
Ann Ponts Chaussees.. ANALES DES PONTS ET CHAUSSEES
ANN PROBAB..... ANNALS OF PROBABILITY
AnnPsych........ ANNEE PSYCHOLOGIQUE
ANN PSYCHOL..... ANNEE PSYCHOLOGIQUE
ANN RADIOL...... ANNALES DE RADIOLOGIE
ANN R ANTHR..... ANNUAL REVIEW OF ANTHROPOLOGY
ANN R ASTRO..... ANNUAL REVIEW OF ASTRONOMY AND ASTROPHYSICS
ANN R BIOCH..... ANNUAL REVIEW OF BIOCHEMISTRY
ANN R BIOPH..... ANNUAL REVIEW OF BIOPHYSICS AND BIOENGINEERING
ANN RC SURG..... ANNALS OF THE ROYAL COLLEGE OF SURGEONS OF ENGLAND
ANN R EARTH..... ANNUAL REVIEW OF EARTH AND PLANETARY SCIENCE
ANN R ECOL...... ANNUAL REVIEW OF ECOLOGY AND SYSTEMATICS
Ann Reg......... AMERICAN ANNUAL REGISTER
ANN R ENTOM..... ANNUAL REVIEW OF ENTOMOLOGY
ANN R FLUID...... ANNUAL REVIEW OF FLUID MECHANICS
ANN R GENET..... ANNUAL REVIEW OF GENETICS
ANN RHEUM D..... ANNALS OF THE RHEUMATIC DISEASES
ANN R INFOR...... ANNUAL REVIEW OF INFORMATION SCIENCE AND TECHNOLOGY
ANN R MATER..... ANNUAL REVIEW OF MATERIALS SCIENCE
ANN R MED....... ANNUAL REVIEW OF MEDICINE

ANN R MICRO . . . . . ANNUAL REVIEW OF MICROBIOLOGY
Ann R Nucl . . . . ANNUAL REVIEW OF NUCLEAR SCIENCE
ANN RP CH A . . . . . ANNUAL REPORTS ON PROGRESS OF CHEMISTRY. SECTION A
ANN RP CH B . . . . . . ANNUAL REPORTS ON THE PROGRESS OF CHEMISTRY. SECTION B
ANN R PHARM . . . . ANNUAL REVIEW OF PHARMACOLOGY
ANN R PH CH . . . . . ANNUAL REVIEW OF PHYSICAL CHEMISTRY
ANN R PHYSL . . . . . ANNUAL REVIEW OF PHYSIOLOGY
ANN R PHYTO . . . . . ANNUAL REVIEW OF PHYTOPATHOLOGY
ANN R PLANT . . . . . ANNUAL REVIEW OF PLANT PHYSIOLOGY
ANN R PSYCH . . . . . ANNUAL REVIEW OF PSYCHOLOGY
AnnS . . . . ANNALES SILESIAE
ANN SCI . . . . ANNALS OF SCIENCE
Ann Sci Agron . . . . . ANNALES DE LA SCIENCE AGRONOMIQUE
ANN SCI EC . . . . . . ANNALES SCIENTIFIQUES DE L' ECOLE NORMALE SUPERIEURE
ANN SCLAVO . . . . . . ANNALI SCLAVO
Ann Scu Archeol Atene . . ANNUARIO DELLA SCUOLA ARCHEOLOGICA DI ATENE E DELLE MISSIONI ITALIANE IN ORIENTE
Ann Seminar Metaf . . ANNALES DEL SEMINARIO DE METAFISICA
Ann Serv . . . . ANNALES DU SERVICE DES ANTIQUITES DE L'EGYPTE
ANN SOC ENT . . . . . ANNALES DE LA SOCIETE ENTOMOLOGIQUE DE FRANCE
Ann Soc Geol Belg . . ANNALES DE LA SOCIETE GEOLOGIQUE DE BELGIQUE
Ann Soc Geol Belg Mem . . ANNALES DE LA SOCIETE GEOLOGIQUE DE BELGIQUE. MEMOIRES
AnnSR . . . . ANNALES DE LA SOCIETA RETORUMANTSCHA
ANN STATIST . . . . . . ANNALS OF STATISTICS
ANN SURG . . . . ANNALS OF SURGERY
ANN TEC AGR . . . . . ANNALES DE TECHNOLOGIE AGRICOLE
ANN TELECOM . . . . . ANNALES DES TELECOMMUNICATIONS
AnnThijm . . . . ANNALEN VAN HET THIJMGENOOTSCHAP
ANN THORAC . . . . . ANNALS OF THORACIC SURGERY
Ann Thorac Surg . . . ANNALS OF THORACIC SURGERY
Ann Trav Publics Belg . . ANNALES DES TRAVAUX PUBLICS DE BELGIQUE
AnnTriest . . . . ANNALI TRIESTINI
ANN TROP M . . . . . . ANNALS OF TROPICAL MEDICINE AND PARASITOLOGY
AnnUA . . . . ANNALS OF THE UKRAINIAN ACADEMY OF ARTS AND SCIENCES IN THE U.S.
AnnUP . . . . ANNALES DE L'UNIVERSITE DE PARIS
Annu Rev Nucl Sci . . ANNUAL REVIEW OF NUCLEAR SCIENCE
ANN UROL . . . . ANNALES D' UROLOGIE
AnnUS . . . . ANNALES UNIVERSITATIS SARAVIENSIS. PHILOSOPHIE-LETTRES
ANN ZOOTECH . . . . . ANNALES DE ZOOTECHNIE
ANOH . . . . AARBOEGER FOER NORDISK OLDKYNDIGHED OG HISTORIE
AnP . . . . ANNE PROPEDEUTIQUE
AnPC . . . . ANNALES DE LA PHILOSOPHIE CHRETIENNE
AnPraem . . . . ANALECTA PRAEMONSTRATENSIA
ANQ . . . . AMERICAN NOTES AND QUERIES
AN QUIMICA . . . . . . ANALES DE QUIMICA
ANS . . . . ARCHIV FUER DAS STUDIUM DER NEUEREN SPRACHEN
ANSDSL . . . . AUSTRALISCH-NEUSEELAENDISCHE STUDIEN ZUR DEUTSCHEN SPRACHE UND LITERATUR
ANSI Stand . . . . ANSI (AMERICAN NATIONAL STANDARDS INSTITUTE) STANDARDS
ANSMusN . . . . AMERICAN NUMISMATIC SOCIETY MUSEUM NOTES
ANSN . . . . AMERICAN NUMISMATIC SOCIETY MUSEUM NOTES
ANSSSR . . . . AKADEMIJA NAUK SSSR

AnST . . . . ANALECTA SACRA TARRACONENSIA
ANT . . . . ALTALANOS NYELVESZETI TANULMANYOK
Ant . . . . ANTAIOS
Ant . . . . ANTIKE
ANTARCTIC J . . . . . ANTARCTIC JOURNAL OF THE UNITED STATES
AntAS . . . . ANTIKE, ALTE SPRACHEN UND DEUTSCHE BILDUNG
Ant Bk . . . . ANTIQUARIAN BOOKMAN
AntC . . . . L'ANTIQUITE CLASSIQUE
AnthL . . . . ANTHROPOLOGICAL LINGUISTICS
AnthQ . . . . ANTHROPOLOGICAL QUARTERLY
Anth Quart . . . . ANTHROPOLOGICAL QUARTERLY
Anthr . . . . ANTHROPOS
ANTHR J CAN . . . . . ANTHROPOLOGICAL JOURNAL OF CANADA
ANTHR KOZL . . . . . . ANTHROPOLOGIAIE KOZLEMENYK-ANTHROPOLOGICAL COMMUNICATIONS
ANTHR LING . . . . . . ANTHROPOLOGICAL LINGUISTICS
Anthrop Gesell Wien Mitt . . ANTHROPOLOGISCHE GESELLSCHAFT IN WIEN. MITTEILUNGEN
Anthrop J . . . . ANTHROPOLOGICAL INSTITUTE. JOURNAL
Anthropol Anz . . . . . ANTHROPOLOGISCHER ANZEIGER
Anthrop Q . . . . ANTHROPOLOGICAL QUARTERLY
Anthrop R . . . . ANTHROPOLOGICAL REVIEW
ANTHR PAP . . . . ANTHROPOLOGICAL PAPERS OF THE AMERICAN MUSEUM OF NATURAL HISTORY
ANTHRPLGICA . . . . . ANTHROPOLOGICA
ANTHR P MIC . . . . . ANTHROPOLOGICAL PAPERS. MUSEUM OF ANTHROPOLOGY. UNIVERSITY OF MICHIGAN
ANTHR Q . . . . ANTHROPOLOGICAL QUARTERLY
ANTHR UCLA . . . . . . ANTHROPOLOGY-UCLA
AntHung . . . . ANTIQUITAS HUNGARICA
ANTI-CORROS . . . . . ANTI-CORROSION METHODS AND MATERIALS
AntigR . . . . ANTIGONISH REVIEW
ANTIM AG CH . . . . . ANTIMICROBIAL AGENTS AND CHEMOTHERAPY
Antioch R . . . . ANTIOCH REVIEW
ANTIQ . . . . ANTIQUES
Antiq . . . . ANTIQUITY
Antiq Bkman . . . . . . ANTIQUARIAN BOOKMAN
Antiq Gesell in Zuerich Mitt . . ANTIQUARISCHE GESELLSCHAFT IN ZUERICH. MITTEILUNGEN
Antiq J . . . . ANTIQUARIES JOURNAL
Antiq Jnl . . . . ANTIQUARIES JOURNAL
Antiq n s . . . . ANTIQUARY (NEW SERIES)
ANTIQUAR J . . . . . . ANTIQUARIES JOURNAL
Antiquary . . . . ANTIQUARY, JEWITT'S
ANTITRUST L & ECON REV . . . . ANTITRUST LAW AND ECONOMICS REVIEW
Antitrust L Sym . . . . ANTITRUST LAW SYMPOSIUM
AntJ . . . . ANTIQUARIES JOURNAL
Anton . . . . ANTONIANUM
ANT R . . . . ANTIOCH REVIEW
Antrol . . . . ANTHROPOLOGICAL INDEX
ANTROPOLOGI . . . . ANTHROPOLOGICA
ANTS . . . . ANGLO-NORMAN TEXT SOCIETY
ANTsW . . . . ALGEMEEN NEDERLANDS TIJDSCHRIFT VOOR WIJSBEGEERTE EN PSYCHOLOGIE
Antw . . . . ANTWERPIENSIA
AnU . . . . ANALES DE LA UNIVERSIDAD
AnuarioF . . . . ANUARIO DE FILOLOGIA

PERIODICAL TITLE ABBREVIATIONS

AnUBLG......... ANALELE UNIVERSITATII BUCURESTI. LIMBI GERMANICE
AnUBLUC........ ANALELE UNIVERSITATII BUCURESTI. LITERATURA UNIVERSALA SI COMPARATA
Anu Filosof....... ANUARIO FILOSOFICO
AnUG.......... ANNALES DE L'UNIVERSITE DE GRENOBLE
AnUILingv........ ANALELE STIINTIFICE ALE UNIVERSITATII 'AL. IL CUZA' DIN IASI. (SERIE NOUA) SECTIUNEA III. (STIINTE SOCIALE) E. LINGVISTICA
AnUILit.......... ANALELE STIINTIFICE ALE UNIVERSITATII 'AI. I. CUZA' DIN IASI. (SERIE NOUA) SECTUINEA III. F. LITERATURA
AnUL........... ANNALES DE L'UNIVERSITE DE LYON
ANU MUS........ ANUARIO MUSICAL
AnUTFil......... ANALELE UNIVERSITATII DIN TIMISOARA. SERIA STIINTE FILOLOGICE
ANVA.......... AVHANDLINGER UTGITT AV NORSK VIDENSKAPS-AKADEMI I OSLO
ANVAO......... AVHANDLINGER UTGITT AV NORSK VIDENSKAPS-AKADEMI I OSLO II
Anz Altertumsw... ANZEIGER FUER ALTERTUMSWISSENSCHAFT
Anz f d Altert..... ANZEIGER FUER DEUTSCHES ALTERTUM
AO............. ALANDSK ODLING: ARSBOK
AO............. AMERICAN OXONIAN
AO............. ARCHIV ORIENTALNI
AOASH......... ACTA ORIENTALIA ACADEMIAE SCIENTIARUM HUNGARICAE
AOAW.......... ANZEIGER DER OESTERREICHISCHEN AKADEMIE DER WISSENSCHAFTEN PHILOSOPHISCH-HISTORISCHE KLASSE
AODNS......... ACTA ORIENTALIA
AOF............ ARCHIV FUER ORIENTFORSCHUNG
AOG........... ARCHIV FUER OESTERREICHISCHE GESCHICHTE
AOH........... ACTA ORIENTALIA ACADEMIAE SCIENTIARUM HUNGARICAE
AOP........... ANALECTES DE L'ORDRE DE PREMONTRE
AOP........... ANALYSER OG PROBLEMER
AOP........... ARCHIVUM ORIENTALE PRAGENSE
AOR........... ANNALS OF ORIENTAL RESEARCH
AOR........... ANUARI DE L'OFICINA ROMANICA
AOrientHung...... ACTA ORIENTALIA ACADEMIAE SCIENTIARUM HUNGARICAE
AORN J......... ASSOCIATION OF OPERATION ROOM NURSES. JOURNAL
AP............. AMERICAN PSYCHOLOGIST
AP............. ANNALEN DER PHILOSOPHIE UND PHILOSOPHISCHEN KRITIK
AP............. ANTHROPOLOGICAL PAPERS (SMITHSONIAN INST.)
Ap............. APRIL
AP............. ARS POETICA
AP............. ARYAN PATH
AP............. AUREA PARMA
APAA.......... ATTI DELLA PONTIFICIA ACCADEMIA ROMANA DI ARCHEOLOGIA
APar........... AUREA PARMA
APARAR........ ATTI DELLA PONTIFICIA ACCADEMIA ROMANA DI ARCHEOLOGIA. RENDICONTI
APAVE......... APAVE, REVUE TECHNIQUE DU GROUPEMENT DES ASSOCIATIONS DE PROPRIETAIRES D' APPAREILS A VAPEUR ET ELECTRIQUES
APAW.......... ABHANDLUNGEN DER PREUSSISCHEN AKADEMIE DER WISSENSCHAFT
APC........... ANNALES DE LA PHILOSOPHIE CHRETIENNE
APen.......... ANIMA PENSIERO
APF............ ARCHIV FUER PAPYRUS FORSCHUNG UND VERWANDTE GEBIETE
APG........... ARCHIV FUER POLITIK UND GESCHICHTE
APh........... ACTA PHILOLOGICA. SOCIETAS ACADEMICA DACOROMANA
APH........... ACTA POLONIAE HISTORICA

APhAP.......... ARCHIVES DE PHILOLOGIE DE L'ACADEMIE POLONAISE DES SCIENCES ET DES LETTRES
APhD........... ACTA PHILOLOGICA SOCIETAS ACADEMICA DACOROMANA
APhilos.......... ARCHIVES DE PHILOSOPHIE
APhS............ ACTA PHILOLOGICA SCANDINAVICA. TIDSSKRIFT FOER NORDISK SPROGFORSKNING
API............. ALTERNATIVE PRESS INDEX
API............. ANNALI DELLA PUBBLICA ISTRUZIONE
APK............ AUFSAETZE ZUR PORTUGIESISCHEN KULTURGESCHICHTE
APL............ ANCIEN PAYS DE 1007
APL............ ANNALES POLITIQUES ET LITTERAIRES
APL............ ANNALES PRINCE DE LIGNE
ApL............ APPRODO LETTERARIO
APL............ ARCHIVO DE PREHISTORIA LEVANTINA
APLA Bull........ ATLANTIC PROVINCES LIBRARY ASSOCIATION. BULLETIN
APM............ ANUARIO DE PREHISTORIA MADRILENA
ApMec.......... APPLIED MECHANICS REVIEW
ApMicrobiol...... APPLIED MICROBIOLOGY
APMS.......... ALTPREUSSISCHE MONATSCHRIFT
Apo............ APOLLO
AP OPTICS....... APPLIED OPTICS
APP............ APPROACH
App Anal........ APPLICABLE ANALYSIS
APPL ECON....... APPLIED ECONOMICS
Appl Electr Phenom.. APPLIED ELECTRICAL PHENOMENA
APPL ERGON...... APPLIED ERGONOMICS
Appleton......... APPLETON'S JOURNAL
Appl Math Mech... APPLIED MATHEMATICS AND MECHANICS
APPL MATH O..... APPLIED MATHEMATICS AND OPTIMIZATION
Appl Mech Rev.... APPLIED MECHANICS REVIEWS
APPL MICROB..... APPLIED MICROBIOLOGY
APPL NEUROP..... APPLIED NEUROPHYSIOLOGY
Appl Opt........ APPLIED OPTICS
APPL PHYS....... APPLIED PHYSICS
APPL PHYS L...... APPLIED PHYSICS LETTERS
Appl Plast........ APPLIED PLASTICS
Appl Polym Symp... APPLIED POLYMER SYMPOSIA
APPL SCI RE...... APPLIED SCIENTIFIC RESEARCH
Appl Sci Res (The Hague).. APPLIED SCIENTIFIC RESEARCH (THE HAGUE)
APPL SPECTR...... APPLIED SPECTROSCOPY
APPL SP REV...... APPLIED SPECTROSCOPY REVIEWS
Appl Stat......... APPLIED STATISTICS
App Math & Mech.. APPLIED MATHEMATICS AND MECHANICS
App Microbiol..... APPLIED MICROBIOLOGY
App Optics....... APPLIED OPTICS
APPP.......... ABHANDLUNGEN ZUR PHILOSOPHIE, PSYCHOLOGIE UND PADAGOGIK
App Phys........ APPLIED PHYSICS
APQ............ AMERICAN PHILOSOPHICAL QUARTERLY
APR............ AMERICAN POETRY REVIEW
APr............ ANALECTA PRAEMONSTRATENSIA
APraem......... ANALECTA PRAEMONSTRATENSIA
APRA J......... APRA (AUSTRALIAN PERFORMING RIGHT ASSOCIATION) JOURNAL
APrF........... ALTPREUSSISCHE FORSCHUNGEN

APS........... ACTA PHILOLOGICA SCANDINAVICA
APS........... AMERICAN PHILOSOPHICAL SOCIETY. PROCEEDINGS
APs........... AMERICAN PSYCHOLOGIST
APS........... HSIN-LI HSUEH-PAO (ACTA PSYCHOLOGICA SINICA)
APSL........... AMSTERDAMER PUBLIKATIONEN ZUR SPRACHE UND LITERATUR
APSR........... AMERICAN POLITICAL SCIENCE REVIEW
APSS........... AMERICAN ACADEMY OF POLITICAL AND SOCIAL SCIENCE. ANNALS
APsych.......... ACTA PSYCHOLOGICA
AQ............. AMAZING STORIES QUARTERLY
AQ............. AMERICAN QUARTERLY
AQ............. ARIZONA QUARTERLY
AQ............. ART QUARTERLY
AQ............. ATLANTIC QUARTERLY
AQ............. AUSTRALIAN QUARTERLY
Aqua Biol Ab...... AQUATIC BIOLOGY ABSTRACTS
AR............. ACCOUNTING REVIEW
AR............. ALABAMA REVIEW
AR............. AMERICAN REVIEW
AR............. ANTIOCH REVIEW
AR............. ANTIQUITAETEN-RUNDSCHAU
AR............. ARCHAEOLOGICAL REPORTS
Ar............. ARCHE
AR............. ARCHITECTURAL REVIEW
AR............. ARCHIV FUER REFORMATIONSGESCHICHTE
Ar............. ARCHIVIO
AR............. ARCHIVUM ROMANICUM
Ar............. ARENA
ARABAn........ ACADEMIE ROYALE D'ARCHEOLOGIE DE BELGIQUE. ANNALES
ARABBull........ ACADEMIE ROYALE D'ARCHEOLOGIE DE BELGIQUE. BULLETIN
ArabW.......... ARAB WORLD
ARAI........... ANNUARIO DELLA R. ACCADEMIA D'ITALIA
ARALNS........ ATTI DELLA R. ACCADEMIA DEI LINCEI. NOTIZIE DEGLI SCAVI ROME
ARAST......... ATTI DELLA R. ACCADEMIA DELLE SCIENZE DI TORINO
Arb............. ARBOR
ARBBull........ ACADEMIE ROYALE DE BELGIQUE. BULLETIN DE LA CLASSE DES LETTRES ET DES SCIENCES
                MORALES ET POLITIQUES ET DE LA CLASSE DES BEAUX-ARTS
ARBITRAT J....... ARBITRATION JOURNAL
ARB J.......... ARBITRATION JOURNAL
ARBRSI......... ANNUAL REPORT OF THE BOARD OF REGENTS OF THE SMITHSONIAN INSTITUTION
ARB U B MAT..... ARBOK FOER UNIVERSITETET I BERGEN. MATEMATISK. NATURVITENSKAPELIG SERIE
Arc............. ARCADIA (BERLIN)
ArCCP.......... ARQUIVOS DO CENTRO CULTURAL PORTUGUES (PARIS)
ARCH........... ARCHAEOLOGIA
Arch........... ARCHIVIO
Arch........... ARCHIVUM (OVIEDO)
Archaeol........ ARCHAEOLOGIA
Archaeol Biblio.... ARCHAEOLOGISCHE BIBLIOGRAPHIE
Archaeol J....... ARCHAEOLOGICAL JOURNAL
Archaeol Phy Anthrop Oceania.. ARCHAEOLOGY AND PHYSICAL ANTHROPOLOGY IN OCEANIA

Archaeol Rep . . . . . . ARCHAEOLOGICAL REPORTS
ARCHAEOMETR . . . . ARCHAEOMETRY
ARCH ANAT M . . . . . ARCHIVES D' ANATOMIE MICROSCOPIQUE ET MORPHOLOGIE EXPERIMENTALE
Arch & Bldg . . . . ARCHITECTURE AND BUILDING
Arch & Eng . . . . ARCHITECT AND ENGINEER
ArchArm . . . . ARCHEOLOGIE ARMORICAINE
Arch Aujourd'hui . . . L'ARCHITECTURE D'AUJOURD'HUI
Arch Automat Telemech . . ARCHIWUM AUTOMATYKI I TELEMECHANIKI
ARCH-BAT-CONSTR . . ARCHITECTURE-BATIMENT-CONSTRUCTION
Arch Begriff . . . . . . ARCHIV FUER BEGRIFFSGESCHICHTE
Arch Bibl . . . . ARCHIVES ET BIBLIOTHEQUES DE BELGIQUE
Arch Bibl et Mus . . . ARCHIVES. BIBLIOTHEQUES ET MUSEES DE BELGIQUE
ARCH BIOCH . . . . . . ARCHIVES OF BIOCHEMISTRY AND BIOPHYSICS
ARCH BIOCHEM BIOPHYS . . ARCHIVES OF BIOCHEMISTRY AND BIOPHYSICS
ARCH BIOL M . . . . . ARCHIVOS DE BIOLOGIA Y MEDICINA EXPERIMENTALES
Arch Budowy Masz . . ARCHIWUM BUDOWY MASZYN
Arch Camb . . . . ARCHAEOLOGIA CAMBRENSIS
Arch Can . . . . ARCHITECTURE CANADA
Arch Cant . . . . ARCHAEOLOGIA CANTIANA
ArchClass . . . . ARCHEOLOGIA CLASSICA
ARCH CONCEPT . . . . ARCHITECTURE CONCEPT
Arch d'Aujourd'hui . . ARCHITECTURE D'AUJOURD'HUI
ARCH DERMAT . . . . ARCHIVES OF DERMATOLOGY
ARCH DERM F . . . . . ARCHIV FUER DERMATOLOGISCHE FORSCHUNG
ARCH DERM R . . . . . ARCHIVES FOR DERMATOLOGICAL RESEARCH
Arch Des . . . . ARCHITECTURAL DESIGN
ARCH DIS CH . . . . . . ARCHIVES OF DISEASE IN CHILDHOOD
ARCH EISENH . . . . . . ARCHIV FUER DAS EISENHUETTENWESEN
ARCH ELEKTR . . . . . ARCHIV FUER ELEKTROTECHNIK
Arch Elektrotech . . . ARCHIWUM ELEKTROTECHNIKI
Arch Elek Uebertragung . . ARCHIV DER ELEKTRISCHEN UEBERTRAGUNG
ARCH ENV HE . . . . . ARCHIVES OF ENVIRONMENTAL HEALTH
ArchEurCO . . . . ARCHIVUM EUROPAE CENTRO-ORIENTALIS
ARCH EUR SO . . . . . ARCHIVES EUROPEENNES DE SOCIOLOGIE
ArchFAr . . . . ARCHIVO DE FILOLOGIA ARAGONESA
Arch Filosof . . . . ARCHIVIO DI FILOSOFIA
ARCH FISCH . . . . . . ARCHIV FUER FISCHEREIWISSENSCHAFT
Arch Forum . . . . ARCHITECTURAL FORUM
ARCH FR MAL . . . . . ARCHIVES FRANCAISE DES MALADIES DE L'APPAREIL DIGESTIF
ARCH FR PED . . . . . . ARCHIVES FRANCAISES DE PEDIATRIE
Arch Gen Psychiatry . . ARCHIVES OF GENERAL PSYCHIATRY
Arch Gesch Phil . . . . ARCHIV FUER GESCHICHTE DER PHILOSOPHIE
ARCH GESCHW . . . . ARCHIV FUER GESCHWULSTFORSCHUNG
Arch Gorn . . . . ARCHIWUM GORNIETWA
ARCH G PSYC . . . . . ARCHIVES OF GENERAL PSYCHIATRY
ARCH GYNAK . . . . . ARCHIV FUER GYNAKOLOGIE
ARCH HIST E . . . . . . ARCHIVE FOR HISTORY OF EXACT SCIENCES
ARCH HIST J . . . . . . ARCHIVUM HISTOLOGICUM JAPONICUM
Arch Hutn . . . . ARCHIWUM HUTNICTWA
ARCH HYDROB . . . . ARCHIV FUER HYDROBIOLOGIE
ArchIA . . . . ARCHIVO IBERO-AMERICANO

ARCH I CARD..... ARCHIVOS DEL INSTITUTO DE CARDIOLOGIA DE MEXICO
Archig.......... ARCHIGINNASIO
ARCH IN MED..... ARCHIVES OF INTERNAL MEDICINE
ARCH INV M...... ARCHIVOS DE INVESTIGACION MEDICA
Arch Inz Ladowej... ARCHIWUM INZYNIERII LADOWEJ
ARCH I PHAR..... ARCHIVES INTERNATIONALES DE PHARMACODYNAMIE ET DE THERAPIE
ARCH I PHYS...... ARCHIVES INTERNATIONALES DE PHYSIOLOGIE ET DE BIOCHIMIE
ARCH IT BIO...... ARCHIVES ITALIENNES DE BIOLOGIE
Archit Des........ ARCHITECTURAL DESIGN
Archit Forum...... ARCHITECTURAL FORUM
Archit R......... ARCHITECTURAL REVIEW
Archit Rec........ ARCHITECTURAL RECORD
Archit Sci Rev..... ARCHITECTURAL SCIENCE REVIEW
Archit Surv....... ARCHITECT AND SURVEYOR
Archlug.......... ARCHAEOLOGIA IUGOSLAVICA
Archiv........... ARCHIV FUER DAS STUDIUM DER NEUEREN SPRACHEN UND LITERATUREN
Archiv........... ARCHIV FUER REFORMATIONSGESCHICHTE
Archiv Anthrop.... ARCHIV FUER ANTHROPOLOGIE UND VOELKERFORSCHUNG
ArchiveP......... THE ARCHIVE (PHILIPPINES)
Archives & Bibl.... ARCHIVES ET BIBLIOTHEQUES DE BELGIQUE
Archives Environ Health.. ARCHIVES OF ENVIRONMENTAL HEALTH
Archives Gen Psychiat.. ARCHIVES OF GENERAL PSYCHIATRY
Archives Ind Hyg & Occup Med.. ARCHIVES OF INDUSTRIAL HYGIENE AND OCCUPATIONAL MEDICINE
Archives Neurol.... ARCHIVES OF NEUROLOGY
Archives Philos.... ARCHIVES DE PHILOSOPHIE
Archives Sociol Relig.. ARCHIVES DE SOCIOLOGIE DES RELIGIONS
Archives Suisses Anthrop Gen.. ARCHIVES SUISSES D' ANTHROPOLOGIE GENERALE
Archiv f Osterr Geschichte.. ARCHIV FUER OESTERREICHISCHE GESCHICHTE
Archiv f Stud...... ARCHIV FUER DAS STUDIUM DER NEUEREN SPRACHEN UND LITERATUREN
Archiv fuer Mus... ARCHIV FUER MUSIKWISSENSCHAFT
Archiv Gesch Buchw.. ARCHIV FUER GESCHICHTE DES BUCHWESENS
Archiv Ling....... ARCHIVUM LINGUISTICUM
Archivo Esp Arq.... ARCHIVO ESPANOL DE ARQUEOLOGIA
Archivo Esp Arte... ARCHIVO ESPANOL DE ARTE
Archiv Oesterr Gesch.. ARCHIV FUER OESTERREICHISCHE GESCHICHTE
Archiv Orientforsch.. ARCHIV FUER ORIENTFORSCHUNG
ArchivPhilos...... ARCHIV FUER PHILOSOPHIE
Archiv Rom....... ARCHIVUM ROMANICUM
Archiv Sci Soc Rel.. ARCHIVES DE SCIENCE SOCIALES DES RELIGIONS
Archiv Soc Rel..... ARCHIVES DE SOCIOLOGIE DES RELIGIONS
Archiv Stor....... ARCHIVIO STORICO
Archivum Hist Soc Iesu.. ARCHIVUM HISTORICUM SOCIETATIS IESU
Archiv Urk....... ARCHIV FUER URKUNDENFORSCHUNG
ArchK........... ARCHIV FUER KULTURGESCHICHTE
ArchL........... ARCHIVUM LINGUISTICUM
Arch Ling........ ARCHIVUM LINGUISTICUM
ArchLit.......... ARCHIV FUER LITERATUR UND VOLKSDICHTUNG
ARCH MAL C...... ARCHIVES DES MALADIES DU COEUR ET DES VAISSEAUX
ARCH MAL PR..... ARCHIVES DES MALADIES PROFESSIONNELLES DE MEDECINE DU TRAVAIL ET DE SECURITE SOCIALE
ARCH MATH...... ARCHIV DER MATHEMATIK

Arch Math Log . . . . . ARCHIV FUER MATHEMATISCHE LOGIK UND GRUNDLAGEN FORSCHUNG
ARCH MECH . . . . . . ARCHIVES OF MECHANICS
Arch Mech-Arch Mech Stosow . . ARCHIVES OF MECHANICS-ARCHIWUM MECHANIKI STOSOWANEJ
Arch Mech Strosowanej . . ARCHIWUM MECHANIKI STROSOWANEJ
ARCH MGB A . . . . . . ARCHIV FUER METEOROLOGIE GEOPHYSIK UND BIOKLIMATOLOGIE. SERIE A
ARCH MGB B . . . . . . ARCHIV FUER METEOROLOGIE GEOPHYSIK UND BIOKLIMATOLOGIE. SERIE B
ARCH MICROB . . . . . ARCHIVES OF MICROBIOLOGY
ARCH MUS . . . . ARCHIV FUER MUSIKWISSENSCHAFT
Arch Neerl Phon Exp . . ARCHIVES NEERLANDAISES DE PHONETIQUE EXPERIMENTALE
ARCH NEUROL . . . . . ARCHIVES OF NEUROLOGY
ArchNPhonExp . . . . . ARCHIVES NEERLANDAISES DE PHONETIQUE EXPERIMENTALE
ARCH OPHTAL . . . . . ARCHIVES D'OPHTALMOLOGIE
ARCH OPHTH . . . . . ARCHIVES OF OPHTHALMOLOGY
Arch Ophthalmol . . . ARCHIVES OF OPHTHALMOLOGY
ARCH ORAL B . . . . . ARCHIVES OF ORAL BIOLOGY
ArchOrient . . . . ARCHIV ORIENTALNI
ARCH ORTHOP . . . . ARCHIV FUER ORTHOPAEDISCHE UND UNFALL CHIRURGIE
ARCH OTOLAR . . . . . ARCHIVES OF OTOLARYNGOLOGY
ARCH OTO-R . . . . . . ARCHIVES OF OTO-RHINO-LARYNGOLOGY
ARCH PATH . . . . . . ARCHIVES OF PATHOLOGY
ARCH PHARM . . . . . ARCHIV DER PHARMAZIE
Arch Phil . . . . ARCHIVES DE PHILOSOPHIE
ARCH PHYS M . . . . ARCHIVES OF PHYSICAL MEDICINE AND REHABILITATION
Arch Phys Med Rehabil . . ARCHIVES OF PHYSICAL MEDICINE AND REHABILITATION
ARCH PSYCH . . . . . . ARCHIVE FUER PSYCHOLOGIE
ARCH PSYCHI . . . . . ARCHIV FUER PSYCHIATRIE UND NERVENKRANKHEITEN
Arch R . . . . ARCHITECTURAL REVIEW
Arch Ration Mech Anal . . ARCHIVE FOR RATIONAL MECHANICS AND ANALYSIS
Arch Rec . . . . ARCHITECTURAL RECORD
Arch Rechts Soz . . . . ARCHIV FUER RECHTS UND SOZIALPHILOSOPHIE
Arch Rev . . . . ARCHITECTURAL REVIEW
ARCH R MECH . . . . . ARCHIVE FOR RATIONAL MECHANICS AND ANALYSIS
Arch Rom . . . . ARCHIVUM ROMANICUM
ARCH S A OF . . . . . . ARCHIVOS DE LA SOCIEDAD AMERICANA OFTALMOLOGIA OPTOMETRIA
ARCH SCI . . . . ARCHIVES DES SCIENCES
ARCH SCI PH . . . . . . ARCHIVES DES SCIENCES PHYSIOLOGIQUES
ARCH SEX BE . . . . . . ARCHIVES OF SEXUAL BEHAVIOR
Arch(Sofia) . . . . ARCHEOLOGIE (SOFIA)
ArchSS . . . . ARCHIVIO STORICO SICILIANO
ARCH SS REL . . . . . . ARCHIVES DE SCIENCES SOCIALES DES RELIGIONS
ARCH SURG . . . . ARCHIVES OF SURGERY
ArchT . . . . ARCHEION THRAKES
Arch Tech Mess/Ind Messtech . . ARCHIV FUER TECHNISCHES MESSEN UND INDUSTRIELLE MESSTECHNIK
Arch Tech Mess Messtech Prax . . ARCHIV FUER TECHNISCHES MESSEN UND MESSTECHNISCHE PRAXIS
ARCH TOXIC . . . . . . ARCHIVES OF TOXICOLOGY
ArchV . . . . ARCHIV FUER VOLKERKUNDE
ARCH VIROL . . . . . . ARCHIVES OF VIROLOGY
Arch Yr . . . . ARCHITECTS' YEARBOOK
Arch Yrbk . . . . ARCHITECT'S YEARBOOK
ArcP . . . . ARCHEION PONTOU
ARD . . . . ARCHITECTURAL RECORD

ArmC . . . . ARMS CONTROL AND DISARMAMENT
ARM KHIM ZH . . . . . ARMYANSKII KHIMICHESKII ZHURNAL
Arnold Arbor J . . . . . HARVARD UNIVERSITY. ARNOLD ARBORETUM JOURNAL
ArNVA . . . . ARBOK DET NORSKE VIDENSKAPSAKADEMI
ArO . . . . ARCHIV ORIENTALNI
ARom . . . . ARCHIVUM ROMANICUM
ARPh . . . . ARCHIV FUER RECHTS- UND WIRTSCHAFTS-PHILOSOPHIE
ARPs . . . . ARCHIV FUER RELIGIONSPSYCHOLOGIE
ArQ . . . . ARIZONA QUARTERLY
ARQ BRAS PS . . . . . . ARQUIVOS BRASILEIROS DE PSICOLOGIA APLICADA
ARDRSP . . . . ARCHIVIO DELLA R. DEPUTAZIONE ROMANA DI STORIA PATRIA
ARDS . . . . ANNUAL REPORT OF THE DANTE SOCIETY
AREA . . . . ASSOCIATION FOR RELIGIOUS EDUCATION ASPECTS OF EDUCATION. BULLETIN
Areth . . . . ARETHUSE
ARG . . . . AMERICAN RECORD GUIDE
ARG . . . . ARCHIV FUER REFORMATIONSGESCHICHTE
Arg . . . . ARGENSOLA
ARGTU . . . . ARCHIV FUER REFORMATIONSGESCHICHTE. TEXTE UND UNTERSUCHUNGEN
ArH . . . . ARCHIVO HISPALENSE
ArHQ . . . . ARKANSAS HISTORICAL QUARTERLY
ArI . . . . ARCHIVO IBEROAMERICANO (MADRID)
ARIPUC . . . . ANNUAL REPORT OF THE INSTITUTE OF PHONETICS. UNIVERSITY OF COPENHAGEN
Aris Soc . . . . THE ARISTOTELIAN SOCIETY: SUPPLEMENTARY VOLUME
Arith Teach . . . . . . ARITHMETIC TEACHER
Ariz Ag Exp . . . . . . ARIZONA AGRICULTURAL EXPERIMENT STATION PUBLICATIONS
Ariz and West . . . . . ARIZONA AND THE WEST
Ariz H . . . . ARIZONA HIGHWAYS
Ariz Hist Rev . . . . . ARIZONA HISTORICAL REVIEW
Ariz Law R . . . . ARIZONA LAW REVIEW
Ariz Libn . . . . ARIZONA LIBRARIAN
Ariz L Rev . . . . ARIZONA LAW REVIEW
Ariz Q . . . . ARIZONA QUARTERLY
Ariz Teach . . . . ARIZONA TEACHER
ArizW . . . . ARIZONA AND THE WEST
Ark Ag Exp . . . . ARKANSAS AGRICULTURAL EXPERIMENT STATION PUBLICATIONS
Arkansas Geol Comm Inform Circ . . ARKANSAS GEOLOGICAL AND CONSERVATION COMMISSION. INFORMATION
                    CIRCULAR
Arkansas Lib . . . . . . ARKANSAS LIBRARIES
Ark Hist Assoc Publ . . ARKANSAS HISTORICAL ASSOCIATION. PUBLICATIONS
Ark Hist Quar . . . . . ARKANSAS HISTORICAL QUARTERLY
ArkHQ . . . . ARKANSAS HISTORICAL QUARTERLY
Arkiv . . . . ARKIV FOER NORDISK FILOLOGI
Arkiv f Nord Filologi . . ARKIV FOER NORDISK FILOLOGI
Ark Law R . . . . ARKANSAS LAW REVIEW
Ark Lib . . . . ARKANSAS LIBRARIES
Ark L Rev . . . . ARKANSAS LAW REVIEW
ARK MATEMAT . . . . ARKIV FOER MATEMATIK
ARKSN . . . . ANNUARIUM DES ROOMSCH-KATHOLIEKE STUDENTEN IN NEDERLAND
ArkUkr . . . . ARKHEOLOGIJA. PUBLIES PAR L'ACADEMIE DES SCIENCES D'UKRAINE
ArL . . . . ARCHIVUM LINGUISTICUM
ARLIS Newsl . . . . . . ARLIS (ART LIBRARIES OF NORTH AMERICA) NEWSLETTER

ArlQ . . . . ARLINGTON QUARTERLY
ArM . . . . ARTE (MILAN)
ArR . . . . ARCHIVI (ROME)
ARS . . . . AUGUSTAN REPRINT SOCIETY
ARSC . . . . ASSOCIATION FOR RECORDED SOUND COLLECTIONS. JOURNAL
ARSCJ . . . . ASSOCIATION FOR RECORDED SOUND COLLECTIONS. JOURNAL
Ars Islam . . . . ARS ISLAMICA
ARS J . . . . ARS JOURNAL
ARSNSP . . . . ATTI DELLA R. SCUOLA NORMALE SUPERIORE DI PISA
Ars Orient . . . . ARS ORIENTALIS
ARSP . . . . ARCHIV FUER RECHTS UND SOZIALPHILOSOPHIE
Arsskr f Modersmalslararnas Foren . . ARSSKRIFT FOER MODERSMALSLARARNAS FORENING
Art Am . . . . ART IN AMERICA
Art & Dec . . . . ART & DECORATION
Art & Ind . . . . ART AND INDUSTRY
ArtArch . . . . ART AND ARCHAEOLOGY TECHNICAL ABSTRACTS
ArtB . . . . ART BULLETIN
Art Bul . . . . ART BULLETIN
ART EDUC . . . . ART EDUCATION
ARTE MUS . . . . ARTE MUSICAL
ArteP . . . . ARTE E POESIA
Arte y Var . . . . ARTE Y VARIEDADES
Arth . . . . ARTHANITI
ARTH RHEUM . . . . . ARTHRITIS AND RHEUMATISM
ArtI . . . . ART INDEX
ARTIC ANTH . . . . . . ARCTIC ANTHROPOLOGY
Artif Intel . . . . ARTIFICIAL INTELLIGENCE
ARTI MUS . . . . ARTI MUSICES
Art in Am . . . . ART IN AMERICA
Art Int . . . . ART INTERNATIONAL
Art J . . . . ART JOURNAL
Art Jnl . . . . ART JOURNAL
Art Jour . . . . ART JOURNAL
Art N . . . . ART NEWS
ART PSYCHOT . . . . . ART PSYCHOTHERAPY
ArtQ . . . . ART QUARTERLY
Arts . . . . ARTS MAGAZINE
Arts & Arch . . . . . . ARTS & ARCHITECTURE
Arts and Dec . . . . . . ARTS AND DECORATION
ARTSCAN . . . . ARTSCANADA
Arts in Soc . . . . ARTS IN SOCIETY
Arts Mag . . . . ARTS MAGAZINE
Arts Reptg Ser . . . . . ARTS REPORTING SERVICE
ArtSt . . . . ARTE STAMPA
ARTU . . . . ARCHIV FUER REFORMATIONSGESCHICHTE. TEXTE UND UNTERSUCHUNGEN
ARW . . . . ARCHIV FUER RELIGIONSWISSENSCHAFT
ARWP . . . . ARCHIV FUER RECHTS UND WIRTSCHAFTSPHILOSOPHIE
ARZNEI-FOR . . . . . . ARZNEIMITTEL-FORSCHUNG
AS . . . . ALTEN SPRACHEN
AS . . . . AMERICAN SCHOLAR
AS . . . . AMERICAN SPEECH

AS............. ANATOLIAN STUDIES
AS............. ANGLISTISCHES SEMINAR
AS............. APOSTOLADO SACERDOTAL
AS............. APPLIED STATISTICS
AS............. ART SCHOLAR
AS............. ARTS IN SOCIETY
As............. ASOMANTE
ASA........... ANZEIGER FUER SCHWEIZERISCHE ALTERTUMSKUNDE
ASAA.......... ANNUARIO DELLA R. SCUOLA ARCHEOLOGICA DI ATENE
ASAAN......... ANNALES DE LA SOCIETE ARCHEOLOGIQUE DE L'ARRONDISSEMENT DE NIVELLES
ASAB.......... ANNALES DE LA SOCIETE D'ARCHEOLOGIE DE BRUXELLES
ASAE.......... ANNALES DU SERVICE DES ANTIQUITES D'EGYPTE
ASAI.......... ANNALES DU SERVICE ARCHEOLOGIQUE DE L'IRAN
ASAK.......... ANZEIGER FUER SCHWEIZERISCHE ALTERTUMSKUNDE
ASal.......... ACTA SALMATICENSIA
ASAL.......... ANNUAIRE DE LA SOCIETE D'HISTOIRE D'ARCHEOLOGIE DE LA LORRAINE
ASAN.......... ANNALES DE LA SOCIETE ARCHEOLOGIQUE DE NAMUR
ASAW.......... ABHANDLUNGEN DER SAECHSISCHEN AKADEMIE DER WISSENSCHAFTEN ZU LEIPZIG. PHILOL.-HIST. KLASSE
ASB........... ACCADEMIA DELLE SCIENZE DI BOLOGNA. MEMORIE
ASB........... AFRICAN STUDIES BULLETIN
ASBA.......... ATAS DO SIMPOSIO SOBRE A BIOTA AMAZONICA
ASBFC......... ARCHIVIO STORICO PER BELLUNO, FELTRE E CADORE
ASc........... AMERICAN SCHOLAR
ASc........... ANNALS OF SCIENCE
ASC........... ARCHIVIO STORICO DI CORSICA
ASCAP......... ASCAP TODAY
ASCBull....... ACADEMIE DES SCIENCES DE CRACOVIE. BULLETIN INTERNATIONAL
ASC COMMUN..... ASC (AMERICAN SOCIETY FOR CYBERNETICS) COMMUNICATIONS
ASCE Combined Sewer Separation Proj Tech Memo.. ASCE (AMERICAN SOCIETY OF CIVIL ENGINEERS). COMBINED SEWER SEPARATION PROJECT. TECHNICAL MEMORANDUM
ASCE Eng Issues J Prof Activ.. ASCE. ENGINEERING ISSUES. JOURNAL OF PROFESSIONAL ACTIVITIES
ASCE J Constr Div.. ASCE. JOURNAL OF THE CONSTRUCTION DIVISION
ASCE J Eng Mech Div.. ASCE. JOURNAL OF THE ENGINEERING MECHANICS DIVISION
ASCE J Prof Activ.. ASCE. JOURNAL OF PROFESSIONAL ACTIVITIES
ASCE J Sanit Eng Div.. ASCE. JOURNAL OF THE SANITARY ENGINEERING DIVISION
ASCE J Soil Mech Found Div.. ASCE. JOURNAL OF THE SOIL MECHANICS AND FOUNDATIONS DIVISION
ASCE J Struct Div... ASCE. JOURNAL OF STRUCTURAL DIVISION
ASCE J Surv Mapp Div.. ASCE. JOURNAL OF THE SURVEYING AND MAPPING DIVISION
ASCE Man Rep Eng Pract   ASCE. MANUALS AND REPORTS ON ENGINEERING PRACTICE
ASch.......... AMERICAN SCHOLAR
ASci.......... AMERICAN SCIENTIST
ASCL.......... ARCHIVIO STORICO PER LA CALABRIA E LA LUCANIA
ASD........... ANNALI DI STORIA DEL DIRITTO
ASD........... ARCHIVIO STORICO PER LA DALMAZIA
ASEA.......... ASIATISCHE STUDIEN/ETUDES ASIATIQUES
ASEB.......... ANNALES DE LA SOCIETE D'EMULATION DE BRUGES
ASEER......... AMERICAN SLAVIC AND EASTERN EUROPEAN REVIEW
ASEF.......... ANNALES DE LA SOCIETE D'EMULATION POUR L'ETUDE DE L'HISTOIRE ET DES ANTIQUITIES DE FLANDRE
ASEG.......... ARQUIVOS DO SEMINARIO DE ESTUDOS GALEGOS

PERIODICAL TITLE ABBREVIATIONS

ASEU . . . . ARCHIVO PER LA STORIA ECCLESIASTICA DELL'UMBRIA
ASF . . . . ANALOG SCIENCE FICTION
ASF . . . . ARCHIVIO DE STORIA DELLA FILOSOFIA
ASF . . . . ASTOUNDING SCIENCE FICTION
ASF . . . . ASTOUNDING STORIES
ASFM . . . . ANUARIO DE LA SOCIEDAD FOLKLORICO DE MEXICO
ASFR . . . . AVON SCIENCE FICTION FANTASY READER
ASG . . . . ABHANDLUNGEN DER PHILOSOPHISCH-HISTORISCHE. KLASSE DER SAECHSISCHEN GESELLSCHAFT
ASGA . . . . NEUES ARCHIV FUER SAECHSISCHE GESCHICHTE UND ALTERTUMSKUNDE
ASGH . . . . ANALES DE LA SOCIEDAD DE GEOGRAFIA E HISTORIA
ASGLM . . . . ATTI DEL SODALIZIO GLOTTOLOGICO MILANESE
ASGM . . . . ATTI DEL SODALIZIO GLOTTOLOGICO MILANESE
Ash . . . . ASTONISHING STORIES
ASHAG . . . . ANNALES DE LA SOCIETE D'HISTOIRE ET D'ARCHEOLOGIE DE GAND
ASHAL . . . . ANNUAIRE DE LA SOCIETE D'HISTOIRE ET D'ARCHEOLOGIE DE LA LORRAINE
ASHAT . . . . ANNALES DE LA SOCIETE HISTORIQUE ET ARCHEOLOGIQUE DE TOURNAI
ASHFY . . . . AMERICAN SWEDISH HISTORICAL FOUNDATION. YEARBOOK
ASHJ . . . . ARCHIVUM HISTORICUM SOCIETATIS JESU
ASHRAE B . . . . AMERICAN SOCIETY OF HEATING, REFRIGERATING AND AIR-CONDITIONING ENGINEERS.
BULLETIN
ASHRAE Handb Fundam . . AMERICAN SOCIETY OF HEATING, REFRIGERATING AND AIR-CONDITIONING ENGINEERS.
HANDBOOK OF FUNDAMENTALS
ASHRAE J . . . . AMERICAN SOCIETY OF HEATING, REFRIGERATING AND AIR-CONDITIONING ENGINEERS.
JOURNAL
ASHRAE Trans . . . . . AMERICAN SOCIETY OF HEATING, REFRIGERATING AND AIR-CONDITIONING ENGINEERS.
TRANSACTIONS
ASHY . . . . AMERICAN SWEDISH HISTORICAL FOUNDATION. YEARBOOK
ASI . . . . ARCHIVIO STORICO ITALIANO
Asia . . . . ASIA AND THE AMERICAS
Asian Aff . . . . ASIAN AFFAIRS
ASIAN PERSP . . . . . ASIAN PERSPECTIVES
Asian R . . . . ASIAN REVIEW
Asian S . . . . ASIAN SURVEY
Asian Stud Prof R . . ASIAN STUDIES PROFESSIONAL REVIEW
Asian Surv . . . . ASIAN SURVEY
Asiatic R . . . . ASIATIC REVIEW
Asiatic R ns . . . . . . ASIATIC REVIEW. NEW SERIES.
Asiatic Soc Japan Trans . . ASIATIC SOCIETY OF JAPAN. TRANSACTIONS
ASILO . . . . ADALBERT STIFTER INSTITUT DES LANDES OBEROESTERREICH: VIERTELJAHRSSCHRIFT
ASIS . . . . ATTI DELLA SOCIETA ITALIANA DI STATISTICA
ASKG . . . . ARCHIV FUER SCHLESISCHE KIRCHENGESCHICHTE
ASL . . . . ARCHIVIO STORICO LOMBARDO
ASLA Pres Newsl . . . ASSOCIATION OF STATE LIBRARY AGENCIES. PRESIDENT'S NEWSLETTER
ASLE Prepr . . . . ASLE (AMERICAN SOCIETY OF LUBRICATION ENGINEERS) PREPRINTS
ASLE Trans . . . . . . ASLE (AMERICAN SOCIETY OF LUBRICATION ENGINEERS) TRANSACTIONS
ASLF . . . . ANNALES DE SAINT-LOUIS DES FRANCAIS
ASLG . . . . ATTI DELLA SOCIETA LINGUISTICA DI SCIENZE E LETTERE DI GENOVA
ASLH . . . . AMERICAN SOCIETY OF THE LEGION OF HONOR MAGAZINE
ASLHM . . . . AMERICAN SOCIETY OF THE LEGION OF HONOR MAGAZINE
ASLIB PROC . . . . . . ASLIB PROCEEDINGS
ASLL . . . . ACTA SOCIETATIS HUMANIORUM LITTERARUM LUNDENSIS

ASLod . . . . ARCHIVIVIO STORICO LODIGIANO
ASLP Bul . . . . ASSOCIATION OF SPECIAL LIBRARIES OF THE PHILIPPINES. BULLETIN
ASLSP . . . . ATTI DELLA SOCIETA LIGURE DI STORIA PATRIA
ASLU . . . . ACTA SOCIETATIS LINGUISTICAE UPSALIENSIS
ASLund . . . . ARSBOK UTGIVEN AV SEMINARIERNA I SLAVISKA SPRAK, JAMFORANDE SPRAKFORSKNING, FINSK-UGRISKA SPRAK OCH OSTASIATISKA SPRAK VID LUNDS UNIVERSITET
ASM . . . . AMERICAN SWEDISH MONTHLY
ASM . . . . ARCHIVIO STORICO MESSINESE
AsM . . . . ASIA MAJOR
ASME Boiler Pressure Vessel Code . . AMERICAN SOCIETY OF MECHANICAL ENGINEERS. BOILER AND PRESSURE VESSEL CODE
ASME Pap . . . . AMERICAN SOCIETY OF MECHANICAL ENGINEERS. PAPERS
ASME Trans . . . . . . AMERICAN SOCIETY OF MECHANICAL ENGINEERS. TRANSACTIONS
ASMG . . . . ATTI E MEMORIE DELLA SOCIETA MAGNA GRECIA
ASM Trans Quart . . . ASM (AMERICAN SOCIETY FOR METALS) TRANSACTIONS QUARTERLY
ASN . . . . ANNALI DELLA SCUOLA NORMALE SUPERIORE DI PISA
ASNP . . . . ANNALI DELLA SCUOLA NORMALE SUPERIORE DI PISA
ASNS . . . . ARCHIV FUER DAS STUDIUM DER NEUEREN SPRACHEN UND LITERATUREN
ASNSL . . . . ARCHIV FUER DAS STUDIUM DER NEUEREN SPRACHEN UND LITERATUREN
ASNSP . . . . ANNALI DELLA SCUOLA NORMALE SUPERIORE DI PISA
Aso . . . . ASOMANTE
ASOC . . . . ANALECTA SACRI ORDINIS CISTERCIENSIS (ROMA)
ASoc . . . . ANNALES SOCIOLOGIQUES
ASoc . . . . ANNEE SOCIOLOGIQUE
ASoc . . . . ARTS IN SOCIETY (U. OF WIS.)
Asco Colombiana Bibl Bol . . ASOCIATION COLOMBIANA DE BIBLIOTECARIOS. BOLETIN
Asoc Cuba Bibl Bol . . ASOCIACION CUBANA DE BIBLIOTECARIOS. BOLETIN
A Soc R . . . . AMERICAN SOCIOLOGICAL REVIEW
ASOL . . . . AMERICAN SYMPHONY ORCHESTRA LEAGUE. NEWSLETTER
ASP . . . . ADVERTISING AND SALES PROMOTION
ASP . . . . ARCHIV FUER SLAVISCHE PHILOLOGIE
ASP . . . . ARCHIVIO STORICO PRATESE
ASP . . . . ARCHIVIO STORICO PUGLIESE
ASPA . . . . ATTI DELLA SOCIETA PIEMONTESE DI ARCHEOLOGIA E BELLE ARTI
ASPABA . . . . ATTI DELLA SOCIETA PIEMONTESE DI ARCHEOLOGIA E BELLE ARTI
ASPECTS ED . . . . ASPECTS OF EDUCATION
Aspects of Ed . . . . . ASPECTS OF EDUCATION
ASPh . . . . ARCHIV FUER SYSTEMATISCHE PHILOSOPHIE
ASPN . . . . ARCHIVIO STORICO PER LE PROVINCIE NAPOLITANE
ASPP . . . . ARCHIVIO STORICO PER LE PROVINCIE PARMENSI
ASPS . . . . ATTI DELLA SOCIETA ITALIANA PER IL PROGRESSO DELLE SCIENZE
ASPu . . . . ARCHIVIO STORICO PUBLIESE
ASR . . . . AMERICAN SCANDINAVIAN REVIEW
ASR . . . . AMERICAN SLAVIC REVIEW
ASR . . . . AMERICAN SOCIOLOGICAL REVIEW
ASR . . . . ANNALES DE LA SOCIETA RETORUMANTSCHA
ASR . . . . ARCHIVES DE SOCIOLOGIE DES RELIGIONS
ASR . . . . AVON SCIENCE FICTION READER
ASRAB . . . . ANNALES DE LA SOCIETE ROYALE D'ARCHEOLOGIE DE BRUXELLES
ASRHAT . . . . ANNALES DE LA SOCIETE ROYALE D'HISTOIRE ET D'ARCHEOLOGIE DE TOURNAI
ASRS . . . . ARCHIVIO DELLA SOCIETA ROMANA DI STORIA PATRIA

ASRSP . . . . ARCHIVIO DELLA SOCIETA ROMANA DI STORIA PATRIA
ASRU . . . . ARCHIVIO STORICO DEL RISORGIMENTO UMBRIO
AsS . . . . ASIATISCHE STUDIEN
ASS . . . . AMAZING SCIENCE STORIES
ASS . . . . ARCHIVIO STORICO SICILIANO
ASSar . . . . ARCHIVIO STORICO SARDO
ASSc . . . . ARCHIVIO DI STORIA DELLA SCIENZA
ASSE J . . . . ASSE JOURNAL
Assist Libn . . . . ASSISTANT LIBRARIAN
Assn Am Ag Coll & Exp Pro . . ASSOCIATION OF AMERICAN AGRICULTURAL COLLEGES AND EXPERIMENT STATIONS.
. . . . PROCEEDINGS
Assn Am Col Bul . . . ASSOCIATION OF AMERICAN COLLEGES. BULLETIN
Assn Am Geog Ann . . ASSOCIATION OF AMERICAN GEOGRAPHERS. ANNALS
Assn Asian Stud Newsletter . . ASSOCIATION FOR ASIAN STUDIES. NEWSLETTER
Ass Naz Ing Architetti Ital Quad . . ASSOCIAZIONE NAZIONALE DEGLE INGEGNERI ED ARCHITETTI ITALIANI.
. . . . QUADERNI
Assn Bar City N Y Rec . . ASSOCIATION OF THE BAR OF THE CITY OF NEW YORK. RECORD
Assn Bibl Francais Bull Inf . . ASSOCIATION DES BIBLIOTHECAIRES FRANCAIS. BULLETIN D'INFORMATIONS
Assn Canadienne Bibl Langue Francaise Bul . . ASSOCIATION CANADIENNE DES BIBLIOTHECAIRES DE LANGUE
. . . . FRANCAISE. BULLETIN
Assn Comp Mach J . . ASSOCIATION FOR COMPUTING MACHINERY. JOURNAL
Assn Ed Radio J . . . . ASSOCIATION FOR EDUCATION BY RADIO. JOURNAL
Assn for Sup & Curric Develop Yearbook . . ASSOCIATION FOR SUPERVISION AND CURRICULUM DEVELOPMENT.
. . . . YEARBOOK
Assn Italiana Bibl Boll Inf . . ASSOCIAZIONE ITALIANA BIBLIOTECHE. BOLLETTINO D' INFORMAZIONI
Assn Men . . . . ASSOCIATION MEN (RURAL MANHOOD)
Assn Offic Ag Chem J . . ASSOCIATION OF OFFICIAL AGRICULTURAL CHEMISTS. JOURNAL
Assn of Gov Bds of State Univ & Allied Insts Proc . . ASSOCIATION OF GOVERNING BOARDS OF STATE UNIVERSITIES
. . . . AND ALLIED INSTITUTIONS. PROCEEDINGS
Assn Sch Bsns Officials U S & Canada Proc . . ASSOCIATION OF SCHOOL BUSINESS OFFICIALS OF THE UNITED STATES
. . . . AND CANADA. PROCEEDINGS.
Assn Stud Teach Yrbk . . ASSOCIATION FOR STUDENT TEACHING. YEARBOOK
Assn Sup & Curric Devel Yrbk . . ASSOCIATION FOR SUPERVISION AND CURRICULUM DEVELOPMENT. YEARBOOK
ASSO . . . . ARCHIVIO STORICO PER LA SICILIA ORIENTALE
Assoc Am Geographers Annals . . ASSOCIATION OF AMERICAN GEOGRAPHERS. ANNALS
Assoc Bibl Francais Bul . . ASSOCIATION DES BIBLIOTHECAIRES FRANCAIS. BULLETIN D'INFORMATIONS
ASSPh . . . . ANNUAIRE DE LA SOCIETE SUISSE DE PHILOSOPHIE
ASS Short-Circuit Test Auth Publ . . ASSOCIATION OF SHORT-CIRCUIT TESTING AUTHORITIES. PUBLICATION
AsSt . . . . ASIAN STUDENT
Asst Libn . . . . ASSISTANT LIBRARIAN
A St . . . . ABERYSTWYTH STUDIES
AST . . . . AMERICAN STRING TEACHER
AST . . . . ANALECTA SACRA TARRACONENSIS
ASt . . . . ASIAN STUDIES
ASt . . . . ASIATISCHE STUDIEN
AST . . . . ASTONISHING STORIES
AST . . . . ATTI E MEMORIE DELLA SOCIETA TIBURTINA DI STORIA E D'ARTE
Ast&AstroAb . . . . . . ASTRONOMY AND ASTROPHYSICS ABSTRACTS
ASTI . . . . APPLIED SCIENCE AND TECHNOLOGY INDEX
ASTic . . . . ARCHIVIO STORICO TICINESE
ASTM Book ASTM Stand . . AMERICAN SOCIETY FOR TESTING AND MATERIALS. BOOK OF ASTM STANDARDS.

ASTM Bul .... AMERICAN SOCIETY FOR TESTING AND MATERIALS. BULLETIN
ASTME/ASM West Metal Tool Conf . . AMERICAN SOCIETY OF TOOL AND MANUFACTURING ENGINEERS. ASTME/ASM WESTERN METAL AND TOOL CONFERENCE
ASTME Collect Papers . . AMERICAN SOCIETY OF TOOL AND MANUFACTURING ENGINEERS. ASTME COLLECTED PAPERS
ASTME Creative Mfg Semin Tech Papers . . AMERICAN SOCIETY OF TOOL AND MANUFACTURING ENGINEERS. CREATIVE MANUFACTURING SEMINARS. TECHNICAL PAPERS
ASTM Spec Tech Publ . . AMERICAN SOCIETY FOR TESTING AND MATERIALS. SPECIAL TECHNICAL PUBLICATIONS
ASTM Stand N . . . . . ASTM STANDARDIZATION NEWS
ASTP . . . . ARCHIVES SUISSES DES TRADITIONS POPULAIRES
ASTRO AERON . . . . . ASTRONAUTICS AND AERONAUTICS
Astron . . . . ASTRONOMY AND ASTRO-PHYSICS
ASTRON ASTR . . . . . ASTRONOMY AND ASTROPHYSICS
Astronaut Acta . . . . ASTRONAUTICA ACTA
Astronaut Aeronaut . . ASTRONAUTICS AND AERONAUTICS
ASTRONOM J . . . . . . ASTRONOMICAL JOURNAL
ASTRONOM ZH . . . . ASTRONOMICHESKII ZHURNAL
ASTROPH J S . . . . . . ASTROPHYSICAL JOURNAL. SUPPLEMENT SERIES
Astrophys J . . . . ASTROPHYSICAL JOURNAL
ASTROPHYS L . . . . . ASTROPHYSICAL LETTERS
ASTRO SP SC . . . . . . ASTROPHYSICS AND SPACE SCIENCE
ASu . . . . ANTHROPONYMICA SUECANA
ASUC . . . . AMERICAN SOCIETY OF UNIVERSITY COMPOSERS. PROCEEDINGS
ASUI . . . . ANALELE STIINTIFICE ALE UNIVERSITATII IASI
ASY . . . . ASTOUNDING STORIES YEARBOOK
AT . . . . AFRICA TODAY
AT . . . . ANALECTA TARRACONENSIA
AT . . . . ANTIK TANULMANYOK
AT . . . . ARCHEOLGRAFO TRIESTINO
At . . . . ATENEA
At . . . . ATLANTIDA
AT . . . . AUTUMN
ATA . . . . ANNEE THEOLOGIQUE AUGUSTINIENNE
ATB . . . . ALTDEUTSCHE TEXTBIBLIOTHEK
ATCP . . . . ATCP (ASOCIACION MEXICANA DE TECNICOS DE LAS INDUSTRIAS DE LA CELULOSA Y DEL PAPEL)
Ate . . . . ATENEA
Ate . . . . NUEVA ATENEA
At Energiya (U.S.S.R.) . . ATOMNAYA ENERGIYA (U.S.S.R.)
At Energy Rev . . . . . ATOMIC ENERGY REVIEW
ATG . . . . ARCHIVO TEOLOGICO GRANADINO
Ath . . . . : . . ATHENAEUM
AThAug . . . . ANNEE THEOLOGIQUE AUGUSTINIENNE
ATHEROSCLER . . . . . ATHEROSCLEROSIS
AThijmG . . . . ANNALEN VAN HET THIJMGENOOTSCHAP
Ath J . . . . ATHLETIC JOURNAL
AThR . . . . ANGLICAN THEOLOGICAL REVIEW
Atl . . . . ATLANTIC MONTHLY
Atl . . . . ATLANTICO
Atla . . . . ATLANTIS
Atl Adv . . . . ATLANTIC ADVOCATE

PERIODICAL TITLE ABBREVIATIONS

Atlan . . . . ATLANTIC MONTHLY
ATLAN ADV . . . . ATLANTIC ADVOCATE
Atlan Com Q . . . . . . ATLANTIC COMMUNITY QUARTERLY
Atlan Mo . . . . ATLANTIC MONTHLY
Atlantic . . . . ATLANTIC MONTHLY
Atl Community Quar . . ATLANTIC COMMUNITY QUARTERLY
ATL ECON R . . . . . . ATLANTA ECONOMIC REVIEW
ATLGT . . . . ARCHEION TOU THRAKIKOU LAOGRAPHIKOU KAI GLOSSIKOU THESAUROU
ATL L J . . . . AMERICAN TRIAL LAWYERS JOURNAL
Atl Mo . . . . ATLANTIC MONTHLY
AtM . . . . ATLANTIC MONTHLY
ATM MESS PR . . . . . ATM MESSTECHNISCHE PRAXIS
Atmos Envir . . . . . . ATMOSPHERIC ENVIRONMENT
ATMTas . . . . ADABIETSUNASLIK VA TILSUNASLIK MASALALARI/VOPROSY LITERATUROVEDENIJA I
                        JAZYKOZNANIJA. TASKENT
ATOM ENER A . . . . . ATOMIC ENERGY IN AUSTRALIA
ATOM ENER R . . . . . ATOMIC ENERGY REVIEW
Atomic Energy L J . . ATOMIC ENERGY LAW JOURNAL
ATOMKERNENE . . . . ATOMKERNENERGIE
ATOMNAYA EN . . . . ATOMNAYA ENERGIYA
ATOM STROM . . . . . ATOM UND STROM
ATOMWIRTSCH . . . . ATOMWIRTSCHAFT-ATOMTECHNIK
ATopPir . . . . ACTAS DE LA PRIMERA REUNION DE TOPONIMIA PIRENAICA
ATP . . . . ARCHIVIO PER LO STUDIO DELLE TRADIZIONI POPULARI
ATP . . . . ARTS ET TRADITIONS POPULAIRES
ATQ . . . . AMERICAN TRANSCENDENTAL QUARTERLY
ATR . . . . ANGLICAN THEOLOGICAL REVIEW
ATR Aust Telecommun Res . . ATR, AUSTRALIAN TELECOMMUNICATION RESEARCH
ATren . . . . ARCHIVIO TRENTINO
ATriest . . . . ARCHEOGRAFO TRIESTINO
ATRJ . . . . ASSOCIATION OF TEACHERS OF RUSSIAN. JOURNAL
ATS . . . . ARBEITEN UND TEXTE ZUR SLAVISTIK
At Strom . . . . ATOM UND STROM
ATT ANL R F . . . . . . ATTI DELLA ACCADEMIA NAZIONALE DEI LINCEI RENDICONTI-CLASSE DI SCIENZE FISICHE-
                        MATHEMATICHE & NATURALI
ATT ASS GEN . . . . . . ATTI ASSOCIAZIONE GENETICA ITALIANA
Atti . . . . ATTI DEL CONGRESSO INTERNAZIONALE DI ESTETICA
AtV . . . . ATENEO VENETO
AU . . . . AFRIKA UND UEBERSEE
AU . . . . ANNALS OF THE UNIVERSITY. GRENOBLE
Au . . . . AUSONIA
AuA . . . . ANGLISTIK UND AMERIKANISTIK
AUA . . . . ANNALS OF THE UKRAINIAN ACADEMY OF ARTS AND SCIENCES IN THE U.S.
AUB . . . . ANALELE UNIVERSITATII BUCURESTI
AUB . . . . ANNALES DE L'UNIVERSITE DE BESANCON
AUBFF . . . . ARQUIVOS DA UNIVERSIDADE DE BAIA. FACULDADE DE FILOSOFIA
AUB-LG . . . . ANALELE UNIVERSITATII BUCURESTI. LIMBI GERMANICE
AUBLL . . . . ANALELE UNIVERSITATII BUCURESTI. LIMBA SI LITERATURA ROMANA
AUB-LLR . . . . ANALELE UNIVERSITATII BUCURESTI. LIMBA LITERARA
AUBLR . . . . ANALELE UNIVERSITATII BUCURESTI. LIMBI ROMANICE
AUB-LUC . . . . ANALELE UNIVERSITATII BUCURESTI. LITERATURA UNIVERSALA COMPARATA

AUBud . . . . ANNALES UNIVERSITATIS SCIENTIARUM BUDAPESTENSIS DE ROLANDO EOTVOS NOMINATAE. SECTIO PHILOLOGICA
AUC . . . . ACTA UNIVERSITATIS CAROLINAE
AUC . . . . ANALES DE LA UNIVERSIDAD DE CHILE
AUC . . . . ANUARUL UNIVERSITATEA CLUJ
AUCal . . . . ANNALI DELLE FACOLTA DI LETTERE. FILOSOFIA E MAGISTERO DELL'UNIVERSITA DI CAGLIARI
AUCC . . . . ANNUARIO DELL'UNIVERSITA CATTOLICA DEL S. CUORE
AUCE . . . . ANALES UNIVERSIDAD CENTRAL DEL ECUADOR
Auckland U L Rev . . . AUCKLAND UNIVERSITY LAW REVIEW
AUCP . . . . ACTA UNIVERSITATIS CAROLINAE PRAGENSIS
AUC-Ph . . . . ACTA UNIVERSITATIS CAROLINAE. PHILOLOGICA
AUD . . . . ACTA ET COMMENTATIONES UNIVERSITATIS DORPATENSIS
AUD . . . . AUDIENCE
Aud . . . . AUDUBON
Audio Engg . . . . AUDIO ENGINEERING
Audio Eng Soc J . . . . AUDIO ENGINEERING SOCIETY. JOURNAL
Audio Visual G . . . . . AUDIO-VISUAL GUIDE
AuE . . . . ARHEOLOGIJA UN ETNOGRAFIJA
AUF . . . . ARCHIV FUER URKUNDENFORSCHUNG
Aufbereit-Tech . . . . AUFBEREITUNGS-TECHNIK
AUG . . . . ANALES DE LA UNIVERSIDAD DE GUAYAQUIL
AUG . . . . ANNALES DE L'UNIVERSITE DE GRENOBLE
Aug . . . . AUGUSTINIANA
Augustin Stud . . . . . AUGUSTINIAN STUDIES
AUH . . . . ANALES DE LA UNIVERSIDAD HISPALENSE
AUHisp . . . . ANALES DE LA UNIVERSIDAD HISPALENSE
AUI . . . . ANALELE UNIVERSITATII AI. I. CUZA. IASI
AUJ . . . . ABERDEEN UNIVERSITY JOURNAL
Aujourd'hui . . . . AUJOURD'HUI: ART ET ARCHITECTURE
AUL . . . . ACTA UNIVERSITATIS LATVIENSIS
AUL . . . . ACTA UNIVERSITATIS LUNDENSIS
AUL . . . . ANNALES DE L'UNIVERSITE DE LYONS
AUL . . . . ANNALI DELL'UNIVERSITA DI LECCE
AUM . . . . ANALES DE LA UNIVERSIDAD DE MURCIA
AUMLA . . . . AUSTRALASIAN UNIVERSITIES MODERN LANGUAGE ASSOCIATION. JOURNAL
AUN . . . . ANNALI DELLA FACOLTA DI LETTERE E FILOSOFIA DELL'UNIVERSITA DI NAPOLI
AUO-Ph . . . . ACTA UNIVERSITATIS PALACKIANAE OLOMUCENSIS, FACULTAS PHILOSOPHICA, PHILOLOGICA
AUP . . . . ANNALES DE L' UNIVERSITE DE PARIS
AUPO . . . . ACTA UNIVERSITATIS PALACKIANAE OLOMUCENSIS
AUR . . . . ABERDEEN UNIVERSITY REVIEW
Aur . . . . AURORA
AUS . . . . ANNALES UNIVERSITATIS SARAVIENSIS
Aus . . . . AUSONIA
AUS AG&R . . . . ACTA UNIVERSITATIS SZEGEDIENSIS. ACTA GERMANICA ET ROMANICA
AUS AHLH . . . . ACTA UNIVERSITATIS SZEGEDIENSIS DE ATTILA JOZSEF NOMINATAE SECTIO: ACTA HISTORIAE LITTERARUM HUNGARICARUM
AUS E&L . . . . ACTA UNIVERSITATIS SZEGEDIENSIS DE ATTILA JOZSEF NOMINATAE SECTIO: ETHNOGRAPHICA ET LINGUISTICA
AUSem St . . . . ANDREWS UNIVERSITY SEMINARY STUDIES

PERIODICAL TITLE ABBREVIATIONS

AUSGRAB FUN..... AUSGRABUNGEN UND FUNDE
AusL........... AUSTRALIAN LETTERS
AusQ.......... AUSTRALIAN QUARTERLY
AUSSEN POLI...... AUSSEN POLITIK
Aust Acad and Res Lib.. AUSTRALIAN ACADEMIC AND RESEARCH LIBRARIES
Aust Bldg Forum... AUSTRALIA BUILDING FORUM
Aust Chem Eng.... AUSTRALIAN CHEMICAL ENGINEERING
Aust Civ Eng...... AUSTRALIAN CIVIL ENGINEERING
Aust Commonw Dept Supply Aeronaut Res Comm Rep.. AUSTRALIA. COMMONWEALTH OF DEPARTMENT OF SUPPLY. AERONAUTICAL RESEARCH COMMITTEE. REPORT
Aust Comput J..... AUSTRALIAN COMPUTER JOURNAL
AUST ECON....... AUSTRALIAN ECONOMIC PAPERS
AUST ECON H..... AUSTRALIAN ECONOMIC HISTORY REVIEW
AUST GEOGR...... AUSTRALIAN GEOGRAPHER
AUST GEOG S...... AUSTRALIAN GEOGRAPHICAL STUDIES
Aust Geomech J... AUSTRALIAN GEOMECHANICS JOURNAL
AUST J AG E...... AUSTRALIAN JOURNAL OF AGRICULTURAL ECONOMICS
AUST J AGR....... AUSTRALIAN JOURNAL OF AGRICULTURAL RESEARCH
AUST J BIOL...... AUSTRALIAN JOURNAL OF BIOLOGICAL SCIENCES
Aust J Bot........ AUSTRALIAN JOURNAL OF BOTANY
AUST J CHEM..... AUSTRALIAN JOURNAL OF CHEMISTRY
AUST J DAIR...... AUSTRALIAN JOURNAL OF DAIRY TECHNOLOGY
AUST J EDUC...... AUSTRALIAN JOURNAL OF EDUCATION
AUST J EX B...... AUSTRALIAN JOURNAL OF EXPERIMENTAL BIOLOGY AND MEDICAL SCIENCE
Aust J Exper Agric.. AUSTRALIAN JOURNAL OF EXPERIMENTAL AGRICULTURE
AUST J INST...... AUSTRALIAN JOURNAL OF INSTRUMENTATION AND CONTROL
AUST J MAR...... AUSTRALIAN JOURNAL OF MARINE AND FRESHWATER RESEARCH
Aust J Phys....... AUSTRALIAN JOURNAL OF PHYSICS
AUST J POLI...... AUSTRALIAN JOURNAL OF POLITICS AND HISTORY
AUST J PSYC...... AUSTRALIAN JOURNAL OF PSYCHOLOGY
AUST J SOC....... AUSTRALIAN JOURNAL OF SOCIAL ISSUES
AUST J SOIL...... AUSTRALIAN JOURNAL OF SOIL RESEARCH
AUST J STAT...... AUSTRALIAN JOURNAL OF STATISTICS
AUST J ZOOL...... AUSTRALIAN JOURNAL OF ZOOLOGY
Aust Law........ AUSTRALIAN LAWYER
Aust Lib J........ AUSTRALIAN LIBRARY JOURNAL
Aust L J......... AUSTRALIAN LAW JOURNAL
Austl J Phil....... THE AUSTRALASIAN JOURNAL OF PHILOSOPHY
Aust Mach Prod Eng.. AUSTRALIAN MACHINERY AND PRODUCTION ENGINEERING
Aust Min........ AUSTRALIAN MINING
AUST NZ J C...... AUSTRALIAN AND NEW ZEALAND JOURNAL OF CRIMINOLOGY
AUST NZ J M...... AUSTRALIAN AND NEW ZEALAND JOURNAL OF MEDICINE
AUST NZ J O...... AUSTRALIAN AND NEW ZEALAND JOURNAL OF OBSTETRICS AND GYNAECOLOGY
AUST NZ J P...... AUSTRALIAN AND NEW ZEALAND JOURNAL OF PSYCHIATRY
AUST NZ J S...... AUSTRALIAN AND NEW ZEALAND JOURNAL OF SURGERY
AUST NZ SOC..... AUSTRALIAN AND NEW ZEALAND JOURNAL OF SOCIOLOGY
AUST OUTLOO..... AUSTRALIAN OUTLOOK
AUST PAEDIA..... AUSTRALIAN PAEDIATRIC JOURNAL
Aust Plast Rubber J.. AUSTRALIAN PLASTICS & RUBBER JOURNAL
AUST PSYCHL..... AUSTRALIAN PSYCHOLOGIST
AUST QUART...... AUSTRALIAN QUARTERLY
AUST RADIOL..... AUSTRALASIAN RADIOLOGY

51

Australas Corros Eng . . AUSTRALASIAN CORROSION ENGINEERING
Australas Eng . . . . . AUSTRALASIAN ENGINEER
Australas Inst Mining Met Proc . . AUSTRALASIAN INSTITUTE OF MINING AND METALLURGY. PROCEEDINGS
Australian and N Z J Sociol . . AUSTRALIAN AND NEW ZEALAND JOURNAL OF SOCIOLOGY
Australian For J . . . . AUSTRALIAN FORESTRY JOURNAL
AUSTRALIAN J MUS ED . . AUSTRALIAN JOURNAL OF MUSIC EDUCATION
Australian J Psychol . . AUSTRALIAN JOURNAL OF PSYCHOLOGY
Australian Lib J . . . . AUSTRALIAN LIBRARY JOURNAL
Aust Road Res . . . . . AUSTRALIAN ROAD RESEARCH
Aust Road Res Board Bull . . AUSTRALIAN ROAD RESEARCH BOARD. BULLETIN
Aust Surv . . . . AUSTRALIAN SURVEYOR
Aust Vet J . . . . AUSTRALIAN VETERINARY JOURNAL
Aust Weld J . . . . AUSTRALIAN WELDING JOURNAL
Aust Weld Res Ass Bull . . AUSTRALIAN WELDING RESEARCH ASSOCIATION. BULLETIN
Aust Yearbook int L . . AUSTRALIAN YEARBOOK OF INTERNATIONAL LAW
AUT . . . . ANALELE UNIVERSITATII DIN TIMISOARA. SERIA, STIINTE FILOLOGICE
AUT . . . . ANNALES UNIVERSITATIS TURKUENSIS
AUT . . . . ANNALI DELLE UNIVERSITA TOSCANE
AUT . . . . AUTHENTIC SCIENCE FICTION
AUT ENG . . . . AUTOMOTIVE ENGINEERING
Auto Eng . . . . AUTOMOBILE ENGINEER
Automat Elec Tech J . . AUTOMATIC ELECTRIC TECHNICAL JOURNAL
Automation (Cleve) . . AUTOMATION (CLEVELAND)
Automat Monit Mea . . AUTOMATIC MONITORING AND MEASURING
Automat Remote Contr . . AUTOMATION AND REMOTE CONTROL
Automobil Tech Z . . AUTOMOBILE TECHNISCHE ZEITSCHRIFT
Automot Des Eng . . . AUTOMOTIVE DESIGN ENGINEERING
Automot Eng . . . . . . AUTOMOTIVE ENGINEERING
Automot Ind . . . . . . AUTOMOTIVE INDUSTRIES
Automotive & Aviation Ind . . AUTOMOTIVE AND AVIATION INDUSTRIES
Autom Remote Control . . AUTOMATION AND REMOTE CONTROL
AUT REMOT R . . . . . AUTOMATION AND REMOTE CONTROL (USSR)
AUT WELD R . . . . . . AUTOMATIC WELDING (USSR)
AuU . . . . AFRIKA UND UEBERSEE
AUV . . . . ANALES DE LA UNIVERSIDAD DE VALENCIA
AUW . . . . ACTA UNIVERSITATIS WRATISLAVIENSIS
AV . . . . ANNALES VALAISANNES
AV . . . . ARCHIVIO VENETO
AV . . . . ARTHA VIJNANA
AV . . . . ATENEO VENETO
AV . . . . AV COMMUNICATION REVIEW
AV . . . . AUS AACHENS VORZEIT
A VAN LEEUW . . . . . ANTONIE VAN LEEUWENHOEK JOURNAL OF MICROBIOLOGY AND SEROLOGY
AVBWKN . . . . ANNALEN DER VEREENIGING TOT HET HEVORDEREN VAN DE BEOEFENING DER WETENSCHAP
ONDER DE KATHOLIEKEN IN NEDERLAND
AVCO Corp Res Rep . . AVCO CORPORATION. RESEARCH REPORTS
Av Comm R . . . . AV COMMUNICATION REVIEW
AVCR . . . . AV COMMUNICATION REVIEW
AVen . . . . ARCHIVIO VENETO

AVF. . . . . ARCHIVOS VENEZOLANOS DE FOLKLORE
AVIAN DIS. . . . . . . AVIAN DISEASES
Aviation N. . . . . AVIATION NEWS
Aviation W. . . . . . . AVIATION WEEK
Aviat Res Monogr. . AVIATION RESEARCH MONOGRAPHS
AVIAT SP EN. . . . . . AVIATION SPACE AND ENVIRONMENTAL MEDICINE
Av Instr. . . . . AUDIOVISUAL INSTRUCTION
AV Media. . . . . AUDIO-VISUAL MEDIA
AVNAG. . . . . ANNALEN DES VEREINS FUER NASSAUISCHE ALTERTUMSKUNDE UND GESCHICHTSFORSCHUNG
AVNAKGF. . . . . . . ANNALEN DES VEREINS FUER NASSAUISCHE ALTERTUMSKUNDE UND GESCHICHTSFORSCHUNG
AVSLK. . . . . ARCHIV DES VEREINS FUER SIEBENBUERGISCHE LANDESKUNDE
AVsLund. . . . . VETENSKAPS-SOCIETETEN I LUND. ARSBOK
AVT. . . . . ARCHIVIO VENETO-TRIDENTINO
Avtomat i Telemekh. . AVTOMATIKA I TELEMEKHANIKA
AW. . . . . AIR WONDER STORIES
AW. . . . . ANNALS OF WYOMING
AWA Tech Rev. . . . . AWA (AMALGAMATED WIRELESS AUSTRALASIA) TECHNICAL REVIEW
AWBAbh. . . . . KOENIGLICH-PREUSSISCHE AKADEMIE DER WISSENSCHAFTEN ZU BERLIN. ABHANDLUNGEN
AWBSb. . . . . KOENIGLICH-PREUSSISCHE AKADEMIE DER WISSENSCHAFTEN ZU BERLIN. SITZUNGSBERICHTE
AWLMGS. . . . . AKADEMIE DER WISSENSCHAFTEN UND LITERATUR (MAINZ): GEISTES- UND SOZIAL-
WISSENSCHAFT-LICHEN KLASSE
AWLML. . . . . AKADEMIE DER WISSENSCHAFTEN UND LITERATURE (MAINZ): KLASSE DER LITERATUR
AWMAbh. . . . . AKADEMIE DER WISSENSCHAFTEN. MUENCHEN. ABHANDLUNGEN
AWMSb. . . . . AKADEMIE DER WISSENSCHAFTEN. MUENCHEN. PHILOSOPHISCHE-HISTORISCHE KLASSE.
SITZUNGSBERICHTE
AWR. . . . . ANGLO-WELSH REVIEW
AWS. . . . . AIR WONDER STORIES
AWWDs. . . . . KOENIGLICHE AKADEMIE DER WISSENSCHAFTEN. WIEN. DENKSCHRIFTEN
AWWSb. . . . . AKADEMIE DER WISSENSCHAFTEN. WIEN. SITZUNGSBERICHTE
AYB. . . . . AMERICAN YEAR REVIEW
AYLR. . . . . AYLESFORD REVIEW
AZ. . . . . ARCHIVALISCHE ZEITSCHRIFT

B

B............. BARCELONA
B............. BIBLIOFILIA
B............. BIBLIOTEKARZ
B............. BIEKORF
B............. BIGAKU
B............. BRAZDA
B............. BROADCASTING
Ba............ BABEL
Ba............ BACONIANA
BA............ BALKAN ARCHIV
BA............ BOLLETTINO D'ARTE
BA............ BOOKS ABROAD
BA............ BUENOS AIRES
BAA........... BULLETIN DES ARCHIVES D'ANVERS
BAABL......... BOLETIN DE LA ACADEMIA ARGENTINA DE BUENAS LETRAS
BAAFLP.........BULLETIN DE L'ASSOCIATION AMICALE DES ANCIENS ELEVES DE LA FACULTE DES LETTRES DE PARIS
BAAJ.......... BRITISH ARCHAEOLOGICAL ASSOCIATION JOURNAL
BAAL.......... BOLETIN DE LA ACADEMIA ARGENTINA DE LETRAS
BAAR.......... BOLLETTINO DELL'ASSOCIAZIONE ARCHEOLOGICA ROMANA
BAARD......... BULLETIN DE L'ASSOCIATION DES AMIS DE RABELAIS ET DE LA DEVINIERE
BAASB......... BRITISH ASSOCIATION FOR AMERICAN STUDIES BULLETIN
BAB........... ACADEMIE ROYALE DE BELGIQUE. BULLETIN DE LA CLASSE DES LETTRES ET DES SCIENCES MORALES ET POLITIQUES
BABA.......... BOLETIN DE LA ACADEMIA DE BELLAS ARTES DE VALLADOLID
BABAT......... BOLETIN DE LA ACADEMIA DE BELLAS ARTES Y CIENCIAS HISTORICAS DE TOLEDO
BABC.......... BOLETIN DE LA ACADEMIA DE BELLAS ARTES DE CORDOBA
BABL.......... BOLETIN DE LA REAL ACADEMIA DE BUENAS LETRAS DE BARCELONA
BABLB......... BOLETIN DE LA REAL ACADEMIA DE BUENAS LETRAS DE BARCELONA
BABN.......... BOLLETTINO DELL'ARCHIVIO STORICO DEL BANCO DI NAPOLI
BAC........... BIBLIOTECA DE AUTORES CRISTIANOS
BAC........... BOLETIN DE LA ACADEMIA COLOMBIANA
BAC........... BOLETIN DE LA REAL ACADEMIA DE CORDOBA
BACA.......... BULLETI DE L'ASSOCIACIO CATALANA D'ANTROPOLOGIA
B ACAD SCI...... BULLETIN OF THE ACADEMY OF SCIENCES OF THE USSR. DIVISION OF CHEMICAL SCIENCE
BACBLNAC...... BOLETIN DE LA ACADEMIA DE CIENCIAS. BELLAS LETRAS Y NOBLES ARTES DE CORDOBA
Bach of Arts...... BACHELOR OF ARTS
BACILg......... BULLETIN SEMESTRIEL DE L'ASSOCIATION DES CLASSIQUES DE L'UNIVERSITES DE LEIGE
BACL.......... BOLETIN DE LA ACADEMIA CUBANA DE LA LENGUA
BACM.......... BULLETIN DE L'ACADEMIE POUR L'HISTOIRE DE LA CULTURE MATERIELLE
BACol.......... BOLETIN DE LA ACADEMIA COLOMBIANA
BACTH......... BULLETIN ARCHEOLOGIQUE DU COMITE DES TRAVAUX HISTORIQUES ET SCIENTIFIQUES (PARIS)
BACTHS........ BULLETIN ARCHEOLOGIQUE DU COMITE DES TRAVAUX HISTORIQUES ET SCIENTIFIQUES (PARIS)
Bact R.......... BACTERIOLOGICAL REVIEWS
BACT REV........ BACTERIOLOGICAL REVIEWS
Bact Rs.......... BACTERIOLOGICAL REVIEWS
Badische Hist Komm Neujahrsbl.. BADISCHE HISTORISCHE KOMMISSION NEUJAHRSBLAETTER
BADL.......... BONNER ARBEITEN ZUR DEUTSCHEN LITERATUR
BADWS......... BAYERISCHE AKADEMIE DER WISSENSCHAFTEN. PHILOSOPHISCH-HISTORISCHE KLASSE. SITZUNGSBERICHTE

BAE. . . . . BIBLIOTECA DE AUTORES ESPANOLES
BAE. . . . . BOLETIN DE LA REAL ACADEMIA ESPANOLA
BAEC. . . . . BULLETIN DE L'ASSOCIATION DES AMIS DES EGLISES ET DE L'ART COPTES
BAEPE. . . . . BOLETIN DE LA ASOCIACION EUROPEA DE PROFESORES DE ESPANOL
BAF. . . . . BAMBERGER ABHANDLUNGEN UND FORSCHUNGEN
BAF. . . . . BULLETIN DES AMIS DE FLAUBERT
BAFA. . . . . BOLETIN DE LA ASOCIACION FOLKLORICA (ARGENTINA)
BAG. . . . . BEITRAEGE ZUR ALTEN GESCHICHTE
BAG. . . . . BOLETIN DE LA ACADEMIA GALLEGA
BAGB. . . . . BULLETIN DE L'ASSOCIATION GUILLAUME BUDE
BAGB(SC). . . . . . . BULLETIN DE L'ASSOCIATION GUILLAUME BUDE. SUPPLEMENT CRITIQUE
BAH. . . . . BOLETIN DE LA ACADEMIA DE LA HISTORIA
BAH. . . . . BULLETIN DE L'ACADEMIE D'HIPPONE
BAH. . . . . BUSINESS ARCHIVES AND HISTORY
BAHD. . . . . BULLETIN D'ARCHEOLOGIE ET D'HISTOIRE DALMATE
BAHist . . . . BOLETIN DE LA R. ACADEMIA DE LA HISTORIA
BIA. . . . . BULLETIN OF THE AMERICAN INSTITUTE OF SWEDISH ARTS, LITERATURE AND SCIENCE
BAIBL. . . . . BULLETIN. ACADEMIE DES INSCRIPTIONS ET BELLES-LETTRES
BAL. . . . . BUENOS AIRES LITERARIA
BALA. . . . . BULLETIN DE L'ASSOCIATION LYONNAISE DE RECHERCHES ARCHEOLOGIQUES
BALA. . . . . BULLETIN OF THE AMERICAN LIBRARY ASSOCIATION
BALAC. . . . . BULLETIN D'ANCIENNE LITTERATURE ET D'ARCHEOLOGIE CHRETIENNES
BALB. . . . . BOLETIN DE LA R. ACADEMIA DE BUENAS LETRAS DE BARCELONA
BALF. . . . . BULLETIN DE L'ACADEMIE ROYALE DE LANGUE ET DE LITTERATURE FRANCAISES
BALI. . . . . BOLLETTINO DELL'ATLANTE LINGUISTICO ITALIANO
BALit. . . . . BIBLIOTEKA ANALIZ LITERACKICH
BalkE. . . . . BALKANSKO EZIKOZNANIJE
Ball Bear J. . . . . . . BALL BEARING JOURNAL
Ball Roller Bear Eng. . BALL AND ROLLER BEARING ENGINEERING
Ball State J. . . . . . . BALL STATE JOURNAL FOR BUSINESS EDUCATORS
BALM. . . . . BOLLETTINO DELL'ATLANTE LINGUISTICO MEDITERRANEO
Bal Sheet. . . . . BALANCE SHEET
Bal St. . . . . BALKAN STUDIES
Baltimore B of Ed. . . BALTIMORE BULLETIN OF EDUCATION
Baltimore Mus Art N. . BALTIMORE MUSEUM OF ART. NEWS
Baltimore Mus N. . . BALTIMORE MUSEUM OF ART. NEWS
BAM. . . . . BUENOS AIRES MUSICAL
BAM. . . . . BULLETIN D'ARCHEOLOGIE MAROCAINE
BAMalgache. . . . . . BULLETIN DE L'ACADEMIE MALGACHE
B AM ANTH A. . . . . BULLETIN OF THE AMERICAN ANTHROPOLOGICAL ASSOCIATION
B AM MATH S. . . . . BULLETIN OF THE AMERICAN MATHEMATICAL SOCIETY
B AM METEOR. . . . . BULLETIN OF THE AMERICAN METEOROLOGICAL SOCIETY
B AM PHYS S. . . . . . BULLETIN OF THE AMERICAN PHYSICAL SOCIETY
BANAZ. . . . . BOLETIN DE LA ACADEMIA ARAGONESA DE NOBLES Y BELLAS ARTES DE SAN LUIS DE ZARAGOZA
B&B. . . . . BOOKS & BOOKMEN
BANHQ. . . . . BOLETIN DE LA ACADEMIA NACIONAL DE LA HISTORIA (QUITO)
Banker-F. . . . . BANKER-FARMER

Bankers M . . . . BANKERS' MAGAZINE
Bankers Mo . . . . BANKERS' MONTHLY
BANK LAW J . . . . . . BANKING LAW JOURNAL
Bank M (L) . . . . BANKERS' MAGAZINE (LONDON)
Bank M (Lond) . . . . . BANKERS' MAGAZINE (LONDON)
Bank M (N.Y.) . . . . . BANKERS' MAGAZINE (NEW YORK)
BANQ . . . . BIBLIONEWS AND AUSTRALIAN NOTES AND QUERIES
BAPC . . . . BULLETIN DE L'ACADEMIE POLONAISE DE CRACOVIE
BAPE . . . . BOLETIM DA ACADEMIA PORTUGUESA DO EX-LIBRIS
BAPEL . . . . BOLETIM DA ACADEMIA PORTUGUESA DO EX-LIBRIS
BAPI . . . . BOLLETTINO DELL'ARCHIVIO PALEOGRAFICO ITALIANO
BAPSL . . . . BULLETIN DE L'ACADEMIE POLONAISE DES SCIENCES ET DES LETTRES
Bapt Hist and Heritage . . BAPTIST HISTORY AND HERITAGE
Bapt Q . . . . BAPTIST QUARTERLY (LONDON)
Bapt Q . . . . BAPTIST QUARTERLY REVIEW
BAR . . . . ASSOCIATION DES AMIS DE RABELAIS ET DE LA DEVINIERE. BULLETIN
Bar . . . . BARETTI
BAR . . . . BIBLIOTECA DELL'ARCHIVUM ROMANICUM
BARAB . . . . BULLETIN DE ACADEMIE ROYALE D'ARCHEOLOGIE DE BELGIQUE
Barat R . . . . BARAT REVIEW
BARB . . . . ACADEMIE ROYALE DE BELGIQUE. BULLETIN DE LA CLASSE DES LETTRES ET DES SCIENCES
MORALES ET POLITIQUES ET DE LA CLASSE DES BEAUX-ARTS
Bar Bull (Boston) . . . BAR BULLETIN OF THE BOSTON BAR ASSOCIATION
Bar Bull (N Y County Law A) . . NEW YORK COUNTY LAWYERS ASSOCIATION BAR BULLETIN
BARD . . . . BULLETIN DES AMIS DE RABELAIS ET DE LA DEVINIERE
BA Rev . . . . BLACK ACADEMY REVIEW
Bar Exam . . . . BAR EXAMINER
BARLLF . . . . BULLETIN DE L'ACADEMIE ROYALE DE LANGUE ET DE LITTERATURE FRANCAISES
B Arn . . . . BIBLIOTHECA ARNAMAGNAEANA
BASD . . . . BOLLETTINO DI ARCHEOLOGIA E STORIA DALMATA
BASI . . . . BULLETIN OF THE AMERICAN SWEDISH INSTITUTE
BASL . . . . BOCHUMER ARBEITEN ZUR SPRACH- UND LITERATURWISSENSCHAFT
Basler Z Gesch & Altertumsk . . BASLER ZEITSCHRIFT FUER GESCHICHTE UND ALTERTUMSKUNDE
BASM . . . . BOLLETTINO DELL'ASSOZIAZIONE PER GLI STUDI MEDITERRANEI
BASO . . . . BULLETIN OF THE AMERICAN SCHOOLS OF ORIENTAL RESEARCH IN JERUSALEM & BAGDAD
BASOR . . . . BULLETIN OF THE AMERICAN SCHOOLS OF ORIENTAL RESEARCH
BASP . . . . BULLETIN OF THE AMERICAN SOCIETY OF PAPYROLOGISTS
BASP . . . . BOLLETTINO DELLA R. ACCADEMIA DE SCIENZE, LETTERE E BELLE ARTI DI PALERMO
BASR . . . . BULLETIN DE L'ACADEMIE DES SCIENCES DE RUSSIE
BAS R CARD . . . . . . BASIC RESEARCH IN CARDIOLOGY
BASS Sound . . . . BASS SOUND POST
B ASTR I CZ . . . . . . BULLETIN OF THE ASTRONOMICAL INSTITUTES OF CZECHOSLOVAKIA
BASURSS . . . . BULLETIN DE L'ACADEMIE DES SCIENCES DE L'U.R.S.S.
BAT . . . . BATAILLE
BAT . . . . BOLETIN ARQUEOLOGICO DE TARRAGONE
BATF . . . . BOLETIN DE LA ASOCIACION TUCUMANA DE FOLKLORE
B ATOM SCI . . . . BULLETIN OF THE ATOMIC SCIENTISTS
Battelle Mem Inst DCIC Rep . . BATTELLE MEMORIAL INSTITUTE, DEFENSE CERAMIC INFORMATION CENTER, DCIC
REPORT
Battelle Mem Inst DMIC Memo . . BATTELLE MEMORIAL INSTITUTE, DEFENSE METALS INFORMATION CENTER, DMIC
MEMORANDUM
Battelle Mem Inst DMIC Rep . . BATTELLE MEMORIAL INSTITUTE, DEFENSE METALS INFORMATION CENTER, DMIC
REPORT

Battelle Res Outlook . . BATTELLE RESEARCH OUTLOOK
BATTELLE MG . . . . . BATTELLE MONOGRAPHS
Battelle Tech R . . . . BATTELLE TECHNICAL REVIEW
Bau & Werk . . . . BAUKUNST UND WERKFORM
Baumasch Bautech . . BAUMASCHINE UND BAUTECHNIK
Bautech-Arch . . . . . BAUTECHNIK-ARCHIV
BAV . . . . BOLETIN DE LA ACADEMIA VENEZOLANA
BAWS . . . . BAYERISCHE AKADEMIE DER WISSENSCHAFTEN. PHILOSOPHISCH HISTORISCHE KLASSE. SITZUNGSBERICHTE
Bax S . . . . ARNOLD BAX SOCIETY BULLETIN
Bayer Akad d Wiss Philos-Philol u Hist Kl Abhandl . . BAYERISCHE AKADEMIE DER WISSENSCHAFTEN. PHILOSOPHISCH-PHILOLOGISCHE UND HISTORISCHE KLASSE. ABHANDLUNGEN
Bayer Akad Wiss Math-Naturw Abt Abh . . BAYERISCHE AKADEMIE DER WISSENSCHAFTEN MATHEMATISCH-NATURWISSENSCHAFTLICHE ABTEILUNG. ABHANDLUNGEN
Bayer Akad Wiss Philos-Hist Abt Abh . . BAYERISCHE AKADEMIE DER WISSENSCHAFTEN. PHILOSOPHISCH-HISTORISCHE ABTEILUNG. ABHANDLUNGEN
BAYER SITZB . . . . . . BAYERISCHEN AKADEMIE DER WISSENSCHAFTEN SITZUNGSBERICHTE
BAYLOR LAW . . . . . BAYLOR LAW REVIEW
Baylor L Rev . . . . . BAYLOR LAW REVIEW
Bay State Libn . . . . BAY STATE LIBRARIAN
Bay State Mo . . . . . BAY STATE MONTHLY
BB . . . . BAYREUTHER BLAETTER
BB . . . . BILLBOARD
BB . . . . BONNER BEITRAEGE
BB . . . . BOOKS AND BOOKMEN
BB . . . . BOSSCHE BIJDRAGEN
BB . . . . BULLETIN DU BIBLIOPHILE ET DU BIBLIOTHECAIRE
BBB . . . . BULLETIN DU BIBLIOPHILE ET DU BIBLIOTHECAIRE
BB . . . . BULLETIN OF BIBLIOGRAPHY
BBA . . . . BERLINER BYZANTINISTISCHE ARBEITEN
BBAA . . . . BOLETIN BIBLIOGRAFICO DE ANTROPOLOGIA AMERICANA
BBB . . . . BOLETIN DE BIBLIOTECAS Y BIBLIOGRAFIA
BBBr . . . . BOLETIM BIBLIOGRAFICO BRASILEIRO
B B C Eng . . . . B B C (BRITISH BROADCASTING CORPORATION) ENGINEERING
B B C Eng Div Monogr . . B B C (BRITISH BROADCASTING CORPORATION) ENGINEERING DIVISION MONOGRAPH
BBCS . . . . BULLETIN OF THE BOARD OF CELTIC STUDIES
BBDI . . . . BULLETIN OF BIBLIOGRAPHY AND DRAMATIC INDEX
BBF . . . . BULLETIN DES BIBLIOTHEQUES DE FRANCE
BBG . . . . BASLER BEITRAEGE ZUR GESCHICHTSWISSENSCHAFT
BBG . . . . BLAETTER FUER DAS BAYERISCHE GYMNASIAL-SCHULWESEN
BBGG . . . . BOLLETTINO DELLA BADIA GRECA DI GROTTAFERRATA
BBH . . . . BULLETIN ANALYTIQUE DE BIBLIOGRAPHIE HELLENIQUE
BBib . . . . BESCHREIBENDE BIBLIOGRAPHIEN
BBibl . . . . BULLETIN DU BIBLIOPHILE
BBK . . . . BIBLIOTEKININKYSTES IR BIBLIOGRAFIJOS KLAUSIMAI
BBKG . . . . BEITRAEGE ZUR BAYERISCHEN KIRCHENGESCHICHTE
BBL . . . . BIBLIOTEKSBLADET
BBLA . . . . BEITRAEGE ZUR BIBLISCHEN LANDES-UND ALTERTUMSKUNDE
BBLAK . . . . BEITRAEGE ZUR BIBLISCHEN LANDES-UND ALTERTUMSKUNDE
BBLG . . . . BASLER BEITRAEGE ZUR DEUTSCHEN LITERATUR-UND GEISTESGESCHICHTE
BBM . . . . BOLETIN BIBLIOGRAFICO MEXICANO

BBMB . . . . BULLETIN BIBLIOGRAPHIQUE DU MUSEE BELGE
BBMP . . . . BOLETIN DE LA BIBLIOTECA DE MENENDEZ PELAYO
BBN . . . . BERLINER BEITRAEGE ZUR NAMENFORSCHUNG
BBNL . . . . BOLETIN DE LA BIBLIOTECA NATIONAL. LIMA
BBNM . . . . BOLETIN DE LA BIBLIOTECA NATIONAL. MEXICO
BBOJ . . . . BERKS, BUCKS AND OXON. ARCHAEOLOGICAL JOURNAL
BBPMB . . . . BULLETIN BIBLIOGRAPHIQUE DU MUSEE BELGE
BBr . . . . BOOKS AT BROWN
BBR . . . . BULETINUL BIBLIOTECII ROMANE
BBRP . . . . BERLINER BEITRAEGE ZUR ROMANISCHEN PHILOLOGIE
B BR PSYCHO . . . . . BULLETIN OF THE BRITISH PSYCHOLOGICAL SOCIETY
BBS . . . . BULLETIN OF BALTIC STUDIES
BBSIA . . . . BULLETIN BIBLIOGRAPHIQUE DE LA SOCIETE INTERNATIONALE ARTHURIENNE
BBSP . . . . BOTETOURT BIBLIOGRAPHICAL SOCIETY PUBLICATIONS
BBST . . . . BIBLIOTHEQUE BONAVENTURIENNE. SERIES "TEXTES"
BBY . . . . BRITANNICA BOOK OF THE YEAR
BByzA . . . . BERLINER BYZANTINISCHE ARBEITEN. DEUTSCHE AKADEMIE DER WISSENSCHAFTEN ZU BERLIN
BByzl . . . . BULLETIN OF THE BYZANTINE INSTITUTE
BC . . . . BIBLIOTHECA CELTICA
BC . . . . BOLETIM CULTURAL. CAMARA MUNICIPAL DO PORTO
BC . . . . BOLLETTINO DELLA CAPITALE
BC . . . . BOOK COLLECTOR
B/C . . . . BROADCASTING
BC . . . . BULLETIN CRITIQUE
BC . . . . BULLETIN OF THE COMEDIANTES. UNIVERSITY OF WISCONSIN
BCA . . . . BLAETTER FUER CHRISTLICHE ARCHAEOLOGIE UND KUNST
BCAC . . . . BOLLETTINO DELLA COMMISSIONE ARCHEOLOGICA COMUNALE DI ROMA
BCACR . . . . BOLLETTINO DELLA COMMISSIONE ARCHEOLOGICA COMUNALE DI ROMA
BCAM . . . . BULLETIN DU CERCLE ARCHEOLOGIQUE, LITTERAIRE ET ARTISTIQUE DE MALINES
BCAN . . . . BULLETIN DE LA COMMISSION ARCHEOLOGIQUE DE NARBONNE
B CANCER . . . . BULLETIN DU CANCER
BCA NEWS . . . . BCA (BUSINESS COMMITTEE FOR THE ARTS) NEWS
BCAR . . . . BOLLETTINO DELLA COMMISSIONE ARCHEOLOGICA COMUALE IN ROMA
BCB . . . . BOLETIN CULTURAL Y BIBLIOGRAFICO (BOGOTA)
BCBA . . . . ACADEMIE ROYALE DE BELGIQUE. BULLETIN DE LA CLASSE DES BEAUX-ARTS
BCBL . . . . BULLETIN DU CERCLE BELGE DE LINGUISTIQUE
BCCCN . . . . BOLLETTINO PER LA COMMEMORAZIONE DEL XVI CENTENARIO DEL CONCILIO DI NICEA
BCCF . . . . BOLLETTINO CRITICO DI COSE FRANCESCANE
BCCMP . . . . BOLETIM CULTURAL, CAMARA, MUNICIPAL DO PORTO
BCDI . . . . BOLLETTINO DELLA CARTA DEI DIALETTI ITALIANI
BCEDLFB . . . . BULLETIN DU CENTRE D'ETUDES ET DE DISCUSSION DE LITTERATURE FRANCAISE DE
L'UNIVERSITE DE BORDEAUX
BCF . . . . BOLETIM TRIMESTRAL SUBCOMISSAO CATARINENSE DE FOLCLORE DA COMISSAO NACIONAL
BRASILEIRA DE FOLCLORE DO INSTITUTO BRASILEIRO DE EDUCACAO, CIENCIA E CULTURA
BCFF . . . . BULLETIN DU COMITE FLAMAND DE FRANCE
BCGuineP . . . . BOLETIM CULTURAL DA GUINE PORTUGUESA
BCH . . . . BULLETIN DI CORRESPONDANCE HELLENIQUE
BCHAC . . . . BULLETIN DU CERCLE HISTORIQUE ET ARCHEOLOGIQUE DE COURTRAI
B CHEM S J . . . . BULLETIN OF THE CHEMICAL SOCIETY OF JAPAN
BCHS . . . . BULLETIN OF THE CINCINNATI HISTORICAL SOCIETY
BC IND & COM L R . . BOSTON COLLEGE INDUSTRIAL & COMMERCIAL LAW REVIEW

BCIRA J......... BCIRA (BRITISH CAST IRON RESEARCH ASSOCIATION) JOURNAL
BCLA Rept........BCLA (BRITISH COLUMBIA LIBRARY ASSOCIATION) REPORTER
BCLC............BULLETIN DU CERCLE LINGUISTIQUE DE COPENHAGUE
BCLF............BULLETIN CRITIQUE DU LIVRE FRANCAIS
B C LIB Q........BRITISH COLUMBIA LIBRARY QUARTERLY
BCLQ...........BRITISH COLUMBIA LIBRARY QUARTERLY
BCLSMP.........ACADEMIE ROYALE DE BELGIQUE. BULLETIN DE LA CLASSE DES LETTRES ET DES SCIENCES MORALES ET POLITIQUES
BCM............BULETINUL COMISIUNII MONUMENTELOR ISTORICE
BCMA...........BULLETIN OF THE CLEVELAND MUSEUM OF ART
BCMB...........BOLETIN DE LA COMISION DE MONUMENTOS DE BURGOS
BCML...........BOLETIN DE LA COMISION DE MONUMENTOS DE LUGO
BCMV...........BOLETIN DE LA COMISION DE MONUMENTOS DE VALLADOLID
BCMVASA........BULLETIN OF THE CENTRAL MISSISSIPPI VALLEY AMERICAN STUDIES ASSOCIATION
BCO............BIBLIOTHECA CLASSICA ORIENTALIS
BCol...........BOOK COLLECTOR
B Com..........BULLETIN OF THE COMEDIANTES
B CON AS SC......BULLETIN OF CONCERNED ASIAN SCHOLARS
B COPYRGT S......BULLETIN OF THE COPYRIGHT SOCIETY OF THE U.S.A.
BCPN...........BOLETIN DE LA COMISION PROVINCIAL DE MONUMENTOS DE NAVARRA
BCPO...........BOLETIN DE LA COMISION PROVINCIAL DE MONUMENTOS DE ORENSE
BCPOrense.......BOLETIN DE LA COMISION PROVINCIAL DE MONUMENTOS DE ORENSE
BCQ............BOOK COLLECTOR'S QUARTERLY
BCr............BULLETIN CRITIQUE DU LIVRE FRANCAIS
BCRAA..........BULLETIN DES COMMISSIONS ROYALES D'ART ET D'ARCHEOLOGIE
BCRALOB........BULLETIN DE LA COMMISSION ROYALES DES ANCIENNES LOIS ET ORDONNANCES DE BELGIQUE
BCRBD..........BOLETIM DA CASA REGIONAL DA BEIRA-DOURO
BCRCA..........BOLETIM DA COMISSAO REGULADORA DE'CEREAIS DO ARQUIPELAGO DOS ACORES
BCRH...........BULLETIN DE LA COMMISSION ROYALE D'HISTOIRE
BCRTD..........BULLETIN DE LA COMMISSION ROYALE DE TOPONYMIE ET DIALECTOLOGIE
BCS............BULLETIN OF CHINESE STUDIES
B CSAR BELG......BULLETIN DE LA CLASSE DES SCIENCES ACADEMIE ROYALE DE BELGIQUE
BCSFLS.........BOLLETTINO DEL CENTRO DI STUDI FILOLOGICI E LINGUISTICI SICILIANI
BCSic..........BOLLETTINO DEL CENTRO DI STUDI FILOLOGICI E LINGUISTICI SICILIANI
BCSO...........BOLLETTINO DEL CENTRO DI STUDI ONOMASTICI (G. D. SERRA)
BCSP...........BOLLETTINO DEL CENTRO DI STUDI DI POESIA ITALIANA E STRANIERA (ROMA)
BCSS...........BOLLETTINO DEL CENTRO DI STUDI FILOLOGICI E LINGUISTICI SICILIANI
BCSV...........BOLLETTINO DEL CENTRO DI STUDI VICHIANI
BCTD...........BULLETIN DE LA COMMISSION ROYALE DE TOPONYMIE ET DE DIALECTOLOGIE
BCTH...........BULLETIN ARCHEOLOGIQUE DU COMITE DES TRAVAUX HISTORIQUES
BCu............BOLETIM CULTURAL
BCURA Gaz.......BCURA (BRITISH COAL UTILIZATION RESEARCH ASSOCIATION) GAZETTE
BD.............BULLETIN DU CANGE
BDAPC..........BULLETIN OF THE DEBATING ASSOCIATION OF PENNSYLVANIA COLLEGES
BDB............BORSENBLATT FUER DEN DEUTSCHEN BUCHHANDEL
BDC............BULLETI DE DIALECTOLOGIA CATALANA
BDC............BULLETIN OF THE DECCAN COLLEGE RESEARCH INSTITUTE
BDE............BOLETIN DE DIALECTOLOGIA ESPANOLA
BDEC...........BULLETIN OF THE DEPARTMENT OF ENGLISH. (CALCUTTA)
B de P..........BIBLIOTHEQUE DE LA PLEIADE
B Dept Ag Trinidad..BULLETIN OF THE DEPARTMENT OF AGRICULTURE TRINIDAD & TOBACO

BdF . . . . BOLETIM DE FILOLOGIA
BDGAB . . . . BOLETIN DE LA DIRECCION GENERAL DE ARCHIVOS Y BIBLIOTECAS
BDI . . . . BEYOND INFINITY
BDial . . . . BALGARSKA DIALEKTOLOGIJA
BdJ . . . . BARRE DU JOUR
BDK . . . . BEITRAEGE ZUR DEUTSCHEN KLASSIK
BDKA . . . . BEITRAEGE ZUR DEUTSCHEN KLASSIK. ABHANDLUNGEN
BDLG . . . . BLAETTER FUER DEUTSCHE LANDESGESCHICHTE
BDLIC . . . . BOLLETI DEL DICCIONARI DE LA LLENGUA CATLANA
BDLM . . . . BIBLIOGRAPHIEN ZUR DEUTSCHEN LITERATUR DES MITTELALTERS
BDM . . . . BOLLETTINO DEL DOMUS MAZZINIANA
BDN . . . . BAUSTEINE ZUM DEUTSCHEN NATIONALTHEATER
BDP . . . . BEITRAEGE ZUR DEUTSCHEN PHILOLOGIE
BDPH . . . . BLAETTER FUER DEUTSCHE PHILOSOPHIE. ZEITSCHRIFT DER DEUTSCHE PHILOSOPHISCHE
GESELLSCHAFT
BDSekt . . . . BJULLETEN DIALEKTOLOGICESKOGO SEKTORA INSTITUTA RUSSKOGO JAZYKA
BDSPU . . . . BOLLETTINO DELLA DEPUTAZIONE DI STORIA PATRIA PER L'UMBRIA
BDVA . . . . BEITRAEGE ZUR DEUTSCHEN VOLKS- UND ALTERTUMSKUNDE
BDW . . . . BULLETIN DU DICTIONNAIRE WALLON
Be . . . . BEALOIDEAS
Be . . . . BELGRADE
BEA . . . . BOLETIN DE ESTUDIOS ASTURIANOS
BEA . . . . BULLETIN DES ETUDES ARABES
BEAUX ARTS INST DES BUL . . BEAUX-ARTS INSTITUTE OF DESIGN BULLETIN
BEC . . . . BIBLIOTHEQUE DE L'ECOLE DES CHARTES
BEC . . . . BOLETIM DE ESTUDOS CLASSICOS
BE . . . . BALGARSKI EZIK
BECh . . . . BIBLIOTHEQUE DE L'ECOLE DES CHARTES
BeCHS . . . . BERKS COUNTY HISTORICAL SOCIETY. PAPERS
BEF . . . . BULLETIN DES ETUDES FRANCAISES
BEFAR . . . . BIBLIOTHEQUE DES ECOLES FRANCAISES D'ATHENES ET DE ROME
BEFEO . . . . BULLETIN DE L'ECOLE FRANCAISE D'EXTREME-ORIENT
BEG . . . . BOLETIN DE ESTUDIOS GERMANICOS
BEHAV BIOL . . . . . . BEHAVIORAL BIOLOGY
BEHAV GENET . . . . . BEHAVIOR GENETICS
Behavioral Sci . . . . . BEHAVIORAL SCIENCE
Behavior Sci Notes . . BEHAVIOR SCIENCE NOTES
BEHAV RES M . . . . . BEHAVIOR RESEARCH METHODS AND INSTRUMENTATION
BEHAV RES T . . . . . . BEHAVIOUR RESEARCH AND THERAPY
BEHAV SCI . . . . BEHAVIORAL SCIENCE
BEHAV SCI N . . . . . . BEHAVIOR SCIENCE NOTES
BEHAV SCI R . . . . . . BEHAVIOR SCIENCE RESEARCH
BEHAV THER . . . . . . BEHAVIOR THERAPY
BEHE . . . . BIBLIOTHEQUE DE L'ECOLE DES HAUTES ETUDES BELFAGOR
Bei . . . . BEIBLATT ZUR ANGLIA
Beibl . . . . BEIBLATT ZUR ANGLIA
Beiblatt . . . . BEIBLATT ZUR ANGLIA
Beitr . . . . BEITRAEGE ZUR GESCHICHTE DER DEUTSCHEN SPRACHE UND LITERATUR
Beitraege Gesch Buchw . . BEITRAEGE ZUR GESCHICHTE DES BUCHWESENS
Beitraege Inkunabelkunde . . BEITRAEGE ZUR INKUNABELKUNDE
Beitr Engl u Nordamerikas . . BEITRAEGE ZUR ERFORSCHUNG DER SPRACHE UND KULTUR ENGLANDS UND
NORDAMERIKAS

BEITR KONFL...... BEITRAEGE ZUR KONFLIKTFORSCHUNG
BEITR MEER....... BEITRAEGE ZUR MEERESKUNDE
BEITR PATH....... BEITRAEGE ZUR PATHOLOGIE
Beitr z Land u Volk v Elsass-loth.. BEITRAEGE ZUR LANDES UND VOLKESKUNDE VON ELSASS-LOTHRINGEN
BEL............. BALGARSKI EZIK I LITERATURA
Bel............. BELFAGOR
Belg Ned Tijdschr Oppervlatke Tech Met.. BELGISCH-NEDERLANDS TIJDSCHRIFT VOOR OPPERVLATKE-TECHNIEKEN
      VAN METALLEN
Belg Plast........ BELGIAN PLASTICS
Belgra........... BELGRAVIA
BELL............ BULLETIN DE LA SOCIETE DES ETUDES DE LETTRES (LAUSANNE)
BELL J ECON...... BELL JOURNAL OF ECONOMICS AND MANAGEMENT SCIENCE
BELL LAB RE...... BELL LABORATORIES RECORD
BELL SYST T...... BELL SYSTEM TECHNICAL JOURNAL
Beloit........... BELOIT POETRY JOURNAL
BELR............ BELL LABORATORIES RECORD
Ben............. BENEDICTINA
Bendix Tech J..... BENDIX TECHNICAL JOURNAL
Bentley.......... BENTLEY'S MISCELLANY
Bent Q.......... BENTLEY'S QUARTERLY REVIEW
B ENT RES....... BULLETIN OF ENTOMOLOGICAL RESEARCH
B ENVIR CON..... BULLETIN OF ENVIRONMENTAL CONTAMINATION AND TOXICOLOGY
BEO............ BULLETIN D'ETUDES ORIENTALES
BEP............ BEITRAEGE ZUR ENGLISCHEN PHILOLOGIE
BEP............. BULLETIN DES ETUDES PORTUGAISES ET DE L'INSTITUT FRANCAIS AU PORTUGAL
BEPh........... BEITRAEGE ZUR ENGLISCHEN PHILOLOGIE
BEPIF........... BULLETIN DES ETUDES PORTUGAISES ET DE L'INSTITUT FRANCAIS AU PORTUGAL
BeR............ BERKELEY REVIEW
BER BUN GES..... BERICHT DER BUNSENGESELLSCHAFT FUER PHYSIKALISCHE CHEMIE
Ber Bunsenges Phys Chem.. BERICHTE DER BUNSENGESELLSCHAFT FUER PHYSIKALISCHE CHEMIE
Berc........... BERCEO
BER DEU BOT..... BERICHTE DER DEUTSCHEN BOTANISCHEN GESELLSCHAFT
Ber Deut Ausschusses Stahlbau.. BERICHTE DES DEUTSCHEN AUSSCHUSSES FUER STAHLBAU
Ber Deut Keram Gesell.. BERICHTE DER DEUTSCHE KERAMISCHE GESELLSCHAFT
BER DW MEER.... BERICHTE DER DEUTSCHEN WISSENSCHAFTLICHEN KOMMISSION FUER MEERESFORSCHUNG
Berg........... BERGONUM
Bergbauwiss...... BERGBAUWISSENSCHAFTEN
Bergbauwiss Verfahrenstech Bergbau Huettenwes.. BERGBAUWISSENSCHAFTEN UND VERFAHRENSTECHNIK IM
      BERGBAU UND HUETTENWESEN
Berg Huettenmaenn Monatsh.. BERG UND HUETTENMAENNISCHE MONATSHEFT
Berk........... BERKELEY
BERKSCoHS...... BERKS COUNTY HISTORICAL SOCIETY. PAPERS
BERUFS-DERM..... BERUFS-DERMATOSEN
Bess........... BESSARIONE
Best Sell........ BEST SELLERS
Bests Ins N...... BEST'S INSURANCE NEWS
BESTS R (Property ed).. BEST'S REVIEW, PROPERTY/LIABILITY EDITION
Bet Hom & Gard... BETTER HOMES & GARDENS
Bet Libns........ BETWEEN LIBRARIANS
Better F........ BETTER FARMING
Betw Libns....... BETWEEN LIBRARIANS. JOURNAL OF THE MARYLAND LIBRARY ASSOCIATION

B EUR S HUM . . . . . . BULLETIN OF THE EUROPEAN SOCIETY OF HUMAN GENETICS
B EXP B MED . . . . . . BULLETIN OF EXPERIMENTAL BIOLOGY AND MEDICINE
B Ez . . . . BALKANSKO EZIKOZNANIE
BF . . . . BIBLIOFILIA
BF . . . . BOLETIN DE FILOLOGIA
BF . . . . BOOKS FROM FINLAND
BFA . . . . BULLETIN OF THE FACULTY OF ARTS (CAIRO)
BFAC . . . . BULLETIN OF THE FACULTY OF ARTS (CAIRO)
BFAM . . . . BULLETIN OF THE FOGG ART MUSEUM
BFC . . . . BOLÈTIN DEL INSTITUTO DO FILOLOGIA DE LA UNIV. DE CHILE
BFC . . . . BOLLETTINO DI FILOLOGIA CLASSICA
BFCL . . . . BULLETIN DES FACULTES CATHOLIQUES DE LYON
BFE . . . . BOLETIN DE FILOLOGIA ESPANOLA
BFF . . . . BEYOND FICTION
BFHA . . . . BULLETIN OF THE FRIENDS HISTORICAL ASSOCIATION
BFIF . . . . BULLETIN FOLKLORIQUE D'ILE-DE-FRANCE
BFL . . . . BULLETIN DE LA FACULTE DES LETTRES DE LILLE
BFLPUL . . . . BIBLIOTHEQUE DE LA FACULTE DE PHILOSOPHIE ET LETTRES DE L'UNIVERSITE DE LIEGE
BFLS . . . . BULLETIN DE LA FACULTE DES LETTRES DE STRASBOURG
BFM . . . . BOLETIN DE FILOLOGIA (MONTEVIDEO)
BFNJ . . . . BIJDRAGEN UITGEGEVEN DOOR EN PHILOSOPHISCHE EN THEOLOGISCHE FACULTEITEN DER
NOORD-EN ZUID-NEDERLANDSE JEZUIETEN
BFo . . . . BIULETYN FONOGRAFICZNY
B FON . . . . BIULETYN FONOGRAFICZNY
BFPhLL . . . . BIBLIOTHEQUE DE LA FACULTE DE PHILOSOPHIE ET LETTRES DE L'UNIVERSITE DE LIEGE
BFPLUL . . . . BIBLIOTHEQUE DE LA FACULTE DE PHILOSOPHIE ET LETTRES DE L'UNIVERSITE DE LIEGE
BFR . . . . BIBLIOTHEQUE FRANCAISE ET ROMANE
BFR . . . . BOLETIN DE FILOLOGIA. RIO DE JANEIRO
BFS . . . . BULLETIN DE LA FACULTE DES LETTRES DE STRASBOURG
BFT . . . . BIZARRE FANTASY TALES
BFU . . . . BOLETIN DE FILOLOGIA. INSTITUTO DE ESTUDIOS SUPERIORES DEL URUGUAY
BFUCH . . . . BOLETIN DE FILOLOGIA. INSTITUTO DE FILOLOGIA DE LA UNIVERSIDADE DE CHILE
BG . . . . BIJDRAGEN TOT DE GESCHIEDENIS
BG . . . . BLUE GUITAR
BG . . . . BOGOSLOVSKI GLASNIK
BG . . . . BUNGAKU
BGB . . . . BULLETIN DE L'ASSOCIATION GUILLAUME BUDE
BGBH . . . . BIJDRAGEN VOOR DE GESCHIEDENIS VAN HET BISDOM VAN HAARLEM
BGCTH . . . . BULLETIN DE LA SECTION DE GEOGRAPHIE DU COMITE DES TRAVAUX HISTORISQUE ET
SCIENTIFIQUE
BGDSL . . . . BEITRAEGE ZUR GESCHICHTE DER DEUTSCHEN SPRACHE UND LITERATUR
BGDSLH . . . . BEITRAEGE ZUR GESCHICHTE DER DEUTSCHEN SPRACHE UND LITERATUR. HALLE
BGDSLT . . . . BEITRAEGE ZUR GESCHICHTE DER DEUTSCHEN SPRACHE UND LITERATURE. TUEBINGEN
BGHB . . . . BIJDRAGEN TOT DE GESCHIEDENIS BIJZONDERLIJK VAN HET ALOUDE HERTOGDOM BRABANT
BGLS . . . . BAUSTEINE ZUR GESCHICHTE DER LITERATUR BEI DEN SLAVEN
BGN . . . . BIJDRAGEN VOOR DE GESCHIEDENIS DER NEDERLANDEN
BGPMN . . . . BIJDRAGEN VOOR DE GESCHIEDENIS VAN DE PROVINCIE DER MINDERBROEDERS IN DE
NEDERLANDEN
BGPTM . . . . BEITRAEGE ZUR GESCHICHTE DER PHILOSOPHIE UND THEOLOGIE DES MITTELALTERS
BGRS . . . . BUNGAKU RONSHU (STUDIES ON LITERATURE)
BGSSE . . . . BEITRAEGE ZUR GESCHICHTE VON STADT UND STIFT ESSEN

BGWK	BOEKENSCHOUW VOOR GODSDIENST, WETENSCHAP EN KUNST
BH	BIBLIOGRAFIA HISPANICA
BH	BULLETIN HISPANIQUE
BH	BUSINESS HISTORY
BHAG	BULLETIN DE LA SOCIETE D'HISTOIRE ET D'ARCHEOLOGIE DE GAND
BHAR	BULLETIN DE LA SECTION HISTORIQUE DE L'ACADEMIE ROUMAINE
BHDL	BULLETIN HISTORIQUE DU DIOCESE DE LYON
B He	BALTISCHE HEFTE
BHEW	BULLETIN DE LA SOCIETE POUR L'HISTOIRE DES EGLISES WALLONNES
BHF	BONNER HISTORISCHE FORSCHUNGEN
BHi	BULLETIN HISPANIQUE
BHis	BIBLIOTECA HISPANA
BHisp	BIBLIOGRAFIA HISPANICA
BHisp	BULLETIN HISPANIQUE
BHM	BULLETIN DE LA SOCIETE FRANCAISE D'HISTOIRE DE LA MEDECINE
BHM	BULLETIN OF THE HISTORY OF MEDICINE
BHPCTHS	BULLETIN HISTORIQUE ET PHILOLOGIQUE, COMITE DES TRAVAUX HISTORIQUES ET SCIENTIFIQUES
BHPF	BULLETIN HISTORIQUE ET LITTERAIRE DE LA SOCIETE DE L'HISTOIRE DU PROTESTANTISME FRANCAIS
B H Points	BULLETIN OF HIGH POINTS
BHPSO	BULLETIN OF THE HISTORICAL AND PHILOSOPHICAL SOCIETY OF OHIO
BHP Tech Bull	BHP (BROKEN HILL PROPRIETARY) TECHNICAL BULLETIN
BHR	BIBLIOTHEQUE D'HUMANISME ET RENAISSANCE
BHR	BUSINESS HISTORY REVIEW
BHS	BIULETYN HISTORII SZTUKI
BHS	BULLETIN OF HISPANIC STUDIES
BHSAM	BULLETIN HISTORIQUE DE LA SOCIETE DES ANTIQUITAIRES DE LA MORINIE
BHSM	BULLETIN OF THE HISTORICAL SOCIETY OF MONTGOMERY COUNTY
BHSMCo	BULLETIN OF THE HISTORICAL SOCIETY OF MONTGOMERY COUNTY
BHTP	BULLETIN D'HISTOIRE DU THEATRE PORTUGAIS
BhV	BHARATIYA VIDYA
BHVBamberg	BERICHT DES HISTORISCHEN. VEREINS FUER DES FUESTBISTUM (BAMBERG)
BHVFB	BERICHT DES HISTORISCHEN. VEREINS FUER DES FUESTBISTUM (BAMBERG)
Bi	BIBLICA
Bi	BIBLIOFILIA
BI	BIBLIOGRAFIA ITALIANA
Bi	BIBLOS
BI	BOOKS AT IOWA
BI	BULLETIN ITALIEN
BiA	BIBLICAL ARCHAEOLOGIST
BIA	BOLLETTINO DEL REALE ISTITUTO DI ARCHEOLOGIA E STORIA DELL'ARTE
BIAA	BOLLETTINO DEL REALE ISTITUTO DI ARCHEOLOGIA E STORIA DELL'ARTE
BIAB	BULLETIN DE L'INSTITUT ARCHEOLOGIQUE BULGARE
Biafra R	BIAFRA REVIEW
BIAL	BULLETIN DE L'INSTITUT ARCHEOLOGIQUE LIEGEOIS
BIAO	BULLETIN DE L'INSTITUT FRANCAIS D'ARCHEOLOGIE ORIENTALE
BIAP	BULLETIN INTERNATIONAL DE L'ACADEMIE POLONAISE DES SCIENCES ET DES LETTRES
BIAPSL	BULLETIN INTERNATIONAL DE L'ACADEMIE POLONAISE DES SCIENCES ET DES LETTRES
Bib	BIBLICA
Bib	BIBLOS

PERIODICAL TITLE ABBREVIATIONS

BIB . . . . BULLETIN DE L'INSTITUT INTERNATIONAL DE BIBLIOGRAPHIE
BibAg . . . . BIBLIOGRAPHY OF AGRICULTURE
Bib Arch . . . . BIBLICAL ARCHAEOLOGIST
Bibl . . . . BIBLIOGRAPHIC INDEX
BiblGeo . . . . BIBLIOGRAPHY AND INDEX OF GEOLOGY
BibL . . . . BIBLIOGRAPHIE LINGUISTIQUE
BIBL ANATOM . . . . . BIBLIOTHECA ANATOMICA
Bibl Archaeolo . . . . . BIBLICAL ARCHAEOLOGIST
BIBLB . . . . BOLETIM INTERNACIONAL DE BIBLIOGRAFIA LUSO-BRASILEIRA (LISBOA)
BIBL CARDIO . . . . . . BIBLIOTHECA CARDIOLOGICA
Bibl Ecole Chartes . . BIBLIOTHEQUE DE L'ECOLE DES CHARTES
Bibl Filol . . . . BIBLIOGRAFIA FILOLOGICA DO CENTRO DE ESTUDOS FILOLOGICA DE LISBOA
BIBL GASTRO . . . . . . BIBLIOTHECA GASTROENTEROLOGICA
BIBL HAEM . . . . BIBLIOTHECA HAEMATOLOGICA
BiblH&R . . . . BIBLIOTHEQUE D'HUMANISME ET RENAISSANCE
Biblio . . . . BIBLIOFILIA
BIBLIOG . . . . BIBLIOGRAPHER
Bibliog Doc Terminology . . BIBLIOGRAPHY, DOCUMENTATION, TERMINOLOGY
Biblio Soc Am . . . . . BIBLIOGRAPHICAL SOCIETY OF AMERICA. PAPERS
BIBL NUTR D . . . . . . BIBLIOTHECA NUTRITO ET DIETA
BIBL PHONET . . . . . . BIBLIOTHECA PHONETICA
BIBL PSYCH . . . . BIBLIOTHECA PSYCHIATRICA
BIBL RADIOL . . . . . . BIBLIOTHECA RADIOLOGICA
Bibl Sac . . . . BIBLIOTHECA SACRA
Bibl Soc Am Pa . . . . BIBLIOGRAPHICAL SOCIETY OF AMERICA. PAPERS
BIBL TUB MET . . . . . BIBLIOTHECA TUBERCULOSEA ET MEDICINAE THORACALIS
BiblZ . . . . BIBLISCHE ZEITSCHRIFT
Bib R . . . . BIBLICAL REVIEW
BIBR . . . . BULLETIN DE L'INSTITUT HISTORIQUE BELGE DE ROME
Bib Res . . . . BIBLICAL RESEARCH
Bib Sac . . . . BIBLIOTHECA SACRA
Bib Sacra . . . . BIBLIOTHECA SACRA
Bib Th Bul . . . . BIBLICAL THEOLOGY BULLETIN
Bib World . . . . BIBLICAL WORLD
Bib Z . . . . BIBLISCHE ZEITSCHRIFT
BICB . . . . INSTITUT ROYAL COLONIAL BELGE. BULLETIN DES SEANCES
BICC . . . . BOLETIN DEL INSTITUO CARO Y CUREVO
BICH . . . . BULLETIN OF THE INTERNATIONAL COMMITTEE OF HISTORICAL SCIENCES
BICHS . . . . BULLETIN OF THE INTERNATIONAL COMMITTEE OF HISTORICAL SCIENCES
BICS . . . . BULLETIN OF THE INSTITUTE OF CLASSICAL STUDIES OF THE UNIVERSITY OF LONDON
BICR . . . . BOLLETTINO DELL'ISTITUTO CENTRALE DI RESTAURO
BIDR . . . . BOLLETTINO DELL'ISTITUTO DI DIRITTO ROMANO
BIE . . . . BOLETIN DEL INSTITUTO DE LAS ESPANAS
BIE . . . . BOLETIN DEL INSTITUTO ESPANOL DE LONDRES
BIE . . . . BULLETIN DE L'INSTITUT D'EGYPTE
BIEA . . . . BOLETIN DEL INSTITUTO DE ESTUDIOS ASTURIANOS
BIF . . . . BOLETIN DEL INSTITUTO FRANCES
BIFAN . . . . BULLETIN DE L'INSTITUT FRANCAIS D'AFRIQUE NOIRE
BIFAO . . . . BULLETIN DE L'INSTITUT FRANCAIS D'ARCHEOLOGIE ORIENTALE
BIFG . . . . BOLETIN DEL INSTITUTO FERNAN GONZALEZ
BIFP . . . . BOLETIN DEL INSTITUTO DE INVESTIGACIONES FOLKLORICAS. UNIVERSIDAD INTERAMERICANA
(PANAMA)

65

B IN SCI T . . . . BULLETIN D'INFORMATIONS SCIENTIFIQUES ET TECHNIQUES DU COMMISSARIAT A L'ENERGIE ATOMIQUE
B INT FIS D . . . . . . BULLETIN FOR INTERNATIONAL FISCAL DOCUMENTATION
BioAb . . . . BIOLOGICAL ABSTRACTS
BioAg . . . . BIOLOGICAL AND AGRICULTURAL INDEX
BIOC . . . . BIOLOGIA CULTURALE
BIOC BIOP A . . . . . . BIOCHIMICA ET BIOPHYSICA ACTA
BIOC BIOP R . . . . . . BIOCHEMICAL AND BIOPHYSICAL RESEARCH COMMUNICATIONS
BIOCHEM . . . . BIOCHEMISTRY
BIOCHEM GEN . . . . . BIOCHEMICAL GENETICS
BIOCHEM J . . . . BIOCHEMICAL JOURNAL
BIOCHEM MED . . . . . BIOCHEMICAL MEDICINE
BIOCHEM SSR . . . . . BIOCHEMISTRY-USSR
BIOCH PHARM . . . . BIOCHEMICAL PHARMACOLOGY
BIOCH SOC T . . . . . BIOCHEMICAL SOCIETY TRANSACTIONS
BIOC PHY PF . . . . . BIOCHEMIE UND PHYSIOLOGIE DER PFLANZEN
BIOELECTR B . . . . . BIOELECTROCHEMISTRY AND BIOENERGETICS
Biol . . . . BIOGRAPHY INDEX
BIOINORG CH . . . . . BIOINORGANIC CHEMISTRY
BIOL B . . . . BIOLOGICAL BULLETIN
Biol Bul . . . . BIOLOGICAL BULLETIN
Biol Conser . . . . . . BIOLOGICAL CONSERVATION
Biol Culturale . . . . . BIOLOGIA CULTURALE
BIOL CYBERN . . . . . BIOLOGICAL CYBERNETICS
BIFP . . . . BULLETIN ET MEMOIRES DE L'INSTITUT DES FOUILLES DE PROVENCE ET DES PREALPES
BIFR . . . . BULETINUL INSTITUTULUI DE FILOLOGIE ROMAINA. ALEXANDRU PHILIPPIDE. IASI
BIFRI . . . . BULETINUL INSTITUTULUI DE FILOLOGIE ROMAINA. ALEXANDRU PHILIPPIDE. IASI
BIFV . . . . BOLETIN DEL INSTITUTO DE FOLKLORE
BiH . . . . BIBLIOGRAFIA HISPANICA
BIH . . . . BULLETIN HISPANICA
BIH . . . . BULLETIN HISPANIQUE
BIHBR . . . . BULLETIN DE L'INSTITUT HISTORIQUE BELGE DE ROME
BIHP . . . . BULLETIN OF THE INSTITUTE OF HISTORY AND PHILOLOGY. ACADEMIA SINICA
BiHR . . . . BIBLIOTHEQUE D'HUMANISME ET RENAISSANCE
BIHR . . . . BULLETIN OF THE INSTITUTE OF HISTORICAL RESEARCH
BIIH . . . . BOLETIN DEL INSTITUTO DE INVESTIGACIONES HISTORICAS
BIIL . . . . BOLETIN DEL INSTITUTO DE INVESTIGACIONES LITERARIAS
BIIRHT . . . . BULLETIN D' INFORMATION DE L' INSTITUT DE RECHERCHE ET D'HISTOIRE DES TEXTES
BIJDRAGEN DIALECTENCOMMISSIE . . BIJDRAGEN EN MEDEDEELINGEN DER DIALECTENCOMMISSIE VAN DE KONINKLIJKE NEDERLANDSCHE AKADEMIE VAN WETENSCHAPPEN TE AMSTERDAM
BIJDRAGEN NEDERL-INDIE . . BIJDRAGEN TOT DE TAAL-, LAND-EN VOLKENKUNDE VAN NEDERLANDSCHE-INDIE
Bijdr Gesch Ndl . . . . BIJDRAGEN VOOR DE GESCHIEDENIS DER NEDERLANDEN
Bijdr Taal- Land- en Volkenk Nederl-Indie . . BIJDRAGEN TOT DE TAAL-, LAND-EN VOLKENKUNDE VAN NEDERLANDSCH-INDIE
BijdrTLV . . . . BIJDRAGEN TOT DE TAAL-, LAND-EN VOLKENKUNDE
BIKEN J . . . . BIKEN JOURNAL
Bil . . . . BILYCHNIS
BIL . . . . BOLLETTINO INTERNAZIONALE DI INFORMAZIONI SUL LATINO
BILAL . . . . BULLETIN D'INFORMATION DU LABORATOIRE D'ANALYSE LEXICOLOGIQUE
BILC . . . . BOLETIM DO INSTITUTO LUIS DE CAMOES
BILE . . . . BOLLETTINO DELL ISTITUTO DI LINGUE ESTERE (GENOVA)

BILEG . . . . BOLLETTINO DELL'ISTITUTO DI LINGUE ESTERE (GENOVA)
BILEUG . . . . BOLLETTINO DELL'ISTITUTO DE LINGUE ESTERE (GENOVA)
BIN . . . . BOLLETTINO ITALIANO DI NUMISMATICA
BIOL GASTRO . . . . . BIOLOGIE ET GASTRO-ENTEROLOGIE
BIOL J LINN . . . . . . BIOLOGICAL JOURNAL OF THE LINNEAN SOCIETY
BIOL NEONAT . . . . . BIOLOGY OF THE NEONATE
BIOL PLANT . . . . . . BIOLOGIA PLANTARUM
BIOL PSYCHI . . . . . . BIOLOGICAL PSYCHIATRY
Biol R . . . . BIOLOGICAL REVIEWS
BIOL REPROD . . . . . BIOLOGY OF REPRODUCTION
Biol Rs . . . . BIOLOGICAL REVIEWS
BIOL ZBL . . . . BIOLOGISCHES ZENTRALBLATT
BIOMAT MED . . . . . BIOMATERIALS MEDICAL DEVICES AND ARTIFICIAL ORGANS
BIOMED ENG . . . . . . BIOMEDICAL ENGINEERING
Bio-Med Eng (Lond) . . BIO-MEDICAL ENGINEERING (LONDON)
Biomed Eng (NY) . . . BIOMEDICAL ENGINEERING (ENGLISH TRANSLATION OF MEDITSINSKAYA TEKHNIKA)
BIOMED EXPR . . . . . BIOMEDICINE EXPRESS
BIOMED MASS . . . . . BIOMEDICAL MASS SPECTROMETRY
BIOMETR Z . . . . BIOMETRISCHE ZEITSCHRIFT
BIOORG CHEM . . . . . BIOORGANIC CHEMISTRY
BIOORG KHIM . . . . . BIOORGANICHESKAYA KHIMIYA
BIOPHYS CH . . . . . . BIOPHYSICAL CHEMISTRY
BIOPHYS J . . . . BIOPHYSICAL JOURNAL
BIOPHYS STR . . . . . . BIOPHYSICS OF STRUCTURE AND MECHANISM
BiOr . . . . BIBLIOTHECA ORIENTALIS
BIOTECH BIO . . . . . . BIOTECHNOLOGY AND BIOENGINEERING
BIOTELEMETR . . . . . BIOTELEMETRY
B I PASTEUR . . . . . . BULLETIN DE L'INSTITUT PASTEUR
BIRD BAND . . . . BIRD-BANDING
Birmingham Univ Chem Eng . . BIRMINGHAM UNIVERSITY CHEMICAL ENGINEER
Birmingham Univ Hist . . BIRMINGHAM UNIVERSITY HISTORICAL JOURNAL
BIRPA . . . . BULLETIN DE L'INSTITUT ROYAL DU PATRIMOINE ARTISTIQUE
BIRS . . . . BRITISH INSTITUTE OF RECORDED SOUND
BIRSC . . . . BULLETIN DE L'INSTITUT DE RECHERCHES SCIENTIFIQUES AU CONGO
BIRT . . . . BULLETIN D'INFORMATION DE L'INSTITUT DE RECHERCHE ET D'HISTOIRE DES TEXTES
BIS . . . . BULLETIN. INSTITUTE OF THE STUDY OF THE U.S.S.R.
BISDP . . . . BOLETIN INFORMATIVO DEL SEMINARIO DE DERECHO POLITICO
BISGM . . . . BOLETIN INFORMATIVO DE LA SECRETARIA GENERAL DEL MOVIMIENTO
BIShk . . . . BULETIN I INSTITUTIT TE SCHKECAVE
BISI . . . . BOLLETTINO DELL'ISTITUTO STORICO ITALIANO
BISIAM . . . . BOLLETTINO DELL'ISTITUTO STORICO ITALIANO E ARCHIVIO MURATORIANO
BISIMAM . . . . BOLLETTINO DELL'ISTITUTO STORICO ITALIANO PER IL MEDIOEVO E ARCHIVIO MURATORIANO
BISO . . . . BULLETIN DE L'INSTITUT POUR L'ETUDE DE L'EUROPE SUD-ORIENTALE
B IST SIER . . . . BOLLETTINO DELL'ISTITUTO SIEROTERAPICO MILANESE
BISV . . . . BOLLETTINO DELL'ISTITUTO DI STORIA DELLA SOCIETA E DELLO STATO VENZIANO
BItal . . . . BULLETIN ITALIEN
B ITAL BIOL . . . . . . BOLLETTINO DELLA SOCIETA ITALIANA DI BIOLOGIA SPERIMENTALE
Bitumen Teere Asphalte Peche . . BITUMEN-TEERE-ASPHALTE-PECHE UND VERWANDTE STOFFE
Biul Ib . . . . BIULETYN INSTYTUTU BIBLIOGRAFICZNEGO
Biul PIK . . . . BIULETYN PANSTWOWEGO INSTYTUTU KSIAZKI
BIV . . . . BOLETIN INDIGENISTA VENEZOLANO

BiZ . . . . BIBLISCHE ZEITSCHRIFT
BIZ . . . . BIZARRE MYSTERY MAGAZINE
B I ZOOL AS . . . . . . BULLETIN OF THE INSTITUTE OF ZOOLOGY ACADEMIA SINICA
BJ . . . . BONNER JAHRBUECHER
BJ . . . . BOOKMAN'S JOURNAL
BJA . . . . BRITISH JOURNAL OF AESTHETICS
B JAP S S F . . . . BULLETIN OF THE JAPANESE SOCIETY OF SCIENTIFIC FISHERIES
BJB . . . . BONNER JAHRBUECHER
B J CRIMINOLOGY . . BRITISH JOURNAL OF CRIMINOLOGY
B J Disorders of Communication . . BRITISH JOURNAL OF DISORDERS OF COMMUNICATION
B J Ednl Psych . . . . . BRITISH JOURNAL OF EDUCATIONAL PSYCHOLOGY
B J Ednl Studies . . . . BRITISH JOURNAL OF EDUCATIONAL STUDIES
B J Ednl Technology . . BRITISH JOURNAL OF EDUCATIONAL TECHNOLOGY
BJES . . . . BRITISH JOURNAL OF EDUCATIONAL STUDIES
BJewPES . . . . BULLETIN OF THE JEWISH PALESTINE EXPLORATION SOCIETY
B J GUIDANCE & COUNSELING . . BRITISH JOURNAL OF GUIDANCE AND COUNSELING
B J In-Service Ed . . . BRITISH JOURNAL OF IN-SERVICE EDUCATION
BJIR . . . . BRITISH JOURNAL OF INDUSTRIAL RELATIONS
B J Math & Stat Psych . . BRITISH JOURNAL OF MATHEMATICAL AND STATISTICAL PSYCHOLOGY
BJMPs . . . . BRITISH JOURNAL OF MEDICAL PSYCHOLOGY
BJP . . . . BRITISH JOURNAL OF PSYCHOLOGY
B J Physical Ed . . . . BRITISH JOURNAL OF PHYSICAL EDUCATION
BJPs . . . . BRITISH JOURNAL OF PSYCHOLOGY
B J Psych . . . . BRITISH JOURNAL OF PSYCHOLOGY
BJR . . . . BULLETIN DES JEUNES ROMANISTES
BJR . . . . BULLETIN OF THE JOHN RYLANDS LIBRARY
BJRL . . . . BULLETIN OF THE JOHN RYLANDS LIBRARY
BJRLM . . . . BULLETIN OF THE JOHN RYLANDS LIBRARY. MANCHESTER.
B JSME . . . . BULLETIN OF THE JSME (JAPAN SOCIETY OF MECHANICAL ENGINEERS)
B J Social and Clinical Psych . . BRITISH JOURNAL OF SOCIAL AND CLINICAL PSYCHOLOGY
B J Sociology . . . . . . BRITISH JOURNAL OF SOCIOLOGY
B J Stat Psych . . . . . BRITISH JOURNAL OF STATISTICAL PSYCHOLOGY
Bjull Akad nauk UzSSR . . BJULLETEN AKADEMIJI NAUK UZBEKSKOJ SSR
BK . . . . BEDI KARTHLISA
Bk . . . . BOOKMAN
Bkbinding & Bk Production . . BOOKBINDING & BOOK PRODUCTION
BKBIRD . . . . BOOKBIRD
Bk Buyer . . . . BOOK BUYER
Bk Collec . . . . BOOK COLLECTOR
Bk Collecting & Lib Mo . . BOOK COLLECTING AND LIBRARY MONTHLY
Bk Collector . . . . . . BOOK COLLECTOR
BKGP . . . . BLAETTER FUER KIRCHENGESCHICHTE POMMERNS
BkIA . . . . BOOKS AT IOWA
BKL . . . . BOOKLIST
BkL . . . . BOOKMAN (LONDON)
Bklegger . . . . BOOKLEGGER MAGAZINE
Bklist . . . . BOOKLIST AND SUBSCRIPTION BOOKS BULLETIN
Bkmark . . . . BOOKMARK
Bkmark (Idaho) . . . . BOOKMARK. UNIVERSITY OF IDAHO
BKMR . . . . BEITRAEGE ZUR KULTURGESCHICHTE DES MITTELALTERS UND DER RENAISSANCE
Bk News . . . . BOOK-NEWS

Bks Abroad . . . . . . BOOKS ABROAD
Bks & Bkmn . . . . . . BOOKS AND BOOKMEN
Bks & Libs . . . . BOOKS AND LIBRARIES AT THE UNIVERSITY OF KANSAS
Bks Today . . . . BOOKS TODAY (CHICAGO SUNDAY TRIBUNE)
BKSTS J . . . . BKSTS (BRITISH KINEMATOGRAPH SOUND AND TELEVISION SOCIETY) JOURNAL
Bk Trolley . . . . BOOK TROLLEY
BKW . . . . A BOOK OF WEIRD TALES
BkW . . . . BOOK WORLD (WASHINGTON POST)
Bk Wk . . . . BOOK WEEK
Bk World . . . . BOOK WORLD (SUNDAY CHICAGO TRIBUNE AND WASHINGTON POST)
BL . . . . BIBLIOGRAPHIE LINGUISTIQUE
BL . . . . BIBLIOTHEEKLEVEN
BL . . . . BOOKLIST
BL . . . . BULLETIN DES LETTRES
BL . . . . BULLETIN LINGUISTIQUE DE LA FACULTE DES LETTRES DE BUCAREST
BLA . . . . BLACK ART (LONDON)
BlackCh . . . . BLACK CHURCH
BlackI . . . . BLACK IMAGES: A CRITICAL QUARTERLY ON BLACK ARTS AND CULTURE
BlackIC . . . . BLACK I: A CANADIAN JOURNAL OF BLACK EXPRESSION
Black L J . . . . BLACK LAW JOURNAL
Black Mag . . . . BLACKWOOD'S MAGAZINE
BlackR . . . . BLACK REVIEW
Blackw . . . . BLACKWOOD'S MAGAZINE
Black W . . . . BLACK WORLD
Blackwood's Mag . . BLACKWOOD'S MAGAZINE
BlakeN . . . . BLAKE NEWSLETTER
BlakeS . . . . BLAKE STUDIES
BLAM . . . . BOLETIN LATINO-AMERICANO DE MUSICA
Blast F & Steel Pl . . . BLAST FURNACE AND STEEL PLANT
Blast Furn Steel Plant . . BLAST FURNACE AND STEEL PLANT
Blatt Technikgesch . . BLAETTER FUER TECHNIKGESCHICHTE
BLB . . . . BULLETIN LINGUISTIQUE DE LA FACULTE DES LETTRES DE BUCAREST
BLC . . . . BULLETIN DE LITTERATURE CHRETIENNE
Bldg Age . . . . BUILDING AGE AND NATIONAL BUILDER
Bldg Mater . . . . BUILDING MATERIALS
Bldg Res (Washington D.C.) . . BUILDING RESEARCH (WASHINGTON D.C.)
Bldg Sci . . . . BUILDING SCIENCE
Bldg Serv Engr . . . . . BUILDING SERVICES ENGINEER
Bldg Systems Design . . BUILDING SYSTEMS DESIGN
Bldg Technol Mgmt . . BUILDING TECHNOLOGY AND MANAGEMENT
BLE . . . . BULLETIN DE LITTERATURE ECCLESIASTIQUE
BLI . . . . BEITRAEGE ZUR LINGUISTIK UND INFORMATIONSVERARBEITUNG
BLM . . . . BOLLETINI DI LITTERATURA MODERNA
BLM . . . . BONNIERS LITTERAERA MAGASIN
BLM . . . . BOOK LEAGUE MONTHLY
BLMag . . . . BONNIERS LITTERAERA MAGASIN
BLOOD VESS . . . . . . BLOOD VESSELS
BLR . . . . BELORUSSIAN REVIEW (MUNICH)
BLR . . . . BODLEIAN LIBRARY RECORD
BLSCR . . . . BOLLETTINO LINGUISTICO PER LA STORIA E LA CULTURA REGIONALE
BLUES . . . . BLUES UNLIMITED

BLux . . . . BULLETIN LINGUISTIQUE ET ETHNOLOGIQUE. INSTITUT GRANDUCAL. LUXEMBOURG
BLVS . . . . BIBLIOTHEK DES LITERARISCHEN VEREINS (STUTTGART)
BL W . . . . BLACK WORLD
BM . . . . BANBER MATENADARANI
BM . . . . BLACKWOOD'S MAGAZINE
BM . . . . BONNIERS MAENADSTIDNING (STOCKHOLM)
BM . . . . BRITISH MUSEUM QUARTERLY
BM . . . . BULLETIN MONUMENTAL
BM . . . . BURLINGTON MAGAZINE
BMA . . . . BERGENS MUSEUMS AARBOK
BMAH . . . . BULLETIN DES MUSEES ROYAUX D'ART ET D'HISTOIRE
B MARIN SCI . . . . . . BULLETIN OF MARINE SCIENCE
B MATH BIOL . . . . . BULLETIN OF MATHEMATICAL BIOLOGY
B MATH STAT . . . . . BULLETIN OF MATHEMATICAL STATISTICS
BMB . . . . BULLETIN BIBLIOGRAPHIQUE DU MUSEE BELGE
BMB . . . . BULLETIN DU MUSEE BASQUE
BMB . . . . BULLETIN DU MUSEE DE BEYROUTH
BM Beyrouth . . . . . . BULLETIN DU MUSEE DE BEYROUTH
BMBL . . . . BERLINER MUNZBLAETTER
BMCR . . . . BOLLETTINO DEL MUSEO DELLA CIVILTA ROMANA
BMD . . . . BIJDRAGEN EN MEDEDEELINGEN DER DIALECTENCOMMISSIE VAN DE KONINKLIJKE AKADEMIE
VAN WETENSCHAPPEN TE AMSTERDAM
BMDial . . . . BIJDRAGEN EN MEDEDEELINGEN DER DIALECTENCOMMISSIE VAN DE KONINKLIJKE AKADEMIE
VAN WETENSCHAPPEN TE AMSTERDAM
B MED LIB A . . . . . . BULLETIN OF THE MEDICAL LIBRARY ASSOCIATION
B MENNINGER . . . . . BULLETIN OF THE MENNINGER CLINIC
BMFEA . . . . BULLETIN OF THE MUSEUM OF FAR EASTERN ANTIQUITIES (STOCKHOLM)
BMFJ . . . . BULLETIN DE LA MAISON FRANCO-JAPONAIS
BMFR . . . . BLAETTER FUER MUNZFREUNDE
BMGeire . . . . BIJDRAGEN EN MEDEDEELINGEN UITGEGEVEN DOOR DE VEREENIGING GEIRE
BMGJW . . . . BIJDRAGEN EN MEDEDEELINGEN VAN HET GENOOTSCHAP VOOR DE JOODSCHE WETENSCHAP
IN NEDERLAND
BMHA . . . . BULLETIN POUR LA CONSERVATION DES MONUMENTS HISTORIQUE D'ALSACE
BMHG . . . . BIJDRAGEN EN MEDEDEELINGEN VAN HET HISTORISCH GENOOTSCHAP
BMI . . . . BMI, THE MANY WORLDS OF MUSIC
BMIR . . . . BOLLETTINO DEL MUSEO DELL'IMPERO ROMANO
BMJH . . . . BOLETIN DEL MUSEO DE MOTIVOS POPULARES ARGENTINOS JOSE HERNANDEZ
BMLA . . . . BULLETIN OF THE MEDICAL LIBRARY ASSOCIATIONS
BMM . . . . BIBLIOTECA MODERNA MONDADORI
BMM . . . . BULLETIN OF THE METROPOLITAN MUSEUM OF ART
BMMA . . . . BULLETIN OF THE METROPOLITAN MUSEUM OF ART
BMNE . . . . BULLETIN OF THE MUSEUM OF MEDITERRANEAN AND NEAR EASTERN ANTIQUITIES
BMod . . . . BIBLIOGRAPHIE MODERNE
BMQ . . . . BRITISH MUSEUM QUARTERLY
BMRAH . . . . BULLETIN DES MUSEES ROYALE D'ART ET D'HISTOIRE
BMRBA . . . . BULLETIN DES MUSEES ROYALE DES BEAUX-ARTS
BMS . . . . BENEDICTINER MONATSSCHRIFT
B M S ANTHR . . . . . . BULLETINS ET MEMOIRES DE LA SOCIETE D'ANTHROPOLOGIE DE PARIS
BMSAO . . . . BULLETIN ET MEMOIRES DE LA SOCIETE DES ANTIQUAIRES DE L'OUEST
BMSLP . . . . BOLETIM MENSAL DA SOCIEDADE DE LINGUA PORTUGUESA
BMus . . . . BERLINER MUSEEN

BMusB . . . . BULLETIN OF THE MUSEUM OF FINE ARTS IN BOSTON
BMusFr . . . . BULLETIN DES MUSEES DE FRANCE
BN . . . . BEITRAEGE ZUR NAMENFORSCHUNG
BN . . . . BIBLIOTHEQUE NATIONALE
BN . . . . BIBLIOTHEQUE NORBERTINE
BN . . . . BOOK NOTES
BN . . . . BROWNING NEWSLETTER
BN . . . . BURKE'S NEWSLETTER
BN&R . . . . BOTSWANA NOTES AND RECORDS
BNAP . . . . BULLETIN OF THE NATIONAL ASSOCIATION OF SECONDARY-SCHOOL PRINCIPALS
B NARCOTICS . . . . . BULLETIN ON NARCOTICS
BNF . . . . BEITRAEGE ZUR NAMENFORSCHUNG
BNJ . . . . BYZANTINISCH-NEUGRIECHISCHE JAHRBUECHER
B NJ ACAD S . . . . . . BULLETIN NEW JERSEY ACADEMY OF SCIENCE
BNL . . . . BANCA NAZIONALE DEL LAVORO. REVIEW
BNL . . . . BEITRAEGE ZUR NEUEREN LITERATURGESCHICHTE
BNOB . . . . BULLETIN VAN DE NEDERLANDSE OUDHEIDKUNDIGE BOND
BNPL . . . . BULLETIN OF THE NEW YORK PUBLIC LIBRARY
B NY AC MED . . . . . BULLETIN OF THE NEW YORK ACADEMY OF MEDICINE
BNYPL . . . . BULLETIN OF THE NEW YORK PUBLIC LIBRARY
BO . . . . BIBLIOTHECA ORIENTALIS
BO . . . . BLACK ORPHEUS
Bo . . . . BOLIVAR
BoAb . . . . BOATING ABSTRACTS
BOCES XVIII . . . . . . BOLETIN DEL CENTRO DE ESTUDIOS DEL SIGLO XVIII, OVIEDO
BODLEIAN LIB REC . . BODLEIAN LIBRARY RECORD
Boek . . . . HET BOEK
B of M . . . . BOOKS OF THE MONTH
B OF SAN PA . . . . . . BOLETIN DE LA OFICIANA SANITARIA PANAMERICANA
BOIA . . . . BULLETIN DE L'OFFICE INTERNATIONAL DES INSTITUTS D'ARCHEOLOGIE ET D'HISTOIRE DE L'ART
BOK OG BIBL . . . . . . BOK OG BIBLIOTEK
Bol . . . . BOLIVAR
Bol Asoc Mex Geol Petrol . . BOLETIN DE LA ASOCIACION MEXICANA DE GEOLOGOS PETROLEROS
Bol Biblio (Peru) . . . BOLETIN BIBLIOGRAFICO
Boletin IF . . . . BOLETIN DEL INSTITUTO DE FOLKLORE
Bol Fac Ing Agrimensura Montevideo . . BOLETIN DE LA FACULTAD DE INGENIERIA Y AGRIMENSURA DE MONTEVIDEO
Bol Ist Pato Lib . . . . BOLLETTINO DELL'ISTITUTO DI PATOLOGIA DEL LIBRO
Boll Arte . . . . BOLLETTINO D'ARTE
Boll Ist Patologia Lib . . BOLLETTINO DELL'ISTITUTO DI PATOLOGIA DEL LIBRO
Boll Psicol App . . . . BOLLETTINO DI PSICOLOGIA APPLICATA
Boll Soc Geog . . . . . BOLLETTINO DELLA SOCIETA GEOGRAFICA ITALIANA
Boll S P . . . . BOLLETTINO STORICO PIACENTINO
Bol Serv Geol Nac Nicaragua . . BOLETIN DEL SERVICIO GEOLOGICO NACIONAL DE NICARAGUA
Bol Soc Nac Mineria Petrol . . BOLETIN DE LA SOCIEDAD NACIONAL DE MINERIA Y PETROLEO
Boll Stor Cat . . . . . . BOLLETTINO STORICO CATANESE
Boll Stran . . . . BOLLETTINO UNIVERSITARIO ITALIANO PER STRANIERI
Booklist . . . . BOOKLIST AND SUBSCRIPTION BOOKS BULLETIN
BOOKLIST AND SBB . . BOOKLIST AND SUBSCRIPTION BOOKS BULLETIN
Booklover's M . . . . . BOOKLOVER'S MAGAZINE
Bookm . . . . BOOKMAN
Bookm (Lond) . . . . . BOOKMAN (LONDON)

Bookmark . . . . (NEW YORK STATE LIBRARY) BOOKMARK
Book R . . . . BOOK REVIEWS
Books . . . . NEW YORK HERALD TRIBUNE BOOKS
BOP . . . . BIBLIOGRAPHIQUE OFFICIEL DES IMPRIMES PUBLIES EN POLOGNE. BULLETIN
BOR . . . . BISERICA ORTHODOXA ROMANA
BoRv . . . . BOOK REVIEW DIGEST
Bost . . . . BOSTONIAN
Bost Mo . . . . BOSTON MONTHLY MAGAZINE
Boston Col Stud Phil . . BOSTON COLLEGE STUDIES IN PHILOSOPHY
Boston Mus Bul . . . . BOSTON MUSEUM OF FINE ARTS. BULLETIN
Boston Pub Lib Quar . . BOSTON PUBLIC LIBRARY. QUARTERLY
Boston Soc C E J . . . BOSTON SOCIETY OF CIVIL ENGINEERS. JOURNAL
Boston Soc of Nat Hist Memoirs . . BOSTON SOCIETY OF NATURAL HISTORY. MEMOIRS
Boston Soc of Nat Hist Occ Papers . . BOSTON SOCIETY OF NATURAL HISTORY. OCCASIONAL PAPERS
Boston Soc of Nat Hist Proc . . BOSTON SOCIETY OF NATURAL HISTORY. PROCEEDINGS
BOSTON U LR . . . . . . BOSTON UNIVERSITY LAW REVIEW
Bost Q . . . . BOSTON QUARTERLY
Bost R . . . . BOSTON REVIEW
Bost Soc Natur Hist Occ Pa . . BOSTON SOCIETY OF NATURAL HISTORY. OCCASIONAL PAPERS
Bost Soc Natur Hist Proc . . BOSTON SOCIETY OF NATURAL HISTORY. PROCEEDINGS
Bost Sym . . . . BOSTON SYMPHONY ORCHESTRA PROGRAM NOTES
Bo Stud . . . . BONNER STUDIEN ZUR ENGLISCHEN PHILOLOGIE
Bost Sym Concert Bul . . BOSTON SYMPHONY ORCHESTRA CONCERT. BULLETIN
BOTAN B A S . . . . . . BOTANICAL BULLETIN OF ACADEMIA SINICA
BOTAN GAZ . . . . . . BOTANICAL GAZETTE
BOTAN J LIN . . . . . . BOTANICAL JOURNAL OF THE LINNEAN SOCIETY
BOTAN MAG . . . . . . BOTANICAL MAGAZINE (TOKYO)
BOTAN MARIN . . . . BOTANICA MARINA
BOTAN NOTIS . . . . . BOTANISKA NOTISER
BOTAN REV . . . . . . BOTANICAL REVIEW
BOTAN TIDS . . . . . . BOTANISK TIDSSKRIFT
Bot Gaz . . . . BOTANICAL GAZETTE
Bot R . . . . BOTANICAL REVIEW
BoV . . . . BOCKERNAS VARLD
Boyce Thompson Inst Contrib . . BOYCE THOMPSON INSTITUTE. CONTRIBUTIONS
Bozart . . . . BOZART AND CONTEMPORARY VERSE
BP . . . . BANASTHALI PATRIKA
BP . . . . BIJDRAGEN VAN DE PHILOSOPHISCHE EN THEOLOGISCHE FACULTEITEN DER NEDERLANDSCHE JEZUIETEN
BPAU . . . . BULLETIN OF THE PAN AMERICAN UNION
BPCTH . . . . BULLETIN PHILOLOGIQUE ET HISTORIQUE DU COMITE DES TRAVAUX HISTORIQUES ET SCIENTIFIQUES
BPEC . . . . BOLLETTINO DEL COMITATO PER LA PREPARAZIONE DELL'EDIZIONE NAZIONALE DEI CLASSICI GRECI E LATINI
BPF . . . . BULLETIN DU PROTESTANTISME FRANCAIS
BPh . . . . BIBLIOGRAPHIE DE LA PHILOSOPHIE
BPH . . . . BULLETIN PHILOLOGIQUE ET HISTORIQUE
BPhC . . . . BIBLIOTHECA PHILOLOGICA CLASSICA
BPHCTHS . . . . BULLETIN PHILOLOGIQUE ET HISTORIQUE DU COMITE DES TRAVAUX HISTORIQUES ET SCIENTIFIQUES
BPHist . . . . BULLETIN PHILOLOGIQUE ET HISTORIQUE

BPHP . . . . BULLETIN PHILOLOGIQUE ET HISTORIQUE DU COMITE DES TRAVAUX HISTORIQUES ET SCIENTIFIQUES (PARIS)
BPhSC . . . . BULLETIN OF THE PHILOLOGICAL SOCIETY OF CALCUTTA
BPhSJ . . . . BULLETIN OF THE PHONETIC SOCIETY OF JAPAN
BPhW . . . . BERLINER PHILOLOGISCHE WOCHENSCHRIFT
B PHYSIO PA . . . . . . BULLETIN DE PHYSIO-PATHOLOGIE RESPIRATOIRE
BPI . . . . BOLLETTINO DELLE PUBLICATIONE ITALIANE
BPI . . . . BOLLETTINO PALEONTOLOGICO ITALIANO
BPJ . . . . BELOIT POETRY JOURNAL
BPKG . . . . BLAETTER FUER PFAELZISCHE KIRCHENGESCHICHTE
BPKS . . . . BERICHTE (AMTLICHE) DER PREUSSISCHEN KUNSTSAMMLUNGEN
BPLQ . . . . BOSTON PUBLIC LIBRARY QUARTERLY
B POL BIOL . . . . BULLETIN DE L' ACADEMIE POLONAISE DES SCIENCES. SERIE DES SCIENCES BIOLOGIQUES
B POL CHIM . . . . . . BULLETIN DE L'ACADEMIE POLONAISE DES SCIENCES. SERIE DES SCIENCES CHIMIQUES
B POL MATH . . . . . . BULLETIN DE L'ACADEMIE POLONAISE DES SCIENCES. SERIE DES SCIENCES MATHEMATIQUES ASTRONOMIQUES ET PHYSIQUES
B POL SCI T . . . . BULLETIN DE L'ACADEMIE POLONAISE DES SCIENCES. SERIE DES SCIENCES DE LA TERRE
B POL TECHN . . . . . . BULLETIN DE L'ACADEMIE POLONAISE DES SCIENCES. SERIE DES SCIENCES TECHNIQUES
BPQ . . . . BOSTON PUBLIC QUARTERLY
B PSIC APPL . . . . . . BOLLETTINO DI PSICOLOGIA APPLICATA
BPSP . . . . BOLLETTINO DELLA SOCIETA PAVESE DI STORIA PATRIA
B PSYCHON S . . . . . . BULLETIN OF THE PSYCHONOMIC SOCIETY
BPTJ . . . . BIULETYN POLSKIEGO TOWARZYSTWA JEZYKOZNAWCZEGO
BPW . . . . BERLINER PHILOLOGISCHE WOCHENSCHRIFT
BQR . . . . BODLEIAN QUARTERLY RECORD
BR . . . . BALTIC REVIEW (NEW YORK)
BR . . . . BENEDICTINE REVIEW
BR . . . . BIBLIOTHECA ROMANA
BR . . . . BUCKNELL REVIEW
BR . . . . BUDAPEST REGISEGEI
BrA . . . . BRASIL ACUCAREIRO: INSTITUTO DO ACUCAR E DO ALCOOL
BRABLB . . . . BOLETIN DE LA REAL ACADEMIA DE BUENAS LETRAS DE BARCELONA
BRAC . . . . BOLETIN DE LA REAL ACADEMIA (CORDOBA)
BRAE . . . . BOLETIN DE LA REAL ACADEMIA ESPANOLA
BRAH . . . . BOLETIN DE LA REAL ACADEMIA DE LA HISTORIA
BRAIN BEHAV . . . . . BRAIN BEHAVIOR AND EVOLUTION
BRAIN LANG . . . . . . BRAIN AND LANGUAGE
Brain Res . . . . BRAIN RESEARCH
Br Alma Comp . . . . . BRITISH ALMANAC COMPANION
Bras . . . . BRASILIA
Brass & Wood Q . . . . BRASS AND WOODWIND QUARTERLY
Brass W . . . . BRASS WORLD AND PLATER'S GUIDE
Brazil Camara Deput Bibl Bol . . BRAZIL. CAMARA DOS DEPUTADOS. BIBLIOTECA. BOLETIM
Brazil Cons Nac Petrol Relat . . BRAZIL. CONSELHO NACIONAL DO PETROLEO. RELATORIO
Brazil Dep Nac Prod Miner Lab Prod Miner Avulso . . BRAZIL. DEPARTMENTO NACIONAL DA PRODUCAO MINERAL. LABORATORIO DA PRODUCAO MINERAL. AVULSO
Brazil Div Geol Mineral Bol . . BRAZIL. DIVISAO DE GEOLOGIA E MINERALOGIA. BOLETIM
Brazil Div Geol Mineral Notas Prelim Estud . . BRAZIL. DIVISAO DE GEOLOGIA E MINERALOGIA. NOTAS PRELIMINARES E ESTUDOS
Br Chem Engng . . . . BRITISH CHEMICAL ENGINEERING
Br Chem Engng Process Technol . . BRITISH CHEMICAL ENGINEERING AND PROCESS TECHNOLOGY

Br Claywkr . . . . BRITISH CLAYWORKER
Br Coal Util Res Ass Mon Bull . . BRITISH COAL UTILISATION RESEARCH ASSOCIATION. MONTHLY BULLETIN
Br Corros J . . . . BRITISH CORROSION JOURNAL
BR DENT J . . . . BRITISH DENTAL JOURNAL
BRDSPL . . . . BOLLETTINO DELLA R. DEPUTAZIONE DI STORIA PATRIA PER LA LIGURIA
BRDSPU . . . . BOLLETTINO DELLA R. DEPUTAZIONE DI STORIA PATRIA PER L'UMBRIA
BrechtH . . . . BRECHT HEUTE—BRECHT TODAY
Breeders Gaz . . . . . BREEDER'S GAZETTE
Brennst-Chem . . . . . BRENNSTOFF-CHEMIE
Brenns-Waerme-Kraft . . BRENNSTOFF-WAERME-KRAFT
BRENN WAERME . . . BRENNSTOFF-WAERME-KRAFT
Bren S . . . . BRENNER-STUDIEN
Breth Life . . . . BRETHREN LIFE AND THOUGHT
Brew Rev . . . . BREWING REVIEW
Brew Trade Rev . . . . BREWING TRADE REVIEW
Br Foundryman . . . . BRITISH FOUNDRYMAN
BRGK . . . . BERICHT DER ROMISCH-GERMANISCHEN KOMMISSION
BR HEART J . . . . BRITISH HEART JOURNAL
Briar Q . . . . BRIARCLIFF QUARTERLY
Brick Clay Rec . . . . . BRICK AND CLAY RECORD
Brief Case . . . . LEGAL AID BRIEF CASE
Br Ink Mkr . . . . BRITISH INK MAKER
Brit & For Evang R . . BRITISH AND FOREIGN EVANGELICAL REVIEW
Brit & For R . . . . BRITISH AND FOREIGN REVIEW
Britannica R For Lang Educ . . BRITANNICA REVIEW OF FOREIGN LANGUAGE EDUCATION
BritArchAb . . . . BRITISH ARCHAEOLOGICAL ABSTRACTS
Brit Assoc Am Studies Bull . . BRITISH ASSOCIATION FOR AMERICAN STUDIES. BULLETIN
Brit Bk News . . . . . . BRITISH BOOK NEWS
Brit Bk Yr . . . . BRITANNICA BOOK OF THE YEAR
Brit Chem Eng . . . . . BRITISH CHEMICAL ENGINEERING
Brit Columbia Dep mines Petrol Resour Bull . . BRITISH COLUMBIA DEPARTMENT OF MINES AND PETROLEUM
RESOURCES. BULLETIN
Brit Columbia Lib Q . . BRITISH COLUMBIA LIBRARY QUARTERLY
Brit Constr Steelworks Ass Publ . . BRITISH CONSTRUCTIONAL STEELWORKS ASSOCIATION. PUBLICATIONS
Brit Corros J . . . . . . BRITISH CORROSION JOURNAL
BritEdI . . . . BRITISH EDUCATION INDEX
Brit Engine Boiler Elec Ins Co Tech Rep . . BRITISH ENGINE, BOILER AND ELECTRICAL INSURANCE COMPANY.
TECHNICAL REPORT
Brit Granite Whinstone Fed J . . BRITISH GRANITE AND WHINSTONE FEDERATION. JOURNAL
Brit Grassland Soc J . . BRITISH GRASSLAND SOCIETY. JOURNAL
Brit Hum . . . . BRITISH HUMANITIES INDEX
Brit J Aes . . . . BRITISH JOURNAL OF AESTHETICS
Brit J Ap Phys . . . . . BRITISH JOURNAL OF APPLIED PHYSICS
Brit J Crim . . . . BRITISH JOURNAL OF CRIMINOLOGY
Brit J Ed Psychol . . . BRITISH JOURNAL OF EDUCATIONAL PSYCHOLOGY
Brit J Ed Studies . . . BRITISH JOURNAL OF EDUCATIONAL STUDIES
Brit J Educ Psychol . . BRITISH JOURNAL OF EDUCATIONAL PSYCHOLOGY
Brit J Educ Stud . . . . BRITISH JOURNAL OF EDUCATIONAL STUDIES
Brit J Hist Sci . . . . . BRITISH JOURNAL FOR THE HISTORY OF SCIENCE
Brit J Math & Stat Psychol . . BRITISH JOURNAL OF MATHEMATICAL AND STATISTICAL PSYCHOLOGY
Brit J Med Psychol . . BRITISH JOURNAL OF MEDICAL PSYCHOLOGY

Brit J Non-Destruct Test . . BRITISH JOURNAL OF NON-DESTRUCTIVE TESTING
Brit J Nutr . . . . BRITISH JOURNAL OF NUTRITION
Brit J Nutr Proc Nutr Soc . . BRITISH JOURNAL OF NUTRITION. PROCEEDINGS OF THE NUTRITION SOCIETY
Brit Jour Sociol . . . . BRITISH JOURNAL OF SOCIOLOGY
Brit J Phil Sci . . . . . . BRITISH JOURNAL FOR THE PHILOSOPHY OF SCIENCE
Brit J Philos Sci . . . . BRITISH JOURNAL FOR THE PHILOSOPHY OF SCIENCE
Brit J Pol Sci . . . . . . BRITISH JOURNAL OF POLITICAL SCIENCE
Brit J Psychiat . . . . . BRITISH JOURNAL OF PSYCHIATRY
Brit J Psychol . . . . . BRITISH JOURNAL OF PSYCHOLOGY
Brit J Social & Clin Psychol . . BRITISH JOURNAL OF SOCIAL AND CLINICAL PSYCHOLOGY
Brit J Social Psychiat . . BRITISH JOURNAL OF SOCIAL PSYCHIATRY
Brit Kinematogr sound telev . . BRITISH KINEMATOGRAPHY SOUND AND TELEVISION
Brit Lib Assoc . . . . . LIBRARY ASSOCIATION OF THE UNITED KINGDOM. MONTHLY NOTES
Brit Med J . . . . BRITISH MEDICAL JOURNAL
Brit Mycol Soc Trans . . BRITISH MYCOLOGICAL SOCIETY. TRANSACTIONS
Brit Plast . . . . BRITISH PLASTICS
Brit Polym J . . . . . . BRITISH POLYMER JOURNAL
Brit Q . . . . BRITISH QUARTERLY REVIEW
Brit Sch Athens Ann . . BRITISH SCHOOL AT ATHENS. ANNUAL
Brit Sch at Rome Papers . . BRITISH SCHOOL AT ROME. PAPERS
Brit Stand Inst Brit Stand . . BRITISH STANDARDS INSTITUTION. BRITISH STANDARD
Brit Steelmaker . . . . BRITISH STEELMAKER
Brit Techl . . . . BRITISH TECHNOLOGY INDEX
Brit Weld J . . . . BRITISH WELDING JOURNAL
BRIT YEAR BOOK INT L . . BRITISH YEARBOOK OF INTERNATIONAL LAW
BR J ADDICT . . . . . . BRITISH JOURNAL OF ADDICTION
BR J ANAEST . . . . . . BRITISH JOURNAL OF ANAESTHESIA
Br J Appl Phys . . . . . BRITISH JOURNAL OF APPLIED PHYSICS
BR J CANC . . . . BRITISH JOURNAL OF CANCER
BR J CLIN P . . . . . . BRITISH JOURNAL OF CLINICAL PRACTICE
BR J CL PH . . . . BRITISH JOURNAL OF CLINICAL PHARMACOLOGY
BR J CRIMIN . . . . . . BRITISH JOURNAL OF CRIMINOLOGY
BR J DERM . . . . BRITISH JOURNAL OF DERMATOLOGY
BR J DIS CH . . . . . . BRITISH JOURNAL OF DISEASES OF THE CHEST
BR J DIS CO . . . . . . BRITISH JOURNAL OF DISORDERS OF COMMUNICATION
BR J ED PSY . . . . . . BRITISH JOURNAL OF EDUCATIONAL PSYCHOLOGY
BR J EDUC S . . . . . . BRITISH JOURNAL OF EDUCATIONAL STUDIES
BR J EDUC T . . . . . . BRITISH JOURNAL OF EDUCATIONAL TECHNOLOGY
BR J EX PAT . . . . . . BRITISH JOURNAL OF EXPERIMENTAL PATHOLOGY
BR J HAEM . . . . BRITISH JOURNAL OF HAEMATOLOGY
BR J HIST S . . . . BRITISH JOURNAL FOR THE HISTORY OF SCIENCE
BR J IND ME . . . . . . BRITISH JOURNAL OF INDUSTRIAL MEDICINE
BR J MATH S . . . . . . BRITISH JOURNAL OF MATHEMATICAL AND STATISTICAL PSYCHOLOGY
BR J MED PS . . . . . . BRITISH JOURNAL OF MEDICAL PSYCHOLOGY
BR J MENT S . . . . . . BRITISH JOURNAL OF MENTAL SUBNORMALITY
Br J Non-Destr Test . . BRITISH JOURNAL OF NON-DESTRUCTIVE TESTING
BR J NUTR . . . . BRITISH JOURNAL OF NUTRITION
BR J OBST G . . . . . . BRITISH JOURNAL OF OBSTETRICS AND GYNAECOLOGY
Br J Occup Saf . . . . . BRITISH JOURNAL OF OCCUPATIONAL SAFETY
BR J OPHTH . . . . . . BRITISH JOURNAL OF OPHTHALMOLOGY
BR J ORAL S . . . . . . BRITISH JOURNAL OF ORAL SURGERY

BR J PHARM...... BRITISH JOURNAL OF PHARMACOLOGY
BR J PHIL S....... BRITISH JOURNAL OF PHILOSOPHY OF SCIENCE
Br J Photogr...... BRITISH JOURNAL OF PHOTOGRAPHY
BR J PHYS O...... BRITISH JOURNAL OF PHYSIOLOGICAL OPTICS
BR J PL SUR......BRITISH JOURNAL OF PLASTIC SURGERY
BR J POLI S....... BRITISH JOURNAL OF POLITICAL SCIENCE
BR J PREV S.......BRITISH JOURNAL OF PREVENTIVE AND SOCIAL MEDICINE
BR J PSYCHI...... BRITISH JOURNAL OF PSYCHIATRY
BR J PSYCHO...... BRITISH JOURNAL OF PSYCHOLOGY
BR J RADIOL...... BRITISH JOURNAL OF RADIOLOGY
BR J SOC CL......BRITISH JOURNAL OF SOCIAL AND CLINICAL PSYCHOLOGY
BR J SOCIOL...... BRITISH JOURNAL OF SOCIOLOGY
BR J SOC PS.......BRITISH JOURNAL OF SOCIAL PSYCHIATRY
BR J SOC W....... BRITISH JOURNAL OF SOCIAL WORK
BR J SURG........ BRITISH JOURNAL OF SURGERY
BR J UROL........BRITISH JOURNAL OF UROLOGY
BR J VEN DI.......BRITISH JOURNAL OF VENEREAL DISEASES
Br Kinnematogr.... BRITISH KINEMATOGRAPHY SOUND AND TELEVISION
BR KNITTING IND.. BRITISH KNITTING INDUSTRY
BRL.............BULLETIN OF THE JOHN RYLANDS LIBRARY
BR MED B....... BRITISH MEDICAL BULLETIN
BR MED J....... BRITISH MEDICAL JOURNAL
BRMMLA........BULLETIN OF THE ROCKY MOUNTAIN MODERN LANGUAGE ASSOCIATION
Broadw.......... BROADWAY
BROB........... BERICHTEN VAN DE RIJKSDIENST VOOR HET OUDHEIDKUNDIG BODEMONDERZOEK
BROILER Prod..... BROILER PRODUCER
Bromma Hembygds-foren Arsskr.. BROMMA HEMBYGDSFORENINGS ARSSKRIFT
BROOKINGS P..... BROOKINGS PAPERS ON ECONOMIC ACTIVITY
Brookings Pa Econ Activ. . BROOKINGS PAPERS ON ECONOMIC ACTIVITY
Brooklyn Bar...... BROOKLYN BARRISTER
Brooklyn L Rev.... BROOKLYN LAW REVIEW
Brooklyn Mus Ann.. BROOKLYN MUSEUM ANNUAL
Brooklyn Mus Bul.. BROOKLYN INSTITUTE OF ARTS AND SCIENCES. MUSEUM BULLETIN
BROOK S BIO...... BROOKHAVEN SYMPOSIA IN BIOLOGY
Brot............ BROTERIA
Brown Boveri Rev.. BROWN BOVERI REVIEW
BROWN BOV R..... BROWN BOVERI REVIEW
Brownson........ BROWNSON'S QUARTERLY REVIEW
BRP........... BEITRAEGE ZUR ROMANISCHEN PHILOLOGIE
BRP........... BOLLETTINO DELLA R. UNIVERSITA ITALIANA PER STRANIERI DI PERUGIA
BRPh........... BEITRAEGE ZUR ROMANISCHEN PHILOLOGIE
Br Plast......... BRITISH PLASTICS
Br Polym J....... BRITISH POLYMER JOURNAL
BR POULT SC...... BRITISH POULTRY SCIENCE
Br Print.......... BRITISH PRINTER
BRSG.......... BOLETIN DE LA REAL SOCIEDAD GEOGRAFICA
Br Steelmaker..... BRITISH STEELMAKER
BRSV.......... BOLETIN DE LA REAL SOCIEDAD VASCONGADA DE AMIGOS DEL PAIS
BRT............ BEHAVIOR RESEARCH AND THERAPY
BRUnesco........ BULLETIN DE LA COMMISSION NATIONALE DE LA REPUBLIQUE POPULAIRE ROUMAINE POUR
L'UNESCO

Brush & P........ BRUSH AND PENCIL
BRUS MUS ROY BEAUX ARTS BULL.. BRUSSELS. MUSEES ROYAUX DES BEAUX-ARTS BELGIQUE. BULLETIN
Brussels Mus Roy Bul.. BRUSSELS. MUSEES ROYAUX D'ART ET D'HISTOIRE. BULLETIN
BR VET J......... BRITISH VETERINARY JOURNAL
Br Wat Supply..... BRITISH WATER SUPPLY
BS.............. BEST SELLERS
BS.............. BOGOSLOVSKA SMOTRA
BS.............. BOLLETTINO SENESE
BS.............. BOLLINGEN SERIES
BS.............. BRIXIA SACRA
BS.............. BULLETIN DES SOMMAIRES DES PERIODIQUES FRANCAIS ET ETRANGERS
BSAA........... BULLETIN DE LA SOCIETE ARCHEOLOGIQUE D'ALEXANDRIE
BSAAV......... BOLETIN DEL SEMINARIO DE ESTUDIOS DE ARTE Y ARQUEOLOGIA. UNIVERSIDAD DE VALLADOLID
BSAB.......... BULLETIN DE LA SOCIETE ARCHEOLOGIQUE DE BORDEAUX
BSAB.......... BULLETIN TRIMESTRIEL DE LA SOCIETE DES ANTIQUAIRES DE PICARDIE
BSAC.......... BULLETIN DE LA SOCIETE D'ARCHEOLOGIE COPTE
BSACorreze...... BULLETIN DE LA SOCIETE ARCHEOLOGIQUE DE LA CORREZE
BSAF........... BULLETIN DE LA SOCIETE NATIONALE DES ANTIQUAIRES DE FRANCE
BSAFrance....... BULLETIN DE LA SOCIETE NATIONALE DES ANTIQUAIRES DE FRANCE
BSAHDL......... BULLETIN DE LA SOCIETE D'ART ET D'HISTOIRE DU DIOCESE DE LIEGE
BSAHLimousin..... BULLETIN DE LA SOCIETE ARCHEOLOGIQUE ET HISTORIQUE DU LIMOUSIN
BSAHNantes...... BULLETIN DE LA SOCIETE ARCHEOLOGIQUE ET HISTORIQUE DE NANTES ET DE LOIRE-ATLANTIQUE
BSAL........... BOLLETI DE LA SOCIETAT ARQUEOLOGICA LUBLIANA
BSAL........... BULLETIN DE LA SOCIETE ARCHEOLOGIQUE DU LIMOUSIN
BSAM.......... BULLETIN DE LA SOCIETE ARCHEOLOGIQUE DU MIDI DE LA FRANCE
BSAM.......... BULLETIN DE LA SOCIETE DES AMIS DE MONTAIGNE
BSAM.......... BULLETIN TRIMESTRIEL DE LA SOCIETE ACADEMIQUE DES ANTIQUAIRES DE LA MORINIE
BSAMorinie....... BULLETIN TRIMESTRIEL DE LA SOCIETE ACADEMIQUE DES ANTIQUAIRES DE LA MORINIE
BSAN.......... BULLETIN DE LA SOCIETE DES ANTIQUAIRES DE NORMANDIE
BSANormandie.... BULLETIN DE LA SOCIETE DES ANTIQUAIRES DE NORMANDIE
BSAO.......... BULLETIN DE LA SOCIETE DES ANTIQUAIRES DE L'OUEST ET DES MUSEES DE POITIERS
BSAOuest........ BULLETIN DE LA SOCIETE DES ANTIQUAIRES DE L'OUEST ET DES MUSEES DE POITIERS
BSAP.......... BIBLIOGRAPHICAL SOCIETY OF AMERICA. PAPERS
BSAP.......... BULLETIN TRIMESTRIEL DE LA SOCIETE DES ANTIQUAIRES DE PICARDIE
BSAPicardie...... BULLETIN TRIMESTRIEL DE LA SOCIETE DES ANTIQUAIRES DE PICARDIE
BSAPR......... BULLETIN DE LA SOCIETE DES AMIS DE PORT-ROYAL
BSAS.......... BULLETIN DE LA SOCIETE ARCHEOLOGIQUE DE SENS
BSASD.......... BULLETIN DE LA SOCIETE D'ARCHEOLOGIQUE ET DE STATISTIQUE DE LA DROME
BSAT.......... BULLETIN DE LA SOCIETE ARCHEOLOGIQUE DE TOURAINE
BSAV.......... BOLETIN DEL SEMINARIO DE ESTUDIOS DE ARTE Y ARQUEOLOGIA. VALLADOLID
BSBBM......... BULLETIN DE LA SOCIETE DES BIBLIOPHILES BELGES SEANT A MONS
BSBF.......... BULLETIN DE LA SOCIETE DES BIBLIOLATRES DE FRANCE
BSBL.......... BULLETIN DE LA SOCIETE DES BIBLIOPHILES LIEGOIS
B S BOT FR I...... BULLETIN DE LA SOCIETE BOTANIQUE DE FRANCE PT I
BSBPP.......... BULLETIN DE LA SOCIETE BIBLIOGRAPHIQUE DES PUBLICATIONS POPULAIRES
BSBR.......... BOLLETTINO SISTEMATICO DI BIBLIOGRAFIA ROMANA
BSBS.......... BOLLETTINO STORICO BIBLIOGRAPHICO SUBALPINO
BSC............ BOLLETTINO STORICO CATANESE
BSC............ BOLLETTINO STORICO CREMONESE
B SC AK MED...... BULLETIN DER SCHWEIZERISCHEN AKADEMIE DER MEDIZINISCHEN WISSENSCHAFTEN

BSCAM . . . . BULLETIN DES SEANCES DU CERCLE ARCHEOLOGIQUE DE MONS
BSCat . . . . BOLLETTINO STORICO CATANESE
BSCC . . . . BOLETIN DE LA SOCIEDAD CASTELLONENSE DE CULTURA
B S CH FR I . . . . BULLETIN DE LA SOCIETE CHIMIQUE DE FRANCE. PART I
B S CH FR II . . . . . . BULLETIN DE LA SOCIETE CHIMIQUE DE FRANCE. PART II
B S CHIM BE . . . . . . BULLETIN DES SOCIETES CHIMIQUES BELGES
BSci . . . . BEHAVIORAL SCIENCE
B SCI MATH . . . . . . BULLETIN DES SCIENCES MATHEMATIQUES
BSDSL . . . . BASLER STUDIEN ZUR DEUTSCHEN SPRACHE UND LITERATUR
BSE . . . . BRNO STUDIES IN ENGLISH
BSEA . . . . BOLETIN DEL SEMINARIO DE ESTUDIOS DE ARTE Y ARQUEOLOGIA
BSEAA . . . . BOLETIN DEL SEMINARIO DE ESTUDIOS DE ARTE Y ARQUEOLOGIA
BSEBourbonnais . . . . BULLETIN DE LA SOCIETE D'EMULATION DU BOURBONNAIS
BSED . . . . BULLETIN DE LA SOCIETE D'ETUDES DANTESQUES DU CENTRE UNIVERSITAIRE MEDITERRANEEN
BSEE . . . . BOLETIN DE LA SOCIETE ESPANOLA DE EXCURSIONES
BSEF . . . . BOLETIM DA SOCIEDADE DE ESTUDOS FILOLOGICOS
BSEIC . . . . BULLETIN DE LA SOCIETE DES ETUDES INDOCHINOISES
B SEIS S AM . . . . . . BULLETIN OF THE SEISMOLOGICAL SOCIETY OF AMERICA
BSELot . . . . BULLETIN DE LA SOCIETE DES ETUDES LITTERAIRES, SCIENTIFIQUES ET ARTISTIQUES DU LOT
BSEM . . . . BOLETIN DA SOCIEDADE DO ESTUDOS DE MOCAMBIQUE BYZANTINOSLAVICA
BSEPC . . . . BULLETIN DE LA SOCIETE D'ETUDES DE LA PROVINCE DE CAMBRAI
BSFF . . . . BOLLETTINO DELLA SOCIETA FILOLOGICA FRIULANA
B S FR CER . . . . BULLETIN DE LA SOCIETE FRANCAISE DE CERAMIQUE
B S FR D SY . . . . . . BULLETIN DE LA SOCIETE FRANCAISE DE DERMATOLOGIE ET DE SYPHILIGRAPHIE
B S FR MIN . . . . BULLETIN DE LA SOCIETE FRANCAISE MINERALOGIE ET DE CRISTALLOGRAPHIE
BSGAE . . . . BOLETIN DE LA SOCIEDAD GENERAL DE AUTORES DE ESPANA
BSGAO . . . . BULLETIN DE LA SOCIETE DE GEOGRAPHIE D'ARCHEOLOGIE D'ORAN
BSHAF . . . . BULLETIN DE LA SOCIETE DE L'HISTOIRE DE L'ART FRANCAIS
BSHAP . . . . PROVINCIA. BULLETIN DE LA SOCIETE D'HISTOIRE ET D'ARCHEOLOGIE DE MARSEILLE ET DE
                        LA PROVENCE
BSHAPerigord . . . . . BULLETIN DE LA SOCIETE HISTORIQUE ET ARCHEOLOGIQUE DU PERIGORD
BSHEW . . . . BULLETIN DE LA SOCIETE POUR L'HISTOIRE DES EGLISES WALLONES
BSHM . . . . BULLETIN DE LA SOCIETE D'HISTOIRE DE LA MEDECINE
BSHM . . . . BULLETIN DE LA SOCIETE D'HISTOIRE MODERNE
BSHPF . . . . BULLETIN DE LA SOCIETE DE L'HISTOIRE DU PROTESTANTISME FRANCAIS
BSHPIF . . . . BULLETIN DE LA SOCIETE HISTORIQUE DE PARIS ET DE L'ILE DE FRANCE
BSHS . . . . BULLETIN DE LA SOCIETE D'HISTOIRE ET DE GEOGRAPHIE DE LA REGION DE SETIF
BSHY . . . . BULLETIN DE LA SOCIETE DES SCIENCES HISTORIQUES DE L'YONNE
BSII . . . . BOLLETTINO DEGLI STUDI INGLESI IN ITALIA
BSJ . . . . BAKER STREET JOURNAL
BSKG . . . . BEITRAEGE ZU SAECHSISCHEN KIRCHENGESCHICHTE
BSL . . . . BOLLETINO STORICO LIVORNESE
BSL . . . . BULLETIN DE LA SOCIETE DE LINGUISTIQUE DE PARIS
BSL . . . . BULLETIN DE LA SOCIETE SCIENTIFIQUE ET LITTERAIRE DU LIMBOURG
BSL . . . . BYZANTINOSLAVICA
BSLLW . . . . BULLETIN DE LA SOCIETE DE LANGUE ET LITTERATURE WALLONNES
BSLP . . . . BULLETIN DE LA SOCIETE DE LINGUISTIQUE DE PARIS
BSM . . . . BEITRAEGE ZUR SCHWEIZERDEUTSCHEN MUNDARTFORSCHUNGEN
BSM . . . . BOLLETTINO DI STUDI MEDITERRANEI
BSM . . . . BOLLETTINO STORICO MANTOVANO
BSM . . . . BRITISH STUDIES MONITOR

B S MATH FR . . . . . . BULLETIN DE LA SOCIETE MATHEMATIQUE DE FRANCE
BSNAF . . . . BULLETIN DE LA SOCIETE NATIONALE DES ANTIQUAIRES DE FRANCE
BSNotes . . . . BROWNING SOCIETY NOTES
BSNS . . . . BOLLETTINO DELLA SEZIONE DI NOVARA DELLA R. DEPUTAZIONE SUBALPINA DI STORIA PATRIA
Bsns Abroad . . . . . . BUSINESS ABROAD
Bsns & Tech Sources . . BUSINESS AND TECHNOLOGY SOURCES
Bsns Automation . . . BUSINESS AUTOMATION
Bsns Ed Forum . . . . . BUSINESS EDUCATION FORUM
Bsns Ed World . . . . . BUSINESS EDUCATION WORLD
Bsns Hist R . . . . . . BUSINESS HISTORY REVIEW
Bsns Lit . . . . BUSINESS LITERATURE
Bsns Mgt . . . . BUSINESS MANAGEMENT
Bsns Mgt (London) . . BUSINESS MANAGEMENT (LONDON)
Bsns W . . . . BUSINESS WEEK
Bsns W . . . . BUSINESS WORLD
BSOA . . . . BULLETIN OF THE SCHOOL OF ORIENTAL AND AFRICAN STUDIES
BSOAS . . . . BULLETIN OF THE SCHOOL OF ORIENTAL AND AFRICAN STUDIES
BSOS . . . . BULLETIN OF THE SCHOOL OF ORIENTAL AND AFRICAN STUDIES
BSP . . . . BIBLIOGRAPHICAL SOCIETY (LONDON). PUBLICATIONS
BSP . . . . BIBLIOGRAPHICAL SOCIETY OF AMERICA. PAPERS
BSP . . . . BOLLETTINO STORICO PIACENTINO
BSP . . . . BOLLETTINO STORICO PISTOIESE
BSP . . . . BRITISH SPACE FICTION MAGAZINE
BSPA . . . . BOLLETTINO DELLA SOCIETA PIEMONTESE DI ARCHEOLOGIA
BSPABA . . . . BOLLETTINO DELLA SOCIETA PIEMONTESE DI ARCHEOLOGIA E BELLE ARTI
BSPi . . . . BOLLETTINO STORICO PISTOIESE
BSPiac . . . . BOLLETTINO DI STORIA PIACENTINA
BSPis . . . . BOLLETTINO STORICO PISANO
BSPL . . . . BULLETIN DE LA SOCIETE POLONAISE DE LINGUISTIQUE
BSPN . . . . BOLLETTINO STORICO PER LA PROVINCIA DE NOVARA
BSPS . . . . BOLLETTINO DELLA SOCIETA PAVESE DI STORIA PATRIA
BSPSP . . . . BOLLETTINO DELLA SOCIETA PAVESE DI STORIA PATRIA
BSPU . . . . BOLLETTINO DELLA REGIA DEPUTAZIONE DI STORIA PATRIA PER L'UMBRIA
BSS . . . . BIRGER SJOBERG SALLSKAPET
BSS . . . . BULETIN PER SHKENCAT SHOQERORE
BSS . . . . BULLETIN OF SPANISH STUDIES
BSSAT . . . . BOLLETTINO DI STUDI STORICI ED ARCHEOLOGICI DI TIVOLI E REGIONE
B S SCI MED . . . . . . BULLETIN DE LA SOCIETE DES SCIENCES MEDICALES DU GRAND-DUCHE DE LUXEMBOURG
BSSHNY . . . . BULLETIN DE LA SOCIETE DES SCIENCES HISTORIQUES ET NATURELLES DE L'YONNE
BSSI . . . . BOLLETTINO STORICO DELLA SVIZZERA ITALIANA
BSSL . . . . BIBLIOGRAPHIEN ZUM STUDIUM DER DEUTSCHEN SPRACHE UND LITERATUR
BSSL . . . . BULLETIN DE LA SOCIETE DES SCIENCES ET DES LETTRES DE LODZ
BSSLL . . . . BULLETIN DE LA SOCIETE SCIENTIFIQUE ET LITTERAIRE DU LIMBOURG
BSSP . . . . BOLLETTINO SENESE DI STORIA PATRIA
BSSS . . . . BULLETIN MENSUEL DE LA SOCIETE DES SCIENCES DE SEMUR
BSSY . . . . BULLETIN DE LA SOCIETE DES SCIENCES HISTORIQUES DE L'YONNE
BST . . . . BRONTE SOCIETY TRANSACTIONS
BSTCF . . . . BALL STATE TEACHERS COLLEGE FORUM
BSTEC . . . . BULLETIN DE LA SOCIETE TOULOUSAINE D'ETUDES CLASSIQUES
BSUF . . . . BALL STATE UNIVERSITY FORUM

BSUSSR . . . . BULLETIN OF THE INSTITUTE FOR THE STUDY OF THE USSR (MUNICH)
BSVAH . . . . BULLETIN DE LA SOCIETE VERVIETOISE D'ARCHEOLOGIE ET D'HISTOIRE
BSVasc . . . . BOLETIN DE LA REAL SOCIEDAD VASCONGADA DE AMIGOS DEL PAIS
B S ZOOL FR . . . . . . BULLETIN DE LA SOCIETE ZOOLOGIQUE DE FRANCE
BT . . . . BIBLE TRANSLATOR
BT . . . . BIG TABLE
BTAM . . . . BULLETIN DE THEOLOGIE ANCIENNE ET MEDIEVALE
BTBS . . . . BOSTON TRANSCRIPT BOOK SECTION
BTD . . . . BULLETIN DE LA COMMISSION ROYALE DE TOPONYMIE ET DIALECTOLOGIE
BTh . . . . BULLETIN DE THEOLOGIE ANCIENNE ET MEDIEVALE
BThom . . . . BULLETIN THOMISTE
BTIAL . . . . BULLETIN TRIMESTRIEL DE L'INSTITUT ARCHEOLOGIQUE DU LUXEMBOURG
BTIALux . . . . BULLETIN TRIMESTRIEL DE L'INSTITUT ARCHEOLOGIQUE DU LUXEMBOURG
BTLV . . . . BIJDRAGEN TOT DE TAAL-LAND-EN VOLKENKUNDE
BTLVNI . . . . BIJDRAGEN TOT DE TAAL-LAND-EN VOLKENKUNDE VAN NEDERLANDSCH INDIE
BTMG . . . . BLAETTER DER THOMAS MANN GESELLSCHAFT
B TOR BOT C . . . . . . BULLETIN OF THE TORREY BOTANICAL CLUB
BTR . . . . BRITISH TAX REVIEW
BTSAAM . . . . BULLETIN TRIMESTRIEL DE LA SOCIETE ACADEMIQUE DES ANTIQUAIRES DE LA MORINIE
BTSAP . . . . BULLETIN TRIMESTRIEL DE LA SOCIETE DES ANTIQUAIRES DE PICARDIE
BU . . . . BLUES UNLIMITED
BuB . . . . BUCHEREI UND BILDUNG
BuCHS . . . . BUCKS COUNTY HISTORICAL SOCIETY. PAPERS
BucksCoHS . . . . BUCKS COUNTY HISTORICAL SOCIETY. PAPERS
BUE . . . . BULLETIN OF THE FACULTY OF ARTS OF THE UNIVERSITY OF EGYPT
BUENOS AIRES MUS . . BUENOS AIRES MUSICAL
Buffalo Gal Notes . . BUFFALO. FINE ARTS ACADEMY. ALBRIGHT ART GALLERY. NOTES
Buffalo Hist Soc Publ . . BUFFALO HISTORICAL SOCIETY. PUBLICATIONS
Buffalo L Rev . . . . . BUFFALO LAW REVIEW
BUFFALO PHIL . . . . . BUFFALO PHILHARMONIC PROGRAM NOTES
BUFF LAW R . . . . . . BUFFALO LAW REVIEW
BUG . . . . BOLETIN DE LA UNIVERSIDAD DE GRANADA
Build Int (Engl Ed) . . BUILD INTERNATIONAL (ENGLISH EDITION)
Build Res . . . . BUILDING RESEARCH
Build Res Estab (sta) Digest . . BUILDING RESEARCH ESTABLISHMENT (STATION) DIGEST
Build Res Pract . . . . BUILDING RESEARCH & PRACTICE
Build Sci . . . . BUILDING SCIENCE
Build Serv Eng . . . . . BUILDING SERVICES ENGINEER
Build Syst Des . . . . . BUILDING SYSTEMS DESIGN
Built Env . . . . BUILT ENVIRONMENT
BUJ . . . . BOSTON UNIVERSITY JOURNAL
Bul Am Repub . . . . . BULLETIN OF INTERNATIONAL BUREAU OF THE AMERICAN REPUBLICS
Bul Atomic Sci . . . . . BULLETIN OF THE ATOMIC SCIENTISTS
Bul Bibl de France . . BULLETIN DES BIBLIOTHEQUES DE FRANCE
Bul Bibliog . . . . BULLETIN OF BIBLIOGRAPHY
BUL BLACK THEATRE . . BULLETIN OF BLACK THEATRE
Bul Child Bks . . . . . . BULLETIN OF THE CENTER FOR CHILDREN'S BOOKS
Bul Corresp Hellenique . . ECOLE FRANCAISE D'ATHENES. BULLETIN DE CORRESPONDANCE HELLENIQUE
Bul Doc Bibliog . . . . BULLETIN DE DOCUMENTATION BIBLIOGRAPHIQUE (PT 2 OF BUL BIBL DE FRANCE)
BULGAR MUZ . . . . . BULGARSKA MUZIKA

PERIODICAL TITLE ABBREVIATIONS

Bul Inst Politeh Bucuresti . . BULETINUL INSTITUTULUI POLITEHNIC BUCURESTI

Bul Inst Politeh Iasi . . BULETINUL INSTITUTULUI POLITEHNIC DIN IASI

Bul Int Fiscal Doc . . . BULLETIN FOR INTERNATIONAL FISCAL DOCUMENTATION

Bull Acad Pol Sci Ser Sci Tech . . BULLETIN DE L'ACADEMIE POLONAISE DES SCIENCES. SERIE DES SCIENCES TECHNIQUES

Bull Acad Sci USSR Phys Ser (Columbia Tech Transl) . . BULLETIN OF THE ACADEMY OF SCIENCES OF THE U.S.S.R. PHYSICAL SERIES (COLUMBIA TECHNICAL TRANSLATIONS)

Bull Ass Suisse Elec . . BULLETIN DE L'ASSOCIATION SUISSE DES ELECTRICIENS

Bull Bibl De France . . BULLETIN DES BIBLIOTHEQUES DE FRANCE

Bull B Psych Soc . . . BULLETIN OF THE BRITISH PSYCHOLOGICAL SOCIETY

Bull Bur Rech Geol Minieres . . BULLETIN DU BUREAU DE RECHERCHES GEOLOGIQUES ET MINIERES (FRANCE)

Bul Bur Rech Geol Minieres Ser 2 Sect 2 . . BULLETIN DU BUREAU DE RECHERCHES GEOLOGIQUES ET MINIERES. SERIE 2, SECTION 2 (FRANCE)

Bull Can Pet Geol . . . BULLETIN OF CANADIAN PETROLEUM GEOLOGY

Bull Chem Soc Japan . . BULLETIN OF THE CHEMICAL SOCIETY OF JAPAN

Bull Classe Sci Acad Roy Belg . . BULLETIN DE LA CLASSE DES SCIENCES. ACADEMIE ROYALE DE BELGIQUE

Bull Comm Geol Finl . . BULLETIN DE LA COMMISSION GEOLOGIQUE DE FINLANDE

Bull Cr Soc . . . . BULLETIN OF THE COPYRIGHT SOCIETY OF THE USA

Bull Doc Bibliog . . . . BULLETIN DE DOCUMENTATION BIBLIOGRAPHIQUE

Bull Earth Miner Sci Exp Sta Pa State Univ . . BULLETIN OF THE EARTH AND MINERAL SCIENCES EXPERIMENT STATION. PENSYLVANIA STATE UNIVERSITY

BULL EARTHQUAKE RES INST UNIV TOKYO . . BULLETIN OF THE EARTHQUAKE RESEARCH INSTITUTE. UNIVERSITY OF TOKYO

Bull Electrotech Lab, Tokyo . . BULLETIN OF THE ELECTROTECHNICAL LABORATORY (TOKYO)

Bull Environ Contam Toxicol . . BULLETIN OF ENVIRONMENTAL CONTAMINATION AND TOXICOLOGY

BULL FAR EASTERN ANTIQUITIES . . BULLETIN OF THE MUSEUM OF FAR EASTERN ANTIQUITIES

Bull Hisp . . . . BULLETIN HISPANIQUE

Bull Hist Med . . . . . BULLETIN OF THE HISTORY OF MEDICINE

Bull Inst Int Froid . . . BULLETIN DE L'INSTITUT INTERNATIONAL DU FROID

BULL INT ASSOC SCI HYDROL . . BULLETIN OF THE INTERNATIONAL ASSOCIATION OF SCIENTIFIC HYDROLOGY

Bull Int Assoc Shell Spat Struct . . BULLETIN OF THE INTERNATIONAL ASSOCIATION FOR SHELL AND SPATIAL STRUCTURES

Bull Int Ass Sci Hydrol . . BULLETIN OF THE INTERNATIONAL ASSOCIATION OF SCIENTIFIC HYDROLOGY

Bull Int Ass Shell Struct . . BULLETIN OF THE INTERNATIONAL ASSOCIATION FOR SHELL STRUCTURES

Bull Int Inst Refrig . . BULLETIN OF THE INTERNATIONAL INSTITUTE OF REFRIGERATION

Bull Int Ry Congr Ass . . BULLETIN OF THE INTERNATIONAL RAILWAY CONGRESS ASSOCIATION

Bull Jap Pet Inst . . . BULLETIN OF THE JAPAN PETROLEUM INSTITUTE

Bull Jap Soc Grinding Eng . . BULLETIN OF JAPAN SOCIETY OF GRINDING ENGINEERS

Bull Jap Soc Precis Eng . . BULLETIN OF THE JAPAN SOCIETY OF PRECISION ENGINEERING

Bull JSAE . . . . BULLETIN OF JSAE (JAPAN SOCIETY OF AUTOMOTIVE ENGINEERS)

Bull JSME . . . . BULLETIN OF JSME (JAPAN SOCIETY OF MECHANICAL ENGINEERS)

Bull Mech Engng Educ . . BULLETIN OF MECHANICAL ENGINEERING EDUCATION

Bull Mon . . . . BULLETIN MONUMENTAL

Bull Narcotics . . . . . BULLETIN ON NARCOTICS

Bull N Z Soc Earthquake Eng . . BULLETIN OF THE NEW ZEALAND SOCIETY OF EARTHQUAKE ENGINEERING

Bull Perma Int Ass Navig Congr . . BULLETIN OF THE PERMANENT INTERNATIONAL ASSOCIATION OF NAVIGATION CONGRESSES

Bull Rijksmus . . . . . . BULLETIN VAN HET RIJKSMUSEUM

Bul Sci AIM . . . . BULLETIN SCIENTIFIQUE DE L'ASSOCIATION DES INGENIEURS ELECTRICIENS SORTIS DE L'INSTITUT ELECTROTECHNIQUE MONTEFIORE

Bull Seismol Soc Amer . . BULLETIN OF THE SEISMOLOGICAL SOCIETY OF AMERICA

Bull SHPF . . . . BULLETIN DE LA SOCIETE DE L'HISTOIRE DU PROTESTANTISME FRANCAIS

Bull Soc Belg Geol Paleontol Hydrol . . BULLETIN DE LA SOCIETE BELGE DE GEOLOGIE, DE PALEONTOLOGIE ET D'HYDROLOGIE
Bull Soc Fr Ceram . . . BULLETIN DE LA SOCIETE FRANCAISE DE CERAMIQUE
Bull Soc Fr Phil . . . . . BULLETIN DE LA SOCIETE FRANCAISE DE PHILOSOPHIE
Bull Soc Fr Photogramm . . BULLETIN DE LA SOCIETE FRANCAISE DE PHOTOGRAMMETRIE
Bull Soc Geol Fr . . . . BULLETIN DE LA SOCIETE GEOLOGIQUE DE FRANCE
Bull Soc Roy Belg Elec . . BULLETIN DE LA SOCIETE ROYALE BELGE DES ELECTRICIENS
Bull Tech Suisse Romande . . BULLETIN TECHNIQUE DE LA SUISSE ROMANDE
Bull Univ Osaka Perfect Ser A . . BULLETIN OF THE UNIVERSITY OF OSAKA, PERFECTURE. SERIES A
Bull Va Polytech Inst Eng Exp Sta Ser . . BULLETIN OF THE VIRGINIA POLYTECHNIC INSTITUTE, ENGINEERING EXPERIMENT STATION SERIES
Bul NHPL . . . . BULLETIN OF THE NEW HAMPSHIRE PUBLIC LIBRARIES
Bul NYPL . . . . BULLETIN OF THE NEW YORK PUBLIC LIBRARY
Bul of Bibliography . . BULLETIN OF BIBLIOGRAPHY AND DRAMATIC INDEX
Bul Pan Am Union . . BULLETIN OF THE PAN AMERICAN UNION
BUL L Rev . . . . BOSTON UNIVERSITY LAW REVIEW
Bul Suicidol . . . . . . BULLETIN OF SUICIDOLOGY
BUM . . . . BOLETIN DE LA UNIVERSIDAD DE MADRID
Bundesminist Bild Wiss Forschungsber . . BUNDESMINISTERIUM FUER BILDUNG UND WISSENSCHAFT, FORSCHUNGSBERICHT
Bundesminist Forsch Technol Forschungsber Weltraumforsch . . BUNDESMINISTERIUM FUER FORSCHUNG UND TECHNOLOGIE, FORSCHUNGSBERICHT, WELTRAUMFORSCHUNG
BundJb . . . . BUNDER JAHRBUCH
BUNDMB . . . . BUNDNERISCHES MONATSBLATT
B Universities Annual . . BRITISH UNIVERSITIES ANNUAL
BUNSEKI KAG . . . . . BUNSEKI KAGAKU
BUP . . . . BULLETIN OF THE UNIVERSITY OF PITTSBURG
BuR . . . . BUCKNELL REVIEW
BUR AM ETHN . . . . . BUREAU OF AMERICAN ETHNOLOGY BULLETIN
Bur Am Ethnol Annual Report . . BUREAU OF AMERICAN ETHNOLOGY. ANNUAL REPORT
Bur Farmer . . . . BUREAU FARMER
BurgHb . . . . BURGENLAENDISCHE HEIMATBLAETTER
BURJL . . . . BULLETIN USTAVU RUSKEHO JAZYKA A LITERATURY
Burl Mag . . . . BURLINGTON MAGAZINE
Burroughs Clear House . . BURROUGHS CLEARING HOUSE
BURS . . . . BIBLIOTHEQUE UNIVERSELLE ET REVUE SUISSE
BUS . . . . BROWN UNIVERSITY STUDIES
BUS . . . . BULLETIN DE L'UNIVERSITE DE STRASBOURG
Bus & Soc R . . . . . . BUSINESS AND SOCIETY REVIEW
BUSC . . . . BOLETIN DE LA UNIVERSIDAD DE SANTIAGO DE COMPOSTELA
Bus Coach . . . . BUS AND COACH
BUSE . . . . BOSTON UNIVERSITY STUDIES IN ENGLISH
Bus Ed Forum . . . . . . BUSINESS EDUCATION FORUM
Bus Ed J . . . . BUSINESS EDUCATION JOURNAL
Bus Ed Observer . . . NEW JERSEY BUSINESS EDUCATION OBSERVER
Bus Ed World . . . . . . BUSINESS EDUCATION WORLD
BUS HISTORY . . . . . . BUSINESS HISTORY
Bus Hist R . . . . BUSINESS HISTORY REVIEW
Bus Hist Soc Bull . . . BUSINESS HISTORY SOCIETY. BULLETIN
BUS HORIZ . . . . BUSINESS HORIZONS
Busl . . . . BUSINESS PERIODICALS INDEX

BUS JAP .... BUSINESS JAPAN
Bus Law .... BUSINESS LAWYER
Bus L Rev .... BUSINESS LAW REVIEW
BUS Q .... BUSINESS QUARTERLY
Bus Transp ...... BUS TRANSPORTATION
Bus W .... BUSINESS WEEK
BUT .... BULETIN I UNIVERSITETIT SHTEREROR TE TIRANES. SERIA SHKENCAT SHOQERORE
BUT .... BULLETIN DE L'UNIVERSITE DE TOULOUSE
Butter & Cheese J . . BUTTER AND CHEESE JOURNAL
BV .... BOGENS VERDEN
BV .... BOGOSLOVNI VESTNIK
BVAB .... BULLETIN VAN DE VEREENIGUNG TOT BEVORDERING DER KENNIS VAN DE ANTIEKE BESCHAVING
BVG .... BIJDRAGEN VOOR VADERLANDSCHE GESCHIEDENIS EN OUDHEIDSKUNDE
BVGO .... BIJDRAGEN VOOR VADERLANDSCHE GESCHIEDENIS EN OUDHEIDSKUNDE
BVSAW .... BERICHTE UEBER DIE VERHANDLUNGEN DER SAECHSISCHEN AKADEMIE DER WISSENSCHAFTEN
ZU LEIPZIG. PHILOLOGISCH-HISTORISCHE KLASSE
BVSAWL .... BERICHTE UEBER DIE VERHANDLUNGEN DER SAECHSISCHEN AKADEMIE DER WISSENSCHAFTEN
ZU LEIPZIG
BVSRJL .... BULLETIN VYSOKE SKOLY RUSSKEHO JAZYKA A LITERATURY
BW .... BETWEEN WORLDS
BW .... BLUES WORLD
BW .... BOOK WORLD (CHICAGO TRIBUNE)
B WHO .... BULLETIN OF THE WORLD HEALTH ORGANIZATION
BWKG .... BLAETTER FUER WUERTTEMBERGISCHE KIRCHENGESCHICHTE
BW (WP) .... BOOK WORLD (WASHINGTON POST)
BYGNIN MEDO ..... BYGNINGSSTATISKE MEDDELELSER
ByJ .... BYZANTINISCH-NEUGRIECHISCHE JAHRBUECHER
Byrsa .... CAHIERS DE BYRSA
ByT .... BARRASIHA-YE TARIKHI
BYUS .... BRIGHAM YOUNG UNIVERSITY STUDIES
ByZ .... BYZANTINISCHE ZEITSCHRIFT
Byz .... BYZANTION
Byz-Met .... BYZANTINA-METABYZANTINA
ByzMetabyz ...... BYZANTINA-METABYZANTINA
BYZ-NEUGR JAHRB . . BYZANTINISCH-NEUGRIECHISCHE JAHRBUECHER
BYZNGJB .... BYZANTINISCH-NEUGRIECHISCHE JAHRBUECHER
ByzS .... BYZANTINO-SLAVICA
ByzSl .... BYZANTINO-SLAVICA
ByzZ .... BYZANTINISCHE ZEITSCHRIFT
BZ .... BIBLISCHE ZEITSCHRIFT
BZ .... BYZANTINISCHE ZEITSCHRIFT
BzdB .... BIBLIOGRAPHIEN ZUR DEUTSCHE BAROCKLITERATUR
BZG .... BASLER ZEITSCHRIFT FUER GESCHICHTE UND ALTERTUMSKUNDE
BZGA .... BASLER ZEITSCHRIFT FUER GESCHICHTE UND ALTERTUMSKUNDE
BZGAK .... BASLER ZEITSCHRIFT FUER GESCHICHTE UND ALTERTUMSKUNDE
BzJA .... BEIHEFTE ZUM JA
BzMW .... BEITRAEGE ZUR MUSIKWISSENSCHAFT
BzNH .... BIZANTION-NEA HELLAS
BZTS .... BONNER ZEITSCHRIFT FUER THEOLOGIE UND SEELSORGE
BZWW .... BEIHEFTE ZUR ZEITSCHRIFT WIRKENDES WORT

C

C..............	CENOBIO
C..............	CENTURY
C..............	COIMBRA
C..............	COMMONWEAL
C..............	CRITICA
C..............	CRITIQUE
CA.............	CRITICA D'ARTE
CA.............	CUADERNOS AMERICANOS
CAAH..........	CAHIERS ALSACIENS D'ARCHEOLOGIE, D'ART ET D'HISTOIRE
CAA J..........	CIVIL AERONAUTICS JOURNAL
CAAS Bull.......	CANADIAN ASSOCIATION OF AMERICAN STUDIES. BULLETIN
Cablecast Cable TV Eng..	CABLECASTING, CABLE TV ENGINEERING
Cables Transm.....	CABLES & TRANSMISSION
CaboV..........	CABO VERDE
CACM..........	COMMUNICATIONS OF THE ASSOCIATION FOR COMPUTING MACHINERY
CACP..........	CAHIERS DE L'AMITIE CHARLES PEGUY
CadB..........	CADERNOS BRASILEIROS
CAE...........	CERCLE ARCHEOLOGIQUE D'ENGHIEN. ANNALES
CAEAn.........	CERCLE ARCHEOLOGIQUE D'ENGHIEN. ANNALES
CAEF..........	CAHIERS DE L'ASSOCIATION INTERNATIONALE DES ETUDES FRANCAISES
CAF...........	CAPTAIN FUTURE
CAfr...........	CONGO-AFRIQUE
CAHA..........	CAHIERS D'ARCHEOLOGIE ET D'HISTOIRE D'ALSACE
CAH BIO MAR.....	CAHIERS DE BIOLOGIE MARINE
CAH ECON BR.....	CAHIERS ECONOMIQUES DE BRUXELLES
CAH ETUD AF.....	CAHIERS D'ETUDES AFRICAINES
Cahiers Droit......	QUEBEC (CITY). UNIVERSITE LAVAL. FACULTE DE DROIT. CAHIERS DE DROIT
CahiersE........	CAHIERS ELISABETHAINS
CahiersF........	CAHIERS FRANCOPHONES
Cahiers Geog Quebec..	CAHIERS DE GEOGRAPHIE DE QUEBEC
Cahiers Herne.....	CAHIERS DE L'HERNE
CAI............	CAIC (COMPUTER ASSISTED INSTRUCTION CENTER) TECHNICAL MEMO. FLORIDA STATE UNIVERSITY
CAIEF..........	CAHIERS DE L'ASSOCIATION INTERNATIONALE DES ETUDES FRANCAISES
CAH INT SOC......	CAHIERS INTERNATIONAUX DE SOCIOLOGIE
CAH MON RUS.....	CAHIERS DU MONDE RUSSE ET SOVIETIQUE
CAH ORST HY.....	CAHIERS ORSTOM HYDROBIOLOGIE
CAH ORST OC.....	CAHIERS ORSTOM OCEANOGRAPHIE
CAH V PARET.....	CAHIERS VILFREDO PARETO
CaiSE..........	CAIRO STUDIES IN ENGLISH
CAJ...........	CENTRAL ASIATIC JOURNAL
CAJ...........	COLLEGE ART JOURNAL
CAL...........	CENTER FOR APPLIED LINGUISTICS (WASH., D.C.)
Cal Ag Exp	UNIVERSITY OF CALIFORNIA. COLLEGE OF AGRICULTURE. AGRICULTURAL EXPERIMENT STATION. PUBLICATIONS
CALC..........	CAHIERS ALGERIENS DE LITTERATURE COMPAREE
CALCIF TISS.......	CALCIFIED TISSUE RESEARCH
Cal Citrograph.....	CALIFORNIA CITROGRAPH
Cal Countryman....	CALIFORNIA COUNTRYMAN
Cal Cultivator.....	CALIFORNIA CULTIVATOR
Calif Ag Bul.......	CALIFORNIA. DEPARTMENT OF AGRICULTURE. BULLETIN

CALIF AGR. . . . . . . CALIFORNIA AGRICULTURE
Calif Bus Ed J. . . . . CALIFORNIA BUSINESS EDUCATION JOURNAL
Calif Ed. . . . . CALIFORNIA EDUCATION
Calif El Sch Adm Assn Mon. . CALIFORNIA ELEMENTARY SCHOOL ADMINISTRATORS ASSOCIATION. MONOGRAPHS
Calif El Sch Adm Assn Yearbook. . CALIFORNIA ELEMENTARY SCHOOL ADMINISTRATORS ASSOCIATION. YEARBOOK
CALIF FISH. . . . . . . CALIFORNIA FISH AND GAME
Calif Folklore Qu. . . CALIFORNIA FOLKLORE QUARTERLY
Calif Hist Soc Q. . . . CALIFORNIA HISTORICAL SOCIETY. QUARTERLY
Calif Hist Soc Quar. . CALIFORNIA HISTORICAL SOCIETY. QUARTERLY
Calif J Ed Res. . . . . CALIFORNIA JOURNAL OF EDUCATIONAL RESEARCH
CALIF J EDU. . . . . . CALIFORNIA JOURNAL OF EDUCATIONAL RESEARCH
Calif J El Ed. . . . . . CALIFORNIA JOURNAL OF ELEMENTARY EDUCATION
Calif J Sec Ed. . . . . CALIFORNIA JOURNAL OF SECONDARY EDUCATION
Calif Libn. . . . . . . CALIFORNIA LIBRARIAN
Calif L Rev. . . . . . . CALIFORNIA LAW REVIEW
Calif M. . . . . CALIFORNIAN ILLUSTRATED MAGAZINE
CALIF MANAG. . . . . CALIFORNIA MANAGEMENT REVIEW
Calif Mgt R. . . . . . . CALIFORNIA MANAGEMENT REVIEW
Calif Pal Leg Hon Bul. . CALIFORNIA PALACE OF THE LEGION OF HONOR. MUSEUM BULLETIN
Calif Q. . . . . CALIFORNIA QUARTERLY
Calif S B. . . . . JOURNAL OF THE STATE BAR OF CALIFORNIA
Calif SBJ. . . . . JOURNAL OF THE STATE BAR OF CALIFORNIA
Calif Sch. . . . . CALIFORNIA SCHOOLS
Calif Sch Lib. . . . . . CALIFORNIA SCHOOL LIBRARIES
Calif Univ Chron. . . CALIFORNIA UNIVERSITY CHRONICLE
Calif Western Int L J. . CALIFORNIA WESTERN INTERNATIONAL LAW JOURNAL
Calif Western L Rev. . CALIFORNIA WESTERN LAW REVIEW
CalN. . . . . CALABRIA NOBILISSIMA
Cal Q Sec Ed. . . . . . CALIFORNIA QUARTERLY OF SECONDARY EDUCATION
CalR. . . . . CALCUTTA REVIEW
Cal SS. . . . . CALIFORNIA SLAVIC STUDIES
Cal State Comm Hort B. . CALIFORNIA. STATE COMMISSION OF HORTICULTURE. MONTHLY BULLETIN
Cal Th J. . . . . CALVIN THEOLOGICAL JOURNAL
Cal Univ Pub. . . . . . U. OF CALIFORNIA. BERKELEY. PUBLICATIONS IN AGRICULTURAL SCIENCE
CAm. . . . . CASA DE LAS AMERICAS (HAVANA)
Cam Abs. . . . . CAMBRIDGE ABSTRACTS
CAMAn. . . . . CERCLE ARCHEOLOGIQUE DE MONS. ANNALES
Camb J. . . . . CAMBRIDGE JOURNAL
Camb L J. . . . . CAMBRIDGE LAW JOURNAL
Camb Philos Soc Trans. . CAMBRIDGE PHILOSOPHICAL SOCIETY. TRANSACTIONS
CAMBull. . . . . CERCLE ARCHEOLOGIQUE DE MALINES. BULLETIN
CamJ. . . . . CAMBRIDGE JOURNAL
Camp Mag. . . . . . . CAMPING MAGAZINE
CamQ. . . . . CAMBRIDGE QUARTERLY
CamR. . . . . CAMBRIDGE REVIEW
CaN. . . . . CALABRIA NOBILISSIMA
Can. . . . . CANONISTE
Canada Ag. . . . . . . DOMINION OF CANADA. DEPARTMENT OF AGRICULTURE. PUBLICATIONS
Canad Bookm. . . . . CANADIAN BOOKMAN
Canad Forum. . . . . CANADIAN FORUM
Canad Geog J. . . . . CANADIAN GEOGRAPHICAL JOURNAL

Canadian Lib Assn Bul. . CANADIAN LIBRARY ASSOCIATION. BULLETIN
Canad J. . . . . CANADIAN JOURNAL OF INDUSTRY
Canad Lib. . . . . CANADIAN LIBRARY
Canad Lib Assn Bul. . CANADIAN LIBRARY ASSOCIATION. BULLETIN
Canad Lib Assn Feliciter. . CANADIAN LIBRARY ASSOCIATION FELICITER
Canad Lib J. . . . . . . CANADIAN LIBRARY JOURNAL
Canad M. . . . . CANADIAN MAGAZINE
Canad Mo. . . . . CANADIAN MONTHLY
Can Aeronaut Space J. . CANADIAN AERONAUTICS AND SPACE JOURNAL
CAN AER SPA. . . . . CANADIAN AERONAUTICS AND SPACE JOURNAL
CAN-AM SLAV. . . . . CANADIAN-AMERICAN SLAVIC STUDIES
CAN ANAE SJ. . . . . . CANADIAN ANAESTHETISTS SOCIETY. JOURNAL
Can & World. . . . . . CANADA AND THE WORLD
Can Ant Coll. . . . . . CANADIAN ANTIQUES COLLECTOR
Can Arch. . . . . CANADIAN ARCHITECT
Can Art. . . . . CANADIAN ART
Can Aud. . . . . CANADIAN AUDUBON
Can Auth & Book. . . CANADIAN AUTHOR AND BOOKMAN
CAN AV. . . . . CANADIAN AVIATION
CAN BANK. . . . . . . CANADIAN BANKER
Can Bar R. . . . . . . CANADIAN BAR REVIEW
CAN B J. . . . . CANADIAN BAR JOURNAL
Can B Rev. . . . . . . CANADIAN BAR REVIEW
Can Bus. . . . . CANADIAN BUSINESS
Can C. . . . . CANONISTE CONTEMPORAIN
CANC BIOC B. . . . . . CANCER BIOCHEMISTRY BIOPHYSICS
CANC CH P 1. . . . . . CANCER CHEMOTHERAPHY REPORTS PART 1
CANC CH P 2. . . . . . CANCER CHEMOTHERAPY REPORTS PART 2
CANC CH P 3. . . . . . CANCER CHEMOTHERAPY REPORTS PART 3
CANCER RES. . . . . . CANCER RESEARCH
CANCER T R. . . . . . CANCER TREATMENT REVIEWS
CAN CHART ACCT. . CANADIAN CHARTERED ACCOUNTANT
Can Chem & Met. . . CANADIAN CHEMISTRY AND METALLURGY
Can Chem & Process Ind. . CANADIAN CHEMISTRY AND PROCESS INDUSTRIES
Can Chem Process. . CANADIAN CHEMICAL PROCESSING
CAN COMMERCE. . . CANADA COMMERCE
CAN COMP. . . . . . . CANADIAN COMPOSER
CAN COMPOSER. . . CANADIAN COMPOSER
CAN CONSUMER. . . CANADIAN CONSUMER
Candid. . . . . CANDID QUARTERLY REVIEW OF PUBLIC AFFAIRS
CAN DIMEN. . . . . . CANADIAN DIMENSION
C&M. . . . . CLASSICA ET MEDIAEVALIA
C&S. . . . . CULTURA E SCUOLA
C&U. . . . . COLLEGE AND UNIVERSITY
C&W. . . . . CHRISTENTUM UND WISSENSCHAFT
CAN ED AND RES. . . CANADIAN EDUCATION AND RESEARCH DIGEST
CanEdI. . . . . CANADIAN EDUCATION INDEX
Can Ed Res Digest. . CANADIAN EDUCATION AND RESEARCH DIGEST
Can Electron Eng. . . CANADIAN ELECTRONICS ENGINEERING
Can Eng. . . . . CANADIAN ENGINEER
Can Entom. . . . . . . CANADIAN ENTOMOLOGIST

Can F. . . . . CANADIAN FORUM
CAN FARM EC. . . . . CANADIAN FARM ECONOMICS
Can Forum. . . . . CANADIAN FORUM
Can Geog. . . . . CANADIAN GEOGRAPHER
Can Geog J. . . . . . . CANADIAN GEOGRAPHICAL JOURNAL
CAN GEOGR. . . . . . . CANADIAN GEOGRAPHER
CAN GEOTECH. . . . . CANADIAN GEOTECHNICAL JOURNAL
CAN HIST ASSN. . . . CANADIAN HISTORICAL ASSOCIATION. HISTORICAL PAPERS
CAN HIST ASSN REP. . CANADIAN HISTORICAL ASSOCIATION. REPORT
Can Hist Assoc Ann Rep. . CANADIAN HISTORICAL ASSOCIATION. ANNUAL REPORT
Can Hist R. . . . . CANADIAN HISTORICAL REVIEW
Can Hort. . . . . CANADIAN HORTICULTURE AND HOME MAGAZINE
CanHR. . . . . CANADIAN HISTORICAL REVIEW
CanI. . . . . CANADIAN PERIODICAL INDEX
CAN I FOOD. . . . . . . CANADIAN INSTITUTE OF FOOD SCIENCE AND TECHNOLOGY JOURNAL
Can Inland Waters Branch Sci Ser. . CANADA. INLAND WATERS BRANCH. SCIENTIFIC SERIES
CAN J AFR S. . . . . . CANADIAN JOURNAL OF AFRICAN STUDIES
Can J Agric Econ. . . CANADIAN JOURNAL OF AGRICULTURAL ECONOMICS
Can J Ag Sci. . . . . . CANADIAN JOURNAL OF AGRICULTURAL SCIENCE
CAN J ANIM. . . . . . CANADIAN JOURNAL OF ANIMAL SCIENCE
CAN J BEH S. . . . . . CANADIAN JOURNAL OF BEHAVIOURAL SCIENCE
CAN J BIOCH. . . . . . CANADIAN JOURNAL OF BIOCHEMISTRY
Can J Bot. . . . . CANADIAN JOURNAL OF BOTANY
CAN J CHEM. . . . . . CANADIAN JOURNAL OF CHEMISTRY
Can J Chem Eng. . . . CANADIAN JOURNAL OF CHEMICAL ENGINEERING
CAN J CH EN. . . . . . CANADIAN JOURNAL OF CHEMICAL ENGINEERING
CAN J COM M. . . . . CANADIAN JOURNAL OF COMPARATIVE MEDICINE
Can J Corr. . . . . CANADIAN JOURNAL OF CORRECTIONS
CAN J CRIM. . . . . . CANADIAN JOURNAL OF CRIMINOLOGY AND CORRECTIONS
CAN J EARTH. . . . . . CANADIAN JOURNAL OF EARTH SCIENCES
Can J Earth Sci. . . . . CANADIAN JOURNAL OF EARTH SCIENCES
CAN J EC. . . . . CANADIAN JOURNAL OF ECONOMICS
Can J Econ. . . . . CANADIAN JOURNAL OF ECONOMICS
Can J Econ & Pol Sci. . CANADIAN JOURNAL OF ECONOMICS AND POLITICAL SCIENCE
CAN J GENET. . . . . . CANADIAN JOURNAL OF GENETICS AND CYTOLOGY
Can J Hist. . . . . CANADIAN JOURNAL OF HISTORY
CanJL. . . . . CANADIAN JOURNAL OF LINGUISTICS
CAN J LINGU. . . . . . CANADIAN JOURNAL OF LINGUISTICS
CAN J MATH. . . . . . CANADIAN JOURNAL OF MATHEMATICS
CAN J MED T. . . . . . CANADIAN JOURNAL OF MEDICAL TECHNOLOGY
CAN J MICRO. . . . . CANADIAN JOURNAL OF MICROBIOLOGY
CAN J OPHTH. . . . . CANADIAN JOURNAL OF OPHTHALMOLOGY
Can Jour Hist. . . . . CANADIAN JOURNAL OF HISTORY
Can J Phil. . . . . CANADIAN JOURNAL OF PHILOSOPHY
CAN J PH SC. . . . . . CANADIAN JOURNAL OF PHARMACEUTICAL SCIENCES
Can J Phys. . . . . . . CANADIAN JOURNAL OF PHYSICS
CAN J PHYSL. . . . . . CANADIAN JOURNAL OF PHYSIOLOGY AND PHARMACOLOGY
CAN J PLANT. . . . . . CANADIAN JOURNAL OF PLANT SCIENCE
CAN J POLI. . . . . . . CANADIAN JOURNAL OF POLITICAL SCIENCE
CAN J POL SCI. . . . . CANADIAN JOURNAL OF POLITICAL SCIENCE
CAN J PSYCH. . . . . . CANADIAN JOURNAL OF PSYCHOLOGY

CAN J PUBL . . . . CANADIAN JOURNAL OF PUBLIC HEALTH
Can J Res . . . . CANADIAN JOURNAL OF RESEARCH
CAN J SOIL . . . . CANADIAN JOURNAL OF SOIL SCIENCE
CAN J SPECT . . . . . . CANADIAN JOURNAL OF SPECTROSCOPY
CAN J SURG . . . . . . CANADIAN JOURNAL OF SURGERY
Can J Th . . . . CANADIAN JOURNAL OF THEOLOGY
Can J Zool . . . . CANADIAN JOURNAL OF ZOOLOGY
CanL . . . . CANADIAN LITERATURE
CAN LAB . . . . CANADIAN LABOUR
CAN LIB . . . . CANADIAN LIBRARY
Can Lib Assn Bul . . . CANADIAN LIBRARY ASSOCIATION. BULLETIN
Can Lib Bull . . . . . . CANADIAN LIBRARY BULLETIN
Can Lib J . . . . CANADIAN LIBRARY JOURNAL
Can Lit . . . . CANADIAN LITERATURE
Can Mach Metalwork . . CANADIAN MACHINERY AND METALWORKING
CAN MATH B . . . . . . CANADIAN MATHEMATICAL BULLETIN
CAN MED A J . . . . . . CANADIAN MEDICAL ASSOCIATION. JOURNAL
Can Med Assn J . . . . CANADIAN MEDICAL ASSOCIATION. JOURNAL
CAN MENT HE . . . . . CANADA'S MENTAL HEALTH
CAN METAL Q . . . . . CANADIAN METALLURGICAL QUARTERLY
Can Metalwork/Mach Prod . . CANADIAN METALWORKING/MACHINE PRODUCTION
Can Metalwork Prod . . CANADIAN METALWORKING PRODUCTION
Can Met Quart . . . . CANADIAN METALLURGICAL QUARTERLY
Can Min & Met Bul . . CANADIAN MINING AND METALLURGICAL BULLETIN
Can Mining Met Bul . . CANADIAN MINING AND METALLURGICAL BULLETIN
Can Min J . . . . CANADIAN MINING JOURNAL
CAN MIN MET . . . . . CANADIAN MINING AND METALLURGICAL BULLETIN
CAN MUS BK . . . . . . CANADA MUSIC BOOK
Can Mus J . . . . CANADIAN MUSIC JOURNAL
Cann Pack . . . . CANNING AND PACKING
CAN PERS . . . . CANADIAN PERSONNEL AND INDUSTRIAL RELATIONS JOURNAL
CAN PLASTICS . . . . . CANADIAN PLASTICS
CAN POETRY . . . . . . CANADIAN POETRY
CAN PSYCHI . . . . . . CANADIAN PSYCHIATRIC ASSOCIATION JOURNAL
CAN PSYCHOL . . . . . CANADIAN PSYCHOLOGIST
CAN PSYCH R . . . . . CANADIAN PSYCHOLOGICAL REVIEW
CAN PUB ADMIN . . . CANADIAN PUBLIC ADMINISTRATION
CAN PUBL AD . . . . . CANADIAN PUBLIC ADMINISTRATION
CAN R AM ST . . . . . . CANADIAN REVIEW OF AMERICAN STUDIES
CAN R SOC . . . . CANADIAN REVIEW OF SOCIOLOGY AND ANTHROPOLOGY
CAN R SOC A . . . . . . CANADIAN REVIEW OF SOCIOLOGY AND ANTHROPOLOGY
CAN SLAV P . . . . . . CANADIAN SLAVONIC PAPERS
CanSP . . . . CANADIAN SLAVONIC PAPERS
CanSS . . . . CANADIAN-AMERICAN SLAVIC STUDIES
Can Stand Ass CSA Stand . . CANADIAN STANDARDS ASSOCIATION. CSA STANDARD
Can Surv . . . . CANADIAN SURVEYOR
Can Tax J . . . . CANADIAN TAX JOURNAL
Canterbury Eng J . . . CANTERBURY ENGINEERING JOURNAL
CAnth . . . . CURRENT ANTHROPOLOGY
CAnthr . . . . CURRENT ANTHROPOLOGY
CANTO GREG . . . . . . CANTO GREGORIANO

CAN VET J . . . . CANADIAN VETERINARY JOURNAL
Can Vet Record . . . . CANADIAN VETERINARY RECORD
CAN WEL . . . . CANADIAN WELFARE
Can Yearbook Int L . . CANADIAN YEARBOOK OF INTERNATIONAL LAW
Cap . . . . CAPITOLI
Cap . . . . CAPITOLIUM
Cap Libn . . . . CAPE LIBRARIAN
Capit . . . . CAPITOLIUM
Capital U L Rev . . . . CAPITAL UNIVERSITY LAW REVIEW
CaPL . . . . CAHIERS DE LA PLEIADE
CAPL . . . . CHRONIQUE ARCHEOLOGIQUE DU PAYS DE LIEGE
CAPWAn . . . . CERCLE ARCHEOLOGIQUE DU PAYS DE WAES. ANNALES
CaQ . . . . CALIFORNIA QUARTERLY
Car . . . . CARAVELLE
CaR . . . . CAKAVSKA RIC
Car . . . . CARMELUS
Car . . . . CAROVANA
Carbide J . . . . CARBIDE JOURNAL
CARBOHY RES . . . . . CARBOHYDRATE RESEARCH
CArch . . . . CAHIERS ARCHEOLOGIQUES
CARDIO RES . . . . . . CARDIOVASCULAR RESEARCH
Carey's Mus . . . . . . CAREY'S AMERICAN MUSEUM
CARIBBEAN S . . . . . CARIBBEAN STUDIES
CARIES RES . . . . CARIES RESEARCH
Carleton Misc . . . . . CARLETON MISCELLANY
CarlN . . . . CARLETON NEWSLETTER
Carnegie Mag . . . . . CARNEGIE MAGAZINE
Carnegie-Mellon Univ Tri Res Rep . . CARNEGIE-MELLON UNIVERSITY. PITTSBURGH. TRANSPORTATION RESEARCH
INSTITUTE. TRI RESEARCH REPORT
CarnM . . . . CARNEGIE MAGAZINE
CarP . . . . CAROLINA PLAYBOOK
CAR Q . . . . CAROLINA QUARTERLY
Carte . . . . CARTE SEGRETE
CasaA . . . . CASA DE LAS AMERICAS
CaSE . . . . CARNEGIE SERIES IN ENGLISH
Case & Com . . . . . . CASE AND COMMENT
CASE W RES . . . . . . CASE WESTERN RESERVE JOURNAL OF INTERNATIONAL LAW
Case W Res J Int L . . CASE WESTERN RESERVE JOURNAL OF INTERNATIONAL LAW
Case W Reserve L Rev . . CASE WESTERN RESERVE LAW REVIEW
CASI Trans . . . . CASI (CANADIAN AERONAUTICS AND SPACE INSTITUTE) TRANSACTIONS
CAsJ . . . . CENTRAL ASIATIC JOURNAL
CAsR . . . . CENTRAL ASIAN REVIEW
CASS . . . . CANADIAN-AMERICAN SLAVIC STUDIES
Cassier . . . . CASSIER'S MAGAZINE
CASURSS . . . . COMPTES RENDUS DE L'ACADEMIE DES SCIENCES DE L'UNION DES REPUBLIQUES SOVIETIQUES
SOCIALISTES
CAT . . . . CAHIERS D'ANALYSE TEXTUELLE, LIEGE. LES BELLES LETTRES
CATAL REV . . . . CATALYSIS REVIEWS
Cath Bib Q . . . . CATHOLIC BIBLICAL QUARTERLY
Cath Choirmaster . . CATHOLIC CHOIRMASTER
Cath Ed R . . . . CATHOLIC EDUCATIONAL REVIEW

Cath Hist R . . . . CATHOLIC HISTORICAL REVIEW
CathHR . . . . CATHOLIC HISTORICAL REVIEW
CathI . . . . CATHOLIC PERIODICAL AND LITERATURE INDEX
Cath Lib W . . . . CATHOLIC LIBRARY WORLD
Catholic Law . . . . . . CATHOLIC LAWYER
Catholic U L Rev . . . CATHOLIC UNIVERSITY LAW REVIEW
Cath Presb . . . . CATHOLIC-PRESBYTERIAN
Cath Rec Soc Pub . . . CATHOLIC RECORD SOCIETY. PUBLICATIONS
Cath Sch J . . . . CATHOLIC SCHOOL JOURNAL
CATH U LAW . . . . . . CATHOLIC UNIVERSITY OF AMERICA LAW REVIEW
Cath Univ Bull . . . . . CATHOLIC UNIVERSITY BULLETIN
Cath Univ Law Rev . . CATHOLIC UNIVERSITY OF AMERICA LAW REVIEW
CathW . . . . CATHOLIC WORLD
CaW . . . . CATHOLIC WORLD
CB . . . . CLASSICAL BULLETIN
CB . . . . COMMENTATIONES BALTICAE
CB . . . . CUADERNOS BIBLIOGRAFICOS (MADRID)
CB . . . . CULTURA BIBLICA
CBA . . . . CRONACA DELLE BELLE ARTI
CBAA . . . . CURRENT BIBLIOGRAPHY ON AFRICAN AFFAIRS
CBalt . . . . COMMENTATIONES BALTICAE
CBC . . . . CAHIERS BENJAMIN CONSTANT
CBC . . . . CESARE BARBIERI COURIER
CBEL . . . . CAMBRIDGE BIBLIOGRAPHY OF ENGLISH LITERATURE
CBKK . . . . CHUBAN KENKYU (STUDIES ON CHINESE LANGUAGE AND LITERATURE)
CBL . . . . CUMULATIVE BOOK LIST
CBQ . . . . CATHOLIC BIBLICAL QUARTERLY
CBr . . . . CADERNOS BRASILEIROS
CBR . . . . CANADIAN BAR REVIEW
CBS . . . . CHUGOKU NO BUNKA TO SHAKAI (CHINESE CULTURE AND SOCIETY)
CBV . . . . COMENIUS-BLAETTER FUER VOLKSERZIEHUNG
CBW . . . . CENTRALBLATT FUER BIBLIOTHEKWESEN
CC . . . . CAHIERS DU CINEMA
CC . . . . CHRISTIAN CENTURY
CC . . . . CIVILTA CATTOLICA
CC . . . . CODRUL COSMINULUI
CC . . . . CONTEMPORARY CHINA
CC . . . . CORPUS CHRISTIANORUM
CC . . . . CROSS CURRENTS
CCa . . . . CIVILTA CATTOLICA
CCanC . . . . CAHIER CANADIEN CLAUDEL
CCatt . . . . CIVILTA CATTOLICA
CCB . . . . CENTER FOR CHILDREN'S BOOKS. BULLETIN
CCB-B . . . . CENTER FOR CHIDREN'S BOOKS. BULLETIN
CCBUC . . . . CURSOS E CONFERENCIAS DA BIBLIOTECA DE UNIVERSIDADE DE COIMBRA
CCC . . . . CITEAUX COMMENTARII CISTERCIENSES
CCC . . . . COLLEGE COMPOSITION AND COMMUNICATION
CCCist . . . . CITEAUX COMMENTARII CISTERCIENSES
CCE . . . . CONTRIBUTIONS TO CANADIAN ECONOMICS
CCE . . . . CUADERNOS DE CULTURA ESPANOLA

CCF . . . . CESKY CASOPIS FILOLOGICKY
CCH . . . . CESKY CASOPIS HISTORICKY
CCHP . . . . CH'UNG CHI HSUEH-PAO
CCist . . . . COLLECTANEA CISTERCIENSIA
CCJ . . . . CHUNG CHI JOURNAL
CCLC . . . . CUADERNOS DEL CONGRESO POR LA LIBERTAD DE LA CULTURA
CCM . . . . CAHIERS DE CIVILISATION MEDIEVALES (X-XII SIECLES)
CCM . . . . CASOPIS CESKENHO MUSEA
CCM . . . . COLBY COLLEGE MONOGRAPHS
CCMe . . . . CAHIERS DE CIVILISATION MEDIEVALE
CCRB . . . . CAHIERS DE LA COMPAGNIE MADELEINE RENAUD-JEAN LOUIS BARRAULT
CCT . . . . CUADERNOS DE CULTURA TEATRAL
CCTE . . . . CONFERENCE OF COLLEGE TEACHERS OF ENGLISH OF TEXAS. PROCEEDINGS
CCU . . . . CUADERNOS DE LA CATEDRA DE UNAMUNO
CCult . . . . CRONACHE CULTURALI
CCV . . . . CENTRO DE CULTURA VALENCIANA
CD . . . . CHILD DEVELOPMENT
CD . . . . CIUDAD DE DIOS
CD . . . . COMPARATIVE DRAMA
CD . . . . CUADERNOS PARA EL DIALOGO
CdA . . . . CAMP DE L'ARPA
CDB . . . . COLECAO DOCUMENTOS BRASILEIROS
CdD . . . . CIUDAD DE DIOS
CdE . . . . CHRONIQUE D'EGYPTE
C de D . . . . CAHIERS DE DROIT
CdF . . . . CUADERNOS DE FILOLOGIA
CdL . . . . CAHIERS DE LEXICOLOGIE
CDMI Bul . . . . CENTRE DE DOCUMENTATION DE MUSIQUE INTERNATIONALE. BULLETIN
CdS . . . . CORRIERE DELLA SERA
CDU . . . . CENTRE DE DOCUMENTATION UNIVERSITAIRE
Ce . . . . CELTICA
CE . . . . CEYLON ECONOMIST
CE . . . . CHILDHOOD EDUCATION
CE . . . . CHRISTIAN EAST
CE . . . . CHRONIQUE D'EGYPTE
CE . . . . COLLEGE ENGLISH
CE . . . . CORNO EMPLUMADO
CE . . . . CORREO ERUDITO
CEA . . . . CEA (COLLEGE ENGLISH ASSOCIATION) CRITIC
CEAAN . . . . CENTER FOR EDITIONS OF AMERICAN AUTHORS. NEWSLETTER
CEAC . . . . CEA (COLLEGE ENGLISH ASSOCIATION) CHAP BOOK
CEACrit . . . . CEA (COLLEGE ENGLISH ASSOCIATION) CRITIC
CEAF . . . . CEA (COLLEGE ENGLISH ASSOCIATION) FORUM
CEAfr . . . . CAHIERS D'ETUDES AFRICAINES
CEAL . . . . CENTRO EDITOR DE AMERICA LATINA
CEBAL . . . . COPENHAGEN SCHOOL OF ECONOMICS AND BUSINESS ADMINISTRATION. LANGUAGE DEPT. PUB.
CEC . . . . CAHIERS D'ETUDES CATHARES
CEC . . . . CONSELHO ESTADUAL DE CULTURA
CEDAM . . . . CASA EDITRICE DOTT. A. MILANI
CeF . . . . CE FASTU ?
CEG . . . . CUADERNOS DE ESTUDIOS GALLEGOS

CEJ. . . . . CALIFORNIA ENGLISH JOURNAL
CELEST MECH. . . . . . CELESTIAL MECHANICS
CELL DIFFER. . . . . . . CELL DIFFERENTIATION
CELL IMMUN. . . . . . CELLULAR IMMUNOLOGY
CELL TIS RE. . . . . . . CELL AND TISSUE RESEARCH
CELL TISS K. . . . . . . CELL AND TISSUE KINETICS
Celt. . . . . CELTIBERIA
CEM. . . . . CAHIERS D'ETUDES MEDIEVALES
CEM. . . . . CUADERNOS DE ESTUDIOS MANCHEGOS
Cem Betong. . . . . . CEMENT OCH BETONG
Cem Concrete Ass Res Rep. . CEMENT AND CONCRETE ASSOCIATION. RESEARCH REPORT
Cem Concr Res. . . . CEMENT AND CONCRETE RESEARCH
Cem Lime Grav. . . . CEMENT, LIME AND GRAVEL
Cem Lime Mf. . . . . . CEMENT AND LIME MANUFACTURE
Cem Technol. . . . . . CEMENT TECHNOLOGY
CEMW. . . . . COLUMBIA ESSAYS ON MODERN WRITERS
CEn. . . . . COLECAO ENSAIO
Cen Eur Hist. . . . . . CENTRAL EUROPEAN HISTORY
CenR. . . . . CENTENNIAL REVIEW
Cent. . . . . CENTURY MAGAZINE
Cent Etud Rech Essais Sci Genie Civ Univ Liege Mem. . CENTRE D'ETUDES DE RECHERCHES ET D'ESSAIS SCIENTIFIQUES DU GENIE CIVIL. UNIVERSITE DE LIEGE. MEMOIRES
CENT EUR H. . . . . . . CENTRAL EUROPEAN HISTORY
Cent Inf Chrome Dur Bull Doc. . CENTRE D'INFORMATION DU CHROME DUR. BULLETIN DE DOCUMENTATION
CentR. . . . . CENTENNIAL REVIEW
CENTRAL OPERA. . . CENTRAL OPERA SERVICE BULLETIN
Centre Inform Chrome Dur Bull Doc. . CENTRE D'INFORMATION DU CHROME DUR. BULLETIN DE DOCUMENTATION
Centre Nat Rech Sci Tech Ind Cimentiere Rapp Rech. . CENTRE NATIONAL DE RECHERCHES SCIENTIFIQUE ET TECHNIQUES POUR L'INDUSTRIE CIMENTIERE. RAPPORT DE RECHERCHE
CENT SS RR. . . . . . . CENTER FOR SETTLEMENT STUDIES RESEARCH REPORTS. UNIVERSITY OF MANITOBA
CENT ST SPE. . . . . . CENTRAL STATES SPEECH JOURNAL
CEP. . . . . CZECHOSLOVAK ECONOMIC PAPERS
CER. . . . . CATHOLIC EDUCATIONAL REVIEW
Ceram Age. . . . . . . CERAMIC AGE
Ceramics Mo. . . . . . CERAMICS MONTHLY
Ceram Ind. . . . . . . CERAMIC INDUSTRY
Cereal Chem. . . . . . CEREAL CHEMISTRY
CEREAL F W. . . . . . . CEREAL FOODS WORLD
Cer Ind. . . . . CERAMIC INDUSTRY
CER-T. . . . . CAHIERS D'ETUDES DE RADIO-TELEVISION
Certif Eng. . . . . . . CERTIFICATED ENGINEER
CES. . . . . CHINESE ECONOMIC STUDIES
CeS. . . . . CULTURA E SCUOLA
CESK C FYS. . . . . . . CESKOSLOVENSKY CASOPIS PRO FYSIKU SEKCE A
CESK PSYCHO. . . . . CESKOSLOVENSKA PSYCHOLOGIE
CEStudies. . . . . . . CANADIAN ETHNIC STUDIES
CF. . . . . CANADA FRANCAIS
CF. . . . . CANADIAN FORUM
CF. . . . . CAPTAIN FUTURE
CF. . . . . CE FASTU?
CF. . . . . CLASSICAL FOLIA

```
CF . . . . . . . . . . . . . COLLECTANEA FRANCISCANA
CFeng . . . . . . . . . . CHING FENG
CFFAn . . . . . . . . . . COMITE FLAMAND DE FRANCE. ANNALES
CFL . . . . . . . . . . . . CLUB FRANCAIS DU LIVRE
CFL . . . . . . . . . . . . CONFLUENCES
CFM . . . . . . . . . . . CANADIAN FICTION MAGAZINE
CFMA . . . . . . . . . . CLASSIQUES FRANCAIS DU MOYEN AGE
CFol . . . . . . . . . . . CLASSICAL FOLIA
CForum . . . . . . . . . CULTURAL FORUM (NEW DELHI)
CFQ . . . . . . . . . . . CALIFORNIA FOLKLORE QUARTERLY
CFS . . . . . . . . . . . . CAHIERS FERDINAND DE SAUSSURE
CFSTI . . . . . . . . . . CLEARINGHOUSE FOR FEDERAL SCIENTIFIC AND TECHNICAL INFORMATION
CG . . . . . . . . . . . . . CHUGOKU GOGAKU
CG . . . . . . . . . . . . . CLASSIQUES GARNIER
CG . . . . . . . . . . . . . COMMON GROUND
CG . . . . . . . . . . . . . COURRIER GRAPHIQUE
CGB . . . . . . . . . . . COLECAO GENERAL BENICIO
CGJ . . . . . . . . . . . CANADIAN GEOGRAPHICAL JOURNAL
CGP . . . . . . . . . . . CARLETON GERMANIC PAPERS
CH . . . . . . . . . . . . . CAHIERS D'HISTOIRE
CH . . . . . . . . . . . . . CHURCH HISTORY
CH . . . . . . . . . . . . . CUADERNOS HISPANOAMERICANOS
CH . . . . . . . . . . . . . CURRENT HISTORY
CHA . . . . . . . . . . . CAHIERS D'HISTOIRE ET D'ARCHEOLOGIE
CHA . . . . . . . . . . . CUADERNOS HISPANOAMERICANOS (MADRID)
CHAC . . . . . . . . . . CERCLE HISTORIQUE ET ARCHEOLOGIQUE DE COURTRAI. BULLETIN
CHACBull . . . . . . . CERCLE HISTORIQUE ET ARCHEOLOGIQUE DE COURTRAI. BULLETIN
Chain Store Age (Adm ed) . . CHAIN STORE AGE (ADMINISTRATION EDITION)
Chal Clim . . . . . . . CHALEUR ET CLIMATS
Chal Climats . . . . . CHALEUR ET CLIMATS
Chalmers Tek Hogsk Handl . . CHALMERS TEKNISKA HOGSKOLAS HANDLINGAR
Chamb J . . . . . . . . CHAMBER'S EDINBURGH JOURNAL
Chang Ed . . . . . . . . CHANGING EDUCATION
Changing T . . . . . . CHANGING TIMES
Chang Times . . . . . CHANGING TIMES
Char . . . . . . . . . . . CHARITIES
Char R . . . . . . . . . CHARITIES REVIEW
Chart Mech Eng . . . . CHARTERED MECHANICAL ENGINEER
Chart Surv . . . . . . . CHARTERED SURVEYOR
CHAS . . . . . . . . . . CAMBRIDGESHIRE AND HUNTINGDONSHIRE ARCHAEOLOGICAL SOCIETY
Chase Econ Bul . . . . CHASE ECONOMIC BULLETIN
Chaucer R . . . . . . . CHAUCER REVIEW
Chaucer Soc . . . . . . CHAUCER SOCIETY
ChauR . . . . . . . . . . CHAUCER REVIEW
Chaut . . . . . . . . . . CHAUTAUQUAN
ChC . . . . . . . . . . . CHINESE CULTURE
ChC . . . . . . . . . . . CHRISTIAN CENTURY
ChCen . . . . . . . . . . CHRISTIAN CENTURY
CHCLG . . . . . . . . . CAHIERS D'HISTOIRE PUBLIES PAR LES UNIVERSITES DE CLERMONT-LYON-GRENOBLE
CHCQ . . . . . . . . . . CALIFORNIA HISTORICAL SOCIETY. QUARTERLY
ChE . . . . . . . . . . . CHIAKE EPITHEORESIS
```

CHE. . . . . CUADERNOS DE HISTORIA DE ESPANA
Chel. . . . . CHELSEA
ChemAb. . . . . CHEMICAL ABSTRACTS
Chem Age. . . . . CHEMICAL AGE
Chem Age India. . . . CHEMICAL AGE OF INDIA
Chem Age Int. . . . . CHEMICAL AGE INTERNATIONAL
Chem Age (Lond). . . CHEMICAL AGE (LONDON)
Chem & Eng N. . . . . CHEMICAL AND ENGINEERING NEWS
Chem & Ind. . . . . . CHEMISTRY AND INDUSTRY
Chem & Met Eng. . . CHEMICAL AND METALLURGICAL ENGINEERING
Chem & Process Eng. . CHEMICAL AND PROCESS ENGINEERING
CHEM BER. . . . . CHEMISCHE BERICHTE
CHEM-BIO IN. . . . . . CHEMICO-BIOLOGICAL INTERACTIONS
CHEM BRIT. . . . . . . CHEMISTRY IN BRITAIN
Chem Can. . . . . CHEMISTRY IN CANADA
Chem Digest. . . . . . CHEMURGIC DIGEST
Chem Eng. . . . . CHEMICAL ENGINEERING
Chem Eng Educ. . . . CHEMICAL ENGINEERING EDUCATION
Chem Eng J. . . . . . . CHEMICAL ENGINEERING JOURNAL
Chem Eng (London). . CHEMICAL ENGINEER (LONDON)
Chem Engng Sci. . . . CHEMICAL ENGINEERING SCIENCE
Chem Eng (N Y). . . . CHEMICAL ENGINEERING (NEW YORK)
CHEM ENG PR. . . . . CHEMICAL ENGINEERING PROGRESS
Chem Eng Progr Symp Ser. . CHEMICAL ENGINEERING PROGRESS SYMPOSIUM SERIES
Chem Engr. . . . . CHEMICAL ENGINEER
CHEM ENG SC. . . . . CHEMICAL ENGINEERING SCIENCE
Chem Geol. . . . . . . CHEMICAL GEOLOGY
Chem in Br. . . . . . . CHEMISTRY IN BRITAIN
Chem Ind. . . . . CHEMICAL INDUSTRIES
Chem Ind. . . . . CHEMISTRY AND INDUSTRY
CHEM IND LOND. . . CHEMISTRY AND INDUSTRY (LONDON)
CHEM ING T. . . . . . CHEMIE INGENIEUR TECHNIK
Chem Ing Tech. . . . . CHEMIE INGENIEUR TECHNIK
CHEM INSTR. . . . . . CHEMICAL INSTRUMENTATION
CHEM LETT. . . . . . . CHEMISTRY LETTERS
CHEM LISTY. . . . . . . CHEMICKE LISTY
Chem Mktg Rep. . . . CHEMICAL MARKETING REPORTER
CHEM NZ. . . . . CHEMISTRY IN NEW ZEALAND
CHEMOTHERA. . . . . CHEMOTHERAPY
Chem Pet Eng. . . . . CHEMICAL AND PETROLEUM ENGINEERING
CHEM PHARM. . . . . CHEMICAL & PHARMACEUTICAL BULLETIN
CHEM PHYS. . . . . . . CHEMICAL PHYSICS
CHEM PHYS L. . . . . CHEMISTRY AND PHYSICS OF LIPIDS
CHEM P LETT. . . . . . CHEMICAL PHYSICS LETTERS
Chem Process. . . . . CHEMICAL PROCESSING
Chem Process Eng. . CHEMICAL AND PROCESS ENGINEERING
Chem R. . . . . CHEMICAL REVIEW
Chem Rec Age. . . . . CHEMICAL RECORD-AGE
CHEM REV. . . . . CHEMICAL REVIEWS
CHEM SCR. . . . . CHEMICA SCRIPTA
CHEM SENSES. . . . . . CHEMICAL SENSES AND FLAVOR

Chem Soc J . . . . CHEMICAL SOCIETY. JOURNAL
CHEM SOC RE . . . . . CHEMICAL SOCIETY REVIEWS
CHEM TECH . . . . CHEMISCHE TECHNIK
CHEMTECH US . . . . . CHEM TECH-CHEMICAL TECHNOLOGY
ChemTitles . . . . CHEMICAL TITLES
Chem W . . . . CHEMICAL WEEK
CHEM ZEITUN . . . . . CHEMIKER-ZEITUNG
CHEM ZVESTI . . . . . CHEMICKE ZVESTI
Chet Soc . . . . CHETHAM SOCIETY
CHF . . . . CAHIERS D'HISTOIRE ET DE FOLKLORE
ChH . . . . CHURCH HISTORY
Chi B Rec . . . . CHICAGO BAR RECORD
Chicago Art Inst Bul . . CHICAGO ART INSTITUTE. BULLETIN
Chicago Art Inst Cal . . CHICAGO ART INSTITUTE. CALENDAR
Chicago Art Inst Q . . CHICAGO ART INSTITUTE. QUARTERLY
Chicago Sch J . . . . . CHICAGO SCHOOLS JOURNAL
Chic R . . . . CHICAGO REVIEW
Chi-Kent L Rev . . . . . CHICAGO-KENT LAW REVIEW
CHILD CARE . . . . . . CHILD CARE QUARTERLY
CHILD DEV . . . . CHILD DEVELOPMENT
ChildDevAb . . . . CHILD DEVELOPMENT ABSTRACTS
Child Ed . . . . CHILDHOOD EDUCATION
Childh Educ . . . . CHILDHOOD EDUCATION
Child Par M . . . . CHILDREN. THE PARENTS' MAGAZINE
CHILD PSYCH . . . . . CHILD PSYCHIATRY AND HUMAN DEVELOPMENT
CHILD PSY Q . . . . . . CHILD PSYCHIATRY QUARTERLY
CHILD ST J . . . . CHILD STUDY JOURNAL
CHILD TODAY . . . . . CHILDREN TODAY
CHILD WEL . . . . CHILD WELFARE
Chimie & Ind . . . . . . CHIMIE ET INDUSTRIE
Chim Ind — Genie Chim . . CHIMIE ET INDUSTRIE — GENIE CHIMIQUE
CHIM IND M . . . . . . CHIMICA E L'INDUSTRIA (MILAN)
China W R . . . . CHINA WEEKLY REVIEW
CHIN ECON S . . . . . . CHINESE ECONOMIC STUDIES
CHIN EDUC . . . . CHINESE EDUCATION
ChinL . . . . CHINESE LITERATURE
CHIN LAW G . . . . . . CHINESE LAW AND GOVERNMENT
CHIN MED J . . . . CHINESE MEDICAL JOURNAL
CHIN SOC A . . . . CHINESE SOCIOLOGY AND ANTHROPOLOGY
Chin Social & Pol Sci R . . CHINESE SOCIAL AND POLITICAL SCIENCE REVIEW
Chin Stud Phil . . . . . CHINESE STUDIES IN PHILOSOPHY
ChiR . . . . CHICAGO REVIEW
CHIR PLAST . . . . CHIRURGIA PLASTICA
CHist . . . . CHURCH HISTORY
CHist . . . . CORSE HISTORIQUE
CHI SYM . . . . CHICAGO SYMPHONY ORCHESTRA PROGRAM NOTES
Chitty's L J . . . . CHITTY'S LAW JOURNAL
CHJ . . . . CAMBRIDGE HISTORICAL JOURNAL
ChL . . . . CHRISTIAN LIBERTY
ChLit . . . . CHINESE LITERATURE
CHLSSF . . . . COMMENTATIONES HUMANARUM LITTERARUM SOCIETATIS SCIENTIARUM FENNICA

CHM . . . . CAHIERS D'HISTOIRE MONDIALE
Chmn . . . . CHURCHMAN
CHO . . . . CHOICE
CHORAL G . . . . CHORAL AND ORGAN GUIDE
CHQ . . . . CALIFORNIA HISTORICAL QUARTERLY
Ch Q R . . . . CHURCH QUARTERLY REVIEW
CHR . . . . CANADIAN HISTORICAL REVIEW
CHR . . . . CATHOLIC HISTORICAL REVIEW
Chr & Cr . . . . CHRISTIANITY AND CRISIS
Chr Cent . . . . CHRISTIAN CENTURY
Chr Cris . . . . CHRISTIANITY AND CRISIS
Chr Disc . . . . CHRISTIAN DISCIPLE
ChrE . . . . CHRONIQUE D'EGYPTE
Chr Exam . . . . CHRISTIAN EXAMINER
CHRF . . . . CAHIERS D'HISTOIRE DE LA REVOLUTION FRANCAISE
Chris Q . . . . CHRISTIAN QUARTERLY REVIEW
Christ Cen . . . . CHRISTIAN CENTURY
Christian Sci Mon Mag . . CHRISTIAN SCIENCE MONITOR. MAGAZINE SECTION
Christ Sci Mon . . . . . CHRISTIAN SCIENCE MONITOR
Chr Lit . . . . CHRISTIAN LITERATURE
Chr Mo Spec . . . . . . CHRISTIAN MONTHLY SPECTATOR
Chr Obs . . . . CHRISTIAN OBSERVER
CHROMATOGR . . . . CHROMATOGRAPHIA
Chron Egypte . . . . . . CHRONIQUE D'EGYPTE
Chronicles Okla . . . . CHRONICLES OF OKLAHOMA
ChronOkla . . . . CHRONICLES OF OKLAHOMA
ChrPer . . . . CHRISTIAN PERSPECTIVES
Chr Q . . . . CHRISTIAN QUARTERLY
Chr Q Spec . . . . CHRISTIAN QUARTERLY SPECTATOR
Chr R . . . . CHRISTIAN REVIEW
Chr Rem . . . . CHRISTIAN REMEMBRANCE
Chr Sch R . . . . CHRISTIAN SCHOLAR'S REVIEW
Chr T . . . . CHRISTIANITY TODAY
Chr Un . . . . CHRISTIAN UNION
ChS . . . . CHRISTIAN SCHOLAR
CHSB . . . . CINCINNATI HISTORICAL SOCIETY. BULLETIN
CHSB . . . . CONNECTICUT HISTORICAL SOCIETY. BULLETIN
Ch Soc . . . . CHURCH AND SOCIETY
CHSQ . . . . CALIFORNIA HISTORICAL SOCIETY. QUARTERLY
CHUM . . . . COMPUTERS AND THE HUMANITIES
Church Hist . . . . CHURCH HISTORY
Church Mus (London) . . CHURCH MUSIC (LONDON)
CHURCH MUS (St. L) . . CHURCH MUSIC (ST. LOUIS)
Church Q R . . . . CHURCH QUARTERLY REVIEW
CI . . . . CUADERNOS DEL IDIOMA
Ciba R . . . . CIBA REVIEW
CIFM . . . . CONTRIBUTI DELL'ISTITUTO DI FILOLOGIA MODERNA
CIG CRYOG INDUS GASES . . CIG, CRYOGENICS AND INDUSTRIAL GASES
CIJE . . . . CURRENT INDEX TO JOURNALS IN EDUCATION
CIL . . . . CONTEMPORARY INDIAN LITERATURE
CILP . . . . CONFERENCES DE L'INSTITUT DE LINGUISTIQUE DE PARIS

CIMAGL......... CAHIERS DE L'INSTITUT DU MOYEN AGE GREC ET LATIN
CimR............CIMARRON REVIEW
Cincinnati Mus Bull.. CINCINNATI ART MUSEUM. BULLETIN
Cincinnati Mus Bul ns.. CINCINNATI ART MUSEUM. BULLETIN. NEW SERIES
Cincinnati Mus N... CINCINNATI ART MUSEUM. NEWS
Cinc Sym Prog Notes.. CINCINNATI SYMPHONY ORCHESTRA. PROGRAM NOTES
CINL............ CUMULATIVE INDEX TO NURSING LITERATURE
CIN SYM......... CINCINNATI SYMPHONY ORCHESTRA. PROGRAM NOTES
Circ Electrotech Lab Tokyo Japan.. CIRCULARS OF THE ELECTROTECHNICAL LABORATORY. TOKYO
CIRC RES......... CIRCULATION RESEARCH
CIRC SHOCK...... CIRCULATORY SHOCK
Cirpho.......... CIRPHO REVIEW
CIR-SP.......... CONGRESO INTERNACIONAL DE FILOSOFIA. ANAIS (SAO PAULO)
CISI............ CIS INDEX
CistC.......... CISTERCIENSERCHRONIK
CiT............ CIENCIA TOMISTA
Cit............ CITEAUX
CitN........... CITEAUX IN DE NEDERLANDE
Citrus Ind........ CITRUS INDUSTRY
Civ Eng.......... CIVIL ENGINEERING
Civ Eng Pub Works Rev.. CIVIL ENGINEERING AND PUBLIC WORKS REVIEW
Civ Eng S Afr...... CIVIL ENGINEERING IN SOUTH AFRICA
Civil Aero J....... CIVIL AERONAUTICS JOURNAL
CIVIL ENG........ CIVIL ENGINEERING
Civ Engng Publ Wks Rev.. CIVIL ENGINEERING AND PUBLIC WORKS REVIEW
Civil War Hist..... CIVIL WAR HISTORY
Civ Rights Digest... CIVIL RIGHTS DIGEST
Civ Serv J........ CIVIL SERVICE JOURNAL
CJ.............. CAMBRIDGE JOURNAL
CJ.............. CANADIAN JOURNAL OF ECONOMICS
CJ.............. CLASSICAL JOURNAL
CJ.............. COYOTE'S JOURNAL
CJa............ CIZI JAZYKY VE SKOLE
CJap........... CONTEMPORARY JAPAN
CJAS........... CANADIAN JOURNAL OF AFRICAN STUDIES
CJE............ CANADIAN JOURNAL OF ECONOMICS AND POLITICAL SCIENCE
CJF............ CHICAGO JEWISH FORUM
CJH............ CANADIAN JOURNAL OF HISTORY
CJL............ CANADIAN JOURNAL OF LINGUISTICS
CJL............ CESKY JAZYK A LITERATURA
CJLit........... CESKY JAZYK A LITERATURA
CJ(Malta)........ CLASSICAL JOURNAL (MALTA)
CJPhil.......... CANADIAN JOURNAL OF PHILOSOPHY
CJPs........... CANADIAN JOURNAL OF PSYCHOLOGY
CJS............ CIZI JAZYKY VE SKOLE
CJVS........... CIZI JAZYKY VE SKOLE
CJZ............ CANADIAN JOURNAL OF ZOOLOGY
CKD............ CASOPIS KATOLICKEKO DUCKOVENSTVA S PRILOHOU
CKYW........... CHUNG-KUO YU-WEN
CL.............. CESKA LITERATURA
CL.............. CLAVILENO

CL.............COMPARATIVE LITERATURE
CL.............CUADERNOS DE LITERATURA
CLA............ COLLECTIONS LITTERATURES AFRICAINES
CLA............ COLLEGE LANGUAGE ASSOCIATION. JOURNAL
CLA Bull......... COLORADO LIBRARY ASSOCIATION. BULLETIN
CLAJ............CLA (COLLEGE LANGUAGE ASSOCIATION) JOURNAL
Clare Q.......... CLAREMONT QUARTERLY
Classic Jnl........CLASSICAL JOURNAL
Classic World..... CLASSICAL WORLD
Class J.......... CLASSICAL JOURNAL
Class Philol....... CLASSICAL PHILOLOGY
Class Q.......... CLASSICAL QUARTERLY
Class R.......... CLASSICAL REVIEW
Class R ns........ CLASSICAL REVIEW. NEW SERIES
Class World....... CLASSICAL WORLD
ClaudelS......... CLAUDEL STUDIES
Clav............ CLAVILENO
CLAY CLAY M..... CLAYS AND CLAY MINERALS
Clay Miner....... CLAY MINERALS
Clays Clay Miner... CLAYS AND CLAY MINERALS
CLC.............COLUMBIA LIBRARY COLUMNS
CLC.............CUADERNOS DE LITERATURA CONTEMPORANEA
CLe.............CAHIERS DE LEXICOLOGIE
Clear H.......... CLEARING HOUSE
CLEB............ COMUNIDAD LATINOAMERICANA DE ESCRITORES BOLETIN
CLEF PAL J....... CLEFT PALATE JOURNAL
Clemson Univ Coll Eng Eng Exp Sta Bull..CLEMSON UNIVERSITY. CLEMSON, S.C. COLLEGE OF ENGINEERING, ENGINEERING EXPERIMENT STATION. BULLETIN
Clev B A J........ CLEVELAND BAR ASSOCIATION. JOURNAL
Cleveland Mus Bull..CLEVELAND MUSEUM OF ART. BULLETIN
Clev-Mar L Rev.... CLEVELAND-MARSHALL LAW REVIEW
CLEV ORCH....... CLEVELAND ORCHESTRA PROGRAM NOTES
CLEV ST L R....... CLEVELAND STATE LAW REVIEW
CLex............ CAHIERS DE LEXICOLOGIE
CLF............. CHRONIQUE DES LETTRES FRANCAISES
CLF............. CLUB DU LIVRE FRANCAIS
CLi............. CUADERNOS DE LITERATURA
CLid............ CESKY LID
CLin............ CERCETARI DE LINGUISTICA
CLIN BIOCH....... CLINICAL BIOCHEMISTRY
CLIN CHEM....... CLINICAL CHEMISTRY
CLIN CHIM A...... CLINICA CHIMICA ACTA
CLIN ELECTR...... CLINICAL ELECTROENCEPHALOGRAPHY
CLIN END ME...... CLINICS IN ENDOCRINOLOGY AND METABOLISM
CLIN ENDOCR..... CLINICAL ENDOCRINOLOGY
CLIN EXP IM...... CLINICAL AND EXPERIMENTAL IMMUNOLOGY
CLIN EXP PH...... CLINICAL AND EXPERIMENTAL PHARMACOLOGY AND PHYSIOLOGY
C Ling........... CERCETARI DE LINGUISTICA
CLIN GASTRO..... CLINICS IN GASTROENTEROLOGY
CLIN GENET....... CLINICAL GENETICS
CLIN HAEMAT..... CLINICS IN HAEMATOLOGY

CLIN IMMUN . . . . . . CLINICAL IMMUNOLOGY AND IMMUNOPATHOLOGY
CLIN MED . . . . CLINICAL MEDICINE
CLIN NEUROL . . . . . . CLINICAL NEUROLOGY AND NEUROSURGERY
CLIN ORTHOP . . . . . CLINICAL ORTHOPAEDICS AND RELATED RESEARCH
CLIN PEDIAT . . . . . . CLINICAL PEDIATRICS
Clin Pediatr (Phila) . CLINICAL PEDIATRICS (PHILADELPHIA)
CLIN PHARM . . . . . . CLINICAL PHARMACOLOGY AND THERAPEUTICS
Clin Pharmacol Ther . CLINICAL PHARMACOLOGY AND THERAPEUTICS
CLIN RADIOL . . . . . . CLINICAL RADIOLOGY
CLIN RES . . . . CLINICAL RESEARCH
CLIN SC MOL . . . . . . CLINICAL SCIENCE AND MOLECULAR MEDICINE
CLIN S WORK . . . . . . CLINICAL SOCIAL WORK JOURNAL
CLIN TOXIC . . . . CLINICAL TOXICOLOGY
CLit . . . . CESKA LITERATURA
CLit . . . . CONVORBIRI LITERARE
CLit . . . . CORREO LITERARIO
CLJ . . . . CLASSICAL JOURNAL
CLJ . . . . CORNELL LIBRARY JOURNAL
CLLA . . . . CAHIERS DE LITTERATURE ET DE LINGUISTIQUE APPLIQUEE
CLLAN . . . . COLLECTION LANGUES ET LITTERATURES DE L'AFRIQUE NOIRE
CLM . . . . CHINESE LITERATURE MONTHLY
CL Med . . . . CLASSICA ET MEDIAEVALIA
CLNL . . . . COMPARATIVE LITERATURE NEWS-LETTER
CLP . . . . CLASSICAL PHILOLOGY
Cl Q . . . . CLASSICAL QUARTERLY
CLQ . . . . COLBY LIBRARY QUARTERLY
Cl R . . . . CLASSICAL REVIEW
ClRh . . . . CLARA RHODOS
CLS . . . . COMPARATIVE LITERATURE STUDIES
CLSB . . . . CHARLES LAMB SOCIETY. BULLETIN
CLS . . . . CHARLES LAMB SOCIETY. BULLETIN
Clt . . . . CULTURE
CLTA . . . . CAHIERS DE LINGUISTIQUE THEORIQUE ET APPLIQUEE
CLU J . . . . CHARTERED LIFE UNDERWRITERS JOURNAL
CLUQ . . . . CAHIERS DE LINGUISTIQUE DE L'UNIVERSITE DU QUEBEC
CLW . . . . CATHOLIC LIBRARY WORLD
Cl Weekly . . . . CLASSICAL WEEKLY
CM . . . . CARLETON MISCELLANY
CM . . . . CIVILTA MODERNA
CM . . . . CLASSICA ET MEDIAEVALIA
CM . . . . COLORADO MAGAZINE
CM . . . . CORNHILL MAGAZINE
CMC . . . . CROSSCURRENTS/MODERN CRITIQUES
CMF . . . . CASOPIS PRO MODERNI FILOLOGII
CMF . . . . CROSSCURRENTS/MODERN FICTION
CMFL . . . . CASOPIS PRO MODERNI FILOLOGII A LITERATURY
CML . . . . CLUB DU MEILLEUR LIVRE
CMLR . . . . CANADIAN MODERN LANGUAGE REVIEW
CMM . . . . CASOPIS MATICE MORAVSKE
CMo . . . . CREATIVE MOMENT
CMP . . . . CMP NEWSLETTER

CMRS.......... CAHIERS DU MONDE RUSSE ET SOVIETIQUE
CMTS.......... CLARENDON MEDIEVAL AND TUDOR SERIES
Cn............ CENTER MAGAZINE
CN............ CULTURA NEOLATINA
CNat........... CAHIERS NATURALISTES
CNM........... CASOPIS NARODNIHO MUZEA
CNRM........... CNRM (CENTRE NATIONAL DE RECHERCHES METALLURGIQUES BENELUX) METALLURGICAL REPORTS
CNRS.......... CENTRE NATIONAL DE LA RECHERCHE SCIENTIFIQUE
CO............ CAHIERS DE L'OUEST
CO............ CHRONICLES OF OKLAHOMA
Co............ CONFERENCE
Co............ CORONA
CoA........... COAT OF ARMS
Coal Min Process... COAL MINING AND PROCESSING
Coal Prep........ COAL PREPARATION
Coastal Eng Japan.. COASTAL ENGINEERING IN JAPAN
COCR.......... COLLECTANEA ORDINIS CISTERCIENSIUM REFORMATORUM
Co Engl.......... COLLEGE ENGLISH
COEUR MED I...... COEUR ET MEDECINE INTERNE
Cog............ COGNITION (THE HAGUE)
COG PSYCHOL..... COGNITIVE PSYCHOLOGY
COH........... CHRISTELIJK OOSTEN EN HERENIGING
COKE CHEM R..... COKE AND CHEMISTRY (USSR)
Coke Chem (USSR).. COKE AND CHEMISTRY (USSR)
Col............ COLLOQUIUM DER FREIEN UNIVERSITAET
ColA........... COLOQUIO ARTES
Col & Res Lib...... COLLEGE & RESEARCH LIBRARIES
Col & Univ........ COLLEGE AND UNIVERSITY
Col & Univ Bsns.... COLLEGE AND UNIVERSITY BUSINESS
Col & Univ J...... COLLEGE AND UNIVERSITY JOURNAL
Colburn.......... COLBURN'S NEW MONTHLY MAGAZINE
ColCM.......... COLBY COLLEGE MONOGRAPHS
Col Comp & Comm.. COLLEGE COMPOSITION AND COMMUNICATION
COLD S HARB..... COLD SPRING HARBOR SYMPOSIA ON QUANTITATIVE BIOLOGY
COLD SPR HARB SYMP.. COLD SPRING HARBOR SYMPOSIA ON QUANTITATIVE BIOLOGY
ColF........... COLUMBIA FORUM
ColGer.......... COLLOQUIA GERMANICA
Col Hist Soc Rec.... COLUMBIA HISTORICAL SOCIETY. RECORDS
CoLi........... COMPARATIVE LITERATURE
ColJR.......... COLUMBIA JOURNALISM REVIEW
ColL........... COLOQUIO (LISBON)
Coll & Res Lib..... COLLEGE AND RESEARCH LIBRARIES
Coll & Res Lib N.... COLLEGE AND RESEARCH LIBRARY NEWS
Coll & Univ....... COLLEGE AND UNIVERSITY
Coll & Univ Bus.... COLLEGE & UNIVERSITY BUSINESS
Coll & Univ J...... COLLEGE & UNIVERSITY JOURNAL
Coll Art J........ COLLEGE ART JOURNAL
ColLat.......... COLLECTION LATOMUS
Coll Cist........ COLLECTANEA CISTERCIENSA
Coll Comp & Comm.. COLLEGE COMPOSITION AND COMMUNICATION

COLL CZECH . . . . . . COLLECTION OF CZECHOSLOVAK CHEMICAL COMMUNICATIONS
CollE . . . . COLLEGE ENGLISH
College & Research Lib . . COLLEGE & RESEARCH LIBRARIES
COLLEGE MUS . . . . . COLLEGE MUSIC SYMPOSIUM
Coll Eng . . . . COLLEGE ENGLISH
Coll Fran . . . . COLLECTANEA FRANCISCANA
Coll G . . . . COLLOQUIA GERMANICA
Collier's . . . . COLLIER'S NATIONAL WEEKLY
Collier's Yrbk . . . . . COLLIER'S ENCYCLOPEDIA YEARBOOK
Colliery Guard . . . . . COLLIERY GUARDIAN
Coll Latomus . . . . . . COLLECTION LATOMUS
COLL MATH . . . . . . COLLOQUIUM MATHEMATICUM
Coll Mgt . . . . COLLEGE MANAGEMENT
Coll N & V . . . . COLLEGIATE NEWS AND VIEWS
COLLOID J . . . . COLLOID JOURNAL (USSR)
Colloid J (USSR) . . . . COLLOID JOURNAL (USSR)
COLLOID P S . . . . . . COLLOID AND POLYMER SCIENCE
COLL RES LI . . . . . . COLLEGE AND RESEARCH LIBRARIES
ColM . . . . COLORADO MAGAZINE
Col Mgt . . . . COLLEGE MANAGEMENT
Colo Ag Exp . . . . . . COLORADO AGRICULTURAL EXPERIMENT STATION. PUBLICATIONS
Colo Farm & Home Res . . COLORADO FARM AND HOME RESEARCH
COLO J RES MUS ED . . COLORADO JOURNAL OF RESEARCH IN MUSIC EDUCATION
Colo Lib Assn Bul . . . COLORADO LIBRARY ASSOCIATION. BULLETIN
ColoM . . . . COLORADO MAGAZINE
Colo Mag . . . . COLORADO MAGAZINE
ColoQ . . . . COLORADO QUARTERLY
Coloquio . . . . COLOQUIO/LETRAS
Color Eng . . . . COLOR ENGINEERING
Color Tr J . . . . COLOR TRADE JOURNAL AND TEXTILE CHEMIST
Colo Sch Mines Miner Ind Bull . . COLORADO SCHOOL OF MINES. MINERAL INDUSTRIES BULLETIN
Colo Sch Mines Q . . . COLORADO SCHOOL OF MINES. QUARTERLY
Colo Sci Soc Proc . . . COLORADO SCIENTIFIC SOCIETY. PROCEEDINGS
Col Phys Ed Assn Proc . . COLLEGE PHYSICAL EDUCATION ASSOCIATION PROCEEDINGS
ColQ . . . . COLORADO QUARTERLY
Col Soc Mass Publ . . COLONIAL SOCIETY OF MASSACHUSETTS. PUBLICATIONS
Col Soc Mass Trans . . COLONIAL SOCIETY OF MASSACHUSETTS. TRANSACTIONS
ColStuAb . . . . COLLEGE STUDENT PERSONNEL ABSTRACTS
Columbia J Transnat Law . . COLUMBIA JOURNAL OF TRANSNATURAL LAW
Columbia Lib C . . . . . COLUMBIA LIBRARY COLUMNS
Columbia U Q . . . . . COLUMBIA UNIVERSITY QUARTERLY
COLUMB J L . . . . . . COLUMBIA JOURNAL OF LAW AND SOCIAL PROBLEMS
COLUMB J TR . . . . . COLUMBIA JOURNAL OF TRANSNATIONAL LAW
COLUMB J W . . . . . . COLUMBIA JOURNAL OF WORLD BUSINESS
COLUMB LAW . . . . . COLUMBIA LAW REVIEW
Columbus Gal Bul . . . COLUMBUS, OHIO. COLUMBUS GALLERY OF FINE ARTS BULLETIN
Colum Forum . . . . . . COLUMBIA FORUM
Colum Human Rights L Rev . . COLUMBIA HUMAN RIGHTS LAW REVIEW
Colum J L & Soc Prob . . COLUMBIA JOURNAL OF LAW AND SOCIAL PROBLEMS
Colum Journalism R . . COLUMBIA JOURNALISM REVIEW
Colum J Transnat L . . COLUMBIA JOURNAL OF TRANSNATIONAL LAW

Colum L Rev . . . . . . COLUMBIA LAW REVIEW
Colum Univ Q . . . . . COLUMBIA UNIVERSITY QUARTERLY
COL UNIV . . . . COLLEGE AND UNIVERSITY
COM . . . . COMET STORIES
Com . . . . COMMENTARI
Com . . . . COMMENTARY
ComAb . . . . COMPUTER ABSTRACTS
Com & Electronics . . COMMUNICATION AND ELECTRONICS
Com & Jr Coll . . . . . COMMUNITY AND JUNIOR COLLEGE JOURNAL
Com & Jr Coll J . . . . COMMUNITY AND JUNIOR COLLEGE JOURNAL
COMB EXPL R . . . . . COMBUSTION EXPLOSION AND SHOCK WAVES (USSR)
COMB FLAME . . . . . COMBUSTION AND FLAME
COMB SCI T . . . . COMBUSTION SCIENCE AND TECHNOLOGY
COM CON PSY . . . . . COMMENTS ON CONTEMPORARY PSYCHIATRY
Com Develop J . . . . COMMUNITY DEVELOPMENT JOURNAL
ComErm . . . . COMMUNICATIONS DU MUSEE NATIONAL DE L'ERMITAGE
COM FOR REV . . . . . COMMONWEALTH FORESTRY REVIEW
Com L J . . . . COMMERCIAL LAW JOURNAL
Comm & Fin . . . . . . COMMERCE AND FINANCE
COMM ACM . . . . . . COMMUNICATIONS OF THE ACM (ASSOCIATION FOR COMPUTING MACHINERY)
COMM ALGEB . . . . . COMMUNICATIONS IN ALGEBRA
Comm & Fin Chron . . COMMERCIAL AND FINANCIAL CHRONICLE
COMM BIOC B . . . . . COMPARATIVE BIOCHEMISTRY AND PHYSIOLOGY. B
COMM BIOC C . . . . . COMPARATIVE BIOCHEMISTRY AND PHYSIOLOGY. C
COMM BROADC . . . . COMMUNICATION AND BROADCASTING
COMM DEN OR . . . . COMMUNITY DENTISTRY AND ORAL EPIDEMIOLOGY
COMM DEV J . . . . . . COMMUNITY DEVELOPMENT JOURNAL
Comm Ed . . . . COMMERCIAL EDUCATION
Com Ment Health J . . COMMUNITY MENTAL HEALTH JOURNAL
Comm Fert . . . . COMMERCIAL FERTILIZER
COMM HEALTH . . . . COMMUNITY HEALTH
Comm M . . . . COMMERCE MONTHLY
COMM MATH H . . . . COMMENTARII MATHEMATICI HELVETICI
COMM MATH P . . . . COMMUNICATIONS IN MATHEMATICAL PHYSICS
COMM MENT H . . . . COMMUNITY MENTAL HEALTH JOURNAL
Comm Mot . . . . COMMERCIAL MOTOR
COMM PHYS-M . . . . COMMENTATIONES PHYSICO-MATHEMATICAE
Comm Rep . . . . COMMERCE REPORTS
COMM RES . . . . COMMUNICATION RESEARCH
COMM SOIL S . . . . . COMMUNICATIONS IN SOIL SCIENCE AND PLANT ANALYSIS
COMM STATIS . . . . . COMMUNICATIONS IN STATISTICS
Comm Today . . . . . . COMMERCE TODAY
Commun . . . . COMMUNION
Commun ACM . . . . . COMMUNICATIONS OF THE ACM (ASSOCIATION FOR COMPUTING MACHINERY)
Commun Eng . . . . . . COMMUNICATION ENGINEERING
Community Dev J . . COMMUNITY DEVELOPMENT JOURNAL
Commutation Electron . . COMMUTATION ET ELECTRONIQUE
Comm Veh . . . . COMMERCIAL VEHICLES
Comp . . . . COMPASS
Comp Air Mag . . . . . COMPRESSED AIR MAGAZINE
COM PA MATH . . . . COMMUNICATIONS ON PURE AND APPLIED MATHEMATICS

Comp & Automation . . COMPUTERS AND AUTOMATION AND PEOPLE
Comparative Ed . . . . COMPARATIVE EDUCATION
Compare . . . . JOURNAL OF THE COMPARATIVE EDUCATION SOCIETY IN EUROPE (BRITISH SECTION)
COMP BIOC A . . . . . COMPARATIVE BIOCHEMISTRY AND PHYSIOLOGY A
CompD . . . . COMPARATIVE DRAMA
CompDr . . . . COMPARATIVE DRAMA
Comp Ed . . . . COMPARATIVE EDUCATION
Comp Ed R . . . . COMPARATIVE EDUCATION REVIEW
COMP EDU RE . . . . . COMPARATIVE EDUCATION REVIEW
COMPENS REV . . . . . COMPENSATION REVIEW
Comp J . . . . COMPUTER JOURNAL
Comp L . . . . COMPARATIVE LITERATURE
CompL . . . . COMPUTATIONAL LINGUISTICS
COM PLAN R . . . . . . COMMUNITY PLANNING REVIEW
Comp Lit . . . . COMPARATIVE LITERATURE
Comp Lit Stud . . . . . COMPARATIVE LITERATURE STUDIES
COMP MATH . . . . . . COMPOSITIO MATHEMATICA
Comp News-Rec . . . . COMPOSERS NEWS-RECORD
Component Technol . . COMPONENT TECHNOLOGY
Compost Sci . . . . . . COMPOST SCIENCE
Comp Pol . . . . COMPARATIVE POLITICS
COMP POLI S . . . . . COMPARATIVE POLITICAL STUDIES
COMP POLIT . . . . . . COMPARATIVE POLITICS
Comp Pol Stud . . . . . COMPARATIVE POLITICAL STUDIES
COMP PSYCHI . . . . . COMPREHENSIVE PSYCHIATRY
COMPRES AIR . . . . . COMPRESSED AIR
COMP STUD S . . . . . COMPARATIVE STUDIES IN SOCIETY AND HISTORY
Comp Stud Soc Hist . . COMPARATIVE STUDIES IN SOCIETY AND HISTORY
Comput Aided Des . . COMPUTER AIDED DESIGN
Comput Biol Med . . . COMPUTERS IN BIOLOGY AND MEDICINE
COMPUT BIOM . . . . COMPUTERS AND BIOMEDICAL RESEARCH
Comput Bull . . . . . . COMPUTER BULLETIN
Comput Des . . . . . . COMPUTER DESIGN
Computer Ed . . . . . . COMPUTER EDUCATION CONFERENCE
COMPUTER HU . . . . COMPUTERS AND THE HUMANITIES
COMPUTER PE . . . . . COMPUTERS AND PEOPLE
COMPUTER PH . . . . COMPUTER PHYSICS COMMUNICATIONS
COMPUTER PR . . . . . COMPUTER PROGRAMS IN BIOMEDICINE
Comput J . . . . COMPUTER JOURNAL
Comput L . . . . COMPUTATIONAL LINGUISTICS
Comput Struct . . . . . COMPUTERS AND STRUCTURES
Comput Surv . . . . . . COMPUTING SURVEYS
ComRev . . . . COMPUTING REVIEWS
Comt . . . . COMMENTARY
Com Via . . . . COMMUNIO VIATORUM
Comw . . . . COMMONWEAL
Con . . . . CONTACT
Con . . . . CONTOUR
Con . . . . CONVIVIUM
Concor . . . . CONCORDIA THEOLOGICAN MONTHLY
Concr Constr . . . . . . CONCRETE CONSTRUCTION

.
Conf . . . . CONFERENCIA
Conf . . . . CONFLUENCE
Conf Bd Bsns Mgt Rec . . CONFERENCE BOARD BUSINESS MANAGEMENT RECORD
Conf Bd Bsns Rec . . . CONFERENCE BOARD BUSINESS RECORD
Conf Bd Rec . . . . . . CONFERENCE BOARD RECORD
Conf Char and Correc . . NATIONAL CONFERENCE OF CHARITIES AND CORRECTION. PROCEEDINGS
Conf City Govt . . . . NATIONAL CONFERENCE FOR GOOD CITY GOVERNMENT. PROCEEDINGS
Conf Int Grands Reseaux Elec Haute Tension . . CONFERENCE INTERNATIONALE DES GRANDS RESEAUX ELECTRIQUES
 A HAUTE TENSION
Conf Pers Fin L Q Rep . . CONFERENCE ON PERSONAL FINANCE LAW. QUARTERLY REPORT
CONF PSYCH . . . . . . CONFINA PSYCHIATRICA
Conf Read Univ Chicago . . CONFERENCE ON READING (UNIVERSITY OF CHICAGO) PROCEEDINGS
Conf on Read Univ Pittsburgh Rep . . CONFERENCE ON READING (UNIVERSITY OF PITTSBURGH) REPORT
Cong . . . . CONGREGATIONALIST
Cong Digest . . . . . . CONGRESSIONAL DIGEST
Cong M . . . . CONGREGATIONAL MAGAZINE
Cong Q . . . . CONGREGATIONAL QUARTERLY
Cong R . . . . CONGREGATIONAL REVIEW
Congres Archeol . . . CONGRES ARCHEOLOGIQUE
Congres Archeol de France . . CONGRES ARCHEOLOGIQUE DE FRANCE
Congres Des Rel Ind . . CONGRES DES RELATIONS INDUSTRIELLES DE L'UNIVERSITE LAVAL. RAPPORT
Congr Int Cybern Actes . . CONGRES INTERNATIONAL DE CYBERNETIQUE ACTES
ConL . . . . CONTEMPORARY LITERATURE
ConLit . . . . CONTEMPORARY LITERATURE
ConLit . . . . CONVORBIRI LITERARE
Conn . . . . CONNOISSEUR
Conn . . . . CONNOTATION
Conn Acad Arts & Sci Trans . . CONNECTICUT ACADEMY OF ARTS AND SCIENCES. TRANSACTIONS
Conn B J . . . . CONNECTICUT BAR JOURNAL
CONNECT TIS . . . . . . CONNECTIVE TISSUE RESEARCH
Conn Geol Natur Hist Surv Bull . . CONNECTICUT. STATE GEOLOGICAL AND NATURAL HISTORY SURVEY. BULLETIN
Conn Hist Soc Bull . . CONNECTICUT HISTORICAL SOCIETY. BULLETIN
Conn Hist Soc Coll . . CONNECTICUT HISTORICAL SOCIETY. COLLECTIONS
ConnHSB . . . . CONNECTICUT HISTORICAL SOCIETY. BULLETIN
Conn Lib . . . . CONNECTICUT LIBRARIES
Conn Lib Assn Bul . . CONNECTICUT LIBRARY ASSOCIAITON. BULLETIN
Conn L Rev . . . . CONNECTICUT LAW REVIEW
Conn R . . . . CONNECTICUT REVIEW
Con(NS) . . . . CONVIVIUM (NEW SERIES)
Conn State Ag Exp . . CONNECTICUT AGRICULTURAL EXPERIMENT STATION. PUBLICATIONS
Conn Woodlands . . . CONNECTICUT WOODLANDS
ConR . . . . CONTEMPORARY REVIEW
Cons . . . . CONSIGNA
Consejo Sup Invest Cient Bibl Bol . . CONSEJO SUPERIOR DE INVESTIGACIONES CIENTIFICAS. BIBLIOTECA GENERAL.
 BOLETIN
Conserv R . . . . CONSERVATIVE REVIEW
Constr Met . . . . CONSTRUCTION METALLIQUE
Constr Metal . . . . . . CONSTRUCTION METALLIQUE
Constr Meth . . . . . . CONSTRUCTION METHODS
Constr Methods Equip . . CONSTRUCTION METHODS AND EQUIPMENT

Constr Plant Equip.. CONSTRUCTION PLANT & EQUIPMENT
Constr Q......... CONSTRUCTIVE QUARTERLY
Constr R......... CONSTRUCTION REVIEW
Constr Rev....... CONSTRUCTIONAL REVIEW
Constr Specifier.... CONSTRUCTION SPECIFIER
Consult Eng (London).. CONSULTING ENGINEER (LONDON)
Consult Eng (St. Joseph Mich.).. CONSULTING ENGINEER (ST. JOSEPH, MICH)
CONT DRUG P..... CONTEMPORARY DRUG PROBLEMS
CONT EDUC....... CONTEMPORARY EDUCATION
Contemp......... CONTEMPORANEO
Contemp......... CONTEMPORARY REVIEW
Contemp Drug..... CONTEMPORARY DRUG PROBLEMS
Contemp Drug Prob.. CONTEMPORARY DRUG PROBLEMS
Contemp Ed....... CONTEMPORARY EDUCATION
Contemp Jewish Rec.. CONTEMPORARY JEWISH RECORD
Contemp Lit...... CONTEMPORARY LITERATURE
Contemp Phys..... CONTEMPORARY PHYSICS
Contemp R....... CONTEMPORARY REVIEW
Contemp Sociol.... CONTEMPORARY SOCIOLOGY
CONT HUM DE..... CONTRIBUTIONS TO HUMAN DEVELOPMENT
Contin Mo........ CONTINENTAL MONTHLY
CONT LEARNING... CONTINUOUS LEARNING
ConTM.......... CONCORDIA THEOLOGICAL MONTHLY
Cont P.......... CONTEMPORARY POETRY
CONT PHYS....... CONTEMPORARY PHYSICS
CONT PSYCHA..... CONTEMPORARY PSYCHOANALYSIS
CONT PSYCHO..... CONTEMPORARY PSYCHOLOGY
CONTRACEPT..... CONTRACEPTION
Contr Eng........ CONTROL ENGINEERING
Contrib Mineral & Petrol.. CONTRIBUTIONS TO MINERALOGY AND PETROLOGY
CONTR INSTR..... CONTROL AND INSTRUMENTATION
Contr Instrum..... CONTROL AND INSTRUMENTATION
CONTR MAR S..... CONTRIBUTIONS IN MARINE SCIENCE
CONTR MIN P..... CONTRIBUTIONS TO MINERALOGY AND PETROLOGY
Control Eng....... CONTROL ENGINEERING
Control Instrum.... CONTROL AND INSTRUMENTATION
CONTR PRIM...... CONTRIBUTIONS TO PRIMATOLOGY
CONT SOCIOL..... CONTEMPORARY SOCIOLOGY
Conv............ CONVIVIUM
Convey.......... CONVEYANCER AND PROPERTY LAWYER
ConvLit.......... CONVORBIRI LITERARE
COO............ CHRONICLE OF OKLAHOMA
Coop............ COOPERATION
Coop Inf........ COOPERATION INFORMATION
Coop Manager & F.. CO-OPERATIVE MANAGER AND FARMER
COORD CH RE..... COORDINATION CHEMISTRY REVIEWS
Coord Res Counc CRC Rep.. COORDINATING RESEARCH COUNCIL. CRC REPORT
Cooper Union Chron.. COOPER UNION MUSEUM CHRONICLE
COPYRIGHT L SYM (ASCAP)..COPYRIGHT LAW SYMPOSIUM. AMERICAN SOCIETY OF COMPOSERS AUTHORS AND
  PUBLISHERS
CoR............ CONTEMPORARY REVIEW

Cor. . . . . CORRESPONDENT
CorL. . . . . CORREO LITERARIO
Cornell Ag Exp. . . . . CORNELL UNIVERSITY. AGRICULTURAL EXPERIMENT STATION. PUBLICATIONS
Cornell Eng. . . . . . . CORNELL ENGINEER
Cornell Hotel & Rest Adm Q. . CORNELL HOTEL AND RESTAURANT ADMINISTRATION QUARTERLY
CORNELL I J. . . . . . . CORNELL INTERNATIONAL LAW JOURNAL
CORNELL J S. . . . . . CORNELL JOURNAL OF SOCIAL RELATIONS
Cornell Lib J. . . . . . CORNELL LIBRARY JOURNAL
Cornell L Q. . . . . . . CORNELL LAW QUARTERLY
CORNELL L R. . . . . . CORNELL LAW REVIEW
Cornell univ Dep Struc Eng Rep. . CORNELL UNIVERSITY. DEPARTMENT OF STRUCTURAL ENGINEERING. REPORT
Cornell Univ Lib Bull. . CORNELL UNIVERSITY LIBRARIES. BULLETIN
Cornell Vet. . . . . . . CORNELL VETERINARIAN
Cornh. . . . . CORNHILL MAGAZINE
Corp J. . . . . CORPORATION JOURNAL
Corp Prac Comm. . . CORPORATE PRACTICE COMMENTATOR
Corros Eng (Tokyo). . CORROSION ENGINEERING (TOKYO)
Corros Pre Contr. . . CORROSION PREVENTION & CONTROL
Corros Sci. . . . . CORROSION SCIENCE
Corros Trait Prot Finition. . CORROSION, TRAITEMENTS, PROTECTION, FINITION
CORR SOC PS. . . . . . CORRECTIVE AND SOCIAL PSYCHIATRY
CORS J. . . . . CORS (CANADIAN OPERATIONAL RESEARCH SOCIETY) JOURNAL
Cos. . . . . COSMIC STORIES
COS. . . . . COSMOS SCIENCE FICTION & FANTASY MAGAZINE
COSM. . . . . COSMIC SCIENCE FICTION
Cosmic Res. . . . . . . COSMIC RESEARCH
Cosmop. . . . . COSMOPOLITAN
Cosmopol. . . . . COSMOPOLITAN
Cost and Man. . . . . COST AND MANAGEMENT
Cost Eng. . . . . COST ENGINEERING
COST MANAGE. . . . COST AND MANAGEMENT
COUNS ED SU. . . . . COUNSELOR EDUCATION AND SUPERVISION
Counsel Ed & Sup. . . COUNSELOR EDUCATION AND SUPERVISION
COUNS PSYCH. . . . . COUNSELING PSYCHOLOGIST
Country Cal. . . . . . . COUNTRY CALENDAR
Country Gent. . . . . COUNTRY GENTLEMAN
Countryside M. . . . . COUNTRYSIDE MAGAZINE AND SUBURBAN LIFE
COUR MUS FRANCE. . COURRIER MUSICAL DE FRANCE
CP. . . . . CASTRUM PEREGRINI
CP. . . . . CLASSICAL PHILOLOGY
CP. . . . . CONCERNING POETRY
CP. . . . . CULTURA POLITICA (RIO DE JANEIRO)
CPAJ. . . . . CPA (AMERICAN INSTITUTE OF CERTIFIED PUBLIC ACCOUNTANTS) JOURNAL
CPe. . . . . CASTRUM PEREGRINI
CPh. . . . . CLASSICAL PHILOLOGY
CPH. . . . . COLECCAO POETAS DE HOJE
CpMF. . . . . CASOPIS PRO MODERNI FILOLOGII
CQ. . . . . CAMBRIDGE QUARTERLY
CQ. . . . . CAROLINA QUARTERLY
CQ. . . . . CLASSICAL QUARTERLY
CQ. . . . . CRITICAL QUARTERLY

CQR............ CHURCH QUARTERLY REVIEW
CR............. CENTENNIAL REVIEW
CR............. CLASSICAL REVIEW
CR............. COMPTES RENDUS
CR............. CONTEMPORARY REVIEW
Cr............. CRITERION
CR............. CRITICAL REVIEW
CRa............ CAHIERS RACINIENS
CRAABull........ COMMISSIONS ROYALES D'ART ET D'ARCHEOLOGIE. BULLETIN
CR ACAD SCI...... COMPTES RENDUS HEBDOMADAIRES DES SEANCES DE L'ACADEMIE DES SCIENCES
CR AC SCI A...... COMPTES RENDUS HEBDOMADAIRES DES SEANCES DE L'ACADEMIE DES SCIENCES. SERIE A
CR AC SCI B...... COMPTES RENDUS HEBDOMADAIRES DES SEANCES DE L'ACADEMIE DES SCIENCES. SERIE B
CR AC SCI C...... COMPTES RENDUS HEBDOMADAIRES DES SEANCES DE L'ACADEMIE DES SCIENCES. SERIE C
CR AC SCI D...... COMPTES RENDUS HEBDOMADAIRES DES SEANCES DE L'ACADEMIE DES SCIENCES. SERIE D
Craft Horiz....... CRAFT HORIZONS
CRAI............ COMPTES RENDUS DE L'ACADEMIE DES INSCRIPTIONS ET BELLES LETTRES
CRAIBL.......... COMPTES-RENDUS DE L'ACADEMIE DES INSCRIPTIONS ET BELLES LETTRES
CRAL........... COMPTE RENDU DE L'ASSOCIATION LYONNAISE DE RECHERCHES ARCHEOLOGIQUES
CraneR.......... CRANE REVIEW
CRAP........... COMPTES RENDUS DE L'ACADEMIE POLONAISE DES SCIENCES ET DES LETTRES
CRAS........... CENTENNIAL REVIEW OF ARTS AND SCIENCES
CRASR.......... COMPTES RENDUS DE L'ACADEMIE DES SCIENCES DE RUSSIE
CRB............ CAHIERS DE LA COMPAGNIE MADELEINE RENAUD-JEAN LOUIS BARRAULT
CrB............ CRITISCH BULLETIN
CRC Crit R Microbiol.. CRC CRITICAL REVIEWS IN MICROBIOLOGY
CREDIF.......... BULLETIN BIBLIOGRAPHIQUE DES C.R.E.D.I.F. (CENTRE DE RECHERCHE ET D'ETUDE POUR LA
                 DIFFUSION DU FRANCAIS SERVICE DE DOCUMENTATION)
Credit M......... CREDIT MONTHLY
Creighton L Rev.... CREIGHTON LAW REVIEW
Cres............ CRESSET
CRESCENDO INT.... CRESCENDO INTERNATIONAL
C Rev AS......... CANADIAN REVIEW OF AMERICAN STUDIES
Cr H............ CRAFT HORIZONS
CRH Acad Sci Ser A Sci Math.. COMPTES RENDUS HEBDOMADAIRES DES SEANCES DE L'ACADEMIE DES SCIENCES.
                 SERIE A. SCIENCES MATHEMATIQUES
CRH Acad Sci Ser B Sci Phys.. COMPTES RENDUS HEBDOMADAIRES DES SEANCES DE L'ACADEMIE DES SCIENCES.
                 SERIE B. SCIENCES PHYSIQUES
CRH Acad Sci Ser C Sci Chim. COMPTES RENDUS HEBDOMADAIRES DES SEANCES DE L'ACADEMIE DES SCIENCES.
                 SERIE C. SCIENCES CHIMIQUES
CRH Acad Sci Ser D Sci Natur.. COMPTES RENDUS HEBDOMADAIRES DES SEANCES DE L'ACADEMIE DES SCIENCES.
                 SERIE D. SCIENCES NATURELLES
CRHBull......... COMMISSION ROYALE D'HISTOIRE. BULLETIN
Cri............. CRITERION
CRIEH.......... CENTRE DE RECHERCHES DE L'INSTITUT D'ETUDES HISPANIQUES
CrimAb.......... ABSTRACTS ON CRIMINOLOGY AND PENOLOGY
CRIME DELIN...... CRIME AND DELINQUENCY
CRIM JUST B...... CRIMINAL JUSTICE AND BEHAVIOR
Crim Law Bul...... CRIMINAL LAW BULLETIN
CRIM LAW Q...... CRIMINAL LAW QUARTERLY
CRIM LAW R...... CRIMINAL LAW REVIEW
CRIM L Q........ CRIMINAL LAW QUARTERLY

CRIM L R . . . . CRIMINAL LAW REVIEW
Crit . . . . CRITERION
Crit . . . . CRITIC
Crit . . . . CRITICA
Crit . . . . CRITIQUE: STUDIES IN MODERN FICTION
Critm . . . . CRITICISM
Crit Q . . . . CRITICAL QUARTERLY
Critq . . . . CRITIQUE
Crit R . . . . CRITICAL REVIEW
CritS . . . . CRITICAL SURVEY
CRL . . . . COLLEGE AND RESEARCH LIBRARIES
CRME . . . . COUNCIL FOR RESEARCH IN MUSIC EDUCATION. BULLETIN
CROAT CHEM . . . . . CROATICA CHEMICA ACTA
CRodSpol . . . . CASOPIS RODOPISNE SPOLECNOSTI CESKOSLOVENSKE
CRom . . . . CUGET ROMANESC
Cron . . . . CRONOS
Crop Sci . . . . CROP SCIENCE
Cross Cur . . . . CROSS CURRENTS
CrQ . . . . CRITICAL QUARTERLY
CrS . . . . CRITICA STORICA
CRSAIBL . . . . COMPTES RENDUS DES SEANCES DE L'ACADEMIE DES INSCRIPTIONS ET BELLES-LETTRES
CRSL . . . . COMPTES RENDUS DE LA SOCIETE DES SCIENCES ET DES LETTRES DE LODZ
CRSLub . . . . COMPTES RENDUS DE LA SOCIETE DES SCIENCES ET DES LETTRES DE L'UNIVERSITE CATHOLIQUE
DE LUBLIN
CR SOC BIOL . . . . . . COMPTES RENDUS DES SEANCES DE LA SOCIETE DE BIOLOGIE ET DE SES FILIALES
C R Som Seances Soc Geol Fr . . COMPTES RENDU SOMMAIRE DES SEANCES DE LA SOCIETE GEOLOGIQUE DE FRANCE
CRSP . . . . COMPTES RENDUS DE LA SOCIETE DES SCIENCES ET DES LETTRES DE POZNAN
CRSVa . . . . COMPTES RENDUS DE LA SOCIETE DES SCIENCES ET DES LETTRES DE VARSOVIE
CRSW . . . . COMPTES RENDUS DE LA SOCIETE DES SCIENCES ET DES LETTRES DE WROCLAW
CR TR LAB C . . . . . . COMPTES RENDUS DES TRAVAUX DU LABORATOIRE CARLSBERG
CRu . . . . CESKOSLOVENSKA RUSISTIKA
CRus . . . . CESKOSLOVENSKA RUSISTIKA
Cr Wtg . . . . CREATIVE WRITING
Cryog Eng News . . . . CRYOGENIC ENGINEERING NEWS
Cryog Technol . . . . . CRYOGENIC TECHNOLOGY
CRYST LATT . . . . CRYSTAL LATTICE DEFECTS
CS . . . . CAHIERS DU SUD
CS . . . . CORNISH STUDIES
CS . . . . CRITICA STORICA
CS . . . . CROATIA SACRA
CSAV . . . . CESKOSLOVENSKA AKADEMIE VED
CSBW . . . . CHICAGO SUN BOOK WEEK
CSCH . . . . CESKOSLOVENSKY CASOPIS HISTORICKY
CSE . . . . CORNELL STUDIES IN ENGLISH
CSEL . . . . CORPUS SCRIPTORUM ECCLESIASTICORUM LATINORUM
CSGH . . . . CHOSEN GAKUNO
CSGLL . . . . CANADIAN STUDIES IN GERMAN LANGUAGE AND LITERATURE
CSHVB . . . . COMPUTER STUDIES IN THE HUMANITIES AND VERBAL BEHAVIOR
CSIC . . . . CONSEJO SUPERIOR DE INVESTIGACIONES CIENTIFICAS
CSJ . . . . CASOPIS PRO SLOVANSKE JAZYKY, LITERATURU A DEJINY SSSR
CSLBull . . . . NEW YORK C.S. LEWIS SOCIETY. BULLETIN

CSLJa . . . . CASOPIS PRO SLOVANSKE JAZYKY. LITERATURU A DEJINY SSSR
CSLP . . . . CANADIAN SLAVONIC PAPERS
CSM . . . . CHRISTIAN SCIENCE MONITOR
CSMF . . . . CARL SCHURZ MEMORIAL FOUNDATION
CSMLT . . . . CAMBRIDGE STUDIES IN MEDIEVAL LIFE AND THOUGHT
CSMMS . . . . CHRISTIAN SCIENCE MONITOR MAGAZINE SECTION
C S Mon Mag . . . . . CHRISTIAN SCIENCE MONITOR MAGAZINE
CSP . . . . CAHIERS SEXTIL PUSCARIU
CSP . . . . CANADIAN SLAVONIC PAPERS
CSp . . . . CESKOSLOVENSKY SPISOVATEL
CSPh . . . . CORNELL STUDIES IN CLASSICAL PHILOLOGY
CsR . . . . CESKOSLOVENSKA RUSISTIKA
CSR . . . . CHRISTIAN SCHOLAR'S REVIEW
C S R Bul . . . . COUNCIL ON THE STUDY OF RELIGION. BULLETIN
CSS . . . . CALIFORNIA SLAVIC STUDIES
CSS . . . . CANADIAN SLAVIC STUDIES
CSSH . . . . COMPARATIVE STUDIES IN SOCIETY AND HISTORY
CSSJ . . . . CENTRAL STATES SPEECH JOURNAL
CST . . . . CHICAGO SUNDAY TRIBUNE
CSt . . . . COLECCAO STUDIUM
CSTA R . . . . CSTA (CANADIAN SOCIETY OF TECHNICAL AGRICULTURISTS) REVIEW
CSTC . . . . CESKOSLOVENSKY TERMINOLOGICKY CASOPIS
CSVAH . . . . CHRONIQUE DE LA SOCIETE VERVIETOISE D'ARCHEOLOGIE ET D'HISTOIRE
CT . . . . CAHIERS-DE TUNISIE
CT . . . . CAHIERS THOMISTES
CT . . . . CHILDREN TODAY
CT . . . . CIENCIA TOMISTA
CT . . . . COLLECTANEA THEOLOGICA
CTA J . . . . CTA JOURNAL (INDIA)
Ctary . . . . COMMENTARY
CTC . . . . CESKOSLOVENSKY TERMINOLOGICKY CASOPIS
CTD . . . . COMMISSION DE TOPONYMIE ET DIALECTOLOGIE
CTHBAr . . . . COMITE DES TRAVAUX HISTORIQUES ET SCIENTIFIQUES. BULLETIN ARCHEOLOGIQUE
CTHBull . . . . COMITE DES TRAVAUX HISTORIQUES ET SCIENTIFIQUES. BULLETIN ARCHEOLOGIQUE
CTHBullH . . . . COMITE DES TRAVAUX HISTORIQUES ET SCIENTIFIQUES. BULLETIN HISTORIQUE ET
                       PHILOLOGIQUE
CTL . . . . CAHIERS—THEATRE LOUVAIN
CTM . . . . CONCORDIA THEOLOGICAL MONTHLY
Ctry Life Am . . . . . . COUNTRY LIFE IN AMERICA
Cuad Filosof . . . . . . CUADERNOS DE FILOSOFIA
CUAPS . . . . CATHOLIC UNIVERSITY OF AMERICA PATRISTIC STUDIES
CUASRL . . . . CATHOLIC UNIVERSITY OF AMERICA STUDIES IN ROMANCE LANGUAGES AND LITERATURES
CUASRLL . . . . CATHOLIC UNIVERSITY OF AMERICA STUDIES IN ROMANCE LANGUAGES AND LITERATURES
CUB . . . . CATHOLIC UNIVERSITY BULLETIN
Cuba Bibl . . . . CUBA BIBLIOTECOLOGICA
CUC . . . . CULTURA UNIVERSITARIA (CARACAS)
CuCanl . . . . CUANDERNOS CANARIOS DE INVESTIGACION
CuCo . . . . CURSOS Y CONFERENCIAS
CUF . . . . COLUMBIA UNIVERSITY FORUM
CUGS . . . . COLUMBIA UNIVERSITY GERMANIC STUDIES
CuH . . . . CUADERNOS HISPANOAMERICANOS

Cu H........... CURRENT HISTORY
CulEA.......... CULTURAL EVENTS IN AFRICA
Cult........... CULTURA
Cult........... CULTURE (MONTREAL)
Cult Hermen...... CULTURAL HERMENEUTICS
Cult Neol........ CULTURA NEOLATINA
Cult Noolat....... CULTURA NEOLATINA
Cumber-Sam L Rev.. CUMBERLAND-SAMFORD LAW REVIEW
Cumb Q......... CUMBERLAND PRESBYTERIAN QUARTERLY REVIEW
CUP........... CAMBRIDGE UNIVERSITY PRESS
CUQ........... COLUMBIA UNIVERSITY QUARTERLY
Cur Anthrop...... CURRENT ANTHROPOLOGY
Cur Bibliog African Affairs.. CURRENT BIBLIOGRAPHY ON AFRICAN AFFAIRS
Cur Biog........ CURRENT BIOGRAPHY
Cur Biog Yrbk..... CURRENT BIOGRAPHY YEARBOOK
Cur Hist........ CURRENT HISTORY
Cur Hist M NY Times.. CURRENT HISTORY MAGAZINE OF THE NEW YORK TIMES
Cur Issues Higher Ed.. CURRENT ISSUES IN HIGHER EDUCATION
Cur Lit.......... CURRENT LITERATURE
Cur Opinion....... CURRENT OPINION
CURR ANTHR...... CURRENT ANTHROPOLOGY
CurrCont........ CURRENT CONTENTS
Current Law...... CURRENT LAW AND SOCIAL PROBLEMS
Current Med...... CURRENT MEDICINE FOR ATTORNEYS
CURRENT MUS..... CURRENT MUSICOLOGY
Curr Hist........ CURRENT HISTORY
Curric Stud and Ed Res B.. CURRICULUM STUDY AND EDUCATIONAL RESEARCH BULLETIN
CURRIC THEO..... CURRICULUM THEORY NETWORK
CURR MUN PR..... CURRENT MUNICIPAL PROBLEMS
CURR SOCIOL..... CURRENT SOCIOLOGY
CURR THER R...... CURRENT THERAPEUTIC RESEARCH-CLINICAL AND EXPERIMENTAL
CUT TOOL EN...... CUTTING TOOL ENGINEERING
CUUCV......... CULTURA UNIVERSITARIA DE LA UNIVERSIDAD CENTRAL DE VENEZUELA
CV............. CERF-VOLANT
CV............. CITTA DI VITA
CV............. CIVILTA FASCISTA
CV............. COMMENTATIONES VINDOBONENSES
CV............. CRKOVEN VESTNIK
CVS........... CLASSIQUES DU XX SIECLE
CVSMO......... CASOPIS VLASTEVECKSEHO SPOLKU MUSEJUIHO V OLOMOUCI
CW............. CATHOLIC WORLD
CW............. CLASSICAL WEEKLY
CW............. CLASSICAL WORLD
CW-CAN WELF..... CW-CANADIAN WELFARE
CWCP.......... CONTEMPORY WRITERS IN CHRISTIAN PERSPECTIVE
Cwd........... CATHOLIC WORLD
Cweal.......... COMMONWEAL
Cwealth........ COMMONWEALTH
CWGV.......... CHRONIK WIENER GOETHEVEREIN
CWH........... CIVIL WAR HISTORY
Cy............. CRAWDADDY

PERIODICAL TITLE ABBREVIATIONS

CyC............ CURSOS Y CONFERENCIAS
Cym Trans........ HONOURABLE SOCIETY OF CYMMRODORION. TRANSACTIONS
CyR............ CRUZ Y RAYA
CYTOG C GEN..... CYTOGENETICS AND CELL GENETICS
CZ............. CELA ZIMES
Cz............. CZYTELNIK
Czech Heavy Ind... CZECHOSLOVAK HEAVY INDUSTRY
CZEC J PHYS...... CZECHOSLOVAK JOURNAL OF PHYSICS. SECTION B
CZEC MATH J..... CZECHOSLOVAK MATHEMATICAL JOURNAL

D

D . . . . DACOROMANIA
D . . . . DANCE
D . . . . DECEMBER
D . . . . DIALECTICA
D . . . . DICKENSIAN
D . . . . DRAMMATURGIA
DA . . . . DEUTSCHES ARCHIV FUER GESCHICHTE
DA . . . . DISSERTATION ABSTRACTS
DAb . . . . DISSERTATION ABSTRACTS
Dac . . . . DACIA
Dac . . . . DACOROMANIA
Dacor . . . . DACOROMANIA
DAEM . . . . DEUTSCHES ARCHIV FUER DIE ERFORSCHUNG DES MITTELALTERS
DaF . . . . DEUTSCH ALS FREMDSPRACHE
DAGM . . . . DEUTSCHES ARCHIV FUER GESCHICHTE DES MITTELALTERS
DAI . . . . DISSERTATION ABSTRACTS INTERNATIONAL
Dairy F . . . . DAIRY FARMER
Dairy Goat J . . . . . . DAIRY GOAT JOURNAL
Dairy Herd Mgt . . . . DAIRY HERD MANAGEMENT
DAIRY IND . . . . DAIRY INDUSTRIES INTERNATIONAL
Dairy Indus . . . . DAIRY INDUSTRIES
DAJ . . . . DERBYSHIRE ARCHAEOLOGICAL SOCIETY. JOURNAL
Dakota F . . . . DAKOTA-FARMER
DALLAS SYM . . . . . . DALLAS SYMPHONY ORCHESTRA PROGRAM NOTES
Dal R . . . . DALHOUSIE REVIEW
DALV . . . . DEUTSCHES ARCHIV FUER LANDES UND VOLKSFORSCHUNG
DAN . . . . DOKLADY AKADEMII NAUK SSSR
DAN BOLG . . . . DOKLADY BOLGARSKOI AKADEMII NAUK
Dance Per . . . . DANCE PERSPECTIVES
D&T . . . . DRAMA AND THEATRE
DanF . . . . DANSKE FOLKEMAAL
DAN MED B . . . . DANISH MEDICAL BULLETIN
DANSK BOTAN . . . . . DANSK BOTANISK ARKIV
DANSK MUS . . . . . . DANSK MUSIKTIDSSKRIFT
DAN SSSR . . . . DOKLADY AKADEMII NAUK SSSR
DanU . . . . DANSK UDSYN
Danv Q . . . . DANVILLE QUARTERLY REVIEW
Dan Yrbk Phil . . . . . DANISH YEARBOOK OF PHILOSOPHY
D Arch . . . . DODEKANESIAKON ARCHEION
Darshana Int . . . . . . DARSHANA INTERNATIONAL
Dart Bi-Mo . . . . DARTMOUTH BI-MONTHLY
DASD . . . . DEUTSCHE AKADEMIE FUER SPRACHE UND DICHTUNG. DARMSTADT. JAHRBUCH
DASDJ . . . . DEUTSCHE AKADEMIE FUER SPRACHE UND DICHTUNG. DARMSTADT. JAHRBUCH
DaSt . . . . DANTE STUDIES
Data Ed . . . . DATA EDUCATION
Data Mgt . . . . DATA MANAGEMENT
DATA PROCES . . . . . DATA PROCESSING
DATA PROCES . . . . DATA PROCESSING (LONDON)
Data Syst . . . . DATA SYSTEMS

Data Systems N . . . . DATA SYSTEMS NEWS
DAUK . . . . DEUTSCHE ARBEITEN DER UNIVERSITAET KOELN
DAWB . . . . DEUTSCHE AKADEMIE DER WISSENSCHAFTEN ZU BERLIN
DAWBIDSL . . . . DEUTSCHE AKADEMIE DER WISSENSCHAFTEN ZU BERLIN. INSTITUT FUER DEUTSCHE SPRACHE UND LITERATUR
Daz . . . . DEUTSCHE ALLGEMEINE ZEITUNG
DB . . . . DOITSU BUNGAKU
DBDK . . . . DAITO BUNKA DAIGAKU KIYO
DBDKK . . . . DAITO BUNKA DAIGAKU KANGAKKAISHI
DBGU . . . . DEUTSCHE BEITRAEGE ZUR GEISTIGEN UEBERLIEFERUNG
Dble Dealer . . . . DOUBLE DEALER
DBNM . . . . DARMSTAEDTER BEITRAEGE ZUR NEUEN MUSIK
DBR . . . . DIALECTES BELGO-ROMANS
DB Sound Eng Mag . . DB, SOUND ENGINEERING MAGAZINE
Dbt . . . . DOWNBEAT
DCB J . . . . D.C. BAR JOURNAL
DC Lib . . . . DISTRICT OF COLUMBIA LIBRARIES
DCNQ . . . . DEVON AND CORNWALL. NOTES AND QUERIES
DD . . . . DANCE AND DANCERS
DD . . . . DEUTSCHE DIALEKTGEOGRAPHIE
DdB . . . . DISTRITO DE BRAGA
DDG . . . . DEUTSCHE DIALEKTGEOGRAPHIE
DDHS . . . . DEUTSCHE HOEHERE SCHULE
DDJ . . . . DEUTSCHES DANTE JAHRBUCH
DE . . . . DEVELOPING ECONOMIES
DE . . . . DIRITTO ECCLESIASTICO
De Bow . . . . DE BOW'S COMMERCIAL REVIEW
Dec . . . . DECADE OF SHORT STORIES
Dec . . . . DECEMBER
Ded . . . . DEDALO
DE Dom Eng . . . . . . DE, DOMESTIC ENGINEERING
DeEc . . . . DE ECONOMIST
DEEP-SEA RE . . . . . . DEEP-SEA RESEARCH
Defense L J . . . . DEFENSE LAW JOURNAL
Defense Sci J . . . . . . DEFENSE SCIENCE JOURNAL
DEF LAW J . . . . DEFENSE LAW JOURNAL
Def Sci J . . . . DEFENCE SCIENCE JOURNAL
DeH . . . . DE HOMINE
DE/J . . . . DE (DOMESTIC ENGINEERING) JOURNAL
Del Ag Exp . . . . DELAWARE COLLEGE. AGRICULTURAL EXPERIMENT STATION. PUBLICATIONS
Delaware Hist Soc Papers . . DELAWARE HISTORICAL SOCIETY. PAPERS
DelH . . . . DELAWARE HISTORY
Del Hist . . . . DELAWARE HISTORY
Delin . . . . DELINEATOR
DelN . . . . DELAWARE NOTES
Del Notes . . . . DELAWARE NOTES
Dem R . . . . DEMOCRATIC REVIEW
DENKI KAG . . . . DENKI KAGAKU
DENT CLIN N . . . . . . DENTAL CLINICS OF NORTH AMERICA
DENVER J INT L & POL . . DENVER JOURNAL OF INTERNATIONAL LAW AND POLICY
DENVER LAW . . . . . . DENVER LAW JOURNAL

Denver LCJ....... DENVER LAW CENTER JOURNAL
DENVER L J....... DENVER LAW JOURNAL
DenverQ........ DENVER QUARTERLY
De Paul L Rev..... DE PAUL LAW REVIEW
Dept El Sch Prin B.. DEPARTMENT OF ELEMENTARY SCHOOL PRINCIPALS. BULLETIN
Dept of Ed and Science Repts.. DEPARTMENT OF EDUCATION AND SCIENCE: REPORTS ON EDUCATION
Dept Sec Sch Prin B.. DEPARTMENT OF SECONDARY-SCHOOL PRINCIPALS. BULLETIN
Dept State Bul..... DEPARTMENT OF STATE BULLETIN
DERMATOLOG..... DERMATOLOGICA
DESALINATN...... DESALINATION
DESB........... DELTA EPSILON SIGMA BULLETIN
Des Compon Engn.. DESIGN AND COMPONENTS IN ENGINEERING
Des Electron...... DESIGN ELECTRONICS
Des Eng......... DESIGN ENGINEERING
Design for Ind..... DESIGN FOR INDUSTRY
Design Ind........ DESIGN FOR INDUSTRY
Detroit Inst Bul.... DETROIT INSTITUTE OF ARTS. BULLETIN
Detroit Law....... DETROIT LAWYER
DETROIT SYM..... DETROIT SYMPHONY ORCHESTRA PROGRAM NOTES
Deut Ausschuss Stahlbeton.. DEUTSCHER AUSSCHUSS FUER STAHLBETON
Deutch Archaeol Inst Jahrb.. DEUTSCHES ARCHAEOLOGISCHES INSTITUT JAHRBUCH
Deut Luft Raumfahrt Forschungsber.. DEUTSCHE LUFT- UND RAUMFAHRT, FORSCHUNGSBERICHT
DEUT MED WO..... DEUTSCHE MEDIZINISCHE WOCHENSCHRIFT
DeutR........... DEUTSCHE REVUE
Deutsch Archaeol Inst Roem Mitt.. DEUTSCHES ARCHAEOLOGISCHES INSTITUT. MITTEILUNGEN. ROEMISCHE
ABTEILUNG
Deutsche Oper.... DEUTSCHE OPER AM RHEIN
Deutsch Jahrb Musikw.. DEUTSCHES JAHRBUCH FUER MUSIKWISSENSCHAFT
Deutsch Zool Ges Verh.. DEUTSCHE ZOOLOGISCHE GESELLSCHAFT. VERHANDLUNGEN
Deut Vier Lit...... DEUTSCHE VIERTELJAHRSSCHRIFT FUER LITERATURWISSENSCHAFT UND GEISTESGESCHICHTE
Deut Z Phil....... DEUTSCHE ZEITSCHRIFT FUER PHILOSOPHIE
Deu Viertel....... DEUTSCHE VIERTELJAHRSSCHRIFT FUER LITERATURWISSENSCHAFT UND GEISTESGESCHICHTE
DevB........... DEVIL'S BOX
DEVELOP BIO...... DEVELOPMENTAL BIOLOGY
DEVELOP CHA..... DEVELOPMENT AND CHANGE
DEVELOP ECO..... DEVELOPING ECONOMIES
DEVELOP GR...... DEVELOPMENT GROWTH & DIFFERENTIATION
DEVELOP MED..... DEVELOPMENTAL MEDICINE AND CHILD NEUROLOGY
DEVELOP PSY..... DEVELOPMENTAL PSYCHOBIOLOGY
Develop Psychol... DEVELOPMENTAL PSYCHOLOGY
DEW Tech Ber..... DEW (DEUTSCHE EDELSTAHLWERKE AKTIENGESELLSCHAFT) TECHNISCHE BERICHTE
DF............. DANDKE FOLKEMAAL
DFBO Mitt........ DFBO MITTEILUNGEN (DEUTSCHE FORSCHUNGSGESELLSCHAFT FUER BLECHVERARBEITUNG UND
OBERFLAECHENBEHANDLUNG)
DFMhe.......... DEUTSCH-FRANZOESISCHE MONATSHEFTE
DFR........... DEUTSCH-FRANZOESISCHE RUNDSCHAU
Dg............. DIALOG (WARSAW)
DGF........... DANMARKS GAMLE FOLKEVISER
DH............. DELAWARE HISTORY
DH............. DOCUMENTS D'HISTOIRE
DHLR.......... D.H. LAWRENCE REVIEW

DHR . . . . DUQUESNE HISPANIC REVIEW
DHS . . . . DIX-HUITIEME SIECLE
Di . . . . DIALOGHI
Di . . . . DIDASKALEION
Dia . . . . DIALOGHI
DIABETE MET . . . . . . DIABETE AND METABOLISME
DIABETOLOG . . . . . . DIABETOLOGIA
Dial (Ch.) . . . . DIAL (CHICAGO)
Dial . . . . DIALOG
Dial . . . . DIALOGHI
DialB . . . . DIALEKTOLOHICNYI BJULETEN
Dial Belg-Rom . . . . . DIALECTES BELGO-ROMANS
Dialec Hum . . . . DIALECTICS AND HUMANISM
Dialogue (Canada) . . DIALOGUE: CANADIAN PHILOSOPHICAL REVIEW
Dailogue (PST) . . . . DIALOGUE (PHI SIGMA TAU)
Dialog W . . . . DIALOG (WARSAW)
DialS . . . . DIALOG: TEATERTIDSKRIFT (STOCKHOLM)
Diap . . . . DIAPASON
Dicht u Volkst . . . . . DICHTUNG UND VOLKSTUM
Dick . . . . DICKENSIAN
DickinsonR . . . . DICKINSON REVIEW
Dick L Rev . . . . DICKINSON LAW REVIEW
Did . . . . DIDASKALEION
Die Cast Eng . . . . . . DIE CASTING ENGINEER
Diesel Eng Users Ass Publ . . DIESEL ENGINEERS AND USERS ASSOCIATION. PUBLICATION
Diesel Equip Supt . . . DIESEL EQUIPMENT SUPERINTENDENT
Diesel Gas Turbine Progr . . DIESEL AND GAS TURBINE PROGRESS
DIFFERENTIA . . . . . . DIFFERENTIATION
DiJ . . . . DZIS I JUTRO
DilR . . . . DILIMAN REVIEW
Dion . . . . DIONISO
Direct Curr . . . . DIRECT CURRENT
DIR GESTION . . . . . . DIRECTION ET GESTION
DiS . . . . DICKENS STUDIES
Dis . . . . DISSENT
DisA . . . . DISSERTATION ABSTRACTS
Dis Abst . . . . DISSERTATION ABSTRACTS
Disc . . . . DISCOVERY
Disco Forum . . . . . . DISCOGRAPHICAL FORUM
DIS COL REC . . . . . . DISEASES OF THE COLON AND RECTUM
DISCR MATH . . . . . . DISCRETE MATHEMATICS
Discuss Faraday Soc . . DISCUSSIONS OF THE FARADAY SOCIETY
DIS NER SYS . . . . . . DISEASES OF THE NERVOUS SYSTEM
Diss Abs . . . . DISSERTATION ABSTRACTS
Diss Abstr Int Sec B . . DISSERTATION ABSTRACTS INTERNATIONAL. SECTION B
DissUW . . . . DISSERTATIONEN DER UNIVERSITAET WIEN
Distrib Age . . . . DISTRIBUTION AGE
Distrib Mgr . . . . DISTRIBUTION MANAGER
Distrib Worldwide . . DISTRIBUTION WORLDWIDE
Div . . . . DIVAN
DJ . . . . DZIS I JUTRO

DjbVk . . . . DEUTSCHES JAHRBUCH FUER VOLKSKUNDE
DJGKN . . . . DOSHIDA JOSHIDAIGAKU GAKUJUTSU KENKYU NENPO
DJV . . . . DEUTSCHES JAHRBUCH FUER VOLKSKUNDE
DK . . . . DIE KULTUR
DK . . . . DUKOVNA KULTURA
DkA . . . . DEUTSCHKUNDLICHE ARBEITEN
DKath . . . . DE KATHOLICK
DKDP . . . . DEUTSCHE KUNST UND DENKMALPFLEGE
DKVS . . . . DET KONEGLIGE VIDENSKAPERS SELSKAP
DL . . . . DETSKAYA LITERATURA
DL . . . . DEUTSCHE LITERATURZEITUNG
DL . . . . DIE LITERATUR
DL . . . . DOURO LITORAL
DLAJ . . . . DEKALB LITERARY ARTS JOURNAL
DLit . . . . DEUTSCHE LITERATUR
DLMov . . . . DOSLIDNENNJA Z LITERATUROZNAVSTAVA TA MOVOZNAVSTVA
DLP . . . . DOURO-LITORAL (PORTUGAL)
DLQ . . . . DREXEL LIBRARY QUARTERLY
DLtz . . . . DEUTSCHE LITERATURZEITUNG
DLZ . . . . DEUTSCHE LITERATURZEITUNG
DM . . . . DANSKE MAGAZIN
DM . . . . DEBATER'S MAGAZINE
DM . . . . DIRECT MARKETING
DM . . . . DISEASE-A-MONTH
DM . . . . DUBLIN MAGAZINE
DmB . . . . DRIEMAANDELIJKSE BLADEN
DMG . . . . DE MAASGOUW. ORGAAN VOOR LIMBRUGSCHE GESCHIEDENIS, TAAL- EN LETTERKUNDE
DMov . . . . DOSLIDZENNJA Z MOVONAVSTVA ZBIRNYK STATEJ ASPIRANTIV I DYSERTANTIV
DMUKrM . . . . DOSLIDZENNJA I MATERIJALY Z UKRJINS'KOJI MOVY
DN . . . . DAGENS NYHETER
DN . . . . DANCE NEWS
DN . . . . DETROIT NEWS
DN . . . . DRUZBA NARODOV
DNav . . . . DE NAVORSCHER
DNB . . . . DICTIONARY OF NATIONAL BIOGRAPHY
DNK . . . . DOKLADY NA NAUCNYCH KONFERENCIJACH
DNL . . . . DIE NEUE LITERATUR
DNS . . . . DIE NEUEREN SPRACHEN
DNT . . . . DE NIEUWE TAGLALGIDS
DNVS . . . . DET NORSKE VIDENKAPERS SELSKAP
DNW . . . . DER NEUE WEG
DO . . . . DANCE OBSERVER
Doc et Bibl . . . . DOCUMENTATION ET BIBLIOTHEQUES
Dock Harb Auth . . . . DOCK AND HARBOUR AUTHORITY
DOC OPHTHAL . . . . . DOCUMENTA OPHTHALMOLOGICA
DOCUM ET BIBLIO . . DOCUMENTATION ET BIBLIOTHEQUES
Dok/Inf . . . . DOKUMENTATION/INFORMATION
Dokl Acad Sci USSR Earth Sci Sect . . DOKLADY. ACADEMY OF SCIENCES OF THE USSR. EARTH SCIENCE SECTIONS
Dokl Chem Technol . . DOKLADY CHEMICAL TECHNOLOGY. ACADEMY OF SCIENCES OF THE USSR. CHEMICAL
TECHNOLOGY SECTION
DoklIRuJa . . . . DOKLADY I SOOBSCENIJA INSTITUTA RUSSKOGO JAZYKA

DokIMU......... DOKLADY I SOOBSCENIJA FILOLOGOCESKOGO FAKUL'TETA MOSKOVSKOGO UNIVERSITETA
Dolmetsch B...... BULLETIN (THE DOLMETSCH FOUNDATION)
Dom Comm....... DOMESTIC COMMERCE
Dom Eng........ DOMESTIC ENGINEERING
DOP UKR A...... DOPOVIDI AKADEMII NAUK UKRAINSKOI RSR. SERIYA A
DOP UKR B...... DOPOVIDI AKADEMII NAUK UKRAINSKOI RSR. SERIYA B
DoR........... DOWNSIDE REVIEW
DOWN BT........ DOWN BEAT
DownR......... DOWNSIDE REVIEW
DP............ DANCE PERSPECTIVES
DP............ DEUTSCHE PHILOLOGIE
DPAA.......... DISSERTAZIONI DELLA PONTIFICIA ACCADEMIA ROMAN DI ARCHEOLOGIA
DPDroh......... DOPOVIDI TA POVIDOMLENNJA. MATERIALY KONFERENCIJ DROHOBYC'KOHO DERZAVNOHO PEDAHOHICNOHO INSTYTUTU IM. I. JA. FRANKA. SERIJA FILOLOHICNYCH NAUK. DROHOBYC
DPL........... DE PROPRIETATIBUS LITTERARUM
DQ............ DENVER QUARTERLY
DQR........... DUTCH QUARTERLY REVIEW OF ANGLO-AMERICAN LETTERS
DR............ DALHOUSIE REVIEW
DR............ DEUTSCHE RUNDSCHAU
DR............ DRAMA: THE QUARTERLY THEATRE REVIEW
DR............ DUBLIN REVIEW
DR............ DUN'S REVIEW
DR............ DUQUESNE REVIEW
DRAE.......... DICCIONARIO DE LA REAL ACADEMIA ESPANOLA
Drake L Rev...... DRAKE LAW REVIEW
Dram.......... DRAMMATURGIA
Drama Surv....... DRAMA SURVEY
DramC......... DRAMA CRITIQUE
DramS......... DRAMA SURVEY
DrB........... DRIEMAANDELIJKSE BLADEN
DreiN.......... DREISER NEWSLETTER
DRev.......... DEUTSCHE REVUE
Drex Lib Q....... DREXEL LIBRARY QUARTERLY
DrG........... DREW GATEWAY
DrN........... DRUZHBA NARODOV
DRs........... DEUTSCHE RUNDSCHAU
DRSPAAJC....... DOCUMENTS ET RAPPORTS DE LA SOCIETE PALEONTOLOGIQUE ET ARCHEOLOGIQUE DE L'ARRONDISSEMENT JUDICIAIRE DE CHARLEROI
DRu........... DEUTSCHE RUNDSCHAU
DRUG ABU MS..... DRUG ABUSE COUNCIL MONOGRAPH SERIES
DRUG ABU PPS.... DRUB ABUSE COUNCIL PUBLIC POLICY SERIES
DRUG COSMET..... DRUG AND COSMETIC INDUSTRY
DRUG DEV C...... DRUG DEVELOPMENT COMMUNICATIONS
DRUG INTEL...... DRUG INTELLIGENCE AND CLINICAL PHARMACY
DRUG METAB..... DRUG METABOLISM REVIEWS
DRUG META D..... DRUG METABOLISM AND DISPOSITION
DS............ DANSKE STUDIER
DS............ DEUTSCHE STUDIEN
DS............ DIDEROT STUDIES
DS............ DOMINICAN STUDIES
DS............ DRAMA SURVEY

PERIODICAL TITLE ABBREVIATIONS

DS . . . . DYNAMIC STORIES
DSA . . . . DICKENS STUDIES ANNUAL
DSARDS . . . . DANTE STUDIES WITH THE ANNUAL REPORT OF THE DANTE SOCIETY
DSF . . . . DYNAMIC SCIENCE FICTION
DSFNS . . . . DEUTSCH-SLAWISCHE FORSCHUNGEN ZUR NAMENKUNDE UND SIEDLUNGSGESCHICHTE
DSG . . . . DEUTSCHE STUDIEN ZUR GEISTESGESCHICHTE
DSH . . . . DSH (DEAFNESS, SPEECH AND HEARING) ABSTRACTS
DSlJa . . . . DOKLADY I SOOBSCENIJA INSTITUTA JAZYKOZANIJA AKADEMIJI NAUK SSSR
DSL . . . . DANSKE SPROG-OG LITERATURSELSKAB
DSN . . . . DICKENS STUDIES NEWSLETTER
DSp . . . . DEUTSCHE SPRACHE
DSPS . . . . DUQUESNE STUDIES. PHILOLOGICAL SERIES
DSS . . . . DYNAMIC SCIENCE STORIES
DSS . . . . XVII SIECLE
DSt . . . . DANSKE STUDIER
DSt . . . . DEUTSCHE STUDIEN
DSUzU . . . . DOKLADY I SOOBSCENIJA UZGORODSKOGO UNIVERSITETA
DT . . . . DAILY TELEGRAPH
DT . . . . DIVUS THOMAS
DT . . . . DUSCEPOLEZNIE TCHTENIE
Dteol T . . . . DANSK TEOLOGISK TIDSSKRIFT
DTh . . . . DIVUS THOMAS
DTM . . . . DEUTSCHE TEXTE DES MITTELALTERS
Dtsch Luft Raumfahrt Mitt . . DEUTSCHE LUFT- UND RAUMFAHRT, MITTEILUNG
DTTid . . . . DANSK TEOLOGISK TIDSSKRIFT
DtVis . . . . DEUTSCHE VIERTELJAHRSSCHRIFT FUER LITERATURWISSENSCHAFT UND GEISTESGESCHICHTE
Dt Vischr . . . . DEUTSCHE VIERTELJAHRSSCHRIFT FUER LITERATURWISSENSCHAFT UND GEISTESGESCHICHTE
DU . . . . DEUTSCHUNTERRICHT
DUA . . . . DEUTSCHUNTERRICHT FUER AUSLAENDER
Dub Mag . . . . DUBLIN MAGAZINE
DubR . . . . DUBLIN Review
Dub Rev . . . . DUBLIN REVIEW
Dub Univ . . . . DUBLIN UNIVERSITY MAGAZINE
Dudley Ednl J . . . . . . DUDLEY EDUCATIONAL JOURNAL
DuE . . . . DICHTUNG UND ERKENNTNIS
Duesseldorfer Jahrb . . DUESSELDORFER JAHRBUCH
DUJ . . . . DURHAM UNIVERSITY JOURNAL
Duke B J . . . . DUKE BAR JOURNAL
Duke Div R . . . . . . DUKE DIVINITY SCHOOL REVIEW
DUKE MATH J . . . . . DUKE MATHEMATICAL JOURNAL
DULN . . . . DUKE UNIVERSITY LIBRARY NOTES
DULR . . . . DUBLIN UNIVERSITY LAW REVIEW
Duns Int R . . . . DUN'S INTERNATIONAL REVIEW
Duns R . . . . DUN'S REVIEW
Dun's Stat R . . . . . . DUN'S STATISTICAL REVIEW
Duquesne L Rev . . . . DUQUESNE LAW REVIEW
Duquesne U L Rev . . DUQUESNE UNIVERSITY LAW REVIEW
DURHAM RES . . . . . DURHAM RESEARCH REVIEW
DuV . . . . DICHTUNG UND VOLKSTUM
DuW . . . . DICHTUNG UND WIRKLICHKEIT
DUZ . . . . DEUTSCHE UNIVERSITAETSZEITUNG

DV . . . . DEUTSCHE VIERTELJAHRSSCHRIFT
DV . . . . DICHTUNG UND VOLKSTUM
DVJS . . . . DEUTSCHE VIERTELJAHRSSCHRIFT FUER LITERATURWISSENSCHAFT UND GEISTESGESCHICHTE
DVLG . . . . DEUTSCHE VIERTELJAHRSSCHRIFT FUER LITERATURWISSENSCHAFT UND GEISTESGESCHICHTE
DVSM . . . . DANSKE VIDENSKABERNES SELSKABS HISTORISHFILOLOGISKE MEDDELELSER
DVSS . . . . DANSKE VIDENSKABERNES SELSKABS SKRIFTER
DW . . . . DEUTSCHE WOCHE
DW . . . . DIE WELTLITERATUR
DWB . . . . DEUTSCHE WARANDE EN BELFORT
DWD . . . . DEUTSCHE WISSENSCHAFTLICHER DIENST
DWD . . . . DREAM WORLD
DWEV . . . . DEUTSCHE WISSENSCHAFT, ERZIEHUNG UND VOLKSBILDUNG
DWZP . . . . DEUTSCHE WISSENSCHAFTLICHE ZEITSCHRIFT FUER POLEN
DYNAM PSYCH . . . . DYNAMISCHE PSYCHIATRIE
DzD . . . . DZEJAS DIENA
DzKarSt . . . . DZVELI KARTULI ENIS K'ATEDRIS STOMEBI
DZKR . . . . DEUTSCHE ZEITSCHRIFT FUER KIRCHENRECHT
Dz Lit . . . . DZIENNIK LITERACKI

E

E..............ENGLISH
E..............EOS. COMMENTARII SOCIETATIS PHILOLOGAE POLONORUM
E..............ERASMUS
E..............ESCORIAL (MADRID)
E..............ESPRIT
EA.............ESTUDIOS AFROCUBANOS
EA.............ETUDES ANGLAISES
EAASN.........EAASN (EUROPEAN ASSOCIATION FOR AMERICAN STUDIES) NEWSLETTER
EADL...........ERLANGER ARBEITEN ZUR DEUTSCHEN LITERATUR
EAER...........EAST AFRICAN ECONOMIC REVIEW
E AFR ECON.......EASTERN AFRICA ECONOMIC REVIEW
E AFR MED J......EAST AFRICAN MEDICAL JOURNAL
E AFR STUD.......EAST AFRICAN STUDIES
EAI............ENGLAND-AMERIKA-INSTITUT
EAJ............EAST AFRICA JOURNAL
EAL............EARLY AMERICAN LITERATURE
EALN...........EARLY AMERICAN LITERATURE NEWSLETTER
EAm............ESTUDIOS AMERICANOS (SEVILLA)
EAn............ETUDES ANGLAISES
E & Ger St........ENGLISH AND GERMANIC STUDIES
E and G Stud......ENGLISH AND GERMANIC STUDIES
E&H............ECONOMY AND HISTORY
E & S............ESSAYS AND STUDIES
E & Th...........EGLISE ET THEOLOGIE
E&W............EAST AND WEST
E ANTHROPOL.....EASTERN ANTHROPOLOGIST
EAP............ENGLISH ASSOCIATION PAMPHLETS
EArch...........ETUDES ARCHEOLOGIQUES
Early Am Lit......EARLY AMERICAN LITERATURE
EArmS...........EREVANSKIJ ARMJANSKIJ GOSUDARSTVENNYK PEDAGOGICESKIJ INSTITUT IM. CHACATUR
                 ABOVJANA. SBORNIK NAUCNYCH TRUDOV. SERIJA RUSSKOGO JAZYKA
EARTH PLAN......EARTH AND PLANETARY SCIENCE LETTERS
Earthquake Eng Struct Dyn.. EARTHQUAKE ENGINEERING AND STRUCTURAL DYNAMICS
EARTH SCI R......EARTH SCIENCE REVIEWS
East Ch R........EASTERN CHURCHES REVIEW
Eastern Anthropol.. EASTERN ANTHROPOLOGIST
East Tenn Hist Soc Publ.. EAST TENNESSEE HISTORICAL SOCIETY. PUBLICATIONS
East Underw......EASTERN UNDERWRITER
EB.............EASTERN BUDDHIST
EB.............EDUCATIONAL BROADCASTING
EB.............ESTUDIOS BIBLICOS
EB.............ETUDES BALZACIENNES
EBB............EIBEI BUNGAKU (BRITISH AND AMERICAN LITERATURE: THE RIKKYO REVIEW OF ARTS AND
                LETTERS)
EBib...........ESTUDIOS BIBLICOS
EBR............EDUCATIONAL BROADCASTING REVIEW
EBS............EDINBURGH BIBLIOGRAPHICAL SOCIETY
EBSC...........EIBUNGAKU SHICHO (THOUGHT CURRENTS IN ENGLISH LITERATURE)
EBSK...........ERLANGER BEITRAGE ZUR SPRACH- UND KUNSTWISSENSCHAFT

EBT . . . . ETUDES BALKANIQUES TCHECOSLOVAQUES
EBTA J . . . . EBTA (EASTERN BUSINESS TEACHERS ASSOCIATION) JOURNAL
EBTA Y . . . . EBTA (EASTERN BUSINESS TEACHERS ASSOCIATION) YEARBOOK
E B Tch . . . . ETUDES BALKANIQUES TCHECOSLOVAQUES
EBU Rev Tech . . . . . EBU (EUROPEAN BROADCASTING UNION) REVIEW. TECHNICAL
EByz . . . . ETUDES BYZANTINES
EC . . . . ECONOMICA
EC . . . . ESSAYS IN CRITICISM
EC . . . . ETUDES CELTIQUES
ECarm . . . . EPHEMERIDES CARMELITICAE
ECB . . . . ESTUDOS DE CASTELO BRANCO
ECelt . . . . ETUDES CELTIQUES
ECh . . . . ENSEIGNEMENT CHRETIEN
ECHC . . . . ETUDES CARMELITAINES HISTORIQUES ET CRITIQUES
EChr . . . . ENSEIGNEMENT CHRETIEN
Eck . . . . ECKART
Eckart J . . . . ECKART JAHRBUCH
E CL . . . . ETUDES CLASSIQUES
ECLA . . . . ETUDES CLASSIQUES
EClas . . . . ESTUDIOS CLASICOS
Ecl Engin . . . . ECLECTIC ENGINEERING MAGAZINE (VAN NOSTRAND'S)
Ecl M . . . . ECLECTIC MAGAZINE
Ecl Mus . . . . ECLECTIC MUSEUM
Ecl R . . . . ECLECTIC REVIEW
ECMM . . . . ETUDES CARMELITAINES MYSTIQUES ET MISSIONNAIRES
ECN . . . . ESTUDIOS DE CULTURA NAHUATL
Ecol . . . . ECOLOGY
ECOL LAW Q . . . . . . ECOLOGY LAW QUARTERLY
ECOL MONOGR . . . . ECOLOGICAL MONOGRAPHS
Ecology L Q . . . . . . ECOLOGY LAW QUARTERLY
Econ . . . . ECONOMIST
EconAb . . . . ECONOMIC ABSTRACTS
ECON APPLIQ . . . . . ECONOMIE APPLIQUEE
Econ Bot . . . . ECONOMIC BOTANY
ECON BOTAN . . . . . . ECONOMIC BOTANY
Econ Comput Econ Cybern Stud Res . . ECONOMIC COMPUTATION AND ECONOMIC CYBERNETICS STUDIES AND
                                        RESEARCH
Econ Cont . . . . CONTENTS OF RECENT ECONOMICS JOURNALS
ECON DEV CU . . . . . ECONOMIC DEVELOPMENT AND CULTURAL CHANGE
Econ Geog . . . . ECONOMIC GEOGRAPHY
Econ Geol . . . . ECONOMIC GEOLOGY
Econ Hist . . . . ECONOMIC HISTORY
Econ Hist R . . . . . . ECONOMIC HISTORY REVIEW
EconHR . . . . ECONOMIC HISTORY REVIEW
ECON INQ . . . . ECONOMIC INQUIRY
Econ Inquiry . . . . . . ECONOMIC INQUIRY
Econ J . . . . ECONOMIC JOURNAL
Econ R . . . . ECONOMIC REVIEW
Econ Rec . . . . ECONOMIC RECORD
ECON SOCIET . . . . . . ECONOMY AND SOCIETY
ECON SOC R . . . . ECONOMIC AND SOCIAL REVIEW

Econ Stud........ ECONOMIC STUDIES
Econ W.......... ECONOMIC WORLD
Ec R........... ECUMENICAL REVIEW
ECr............ L'ESPRIT CREATEUR
ECr............ ESSAYS IN CRITICISM
ECS............ EIGHTEENTH CENTURY STUDIES
Fcumen Rev....... ECUMENICAL REVIEW
Ecum R......... ECUMENICAL REVIEW
Ed............. EDDA; REVUE DE LITTERATURE
Ed............. EDUCATION
ED............ EPHEMERIS DACOROMANA
EdAb........... EDUCATION ABSTRACTS
EdAd.......... EDUCATIONAL ADMINISTRATION ABSTRACTS
Ed Adm & Sup..... EDUCATIONAL ADMINISTRATION AND SUPERVISION
Ed Adm Q........ EDUCATIONAL ADMINISTRATION QUARTERLY
Ed & Psychol M.... EDUCATIONAL AND PSYCHOLOGICAL MEASUREMENT
Ed & Pub........ EDITOR AND PUBLISHER
Ed & Training..... EDUCATION AND TRAINING
Ed & Train Men Retard.. EDUCATION AND TRAINING OF THE MENTALLY RETARDED
Ed Arn.......... EDITIONES ARNAMAGNAENAE
EDB............ EMILY DICKINSON BULLETIN
Ed Can......... EDUCATION CANADA
Ed Cat.......... EDICIONES CATEDRA
EDCC.......... ECONOMIC DEVELOPMENT AND CULTURAL CHANGE
Ed Digest....... EDUCATION DIGEST
EDESA.......... EDICIONES ESPANOLAS S.A.
Ed Exec Overview.. EDUCATIONAL EXECUTIVE'S OVERVIEW
Ed for Dev....... EDUCATION FOR DEVELOPMENT
Ed for Teaching.... EDUCATION FOR TEACHING
Ed Forum........ EDUCATIONAL FORUM
EDH............ ESSAYS BY DIVERS HANDS
Ed Horiz........ EDUCATIONAL HORIZONS
EdI............. EDUCATION INDEX
EDICUDA........ EDITORIAL CUADERNOS PARA EL DIALOGO
Ed in Chem....... EDUCATION IN CHEMISTRY
Edin Rev......... EDINBURGH REVIEW
Ed in the North.... EDUCATION IN THE NORTH
EdL............ EDUCATIONAL LEADERSHIP
EdL............ ETUDES DE LETTRES (U. DE LAUSANNE)
Ed Lead......... EDUCATIONAL LEADERSHIP
Ed Lib Bulletin..... EDUCATION LIBRARIES BULLETIN
Ed Meth......... EDUCATIONAL METHOD
Ed Mo.......... EDINBURGH MONTHLY REVIEW
ED MUS.......... EDUCAZIONE MUSICALE
Ed Mus Mag...... EDUCATION MUSIC MAGAZINE
Ed New Philos J.... EDINBURGH NEW PHILOSOPHICAL JOURNAL
Ednl Administration Bull.. EDUCATIONAL ADMINISTRATION BULLETIN
Ednl Dev........ EDUCATIONAL DEVELOPMENT
Ednl Dev International.. EDUCATIONAL DEVELOPMENT INTERNATIONAL
Ednl R.......... EDUCATIONAL REVIEW
Ednl Studies in Maths.. EDUCATIONAL STUDIES IN MATHEMATICS

Ed Outl . . . . EDUCATIONAL OUTLOOK
Ed Philos J . . . . EDINBURGH PHILOSOPHICAL JOURNAL
Ed Prod Rep . . . . EDUCATIONAL PRODUCT REPORT
Ed R . . . . EDINBURGH REVIEW
Ed R . . . . EDUCATIONAL REVIEW (BRITISH)
Ed R China . . . . EDUCATIONAL REVIEW (CHINA)
Ed Rec . . . . EDUCATIONAL RECORD
Ed Rec Bur Bul . . . . . EDUCATIONAL RECORDS BUREAU BULLETINS
Ed Res . . . . EDUCATIONAL RESEARCH (BRITISH)
Ed Res B . . . . EDUCATIONAL RESEARCH BULLETIN
Ed Res Record . . . . . EDUCATIONAL RESEARCH RECORD
EDRS . . . . ERIC DOCUMENT REPRODUCTION SERVICE
EdS . . . . ECRITS DES SAINTS
EDS . . . . ENGLISH DANCE AND SONG
EDS . . . . ESSAYS BY DIVERS HANDS
Ed Screen . . . . EDUCATIONAL SCREEN
Ed Screen AV G . . . . EDUCATIONAL SCREEN AV GUIDE
Ed Survey . . . . EDUCATIONAL SURVEY
Ed Tech . . . . EDUCATIONAL TECHNOLOGY
Ed Theatre J . . . . . . EDUCATIONAL THEATRE JOURNAL
Ed Theory . . . . EDUCATIONAL THEORY
Ed TV Int . . . . EDUCATIONAL TELEVISION INTERNATIONAL
Educ . . . . EDUCATION
Educa . . . . EDUCATION
Educ Adm & Sup . . . . EDUCATIONAL ADMINISTRATION AND SUPERVISION
EDUC ADMIN . . . . . . EDUCATIONAL ADMINISTRATION QUARTERLY
Educ Adm Q . . . . EDUCATIONAL ADMINISTRATION QUARTERLY
Educ & Psychol Meas . . EDUCATIONAL AND PSYCHOLOGICAL MEASUREMENT
Educ & Train . . . . . . EDUCATION & TRAINING
Educ & Train Mentally Retard . . EDUCATION AND TRAINING OF THE MENTALLY RETARDED
Educa R . . . . EDUCATIONAL REVIEW
Educ Broad Int . . . . . EDUCATIONAL BROADCASTING INTERNATIONAL
Educ Can . . . . EDUCATION CANADA
Educ Digest . . . . EDUCATION DIGEST
EducF . . . . EDUCATIONAL FORUM
Educ Horiz . . . . EDUCATIONAL HORIZONS
Educ Lead . . . . EDUCATIONAL LEADERSHIP
EDUC LG CIT . . . . . . EDUCATION IN LARGE CITIES
Educ Media Int . . . . EDUCATIONAL MEDIA INTERNATIONAL
Educ Mus Mag . . . . . EDUCATIONAL MUSIC MAGAZINE
Educ Outl . . . . EDUCATIONAL OUTLOOK
Educ Phil Theor . . . . EDUCATIONAL PHILOSOPHY AND THEORY
Educ Prod Rept . . . . EDUCATIONAL PRODUCT REPORT
EDUC PSYC M . . . . . EDUCATIONAL AND PSYCHOLOGICAL MEASUREMENT
Educ R . . . . EDUCATIONAL REVIEW
EDUC REC . . . . EDUCATIONAL RECORD
Educ Rec Bur Bull . . . EDUCATIONAL RECORDS BUREAU. BULLETINS
Educ Res . . . . EDUCATIONAL RESEARCH
Educ Res Bul . . . . . . EDUCATIONAL RESEARCH BULLETIN
Educ Rev . . . . EDUCATION REVIEW
Educ Screen . . . . . . EDUCATIONAL SCREEN

Educ Tech . . . . EDUCATIONAL TECHNOLOGY
Educ Theatre J . . . . . EDUCATIONAL THEATRE JOURNAL
Educ Theor . . . . EDUCATIONAL THEORY
Educ Theory . . . . . . EDUCATIONAL THEORY
EDUC TRAIN . . . . . . EDUCATION AND TRAINING OF THE MENTALLY RETARDED
EDUC URBAN . . . . . . EDUCATION AND URBAN SOCIETY
Educ Urb Soc . . . . . . EDUCATION AND URBAN SOCIETY
Educ Vict . . . . EDUCATION FOR VICTORY
Ed Vis Hand . . . . EDUCATION OF THE VISUALLY HANDICAPPED
EDUC VISUAL . . . . . EDUCATION OF THE VISUALLY HANDICAPPED
EE . . . . EAST EUROPE
EE . . . . ELEMENTARY ENGLISH
EE . . . . ENLIGHTENMENT ESSAYS
EE . . . . ERASMUS IN ENGLISH
EE . . . . ESTUDIOS ECCLESIASTICO
EE . . . . ESTUDIOS ERUDITOS EN MEMORIAM DE BONILLA Y SAN MARTIN
EEE . . . . EASTERN EUROPEAN ECONOMICS
EEG CL NEUR . . . . . . ELECTROENCEPHALOGRAPHY AND CLINICAL NEUROPHYSIOLOGY-EEG JOURNAL
EEH . . . . EXPLORATIONS IN ENTREPRENEURIAL HISTORY
EEI Bul . . . . EDISON ELECTRIC INSTITUTE BULLETIN
EEMB . . . . ESTUDIOS EN MEMORIAM DE BONILLA Y SAN MARTIN
EEMCA . . . . ESTUDIOS DE EDAD MEDIA DE LA CORONA DE ARAGON
EEPSAPT . . . . EPISTEMONIKE EPETERIS PHILOSOPHIKES SCHOLES ARISTOTELEIOU PANEPISTEMIOU THES-
SALONIKES
EEPSPA . . . . EPISTEMONIKE EPETERIS TES PHILOLOPHIKES SCHOLES TOU PANEPISTEMIOU ATHENON
EESB . . . . EXPRESSION: JOURNAL OF THE ENGLISH SOCIETY
EE/Systems Eng . . . . EE/SYSTEMS ENGINEERING TODAY
EETS . . . . EARLY ENGLISH TEXT SOCIETY
E EUR ECON . . . . . . EASTERN EUROPEAN ECONOMICS
E EUROPE Q . . . . . . EASTERN EUROPEAN QUARTERLY
E Eur Q . . . . EAST EUROPEAN QUARTERLY
EF . . . . ESTUDIS FRANCISCANS
EF . . . . ETUDES FRANCISCAINES
EFF WAT TRE . . . . . . EFFLUENT AND WATER TREATMENT JOURNAL
EFil . . . . ESTUDIOS FILOLOGICOS
EFL . . . . ESSAYS IN FRENCH LITERATURE (U OF WESTERN AUSTRALIA)
EFR . . . . EDITEURS FRANCAIS REUNIS
EFran . . . . ETUDES FRANCISCAINES
EFT . . . . ENGLISH FICTION IN TRANSITION (1880-1920)
EG . . . . ECONOMIC GEOGRAPHY
EG . . . . ENGLISH AND GERMANIC STUDIES
EG . . . . ESTUDIOS GEOGRAFICOS
EG . . . . ETUDES GERMANIQUES
EgC . . . . EGYPTE CONTEMPORAINE
EGerm . . . . ETUDES GERMANIQUES
Egg Prod . . . . EGG PRODUCER
Eglise Th . . . . EGLISE ET THEOLOGIE
EgR . . . . EGYPTIAN RELIGION
EGS . . . . ENGLISH AND GERMANIC STUDIES
EGYPT J CH . . . . . . EGYPTIAN JOURNAL OF CHEMISTRY
EH . . . . EASTERN HORIZON (HONG KONG)

EH . . . . ECONOMIC HISTORY
EH . . . . EUROPAEISCHE HOCHSCHULSCHRIFTEN
EHBS . . . . EPETERIS TES HETAIREIAS BYZANTINON SPOUDON
EHJ . . . . ECONOMISCH-HISTORISCH JAARBOEK
EHKM . . . . EPETERIS HETAIREIAS KYKLADIKON MELETON
EHR . . . . ECONOMIC HISTORY REVIEW
EHR . . . . ENGLISH HISTORICAL REVIEW
EHSE . . . . ESTUDIOS DE HISTORIA SOCIAL DE ESPANA
EHSM . . . . EPETERIS HETAIREIAS STEREOELLADIKON MELETON
EI . . . . ECONOMIA INTERNAZIONALE
EI . . . . ETUDES ITALIENNES
EIB . . . . EDUCATIONAL/INSTRUCTIONAL BROADCASTING
EIC . . . . EPHEMERIDES IURIS CANONICI
EIC . . . . ESSAYS IN CRITICISM
Eidg Tech Hochsch Versuchsanst Wasserbau Erdbau Mitt . . EIDGENOESSISCHE TECHNISCHE HOCHSCHULE,
. . . . VERSUCHSANSTALT FUER WASSERBAU UND ERDBAU, MITTEILUNGEN (ZURICH)
EIE . . . . ENGLISH INSTITUTE ESSAYS
Eig . . . . EIGSE
18th Cent Stud . . . . EIGHTEENTH-CENTURY STUDIES
Eigo S . . . . EIGO SEINEN
EIHC . . . . ESSEX INSTITUTE HISTORICAL COLLECTIONS
EiL . . . . EZIK I LITERATURA
EIP . . . . ESTUDOS ITALIANOS EM PORTUGAL
Eire . . . . IRELAND: A JOURNAL OF IRISH STUDIES
EIRJa . . . . ETIMOLOGICESKIE ISSLEDOVANIJA PO RUSSKOMU JAZYKU
EIUES . . . . ENGLISH INSTITUTE OF THE UNIVERSITY OF UPPSALA. ESSAYS AND STUDIES ON ENGLISH
. . . . LANGUAGE AND LITERATURE
EJ . . . . ECONOMIC JOURNAL
EJ . . . . EDOTH (JERUSALEM)
EJ . . . . ENGLISH JOURNAL
EJ . . . . ESTUDIOS JOSEFINOS
EJEV . . . . EUSKO-JAKINTZA. REVISTA DE ESTUDIOS VASCOS
EKEEK . . . . EPETERIS TOU KENTROU EPISTEMONIKON EREUNON KYPROU
EKEHL . . . . EPETERIS TOU KENTROU EREUNES TES HELLENIKES LAOGRAPHIAS
EKI . . . . EKISTIC INDEX
EKI . . . . EKONOMI DAN KEUANGAN INDONESIA
EKON CAS . . . . EKONOMICKY CASOPIS
EKON-MATH O . . . . . EKONOMICKO-MATEMATICKY OBZOR
EKON SAMF T . . . . . EKONOMISKA SAMFUNDETS TIDSKRIFT
EL . . . . EDUCATIONAL LEADERSHIP
EL . . . . EPHEMERIDES LITURGICAE
EL . . . . ETUDES DE LETTRES
EI . . . . ETUDES ITALIENNES
EL . . . . EUROPA LETTERARIA
EL . . . . EUROPAEISCHE LITERATUR
EL . . . . EZIK I LITERATURA
ELA . . . . ETUDES DE LINGUISTIQUE APPLIQUEE
ELCFR . . . . ENGLISH LINGUISTICS, 1500-1800: A COLLECTION OF FACSIMILE REPRINTS
ELEC . . . . ENGLISH LANGUAGE EDUCATION COUNCIL. BULLETIN
ELEC . . . . ETUDES DE LITTERATURE ETRANGERE ET COMPAREE
Elec Com . . . . ELECTRICAL COMMUNICATION

ELEC COMMUN.... ELECTRICAL COMMUNICATION
Elec Constr Maint.. ELECTRICAL CONSTRUCTION AND MAINTENANCE
Elec Eng......... ELECTRICAL ENGINEERING
Elec Eng Japan..... ELECTRICAL ENGINEERING IN JAPAN
Elec Eng (Melbourne).. ELECTRICAL ENGINEER (MELBOURNE)
Elec Eng Rev...... ELECTRICAL ENGINEERING REVIEW
ELEC EN JAP...... ELECTRICAL ENGINEERING IN JAPAN
Elec Fr Bull Dir Etud Rech Ser A Nucl Hydraul Therm.. ELECTRICITE DE FRANCE. BULLETIN DE LA DIRECTION DES ETUDES ET RECHERCHES. SERIE A. NUCLEAIRE, HYDRAULIQUE, THERMIQUE
Elec Fr Bull Dir Etud Rech Ser B Reseaux Elec Mater Elec.. ELECTRICITE DE FRANCE. BULLETIN DE LA DIRECTION DES ETUDES ET RECHERCHES. SERIE B. RESEAUX ELECTRIQUES, MATERIELS ELECTRIQUES
Elec Furnace Conf Proc AIME.. ELECTRIC FURNACE CONFERENCE PROCEEDINGS. METALLURGICAL SOCIETY OF AIME. IRON AND STEEL DIVISION
Elec J........... ELECTRICAL JOURNAL
Elec Manuf....... ELECTRICAL MANUFACTURING
Elec Merch....... ELECTRICAL MERCHANDISING
Elec Merch W..... ELECTRICAL MERCHANDISING WEEK
Elec Mus R....... ELECTRONIC MUSIC REVIEW
Elec News Eng..... ELECTRICAL NEWS AND ENGINEERING
Elec r.......... ELECTRICAL REVIEW
Elec Res Ass ERA Rep.. ELECTRICAL RESEARCH ASSOCIATION. ERA REPORT
ELEC REV......... ELECTRICAL REVIEW
Elec Ry J......... ELECTRIC RAILWAY JOURNAL
Elec Technol USSR.. ELECTRIC TECHNOLOGY (USSR)
ELEC TECH R...... ELECTRIC TECHNOLOGY (USSR)
Elect Electron Mfr.. ELECTRICAL AND ELECTRONICS MANUFACTURER
Elect J........... ELECTRIC JOURNAL
Elect Pwr........ ELECTRICAL POWER ENGINEER
Elect Pwr Engr..... ELECTRICAL POWER ENGINEER
ELECTR ACT....... ELECTROCHIMICA ACTA
ELECTR CO J...... ELECTRONICS AND COMMUNICATIONS IN JAPAN
Electr Commun.... ELECTRICAL COMMUNICATION
ELECTR ENG....... ELECTRONIC ENGINEERING
Electr Eng Jap..... ELECTRICAL ENGINEERING IN JAPAN
Electr Eng (Melb)... ELECTRICAL ENGINEER (MELBOURNE)
Electr Eng Rev..... ELECTRICAL ENGINEERING REVIEW
Elect Rev......... ELECTRICAL REVIEW
Electr Fr Bull Dir Etud Rech Ser A Nucl Hydraul Therm.. ELECTRICITE DE FRANCE, BULLETIN DE LA DIRECTION DES ETUDES ET RECHERCHES. SERIE A. NUCLEAIRE, HYDRAULIQUE, THERMIQUE
Electr Fr Bull Dir Etud Rech Ser B Reseaux Electr Mater Electr.. ELECTRICITE DE FRANCE. BULLETIN DE LA DIRECTION DES ETUDES ET RECHERCHES. SERIE B. RESEAUX ELECTRIQUES, MATERIELS ELECTRIQUES
Electr Furn Proc Metall Soc AIME.. ELECTRIC FURNACE PROCEEDINGS. METALLURGICAL SOCIETY OF AIME. IRON AND STEEL DIVISION
ELECTR LETT...... ELECTRONICS LETTERS
Electrochem Soc J.. ELECTROCHEMICAL SOCIETY. JOURNAL
Electrochem Tech.. ELECTROCHEMICAL TECHNOLOGY
Electrochim Acta... ELECTROCHIMICA ACTA
Electrochim Metal.. ELECTROCHIMICA METALLORUM
Electromech Des... ELECTROMECHANICAL DESIGN
Electron Appl...... ELECTRONIC APPLICATIONS
Electron Appl Bull.. ELECTRONIC APPLICATIONS BULLETIN

Electron Commun Japan . . ELECTRONICS AND COMMUNICATIONS IN JAPAN
Electron Compon . . . ELECTRONIC COMPONENTS
Electron Des . . . . . . ELECTRONIC DESIGN
Electron Eng (Lond) . . ELECTRONIC ENGINEERING (LONDON)
Electron Eng (Phila) . . ELECTRONIC ENGINEER (PHILADELPHIA)
Electronic & Radio Eng . . ELECTRONIC AND RADIO ENGINEER
Electronic Ind & Tele-Tech . . ELECTRONIC INDUSTRIES AND TELE-TECH
Electronic N . . . . . . ELECTRONIC NEWS
Electron Ind Ass Eng Dep EIA Stand . . ELECTRONIC INDUSTRIES ASSOCIATION, ENGINEERING DEPARTMENT.
EIA STANDARD
Electron Lett . . . . . . ELECTRONICS LETTERS
Electron Med . . . . . . ELECTRONIQUE MEDICALE
Electron Mfr . . . . . . ELECTRONICS MANUFACTURER
Electron Nouv . . . . . ELECTRONIQUE NOUVELLE
Electron Packag Prod . . ELECTRONIC PACKAGING AND PRODUCTION
Electron Power . . . . ELECTRONICS AND POWER
Electron Prod . . . . . ELECTRONIC PRODUCTS
Electron Pwr . . . . . . ELECTRONICS AND POWER
Electron Technol . . . ELECTRON TECHNOLOGY
Electron Technol Q . . ELECTRON TECHNOLOGY QUARTERLY
Electron Wkly . . . . . ELECTRONICS WEEKLY
Electro-Opt Syst Des . . ELECTRO-OPTICAL SYSTEMS DESIGN
Electroplat Met Finish . . ELECTROPLATING AND METAL FINISHING
Electro-Tech . . . . . . ELECTRO-TECHNIEK
Electro-Tech . . . . . . ELECTRO-TECHNOLOGY
ELECTR POW . . . . . . ELECTRONICS AND POWER
ELECTR PROD . . . . . ELECTRONIC PRODUCTS MAGAZINE
Electr Technol (USSR) . . ELECTRIC TECHNOLOGY (USSR)
Elect Supervis . . . . . ELECTRICAL SUPERVISOR
Elect Times . . . . . . ELECTRICAL TIMES
Elec West . . . . ELECTRICAL WEST
Elec World . . . . ELECTRICAL WORLD
Elek Bahnen . . . . . . ELEKTRISCHE BAHNEN
Elektr Bahnen . . . . . ELEKTRISCHE BAHNEN
Elektron Datenverarb . . ELEKTRONISCHE DATENVERARBEITUNG
Elektron Obrab Mater . . ELEKTRONNAYA OBRABOTKA MATERIALOV
Elektron Rechenanlagen . . ELEKTRONISCHE RECHENANLAGEN
Electro-Tech . . . . . . ELECTRO-TECHNIEK
Elektrotech Maschinenbau . . ELEKTROTECHNIK UND MASCHINENBAU
Elektrotech Obz . . . . ELEKTROTECHNICKY OBZOR
Elektrotech Z Ausg A . . ELEKTROTECHNISCHE ZEITSCHRIFT. AUSGABE A
Elektrotech Z Ausg B . . ELEKTROTECHNISCHE ZEITSCHRIFT. AUSGABE B
Elektrotech Zeit . . . ELEKTROTECHNISCHE ZEITSCHRIFT
Elektroteh Vestn . . . ELEKTROTEHNISKI VESTNIK
Elektrotek Tidsskr . . ELEKTROTEKNISK TIDSSKRIFT
Elektrowaerme Int . . ELEKTROWAERME INTERNATIONAL
ELEKTR Z B . . . . ELEKTROTECHNISCHE ZEITSCHRIFT. AUSGABE B
ELEM SCH J . . . . ELEMENTARY SCHOOL JOURNAL
El Engl . . . . ELEMENTARY ENGLISH
El Engl R . . . . ELEMENTARY ENGLISH REVIEW
ELet . . . . EUROPA LETTERARIA

ELETTROTECN . . . . . ELETTROTECNICA
ELF . . . . ETUDE DE LA LANGUE FRANCAISE
Elin-Z . . . . ELIN-ZEITSCHRIFT
ELiT . . . . ENGLISH LITERATURE IN TRANSITION
ELit . . . . ESTAFETA LITERARIA
ELit . . . . ETUDES LITTERAIRES
ElizS . . . . ELIZABETHAN STUDIES
ELkT . . . . EPITHEORESE LOGOU KAI TECHNES
ELL . . . . ENGLISH LANGUAGE AND LITERATURE (KOREA)
ELLF . . . . ETUDES DE LANGUE ET DE LITTERATURE FRANCAISES
ELL . . . . ENGLISH LITERATURE AND LANGUAGE (TOKYO)
ELM . . . . EL UROGALLO (MADRID)
ELN . . . . ENGLISH LANGUAGE NOTES
El Pal . . . . EL PALACIO
ELR . . . . ENGLISH LITERARY RENAISSANCE
Els . . . . ELSINORE
El Sch Guid & Counsel . . ELEMENTARY SCHOOL GUIDANCE AND COUNSELING
El Sch J . . . . ELEMENTARY SCHOOL JOURNAL
El School T . . . . ELEMENTARY SCHOOL TEACHER
ELSM . . . . ELS MARGES (BARCELONA)
ELT . . . . ENGLISH LANGUAGE TEACHING
ELT . . . . ENGLISH LITERATURE IN TRANSITION (1800-1920)
ELu . . . . ESTUDIOS LULIANOS
ELul . . . . ESTUDIOS LULIANOS
EM . . . . ECONOMETRICA
Em . . . . EMERITA
EM . . . . ENGLISH MISCELLANY
EM . . . . ESPANA MISIONERA
EM . . . . ETHNOMUSICOLOGY
EMAAA . . . . EPETERIS MESAIONIKOU ARCHEIOU AKADEMIAS ATHENON
EmAb . . . . EMPLOYMENT RELATIONS ABSTRACTS
EM&D J Eng Mater Compon Des . . EM&D. JOURNAL OF ENGINEERING MATERIALS COMPONENTS AND DESIGN
EM&D Prod Data . . . EM&D PRODUCT DATA
EMC . . . . EL MONTE CARMELO
EMC . . . . EL MUSEO CANARIO
EMD . . . . ENGLISH MISCELLANY. ST. STEPHEN'S COLLEGE (DELHI)
Emer . . . . EMERITA
EMM . . . . ETUDES DE METAPHYSIQUE ET DE MORALE
Emp For J . . . . EMPIRE FORESTRY JOURNAL
Emp J Exp Ag . . . . . . EMPIRE JOURNAL OF EXPERIMENTAL AGRICULTURE
Emporia St Res Stud . . EMPORIA STATE RESEARCH STUDIES
EmSA . . . . EMAKEELE SELTSI AASTARAAMAT
EMSCD . . . . ENGLISH MISCELLANY. ST. STEPHEN'S COLLEGE (DELHI)
EMW . . . . ENQUETES DU MUSEE DE LA VIE WALLONNE
En . . . . ENCOUNTER
EN . . . . EDUCATION NATIONALE
ENC . . . . ELS NOSTRES CLASSICS
ENC . . . . ENCOUNTER
Encount . . . . ENCOUNTER
ENDOCR EXP . . . . . ENDOCRINOLOGIA EXPERIMENTALIS
ENDOCRINOL . . . . . ENDOCRINOLOGY

ENDOCR JAP...... ENDOCRINOLOGIA JAPONICA
ENDOCR RES...... ENDOCRINE RESEARCH COMMUNICATIONS
ENDOKRINOL...... ENDOKRINOLOGIE
ENERGA ATOM.... ENERGIA ES ATOMTECHNIKA
ENERGA NU....... ENERGIA NUCLEARE
ENERGA NUCL..... ENERGIA NUCLEARE
Energ Elet........ ENERGIA ELETTRICA
Energ Fluide...... ENERGIE FLUIDE
Energietech....... ENERGIETECHNIK
Energ Nucl (Milan).. ENERGIA NUCLEARE (MILAN)
Energ Nucl (Paris).. ENERGIE NUCLEAIRE (PARIS)
ENERG POLIC...... ENERGY POLICY
Energ Technik..... ENERGIE UND TECHNIK
ENERGY CONV..... ENERGY CONVERSION
Energy Dig....... ENERGY DIGEST
EnF............. ENCONTRO COM O FOLCLORE
Eng............. ENGLISH
Engage/Soc Act.... ENGAGE/SOCIAL ACTION
Eng & Contr....... ENGINEERING AND CONTRACTING
Eng & Instrumentation.. ENGINEERING AND INSTRUMENTATION
Eng & Min J....... ENGINEERING AND MINING JOURNAL
Eng Boilerhouse Rev.. ENGINEERING AND BOILERHOUSE REVIEW
Eng Contract Rec... ENGINEERING AND CONTRACT RECORD
Eng Cybern....... ENGINEERING CYBERNETICS
ENG DANCE....... ENGLISH DANCE AND SONG
Eng Dig.......... ENGINEERS' DIGEST
Eng Dom M....... ENGLISHWOMAN'S DOMESTIC MAGAZINE
Eng Economist..... ENGINEERING ECONOMIST
Eng Educ......... ENGINEERING EDUCATION
Engelhard Ind Tech Bull.. ENGELHARD INDUSTRIES. TECHNICAL BULLETIN
Eng FD&S Soc Jl.... ENGLISH FOLK DANCE AND SONG SOCIETY. JOURNAL
Eng Fract Mech.... ENGINEERING FRACTURE MECHANICS
Eng Geol......... ENGINEERING GEOLOGY
Eng Hist R........ ENGLISH HISTORICAL REVIEW
Engl............. ENGINEERING INDEX
Eng Illust......... ENGLISH ILLUSTRATED MAGAZINE
Engin M.......... ENGINEERING MAGAZINE
Engin N.......... ENGINEERING NEWS RECORD
ENG J........... ENGINEERING JOURNAL OF THE AMERICAN INSTITUTE OF STEEL CONSTRUCTION
Eng J............ ENGLISH JOURNAL
Eng J (Montreal)... ENGINEERING JOURNAL (MONTREAL)
Eng Lang Notes.... ENGLISH LANGUAGE NOTES
Eng Lang Teach J... ENGLISH LANGUAGE TEACHING JOURNAL
Engl Elec J........ ENGLISH ELECTRIC JOURNAL
Engl Hist R....... ENGLISH HISTORICAL REVIEW
ENGLISH HIS...... ENGLISH HISTORICAL REVIEW
English in Ed...... ENGLISH IN EDUCATION
Eng Lit In Trans.... ENGLISH LITERATURE IN TRANSITION
Engl J........... ENGLISH JOURNAL
Engl J (Col Ed)..... ENGLISH JOURNAL (COLLEGE EDITION)
Engl J (H S ED)..... ENGLISH JOURNAL (HIGH SCHOOL EDITION)

Engl Lang notes. . . . ENGLISH LANGUAGE NOTES
Engl Lang Teach. . . . ENGLISH LANGUAGE TEACHING
Engl Rec. . . . . ENGLISH RECORD
Engl Rev. . . . . ENGLISH REVIEW
Engl Stud. . . . . ENGLISCHE STUDIEN
Engl Stud. . . . . ENGLISH STUDIES
Eng M. . . . . ENGINEERING MAGAZINE
ENG MAT DES. . . . . ENGINEERING MATERIALS AND DESIGN
Eng Mater Des. . . . . ENGINEERING MATERIALS AND DESIGN
Eng Med. . . . . ENGINEERING IN MEDICINE
Eng Mineracao Met. . ENGENHARIA, MINERACAO, METALURGIA
Eng Min J. . . . . ENGINEERING AND MINING JOURNAL
Eng N. . . . . ENGINEERING NEWS-RECORD
Eng News-Rec. . . . . ENGINEERING NEWS-RECORD
Engng Des. . . . . ENGINEERING DESIGNER
Engng Mater Des. . . ENGINEERING MATERIALS AND DESIGN
Engng Prod. . . . . . . ENGINEERING PRODUCTION
Eng Prod. . . . . ENGINEERING PRODUCTION
Eng Progr Univ Fla Bull. . ENGINEERING PROGRESS. UNIVERSITY OF FLORIDA. BULLETIN
Eng Progr Univ Fla Tech Progr Rep. . ENGINEERING PROGRESS. UNIVERSITY OF FLORIDA. TECHNICAL PROGRESS
REPORT
EngR. . . . . ENGLISH RECORD
EngR. . . . . ENGLISH REVIEW
Engrs Dig. . . . . ENGINEERS' DIGEST
EngS. . . . . ENGLISH STUDIES (AMSTERDAM)
Eng Soc Libr ESL Bibliogr. . ENGINEERING SOCIETIES LIBRARY. ESL BIBLIOGRAPHY
Eng Soc W Pa. . . . . . PROCEEDINGS OF THE ENGINEERS' SOCIETY OF WESTERN PENNSYLVANIA
Eng St. . . . . ENGLISH STUDIES
Eng Stud. . . . . ENGLISCHE STUDIEN
Eng Stud. . . . . ENGLISH STUDIES
Eng Studn. . . . . ENGLISCHE STUDIEN
Enl E. . . . . ENLIGHTENMENT ESSAYS
Ensay Estud. . . . . . . ENSAYOS Y ESTUDIOS
ENT EXP APP. . . . . . ENTOMOLOGIA EXPERIMENTALIS ET APPLICATA
Entom N. . . . . ENTOMOLOGICAL NEWS
Entom News. . . . . . ENTOMOLOGICAL NEWS
Entom Soc Am Ann. . ENTOMOLOGICAL SOCIETY OF AMERICA. ANNALS
Env. . . . . ENVIRONMENT INFORMATION ACCESS
ENV ENTOMOL. . . . . ENVIRONMENTAL ENTOMOLOGY
Envl. . . . . ENVIRONMENT INDEX
ENVIR BEHAV. . . . . ENVIRONMENT AND BEHAVIOR
ENVIR GEOL. . . . . . . ENVIRONMENTAL GEOLOGY
ENVIR LETT. . . . . . . ENVIRONMENTAL LETTERS
Environ Aff. . . . . . . ENVIRONMENTAL AFFAIRS
Environ Behav. . . . . ENVIRONMENT AND BEHAVIOR
Environ Contr Manage. . ENVIRONMENTAL CONTROL MANAGEMENT
Environ Contr Safety Manage. . ENVIRONMENTAL CONTROL AND SAFETY MANAGEMENT
Environ Eng. . . . . . . ENVIRONMENTAL ENGINEERING
Environ Health. . . . . ENVIRONMENTAL HEALTH
Environ Lett. . . . . . . ENVIRONMENTAL LETTERS

Environ Pollut . . . . . ENVIRONMENTAL POLLUTION
Environ Quart . . . . . ENVIRONMENTAL QUARTERLY
Environ Res . . . . ENVIRONMENTAL RESEARCH
Environ Sci Technol . . ENVIRONMENTAL SCIENCE & TECHNOLOGY
Environ Space Sci . . . ENVIRONMENTAL SPACE SCIENCES
ENVIR PLANN . . . . . ENVIRONMENT AND PLANNING
ENVIR POLLU . . . . . . ENVIRONMENTAL POLLUTION
ENVIR RES . . . . ENVIRONMENTAL RESEARCH
Envir Sci & Tech . . . . ENVIRONMENTAL SCIENCE & TECHNOLOGY
ENV PHYS BI . . . . . . ENVIRONMENTAL PHYSIOLOGY & BIOCHEMISTRY
ENV SCI TEC . . . . . . ENVIRONMENTAL SCIENCE & TECHNOLOGY
EO . . . . EOHOS D'ORIENT
EO . . . . EUROPAISCHE OSTEN
EO . . . . EUROPE ORIENTALE
EOMC . . . . ESTUDIOS ORIENTALES (MEXICO CITY)
EOP . . . . ECONOMICS OF PLANNING
EP . . . . ECONOMIC PAPERS
EP . . . . EDITOR AND PUBLISHER
EP . . . . ETUDES PAPYROLOGIQUES
EP . . . . ETUDES PHILOSOPHIQUES
EPap . . . . ETUDES DE PAPYROLOGIE
EPESA . . . . EDICIONES Y PUBLICACIONES ESPANOLAS S.A.
EPh . . . . ECCLESIASTICOS PHAROS
EpH . . . . EPEIROTIKE HESTIA
EPh . . . . ETUDES PHILOSOPHIQUES
EphC . . . . EPHEMERIDES CARMELITICAE
EPhK . . . . EGYETEMES PHILOLOGIAI KOZLONY
EphL . . . . EPHEMERIDES LITURGICAE (ROMA)
Eph Th L . . . . EPHEMERIDES THEOLOGICAE LOVANIENSES
EPM . . . . EDUCATIONAL AND PSYCHOLOGICAL MEASUREMENT
EPM . . . . ETUDES DE PHILOSOPHIE MEDIEVALE
EPNS . . . . ENGLISH PLACE-NAME SOCIETY
EPo . . . . ESPERIENZA POETICA
EPr . . . . ETUDES DE PRESSE
EPS . . . . ENGLISH PHILOLOGICAL STUDIES
EPsM . . . . EDUCATIONAL AND PSYCHOLOGICAL MEASUREMENT
EPubl . . . . ENSEIGNEMENT PUBLIC
ER . . . . ECCLESIASTICAL REVIEW
ER . . . . ECONOMIC RECORD
ER . . . . ECUMENICAL REVIEW
ER . . . . EDINBURGH REVIEW
ER . . . . EDUCATIONAL REVIEW
ER . . . . ENGLISH REVIEW
Er . . . . ERANOS
Er . . . . ERIU
ER . . . . ESTUDIS ROMANICS
ER . . . . ETERNELLE REVUE
ER . . . . ETUDES RABELAISIENNES
ER . . . . ETUDES RHODANIENNES
ER . . . . EVERGREEN REVIEW
ERab . . . . ETUDES RABELAISIENNES

PERIODICAL TITLE ABBREVIATIONS

Eranos-Jb . . . . ERANOS-JAHRBUCH
Erasmus E . . . . ERASMUS IN ENGLISH
ErasmusR . . . . ERASMUS REVIEW
ErasR . . . . ERASMUS REVIEW
ERB . . . . EDUCATIONAL RESEARCH BULLETIN
ERB . . . . ETUDES ROMANES DE BRNO
Erbe der B . . . . ERBE DER VERGANGENHEIT
ERBr . . . . ETUDES ROMANES DE BRNO
ERD KOH EPB . . . . . . ERDOL UND KOHLE ERDAS PETROCHEMIE VEREINIGT MIT BRENNSTOFFCHEMIE
Erdoel-Erdgas-Z . . . . ERDOEL-ERDGAS-ZEITSCHRIFT
ERec . . . . ENGLISH RECORD
ERGS . . . . ETC: A REVIEW OF GENERAL SEMANTICS
ERIC . . . . EDUCATIONAL RESOURCES INFORMATION CENTER
ERICSSON TE . . . . . . ERICSSON TECHNICS
ERL . . . . ETUDES ROMANES DE LUND
ERS . . . . ENGLISH REPRINT SERIES
ES . . . . ENGLISCHE STUDIEN
ES . . . . ENGLISCHES SEMINAR
ES . . . . ENGLISH STUDIES
Es . . . . ESCORIAL
ES . . . . ESSAYS AND STUDIES
ES . . . . ESTUDIOS SEGOVIANOS
ESA . . . . EMAKEELE SELTSI AASTARAAMAT
ESA . . . . ENGLISH STUDIES IN AFRICA
ESAfr . . . . ENGLISH STUDIES IN AFRICA
ESB . . . . EIGEN SCHOON EN DE BRABANDER
ESBP . . . . EZIK I STIL NA BALGARSKITE PITSATELI
Esc . . . . ESCORIAL
EsC . . . . ESPRIT CREATEUR
EsCl . . . . ESTUDIOS CLASICOS
ESDU Data Items . . . ENGINEERING SCIENCES DATA UNIT, DATA ITEMS
E Sec . . . . L'ENSEIGNEMENT SECONDAIRE
ESELL . . . . ESSAYS AND STUDIES IN ENGLISH LANGUAGE AND LITERATURE
ESHG . . . . ETUDES SUISSES D'HISTOIRE GENERALE
ESI . . . . EDIZIONI SCIENTIFICHE ITALIANE
ESI . . . . ETUDES SLAVES ET EST-EUROPEENNES
ESLR . . . . ETUDES STAVES ET ROUMAINES
ESn . . . . ENGLISCHE STUDIEN
ESov . . . . ETUDES SOVIETIQUES
ESP . . . . ENGLISH SYMPOSIUM PAPERS
EspA . . . . ESPANOL ACTUAL
ESPSL . . . . O ESTADO DE SAO PAULO. SUPLEMENTO LITERARIO
ESQ . . . . EMERSON SOCIETY QUARTERLY
ESQ . . . . ESQ: A JOURNAL OF THE AMERICAN RENAISSANCE
ESQ . . . . ESQUIRE
ESR . . . . EMORY SOURCES AND REPRINTS
ESR . . . . ETUDES SLAVES ET ROUMAINES
ESR . . . . EUROPEAN STUDIES REVIEW
ESRS . . . . EMPORIA STATE RESEARCH STUDIES
ESs . . . . ENGLISH STUDIES

Ess . . . . ESSENCE
Essays Crit . . . . . . ESSAYS IN CRITICISM
Ess Crit . . . . ESSAYS IN CRITICISM
Essex Inst Hist Coll . . ESSEX INSTITUTE. HISTORICAL COLLECTIONS
Esso Mag . . . . ESSO MAGAZINE
Ess R . . . . ESSEX REVIEW
ESt . . . . ENGLISCHE STUDIEN
ESt . . . . ENGLISH STUDIES
Est . . . . ESTUDIOS
EST COAS M . . . . . . ESTUARINE AND COASTAL MARINE SCIENCE
EstD . . . . ESTUDIOS. DUQUESNE UNIVERSITY
EstdH . . . . ESTUDIOS DE HISPANOFILA
EstE . . . . ESTUDIOS ESCENICOS
EstF . . . . ESTUDIOS FRANCISCANOS
EstHM . . . . ESTUDIOS DE HISTORIA MODERNA
EstLit . . . . ESTAFETA LITERARIA
EStn . . . . ENGLISCHE STUDIEN
ESTS . . . . EARLY SCOTTISH TEXT SOCIETY
EStud . . . . ENGLISH STUDIES
Estud Filosof . . . . . ESTUDIOS FILOSOFICOS
E Studien . . . . ENGLISCHE STUDIEN
E Studies . . . . ENGLISH STUDIES
ESTUD SOC C . . . . . ESTUDIOS SOCIALES CENTROAMERICANOS
ET . . . . EDUCATIONAL TELEVISION
ET . . . . EKONOMISK TIDSKRIFT
ET . . . . EPITHEORESE TECHNES
Et . . . . ETHICS
Et . . . . ETOILES
Et . . . . ETUDES
ET . . . . ETUDES TRADITIONNELLES
ET . . . . EXPOSITORY TIMES
EtA . . . . ETUDES ANGLAISES
ETAb . . . . ENGLISH TEACHING ABSTRACTS
Et Angl . . . . ETUDES ANGLAISES
ETAT . . . . EESTI NSV TEADUSTE AKADEEMIA TOIMETISED, UHISKONNATEADUSTE SEERIA
Et Celt . . . . ETUDES CELTIQUES
ETC REV GEN . . . . . . ETC-REVIEW OF GENERAL SEMANTICS
EtF . . . . ETUDES FRANCISCAINES
Et Germ . . . . ETUDES GERMANIQUES
EThL . . . . EPHEMERIDES THEOLOGICAE LOVANIENSES
ETHMUS . . . . ETHNOMUSICOLOGY
Ethnic Stud . . . . . . ETHNIC STUDIES
EthnoE . . . . ETHNOLOGIA EUROPAEA
EthnoF . . . . ETHNOLOGIE FRANCAISE
ETHNOMUSIC . . . . . ETHNOMUSICOLOGY
EThR . . . . ETUDES THEOLOGIQUES ET RELIGIEUSES
Eth Rec . . . . ETHICAL RECORD
ETI . . . . EN TERRE D'ISLAM
ETiM . . . . ECHO TEATROLNE I MUZYCZNE
ETJ . . . . EDUCATIONAL THEATRE JOURNAL
EtK . . . . EPETERIS TON KALABRYTON

ETL . . . . EPHEMERIDES THEOLOGICAE LOVANIENSES
EtL . . . . ETUDES DE LETTRES
ETL . . . . EXPLICACION DE TEXTOS LITERARIOS (SACRAMENTO)
ETLA . . . . EPETERIS TOU LAOGRAPHIKOV ARKHEIOV
EtP . . . . ETNOLOSKI PREGLED
EtPol . . . . ETNOGRAFIA POLSKA
ETR . . . . ETERNITY
ETR . . . . ETUDES THEOLOGIQUES ET RELIGIEUSES
E T Rel . . . . ETUDES THEOLOGIQUES ET RELIGIEUSES
ETs . . . . ETUDES TSIGANES
Etud Ang . . . . ETUDES ANGLAISES
Etud Anglaises . . . . . ETUDES ANGLAISES
Etud Germaniques . . ETUDES GERMANIQUES
ETUD INT . . . . ETUDES INTERNATIONALES
Etud Ital . . . . ETUDES ITALIENNES
Etud Phil . . . . ETUDES PHILOSOPHIQUES
ETUD SLAV E . . . . . ETUDES SLAVES ET EST-EUROPEENNES
EU . . . . EAST EUROPE
EU . . . . ESTUDOS UNIVERSITARIOS
Eu . . . . EUPHORION
EUC . . . . ESTUDIS UNIVERSITARIS CATALANS
EUDEBA . . . . EDITORIAL UNIVERSITARIA DE BUENOS AIRES
Eug R . . . . EUGENICS REVIEW
Eul J . . . . EULENSPIEGEL-JAHRBUCH
EUP . . . . EXTENSION (O INTERCAMBIO) UNIVERSITARIA DE LA PLATA
Euph . . . . EUPHORION (HEIDELBERG)
EUQ . . . . EMORY UNIVERSITY QUARTERLY
EUR ARCH . . . . EUROPA-ARCHIV
EURCUP . . . . ESTUDOS UNIVERSITARIOS: REVISTA DE CULTURA DA UNIVERSIDADE DE PERNAMBUCO
Eur Econ R . . . . EUROPEAN ECONOMIC REVIEW
EurH . . . . EUROPAEISCHE HOCHSCHULSCHRIFTEN
EUR J A PHY . . . . . . EUROPEAN JOURNAL OF APPLIED PHYSIOLOGY AND OCCUPATIONAL PHYSIOLOGY
EUR J APP M . . . . . . EUROPEAN JOURNAL OF APPLIED MICROBIOLOGY
EUR J BIOCH . . . . . . EUROPEAN JOURNAL OF BIOCHEMISTRY
EUR J CANC . . . . . . EUROPEAN JOURNAL OF CANCER
EUR J CL IN . . . . . . EUROPEAN JOURNAL OF CLINICAL INVESTIGATION
EUR J CL PH . . . . . . EUROPEAN JOURNAL OF CLINICAL PHARMACOLOGY
EUR J I CAR . . . . . . EUROPEAN JOURNAL OF INTENSIVE CARE MEDICINE
EUR J IMMUN . . . . . EUROPEAN JOURNAL OF IMMUNOLOGY
EUR J MED C . . . . . . EUROPEAN JOURNAL OF MEDICINAL CHEMISTRY-CHIMICA THERAPEUTICA
EUR J PED . . . . EUROPEAN JOURNAL OF PEDIATRICS
EUR J PHARM . . . . . EUROPEAN JOURNAL OF PHARMACOLOGY
Eur J Sociol . . . . EUROPEAN JOURNAL OF SOCIOLOGY
EUR J SOC P . . . . . . EUROPEAN JOURNAL OF SOCIAL PSYCHOLOGY
EUR NEUROL . . . . . . EUROPEAN NEUROLOGY
Eur Nouv . . . . L'EUROPE NOUVELLE
Europ Econ and Pol Survey . . EUROPEAN ECONOMIC AND POLITICAL SURVEY
Europlast Mon . . . . . EUROPLASTICS MONTHLY
EURO SPECTR . . . . . EURO-SPECTRA
Eur Plast News . . . . EUROPEAN PLASTICS NEWS
EUR POLYM J . . . . . EUROPEAN POLYMER JOURNAL

Eur Rubb J . . . . EUROPEAN RUBBER JOURNAL
Eur Shipbldg . . . . . . EUROPEAN SHIPBUILDING
Eur Stud R . . . . EUROPEAN STUDIES REVIEW
EUR SURG RE . . . . . . EUROPEAN SURGICAL RESEARCH
EV . . . . ECOS DE VALVANERA
EV . . . . EPEGRAFIKA VOSTIKA
EV . . . . EVERGREEN REVIEW
Eval Eng . . . . EVALUATION ENGINEERING
Evang Q . . . . EVANGELICAL QUARTERLY
Evang R . . . . EVANGELICAL REVIEW
Evang Th . . . . EVANGELISCHE THEOLOGIE
Evan Kirchor . . . . . EVANGELISCHE KIRCHENCHOR
EvR . . . . EVERGREEN REVIEW
Ev Sat . . . . EVERY SATURDAY
EWD . . . . EUROPAEISCHER WISSENSCHAFTSDIENST
EWN . . . . EVELYN WAUGH NEWSLETTER
EWR . . . . EAST-WEST REVIEW
Ex . . . . EXPLICATOR
Excep Child . . . . . . EXCEPTIONAL CHILDREN
EXCEPT CHIL . . . . . EXCEPTIONAL CHILDREN
ExChAb . . . . EXCEPTIONAL CHILD EDUCATION ABSTRACTS
Exec . . . . EXECUTIVE
Ex H Lec . . . . EXETER HALL LECTURES
Exist Psychiat . . . . . EXISTENTIAL PSYCHIATRY
Exp . . . . EXPERIMENT
Exp . . . . EXPLICATOR
Exp . . . . EXPOSITOR
Exp Ag . . . . EXPERIMENTAL AGRICULTURE
EXP BRAIN R . . . . . EXPERIMENTAL BRAIN RESEARCH
EXP CELL RE . . . . . EXPERIMENTAL CELL RESEARCH
Exped . . . . EXPEDITION
Exper Agric . . . . . . EXPERIMENTAL AGRICULTURE
EXP EYE RES . . . . . EXPERIMENTAL EYE RESEARCH
EXP GERONT . . . . . EXPERIMENTAL GERONTOLOGY
EXP HEMATOL . . . . EXPERIMENTAL HEMATOLOGY
Expl . . . . EXPLICATOR
EXPL EC HIS . . . . . . EXPLORATIONS IN ECONOMIC HISTORY
Explor . . . . EXPLORATIONS
Explor Econ Petrol Ind . . EXPLORATION AND ECONOMICS OF THE PETROLEUM INDUSTRY
Explosives Eng . . . . . EXPLOSIVES ENGINEER
Exp Mech . . . . EXPERIMENTAL MECHANICS
EXP MOL PAT . . . . . EXPERIMENTAL AND MOLECULAR PATHOLOGY
EXP NEUROL . . . . . . EXPERIMENTAL NEUROLOGY
Expos . . . . EXPOSITOR
Expos T . . . . EXPOSITORY TIMES
EXP PARASIT . . . . . . EXPERIMENTAL PARASITOLOGY
EXP PATH . . . . EXPERIMENTELLE PATHOLOGIE
Exp Sta Record . . . . EXPERIMENT STATION RECORD
ExpT . . . . EXPOSITORY TIMES
EXT . . . . EXTRAPOLATION
EXT AFFAIRS . . . . . . EXTERNAL AFFAIRS

ExTL . . . . EXPLICACION DE TEXTOS LITERARIOS
Ext Serv R . . . . EXTENSION SERVICE REVIEW
EYE EAR NOS . . . . . . EYE EAR NOSE AND THROAT MONTHLY

F

F . . . . FEBRUARY
F . . . . FOLIO
F . . . . FONTAINE
F . . . . FORTNIGHTLY
Fa . . . . FABULA
FA . . . . FANTASTIC ADVENTURES
FA . . . . FASTI ARCHAEOLOGICI
FA . . . . FILOLOGISKT ARKIV
FA . . . . FINANZ-ARCHIV
FA . . . . FOLKLORE AMERICANO
FA . . . . FOLKLORE AMERICAS
FA . . . . FRANCE-AMERIQUE
FAA . . . . OFFICE OF AVIATION MEDICINE REPORT (FEDERAL AVIATION AGENCY)
Fab . . . . FABULA
FAC . . . . FRANCE AU COMBAT
FACI . . . . FOLKLORE AMERICANO; ORGANO DEL COMITE INTERAMERICANO DE FOLKLORE
Fac L Rev . . . . FACULTY OF LAW REVIEW
Factory and Ind Management . . FACTORY AND INDUSTRIAL MANAGEMENT
Factory Mgt . . . . . . FACTORY MANAGEMENT AND MAINTENANCE
Fact Plant . . . . FACTORY AND PLANT
FAD . . . . FANTASTIC ADVENTURES (1939-1953)
FAGASS . . . . FRANKFURTER ARBEITEN AUS DEM GEBIETE DER ANGLISTIK UND DER AMERIKA-STUDIEN
FAM . . . . FANTASY FICTION
FAm . . . . FOLKLORE AMERICANO (LIMA)
FAm . . . . FOLKLORE AMERICAS
FAM COORD . . . . . . FAMILY COORDINATOR
Family LQ . . . . FAMILY LAW QUARTERLY
FAM PLAN PE . . . . . FAMILY PLANNING PERSPECTIVES
FAM PROCESS . . . . . FAMILY PROCESS
F&D . . . . FONETICA SI DIALECTOLOGIE
F&F . . . . FORSCHUNGEN UND FORTSCHRITTE
F & G Rundsch . . . . . F & G (FELTEN & GUILLEAUME) RUNDSCHAU
F&SF . . . . MAGAZINE OF FANTASY AND SCIENCE FICTION
FanF . . . . FANTASY FICTION
FanS . . . . FANTASY STORIES
FANS . . . . FANTASY, THE MAGAZINE OF SCIENCE FICTION
FANT . . . . FANTASY
Fant & Sci Fict . . . . . FANTASY AND SCIENCE FICTION
FAO Mo Bul Ag Econ & Stat . . FAO (FOOD AND AGRICULTURE ORGANIZATION) MONTHLY BULLETIN OF AGRICULTURAL ECONOMICS AND STATISTICS
FAO PLANT . . . . FAO(FOOD AND AGRICULTURE ORGANIZATION) PLANT PROTECTION BULLETIN
FAR . . . . FRANCO-AMERICAN REVIEW
FAR . . . . FRENCH AMERICAN REVIEW
FARADAY DIS . . . . . FARADAY DISCUSSIONS OF THE CHEMICAL SOCIETY
Far East Q . . . . FAR EASTERN QUARTERLY
Far East R . . . . FAR EASTERN REVIEW
Far East S . . . . FAR EASTERN SURVEY
Far E Econ R . . . . FAR EASTERN ECONOMIC REVIEW
FARMAKOL T . . . . . . FARMAKOLOGIYA I TOKSIKOLOGIYA
FARMACO PRA . . . . FARMACO-EDIZIONE PRATICA
FARMACO SCI . . . . . FARMACO-EDIZIONE SCIENTIFICA

Farm & Home Sci... FARM & HOME SCIENCE
Farm Chem....... FARM CHEMICALS
Farm Econ........ FARM ECONOMICS
Farm Eng......... FARM ENGINEERING
Farmers' B....... FARMERS' BULLETIN
Farm J.......... FARM JOURNAL
Farm Q.......... FARM QUARTERLY
F Arts Q........ FINE ARTS QUARTERLY
FAS............. FANTASTIC STORIES
FASF........... FANTASTIC SCIENCE FICTION
FAU............ FANTASTIC UNIVERSE SCIENCE FICTION
FAY............ FANTASTIC ADVENTURES YEARBOOK
FB............. FABULA
FB............. FANTASY BOOK
FB............. FOLKLORE BRABANCON
FB............. FONTANE BLAETTER
FB............. FRANSE BOEK
FBAA........... FRANKFURTER BEITRAEGE ZUR ANGLISTIK UND AMERIKANISTIK
FBG........... FRANKFURTER BEITRAEGE ZUR GERMANISTIK
FBK............ FANTASY BOOK
FBPG.......... FORSCHUNGEN ZUR BRANDENBURGISCH-PREUSSISCHEN GESCHICHTE
F Brab.......... FOLKLORE BRABANCON
FC............. FATHERS OF THE CHURCH
FCE............ FONDO DE CULTURA ECONOMICA (MEXICO)
FCHQ.......... FILSON CLUB HISTORICAL QUARTERLY
FCR........... FREE CHINA REVIEW
FD............ FANETICA SI DIALECTOLOGIE
FD............ FANFULLA DELLA DOMENICA
FD............ FILOSOFS'KA DUMKA
FDA........... FREIBURGER DIOZESANARCHIV
FDA CONSUM..... FDA CONSUMER
FDG........... FOLK DANCE GUIDE
FDGK.......... FUKUI DAIGAKU GAKUGEIGAKUBU KIYO
FDHRS......... FREIES DEUTSCHES HOCHSTIFT: REIHE DER SCHRIFTEN
FdL........... FORUM DER LETTEREN
Fd Mf.......... FOOD MANUFACTURE
Fd Process Ind..... FOOD PROCESSING INDUSTRY
Fd Process Market.. FOOD PROCESSING AND MARKETING
FDS........... FOUNTAINWELL DRAMA SERIES
FDSD.......... FORSCHUNGEN ZUR DEUTSCHEN SPRACHE UND DICHTUNG
Fd Trade Rev..... FOOD TRADE REVIEW
FDTSC.......... FOLGER DOCUMENTS OF TUDOR AND STUART CIVILIZATION
FE............ FRANCE-EURAFRIQUE
FE............ ORGANO DE FALANGE ESPANOLA
Fed B J......... FEDERAL BAR JOURNAL
Fed Com B J...... FEDERAL COMMUNICATIONS BAR JOURNAL
FEDERATION INS COUNS Q.. FEDERATION OF INSURANCE COUNSEL. QUARTERLY
FED P.......... FEDERATION PROCEEDINGS
Fed Prob........ FEDERAL PROBATION
Fed Proc........ FEDERATION PROCEEDINGS
Fed R D......... FEDERAL RULES DECISIONS

Fed Res Bull . . . . . . FEDERAL RESERVE BULLETIN
FeL . . . . FILOLOGIA E LETTERATURA
FEQ . . . . FAR EASTERN QUARTERLY
FER . . . . , FEAR
FER . . . . FEDERAL ECONOMIC REVIEW
FERROELECTR . . . . . FERROELECTRICS
Fert Green Bk . . . . . FERTILIZER GREEN BOOK
Fert R . . . . FERTILIZER REVIEW
FERT STERIL . . . . FERTILITY AND STERILITY
FET SEI ANS . . . . FETTE SEIFEN ANSTRICHMITTEL VERBUNDEN MIT DER ZEITSCHRIFT DIE ERNAHRUNGSINDUSTRIE
FEUFJ . . . . FAR EASTERN UNIVERSITY FACULTY JOURNAL
FF . . . . FOLKLORE
FF . . . . FOLKLORE FORUM
FF . . . . FORGOTTEN FANTASY
FF . . . . FORSCHUNGEN UND FORTSCHRITTE
FF . . . . FRANCE FRANCISCAINE
FF . . . . FRANKISCHE FORSCHUNGEN
FF . . . . FRATE FRANCESCO
FFC . . . . FOLKLORE FELLOWS COMMUNICATIONS
FFKL . . . . FREIBURGER FORSCHUNGEN ZUR KUNST UND LITERATURGESCHICHTE
FFLR . . . . FLORIDA FOREIGN LANGUAGE REPORTER
FFM . . . . FAMOUS FANTASTIC MYSTERIES
FFMA . . . . FOLKLORE AND FOLK MUSIC ARCHIVIST
FFN . . . . FANTASY STORIES
FForum . . . . FOLKLORE FORUM
FForumB . . . . FOLKLORE FORUM BIBLIOGRAPHIC AND SPECIAL SERIES
FFR . . . . FILM FORUM REVIEW
FG . . . . FORM UND GEIST
FGO . . . . FORSCHUNGEN ZUR GESCHICHTE OBEROESTERREICHS
FH . . . . FEUILLES D'HISTOIRE
FH . . . . FRANKFURTER HEFTE
FHA . . . . FITZGERALD-HEMINGWAY ANNUAL
FHP . . . . FORT HARE PAPERS
FHQ . . . . FLORIDA HISTORICAL QUARTERLY
FHS . . . . FRENCH HISTORICAL STUDIES
fi . . . . FILOLOGIA
FI . . . . FOLKLORE ITALIANO
FI . . . . FORUM ITALICUM
FIBONACCI Q . . . . . . FIBONACCI QUARTERLY
Fibre Chem . . . . FIBRE CHEMISTRY
Fibre Containers . . . FIBRE CONTAINERS AND PAPERBOARD MILLS
Fibre Sci Technol . . . FIBRE SCIENCE AND TECHNOLOGY
FICU . . . . FOLKLORE. BOLETIN DEL DEPARTAMENTO DE FOLKLORE DEL INSTITUTO DE COOPERACION
                        UNIVERSITARIA
FID R Doc . . . . FEDERATION INTERNATIONALE DE DOCUMENTATION. REVUE DE LA DOCUMENTATION
Field & S . . . . FIELD & STREAM
Field Il . . . . FIELD ILLUSTRATED
Field Nat . . . . FIELD NATURALIST
FIELD W FIE . . . . . . FIELDS WITHIN FIELDS WITHIN FIELDS
Fiji Geol Surv Dep Bull . . FIJI, GEOLOGICAL SURVEY DEPARTMENT. BULLETIN
Fil . . . . FILOSOFIA
Film J . . . . FILM JOURNAL

Film Lib Q........ FILM LIBRARY QUARTERLY
Film Mus......... FILM MUSIC
Film Mus Notes.... FILM MUSIC NOTES
Film Q.......... FILM QUARTERLY
Films in R........ FILMS IN REVIEW
Filo............. FILOLOGICA
Filosof Cas Csav... FILOSOFICKY CASOPIS CSAV
FILS............ FILOLOGICKE STUDIE
FilSbAlm......... FILOLOGICESKIJ SBORNIK (STAT'I ASPIRANTOV I SOISKATELEJ). ALMA-ATA
Filtr Sep......... FILTRATION AND SEPARATION
FilZ............ FILOLOGIJA (ZAGREB)
FiM............. FILOLOGIA MODERNA
FIMS........... FOLKLORE INSTITUTE MONOGRAPH SERIES
Fin Analysts J..... FINANCIAL ANALYSTS JOURNAL
Finance & Dev..... FINANCE AND DEVELOPMENT
FINAN MANAG.... FINANCIAL MANAGEMENT
Fin Exec........ FINANCIAL EXECUTIVE
FINN CHEM L..... FINNISH CHEMICAL LETTERS
FIN POST........ FINANCIAL POST
Fin World....... FINANCIAL WORLD
FiR............ FILOLOGIA ROMANZA
Fire Eng........ FIRE ENGINEERING
Fire Eng J........ FIRE ENGINEERS JOURNAL
Fire J........... FIRE JOURNAL
Fire Tech........ FIRE TECHNOLOGY
First Nat City Bank.. FIRST NATIONAL CITY BANK OF NEW YORK. MONTHLY ECONOMIC LETTER
FISH B.......... FISHERY BULLETIN
Fishg News Int..... FISHING NEWS INTERNATIONAL
FiTs............ FINSK TIDSKRIFT
FitzN........... FITZGERALD NEWSLETTER
FIZ............ FARHANG-E IRAN-ZAMIN (REVUE TRIMESTRIELLE DES ETUDES IRANOLOGIQUES)
Fiz Metallov Metalloved.. FIZIKA METALLOV I METALLOVEDENIE
FIZ METAL M..... FIZIKA METALLOV I METALLOVEDENIE
Fiz-Tekh Probl Razrab Polez Iskop.. FIZIKO-TEKHNICHESKIE PROBLEMY RAZRABOTKI POLEZYNKH ISKOPAEMYKH
FIZ TVERD T...... FIZIKA TVERDOGO TELA
FIZ ZEMLI....... FIZIKA ZEMLI
FK............ FILOLOGIAI KOEZLOENY
FKG(NF)......... FORSCHUNGEN ZUR KIRCHEN- UND GEISTESGESCHICHTE. NEUE FOLGE
FL............. FALL
FL............. FIGARO LITTERAIRE
FL............. FOLKLORE
FL............. FORUM DER LETTEREN
FL............. FRANCE LIBRE
FL............. FRANCISCANSCH LEVEN
FLA............ FOREIGN LANGUAGE ANNALS
Fla Acad Sci Q J.... FLORIDA ACADEMY OF SCIENCES. QUARTERLY JOURNAL
Fla Ag Dept Quar B.. FLORIDA DEPARTMENT OF AGRICULTURE. QUARTERLY BULLETIN
Fla Ag Exp....... UNIVERSITY OF FLORIDA. AGRICULTURAL EXPERIMENT STATION. PUBLICATIONS
Fla B J.......... FLORIDA BAR JOURNAL
Fla Geol Surv Geol Bull.. FLORIDA GEOLOGICAL SURVEY. GEOLOGICAL BULLETIN
Fla Geol Surv Inform Circ.. FLORIDA GEOLOGICAL SURVEY. INFORMATION CIRCULAR

Fla Geol Surv Rep Invest. . FLORIDA GEOLOGICAL SURVEY. REPORT OF INVESTIGATIONS
Fla Hist Quar. . . . . . FLORIDA HISTORICAL QUARTERLY
Fla Lib. . . . . FLORIDA LIBRARIES
F Lang. . . . . FOUNDATIONS OF LANGUAGE
Fla State Board Conserv Bien Rep. . FLORIDA STATE BOARD OF CONSERVATION. BIENNIAL REPORT
Fla State Plant Bd. . FLORIDA STATE PLANT BOARD. PUBLICATIONS
Fla St U L Rev. . . . . FLORIDA STATE UNIVERSITY LAW REVIEW
Fla Univ Eng Exp Sta Bull. . FLORIDA UNIVERSITY. ENGINEERING AND INDUSTRIAL EXPERIMENT STATION. BULLETIN
Flavour Ind. . . . . . . FLAVOUR INDUSTRY
FLC. . . . . FOLK-LORE (CALCUTTA)
FLe. . . . . FIERA LETTERARIA
FLett. . . . . FIERA LETTERARIA
Flight Int (London). . FLIGHT INTERNATIONAL (LONDON)
FLin. . . . . FOLIA LINGUISTICA
FLiv. . . . . FOLK-LIV
FloQ. . . . . FLORIDA QUARTERLY
FlorQ. . . . . FLORIDA QUARTERLY
F L Rev. . . . . FEDERAL LAW REVIEW
Fluid Contr Inst FCI Stand. . FLUID CONTROLS INSTITUTE. FCI STANDARDS
Fluid Dyn. . . . . FLUID DYNAMICS
Fluid Mech Sov Res. . FLUID MECHANICS. SOVIET RESEARCH
Fluid Pwr Int. . . . . . FLUID POWER INTERNATIONAL
Fly. . . . . FLYING
Flygtek Forsoksanst Medd. . FLYGTEKNISKA FORSOKSANSTALTEN, MEDDELANDE
FM. . . . . FILOSOFSKA MISUL
FM. . . . . FRANCAIS MODERNE
FMAS. . . . . FRUEHMITTELALTERLICHE STUDIEN
FMF. . . . . FAMOUS SCIENCE FICTION
F M-FEINW M. . . . . . F&M-FEINWERKTECHNIK & MESSTECHNIK
FMJ. . . . . FOLK MUSIC JOURNAL
FMLS. . . . . FORUM FOR MODERN LANGUAGE STUDIES
FMod. . . . . FILOLOGIA MODERNA (MADRID)
FMonde. . . . . FRANCAIS DANS LE MONDE
FMSt. . . . . FOLKMALSSTUDIER
FN. . . . . FANTASTIC NOVELS
FN. . . . . FILOLOGICESKIE NAUKI
FN. . . . . FOLKLORE; RIVISTA DI TRADIZIONI POPOLARI (NAPLES)
FN. . . . . FORTID OG NUTID
Fn. . . . . FORTNIGHTLY
F NEUR PSYC. . . . . . FORTSCHRITTE DER NEUROLOGIE UND PSYCHIATRIE UND IHRER GRENZGEBIETE
FNL. . . . . FITZGERALD NEWSLETTER
FNLG. . . . . FORSCHUNGEN ZUR NEUEREN LITERATURGESCHICHTE
FNM. . . . . FANTASTIC NOVELS MAGAZINE
FNT. . . . . FOILSEACHAIN NAISIUNTA TTA
FO. . . . . FOLIA ORIENTALIA
Fo. . . . . FOLKLORE
Fo. . . . . FORNVANNEN
FOB. . . . . FLANNERY O'CONNER BULLETIN
FOC EXC CHI. . . . . . FOCUS ON EXCEPTIONAL CHILDREN
Focus. . . . . FOCUS ON INDIANA LIBRARIES
FOEG. . . . . FORSCHUNGEN ZUR OSTEUROPAEISCHEN GESHICHTE

Foerdern Heben. . . . FOERDERN UND HEBEN
FOG. . . . . FORSCHUNGEN ZUR OSTEUROPAEISCHEN GESCHICHTE
Fogg Mus Bul. . . . . . HARVARD UNIVERSITY. FOGG ART MUSEUM. BULLETIN
Fol. . . . . FORUM ITALICUM
Foi Vie. . . . . FOI ET VIE
FoL. . . . . FOLK LIFE (CARDIFF)
FoL. . . . . FOUNDATIONS OF LANGUAGE
FOL BIOL. . . . . FOLIA BIOLOGICA
FOL HIST CY. . . . . . FOLIA HISTOCHEMICA ET CYTOCHEMICA
FOL HUMANIS. . . . . FOLIA HUMANISTICA
Fo Li. . . . . FOLIA LINGUISTICA
Folk. . . . . FOLKLORE
Folk Inst. . . . . JOURNAL OF THE FOLKLORE INSTITUTE
Folklore C. . . . . FOLKLORE (CALCUTTA)
Folk-Lore J. . . . . . . FOLK-LORE JOURNAL
Folk Mus Arch. . . . . FOLKLORE AND FOLK MUSIC ARCHIVIST
FolkS. . . . . FOLKLORE STUDIES (TOKYO)
FOL MICROB. . . . . . FOLIA MICROBIOLOGICA
FOL PHARM J. . . . . FOLIA PHARMACOLOGICA JAPONICA
FOL PHONIAT. . . . . FOLIA PHONIATRICA
FOL PRIMAT. . . . . . FOLIA PRIMATOLOGICA
FoN. . . . . FORTID OG NUTID
Font. . . . . FONTAINE
FONTES. . . . . FONTES ARTIS MUSICAE
FOOD COSMET. . . . . FOOD AND COSMETICS TOXICOLOGY
FOOD DRUG C. . . . . FOOD, DRUG, COSMETIC LAW JOURNAL
Food Eng. . . . . FOOD ENGINEERING
FOOD MANUF. . . . . FOOD MANUFACTURE
Food Processing-Mktg. . FOOD PROCESSING-MARKETING
Food Res. . . . . FOOD RESEARCH
Food Tech. . . . . . . FOOD TECHNOLOGY
For Aff. . . . . FOREIGN AFFAIRS
For Agric. . . . . FOREIGN AGRICULTURE
For Comm. . . . . . . FOREIGN COMMERCE WEEKLY
Fordham L Rev. . . . . FORDHAM LAW REVIEW
Fordham Urban L J. . FORDHAM URBAN LAW JOURNAL
FOREIGN AFF. . . . . . FOREIGN AFFAIRS
FOREIGN LAN. . . . . FOREIGN LANGUAGE ANNALS
FOREIGN POL. . . . . FOREIGN POLICY
FOREIGN TR. . . . . . FOREIGN TRADE
FOREST CHRO. . . . . FORESTRY CHRONICLE
Forest Hist. . . . . . . FOREST HISTORY
Forest Ind. . . . . . . FOREST INDUSTRIES
Forest Prod J. . . . . . FOREST PRODUCTS JOURNAL
FOREST SCI. . . . . . FOREST SCIENCE
For Pol. . . . . FOREIGN POLICY
For Policy Bul. . . . . FOREIGN POLICY BULLETIN
For Policy Rep. . . . . FOREIGN POLICY REPORTS
For Q. . . . . FOREIGN QUARTERLY REVIEW
For Quar. . . . . FOREST QUARTERLY
For R. . . . . FOREIGN REVIEW

Forsch Ingenieurw . . FORSCHUNG IM INGENIEURWESEN
Forschungsh Geb Stahlbaues . . FORSCHUNGSHEFTE AUS DEM GEBIETE DES STAHLBAUES
For Sci . . . . FOREST SCIENCE
Fortn . . . . FORTNIGHTLY REVIEW
FortnR . . . . FORTNIGHTLY REVIEW
Fort Rev . . . . FORTNIGHTLY REVIEW
Fortschr Ber VDIZ . . FORTSCHRITT BERICHTE, VDI ZEITSCHRIFT
FORTSCHR PH . . . . . FORTSCHRITTE DER PHYSIK
Forum . . . . FORUM FOR THE DISCUSSION OF NEW TRENDS IN EDUCATION
Forum Ed . . . . FORUM OF EDUCATION
ForumH . . . . FORUM (HOUSTON)
ForumS . . . . FORUM: A UKRAINIAN REVIEW (SCRANTON, PA.)
ForumZ . . . . FORUM (ZAGREB)
Foster Mo Ref . . . . . FOSTER'S MONTHLY REFERENCE LISTS
FOU . . . . FOUNDATION
Foun . . . . FOUNDATIONS (BAPTIST)
Found Facts . . . . FOUNDATION FACTS
Founding Weld Prod Eng J Metal Ind Dig . . FOUNDING, WELDING, PRODUCTION ENGINEERING JOURNAL AND METAL
INDUSTRY DIGEST
Found Lang . . . . FOUNDATIONS OF LANGUAGE
FOUND PHYS . . . . . . FOUNDATIONS OF PHYSICS
Found Trade J . . . . . FOUNDRY TRADE JOURNAL
FP . . . . FILOLOSKI PREGLED (BELGRADE)
F Phon . . . . FOLIA PHONIATRICA
FPL . . . . FOLKLORE, TRIBUNA DEL PENSAMIENTO PERUANO
FPn . . . . FRYSKE PLAKNAMMEN
FPt . . . . FAR POINT
FQ . . . . FAERIE QUEENE
FQ . . . . FILM QUARTERLY
FQ . . . . FLORIDA QUARTERLY
FQ . . . . FOUR QUARTERS
FQ . . . . FRENCH QUARTERLY
FR . . . . FELIX RAVENNA
FR . . . . FORTNIGHTLY REVIEW
FR . . . . FRENCH REVIEW
FrA . . . . FRANCE-ASIE
Franc . . . . FRANCISCANA
France Illus . . . . FRANCE ILLUSTRATION
France Illus Sup . . . . FRANCE ILLUSTRATION SUPPLEMENT
Frankf Hist Forsch . . FRANKFURTER HISTORISCHE FORSCHUNGEN
FranS . . . . FRANCISCAN STUDIES
Fran Stud . . . . FRANCISCAN STUDIES
Fraser . . . . FRASER'S MAGAZINE
FRD . . . . FEDERAL RULES DECISIONS
Frei Z Phil Theol . . . FREIBURGER ZEITSCHRIFT FUER PHILOSOPHIE UND THEOLOGIE
French Am Rev . . . . FRENCH AMERICAN REVIEW
FRESHW BIOL . . . . . FRESHWATER BIOLOGY
FRG . . . . REVISTA DE FILOLOGIE ROMANICA SI GERMANICA
Fr Hist Stud . . . . . . FRENCH HISTORICAL STUDIES
Frict Wear Mach . . . FRICTION AND WEAR IN MACHINERY
Friends' Hist Assoc Bull . . FRIENDS' HISTORICAL ASSOCIATION. BULLETIN

PERIODICAL TITLE ABBREVIATIONS

FRIS . . . . STANFORD UNIVERSITY. FOOD RESEARCH INSTITUTE. STUDIES
Fr LM . . . . FRENCH LITERATURE ON MICROFICHE
F ROENT NUK . . . . . . FORTSCHRITTE AUF DEM GEGIETE DER ROENTGENSTRAHLEN UND DER NUKLEARMEDIZIN
Froid Clim . . . . FROID ET LA CLIMATISATION
FRom . . . . FILOLOGIA ROMANZA
Front . . . . FRONTIER
Frozen Fds . . . . FROZEN FOODS
Fr Railw Tech . . . . . . FRENCH RAILWAY TECHNIQUES
FrSM . . . . FRANZISKANISCHE STUDIEN. MUENSTER
FrSt . . . . FRANZISKANISCHE STUDIEN
Fr St . . . . FRENCH STUDIES
F:RTP . . . . RIVISTA DE TRADIZIONI POPOLARI
FryskJb . . . . FRYSK JIERBOEK
FS . . . . FRANCISCAN STUDIES
FS . . . . FRANZISKANISCHE STUDIEN
FS . . . . FRENCH STUDIES
FS . . . . FUNBERICHT AUS SCHWABEN
FS . . . . FURMAN STUDIES
FsD . . . . FONETICA SI DIALECTOLOGIE
FSF . . . . MAGAZINE OF FANTASY & SCIENCE FICTION
FSM . . . . FANTASTIC STORY MAGAZINE
FSO . . . . FLYING SAUCERS FROM OTHER WORLDS
FSQ . . . . FANTASTIC STORY QUARTERLY
FSRTS . . . . FYRA SVENSKA REFORMATIONSKRIFTER TRYCKTA I STOCKHOLM AR 1562
FSt . . . . FRANCISCAN STUDIES
FSUS . . . . FLORIDA STATE UNIVERSITY STUDIES
FSUSP . . . . FLORIDA STATE UNIVERSITY SLAVIC PAPERS
FT . . . . FINSK TIDSKRIFT
FTDP . . . . FOLKLORE: TRIBUNA DEL PENSAMIENTO PERUANO
FTS . . . . FACSIMILE TEXT SOCIETY
FTT . . . . FANCIFUL TALES OF TIME AND SPACE
FUB . . . . FURMAN UNIVERSITY BULLETIN
FUBA . . . . FILOLOGIA. INSTITUTO DE FILOLOGIA ROMANCIA FACULTAD DE FILOSOFIA Y LETRAS.
          UNIVERSIDAD DE BUENOS AIRES
FUF . . . . FINNISCH-UGRISCHE FORSCHUNGEN
FuF . . . . FORSCHUNGEN UND FORTSCHRITTE
FUN . . . . FROM UNKNOWN WORLDS
Fur . . . . FURIOSO
FurmS . . . . FURMAN STUDIES
Fut . . . . FUTURE FICTION
FUT . . . . FUTURES
FUTF . . . . FUTURE SCIENCE FICTION
FUTS . . . . FUTURISTIC STORIES
FVL . . . . FORSCHUNGEN ZUR VOLKS UND LANDESKUNDE
FW . . . . FOLKTALES OF THE WORLD
FyL . . . . FILOSOFIA Y LETRAS
FzG . . . . FORSCHUNGSBERICHTE ZUR GERMANISTIK (OSAKA-KOBE)
FZPT . . . . FREIBURGER ZEITSCHRIFT FUER PHILOSOPHIE UND THEOLOGIE

G

G.............. GERMANOSLAVICA
G.............. GIDS
GA............. GEISTIGE ARBEIT
GA............. GEOGRAPHISCHER ANZEIGER
GA............. GERMANISTISCHE ABHANDLUNGEN
GA............. GERMANISTISCHE ARBEITSHEFTE
GA............. GLOS ANGLII
GA............. GRAPHIC ARTS MONTHLY
GAA............ SKRIFTER UTGIVNA AV KUNGLIGA. GUSTAV ADOLFS AKADEMIEN
Ga Ag Coll........ GEORGIA STATE COLLEGE OF AGRICULTURE PUBLICATIONS
Ga Ag Exp........ GEORGIA AGRICULTURAL EXPERIMENT STATION PUBLICATIONS
GAB............ GEOPPINGER AKADEMISCHE BEITRAEGE
Ga B J........... GEORGIA BAR JOURNAL
Ga Dep Mines Mining Geol Geol Surv Bull..GEORGIA DEPARTMENT OF MINES, MINING AND GEOLOGY, GEOLOGICAL SURVEY BULLETIN
GAf............ GENEVE-AFRIQUE
GAG............ GOPPINGER ARBEITEN ZUR GERMANISTIK
Ga Hist Quart..... GEORGIA HISTORICAL QUARTERLY
Ga Hist Soc Coll.... GEORGIA HISTORICAL SOCIETY, COLLECTIONS
GaHQ........... GEORGIA HISTORICAL QUARTERLY
GAI............ GLI ARCHIVI ITALIANI
Ga Inst Technol Eng Exp Sta Bull..GEORGIA INSTITUTE OF TECHNOLOGY, ENGINEERING EXPERIMENT STATION, BULLETIN
Ga Inst Technol Environ Resour Cent Rep..GEORGIA INSTITUTE OF TECHNOLOGY, ENVIRONMENTAL RESOURCES CENTER, REPORT
GaiS........... LO GAI SABER (TOULOUSE)
Ga J Int & Comp L.. GEORGIA JOURNAL OF INTERNATIONAL AND COMPARATIVE LAW
GAKS.......... GESAMMELTE AUFSAETZE ZUR KULTURGESCHICHTE SPANIENS
GAL........... GALAXY
GAlb........... GJURMIME ALBANOLOGIJIKE
Ga Libn......... GEORGIA LIBRARIAN
GALPIN S J....... GALPIN SOCIETY JOURNAL
Ga L Rev........ GEORGIA LAW REVIEW
Gam........... GAMBIT
GAM........... GAMMA
G & BS......... GREEK AND BYZANTINE STUDIES
G&R........... GREECE AND ROME
G&S........... GRAI SI SUFLET
GAP........... GAP (GROUP FOR THE ADVANCEMENT OF PSYCHIATRY) REPORT
Ga R........... GEORGIA REVIEW
GArb........... GEISTIGE ARBEIT
Gard & Home B.... GARDEN AND HOME BUILDER
Gard Chron Am.... GARDENERS' CHRONICLE OF AMERICA
Gard Chron (Lond).. GARDENERS' CHRONICLE (LONDON)
Gard Digest....... GARDEN DIGEST
Garden & F....... GARDEN AND FOREST
Gard J........... GARDEN JOURNAL
Gard J N Y Bot Gard..GARDEN JOURNAL OF THE NEW YORK BOTANICAL GARDEN
Gard M......... GARDEN MAGAZINE

GAS............ GERMAN-AMERICAN STUDIES
Ga SBJ.......... GEORGIA STATE BAR JOURNAL
Gas Counc (Gt Brit) Res Commun. . GAS COUNCIL (GREAT BRITAIN) RESEARCH COMMUNICATIONS
Gas Engng Mgmt. . . GAS ENGINEERING AND MANAGEMENT
Gas J........... GAS JOURNAL
Gas Oil Pwr....... GAS AND OIL POWER
Gas (Phila)....... GAS (PHILADELPHIA)
GASTROENTY...... GASTROENTEROLOGY
GASTROIN EN..... GASTROINTESTINAL ENDOSCOPY
Gas Turbine Int.... GAS TURBINE INTERNATIONAL
Gas Waerme Int. . . GAS WAERME INTERNATIONAL
Gas Wasserfach. . . GAS UND WASSERFACH
Gas Wasserfach Gas Erdgas. . GAS UND WASSERFACH, GAS ERDGAS
Gas Wasserfach Wasser Abwasser. . GAS UND WASSERFACH, WASSER ABWASSER
Gas Wld......... GAS WORLD
Gas World Gas Coke. . GAS WORLD AND GAS AND COKE
Gas World Gas J. . . GAS WORLD AND GAS JOURNAL
GAV............ GAVROCHE
Gavel.......... MILWAUKEE BAR ASSOCIATION GAVEL
GAZ CHIM IT...... GAZZETTA CHIMICA ITALIANA
Gaz Mus......... GAZETA MUSICAL E DE TODAS LAS ARTES
GB............. GESCHIEDKUNDIGE BLADEN
GB............. GILDEBOEK
GBA........... GAZETTE DES BEAUX-ARTS
GBDP.......... GIESSENER BEITRAEGE ZUR DEUTSCHEN PHILOLOGIE
GBKG.......... GENTSCHE BIJDRAGEN TOT DE KUNSTGESCHIEDENIS
GBM........... GELRE. BIJDRAGEN EN MEDEDEELINGEN
GBM........... GOLDEN BOOK MAGAZINE
GB Minist Power Saf Mines Res Establ Res Rep. . GREAT BRITAIN. MINISTRY OF POWER. SAFETY IN MINES
        RESEARCH ESTABLISHMENT. RESEARCH REPORT
GB Minist Transp Road Res Lab RRL Rep. . GREAT BRITAIN. MINISTRY OF TRANSPORT. ROAD RESEARCH
        LABORATORY. RRL REPORT
GBRP.......... GIESSENER BEITRAEGE ZUR ROMANISCHEN PHILOLOGIE
GBS........... GLASGOW BIBLIOGRAPHICAL SOCIETY
GCFI.......... GIORNALE CRITICO DELLA FILOSOFIA ITALIANA
GCNA......... GUILD OF CARILLONNEURS IN NORTH AMERICA. BULLETIN
GCR........... GERMAN CANADIAN REVIEW
G Crit Filosof Ital. . . GIORNALE CRITICO DELLA FILOSOFIA ITALIANA
GD............ GIORNALE DANTESCO
GdB........... GIORNALE DI BORDO: MENSILE DI STORIA, LETTERATURA ED ARTE
GdD........... GEGENWART DER DICHTUNG
GdG........... GRUNDLAGEN DER GERMANISTIK
GdI........... GIORNALE D'ITALIA
GdiM.......... GIORNALE DI METAFISICA
GDM........... GADS DANSKE MAGASIN
GdM........... GAZZETTA DEL MEZZOGIORNO
Ge............ GEGENWART
GE............ GIORNALE DEGLI ECONOMISTI E ANNALI DI ECONOMIA
Gebrauchs....... GEBRAUCHSGRAPHIK
Gebrauchs Novum. . GEBRAUCHSGRAPHIK NOVUM
GEBURTSH FR..... GEBURTSHILFE UND FRAUENHEILKUNDE

GEDRAG T P . . . . . . GEDRAG-TIJDSCHRIFT VOOR PSYCHOLOGIE
GEG G S ERZ . . . . . . GEGENWARTSKUNDE GESELLSCHAFT STAAT ERZIEHUNG
GeM . . . . GEOGRAPHICAL MAGAZINE
Gen . . . . GENAVA
Gen Arm . . . . GENERALS OF THE ARMY AND THE AIR FORCE AND ADMIRALS OF THE NAVY
GEN C ENDOC . . . . . GENERAL AND COMPARATIVE ENDOCRINOLOGY
Gen Elec R . . . . GENERAL ELECTRICAL REVIEW
General Ed . . . . . . GENERAL EDUCATION
GENET POL . . . . . . GENETICA POLONICA
GENET PSYCH . . . . GENETIC PSYCHOLOGY MONOGRAPHS
Genet Res . . . . GENETICAL RESEARCH
Genie Biol Med . . . . GENIE BIOLOGIQUE ET MEDICAL
Genie Civ . . . . GENIE CIVIL
GEN LINGUIS . . . . . . GENERAL LINGUISTICS
GEN PHARM . . . . . . GENERAL PHARMACOLOGY
GEN RELAT G . . . . . . GENERAL RELATIVITY AND GRAVITATION
Gen Repos . . . . GENERAL REPOSITORY
GEN SYST . . . . GENERAL SYSTEMS BULLETIN
Gent M . . . . GENTLEMAN'S MAGAZINE
Gent M n.s. . . . . GENTLEMAN'S MAGAZINE, NEW SERIES
GeoAb . . . . GEOGRAPHICAL ABSTRACTS
GEOCH COS A . . . . . GEOCHIMICA ET COSMOCHIMICA ACTA
GEOEXPLOR . . . . GEOEXPLORATION
GEOG BUL . . . . GEOGRAPHICAL BULLETIN
Geog J . . . . GEOGRAPHICAL JOURNAL
Geog Jnl . . . . GEOGRAPHICAL JOURNAL
Geog M . . . . GEOGRAPHICAL MAGAZINE
GEOGR ANAL . . . . . . GEOGRAPHICAL ANALYSIS
GEOGR ANN B . . . . . GEOGRAFISKA ANNALER B. HUMAN GEOGRAPHY
Geog Rev . . . . GEOGRAPHICAL REVIEW
Geogr Helv . . . . . . GEOGRAPHICA HELVETICA
Geogr J . . . . GEOGRAPHICAL JOURNAL
Geogr R . . . . GEOGRAPHICAL REVIEW
GEOGR REV . . . . . . GEOGRAPHICAL REVIEW
GEOGR Z . . . . GEOGRAPHISCHE ZEITSCHRIFT
GeoL . . . . GEOGRAPHICA (LISBON)
Geol Geofiz Akad Nauk SSSR Sibirsk Otd . . GEOLOGIYA I GEOFIZIKA, AKADEMIYA NAUK SSSR, SIBIRSKOE OTDELENIE
Geo LJ . . . . GEORGETOWN LAW JOURNAL
Geol Mag . . . . GEOLOGICAL MAGAZINE
Geol Met Bol . . . . . . GEOLOGIA E METALURGIA. BOLETIM. ESCOLA POLITECNICA. UNIVERSIDADE DE SAO PAULO
Geol Mijnbouw . . . . GEOLOGIE EN MIJNBOUW
Geol Nefti i Gaza . . . GEOLOGIY A NEFTI I GAZA
Geol Rudn Mestorozhd Akad Nauk SSSR . . GEOLOGIYA RUDNYKH MESTOROZHDENII. AKADEMIYA NAUK SSSR
Geol Rundsch . . . . . GEOLOGISCHE RUNDSCHAU
GEOL S AM B . . . . . . GEOLOGICAL SOCIETY OF AMERICA. BULLETIN
Geol Soc Amer Eng Geol Case Hist . . GEOLOGICAL SOCIETY OF AMERICA. ENGINEERING GEOLOGY CASE HISTORIES
Geol Soc Am Proc . . GEOLOGICAL SOCIETY OF AMERICA. PROCEEDINGS
Geol Soc Australia J . . GEOLOGICAL SOCIETY OF AUSTRALIA. JOURNAL
Geol Soc Bull . . . . . . GEOLOGICAL SOCIETY OF AMERICA. BULLETIN
Geol Soc Lond J . . . . GEOLOGICAL SOCIETY OF LONDON. JOURNAL
Geol Soc Lond Q J . . GEOLOGICAL SOCIETY OF LONDON. QUARTERLY JOURNAL

Geol Soc Proc..... GEOLOGICAL SOCIETY OF AMERICA. PROCEEDINGS
Geol Soc So Africa Trans. . GEOLOGICAL SOCIETY OF SOUTH AFRICA. TRANSACTIONS AND PROCEEDINGS
Geol Surv Can Bull. . GEOLOGICAL SURVEY OF CANADA. BULLETIN
Geol Surv Can Mem. . GEOLOGICAL SURVEY OF CANADA. MEMOIR
Geol Surv Can Pap. . GEOLOGICAL SURVEY OF CANADA. PAPER
Geol Surv Guyana Bull. . GEOLOGICAL SURVEY OF GUYANA. BULLETIN
Geol Surv Jap Hydrogeol Maps Jap. . GEOLOGICAL SURVEY OF JAPAN. HYDROGEOLOGICAL MAPS OF JAPAN
Geol Surv Jap Rep. . GEOLOGICAL SURVEY OF JAPAN. REPORT
Geol Surv NSW Geol Surv Rep. . GEOLOGICAL SURVEY OF NEW SOUTH WALES. GEOLOGICAL SURVEY REPORT
Geol Surv of NSW Miner Ind NSW. . GEOLOGICAL SURVEY OF NEW SOUTH WALES. DEPARTMENT OF MINES. THE
    MINERAL INDUSTRY OF NEW SOUTH WALES
Geol Surv W Aust Bull. . GEOLOGICAL SURVEY OF WESTERN AUSTRALIA. BULLETIN
Geol Surv W Aust Geol Ser Explan Notes. . GEOLOGICAL SURVEY OF WESTERN AUSTRALIA. GEOLOGICAL SERIES.
    EXPLANATORY NOTES
Geol Surv Wyo Bull. . GEOLOGICAL SURVEY OF WYOMING. BULLETIN
Geol Surv Wyo Prelim Rep. . GEOLOGICAL SURVEY OF WYOMING. PRELIMINARY REPORT
Geol Tutkimuslaitos Geotek Julk. . GEOLOGINEN TUTKIMUSLAITOS. GEOTEKNILLISIA JULKAISUJA
GEOMAG AER..... GEOMAGNETIZM I AERONOMIYA
Geophys Inst Fac Sci Tokyo Univ Geophys Notes Suppl. . GEOPHYSICAL INSTITUTE, FACULTY OF SCIENCE TOKYO
    JAPAN. GEOPHYSICAL NOTES. SUPPLEMENT
GEOPHYS J R...... GEOPHYSICAL JOURNAL OF THE ROYAL ASTRONOMICAL SOCIETY
Geophys Prospect. . GEOPHYSICAL PROSPECTING
GEOPHYS R B...... GEOPHYSICAL RESEARCH BULLETIN
GEOPHYS R L...... GEOPHYSICAL RESEARCH LETTERS
GeoR.......... GEOGRAPHICAL REVIEW
GEORGET LAW..... GEORGETOWN LAW JOURNAL
GEORGE WASH..... GEORGE WASHINGTON LAW REVIEW
GEOSCI CAN...... GEOSCIENCE CANADA
GEOTECHNIQ...... GEOTECHNIQUE
Geoteknisk Inst Bull. . GEOTEKNISK INSTITUT. BULLETIN
Geo Wash L Rev.... GEORGE WASHINGTON LAW REVIEW
GeR........... GENGOGAKU RONSO
Ger........... GERMAN ECONOMIC REVIEW
Ger........... GERMANIA
Ger........... GERMANISTIK
GER ECON RE...... GERMAN ECONOMIC REVIEW
Ger L & L........ GERMAN LIFE AND LETTERS
GermL.......... GERMANISTISCHE LINGUISTIK
Germ R......... GERMANIC REVIEW
Germ Rom Monat. . GERMANISCH-ROMANISCHE MONATSCHRIFT
GERONTOL....... GERONTOLOGIST
Ger Q.......... GERMAN QUARTERLY
Ger Rev......... GERMANIC REVIEW
Gesell Erdk Leipz Mitt. . GESELLSCHAFT FUER ERDKUNDE ZU LEIPZIG. MITTEILUNGEN
Gesell f Kieler Stadtgesch Mitt. . GESELLSCHAFT FUER KIELER STADTGESCHICHTE. MITTEILUNGEN
Gesell Kieler Stadtgesch Mitt. . GESELLSCHAFT FUER KIELER STADTGESCHICHTE. MITTEILUNGEN
Gesundheits-Ing... GESUNDHEITS-INGENIEUR
GeW........... GERMANICA WRATISLAVIENSIA
GF............. GRAFISKT FORUM
GF............. GUTENBERG-JAHRBUCH
GFB........... GUSTAV FREYTAG BLAETTER

GFF . . . . GRILLPARZER FORUM FORCHTENSTEIN
GFFNS . . . . GODISNJAK FILOZOFSKOG FAKULTETA U NOVOM SADU
GFI . . . . GIORNALE CRITICO DELLA FILOSOFIA ITALIANA
G FIS SANIT . . . . . . GIORNALE DI FISICA SANITARIA E PROTEZIONE CONTRO LE RADIAZIONI
GGPI . . . . PEDAGOGICAL INSTITUTE IN GORKI. TRANSACTIONS
GH . . . . GELBE HEFTE
GH . . . . GURE HERRIA
GG . . . . GOLDEN GOOSF
GGA . . . . GOETTINGISCHE GELEHRTE ANZEIGER
G Genio Civ . . . . . . GIORNALE DEL GENIO CIVILE
GGK . . . . GAIGOKUGO GAIGOKU BUNGAKU KENKYU
GHA . . . . GOETEBORGS HOGSKOLAS ARSSKRIFT
GHANA SOC S . . . . . GHANA SOCIAL SCIENCE JOURNAL
GHQ . . . . GEORGIA HISTORICAL QUARTERLY
GHT . . . . GOETEBORGS HANDELSTIDNING
Gidrotekh Stroit . . . GIDROTEKHNICHESKOE STROITEL'STVO
Gids . . . . DE GIDS
GIF . . . . GIORNALE ITALIANO DI FILOLOGIA
GIFT CHILD . . . . . . GIFTED CHILD QUARTERLY
GInd . . . . GUIDE TO INDIAN PERIODICAL LITERATURE
GIOR GERONT . . . . . GIORNALE DI GERONTOLOGIA
Gior storico . . . . . . GIORNALE STORICO DELLA LETTERATURA ITALIANA
GJ . . . . GEOGRAPHICAL JOURNAL
GJ . . . . GUTENBERG-JAHRBUCH
GjA . . . . GJURMIME ALBANOLOGJIKE (PRISHTINA)
GJb . . . . GEOGRAPHISCHES JAHRBUCH
GK . . . . GENGO KENKYU
GK . . . . GEOTHE-KALENDER
GKVVH . . . . GOETEBORGS KUNGL. VETENSKAPS OCH VITTERHETS SAMHAELLES HANDLINGAR
GL . . . . GAZETTE DES LETTRES
GL . . . . GENERAL LINGUISTICS
GI . . . . GLASNIK
GL . . . . GLOSSA
GL . . . . GLOTTA
GLa . . . . GAZETTE DE LAUSANNE
GLAIU . . . . GLEDALISKI LIST AKADEMIJE ZA IGRALSKO UMETNOST
GL&L . . . . GERMAN LIFE AND LETTERS
Glasers Ann . . . . . . GLASERS ANNALEN
Glasgow Art R . . . . . GLASGOW ART GALLERY AND MUSEUMS ASSOCIATION. REVIEW
GLAS MATH J . . . . . GLASGOW MATHEMATICAL JOURNAL
GlasSAN . . . . GLAS SRPSKE AKADEMIJE NAUKA
Glass Ceram . . . . . . GLASS AND CERAMICS
Glass Ind . . . . GLASS INDUSTRY
GLASS TECH . . . . . . GLASS TECHNOLOGY
Glastech Ber . . . . . . GLASTECHNISCHE BERICHTE
GLC . . . . GLOSSARI DI LINGUA CONTEMPORANEA
GLECS . . . . GROUPE LINGUISTIQUE D'ETUDES CHAMITO-SEMITIQUES. COMPTES RENDUS
GIH . . . . GLASS HILL
GLit . . . . GAZETA LITERARA
GLL . . . . GERMAN LIFE AND LETTERS
GLLNS . . . . GERMAN LIFE AND LETTERS. NEW SERIES

GISAN . . . . GLAS SRPSKA AKADEMIJA NAUKA
GLSNG-L . . . . GLEDALISKI LIST SLOVENSKEGA NARODNEGA GLEDALISCA V LJUBLJANE
GLSNG-M . . . . GLEDALISKI LIST SLOVENSKEGA NARODNEGA GLEDALISCA V MARIBORU
GM . . . . GANDHI MARG
GM . . . . GAZETA MUSICAL
GM . . . . GEOGRAPHICAL MAGAZINE
GM . . . . GIORNALE DI METAFISICA
G Metaf . . . . GIORNALE DI METAFISICA
GMSLL . . . . GEORGETOWN MONOGRAPH SERIES ON LANGUAGE AND LINGUISTICS
GN . . . . GERMANIC NOTES
Gn . . . . GNOMON
GNDBiH . . . . GODISNJAK NAUCNOG DRUSTVA NR BOSNE I HERCEGOVINE
GNS . . . . GAZETTE NUMISMATIQUE SUISSE
God . . . . ,. . . . . . . GODISNIK N SOFILSKIYA UNIVERSITET. ISTORIKOFILOLOGICESKI FAKULTET
Godey . . . . GODEY'S LADY'S BOOK
GodFFNS . . . . GODISNJAK FILOZOFSKOG FAKULTETA U NOVOM SADU
GodSU . . . . GODISNIK NA SOFIJSKIJA UNIVERSITET: FAKULTET PO SLAVJANSKI FILOLOGII
Goe . . . . GOETHE, VIERTELJAHRSSCHRIFT DER GOETHE-GESELLSCHAFT
Goethe-Al . . . . GOETHE-ALMANACH
GOF . . . . GOLDEN FLEECE
Golden Bk . . . . GOLDEN BOOK MAGAZINE
Golden Gate L Rev . . GOLDEN GATE LAW REVIEW
Gold K . . . . GOLDENE KEYT
Gonzaga L Rev . . . . GONZAGA LAW REVIEW
Good H . . . . GOOD HOUSEKEEPING
Good House . . . . . . GOOD HOUSEKEEPING
Gorn Zh . . . . GORNYI ZHURNAL
Gor R . . . . GORDON REVIEW
Gospod Wodna . . . . GOSPODARKA WODNA
Goth SE . . . . GOTHENBURG STUDIES IN ENGLISH
Gott Abh . . . . ABHANDLUNGEN DER KUNGLIGA. GESSELSCHAFT DER WISSENSCHAFTEN ZU GOETTINGEN
Gottesd U Kir . . . . . GOTTESDIENST UND KIRCHENMUSIK
Govt & Oppos . . . . . GOVERNMENT AND OPPOSITION
GOVT OPPOS . . . . . . GOVERNMENT AND OPPOSITION
Govt Pub R . . . . GOVERNMENT PUBLICATIONS REVIEW
GP . . . . GIORNALE DEI POETI
GP . . . . GREGORIOS HO PALAMAS
GP . . . . GULDEN PASSER
GPerfArts . . . . GUIDE TO PERFORMING ARTS
GPJ . . . . GREAT PLAINS JOURNAL
GPM . . . . GENETIC PSYCHOLOGY MONOGRAPHS
GPrag . . . . GERMANISTICA PRAGENSIA
GPSR . . . . GLOSSAIRE DES PATOIS DE LA SUISSE ROMANDE
GPTKS . . . . GLASNIK PRAVOSLAVNE TZRKVE U KRALJEVINI SRBIJI
GQ . . . . GERMANIC QUARTERLY
GQ . . . . GERMAN QUARTERLY
GR . . . . GEOGRAPHICAL REVIEW
GR . . . . GEORGIA REVIEW
GR . . . . GERMANIC REVIEW
GR . . . . GERMAN REVIEW
GR . . . . GRANDE REVUE

Grade Teach...... GRADE TEACHER
Gradja......... GRADJA ZA POVIJEST KNJIZEVNOSTI HRVATSKE
Grad Res Ed...... GRADUATE RESEARCH IN EDUCATION AND RELATED DISCIPLINES
GR&BS......... GREEK, ROMAN AND BYZANTINE STUDIES
Granite Mo...... GRANITE MONTHLY
Graphic Sci...... GRAPHIC SCIENCE
GRBS.......... GREEK, ROMAN AND BYZANTINE STUDIES
Greece & Rome New Surv Class.. GREECE AND ROME: NEW SURVEYS IN THE CLASSICS
Greek Rom & Byz Stud.. GREEK, ROMAN AND BYZANTINE STUDIES
Greg........... GREGORIANUM
GREGOR........ GREGORIUSBLAD
Grenoble Univ Lett Ann.. UNIVERSITE DE GRENOBLE. LETTRES-DROIT. ANNALES
Grenoble Univ Sci Ann.. UNIVERSITE DE GRENOBLE. SCIENCES-MEDECINE. ANNALES
GRM........... GERMANISCH-ROMANISCHE MONATSSCHRIFT
G-R Mon........ GERMANISCH-ROMANISCHE MONATSSCHRIFT
GRMS.......... GERMANISCH-ROMANISCHE MONATSSCHRIFT
Gr Orth Th R...... GREEK ORTHODOX THEOLOGICAL REVIEW
GROUND WAT..... GROUND WATER AGE
Group Avan Mec Ind.. GROUPEMENT POUR L'AVANCEMENT DE LA MECANIQUE INDUSTRIELLE
GROUP PSYCH..... GROUP PSYCHOTHERAPY AND PSYCHODRAMA
GROWTH CHAN.... GROWTH AND CHANGE
GrSt........... GRUNDTVIG STUDIER
Grund Kyber Geist.. GRUNDLAGESTUDIEN AUS KYBERNETIK UND GEISTESWISSENSCHAFT
GRUPPENPSYC.... GRUPPENPSYCHOTHERAPIE UND GRUPPENDYNAMIK
GS............. GENGO SEIKATSU
GS............. GERMANISTISCHE STUDIEN
GS............. GRAI SI SUFLET
GSA........... GERMAN STUDIES IN AMERICA
GSAI........... GIORNALE DELLA SOCIETA ASIATICA ITALIANA
GSB........... GENERAL SEMANTICS BULLETIN
GSD........... GEISTES-UND SOZIALWISSENSCHAFTLICHE DISSERTATIONEN
GSE........... GOTHENBURG STUDIES IN ENGLISH
GSE........... GRADUATE STUDENT OF ENGLISH
GSF........... GALAXY SCIENCE FICTION
GSFN.......... GALAXY SCIENCE FICTION NOVELS
GSFS.......... GREAT SCIENCE FICTION STORIES
GSL........... GERMANO-SLAVICA
GSL........... MEDIEVAL STUDIES IN MEMORY OF GERTRUDE SCHOEPPERLE LOOMIS
GSLI........... GIORNALE STORICO DELLA LETTERATURA ITALIANA
GSLL.......... GIORNALE STORICO E LETTERARIO DELLA LIGURIA
GSt........... GERMANISCHE STUDIEN
GSU........... GODISNIK NA SOFIJSKIYA UNIVERSITET. FILOLOGICESKI FAKULTET
GSUF.......... GODISNIK NA SOFIJSKIYA UNIVERSITET. FILOLOGICESKI FAKULTET
GSUFZF......... GODISNIK NA SOFIJSKIYA UNIVERSITET. FAKULTET PO ZAPADNI FILOLOGII
GT............ GEOGRAFISK TIDSKRIFT
Gt Brit & East..... GREAT BRITAIN AND THE EAST
Gt Plains Jour..... GREAT PLAINS JOURNAL
GTT........... GEREFORMEERD THEOLOGISCH TIJDSCHRIFT
GUA........... GOETEBORGS UNIVERSITETS ARSSKRIFT
Guam Ag Exp...... GUAM AGRICULTURAL EXPERIMENT STATION PUBLICATIONS
GuG........... GESTALT UND GEDANKE: EIN JAHRBUCH

GUILD PRAC...... GUILD PRACTITIONER
GUITAR R........ GUITAR REVIEW
Gummi Asbest Kunstst.. GUMMI, ASBEST, KUNSTSTOFFE
GUMSL.......... GEORGETOWN UNIVERSITY MONOGRAPH SERIES ON LANGUAGES AND LINGUISTICS
Gunton.......... GUNTON'S MAGAZINE
GuT............ GEIST UND TAT
GuZ............ GEIST UND ZEIT
GV............. GIL VICENTE
GVA............ GRONINGSCHE VOLKSALMANACH
GW............. GENESIS WEST
GW............. GERMANICA WRATISLAVIENSIA
GW............. GUARDIAN WEEKLY
GW............. GYMNASIUM UND WISSENSCHAFT
Gym............ GYMNASIUM
GYNECOL INV..... GYNECOLOGIC INVESTIGATION
GZ............. GEOGRAPHISCHE ZEITSCHRIFT
GZH............ GDANSKIE ZESZYTY HUMANISTYCZNE
GZM............ GLASNIK ZEMALJSKOG MUZEJA (SUBSERIES) ETNOLOGIJA

PERIODICAL TITLE ABBREVIATIONS

H

H.............. HERMES. ZEITSCHRIFT FUER KLASSISCHE PHILOLOGIE
H.............. HISPANIA
H.............. HISTORY
HA............. HANDES AMSORIAY
HA............. HEIDELBERGER ABHANDLUNGEN
Ha............. HERMATHENA
HAB............ HUMANITIES ASSOCIATION BULLETIN
HACETT B SS...... HACETTEPE BULLETIN OF SOCIAL SCIENCES AND HUMANITIES
HAEK........... HISTORISCHE. ARCHIV FUER DIE ERZBISTUM KOELN
Haerterei-Tech Mitt.. HAERTEREI-TECHNISCHE MITTEILUNGEN
HAHGG.......... HISTORICHE AVONDEN, UITGEGEVEN DOOR HET HISTORICHE GENOOTSCHAP TE GRONINGEN
              TER GELEGENHEID VAN ZIJN TWINTIGJARIG BESTAAN
HAHR.......... HISPANIC AMERICAN HISTORICAL REVIEW
Halle Beitr....... BEITRAEGE ZUR GESCHICHTE DER DEUTSCHEN SPRACHE UND LITERATUR (HALLE)
Halle Univ Wiss Z Gesellsch & Sprachw Reihe.. HALLE. UNIVERSITAET. WISSENSCHAFTLICHE ZEITSCHRIFT
              GESELLSCHAFTS UND SPRACHWISSENSCHAFTLICHE REIHE
Hamb Zool Staatsinst u Zool Mus Mitt.. HAMBURG. ZOOLOGISCHES STAATSINSTITUT UND ZOOLOGISCHES
              MUSEUM. MITTEILUNGEN
Hampton......... HAMPTON'S MAGAZINE
Handelingen Commissie Toponymie & Dialectologie.. HANDELINGEN VAN DE KONINKLIJKE COMMISSIE VOOR
              TOPONYMIE EN DIALECTOLOGIE
Handelingen Ned Phonol Werkgemeenschap.. HANDELINGEN VAN DE NEDERLANDSE PHONOLOGISCHE
              WERKGEMEENSCHAP
H & Home........ HOUSE AND HOME
HandKonCommTop-Dial.. HANDELINGEN VAN DE KONINKLIJKE COMMISSIE VOOR TOPONYMIE EN DIALECTOLOGIE
H&M........... HOMMES ET MONDES
H&N............ HERE AND NOW
HandNFC........ HANDELINGEN VAN HET NEDERLANDS FILOLOGENCONGRES
H & R.......... HUMANISME ET RENAISSANCE
Hand VIFC....... HANDELINGEN VAN HET VLAAMSE FILOLOGENCONGRES
HAR............ HAMBURGER AKADEMISCHE RUNDSCHAU
Harp B......... HARPER'S BAZAAR
Harper......... HARPER'S MAGAZINE
Harp N......... HARP NEWS
Harp W......... HARPER'S WEEKLY
Hartf Sem Rec..... HARTFORD SEMINARY RECORD
Hart Q......... HARTFORD QUARTERLY
Hart R......... HARTWICK REVIEW
HarvardA....... HARVARD ADVOCATE
Harvard Bsns R.... HARVARD BUSINESS REVIEW
Harvard Ed R...... HARVARD EDUCATIONAL REVIEW
Harvard Lib Bul.... HARVARD LIBRARY BULLETIN
Harvard Univ Dep Eng Publ..HARVARD UNIVERSITY. DEPARTMENT OF ENGINEERING. PUBLICATIONS
Harvard Univ Harvard Soil Mech Ser..HARVARD UNIVERSITY. HARVARD SOIL MECHANICS SERIES
HARV BUS RE..... HARVARD BUSINESS REVIEW
HARV CIV RI...... HARVARD CIVIL RIGHTS
Harv Div B....... HARVARD DIVINITY BULLETIN
HARV EDU RE..... HARVARD EDUCATIONAL REVIEW
Harv Grad M...... HARVARD GRADUATES' MAGAZINE
Harv Int L J....... HARVARD INTERNATIONAL LAW JOURNAL
Harv J Asiatic Stud.. HARVARD JOURNAL OF ASIATIC STUDIES

HARV J LEG . . . . . . HARVARD JOURNAL ON LEGISLATION
Harv Law R . . . . . . HARVARD LAW REVIEW
Harv Lib Bull . . . . . . HARVARD LIBRARY BULLETIN
Harv LS Bull . . . . . . HARVARD LAW SCHOOL BULLETIN
Harv Mo . . . . HARVARD MONTHLY
Harv R . . . . HARVARD REVIEW
Harv Stud Class Philol . . HARVARD STUDIES IN CLASSICAL PHILOLOGY
Harv Th R . . . . HARVARD THEOLOGICAL REVIEW
Hasler Mitt . . . . HASLER MITTEILUNGEN
Hasler Rev . . . . HASLER REVIEW
HAST CEN ST . . . . . . HASTINGS CENTER STUDIES
Hast Cent Rpt . . . . . HASTINGS CENTER REPORT
Hast Cent St . . . . . . HASTINGS CENTER STUDIES
Hastings L J . . . . . . HASTINGS LAW JOURNAL
HAST LAW J . . . . . . HASTINGS LAW JOURNAL
Hausmus . . . . HAUSMUSIK
Havana Bibl Nac R . . HAVANA. BIBLIOTECA NACIONAL. REVISTA
Hawaii Ag Exp . . . . . HAWAII AGRICULTURAL EXPERIMENT STATION. PUBLICATIONS
Hawaiian For . . . . . . HAWAIIAN FORESTER AND AGRICULTURIST
Hawaii B J . . . . HAWAII BAR JOURNAL
Hawaii Lib Assn J . . . HAWAII LIBRARY ASSOCIATION. JOURNAL
Hawaii Univ Look Lab Oceanogr Eng Tech Rep . . HAWAII UNIVERSITY. LOOK LABORATORY OF OCEANOGRAPHIC
       ENGINEERING. TECHNICAL REPORT
HB . . . . HET BOEK
HB . . . . HISTORICAL BULLETIN
HB . . . . HORN BOOK
HB . . . . HUMAN BEHAVIOR
HBA . . . . HISTORIOGRAFIA Y BIBLIOGRAFIA AMERICANISTAS
HBalt . . . . HISPANIA (BALTIMORE)
HBd . . . . HAARLEMSCH BIJDRAGEN
HBL . . . . HOFMANNSTHAL BLAETTER
HBM . . . . DIE HAGHE. BIJDRAGEN EN MEDEDEELINGEN
HBR . . . . HARVARD BUSINESS REVIEW
HBSA . . . . HJALMAR BERGMAN SAMFUNDET ARSBOK
HBV . . . . HESSISCHE BLAETTER FUER VOLKSKUNDE
HBVk . . . . HESSISCHE BLAETTER FUER VOLKSKUNDE
HC . . . . HESSISCHE CHRONIK
HC . . . . HISTORICKY CASOPIS
HC . . . . HOLLINS CRITIC
HC . . . . HRISTIANSKOE CTENIE
HCal . . . . HISPANIA (CALIFORNIA)
HCompL . . . . HEBREW COMPUTATIONAL LINGUISTICS
HD . . . . HECHOS Y DICHOS
HD . . . . HUMAN DEVELOPMENT
HDL . . . . HANDBUCH DER DEUTSCHEN LITERATURGESCHICHTE
HDZ . . . . HRVATSKI DIJALEKTOLOSKI ZBORNIK
HDZb . . . . HRVATSKI DIJALEKTOLOSKI ZBORNIK
HE . . . . HUMAN EVENTS
HEAL ED MON . . . . . HEALTH EDUCATION MONOGRAPHS
Health Ed J . . . . HEALTH EDUCATION JOURNAL

HEALTH EDUC . . . . . HEALTH EDUCATION JOURNAL
HEALTH LAB . . . . . . HEALTH LABORATORY SCIENCE
HEALTH PHYS . . . . . HEALTH PHYSICS
HEALTH SERV . . . . . HEALTH SERVICES REPORT
Health Serv Res . . . . HEALTH SERVICES RESEARCH (CHICAGO)
HEARST'S M . . . . . . HEARST'S MAGAZINE
HEAS . . . . HARVARD EAST ASIAN SERIES
Heat Air Cond Contr . . HEATING AND AIR CONDITIONING CONTRACTOR
Heat Air Condit J . . . HEATING AND AIR CONDITIONING JOURNAL
Heat & Vent . . . . . . HEATING AND VENTILATING
Heating Piping . . . . . HEATING, PIPING AND AIR CONDITIONING
Heat Transfer Jap Res . . HEAT TRANSFER. JAPANESE RESEARCH
Heat Transfer Sov Res . . HEAT TRANSFER. SOVIET RESEARCH
Heat Vent Engr . . . . HEATING AND VENTILATING ENGINEER
HebrUCA . . . . HEBREW UNION COLLEGE ANNUAL
Hegel-Jrbh . . . . HEGEL-JAHRBUCH
HeidJb . . . . HEIDELBERGER JAHRBUECHER
Heid Stizb . . . . HEIDELBERGER AKADEMIE DER WISSENSCHAFTEN, SITZUNGSBERICHTE
HEILPAED FOR . . . . . HEILPAEDAGOGISCHE FORSCHUNG
HeineJ . . . . HEINE JAHRBUCH
Hel . . . . HELICON
Hel . . . . HELLAS-JAHRBUCH
Helicop Wld . . . . . . HELICOPTER WORLD
HELG W MEER . . . . . HELGOLANDER WISSENSCHAFTLICHE MEERESUNTERSUCHUNGEN
HellasJB . . . . HELLAS-JAHRBUCH
Hellen . . . . HELLENIKA
Hellenika S . . . . HELLENIKA (SALONIKA)
HELV CHIM A . . . . . HELVETICA CHIMICA ACTA
HELV ODON A . . . . . HELVETICA ODONTOLOGICA ACTA
HELV PAED A . . . . . HELVETICA PAEDIATRICA ACTA
HELV PHYS A . . . . . HELVETICA PHYSICA ACTA
Hem . . . . ONS HEMECHT
Hennepin Law . . . . . HENNEPIN LAWYER
HEP . . . . HONG KONG ECONOMIC PAPERS
HER . . . . HARVARD EDUCATIONAL REVIEW
Herald Lib Sci . . . . . HERALD OF LIBRARY SCIENCE
Heron Engl Ed . . . . . HERON (ENGLISH EDITION)
HERZ KREISL . . . . . . HERZ KREISLAUF
Hesp . . . . HESPERIAN
Heythrop J . . . . HEYTHROP JOURNAL
HF . . . . HAMBURGER FREMDENBLATT
HF . . . . HEIDELBERGER FORSCHUNGEN
HF . . . . HOOSIER FOLKLORE
HFB . . . . HOOSIER FOLKLORE BULLETIN
HFC . . . . HANTS FIELD CLUB AND ARCHAEOLOGICAL SOCIETY
HFM . . . . HISTORISK-FILOSOFISKE MEDDELELSER UDGIVET AF DET KONGELINGE DANSKE VIDENSKABERNES SELSKAB
HFMKDVS . . . . HISTORISK-FILOSOFISKE MEDDELELSER UDGIVET AF DET KONGELINGE DANSKE VIDENSKABERNES SELSKAB
HG . . . . HANNOVERSCHE GESCHICHTSBLAETTER
HG . . . . HUMANISTISCHES GYMNASIUM

HGB. . . . . HANSISCHE GESCHICHTSBLAETTER
HGB. . . . . HET GILDEBOEK. TIJDSCHRIFT VOOR KERKELIJKE KUNST EN OUDHEIDKUNDE
HGGSEB. . . . . HANDELINGEN VAN HET GENOOTSCHAP VOOR GESCHIEDENIS GESTICHT ONDER DE BENAMING
  SOCIETE D'EMULATION DE BRUGES
HGH. . . . . HANSISCHE GESCHICHTBLAETTER
HGKV. . . . . HEFTE FUER GESCHICHTE, KUNST UND VOLKSKUNDE
HGS. . . . . HARVARD GERMANIC STUDIES
Hi. . . . . HID
Hi. . . . . HISPANIA
HI. . . . . HISTORICA IBERICA
HIAR. . . . . HAMBURGER IBERO-AMERIKANISCHE REIHE
HibbJ. . . . . HIBBERT JOURNAL
HibJ. . . . . HIBBERT JOURNAL
HICL. . . . . HISTOIRE DES IDEES ET CRITIQUE LITTERAIRE
Hi Fi. . . . . HIGH FIDELITY
HIGH EDUC. . . . . . . HIGHER EDUCATION
HIGH EDUC R. . . . . . HIGHER EDUCATION REVIEW
Higher Ed. . . . . HIGHER EDUCATION
High Polym. . . . . . . HIGH POLYMERS
High Sch J. . . . . HIGH SCHOOL JOURNAL
High Temp. . . . . HIGH TEMPERATURE
High Temp High Pressures. . HIGH TEMPERATURES HIGH PRESSURES
HIGH TEMP R. . . . . HIGH TEMPERATURE-USSR
HIGH TEMP S. . . . . . HIGH TEMPERATURE SCIENCE
Highw Des Constr. . HIGHWAYS DESIGN AND CONSTRUCTION
Highw Eng. . . . . HIGHWAY ENGINEER
Highw Publ Wks. . . . HIGHWAYS AND PUBLIC WORKS
Highw Rd Constr. . . HIGHWAYS AND ROAD CONSTRUCTION
Highw Res Bd Nat Coop Highw Res Program Rep. . HIGHWAY RESEARCH BOARD. NATIONAL COOPERATIVE
  HIGHWAY RESEARCH PROGRAM. REPORT
Highw Res Board Spec Rep. . HIGHWAY RESEARCH BOARD. SPECIAL REPORT
Highw Res News. . . HIGHWAY RESEARCH NEWS
Highw Res Rec. . . . . HIGHWAY RESEARCH RECORD
Highw Road Const. . HIGHWAYS AND ROAD CONSTRUCTION
Highw Traff Engng. . HIGHWAYS OF TRAFFIC ENGINEERING
HiM. . . . . HISPANIA (MADRID)
HINL. . . . . HISTORY OF IDEAS NEWSLETTER
HIR. . . . . HISPANIC REVIEW
HiroBK. . . . . HIROSHIMA DAIGAKU BUNGAKUBU KIYO
HIROS J MED. . . . . . HIROSHIMA JOURNAL OF MEDICAL SCIENCES
His. . . . . HISPANIA
HisK. . . . . HISPANIA (UNIVERSITY OF KANSAS. LAWRENCE)
HisL. . . . . HISPANIA (UNIVERSITY OF KANSAS. LAWRENCE)
Hisp. . . . . HISPANIA (MADRID)
Hisp. . . . . HISPANIA (STANFORD UNIVERSITY)
Hispano. . . . . HISPANOFILA (MADRID)
Hispan R. . . . . HISPANIC REVIEW
HispCal. . . . . HISPANIA (STANFORD, CALIFORNIA)
Hispl. . . . . HISPANOFILA (MADRID AND ILLINOIS)
HispM. . . . . HISPANIA (MADRID)
Hisp Rev. . . . . HISPANIC REVIEW

Hist............ HISTORICA
Hist............ HISTORY
HistAb.......... HISTORICAL ABSTRACTS
Hist Ag.......... HISTORIA AGRICULTURAE
Hist and Phil Soc of Ohio Trans.. HISTORICAL AND PHILOSOPHICAL SOCIETY OF OHIO. TRANSACTIONS
Hist and Theory.... HISTORY AND THEORY
Hist Bull......... HISTORICAL BULLETIN
Hist Educ Jour..... HISTORY OF EDUCATION JOURNAL
Hist Educ Q....... HISTORY OF EDUCATION QUARTERLY
Hist J........... HISTORICAL JOURNAL
HistL...........HISTORIOGRAPHIA LINGUISTICA
Hist M.......... HISTORICAL MAGAZINE (DAWSON'S)
Hist Mag........ HISTORICAL MAGAZINE OF THE PROTESTANT EPISCOPAL CHURCH
Hist Mex........ HISTORIA MEXICANA
Hist N H........ HISTORICAL NEW HAMPSHIRE
HISTOCHEMIS..... HISTOCHEMISTRY
HISTOCHEM J..... HISTOCHEMICAL JOURNAL
History of Ed Soc Bull.. HISTORY OF EDUCATION SOCIETY BULLETIN
Hist Outl........ HISTORICAL OUTLOOK
Hist Pol Ec....... HISTORY OF POLITICAL ECONOMY
HIST POLIT...... HISTORY OF POLITICAL ECONOMY
Hist Pres........ HISTORIC PRESERVATION
Hist Rel......... HISTORY OF RELIGIONS
HIST SOC........ HISTOIRE SOCIALE/SOCIAL HISTORY
Hist Stud........ HISTORICAL STUDIES
Hist Theor....... HISTORY AND THEORY
Hist Tidskr....... HISTORISK TIDSKRIFT
Hist Today....... HISTORY TODAY
Hist Verein Oberpfalz & Regensburg Verh..HISTORISCHER VEREIN FUER OBERPFALZ UND REGENSBURG VERHANDLUNGEN
Hist Ver f d Grafsch Ravensberg Jahresber..HISTORISCHER VEREIN FUER DIE GRAFSCHAFT RAVENSBERG ZU BIELEFELD. JAHRESBERICHTF
Hist Ver f Mittelfranken Jahresber..HISTORISCHER VEREIN FUER MITTELFRANKEN. JAHRESBERICHTE
Hist Ver v Oberpfalz u Regensburg Verhandl..HISTORISCHER VEREIN VON OBERPFALZ UND REGENSBURG. VERHANDLUNGEN
Hist Z.......... HISTORISCHE ZEITSCHRIFT
Hist Ztsch....... HISTORISCHE ZEITSCHRIFT
Hitachi Rev....... HITACHI REVIEW
HITOTS J ECON.... HITOTSUBASHI JOURNAL OF ECONOMICS
HiUS........... HISPANIA (U.S.A.)
HJ............. HIBBERT JOURNAL
HJ............. HISTORIA JUDAICA
HJ............. HISTORISCHES JAHRBUCH
HJAS...........HARVARD JOURNAL OF ASIATIC STUDIES
HJAS...........HITOTSUBASHI JOURNAL OF ARTS AND SCIENCES
HJb............HEBBEL-JAHRBUCH
HJC........... HITOTSUBASHI JOURNAL OF COMMERCE & MANAGEMENT
HJE............ HITOTSUBASHI JOURNAL OF ECONOMICS
HJI............ HIBBERT JOURNAL
HJSS........... HITOTSUBASHI JOURNAL OF SOCIAL STUDIES
HJud........... HISTORIA JUDAICA

PERIODICAL TITLE ABBREVIATIONS

HK............. HRVATSKO KOLO
HKCTD.......... HANDELINGEN VAN DE KONINKLIJKE COMMISSIE VOOR TOPONYMIE EN DIALECTOLOGIE
HKDBK.......... HOKKAIDO DAIGAKU BUNGAKUBU KIYO
HKN............ HOGEN KENKYU NENPO
HL............. HANGING LOOSE
HL............. HARVARD LIBRARY BULLETIN
HL............. HOCHLAND
HL............. HUMANISTICA LOVANIENSIA
HLB............ HARVARD LIBRARY BULLETIN
HLB............ HISTORISCHES LITTERATURBLATT
HLB............ HUNTINGTON LIBRARY BULLETIN
HLF............ HISTOIRE LITTERAIRE DE LA FRANCE
HLH ZEIT HEIZUNG LUEFTUNG KLIM HAUSTECH..HLH. ZEITSCHRIFT FUER HEIZUNG, LUEFTUNG, KLIMATECHNIK, HAUSTECHNIK
HLK............ HEFTE FUER LITERATUR UND KRITIK
HLQ............ HUNTINGTON LIBRARY QUARTERLY
HLR............ HARVARD LAW REVIEW
HLS............ HISTORISKA OCH LITTERATURHISTORISKA STUDIER
HM............. HARPER'S MAGAZINE
HM............. HERMES
HM............. HOMMES ET MONDES
HMad.......... HISPANIA (MADRID)
HME............ HISTORICAL MAGAZINE OF THE PROTESTANT EPISCOPAL CHURCH
H MEX......... HISTORIA MEXICANA
HMGOG........ HANDELINGEN DER MAATSCHAPPIJ VOOR GESCHIEDENIS EN OUDHEIDKUNDE TE GENT
HMMNL........ HANDELINGEN EN MEDEDEELINGEN VAN DE MAATSCHAPPIJ DER NEDERLANDSCHE LETTERKUNDE TE LEIDEN
HMP............ HOMENAJE A MENENDEZ PIDAL
HMPEC......... HISTORICAL MAGAZINE OF THE PROTESTANT EPISCOPAL CHURCH
HN............. HAMANN NEWSLETTER
HN............. HEMINGWAY NOTES
HN............. HERE AND NOW
HN............. HOCHSCHULNACHRICHTEN
HNH............ HISTORICAL NEW HAMPSHIRE
HNK............ HO NEOS KOUBARAS
HNorv.......... HUMANIORA NORVEGICA
HNO WEG FAC..... HNO. WEGEISER FUER DIE FACHARZLICHE PRAXIS
HNR............ HIKONE RONSO
Ho............. HOCHLAND
Ho & For R....... HOME AND FOREIGN REVIEW
Hoards D........ HOARD'S DAIRYMAN
Hob............ HOBBIES
Hochl.......... HOCHLAND
HoE............ HO ERANISTES
Hoesch Ber Forsch Entwickl Werke..HOESCH, ARBEITSKREIS FORSCHUNG UND ENTWICKLUNG, BERICHTE AUS FORSCHUNG UND ENTWICKLUNG UNSERER WERKE
Hofstra L Rev..... HOFSTRA LAW REVIEW
Hogg.......... HOGG'S INSTRUCTOR
HOH........... HAUNT OF HORROR
HoJb.......... HOLDERLIN-JAHRBUCH
Holb Rev........ HOLBORN REVIEW

HOLZF HOLZV	HOLZFORSCHUNG UND HOLZVERWERTUNG
HOLZFORSCH	HOLZFORSCHUNG
Holstein World	HOLSTEIN-FRIESIAN WORLD
HOLZ ROH WE	HOLZ ALS ROH- UND WERKSTOFF
Home Econ News . . .	HOME ECONOMICS NEWS
Home Gard	HOME GARDEN
Home Geog Mo	HOME GEOGRAPHIC MONTHLY
Home Prog	HOME PROGRESS
HOMME SOC	HOMME ET LA SOCIETE
Hoosier Sch Lib	HOOSIER SCHOOL LIBRARIES
Hop R	HOPKINS REVIEW
HOR	HORIZON
HORMONE BEH	HORMONES AND BEHAVIOR
HORMONE MET	HORMONE AND METABOLIC RESEARCH
HORMONE RES	HORMONE RESEARCH
Horn Bk	HORN BOOK
Horol J	HOROLOGICAL JOURNAL
HorsAb	HORSEMAN'S ABSTRACTS
Hort	HORTICULTURE
Hort N	HORTICULTURAL NEWS
Hort Res	HORTICULTURAL RESEARCH
HospAb	HOSPITAL ABSTRACTS
HOSP COMMUN	HOSPITAL AND COMMUNITY PSYCHIATRY
Hospital Mus News . .	HOSPITAL MUSIC NEWSLETTER
House & Gard	HOUSE AND GARDEN
House B	HOUSE BEAUTIFUL
House Words	HOUSEHOLD WORDS
HousP	HOUSING AND PLANNING REFERENCES
HOUSTON LAW	HOUSTON LAW REVIEW
HOUSTON L REV	HOUSTON LAW REVIEW
HOUSTON SYM	HOUSTON SYMPHONY PROGRAM NOTES
Hov Craft Hydrof . . .	HOVERING CRAFT AND HYDROFOIL
Hovercr Wld	HOVERCRAFT WORLD
Howard L J	HOWARD LAW JOURNAL
Howitt	HOWITT'S JOURNAL
HPB	HISTORISCH-POLITISCHE BLAETTER FUER DAS KATHOLISCHE DEUTSCHLAND
HPBKD	HISTORISCH-POLITISCHE BLAETTER FUER DAS KATHOLISCHE DEUTSCHLAND
HPBL	HISTORISCH-POLITISCHE BLAETTER FUER DAS KATHOLISCHE DEUTSCHLAND
HPEN	P.E.N. HONGROIS
H Points	HIGH POINTS
HPR	HOMILETIC AND PASTORAL REVIEW
HPS	HAMBURGER PHILOLOGISCHE STUDIEN
HPSO	HISTORICAL AND PHILOSOPHICAL SOCIETY OF OHIO. BULLETIN
HR	HERMES, MESSAGER SCIENTIFIQUE ET POPULAIRE DE L'ANTIQUITE CLASSIQUE EN RUSSIE
HR	HISPANIC REVIEW
HR	HUDSON REVIEW
HR	HUMAN RELATIONS
HR	HUMANISME ET RENAISSANCE
HRB	HOPKINS RESEARCH BULLETIN
HRBC	HISTORICAL REVIEW OF BERKS COUNTY
HRD	HAMBURGER ROMANISTISCHE DISSERTATIONEN

HRen.......... HUMANISME ET RENAISSANCE
HRPV.......... HERMES. REVISTA DEL PAIS VASCO
HRS........... HISTORICAL RECORDS AND STUDIES
HS............ HEMISPHERES
HS............ HISPANIA SACRA
HS............ HUMANITIES IN THE SOUTH
HSan.......... HELSINGIN SANOMAT
H Sch.......... HIGH SCHOOL
H Sch J......... HIGH SCHOOL JOURNAL
H Sch Q......... HIGH SCHOOL QUARTERLY
H Sch Teach...... HIGH SCHOOL TEACHER
HSCL.......... HARVARD STUDIES IN COMPARATIVE LITERATURE
HSCP.......... HARVARD STUDIES IN CLASSICAL PHILOLOGY
HSE............ HUNGARIAN STUDIES IN ENGLISH
HSELL.......... HIROSHIMA STUDIES IN ENGLISH LANGUAGE AND LITERATURE
HSL........... HARTFORD STUDIES IN LITERATURE
HSLS........... HARVARD SLAVIC STUDIES
HSNPL.......... HARVARD STUDIES AND NOTES IN PHILOLOGY AND LITERATURE
HSPh........... HARVARD STUDIES IN CLASSICAL PHILOLOGY
HSPL.......... HARVARD STUDIES AND NOTES IN PHILOLOGY AND LITERATURE
HSRL.......... HARVARD STUDIES IN ROMANCE LANGUAGES
HSS........... HARVARD SLAVIC STUDIES
HSSCQ.......... HISTORICAL SOCIETY OF SOUTHERN CALIFORNIA QUARTERLY
H-S Z PHYSL...... HOPPE-SEYLER ZEITSCHRIFT FUER PHYSIOLOGISCHE CHEMIE
H-T............ HESPERIS-TAMUDA
HT............ HISTORISK TIDSKRIFT
HT............ HISTORY TODAY
HTB........... NEW YORK HERALD-TRIBUNE BOOKS
HTD........... DANSK HISTORISK TIDSKRIFT
HTF........... HISTORISK TIDSKRIFT FOER FINLAND
HThR.......... HARVARD THEOLOGICAL REVIEW
HTK........... HISTORISK TIDSKRIFT
HTLStu......... HISTORIA I TEORIA LITERATURY-STUDIA
HTM........... HISTORY TEACHER'S MAGAZINE
HTO........... HISTORISK TIDSKRIFT (OSLO)
HTR........... HARVARD THEOLOGICAL REVIEW
HTS........... HISTORISK TIDSKRIFT (STOCKHOLM)
HTsFi.......... HISTORISK TIDSKRIFT FOER FINLAND
Hub Roz........ HUDEBNI ROZHLEDY
HUCA.......... HEBREW UNION COLLEGE ANNUAL
Hud R.......... HUDSON REVIEW
Hud Veda....... HUDEBNI VEDA
Hum........... HUMANIST
HUM........... HUMANIDADES
Hum........... HUMANITAS
HUMAN BIOL..... HUMAN BIOLOGY
HUMAN CONT..... HUMAN CONTEXT
HUMAN DEV...... HUMAN DEVELOPMENT
HUMAN ECOL..... HUMAN ECOLOGY
HUMAN FACT..... HUMAN FACTORS
HUMANGENET..... HUMANGENETIK

HUMAN HERED . . . . HUMAN HEREDITY
HUMAN ORG . . . . . . HUMAN ORGANIZATION
HUMAN PATH . . . . . HUMAN PATHOLOGY
HUMAN RELAT . . . . HUMAN RELATIONS
HumB . . . . HUMANITAS (BRESCIA)
Hum(Ba) . . . . HUMANIDADES (BUENOS-AIRES)
Hum Ecol Forum . . . . HUMAN ECOLOGY FORUM
Hume Stud . . . . . . HUME STUDIES
Hum Factors . . . . . . HUMAN FACTORS
HumNL . . . . HUMANITAS (NUEVO LEON)
Hum(NRH) . . . . HUMANITAS. LA NOUVELLE REVUE DES HUMANITES
Hum Org . . . . HUMAN ORGANIZATION
Hum Relat . . . . HUMAN RELATIONS
Hum (RES) . . . . HUMANITES. REVUE D'ENSEIGNEMENT SECONDAIRE ET D'EDUCATION
Hum (RIPh) . . . . HUMANITAS. REVUE INTERNATIONALE DE PHILOLOGIE CLASSIQUE ET HUMANITES
HumT . . . . HUMANITAS (TUCUMAN, ARGENTINA)
Hum Vetensk Samf i Lund Arsberatt . . HUMANISTISKA VETENSKAPS-SAMFUNDET I LUND ARSBERATTELSE
Hung Heavy Ind . . . . HUNGARIAN HEAVY INDUSTRIES
Hung S . . . . HUNGARIAN SURVEY
HunQ . . . . HUNGARIAN QUARTERLY (NEW YORK)
Hunt . . . . HUNT'S MERCHANTS' MAGAZINE
HuR . . . . HUDSON REVIEW
HuR . . . . HUMANISME ET RENAISSANCE
HussR . . . . HUSSON REVIEW (BANGOR, MAINE)
Hutn Listy . . . . HUTNICKE LISTY
HV . . . . HISTORISCHE VIERTELJAHRSCHRIFT
HVJ . . . . HISTORISCHE VIERTELJAHRSCHRIFT
HVJS . . . . HISTORISCHE VIERTELJAHRSCHRIFT
HvM . . . . HONAR VA MARDOM
HVNU . . . . HISTORISCHER VEREIN FUER NORDINGEN UND UMGEBUNG
HW . . . . HISTORICAL WYOMING
HWS . . . . HORACE WALPOLE SOCIETY
HwyResAb . . . . HIGHWAY RESEARCH ABSTRACTS
HYDRA PNEUM . . . . HYDRAULICS AND PNEUMATICS
Hydraul Pneum Pwr . . HYDRAULIC PNEUMATIC POWER
HYDROBIOL . . . . . . HYDROBIOLOGIA
HYDROC PROC . . . . HYDROCARBON PROCESSING
Hydrol Sci BULL Sci Hydrol . . HYDROLOGICAL SCIENCES. BULLETIN DES SCIENCES HYDROLOGIQUES
Hydrotech Constr . . HYDROTECHNICAL CONSTRUCTION
HYHN . . . . HSIN-YA SHU-YUAN HSUEH-SHY NIEN-K'AN
HYMN S . . . . HYMN SOCIETY OF GREAT BRITAIN AND IRELAND
HZ . . . . HISTORISCHE ZEITSCHRIFT
HZKP . . . . HERMES. ZEITSCHRIFT FUER KLASSISCHE PHILOLOGIE
HZM . . . . HANDLINGEN DER ZUIDNEDERLANDSE MAATSCHAPPIJ VOOR TAAL-EN LETTERKUNDE EN GESCHIEDENIS
HZMTLG . . . . HANDLINGEN DER ZUIDNEDERLANDSE MAATSCHAPPIJ VOOR TAAL-EN LETTERKUNDE EN GESCHIEDENIS
HZnMTL . . . . HANDLINGEN DER ZUIDNEDERLANDSE MAATSCHAPPIJ VOOR TAAL-EN LETTERKUNDE EN GESCHIEDENIS

I

I . . . . ISIS
I . . . . ITALICA
IA . . . . IBSEN-AARBOKEN
IA . . . . IBSENFORBUNDET: AARBOK
IA . . . . INSEL-ALMANACH
IA . . . . IRANICA ANTIQUA
IA . . . . ITALIA ANTICHISSIMA
IAA . . . . IBERO-AMERIKANISCHES ARCHIV
Ia Ag Exp . . . . IOWA STATE COLLEGE OF AGRICULTURE AND MECHANIC ARTS. AGRICULTURAL EXPERIMENT STATION. PUBLICATIONS
IAALD Q BULL . . . . . INTERNATIONAL ASSOCIATION OF AGRICULTURAL LIBRARIANS AND DOCUMENTALISTS. QUARTERLY BULLETIN
IAB . . . . INSTITUT FUER AUSLANDSBEZIEHUNGEN
IAC . . . . INDO-ASIAN CULTURE
IADD . . . . INDEX TO AMERICAN DOCTORAL DISSERTATIONS
IAE . . . . INTERNATIONALES ARCHIV FUER ETHNOGRAPHIE
IAHI . . . . INTERNATIONAL ARCHIVES OF THE HISTORY OF IDEAS
IAI . . . . IZVESTIJA NA BALGARSKIJA ARHEOLOGICESKI INSTUTUT
IAJRC . . . . IAJRC (INTERNATIONAL ASSOCIATION OF JAZZ RECORD COLLECTORS) JOURNAL
IA LAW REV . . . . IOWA LAW REVIEW
IALBull . . . . INSTITUT ARCHEOLOGIQUE LIEGEOIS. BULLETIN
IALR . . . . INTERNATIONAL ANTHROPOLOGICAL AND LINGUISTIC REVIEW
Ia L Rev . . . . IOWA LAW REVIEW
IAM . . . . ISTANBUL ASARIATIKA MUZELERI NESRIYATI
IAN . . . . IZVESTIYA AKADEMII NAUK SSSR. SERIJA LITERATURY I JAZYKA (MOSCOW)
I&L . . . . IAZYK I LITERATURA
I&V . . . . IDEAS Y VALORES
IAN-OGN . . . . IZVESTIYA AKADEMII NAUK SSSR. OTDELENIYA GUMANITARNYX NAUK
IAN-OLJa . . . . IZVESTIYA AKADEMII NAUK OTDELENIYA LITERATURY I JAZYKA
IAG J . . . . IAG (INTERNATIONAL FEDERATION FOR INFORMATION PROCESSING ADMINISTRATIVE DATA PROCESSING GROUP) JOURNAL
IAN OON . . . . IZVESTIYA AKADEMII NAUK SSSR. OTDELENIYA OBSCESTVENNYX NAUK
IAN ORJaSL . . . . . . IZVESTIYA AKADEMII NAUK SSSR. OTDELENIYA RUSSKOGO JAZYKA I SLAVESNOSTI AKADEMII NAUK
IAN SSS BIO . . . . . . IZVESTIYA AKADEMII NAUK SSSR. SERIYA BIOLOGICHESKAYA
IAN SSS FAO . . . . . . IZVESTIYA AKADEMII NAUK SSSR. SERIYA FIZIKA ATMOSFERY I OKEANA
IAN SSS FIZ . . . . IZVESTIYA AKADEMII NAUK SSSR. SERIYA FIZICHESKAYA
IANUz . . . . IZVESTIYA AKADEMII NAUK. UZBEKISTANSKOJ SSSR
IARB . . . . INTER-AMERICAN REVIEW OF BIBLIOGRAPHY
IASOP . . . . INSTITUTE OF AFRICAN STUDIES. OCCASIONAL PUBLICATIONS
IAT . . . . IZVESTIYA AKADEMII NAUK TURKMENSKOJ SSSR. SERIYA OBSCESTVENNYX NAUK
Ib . . . . IBERO-ROMANIA
IB . . . . INDOGERMANISCHE BIBLIOTHEK
IB . . . . IRISH BOOK (BIBLIOGRAPHICAL SOCIETY OF IRELAND)
IBA of A . . . . INVESTMENT BANKERS ASSOCIATION OF AMERICA. BULLETIN
Ibero . . . . IBERO-ROMANIA
IBHS . . . . INTERNATIONAL BIBLIOGRAPHY OF HISTORICAL SCIENCES
IBi . . . . ILLUSTRAZIONE BIELLESE
IBk . . . . INDEX TO BOOK REVIEWS IN THE HUMANITIES

```
IBK . . . . . . . . . . . . INNSBRUECKER BEITRAEGE ZUR KULTURWISSENSCHAFT
IBL . . . . . . . . . . . . INSTYTUT BADAN LITERACKICK POLSKIEJ AKADEMII NAUK
IBLA . . . . . . . . . . . INSTITUT BELLES-LETTRES ARABES. REVUE (TUNIS)
IBM J RES . . . . . . . IBM JOURNAL OF RESEARCH AND DEVELOPMENT
IBM J Res Dev . . . . . IBM JOURNAL OF RESEARCH AND DEVELOPMENT
IBM Syst J . . . . . . . IBM SYSTEMS JOURNAL
IbNY . . . . . . . . . . . IBERICA (NEW YORK)
IBOJ . . . . . . . . . . . INFORMACNI BULLETIN PRO OTAZKY JAZYKOVEDNE
IBS . . . . . . . . . . . . INNSBRUECKER BEITRAEGE ZUR SPRACHWISSENSCHAFT
IBZ . . . . . . . . . . . . INTERNATIONALE BIBLIOGRAPHIE DER ZEITSCHRIFTENLITERATUR
IC . . . . . . . . . . . . . ICELANDIC CANADIAN
IC . . . . . . . . . . . . . INDIAN CULTURE
IC . . . . . . . . . . . . . INSTITUTO COIMBRA
IC . . . . . . . . . . . . . ISLAMIC CULTURE
IC . . . . . . . . . . . . . ISTORISKI CASOPIS
ICC . . . . . . . . . . . . INFORMATION DES COURS COMPLEMENTAIRES
ICC . . . . . . . . . . . . INSTITUTO CARO Y CUERVO
ICC . . . . . . . . . . . . INTERMEDIAIRE DES CHERCHEURS ET DES CURIEUX
ICC Pract J . . . . . . ICC (INTERSTATE COMMERCE COMMISSION) PRACTITIONERS' JOURNAL
ICE . . . . . . . . . . . . INFORMACION COMERCIAL ESPANOL
Ice Cream R . . . . . . ICE CREAM REVIEW
ICFTU Econ & Social Bul . . ICFTU (INTERNATIONAL CONFEDERATION OF FREE TRADE UNIONS) ECONOMIC AND
                            SOCIAL BULLETIN
ICHCA J . . . . . . . . ICHCA (INTERNATIONAL CARGO HANDLING COORDINATION ASSOCIATION) JOURNAL
ICHCA Mon J . . . . . . ICHCA (INTERNATIONAL CARGO HANDLING COORDINATION ASSOCIATION) MONTHLY
                        JOURNAL
IChildMag . . . . . . . SUBJECT INDEX TO CHILDREN'S MAGAZINES
ICHR . . . . . . . . . . . ILLINOIS CATHOLIC HISTORICAL REVIEW
ICLM . . . . . . . . . . . INDEX TO COMMONWEALTH LITTLE MAGAZINES
ICP . . . . . . . . . . . . INFORMACAO CULTURAL PORTUGUES
ICS . . . . . . . . . . . . ITALIA CHE SCRIVE
ID . . . . . . . . . . . . . INTELLECTUAL DIGEST
ID . . . . . . . . . . . . . IRISH DIGEST
ID . . . . . . . . . . . . . ITALIA DIALETTALE
Idaho Ag Exp . . . . . . UNIVERSITY OF IDAHO. AGRICULTURAL EXPERIMENT STATION. PUBLICATIONS
Idaho Bur Mines Geol Bull . . IDAHO BUREAU OF MINES AND GEOLOGY. BULLETIN
Idaho Bur Mines Geol County Rep . . IDAHO BUREAU OF MINES AND GEOLOGY. COUNTY REPORT
Idaho Bur Mines Geol Pam . . IDAHO BUREAU OF MINES AND GEOLOGY. PAMPHLET
Idaho L Rev . . . . . . IDAHO LAW REVIEW
Idaho Univ Eng Exp Sta Bull . . IDAHO UNIVERSITY. ENGINEERING EXPERIMENT STATION. BULLETIN
Ideal Stud . . . . . . . IDEALISTIC STUDIES
IDD . . . . . . . . . . . . IOWA. STATE UNIVERSITY. DOCTORAL DISSERTATIONS: ABSTRACTS AND REFERENCES
Idg Anz . . . . . . . . . ANZEIGER FUER INDOGERM
Idg Forsch . . . . . . . INDOGERMANISCHE FORSCHUNGEN
IDL . . . . . . . . . . . . INDICES ZUR DEUTSCHEN LITERATUR
IDOC Bul . . . . . . . . IDOC (INTERNATIONAL DOCUMENTATION) BULLETIN
IDS . . . . . . . . . . . . IZVESTIYA NA DRUZESTOVOTO NA FILOLOZITE-SLAVISTI V BALGARIJA. SOFIJA
IEBY . . . . . . . . . . . IOWA ENGLISH BULLETIN. YEARBOOK
IEc . . . . . . . . . . . . INDEX OF ECONOMIC ARTICLES
IEC . . . . . . . . . . . . INSTITUT D'ESTUDIS CATALANS
I ECON J . . . . . . . . INDIAN ECONOMIC JOURNAL
```

IEE Conf Publ (Lond). . IEE CONFERENCE PUBLICATION (INSTITUTION OF ELECTRICAL ENGINEERS, LONDON)
IEEE ACOUST. . . . . . IEEE (INSTITUTE OF ELECTRICAL AND ELECTRONICS ENGINEERS) TRANSACTIONS ON ACOUSTICS
      SPEECH AND SIGNAL PROCESSING
IEEE AER EL. . . . . . . IEEE TRANSACTIONS ON AEROSPACE AND ELECTRONIC SYSTEMS
IEEE ANTENN. . . . . . IEEE TRANSACTIONS ON ANTENNAS AND PROPAGATION
IEEE AUTO C. . . . . . IEEE TRANSACTIONS ON AUTOMATIC CONTROL
IEEE BIOMED. . . . . . IEEE TRANSACTIONS ON BIO MEDICAL ENGINEERING
IEEE BROADC. . . . . . IFFF TRANSACTIONS ON BROADCASTING
IEEE CIRC S. . . . . . . IEEE TRANSACTIONS ON CIRCUITS AND SYSTEMS
IEEE COMMUN. . . . . IEEE TRANSACTIONS ON COMMUNICATIONS
IEEE COMPUT. . . . . IEEE TRANSACTIONS ON COMPUTERS
IEEE Comput Group News. . IEEE COMPUTER GROUP NEWS
IEEE Conf Rec Thermion Convers Spec Conf. . IEEE CONFERENCE RECORDS OF THE THERMIONIC CONVERSION
      SPECIALIST CONFERENCE
IEEE CONS E. . . . . . . IEEE TRANSACTIONS ON CONSUMER ELECTRONICS
IEEE DEVICE. . . . . . . IEEE TRANSACTIONS ON ELECTRON DEVICES
IEEE EDUCAT. . . . . . IEEE TRANSACTIONS ON EDUCATION
IEEE EL INS. . . . . IEEE TRANSACTIONS ON ELECTRICAL INSULATION
IEEE ELMAGN. . . . . . IEEE TRANSACTIONS ON ELECTROMAGNETIC COMPATIBILITY
IEEE ENG MANAGE REV. . IEEE ENGINEERING MANAGEMENT REVIEW
IEEE GEOSCI. . . . . . . IEEE TRANSACTIONS ON GEOSCIENCE ELECTRONICS
IEEE IND AP. . . . . . . IEEE TRANSACTIONS ON INDUSTRY APPLICATIONS
IEEE IND EL. . . . . . . IEEE TRANSACTIONS ON INDUSTRIAL ELECTRONICS AND CONTROL INSTRUMENTATION
IEEE INFO T. . . . . . . IEEE TRANSACTIONS ON INFORMATION THEORY
IEEE INSTR. . . . . IEEE TRANSACTIONS ON INSTRUMENTATION AND MEASUREMENT
IEEE Int Conv Rec. . . IEEE INTERNATIONAL CONVENTION RECORD
IEEE Intercon Tech Pap. . IEEE INTERCON TECHNICAL PAPERS
IEEE J Q EL. . . . . IEEE JOURNAL OF QUANTUM ELECTRONICS
IEEE J SOLI. . . . . IEEE JOURNAL OF SOLID-STATE CIRCUITS
IEEE MAGNET. . . . . . IEEE TRANSACTIONS ON MAGNETICS
IEEE MANAGE. . . . . IEEE TRANSACTIONS ON ENGINEERING MANAGEMENT
IEEE MICR T. . . . . . . IEEE TRANSACTIONS ON MICROWAVE THEORY AND TECHNIQUES
IEEE NUCL S. . . . . . . IEEE TRANSACTIONS ON NUCLEAR SCIENCE
IEEE PARTS. . . . . . . IEEE TRANSACTIONS ON PARTS HYBRIDS AND PACKAGING
IEEE PLAS S. . . . . . . IEEE TRANSACTIONS ON PLASMA SCIENCE
IEEE POWER. . . . . . . IEEE TRANSACTIONS ON POWER APPARATUS AND SYSTEMS
IEEE Proc. . . . . IEEE (INSTITUTE OF ELECTRICAL AND ELECTRONICS ENGINEERS) PROCEEDINGS
IEEE Proc Annu Symp Rel. . IEEE PROCEEDINGS ANNUAL SYMPOSIUM ON RELIABILITY
IEEE Proc Conf Elec Appl Text Ind. . IEEE PROCEEDINGS OF THE CONFERENCE ON ELECTRICAL APPLICATIONS FOR THE
      TEXTILE INDUSTRY
IEEE Proc Conf Eng Med Biol. . IEEE PROCEEDINGS OF THE CONFERENCE ON ENGINEERING IN MEDICINE AND BIOLOGY
IEEE Proc Electron Components Conf. . IEEE PROCEEDINGS. ELECTRONIC COMPONENTS CONFERENCE
IEEE Proc Intermag Conf. . IEEE INTERNATIONAL CONFERENCE ON MAGNETICS. PROCEEDINGS OF THE INTERMAG
      CONFERENCE
IEEE Proc Nat Aerosp Electron Conf. . IEEE PROCEEDINGS OF THE NATIONAL AEROSPACE AND ELECTRONICS
      CONFERENCE
IEEE Proc Natl Aerosp Electron Conf. . IEEE PROCEEDINGS OF THE NATIONAL AEROSPACE AND ELECTRONICS
      CONFERENCE
IEEE PROF C. . . . . . . IEEE TRANSACTIONS ON PROFESSIONAL COMMUNICATION
IEEE RELIAB. . . . . . . IEEE TRANSACTIONS ON RELIABILITY
IEEE SON UL. . . . . . . IEEE TRANSACTIONS ON SONICS AND ULTRASONICS

IEEE SPECTR . . . . IEEE SPECTRUM
IEEE Stand Publ . . . . IEEE STANDARDS PUBLICATIONS
IEEE SYST M . . . . IEEE TRANSACTIONS ON SYSTEMS, MAN AND CYBERNETICS
IEEE Trans Aerosp Electron Syst . . IEEE TRANSACTIONS ON AEROSPACE AND ELECTRONIC SYSTEMS
IEEE Trans Antennas Propagat . . IEEE TRANSACTIONS ON ANTENNAS AND PROPAGATION
IEEE Trans Audio Electroacoust . . IEEE TRANSACTIONS ON AUDIO AND ELECTROACOUSTICS
IEEE Trans Automat Contr . . IEEE TRANSACTIONS ON AUTOMATIC CONTROL
IEEE Trans Autom Control . . IEEE TRANSACTIONS ON AUTOMATIC CONTROL
IEEE Trans Bio-Med Eng . . IEEE TRANSACTIONS ON BIO-MEDICAL ENGINEERING
IEEE Trans Broadcast . . IEEE TRANSACTIONS ON BROADCASTING
IEEE Trans Broadcast Telev Receivers . . IEEE TRANSACTIONS ON BROADCAST AND TELEVISION RECEIVERS
IEEE Trans Com . . . . IEEE TRANSACTIONS ON COMMUNICATIONS
IEEE Trans Comput . . IEEE TRANSACTIONS ON COMPUTERS
IEEE Trans Com Tech . . IEEE TRANSACTIONS ON COMMUNICATION TECHNOLOGY
IEEE Trans Educ . . . . IEEE TRANSACTIONS ON EDUCATION
IEEE Trans Elec Insul . . IEEE TRANSACTIONS ON ELECTRICAL INSULATION
IEEE Trans Electromagn Compat . . IEEE TRANSACTIONS ON ELECTROMAGNETIC COMPATIBILITY
IEEE Trans Electron Devices . . IEEE TRANSACTIONS ON ELECTRON DEVICES
IEEE Trans Eng Manage . . IEEE TRANSACTIONS ON ENGINEERING MANAGEMENT
IEEE Trans Eng Writing Speech . . IEEE TRANSACTIONS ON ENGINEERING WRITING AND SPEECH
IEEE Trans Geosci Electron . . IEEE TRANSACTIONS ON GEOSCIENCE ELECTRONICS
IEEE Trans Ind Appl . . IEEE TRANSACTIONS ON INDUSTRY APPLICATIONS
IEEE Trans Ind Electron Control Instrum . . IEEE TRANSACTIONS ON INDUSTRIAL ELECTRONICS AND CONTROL INSTRUMENTATION
IEEE Trans Ind Gen Appl . . IEEE TRANSACTION ON INDUSTRY AND GENERAL APPLICATIONS
IEEE Trans Inf Theory . . IEEE TRANSACTIONS ON INFORMATION THEORY
IEEE Trans Instrum Meas . . IEEE TRANSACTIONS ON INSTRUMENTATION AND MEASUREMENT
IEEE Trans Magn . . . IEEE TRANSACTIONS ON MAGNETICS
IEEE Trans Man-Mach Syst . . IEEE TRANSACTIONS ON MAN-MACHINE SYSTEMS
IEEE Trans Manuf Technol . . IEEE TRANSACTIONS ON MANUFACTURING TECHNOLOGY
IEEE Trans Microwave Theory Tech . . IEEE TRANSACTIONS ON MICROWAVE THEORY AND TECHNIQUES
IEEE Trans Nucl Sci . . IEEE TRANSACTIONS ON NUCLEAR SCIENCE
IEEE Trans Parts Hybrids Packag . . IEEE TRANSACTIONS ON PARTS, HYBRIDS AND PACKAGING
IEEE Trans Parts Mater Packag . . IEEE TRANSACTIONS ON PARTS, MATERIALS AND PACKAGING
IEEE Trans Power App Syst . . IEEE TRANSACTIONS ON POWER APPARATUS AND SYSTEMS
IEEE Trans Prof Commun . . IEEE TRANSACTIONS ON PROFESSIONAL COMMUNICATIONS
IEEE Trans Rel . . . . . IEEE TRANSACTIONS ON RELIABILITY
IEEE Trans Sonics Ultrason . . IEEE TRANSACTIONS ON SONICS AND ULTRASONICS
IEEE Trans Syst Man Cybern . . IEEE TRANSACTIONS ON SYSTEMS, MAN AND CYBERNETICS
IEEE Trans Syst Sci Cybern . . IEEE TRANSACTIONS ON SYSTEMS SCIENCE AND CYBERNETICS
IEEE Trans Ultrasonics Eng . . IEEE TRANSACTIONS ON ULTRASONICS ENGINEERING
IEEE Trans Veh Technol . . IEEE TRANSACTIONS ON VEHICULAR TECHNOLOGY
IEEE VEH T . . . . IEEE TRANSACTIONS ON VEHICULAR TECHNOLOGY
IEEE Wescon Conven Rec . . IEEE WESCON CONVENTION RECORD
IEEE Wescon Tech Pap . . IEEE WESCON TECHNICAL PAPERS
IEE-IERE Proc-India . . IEE (INSTITUTION OF ELECTRICAL ENGINEERS)-IERE (INSTITUTION OF ELECTRONIC AND RADIO ENGINEERS) PROCEEDINGS (INDIA)
IEIM . . . . IZVESTIYA NA ETNOGRAFSKIJA INSTITUT MUZEJ
IE Ind Eng . . . . IE, INDUSTRIAL ENGINEERING
IEJ . . . . INDIANA ENGLISH JOURNAL
IEJ . . . . INDIAN ECONOMIC JOURNAL

IEJ . . . . ISRAEL EXPLORATION JOURNAL
IER . . . . INDIAN ECONOMIC REVIEW
IER . . . . IRISH ECCLESIASTICAL RECORD
IERE Conf Proc (Lond) . . IERE (INSTITUTION OF ELECTRONIC AND RADIO ENGINEERS) CONFERENCE PROCEEDINGS
　　　　　　　　　　　　 (LONDON)
IESH . . . . INDIAN ECONOMIC AND SOCIAL HISTORY REVIEW
IEY . . . . IOWA ENGLISH YEARBOOK
IF . . . . INDOGERMANISCHE FORSCHUNGEN
IFDAI . . . . ISTANBULER FORSCHUNGEN DES DEUTSCHEN ARCHAEOLOGISCHEN INSTITUTS
IFiS . . . . INSTYTUT FILOZOFII I SOCJOLOGII PAN
IFMCJ . . . . INTERNATIONAL FOLK MUSIC COUNCIL. JOURNAL
IFMCY . . . . INTERNATIONAL FOLK MUSIC COUNCIL. YEARBOOK
IFMLL . . . . INTERNATIONAL FEDERATION FOR MODERN LANGUAGES AND LITERATURES
IFP . . . . INTERNATIONAL JOURNAL OF PSYCHOLINGUISTICS
IFr . . . . ITALIA FRANCESCANA
IFSSykt . . . . ISTORIKO-FILOLOGICESKIJ SBORNIK. SYKTYVBAR
IFZ . . . . ISTORIKO-FILOLOGICESKIJ ZURNAL
IH . . . . INFORMATION HISTORIQUE
IH . . . . ITA HUMANIDADES
IHA . . . . INFORMATION D'HISTOIRE DE L'ART
IHB . . . . INDIANA HISTORY BULLETIN
IHE . . . . INDICE HISTORICO ESPANOL
IHI Eng Rev . . . . IHI (ISHIKAWAJIMA-HARIMA HEAVY INDUSTRIES) ENGINEERING REVIEW
I HIST . . . . INDIAN HISTORIAN
IHML . . . . INTERNATIONAL HENRY MILLER LETTER
IHQ . . . . INDIAN HISTORICAL QUARTERLY
IHRB . . . . INSTITUTE OF HISTORICAL RESEARCH. BULLETIN
IHS . . . . IRISH HISTORICAL STUDIES
IHVE J . . . . IHVE (INSTITUTION OF HEATING AND VENTILATING ENGINEERS) JOURNAL
II . . . . ILLUSTRAZIONE ITALIANA
II . . . . ITALIA INTELLETTUALE
IIBE . . . . IZVESTIYA NA INSTITUTA ZA BELGARSKI EZIK
IIBL . . . . IZVESTIYA NA INSTITUTA ZA BELGARSKA LITERATURA
IID . . . . IZVESTIYA NA ISTORISESKOTO DRUZESTVO
IIJ . . . . INDO-IRANIAN JOURNAL
IIn . . . . INDEX INDIA
IIRB . . . . IIRB-INSTITUT INTERNATIONAL DE RECHERCHES BETTERAVIERES
IJ . . . . INDOGERMANISCHE JAHRBUCH
I J AGR SCI . . . . INDIAN JOURNAL OF AGRICULTURAL SCIENCE
IJAL . . . . INTERNATIONAL JOURNAL OF AMERICAN LINGUISTICS
IJAS . . . . INDIAN JOURNAL OF AMERICAN STUDIES
IJaS . . . . INOSTRANNY JE JAZYKI V SKOLE
I J BIOCH B . . . . INDIAN JOURNAL OF BIOCHEMISTRY AND BIOPHYSICS
I J CHEM . . . . INDIAN JOURNAL OF CHEMISTRY
IJCIS . . . . INTERNATIONAL JOURNAL OF COMPUTER AND INFORMATION SCIENCES
IJE . . . . INDIAN JOURNAL OF ECONOMICS
IJES . . . . INDIAN JOURNAL OF ENGLISH STUDIES (CALCUTTA)
IJewAr . . . . INDEX OF ARTICLES ON JEWISH STUDIES
IJewPer . . . . INDEX TO JEWISH PERIODICALS
I J EX BIOL . . . . INDIAN JOURNAL OF EXPERIMENTAL BIOLOGY
I J GENET P . . . . INDIAN JOURNAL OF GENETICS AND PLANT BREEDING

IJH . . . . IOWA JOURNAL OF HISTORY
IJHP . . . . IOWA JOURNAL OF HISTORY AND POLITICS
I J IND REL . . . . INDIAN JOURNAL OF INDUSTRIAL RELATIONS
I J MED RES . . . . INDIAN JOURNAL OF MEDICAL RESEARCH
IJMES . . . . INTERNATIONAL JOURNAL OF MIDDLE EAST STUDIES
I J NUTR D . . . . . . INDIAN JOURNAL OF NUTRITION AND DIETETICS
IJOAR . . . . INTERNATIONAL JOURNAL OF OPINION AND ATTITUDE RESEARCH
IJP . . . . INTERNATIONAL JOURNAL OF PARAPSYCHOLOGY
I J PA PHYS . . . . . . INDIAN JOURNAL OF PURE & APPLIED PHYSICS
I J PHYSICS . . . . . . INDIAN JOURNAL OF PHYSICS
IJPsa . . . . INTERNATIONAL JOURNAL OF PSYCHOANALYSIS
I J PSYCHOL . . . . . . INDIAN JOURNAL OF PSYCHOLOGY
IJS . . . . INOSTRANNYE JAZYKI V SKOLE
IJS . . . . INTERNATIONAL JOURNAL OF SEXOLOGY
IJSLP . . . . INTERNATIONAL JOURNAL OF SLAVIC LINGUISTICS AND POETICS
I J SOC RES . . . . . . INDIAN JOURNAL OF SOCIAL RESEARCH
I J TECHN . . . . INDIAN JOURNAL OF TECHNOLOGY
I J THEOR P . . . . . . INDIAN JOURNAL OF THEORETICAL PHYSICS
IK . . . . IRODALOMTORTENETI KOZLEMENYEK
IKE . . . . IBERIUL-K'AVK'ASIURI ENATMECNIEREBA
IKV . . . . INTERNATIONAL KONGRESS DER VOLKSERZAEHLUNGSFORSCHER
IKZ . . . . INTERNATIONALE KIRCHLICHE ZEITSCHRIFT
IL . . . . INDIAN LINGUISTICS
IL . . . . L'INFORMATION LITTERAIRE
IL . . . . INTERNATIONAL LITERATURE (U.S.S.R.)
ILA . . . . INTERNATIONAL LITERARY ANNUAL (LONDON)
ILA Rec . . . . ILLINOIS LIBRARY ASSOCIATION. RECORD
IIATos . . . . ILMIJ ASARLARI. V.I. LENIN MONIDAGI TOSKENT DAVLAT UNIVERSITETI
Ile . . . . ILERDA
ILF . . . . STUDII SE CERCETARI DE ISTORIE LITERARA SI FOLCLOR
ILGU . . . . IZVESTIJA LENINGRADSKOGO GOSUDARSTVENNOGO UNIVERSITETA
I Ling . . . . INITIATION A LA LINGUISTIQUE
I Lit . . . . IASUL LITERAR
Ill . . . . ILLITERATI
Ill . . . . ILLUSTRATION
Ill Ag Exp . . . . UNIVERSITY OF ILLINOIS. AGRICULTURAL EXPERIMENT STATION. PUBLICATIONS
Ill B J . . . . ILLINOIS BAR JOURNAL
Ill CLE . . . . ILLINOIS CONTINUING LEGAL EDUCATION
Ill Educ . . . . ILLINOIS EDUCATION
Ill Hist Coll . . . . . . ILLINOIS STATE HISTORICAL LIBRARY. COLLECTIONS
Illinois F . . . . ILLINOIS FARMER
ILL J MATH . . . . ILLINOIS JOURNAL OF MATHEMATICS
Ill Law Rev . . . . ILLINOIS LAW REVIEW
Ill Lib . . . . ILLINOIS LIBRARIES
Ill Mo . . . . ILLINOIS MONTHLY MAGAZINE
Ill Q . . . . ILLINOIS QUARTERLY
Ill Sch J . . . . ILLINOIS SCHOOLS JOURNAL
Ill State Geol Surv Bull . . ILLINOIS STATE GEOLOGICAL SURVEY. BULLETIN
Ill State Geol Surv Circ . . ILLINOIS STATE GEOLOGICAL SURVEY. CIRCULAR
Ill State Geol Surv Ill Petrol . . ILLINOIS STATE GEOLOGICAL SURVEY. ILLINOIS PETROLEUM
Ill State Geol Surv Rep Invest . . ILLINOIS STATE GEOLOGICAL SURVEY. REPORT OF INVESTIGATIONS

Ill State Hist Soc Jour . . ILLINOIS STATE HISTORICAL SOCIETY. JOURNAL
Ill State Hort Soc N L . . ILLINOIS STATE HORTICULTURAL SOCIETY. NEWSLETTER
Ill State Univ Jour . . ILLINOIS STATE UNIVERSITY. JOURNAL
Ill State Water Surv Bull . . ILLINOIS STATE WATER SURVEY. BULLETIN
Ill State Water Surv Rep Invest . . ILLINOIS STATE WATER SURVEY. REPORT OF INVESTIGATION
Ill Teach . . . . ILLINOIS TEACHER
Ill U Eng Exp Sta Bul . . ILLINOIS UNIVERSITY ENGINEERING EXPERIMENT STATION BULLETIN
Ill U Eng Exp Sta Circ . . ILLINOIS UNIVERSITY ENGINEERING EXPERIMENT STATION CIRCULAR
Illum Eng . . . . ILLUMINATING ENGINEERING
Illum Eng Soc J . . . . . ILLUMINATING ENGINEERING SOCIETY. JOURNAL
Illum Eng Soc Trans . . ILLUMINATING ENGINEERING SOCIETY. TRANSACTIONS
Ill Univ Civ Eng Stud Constr Res Ser . . ILLINOIS UNIVERSITY. CIVIL ENGINEERING STUDIES. CONSTRUCTION
RESEARCH SERIES
Ill Univ Civ Eng Stud Hydraul Eng Ser . . ILLINOIS UNIVERSITY. CIVIL ENGINEERING STUDIES. HYDRAULIC
ENGINEERING SERIES
Ill Univ Civ Eng Stud Soil Mech Ser . . ILLINOIS UNIVERSITY. CIVIL ENGINEERING STUDIES. SOIL MECHANICS SERIES
Ill Univ Civ Eng Stud Struct Res Ser . . ILLINOIS UNIVERSITY. CIVIL ENGINEERING STUDIES. STRUCTURAL RESEARCH
SERIES
Ill Univ Dep Elec Eng Aeron Lab Aeron Rep . . ILLINOIS UNIVERSITY. DEPARTMENT OF ELECTRICAL ENGINEERING
AERONOMY LABORATORY. AERONOMY REPORT
Ill Univ Eng Exp Sta Bull . . ILLINOIS UNIVERSITY. ENGINEERING EXPERIMENT STATION. BULLETIN
Ill Univ Proc Sanit Eng Conf . . ILLINOIS UNIVERSITY. PROCEEDINGS OF THE SANITARY ENGINEERING CONFERENCE
Ill Univ Tam Rep . . . ILLINOIS UNIVERSITY. DEPARTMENT OF THEORETICAL AND APPLIED MECHANICS. T.&A.M.
REPORT
Illus Archaeol . . . . . ILLUSTRATED ARCHAEOLOGIST
Illus Lond N . . . . ILLUSTRATED LONDON NEWS
Ilmenau Tech Hochsch Wiss Z . . ILMENAU, TECHNISCHE HOCHSCHULE, WISSENSCHAFTLICHE ZEITSCHRIFT
ILML . . . . ISTITUTO LOMBARDO. ACCADEMIA DI SCIENZE E LETTERE. MEMORIE DELLA CLASSE DI LETTERE
ILN . . . . ILLUSTRATED LONDON NEWS
ILP . . . . IL PONTE
ILR . . . . INTERNATIONAL LABOUR REVIEW
ILR . . . . INTERNATIONAL LANGUAGE REPORTER
ILRL . . . . ISTITUTO LOMBARDO. ACCADEMIA DI SCIENZE E LETTERE RENDICONTI DELLA CLASSE DI
LETTERE
ILRR . . . . INDUSTRIAL AND LABOR RELATIONS REVIEW
ILT . . . . IL TESAUR
IM . . . . ILLUMINARE
Im . . . . IMAGINATION
Im . . . . IMAGO
IM . . . . IMAGO MUNDI
IM . . . . INCONTRI MUSICALI
IMB . . . . INTERNATIONAL MEDIEVAL BIBLIOGRAPHY
IMed . . . . INDEX MEDICUS
IMF . . . . INTERNATIONAL MONETARY FUND. STAFF PAPERS
IMH . . . . INDIANA MAGAZINE OF HISTORY
IMMUNOCHEM . . . . IMMUNOCHEMISTRY
IMMUNOGENET . . . . IMMUNOGENETICS
IMMUNOL COM . . . . IMMUNOLOGICAL COMMUNICATIONS
IMN . . . . IRISLEABHAR MHA NUAD
IMPACT SCI . . . . IMPACT OF SCIENCE ON SOCIETY
Impact Sci Soc . . . . . IMPACT OF SCIENCE ON SOCIETY
Imp Coll Sci Technol Rock Mech Res Rep . . IMPERIAL COLLEGE OF SCIENCE AND TECHNOLOGY. ROCK MECHANICS
RESEARCH REPORT

IMP OIL R . . . . IMPERIAL OIL REVIEW
IMPR HUM P . . . . . . IMPROVING HUMAN PERFORMANCE
Improv Coll & Univ Teach . . IMPROVING COLLEGE AND UNIVERSITY TEACHING
Imp Univ Tokyo Fac Sci J . . TOKYO. IMPERIAL UNIVERSITY. FACULTY OF SCIENCE. JOURNAL
IMR Ind Manage Rev . . IMR, INDUSTRIAL MANAGEMENT REVIEW
IMS . . . . INTERNATIONAL MUSICOLOGICAL SOCIETY. REPORT OF THE CONGRESS
IMS . . . . INTERNATIONALE MONATSSCHRIFT
IMU . . . . ITALIA MEDIOEVALE E UMANISTICA
IN . . . . INDIANA NAMES (INDIANA STATE UNIV.)
In . . . . INSULA
IncL . . . . INCORPORATED LINGUIST (LONDON)
Ind . . . . INDEPENDENT
Ind . . . . INDICE DE ARTE Y LETRAS
Ind Ag Exp . . . . PURDUE UNIVERSITY. INDIANA AGRICULTURAL EXPERIMENT STATION PUBLICATIONS
Ind & Eng Chem . . . . INDUSTRIAL AND ENGINEERING CHEMISTRY
Ind & Eng Chem Process Design . . INDUSTRIAL AND ENGINEERING CHEMISTRY PROCESS DESIGN AND DEVELOPMENT
Ind & Lab Rel Rev . . INDUSTRIAL AND LABOR RELATIONS REVIEW
Ind-Anz . . . . INDUSTRIE-ANZEIGER
Ind Arts & Voc Ed . . INDUSTRIAL ARTS AND VOCATIONAL EDUCATION/TECHNICAL EDUCATION
Ind Arts M . . . . INDUSTRIAL-ARTS MAGAZINE
Ind At Spatiales . . . . INDUSTRIES ATOMIQUE ET SPATIALES
Ind Bldg . . . . INDUSTRIALISED BUILDING
IND CAN . . . . INDUSTRIAL CANADA
Ind Chem . . . . INDUSTRIAL CHEMIST
Ind Ch HR . . . . INDIAN CHURCH HISTORY REVIEW
Ind Comm Gas . . . . . INDUSTRIAL AND COMMERCIAL GAS
Ind Des . . . . INDUSTRIAL DESIGN
Ind Dev . . . . INDUSTRIAL DEVELOPMENT AND MANUFACTURERS RECORD
IND DIAM RE . . . . . . INDUSTRIAL DIAMOND REVIEW
Ind Distrib . . . . INDUSTRIAL DISTRIBUTION
Ind Ed M . . . . INDUSTRIAL EDUCATION MAGAZINE
Ind Educ . . . . INDUSTRIAL EDUCATION
Ind Educ M . . . . INDUSTRIAL EDUCATION MAGAZINE
Ind Electr Electron . . INDUSTRIES ELECTRIQUES ET ELECTRONIQUES
Ind Electron . . . . INDUSTRIES ELECTRONIQUES
Ind Eng . . . . INDUSTRIAL ENGINEERING
Ind Eng Chem . . . . . INDUSTRIAL AND ENGINEERING CHEMISTRY
IND ENG F . . . . INDUSTRIAL AND ENGINEERING CHEMISTRY FUNDAMENTALS
IND ENG PDD . . . . . INDUSTRIAL AND ENGINEERING CHEMISTRY PROCESS DESIGN AND DEVELOPMENT
IND ENG PRD . . . . . . INDUSTRIAL AND ENGINEERING CHEMISTRY PRODUCT RESEARCH AND DEVELOPMENT
Indep . . . . INDEPENDENT
Indep Ed . . . . INDEPENDENT EDUCATION
Ind F . . . . INDIAN FARMING
IndF . . . . INDIANA FOLKLORE
Ind Finish . . . . INDUSTRIAL FINISHING
Ind Gas . . . . INDUSTRIAL GAS
IND GERONT . . . . . . INDUSTRIAL GERONTOLOGY
Ind Heat . . . . INDUSTRIAL HEATING
Ind Hist Soc Publ . . . INDIANA HISTORICAL SOCIETY. PUBLICATIONS
Indian Acad Sci Pro . . INDIAN ACADEMY OF SCIENCE. PROCEEDINGS
INDIANA LAW . . . . . INDIANA LAW JOURNAL

Indiana Univ Ed Bul. . INDIANA UNIVERSITY. SCHOOL OF EDUCATION. BULLETIN
Indian Concr J. . . . . INDIAN CONCRETE JOURNAL
Indian Hist. . . . . . . INDIAN HISTORIAN
Indian J Chem. . . . . INDIAN JOURNAL OF CHEMISTRY
Indian J Power River Val Develop. . INDIAN JOURNAL OF POWER AND RIVER VALLEY DEVELOPMENT
Indian J Psychol. . . INDIAN JOURNAL OF PSYCHOLOGY
Indian J Pure Appl Phys. . INDIAN JOURNAL OF PURE AND APPLIED PHYSICS
Indian J Technol. . . INDIAN JOURNAL OF TECHNOLOGY
Indian Lib Assn J. . . INDIAN LIBRARY ASSOCIATION. JOURNAL
Indian L Rev. . . . . . INDIAN LAW REVIEW
Indian Miner. . . . . . INDIAN MINERALS
INDIAN MS. . . . . . . INDIAN MUSICOLOGICAL SOCIETY. JOURNAL
Indian Mus Q. . . . . . INDIAN MUSIC QUARTERLY
Indian Phil Cult. . . . INDIAN PHILOSOPHY AND CULTURE
Indian Phil Quart. . . INDIAN PHILOSOPHICAL QUARTERLY
Indian Psychol R. . . INDIAN PSYCHOLOGICAL REVIEW
Indian Weld J. . . . . INDIAN WELDING JOURNAL
India Quar. . . . . INDIA QUARTERLY
INDI MATH J. . . . . . INDIANA UNIVERSITY MATHEMATICS JOURNAL
Indiv Inst. . . . . INDIVIDUAL INSTRUCTION
INDIV PSYCH. . . . . . INDIVIDUAL PSYCHOLOGIST
Ind J Ag Sci. . . . . . INDIAN JOURNAL OF AGRICULTURAL SCIENCE
Ind J Th. . . . . INDIAN JOURNAL OF THEOLOGY
Ind J Vet Sci. . . . . . INDIAN JOURNAL OF VETERINARY SCIENCE
Ind L. . . . . INDIAN LITERATURE
Ind Lab. . . . . INDUSTRIAL LABORATORIES
IND LAB REL. . . . . . INDUSTRIAL AND LABOR RELATIONS REVIEW
Ind Lab (USSR). . . . . INDUSTRIAL LABORATORY (USSR)
Ind Law Jour. . . . . . INDIANA LAW JOURNAL
Ind Legal F. . . . . . . INDIANA LEGAL FORUM
Ind Ling. . . . . INDIAN LINGUISTICS
IndLit. . . . . INDIAN LITERATURE
Ind L J. . . . . INDIANA LAW JOURNAL
Ind L Rev. . . . . INDIANA LAW REVIEW
Ind Lubric. . . . . . . INDUSTRIAL LUBRICATION
Ind Lubric Tribology. . INDUSTRIAL LUBRICATION AND TRIBOLOGY
Ind Mag Hist. . . . . . INDIANA MAGAZINE OF HISTORY
Ind Management. . . INDUSTRIAL MANAGEMENT (NEW YORK)
Ind Management (London). . INDUSTRIAL MANAGEMENT (LONDON)
Ind Management R. . INDUSTRIAL MANAGEMENT REVIEW
Ind Market. . . . . . . INDUSTRIAL MARKETING
Ind Math. . . . . INDUSTRIAL MATHEMATICS
Ind Med. . . . . INDUSTRIAL MEDICINE AND SURGERY
Ind Mgt. . . . . INDUSTRIAL MANAGEMENT
Ind Mgt R. . . . . INDUSTRIAL MANAGEMENT REVIEW
Ind Miner. . . . . INDUSTRIE MINERALE
Ind Miner Mine. . . . INDUSTRIE MINERALE. MINE
Ind Miner Mineralurgie. . INDUSTRIE MINERALE. MINERALURGIE
Ind Mktg. . . . . INDUSTRIAL MARKETING
IND MKT MAN. . . . . INDUSTRIAL MARKETING MANAGEMENT
Ind Phot. . . . . INDUSTRIAL PHOTOGRAPHY

IND PHOTOGR..... INDUSTRIAL PHOTOGRAPHY
Ind Quality Control.. INDUSTRIAL QUALITY CONTROL
Ind Rel.......... INDUSTRIAL RELATIONS
Ind Res.......... INDUSTRIAL RESEARCH
Ind S............ INDIAN STUDIES: PAST AND PRESENT
Ind Saf.......... INDUSTRIAL SAFETY
Ind Sch Bull....... INDEPENDENT SCHOOL BULLETIN
Ind Stand........ INDUSTRIAL STANDARDIZATION
Ind Therm Aerauliques.. INDUSTRIES THERMIQUES ET AERAULIQUES
Ind Univ Extension Division Bull.. INDIANA UNIVERSITY. EXTENSION DIVISION BULLETIN
Ind Univ Sch Ed B... INDIANA UNIVERSITY. SCHOOL OF EDUCATION. BULLETIN
Industrial & Labor Rel Rev.. INDUSTRIAL AND LABOR RELATIONS REVIEW
Industrial L Rev Q.. INDUSTRIAL LAW REVIEW QUARTERLY
Ind Water Eng..... INDUSTRIAL WATER ENGINEERING
Ind Week........ INDUSTRY WEEK
Ind Woman....... INDEPENDENT WOMAN
INeg............ INDEX TO PERIODICALS BY AND ABOUT NEGROES
INF............. INFINITY SCIENCE FICTION
InF............. INOZEMNA FILOLOGIYA. L'VOV
Inf C............ INFORMATION AND CONTROL
INF CONTR....... INFORMATION AND CONTROL
INF DISPLAY...... INFORMATION DISPLAY
INFEC IMMUN..... INFECTION AND IMMUNITY
Inf Hist.......... INFORMATION HISTORIQUE
Inf Litt.......... INFORMATION LITTERAIRE
INFOR J..........INFOR JOURNAL (CANADIAN JOURNAL OF OPERATIONAL RESEARCH AND INFORMATION
     PROCESSING)
Inform Contr...... INFORMATION AND CONTROL
Inform Sci........ INFORMATION SCIENCES
Inform Stor Retrieval.. INFORMATION STORAGE AND RETRIEVAL
InfoS............ INFORMATION SCIENCES
InfP............ INFORMATION PROCESSING JOURNAL
INF PR MAN...... INFORMATION PROCESSING AND MANAGEMENT
Inf Process Lett.... INFORMATION PROCESSING LETTERS
Inf: Pt 1......... INFORMATION: PART 1: NEWS/SOURCES/PROFILES
Inf: Pt 2......... INFORMATION: PART 2: REPORTS/BIBLIOGRAPHIES
INFRAR PHYS..... INFRARED PHYSICS
Inf Sci........... INFORMATION SCIENCES
InfSciAb......... INFORMATION SCIENCE ABSTRACTS
INF SCIENT....... INFORMATION SCIENTIST
Inf Serv..........NATIONAL COUNCIL OF THE CHURCHES OF CHRIST IN THE UNITED STATES OF AMERICA.
     INFORMATION SERVICE
INF STORAGE...... INFORMATION STORAGE AND RETRIEVAL
Inf Stor Retr...... INFORMATION STORAGE AND RETRIEVAL
Ing-Arch......... INGENIEUR-ARCHIV
Ing Auto......... INGENIEURS DE L'AUTOMOBILE
ING CHIM IT...... QUADERNI DELL INGEGNERE CHIMICO ITALIANO
ING ENG PRD..... INDUSTRIAL AND ENGINEERING CHEMISTRY PRODUCT RESEARCH AND DEVELOPMENT
Ing Ferrov........ INGEGNERIA FERROVIARIA
Ing Mecc......... INGEGNERIA MECCANICA
Ing Nav (Madrid)... INGENIERIA NAVAL (MADRID)

Ing Vetenskaps Akad Medd . . INGENIORS VETENSKAPS AKADEMIEN, MEDDELANDE
Iniz . . . . INIZIATIVE
InL . . . . INDIAN LITERATURE
InL . . . . INOSTRANNAYA LITERATURA (MOSCOW)
Inland & Ptr & Lithog . . INLAND AND AMERICAN PRINTER AND LITHOGRAPHER
Inland Ptr . . . . INLAND PRINTER
INORG CHEM . . . . . . INORGANIC CHEMISTRY
INORG CHIM . . . . . . INORGANICA CHIMICA ACTA
INORG CHIM . . . . . . INORGANICA CHIMICA ACTA
INORG NUCL . . . . . . INORGANIC AND NUCLEAR CHEMISTRY LETTERS
InostrJazyki . . . . . . INOSTRANNI JAZYKI V SKOLE
InPEN . . . . INDIAN P.E.N.
InS . . . . INLAND SEAS
Ins . . . . INSULA
Ins . . . . INSURANCE
Ins Counsel J . . . . . . INSURANCE COUNSEL JOURNAL
INSECT BIOC . . . . . . INSECT BIOCHEMISTRY
INSECT SOC . . . . . . INSECTES SOCIAUX
Ins Field (Fire ed) . . INSURANCE FIELD (FIRE AND CASUALTY EDITION)
Ins Field (Life ed) . . INSURANCE FIELD (LIFE EDITION)
INS L J . . . . INSURANCE LAW JOURNAL
INSPEL . . . . INSPEL (INTERNATIONAL NEWSLETTER OF SPECIAL LIBRARIES)
Inst . . . . INSTRUCTOR
Inst Alatne Masine Alate Monogr . . INSTITUT ZA ALATNE MASINE I ALATE. MONOGRAFIJE
Inst Alatne Masine Alate Saopstenja . . INSTITUT ZA ALATNE MASINE I ALATE. SAOPSTENJA
INSTANT RES . . . . . . INSTANT RESEARCH ON PEACE AND VIOLENCE
Inst Arch Ethnog . . . INTERNATIONALES ARCHIV FUER ETHNOGRAPHIE
Inst Bauwissenschaftliche Forsch Publ . . INSTITUT FUER BAUWISSENSCHAFTLICHE FORSCHUNG. PUBLIKATION
Inst Chem Eng Trans . . INSTITUTION OF CHEMICAL ENGINEERS. TRANSACTIONS
Inst E B . . . . INSTITUTO DE ESTUDOS BRASILEIROS
Inst E E J . . . . INSTITUTION OF ELECTRICAL ENGINEERS. JOURNAL
Inst E E Proc . . . . . . INSTITUTION OF ELECTRICAL ENGINEERS. PROCEEDINGS
Inst Elec Eng Conf Publ . . INSTITUTION OF ELECTRICAL ENGINEERS. CONFERENCE PUBLICATION
Inst Elec Eng J . . . . . INSTITUTION OF ELECTRICAL ENGINEERS. JOURNAL
Inst Eng Aust Civ Eng Trans . . INSTITUTION OF ENGINEERS. AUSTRALIA. CIVIL ENGINEERING TRANSACTIONS
Inst Eng Aust Elec Eng Trans . . INSTITUTION OF ENGINEERS. AUSTRALIA. ELECTRICAL ENGINEERING TRANSACTIONS
Inst Eng Aust Mech Chem Eng Trans . . INSTITUTION OF ENGINEERS. AUSTRALIA. MECHANICAL AND CHEMICAL
ENGINEERING TRANSACTIONS
Inst Eng Ceylon Trans . . INSTITUTION OF ENGINEERS OF CEYLON. TRANSACTIONS
Inst Estate Plan . . . . INSTITUTE ON ESTATE PLANNING
Inst Ethmus Sel Repts . . INSTITUTE OF ETHNOMUSICOLOGY. SELECTED REPORTS
Inst Fire Eng Q . . . . . INSTITUTION OF FIRE ENGINEERS QUARTERLY
Inst Folk . . . . BOLETIN DEL INSTITUTO DE FOLKLORE
Inst Gas Eng J . . . . . INSTITUTION OF GAS ENGINEERS. JOURNAL
Inst Int Educ N Bul . . INSTITUTE OF INTERNATIONAL EDUCATION. NEWS BULLETIN
Inst Int Rel Proc . . . INSTITUTE OF INTERNATIONAL RELATIONS. PROCEEDINGS
Inst Int Stat R . . . . . INSTITUT INTERNATIONAL DE STATISTIQUE. REVUE
Inst Locomotive Eng J . . INSTITUTION OF LOCOMOTIVE ENGINEERS. JOURNAL
Inst Mech Eng J & Proc . . INSTITUTION OF MECHANICAL ENGINEERS. JOURNAL AND PROCEEDINGS
Inst Mech Eng (Lond) Proc . . INSTITUTION OF MECHANICAL ENGINEERS (LONDON). PROCEEDINGS
Inst Mech Eng Proc . . INSTITUTION OF MECHANICAL ENGINEERS. PROCEEDINGS

Inst Mech Eng Ry Div J . . INSTITUTION OF MECHANICAL ENGINEERS (LONDON). RAILWAY DIVISION JOURNAL
Inst Metals J . . . . . . INSTITUTE OF METALS. JOURNAL
Inst Mex Petrol Rev . . INSTITUTE MEXICANO DEL PETROLEO. REVISTA
Inst Min & Met Trans . . INSTITUTION OF MINING AND METALLURGY. TRANSACTIONS
Inst Min L . . . . INSTITUTE ON MINERAL LAW
Inst Munic Eng S Afr Dist Annu J . . INSTITUTION OF MUNICIPAL ENGINEERS. SOUTH AFRICAN DISTRICT. ANNUAL
      JOURNAL
Inst Napoleon R . . . . INSTITUT NAPOLEON (PARIS) REVUE
Inst Nat Ind Charbonniere Bull Tech-Mines . . INSTITUT NATIONAL DE L'INDUSTRIE CHARBONNIERE. BULLETIN
      TECHNIQUE-MINES
Inst Nat Ind Extr Bull Tech-Mines Carrieres . . INSTITUT NATIONAL DES INDUSTRIES EXTRACTIVES. (LIEGE) BULLETIN
      TECHNIQUE-MINES ET CARRIERES
Inst N L . . . . INSTITUTO NACIONAL DO LIVRO
Inst Oil & Gas L & Taxation . . INSTITUTE ON OIL AND GAS LAW AND TAXATION
Inst Pet J . . . . INSTITUTE OF PETROLEUM. JOURNAL
Inst Post Office Elec Eng Paper . . INSTITUTION OF POST OFFICE ELECTRICAL ENGINEERS. PAPER
Inst Private Investments . . INSTITUTE ON PRIVATE INVESTMENTS ABROAD AND FOREIGN TRADE
Instr . . . . INSTRUCTOR
Inst Radio Eng Proc . . INSTITUTE OF RADIO ENGINEERS. PROCEEDINGS
Instr & Autom . . . . . INSTRUMENTS AND AUTOMATION
INSTR CONTR . . . . . INSTRUMENTS AND CONTROL SYSTEMS
Inst Roy Sci Natur Belgique Bul . . INSTITUT ROYAL DES SCIENCES NATURELLES DE BELGIQUE. BULLETIN
INSTR SCI . . . . INSTRUCTIONAL SCIENCE
INSTR TECH . . . . INSTRUMENTATION TECHNOLOGY
Instrum Control Engng . . INSTRUMENT AND CONTROL ENGINEERING
Instrum Contr Syst . . INSTRUMENTS AND CONTROL SYSTEMS
INSTRUMENT . . . . . . INSTRUMENTALIST
Instrumentation Tech . . INSTRUMENTATION TECHNOLOGY
Instrum Exp Tech . . . INSTRUMENTS AND EXPERIMENTAL TECHNIQUES
Instrum Pract . . . . . INSTRUMENT PRACTICE
Instrum Soc Amer Conf Preprint . . INSTRUMENT SOCIETY OF AMERICA. CONFERENCE PREPRINT
Instrum Technol . . . INSTRUMENTATION TECHNOLOGY
INST SECURITIES REG . . INSTITUTE ON SECURITIES REGULATION
Inst Stud Project Energ Bul . . INSTITUTUL DE STUDII SI PROIECTARI ENERGETICE. BULETINUL (ROMANIA)
Inst Verkstadstek Forsk IVF Resultat . . INSTITUTET FOR VERKSTADSTEKNISK FORSKNING. IVF RESULTAT
Inst/Vol Feeding Mgt . . INSTITUTIONS/VOLUME FEEDING
Inst World Affairs Proc . . INSTITUTE OF WORLD AFFAIRS. PROCEEDINGS
Insul . . . . INSULANA
Insul/Circuits . . . . . INSULATION/CIRCUITS
INT . . . . INTERNATIONAL SCIENCE FICTION
INT A ALLER . . . . . . INTERNATIONAL ARCHIVES OF ALLERGY AND APPLIED IMMUNOLOGY
Int Advertiser . . . . . INTERNATIONAL ADVERTISER
IntAe . . . . INTERNATIONAL AEROSPACE ABSTRACTS
Int Aff . . . . INTERNATIONAL AFFAIRS
Intam Inst Mus Res . . INTER-AMERICAN INSTITUTE FOR MUSICAL RESEARCH YEARBOOK
INTAM MUS B . . . . . BOLETIN INTERAMERICANO DE MUSICA
INTAM MUS B (Eng ed) . . INTER-AMERICAN MUSIC BULLETIN (ENGLISH EDITION)
INTAM MUS RES YRBK . . . . INTER-AMERICAN MUSICAL RESEARCH. YEARBOOK
INT & COMP L Q . . . INTERNATIONAL AND COMPARATIVE LAW QUARTERLY
INT A OCCUP . . . . . . INTERNATIONAL ARCHIVES OF OCCUPATIONAL AND ENVIRONMENTAL HEALTH
Int Archiv Ethnog . . . INTERNATIONALES ARCHIV FUER ETHNOGRAPHIE

PERIODICAL TITLE ABBREVIATIONS

INT ASIENF....... INTERNATIONALES ASIENFORUM
Int Ass Bridge Struct Eng Publ.. INTERNATIONAL ASSOCIATION FOR BRIDGE AND STRUCTURAL ENGINEERING. PUBLICATIONS
Int Astronaut Congr Proc.. INTERNATIONAL ASTRONAUTICAL CONGRESS PROCEEDINGS
Int At Energy Ag Bibliogr Ser.. INTERNATIONAL ATOMIC ENERGY AGENCY. BIBLIOGRAPHICAL SERIFS
Int At Energy Agency Tech Rep Ser.. INTERNATIONAL ATOMIC ENERGY AGENCY. TECHNICAL REPORT SERIES
Int At Energy Ag Proc Ser.. INTERNATIONAL ATOMIC ENERGY AGENCY. PROCEEDINGS SERIES
INT BIOD B....... INTERNATIONAL BIODETERIORATION BULLETIN
Int Broadc Engr.... INTERNATIONAL BROADCAST ENGINEER
Int Bur Ed B...... INTERNATIONAL BUREAU OF EDUCATION. BULLETIN
INT CATALOGUING.. INTERNATIONAL CATALOGUING
INT CHEM EN...... INTERNATIONAL CHEMICAL ENGINEERING
Int Civ Eng Mon.... INTERNATIONAL CIVIL ENGINEERING MONTHLY
Int Comm....... INTERNATIONAL COMMERCE
Int Comm Illum Proc.. INTERNATIONAL COMMISSION ON ILLUMINATION. PROCEEDINGS
Int Concil........ INTERNATIONAL CONCILIATION
Int Congr Large Dams.. INTERNATIONAL CONGRESS ON LARGE DAMS
Int Constr........ INTERNATIONAL CONSTRUCTION
Int Curr Meter Group Rep.. INTERNATIONAL CURRENT METER GROUP. REPORT
INT DENT J....... INTERNATIONAL DENTAL JOURNAL
Int Des.......... INTERIOR DESIGN
INT DEV REV...... INTERNATIONAL DEVELOPMENT REVIEW
Int Dialog Z....... INTERNATIONALE DIALOG ZEITSCHRIFT
Int Dig.......... INTERNATIONAL DIGEST
Int Econ R........ INTERNATIONAL ECONOMIC REVIEW
Int Ed & Cul Exch... INTERNATIONAL EDUCATIONAL AND CULTURAL EXCHANGE
Integ Ed......... INTEGRATED EDUCATION: RACE AND SCHOOLS
Int Electrotech Comm Publ.. INTERNATIONAL ELECTROTECHNICAL COMMISSION. PUBLICATIONS
INT ELEKTR....... INTERNATIONALE ELEKTRONISCHE RUNDSCHAU
Intel Obs......... INTELLECTUAL OBSERVER
IntER........... INTERNATIONAL ECONOMIC REVIEW
Inter-Am......... INTER-AMERICAN
INTERAM J P...... INTER-AMERICAN JOURNAL OF PSYCHOLOGY
Inter-Am L Rev.... INTER-AMERICAN LAW REVIEW
Inter-Am Q....... INTER-AMERICAN QUARTERLY
Interchurch N..... INTERCHURCH NEWS
INTERIOR DES..... INTERIOR DESIGN
Internat......... INTERNATIONAL QUARTERLY
Internat Archiv f Ethno.. INTERNATIONALES ARCHIV FUER ETHNOLOGIE
Internatl Cong Hist Sci Proc.. INTERNATIONAL CONGRESS OF HISTORICAL SCIENCES. PROCEEDINGS
Internatl Jour..... INTERNATIONAL JOURNAL
Internatl Organ.... INTERNATIONAL ORGANIZATION
Internat M....... INTERNATIONAL MAGAZINE
Internat Mo...... INTERNATIONAL MONTHLY
Internat R........ INTERNATIONAL REVIEW
Interp........... INTERPRETATION
INTERPERS D...... INTERPERSONAL DEVELOPMENT
INTERVIROLO..... INTERVIROLOGY
Int Folk Mus Council JL.. INTERNATIONAL FOLK MUSIC COUNCIL. JOURNAL
IntGuC.......... INTERNATIONAL GUIDE TO CLASSICAL STUDIES
INT HYD REV...... INTERNATIONAL HYDROGRAPHIC REVIEW

Int Inst Land Reclam Impr Netherlands Bibliogr. . INTERNATIONAL INSTITUTE FOR LAND RECLAMATION AND
    IMPROVEMENT. NETHERLANDS. BIBLIOGRAPHY
Int Inst Land Reclam Impr Netherlands Bull. . INTERNATIONAL INSTITUTE FOR LAND RECLAMATION AND
    IMPROVEMENT. NETHERLANDS. BULLETIN
Int Inst Land Reclam Impr Netherlands Publ. . INTERNATIONAL INSTITUTE FOR LAND RECLAMATION AND
    IMPROVEMENT. NETHERLANDS. PUBLICATION
INT J. . . . . INTERNATIONAL JOURNAL
INT J A AFF. . . . . . . INTERNATIONAL JOURNAL OF AGRARIAN AFFAIRS
INT J ADDIC. . . . . . INTERNATIONAL JOURNAL OF THE ADDICTIONS
Int J Adult Youth Ed. . INTERNATIONAL JOURNAL OF ADULT AND YOUTH EDUCATION
INT J AFR H. . . . . . . INTERNATIONAL JOURNAL OF AFRICAN HISTORICAL STUDIES
Int J Ag Affairs. . . . INTERNATIONAL JOURNAL OF AGRARIAN AFFAIRS
INT J AGING. . . . . . INTERNATIONAL JOURNAL OF AGING AND HUMAN DEVELOPMENT
INT J AMER. . . . . . . INTERNATIONAL JOURNAL OF AMERICAN LINGUISTICS
Int J Am Ling. . . . . . INTERNATIONAL JOURNAL OF AMERICAN LINGUISTICS
INT J A RAD. . . . . . INTERNATIONAL JOURNAL OF APPLIED RADIATION AND ISOTOPES
INT J BIOCH. . . . . . INTERNATIONAL JOURNAL OF BIOCHEMISTRY
INT J BIO-M. . . . . . INTERNATIONAL JOURNAL OF BIO-MEDICAL COMPUTING
INT J BIOM. . . . . . . INTERNATIONAL JOURNAL OF BIOMETEOROLOGY
INT J CANC. . . . . . INTERNATIONAL JOURNAL OF CANCER
INT J CE HY. . . . . . INTERNATIONAL JOURNAL OF CLINICAL AND EXPERIMENTAL HYPNOSIS
Int J Chem Kinet. . . INTERNATIONAL JOURNAL OF CHEMICAL KINETICS
INT J CHILD. . . . . . INTERNATIONAL JOURNAL OF CHILD PSYCHOTHERAPY
INT J CH K. . . . . . . INTERNATIONAL JOURNAL OF CHEMICAL KINETICS
INT J C INF. . . . . . . INTERNATIONAL JOURNAL OF COMPUTER AND INFORMATION SCIENCES
INT J CLIN. . . . . INTERNATIONAL JOURNAL OF CLINICAL PHARMACOLOGY AND BIOPHARMACY
Int J Clin & Exp Hypnosis. . INTERNATIONAL JOURNAL OF CLINICAL AND EXPERIMENTAL HYPNOSIS
INT J COM M. . . . . . INTERNATIONAL JOURNAL OF COMPUTER MATHEMATICS
INT J COM P. . . . . . INTERNATIONAL JOURNAL OF COMMUNITY PSYCHIATRY AND EXPERIMENTAL PSYCHO-
    THERAPY
INT J COMP. . . . . . . INTERNATIONAL JOURNAL OF COMPARATIVE SOCIOLOGY
Int J Comput Math. . INTERNATIONAL JOURNAL OF COMPUTER MATHEMATICS
INT J CON S. . . . . . . INTERNATIONAL JOURNAL OF CONTEMPORARY SOCIOLOGY
Int J Contr. . . . . . . INTERNATIONAL JOURNAL OF CONTROL
Int J Elec Eng Educ. . INTERNATIONAL JOURNAL OF ELECTRICAL ENGINEERING EDUCATION
INT J ELECT. . . . . . . INTERNATIONAL JOURNAL OF ELECTRONICS
Int J Electron. . . . . . INTERNATIONAL JOURNAL OF ELECTRONICS
INT J EL EN. . . . . . . INTERNATIONAL JOURNAL OF ELECTRICAL ENGINEERING EDUCATION
INT J ENG S. . . . . . . INTERNATIONAL JOURNAL OF ENGINEERING SCIENCE
INT J ENV S. . . . . . . INTERNATIONAL JOURNAL OF ENVIRONMENTAL STUDIES
INT J EPID. . . . . . . INTERNATIONAL JOURNAL OF EPIDEMIOLOGY
Int J Ethics. . . . . . . INTERNATIONAL JOURNAL OF ETHICS
INT J FERT. . . . . . . INTERNATIONAL JOURNAL OF FERTILITY
Int J Fract. . . . . INTERNATIONAL JOURNAL OF FRACTURE
Int J Fract Mech. . . INTERNATIONAL JOURNAL OF FRACTURE MECHANICS
INT J GEN S. . . . . . . INTERNATIONAL JOURNAL OF GENERAL SYSTEMS
INT J GRP P. . . . . . . INTERNATIONAL JOURNAL OF GROUP PSYCHOTHERAPY
INT J GRP T. . . . . . . INTERNATIONAL JOURNAL OF GROUP TENSIONS
INT J HEALT. . . . . . INTERNATIONAL JOURNAL OF HEALTH EDUCATION
INT J HEAT. . . . . . . INTERNATIONAL JOURNAL OF HEAT AND MASS TRANSFER
INT J HE SE. . . . . . . INTERNATIONAL JOURNAL OF HEALTH SERVICES

INT J LEPR . . . . INTERNATIONAL JOURNAL OF LEPROSY
INT J MACH . . . . . . INTERNATIONAL JOURNAL OF MACHINE TOOL DESIGN & RESEARCH
Int J Magn . . . . INTERNATIONAL JOURNAL OF MAGNETISM
INT J MAN M . . . . . . INTERNATIONAL JOURNAL OF MAN-MACHINE STUDIES
INT J MASS . . . . INTERNATIONAL JOURNAL OF MASS SPECTROMETRY AND ION PHYSICS
INT J MECH . . . . . . INTERNATIONAL JOURNAL OF MECHANICAL SCIENCES
INT J MENT . . . . . . INTERNATIONAL JOURNAL OF MENTAL HEALTH
INT J ME ST . . . . . . INTERNATIONAL JOURNAL OF MIDDLE EAST STUDIES
INT J NEURO . . . . . . INTERNATIONAL JOURNAL OF NEUROLOGY
INT J NEURS . . . . . . INTERNATIONAL JOURNAL OF NEUROSCIENCE
Int J Nondestruct Test . . INTERNATIONAL JOURNAL OF NONDESTRUCTIVE TESTING
Int J Non-Linear Mech . . INTERNATIONAL JOURNAL OF NON-LINEAR MECHANICS
INT J NUC M . . . . . . INTERNATIONAL JOURNAL OF NUCLEAR MEDICINE & BIOLOGY
Int J Numer Methods Eng . . INTERNATIONAL JOURNAL FOR NUMERICAL METHODS IN ENGINEERING
INT J NURS . . . . . . INTERNATIONAL JOURNAL OF NURSING STUDIES
INT J OCC H . . . . . . INTERNATIONAL JOURNAL OF OCCUPATIONAL HEALTH AND SAFETY
INT J OFFEN . . . . . . INTERNATIONAL JOURNAL OF OFFENDER THERAPY
INT J OR SU . . . . . . INTERNATIONAL JOURNAL OF ORAL SURGERY
INT J PARAS . . . . . . INTERNATIONAL JOURNAL FOR PARASITOLOGY
INT J PEPT . . . . INTERNATIONAL JOURNAL OF PEPTIDE AND PROTEIN RESEARCH
Int J Phil Relig . . . . . INTERNATIONAL JOURNAL FOR PHILOSOPHY OF RELIGION
INT J POLIT . . . . . . INTERNATIONAL JOURNAL OF POLITICS
INT J POWD . . . . . . INTERNATIONAL JOURNAL OF POWDER METALLURGY
Int J Prod Res . . . . . INTERNATIONAL JOURNAL OF PRODUCTION RESEARCH
INT J PS PS . . . . INTERNATIONAL JOURNAL OF PSYCHOANALYTIC PSYCHOTHERAPY
INT J PSYCH . . . . . . INTERNATIONAL JOURNAL OF PSYCHOANALYSIS
Int J Psychiat . . . . . INTERNATIONAL JOURNAL OF PSYCHIATRY
Int J Psychoanal . . . INTERNATIONAL JOURNAL OF PSYCHOANALYSIS
INT J PSYCI . . . . . . INTERNATIONAL JOURNAL OF PSYCHIATRY
INT J PSYCO . . . . . . INTERNATIONAL JOURNAL OF PSYCHOLOGY
INT J PSY M . . . . . . INTERNATIONAL JOURNAL OF PSYCHIATRY IN MEDICINE
INT J QUANT . . . . . . INTERNATIONAL JOURNAL OF QUANTUM CHEMISTRY
INT J RAD B . . . . . . INTERNATIONAL JOURNAL OF RADIATION BIOLOGY
INT J RAD O . . . . . . INTERNATIONAL JOURNAL OF RADIATION ONCOLOGY, BIOLOGY, AND PHYSICS
INT J RAD P . . . . . . INTERNATIONAL JOURNAL FOR RADIATION PHYSICS AND CHEMISTRY
Int J Relig Ed . . . . . . INTERNATIONAL JOURNAL OF RELIGIOUS EDUCATION
INT J ROCK . . . . INTERNATIONAL JOURNAL OF ROCK MECHANICS
INT J SOC F . . . . INTERNATIONAL JOURNAL OF SOCIOLOGY OF THE FAMILY
Int J Social Psychiat . . INTERNATIONAL JOURNAL OF SOCIAL PSYCHIATRY
INT J SOC L . . . . INTERNATIONAL JOURNAL OF THE SOCIOLOGY OF LANGUAGE
INT J SOC P . . . . . . INTERNATIONAL JOURNAL OF SOCIAL PSYCHIATRY
Int J Solids Struct . . INTERNATIONAL JOURNAL OF SOLIDS AND STRUCTURES
INT J SP PS . . . . INTERNATIONAL JOURNAL OF SPORT PSYCHOLOGY
INT J SY B . . . . INTERNATIONAL JOURNAL OF SYSTEMATIC BACTERIOLOGY
INT J SYMB . . . . INTERNATIONAL JOURNAL OF SYMBOLOGY
INT J SYST . . . . INTERNATIONAL JOURNAL OF SYSTEMS SCIENCE
INT J THEOR . . . . . . INTERNATIONAL JOURNAL OF THEORETICAL PHYSICS
INT J VIT N . . . . INTERNATIONAL JOURNAL FOR VITAMIN AND NUTRITION RESEARCH
Int Labour R . . . . . . INTERNATIONAL LABOUR REVIEW
Int Labour R Stat Sup . . INTERNATIONAL LABOUR REVIEW. STATISTICAL SUPPLEMENT
INT LAB REV . . . . . . INTERNATIONAL LABOUR REVIEW

Int Law.......... INTERNATIONAL LAWYER
Int Lib R......... INTERNATIONAL LIBRARY REVIEW
INT LIBR RE....... INTERNATIONAL LIBRARY REVIEW
Intl Jnl Rel Ed..... INTERNATIONAL JOURNAL OF RELIGIOUS EDUCATION
Int Log Rev....... INTERNATIONAL LOGIC REVIEW
Int Metall Revs.... INTERNATIONAL METALLURGICAL REVIEWS
Int Mgt.......... INTERNATIONAL MANAGEMENT
INT MIGR RE...... INTERNATIONAL MIGRATION REVIEW
Int Min Equip...... INTERNATIONAL MINING EQUIPMENT
INT MONETAR..... INTERNATIONAL MONETARY FUND. STAFF PAPERS
Int Mus.......... INTERNATIONAL MUSICIAN
INT MUS ED....... INTERNATIONAL MUSIC EDUCATOR
Int Nickel........ INTERNATIONAL NICKEL
IntNurl.......... INTERNATIONAL NURSING INDEX
INT NURS RE...... INTERNATIONAL NURSING REVIEW
Int Org.......... INTERNATIONAL ORGANIZATION
Int Organ........ INTERNATIONAL ORGANIZATION
INT PERSPECT..... INTERNATIONAL PERSPECTIVES
Int Pest Control.... INTERNATIONAL PEST CONTROL
Int Petrol Annu.... INTERNATIONAL PETROLEUM ANNUAL
INT PHARMAC..... INTERNATIONAL PHARMACOPSYCHIATRY
Int Phil Quart..... INTERNATIONAL PHILOSOPHICAL QUARTERLY
INT POLIT O...... INTERNASJONAL POLITIKK (OSLO)
IntPolSc......... INTERNATIONAL POLITICAL SCIENCE ABSTRACTS
Intpr............ INTERPRETATION: A JOURNAL OF BIBLE AND THEOLOGY
Int R Aesthetics & Soc Mus.. INTERNATIONAL REVIEW OF THE AESTHETICS AND SOCIOLOGY OF MUSIC
Int R Ag......... INTERNATIONAL REVIEW OF AGRICULTURE
Int R Ag Econ...... INTERNATIONAL REVIEW OF AGRICULTURAL ECONOMICS
Intra L Rev (Am U).. INTRAMURAL LAW REVIEW OF AMERICAN UNIVERSITY
Intra L Rev (NYU).. INTRAMURAL LAW REVIEW OF NEW YORK UNIVERSITY
Intra L Rev (UCLA).. INTRAMURAL LAW REVIEW OF UNIVERSITY OF CALIFORNIA AT LOS ANGELES
Int Read Assn Conf Pa.. INTERNATIONAL READING ASSOCIATION CONFERENCE. PAPERS
Int R Ed.......... INTERNATIONAL REVIEW OF EDUCATION
Int R Ed Cinemat... INTERNATIONAL REVIEW OF EDUCATIONAL CINEMATOGRAPHY
Int R Educ........ INTERNATIONAL REVIEW OF EDUCATION
INT REV CYT...... INTERNATIONAL REVIEW OF CYTOLOGY
INT REV EDU...... INTERNATIONAL REVIEW OF EDUCATION
INT REV HIS....... INTERNATIONAL REVIEW OF HISTORY AND POLITICAL SCIENCE
INT REV MOD..... INTERNATIONAL REVIEW OF MODERN SOCIOLOGY
INT REV S H....... INTERNATIONAL REVIEW OF SOCIAL HISTORY
Int R Miss........ INTERNATIONAL REVIEW OF MISSIONS
Int R Mod Sociol... INTERNATIONAL REVIEW OF MODERN SOCIOLOGY
Int Ropeway Rev... INTERNATIONAL ROPEWAY REVIEW
Int R Sci & Prac Ag.. INTERNATIONAL REVIEW OF THE SCIENCE AND PRACTICE OF AGRICULTURE
Int R Soc Hist..... INTERNATIONAL REVIEW OF SOCIAL HISTORY
Int Shipbldg Progr.. INTERNATIONAL SHIPBUILDING PROGRESS
INT SOC DEV...... INTERNATIONAL SOCIAL DEVELOPMENT REVIEW
INT SOC SCI....... INTERNATIONAL SOCIAL SCIENCE JOURNAL
Int Soc Sci J....... INTERNATIONAL SOCIAL SCIENCE JOURNAL
Int Stat R........ INTERNATIONAL STATISTICAL REVIEW
INT ST E AS....... INTERNATIONAL STUDIES. EAST ASIAN SERIES RESEARCH PUBLICATION

Int Stud.........INTERNATIONAL STUDIES (NEW DELHI)
Int Studio........INTERNATIONAL STUDIO
Int Stud Phil......INTERNATIONAL STUDIES IN PHILOSOPHY
Int Stud Q........INTERNATIONAL STUDIES QUARTERLY
Int Sug J.........INTERNATIONAL SUGAR JOURNAL
INT SURG........INTERNATIONAL SURGERY
Int Yearbook Ag Leg..INTERNATIONAL YEARBOOK OF AGRICULTURAL LEGISLATION
Int Yearbook of Ed..INTERNATIONAL YEARBOOK OF EDUCATION
Int Yrbk Ed.......INTERNATIONAL YEARBOOK OF EDUCATION
Int Z Erzieh.......INTERNATIONALE ZEITSCHRIFT FUER ERZIEHUNGSWISSENSCHAFT
Inv.............INVENTARIO
Inv Banking.......INVESTMENT BANKING
INVENT MATH.....INVENTIONES MATHEMATICAE
INV OPHTH......INVESTIGATIVE OPHTHALMOLOGY
INV PESQ........INVESTIGACION PESQUERA
INV RADIOL......INVESTIGATIVE RADIOLOGY
INV UROL........INVESTIGATIVE UROLOGY
Inz Budownictwo...INZYNIERIA I BUDOWNICTWO
Inzh-Fiz Zh Akad Nauk Belorus SSR..INZHENERNO-FIZICHESKII ZHURNAL. AKADEMIYA NAUK BELORUSKOI S.S.R.
Inzh Zh Mekh Tverd Tela..INZHENERNYI ZHURNAL, MEKHANIKA TVERDOGO TELA
Inz Stavby........INZENYRSKE STAVBY
Iowa Geol Surv Rep Invest..IOWA GEOLOGICAL SURVEY. REPORT OF INVESTIGATIONS
Iowa Jour Hist and Pol..IOWA JOURNAL OF HISTORY AND POLITICS
Iowa Lib Q........IOWA LIBRARY QUARTERLY
IowaR...........IOWA REVIEW
Iowa State Univ Ames Eng Res Inst Rep..IOWA STATE UNIVERSITY, AMES. ENGINEERING RESEARCH INSTITUTE. REPORT
Iowa State Univ Eng Exp Sta Bull..IOWA STATE UNIVERSITY, AMES. IOWA ENGINEERING EXPERIMENT STATION. BULLETIN
IP.............INVESTIGACION Y PROGRESO
IPAJ...........INTERNATIONAL PHONETIC ASSOCIATION JOURNAL
IPC MG.........IPC (INSTITUTE OF PHILIPPINE CULTURE) MONOGRAPHS
IPC PAP........IPC (INSTITUTE OF PHILIPPINE CULTURE) PAPERS
IPEN...........INDIAN P.E.N.
IPLL...........ILLINOIS PUBLICATIONS IN LANGUAGE AND LITERATURE
IPLO Q.........IPLO (INSTITUTE OF PROFESSIONAL LIBRARIANS OF ONTARIO) QUARTERLY
IPNA...........INSTITUTO PERUANO-NORTE AMERICANO
I POLIT SCI.......INDIAN POLITICAL SCIENCE REVIEW
IPQ............INTERNATIONAL PHILOSOPHICAL QUARTERLY
I PSYCHOL R......INDIAN PSYCHOLOGICAL REVIEW
IQ.............ISLAMIC QUARTERLY
IQ.............ITALIAN QUARTERLY
IqR............IQBAL REVIEW
IR.............ILIFF REVIEW
IR.............INDUSTRIAL RELATIONS
IR.............INNERE REICH
IRAL...........INTERNATIONAL REVIEW OF APPLIED LINGUISTICS IN LANGUAGE TEACHING
Iran Antiq........IRANICA ANTIQUA
Iran J Sci Technol...IRANIAN JOURNAL OF SCIENCE AND TECHNOLOGY
IranS...........IRANIAN STUDIES
IRCD Bul........YESHIVA UNIVERSITY. INFORMATION RETRIEVAL CENTER ON THE DISADVANTAGED. BULLETIN

IrEccRec......... IRISH ECCLESIASTICAL RECORD
Iren............ IRENIKON
IRISH ASTR....... IRISH ASTRONOMICAL JOURNAL
Irish Econ........ IRISH ECONOMIST
Irish Hist Stud..... IRISH HISTORICAL STUDIES
IRISH J AGR...... IRISH JOURNAL OF AGRICULTURAL RESEARCH
Irish J Ed......... IRISH JOURNAL OF EDUCATION
IRISH J MED...... IRISH JOURNAL OF MEDICAL SCIENCE
IRISH J PSY....... IRISH JOURNAL OF PSYCHOLOGY
Irish Jur......... IRISH JURIST
Irish Lib Bul...... IRISH LIBRARY BULLETIN
IRISH MED J...... IRISH MEDICAL JOURNAL
Irish Mo......... IRISH MONTHLY
Irish Q......... IRISH QUARTERLY REVIEW
Irish S.......... IRISH SWORD
IRJaSl.......... INSTITUT RUSSKOGO JAZYKA I SLOVESNOSTI PRI AKADEMII NAUK SSSR
Ir Jur.......... IRISH JURIST
IRLI........... ITALIANISTICA: RIVISTA DI LETTERATURA ITALIANA
Ir L T........... IRISH LAW TIMES
IrM............ IRISH MONTHLY
Irodal F......... IRODALOMTORTENETI FUZETEK
Ironmaking Proc AIME.. IRONMAKING PROCEEDINGS. METALLURGICAL SOCIETY OF AIME. IRON AND STEEL DIVISION
Iron St.......... IRON AND STEEL
Iron Steel........ IRON AND STEEL (LONDON)
Iron Steel Eng..... IRON AND STEEL ENGINEER
Iron Steel Inst (London) Publ.. IRON AND STEEL INSTITUTE (LONDON) PUBLICATION
Iron St Int....... IRON AND STEEL INTERNATIONAL
Iron Tr R........ IRON TRADE REVIEW
IRRA........... INDUSTRIAL RELATIONS RESEARCH ASSOCIATION. PROCEEDINGS
Irr Age......... IRRIGATION AGE
Irrig Power...... IRRIGATION AND POWER
IRSH.......... INTERNATIONAL REVIEW OF SOCIAL HISTORY
IRV........... ISTITUTO TECNICO STATALE COMMERCIALE E PER GEOMETRI ROBERTO VALTURIO (RIMINI)
IS............. IRISH STATESMAN
Is............. ISIS
IS............. ITALIAN STUDIES
IS............. ITALIENISCHE STUDIEN
ISA J........... ISA (INSTRUMENT SOCIETY OF AMERICA) JOURNAL
ISA Prepr........ ISA (INSTRUMENT SOCIETY OF AMERICA) CONFERENCE PREPRINT
ISA Trans........ ISA (INSTRUMENT SOCIETY OF AMERICA) TRANSACTIONS
ISB........... INDEPENDENT SCHOOL BULLETIN
ISE........... IBADAN STUDIES IN ENGLISH
ISF........... IMAGINATION SCIENCE FICTION
ISHS.......... ILLINOIS STATE HISTORICAL SOCIETY. JOURNAL
ISHSJ......... ILLINOIS STATE HISTORICAL SOCIETY. JOURNAL
ISLL.......... ILLINOIS STUDIES IN LANGUAGE AND LITERATURE
ISLS.......... INFORMATION SYSTEM LANGUAGE STUDIES
ISM........... MITTEILUNGEN DER INTERNATIONALEN STIFTUNG MOZARTEUM
ISO........... INTERNATIONAL SOCIETY OF ORGANBUILDERS
Isotop Radiat Technol.. ISOTOPES AND RADIATION TECHNOLOGY
IsQ........... ISLAMIC QUARTERLY

ISR ANN PSY . . . . . . ISRAEL ANNALS OF PSYCHIATRY AND RELATED DISCIPLINES
ISR EXPL J . . . . ISRAEL EXPLORATION JOURNAL
ISR J BOT . . . . ISRAEL JOURNAL OF BOTANY
ISR J CHEM . . . . ISRAEL JOURNAL OF CHEMISTRY
ISR J EARTH . . . . . . ISRAEL JOURNAL OF EARTH SCIENCES
ISR J MATH . . . . ISRAEL JOURNAL OF MATHEMATICS
ISR J MED S . . . . ISRAEL JOURNAL OF MEDICAL SCIENCES
ISR J TECH . . . . ISRAEL JOURNAL OF TECHNOLOGY
ISR J ZOOL . . . . ISRAEL JOURNAL OF ZOOLOGY
ISR LAW REV . . . . . . ISRAEL LAW REVIEW
Isr Min Agr Water Comm Hydrol Serv Hydrol Paper . . ISRAEL MINISTRY OF AGRICULTURE. WATER COMMISSION.
    HYDROLOGICAL SERVICE. HYDROLOGICAL PAPER
ISS . . . . INDIANA SLAVIC STUDIES
ISSJ . . . . INTERNATIONAL SOCIAL SCIENCE JOURNAL (UNESCO)
ISSUES CRIM . . . . . . ISSUES IN CRIMINOLOGY
ISt . . . . INSEMNARI STIINTIFICE
ISt . . . . ITALIAN STUDIES
Istanbul Univ Edebiyat Fak Turk ve Edebiyat Dergisi . . ISTANBUL UNIVERSITESI EDEBIYAT FAKULTESI TURK VE
    EDEBIYAT DERGISI
Istoria Artei . . . . . . STUDII SI CERCETARI DE ISTORIA ARTEI
Ist Patologia Libro Boll . . ISTITUTO DI PATOLOGIA DEL LIBRO. BOLLETTINO
IstZap . . . . ISTORICESKII ZAPISKI
I Sz . . . . IRODALMI SZEMLE
IT . . . . ISLENZK TUNGA
It . . . . ITALIA CHE SCRIVE
It . . . . ITALICA
Ital . . . . ITALIANISTICA
Ital . . . . ITALICA
Italamer . . . . ITALAMERICAN
ITAL J BIOC . . . . ITALIAN JOURNAL OF BIOCHEMISTRY
ItB . . . . IT BEAKEN
ItF . . . . ITALYAN FILOLOJISI
Itin . . . . ITINERARI
ITQ . . . . IRISH THEOLOGICAL QUARTERLY
ItQ . . . . ITALIAN QUARTERLY
ITS . . . . IRISH TEXTS SOCIETY
IUB . . . . INDIANA UNIVERSITY BOOKMAN
IUFS . . . . INDIANA UNIVERSITY FOLKLORE SERIES
IUHS . . . . INDIANA UNIVERSITY HUMANITIES SERIES
IUP . . . . IRISH UNIVERSITY PRESS
IUPAL . . . . INDIANA UNIVERSITY. PUBLICATIONS IN ANTHROPOLOGY AND LINGUISTICS
IUPFS . . . . INDIANA UNIVERSITY. PUBLICATIONS. FOLKLORE SERIES
IUPHS . . . . INDIANA UNIVERSITY. PUBLICATIONS. HUMANISTIC SERIES
IUPLSM . . . . INDIANA UNIVERSITY. PUBLICATIONS. LANGUAGE SCIENCE MONOGRAPHS
IUPSEES . . . . INDIANA UNIVERSITY. PUBLICATIONS. SLAVIC AND EAST EUROPEAN SERIES
IUPUAS . . . . INDIANA UNIVERSITY. PUBLICATIONS. URALIC AND ALTAIC SERIES
IUR . . . . IRISH UNIVERSITY REVIEW
IURCAFL . . . . INDIANA UNIVERSITY RESEARCH CENTER IN ANTHROPOLOGY, FOLKLORE, AND LINGUISTICS
IUSHTL . . . . INDIANA UNIVERSITY STUDIES IN THE HISTORY AND THEORY OF LINGUISTICS
IV . . . . ILLUSTRAZIONE VATICANA
IV . . . . ISTORITCHESKII VIESTNIK

IVat............ ILLUSTRAZIONE VATICANA
IVA Tidskr Tek-Vetenskaplig Forsk.. IVA TIDSKRIFT FOER TEKNISK-VETENSKAPLIG FORSKNING
IVGPI.......... IZVESTIYA VORONEZSKOGO GOSUDARSTENNOGO PEDAGOGICESKOGO INSTITUTA
IVI............. IKUSKA. INSTITUTO VASCO DE INVESTIGACIONES
IVN............. INTERNATIONALE VERENIGING VOOR NEDERLANDISTIEK
IVUZ FIZ........ IZVESTIYA VYSSHIKH UCHEBNYKH ZAVEDENII FIZIKA
IWT............ INDIANA WRITING TODAY
IYaSh........... INOSTRANNYE YAZYKI V SHKOLE (MOSCOW)
IZ.............. INSTRUMENTENBAU-ZEITSCHRIFT
Iz.............. IZVESTIYA (MOSCOW)
Izv Akad Nauk SSSR Energ Transp.. IZVESTIYA AKADEMII NAUK SSSR. ENERGETIKA I TRANSPORT
Izv Akad Nauk SSSR Fiz Atmos Okeana.. IZVESTIYA AKADEMII NAUK SSSR. FIZIKA ATMOSFERY I OKEANA
Izv Akad Nauk SSSR Fiz Zemli.. IZVESTIYA AKADEMII NAUK SSSR. FIZIKA ZEMLI
Izv Akad Nauk SSSR Mekh Tverd Tela.. IZVESTIYA AKADEMII NAUK SSSR. MEKHANIKA TVERDOGO TELA
Izv Akad Nauk SSSR Mekh Zhidk Gaza.. IZVESTIYA AKADEMII NAUK SSSR. MEKHANIKA ZHIDROSTI I GAZA
Izv Akad Nauk SSSR Metally.. IZVESTIYA AKADEMII NAUK SSSR. METALLY
IzvAN.......... IZVESTIYA AKADEMII NAUK SSSR. OTDELENIE LITERATURY I JAZYKA
IzvANArm........ IZVESTIYA AKADEMII NAUK ARMJANSKOJ SSR. OBSCESTVENNYH NAUK
IzvANAzerb....... IZVESTIYA AKADEMII NAUK AZERBAJDZANSKOJ SSR. SERIYA OBSCESTYENNYCH NAUK
IzvANKaz........ IZVESTIYA AKADEMII NAUK KAZACHSKOJ SSR. SERIYA FILOLOGII I ISKUSSTVOVEDENIYA
IzvANTadz....... IZVESTIYA AKADEMII NAUK TADZICKOJ SSR. OTDELENIE OBSOESTVENNYCH NAUK
IzvANTurkm...... IZVESTIYA AKADEMII NAUK TURKMENSKOJ SSR. SERIYA OBSCESTVENNYCH NAUK
IzvArmZPI....... IZVESTIYA ARMYANSKOGO GOSUDARSTVENNOGO ZAOCNOGO PEDAGOGICESKOGO INSTITUTA
IzvBAI.......... IZVESTIYA NA BALGARSKIYA ARCHEOLOGICESKI INSTITUT
IzvCIngNII....... IZVESTIYA CECENO-INGUSSKOGO NAUCNO-ISSLEDOVATEL-SKOGO INSTITUTA ISTORII, JAZYKA
                  I LITERATURY
IzvDS.......... IZVESTIYA NA DRUZESTVOTO NA FILOLOZITE-SLAVISTI V BALGARIJA (SOFIA)
IZVESTIYA AKAD NAUK SSSR.. IZVESTIYA AKADEMII NAUK SSSR OTDELENIE LITERATURY I JAZYKA
Izvestiya Jugo-Oset Nauc Issl Inst.. IZVESTIYA JUGO-OSETINSKOGO NAUCNO-ISSLEDOVATEL'SKOGO INSTITUTA
                  AKADEMII NAUK-GRUZINSKOJ SSR
Izvestiya Kirgiz Filiala Akad nauk SSSR.. IZVESTIYA KIRGIZSKOGO FILIALA AKADEMII NAUK SSR
Izvestiya Turkm Filiala Akad nauk SSSR.. IZVESTIYA TURKMENSKOGO FILIALA AKADEMII NAUK SSSR
Izvestiya Voronezskogo gos ped inst.. IZVESTIYA VORONEZSKOGO GOSUD. PEDAGOGICESKOGO INSTITUTA
IzvIBE.......... IZVESTIYA INSTITUTA ZA BALGARSKI EZIK
IzvIRGruz........ IZVESTIYA INSTITUT RUKOPISEJ AKADEMII NAUK GRUZINSKOJ SSR
IzvJOsNII........ IZVESTIYA JUGO-OSETINSKOGO NAUCNO-ISSLEDOVATEL' SKOGO INSTITUTA
IzvJuOsl........ IZVESTIYA JUGO-OSETINSKOGO NAUCNO-ISSLEDOVATEL'SKOGO INSTITUTA AKADEMII NAUK
                  GRUZINSKOJ SSR
IzvSLF.......... IZVESTIYA SEMINARA PO SLAVJANSKE FILOLOGIJA
IzvSOsNII........ IZVESTIYA SEVERO-OSETINSKOGO NAUCNO-ISSLEDOVATEL'SKOGO INSTITUTA
IzvTadzikAN...... IZVESTIYA TADZIKSKOGO FILIALA AKADEMII NAUK
IzvVorPI........ IZVESTIYA VORONEZSKOGO GOSUDARSTVENNOGO PEDAGOGICESKOGO INSTITUTA
Izv Vyssh Uchebn Zaved Mashinostr.. IZVESTIYA VYSSHIKH UCHEBNYKH ZAVEDENII. MASHINOSTROENIE
Izv Vyssh Uchebn Zaved Radioelektron.. IZVESTIYA VYSSHIKH UCHEBNYKH ZAVEDENII. RADIOELEKTRONIKA
Izv Vyssh Ucheb Zaved Chern Met.. IZVESTIYA VYSSHIKH UCHEBNYKH ZAVEDENII. CHERNAYA METALLURGIYA
Izv Vyssh Ucheb Zabed Elektromekh.. IZVESTIYA VYSSHIKH UCHEBNYKH ZAVEDENII. ELEKTROMEKHANIKA
Izv Vyssh Ucheb Zaved Energ.. IZVESTIYA VYSSHIKH UCHEBNYKH ZAVEDENII. ENERGETIKA
Izv Vyssh Ucheb Zaved Geol i Razved.. IZVESTIYA VYSSHIKH UCHEBNYKH ZAVEDENII. GEOLOGIYA I RAZVEDKA
Izv Vyssh Ucheb Zaved Gorn Zh.. IZVESTIYA VYSSHIKH UCHEBNYKH ZAVEDENII. GORNYI ZHURNAL
Izv Vyssh Ucheb Zaved Khim i Khim.. IZVESTIYA VYSSHIKH UCHEBNYKH ZAVEDENII. KHIMIYA I KHIMICHESKAYA
Izv Vyssh Ucheb Zaved Neft i Gaz.. IZVESTIYA VYSSHIKH UCHEBNYKH ZAVEDENII. NEFT I GAZ

Izv Vyssh Uchob Zaved Tsvet Met . . IZVESTIYA VYSSHIKH UCHEBNYKH ZAVEDENII. TSVETNAYA METALLURGIYA

J

J	JEUNESSE
J	JEZIK
JA	JAHRBUCH FUER AMERIKASTUDIEN
JA	JANUARY
JA	JAPAN ARCHITECT
JA	JOURNAL ASIATIQUE
JA	JOURNAL OF AESTHETICS
JA	JOURNAL OF AESTHETICS AND ART CRITICISM
JAAC	JOURNAL OF AESTHETICS AND ART CRITICISM
JAAK	JAHRBUCH FUER AESTHETIK UND ALLGEMEINE KUNSTWISSENSCHAFT
J Abnorm Psychol . .	JOURNAL OF ABNORMAL AND SOCIAL PSYCHOLOGY
J ABN PSYCH	JOURNAL OF ABNORMAL PSYCHOLOGY
JABS	JOURNAL OF APPLIED BEHAVIORAL SCIENCE
JAC	JAHRBUCH FUER ANTIKE UND CHRISTENTUM
J Account	JOURNAL OF ACCOUNTANCY
J ACCOUNTIN	JOURNAL OF ACCOUNTING RESEARCH
J Accounting Res . . .	JOURNAL OF ACCOUNTING RESEARCH
J Accy	JOURNAL OF ACCOUNTANCY
J ACM	JOURNAL OF THE ASSOCIATION FOR COMPUTING MACHINERY
J ACOUST SO	JOURNAL OF THE ACOUSTICAL SOCIETY OF AMERICA
J Acoust Soc Am . . .	JOURNAL OF THE ACOUSTICAL SOCIETY OF AMERICA
JAcS	JOURNAL OF THE ACOUSTICAL SOCIETY OF AMERICA
J Adhes	JOURNAL OF ADHESION
J ADHESION	JOURNAL OF ADHESION
J Adult Ed	JOURNAL OF ADULT EDUCATION
J Adv Res	JOURNAL OF ADVERTISING RESEARCH
JAe	JAHRBUCH FUER AESTHETIK UND ALLGEMEINE KUNSTWISSENSCHAFT
JAE	JOURNAL OF AESTHETIC EDUCATION
J Aero Sci	JOURNAL OF THE AERONAUTICAL SCIENCES
J Aerosol Sci	JOURNAL OF AEROSOL SCIENCE
J Aero/Space Sci . . .	JOURNAL OF THE AERO/SPACE SCIENCES
JAERT	JOURNAL OF THE ASSOCIATION FOR EDUCATION BY RADIO-TELEVISION
J Aes Art Crit	JOURNAL OF AESTHETICS AND ART CRITICISM
J Aes Educ	JOURNAL OF AESTHETIC EDUCATION
J Aesth	JOURNAL OF AESTHETICS AND ART CRITICISM
J AESTHET E	JOURNAL OF AESTHETIC EDUCATION
J AESTHETICS	JOURNAL OF AESTHETICS AND ART CRITICISM
JAF	JOURNAL OF AMERICAN FOLKLORE
JAFL	JOURNAL OF AMERICAN FOLKLORE
JAfrH	JOURNAL OF AFRICAN HISTORY
J AFR HIST	JOURNAL OF AFRICAN HISTORY
JAfrL	JOURNAL OF AFRICAN LANGUAGES
J Ag & Food Chem . .	JOURNAL OF AGRICULTURE AND FOOD CHEMISTRY
JAG	JAG (JUDGE ADVOCATE GENERAL, U.S. AIR FORCE) BULLETIN
J Ag Econ	JOURNAL OF AGRICULTURAL ECONOMICS
JAG J	JAG (JUDGE ADVOCATE GENERAL, U.S. NAVY) JOURNAL
J Ag New Zealand . .	NEW ZEALAND JOURNAL OF AGRICULTURE
J Ag Pratique	JOURNAL D'AGRICULTURE PRATIQUE
J Ag (Quebec)	JOURNAL OF AGRICULTURE AND HORTICULTURE
J AGR CHE J	AGRICULTURAL CHEMICAL SOCIETY OF JAPAN. JOURNAL

J AGR ECON . . . . . . JOURNAL OF AGRICULTURAL ECONOMICS
J AGR ENG R . . . . . . JOURNAL OF AGRICULTURAL ENGINEERING RESEARCH
J Ag Res . . . . JOURNAL OF AGRICULTURAL RESEARCH
J AGR FOOD . . . . . . JOURNAL OF AGRICULTURAL AND FOOD CHEMISTRY
J Agric Engin Res . . . JOURNAL OF AGRICULTURAL ENGINEERING RESEARCH
J AGR SCI . . . . JOURNAL OF AGRICULTURAL SCIENCE
J Ag Univ Puerto Rico . . JOURNAL OF AGRICULTURE. UNIVERSITY OF PUERTO RICO
JAH . . . . JOURNAL OF AMERICAN HISTORY
JahAs . . . . JAHRBUCH FUER AMERIKASTUDIEN
Jahrb Amerikastud . JAHRBUCH FUER AMERIKASTUDIEN
Jahr Berliner Mus . . JAHRBUCH DER BERLINER MUSEEN
Jahrb d Kunsthist Samml d Kaiserhauses . . JAHRBUCH DER KUNSTHISTORISCHEN SAMMLUNGEN DES ALLERHOCHSTEN
KAISERHAUSES
Jahrb d Preuss Kunstsamml . . JAHRBUCH DER PREUSSISCHEN KUNSTSAMMLUNGEN
Jahrb Gesch & Kunst Mittelrheins & Nachbargeb . . JAHRBUCH FUER GESCHICTE UND KUNST DES MITTELRHEINS UND
SEINER NACHBARGEBIETE
Jahrb Gesch Osteurop . . JAHRBUECHER FUER GESCHICHTE OSTEUROPAS
Jahrb Kunsth Samml Kaiserh n s . . JAHRBUCH DER KUNSTHISTORISCHEN SAMMLUNGEN DES ALLERHOCHSTEN
KAISERHAUSES
Jahrb Liturg & Hymnol . . JAHRBUCH FUER LITURGIK UND HYMNOLOGIE
JAHRB N ST . . . . . . JAHRBUCHER FUER NATIONAL EKONOMIE UND STATISTIK
Jahrb Preuss Kunstsamml . . JAHRBUCH DER PREUSSISCHEN KUNSTSAMMLUNGEN
Jahrb Schiffbautech Ges . . JAHRBUCH DER SCHIFFBAUTECHNISCHEN GESSELSCHAFT
JAHRB SOZIA . . . . . JAHRBUCH FUER SOZIALWISSENSCHAFT
Jahrbuch Hamburger Kunstsam . . JAHRBUCH DER HAMBURGER KUNSTSAMMLUNGEN
Jahrbuch Niederdonau . . JAHRBUCH FUER LANDESKUNDE VON NIEDERDONAU
Jahr Deutsch Archaeol Inst . . JAHRBUCH DES DEUTSCHEN ARCHAEOLOGISCHEN INSTITUTS
Jahresbericht Grabunden . . JAHRESBERICHT DER HISTORISCH-ANTIQUARISCHEN GESELL SCHAFT VON GRABUNDEN
Jahr Hamburger Kunstsam . . JAHRBUCH DER HAMBURGER KUNSTSAMMLUNGEN
Jahr Kunsthist Sam Wien . . JAHRBUCH DER KUNSTHISTORISCHEN SAMMLUNGEN IN WIEN
JAHum . . . . JOURNAL OF AMERICAN HUMOR
JAI . . . . JOURNAL OF THE ROYAL ANTHROPOLOGICAL INSTITUTE OF GREAT BRITAIN AND IRELAND
JAIA . . . . JOURNAL OF THE ARCHAEOLOGICAL INSTITUTE OF AMERICA
JAIB . . . . JOURNAL OF THE ROYAL ANTHROPOLOGICAL INSTITUTE OF GREAT BRITAIN AND IRELAND
JaiL . . . . JAZYK I LITERATURA
J Aircraft . . . . JOURNAL OF AIRCRAFT
J Air L . . . . JOURNAL OF AIR LAW AND COMMERCE
J AIR POLLU . . . . . . JOURNAL OF THE AIR POLLUTION CONTROL ASSOCIATION
J Air Pollut Contr Ass . . JOURNAL OF THE AIR POLLUTION CONTROL ASSOCIATION
Ja J . . . . JUDGE ADVOCATE JOURNAL
JAk . . . . JAZYKOVEDNE AKTUALITY
JAL . . . . JOURNAL OF AFRICAN LANGUAGES
J ALC . . . . JOURNAL OF ALCOHOLISM
J ALC DRUG . . . . . JOURNAL OF ALCOHOL AND DRUG EDUCATION
J ALGEBRA . . . . . . JOURNAL OF ALGEBRA
J ALLERG CL . . . . . JOURNAL OF ALLERGY AND CLINICAL IMMUNOLOGY
J Allergy . . . . JOURNAL OF ALLERGY AND CLINICAL IMMUNOLOGY
JAM . . . . JOURNAL OF AMERICAN MUSICOLOGY
J AMA . . . . JOURNAL OF THE AMERICAN MEDICAL ASSOCIATION
J AM ACAD P . . . . JOURNAL OF THE AMERICAN ACADEMY OF PSYCHOANALYSIS

J AM A CHIL . . . . . . JOURNAL OF THE AMERICAN ACADEMY OF CHILD PSYCHIATRY
Jamaica Ag Soc J . . . JAMAICA AGRICULTURAL SOCIETY. JOURNAL
J AM A REL . . . . JOURNAL OF THE AMERICAN ACADEMY OF RELIGION
J AM CERAM . . . . . . JOURNAL OF THE AMERICAN CERAMIC SOCIETY
J AM CHEM S . . . . . . JOURNAL OF THE AMERICAN CHEMICAL SOCIETY
J AM COLL H . . . . . . JOURNAL OF THE AMERICAN COLLEGE OF HEALTH ASSOCIATION
J Am Concr Inst . . . . JOURNAL OF THE AMERICAN CONCRETE INSTITUTE
J AM DENT A . . . . . . JOURNAL OF THE AMERICAN DENTAL ASSOCIATION
J AM DIET A . . . . . . JOURNAL OF THE AMERICAN DIETETIC ASSOCIATION
J Amer Ceram Soc . . JOURNAL OF THE AMERICAN CERAMIC SOCIETY
J Amer Chem Soc . . . JOURNAL OF THE AMERICAN CHEMICAL SOCIETY
J Amer Leather Chem Ass . . JOURNAL OF THE AMERICAN LEATHER CHEMISTS ASSOCIATION
J Amer Soc Inform Sci . . JOURNAL OF THE AMERICAN SOCIETY FOR INFORMATION SCIENCE
J Amer Soc Safety Eng . . JOURNAL OF THE AMERICAN SOCIETY OF SAFETY ENGINEERS
James Sprunt Hist Publ . . JAMES SPRUNT HISTORICAL PUBLICATIONS
J Am Folk . . . . JOURNAL OF AMERICAN FOLKLORE
J AM FOLKLO . . . . . . JOURNAL OF AMERICAN FOLKLORE
J AM GER SO . . . . . . JOURNAL OF THE AMERICAN GERIATRICS SOCIETY
J Am Hist . . . . JOURNAL OF AMERICAN HISTORY
J Am Indian Ed . . . . JOURNAL OF AMERICAN INDIAN EDUCATION
J AM INST P . . . . . . JOURNAL OF THE AMERICAN INSTITUTE OF PLANNERS
J Am Jud Soc . . . . . . JOURNAL OF THE AMERICAN JUDICATURE SOCIETY
J AM LEATH . . . . . . JOURNAL OF THE AMERICAN LEATHER CHEMISTS ASSOCIATION
J AM MED A . . . . . . JOURNAL OF THE AMERICAN MEDICAL ASSOCIATION
J AM OIL CH . . . . . . JOURNAL OF THE AMERICAN OIL CHEMISTS SOCIETY
J AM PHARM . . . . . JOURNAL OF THE AMERICAN PHARMACEUTICAL ASSOCIATION
J Am PSYCHO . . . . . JOURNAL OF THE AMERICAN PSYCHOANALYTIC ASSOCIATION
JAmS . . . . JOURNAL OF AMERICAN STUDIES
JAMS . . . . JOURNAL OF THE AMERICAN MUSICOLOGICAL SOCIETY
J AM S HORT . . . . . . JOURNAL OF THE AMERICAN SOCIETY FOR HORTICULTURAL SCIENCE
J AM S INFOR . . . . . JOURNAL OF THE AMERICAN SOCIETY FOR INFORMATION SCIENCE
J Am Soc CLU . . . . . JOURNAL OF THE AMERICAN SOCIETY OF CHARTERED LIFE UNDERWRITERS
J Am Soc Inf Sci . . . . JOURNAL OF THE AMERICAN SOCIETY FOR INFORMATION SCIENCE
J AM S PSYC . . . . . . JOURNAL OF THE AMERICAN SOCIETY FOR PSYCHICAL RESEARCH
J AM STAT A . . . . . . JOURNAL OF THE AMERICAN STATISTICAL ASSOCIATION
J Am Stud . . . . JOURNAL OF AMERICAN STUDIES
J AM VET ME . . . . . . JOURNAL OF THE AMERICAN VETERINARY MEDICAL ASSOCIATION
J AM VET RA . . . . . . JOURNAL OF THE AMERICAN VETERINARY RADIOLOGY SOCIETY
J AM WATER . . . . . . JOURNAL AMERICAN WATER WORKS ASSOCIATION
Jan . . . . JANUS. ARCHIVES INTERNATIONALES POUR L'HISTOIRE DE LA MEDECINE
JAN . . . . JOURNAL INTERNATIONAL D'ARCHEOLOGIE NUMISMATIQUE
J ANAL CHEM . . . . . JOURNAL OF ANALYTICAL CHEMISTRY OF THE USSR
J ANAL MATH . . . . . JOURNAL D'ANALYSE MATHEMATIQUE
J Anal Psych . . . . . . JOURNAL OF ANALYTICAL PSYCHOLOGY
J ANAT . . . . JOURNAL OF ANATOMY
J Animal Ecol . . . . . . JOURNAL OF ANIMAL ECOLOGY
J Animal Sci . . . . . . JOURNAL OF ANIMAL SCIENCE
J ANIM ECOL . . . . . . JOURNAL OF ANIMAL ECOLOGY
J ANIM SCI . . . . JOURNAL OF ANIMAL SCIENCE
JanL . . . . JANUA LINGUARUM
JAnthrI . . . . JOURNAL OF THE ROYAL ANTHROPOLOGICAL INSTITUTE OF GREAT BRITAIN AND IRELAND

J Anthrop Res . . . . . JOURNAL OF ANTHROPOLOGICAL RESEARCH
J ANTHR RES . . . . . . JOURNAL OF ANTHROPOLOGICAL RESEARCH
J ANTHR S N . . . . . . JOURNAL OF THE ANTHROPOLOGICAL SOCIETY OF NIPPON
J ANTIBIOT . . . . JOURNAL OF ANTIBIOTICS
J AOAC . . . . JOURNAL OF THE ASSOCIATION OF OFFICIAL ANALYTICAL CHEMISTS
JAOS . . . . JOURNAL OF THE AMERICAN ORIENTAL SOCIETY
JAP . . . . JOURNAL OF APPLIED PSYCHOLOGY
Japan Arch . . . . JAPAN ARCHITECT
JAPAN INTER . . . . . JAPAN INTERPRETER
Japan J Geol & Geog . . JAPANESE JOURNAL OF GEOLOGY AND GEOGRAPHY
J Ap Behav Sci . . . . . JOURNAL OF APPLIED BEHAVIORAL SCIENCE
Jap Chr Q . . . . JAPAN CHRISTIAN QUARTERLY
JAP CIRC J . . . . JAPANESE CIRCULATION JOURNAL-ENGLISH EDITION
J Ap Ecol . . . . JOURNAL OF APPLIED ECOLOGY
JAP ECON ST . . . . . . JAPANESE ECONOMIC STUDIES
JAP HEART J . . . . . . JAPANESE HEART JOURNAL
JAP J A PHY . . . . . . JAPANESE JOURNAL OF APPLIED PHYSICS
JAP J BOTAN . . . . . . JAPANESE JOURNAL OF BOTANY
JAP J CHILD . . . . . . JAPANESE JOURNAL OF CHILD PSYCHIATRY
JAP J EDU P . . . . . . JAPANESE JOURNAL OF EDUCATIONAL PSYCHOLOGY
JAP J EXP M . . . . . . JAPANESE JOURNAL OF EXPERIMENTAL MEDICINE
JAP J GENET . . . . . . JAPANESE JOURNAL OF GENETICS
JAP J HUM G . . . . . . JAPANESE JOURNAL OF HUMAN GENETICS
JAP J MED S . . . . . . JAPANESE JOURNAL OF MEDICAL SCIENCE AND BIOLOGY
JAP J MICRO . . . . . . JAPANESE JOURNAL OF MICROBIOLOGY
JAP J PHARM . . . . . JAPANESE JOURNAL OF PHARMACOLOGY
JAP J PHYSL . . . . . . JAPANESE JOURNAL OF PHYSIOLOGY
JAP J PSYCH . . . . . . JAPANESE JOURNAL OF PSYCHOLOGY
JAP J VET R . . . . JAPANESE JOURNAL OF VETERINARY RESEARCH
JAP J VET S . . . . JAPANESE JOURNAL OF VETERINARY SCIENCE
JAP J ZOOL . . . . JAPANESE JOURNAL OF ZOOLOGY
J Ap Meterol . . . . . . JOURNAL OF APPLIED METEOROLOGY
Jap Nat Ry Ry Tech Res . . JAPANESE NATIONAL RAILWAYS. RAILWAY TECHNICAL RESEARCH
J Ap Nutrition . . . . . JOURNAL OF APPLIED NUTRITION
J App Bact . . . . JOURNAL OF APPLIED BACTERIOLOGY
J App Behav Anal . . JOURNAL OF APPLIED BEHAVIOR ANALYSIS
J App Behav Sci . . . . JOURNAL OF APPLIED BEHAVIORAL SCIENCE
J App Ecol . . . . JOURNAL OF APPLIED ECOLOGY
J APPL BACT . . . . . . JOURNAL OF APPLIED BACTERIOLOGY
J APPL BE A . . . . . . JOURNAL OF APPLIED BEHAVIOR ANALYSIS
J APPL BEH . . . . JOURNAL OF APPLIED BEHAVIORAL SCIENCE
J APPL CH B . . . . . . JOURNAL OF APPLIED CHEMISTRY AND BIOTECHNOLOGY
J Appl Chem . . . . . . JOURNAL OF APPLIED CHEMISTRY
J APPL CHEM . . . . . JOURNAL OF APPLIED CHEMISTRY OF THE USSR
J Appl Chem Biotechnol . . JOURNAL OF APPLIED CHEMISTRY AND BIOTECHNOLOGY
J Appl Chem (London) . . JOURNAL OF APPLIED CHEMISTRY (LONDON)
J Appl Chem USSR . . JOURNAL OF APPLIED CHEMISTRY OF THE USSR
J APPL CRYS . . . . . . JOURNAL OF APPLIED CRYSTALLOGRAPHY
J APPL ECOL . . . . . . JOURNAL OF APPLIED ECOLOGY
J APPL ELEC . . . . . . JOURNAL OF APPLIED ELECTROCHEMISTRY
J Applied Ednl Studies . . JOURNAL OF APPLIED EDUCATIONAL STUDIES

J APPL MECH. . . . . JOURNAL OF APPLIED MECHANICS. TRANSACTIONS. ASME
J Appl Mech Trans ASME . . JOURNAL OF APPLIED MECHANICS. TRANSACTIONS. ASME
J Appl Met . . . . . . JOURNAL OF APPLIED METEOROLOGY
J Appl Phys . . . . . . JOURNAL OF APPLIED PHSYICS
J APPL POLY . . . . . JOURNAL OF APPLIED POLYMER SCIENCE
J APPL PROBAB . . . . JOURNAL OF APPLIED PROBABILITY
J APPL PSYC . . . . . JOURNAL OF APPLIED PSYCHOLOGY
J APPL SO P . . . . . IOURNAL OF APPLIED SOCIAL PSYCHOLOGY
J App Mech . . . . . . JOURNAL OF APPLIED MECHANICS
J App Meteor . . . . . JOURNAL OF APPLIED METEOROLOGY
J App Nutr . . . . . . JOURNAL OF APPLIED NUTRITION
J App Physiol . . . . . JOURNAL OF APPLIED PHYSIOLOGY
J App Psychol . . . . . JOURNAL OF APPLIED PSYCHOLOGY
J APPROX TH . . . . . JOURNAL OF APPROXIMATION THEORY
J Ap Psychol . . . . . . JOURNAL OF APPLIED PSYCHOLOGY
JAP PSY RES . . . . . . JAPANESE PSYCHOLOGICAL RESEARCH
Jap Q . . . . JAPAN QUARTERLY
JAP QUART . . . . . . JAPAN QUARTERLY
JAPs . . . . JOURNAL OF APPLIED PSYCHOLOGY
Jap Shipbldg Mar Eng . . JAPAN SHIPBUILDING AND MARINE ENGINEERING
J Ap Sociol . . . . JOURNAL OF APPLIED SOCIOLOGY
Jap Soc Promot Sci Sub-Comm Phys Chem Steelmaking Spec Rep . . JAPAN SOCIETY FOR THE PROMOTION OF SCIENCE. SUB-COMMITTEE FOR PHYSICAL CHEMISTRY OF STEELMAKING. SPECIAL REPORT
JAP TELECOM . . . . . JAPAN TELECOMMUNICATIONS REVIEW
Jap Weld Soc Trans . . JAPAN WELDING SOCIETY. TRANSACTIONS
JArabL . . . . JOURNAL OF ARABIC LITERATURE
JARCE . . . . JOURNAL OF THE AMERICAN RESEARCH CENTER IN EGYPT
J ARCH SCI . . . . . . JOURNAL OF ARCHAEOLOGICAL SCIENCE
JARGV . . . . JAHRBUCH DER ARBEITSGEMEINSCHAFT DER RHEINISCHEN GESCHICHTSVEREINE
JArizH . . . . JOURNAL OF ARIZONA HISTORY
J ARN ARBOR . . . . . JOURNAL OF THE ARNOLD ARBORETUM
JARS . . . . JOURNAL OF THE ASSAM RESEARCH SOCIETY
JAS . . . . JAHRBUCH FUER AMERIKASTUDIEN
JAS . . . . JOURNAL OF AMERICAN STUDIES
JAS . . . . JOURNAL OF ASIAN STUDIES
JAS . . . . JOURNAL OF AUSTRONESIAN STUDIES
JAS . . . . JOURNAL OF THE ACOUSTICAL SOCIETY
JAS . . . . JOURNAL OF THE ASIATIC SOCIETY OF GREAT BRITAIN AND IRELAND
JASA . . . . JOURNAL OF THE AMERICAN STATISTICAL ASSOCIATION
JASAT . . . . JOURNAL OF THE AMERICAN STUDIES ASSOCIATION OF TEXAS
JAS B . . . . JOURNAL OF THE ASIATIC SOCIETY OF BOMBAY
J ASIAN AFR . . . . . . JOURNAL OF ASIAN AND AFRICAN STUDIES
J Asian & Afric Stud . . JOURNAL OF ASIAN AND AFRICAN STUDIES
J ASIAN HIS . . . . JOURNAL OF ASIAN HISTORY
J ASIAN ST . . . . JOURNAL OF ASIAN STUDIES
J Asiat . . . . JOURNAL ASIATIQUE
JASIS . . . . JOURNAL OF THE AMERICAN SOCIETY FOR INFORMATION SCIENCE
JASL . . . . JOURNAL OF THE ASIATIC SOCIETY. LETTERS
JASP . . . . JOURNAL OF ABNORMAL AND SOCIAL PSYCHOLOGY
J Ass Advan Med Instrum . . JOURNAL OF THE ASSOCIATION FOR THE ADVANCEMENT OF MEDICAL INSTRUMENTATION

J Ass Comput Mach . . JOURNAL OF THE ASSOCIATION FOR COMPUTING MACHINERY
J Assoc Adv Med Instrum . . JOURNAL OF THE ASSOCIATION FOR THE ADVANCEMENT OF MEDICAL INSTRUMENTATION
J Assoc Comput Mach . . JOURNAL OF THE ASSOCIATION FOR COMPUTING MACHINERY
J AS STUD P . . . . . . JOURNAL OF THE ASSOCIATION FOR THE STUDY OF PERCEPTION
JASt . . . . JOURNAL OF ASIAN STUDIES
J ASTRONAUT . . . . . JOURNAL OF THE ASTRONAUTICAL SCIENCES
J Astronaut Sci . . . . JOURNAL OF THE ASTRONAUTICAL SCIENCES
JAStud . . . . JOURNAL OF AMERICAN STUDIES
JAT . . . . JAARBOEKJE VAN J.A. ALBERDINGK-THYM
JATI . . . . JOURNAL OF THE ASSOCIATION OF TEACHERS OF ITALIAN
JATJ . . . . JOURNAL-NEWSLETTER OF THE ASSOCIATION OF TEACHERS OF JAPANESE
J Atmos Sci . . . . JOURNAL OF THE ATMOSPHERIC SCIENCES
J ATM TER P . . . . . . JOURNAL OF ATMOSPHERIC AND TERRESTRIAL PHYSICS
J AUD ENG S . . . . . . JOURNAL OF THE AUDIO ENGINEERING SOCIETY
J Audio Eng Soc . . . . JOURNAL OF THE AUDIO ENGINEERING SOCIETY
J AUD RES . . . . JOURNAL OF AUDITORY RESEARCH
JAUK . . . . JAHRBUCH DER ALBERTUS UNIVERSITAET ZU KOENIGSBERG
JAUMLA . . . . JOURNAL OF THE AUSTRALASIAN UNIVERSITIES MODERN LANGUAGE ASSOCIATION
J AUS I AGR . . . . . . JOURNAL OF THE AUSTRALIAN INSTITUTE OF AGRICULTURAL SCIENCE
J AUS I MET . . . . . . JOURNAL OF THE AUSTRALIAN INSTITUTE OF METALS
J Aust Inst Met . . . . JOURNAL OF THE AUSTRALIAN INSTITUTE OF METALS
J AUTISM CH . . . . . . JOURNAL OF AUTISM AND CHILDHOOD SCHIZOPHRENIA
J Automot Eng . . . . . JOURNAL OF AUTOMOTIVE ENGINEERING
JAW . . . . JAHRESBERICHT UEBER DIE FORTSCHRITTE DER KLASSISCHEN ALTERTUMSWISSENSCHAFT
JazA . . . . JAZYKOVEDNY AKTUALITY. ZPRAVODAJ JAZYKOVEDNEHO SDRUZENI PRI CESKOSLOVENSKE AKADEMII VED
JazS . . . . JAZYKOVEDNY STUDIE
JazSB . . . . JAZYKOVEDNY SBORNIK
JAZU . . . . JUGOSLAVENS KE AKADEMIJE ZNANOSTI I UMJETNOSTI
Jazz Ieri . . . . JAZZ DI IERI E DI OGGI
Jazz J . . . . JAZZ JOURNAL
Jazz Jl . . . . JAZZ JOURNAL
JAZZ MAG . . . . JAZZ MAGAZINE
Jazz Mo . . . . JAZZ MONTHLY
Jazz R . . . . JAZZ REVIEW
JAZZ REPT . . . . JAZZ REPORT
JAZZ RYTM . . . . . . JAZZ RYTM I PIOSENKA
JB . . . . JOURNAL OF BROADCASTING
JB . . . . JOURNAL OF BUSINESS
JBAA . . . . JOURNAL OF THE BRITISH ARCHAEOLOGICAL ASSOCIATION
JbAC . . . . JAHRBUCH FUER ANTIKE UND CHRISTENTUM
JbAChr . . . . JAHRBUCH FUER ANTIKE UND CHRISTENTUM
J Bact . . . . JOURNAL OF BACTERIOLOGY
J BADC . . . . JOURNAL OF THE BAR ASSOCIATION OF THE DISTRICT OF COLUMBIA
J BA Kan . . . . JOURNAL OF THE BAR ASSOCIATION OF THE STATE OF KANSAS
JBaIS . . . . JOURNAL OF BALTIC STUDIES
J BAND RES . . . . . : . JOURNAL OF BAND RESEARCH
Jb AS . . . . JAHRBUCH FUER AMERIKASTUDIEN
J Basic Eng . . . . JOURNAL OF BASIC ENGINEERING
J Basic Eng Trans ASME . . JOURNAL OF BASIC ENGINEERING. TRANSACTIONS OF THE ASME

JBAW . . . . JAHRBUCH DER BAYERISCHEN AKADEMIE DER WISSENSCHAFTEN
JbAWG . . . . JAHRBUCH DER AKADEMIE DER WISSENSCHAFTEN IN GOETTINGEN
JbAWL . . . . JAHRBUCH DER AKADEMIE DER WISSENSCHAFTEN UND DER LITERATUR IN MAINZ
JbBAW . . . . JAHRBUCH DER BAYERISCHEN AKADEMIE DER WISSENSCHAFTEN
J Bd Ag . . . . JOURNAL OF THE BOARD OF AGRICULTURE (GREAT BRITAIN)
JbDAW . . . . JAHRBUCH DER DEUTSCHEN AKADEMIE DER WISSENSCHAFTEN ZU BERLIN
JbDG . . . . JAHRBUCH DER DANTE GESELLSCHAFT
JBE . . . . JOURNAL OF BUSINESS EDUCATION
J BEHAV EXP . . . . . . JOURNAL OF BEHAVIOR THERAPY AND EXPERIMENTAL PSYCHIATRY
J BELG RAD . . . . JOURNAL BELGE DE RADIOLOGIE
J Beverly Hills Ba . . JOURNAL OF THE BEVERLY HILLS BAR ASSOCIATION
JbFL . . . . JAHRBUCH FUER FRANKISCHE LANDESFORSCHUNG
Jb f niederdeut Spr . . JAHRBUCH FUER NIEDERDEUTSCHE SPRACHFORSCHUNG
Jb f niederdt Spr . . . JAHRBUCH FUER NIEDERDEUTSCHE SPRACHFORSCHUNG
JBG . . . . JAHRBUCH DER BARLACH-GESELLSCHAFT
JBG . . . . JINBUNGAKU (STUDIES IN HUMANITIES)
JBGH . . . . JINBUN GAKUHO (JOURNAL OF SOCIAL SCIENCE AND HUMANITIES)
JBHVMF . . . . JAHRESBERICHT DES HISTORISCHEN. VEREINS FUER MITTELFRANKEN
J Bib Lit . . . . JOURNAL OF BIBLICAL LITERATURE
J BIOCHEM . . . . JOURNAL OF BIOCHEMISTRY
J BIOENERG . . . . JOURNAL OF BIOENERGETICS
J BIOL BUCC . . . . . . JOURNAL DE BIOLOGIE BUCCALE
J Biol Chem . . . . JOURNAL OF BIOLOGICAL CHEMISTRY
J Biological Ed . . . . . JOURNAL OF BIOLOGICAL EDUCATION
J BIOL PHOT . . . . . . JOURNAL OF THE BIOLOGICAL PHOTOGRAPHIC ASSOCIATION
J BIOL STAN . . . . . . JOURNAL OF BIOLOGICAL STANDARDIZATION
J Biomech . . . . JOURNAL OF BIOMECHANICS
J BIOMECHAN . . . . . JOURNAL OF BIOMECHANICS
J Biomed Mater Res . . JOURNAL OF BIOMEDICAL MATERIALS RESEARCH
J Biomed Mater Res Biomed Mater Symp . . JOURNAL OF BIOMEDICAL MATERIALS RESEARCH. BIOMEDICAL
    MATERIALS SYMPOSIUM
J BIOMED MR . . . . . JOURNAL OF BIOMEDICAL MATERIALS RESEARCH
J BIOSOC SC . . . . . . JOURNAL OF BIOSOCIAL SCIENCE
JBIRS . . . . JOURNAL OF THE BIHAR RESEARCH SOCIETY
JbKAF . . . . JAHRBUCH FUER KLEINASIATISCHE FORSCHUNG
JBKG . . . . JAHRBUCH FUER BRANDENBURGISCHE KIRCHENGESCHICHTE
JBKK . . . . JINBUN KENKYU (STUDIES IN HUMANITIES)
JbKNA . . . . JAARBOEK DER KONINKLIJKE NEDERLANDSCHE AKADEMIE VAN WETENSCHAPPEN
JbKVA . . . . JAARBOEK DER KONINKLIJKE VLAAMSE ACADEMIE VOOR TAAL-EN LETTERKUNDE
JbKVAW . . . . JAARBOEK VAN DE KONINKLIJKE VLAAMSE ACADEMIE VOOR WETENSCHAPPEN
JBL . . . . JOURNAL OF BIBLICAL LITERATURE
J Black Poetry . . . . . JOURNAL OF BLACK POETRY
J BLACK ST . . . . JOURNAL OF BLACK STUDIES
JBLG . . . . JAHRESBERICHTE DER BERLINER LITERATUR GESELLSCHAFT
JBM . . . . JAHRBUCH DER BERLINER MUSEEN
JBM . . . . JAHRBUCH DES BERNISCHEN HISTORISCHEN MUSEUMS
JBM . . . . JAHRBUCH FUER DAS BISTUM (MAINZ)
JbMNL . . . . JAARBOEK VAN DE MAATSCHAPPIJ DER NEDERLANDSE LETTERKUNDE TE LEIDEN
JbMu . . . . JAHRBUCH: MARBURGER UNIVERSITAETSBUND
JbNo . . . . JAHRBUCH FUER LANDESKUNDE VON NIEDEROESTERREICH
J BONE-AM V . . . . . JOURNAL OF BONE AND JOINT SURGERY (AMERICAN VOLUME)

J BONE-BR V . . . . . . JOURNAL OF BONE AND JOINT SURGERY (BRITISH VOLUME)
J BONE JOINT SURG . . JOURNAL OF BONE AND JOINT SURGERY
J Bone Joint Surg (Am) . . JOURNAL OF BONE AND JOINT SURGERY (AMERICAN VOLUME)
J Bone Joint Surg (Br) . . JOURNAL OF BONE AND JOINT SURGERY (BRITISH VOLUME)
JBORS . . . . JOURNAL OF THE BIHAR AND ORISSA RESEARCH SOCIETY
J Boston Soc Civ Eng . . JOURNAL OF THE BOSTON SOCIETY OF CIVIL ENGINEERS
JBR . . . . JOURNAL OF BIBLE AND RELIGION
JBRAS . . . . JOURNAL OF THE BOMBAY BRANCH OF THE ROYAL ASIATIC SOCIETY
J Br Boot Shoe Instn . . JOURNAL OF THE BRITISH BOOT AND SHOE INSTITUTION
J BR GRASSL . . . . . . JOURNAL OF THE BRITISH GRASSLAND SOCIETY
J Brit Ceram Soc . . . JOURNAL OF THE BRITISH CERAMIC SOCIETY
J Brit Interplanet Soc . . JOURNAL OF THE BRITISH INTERPLANETARY SOCIETY
J Brit Nucl Energy Soc . . JOURNAL OF THE BRITISH NUCLEAR ENERGY SOCIETY
J Brit Ship Res Ass . . JOURNAL OF THE BRITISH SHIP RESEARCH ASSOCIATION
J Brit Soc Phenomenol . . THE JOURNAL OF THE BRITISH SOCIETY FOR PHENOMENOLOGY
J Brit Stud . . . . JOURNAL OF BRITISH STUDIES
J BR NUCL E . . . . . . JOURNAL OF THE BRITISH NUCLEAR ENERGY SOCIETY
J BROADCAST . . . . . JOURNAL OF BROADCASTING
JBRS . . . . JOURNAL OF THE BURMA RESEARCH SOCIETY
J BR SOC PH . . . . . . JOURNAL OF THE BRITISH SOCIETY OF PHENOMENOLOGY
J BRYOL . . . . JOURNAL OF BRYOLOGY
JBS . . . . JOURNAL OF BRITISH STUDIES
JBS . . . . JOURNAL OF BYELORUSSIAN STUDIES
JbSAW . . . . JAHRBUCH. SAECHSISCHE AKADEMIE DER WISSENSCHAFTEN ZU LEIPZIG
JbShG . . . . JAHRBUCH DER SHAKESPEARE GESELLSCHAFT
J Bsns . . . . JOURNAL OF BUSINESS
J Bsns Ed . . . . JOURNAL OF BUSINESS EDUCATION
J Bsns Educ . . . . JOURNAL OF BUSINESS EDUCATION
Jb u Ersch ger Lit . . . JAHRESBERICHTE UEBER DIE ERSCHEINUNGEN AUF DEM GEBIETE DER GERMANISCHEN
LITERATURGESCHICHTE
J Bus . . . . JOURNAL OF BUSINESS
J Bus Ed . . . . JOURNAL OF BUSINESS EDUCATION
J Bus L . . . . JOURNAL OF BUSINESS LAW
J BUS RES . . . . JOURNAL OF BUSINESS RESEARCH
JbVH . . . . JAHRBUCH FUER VOLKSKUNDE DER HEIMATVERTRIEBENEN
JByelS . . . . JOURNAL OF BYELORUSSIAN STUDIES
JC . . . . JAZYKOVEDNY CASOPIS
JC . . . . JOURNAL OF COMMUNICATION
J Can Ba . . . . JOURNAL OF THE CANADIAN BAR ASSOCIATION
J Can Petrol Technol . . JOURNAL OF CANADIAN PETROLEUM TECHNOLOGY
J CAN PET T . . . . . . JOURNAL OF CANADIAN PETROLEUM TECHNOLOGY
J Can Stud . . . . JOURNAL OF CANADIAN STUDIES
J CARB-NUCL . . . . . JOURNAL OF CARBOHYDRATES-NUCLEOSIDES-NUCLEOTIDES
J CARD SURG . . . . . JOURNAL OF CARDIOVASCULAR SURGERY
J Catal . . . . JOURNAL OF CATALYSIS
J Cat & Class . . . . . . JOURNAL OF CATALOGING AND CLASSIFICATION
JCEA . . . . JOURNAL OF CENTRAL EUROPEAN AFFAIRS
J Cell Biol . . . . JOURNAL OF CELL BIOLOGY
J CELL PHYS . . . . . . JOURNAL OF CELLULAR PHYSIOLOGY
J Cell Plast . . . . JOURNAL OF CELLULAR PLASTICS
J Cell Sci . . . . JOURNAL OF CELL SCIENCE

JCeltS . . . . JOURNAL OF CELTIC STUDIES
J Cent Eur Affairs . . JOURNAL OF CENTRAL EUROPEAN AFFAIRS
J Cer Soc Jap . . . . . . JOURNAL OF THE CERAMIC SOCIETY OF JAPAN
JCF . . . . JOURNAL OF CANADIAN FICTION
J Chart Inst Transp . . CHARTERED INSTITUTE OF TRANSPORT JOURNAL
JCHAS . . . . JOURNAL OF THE CORK HISTORICAL AND ARCHAEOLOGICAL SOCIETY
J Chem Doc . . . . JOURNAL OF CHEMICAL DOCUMENTATION
J Chem Educ . . . . . . JOURNAL OF CHEMICAL EDUCATION
J CHEM EN D . . . . . . JOURNAL OF CHEMICAL AND ENGINEERING DATA
J Chem Eng Data . . . JOURNAL OF CHEMICAL AND ENGINEERING DATA
J Chem Eng Jap . . . . JOURNAL OF CHEMICAL ENGINEERING OF JAPAN
J CHEM INF . . . . JOURNAL OF CHEMICAL INFORMATION AND COMPUTER SCIENCES
J CHEM PHYS . . . . . JOURNAL OF CHEMICAL PHYSICS
J CHEM S CH . . . . . . JOURNAL OF THE CHEMICAL SOCIETY. CHEMICAL COMMUNICATIONS
J CHEM S DA . . . . . . JOURNAL OF THE CHEMICAL SOCIETY. DALTON TRANSACTIONS
J CHEM S F1 . . . . . . JOURNAL OF THE CHEMICAL SOCIETY. FARADAY TRANSACTIONS 1
J CHEM S F2 . . . . . . JOURNAL OF THE CHEMICAL SOCIETY. FARADAY TRANSACTIONS 2
J CHEM SOC . . . . . . JOURNAL OF THE CHEMICAL SOCIETY
J Chem Soc Japan . . JOURNAL OF THE CHEMICAL SOCIETY OF JAPAN. INDUSTRIAL CHEMISTRY SECTION
J CHEM S P1 . . . . . . JOURNAL OF THE CHEMICAL SOCIETY. PERKIN TRANSACTIONS 1
J CHEM S P2 . . . . . . JOURNAL OF THE CHEMICAL SOCIETY. PERKIN TRANSACTIONS 2
J CHEM THER . . . . . JOURNAL OF CHEMICAL THERMODYNAMICS
J Child Language . . . JOURNAL OF CHILD LANGUAGE
J CHILD PSY . . . . . . JOURNAL OF CHILD PSYCHOLOGY AND PSYCHIATRY AND ALLIED DISCIPLINES
J Child Psych & Psychiatry . . JOURNAL OF CHILD PSYCHOLOGY AND PSYCHIATRY
J Child Psychol . . . . JOURNAL OF CHILD PSYCHOLOGY AND PSYCHIATRY AND ALLIED DISCIPLINES
J Child Psychotherapy . . JOURNAL OF CHILD PSYCHOTHERAPY
J CHIM PHYS . . . . . . JOURNAL DE CHIMIE PHYSIQUE ET DE PHYSICO-CHIMIE BIOLOGIQUE
J CHIN CHEM . . . . . . JOURNAL OF THE CHINESE CHEMICAL SOCIETY
J Chin Phil . . . . JOURNAL OF CHINESE PHILOSOPHY
J CHIR . . . . JOURNAL DE CHIRURGIE
J CHROMAT . . . . . . JOURNAL OF CHROMATOGRAPHY
J Chromatogr Sci . . . JOURNAL OF CHROMATOGRAPHIC SCIENCE
J CHROM SCI . . . . . . JOURNAL OF CHROMATOGRAPHIC SCIENCE
J CHRON DIS . . . . . . JOURNAL OF CHRONIC DISEASES
J Chr Philos . . . . JOURNAL OF CHRISTIAN PHILOSOPHY
J Ch St . . . . JOURNAL OF CHURCH AND STATE
J Church & State . . . JOURNAL OF CHURCH AND STATE
J CHURCH MUS . . . . JOURNAL OF CHURCH MUSIC
J Civ Eng (Taipei) . . . JOURNAL OF CIVIL ENGINEERING (TAIPEI)
JCL . . . . JOURNAL OF COMMONWEALTH LITERATURE
JCLA . . . . JOURNAL OF THE CANADIAN LANGUAGE ASSOCIATION
JCLA . . . . JOURNAL OF THE CANADIAN LINGUISTIC ASSOCIATION (EDMONTON)
J CLIN CHIL . . . . JOURNAL OF CLINICAL CHILD PSYCHOLOGY
J CLIN END . . . . JOURNAL OF CLINICAL ENDOCRINOLOGY AND METABOLISM
J CLIN INV . . . . JOURNAL OF CLINICAL INVESTIGATION
J CLIN MICR . . . . . . JOURNAL OF CLINICAL MICROBIOLOGY
J CLIN PATH . . . . . . JOURNAL OF CLINICAL PATHOLOGY
J CLIN PHAR . . . . . . JOURNAL OF CLINICAL PHARMACOLOGY
J CLIN PSYC . . . . . . JOURNAL OF CLINICAL PSYCHOLOGY
JCLTA . . . . JOURNAL OF THE CHINESE LANGUAGE TEACHERS ASSOCIATION

JCMVASA . . . . JOURNAL OF THE CENTRAL MISSISSIPPI VALLEY AMERICAN STUDIES ASSOCIATION
J Coated Fibrous Mater . . JOURNAL OF COATED FIBROUS MATERIALS
J Coll Ag Tokyo . . . . JOURNAL OF THE COLLEGE OF AGRICULTURE. TOKYO IMPERIAL UNIVERSITY
J Coll & Univ Personnel Assn . . JOURNAL OF THE COLLEGE AND UNIVERSITY PERSONNEL ASSOCIATION
J COLL I SC . . . . JOURNAL OF COLLOID AND INTERFACE SCIENCE
J Colloid Sci . . . . . . JOURNAL OF COLLOID SCIENCE
J Coll Placement . . . JOURNAL OF COLLEGE PLACEMENT
J COLL STUD . . . . . . JOURNAL OF COLLEGE STUDENT PERSONNEL
J Coll Stud Personnel . . JOURNAL OF COLLEGE STUDENT PERSONNEL
J COLL UNIV . . . . . . JOURNAL OF THE COLLEGE AND UNIVERSITY PERSONNEL ASSOCIATION
J Color Appearance . . JOURNAL OF COLOR AND APPEARANCE
J Col Placement . . . . JOURNAL OF COLLEGE PLACEMENT
J Col Stud Personnel . . JOURNAL OF COLLEGE STUDENT PERSONNEL
J COMB TH A . . . . . . JOURNAL OF COMBINATORIAL THEORY. SERIES A
J COMB TH B . . . . . . JOURNAL OF COMBINATORIAL THEORY. SERIES B
JComLit . . . . JOURNAL OF COMMONWEALTH LITERATURE
J Comm . . . . JOURNAL OF COMMUNICATION
J Comm Bank Lending . . JOURNAL OF COMMERCIAL BANK LENDING
J COMM DIS . . . . . . JOURNAL OF COMMUNICATION DISORDERS
J COM MKT S . . . . . . JOURNAL OF COMMON MARKET STUDIES
J Commonwealth Lit . . JOURNAL OF COMMONWEALTH LITERATURE
J Comp & Physiol Psychol . . JOURNAL OF COMPARATIVE AND PHYSIOLOGICAL PSYCHOLOGY
J COM PHYSL . . . . . JOURNAL OF COMPARATIVE AND PHYSIOLOGICAL PSYCHOLOGY
J COMP NEUR . . . . . JOURNAL OF COMPARATIVE NEUROLOGY
J COMPOS MA . . . . . JOURNAL OF COMPOSITE MATERIALS
J Compos Mater . . . JOURNAL OF COMPOSITE MATERIALS
J COMP PATH . . . . . JOURNAL OF COMPARATIVE PATHOLOGY
J COMP PHYS . . . . . JOURNAL OF COMPARATIVE PHYSIOLOGY
J Comp Psychol . . . . JOURNAL OF COMPARATIVE PSYCHOLOGY
J COMPUT PH . . . . . JOURNAL OF COMPUTATIONAL PHYSICS
J COMPUT SY . . . . . JOURNAL OF COMPUTER AND SYSTEM SCIENCES
J Comput Syst Sci . . JOURNAL OF COMPUTER AND SYSTEM SCIENCES
J CONFL RES . . . . . . JOURNAL OF CONFLICT RESOLUTION
J CONS ASCE . . . . . . JOURNAL OF THE CONSTRUCTION DIVISION-ASCE
J CONS CLIN . . . . . . JOURNAL OF CONSULTING AND CLINICAL PSYCHOLOGY
J CONSEIL . . . . JOURNAL DU CONSEIL
J Consult Clin Psychol . . JOURNAL OF CONSULTING AND CLINICAL PSYCHOLOGY
J Consult Psychol . . JOURNAL OF CONSULTING PSYCHOLOGY
J CONSUM AF . . . . . JOURNAL OF CONSUMER AFFAIRS
J CONT BUS . . . . . . JOURNAL OF CONTEMPORARY BUSINESS
J Contemp Asia . . . . JOURNAL OF CONTEMPORARY ASIA
J Contemp Hist . . . . JOURNAL OF CONTEMPORARY HISTORY
J CONT HIST . . . . . . JOURNAL OF CONTEMPORARY HISTORY
J CONT PSYT . . . . . . JOURNAL OF CONTEMPORARY PSYCHOTHERAPY
J COORD CH . . . . . . JOURNAL OF COORDINATION CHEMISTRY
J CORP TAX . . . . . . JOURNAL OF CORPORATE TAXATION
J COUN PSYC . . . . . JOURNAL OF COUNSELING PSYCHOLOGY
JCP . . . . JOURNAL OF CLINICAL PSYCHOLOGY
JCP . . . . JOURNAL OF COUNSELING PSYCHOLOGY
JCPs . . . . JOURNAL OF CLINICAL PSYCHOLOGY
JCQ . . . . JAPAN CHRISTIAN QUARTERLY

JCRAS . . . . JOURNAL OF THE CEYLON BRANCH OF THE ROYAL ASIATIC SOCIETY
J CREAT BEH . . . . . . JOURNAL OF CREATIVE BEHAVIOR
J CRIM JUS . . . . JOURNAL OF CRIMINAL JUSTICE
J Crim Law . . . . JOURNAL OF CRIMINAL LAW AND CRIMINOLOGY
J Crim L (Eng) . . . . . JOURNAL OF CRIMINAL LAW (ENGLISH)
J Crit Anal . . . . JOURNAL OF CRITICAL ANALYSIS
J CROSS-CUL . . . . . . JOURNAL OF CROSS CULTURAL PSYCHOLOGY
J CRYST GR . . . . JOURNAL OF CRYSTAL GROWTH
J CRYST MOL . . . . . . JOURNAL OF CRYSTAL AND MOLECULAR STRUCTURE
JCS . . . . JOURNAL OF CELTIC STUDIES
JCS . . . . JOURNAL OF CLASSICAL STUDIES (KYOTO UNIVERSITY)
JCS . . . . JOURNAL OF CROATIAN STUDIES
JCS . . . . JOURNAL OF CUNEIFORM STUDIES
JCSA . . . . JOURNAL OF THE CATCH SOCIETY OF AMERICA
JcSH . . . . JIHOCESKY SBORNIK HISTORICKY
J Cun S . . . . JOURNAL OF CUNEIFORM STUDIES
J CURRIC ST . . . . . . JOURNAL OF CURRICULUM STUDIES
J CUT PATH . . . . . . JOURNAL OF CUTANEOUS PATHOLOGY
J Cybern . . . . JOURNAL OF CYBERNETICS
J CYCL NUCL . . . . . JOURNAL OF CYCLIC NUCLEOTIDE RESEARCH
JD . . . . JOURNAL OF DOCUMENTATION
JDAI . . . . JAHRBUCH DES DEUTSCHEN ARCHAEOLOGISCHEN INSTITUTS
J DAIRY RES . . . . . JOURNAL OF DAIRY RESEARCH
J DAIRY SCI . . . . . . JOURNAL OF DAIRY SCIENCE
JDASD . . . . JAHRBUCH DER DEUTSCHEN AKADEMIE FUER SPRACHE UND DICHTUNG IN DARMSTADT
J Data Mgt . . . . JOURNAL OF DATA MANAGEMENT
J Debats . . . . JOURNAL DES DEBATS
J DENT CHIL . . . . . JOURNAL OF DENTISTRY FOR CHILDREN
J DENT RES . . . . . . JOURNAL OF DENTAL RESEARCH
J Dept Ag Ireland . . IRISH FREE STATE DEPARTMENT OF AGRICULTURE JOURNAL
J Dept Ag Puerto Rico . . JOURNAL OF THE DEPARTMENT OF AGRICULTURE OF PUERTO RICO
J Dept Ag S Africa . . JOURNAL OF THE DEPARTMENT OF AGRICULTURE OF SOUTH AFRICA
J Dept Ag S Australia . . JOURNAL OF THE DEPARTMENT OF AGRICULTURE OF SOUTH AUSTRALIA
J Dept Ag Victoria . . JOURNAL OF THE DEPARTMENT OF AGRICULTURE OF VICTORIA
J DEV AREAS . . . . . JOURNAL OF DEVELOPING AREAS
J Develop Areas . . . JOURNAL OF DEVELOPING AREAS
J Develop Plan . . . . JOURNAL OF DEVELOPMENT PLANNING
J Develop Read . . . . JOURNAL OF DEVELOPMENTAL READING
J Develop Stud . . . . JOURNAL OF DEVELOPMENT STUDIES
J DEV STUD . . . . . . JOURNAL OF DEVELOPMENT STUDIES
JDG . . . . JAHRBUCH DER DROSTE-GESELLSCHAFT
J DIFF EQUA . . . . . JOURNAL OF DIFFERENTIAL EQUATIONS
JdL . . . . JORNAL DE LETRAS
JDM . . . . JAHRBUCH DER MUSIKWELT
J Doc . . . . JOURNAL OF DOCUMENTATION
JDPL . . . . JOURNAL DES DEBATS POLITIQUES ET LITTERAIRES
J DRUG ISS . . . . . . JOURNAL OF DRUG ISSUES
JDS . . . . JACOBEAN DRAMA STUDIES
JdS . . . . JOURNAL DES SAVANTS
JDS . . . . JOURNAL OF DEVELOPMENT STUDIES
JDSG . . . . JAHRBUCH DER DEUTSCHEN SCHILLER-GESELLSCHAFT

J Dyn Syst Meas Control . . JOURNAL OF DYNAMIC SYSTEMS, MEASUREMENT AND CONTROL
JE . . . . JUNE
JEA . . . . JOURNAL OF EGYPTIAN ARCHAEOLOGY
JEAfrSC . . . . JOURNAL OF THE EAST AFRICAN SWAHILI COMMITTEE
Jean-Paul-Gesellsch Jahrb . . JEAN-PAUL-GESELLSCHAFT. JAHRBUCH
JEAS . . . . JOURNAL OF EAST ASIATIC STUDIES
JEB . . . . JOURNAL OF ECONOMIC BEHAVIOR
JEBH . . . . JOURNAL OF ECONOMIC AND BUSINESS HISTORY
J Eccl H . . . . JOURNAL OF ECCLESIASTICAL HISTORY
J Ecol . . . . JOURNAL OF ECOLOGY
J Econ . . . . JOURNAL DES ECONOMISTES
J ECON BUS . . . . JOURNAL OF ECONOMICS AND BUSINESS
J Econ Ed . . . . JOURNAL OF ECONOMIC EDUCATION
J ECON ENT . . . . JOURNAL OF ECONOMIC ENTOMOLOGY
J Econ H . . . . JOURNAL OF ECONOMIC HISTORY
J Econ Iss . . . . JOURNAL OF ECONOMIC ISSUES
JEconLit . . . . JOURNAL OF ECONOMIC LITERATURE
J Economistes . . . . . JOURNAL DE ECONOMISTES
J ECON THEO . . . . . JOURNAL OF ECONOMIC THEORY
J Ec St . . . . JOURNAL OF ECUMENICAL STUDIES
J Ecum Stud . . . . . . JOURNAL OF ECUMENICAL STUDIES
J Ed . . . . JOURNAL OF EDUCATION
J Ed Data Process . . JOURNAL OF EDUCATIONAL DATA PROCESSING
J Ed London . . . . . . JOURNAL OF EDUCATION (LONDON)
J Ed M . . . . JOURNAL OF EDUCATIONAL MEASUREMENT
J Ednl Admin and History . . JOURNAL OF EDUCATIONAL ADMINISTRATION AND HISTORY
J Ed Psychol . . . . . . JOURNAL OF EDUCATIONAL PSYCHOLOGY
J Ed Res . . . . JOURNAL OF EDUCATIONAL RESEARCH
J Ed Soc . . . . JOURNAL OF EDUCATIONAL SOCIOLOGY
J Educ . . . . JOURNAL OF EDUCATION
J EDUC ADM . . . . . . JOURNAL OF EDUCATIONAL ADMINISTRATION
J Educ Data Proc . . . JOURNAL OF EDUCATIONAL DATA PROCESSING
J EDUC LIBR . . . . . . JOURNAL OF EDUCATION FOR LIBRARIANSHIP
J Educ (Lond) . . . . . . JOURNAL OF EDUCATION (LONDON)
J Educ M . . . . JOURNAL OF EDUCATIONAL MEASUREMENT
J Educ Method . . . . . JOURNAL OF EDUCATIONAL METHOD
J EDUC PSYC . . . . . . JOURNAL OF EDUCATIONAL PSYCHOLOGY
J Educ Res . . . . JOURNAL OF EDUCATIONAL RESEARCH
J EDUC SOC . . . . . . JOURNAL OF EDUCATION FOR SOCIAL WORK
J Educ Sociol . . . . . . JOURNAL OF EDUCATIONAL SOCIOLOGY
J EDUC TH . . . . JOURNAL OF EDUCATIONAL THOUGHT
JEE . . . . JOURNAL OF EXPERIMENTAL EDUCATION
JEFDS . . . . JOURNAL OF THE ENGLISH FOLK DANCE AND SONG SOCIETY
JEFDSS . . . . JOURNAL OF THE ENGLISH FOLK DANCE AND SONG SOCIETY
JEFS . . . . JOURNAL OF THE ENGLISH FOLK DANCE AND SONG SOCIETY
JEGP . . . . JOURNAL OF ENGLISH AND GERMANIC PHILOLOGY
JEG PH . . . . JOURNAL OF ENGLISH AND GERMANIC PHILOLOGY
JEG Phil . . . . JOURNAL OF ENGLISH AND GERMANIC PHILOLOGY
J Egypt Archaeol . . . JOURNAL OF EGYPTIAN ARCHAEOLOGY
JEH . . . . JOURNAL OF ECCLESIASTICAL HISTORY

JEH . . . . JOURNAL OF ECONOMIC HISTORY
JEH/S . . . . JOURNAL OF ECONOMIC HISTORY (SUPPLEMENT) THE TASKS OF ECONOMIC HISTORY
JEI . . . . JEI/JOURNAL OF ECONOMIC ISSUES
JEL . . . . JOURNAL OF ECONOMIC LITERATURE
JEL . . . . JOURNAL OF ENGLISH LINGUISTICS
J ELAST . . . . JOURNAL OF ELASTICITY
J Elastoplast . . . . . . JOURNAL OF ELASTOPLASTICS
J ELCHEM SO . . . . . . JOURNAL OF THE ELECTROCHEMICAL SOCIETY
J Elec . . . . JOURNAL OF ELECTRICITY
J ELCARDIOL . . . . . . JOURNAL OF ELECTROCARDIOLOGY
J ELCHEM SO . . . . . . JOURNAL OF THE ELECTROCHEMICAL SOCIETY
J ELEC CHEM . . . . . . JOURNAL OF ELECTROANALYTICAL CHEMISTRY AND INTERFACIAL ELECTROCHEMISTRY
J ELEC MAT . . . . JOURNAL OF ELECTRONIC MATERIALS
J ELEC MICR . . . . . . JOURNAL OF ELECTRON MICROSCOPY
J ELEC SPEC . . . . JOURNAL OF ELECTRON SPECTROSCOPY AND RELATED PHENOMENA
J Electroanal Chem Interfacial Electrochem . . JOURNAL OF ELECTROANALYTICAL CHEMISTRY AND INTERFACIAL
        ELECTROCHEMISTRY
J Electrochem Soc . . JOURNAL OF THE ELECTROCHEMICAL SOCIETY
J Electrochem Soc Japan . . JOURNAL OF THE ELECTROCHEMICAL SOCIETY OF JAPAN
J Electron Mater . . . JOURNAL OF ELECTRONIC MATERIALS
J EMB EXP M . . . . . . JOURNAL OF EMBRYOLOGY AND EXPERIMENTAL MORPHOLOGY
JEMFQ . . . . JOHN EDWARDS MEMORIAL FOUNDATION. QUARTERLY
J EMPL COUN . . . . . JOURNAL OF EMPLOYMENT COUNSELING
Jena Rev . . . . JENA REVIEW
J ENDOCR . . . . JOURNAL OF ENDOCRINOLOGY
J Eng and Germ Philol . . JOURNAL OF ENGLISH AND GERMANIC PHILOLOGY
J Eng Ed . . . . JOURNAL OF ENGINEERING EDUCATION
J Eng Educ . . . . JOURNAL OF ENGINEERING EDUCATION
J Eng Ind . . . . JOURNAL OF ENGINEERING FOR INDUSTRY
J Eng Ind Tran ASME . . JOURNAL OF ENGINEERING FOR INDUSTRY. TRANSACTIONS ASME
J Eng L . . . . JOURNAL OF ENGLISH LINGUISTICS
J Engl & Germ Philol . . JOURNAL OF ENGLISH AND GERMANIC PHILOLOGY
J ENG MATER . . . . . JOURNAL OF ENGINEERING MATERIALS AND TECHNOLOGY
J Eng Math . . . . JOURNAL OF ENGINEERING MATHEMATICS
J ENG MECH . . . . . . JOURNAL OF THE ENGINEERING MECHANICS
J Eng Power . . . . . . JOURNAL OF ENGINEERING FOR POWER
J Eng Power Trans ASME . . JOURNAL OF ENGINEERING FOR POWER. TRANSACTIONS ASME
J Eng Psychol . . . . . JOURNAL OF ENGINEERING PSYCHOLOGY
J ENTOMOL A . . . . . JOURNAL OF ENTOMOLOGY. SERIES A. GENERAL ENTOMOLOGY
J ENTOMOL B . . . . . JOURNAL OF ENTOMOLOGY. SERIES B. TAXONOMY
J ENV EDUC . . . . . . JOURNAL OF ENVIRONMENTAL EDUCATION
J ENVIR ENG . . . . . . JOURNAL OF THE ENVIRONMENTAL ENGINEERING DIVISION. ASCE (AMERICAN SOCIETY OF
        CIVIL ENGINEERS)
J ENVIR MGM . . . . . JOURNAL OF ENVIRONMENTAL MANAGEMENT
J Environ Sci . . . . . . JOURNAL OF ENVIRONMENTAL SCIENCES
J Environ Syst . . . . . JOURNAL OF ENVIRONMENTAL SYSTEMS
J ENVIR Q . . . . JOURNAL OF ENVIRONMENTAL QUALITY
J ENVIR SCI . . . . JOURNAL OF ENVIRONMENTAL SCIENCES
JEOL . . . . JAARBERICHT VAN HET VOORAZIATISCH-EGYPTISCH GENOOTSCHAP EX ORIENTE LUX
JEP . . . . JOURNAL OF EDUCATIONAL PSYCHOLOGY
JEPs . . . . JOURNAL OF EDUCATIONAL PSYCHOLOGY

JER . . . . JOURNAL OF EDUCATIONAL RESEARCH
JERNKON ANN . . . . . JERNKONTORETS ANNALER
Jersey B . . . . JERSEY BULLETIN AND DAIRY WORLD
Jersey Bul . . . . JERSEY BULLETIN
Jersey J . . . . JERSEY JOURNAL
JES . . . . JOURNAL OF ECONOMIC STUDIES
JES . . . . JOURNAL OF ECUMENICAL STUDIES
JES . . . . JOURNAL OF EUROPEAN STUDIES
JESHO . . . . JOURNAL OF ECONOMIC AND SOCIAL HISTORY OF THE ORIENT
JEthS . . . . JOURNAL OF ETHOPIAN STUDIES
JETP Lett . . . . JETP LETTERS (TRANSLATION OF JETP PIS'MA V REDAKTSIYU)
JeuneA . . . . JEUNE AFRIQUE
J Eur Stud . . . . JOURNAL OF EUROPEAN STUDIES
J Evang Th S . . . . . . JOURNAL OF THE EVANGELICAL THEOLOGICAL SOCIETY
JEVWK . . . . JAHRBUCH DES EVANGELISCHEN VEREINS FUER WESTFAELISCHE KIRCHENGESCHICHTE
Jew Hist Soc Engl Trans . . JEWISH HISTORICAL SOCIETY OF ENGLAND. TRANSACTIONS
Jewish Ed . . . . JEWISH EDUCATION
Jewish Hist Soc of England Trans . . JEWISH HISTORICAL SOCIETY OF ENGLAND. TRANSACTIONS
Jewish Soc Stud . . . . JEWISH SOCIAL STUDIES
JEW J SOCIO . . . . . . JEWISH JOURNAL OF SOCIOLOGY
JewQ . . . . JEWISH QUARTERLY REVIEW
Jew Q R . . . . JEWISH QUARTERLY REVIEW
JEW SOC STU . . . . . . JEWISH SOCIAL STUDIES
J EX AN BEH . . . . . . JOURNAL OF THE EXPERIMENTAL ANALYSIS OF BEHAVIOR
J Excep Child . . . . . . JOURNAL OF EXCEPTIONAL CHILDREN
JExP . . . . JOURNAL OF EXPERIMENTAL PSYCHOLOGY
J EXP BIOL . . . . JOURNAL OF EXPERIMENTAL BIOLOGY
J EXP BOT . . . . JOURNAL OF EXPERIMENTAL BOTANY
J Exp Child Psy . . . . JOURNAL OF EXPERIMENTAL CHILD PSYCHOLOGY
J EXP C PSY . . . . . . JOURNAL OF EXPERIMENTAL CHILD PSYCHOLOGY
J Exp Ed . . . . JOURNAL OF EXPERIMENTAL EDUCATION
J Exper Biol . . . . . . JOURNAL OF EXPERIMENTAL BIOLOGY
J Exper Bot . . . . . . JOURNAL OF EXPERIMENTAL BOTANY
J Exper Educ . . . . . . JOURNAL OF EXPERIMENTAL EDUCATION
J Exper Marine Biol & Ecol . . JOURNAL OF EXPERIMENTAL MARINE BIOLOGY AND ECOLOGY
J Exper Zool . . . . . . JOURNAL OF EXPERIMENTAL ZOOLOGY
J EXP MAR B . . . . . . JOURNAL OF EXPERIMENTAL MARINE BIOLOGY AND ECOLOGY
J EXP MED . . . . JOURNAL OF EXPERIMENTAL MEDICINE
J EXP PSY A . . . . . . JOURNAL OF EXPERIMENTAL PSYCHOLOGY. ANIMAL BEHAVIOR PROCESSES
J EXP PSYCH . . . . . . JOURNAL OF EXPERIMENTAL PSYCHOLOGY
J Exp Psychol (Animal Behav Proc) . . JOURNAL OF EXPERIMENTAL PSYCHOLOGY: ANIMAL BEHAVIORAL PROCESSES
J Exp Psychol (Gen) . . JOURNAL OF EXPERIMENTAL PSYCHOLOGY: GENERAL
J Exp Psychol (Hum Learn Mem) . . JOURNAL OF EXPERIMENTAL PSYCHOLOGY: HUMAN LEARNING AND MEMORY
J Exp Psychol (Hum Perc Perf) . . JOURNAL OF EXPERIMENTAL PSYCHOLOGY: HUMAN PERCEPTION AND PERFORMANCE
J Exp Psy G . . . . . . JOURNAL OF EXPERIMENTAL PSYCHOLOGY. GENERAL
J Exp Psy H . . . . . . JOURNAL OF EXPERIMENTAL PSYCHOLOGY. HUMAN LEARNING AND MEMORY
J EXP PSY P . . . . . . JOURNAL OF EXPERIMENTAL PSYCHOLOGY. HUMAN PERCEPTION AND PERFORMANCE
J Exp Soc Psychol . . . JOURNAL OF EXPERIMENTAL SOCIAL PSYCHOLOGY
J EXP S PSY . . . . . . JOURNAL OF EXPERIMENTAL SOCIAL PSYCHOLOGY
J EXP ZOOL . . . . JOURNAL OF EXPERIMENTAL ZOOLOGY

J EXT . . . . JOURNAL OF EXTENSION
JF . . . . JORNAL DE FILOLOGIA
JF . . . . JOURNAL OF FINANCE
JF . . . . JUZNOSLOVENSKI FILOLOG
JFA . . . . JAHRESBERICHT UEBER DIE FORTSCHRITTE DER KLASSISCHEN ALTERTUMSWISSENSCHAFT
JfAaK . . . . JAHRBUCH FUER AESTHETIK UND ALLGEMEINE KUNSTWISSENSCHAFT
J Fac Eng Univ Tokyo Ser B . . JOURNAL OF THE FACULTY OF ENGINEERING. UNIVERSITY OF TOKYO. SERIES B
J FAC TOK 1 . . . . JOURNAL OF THE FACULTY OF SCIENCE. UNIVERSITY OF TOKYO. SECTION 1. MATHEMATICS
ASTRONOMY PHYSICS CHEMISTRY
J FAM COUNS . . . . . JOURNAL OF FAMILY COUNSELING
J Family L . . . . JOURNAL OF FAMILY LAW
J FAM LAW . . . . . . JOURNAL OF FAMILY LAW
J FAM WELF . . . . . . JOURNAL OF FAMILY WELFARE
J Farm Econ . . . . . . JOURNAL OF FARM ECONOMICS
JFCAW . . . . JAHRESBERICHT UEBER DIE FORTSCHRITTE DER KLASSISCHEN ALTERTUMSWISSENSCHAFT
JFDH . . . . JAHRBUCH DES FREIEN DEUTSCHEN HOCHSTIFTS
JFE . . . . JOURNAL OF FARM ECONOMICS
J FERM TECH . . . . . JOURNAL OF FERMENTATION TECHNOLOGY
JFG . . . . JAHRBUCH DER PHILOSOPHISCHEN FAKULTAET DER UNIVERSITAET ZU GOETTINGEN
JFI . . . . JOURNAL OF THE FOLKLORE INSTITUTE
JFI . . . . JOURNAL OF THE FRANKLIN INSTITUTE
J Finance . . . . JOURNAL OF FINANCE
J FIN QU AN . . . . . . JOURNAL OF FINANCIAL AND QUANTITATIVE ANALYSIS
J Fire Flammability . . JOURNAL OF FIRE AND FLAMMABILITY
J FISH BIOL . . . . JOURNAL OF FISH BIOLOGY
J FISH RES . . . . JOURNAL OF THE FISHERIES RESEARCH BOARD OF CANADA
JFKAW . . . . JAHRESBERICHTE UEBER DIE FORTSCHRITTE DER KLASSISCHEN ALTERTUMSWISSENSCHAFT
JFL . . . . JAHRBUCH FUER FRANKISCHE LANDESFORSCHUNG
JFLF . . . . JAHRBUCH FUER FRANKISCHE LANDESFORSCHUNG
J Flour Anim Feed Milling . . JOURNAL OF FLOUR AND ANIMAL FEED MILLING
J FLUID ENG . . . . . . JOURNAL OF FLUIDS ENGINEERING. TRANSACTIONS OF THE ASME
J Fluid Eng Trans ASME . . JOURNAL OF FLUIDS ENGINEERING TRANSACTIONS OF THE ASME
J FLUID MEC . . . . . . JOURNAL OF FLUID MECHANICS
J Fluids Eng . . . . JOURNAL OF FLUIDS ENGINEERING
J FLUORINE . . . . . . JOURNAL OF FLUORINE CHEMISTRY
J FOOD SCI . . . . JOURNAL OF FOOD SCIENCE
J For . . . . JOURNAL OF FORESTRY
J Forest . . . . JOURNAL OF FORESTRY
J For Med . . . . JOURNAL OF FORENSIC MEDICINE
J For Sci . . . . JOURNAL OF FORENSIC SCIENCES
J For Suisse . . . . JOURNAL FORESTIER SUISSE
J Four Elec . . . . JOURNAL DU FOUR ELECTRIQUE
J f Psychol u Neurol . . JOURNAL FUER PSYCHOLOGIE UND NEUROLOGIE
JFQA . . . . JOURNAL OF FINANCIAL AND QUANTITATIVE ANALYSIS
J FRANKL I . . . . JOURNAL OF THE FRANKLIN INSTITUTE
JFSGW . . . . JOURNAL OF THE FOLKLORE SOCIETY OF GREATER WASHINGTON
J Fuel Heat Technol . . JOURNAL OF FUEL AND HEAT TECHNOLOGY
J Fuel Soc Jap . . . . . JOURNAL OF THE FUEL SOCIETY OF JAPAN (NENRYO KYOKAI-SHI)
J FUNCT ANA . . . . . JOURNAL OF FUNCTIONAL ANALYSIS
JG . . . . JOURNAL DE GENEVE
JG . . . . JOURNAL OF GEOGRAPHY

J Ga . . . . JAUNA GAITA

J Gas Chromatogr . . JOURNAL OF GAS CHROMATOGRAPHY

JGE . . . . JOL'RNAL OF GENERAL EDUCATION

J GEN A MIC . . . . . . JOURNAL OF GENERAL AND APPLIED MICROBIOLOGY

J Gen Ed . . . . JOURNAL OF GENERAL EDUCATION

J Genet . . . . JOURNAL OF GENETICS

J GENET HUM . . . . . JOURNAL DE GENETIQUE HUMAINE

J GENET PSY . . . . . . JOURNAL OF GENETIC PSYCHOLOGY

J GEN MANAG . . . . . JOURNAL OF GENERAL MANAGEMENT

J GEN MICRO . . . . . . JOURNAL OF GENERAL MICROBIOLOGY

J Gen Physiol . . . . . JOURNAL OF GENERAL PHYSIOLOGY

J GEN PHYSL . . . . . . JOURNAL OF GENERAL PHYSIOLOGY

J Gen Ps . . . . PEDAGOGICAL SEMINARY AND JOURNAL OF GENETIC PSYCHOLOGY

J GEN PSYCH . . . . . . JOURNAL OF GENERAL PSYCHOLOGY

J Gen Psychol . . . . . JOURNAL OF GENERAL PSYCHOLOGY

J GEN VIROL . . . . . . JOURNAL OF GENERAL VIROLOGY

J Geo . . . . JOURNAL OF GEOLOGY

J GEOCHEM E . . . . . . JOURNAL OF GEOCHEMICAL EXPLORATION

J GEOG . . . . JOURNAL OF GEOGRAPHY

J Geol . . . . JOURNAL OF GEOLOGY

J GEOL S IN . . . . JOURNAL OF THE GEOLOGICAL SOCIETY OF INDIA

J GEOMAGN G . . . . . JOURNAL OF GEOMAGNETISM AND GEOELECTRICITY

J GEOPH RES . . . . . . JOURNAL OF GEOPHYSICAL RESEARCH

J GEOPHYS . . . . JOURNAL OF GEOPHYSICS

J Geophys Res . . . . . JOURNAL OF GEOPHYSICAL RESEARCH

J GEO R-O A . . . . . . JOURNAL OF GEOPHYSICAL RESEARCH. OCEANS AND ATMOSPHERE

J GEO R-S P . . . . JOURNAL OF GEOPHYSICAL RESEARCH. SPACE PHYSICS

JGEPs . . . . JOURNAL OF GENETIC PSYCHOLOGY

J GERIAT PS . . . . . . JOURNAL OF GERIATRIC PSYCHIATRY

J Geront . . . . JOURNAL OF GERONTOLOGY

J Gerontol . . . . JOURNAL OF GERONTOLOGY

JGF . . . . JENAER GERMANISTISCHE FORSCHUNGEN

JGG . . . . JAHRBUCH DER GOETHE-GESELLSCHAFT

JGG . . . . JAHRBUCH DER GRILLPARZER-GESELLSCHAFT

JGGPO . . . . JAHRBUCH DER GESELLSCHAFT FUER DIE GESCHICHTE DES PROTESTANTISMUS IN OESTERREICH

JGGPOes . . . . JAHRBUCH DER GESELLSCHAFT FUER DIE GESCHICHTE DES PROTESTANTISMUS IN OESTERREICH

JGJRI . . . . JOURNAL OF THE GANGANATHAN JHA RESEARCH INSTITUTE

J GLACIOL . . . . JOURNAL OF GLACIOLOGY

JGLGA . . . . JAHRBUCH DER GESELLSCHAFT FUER LOTHRINGISCHE GESCHICHTE UND ALTERTUMSKUNDE

JGLGAK . . . . JAHRBUCH DER GESELLSCHAFT FUER LOTHRINGISCHE GESCHICHTE UND ALTERTUMSKUNDE

JGLS . . . . JOURNAL OF THE GYPSY LORE SOCIETY

JGMOD . . . . JAHRBUCH FUER DIE GESCHICHTE MITTEL- UND OSTDEUTSCHLANDS

JGNSKG . . . . JAHRBUCH DER GESELLSCHAFT FUER NIEDERSAECHSISCHE KIRCHENGESCHICHTE

JGO . . . . JAHRBUECHER FUER GESCHICHTE OSTEUROPAS

JGOE . . . . JAHRBUECHER FUER GESCHICHTE OSTEUROPAS

JGOLR . . . . JAARBOEKJE VOOR GESCHIEDENIS EN OUDHEIDKUNDE VAN LEIDEN EN RIJNLAND

JGP . . . . JOURNAL OF GENERAL PSYCHOLOGY

JGPs . . . . JOURNAL OF GENERAL PSYCHOLOGY

JGrG . . . . JAHRBUCH DER GRILLPARZER-GESELLSCHAFT

JGRI . . . . JOURNAL OF THE GANGANATHA JHA RESEARCH INSTITUTE

JGW . . . . JAHRESBERICHT FUER GESCHICHTSWISSENSCHAFT

JGWT . . . . JAHRBUCH DER GESELLSCHAFT FUER WIENER THEATER-FORSCHUNG
JGyLS . . . . JOURNAL OF THE GYPSY LORE SOCIETY
J H Clearing House . . JUNIOR HIGH CLEARING HOUSE
JHE . . . . JOURNAL OF HIGHER EDUCATION
J Health & Soc Behav . . JOURNAL OF HEALTH AND SOCIAL BEHAVIOR
J Health Phys Ed Rec . . JOURNAL OF HEALTH, PHYSICAL EDUCATION, RECREATION
J HEALTH SO . . . . . . JOURNAL OF HEALTH AND SOCIAL BEHAVIOR
J Heat Tran . . . . JOURNAL OF HEAT TRANSFER
J Heat Transfer Trans ASME . . JOURNAL OF HEAT TRANSFER. TRANSACTIONS OF ASME
J Hellen Stud . . . . . . JOURNAL OF HELLENIC STUDIES
J Hell Stud . . . . JOURNAL OF HELLENIC STUDIES
J HELMINTH . . . . . . JOURNAL OF HELMINTHOLOGY
J Hel Stud . . . . JOURNAL OF HELLENIC STUDIES
J HETERO CH . . . . . . JOURNAL OF HETEROCYCLIC CHEMISTRY
JHGA . . . . JAHRBUCH DER K. K. HERALDISCHEN GESELLSCHAFT, "ADLER"
JHI . . . . JOURNAL OF THE HISTORY OF IDEAS
J Hi E . . . . JOURNAL OF HIGHER EDUCATION
J HIGH EDUC . . . . . . JOURNAL OF HIGHER EDUCATION
J HIST BEH . . . . JOURNAL OF THE HISTORY OF THE BEHAVIORAL SCIENCES
J Hist Biol . . . . JOURNAL OF THE HISTORY OF BIOLOGY
J HIST CYTO . . . . . . JOURNAL OF HISTOCHEMISTRY AND CYTOCHEMISTRY
J Hist Ideas . . . . JOURNAL OF THE HISTORY OF IDEAS
J Hist Phil . . . . JOURNAL OF THE HISTORY OF PHILOSOPHY
JHM . . . . JOURNAL OF THE HISTORY OF MEDICINE
JHMa . . . . JOHNS HOPKINS MAGAZINE
JhOAI . . . . JAHRESHEFTE DES OESTERREICHISCHEN ARCHAEOLOGISCHEN INSTITUTS IN WIEN
J Ho E . . . . JOURNAL OF HOME ECONOMICS
J Hort Sci . . . . JOURNAL OF HORTICULTURAL SCIENCE
J Housing . . . . JOURNAL OF HOUSING
JHP . . . . JOURNAL OF THE HISTORY OF PHILOSOPHY
JHPh . . . . JOURNAL OF THE HISTORY OF PHILOSOPHY
JHR . . . . JOURNAL OF HUMAN RESOURCES
JHS . . . . JOURNAL OF HELLENIC STUDIES
JHS . . . . JOURNAL OF HISTORICAL STUDIES
JHSch . . . . JAHRESBERICHTE UEBER DAS HOEHRE SCHULWESEN
JHSCW . . . . JOURNAL OF THE HISTORICAL SOCIETY OF THE CHURCH IN WALES
JHSRLL . . . . JOHNS HOPKINS STUDIES IN ROMANCE LANGUAGE AND LITERATURE
JHStud . . . . JOURNAL OF HISTORICAL STUDIES
J Humanistic Psychol . . JOURNAL OF HUMANISTIC PSYCHOLOGY
J HUM EVOL . . . . . . JOURNAL OF HUMAN EVOLUTION
J HUM PSY . . . . JOURNAL OF HUMANISTIC PSYCHOLOGY
J HUM RELAT . . . . . JOURNAL OF HUMAN RELATIONS
J Hum Resources . . . JOURNAL OF HUMAN RESOURCES
J H U Studies . . . . . . JOHNS HOPKINS UNIVERSITY STUDIES IN HISTORICAL AND POLITICAL SCIENCE
JHVD . . . . JAHRBUCH DES HISTORISCHEN VEREIN DILLINGEN
JHVFB . . . . JAHRBUCH DES HISTORISCHEN VEREINS FUER DAS FUERSTBISTUM BAMBERG
J HYDR-ASCE . . . . . . JOURNAL OF THE HYDRAULICS DIVISION. ASCE (AMERICAN SOCIETY OF CIVIL ENGINEERS)
J Hydraul Eng (Peking) . . JOURNAL OF HYDRAULIC ENGINEERING (PEKING)
J Hydraul Res . . . . . JOURNAL OF HYDRAULIC RESEARCH
J Hydrol . . . . JOURNAL OF HYDROLOGY
J Hydrol NZ . . . . JOURNAL OF HYDROLOGY (NEW ZEALAND)

J Hydronaut . . . . . . JOURNAL OF HYDRONAUTICS
J Hyg . . . . JOURNAL OF HYGIENE
J HYG EP MI . . . . . . JOURNAL OF HYGIENE, EPIDEMIOLOGY, MICROBIOLOGY AND IMMUNOLOGY
JI . . . . JAPAN INTERPRETER
JIA . . . . JOURNAL OF INDUSTRIAL ARCHAEOLOGY
JIAS . . . . JOURNAL OF INTER-AMERICAN STUDIES
JIASRA . . . . JOURNAL OF THE INTERNATIONAL ARTHUR SCHNITZLER RESEARCH ASSOCIATION
J I BREWING . . . . . . JOURNAL OF THE INSTITUTE OF BREWING
JIE . . . . JOURNAL OF INDUSTRIAL ECONOMICS
JIES . . . . JOURNAL OF INDO-EUROPEAN STUDIES
JIFC . . . . JOURNAL OF THE INTERNATIONAL FOLK MUSIC COUNCIL
JIFM . . . . JOURNAL OF THE INTERNATIONAL FOLK MUSIC COUNCIL
JIFMC . . . . JOURNAL OF THE INTERNATIONAL FOLK MUSIC COUNCIL
J I FUEL . . . . JOURNAL OF THE INSTITUTE OF FUEL
JIG . . . . JAHRBUCH FUER INTERNATIONALE GERMANISTIK
JIHS . . . . JOURNAL OF THE ILLINOIS STATE HISTORICAL SOCIETY
JIL . . . . JOURNAL OF IRISH LITERATURE
JILLHS . . . . JOURNAL OF THE ILLINOIS STATE HISTORICAL SOCIETY
J Illum Eng Soc . . . . . JOURNAL OF THE ILLUMINATING ENGINEERING SOCIETY
J I MATH AP . . . . . . JOURNAL OF THE INSTITUTE OF MATHEMATICS AND ITS APPLICATION
J IMMUNOGEN . . . . JOURNAL OF IMMUNOGENETICS
J IMMUNOL . . . . JOURNAL OF IMMUNOLOGY
J IMMUNOL M . . . . . JOURNAL OF IMMUNOLOGICAL METHODS
J IND AERO . . . . JOURNAL OF INDUSTRIAL AERODYNAMICS
J Ind Arts Ed . . . . . . JOURNAL OF INDUSTRIAL ARTS EDUCATION
J Ind Bot Soc . . . . . . JOURNAL OF THE INDIAN BOTANICAL SOCIETY
J IND CH S . . . . JOURNAL OF THE INDIAN CHEMICAL SOCIETY
J Ind Econ . . . . JOURNAL OF INDUSTRIAL ECONOMICS
J Ind Eng . . . . JOURNAL OF INDUSTRIAL ENGINEERING
J Ind Hyg . . . . JOURNAL OF INDUSTRIAL HYGIENE AND TOXICOLOGY
J Indian Acad Phil . . JOURNAL OF THE INDIAN ACADEMY OF PHILOSOPHY
J INDIAN I . . . . JOURNAL OF THE INDIAN INSTITUTE OF SCIENCE
J Indian Nat Soc Soil Mech Found Eng . . JOURNAL OF THE INDIAN NATIONAL SOCIETY OF SOIL MECHANICS AND
            FOUNDATION ENGINEERING
J Indian Phil . . . . . . JOURNAL OF INDIAN PHILOSOPHY
J Indian Roads Congr . . JOURNAL OF THE INDIAN ROADS CONGRESS
J INDIV PSY . . . . . . JOURNAL OF INDIVIDUAL PSYCHOLOGY
J INFEC DIS . . . . JOURNAL OF INFECTIOUS DISEASES
J INORG NUC . . . . . . JOURNAL OF INORGANIC AND NUCLEAR CHEMISTRY
J INSECT PH . . . . . . JOURNAL OF INSECT PHYSIOLOGY
J Inst Brew . . . . JOURNAL OF THE INSTITUTE OF BREWING
J Inst Eng Aust . . . . JOURNAL OF THE INSTITUTION OF ENGINEERS (AUSTRALIA)
J Inst Eng (India) Chem Eng Div . . JOURNAL OF THE INSTITUTION OF ENGINEERS (INDIA). CHEMICAL ENGINEERING
            DIVISION
J Inst Eng (India) Civ Eng Div . . JOURNAL OF THE INSTITUTION OF ENGINEERS (INDIA). CIVIL ENGINEERING DIVISION
J Inst Eng (India) Elec Eng Div . . JOURNAL OF THE INSTITUTION OF ENGINEERS (INDIA). ELECTRICAL ENGINEERING
            DIVISION
J Inst Eng (India) Electron Telecommun Eng Div . . JOURNAL OF THE INSTITUTION OF ENGINEERS (INDIA).
            ELECTRONICS & TELECOMMUNICATION ENGINEERING DIVISION
J Inst Eng (India) Gen Eng . . JOURNAL OF THE INSTITUTION OF ENGINEERS (INDIA). GENERAL ENGINEERING
            DIVISION
J Inst Eng (India) Ind Dev Gen Eng Div . . JOURNAL OF THE INSTITUTION OF ENGINEERS (INDIA). INDUSTRIAL
            DEVELOPMENT AND GENERAL ENGINEERING DIVISION

J Inst Eng (India) Mech Eng Div..JOURNAL OF THE INSTITUTION OF ENGINEERS (INDIA). MECHANICAL ENGINEERING DIVISION

J Inst Eng (India) Mining Met Div..JOURNAL OF THE INSTITUTION OF ENGINEERS (INDIA). MINING & METALLURGY DIVISION

J Inst Eng (India) Pub Health Eng Div..JOURNAL OF THE INSTITUTION OF ENGINEERS (INDIA). PUBLIC HEALTH ENGINEERING DIVISION

J Inst Eng Malaysia..JOURNAL OF THE INSTITUTION OF ENGINEERS (MALAYSIA)

J Inst Fuel........JOURNAL OF THE INSTITUTE OF FUEL

J Inst Highw Eng...JOURNAL OF THE INSTITUTE OF HIGHWAY ENGINEERS

J Inst (India) Electron Telecommun Eng Div..JOURNAL OF THE INSTITUTION OF ENGINEERS (INDIA). ELECTRONICS & TELECOMMUNICATION ENGINEERING DIVISION

J Inst Math Applic..JOURNAL OF THE INSTITUTE OF MATHEMATICS AND ITS APPLICATIONS

J Inst Met (Lond)...JOURNAL OF THE INSTITUTE OF METALS (LONDON)

J Inst Mine Surv S Afr..JOURNAL OF THE INSTITUTE OF MINE SURVEYORS OF SOUTH AFRICA

J Inst Munic Eng...JOURNAL OF THE INSTITUTION OF MUNICIPAL ENGINEERS

J Inst Navig.......JOURNAL OF THE INSTITUTE OF NAVIGATION

J Instn Gas Engrs...JOURNAL OF THE INSTITUTION OF GAS ENGINEERS

J Instn Heat Vent Engrs..JOURNAL OF THE INSTITUTION OF HEATING AND VENTILATING ENGINEERS

J Instn Highw Engrs..JOURNAL OF THE INSTITUTION OF HIGHWAY ENGINEERS

J Instn Loco Engrs..JOURNAL OF THE INSTITUTION OF LOCOMOTIVE ENGINEERS

J Instn Munic Engrs..JOURNAL OF THE INSTITUTION OF MUNICIPAL ENGINEERS

J Instn Nucl Engrs..JOURNAL OF THE INSTITUTION OF NUCLEAR ENGINEERS

J Instn Rubb Ind...JOURNAL OF THE INSTITUTION OF THE RUBBER INDUSTRY

J Inst Nucl Eng.....JOURNAL OF THE INSTITUTION OF NUCLEAR ENGINEERS

J Instn Wat Engrs..JOURNAL OF THE INSTITUTION OF WATER ENGINEERS

J Inst Pet........JOURNAL OF THE INSTITUTE OF PETROLEUM

J Inst Rubber Ind...JOURNAL OF THE INSTITUTION OF THE RUBBER INDUSTRY

J Inst Telecommun Eng New Delhi..JOURNAL OF THE INSTITUTION OF TELECOMMUNICATION ENGINEERS (NEW DELHI)

J Inst Transp......JOURNAL OF THE INSTITUTE OF TRANSPORT

J Inst Water Eng...JOURNAL OF THE INSTITUTION OF WATER ENGINEERS

J INT AFF........JOURNAL OF INTERNATIONAL AFFAIRS

J INT A MAT......JOURNAL OF THE INTERNATIONAL ASSOCIATION FOR MATHEMATICAL GEOLOGY

J INT-AM ST......JOURNAL OF INTERAMERICAN STUDIES AND WORLD AFFAIRS

J Int Econ........JOURNAL OF INTERNATIONAL ECONOMICS

J Interam Stud.....JOURNAL OF INTERAMERICAN STUDIES AND WORLD AFFAIRS

J INTERD CY......JOURNAL OF INTERDISCIPLINARY CYCLE RESEARCH

J Interdiscip Hist...JOURNAL OF INTERDISCIPLINARY HISTORY

J Int Law & Econ...JOURNAL OF INTERNATIONAL LAW AND ECONOMICS

J INT LAW E.......JOURNAL OF INTERNATIONAL LAW AND ECONOMICS

J INT MED R......JOURNAL OF INTERNATIONAL MEDICAL RESEARCH

J Int Relations.....JOURNAL OF INTERNATIONAL RELATIONS

J Int Th C........JOURNAL OF THE INTERDENOMINATIONAL THEOLOGICAL CENTER

J I NUCL EN.......JOURNAL OF THE INSTITUTION OF NUCLEAR ENGINEERS

J INVER PAT......JOURNAL OF INVERTEBRATE PATHOLOGY

J INVES DER......JOURNAL OF INVESTIGATIVE DERMATOLOGY

JIP.............JOURNAL OF INDIAN PHILOSOPHY

JIPA............JOURNAL OF THE INTERNATIONAL PHONETIC ASSOCIATION

JIR.............JOURNAL OF INDUSTRIAL RELATIONS

J IRISH C P.......JOURNAL OF THE IRISH COLLEGES OF PHYSICIANS AND SURGEONS

J Iron St Inst......JOURNAL OF THE IRON AND STEEL INSTITUTE

JiS............. JEZIK IN SLOVSTVO
JISHS........... JOURNAL OF THE ILLINOIS STATE HISTORICAL SOCIETY
J I WOOD SC...... JOURNAL OF THE INSTITUTE OF WOOD SCIENCE
J Jap Inst Light Metals.. JOURNAL OF THE JAPAN INSTITUTE OF LIGHT METALS
J Jap Inst Met..... JOURNAL OF THE JAPAN INSTITUTE OF LIGHT METALS
J JAP S LUB....... JOURNAL OF THE JAPAN SOCIETY OF LUBRICATION ENGINEERS
J Jap Soc Civ Eng... JOURNAL OF THE JAPAN SOCIETY OF CIVIL ENGINEERS
J Jap Soc Mech Eng.. JOURNAL OF THE JAPAN SOCIETY OF MECHANICAL ENGINEERS
J Jap Soc Powder Met.. JOURNAL OF THE JAPAN SOCIETY OF POWDER AND POWDER METALLURGY
JJCL............ JADAVPUR JOURNAL OF COMPARATIVE LITERATURE
JJewS........... JOURNAL OF JEWISH STUDIES
J Joint Panel Nucl Mar Propul.. JOURNAL OF THE JOINT PANEL ON NUCLEAR MARINE PROPULSION
JJP............. JOURNAL OF JURISTIC PAPYROLOGY
JJPG............ JAHRBUCH DER JEAN-PAUL-GESELLSCHAFT
JJQ............. JAMES JOYCE QUARTERLY
JJR............. JAMES JOYCE REVIEW
JJS............. JOURNAL OF JEWISH STUDIES
J Juvenile Res..... JOURNAL OF JUVENILE RESEARCH
JKAF............ JAHRBUCH FUER KLEINASIATISCHE FORSCHUNG. INTERNATIONALE ORIENTALISTISCHE
               ZEITSCHRIFT
JKAHS........... JOURNAL OF THE KERRY ARCHAEOLOGICAL AND HISTORICAL SOCIETY
J Kan BA........ JOURNAL OF THE KANSAS BAR ASSOCIATION
JKAWA.......... JAARBOEK VAN DE KONINKLIJKE AKADEMIE VAN WETENSCHAPPEN. AMSTERDAM
JKG............ JAHRBUCH DER KLEIST-GESELLSCHAFT
JKGS........... JAHRBUECHER FUER KULTUR UND GESCHICHTE DER SLAVEN
JKGV........... JAHRBUCH DES KOELNISCHEN GESCHICHTSVEREINS
JKNA........... JAARBOEK VAN DE KONINKLIJKE NEDERLANDSE AKADEMIE
JKSW........... JAHRBUCH DER KUNSTHISTORISCHEN SAMMLUNGEN IN WIEN
JKUR........... JAMMU AND KASHMIR UNIVERSITY REVIEW
JKVA........... JAARBOEK KONINKLIJKE VLAAMSE ACADEMIE VOOR WETENSCHAPPEN. LETTEREN EN SCHONE
               KUNSTEN VAN BELGIE
JKW............ JAHRBUCH FUER KUNSTWISSENSCHAFT
JL............. JORNAL DE LETRAS
JL............. JOURNAL OF LINGUISTICS
JL............. JULY
JLA............ JORNAL DE LETRAS E ARTES
J LAB CLIN MED.... JOURNAL OF LABORATORY AND CLINICAL MEDICINE
J LABEL COM...... JOURNAL OF LABELLED COMPOUNDS
J LA CL MED...... JOURNAL OF LABORATORY AND CLINICAL MEDICINE
JLAEA........... JOURNAL OF THE LANGUAGE ASSOCIATION OF EASTERN AFRICA
Jl Aesthetics...... JOURNAL OF AESTHETICS AND ART CRITICISM
J Land & Pub Util Econ.. JOURNAL OF LAND AND PUBLIC UTILITIES ECONOMICS
J L & Econ........ JOURNAL OF LAW AND ECONOMICS
J L & Econ Develop.. JOURNAL OF LAW AND ECONOMIC DEVELOPMENT
J L & Educ........ JOURNAL OF LAW AND EDUCATION
J Laryngol Otol.... JOURNAL OF LARYNGOLOGY AND OTOLOGY
J LARYNG OT...... JOURNAL OF LARYNGOLOGY AND OTOLOGY
J Lat Am Stud..... JOURNAL OF LATIN AMERICAN STUDIES
J Law & Econ...... JOURNAL OF LAW AND ECONOMICS
J LAW ECON...... JOURNAL OF LAW AND ECONOMICS
JLDS........... JOURNAL OF THE LANCASHIRE DIALECT SOCIETY

JLE . . . . JOURNAL OF LAW AND ECONOMICS
J LEARN DI . . . . JOURNAL OF LEARNING DISABILITIES
J Legal Ed . . . . JOURNAL OF LEGAL EDUCATION
J LEG EDUC . . . . JOURNAL OF LEGAL EDUCATION
J LEG STUD . . . . JOURNAL OF LEGAL STUDIES
J Leis Res . . . . JOURNAL OF LEISURE RESEARCH
J LEISURE . . . . JOURNAL OF LEISURE RESEARCH
J LESS C MET . . . . . JOURNAL OF THE LESS-COMMON METALS
JLH . . . . JOURNAL OF LIBRARY HISTORY
J Lib Automation . . . JOURNAL OF LIBRARY AUTOMATION
J Lib Hist . . . . JOURNAL OF LIBRARY HISTORY
J Libnship . . . . JOURNAL OF LIBRARIANSHIP
J LIBR . . . . JOURNAL OF LIBRARIANSHIP
J LIBR AUT . . . . JOURNAL OF LIBRARY AUTOMATION
J Ling . . . . JOURNAL OF LINGUISTICS
J LIPID RES . . . . JOURNAL OF LIPID RESEARCH
JLKNO . . . . JAHRBUCH FUER LANDESKUNDE VON NIEDEROESTERREICH
Jl Musicology . . . . . JOURNAL OF MUSICOLOGY
Jl of Research . . . . . JOURNAL OF RESEARCH IN MUSIC EDUCATION
J LOND MATH . . . . . JOURNAL OF THE LONDON MATHEMATICAL SOCIETY
J Low Temp Phys . . . JOURNAL OF LOW TEMPERATURE PHYSICS
JLRU . . . . JOURNAL OF THE LIBRARY OF RUTGERS UNIVERSITY
JLS . . . . JOURNAL OF LITERARY SEMANTICS
J L TEMP PH . . . . . . JOURNAL OF LOW TEMPERATURE PHYSICS
J Lubric Technol Trans ASME . . JOURNAL OF LUBRICATION TECHNOLOGY. TRANSACTIONS ASME
J LUB TECH . . . . . . JOURNAL OF LUBRICATION TECHNOLOGY. TRANSACTIONS ASME
J Lumin . . . . JOURNAL OF LUMINESCENCE
J LUMINESC . . . . . . JOURNAL OF LUMINESCENCE
JLW . . . . JAHRBUCH FUER LITURGIEWISSENSCHAFT
JLZ . . . . JAHRESBERICHTE DES LITERARISCHEN ZENTRALBLATTES
JM . . . . JOURNAL OF MARKETING
J MACR S CH . . . . . . JOURNAL OF MACROMOLECULAR SCIENCE. CHEMISTRY
J MACR S PH . . . . . . JOURNAL OF MACROMOLECULAR SCIENCE. PHYSICS
J MACR S RM . . . . . JOURNAL OF MACROMOLECULAR SCIENCE. REVIEWS IN MACROMOLECULAR CHEMISTRY
J MAGN RES . . . . . . JOURNAL OF MAGNETIC RESONANCE
J MAMMAL . . . . JOURNAL OF MAMMALOGY
J MANAG STU . . . . . JOURNAL OF MANAGEMENT STUDIES
J MARINE BI . . . . . . JOURNAL OF THE MARINE BIOLOGICAL ASSOCIATION OF THE UNITED KINGDOM
J MARINE RE . . . . . . JOURNAL OF MARINE RESEARCH
J Maritime L . . . . . . JOURNAL OF MARITIME LAW AND COMMERCE
J MARKET . . . . JOURNAL OF MARKETING
J Marketing . . . . . . JOURNAL OF MARKETING
J MARKET L . . . . JOURNAL OF THE MARKET RESEARCH SOCIETY (LONDON)
J MARKET R . . . . . . JOURNAL OF MARKETING RESEARCH
J Marr & Fam . . . . . JOURNAL OF MARRIAGE AND THE FAMILY
J Mar Res . . . . JOURNAL OF MARINE RESEARCH
J MARRIAGE . . . . . . JOURNAL OF MARRIAGE AND THE FAMILY
JMAS . . . . JOURNAL OF MODERN AFRICAN STUDIES
J Mater . . . . JOURNAL OF MATERIALS
J Mater Sci . . . . JOURNAL OF MATERIALS SCIENCE
J MATH ANAL . . . . JOURNAL OF MATHEMATICAL ANALYSIS AND APPLICATIONS

J Math Anal Appl . . . JOURNAL OF MATHEMATICAL ANALYSIS AND APPLICATION
J Math & Phys . . . . . JOURNAL OF MATHEMATICS AND PHYSICS
J MATH BIOL . . . . . . JOURNAL OF MATHEMATICAL BIOLOGY
J MATH JAP . . . . . . JOURNAL OF THE MATHEMATICAL SOCIETY OF JAPAN
J Math Mech . . . . . . JOURNAL OF MATHEMATICS AND MECHANICS
J MATH P A . . . . JOURNAL DE MATHEMATIQUES PURES ET APPLIQUEES
J Math Phys . . . . . . JOURNAL OF MATHEMATICS AND PHYSICS
J MATH PSYC . . . . . JOURNAL OF MATHEMATICAL PSYCHOLOGY
J Math Psychol . . . . JOURNAL OF MATHEMATICAL PSYCHOLOGY
J MATH SOCI . . . . . . JOURNAL OF MATHEMATICAL SOCIOLOGY
J Mec . . . . JOURNAL DE MECANIQUE
J MECANIQUE . . . . . JOURNAL DE MECANIQUE
J Mech . . . . JOURNAL OF MECHANISMS
J MECH ENG . . . . . . JOURNAL OF MECHANICAL ENGINEERING SCIENCE
J Mech Eng Sci . . . . . JOURNAL OF MECHANICAL ENGINEERING SCIENCE
J Mech Lab Jap . . . . JOURNAL OF MECHANICAL LABORATORY OF JAPAN
J MECH PHYS . . . . . JOURNAL OF THE MECHANICS AND PHYSICS OF SOLIDS
J Mech Phys Solids . . JOURNAL OF THE MECHANICS AND PHYSICS OF SOLIDS
J MED . . . . JOURNAL OF MEDICINE
J MED CHEM . . . . . . JOURNAL OF MEDICINAL CHEMISTRY
J MED EDUC . . . . . . JOURNAL OF MEDICAL EDUCATION
J MED ENT . . . . JOURNAL OF MEDICAL ENTOMOLOGY
J MED GENET . . . . . . JOURNAL OF MEDICAL GENETICS
J MED MICRO . . . . . JOURNAL OF MEDICAL MICROBIOLOGY
J MED PRIM . . . . . . JOURNAL OF MEDICAL PRIMATOLOGY
J MEMBR BIO . . . . . JOURNAL OF MEMBRANE BIOLOGY
J Mental Def Research . . JOURNAL OF MENTAL DEFICIENCY RESEARCH
J MENT DEF . . . . JOURNAL OF MENTAL DEFICIENCY RESEARCH
J Met . . . . JOURNAL OF METALS
J Mex Am Hist . . . . . JOURNAL OF MEXICAN AMERICAN HISTORY
JMF . . . . JOURNAL OF MARRIAGE AND THE FAMILY
JMH . . . . JOURNAL OF MISSISSIPPI HISTORY
JMH . . . . JOURNAL OF MODERN HISTORY
J Microgr . . . . JOURNAL OF MICROGRAPHICS
J Micros . . . . JOURNAL OF MICROSCOPY (OXFORD)
J MICROSC B . . . . . . JOURNAL DE MICROSCOPIE ET DE BIOLOGIE CELLULAIRE
J MICROSC O . . . . . . JOURNAL OF MICROSCOPY (OXFORD)
J Microwave Power . . JOURNAL OF MICROWAVE POWER
JMiH . . . . JOURNAL OF MISSISSIPPI HISTORY
J Milk & Food Tech . . JOURNAL OF MILK AND FOOD TECHNOLOGY
J MILK FOOD . . . . . . JOURNAL OF MILK AND FOOD TECHNOLOGY
J Milk Tech . . . . JOURNAL OF MILK TECHNOLOGY
J Mil Serv Inst . . . . . JOURNAL OF THE MILITARY SERVICE INSTITUTION
J Mines Met Fuels . . JOURNAL OF MINES, METALS & FUELS
J Mine Vent Soc S Afr . . JOURNAL OF THE MINE VENTILATION SOCIETY OF SOUTH AFRICA
J Mining Met Inst Jap . . JOURNAL OF THE MINING AND METALLURGICAL INSTITUTE OF JAPAN
J Ministry Ag . . . . . AGRICULTURE (JOURNAL OF THE MINISTRY OF AGRICULTURE)
J Min Metall Inst Jap . . JOURNAL OF THE MINING AND METALLURGICAL INSTITUTE OF JAPAN
JMIR . . . . JOURNAL DU MINISTERE DE L'INSTRUCTION PUBLIQUE EN RUSSIE
JMissH . . . . JOURNAL OF MISSISSIPPI HISTORY
J Mktg . . . . JOURNAL OF MARKETING

J Mktg Res . . . . JOURNAL OF MARKETING RESEARCH
JML . . . . JOURNAL OF MODERN LITERATURE
JMM . . . . JOURNAL OF THE MANX MUSEUM
J Mod Afric Stud . . . JOURNAL OF MODERN AFRICAN STUDIES
J MOD AFR S . . . . . . JOURNAL OF MODERN AFRICAN STUDIES
J Mod Hist . . . . JOURNAL OF MODERN HISTORY
J Mod Lit . . . . JOURNAL OF MODERN LITERATURE
J MOL BIOL . . . . JOURNAL OF MOLECULAR BIOLOGY
J MOL CATAL . . . . . JOURNAL OF MOLECULAR CATALYSIS
J MOL CEL C . . . . . . JOURNAL OF MOLECULAR AND CELLULAR CARDIOLOGY
J MOL EVOL . . . . JOURNAL OF MOLECULAR EVOLUTION
J MOL MED . . . . JOURNAL OF MOLECULAR MEDICINE
J MOL SPECT . . . . . . JOURNAL OF MOLECULAR SPECTROSCOPY
J MOL STRUCT . . . . . JOURNAL OF MOLECULAR STRUCTURE
J Money Cred Bank . . JOURNAL OF MONEY, CREDIT AND BANKING
J Moral Ed . . . . JOURNAL OF MORAL EDUCATION
J MORPH . . . . JOURNAL OF MORPHOLOGY
J MOTOR BEH . . . . . JOURNAL OF MOTOR BEHAVIOR
JMRAS . . . . JOURNAL OF THE MALAYAN BRANCH OF THE ROYAL ASIATIC SOCIETY
JMRS . . . . JOURNAL OF MEDIEVAL AND RENAISSANCE STUDIES
JMS . . . . JOURNAL OF MALTESE STUDIES
JMS . . . . JOURNAL OF MANAGEMENT STUDIES
JMSUB . . . . JOURNAL OF THE MAHARAJA SAYAJIRAO UNIVERSITY OF BARODA
JMT . . . . JOURNAL OF MUSIC THERAPY
J Multivar Anal . . . . JOURNAL OF MULTIVARIATE ANALYSIS
J Mus Francais . . . . JOURNAL MUSICAL FRANCAIS
J Mus Theory . . . . . JOURNAL OF MUSIC THEORY
J Mus Therapy . . . . . JOURNAL OF MUSIC THERAPY
JNALA . . . . JOURNAL OF THE NEW AFRICAN LITERATURE AND THE ARTS
J Nat Assn Col Adm Counsel . . JOURNAL OF THE NATIONAL ASSOCIATION OF COLLEGE ADMISSIONS COUNSELORS
J NAT CANC . . . . . . JOURNAL OF THE NATIONAL CANCER INSTITUTE
J NAT HIST . . . . JOURNAL OF NATURAL HISTORY
J Natl Assn Coll Adm Counsel . . THE JOURNAL OF THE NATIONAL ASSOCIATION OF COLLEGE ADMISSIONS COUNSELORS
J Natl Assn Women Deans Adm & Counsel . . THE JOURNAL OF THE NATIONAL ASSOCIATION FOR WOMEN DEANS, ADMINISTRATORS, AND COUNSELORS
J Natural Hist . . . . . JOURNAL OF NATURAL HISTORY
J NAVIG . . . . JOURNAL OF NAVIGATION
JNE . . . . JOURNAL OF NEAR EASTERN STUDIES
JNE . . . . JOURNAL OF NEGRO EDUCATION
J Near East Stud . . . JOURNAL OF NEAR EASTERN STUDIES
J NEAR E ST . . . . JOURNAL OF NEAR EASTERN STUDIES
J NE EXP NE . . . . JOURNAL OF NEUROPATHOLOGY AND EXPERIMENTAL NEUROLOGY
J Negro Ed . . . . JOURNAL OF NEGRO EDUCATION
J Negro Hist . . . . . . JOURNAL OF NEGRO HISTORY
J NEMATOL . . . . JOURNAL OF NEMATOLOGY
J NE NE PSY . . . . JOURNAL OF NEUROLOGY NEUROSURGERY AND PSYCHIATRY
J N Engl Water Works Assoc . . JOURNAL OF THE NEW ENGLAND WATER WORKS ASSOCIATION
J NERV MENT . . . . . JOURNAL OF NERVOUS AND MENTAL DISEASE
J Nerv Ment Dis . . . JOURNAL OF NERVOUS AND MENTAL DISEASE
JNES . . . . JOURNAL OF NEAR EASTERN STUDIES

J NEURAL TR . . . . . . JOURNAL OF NEURAL TRANSMISSION
J NEUROBIOL . . . . . . JOURNAL OF NEUROBIOLOGY
J NEUROCHEM . . . . . JOURNAL OF NEUROCHEMISTRY
J NEUROCYT . . . . . . JOURNAL OF NEUROCYTOLOGY
J NEUROL . . . . JOURNAL OF NEUROLOGY
J NEUROSURG . . . . . JOURNAL OF NEUROSURGERY
J NEURPHYSL . . . . . JOURNAL OF NEUROPHYSIOLOGY
J NEUR SCI . . . . JOURNAL OF THE NEUROLOGICAL SCIENCES
J New Engl Water Works Ass . . JOURNAL OF THE NEW ENGLAND WATER WORKS ASSOCIATION
JNG . . . . JAHRBUCH FUER NUMISMATIK UND GELDGESCHICHTE
JNGG . . . . JAHRBUCH FUER NUMISMATIK UND GELDGESCHICHTE
JNH . . . . JOURNAL OF NEGRO HISTORY
JNI . . . . JAHRBUCH DES NORDFRIESISCHEN INSTITUTS
JNL . . . . JOHNSONIAN NEWS LETTER
Jnl Aesthetics . . . . . JOURNAL OF AESTHETICS AND ART CRITICISM
Jnl Aesthetics & Art Crit . . JOURNAL OF AESTHETICS AND ART CRITICISM
Jnl Am Folklore . . . . JOURNAL OF AMERICAN FOLKLORE
Jnl Am Hist . . . . JOURNAL OF AMERICAN HISTORY
Jnl Asian Stu . . . . . . JOURNAL OF ASIAN STUDIES
Jnl Business Ed . . . . JOURNAL OF BUSINESS EDUCATION
Jnl Counsel Psych . . JOURNAL OF COUNSELING PSYCHOLOGY
Jnl Econ Hist . . . . . . JOURNAL OF ECONOMIC HISTORY
Jnl Engl Ger Philol . . JOURNAL OF ENGLISH AND GERMANIC PHILOLOGY
Jnl Gen Ed . . . . JOURNAL OF GENERAL EDUCATION
Jnl Higher Ed . . . . . . JOURNAL OF HIGHER EDUCATION
Jnl Hist Ideas . . . . . JOURNAL OF THE HISTORY OF IDEAS
Jnl Home Econ . . . . . JOURNAL OF HOME ECONOMICS
Jnl Lib Hist . . . . JOURNAL OF LIBRARY HISTORY
Jnl Marketing . . . . . JOURNAL OF MARKETING
Jnl Marr & Fam . . . . JOURNAL OF MARRIAGE AND FAMILY
Jnl Mod Hist . . . . . . JOURNAL OF MODERN HISTORY
Jnl Negro Ed . . . . . . JOURNAL OF NEGRO EDUCATION
Jnl Negro Hist . . . . . JOURNAL OF NEGRO HISTORY
Jnl Philos . . . . JOURNAL OF PHILOSOPHY
Jnl Polit Econ . . . . . . JOURNAL OF POLITICAL ECONOMY
Jnl Politics . . . . JOURNAL OF POLITICS
Jnl Relig . . . . JOURNAL OF RELIGION
JNMD . . . . JOURNAL OF NERVOUS AND MENTAL DISEASES
J NON-CRYST . . . . . JOURNAL OF NON-CRYSTALLINE SOLIDS
JNPS . . . . JOURNAL OF THE NAGARI PRACARINI SABHA
JNT . . . . JOURNAL OF NARRATIVE TECHNIQUE
J NUCL BIOL . . . . . . JOURNAL OF NUCLEAR BIOLOGY AND MEDICINE
J Nucl Energy . . . . . JOURNAL OF NUCLEAR ENERGY
J NUCL MAT . . . . . . JOURNAL OF NUCLEAR MATERIALS
J NUCL MED . . . . . . JOURNAL OF NUCLEAR MEDICINE
J Nucl Sci Technol . . JOURNAL OF NUCLEAR SCIENCE AND TECHNOLOGY
J NUC SCI T . . . . JOURNAL OF NUCLEAR SCIENCE AND TECHNOLOGY
J NUMBER TH . . . . . JOURNAL OF NUMBER THEORY
J Nurs Ed . . . . THE JOURNAL OF NURSERY EDUCATION
J Nutr . . . . JOURNAL OF NUTRITION
J NUTR SC V . . . . . . JOURNAL OF NUTRITIONAL SCIENCE AND VITAMINOLOGY

J NY ENT SO . . . . . . JOURNAL OF THE NEW YORK ENTOMOLOGICAL SOCIETY
JoA . . . . JEWEL OF AFRICA (ZAMBIA)
JOAI . . . . JAHRESHEFTE DES OESTERREICHISCHEN INSTITUTS IN WIEN
JOBG . . . . JAHRBUCH DER OESTERREICHISCHEN BYZANTINISCHEN GESELLSCHAFT
J Obstet Gynaecol Br Commonw . . JOURNAL OF OBSTETRICS AND GYNAECOLOGY OF THE BRITISH COMMONWEALTH
J OCCUP MED . . . . . JOURNAL OF OCCUPATIONAL MEDICINE
J Ocean Technol . . . JOURNAL OF OCEAN TECHNOLOGY
JOEAI . . . . JAHRESHEFTE DES OESTERREICHISCHEN ARCHAEOLOGISCHEN INSTITUTS IN WIEN
J of Phys B (At Mol Phys) . . JOURNAL OF PHYSICS B (ATOMIC AND MOLECULAR PHYSICS)
John Dewey Soc Yrbk . . JOHN DEWEY SOCIETY. YEARBOOK
John Herron Art Inst Bul . . JOHN HERRON ART INSTITUTE. INDIANAPOLIS. BULLETIN
John Marshall J . . . . JOHN MARSHALL JOURNAL OF PRACTICE AND PROCEDURE
John Rylands Lib Bul . . JOHN RYLANDS LIBRARY BULLETIN
JOHNS H MED . . . . . JOHNS HOPKINS MEDICAL JOURNAL
Johns Hopkins Univ Stud . . JOHNS HOPKINS UNIVERSITY STUDIES IN HISTORICAL AND POLITICAL SCIENCE
Johns H U Stud . . . . JOHNS HOPKINS UNIVERSITY STUDIES IN HISTORICAL AND POLITICAL SCIENCE
JOHPER . . . . JOURNAL OF HEALTH, PHYSICAL EDUCATION AND RECREATION
JoHS . . . . JOURNAL OF HELLENIC STUDIES
JOIB . . . . JOURNAL OF THE ORIENTAL INSTITUTE (BARODA)
J OIL COL C . . . . JOURNAL OF THE OIL AND COLOUR CHEMISTS ASSOCIATION
Joint Automat Contr Conf Prepr Tech Pap . . JOINT AUTOMATIC CONTROL CONFERENCE. PREPRINTS OF TECHNICAL
PAPERS
JOL . . . . JOURNAL OF ORIENTAL LITERATURE
JOMV . . . . JAHRBUCH DES OBEROESTERREICHISCHEN MUSEALVEREINS
JOMV . . . . JAHRBUCH DES VEREINS FUER LANDESKUNDE UND HEIMATPFLEGE IM GAU OBERDONAU
J Oper Res Soc Jap . . JOURNAL OF THE OPERATIONS RESEARCH SOCIETY OF JAPAN
J OP RES SO . . . . JOURNAL OF THE OPERATIONS RESEARCH SOCIETY OF JAPAN
J OPTIM TH . . . . JOURNAL OF OPTIMIZATION THEORY AND APPLICATIONS
J Optim Theory Appl . . JOURNAL OF OPTIMIZATION THEORY AND APPLICATIONS
J OPT SOC . . . . JOURNAL OF THE OPTICAL SOCIETY OF AMERICA
J Opt Soc Am . . . . . . JOURNAL OF THE OPTICAL SOCIETY OF AMERICA
JOR . . . . JOURNAL OF ORIENTAL RESEARCH
J ORAL SURG . . . . . . JOURNAL OF ORAL SURGERY
J Org Chem . . . . . . JOURNAL OF ORGANIC CHEMISTRY
J ORGMET CH . . . . . JOURNAL OF ORGANOMETALLIC CHEMISTRY
JOS . . . . JEZYKI OBCE W SZKOLE
J OTTO RANK . . . . . JOURNAL OF THE OTTO RANK ASSOCIATION
Jour Acoust Soc . . . . JOURNAL OF THE ACOUSTICAL SOCIETY OF AMERICA
Jour Aesthetics and Art Crit . . JOURNAL OF AESTHETICS AND ART CRITICISM
Jour Am Folklore . . . JOURNAL OF AMERICAN FOLKLORE
Jour Am Inst Archit . . JOURNAL OF THE AMERICAN INSTITUTE OF ARCHITECTURE
Jour Am Studies . . . JOURNAL OF AMERICAN STUDIES
Jour Brit Studies . . . JOURNAL OF BRITISH STUDIES
Jour Church and State . . JOURNAL OF CHURCH AND STATE
Jour Conflict Resolution . . JOURNAL OF CONFLICT RESOLUTION
Jour Contemp Hist . . JOURNAL OF CONTEMPORARY HISTORY
Jour Crim Law . . . . . JOURNAL OF CRIMINAL LAW, CRIMINOLOGY AND POLICE SCIENCE
Jour Devel Areas . . . JOURNAL OF DEVELOPMENTAL AREAS
Jour Eccl Hist . . . . . JOURNAL OF ECCLESIASTICAL HISTORY
Jour Econ and Bus Hist . . JOURNAL OF ECONOMIC AND BUSINESS HISTORY
Jour Econ Hist . . . . . JOURNAL OF ECONOMIC HISTORY

Jour Farm Hist . . . . . JOURNAL OF FARM HISTORY
Jour Folklore Inst . . JOURNAL OF THE FOLKLORE INSTITUTE
Jour f Psychol u Neurol . . JOURNAL FUER PSYCHOLOGIE UND NEUROLOGIE
Jour Hist Ideas . . . . JOURNAL OF THE HISTORY OF IDEAS
Jour Hist Med . . . . . JOURNAL OF THE HISTORY OF MEDICINE
Jour Hist Phil . . . . . JOURNAL OF THE HISTORY OF PHILOSOPHY
Jour Human Rel . . . . JOURNAL OF HUMAN RELATIONS
Jour Inter-Am Studies . . JOURNAL OF INTER-AMERICAN STUDIES AND WORLD AFFAIRS
Jour Land Public Utility Econ . . JOURNAL OF LAND AND PUBLIC UTILITY ECONOMICS
Jour Law and Econ . . JOURNAL OF LAW AND ECONOMIC DEVELOPMENT
Jour Legal Ed . . . . . . JOURNAL OF LEGAL EDUATION
Jour Lib Hist . . . . . . JOURNAL OF LIBRARY HISTORY
Jour Miss Hist . . . . . JOURNAL OF MISSISSIPPI HISTORY
Jour Mod Hist . . . . . JOURNAL OF MODERN HISTORY
Journal Cork Hist Soc . . JOURNAL OF THE CORK HISTORICAL AND ARCHAEOLOGICAL SOCIETY
Journal Greater India Soc . . JOURNAL OF THE GREATER INDIA SOCIETY
Journal Gujarat Research Soc . . JOURNAL OF THE GUJARAT RESEARCH SOCIETY
Journal Sadul Rajasthani Research Inst . . JOURNAL OF THE SADUL RAJASTHANI RESEARCH INSTITUTE
Journal Soc Antiq . . . JOURNAL OF THE ROYAL SOCIETY OF ANTIQUARIES OF IRELAND
Journal Soc Finno-Ougr . . JOURNAL DE LA SOCIETE FINNO-OUGRIENNE
Journ Hist Behavioral Sci . . JOURNAL OF THE HISTORY OF THE BEHAVIORAL SCIENCES
JOURN Q . . . . JOURNALISM QUARTERLY
Jour of Folklore Inst . . FOLKLORE INSTITUTE JOURNAL
Jour of Indian Art and Ind . . JOURNAL OF INDIAN ART AND INDUSTRY
Jour of Int Affairs . . JOURNAL OF INTERNATIONAL AFFAIRS
Jour of Relig . . . . . . JOURNAL OF RELIGION
Jour of Soc Issues . . JOURNAL OF SOCIAL ISSUES
Jour of West . . . . . . JOURNAL OF THE WEST
Jour Pac Hist . . . . . . JOURNAL OF PACIFIC HISTORY
Jour Philos . . . . JOURNAL OF PHILOSOPHY
Jour Pol Econ . . . . . . JOURNAL OF POLITICAL ECONOMY
Jour Politics . . . . . . JOURNAL OF POLITICS
Jour Presby Hist . . . JOURNAL OF PRESBYTERIAN HISTORY
Jour Pub Law . . . . . . JOURNAL OF PUBLIC LAW
Jour Relig Hist . . . . . JOURNAL OF RELIGIOUS HISTORY
Jour Soc Hist . . . . . . JOURNAL OF SOCIAL HISTORY
Jour Society Archit Historians . . JOURNAL OF THE SOCIETY OF ARCHITECTURAL HISTORIANS
Jour Soc Philos . . . . JOURNAL OF SOCIAL PHILOSOPHY
Jour Soc Sci . . . . . . JOURNAL OF SOCIAL SCIENCES
Jour Speech Disorders . . JOURNAL OF SPEECH DISORDERS
JOV . . . . JAHRBUCH DES OESTERREICHISCHEN VOLKSLIEDWERKES
JOV . . . . JAHRBUCH FUER OSTDEUTSCHE VOLKSKUNDE
JP . . . . JAHRBUCH FUER PHILOLOGIE
JP . . . . JEZKY POLSKI
JP . . . . JOURNAL DE PSYCHOLOGIE NORMALE ET PATHOLOGIQUE
JP . . . . JOURNAL OF PHILOSOPHY
JP . . . . JOURNAL OF POLITICS
J Pac Hist . . . . JOURNAL OF PACIFIC HISTORY
J PAINT TEC . . . . . . JOURNAL OF PAINT TECHNOLOGY
J Paleont . . . . JOURNAL OF PALEONTOLOGY
J PALES STU . . . . . . JOURNAL OF PALESTINE STUDIES

J PARAPSYCH. . . . . JOURNAL OF PARAPSYCHOLOGY
J PARASITOL. . . . . . JOURNAL OF PARASITOLOGY
J Past Care. . . . . . . JOURNAL OF PASTORAL CARE
J Past Coun. . . . . . . JOURNAL OF PASTORAL COUNSELING
J PATHOLOGY. . . . . JOURNAL OF PATHOLOGY
J PAT OF SO. . . . . . JOURNAL OF THE PATENT OFFICE SOCIETY
JPB. . . . . JOURNAL DES POETES (BRUSSELS)
JPC. . . . . JOURNAL OF POPULAR CULTURE
JPE. . . . . JOURNAL OF POLITICAL ECONOMY
J Peace Res. . . . . . . JOURNAL OF PEACE RESEARCH
J PEDIAT. . . . . JOURNAL OF PEDIATRICS
J PED SURG. . . . . . . JOURNAL OF PEDIATRIC SURGERY
JPer. . . . . JOURNAL OF PERSONALITY
J PERIODONT. . . . . JOURNAL OF PERIODONTOLOGY
J PERIOD RE. . . . . . JOURNAL OF PERIODONTAL RESEARCH
J Perm Way Instn. . PERMANENT WAY INSTITUTION JOURNAL
JPers. . . . . JOURNAL OF PERSONALITY
J PERS ASSE. . . . . . . JOURNAL OF PERSONALITY ASSESSMENT
J PERSONAL. . . . . . JOURNAL OF PERSONALITY
J PERS SOC. . . . . . . JOURNAL OF PERSONALITY AND SOCIAL PSYCHOLOGY
J Pers Soc Psychol. . JOURNAL OF PERSONALITY AND SOCIAL PSYCHOLOGY
J Petrol. . . . . JOURNAL OF PETROLOGY
J PETRO TEC. . . . . . JOURNAL OF PETROLEUM TECHNOLOGY
J Pet Tech. . . . . JOURNAL OF PETROLEUM TECHNOLOGY
JPh. . . . . JOURNAL OF PHILOSOPHY
JPh. . . . . JOURNAL OF PHONETICS
J PHAR BIOP. . . . . . JOURNAL OF PHARMACOKINETICS AND BIOPHARMACEUTICS
J PHARMACOL. . . . . JOURNAL DE PHARMACOLOGIE
J PHARM EXP. . . . . JOURNAL OF PHARMACOLOGY AND EXPERIMENTAL THERAPEUTICS
J PHARM PHA. . . . . JOURNAL OF PHARMACY AND PHARMACOLOGY
J PHARM SCI. . . . . . JOURNAL OF PHARMACEUTICAL SCIENCES
J PHENOMEN. . . . . . JOURNAL OF PHENOMENOLOGICAL PSYCHOLOGY
J Phil. . . . . JOURNAL OF PHILOSOPHY
J Phil Log. . . . . JOURNAL OF PHILOSOPHICAL LOGIC
J Philos. . . . . JOURNAL OF PHILOSOPHY
J PHILOS LO. . . . . . JOURNAL OF PHILOSOPHICAL LOGIC
J Phil Sport. . . . . . . JOURNAL OF THE PHILOSOPHY OF SPORT
J PHOTOCHEM. . . . . JOURNAL OF PHOTOCHEMISTRY
J Photogr Sci. . . . . . JOURNAL OF PHOTOGRAPHIC SCIENCE
J PHOT SCI. . . . . . . JOURNAL OF PHOTOGRAPHIC SCIENCE
JPHS. . . . . JOURNAL OF THE PRESBYTERIAN HISTORICAL SOCIETY
JPhV. . . . . JAHRESBERICHT DES PHILOLOGISCHEN VEREINS
J PHYCOLOGY. . . . . JOURNAL OF PHYCOLOGY
J Phys A (Math Nucl Gen). . JOURNAL PHYSICS. A (MATHEMATICAL, NUCLEAR AND GENERAL)
J Phys & Colloid Chem. . JOURNAL OF PHYSICAL AND COLLOID CHEMISTRY
J PHYS B. . . . . JOURNAL OF PHYSICS. B (ATOMIC AND MOLECULAR PHYSICS)
J PHYS C. . . . . JOURNAL OF PHYSICS. C (SOLID STATE PHYSICS)
J Phys Chem. . . . . . JOURNAL OF PHYSICAL CHEMISTRY
J Phys Chem Solids. . JOURNAL OF PHYSICS AND CHEMISTRY OF SOLIDS
J PHYS CH S. . . . . . JOURNAL OF PHYSICS AND CHEMISTRY OF SOLIDS
J Phys D (Appl Phys). . JOURNAL OF PHYSICS. D (APPLIED PHYSICS)

J PHYS E . . . . JOURNAL OF PHYSICS. E (SCIENTIFIC INSTRUMENTS)
J Phys Ed . . . . JOURNAL OF PHYSICAL EDUCATION
J PHYS F . . . . JOURNAL OF PHYSICS. F (METAL PHYSICS)
J PHYS G-NU . . . . . . JOURNAL OF PHYSICS. G (NUCLEAR PHYSICS)
J PHYSIQUE . . . . JOURNAL DE PHYSIQUE
J PHYS JAP . . . . JOURNAL OF THE PHYSICAL SOCIETY OF JAPAN
J PHYS LETT . . . . . . JOURNAL DE PHYSIQUE LETTRES
J PHYSL LON . . . . . . JOURNAL OF PHYSIOLOGY (LONDON)
J PHYSL PAR . . . . . . JOURNAL DE PHYSIOLOGIE (PARIS)
J PHYS OCEA . . . . . . JOURNAL OF PHYSICAL OCEANOGRAPHY
J Phys (Paris) . . . . . JOURNAL DE PHYSIQUE (PARIS)
J Phys (Paris) Colloq . . JOURNAL DE PHYSIQUE (PARIS) COLLOQUE
J Phys Soc Jap . . . . . JOURNAL OF THE PHYSICAL SOCIETY OF JAPAN
JPKS . . . . JAHRBUCH DES PREUSSISCHEN KUNSTSAMMLUNGEN
J P L . . . . JOURNAL OF PLANNING LAW
J PLASMA PH . . . . . JOURNAL OF PLASMA PHYSICS
JPL Q Tech Rev . . . . JPL QUARTERLY TECHNICAL REVIEW (JET PROPULSION LABORATORY, PASADENA CALIFORNIA)
JPNP . . . . JOURNAL DE PSYCHOLOGIE NORMALE ET PATHOLOGIQUE
JPol . . . . JEZYK POLSKI
JPol . . . . JOURNAL OF POLITICS
J Pol Econ . . . . JOURNAL OF POLITICAL ECONOMY
J Police Sci Adm . . . JOURNAL OF POLICE SCIENCE AND ADMINISTRATION
J POLIC SCI . . . . JOURNAL OF POLICE SCIENCE AND ADMINISTRATION
J POLIT . . . . JOURNAL OF POLITICS
J POLIT EC . . . . JOURNAL OF POLITICAL ECONOMY
J POLIT MIL . . . . JOURNAL OF POLITICAL AND MILITARY SOCIOLOGY
J POL SCI C . . . . JOURNAL OF POLYMER SCIENCE. PART C. POLYMER SYMPOSIA
J POL SC PC . . . . . . JOURNAL OF POLYMER SCIENCE. POLYMER CHEMISTRY EDITION
J POL SC PL . . . . . . JOURNAL OF POLYMER SCIENCE. POLYMER LETTERS EDITION
J POL SC PP . . . . . . JOURNAL OF POLYMER SCIENCE. POLYMER PHYSICS EDITION
J Polym Sci Part A-1: Polym Chem . . JOURNAL OF POLYMER SCIENCE. PART A-1: POLYMER CHEMISTRY
J Polym Sci Part A-2: Polym Phys . . JOURNAL OF POLYMER SCIENCE. PART A-2: POLYMER PHYSICS
J Polym Sci Part B: Polym Lett . . JOURNAL OF POLYMER SCIENCE. PART B: POLYMER LETTERS
J Polym Sci Part C: Polym Symp . . JOURNAL OF POLYMER SCIENCE. PART C: POLYMER SYMPOSIA
J Polym Sci Part D: Macromol Rev . . JOURNAL OF POLYMER SCIENCE. PART D: MACROMOLECULAR REVIEWS
J Polym Sci Polym Chem Ed . . JOURNAL OF POLYMER SCIENCE. POLYMER CHEMISTRY EDITION
J POLYNESIA . . . . . . JOURNAL OF THE POLYNESIAN SOCIETY
J Pomology . . . . JOURNAL OF POMOLOGY AND HORTICULTURAL SCIENCE
J Pop Cult . . . . JOURNAL OF POPULAR CULTURE
JPOS . . . . JOURNAL OF THE PALESTINE ORIENTAL SOCIETY
J POS . . . . JOURNAL OF THE PATENT OFFICE SOCIETY
J POWER-ASC . . . . . JOURNAL OF THE POWER DIVISION-ASCE
JPR . . . . JOURNAL OF PSYCHOLINGUISTIC RESEARCH
J PRAK CHEM . . . . . JOURNAL FUER PRAKTISCHE CHEMIE
J PRE CONCR . . . . . . JOURNAL PRESTRESSED CONCRETE INSTITUTE
J Pres H . . . . JOURNAL OF PRESBYTERIAN HISTORY
J Proc Inst Rd Transp Engrs . . JOURNAL AND PROCEEDINGS OF THE INSTITUTE OF ROAD TRANSPORT ENGINEERS
J Proc Roy Soc N S W . . JOURNAL AND PROCEEDINGS OF THE ROYAL SOCIETY OF NEW SOUTH WALES
J Project Techniques . . JOURNAL OF PROJECTIVE TECHNIQUES AND PERSONALITY ASSESSMENT
J PROS DENT . . . . . . JOURNAL OF PROSTHETIC DENTISTRY

J PROTOZOOL.... JOURNAL OF PROTOZOOLOGY
JPs............. JOURNAL DE PSYCHOLOGIE
JPs............. JOURNAL OF PSYCHOLOGY
JPS............. JOURNAL OF THE POLYNESIAN SOCIETY
JPsNP.......... JOURNAL DE PSYCHOLOGIE NORMALE ET PATHOLOGIQUE
JPSP........... JOURNAL OF PERSONALITY AND SOCIAL PSYCHOLOGY
JPST........... JAHRBUCH FUER PHILOSOPHIE UND SPEKULATIVE THEOLOGIE
JPsy........... JOURNAL OF PSYCHOLOGY
JPsych......... JOURNAL DE PSYCHOLOGIE NORMALE ET PATHOLOGIQUE
J Psychedel Drugs.. JOURNAL OF PSYCHEDELIC DRUGS
J PSYCH LAW..... JOURNAL OF PSYCHIATRY AND LAW
J PSYCHOL....... JOURNAL OF PSYCHOLOGY
J PSYCHOLIN...... JOURNAL OF PSYCHOLINGUISTIC RESEARCH
J Psychol u Neurol.. JOURNAL FUER PSYCHOLOGIE UND NEUROLOGIE
J PSYCHOSOM..... JOURNAL OF PSYCHOSOMATIC RESEARCH
J PSYCH RES...... JOURNAL OF PSYCHIATRIC RESEARCH
J Psych Th....... JOURNAL OF PSYCHOLOGY AND THEOLOGY
JPsyR.......... JOURNAL OF PSYCHOLINGUISTIC RESEARCH
JPT............ JAHRBUCH FUER PHILOSOPHIE UND SPEKULATIVE THEOLOGIE
JPT J Pet Technol.. JPT, JOURNAL OF PETROLEUM TECHNOLOGY
J Pub L.......... JOURNAL OF PUBLIC LAW
JQ............. JOURNALISM QUARTERLY
JQR........... JEWISH QUARTERLY REVIEW
J Qual Technol..... JOURNAL OF QUALITY TECHNOLOGY
J QUAN SPEC...... JOURNAL OF QUANTITATIVE SPECTROSCOPY AND RADIATIVE TRANSFER
JR............. JEZYK ROSYJSKI
JR............. JOURNAL OF RELIGION
J RAD CHEM...... JOURNAL OF RADIOANALYTICAL CHEMISTRY
J RADIOL........ JOURNAL DE RADIOLOGIE D'ELECTROLOGIE ET DE MEDECINE NUCLEAIRE
J Radio Res Lab.... JOURNAL OF THE RADIO RESEARCH LABORATORIES (JAPAN)
J RAD RES L....... JOURNAL OF THE RADIO RESEARCH LABORATORIES (JAPAN)
J RAMAN SP...... JOURNAL OF RAMAN SPECTROSCOPY
J RANGE MAN..... JOURNAL OF RANGE MANAGEMENT
JRAS........... JOURNAL OF THE ROYAL ASIATIC SOCIETY OF GREAT BRITAIN AND IRELAND
JRASBengal....... JOURNAL OF THE ROYAL ASIATIC SOCIETY OF BENGAL
JRASM.......... JOURNAL OF THE ROYAL ASIATIC SOCIETY, MALAYAN BRANCH
Jr Bkshelf........ JUNIOR BOOKSHELF
Jr Coll J......... JUNIOR COLLEGE JOURNAL
Jr Coll Jnl........ JUNIOR COLLEGE JOURNAL
JRD............ JAHRBUCH DER RHEINISCHEN DENKMALPFLEGE
JRDP........... JAHRBUCH DER RHEINISCHEN DENKMALPFLEGE
J Read.......... JOURNAL OF READING
J READ BEH....... JOURNAL OF READING BEHAVIOR
J Refrig......... JOURNAL OF REFRIGERATION
J REG SCI........ JOURNAL OF REGIONAL SCIENCE
J REHABIL........ JOURNAL OF REHABILITATION
J REHABIL D...... JOURNAL OF REHABILITATION OF THE DEAF
J REIN MATH...... JOURNAL FUER DIE REINE UND ANGEWANDTE MATHEMATIK
J Rel........... JOURNAL OF RELIGION
J Rel Africa....... JOURNAL OF RELIGION IN AFRICA
J Rel Ethics....... JOURNAL OF RELIGIOUS ETHICS

J Rel H . . . . JOURNAL OF RELIGIOUS HISTORY
J Rel Health . . . . . . JOURNAL OF RELIGION AND HEALTH
J Relig . . . . JOURNAL OF RELIGION
J Relig Ethics . . . . . . JOURNAL OF RELIGIOUS ETHICS
J Rel Thot . . . . JOURNAL OF RELIGIOUS THOUGHT
J Remote Sensing . . JOURNAL OF REMOTE SENSING
J Ren & Bar Mus . . . JOURNAL OF RENAISSANCE AND BAROQUE MUSIC
J Reprd & Fert . . . . . JOURNAL OF REPRODUCTION AND FERTILITY
J REPR FERT . . . . . . JOURNAL OF REPRODUCTION AND FERTILITY
J REPRO MED . . . . . JOURNAL OF REPRODUCTIVE MEDICINE FOR THE OBSTETRICIAN AND GYNECOLOGIST
J Res & Devel Educ . JOURNAL OF RESEARCH AND DEVELOPMENT IN EDUCATION
J RES CRIME . . . . . . JOURNAL OF RESEARCH IN CRIME AND DELINQUENCY
J RES DEV E . . . . JOURNAL OF RESEARCH AND DEVELOPMENT IN EDUCATION
J Res Develop Educ . JOURNAL OF RESEARCH AND DEVELOPMENT IN EDUCATION
J Res Math Educ . . . JOURNAL FOR RESEARCH IN MATHEMATICS EDUCATION
J Res Mus Ed . . . . . . JOURNAL OF RESEARCH IN MUSIC EDUCATION
J RES MUSIC . . . . . . JOURNAL OF RESEARCH IN MUSIC EDUCATION
J Res Nat Bur Stand . JOURNAL OF RESEARCH OF THE NATIONAL BUREAU OF STANDARDS
J Res Nat Bur Stand Sect A Phys Chem . . JOURNAL OF RESEARCH OF THE NATIONAL BUREAU OF STANDARDS. SECTION A. PHYSICS AND CHEMISTRY
J Res Nat Bur Stand Sect B Math Sci . . JOURNAL OF RESEARCH OF THE NATIONAL BUREAU OF STANDARDS. SECTION B. MATHEMATICAL SCIENCES
J Res Nat Bur Stand Sect C Eng Instrum . . JOURNAL OF RESEARCH OF THE NATIONAL BUREAU OF STANDARDS. SECTION C. ENGINEERING AND INSTRUMENTATION
J RES NBS A . . . . JOURNAL OF RESEARCH OF THE NATIONAL BUREAU OF STANDARDS. SECTION A. PHYSICS AND CHEMISTRY
J RES NBS B . . . . JOURNAL OF RESEARCH OF THE NATIONAL BUREAU OF STANDARDS. SECTION B. MATHEMATICAL SCIENCES
J RES PERS . . . . JOURNAL OF RESEARCH IN PERSONALITY
J RES SCI TEACH . . . JOURNAL OF RESEARCH IN SCIENCE TEACHING
J Res US Geol Surv . . JOURNAL OF RESEARCH OF THE UNITED STATES GEOLOGICAL SURVEY
J RES US GS . . . . JOURNAL OF RESEARCH OF THE US GEOLOGICAL SURVEY
J Retail . . . . JOURNAL OF RETAILING
J RETIC SOC . . . . JOURNAL OF THE RETICULOENDOTHELIAL SOCIETY
JRG . . . . JAHRBUCH DER RAABE-GESELLSCHAFT
JRGZ . . . . JAHRBUCH DES ROEMISCH-GERMANISCHEN ZENTRALMUSEUMS (MAINZ)
JRGZMainz . . . . JAHRBUCH DES ROEMISCH-GERMANISCHEN ZENTRALMUSEUMS (MAINZ)
JRH . . . . JOURNAL OF RELIGIOUS HISTORY
J RHEUMATOL . . . . JOURNAL OF RHEUMATOLOGY
J R Inst Br Archit . . . ROYAL INSTITUTE OF BRITISH ARCHITECTS JOURNAL
J RISK INS . . . . JOURNAL OF RISK AND INSURANCE
JRLB . . . . JOHN RYLANDS LIBRARY BULLETIN
Jr Lib . . . . JUNIOR LIBRARIES
J Rly Div Instn Mech Engrs . . INSTITUTION OF MECHANICAL ENGINEERS RAILWAY DIVISION. JOURNAL
JRME . . . . JOURNAL OF RESEARCH IN MUSIC EDUCATION
J Roman Stud . . . . . JOURNAL OF ROMAN STUDIES
J Rom Stud . . . . JOURNAL OF ROMAN STUDIES
J ROY AGR S . . . . . . JOURNAL OF THE ROYAL AGRICULTURAL SOCIETY OF ENGLAND
J ROY ASTRO . . . . . . JOURNAL OF THE ROYAL ASTRONOMICAL SOCIETY OF CANADA
J ROY STA A . . . . . . JOURNAL OF THE ROYAL STATISTICAL SOCIETY. SERIES A. GENERAL
J ROY STA B . . . . . . JOURNAL OF THE ROYAL STATISTICAL SOCIETY. SERIES B. METHODOLOGICAL

```
J ROY STA C . . . . . .  JOURNAL OF THE ROYAL STATISTICAL SOCIETY. SERIES C. APPLIED STATISTICS
J Roy Statis . . . . . . .  JOURNAL OF THE ROYAL STATISTICAL SOCIETY
JRS . . . . . . . . . . . . .  JOURNAL OF REGIONAL SCIENCE
JRS . . . . . . . . . . . .  JOURNAL OF ROMAN STUDIES
JRS . . . . . . . . . . . .  JOURNAL OF RUSSIAN STUDIES
JRSAI . . . . . . . . . .  JOURNAL OF THE ROYAL SOCIETY OF ANTIQUARIES OF IRELAND
JRSAntl . . . . . . . . .  JOURNAL OF THE ROYAL SOCIETY OF ANTIQUARIES OF IRELAND
J RS NZ . . . . . . . . .  JOURNAL OF THE ROYAL SOCIETY OF NEW ZEALAND
J R Soc Hlth . . . . . .  JOURNAL OF THE ROYAL SOCIETY OF HEALTH
JRSS . . . . . . . . . . .  JOURNAL OF THE ROYAL STATISTICAL SOCIETY
JRT . . . . . . . . . . . .  JOURNAL OF RELIGIOUS THOUGHT
JR Telev Soc . . . . . .  JOURNAL OF THE ROYAL TELEVISION SOCIETY
JRUL . . . . . . . . . . .  JOURNAL OF THE RUTGERS UNIVERSITY LIBRARY
J Rural Educ . . . . . .  JOURNAL OF RURAL EDUCATION
JRuS . . . . . . . . . . .  JOURNAL OF RUSSIAN STUDIES
JS . . . . . . . . . . . . .  JAZYKOVEDNY STUDIE
JS . . . . . . . . . . . . .  JAZYKOVEDNY SBORNIK
JS . . . . . . . . . . . . .  JOURNAL DES SAVANTS
JSA . . . . . . . . . . . .  JOURNAL DE LA SOCIETE DES AMERICANISTES
J SA CHEM I . . . . . .  JOURNAL OF THE SOUTH AFRICAN CHEMICAL INSTITUTE
JSAf . . . . . . . . . . . .  JOURNAL DE LA SOCIETE DES AFRICANISTES
J SAFE RES . . . . . . .  JOURNAL OF SAFETY RESEARCH
JSAfr . . . . . . . . . . .  JOURNAL DE LA SOCIETE DES AFRICANISTES
J S Afr Inst Mining Met . .  JOURNAL OF THE SOUTH AFRICAN INSTITUTE MINING AND METALLURGY
JSAH . . . . . . . . . . .  JOURNAL OF THE SOCIETY OF ARCHITECTURAL HISTORIANS
J SA I MIN . . . . . . .  JOURNAL OF THE SOUTH AFRICAN INSTITUTE OF MINING AND METALLURGY
JSAm . . . . . . . . . . .  JOURNAL DE LA SOCIETE DES AMERICANISTES DE PARIS
JSAmP . . . . . . . . . .  JOURNAL DE LA SOCIETE DES AMERICANISTES DE PARIS
JSAP . . . . . . . . . . .  JOURNAL DE LA SOCIETE DES AMERICANISTES DE PARIS
J Savants . . . . . . . .  JOURNAL DES SAVANTS
J SCH HEALT . . . . . .  JOURNAL OF SCHOOL HEALTH
J SCH PSYCH . . . . . .  JOURNAL OF SCHOOL PSYCHOLOGY
J Sci . . . . . . . . . . . .  JOURNAL OF SCIENCE
J Sci and Technol . . .  JOURNAL OF SCIENCE AND TECHNOLOGY
J Scient Instrum . . .  JOURNAL OF SCIENTIFIC INSTRUMENTS
J Sci Fd Agric . . . . . .  JOURNAL OF SCIENCE OF FOOD AND AGRICULTURE
J SCI FOOD . . . . . . .  JOURNAL OF SCIENCE OF FOOD AND AGRICULTURE
J SCI IND R . . . . . . .  JOURNAL OF SCIENTIFIC AND INDUSTRIAL RESEARCH
J Sci Instr . . . . . . . .  JOURNAL OF SCIENTIFIC INSTRUMENTS
J SCI LAB D . . . . . . .  JOURNAL OF THE SCIENTIFIC LABORATORIES-DENISON UNIVERSITY
J SCI ST RE . . . . . . .  JOURNAL FOR THE SCIENTIFIC STUDY OF RELIGION
J Sci Tech . . . . . . . .  JOURNAL OF SCIENCE AND TECHNOLOGY
J S COSM CH . . . . . .  JOURNAL OF THE SOCIETY OF COSMETIC CHEMISTS
J S DYE COL . . . . . . .  JOURNAL OF THE SOCIETY OF DRYERS AND COLOURISTS
J SE Asian Hist . . . . .  JOURNAL OF SOUTHEAST ASIAN HISTORY
J SE ASIA S . . . . . . .  JOURNAL OF SOUTHEAST ASIAN STUDIES
J Sec Ed . . . . . . . . .  JOURNAL OF SECONDARY EDUCATION
J Sed Petrol . . . . . . .  JOURNAL OF SEDIMENTARY PETROLOGY
J Sem St . . . . . . . . .  JOURNAL OF SEMITIC STUDIES
J SEX RES . . . . . . . .  JOURNAL OF SEX RESEARCH
JSFOu . . . . . . . . . . .  JOURNAL DE LA SOCIETE FINNO-OUGRIENNE
```

JSFWUB . . . . JAHRBUCH DER SCHLESISCHEN FRIEDRICH-WILHELM-UNIVERSITAET ZU BRESLAU
JSG . . . . JAHRBUCH DER SCHILLER-GESELLSCHAFT
JSGLL . . . . JAPANESE STUDIES IN GERMAN LANGUAGE AND LITERATURE
JSGU . . . . JAHRBUCH DER SCHWEIZERISCHEN GESELLSCHAFT FUER URGESCHICHTE
JSH . . . . JIHOCESKY SBORNIK HISTORICKY
JSH . . . . JOURNAL OF SOUTHERN HISTORY
JSHD . . . . JOURNAL OF SPEECH AND HEARING DISORDERS
J Sheffield Univ Met Soc . . JOURNAL OF THE SHEFFIELD UNIVERSITY METALLURGICAL SOCIETY
J Ship Res . . . . JOURNAL OF SHIP RESEARCH
JSHR . . . . JOURNAL OF SPEECH AND HEARING RESEARCH
J-S H Sch Clearing House . . JUNIOR-SENIOR HIGH SCHOOL CLEARING HOUSE
JSI . . . . JEZIK IN SLOVSTVO
JSI . . . . JOURNAL OF SOCIAL ISSUES
JSJHS . . . . JOURNAL OF THE SOUTHERN JEWISH HISTORICAL SOCIETY
JSK . . . . JAHRBUCH DER SAMMLUNG KIPPENBERG DUESSELDORF
JslF . . . . JUZNOSLOVENSKI FILOLOG
J SM ANIM P . . . . . . JOURNAL OF SMALL ANIMAL PRACTICE
J SMPTE . . . . JOURNAL OF THE SMPTE (SOCIETY OF MOTION PICTURE AND TELEVISION ENGINEERS)
JSO . . . . JOURNAL DE LA SOCIETE DES OCEANISTES
JSOc . . . . JOURNAL DE LA SOCIETE DES OCEANISTES
J SOC AMER . . . . . . JOURNAL DE LA SOCIETE DES AMERICANISTES
J Soc Arts . . . . JOURNAL OF THE SOCIETY OF ARTS
J Soc Dy Colour . . . . JOURNAL OF THE SOCIETY OF DYERS AND COLOURISTS
J Soc Eng (Lond) . . . JOURNAL OF THE SOCIETY OF ENGINEERS (LONDON)
J Soc Env Engrs . . . . JOURNAL OF THE SOCIETY OF ENVIRONMENTAL ENGINEERS
J Soc Hist . . . . JOURNAL OF SOCIAL HISTORY
J Soc Hygiene . . . . . JOURNAL OF SOCIAL HYGIENE
J Social Casework . . JOURNAL OF SOCIAL CASEWORK
J Social Forces . . . . . JOURNAL OF SOCIAL FORCES
J Social Hyg . . . . . . JOURNAL OF SOCIAL HYGIENE
J Social Psychol . . . . JOURNAL OF SOCIAL PSYCHOLOGY
J SOC ISSUE . . . . JOURNAL OF SOCIAL ISSUES
J Soc Leath Technol Chem . . JOURNAL OF THE SOCIETY OF LEATHER TECHNOLOGISTS AND CHEMISTS
J Soc Leath Trades Chem . . JOURNAL OF THE SOCIETY OF LEATHER TRADES CHEMISTS
J Soc Motion Pict Telev Eng . . JOURNAL OF THE SOCIETY OF MOTION PICTURE AND TELEVISION ENGINEERS
J Soc Phil . . . . JOURNAL OF SOCIAL PHILOSOPHY
J SOC POLIC . . . . . . JOURNAL OF SOCIAL POLICY
J SOC PSYCH . . . . . . JOURNAL OF SOCIAL PSYCHOLOGY
J Soc Pub Teach Law n. s. . . JOURNAL OF THE SOCIETY OF PUBLIC TEACHERS OF LAW. NEW SERIES
J Soc Pub T L . . . . . . JOURNAL OF THE SOCIETY OF PUBLIC TEACHERS OF LAW
J So Hist . . . . JOURNAL OF SOUTHERN HISTORY
J SOIL SCI . . . . JOURNAL OF SOIL SCIENCE
J SOIL WAT . . . . JOURNAL OF SOIL AND WATER CONSERVATION
J SOL CHEM . . . . JOURNAL OF SOLUTION CHEMISTRY
J Solid State Chem . . JOURNAL OF SOLID STATE CHEMISTRY
J SOL ST CH . . . . JOURNAL OF SOLID STATE CHEMISTRY
JSOR . . . . JOURNAL OF THE SOCIETY OF ORIENTAL RESEARCH
J Sound Vib . . . . JOURNAL OF SOUND AND VIBRATION
J SOUTH HIS . . . . . . JOURNAL OF SOUTHERN HISTORY
JSP . . . . JOURNAL OF SOCIAL PSYCHOLOGY
J Spacecr Rockets . . JOURNAL OF SPACECRAFT AND ROCKETS

J SPAC ROCK . . . . . . JOURNAL OF SPACECRAFT AND ROCKETS
J Sp Disorders . . . . . JOURNAL OF SPEECH AND HEARING DISORDERS
J Spec Ed . . . . JOURNAL OF SPECIAL EDUCATION
J Spec Ed Men Retard . . JOURNAL FOR SPECIAL EDUCATORS OF THE MENTALLY RETARDED
J Spec Philos . . . . . . JOURNAL OF THE SPECULATIVE PHILOSOPHY
J Sp Educ . . . . JOURNAL OF SPECIAL EDUCATION
J Sp Educ Men Retard . . JOURNAL FOR SPECIAL EDUCATORS OF THE MENTALLY RETARDED
J Speech & Hear Dis . JOURNAL OF SPEECH AND HEARING DISORDERS
J Speech & Hear Res . . JOURNAL OF SPEECH AND HEARING RESEARCH
J SPEECH D . . . . JOURNAL OF SPEECH AND HEARING DISORDERS
J SPEECH HE . . . . . . JOURNAL OF SPEECH AND HEARING RESEARCH
JSPs . . . . JOURNAL OF SOCIAL PSYCHOLOGY
JSR . . . . JAPAN SCIENCE REVIEW
JSS . . . . JEWISH SOCIAL STUDIES
JSS . . . . JOURNAL OF SEMITIC STUDIES
JSS . . . . JOURNAL OF SIAM SOCIETY
JSS . . . . JOURNAL OF SPANISH STUDIES: TWENTIETH CENTURY
JSSB . . . . JOURNAL OF SIAM SOCIETY (BANGKOK)
JSSR . . . . JOURNAL FOR THE SCIENTIFIC STUDY OF RELIGION
JSSRel . . . . JOURNAL FOR THE SCIENTIFIC STUDY OF RELIGION
J Statis Soc . . . . JOURNAL OF THE STATISTICAL SOCIETY
J STAT PHYS . . . . . . JOURNAL OF STATISTICAL PHYSICS
J STEROID B . . . . . . JOURNAL OF STEROID BIOCHEMISTRY
J St Jud . . . . JOURNAL FOR THE STUDY OF JUDAISM
J STORED PR . . . . . . JOURNAL OF STORED PRODUCTS RESEARCH
J Strain Anal . . . . . . JOURNAL OF STRAIN ANALYSIS
J STRUC MEC . . . . . . JOURNAL OF STRUCTURAL MECHANICS
J STRUCT CH . . . . . . JOURNAL OF STRUCTURAL CHEMISTRY
J STRUCT DI . . . . . . JOURNAL OF THE STRUCTURAL DIVISION. ASCE (AMERICAN SOCIETY OF CIVIL ENGINEERS)
J STRUCT LE . . . . . . JOURNAL OF STRUCTURAL LEARNING
J STUD ALC . . . . JOURNAL OF STUDIES ON ALCOHOL
JSUB . . . . JAHRBUCH DER SCHLESISCHEN FRIEDRICH-WILHELM UNIVERSITAET ZU BRESLAU
J SUBMIC CY . . . . . . JOURNAL OF SUBMICROSCOPIC CYTOLOGY
J SUPRAM ST . . . . . JOURNAL OF SUPRAMOLECULAR STRUCTURE
J SURG RES . . . . JOURNAL OF SURGICAL RESEARCH
J SURV MAPP . . . . . JOURNAL OF THE SURVEYING AND MAPPING DIVISION. ASCE (AMERICAN SOCIETY OF CIVIL ENGINEERS)
J SYMB LOG . . . . . . JOURNAL OF SYMBOLIC LOGIC
J Sym Log . . . . JOURNAL OF SYMBOLIC LOGIC
J SYN ORG J . . . . . . JOURNAL OF SYNTHETIC ORGANIC CHEMISTRY (JAPAN)
J Systems Mgt . . . . . JOURNAL OF SYSTEMS MANAGEMENT
J SYST MAN . . . . . . JOURNAL OF SYSTEMS MANAGEMENT
J Tam S . . . . JOURNAL OF TAMIL STUDIES
J Teach Ed . . . . JOURNAL OF TEACHER EDUCATION
J Technol . . . . JOURNAL OF TECHNOLOGY
J Tech Writ Commun . . JOURNAL OF TECHNICAL WRITING AND COMMUNICATION
J Terramech . . . . . . JOURNAL OF TERRAMECHANICS
J TEST EVAL . . . . . . JOURNAL OF TESTING AND EVALUATION
J Text Inst . . . . JOURNAL OF THE TEXTILE INSTITUTE
J Text Mach Soc Jap . . JOURNAL OF THE TEXTILE MACHINERY SOCIETY OF JAPAN
J Thanatol . . . . JOURNAL OF THANATOLOGY

J THEOR BIO . . . . . . JOURNAL OF THEORETICAL BIOLOGY
J Theor Soc Behav . . JOURNAL FOR THE THEORY OF SOCIAL BEHAVIOR
J THERM ANA . . . . . JOURNAL OF THERMAL ANALYSIS
J THERM BIO . . . . . . JOURNAL OF THERMAL BIOLOGY
J THOR SURG . . . . . JOURNAL OF THORACIC AND CARDIOVASCULAR SURGERY
J Thought . . . . JOURNAL OF THOUGHT
JThS . . . . JOURNAL OF THEOLOGICAL STUDIES
J Th St . . . . JOURNAL OF THEOLOGICAL STUDIES
J TOWN PL I . . . . . . JOURNAL OF TOWN PLANNING INSTITUTE
J TOX ENV H . . . . . . JOURNAL OF TOXICOLOGY AND ENVIRONMENTAL HEALTH
JTR . . . . JOURNAL OF TYPOGRAPHIC RESEARCH
J TRANSP EC . . . . . . JOURNAL OF TRANSPORT ECONOMICS AND POLICY
J TRAUMA . . . . JOURNAL OF TRAUMA
J TROP GEOG . . . . . JOURNAL OF TROPICAL GEOGRAPHY
J TROP MED . . . . . . JOURNAL OF TROPICAL MEDICINE AND HYGIENE
JTS . . . . JOURNAL OF THEOLOGICAL STUDIES
J T S BEHAV . . . . . . JOURNAL FOR THE THEORY OF SOCIAL BEHAVIOR
JUAG . . . . JAHRBUCH DER UNGARISCHEN ARCHAEOLOGISCHEN GESELLSCHAFT
Jud . . . . JUDAISM
Juilliard R . . . . JUILLIARD REVIEW
J ULTRA RES . . . . . . JOURNAL OF ULTRASTRUCTURE RESEARCH
Jun Col J . . . . JUNIOR COLLEGE JOURNAL
Junior Coll J . . . . . . JUNIOR COLLEGE JOURNAL
Junior Inst Eng London J Rec Trans . . JUNIOR INSTITUTION OF ENGINEERS. LONDON. JOURNAL AND RECORD OF
 TRANSACTIONS
J URBAN EC . . . . . . JOURNAL OF URBAN ECONOMICS
J Urban L . . . . JOURNAL OF URBAN LAW
J URBAN PLA . . . . . JOURNAL OF THE URBAN PLANNING AND DEVELOPMENT DIVISION. ASCE (AMERICAN SOCIETY
 OF CIVIL ENGINEERS)
Jurid R . . . . JURIDICAL REVIEW
Jurimetrics . . . . JURIMETRICS JOURNAL
J UROL . . . . JOURNAL OF UROLOGY
J UROL NEPH . . . . . . JOURNAL D'UROLOGIE ET DE NEPHROLOGIE
Just P . . . . JUSTICE OF THE PEACE
JUST SYST J . . . . . . JUSTICE SYSTEM JOURNAL
Juv Ct Judges J . . . . JUVENILE COURT JUDGES JOURNAL
JUVEN JUST . . . . . . JUVENILE JUSTICE
JVA . . . . JAARBOEK DER VEREENIGING AMSTELODANUM
JVA . . . . JAHRBUCH DES VEREINS VON ALTERTUMSFREUNDEN IM RHEINLANDE
J VAC SCI T . . . . . . JOURNAL OF VACUUM SCIENCE AND TECHNOLOGY
J Value Eng . . . . . . JOURNAL OF VALUE ENGINEERING
J Value Inq . . . . . . JOURNAL OF VALUE INQUIRY
JVARh . . . . JAHRBUCH DES VEREINS VON ALTERTUMSFREUNDEN IM RHEINLANDE
JVEG . . . . JAARBERICHT VAN HET VOORAZIATISCHE-EGIPTISCH GEZELSCHAP EX ORIENTE LUX
J Verb Learn . . . . . . JOURNAL OF VERBAL LEARNING AND VERBAL BEHAVIOR
JVF . . . . JAHRBUCH FUER VOLKSLIEDFORSCHUNG
JVH . . . . JAHRBUCH FUER VOLKSKUNDE DER HEIMATVERTRIEBENEN
J VIROLOGY . . . . . . JOURNAL OF VIROLOGY
JVLHOD . . . . JAHRBUCH DES VEREINS FUER LANDESKUNDE UND HEIMATPFLEGE IM GAU OBERDONAU
JVLVB . . . . JOURNAL OF VERBAL LEARNING AND VERBAL BEHAVIOR
JVNS . . . . JAHRBUCH DES VEREINS FUER NIEDERDEUTSCHE SPRACHFORSCHUNG

J VOLUN ACT..... JOURNAL OF VOLUNTARY ACTION RESEARCH
J VOCAT BEH...... JOURNAL OF VOCATIONAL BEHAVIOR
JVSch........... JAHRBUCH DES VEREINS SCHWEIZERISCHER GYMNASIAL-LEHRER
JVWK........... JAHRBUCH DES VEREINS FUER WESTFAELISCHE KIRCHENGESCHICHTE
JWAfrL.......... JOURNAL OF WEST AFRICAN LANGUAGES
JWAG........... JOURNAL OF THE WALTERS ART GALLERY
JWAL........... JOURNAL OF WEST AFRICAN LANGUAGES
J Warburg and Courtauld Inst.. JOURNAL OF THE WARBURG AND COURTAULD INSTITUTES
J Wash Acad Sci.... JOURNAL OF THE WASHINGTON ACADEMY OF SCIENCES
J WATER P C...... JOURNAL WATER POLLUTION CONTROL FEDERATION
J Water Pollut Control Fed.. JOURNAL WATER POLLUTION CONTROL FEDERATION
J WATERWAY..... JOURNAL OF THE WATERWAYS HARBORS AND COASTAL ENGINEERING DIVISION. ASCE
(AMERICAN SOCIETY OF CIVIL ENGINEERS)
JWB........... JAHRBUCH DER WITTHEIT ZU BREMEN
JWBS........... JOURNAL OF THE WELSH BIBLIOGRAPHIC SOCIETY
JWCI........... JOURNAL OF THE WARBURG AND COURTAULD INSTITUTE
J West.......... JOURNAL OF THE WEST
J West Scot Iron Steel Inst.. JOURNAL OF THE WEST OF SCOTLAND IRON AND STEEL INSTITUTE
JWG........... JAHRBUCH FUER WIRTSCHAFTSGESCHICHTE
JWGV........... JAHRBUCH DES WIENER GOETHE-VEREINS
JWH........... JOURNAL OF WORLD HISTORY
JWI............ JOURNAL OF THE WARBURG AND COURTAULD INSTITUTE (LONDON)
JWI............ JOURNAL OF THE WARBURG INSTITUTE
J WILDL MAN..... JOURNAL OF WILDLIFE MANAGEMENT
JWMS.......... JOURNAL OF THE WILLIAM MORRIS SOCIETY
J World Hist...... JOURNAL OF WORLD HISTORY
J WORLD TR...... JOURNAL OF WORLD TRADE LAW
JWS........... JOURNAL OF WESTERN SPEECH
J W Vir Phil Soc.... JOURNAL OF THE WEST VIRGINIA PHILOSOPHICAL SOCIETY
J YOUTH ADO..... JOURNAL OF YOUTH AND ADOLESCENCE
JZ............. JAZYKOVEDNY ZBORNIK
Jz............. JEZYKOZNAWCA
JZ............. JINRUIGAKU ZASSHI (ANTHROPOLOGICAL JOURNAL)
J Zool.......... JOURNAL OF ZOOLOGY

PERIODICAL TITLE ABBREVIATIONS

K

K. . . . . KLIO. BEITRAGE ZUR ALTEN GESCHICHTE
K. . . . . KNJIZEVNOST
K. . . . . KULTUR
KA. . . . . KOREAN AFFAIRS
KA. . . . . KULTURA
KA. . . . . KUNSTMUSEETS AARSSKRIFT
KA. . . . . KYRKOHISTORISK AARSSKRIFT
Kadel R. . . . . KADELPIAN REVIEW
Kaeltetech-Klim. . . . KAELTETECHNIK-KLIMATISIERUNG
KAF. . . . . KLEINASIATISCHE FORSCHUNGEN
KagoBH. . . . . KAGOSHIMA DAIGAKU BUNKA HOKOKU (CULTURAL SCIENCE REPORTS OF KAGOSHIMA
UNIVERSITY)
Kais Akad d Wiss Denksch Philos-Hist Kl. . KAISERLICHE AKADEMIE DER WISSENSCHAFTEN IN WIEN.
PHILOSOPHISCH-HISTORISCHE KLASSE. DENKSCHRIFTEN
Kais Akad d Wissensch Sitzungsb Philos-Hist Klasse. . KAISERLICHE AKADEMIE DER WISSENSCHAFTEN IN WIEN.
PHILOSOPHISCH-HISTORISCHE KLASSE. SITZUNGSBERICHTE
Kais-Deutsch Archaol Inst Jahrb. . KAISERLICH-DEUTSCHES ARCHAOLOGISCHES INSTITUT. JAHRBUCH
KAL. . . . . KYUSHA AMERICAN LITERATURE (FUKUOKA, JAPAN)
KAM. . . . . KAMENA
Kan Acad Sci Trans. . TRANSACTIONS OF THE KANSAS ACADEMY OF SCIENCE
Kan Ag Exp. . . . . . . KANSAS STATE AGRICULTURAL COLLEGE. AGRICULTURAL EXPERIMENT STATION.
PUBLICATIONS
KanazHB. . . . . KANAZAWA DAIGAKU HOBUNGAKUBU RONSHU, BUNGAKUHEN (STUDIES AND ESSAYS BY THE
FACULTY OF LAW AND LITERATURE, KANAZAWA UNIVERSITY, LITERATURE)
KanazJK. . . . . KANAZAWA DAIGAKU KYOYOBU RONSHU JINBUNKAGAKUHEN (STUDIES IN HUMANITIES,
COLLEGE OF LIBERAL ARTS, KANAZAWA UNIVERSITY)
K&K. . . . . KUNST UND KUNSTLER
K&S. . . . . KUNST UND SPRACHE
Kan Hist Quar. . . . . KANSAS HISTORICAL QUARTERLY
Kan Jud Council Bull. . KANSAS JUDICIAL COUNCIL. BULLETIN
Kan Law Rev. . . . . . KANSAS LAW REVIEW
Kan Lib Bull. . . . . . . KANSAS LIBRARY BULLETIN
Kan L Rev. . . . . KANSAS LAW REVIEW
Kano S. . . . . KANO STUDIES (NIGERIA)
KanQ. . . . . KANSAS QUARTERLY
KANSAS BUS TCHR. . KANSAS BUSINESS TEACHER
Kansas Lib Bul. . . . . KANSAS LIBRARY BULLETIN
Kansas R. . . . . KANSAS CITY REVIEW
Kans State Geol Surv Bull. . KANSAS STATE GEOLOGICAL SURVEY. BULLETIN
Kans State Geol Surv Comput Contrib. . KANSAS STATE GEOLOGICAL SURVEY. COMPUTER CONTRIBUTION
Kans State Geol Surv Spec Distrib Publ. . KANSAS STATE GEOLOGICAL SURVEY. SPECIAL DISTRIBUTION
PUBLICATION
Kan State Univ Bull Kans Eng Exp Sta Bull. . KANSAS STATE UNIVERSITY BULLETIN. KANSAS ENGINEERING
EXPERIMENT STATION BULLETIN
Kan State Hist Soc Coll. . KANSAS STATE HISTORICAL SOCIETY. COLLECTIONS
Kan State Univ Inst Syst Des Optim Rep. . KANSAS STATE UNIVERSITY. INSTITUTE FOR SYSTEMS DESIGNS AND
OPTIMIZATION. REPORT
Kans Teach. . . . . . . KANSAS TEACHER AND WESTERN SCHOOL JOURNAL
Kans Univ B Ed. . . . UNIVERSITY OF KANSAS. BULLETIN OF EDUCATION

KantStud . . . . KANT-STUDIEN
Kan Univ Kan Studies Ed . . KANSAS. UNIVERSITY. KANSAS STUDIES IN EDUCATION
KAnz . . . . KUNSTGESCHICHTLICHE ANZEIGEN
Kat . . . . KATHOLIEK
Katal . . . . KATALLAGETE
Kath . . . . KATHOLIEK
KAUT GUM KU . . . . . KAUTSCHUNK UND GUMMI KUNSTSTOFFE
KB . . . . KOMUNIST (BELGRADE)
KBAA . . . . LIELER BEITRAEGE ZUR ANGLISTIK UND AMERIKANISTIK
KBB . . . . KULTURAS BIROJA BILETINS (BULLETIN OF THE CULTURAL BUREAU OF THE AMERICAN
LATVIAN ASSOCIATION IN THE U.S.)
KBDA . . . . KORRESPONDENZBLATT DES GESAMTVEREINS DER DEUTSCHEN GESCHICHTE UND
ALTERTUMSVEREINE
KBKL . . . . KRITISCHE BERICHTE ZUR KUNSTGESCHICHTLICHEN LITERATUR
Kbl . . . . KORRESPONDENZBLATT DES VEREINS FUER NIEDERDEUTSCHE SPRACHFORSCHUNG
KBLG . . . . KRITISCHE BLAETTER ZUR LITERATUR DER GEGENWART
KBP Q . . . . KAPPA BETA PI QUARTERLY
KBR . . . . KEIO BUSINESS REVIEW
KBW . . . . KORRESPONDENZ-BLATT FUER DIE HOEHEREN SCHULEN WUERTTEMBERGS
KC . . . . KRETIKA CHRONIKA
KC . . . . KUNSTCHRONIK
KC PHIL . . . . KANSAS CITY PHILHARMONIC PROGRAM NOTES
KCT . . . . KATHOLIEK CULTUREEL TIJDSCHRIFT
KDF . . . . KOENIGSBERGER DEUTSCHE FORSCHUNGEN
KDPM . . . . KLEINE DEUTSCHE PROSADENKMAELER DES MITTELALTERS
KDVS . . . . KONGELIGE DANSKE VIDENSKABERNES SELSKAB. HISTORISK-FILOSOFISKE MEDDELELSER
(COPENHAGEN)
Keats-Shelley J . . . . KEATS-SHELLEY JOURNAL
KEBR . . . . KOBE ECONOMIC AND BUSINESS REVIEW
KEIO ECON S . . . . . . KEIO ECONOMIC STUDIES
Ke K . . . . KEIRYO KOKUGOGAKU (MATHEMATICAL LINGUISTICS)
KEM KOZLEM . . . . . . KEMIAI KOZLEMENYEK
Kem Teollisuus . . . . KEMIAN TEOLLISUUS
KEM TIDSKR . . . . . . KEMISK TIDSKRIFT
Kenyon R . . . . KENYON REVIEW
Keram Z . . . . KERAMISCHE ZEITSCHRIFT
KerC . . . . KERKYRAIKA CHRONIKA
KerDo . . . . KERYGMA UND DOGMA
Kerntechnik Isotopentech Chem . . KERNTECHNIK, ISOTOPENTECHNIK UND CHEMIE
KES . . . . KEIO ECONOMIC STUDIES
KESS . . . . KARTVELUR ENATA ST'RUKT'URIS SAK'ITXEBI
KFLQ . . . . KENTUCKY FOREIGN LANGUAGE QUARTERLY
KFQ . . . . KEYSTONE FOLKLORE QUARTERLY
KFR . . . . KENTUCKY FOLKLORE RECORD
KFS . . . . KENTUCKY FOLKLORE SERIES
KG . . . . KATHOLISCHE GEDANKE
KGA . . . . KUNSTGESCHICHTLICHE ANZEIGEN
KGAAM . . . . KUNGL GUSTAV ADOLFS AKADEMIENS MINNESBOK
KGH . . . . KANBUM GAKKAI KAIHO (JOURNAL OF THE SINOLOGICAL SOCIETY)
KGKK . . . . KANGAKU KENKYU (SINOLOGICAL STUDIES)
KGKR . . . . KANSAI GAIDAI KENKYU RONSHU (JOURNAL OF THE KANSAI UNIVERSITY OF FOREIGN STUDIES)

KGR . . . . KOBE GAIDAI RONSO (KOBE CITY UNIVERSITY JOURNAL)
KGS . . . . KOELNER GERMANISTISCHE STUDIEN
KGUAS . . . . KWANSEI GAKUIN UNIVERSITY. ANNUAL STUDIES
KH . . . . KWARTALNIK HISTORYCZNY
KHIM FAR ZH . . . . . KHIMIKO-FARMATSEVTICAESKII ZHURNAL
KHIM GETERO . . . . . KHIMIYA GETEROTSIKLICHESKIKH SOEDINENIYA
Khim I Neft Mashinostr . . KHIMICHESKOE I NEFTYANOE MASHINOSTROENIE
Khim i Tekhnol Topliv i Masel . . KHIMIYA I TEKHNOLOGIYA TOPLIV I MASEL
KHIM PRIR S . . . . . . KHIMIYA PRIRODNYIKH SOEDINENII
Khim Prom . . . . KHIMICHESKAYA PROMYSHLENNOST
KHQ . . . . KANSAS HISTORICAL QUARTERLY
KHS . . . . KENTUCKY HISTORICAL SOCIETY. REGISTER
KHSR . . . . KENTUCKY HISTORICAL SOCIETY. REGISTER
KHVSU . . . . KUNGL. HUMANISTIKA VETENSKAPSSAMFUNDET I UPPSALA
Ki . . . . KIERUNKI
KIDNEY INT . . . . . . KIDNEY INTERNATIONAL
Kie . . . . KIERKEGAARDIANA
KiJ . . . . KNJIZEVNOST I JEZIK
Kimball's D F . . . . . . KIMBALL'S DAIRY FARMER
Kind and First Grade . . KINDERGARTEN AND FIRST GRADE
Kind M . . . . KINDERGARTEN PRIMARY MAGAZINE
Kinet Catal . . . . KINETICS AND CATALYSIS
KIPR . . . . KWARTALNIK INSTITUTU POLSKO-RADZIECKIEGO
KiR . . . . KNIGA I REVOLJUCIJA
KIRCHOR . . . . KIRCHENCHOR
Kirkus . . . . VIRGINIA KIRKUS' SERVICE. BULLETIN
KIR MUS . . . . KIRCHENMUSIKER
KiS . . . . KULTURA I SPOLECZENSTWO
Kitto . . . . KITTO'S JOURNAL OF SACRED LITERATURE
KiW . . . . KSIAZKA I WIEDZA
KJ . . . . KIPLING JOURNAL
KJ . . . . KNJIZEVNOST I JEZIK
KJG . . . . KUNSTWISSENSCHAFTLICHES JAHRBUCH DER GORRESGESELLSCHAFT
KjK . . . . KEEL JA KIRJANDUS
KJS . . . . KNJIZEVNOST I JEZIK U SKOLI
KK . . . . KIRKE OG KULTUR
KK . . . . KWARTALNIK KLASYCZNY
KKIU . . . . KEELE JA KIRJANDUSE INSTITUUDI UURIMUSED
KKK . . . . KOKUGO KOKUBUN NO KENKYU (STUDIES IN JAPANESE LANGUAGE AND LITERATURE)
KI . . . . KLIO. BEITRAGE ZUR ALTEN GESCHICHTE
KL . . . . KULTUR IN LITERATUR
KL . . . . KUNSTLITERATUR
KL . . . . KYPRIAKOS LOGOS
Klim Kaelte Ing . . . . KLIMA & KAELTE INGENIEUR
KLIN MONATS . . . . . KLINISCHE MONATSBLAETTER FUER AUGENHEILKUNDE
KLIN PADIAT . . . . . . KLINISCHE PADIATRIE
KLIN WOCH . . . . KLINISCHE WOCHENSCHRIFT
KM . . . . KANSAS MAGAZINE
KMHP . . . . K'UNG MENG MSUEH-PAO (JOURNAL OF THE CONFUCIUS MENCIUS SOCIETY)
KN . . . . KRASNAJA NOV'
KN . . . . KUNST DER NEDERLANDEN

KN . . . . KWARTALNIK NEOFILOLOGICZNY
KNAW . . . . KONINKLIJKE NEDERLANDSE AKADEMIE VAN WETENSCHAPPEN
KNf . . . . KWARTALNIK NEOFILOLOGICZNY
Knick . . . . KNICKERBOCKER MAGAZINE
Knitting Int . . . . KNITTING INTERNATIONAL
Knji . . . . KNJIZEVNOST
KnjiNov . . . . KNJIZEVNE NOVINE
KnjIst . . . . KNJIZEVNA ISTORIJA
KnN . . . . KNJIZEVNE NOVINE
KNO . . . . KWARTALNIK NAUCYZCIELA OPOLSKIEGO
Knowl . . . . KNOWLEDGE
KNVS . . . . KONGELIGE NORSKE VIDENSKAPERS SELSKAP
KO . . . . KONGO-OVERZEE. TIJDSCHRIFT VOOR EN OVER BELGISCH-KONGO EN ANDERE OVERZEESE
               GEWESTEN
Ko . . . . KOVCEZIC
KOBUNSH RON . . . . KOBUNSHI RONBUNSHU
Koelner Z Soz . . . . . KOELNER ZEITSCHRIFT FUER SOZIOLOGIE UND SOZIAL-PSYCHOLOGIE
KOF . . . . KULTUR OG FOLKEMINDER
KoJ . . . . KOREA JOURNAL
KoK . . . . KIRKE OG KULTUR
KOK GAK ZAS . . . . . KOKKA GAKKAI ZASSI (JOURNAL OF THE ASSOCIATION OF POLITICAL AND SOCIAL SCIENCE)
KOLLOID-Z & Z Polym . . KOLLOID-ZEITSCHRIFT UND ZEITSCHRIFT FUER POLYMERE
KOLNER Z SO . . . . . . KOELNER ZEITSCHRIFT FUER SOZIOLOGIE UND SOZIAL PSYCHOLOGIE
Kon-Bayer Akad d Wiss Philol u Hist Kl Abhandl . . KOENIGLICH-BAYERISCHE AKADEMIE DER WISSENSCHAFTEN,
               PHILOSOPHISCH-PHILOLOGISCHE UND HISTORISCHE KLASSE. ABHANDLUNGEN
Konigsberg Univ Jahrb . . KOENIGSBERG UNIVERSITAET. JAHRBUCH
Konsthist Tidskrift . . KONSTHISTORISK TIDSKRIFT
Konstr Ingenieurbau Ber . . KONSTRUKTIVER INGENIEURBAU BERICHTE
Konstr Masch App Geraetebau . . KONSTRUKTION IM MASCHINEN-APPARATE-UND-GERAETEBAU
KopGS . . . . KOPENHAGENER GERMANISTISCHE STUDIEN
KOSM B AV M . . . . . KOSMICHESKAYA BIOLOGIYA I AVIAKOSMICHESKAYA MEDITSINA
Kov . . . . KOVCEZIC
Kovove Mater . . . . . KOVOVE MATERIALY
KP . . . . KRITIKA PHYLLA
KP . . . . KULTURNI POLITIKA
KP . . . . KWARTALNIK PRASOZNAWCZY
KPG . . . . KLIATT PAPERBACK BOOK GUIDE
KPR . . . . KNIGA I PROLETARSKAYA REVOLYUTSIYA
KQ . . . . KANSAS QUARTERLY
KQ . . . . KOREANA QUARTERLY
KR . . . . KENYON REVIEW
KR . . . . KIRKUS REVIEWS
KRA . . . . KOELNER ROMANISTISCHE ARBEITEN
Kratkije soobscenija Inst Eth . . KRATKIJE SOOBSCENIJA INSTITUTA ETHNOGRAFIJI. AKADEMIJI NAUK SSSR
KRISTALLOGR . . . . . KRISTALLOGRAFIYA
Krit . . . . KRITERION
KritC . . . . KRITIK (COPENHAGEN)
Kron . . . . KRONIKA
KRQ . . . . KENTUCKY ROMANCE QUARTERLY
KrSoob(Kiev) . . . . . . KRATKIE SOOBSCENIJA. BREVES COMMUNICATIONS DE L'INSTITUTE D'ARCHEOLOGIE (KIEV)
KS . . . . KANT-STUDIEN

KS . . . . KULTURA SLOVA
KSBurNII . . . . KRATKIR SOOBSCENIJA BURJATSKOGO KOMPLEKSNOGO NAUCNOISSLEDOVATEL'SKOGO
INSTITUTA. SERIJA ISTORIKO-FILOLOGICESKAJA
KSCGH . . . . KYUSHU CHUGOKUGAKKAIHO (JOURNAL OF THE SINOLOGICAL SOCIETY OF KYUSHU)
KSDL . . . . KIELER STUDIEN ZUR DEUTSCHEN LITERATURGESCHICHTE
KSGT . . . . KLEINE SCHRIFTEN DER GESELLSCHAFT FUER THEATERGESCHICHTE
KSHSR . . . . KENTUCKY STATE HISTORICAL SOCIETY. REGISTER
KSINA . . . . KRATKIJE SOOBSCENIJA INSTITUTA NARODOV AZII
KSISL . . . . KRATKIJE SOOBSCENIJA INSTITUTA SLAJANOVEDNIJA. AKADEMIJA NAUK SSSR
KSIV . . . . KRATKIJE SOOBSCENIJA INSTITUTA VOSTOKOVEDENIJA. AKADEMIJA NAUK SSSR
KSJ . . . . KEATS-SHELLEY JOURNAL
KSMB . . . . KEATS-SHELLEY MEMORIAL BULLETIN (ROME)
KSMRB . . . . KEATS-SHELLEY MEMORIAL BULLETIN (ROME)
KSt . . . . KANT-STUDIEN
KSV . . . . KIRJALLISUUDENTUTKIJAIN SEURAN VUOSIKIRJA
KSVK . . . . KALEVALASEURAN VUOSIKIRJA
KT . . . . KHRISTIANSKOE TCHTENIE
KtoK . . . . KOKUGO TO KOKUBUNGAKY (JAPANESE LANGUAGE AND LITERATURE)
KUER . . . . KOBE UNIVERSITY ECONOMIC REVIEW
KuL . . . . KUNST UND LITERATUR
KulturaW . . . . KULTURA (WARSAW)
Kunstst-Plast . . . . . KUNSTSTOFFE-PLASTICS
Kunstst-Rundsch . . . KUNSTSTOFF-RUNDSCHAU
Kunst u Lit . . . . KUNST UND LITERATUR
Kuz . . . . KUZNICA
KV . . . . KALEVALASEURAN VUOSIKIRJA
KV . . . . KIRKENS VERDEN
KVAN ELEKTR . . . . . KVANTOVIA ELEKTRONIKA
KVATL . . . . KONINKLIJKE ACADEMIE VOOR TAAL- EN LETTERKUNDE
KVATL . . . . KONINKLIJKE VLAAMSE ACADEMIE VOOR TAAL- EN LETTERKUNDE
KVG . . . . KRITISCHE VIERTELJAHRESSCHRIFT FUER GESETZGEBUNG
KVHAAH . . . . KUNGL. VITTERHETS HISTORIE OCH ANTIKVITETS AKADEMIENS HANDLINGAR
KVJS . . . . KRITISCHE VIERTELJAHRESSCHRIFT
KVKEK . . . . KRONIEK VAN KUNST EN KULTUR
KVNS . . . . KORRESPONDENZBLATT DES VEREINS FUER NIEDERDEUTSCHE SPRACHEFORSCHUNG
KwO . . . . KWARTALNIK OPOLSKI
Ky Ag Exp . . . . KENTUCKY AGRICULTURAL EXPERIMENT STATION. PUBLICATIONS
Kyb . . . . KYBERNETIKA
Ky B J . . . . KENTUCKY BAR JOURNAL
KyC . . . . KYPRIAKA CHRONIKA
Ky Folk Rec . . . . KENTUCKY FOLKLORE RECORD
Ky Hist Soc Reg . . . . KENTUCKY HISTORICAL SOCIETY. REGISTER
KyHS . . . . KENTUCKY HISTORICAL SOCIETY. REGISTER
Kyk . . . . KYKLOS
Ky Law J . . . . KENTUCKY LAW JOURNAL
Ky Lib Assn Bull . . . . KENTUCKY LIBRARY ASSOCIATION BULLETIN
Ky L J . . . . KENTUCKY LAW JOURNAL
Kyo . . . . KYOTO UNIVERSITY ECONOMIC REVIEW
KyR . . . . KENTUCKY REVIEW
Kyrkohist Arsskr . . . KYRKOHISTORISK ARSSKRIFT
KyS . . . . KYPRIAKAI SPOUDAI

Ky Sch J......... KENTUCKY SCHOOL JOURNAL
Ky Univ Office Res Eng Services Bull..KENTUCKY. UNIVERSITY. OFFICE OF RESEARCH AND ENGINEERING SERVICES.
BULLETIN
KZ............. KIRCHLICHE ZEITSCHRIFT
KZ............. KULTURNY ZIVOT (BRATISLAVA)
KZ............. ZEITSCHRIFT FUER VERGLEICHENDE SPRACHFORSCHUNG (KUHN'S ZEITSCHRIFT)
KZMTLG........ KONINKLIJKE ZUIDNEDERLANDSE MAATSCHAPPIJ VOOR TAAL- EN LETTERKUNDE EN
GESCHIEDENIS

L

L . . . . LANGUAGE
L . . . . LATOMUS. REVUE D'ETUDES LATINES
L . . . . LEODIUM
LA . . . . LE ARTI
LA . . . . LETTERATURA
LA . . . . LINCOLN ANNEX
LA . . . . LINGUISTICA ANTVERPIENSIA
LA . . . . LINGUISTISCHE ARBEITEN
LA . . . . LISAN AL-'ARABI
LA . . . . LITERARISCHE ANZEIGER
LA . . . . LIVING AGE
La Ag Exp . . . . LOUISIANA AGRICULTURAL EXPERIMENT STATION. PUBLICATIONS
LAAW . . . . LOTUS. AFRO-ASIAN WRITINGS
LAB ANIM SC . . . . . . LABORATORY ANIMAL SCIENCE
LABB . . . . LOS ANGELES BAR BULLETIN
Lab Cent Ponts Chaussees Bull Liaison Lab Ponts Chaussees . . LABORATOIRE CENTRAL DES PONTS ET CHAUSSEES.
    BULLETIN DE LIAISON DES LABORATOIRES DES PONTS ET CHAUSSEES
Lab Cent Ponts Chaussees Rapp Rech . . LABORATOIRE CENTRAL DES PONTS ET CHAUSSEES. RAPPORT DE RECHERCHE
Lab Central Ensayo Mater Constr Madrid Publ . . LABORATORIO CENTRAL DE ENSAYO DE MATERIALES DE
    CONSTRUCCION. MADRID. PUBLICACION
LAB GAZ . . . . LABOUR GAZETTE
Lab Hist . . . . LABOR HISTORY
LAB INV . . . . LABORATORY INVESTIGATION
La B J . . . . LOUISIANA BAR JOURNAL
Lab L J . . . . LABOR LAW JOURNAL
Lab Mo . . . . LABOUR MONTHLY
Labor Hist . . . . LABOR HISTORY
Labor Law J . . . . . . LABOR LAW JOURNAL
Labor L J . . . . LABOR LAW JOURNAL
Labour Gaz . . . . LABOUR GAZETTE
Labour Mo . . . . LABOUR MONTHLY
Lab Pract . . . . LABORATORY PRACTICE
LAC . . . . LETTERATURA ED ARTE CONTEMPORANEA
Lacuny J . . . . LACUNY JOURNAL
Ladies' H J . . . . . . LADIES' HOME JOURNAL
LaF . . . . LANGUE FRANCAISE
LaG . . . . LA GIUSTIZIA
La Geol Surv Geol Bull . . LOUISIANA. GEOLOGICAL SURVEY. GEOLOGICAL BULLETIN
La Geol Surv Water Resour Bull . . LOUISIANA. GEOLOGICAL SURVEY AND DEPARTMENT OF PUBLIC WORKS. WATER
    RESOURCES BULLETIN
La Geol Surv Water Resour Pam . . LOUISIANA. GEOLOGICAL SURVEY AND DEPARTMENT OF PUBLIC WORKS. WATER
    RESOURCES PAMPHLET
LaH . . . . LOUISIANA HISTORY
La Hist . . . . LOUISIANA HISTORY
La Hist Quar . . . . . . LOUISIANA HISTORICAL QUARTERLY
LaK . . . . LITERATUR ALS KUNST
Lakeside . . . . LAKESIDE MONTHLY
La Law Rev . . . . LOUISIANA LAW REVIEW
La Lib Assn Bull . . . . LOUISIANA LIBRARY ASSOCIATION. BULLETIN

La Lib Bul . . . . LOUISIANA LIBRARY ASSOCIATION. BULLETIN
LALR . . . . LATIN-AMERICAN LITERARY REVIEW
La L Rev . . . . LOUISIANA LAW REVIEW
LaM . . . . LANGUES MODERNES
LANBAU VOL . . . . . . LANBAUFORSCHUNG VOLKENRODE
Land . . . . LAND AND LAND NEWS
Land & Water L Rev . . LAND AND WATER LAW REVIEW
Land Econ . . . . LAND ECONOMICS
L & I . . . . LITERATURE AND IDEOLOGY
L&L . . . . LEHRPROBEN UND LEHRGANGE
L&L . . . . LIMBA SI LITERATURA
L&L . . . . LINGUISTICA ET LITTERARIA
Land of Sun . . . . LAND OF SUNSHINE
L&P . . . . LITERATURE AND PSYCHOLOGY
Land Reform . . . . . . LAND REFORM, LAND SETTLEMENT AND COOPERATIVES
L&S . . . . LANGUAGE AND SPEECH
Landscape Arch . . . . LANDSCAPE ARCHITECT
L & Soc Order . . . . . LAW AND THE SOCIAL ORDER
Lang . . . . LANGUAGE
LangA . . . . LANGUAGE AND AUTOMATION
LangAb . . . . LANGUAGE AND LANGUAGE BEHAVIOR ABSTRACTS
Lang&L . . . . LANGUAGE AND LITERATURE
Lang&S . . . . LANGUAGE AND STYLE
Lang & Speech . . . . . LANGUAGE AND SPEECH
LANGENBECK . . . . . . LANGENBECKS ARCHIV FUER CHIRURGIE
LangL . . . . LANGUAGE LEARNING
Lang Learn . . . . LANGUAGE LEARNING
Lang Mod . . . . LANGUES MODERNES
LangMono . . . . LANGUAGE MONOGRAPHS
LangQ . . . . LANGUAGE QUARTERLY
LangS . . . . LANGUAGE AND STYLE
LangS . . . . LANGUAGE SCIENCES
LANG SPEECH . . . . . LANGUAGE AND SPEECH
LangTAb . . . . LANGUAGE TEACHING ABSTRACTS
LanM . . . . LANGUES MODERNES
L A OF ALTA BUL . . . LIBRARY ASSOCIATION OF ALBERTA BULLETIN
LaPar . . . . LA PARISIENNE
LA PHIL . . . . LOS ANGELES PHILHARMONIC PROGRAM NOTES
LA Phil Sym Mag . . . LOS ANGELES PHILHARMONIC ORCHESTRA SYMPHONY MAGAZINE
LaR . . . . LA RASSEGNA
LAR . . . . LIBRARY ASSOCIATION RECORD
LARC Rep . . . . LARC REPORTS
LARYNGOSCOP . . . . LARYNGOSCOPE
LaS . . . . LOUISIANA STUDIES
La State Univ Div Eng Res Bull . . LOUISIANA STATE UNIVERSITY. DIVISION OF ENGINEERING RESEARCH. BULLETIN
Lat . . . . LATOMUS
LaT . . . . LA TORRE
LatAm . . . . INDEX TO LATIN AMERICAN PERIODICALS
LAT AMER MG . . . . . LATIN AMERICAN MONOGRAPHS
LAT AM RES . . . . LATIN AMERICAN RESEARCH REVIEW
Lat Am Res R . . . . . . LATIN AMERICAN RESEARCH REVIEW

LATR . . . . LATIN AMERICAN THEATER REVIEW
LatT . . . . LATIN TEACHING
Lau R . . . . LAUREL REVIEW
Laval Theol Phil . . . . LAVAL THEOLOGIQUE ET PHILOSOPHIQUE
LavTP . . . . LAVAL THEOLOGIQUE ET PHILOSOPHIQUE
Law Am . . . . LAWYER OF THE AMERICAS
Law & Contemp Prob . . LAW AND CONTEMPORARY PROBLEMS
Law & L N . . . . LAWYER AND LAW NOTES
Law & Pol Int'l Bus . . LAW AND POLICY IN INTERNATIONAL BUSINESS
Law & Soc Order . . . LAW AND THE SOCIAL ORDER
Law & Soc R . . . . . . LAW AND SOCIETY REVIEW
LAW CONT PR . . . . . LAW AND CONTEMPORARY PROBLEMS
Law Guild Rev . . . . . LAWYERS GUILD REVIEW
Law J . . . . LAWYERS JOURNAL
Law Lib J . . . . LAW LIBRARY JOURNAL
Law Libn . . . . LAW LIBRARIAN
LAW LIBR J . . . . LAW LIBRARY JOURNAL
Law Off Econ & Management . . LAW OFFICE ECONOMICS AND MANAGEMENT
Law Q . . . . LAW QUARTERLY REVIEW
Law Q R . . . . LAW QUARTERLY REVIEW
LAW QUART . . . . . . LAW QUARTERLY REVIEW
LAW STATE . . . . LAW AND STATE
LB . . . . LEUVENSE BIJDRAGEN (BIJBLAD)
LBB . . . . LEUVENSE BIJDRAGEN (BIJBLAD)
LBer . . . . LINGUISTISCHE BERICHTE
LBIB . . . . LINGUISTICA BIBLICA
LBj . . . . LEKSYKOHRAFICNYJ BJULETEN
LBL . . . . LITERATURBLATT FUER GERMANISCHE UND ROMANISCHE PHILOLOGIE
LbR . . . . LIMBA ROMINA
LBR . . . . LLOYD'S BANK REVIEW
LBR . . . . LUSO-BRAZILIAN REVIEW
LC . . . . LETTERATURE CONTEMPORANEA
LC . . . . LIBRARY CHRONICLE
LCCP . . . . LINGUISTIC CIRCLE OF CANBERRA PUBLICATIONS
LCD . . . . LITTERARISCHES CENTRALBLATT FUER DEUTSCHLAND
LCh . . . . LIBERTE CHRETIENNE
LCHP . . . . LANCASTER COUNTY HISTORICAL SOCIETY. PAPERS
LChQ . . . . LUTHERAN CHURCH QUARTERLY
LChr . . . . LOGOTECHNIKA CHRONIKA
LCHS . . . . LANCASTER COUNTY HISTORICAL SOCIETY. PAPERS
LC Inf Bul . . . . UNITED STATES. LIBRARY OF CONGRESS. INFORMATION BULLETIN
LCM . . . . LITERARY CRITERION (MYSORE)
LCrit . . . . LITERARY CRITERION (MYSORE)
LCSCF . . . . LIBERA CATTEDRA DI STORIA DELLA CIVILTA FIORENTINA
LCUP . . . . LIBRARY CHRONICLE OF THE UNIVERSITY OF PENNSYLVANIA
LCUT . . . . LIBRARY CHRONICLE OF THE UNIVERSITY OF TEXAS
LD . . . . LITERARY DIGEST
LD . . . . LITHUANIAN DAYS
LD . . . . LITUANISTIKOS DARBAI (CHICAGO)
LDAA . . . . LEXIKOGRAPHIKON DELTION AKADEMIAS ATHENON
LdD . . . . LETRAS DE DEUSTO

L DE MUZ . . . . LUCRARI DE MUZICOLOGIE
LDL . . . . LETOPIS DOMA LITERATOROV
LdM . . . . LAUTBIBLIOTHEK DER DEUTSCHEN MUNDARTEN
LDM . . . . LINGUE DEL MONDE
LdP . . . . LIVROS DE PORTUGAL
LdProv . . . . LETTORE DE PROVINCIA
LE . . . . LAGINA EPHEMERIS AEGYPTIACA ET UNIVERSA
LE . . . . LAND ECONOMICS
LE . . . . LITERARISCHES ECHO
LE&W . . . . LITERATURE EAST AND WEST
LEARN MOTIV . . . . . LEARNING AND MOTIVATION
LEBENSM IND . . . . . LEBENSMITTEL INDUSTRIE
LEBER MAG D . . . . . LEBER MAGEN DARM
LEC . . . . LES ETUDES CLASSIQUES
LeC . . . . LINGUA E CULTURA
Lect . . . . LECTURAS
LeedsSE . . . . LEEDS STUDIES IN ENGLISH
LegPer . . . . INDEX TO LEGAL PERIODICALS
Lei . . . . LEITURA
Leis Hour . . . . LEISURE HOUR
LeMo . . . . LETTERATURE MODERNE
LenauA . . . . LENAU ALMANACH
LenauF . . . . LENAU FORUM
LenC . . . . LENGUAJE Y CIENCIAS
Lend a H . . . . LEND A HAND
Leo . . . . LEONARDO
Leo Baeck Inst Jews Germ Yrbk . . LEO BAECK INSTITUTE OF JEWS FROM GERMANY. YEARBOOK
Leon . . . . LEONARDO
Les . . . . LESONENU. QUARTERLY OF HEBREW
LeS . . . . LINGUA E STILE (BELOGNA)
LEst . . . . LE LINGUE ESTERE
Let . . . . LETTERATURA
LetD . . . . LETRAS DE DEUSTO
Let It . . . . LETTERE ITALIANE
LetM . . . . LETTRES MODERNES
LetMs . . . . LETOPIS MATICE SRPSKE
LetN . . . . LETTRES NOUVELLES
Let Rom . . . . LETTRES ROMANES
Lett . . . . LETTERATURA
Lett Mod . . . . LETTERATURE MODERNE
LETT NUOV C . . . . . LETTERE AL NUOVO CIMENTO
LeuB . . . . LEUVENSE BIJDRAGEN
Leu Bij . . . . LEUVENSE BIJDRAGEN
Leuv Bijdr . . . . LEUVENSE BIJDRAGEN
LevT . . . . LEVENDE TALEN
Lex . . . . LEXIS
Lex Th Q . . . . LEXINGTON THEOLOGICAL QUARTERLY
LF . . . . LETTERS FRANCAISES
LF . . . . LIA FAIL
LF . . . . LISTY FILOLOGICKE
LF . . . . LITERATUREN FRONT (SOFIA)

LFil . . . . LISTY FILOLOGICKE
LFr . . . . LANGUE FRANCAISE
LF(RA) . . . . LISTY FILOLOGICKE. SUPPLEMENT: REVUE ARCHEOLOGIQUE
LFS . . . . LETTRES FRANCAISES
Lg . . . . LANGUAGE
LG . . . . LITERARY GUIDE
LG . . . . LITERATURNAYA GAZETA
LGF . . . . LUNDER GERMANISTISCHE FORSCHUNGEN
LGPIT . . . . LENINGRAD PEDAGOGICAL INSTITUTE OF FOREIGN LANGUAGES. TRANSACTIONS
LGr . . . . LITERATURNAYA GRUZIYA (TBILISI)
LGRP . . . . LITERATURBLATT FUER GERMANISCHE UND ROMANISCHE PHILOLOGIE
LGRPh . . . . LITERATURBLATT FUER GERMANISCHE UND ROMANISCHE PHILOLOGIE
LGU . . . . LENINGRAD STATE UNIVERSITY. PHILOLOGY SERIES. TRANSACTIONS
LH . . . . LINCOLN HERALD
LH . . . . LITERARISCHER HANDWEISER
LHB . . . . LOCK HAVEN BULLETIN
LHQ . . . . LOUISIANA HISTORICAL QUARTERLY
LHR . . . . LOCK HAVEN REVIEW
LHSb . . . . LITERARNOHISTORICKY SBORNIK
LHSl . . . . LITTERARIA HISTORICA SLOVACA
LHW . . . . LITERARISCHER HANDWEISER
LHY . . . . LITERARY HALF-YEARLY
Li . . . . BRITISH BROADCASTING CORPORATION LISTENER
LI . . . . LETTERE ITALIANE
LI . . . . LIBRO ITALIANO
Li . . . . LINGUA
Li . . . . LISTENER
LI . . . . LUCE INTELLETTUALE
LI . . . . (RUSSIAN) LITERATURE AND ART
LIal . . . . LETTERE ITALIANE
Lib . . . . LIBRARY
Lib . . . . LIBRARY
Lib . . . . LIBYA
LibAnt . . . . LIBYA ANTIQUA
Lib Assn Alta Bull . . LIBRARY ASSOCIATION OF ALBERTA. BULLETIN
Lib Assn Rec . . . . . . LIBRARY ASSOCIATION RECORD
Lib Assn Yrbk . . . . . LIBRARY ASSOCIATION. YEARBOOK
Lib Binder . . . . LIBRARY BINDER
LibC . . . . LIBRARY CHRONICLE
Lib Chron . . . . LIBRARY CHRONICLE
Lib Coll J . . . . LIBRARY COLLEGE JOURNAL
Lib Cong Inf Bull . . . LIBRARY OF CONGRESS. INFORMATION BULLETIN
Lib Cong Q J . . . . . . LIBRARY OF CONGRESS. QUARTERLY JOURNAL
Lib Cong Q J Cur Acq . . LIBRARY OF CONGRESS. QUARTERLY JOURNAL OF CURRENT ACQUISITIONS
Liberal Ed . . . . LIBERAL EDUCATION
LiberianSJ . . . . LIBERIAN STUDIES JOURNAL
Lib Hist . . . . LIBRARY HISTORY
Lib Inf Bull . . . . LIBRARY INFORMATION BULLETIN
Lib Inf Sci . . . . LIBRARY AND INFORMATION SCIENCE
LibJ . . . . LIBRARY JOURNAL
Lib Leaves . . . . LIBRARY LEAVES FROM THE LIBRARY OF LONG ISLAND UNIVERSITY

LibLit . . . . LIBRARY LITERATURE
Lib (London) . . . . . . LIBRARY (TRANSACTIONS OF THE BIBLIOGRAPHICAL SOCIETY)
Libn & Bk W . . . . LIBRARIAN AND BOOK WORLD
Lib News Bul . . . . . . LIBRARY NEWS BULLETIN
Lib Occurrent . . . . . LIBRARY OCCURRENT
Lib Period Round Table Newsletter . . LIBRARY PERIODICALS ROUND TABLE. NEWSLETTER
Lib Q . . . . LIBRARY QUARTERLY
LIB RES TEC . . . . LIBRARY RESOURCES AND TECHNICAL SERVICES
Lib Rev . . . . LIBRARY REVIEW
Lib Scene . . . . LIBRARY SCENE
LibSciAb . . . . LIBRARY AND INFORMATION SCIENCE ABSTRACTS
Lib Sci Slant Doc . . . LIBRARY SCIENCE WITH A SLANT TO DOCUMENTATION
Lib Tech Rep . . . . . . LIBRARY TECHNOLOGY REPORTS
Lib Trends . . . . LIBRARY TRENDS
Lib W . . . . LIBRARY WORLD
LICHTTECH . . . . LICHTTECHNIK
LicP . . . . LICEUS DE PORTUGAL
LiD . . . . LITERATUR IM DIALOG
Life & Lett . . . . LIFE AND LETTERS
Life Ins Courant . . . . LIFE INSURANCE COURANT
LIFE SCI . . . . LIFE SCIENCES
LIFE-THREAT . . . . . . LIFE-THREATENING BEHAVIOR
Life With Mus . . . . . LIFE WITH MUSIC
Lift Elevator Lift Ropeway Eng . . LIFT ELEVATOR LIFT AND ROPEWAY ENGINEERING
LiG . . . . LITERATUR IN DER GESELLSCHAFT
Light Des Appl . . . . . LIGHTING DESIGN AND APPLICATION
Light Light . . . . LIGHT AND LIGHTING
Light Met Age . . . . . LIGHT METAL AGE
Light Res Technol . . LIGHTING RESEARCH AND TECHNOLOGY
LI Hist Soc Memoirs . . LONG ISLAND HISTORICAL SOCIETY. MEMOIRS
LiK . . . . LIAUDIES KURYBA
LiK . . . . LITERATURA IR KALBA
LiL . . . . LIMBA SI LITERATURA
LiLi . . . . ZEITSCHRIFT FUER LITERATURWISSENSCHAFT UND LINGUISTIC
LILLE MED . . . . LILLE MEDICAL
LiM . . . . LINGUE DEL MONDO
LiM . . . . LITERATURA I MARKSIZM
LIMN OCEAN . . . . . . LIMNOLOGY AND OCEANOGRAPHY
LimR . . . . LIMBA ROMANA (BUCURESTI)
LIN ALG APP . . . . . . LINEAR ALGEBRA AND ITS APPLICATIONS
Lincoln L Rev . . . . . . LINCOLN LAW REVIEW
LINCS . . . . LANGUAGE INFORMATION NETWORK AND CLEARINGHOUSE SYSTEM. CENTER FOR APPLIED LINGUISTICS
Linde Rep Sci Technol . . LINDE REPORTS ON SCIENCE AND TECHNOLOGY
Linear Algebra Its Appl . . LINEAR ALGEBRA AND ITS APPLICATIONS
Ling . . . . LINGUISTICA
LingB . . . . LINGUISTISCHE BERICHTE
LingC . . . . LINGUISTIC COMMUNICATIONS
Ling Est . . . . LINGUE ESTERE
LingH . . . . LINGUISTICS (THE HAGUE)
LingI . . . . LINGUISTIC INQUIRY

Lingnan Sci J . . . . . . LINGNAN SCIENCE JOURNAL
LingP . . . . LINGUISTIQUE (PARIS)
Ling R . . . . LINGUISTIC REPORTER
Linnean Soc Biol J . . LINNEAN SOCIETY. BIOLOGICAL JOURNAL
L Inst J . . . . LAW INSTITUTE JOURNAL
L in Trans . . . . LAW IN TRANSITION
Lippinc . . . . LIPPINCOTT'S MAGAZINE
LiR . . . . LIMBA ROMANA
LIs . . . . LINGUA ISLANDICA
Lis . . . . LISTENER
LISL . . . . LETOPIS INSTITUTA ZA SERBSKI IUDOSPYT W BUDYSINJE PRI NEMSKEJ AKADEMIJI WEDO-
MOSCOW W BERLINJE RJAD A. REC A LITERATURA
List . . . . LISTENER
List . . . . LIST SDRUZENI MORAVSKYCH SPISOVATELU
LIt . . . . LETTERE ITALIANE
LIt . . . . LIBRO ITALIANO
LIT . . . . LITERARISCHES
Lit . . . . LITERATUR
Lit . . . . LITTERATURE (U. OF PARIS)
Lit . . . . LITTERIS
LitA . . . . LITERATURNAYA ARMENIYA (EREVAN)
LItal . . . . LETTERE ITALIANAE
Lit & Psychol . . . . . . LITERATURE AND PSYCHOLOGY
Lit & Theo R . . . . . . LITERARY AND THEOLOGICAL REVIEW
LitAP . . . . LITERARNI ARCHIV PAMATNIKU NARODNIHO PISEMNICTVI
Lit D . . . . LITERARY DIGEST
Lit Dig . . . . LITERARY DIGEST
LitEW . . . . LITERATURE EAST AND WEST
Lithol Miner Resour . . LITHOLOGY AND MINERAL RESOURCES
LItL . . . . LETTERATURA ITALIANA LATERZA
LitL . . . . LITERARNI LISTY
LitL . . . . LITERATURA LUDOWA
LitM . . . . LITERARNI MESICNIK
LitM . . . . LITERATURNAJA MYSL
LitN . . . . LITERARNI NOVINY (PRAHA)
Litol i Polez Iskop . . LITOLOGIYA I POLEZNYE ISKOPAEMYE
LitP . . . . LITERATURE AND PSYCHOLOGY
LitP . . . . LITERATURE IN PERSPECTIVE
Lit R . . . . LITERARY REVIEW
LitS . . . . LITERATURA I SUCANIST
Litt . . . . LITTERARIA
Litt . . . . LITTERIS
LittK . . . . LITTERAE (KUEMMERLE)
LittleR . . . . LITTLE REVIEW
LittW . . . . LITTERARIA (WARSAW)
Liturg Arts . . . . LITURGICAL ARTS
LitW . . . . LITERATURA (WARSAW)
Lit W (Bost) . . . . . . LITERARY WORLD (BOSTON)
Lit ZentB . . . . LITERARISCHES ZENTRALBLATT
Liv Age . . . . LITTELL'S LIVING AGE
LIV BLUES . . . . LIVING BLUES

Liv for Young Home. . LIVING FOR YOUNG HOMEMAKERS
Liv Wild. . . . . LIVING WILDERNESS
L J. . . . . LAW JOURNAL
LJ. . . . . LIBRARY JOURNAL
LJ. . . . . LIMBURG'S JAARBOEK
LJ. . . . . LITURGISCHES JAHRBUCH
LJA. . . . . LJETOPIS JUGOSLAVENSKE AKADEMIJE
LJb. . . . . LITERATURWISSENSCHAFTLICHES JAHRBUCH DER GOERRES-GESELLSCHAFT
LJb. . . . . LUTHER JAHRBUCH
LJGG. . . . . LITERATURWISSENSCHAFTLICHES JAHRBUCH DER GOERRES-GESELLSCHAFT
LK. . . . . LITERATURA IR KALBA
LK. . . . . LITERATUR UND KRITIK. OESTERREICHISCHE MONATSSCHRIFT
LK. . . . . LITERATURNYJ KRITIK
LKI. . . . . IS LIETUVIU KULTUROS ISTORIJOS
LKK. . . . . LIETUVIU KALBOTYROS KLAUSIMAI
LL. . . . . LANGUAGE LEARNING
LL. . . . . LETRAS (LIMA)
LL. . . . . LIFE AND LETTERS
LL. . . . . LITERATUR UND LEBEN
LLA. . . . . LESHONENU LA'AM
LLBA. . . . . LANGUAGE AND LANGUAGE BEHAVIOR ABSTRACTS
LIC. . . . . LLEN CYMRU
L Lib J. . . . . LAW LIBRARY JOURNAL
LLM. . . . . LANGUES ET LETTRES MODERNES
LLM. . . . . LIMBA SI LITERATURA MOLDOVENEASCA CHISINAU
LLud. . . . . LITERATURA LUDOWA
LM. . . . . LANGUAGE MONOGRAPHS
LM. . . . . LANGUES MODERNES
LM. . . . . LETTERATURE MODERNE
LM. . . . . LONDON MAGAZINE
LM. . . . . LONDON MERCURY
LM. . . . . LUNA MONTHLY
LMA. . . . . LE MOYEN AGE
LMAD. . . . . LIETUVOS TSR MOKSLU AKADEMIJOS DARBAI. SERIJA A (VILNIUS)
LMags. . . . . INDEX TO LITTLE MAGAZINES
LMAS. . . . . LONDON AND MIDDLESEX ARCHAEOLOGICAL SOCIETY
LMD. . . . . LA MAISON-DIEU
L Mer. . . . . LONDON MERCURY
LMi. . . . . LITERATURNA MISEL (SOFIA)
LMLG. . . . . LUTHER. MITTEILUNGEN DER LUTHERGESELLSCHAFT
LMLP. . . . . LA MONDA LINGVO-PROBLEMO
LMLSA. . . . . LANGUAGE MONOGRAPHS OF THE LINGUISTIC SOCIETY OF AMERICA
L Mod. . . . . LANGUES MODERNES
LMod. . . . . LETTRES MODERNES
LMold. . . . . LIMBA SI LITERATURA MOLDOVENEASCA
LMS. . . . . LETOPIS MATICE SRPSKE (NOVI SAD)
LMS. . . . . LONDON MEDIAEVAL STUDIES
LN. . . . . LIBRARY NOTES
LN. . . . . LINGUA NOSTRA
LN. . . . . LITERATURNOE NASLEDSTVO
LnA. . . . . LONDON APHRODITE

LNB . . . . LEIPZIGER NAMENKUNDLICHE BEITRAEGE
LNI . . . . LA NUOVA ITALIA
LNL . . . . LANGUES NEO-LATINES
LNLJ . . . . LINGUISTIC NOTES FROM LA JOLLA
LnM . . . . LONDON MERCURY
LNN . . . . LEIPZIGER NEUESTE NACHRICHTEN
LNo . . . . LINGUA NOSTRA
LNos . . . . LINGUA NOSTRA
LNouv . . . . LETTRES NOUVELLES
LNQ . . . . LINCOLNSHIRE NOTES AND QUERIES
LNS . . . . LUNDASTUDIER I NORDISK SPRAKVETENSKAP
LO . . . . LITERATURNOE OBOZRENIE
Lo . . . . LOCHLANN
Locke News . . . . LOCKE NEWSLETTER
L Off Econ & Man . . . LAW OFFICE ECONOMICS AND MANAGEMENT
Log . . . . LOGOS. INTERNATIONALE ZEITSCHRIFT FUER PHILOSOPHIE UND KULTUR
Log Anal . . . . LOG ANALYST
Log Anal . . . . LOGIQUE ET ANALYSE
Logist Spectrum . . . . LOGISTICS SPECTRUM
Lond M . . . . LONDON MAGAZINE
Lond Med St . . . . . . LONDON MEDIAEVAL STUDIES
London Ednl R . . . . . LONDON EDUCATIONAL REVIEW
Lond Q . . . . LONDON QUARTERLY REVIEW
Lond QHR . . . . LONDON QUARTERLY AND HOLBORN REVIEW
Lond Q R . . . . LONDON QUARTERLY AND HOLBORN REVIEW
Lond Soc . . . . LONDON SOCIETY
Lond Topog Rec . . . . LONDON TOPOGRAPHICAL RECORD
Longm . . . . LONGMAN'S MAGAZINE
LONG RANG P . . . . . LONG RANGE PLANNING
LonM . . . . LONDON MAGAZINE
Lon Mag . . . . LONDON MAGAZINE
Los Angeles Ed Res B . . LOS ANGELES EDUCATIONAL RESEARCH BULLETIN
Los Angeles Mus Bul . . LOS ANGELES COUNTY MUSEUM. ART DIVISION. BULLETIN
Los Angeles Mus Q . . LOS ANGELES COUNTY MUSEUM OF HISTORY, SCIENCE AND ART. QUARTERLY
Loughborough Univ Technol Chem Eng J . . LOUGHBOROUGH UNIVERSITY OF TECHNOLOGY. CHEMICAL ENGINEERING
        JOURNAL
Loughborough Univ Technol Dep Transp Technol . . LOUGHBOROUGH UNIVERSITY OF TECHNOLOGY. DEPARTMENT OF
        TRANSPORT TECHNOLOGY
Loyola L Rev . . . . . . LOYOLA LAW REVIEW
Loyola ULJ (Chicago) . . LOYOLA UNIVERSITY LAW JOURNAL (CHICAGO)
Loyola UL Rev (LA) . . LOYOLA UNIVERSITY OF LOS ANGELES LAW REVIEW
LP . . . . LINGUA PORTUGUESA
LP . . . . LINGUA POSNANIENSIS
LP . . . . LITERATURE AND PSYCHOLOGY
LPosn . . . . LINGUA POSNANIENSIS
LPP . . . . LA PAROLA DEL PASSATO
LQ . . . . LIBRARY QUARTERLY
LQ . . . . LONDON QUARTERLY
LQHR . . . . LONDON QUARTERLY AND HOLBORN REVIEW
LQR . . . . LONDON QUARTERLY REVIEW
L Q Rev . . . . LAW QUARTERLY REVIEW

LR . . . . LES LETTRES ROMANES
LR . . . . LIBRARY REVIEW
LR . . . . LITERARY REVIEW
LR . . . . LITERATURNAYA ROSSIYA
LRB . . . . LA REVUE BIBLIOGRAPHIQUE
LRe . . . . LINGUISTISCHE REIHE
LRI . . . . LIBRI E RIVISTE D'ITALIA
LRIF . . . . LOGOS. RIVISTA INTERNAZIONALE DI FILOSOFIA
LRKD . . . . LITERARISCHE RUNDSCHAU FUER DAS KATHOLISCHE DEUTSCHLAND
LRS . . . . LEIPZIGER ROMANISTISCHER STUDIEN
LRS . . . . LINCOLN RECORD SOCIETY
LRTS . . . . LIBRARY RESOURCES AND TECHNICAL SERVICES
LS . . . . LANGUAGE AND SPEECH
LS . . . . LINGUA E STILE
LS . . . . LINGUE STRANIERE
LS . . . . LINGUISTICA SLOVACA
LS . . . . LITERATURNY SOVREMENNIK
LS . . . . LUSITANIA SACRA
LS . . . . SPECTATOR (LONDON)
LSa . . . . LUSITANIA SACRA
LSAB . . . . LINGUISTIC SOCIETY OF AMERICA. BULLETIN
LSb . . . . LEKSIKOGRAFICESKIJ SBORNIK
LSB . . . . LINGUISTIC SURVEY BULLETIN
LSci . . . . LANGUAGE SCIENCES
LSE . . . . LEEDS STUDIES IN ENGLISH AND KINDRED LANGUAGES
LSE . . . . LUND STUDIES IN ENGLISH
LSh . . . . LITERATURA V SHKOLE (MOSCOW)
LsL . . . . LIMBA SI LITERATURA
LSI . . . . LINGUISTICA SLOVACA
LSlov . . . . LIVRE SLOVENE (YUGOSLAVIA)
LSLT . . . . LI-SHIH LUN-TS'UNG (COLLECTION OF ARTICLES ON HISTORY)
LSNS . . . . LUNDASTUDIER I NORDISK SPRAKVETENSKAP
LSoc . . . . LANGUAGE IN SOCIETY
L Soc Gaz . . . . LAW SOCIETY'S GAZETTE
LSp . . . . LANGUAGE AND SPEECH
LSp . . . . LEBENDE SPRACHEN
LSP . . . . LINGVISTICESKIJ SBORNIK. PETROZAVODSK
LSR . . . . LUTTRELL SOCIETY REPRINTS
LSS . . . . LEYTE-SAMAR STUDIES
LSty . . . . LANGUAGE AND STYLE
LSUHS . . . . LOUISIANA STATE UNIVERSITY HUMANISTIC SERIES
LSUSHS . . . . LOUISIANA STATE UNIVERSITY STUDIES. HUMANITIES SERIES
LSVL ORCH . . . . LOUISVILLE ORCHESTRA PROGRAM NOTES
LSW . . . . LUDOWA SPOLDZIELNIA WYDAWNICZA
LT . . . . LA TORRE
L T . . . . LAW TIMES
LT . . . . LEVENDE TALEN
LThPh . . . . LAVAL THEOLOGIQUE ET PHILOSOPHIQUE
LTLS . . . . (LONDON) TIMES LITERARY SUPPLEMENT
Lt Ltg . . . . LIGHT AND LIGHTING
LTM . . . . LEEDS TEXTS AND MONOGRAPHS

LTP . . . . LAVAL THEOLOGIQUE ET PHILOSOPHIQUE
Lt Prod Engng . . . . . LIGHT PRODUCTION ENGINEERING
LTS . . . . (LONDON) TIMES LITERARY SUPPLEMENT
Lit Steam Pwr . . . . . LIGHT STEAM POWER
Lu . . . . LUSIADA
LUA . . . . LUNDS UNIVERSITETS ARSSKRIFT
Lubr Eng . . . . LUBRICATION ENGINEERING
Luc . . . . LUCEAFARUL
Lucas Eng Rev . . . . . LUCAS ENGINEERING REVIEW
LuD . . . . LINGUISTIK UND DIDAKTIK
LUF . . . . LIBRARIE UNIVERSELLE DE FRANCE
Luftfahrtech Raumfahrttech . . LUFTFAHRTTECHNIK, RAUMFAHRTTECHNIK
Luft Kaeltetech . . . . LUFT- UND KAELTETECHNIK
LUK . . . . LITERATUR UND KRITIK (WIEN)
LuL . . . . LITERATUR UND LEBEN
LuM . . . . LITERATURA UN MAKSLA
LuQ . . . . LUTHERAN QUARTERLY
LuR . . . . LITERATURE UND REFLEXION
LUR . . . . PETERA STUCKAS LATVIJAS VALSTS UNIV. ZINATNISKIE RAKSTI. FILOLOGIJAS ZINATNES. A
               SERIJA (RIGA)
LuthChQ . . . . LUTHERAN CHURCH QUARTERLY
Luther-Jahrb . . . . . . LUTHER-JAHRBUCH
LuthQ . . . . LUTHERAN QUARTERLY
LuthW . . . . LUTHERAN WORLD
LuW . . . . LITERATUR UND WIRKLICHKEIT
LUZR . . . . PETERA STUCKAS LATVIJAS VALSTS UNIVERSITATE ZINATNISKIE RAKSTI
LV . . . . LENINGRADSKIJ UNIVERSITET. VESTNIK. SERIJA ISTORIL, LITERATURY I JAZYKA
LV . . . . LUMEN VITAE
LVKJ . . . . LATVIESU VALODAS KULTURAS JAUTAJUMI
LVLG . . . . LUTHER. VIERTELJAHRSCHRIFT DER LUTHER-GESELLSCHAFT
LvS . . . . LITERATURA V SKOLE
LvSK . . . . LITERATURA V SKOLE
LW . . . . LITERARISCHE WOCHENSCHRIFT
LW . . . . LIVING WILDERNESS
LWU . . . . LITERATUR IN WISSENSCHAFT UND UNTERRICHTE
LY . . . . LESSING YEARBOOK
Ly . . . . LYCHNOS
LyC . . . . LENGUAJEY CIENCIAS (UNIV. NACIONAL DE TRUJILLO)
LydgN . . . . LYDGATE NEWSLETTER
LYON CHIR . . . . LYON CHIRURGICAL
LYON MED . . . . LYON MEDICAL
LYON PHARM . . . . . LYON PHARMACEUTIQUE
LyP . . . . LIBRO Y PUEBLO
LZ . . . . LITERARISCHES ZENTRALBLATT FUER DEUTSCHLAND
LZ . . . . LITERATUREN ZBOR
LZ . . . . LITERATURNYE ZAPISKI
LZAV . . . . LATVIJAS PSR ZINATNU AKADEMIJAS VESTIS (RIGA)
LZB . . . . LITERARISCHES ZENTRALBLATT FUER DEUTSCHLAND
LZD . . . . LITERARISCHES ZENTRALBLATT FUER DEUTSCHLAND
LzT . . . . LISTY Z TEATRU

M

M.............. MANUSCRIPTS
M.............. MERKUR
M.............. MNEMOSYNE
M.............. MONDE
M.............. MUSEON
M.............. MUSICA
M.............. MUSICOLOGY
MA............. MADISON AVENUE
MA............. MAGAZINE OF ART
MA............. MEDIUM AEVUM
MA............. MICROFILM ABSTRACTS
M-A............ MID-AMERICA
MA............. MODERN AGE
MA............. MOYEN AGE
MAAL........... MONUMENTI ANTICHI DELLA R. ACCADEMIA NAZIONALE DIE LINCEI
MAAN........... MEMORIE DELLA R. ACCADEMIA DI ARCHEOLOGIA, LETTERE E BELLE ARTI DI NAPOLI
MAAR........... MEMOIRS OF THE AMERICAN ACADEMY IN ROME
MAb............ MASTERS ABSTRACTS
MAB............ MEMOIRES DE L'ACADEMIE ROYALE DE BELGIQUE
MAC............ MACABRE
MAC............ MAC/WESTERN ADVERTISING
MAC............ MEMORIAS DA ACADEMIA DAS CIENCIAS DE LISBOA. CLASSE DE LETRAS
Mach........... MACHINERY
Mach Des....... MACHINE DESIGN
Mach Market..... MACHINERY MARKET
MACH PROD E..... MACHINERY AND PRODUCTION ENGINEERING
Mach Shop....... MACHINE SHOP
Mach Tool....... MACHINES AND TOOLING (ENGLISH TRANSLATION OF STANKI I INSTRUMENT)
Mach Tool Blue Book.. MACHINE AND TOOL BLUE BOOK
Mach Tool Eng..... MACHINE TOOL ENGINEERING
MACH TOOL R..... MACHINE TOOL REVIEW
MACL........... MEMORIAS DA ACADEMIA DAS CIENCIAS DE LISBOA. CLASSE DE LETRAS
MACL........... MEMOIRES DE L'ACADEMIE D'HISTOIRE DE LA CULTURE DE LENINGRAD
MACLCL......... MEMORIAS DA ACADEMIA DAS CIENCIAS DE LISBOA. CLASSE DE LETRAS
MACLL.......... MEMORIAS DA ACADEMIA DAS CIENCIAS DE LISBOA. CLASSE DE LETRAS
MACL MAG....... MACLEAN'S MAGAZINE
Macmil......... MACMILLAN'S MAGAZINE
MACROMOLEC..... MACROMOLECULES
MACROMOL R..... MACROMOLECULAR REVIEWS PART D-JOURNAL OF POLYMER SCIENCE
MAC/WA......... MAC/WESTERN ADVERTISING
MAD............ MEMOIRES DE L'ACADEMIE DES SCIENCES, ARTS ET BELLES-LETTRES DE DIJON
MADNV......... MITTEILUNGSBLATT DES ALLGEMEINER DEUTSCHER NEUPHILOLOGENVERBAND
Mad Q.......... MADISON QUARTERLY
MAE............ MEDIUM AEVUM
MAev........... MEDIUM AEVUM
MAFS........... MEMOIRS OF THE AMERICAN FOLKLORE SOCIETY
Mag Art......... MAGAZINE OF ART
Mag Bank Adm.... MAGAZINE OF BANK ADMINISTRATION
Mag Bldg........ MAGAZINE OF BUILDING

MAG CONCR R . . . . . MAGAZINE OF CONCRETE RESEARCH
Mag Fantasy & Sci Fict . . MAGAZINE OF FANTASY AND SCIENCE FICTION
MAG MACL . . . . MAGAZINE MACLEAN
MagN . . . . MAGYAR NYELVOR
Mag of Art . . . . MAGAZINE OF ART
Mag of Business . . . MAGAZINE OF BUSINESS
Mag of Hist . . . . . . MAGAZINE OF HISTORY
Mag of Stand . . . . . MAGAZINE OF STANDARDS
Mag of Wall St . . . . MAGAZINE OF WALL STREET
Mag Stand . . . . MAGAZINE OF STANDARDS
MAGW . . . . MITTEILUNGEN DER ANTHROPOLOGISCHEN GESELLSCHAFT IN WIEN
Mag Wall St . . . . . . MAGAZINE OF WALL STREET
MAGY KEM FO . . . . MAGYAR KEMIAI FOLYOIRAT
MAGZ . . . . MITTEILUNGEN DER ANTIQUARISCHEN GESELLSCHAFT IN ZURICH
MAH . . . . MELANGES D' ARCHEOLOGIE ET D'HISTOIRE
MAHR . . . . MID-AMERICA, AN HISTORICAL REVIEW
MAI . . . . MEMOIRES DE L'INSTITUT NATIONAL DE FRANCE. ACADEMIE DES INSCRIPTIONS ET BELLES-
LETTRES
MAIN CURR M . . . . . MAIN CURRENTS IN MODERN THOUGHT
Maine Ag Dept B . . . MAINE DEPARTMENT OF AGRICULTURE. QUARTERLY BULLETIN
Maine Ag Exp . . . . . MAINE AGRICULTURAL EXPERIMENT STATION. PUBLICATIONS
Maine Geol Surv Spec Econ Stud Ser Bull . . MAINE GEOLOGICAL SURVEY. SPECIAL ECONOMIC STUDIES SERIES.
BULLETIN
Maine Hist Soc Coll . . MAINE HISTORICAL SOCIETY. COLLECTIONS
Maine Lib Assn Bul . . MAINE LIBRARY ASSOCIATION. BULLETIN
Maine L R . . . . MAINE LAW REVIEW
MAIR . . . . MEMORIE DELLA CLASSE DI SCIENZE MORALI, STORICHE E FILOLOGICHE DELL'ACCADEMIA
D'ITALIA. ROMA
MaitrePhon . . . . MAITRE PHONETIQUE
MAKING MUS . . . . . MAKING MUSIC
MAKROM CHEM . . . MAKROMOLEKULARE CHEMIE
MAKW . . . . MITTEILUNGEN DER ALTERTUMSKOMISSION FUER WESTPHALEN
MAL . . . . ATTI DELLA ACCADEMIA NAZIONALE DEI LINCEI. MEMORIE DELLA CLASSE DI SCIENZE MORALE,
STORICHE E FILOLOGICHE
MAL . . . . MODERN AUSTRIAN LITERATURE
MALA ECON R . . . . . MALAYAN ECONOMIC REVIEW
MalaR . . . . MALAHAT REVIEW
Malawi Geol Surv Dep Bull . . MALAWI. GEOLOGICAL SURVEY DEPARTMENT. BULLETIN
Malawi Geol Surv Dep Mem . . MALAWI. GEOLOGICAL SURVEY DEPARTMENT. MEMOIR
Malayan Ag J . . . . . MALAYAN AGRICULTURAL JOURNAL
Malayan Lib J . . . . . MALAYAN LIBRARY JOURNAL
MALHC . . . . MENSUARIO DE ARTE, LITERATURE, HISTORIA Y CIENCIA
MALinc . . . . ATTI DELLA ACCADEMIA NAZIONALE DEI LINCEI. MEMORIE DELLA CLASSE DI SCIENZE MORALE,
STORICHE E FILOLOGICHE
MALincei . . . . ATTI DELLA ACCADEMIA NAZIONALE DEI LINCEI. MEMORIE DELLA CLASSE DI SCIENZE MORALI,
STORICHE E FILOLOGICHE
M Am Hist . . . . MAGAZINE OF AMERICAN HISTORY
Man . . . . MANNUS. ZEITSCHRIFT FUER VORGESCHICHTE
Man . . . . MANUSCRIPTA
Manage Account . . . MANAGEMENT ACCOUNTING
Manage Inf . . . . MANAGEMENT INFORMATICS

Management Inf Serv. . MANAGEMENT INFORMATION SERVICES
Managements Bibliog Data. . MANAGEMENT'S BIBLIOGRAPHIC DATA
Management Servs. MANAGEMENT SERVICES
Manage Sci. . . . . . . MANAGEMENT SCIENCE
MANAG INT R. . . . . MANAGEMENT INTERNATIONAL REVIEW
MANAG SCI A. . . . . MANAGEMENT SCIENCE. SERIES A. THEORY
MANAG SCI B. . . . . MANAGEMENT SCIENCE. SERIES B. APPLICATION
Man B New. . . . . . . MANITOBA BAR NEWS
Manch. . . . . MANCHESTER LITERARY CLUB. PAPERS
Manchester Sch Econ Soc Stud. . MANCHESTER SCHOOL OF ECONOMIC AND SOCIAL STUDIES
Manchester Sch Ed Gazette. . UNIVERSITY OF MANCHESTER. SCHOOL OF EDUCATION. GAZETTE
Manch Guard. . . . . . MANCHESTER GUARDIAN WEEKLY
Manch Q. . . . . MANCHESTER QUARTERLY
M & Eval Guid. . . . . MEASUREMENT AND EVALUATION IN GUIDANCE
M&H. . . . . MEDIEVALIA ET HUMANISTICA
M&L. . . . . MUSIC AND LETTERS
M & R. . . . . MEDIAEVAL AND RENAISSANCE STUDIES
M&RS. . . . . MEDIAEVAL AND RENAISSANCE STUDIES
Manhat. . . . . MANHATTAN
MAN INDIA. . . . . . . MAN IN INDIA
Manitoba Dep Mines Natur Resour Mines Br Publ. . MANITOBA. DEPARTMENT OF MINES AND NATURAL RESOURCES. MINES BRANCH. PUBLICATION
Man L J. . . . . MANITOBA LAW JOURNAL
Man LSJ. . . . . MANITOBA LAW SCHOOL JOURNAL
Man Q. . . . . MANCHESTER QUARTERLY
ManR. . . . . MANCHESTER REVIEW
MAN/SOC/TECH. . . . MAN/SOCIETY/TECHNOLOGY
Manual Train. . . . . . MANUAL TRAINING MAGAZINE
Manufacturing Ind. . MANUFACTURING INDUSTRIES
MANUF CH AE. . . . . MANUFACTURING CHEMIST AND AEROSOL NEWS
Manuf Chem. . . . . . MANUFACTURING CHEMIST AND AEROSOL NEWS
MANUF ENG. . . . . . MANUFACTURING ENGINEERING
Manuf Eng & Mgt. . . MANUFACTURING ENGINEERING AND MANAGEMENT
Manuf Rec. . . . . . . MANUFACTURERS RECORD
MANUSC MATH. . . . MANUSCRIPTA MATHEMATICA
Man World. . . . . . . MAN AND WORLD
MaNy. . . . . MAGYAR NYELVOR
MAP. . . . . MEDIAEVAL ACADEMY PUBLICATIONS
MAPS. . . . . MEDIUM AEVUM. PHILOLOGISCHE STUDIEN
MAPS. . . . . MEMOIRS OF THE AMERICAN PHILOSOPHICAL SOCIETY
MAQR. . . . . MICHIGAN ALUMNUS QUARTERLY REVIEW
Mar. . . . . MAR DEL SUR
Mar. . . . . MARIANUM
MArch. . . . . MEDIEVAL ARCHAEOLOGY
Mar Eng/ Log. . . . . . MARINE ENGINEERING/LOG
Mar Eng Nav Architect. . MARINE ENGINEER AND NAVAL ARCHITECT
Mar Eng Rev. . . . . . MARINE ENGINEERS REVIEW
Mar Engrs J. . . . . . . MARINE ENGINEERS JOURNAL
Mar Engrs Rev. . . . . MARINE ENGINEERS REVIEW
MAR FISH RE. . . . . . MARINE FISHERIES REVIEW
Mar Geol. . . . . MARINE GEOLOGY

MAR GEOTECH . . . . . MARINE GEOTECHNOLOGY
Marine Bio . . . . MARINE BIOLOGY
Marine Biol Assn UK J . . MARINE BIOLOGICAL ASSOCIATION OF THE UNITED KINGDOM. JOURNAL
Marine Eng . . . . MARINE ENGINEERING
Marine Eng/Log . . . . MARINE ENGINEERING/LOG
Marine Tech Soc J . . MARINE TECHNOLOGY SOCIETY. JOURNAL
MarkR . . . . MARKHAM REVIEW
Marq L Rev . . . . MARQUETTE LAW REVIEW
MArt . . . . MAGAZINE OF ART
MArt . . . . MUNDUS ARTIUM
Mar Technol . . . . . . MARINE TECHNOLOGY
Mar Technol Soc J . . MARINE TECHNOLOGY SOCIETY. JOURNAL
MAR TECH SJ . . . . . . MARINE TECHNOLOGY SOCIETY. JOURNAL
Marxist Quar . . . . . . MARXIST QUARTERLY
MASCHIN TEC . . . . . MASCHINENBAUTECHNIK
MASJ . . . . MIDCONTINENT AMERICAN STUDIES. JOURNAL
MASO . . . . MEIJERBERGS ARKIV FOER SVENSK ORDFORSKNING
Mass Ag Exp . . . . . . MASSACHUSETTS AGRICULTURAL EXPERIMENT STATION. PUBLICATIONS
Mass Hist Soc Coll . . MASSACHUSETTS HISTORICAL SOCIETY. COLLECTIONS
Mass Hist Soc Proc . MASSACHUSETTS HISTORICAL SOCIETY. PROCEEDINGS
Mass Inst Tech Dep Civ Eng Hydrodyn Lab Rep . . MASSACHUSETTS INSTITUTE OF TECHNOLOGY. SCHOOL OF ENGINEERING. DEPARTMENT OF CIVIL ENGINEERING HYDRODYNAMICS LABORATORY. REPORT
Mass Inst Tech Dep Civ Eng Res Earth Phys Res Rep . . MASSACHUSETTS INSTITUTE OF TECHNOLOGY. SCHOOL OF ENGINEERING. DEPARTMENT OF CIVIL ENGINEERING. RESEARCH IN EARTH PHYSICS. RESEARCH REPORT
Mass Inst Tech Dep Civ Eng Soils Publ . . MASSACHUSETTS INSTITUTE OF TECHNOLOGY. SCHOOL OF ENGINEERING. DEPARTMENT OF CIVIL ENGINEERING. SOILS PUBLICATION
Mass Inst Tech Dep Nav Architect Mar Eng Rep . . MASSACHUSETTS INSTITUTE OF TECHNOLOGY. DEPARTMENT OF NAVAL ARCHITECTURE AND MARINE ENGINEERING. REPORT
Mass Inst Tech Fluid Mech Lab Publ . . MASSACHUSETTS INSTITUTE OF TECHNOLOGY. FLUID MECHANICS LABORATORY. PUBLICATION
Mass Inst Tech Res Lab Electron Tech Rep . . MASSACHUSETTS INSTITUTE OF TECHNOLOGY. RESEARCH LABORATORY OF ELECTRONICS. TECHNICAL REPORT
Mass Lib Assn Bul . . MASSACHUSETTS LIBRARY ASSOCIATION. BULLETIN
Mass L Q . . . . MASSACHUSETTS LAW QUARTERLY
Mass Prod . . . . MASS PRODUCTION
Mass Q . . . . MASSACHUSETTS QUARTERLY REVIEW
Mass R . . . . MASSACHUSETTS REVIEW
Mass Transp . . . . . . MASS TRANSPORTATION
MAST . . . . MEMORIE DELLA REALE ACCADEMIA DELLE SCIENZE DI TORINO
Mast Draw . . . . MASTER DRAWINGS
Master Bldr . . . . MASTER BUILDER
Mast in Art . . . . MASTERS IN ART
Mast in Music . . . . MASTERS IN MUSIC
Mat . . . . MATRIX
MAT . . . . MEMORIE DELLA REALE ACCADEMIA DELLE SCIENZE DI TORINO
Mater Constr Mater Struct . . MATERIAUX ET CONSTRUCTION MATERIALS AND STRUCTURES
Mater Eng . . . . MATERIALS ENGINEERING
Mater Eval . . . . MATERIALS EVALUATION
Mater Handl Eng . . . MATERIAL HANDLING ENGINEERING
Mater Handl Mgmt . . MATERIALS HANDLING AND MANAGEMENT

Materials Eng . . . . . MATERIALS ENGINEERING
Mater J SAMPE Quart . . MATERIALS JOURNAL. SAMPE QUARTERLY
MATER PERF . . . . . . MATERIALS PERFORMANCE
Mater Plast Elastomeri Fibre Sint . . MATERIALE PLASTICE, ELASTOMERI, FIBRE SINTETICE
Mater Process Technol . . MATERIALS AND PROCESS TECHNOLOGY
Mater Prot . . . . MATERIALS PROTECTION
Mater Prot Performance . . MATERIALS PROTECTION AND PERFORMANCE
Materpruefengsamt Bauw Tech Hochsch Muenchen Der . . MATERIALPRUEFENGSAMT FUER DAS BAUWESEN DER
        TECHNISCHEN HOCHSCHULE MUENCHEN. BERICHT
Mater Res Bull . . . . MATERIALS RESEARCH BULLETIN
Mater Res Stand . . . MATERIALS RESEARCH AND STANDARDS
MATER SCI E . . . . . . MATERIALS SCIENCE AND ENGINEERING
Mater Tech . . . . MATERIAUX ET TECHNIQUES
MAT FYS MED . . . . . MATEMATISK-FYSISKE MEDDELELSER KONGELIGE DANSKE VIDENSKABERNES SELSKAB
MATH ANNAL . . . . . MATHEMATISCHE ANNALEN
MATH COMPUT . . . . MATHEMATICS OF COMPUTATION
Math Ed for Teaching . . MATHEMATICAL EDUCATION FOR TEACHING
Math Gazette . . . . . MATHEMATICAL GAZETTE
Math in School . . . . . MATHEMATICS IN SCHOOL
Math Mo . . . . MATHEMATICAL MONTHLY
MATH NACHR . . . . . MATHEMATISCHE NACHRICHTEN
Math of Comput . . . MATHEMATICS OF COMPUTATION
MATH PROC C . . . . . MATHEMATICAL PROCEEDINGS OF THE CAMBRIDGE PHILOSOPHICAL SOCIETY
MATH PROGR . . . . . MATHEMATICAL PROGRAMMING
MathR . . . . MATHEMATICAL REVIEWS
MATH SCAND . . . . . MATHEMATICA SCANDINAVICA
Math Sci . . . . MATHEMATICAL SCIENCES
MATH SYST T . . . . . . MATHEMATICAL SYSTEMS THEORY
Math Teach . . . . MATHEMATICS TEACHER
Math Teaching . . . . MATHEMATICS TEACHING
MATH Z . . . . MATHEMATISCHE ZEITSCHRIFT
MatIRJa . . . . MATERIALY I ISSLEDOVANIJA PO ISTORII RUSSKOGO JAZYKA
MatRD . . . . MATERIALY I ISSLEDOVANIJA PO RUSSKOJ DIALEKTOLOGII
MATR TENS Q . . . . . MATRIX AND TENSOR QUARTERLY
MatSL . . . . MATICA SLOVENSKA
Maur . . . . MAURETANIA
MAW . . . . MEDEDEELINGEN DER AKADEMIE VAN WETENSCHAPPEN
MAWA . . . . MEDEDEELINGEN DER AKADEMIE VAN WETENSCHAPPEN
MAYO CLIN P . . . . . MAYO CLINIC PROCEEDINGS
Maz . . . . MAZUNGUMZO
MB . . . . MAGAZINE OF BUILDING
MB . . . . MARE BALTICUM
MB . . . . MEDIAEVALIA BOHEMICA
MB . . . . MELANGES BALDENSPERGER
MB . . . . MORE BOOKS
MB . . . . MUSEE BELGE
MBBull . . . . BULLETIN BIBLIOGRAPHIQUE DU MUSEE BELGE
MBDL . . . . MUENSTERSCHE BEITRAEGE ZUR DEUTSCHEN LITERATUR
MBG . . . . MARBURGER BEITRAEGE ZUR GERMANISTIK
MbJb . . . . MECKLENBURGER JAHRBUCH SCHWERIN
MBOP . . . . MONITEUR BIBLIOGRAPHIQUE. BULLETIN OFFICIEL DES IMPRIMES PUBLIES EN POLOGNE

MBP . . . . MUENCHENER BEITRAEGE ZUR PAPYRUSFORSCHUNG
M/C . . . . MARKETING/COMMUNICATIONS
MC . . . . MONDO CLASSICO
MC . . . . MONTE CARMELO
MC . . . . MONTHLY CRITERION
MCACO . . . . MEMOIRES DE LA COMMISSION DES ANTIQUITES DE LA COTE D'OR
MCar . . . . MONTE CARMELO
McBride's . . . . MCBRIDE'S MAGAZINE
McClure . . . . MCCLURE'S MAGAZINE
McCQ . . . . MCCORMICK QUARTERLY
MCG . . . . MONATSHEFTE DER COMENIUS-GESELLSCHAFT
MCGILL L J . . . . MCGILL LAW JOURNAL
MCh . . . . MIKRASIATIKI CHRONIKA
MCHAC . . . . MEMOIRES DU CERCLE HISTORIQUE ET ARCHEOLOGIQUE DE COURTRAI
M Chr Lit . . . . MAGAZINE OF CHRISTIAN LITERATURE
MCJ . . . . MENSAJERO DEL CORAZON DE JESUS
MCL . . . . MARTIN CLASSICAL LECTURES
MCLB . . . . MODERN AND CLASSICAL LANGUAGE BULLETIN
MCM . . . . MAGIC CARPET MAGAZINE
MCMT . . . . MAIN CURRENTS IN MODERN THOUGHT
McN R . . . . MCNEESE REVIEW
MCom . . . . MISCELANEA COMILLAS
MCR . . . . MELBOURNE CRITICAL REVIEW (UNIVERSITY OF MELBOURNE)
MCRHAC . . . . MEMOIRES DU CERCLE ROYAL HISTORIQUE ET ARCHEOLOGIQUE DE COURTRAI
MCS . . . . MANCHESTER CUNEIFORM STUDIES
MCV . . . . MELANGES DE LA CASA DE VELAZQUEZ
MD . . . . MEDIA DECISIONS
MD . . . . MODERN DRAMA
MD . . . . MUSICA DISCIPLINA
MDAC . . . . MYSTERY AND DETECTION ANNUAL
Md Ag Exp . . . . MARYLAND AGRICULTURAL EXPERIMENT STATION. PUBLICATIONS
MDAI . . . . MITTEILUNGEN DES DEUTSCHEN ARCHAOLOGISCHEN INSTITUTS
MDAI(A) . . . . MITTEILUNGEN DES DEUTSCHEN ARCHAOLOGISCHEN INSTITUTS. ABTEILUNG (ATHENS)
MDAI(K) . . . . MITTEILUNGEN DES DEUTSCHEN ARCHAOLOGISCHEN INSTITUTS. ABTEILUNG (KAIRO)
MDAI(M) . . . . MITTEILUNGEN DES DEUTSCHEN ARCHAOLOGISCHEN INSTITUTS. ABTEILUNG(MADRID)
MDAI(R) . . . . MITTEILUNGEN DER DEUTSCHEN ARCHAOLOGISCHEN INSTITUTS. ABTEILUNG (ROME)
MDAM . . . . MAJALLE(H)-YE DANESHKADE(H)-YE ADABIYYAT-E MASHHAD
MDan . . . . MEDDELESER FRA DANSKLAERERFORENINGEN
MDA (Tehran) . . . . . MAJAALE (H)-YE DANESHKADE (H)-YE ADABIYYAT VA OLUN-E ENSANIE-YE
MdF . . . . MERCURE DE FRANCE
MDF . . . . MITTELDEUTSCHE FORSCHUNGEN
MDG . . . . MONATSSCHRISFT FUER DAS DEUTSCHE GEISTESLEBEN
Md Geol Surv Bull . . MARYLAND GEOLOGICAL SURVEY. BULLETIN
Md Geol Surv Rep Invest . . MARYLAND GEOLOGICAL SURVEY. REPORT OF INVESTIGATIONS
Md Hist Mag . . . . . . MARYLAND HISTORICAL MAGAZINE
Md Hist Soc Fund-Publ . . MARYLAND HISTORICAL SOCIETY. FUND-PUBLICATIONS
MdHM . . . . MARYLAND HISTORICAL MAGAZINE
MdJb . . . . MITTELDEUTSCHES JAHRBUCH
MDL . . . . MATERIALIEN ZUR DEUTSCHEN LITERATUR
MD L REV . . . . MARYLAND LAW REVIEW
MDOG . . . . MITTEILUNGEN DER DEUTSCHEN ORIENT-GESELLSCHAFT ZU BERLIN

MDtShG . . . . MITTEILUNGEN DER DEUTSCHEN SHAKESPEARE-GESELLSCHAFT
MDU . . . . MONATSHEFTE FUER DEN DEUTSCHEN UNTERRICHT
Me . . . . MEANDER
Me . . . . MEANING
ME . . . . MUSIKERZIEHUNG
Mea . . . . MEANDER
MEAH . . . . MISCELANEA DE ESTUDIOS ARABES Y HEBRAICOS
Meanjin . . . . MEANJIN QUARTERLY (UNIVERSITY OF MELBOURNE)
Meas Contr . . . . MEASUREMENT AND CONTROL
MEAS EVAL G . . . . . MEASUREMENT AND EVALUATION IN GUIDANCE
Meas Tech . . . . MEASUREMENT TECHNIQUES
MEAS TECH R . . . . . MEASUREMENT TECHNIQUES USSR
MEB . . . . MISSOURI ENGLISH BULLETIN
MEC . . . . MINISTERIO DE EDUCACAO E CULTURA
Mec Elec . . . . MECANIQUE ELECTRICITE
MECH AGE D . . . . . . MECHANISMS OF AGEING AND DEVELOPMENT
MECHANIK . . . . MECHANIK MIESIECZNIK NAUKOWO-TECHNICZNY
Mech Eng . . . . MECHANICAL ENGINEERING
Mech Eng Bull . . . . . MECHANICAL ENGINEERING BULLETIN
Mech Eng Sci Monogr . . MECHANICAL ENGINEERING SCIENCE MONOGRAPH. INSTITUTION OF MECHANICAL
ENGINEERS (LONDON)
Mech Handl . . . . MECHANICAL HANDLING
Mech Illus . . . . MECHANIX ILLUSTRATED
MECH MACH T . . . . . MECHANISM AND MACHINE THEORY
Mec Mat Elec . . . . . MECANIQUE-MATERIAUX-ELECTRICITE
Mech Miesiecznik Nauk-Tech . . MECHANIK, MIESIECZNIK NAUKOWO-TECHNICZNY
Mech Teor i Stoso . . MECHANIKA TEORETYCZNA I STOSOWANA
Med . . . . MEDITERRANEO
MED . . . . MIDDLE ENGLISH DICTIONARY
MedAE . . . . MEDIUM AEVUM
MedAev . . . . MEDIUM AEVUM
Med and Biol Eng . . . MEDICAL AND BIOLOGICAL ENGINEERING
Med Arch . . . . MEDIEVAL ARCHAEOLOGY
MED BIO ENG . . . . . MEDICAL AND BIOLOGICAL ENGINEERING
MED BIO ILL . . . . . . MEDICAL AND BIOLOGICAL ILLUSTRATION
MED BIOL . . . . MEDICAL BIOLOGY
Med Biol Eng . . . . . MEDICAL AND BIOLOGICAL ENGINEERING
MED CARE . . . . MEDICAL CARE
MED CLIN NA . . . . . MEDICAL CLINICS OF NORTH AMERICA
MED C VIRG . . . . . . MEDICAL COLLEGE OF VIRGINIA QUARTERLY
Medd Kgl Tek Hogsk Inst Elek Anlaggnings-tek Elektromaskinlara . . MEDDELANDE FRAN KUNGL. TEKNISKA
HOGSKOLANS INSTITUTIONER FOR ELEKTRISK ANLAGGNINSTEKNIK OCH ELEKTROMASKINLARA
MEDD NOR SK . . . . . MEDDELELSER FRA DET NORSKE SKOGFORSOKSVESEN
Medd Statens Skeppsprovningsanst . . MEDDELANDEN FRAN STATENS SKEPPSPROVNINGSANSTALT
Meded Kon Nederl Ak Wetensch . . MEDEDEELINGEN DER KONINKLIJKE NEDERLANDSCHE AKADEMIE VAN
WETENSCHAPPEN
Meded Kon Vl Ak Wetensch . . MEDEDEELINGEN DER KONINKLIJKE VLAAMSCHE AKADEMIE VAN WETENSCHAPPEN
Meded Vl Topon Ver . . MEDEDEELINGEN UITGEGEVEN DOOR DE VLAAMSCHE TOPONYMISCHE VEREENIGING
Meded Zuid-Nederl Dial Centr . . MEDEDEELINGEN VAN DE ZUID-NEDERLANDSCHE DIALECT CENTRALE
Med et Hum . . . . . . MEDIAEVALIA ET HUMANISTICA
MedHum . . . . MEDIAEVALIA ET HUMANISTICA

Med Instrum...... MEDICAL INSTRUMENTATION
Medit.......... MEDITERRANEO
M ED J......... MUSIC EDUCATORS JOURNAL
MED J AUST...... MEDICAL JOURNAL OF AUSTRALIA
MED KLIN........ MEDIZINISCHE KLINIK
MED LAB TEC...... MEDICAL LABORATORY TECHNOLOGY
Med Lett Drugs Ther.. MEDICAL LETTER ON DRUGS AND THERAPEUTICS
Med Lib Assn Bul... MEDICAL LIBRARY ASSOCIATION. BULLETIN
MED MICROBI..... MEDICAL MICROBIOLOGY AND IMMUNOLOGY
MED PR TECH..... MEDICAL PROGRESS THROUGH TECHNOLOGY
MedR........... MEDITERRANEAN REVIEW
Med Res Eng...... MEDICAL RESEARCH ENGINEERING
MedRom......... MEDIOEVO ROMANZO
MedS........... MEDICAL SOCIOECONOMIC RESEARCH SOURCES
MedS........... MEDIAEVAL STUDIES
MED SCI & L...... MEDICINE, SCIENCE AND THE LAW
MED SCI LAW..... MEDICINE, SCIENCE AND THE LAW
MED SCI SPT...... MEDICINE AND SCIENCE IN SPORTS
Med St.......... MEDIAEVAL STUDIES
Med Tr TQ........ MEDICAL TRIAL TECHNIQUE QUARTERLY
MEEP........... MIDDLE EAST ECONOMIC PAPERS
Meerestech Mar Tech.. MEERESTECHNIK, MARINE TECHNOLOGY
MEFO.......... MISCELANEA DE ESTUDIOS DEDICADOS A FERNANDO ORTIZ POR SUS DISCIPULOS
MEFR.......... MELANGES D'ARCHEOLOGIE ET D'HISTOIRE DE L'ECOLE FRANCAISE DE ROME
MEJ........... MIDDLE EAST JOURNAL
MEJC.......... MISCELANEA DE ESTUDOS A JOAQUIM DE CARVALHO
Mel........... MELANGES
Melanges Chamard.. MELANGES D'HISTOIRE LITTERAIRE DE LA RENAISSANCE OFFERTS A HENRI CHAMARD
Melanges Hoepffner.. MELANGES DE PHILOLOGIE ROMANE ET DE LITTERATURE MEDIEVALE OFFERTS A ERNEST
        HOEPFFNER
Melanges Roques.. MELANGES DE LINGUISTIQUE ET DE LITTERATURE ROMANES OFFERTS A MARIO ROQUES
MelbSS......... MELBOURNE SLAVONIC STUDIES
MEL MAKER...... MELODY MAKER
MeM........... MENS EN MUZIEK
MEM AM MATH.... MEMOIRS OF THE AMERICAN MATHEMATICAL SOCIETY
Mem Bur Rech Geol Minieres.. MEMOIRES DU BUREAU DE RECHERCHES GEOLOGIQUES ET MINIERES (FRANCE)
MEM COGNIT..... MEMORY AND COGNITION
Mem Coll Sci Univ Kyoto Ser A Math.. MEMOIRS OF THE COLLEGE OF SCIENCE. UNIVERSITY OF KYOTO. SERIES A.
        MATHEMATICS
Mem Coll Sci Univ Kyoto Ser B Geol Biol.. MEMOIRS OF THE COLLEGE OF SCIENCE. UNIVERSITY OF KYOTO. SERIES B.
        GEOLOGY AND BIOLOGY
Mem Def Acad Jap.. MEMOIRS OF THE DEFENSE ACADEMY. JAPAN
MEM ENT S C...... MEMOIRS OF THE ENTOMOLOGICAL SOCIETY OF CANADA
Mem Fac Eng Hokkaido Univ Sapporo Jap.. MEMOIRS OF THE FACULTY OF ENGINEERING. HOKKAIDO UNIVERSITY.
        SAPPORO,JAPAN
Mem Fac Eng Kumamoto Univ.. MEMOIRS OF THE FACULTY OF ENGINEERING. KUMAMOTO UNIVERSITY
Mem Fac Eng Kyoto Univ.. MEMOIRS OF THE FACULTY OF ENGINEERING. KYOTO UNIVERSITY
Mem Fac Eng Kyushu Univ.. MEMOIRS OF THE FACULTY OF ENGINEERING. KYUSHU UNIVERSITY
Mem Geol Surv India.. MEMOIRS OF THE GEOLOGICAL SURVEY OF INDIA
Mem Geol Surv of NSW Geol.. MEMOIRS OF THE GEOLOGICAL SURVEY OF NEW SOUTH WALES. DEPARTMENT OF
        MINES. GEOLOGY

PERIODICAL TITLE ABBREVIATIONS

Memphis St U L Rev . . MEMPHIS STATE UNIVERSITY LAW REVIEW
MenJ . . . . MENORAH JOURNAL
Menabo . . . . MENABO DI LETTERATURA
MEM S R MET . . . . . MEMOIRES SCIENTIFIQUES DE LA REVUE DE METALLURGIE
Mem Sci Rev Met . . . MEMOIRES SCIENTIFIQUES DE LA REVUE DE METALLURGIE
MENNL . . . . MENNONITE LIFE
Mennonite Q R . . . . MENNONITE QUARTERLY REVIEW
Menorah J . . . . MENORAH JOURNAL
MENS EN MEL . . . . . MENS EN MELODIE
Mental Hyg . . . . . . MENTAL HYGIENE
MENTAL RETA . . . . . MENTAL RETARDATION
MeP . . . . MEKEDONSKI PREGLED. SPISANIE ZA NAUKA. LITERATURA I OBSTEOSTVEN ZIVOT
MER . . . . MALAYAN ECONOMIC REVIEW
MER . . . . MIDWEST ENGLISH REVIEW
Merc . . . . LONDON MERCURY
MERCER LAW . . . . . . MERCER LAW REVIEW
Mercersb . . . . MERCERSBURG REVIEW
Merch W . . . . MERCHANDISING WEEK
MERC S ARCH . . . . . MERCURY SERIES. ARCHAEOLOGICAL SURVEY OF CANADA. PAPERS
MERC S ETHN . . . . . . MERCURY SERIES. ETHNOLOGY DIVISION. PAPERS
Mercure . . . . MERCURE DE FRANCE
Meres Autom . . . . . MERES ES AUTOMATIKA
MERF . . . . MELANGES DE L'ECOLE ROUMAINE EN FRANCE
MerP . . . . MERCURIO PERUANO
MERRIL-PAL . . . . . . MERRILL-PALMER QUARTERLY
MES REG AUT . . . . . MESURES REGULATION AUTOMATISME
Mes Regul Automat . . MESURES, REGULATION, AUTOMATISME
Mes Steuern Regeln . . MESSEN, STEUERN, REGELN
Met . . . . METROECONOMICA
MetAb . . . . METALS ABSTRACTS
Met ABM . . . . METALURGIA, ABM (ASSOCIACAO BRASILERIRA DE METAIS)
METABOLISM . . . . . METABOLISM-CLINICAL AND EXPERIMENTAL
Metal ABM . . . . METALURGIA, ABM (ASSOCIACAO BRASILEIRA DE METAIS)
METAL CONS . . . . . . METAL CONSTRUCTION
Metal Constr Br Weld J . . METAL CONSTRUCTION AND BRITISH WELDING JOURNAL
METAL ENG Q . . . . . METALS ENGINEERING QUARTERLY
Metal Finish . . . . . . METAL FINISHING
Metal Form . . . . . . METAL FORMING
Metal Ind . . . . METAL INDUSTRY
Metall Constr Mec . . METALLURGIE ET LA CONSTRUCTION MECANIQUE
Metallges Rev Activ . . METALLGESELLSCHAFT AG. FRANKFURT/MAIN. REVIEW OF THE ACTIVITIES
METALL ITAL . . . . . . METALLURGIA ITALIANA
METALL MET . . . . . . METALLURGIA AND METAL FORMING
Metall Met Form . . . METALLURGIA AND METAL FORMING
Metallogr Rev . . . . . METALLOGRAPHIC REVIEW
Metallov i Term Obrab Metal . . METALLOVEDENIE I TERMICHESKAYA OBRABOTKA METALLOV
Metall Rep CRM . . . METALLURGICAL REPORTS CRM (CENTRE DE RECHERCHES METALLURGIQUES)
Metall Rev . . . . METALLURGICAL REVIEWS
METALL T-A . . . . METALLURGICAL TRANSACTIONS A. PHYSICAL METALLURGY AND MATERIALS SCIENCE
METALL T-B . . . . METALLURGICAL TRANSACTIONS B. PROCESS METALLURGY
Metall Trans . . . . . . METALLURGICAL TRANSACTIONS

Metal Powder Ind Fed Stand . . METAL POWDER INDUSTRIES FEDERATION. MPIF STANDARD
Metal Prog . . . . METAL PROGRESS
METAL SCI H . . . . . . METAL SCIENCE AND HEAT TREATMENT
Metal Sci J . . . . METAL SCIENCE JOURNAL
Metals Eng Quart . . . METALS ENGINEERING QUARTERLY
Metals Mater . . . . . METALS AND MATERIALS
METAL STAMP . . . . . METAL STAMPING
Metal Treat . . . . METAL TREATING
Metalwrkg Prod . . . METALWORKING PRODUCTION
Met&GeoAb . . . . . . METEOROLOGICAL AND GEOASTROPHYSICAL ABSTRACTS
Metaux (Corros-Ind) . . METAUX (CORROSION-INDUSTRIES)
Met Constr Br Weld J . . METAL CONSTRUCTION AND BRITISH WELDING JOURNAL
Met Constr Mec . . . METALLURGIE ET LA CONSTRUCTION MECANIQUE
Met (Corros Ind) . . . METAUX (CORROSION-INDUSTRIES)
Met Eng Q . . . . METALS ENGINEERING QUARTERLY
METEOR MAG . . . . . METEOROLOGICAL MAGAZINE
METEOR RUND . . . . . METEOROLOGISCHE RUNDSCHAU
Met Finish J . . . . . . METAL FINISHING JOURNAL
MetH . . . . MEDIEVALIA ET HUMANISTICA
MethH . . . . METHODIST HISTORY
Meth M . . . . METHODIST MAGAZINE
Meth Q . . . . METHODIST QUARTERLY
Meth Q R . . . . METHODIST QUARTERLY REVIEW
Meth R . . . . METHODIST REVIEW
MET INF MED . . . . . METHODS OF INFORMATION IN MEDICINE
Met Ital . . . . METALLURGIA ITALIANA
Met J Univ Strathclyde Glasgow . . METALLURGICAL JOURNAL. UNIVERSITY OF STRATHCLYDE, GLASGOW
Met Mater . . . . METALS AND MATERIALS
Met Mus Bul . . . . . . METROPOLITAN MUSEUM OF ART. BULLETIN
Met Mus J . . . . METROPOLITAN MUSEUM JOURNAL
Met Prog . . . . METAL PROGRESS
Met Rev (Suppl Metals Mater) . . METALLURGICAL REVIEWS (SUPPLEMENT TO METALS AND MATERIALS)
Metro . . . . METRONOME
Metrop . . . . METROPOLITAN
Metropolitan Life Stat Bul . . METROPOLITAN LIFE INSURANCE COMPANY. STATISTICAL BULLETIN
Met Sci Heat Treat . . METAL SCIENCE AND HEAT TREATMENT
Met Sci J . . . . METAL SCIENCE JOURNAL
Met Soc AIME Conf . . METALLURGICAL SOCIETY. AMERICAN INSTITUTE OF MINING, METALLURGICAL AND PETROLEUM ENGINEERS. CONFERENCES
Met Soc AIME Inst Metals Div Spec Rep . . METALLURGICAL SOCIETY. AMERICAN INSTITUTE OF MINING, METALLURGICAL AND PETROLEUM ENGINEERS. INSTITUTE OF METALS DIVISION. SPECIAL REPORT
Met Soc AIME TMS Pap . . METALLURGICAL SOCIETY. AMERICAN INSTITUTE OF MINING, METALLURGICAL AND PETROLEUM ENGINEERS. TMS PAPERS
Met Trans . . . . METALLURGICAL TRANSACTIONS
Met Treat . . . . METAL TREATING
Metwork Prod . . . . . METALWORKING PRODUCTION
Mex Folkways . . . . . MEXICAN FOLKWAYS
MF . . . . MAKEDONSKI FOLKLOR
MF . . . . MERCURE DE FRANCE
MF . . . . MIDWEST FOLKLORE

MF . . . . MISCELLANEA FRANCESCANA
MF . . . . MISIONES FRANCISCANOS
MF . . . . MODERN PHILOLOGY
MF . . . . MUSIKFORSCHUNG
MfAb . . . . MICROFILM ABSTRACTS
MFCG . . . . MITTEILUNGEN UND FORSCHUNGSBEITRAEGE DER CUSANUS-GESELLSCHAFT
MFCL . . . . MEMOIRE ET TRAVAUX PUBLIES PAR LES FACULTES CATHOLIQUES DE LILLE
MFCusanusG . . . . . . MITTEILUNGEN UND FORSCHUNGSBEITRAEGE DER CUSANUS-GESELLSCHAFT
MFDU . . . . MONATSHEFTE FUER DEUTSCHEN UNTERRICHT
Mfg Chem . . . . MANUFACTURING CHEMIST
Mfg Eng Manage . . . MANUFACTURING ENGINEERING AND MANAGEMENT
MFI . . . . MIDWEST FOLKLORE (INDIANA UNIVERSITY)
MFN . . . . MITTEILUNGEN FUER NAMENKUNDE (AACHEN)
MFR . . . . MALTESE FOLKLORE REVIEW (BALZAN)
MFr . . . . MERCURE DE FRANCE
MFr . . . . MISCELLANEA FRANSCESCANA
MFS . . . . MEDDELANDEN FRAN STRINDBERGSSAELLSKAPET
MFS . . . . MODERN FICTION STUDIES
MFSF . . . . MAGAZINE OF FANTASY AND SCIENCE FICTION
MG . . . . MANCHESTER GUARDIAN
MG . . . . MOLODAYA GVARDIYA (MOSCOW)
MGATC . . . . MODERN GERMAN AUTHORS, TEXTS AND CONTEXTS
MGB . . . . MUENCHENER GERMANISTISCHE BEITRAEGE
MGBL . . . . MUEHLHAUSER GESCHICHTSBLAETTER
MG C POP CR . . . . . MONOGRAPHS OF THE CAROLINA POPULATION CENTER
MGGW . . . . MITTEILUNGEN DER GEOGRAPHISCHEN GESELLSCHAFT IN WIEN
MGH . . . . MONUMENTA GERMANIAE HISTORICA
MGJ . . . . MONATSSCHRIFT FUER DIE GESCHICHTE UND WISSENSCHAFT DES JUDENTUMUS
MGM . . . . MITTEILUNGEN ZUR GESCHICHTE DER MEDIZIN UND DER NATURWISSENSCHAFT
MGNM . . . . MITTEILUNGEN AUS DEM GERMANISCHEN NATIONALMUSEUM
MGOKL . . . . MEDEDEELINGEN VAN DE GESCHIED- EN OUDHEIDKUNDIGE KRING VOOR LEUVEN EN OMGEVING
MGOKLeuven . . . . . MEDEDEELINGEN VAN DE GESCHIED- EN OUDHEIDKUNDIGE KRING VOOR LEUVEN EN OMGEVING
MGPGA . . . . MONATSBLAETTER DIE GESELLSCHAFT FUER POMMERSCHE GESCHICHTE UND ALTERTUMS-KUNDE
MGSL . . . . MINAS GERAIS. SUPLEMENTO LITERARIO
MGSLK . . . . MITTEILUNGEN DER GESELLSCHAFT FUER SALZBURGER LANDESKUNDE
MG SOC ANTH . . . . . MONOGRAPHS ON SOCIAL ANTHROPOLOGY
MG S WLD . . . . MONOGRAPH SERIES IN WORLD AFFAIRS. UNIVERSITY OF DENVER
Mgt Accounting . . . . MANAGEMENT ACCOUNTING
Mgt Adviser . . . . . . MANAGEMENT ADVISER
Mgt Int R . . . . MANAGEMENT INTERNATIONAL REVIEW
Mgt Methods . . . . . MANAGEMENT METHODS
Mgt R . . . . MANAGEMENT REVIEW
Mgt Rec . . . . MANAGEMENT RECORD
Mgt Sci . . . . MANAGEMENT SCIENCE
Mgt Services . . . . . . MANAGEMENT SERVICES
MGW . . . . MANCHESTER GUARDIAN WEEKLY
MGWJ . . . . MONATSSCHRIFT FUER GESCHICHTE UND WISSENSCHAFT DES JUDENTUMS
MH . . . . MEDIAEVALIA ET HUMANISTICA

MH............. MICHIGAN HISTORY
MH............. MINNESOTA HISTORY
MH............. MISSIONALIA HISPANICA
MH............. MUSEUM HELVETICUM
MH............. MUSICHANDEL
MHAR........... MEMOIRES DE LA SECTION HISTORIQUE DE L'ACADEMIE ROUMAINE
MHB........... MENNONITE HISTORICAL BULLETIN
MHF........... MATERIALY DO HISTORII FILOZOFII STREDNIOWIECZNEJ W POLSCE
MHF........... MONUMENTS HISTORIQUES DE LA FRANCE
MHG........... MITTEILUNEN DER E.T.A. HOFFMAN-GESELLSCHAFT
MHis........... MUNDO HISPANICO
MHL........... MITTEILUNGEN AUS DER HISTORISCHEN LITERATUR
MHM........... MARYLAND HISTORICAL MAGAZINE
MHM........... MICHIGAN HISTORY MAGAZINE
MHR........... MISSOURI HISTORICAL REVIEW
MHRA Bull....... MODERN HUMANITIES RESEARCH ASSOCIATION. BULLETIN
MHRADS........ MODERN HUMANITIES RESEARCH ASSOCIATION. DISSERTATION SERIES
MHRev.......... MALAHAT REVIEW
MHRKG......... MONATSHEFTE FUER RHEINISCHE KIRCHENGESCHICHTE
MHS........... MELANGES D'HISTOIRE SOCIALE
MHS........... MORAVIAN HISTORICAL SOCIETY. TRANSACTIONS
MHSB.......... MISSOURI HISTORICAL SOCIETY. BULLETIN
MHSch......... MONATSCHRIFT FUER HOEHERE SCHULEN
MHSJ.......... MONUMENTA HISTORICA SOCIETATIS JESU
MHum.......... MEDIAEVALIA ET HUMANISTICA
MHVP.......... MITTEILUNGEN DER HISTORISCHER VEREIN FUER DIE PFALZ
MI............. MAN IN INDIA
MI............. MARKETING INSIGHTS
Mi............. MIND
MIA........... MITTEILUNGEN. INSTITUT FUER AUSLANDSBEZIEHUNGEN (STUTTGART)
MichA.......... MICHIGAN ACADEMICIAN
Mich Ag Exp...... MICHIGAN AGRICULTURAL COLLEGE. AGRICULTURAL EXPERIMENT STATION. PUBLICATIONS
Mich Alumni Quar Rev.. MICHIGAN ALUMNI QUARTERLY REVIEW
Mich Bus R....... MICHIGAN BUSINESS REVIEW
Mich Ed J........ MICHIGAN EDUCATION JOURNAL
Mich Geol Surv Bull.. MICHIGAN GEOLOGICAL SURVEY. BULLETIN
MichH.......... MICHIGAN HISTORY MAGAZINE
MICH LAW R...... MICHIGAN LAW REVIEW
MICH LIBN....... MICHIGAN LIBRARIAN
Mich Lib News..... MICHIGAN LIBRARY NEWS
MICH L REV....... MICHIGAN LAW REVIEW
MICH MATH J..... MICHIGAN MATHEMATICAL JOURNAL
Mich Munic R..... MICHIGAN MUNICIPAL REVIEW
MichQR......... MICHIGAN QUARTERLY REVIEW
Mich S B J........ MICHIGAN STATE BAR JOURNAL
Mich Univ Dep Nav Architect Mar Eng Rep.. MICHIGAN UNIVERSITY. DEPARTMENT OF NAVAL ARCHITECTURE AND
                    MARINE ENGINEERING. REPORT
MICROBIOLOG..... MICROBIOLOGY
MICROBIOS L...... MICROBIOS LETTERS
MICROCHEM J..... MICROCHEMICAL JOURNAL
MICROEL REL...... MICROELECTRONICS AND RELIABILITY

MICROSC ACT..... MICROSCOPICA ACTA
MICROVASC R..... MICROVASCULAR RESEARCH
MidA........... MID-AMERICA
MidAm.......... MID-AMERICA
Mid Cont........ MID-CONTINENT
Midcontinent Am Studies Jour.. MIDCONTINENT AMERICAN STUDIES JOURNAL
MIDDLE E J....... MIDDLE EAST JOURNAL
MIDDLE E MG..... MIDDLE EASTERN MONOGRAPHS
MIDDLE E ST...... MIDDLE EASTERN STUDIES
Middle States Assn Col & Sec Sch Proc.. MIDDLE STATES ASSOCIATION OF COLLEGES AND SECONDARY SCHOOLS. PROCEEDINGS
Middle States Council for Social Studies Proc.. MIDDLE STATES COUNCIL FOR THE SOCIAL STUDIES. PROCEEDINGS
Mid E J.......... MIDDLE EAST JOURNAL
MIDEO.......... MELANGES DE L'INSTITUT DOMINICAIN DE'ETUDES ORIENTALES
Mid E Studies...... MIDDLE EASTERN STUDIES
Midland........ MIDLAND MONTHLY
Midland Sch...... MIDLAND SCHOOLS
MidM........... MIDWEST MONOGRAPHS
MidQ........... MIDWEST QUARTERLY
MidR........... MIDWEST REVIEW
Midwest Eng...... MIDWEST ENGINEER
Midwest J Phil..... MIDWEST JOURNAL OF PHILOSOPHY
Midw Jour Pol Sci.. MIDWEST JOURNAL OF POLITICAL SCIENCE
Midw Quar....... MIDWEST QUARTERLY
MIGFW.......... MITTEILUNGEN DES INSTITUTS FUER GESCHICHTSFORSCHUNG UND ARCHIVWISSENSCHAFT IN WIEN
MIKROCH ACT..... MIKROCHIMICA ACTA
MIL............. MEMORIE DELL'ISTITUTO LOMBARDO
Mil Aff.......... MILITARY AFFAIRS
MILBANK MEM.... MILBANK MEMORIAL FUND QUARTERLY
Mil Eng.......... MILITARY ENGINEER
MILIT MED....... MILITARY MEDICINE
Milk Plant Mo..... MILK PLANT MONTHLY
Mill News........ MILL NEWS-LETTER
Mil L Rev......... MILITARY LAW REVIEW
Mil Rev.......... MILITARY REVIEW
MILT LAW R...... MILITARY LAW REVIEW
Milton N......... MILTON NEWSLETTER
Milton Q........ MILTON QUARTERLY
Milton S........ MILTON STUDIES
Min............. MINERVA
Min & Met........ MINING AND METALLURGY
Min Cong J....... MINING CONGRESS JOURNAL
MIN DEPOSIT...... MINERALIUM DEPOSITA
Min Eng.......... MINING ENGINEERING
Min Eng (Lond).... MINING ENGINEER (LONDON)
Min Eng (NY)...... MINING ENGINEERING (NEW YORK)
Mine Quarry...... MINE AND QUARRY
Min Equip Int...... MINING EQUIPMENT INTERNATIONAL
MINERAL MAG.... MINERALOGICAL MAGAZINE
Miner Deposita.... MINERALIUM DEPOSITA

Mineria Met (Mexico City). . MINERIA Y METALURGIA (MEXICO CITY)
Miner Process. . . . . MINERALS PROCESSING
Miner Sci Eng. . . . . . MINERALS SCIENCE AND ENGINEERING
MINERVA PED. . . . . MINERVA PEDIATRICA
Mines Met. . . . . . . MINES ET METALLURGIE
Mines Metall. . . . . . MINES ET METALLURGIE
Mining Congr J. . . . MINING CONGRESS JOURNAL
Mining Elec Mech Eng. . MINING ELECTRICAL & MECHANICAL ENGINEER
Mining Eng (London). . MINING ENGINEER (LONDON)
Mining Eng (NY). . . MINING ENGINEERING (NEW YORK)
Mining Mag. . . . . . MINING MAGAZINE
Mining Met Quart. . MINING AND METALLURGY QUARTERLY
Mining Miner Eng. . . MINING AND MINERALS ENGINEERING
Mining Technol. . . . MINING TECHNOLOGY
Min Mag. . . . . MINING MAGAZINE
Min Miner Engng. . . MINING AND MINERALS ENGINEERING
Minn Ag Exp. . . . . . MINNESOTA UNIVERSITY. AGRICULTURAL EXPERIMENT STATION. PUBLICATIONS
Minneapolis Inst Bul. . MINNEAPOLIS INSTITUTE OF ARTS. BULLETIN
Minn Farm & Home Sci. . MINNESOTA FARM AND HOME SCIENCE
Minn Geol Surv Bull. . MINNESOTA GEOLOGICAL SURVEY. BULLETIN
Minn Geol Surv Rep Invest. . MINNESOTA GEOLOGICAL SURVEY. REPORT OF INVESTIGATIONS
Minn H. . . . . MINNESOTA HISTORY
Minn Hort. . . . . . . MINNESOTA HORTICULTURIST
Minn Inst Arts Bul. . MINNEAPOLIS INSTITUTE OF ARTS. BULLETIN
Minn Inst Bul. . . . . MINNEAPOLIS INSTITUTE OF ARTS. BULLETIN
Minn J Ed. . . . . . . MINNESOTA JOURNAL OF EDUCATION
Minn J of Ed. . . . . . MINNESOTA JOURNAL OF EDUCATION
Minn L Rev. . . . . . . MINNESOTA LAW REVIEW
Minn Lib. . . . . MINNESOTA LIBRARIES
MINN MED. . . . . . MINNESOTA MEDICINE
MinnR. . . . . MINNESOTA REVIEW
Minn Univ St Anthony Falls Hydraul Lab Proj Rep. . MINNESOTA UNIVERSITY. ST. ANTHONY FALLS HYDRAULIC
LABORATORY. PROJECT REPORT
Minn Univ St Anthony Falls Hydraul Lab Tech Pap. . MINNESOTA UNIVERSITY. ST. ANTHONY FALLS HYDRAULIC
LABORATORY. TECHNICAL PAPER
Minn Univ Water Resour Res Cent Bull. . MINNESOTA UNIVERSITY. WATER RESOURCES RESEARCH CENTER. BULLETIN
Min St. . . . . MINISTRY STUDIES
Min Technol. . . . . . MINING TECHNOLOGY
Minutes. . . . . MINUTES OF THE SEMINAR IN UKRAINIAN STUDIES
MINZOKUGAKU. . . . MINZOKUGAKU-KENKYU. THE JAPANESE JOURNAL OF ETHNOLOGY
MIO. . . . . MITTEILUNGEN DES INSTITUTS FUER ORIENTFORSCHUNG DER DEUTSCHEN AKADEMIE DER
WISSENSCHAFTEN ZU BERLIN
MIO. . . . . MITTEILUNGEN DES INSTITUTS FUER ORIENTFORSCHUNG GESCHICHTSFORSCHUNG
MIOEG. . . . . MITTEILUNGEN DES INSTITUTS FUER OESTERREICHISCHE GESCHICHTSFORSCHUNG
MIOG. . . . . MITTEILUNGEN DES INSTITUTS FUER OESTERREICHISCHE GESCHICHTSFORSCHUNG
MIOGF. . . . . MITTEILUNGEN DES INSTITUTS FUER OESTERREICHISCHE GESCHICHTSFORSCHUNG
Mi R. . . . . MINNESOTA REVIEW
MiscBare. . . . . MISCELLANEA BARCINONENSIA
Misc Fr. . . . . MISCELLANEA FRANCESCANA
Misc Med. . . . . . . MISCELLANEA MEDIAVALIA
MISC MUS. . . . . . . MISCELLANEA MUSICOLOGICA

PERIODICAL TITLE ABBREVIATIONS

MisEAH......... MISCELANEA DE ESTUDIOS ARABES Y HEBREOS
MisP............ MISCELLANEA PHONETICA
Mis R........... MISSIONARY REVIEW OF THE WORLD
Miss Ag Exp...... MISSISSIPPI AGRICULTURAL EXPERIMENT STATION. PUBLICATIONS
Miss & Roc....... MISSILES AND ROCKETS
MissFR.......... MISSISSIPPI FOLKLORE REGISTER
Miss Geol Surv Bull.. MISSISSIPPI GEOLOGICAL, ECONOMIC AND TOPOGRAPHICAL SURVEY. BULLETIN
MissHisp......... MISSIONALIA HISPANICA
Miss Hist Soc Publ.. MISSISSIPPI HISTORICAL SOCIETY. PUBLICATIONS
Missio.......... MISSIOLOGY
MISS LAW J....... MISSISSIPPI LAW JOURNAL
MISS LIB NEWS.... MISSISSIPPI LIBRARY NEWS
MISS L J......... MISSISSIPPI LAW JOURNAL
MissQ.......... MISSISSIPPI QUARTERLY
Miss Val Hist R.... MISSISSIPPI VALLEY HISTORICAL REVIEW
MIT Fluid Mech Lab Publ.. MASSACHUSETTS INSTITUTE OF TECHNOLOGY. FLUID MECHANICS LABORATORY. PUBLICATION
Mit J........... MITTELLATEINISCHES JAHRBUCH
MIT Ralph M. Parsons Lab Water Resour Hydrodyn Rep.. MASSACHUSETTS INSTITUTE OF TECHNOLOGY. SCHOOL OF ENGINEERING. RALPH M. PARSONS LABORATORY FOR WATER RESOURCES AND HYDRODYNAMICS. REPORT
Mitsubishi Denki Lab Rep.. MITSUBISHI DENKI LABORATORY REPORTS
Mitt AGEN........ MITTEILUNGEN AGEN
MITT B FORS...... MITTEILUNGEN DER BUNDESFORSCHUNGSTALT FUER FORST- UND HOLZWIRTSCHAFT
Mitt Forsch Konstr Stahlbau.. MITTEILUNGEN UEBER FORSCHUNG UND KONSTRUKTION IM STAHLBAU
Mitt Inst Aerodyn.. MITTEILUNGEN AUS DEM INSTITUT FUER AERODYNAMIK AN DER EI˜GENOESSISCHEN TECHNISCHEN HOCHSCHULE IN ZUERICH
Mitt Inst Baustatik.. MITTEILUNGEN AUS DEM INSTITUT FUER BAUSTATIK AN DER EIDGENOESSISCHEN TECHNISCHEN HOCHSCHULE IN ZUERICH
Mitt Inst Hydraul Gewaesserkd.. MITTEILUNGEN INSTITUT FUER HYDRAULIK UND GEWAESSERKUNDE, TECHNISCHER HOCHSCHULE (MUENCHEN)
Mitt Inst Therm Turbomasch.. MITTEILUNGEN INSTITUT FUER THERMISCHE TURBOMASCHINEN AN DER EIDGENOESSISCHEN TECHNISCHEN HOCHSCHULE (ZUERICH)
Mitt Max-Planck-Inst Stroemungsforsch Aerodyn Versuchsanst.. MITTEILUNGEN AUS DEM MAX-PLANCK-INSTITUT FUER STROEMUNGSFORSCHUNG UND DER AERODYNAMISCHEN VERSUCHSANSTALT
MITT O GEOG..... MITTEILUNGEN DER OESTERREICHISCHEN GEOGRAPHISCHEN GESELLSCHAFT
Mitt Vaterl Gesch St Gall.. MITTEILUNGEN ZUR VATERLANDISCHEN GESCHICHTE. HRSG. VOM HISTORISCHEN VEREIN IN ST. GALLEN
Mitt Ver Grosskesselbesitzer.. MITTEILUNGEN DER VEREINIGUNG DER GROSSKESSELBESITZER
Mitt Ver Grosskesselbetr.. MITTEILUNGEN DER VEREINIGUNG DER GROSSKESSELBETREIBER
MJ............. MAKEDONSKI JAZIK
MJ............. MIDWEST JOURNAL
MJ............. MITTELLATEINISCHES JAHRBUCH
MJ............. MUSEUM JOURNAL
MJB............ MINDENER JAHRBUCH
MJBK.......... MUENCHENER JAHRBUCH FUER BILDENDE KUNST
MJPS.......... MIDWEST JOURNAL OF POLITICAL SCIENCE
MK............. MAGYAR KONYVSZEMLE
MK............. MIESIECZNIK KOSCIELNY
MK............. MINZOKUGAKU KNEKYU (JAPANESE JOURNAL OF ETHNOLOGY)
MK............. MYSL KARAIMSKA

MKAI . . . . MAJALLAT KULLIYAT AL-ADAB, AL-ISKANDARIYYAH
MKAW . . . . MEDEDEELINGEN DER KONIKLIJKE NEDERLANDSCHE AKADEMIE VAN WETENSCHAPPEN. AFDELING LETTERKUNDE
MKK . . . . MAL KWA KUL (SPEECH AND LANGUAGE)
MKNA . . . . MEDEDEELINGEN DER KONIKLIJKE NEDERLANDSCHE AKADEMIE VAN WETENSCHAPPEN. AFDELING LETTERKUNDE
MKNAL . . . . MEDEDEELINGEN DER KONINKLIJKE NEDERLANDSCHE AKADEMIE VAN WETENSCHAPPEN. AFDELING LETTERKUNDE
MKNAWL . . . . MEDEDEELINGEN DER KONINKLIJKE NEDERLANDSCHE AKADEMIE VAN WETENSCHAPPEN. AFDELING LETTERKUNDE
MKOH . . . . MEDEDEELINGEN VAN DEN KUNST- EN OUDHEIDKUNDIGEN KRING VAN HERENTHALS
MKVAB . . . . MEDEDEELINGEN VAN DE KONINKLIJKE VLAAMSE AKADEMIE VAN WETENSCHAPPEN, LETTEREN EN SCHONE KUNSTEN V BELGIE
ML . . . . MENNONITE LIFE
MI . . . . MLADOST
ML . . . . MODERN LANGUAGES
ML . . . . MUSIC AND LETTERS
MLA . . . . MODERN LANGUAGE ASSOCIATION. INTERNATIONAL BIBLIOGRAPHY
MLA Int Bibl . . . . . MODERN LANGUAGE ASSOCIATION. INTERNATIONAL BIBLIOGRAPHY
MLAN . . . . MUSIC LIBRARY ASSOCIATION NOTES
M Lang . . . . MODERN LANGUAGES
MLA Q . . . . MISSOURI LIBRARY ASSOCIATION QUARTERLY
MLatJb . . . . MITTELLATEINISCHES JAHRBUCH
MLF . . . . MODERN LANGUAGE FORUM
MLF . . . . MODERSMALSLARARNAS FORENING: ARSSKRIFT
MLFA . . . . MODERSMALSLARARNAS FORENINGS: ARSSKRIFT
MLG . . . . MITTEILUNGEN AUS DER LIVLANDISCHEN GESCHICHTE
MLit . . . . MIESIECZNIK LITERACKI
MLJ . . . . MODERN LANGUAGE JOURNAL
Mlle . . . . MADEMOISELLE
MLN . . . . MODERN LANGUAGE NOTES
MLQ . . . . MODERN LANGUAGE QUARTERLY
MIR . . . . MLADINSKA REVIJA
MLR . . . . MODERN LANGUAGE REVIEW
MLS . . . . MODERN LANGUAGE STUDIES
MLW . . . . MOUNTAIN LIFE AND WORK
MM . . . . MAAL OG MINNE
MM . . . . MACLEAN'S MAGAZINE
MM . . . . MARINER'S MIRROR
MM . . . . MASSES AND MAINSTREAM
MM . . . . MISCELLANEOUS MAN
MM . . . . MONUMENTS ET MEMOIRES PUBLIES PAR L'ACADEMIE DES INSCRIPTIONS ET BELLES-LETTRES
MM . . . . MUENCHENER MUSEUM
MMAD . . . . MACALLAT AL-MACMA AL-ILMI AL-ARABI DIMASQ
MMAI . . . . MONUMENTS ET MEMOIRES PUBLIES PAR L'ACADEMIE DES INSCRIPTIONS ET BELLES-LETTRES
MMGS . . . . MELBOURNE MONOGRAPHS IN GERMANIC STUDIES
MMH . . . . MONTANA MAGAZINE OF HISTORY
MMII . . . . MAJALLAT AL-MAJMA AL-ILMI AL-IRAQI
MMLA . . . . MAJALLAT MAJMA AL-LUGHAH AL-ARABIYAH (CAIRO)
MMLMP . . . . MATERIALY PO MATEMATICESKOJ LINGVISTIKE I MASINNOMU PEREVODU
MMMSM . . . . MILLENAIRE MONASTIQUE DU MONT SAINT-MICHEL

MMR . . . . MONTHLY MUSICAL RECORD
MMS . . . . METROPOLITAN MUSEUM STUDIES
MMS . . . . MUENSTERSCHE MITTELALTER-SCHRIFTEN
MN . . . . MISCELLANEA NUMISMATICA
Mn . . . . MNEMOSYNE
MN . . . . MONUMENTA NIPPONICA
MN . . . . MUSEUM NEWS
MNAWL . . . . MEDEDEELINGEN DER KONINKLIJKE NEDERLANDSE AKADEMIE VAN WETENSCHAPPEN. AFDELING LETTERKUNDE
MNCDN . . . . MEDEDEELINGEN VAN DE NIJMEEGSE CENTRALE VOOR DIALECTEN NAAMKUNDE
MNDPV . . . . MITTEILUNGEN UND NACHRICHTEN DES DEUTSCHEN PALAESTINA VEREINS
MNFS . . . . MEDDELELSER FRA NORSK FORENING FOR SPROGVIDENSKAP
MnH . . . . MINNESOTA HISTORY
MNHIR . . . . MEDEDEELINGEN VAN HET NEDERLANDSCH-HISTORISCH INSTITUT LE ROME
MNip . . . . MONUMENTA NIPPONICA
MNIR . . . . MEDEDEELINGEN VAN HET NEDERLANDSCH-HISTORISCH INSTITUT LE ROME
MNN . . . . MUENCHENER NEUESTE NACHRICHTEN
M NOT R AST . . . . . MONTHLY NOTICES OF THE ROYAL ASTRONOMICAL SOCIETY
MNP . . . . MONDE NOUVEAU-PARU
MNSV . . . . MEDDELELSER FRA NORSK FORENING FOR SPROG-VIDENSKAP
Mnu . . . . MUNDO NUEVO
MNy . . . . MAGYAR NYELV
MNy . . . . MAGYAR NYELVJARASOK
MNY . . . . MESSAGER DE NEW YORK
MNyj . . . . MAGYAR NYELVJARASOK
MO . . . . MISSIONERSKOE OBOZRIENIE
Mo . . . . MONAT
MO . . . . MONATSHEFTE
MO . . . . MONDE ORIENTAL
Mo . . . . MONEY
Mo . . . . MOSKVA
MO . . . . MOVIMENTO OPERAIO
Mo Ag Bd . . . . MISSOURI STATE BOARD OF AGRICULTURE. PUBLICATIONS
Mo Ag Exp . . . . UNIVERSITY OF MISSOURI. COLLEGE OF AGRICULTURE. AGRICULTURAL EXPERIMENT STATION. PUBLICATIONS
MO B J . . . . JOURNAL OF THE MISSOURI BAR
Mo Bot Gard Ann . . . MISSOURI BOTANICAL GARDEN. ANNALS
Moccasin Tel . . . . . . MOCCASIN TELEGRAPH
Mod A . . . . MODERN AGE
MOD ASIAN S . . . . . MODERN ASIAN STUDIES
Mod Cast . . . . MODERN CASTING
MOD C CARDI . . . . . MODERN CONCEPTS OF CARDIOVASCULAR DISEASE
Mod Ch . . . . MODERN CHURCHMAN
Mod Concr . . . . MODERN CONCRETE
ModD . . . . MODERN DRAMA
ModDr . . . . MODERN DRAMA
Mod Ed . . . . MODERN EDUCATION
Modern L Rev . . . . . MODERN LAW REVIEW
Mod Fict Stud . . . . . MODERN FICTION STUDIES
Mod Geol . . . . MODERN GEOLOGY
Mod Ind . . . . MODERN INDUSTRY

Mo Div Geol Surv Water Resour (Rep)..MISSOURI. DIVISION OF GEOLOGICAL SURVEY AND WATER RESOURCES. REPORT
Mod Lang........MODERN LANGUAGES
Mod Lang Assn Pub..MODERN LANGUAGE ASSOCIATION OF AMERICA. PUBLICATION
Mod Lang Forum...MODERN LANGUAGE FORUM
Mod Lang J.......MODERN LANGUAGE JOURNAL
Mod Lang N.......MODERN LANGUAGE NOTES
Mod Lang Q.......MODERN LANGUAGE QUARTERLY
Mod Lang R.......MODERN LANGUAGE REVIEW
MOD LAW SOC.....MODERN LAW AND SOCIETY
Mod Libn.........MODERN LIBRARIAN
Mod Mater Handl..MODERN MATERIALS HANDLING
Mod Metals.......MODERN METALS
Mod Mfg........MODERN MANUFACTURING
Mod Mus.........MODERN MUSIC
Mod Packag......MODERN PACKAGING
Mod Phil........MODERN PHILOLOGY
Mod Phot........MODERN PHOTOGRAPHY
Mod Plast........MODERN PLASTICS
Mod Poetry Stud...MODERN POETRY STUDIES
Mod Quart Misc....MODERN QUARTERLY MISCELLANY
Mod R...........MODERN REVIEW
Mod Refrig Air Cond..MODERN REFRIGERATION AND AIR CONDITIONING
ModRev.........MODERN REVIEW (CALCUTTA)
Mod Sch.........MODERN SCHOOLMAN
Mod Sp..........MODERNE SPRACHEN
Mod Text........MODERN TEXTILES
Mod Text Mag.....MODERN TEXTILES MAGAZINE
Mod Tramway.....MODERN TRAMWAY
MOEIG...........MITTEILUNGEN DES OESTERREICHISCHEN INSTITUTS ZUR GESCHICHTSFORSCHUNG
M of Art.........MAGAZINE OF ART (CASSELL'S)
M of Hist........MAGAZINE OF HISTORY
MOGA...........MITTEILUNGEN DER OESTERREICHISCHEN GESELLSCHAFT FUER ANTHROPOLOGIE, ETHNOLOGIE UND PRAHISTORIE
Mo Geol Surv Water Resour Inform Circ..MISSOURI. DIVISION OF GEOLOGICAL SURVEY AND WATER RESOURCES. INFORMATION CIRCULAR
Mo Geol Surv Water Resour (Rep)..MISSOURI. DIVISION OF GEOLOGICAL SURVEY AND WATER RESOURCES. REPORT
Mo Geol Surv Water Resour Rep Invest..MISSOURI. DIVISION OF GEOLOGICAL SURVEY AND WATER RESOURCES. REPORT OF INVESTIGATIONS
MOH............MAGAZINE OF HORROR
MoH............MONATSHEFTE
Mo Hist Rev......MISSOURI HISTORICAL REVIEW
Mo Hist Soc Bull...MISSOURI HISTORICAL SOCIETY. BULLETIN
MOIGF..........MITTEILUNGEN DES OESTERREICHISCHEN INSTITUTS FUER GESCHICHTSFORSCHUNG
Mo Illust.........MONTHLY ILLUSTRATOR
Mo J Res Mus Ed...MISSOURI JOURNAL OF RESEARCH IN MUSIC EDUCATION
Mo Labor R.......MONTHLY LABOR REVIEW
MOL BIOL........MOLECULAR BIOLOGY
MOL BIOL RP......MOLECULAR BIOLOGY REPORT
MOL C BIOCH.....MOLECULAR AND CELLULAR BIOCHEMISTRY
MOL C ENDOC.....MOLECULAR AND CELLULAR ENDOCRINOLOGY

Mol Cryst Liq Cryst. . MOLECULAR CRYSTALS AND LIQUID CRYSTALS
Molec Biol. . . . . . . MOLECULAR BIOLOGY
MOLEC CRYST. . . . . MOLECULAR CRYSTALS AND LIQUID CRYSTALS
MOLEC PHARM. . . . MOLECULAR PHARMACOLOGY
MOLEC PHYS. . . . . . MOLECULAR PHYSICS
MOL G GENET. . . . . MOLECULAR & GENERAL GENETICS
Mo Lib Assn Newsl. . MISSOURI LIBRARY ASSOCIATION. NEWSLETTER
Mo Lib Assn Q. . . . . MISSOURI LIBRARY ASSOCIATION. QUARTERLY
MOL PHOTOCH. . . . MOLECULAR PHOTOCHEMISTRY
Mo L Rev. . . . . MISSOURI LAW REVIEW
MO MED. . . . . MISSOURI MEDICINE
Mo Mus Rec. . . . . . MONTHLY MUSICAL RECORD
MON. . . . . MINISTERSTWO OBRONY NARODOWEJ
Monat f deut Unt. . . MONATSHEFTE FUER DEN DEUTSCHEN UNTERRICHT
Monatsber Deut Akad Wiss Berlin. . MONATSBERICHTE DER DEUTSCHEN AKADEMIE DER WISSENSCHAFTEN ZU BERLIN
MONATS CHEM. . . . MONATSHEFTE FUER CHEMIE
Monatshefte. . . . . . MONATSHEFTE FUER DEUTSCHEN UNTERRICHT, DEUTSCHE SPRACHE UND LITERATUR
MONATS KIND. . . . . MONATSSCHRIFT FUER KINDERHEILKUNDE
MONATS MATH. . . . MONATSHEFTE FUER MATHEMATIK
MONATS UNFA. . . . MONATSSCHRIFT FUER UNFALLHEILKUNDE
Mon Bull Int Ry Congr Ass Cybern Electron Ry. . MONTHLY BULLETIN OF THE INTERNATIONAL RAILWAY CONGRESS ASSOCIATION. CYBERNETICS AND ELECTRONICS OF THE RAILWAYS
MonF. . . . . MONDE FRANCAIS
MON LAB RE. . . . . . MONTHLY LABOR REVIEW
MON NIPP. . . . . . . MONUMENTA NIPPONICA
MON PAEDIAT. . . . . MONOGRAPHS IN PAEDIATRICA
MON S RES C. . . . . . MONOGRAPHS OF THE SOCIETY FOR RESEARCH IN CHILD DEVELOPMENT
Mont. . . . . MONTANA MAGAZINE OF HISTORY
Mont Ag Exp. . . . . . MONTANA AGRICULTURAL EXPERIMENT STATION. PUBLICATIONS
Montana Lib. . . . . . MONTANA LIBRARIES
Montana Lib Q. . . . . MONTANA LIBRARY QUARTERLY
Montana L Rev. . . . MONTANA LAW REVIEW
Mont Bur Mines Geol Bull. . MONTANA. BUREAU OF MINES AND GEOLOGY. BULLETIN
Mont Bur Mines Geol Mem. . MONTANA. BUREAU OF MINES AND GEOLOGY. MEMOIR
Mont Bur Mines Geol Spec Publ. . MONTANA. BUREAU OF MINES AND GEOLOGY. SPECIAL PUBLICATION
Mont Ed. . . . . MONTANA EDUCATION
Monthly Crop Rep. . MONTHLY CROP REPORT
Monthly Labor R. . . MONTHLY LABOR REVIEW
Monthly R. . . . . . . MONTHLY REVIEW
MON TIMES. . . . . . MONETARY TIMES
MONT LAW RE. . . . . MONTANA LAW REVIEW
Mont Mag Hist. . . . MONTANA. THE MAGAZINE OF WESTERN HISTORY
Monuments Piot. . . ACADEMIE DES INSCRIPTIONS ET BELLES LETTRES, PARIS. FONDATION EUGENE PIOT. MONUMENTS ET MEMOIRES
Moody. . . . . MOODY'S MAGAZINE
Moody's Inv Serv. . . MOODY'S INVESTORS SERVICE
MOORG WAL S. . . . . MOORGATE AND WALL STREET
Mo R. . . . . MONTHLY REVIEW
MORAVIAN MUS. . . MORAVIAN MUSIC FOUNDATION BULLETIN
Mo Rel M. . . . . MONTHLY RELIGIOUS MAGAZINE

MOSA . . . . MITTEILUNGEN DES OESTERREICHISCHEN STAATSARCHIVS
Moslem W . . . . MOSLEM WORLD
MOSQUITO NE . . . . . MOSQUITO NEWS
MOstf . . . . MARBURGER OSTFORSCHUNGEN
Mot Boat . . . . MOTOR BOAT
Mot Boat Yacht . . . . MOTOR BOAT AND YACHTING
Mot Cycle . . . . MOTOR CYCLE
Motor B . . . . MOTOR BOATING
Motor T . . . . MOTOR TREND
Mot Ship . . . . MOTOR SHIP
Mo U Sch Mines & Met Bul tech ser . . UNIVERSITY OF MISSOURI. SCHOOL OF MINES AND METALLURGY. BULLETIN. TECHNICAL SERIES
Mov . . . . MOVOZNAVSTVO
MOVB . . . . MITTEILUNGEN DES OESTERREICHISCHES. VEREINS FUER BIBLIOTHEKWESEN
MOVBW . . . . MITTEILUNGEN DES OESTERREICHISCHES. VEREINS FUER BIBLIOTHEKWESEN
MP . . . . MASINNYJ PEREVOD. TRUDY INSTITUTA TOCNOJ MECHANIKI I VYCISLITEL HOJ TECHNIKI AKADEMIY NAUK SSR
MP . . . . MODERN PACKAGING
MP . . . . MODERN PHILOLOGY
M Pad . . . . MEMORIE DELLA REALE ACCADEMIA DI SCIENZE, LETTERE ED ARTI IN PADOVA
MPh . . . . MAITRE PHONETIQUE
MPh . . . . MODERN PHILOLOGY
MPh . . . . MUSEUM. MAANBLAD VOOR PHILOLOGIE EN GESCHIEDENIS
M Phil . . . . MODERN PHILOLOGY
MPhon . . . . MAITRE PHONETIQUE
MPhP . . . . MEDIAEVALIA PHILOSOPHICA POLONORUM
MPI . . . . MILITAERPSYKOLOGISKA INSTITUTET
MPiKL . . . . MASINNYJ PEREVOD I PRIKLADNAJA LINGVISTIKA
MPP . . . . MEDIAEVALIA PHILOSOPHICA POLONORUM
MPS . . . . MODERN POETRY STUDIES
MQ . . . . MIDWEST QUARTERLY
MQ . . . . MILTON QUARTERLY
MQ . . . . MODERN QUARTERLY
MQ . . . . MUSICAL QUARTERLY
MQ . . . . MUSIC QUARTERLY
MQR . . . . MENNONITE QUARTERLY REVIEW
MQR . . . . MICHIGAN QUARTERLY REVIEW
MR . . . . MARCH
MR . . . . MARCHE ROMANE
MR . . . . MASSACHUSETTS REVIEW
Mr . . . . MEANDER
MR . . . . MINNESOTA REVIEW
MR . . . . MISSIONSWISSENSCHAFT UND RELIGIONSWISSENSCHAFT
MR . . . . MUSIC REVIEW
MR . . . . MUSIKREVY
MRD . . . . MEMOIRS OF THE RESEARCH DEPARTMENT. TOYO BUNKO
Mr Eng/Log . . . . . . MARINE ENGINEERING/LOG
MRev . . . . MEDITERRANEAN REVIEW
MRG . . . . MITTEILUNGEN DER RAABE-GESELLSCHAFT
MRGB . . . . MITTELRHEINSICHE GESCHICHTSBLAETTER
MRo . . . . MARCHE ROMANE

MRom . . . . MARCHE ROMANE
MRR . . . . MAD RIVER REVIEW
MRS . . . . MEDIAEVAL AND RENAISSANCE STUDIES
MS . . . . MANCHESTER SCHOOL OF ECONOMICS AND SOCIAL STUDIES
MS . . . . MAR DEL SUR
MS . . . . MEDIAEVAL STUDIES
M/S . . . . MEDIA/SCOPE
MS . . . . MODERNA SPRAK (STOCKHOLM)
MS . . . . MONDE SLAVE
MS . . . . MOUVEMENT SOCIOLOGIQUE
Ms . . . . MS MAGAZINE
MS . . . . MS (MANUSCRIPT) (LOS ANGELES)
MS . . . . MUSIC SURVEY
MSAF . . . . MEMOIRES DE LA SOCIETE NATIONALE DES ANTIQUAIRES DE FRANCE
MSAM . . . . MEMOIRES DE LA SOCIETE DES ANTIQUAIRES DE LA MORINIE
MSAO . . . . MEMOIRES DE LA SOCIETE DES ANTIQUAIRES DE L'OUEST
MSAP . . . . MEMOIRES DE LA SOCIETE DES ANTIQUAIRES DE PICARDIE
MSB . . . . MONGOLIA SOCIETY BULLETIN
MSBGK . . . . MIN SHIN GENGO KENKYUKAI KAIHO (JOURNAL OF THE SOCIETY OF MING AND CH'ING
          LITERARY LANGUAGE STUDIES)
MScan . . . . MEDIAEVAL SCANDINAVIA
MSch . . . . MODERN SCHOOLMAN
M Sci Rel . . . . MELANGES DE SCIENCE RELIGIEUSE
MSCS . . . . MANKATO STATE COLLEGE STUDIES
MS Diss . . . . MANUSCRIPT DISSERTATION
MSE . . . . MASSACHUSETTS STUDIES IN ENGLISH
MSE . . . . MATHEMATICAL STUDIES IN ECONOMICS AND STATISTICS IN THE USSR AND EASTERN EUROPE
MSEC . . . . MEMOIRES DE LA SOCIETE D'EMULATION DE CAMBRAI
MSER . . . . MEMOIRES DE LA SOCIETE D'EMULATION DE ROUBAIX
MSer . . . . MONUMENTA SERICA
MSF . . . . MARVEL SCIENCE FICTION
MSF . . . . MEMOIRE STORICHE FOROGIULIESI
MSFO . . . . MEMOIRES DE LA SOCIETE FINNO-OUGRIENNE
MSForogiuliesi . . . . . MEMOIRE STORICHE FOROGIULIESI
MSFOu . . . . MEMOIRES DE LA SOCIETE FINNO-OUGRIENNE
MSGV . . . . MITTEILUNGEN DER SCHLESISCHEN GESELLSCHAFT FUER VOLKSKUNDE
MSHDI . . . . MEMOIRES DE LA SOCIETE POUR L'HISTOIRE DU DROIT ET DES INSTITUTIONS DES ANCIENS
          PAYS BOURGUIGNONS, COMTOIS ET ROMANDS
MSK . . . . MITTEILUNGEN AUS DEM STADTARCHIV VON KOELN
MSL . . . . MEMOIRES DE LA SOCIETE DE LINGUISTIQUE DE PARIS
MSL . . . . MISCELLANEA DI STORIA LIGURE
MSLC . . . . MISCELLANEA DI STUDI LETTERATURA CRISTIANA ANTICA
MSLL . . . . MONOGRAPH SERIES ON LANGUAGES AND LINGUISTICS. GEORGETOWN UNIVERSITY
MSLP . . . . MEMOIRES DE LA SOCIETE LINGUISTIQUE DE PARIS
MSLund . . . . MEDDELANDEN FRAN SEMINARIERNA FOER SLAVISKA SPRAK, JAMFORANDE SPRAKFORSNING
          OCH FINSK-UGRISKA SPRAK VID LUNDS UNIVERSITET
MsM . . . . MS MAGAZINE
MSMarne . . . . MEMOIRES DE LA SOCIETE D'AGRICULTURE, COMMERCE, SCIENCES ET ARTS, DU DEPARTEMENT
          DE LA MARINE
MSMC . . . . MASTERKEY. SOUTHWEST MUSEUM. LOS ANGELES, CALIFORNIA

MSNAF . . . . MEMOIRES DE LA SOCIETE NATIONALE DES ANTIQUAIRES DE FRANCE
MSNH . . . . MEMOIRES DE LA SOCIETE NEOPHILOLOGIQUE DE HELSINKI
MSp . . . . MUTTERSPRACHE
MSPP . . . . MAHARASTRA SAHITYA PARISAD PATRIKA
MSpr . . . . MODERNA SPRAK
MSprak . . . . MODERNA SPRAK
MSR . . . . MALONE SOCIETY REPRINTS
MSR . . . . MELANGES DE SCIENCE RELIGIEUSE
MSRC . . . . MEMOIRES DE LA SOCIETE ROYALE DU CANADA
MSS . . . . MANUSCRIPTS
MSS . . . . MARVEL SCIENCE STORIES
MSS . . . . MUENCHENER STUDIEN ZUR SPRACHWISSENSCHAFT
MSt . . . . MITTELDEUTSCHE STUDIEN
MSt . . . . MONASTIC STUDIES
MStud . . . . MILTON STUDIES
MSU BUS TO . . . . . . MICHIGAN STATE UNIVERSITY. MSU BUSINESS TOPICS
MSV . . . . MISCELLANEA STORICA DELLA VALDELSA
MSZS . . . . MUENCHENER STUDIEN ZUR SPRACHWISSENSCHAFT
MT . . . . MACHINE TRANSLATION
MT . . . . MARVEL TALES
MT . . . . MATEMATISK TIDSSKRIFT
MT . . . . MECHANICAL TRANSLATION
MT . . . . MUSICAL TIMES
MTA . . . . MAGYAR TUDOMANYOS AKADEMIA NYELV-ES IRODA-LOMTUDOMANYI OSTALYANAK KOZLEMENYEI
MTAK . . . . MAGYAR TUDOMANYOS AKADEMIA NYELV-ES IRODALOMTUDOMANYI OSTALYANAK KOZLEMENYEI
MTatD . . . . MATERIALY PO TATARSKOJ DIALEKTOLOGII
MTJ . . . . MARK TWAIN JOURNAL
Mt Plains Lib Assn Q . . . . MOUNTAIN PLAINS LIBRARY ASSOCIATION QUARTERLY
MTQ . . . . MARK TWAIN QUARTERLY
MTS . . . . MOST THRILLING SCIENCE EVER TOLD
MT SINAI J . . . . MOUNT SINAI JOURNAL OF MEDICINE
MTU . . . . MUENCHENER TEXTE UND UNTERSUCHUNGEN ZUR DEUTSCHEN LITERATUR DES MITTELALTERS
MTUDLM . . . . MUENCHENER TEXTE UND UNTERSUCHUNGEN ZUR DEUTSCHEN LITERATUR DES MITTELALTERS
MTZ Motortech Z . . MTZ MOTORTECHNISCHE ZEITSCHRIFT
MTZ . . . . MUENCHENER THEOLOGISCHE ZEITSCHRIFT
Mu . . . . MULINO
Mu . . . . MUTTERSPRACHE. ZEITSCHRIFT ZUR PFLEGE UND ERFORSCHUNG DER DEUTSCHEN SPRACHE
Muanyag Gumi . . . . MUANYAG ES GUMI
MUB . . . . MELANGES DE L'UNIVERSITE SAINT-JOSEPH (BEYROUTH)
Muench Jahr Bild Kunst . . MUENCHENER JAHRBUCH DER BILDENDEN KUNST
MuK . . . . MASKE UND KOTHURN
MuL . . . . MUSIC AND LETTERS
Mullard Tech Commun . . MULLARD TECHNICAL COMMUNICATIONS
MULR . . . . MELBOURNE UNIVERSITY LAW REVIEW
MULTIV BE R . . . . . MULTIVARIATE BEHAVIORAL RESEARCH
Munch Beitr . . . . . . MUENCHENER BEITAEGE ZUR ROMANISCHEN UND ENGLISCHEN PHILOLOGIE
MundusA . . . . MUNDUS ARTIUM
Munic Aff . . . . MUNICIPAL AFFAIRS
Munic & Co Eng . . . . MUNICIPAL AND COUNTY ENGINEERING

Munic Eng J . . . . MUNICIPAL ENGINEERS JOURNAL
Munic Engng . . . . . . MUNICIPAL ENGINEERING
Munic J . . . . MUNICIPAL JOURNAL
Munic Ref & Res Center Notes . . NEW YORK (CITY). MUNICIPAL REFERENCE AND RESEARCH CENTER. NOTES
Munic Ref Lib Notes . . NEW YORK (CITY). PUBLIC LIBRARY. MUNICIPAL REFERENCE LIBRARY. NOTES
Munic Util . . . . MUNICIPAL UTILITIES
Munsey . . . . MUNSEY'S MAGAZINE
Murray . . . . MURRAY'S MAGAZINE
Mus . . . . MUSEON. REVUE D'ETUDES ORIENTALES
Mus . . . . MUSEUM. MAANBLAD VOOR PHILOLOGIE EN GESCHIEDENIS
Mus . . . . MUSEUM OF FOREIGN LITERATURE, LITTELL'S
Mus Academy Jl . . . MUSIC ACADEMY JOURNAL
Mus Am . . . . MUSICAL AMERICA
MUS ANAL . . . . MUSICAL ANALYSIS
MUS & ARTISTS . . . . MUSIC AND ARTISTS
Mus & Dance . . . . . . MUSIC AND DANCE
Mus & Lett . . . . MUSIC AND LETTERS
MUS & MUS . . . . MUSIC AND MUSICIANS
Mus at Home . . . . . . MUSIC AT HOME
Muscan . . . . MUSICANADA (ENGLISH EDITION)
Mus Clubs Mag . . . . MUSIC CLUBS MAGAZINE
Mus Comp Zool Mem . . HARVARD UNIVERSITY. MUSEUM OF COMPARATIVE ZOOLOGY. MEMOIRS
Mus Cour . . . . MUSICAL COURIER
Mus Dealer . . . . MUSIC DEALER
MUS DISC . . . . MUSICA DISCIPLINA
Mus D'Oggi . . . . MUSICA D'OGGI; RASSEGNA DI VITA E DI CULTURA MUSICALE
Mus Ed J . . . . MUSIC EDUCATORS JOURNAL
Musee Guimet Annales Bibl d'Etudes . . MUSEE GUIMET. ANNALES. BIBLIOTHEQUE D'ETUDES
Musee Guimet Annales Bibl de Vulg . . MUSEE GUIMET. ANNALES. BIBLIOTHEQUE DE VULGARISATION
Museo Nac de Hist Nat de Buenos Aires Anales . . MUSEO NACIONAL DE HISTORIA NATURAL DE BUENOS AIRES. ANALES
Mus Et Lit . . . . MUSIQUE ET LITURGIE
Museum Comp Zool Memoirs . . HARVARD UNIVERSITY. MUSEUM OF COMPARATIVE ZOOLOGY. MEMOIRS
Museum d'Hist Nat de Lyon Archives . . MUSEUM D'HISTOIRE NATURELLE DE LYON. ARCHIVES
Museum Stud . . . . . MUSEUM STUDIES
Mus Events . . . . MUSICAL EVENTS
Mus Guimet Ann Bibl Etudes . . MUSEE GUIMET. ANNALES. BIBLIOTHEQUE D'ETUDES
Mus Guimet Ann Bibl Vulg . . MUSEE GUIMET. ANNALES. BIBLIOTHEQUE DE VULGARISATION
Music Ed Jnl . . . . . . MUSIC EDUCATORS JOURNAL
Musicl . . . . MUSIC INDEX
Music in Ed . . . . MUSIC IN EDUCATION
Music Man . . . . MUSIC AND MAN
Music (SMA) . . . . . . MUSIC (SCHOOLS OF MUSIC ASSOCIATION)
Mus Industry . . . . . MUSIC INDUSTRY
MUS IN ED . . . . MUSIC IN EDUCATION
MUS IN SCHULE . . . . MUSIK IN DER SCHULE
MUSIP . . . . MARQUETTE UNIVERSITY SLAVIC INSTITUTE. PAPERS
MUSJ . . . . MELANGES DE L'UNIVERSITE SAINT-JOSEPH
Mus J . . . . MUSEUMS JOURNAL
MUS J . . . . MUSIC JOURNAL
Mus Jazz . . . . MUSICA JAZZ

Mus Jl . . . . MUSIC JOURNAL
MusL . . . . MUSIC AND LETTERS
Mus Leader . . . . MUSICAL LEADER
Mus Lib Assn Notes . . MUSIC LIBRARY ASSOCIATION. NOTES
Muslim W . . . . MUSLIM WORLD
Mus Min . . . . MUSIC MINISTRY
Mus Mod Art Bul . . . NEW YORK (CITY). MUSEUM OF MODERN ART. BULLETIN
Mus N . . . . MUSEUM NEWS
Mus Nac Hist Natur Buenos Aires An . . MUSCO NACIONAL DE HISTORIA NATURAL DE BUENOS AIRES. ANALES
Mus News . . . . MUSIC NEWS
MUS NEWS . . . . MUSICAL NEWSLETTER
MUS NEWS PRAGUE . . MUSIC NEWS FROM PRAGUE
Mus Oggi . . . . MUSICA D'OGGI. RASSEGNA DI VITA E DI CULTURA MUSICALE
MUS OP . . . . MUSICAL OPINION
Mus Parade . . . . MUSIC PARADE
Mus Q . . . . MUSICAL QUARTERLY
Mus Qu . . . . MUSICAL QUARTERLY
Mus R . . . . MUSIC REVIEW
Mus Rev . . . . MUSIC REVIEW
MusS . . . . MUSEES SUISSES
Mus Sacra . . . . MUSICA SACRA
MUS SCENE . . . . MUSIC SCENE
Mus Schall . . . . MUSICA SCHALLPLATTE. ZEITSCHRIFT FUER SCHALLPLATTENFREUNDE
Mus Stud . . . . MUSEUM STUDIES. ART INSTITUTE OF CHICAGO
Mus Superv J . . . . . . MUSIC SUPERVISORS JOURNAL
Mus Survey . . . . MUSIC SURVEY
MUS T . . . . MUSICAL TIMES
MUS TCR . . . . MUSIC TEACHER AND PIANO STUDENT
Mus Teach Nat Assn Proc . . MUSIC TEACHERS NATIONAL ASSOCIATION. PROCEEDINGS
Mus Teyler Archiv . . MUSEE TEYLER. ARCHIVES
Mus Times . . . . MUSICAL TIMES
Mus Today NL . . . . . MUSIC TODAY NEWSLETTER
Mus Trade Rev . . . . MUSIC TRADE REVIEW
Mus Trades . . . . MUSIC TRADES
MUS U BILD . . . . . . MUSIK UND BILDUNG
MUS U GES . . . . MUSIK UND GESELLSCHAFT
Mus U Gottesd . . . . MUSIK UND GOTTESDIENST
MUS U KIR . . . . MUSIK UND KIRCHE
Mus West . . . . MUSIC OF THE WEST MAGAZINE
Mus y Artes . . . . . . BOLETIN DE MUSICA Y ARTES VISUALES
Mut . . . . MUTTERSPRACHE
MUTAT RES . . . . MUTATION RESEARCH
Mutech Chem Eng J . . MUTECH CHEMICAL ENGINEERING JOURNAL
Muz . . . . MUZEON
MUZ ZBORNIK . . . . . MUZIKOLOSKI ZBORNIK-MUSICOLOGICAL ANNUAL
MVGDB . . . . MITTEILUNGEN DES VEREINS FUER GESCHICHTE DER DEUTSCHEN IN BOHMEN
MVGOW . . . . MITTEILUNGEN DES VEREINS FUER DIE GESCHICHTE VON OST- UND WEST-PREUSSEN
MVGSN . . . . MITTEILUNGEN DES VEREINS FUER GESCHICHTE DER STADT NURNBERG
MVHG . . . . MITTEILUNGEN DES VEREINS DER FREUNDE DES HUMANISTISCHEN GYMNASIUMS
MVHR . . . . MISSISSIPPI VALLEY HISTORICAL REVIEW
MVL . . . . MONOGRAFIEEN OVER VLAAMSE LETTERKUNDE

MVKAUO .... MITTEILUNGEN DES VEREINS FUER KUNST UND ALTERTUM IN ULM UND OBERSCHWABEN ULM

MVL .... MAANDSCHRIFT VOOR LITURGIE

MVN .... MEDEDEELINGEN UITGEGEVEN DOOR DE VERENIGING VOOR NAAMKUNDE TE LEUVEN

MVN .... MEDEDEELINGEN VAN DE VERENIGING VOOR NAAMKUNDE TE LEUVEN EN DE COMMISSIEE NAAMKUNDE TE AMSTERDAM

MVNAG .... MITTEILUNGEN DES VEREINS FUER NASSAUISCHE ALTERTUMSKUNDE UND GESCHICHTS-FORSCHUNG

MVNLA .... MEDEDEELINGEN VAN DE VEREENIGING VOOR NAAMKUNDE TE LEUVEN EN DE COMMISSIE VOOR NAAMKUNDE TE AMSTERDAM

MVPhW .... MITTEILUNGEN DES VEREINS KLASSISCHER PHILOLOGEN IN WIEN

MW .... MUSLIM WORLD

M WEATH REV ..... MONTHLY WEATHER REVIEW

M West Hist ...... MAGAZINE OF WESTERN HISTORY

MWQ .... MIDWEST QUARTERLY

MY .... MAY

Mycol .... MYCOLOGIA

MYCOPATHOLO .... MYCOPATHOLOGIA

Mysore Dep Mines Geol Geol Stud .. MYSORE, INDIA. DEPARTMENT OF MINES AND GEOLOGY. GEOLOGICAL STUDIES

MYT .... MYSTERIOUS TRAVELER MYSTERY READER

MZ .... MAINZER ZEITSCHRIFT

N

N	NATION
N	NEOPHILOLOGUS
N	NOVEMBER
NA	NAMES
NA	NATION AND ATHENAEUM
NA	NEDERLANDSCH ARCHIEVENBLAD
NA	NEUES ARCHIV DER GESELLSCHAFT FUER AELTERE DEUTSCHE GESCHICHTSKUNDE
NA	NEW ADELPHI
NA	NOTES AFRICAINES
NA	NUOVA ANTOLOGIA
NAA	NARODY AZII I AFRIKI
NAA	NOTICES D'ARCHEOLOGIE ARMORICAINE
N A A Bul	NATIONAL ASSOCIATION OF ACCOUNTANTS. BULLETIN
NAAS	NEWSLETTER OF THE ASSOCIATION FOR ASIAN STUDIES
NAB	NEDERLANDSCH ARCHIEVENBLAD
NAb	NEUES ABENDLAND
Nac	NACION
NacC	NACIONAL (CARACAS)
Nachr Dok	NACHRICHTEN FUER DOKUMENTATION
Nachrichtentech Elektron	NACHRICHTENTECHNIK-ELEKTRONIK
Nachrichtentech Fachber Beih NTZ	NACHRICHTENTECHNISCHE FACHBERICHTE, BEIHEFTE DER NTZ
NACHRTECH Z	NACHRICHTENTECHNISCHE ZEITSCHRIFT
Nachr Verein Schweizer Bibl	NACHRICHTEN VEREINIGUNG SCHWEIZERISCHER BIBLIOTEHKARE
NADA	NATIVE AFFAIRS DEPARTMENT ANNUAL
NADS	NEWSLETTER OF THE AMERICAN DIALECT SOCIETY
NAEBJ	NATIONAL ASSOCIATION OF EDUCATIONAL BROADCASTERS. JOURNAL
NAfr	NOTES AFRICAINES
NAGADGK	NEUES ARCHIV DER GESELLSCHAFT FUER AELTERE DEUTSCHE GESCHICHTSKUNDE
NAG MATH J	NAGOYA MATHEMATICAL JOURNAL
NagoKR	NAGOYA DAIGAKU BUNGAKUBU KENKYU RONSHU (JOURNAL OF THE FACULTY OF (LITERATURE, NAGOYA UNIVERSITY)
NAGSHKP	NEUES ARCHIV FUER DIE GESCHICHTE DER STADT HEIDELBERG UND DER KURPFALZ
NAGSHRP	NEUES ARCHIV FUER DIE GESCHICHTE DER STADT HEIDELBERG UND DER RHEINISCHEN PFALZ
NAk	NARODOPISNE AKTUALITY
NAKG	NEDERLANDSCH ARCHIEF VOOR KERKGESCHIEDENIS
NALF	NEGRO AMERICAN LITERATURE FORUM
NAMC	NOTIZIARIO ARCHEOLOGICO DEL MINISTERO DELLE COLONIE
NAmerR	NORTH AMERICAN REVIEW
N Am R	NORTH AMERICAN REVIEW
NAN	NASSAUISCHE ANNALEN
N&A	NATION AND ATHENAEUM
N&Q	NOTES AND QUERIES
N&V	NOVA ET VETERA
NAnt	NUOVA ANTOLOGIA DI SCIENZE, LETTERE ED ARTI
NaR	NASA REC (PARIS)
NAR	NORTH AMERICAN REVIEW
NAr	NUOVI ARGOMENTI
Narrag Reg	NARRAGANSETT HISTORICAL REGISTER
NAS	NORWEGIAN-AMERICAN STUDIES

NAS. . . . . NOTIZIE DEGLI ARCHIVI DI STATO
NASGA. . . . . NEUES ARCHIV FUER SAECHSISCHE GESCHICHTE UND ALTERTHUMSKUNDE
NASGAK. . . . . NEUES ARCHIV FUER SAECHSISCHE GESCHICHTE UND ALTERTHUMSKUNDE
NASPA J. . . . . NASPA (NATIONAL ASSOCIATION OF STUDENT PERSONNEL ADMINISTRATORS) JOURNAL
NASR. . . . . NORWEGIAN-AMERICAN STUDIES AND RECORDS
NASSP-B. . . . . NATIONAL ASSOCIATION OF SECONDARY SCHOOL PRINCIPALS. BULLETIN
NAT. . . . . NATION
Nat Acad Sci Biog Mem. . NATIONAL ACADEMY OF SCIENCES OF THE UNITED STATES OF AMERICA. BIOGRAPHICAL
　　　　MEMOIRS
Nat Acad Sci Nat Res Counc Publ. . NATIONAL ACADEMY OF SCIENCES. NATIONAL RESEARCH COUNCIL.
　　　　PUBLICATION
Nat Acad Sci Proc. . NATIONAL ACADEMY OF SCIENCES OF THE UNITED STATES OF AMERICA. PROCEEDINGS
Nat Art Ed Assn Yrbk. . NATIONAL ART EDUCATION ASSOCIATION. YEARBOOK
Nat Assn Deans Women J. . NATIONAL ASSOCIATION OF DEANS OF WOMEN. JOURNAL
Nat Assn Sec Sch Prin Bul. . NATIONAL ASSOCIATION OF SECONDARY SCHOOL PRINCIPALS. BULLETIN
Nat Assn State Univs Trans & Proc. . NATIONAL ASSOCIATION OF STATE UNIVERSITIES. TRANSACTIONS AND
　　　　PROCEEDINGS
Nat Assn Stud Council Yrbk. . NATIONAL ASSOCIATION OF STUDENT COUNCILS. YEARBOOK
Nat Assoc of Inspectors and Ednl Advisers J. . NATIONAL ASSOCIATION OF INSPECTORS AND EDUCATIONAL
　　　　ADVISERS JOURNAL
Nat Banking R. . . . . NATIONAL BANKING REVIEW
Nat Bsns Ed Q. . . . . NATIONAL BUSINESS EDUCATION QUARTERLY
Nat Bsns Ed Yrbk. . . NATIONAL BUSINESS EDUCATION YEARBOOK
Nat Bsns Woman. . . NATIONAL BUSINESS WOMAN
Nat Bur Stand Appl Math Ser. . NATIONAL BUREAU OF STANDARDS. APPLIED MATHEMATICS SERIES
Nat Bur Stand Bldg Sci Ser. . NATIONAL BUREAU OF STANDARDS. BUILDING SCIENCE SERIES
Nat Bur Stand Handb. . NATIONAL BUREAU OF STANDARDS. HANDBOOK
Nat Bur Stand Monogr. . NATIONAL BUREAU OF STANDARDS. MONOGRAPHS
Nat Bur Stand Spec Publ. . NATIONAL BUREAU OF STANDARDS. SPECIAL PUBLICATION
Nat Bur Stand Tech News Bull. . NATIONAL BUREAU OF STANDARDS. TECHNICAL NEWS BULLETIN
Nat Bus Educ Yrbk. . NATIONAL BUSINESS EDUCATION. YEARBOOK
Nat Butter & Cheese J. . NATIONAL BUTTER AND CHEESE JOURNAL
Nat Butter J. . . . . . NATIONAL BUTTER JOURNAL
NAT CAN. . . . . NATURE CANADA
NAT CAN I M. . . . . . NATIONAL CANCER INSTITUTE MONOGRAPHS
Nat Cath Ed Assn Bul. . NATIONAL CATHOLIC EDUCATIONAL ASSOCIATION. BULLETIN
Nat Cath Ed Assn Proc. . NATIONAL CATHOLIC EDUCATIONAL ASSOCIATION. PROCEEDINGS
Nat Cheese J. . . . . . NATIONAL CHEESE JOURNAL
Nat Child Labor Com Proc. . NATIONAL CHILD LABOR COMMITTEE PROCEEDINGS
Nat Cities. . . . . NATION'S CITIES
Nat City Bank. . . . . NATIONAL CITY BANK OF NEW YORK
Nat Civic R. . . . . . . NATIONAL CIVIC REVIEW
Nat Comm Teach Ed & Prof Stand Off Rep. . NATIONAL COMMISSION ON TEACHER EDUCATION AND PROFESSIONAL
　　　　STANDARDS. OFFICIAL REPORT
Nat Conf City Govt. . NATIONAL CONFERENCE FOR GOOD CITY GOVERNMENT. PROCEEDINGS
Nat Conf Soc Work. . NATIONAL CONFERENCE OF SOCIAL WORK. PROCEEDINGS
Nat Council O. . . . . NATIONAL COUNCIL OUTLOOK
Nat Council Social Stud Yrbk. . NATIONAL COUNCIL FOR THE SOCIAL STUDIES. YEARBOOK
Nat Council Teach Math Yrbk. . NATIONAL COUNCIL OF TEACHERS OF MATHEMATICS. YEARBOOK
Nat Ed Assn Proc. . . NATIONAL EDUCATION ASSOCIATION. ADDRESSES AND PROCEEDINGS
Nat Ed Assn Res Bul. . NATIONAL EDUCATION ASSOCIATION. RESEARCH BULLETIN

Nat Educ Assn J .... NATIONAL EDUCATION ASSOCIATION. JOURNAL
Nat Elec Mfr Ass Stand Publ . . NATIONAL ELECTRICAL MANUFACTURERS ASSOCIATION. STANDARDS PUBLICATION
Nat El Prin .... NATIONAL FI FMENTARY PRINCIPAL
NAtenea .... NUEVA ATENEA (CHILE)
Nat Eng .... NATIONAL ENGINEER
Nat Gal Rep ...... NATIONAL GALLERY OF ART. REPORT
Nat Geog M ...... NATIONAL GEOGRAPHIC MAGAZINE
Nat Hist .... NATURAL HISTORY
Nat Hort M ...... NATIONAL HORTICULTURAL MAGAZINE
NAT I ANIM ...... NATIONAL INSTITUTE OF ANIMAL HEALTH. QUARTERLY
Nat Inst Arch Ed Bul . . NATIONAL INSTITUTE FOR ARCHITECTURAL EDUCATION. BULLETIN
Nat Inst Econ R .... NATIONAL INSTITUTE ECONOMIC REVIEW
Nation and Ath .... NATION AND ATHENAEUM
Nation-Athen ..... NATION AND ATHENAEUM
Nation (Lond) ..... NATION AND ATHENAEUM
Nations Ag .... NATION'S AGRICULTURE
Nation's Bus ...... NATION'S BUSINESS
Nation's Sch ...... NATION'S SCHOOLS
Natl Assn Sec-Schl Princ . . NATIONAL ASSOCIATION OF SECONDARY-SCHOOL PRINCIPALS. BULLETIN
Natl Bus Educ Yrbk . . NATIONAL BUSINESS EDUCATION YEARBOOK
Natl Civic Rev ..... NATIONAL CIVIC REVIEW
Natl Council Social Stud Yrbk . . NATIONAL COUNCIL FOR THE SOCIAL STUDIES. YEARBOOK
Natl Council Teach Math Yrbk . . NATIONAL COUNCIL OF TEACHERS OF MATHEMATICS YEARBOOK
Natl El Prin .... NATIONAL ELEMENTARY PRINCIPAL
Nat Lime Ass Bull . . NATIONAL LIME ASSOCIATION. BULLETIN
Nat'l M (Bost) ..... NATIONAL MAGAZINE (BOSTON)
Natl Observer ..... NATIONAL OBSERVER
Natl Parks .... NATIONAL PARKS MAGAZINE
Natl Pet Refiners Assoc Pap . . NATIONAL PETROLEUM REFINERS ASSOCIATION. PAPERS
Natl Ready Mixed Concr Assoc Publ . . NATIONAL READY MIXED CONCRETE ASSOCIATION. PUBLICATION
Natl Res Counc Build Res Advis Board Tech Rep . . NATIONAL RESEARCH COUNCIL. BUILDING RESEARCH ADVISORY BOARD. TECHNICAL REPORT
Natl Rev .... NATIONAL REVIEW
Natl Sand Gravel Assoc NSGA Circ . . NATIONAL SAND AND GRAVEL ASSOCIATION. NSGA CIRCULAR
Natl Soc Stud Educ Yrbk . . NATIONAL SOCIETY FOR THE STUDY OF EDUCATION. YEARBOOK
Natl Swed Build Res Doc . . NATIONAL SWEDISH BUILDING RESEARCH. DOCUMENT (STATENS INST FOER BYGGNADSFORSKNING)
NATL SYM .... NATIONAL SYMPHONY PROGRAM NOTES
Natl Tech Rep Matsushita Electr Ind . . NATIONAL TECHNICAL REPORT (MATSUSHITA ELECTRIC INDUSTRY, CO., OSAKA)
NAT LUCHT-RUIMTEVAARTLAB VERSLAGEN EN VERHANDEL ..... NATIONAAL LUCHT-EN RUIMTEVAARTLABOR- ATORIUM, VERSLAGEN EN VERHANDELINGEN
Nat M .... NATIONAL MAGAZINE
Nat Munic R ...... NATIONAL MUNICIPAL REVIEW
Nat Mus Council Bul . . NATIONAL MUSIC COUNCIL. BULLETIN
Natn Bldr .... NATIONAL BUILDER
Nat Parent Teach . . NATIONAL PARENT-TEACHER
Nat Parks .... NATIONAL PARKS MAGAZINE
Nat Pet N .... NATIONAL PETROLEUM NEWS
Nat Petrol Refiners Ass Tech Papers . . NATIONAL PETROLEUM REFINERS ASSOCIATION. TECHNICAL PAPERS
Nat Phys Lab Gt Brit Notes Appl Sci . . NATIONAL PHYSICAL LABORATORY. GREAT BRITAIN. DEPARTMENT OF SCIENTIFIC AND INDUSTRIAL RESEARCH. NOTES ON APPLIED SCIENCE

Nat Probation Assn Yrbk . . NATIONAL PROBATION AND PAROLE ASSOCIATION. YEARBOOK
Nat Q . . . . NATIONAL QUARTERLY REVIEW
Nat R . . . . NATIONAL REVIEW
Nat Rep . . . . NATIONAL REPUBLIC
Nat Res Counc Bldg Res Adv Bd Tech Rep . . NATIONAL RESEARCH COUNCIL. BUILDING RESEARCH ADVISORY
    BOARD. TECHNICAL REPORT
Nat Res Counc Can Aeronaut Rep . . NATIONAL RESEARCH COUNCIL OF CANADA. AERONAUTICAL REPORT
Nat Res Counc Can Ass Comm Geod Geophys Proc Hydrol Symp . . NATIONAL RESEARCH COUNCIL OF CANADA.
    ASSOCIATE COMMITTEE ON GEODESY AND GEOPHYSICS. PROCEEDINGS OF HYDROLOGY
    SYMPOSIUM
Nat Res Counc Can Ass Comm Geotech Res Tech Memo . . NATIONAL RESEARCH COUNCIL OF CANADA. ASSOCIATE
    COMMITTEE ON GEOTECHNICAL RESEARCH. TECHNICAL MEMORANDUM
Nat Res Counc Can Div Bldg Res Bibliogr . . NATIONAL RESEARCH COUNCIL OF CANADA. DIVISION OF BUILDING
    RESEARCH. BIBLIOGRAPHY
Nat Res Counc Can Div Mech Eng Mech Eng Rep . . NATIONAL RESEARCH COUNCIL OF CANADA. DIVISION OF
    MECHANICAL ENGINEERING, MECHANICAL ENGINEERING REPORT
Nat Res Counc Conf Elec Insul Annu Rep . . NATIONAL RESEARCH COUNCIL. CONFERENCE ON ELECTRICAL
    INSULATION. ANNUAL REPORT
Nat Rev . . . . NATIONAL REVIEW
NATS . . . . NATIONAL ASSOCIATION OF TEACHERS OF SINGING. BULLETIN
Nat Saf News . . . . . NATIONAL SAFETY NEWS
Nat Sand Gravel Ass NSGA Circ . . NATIONAL SAND AND GRAVEL ASSOCIATION. NSGA CIRCULAR
Nat Sanit Found Bd Consult Superv Inter-County Comm Rep Sewage Disposal Probl . . NATIONAL SANITATION
    FOUNDATION. BOARD OF CONSULTANTS, SUPERVISORS INTER-COUNTY COMMITTEE. REPORT
    ON SEWAGE DISPOSAL PROBLEMS
NATS Bull . . . . NATIONAL ASSOCIATION OF TEACHERS OF SINGING. BULLETIN
Nat Sch . . . . NATION'S SCHOOLS
Nat Sci . . . . NATURAL SCIENCE
Nat Sculp R . . . . . . NATIONAL SCULPTURE REVIEW
Nat Seedsman . . . . . NATIONAL SEEDSMAN
Nat Soc Study Ed Yrbk . . NATIONAL SOCIETY FOR THE STUDY OF EDUCATION. YEARBOOK
Nat Stock & F . . . . . NATIONAL STOCKMAN AND FARMER
NAT TAX J . . . . NATIONAL TAX JOURNAL
Nat Tech Rep . . . . . . NATIONAL TECHNICAL REPORT (MATSUSHITA ELECTRIC INDUSTRIAL CO., OSAKA)
Nat Underw . . . . NATIONAL UNDERWRITER
Nat Underw (Fire ed) . . NATIONAL UNDERWRITER (FIRE AND CASUALTY INSURANCE EDITION)
Nat Underw (Life) . . NATIONAL UNDERWRITER (LIFE AND HEALTH INSURANCE EDITION)
Nat Underw (Property ed) . . NATIONAL UNDERWRITER. (PROPERTY AND CASUALTY INSURANCE EDITION)
Natural Gard . . . . . . NATURAL GARDENING
NATURAL HI . . . . . . NATURAL HISTORY
Natural L F . . . . NATURAL LAW FORUM
Natural Resources Jnl . . NATURAL RESOURCES JOURNAL
Natural Resources Law . . NATURAL RESOURCES LAWYER
Nature and Sci Ed R . . NATURE AND SCIENCE EDUCATION REVIEW
Nature: Phys Sci . . . NATURE: PHYSICAL SCIENCE
Naturf Gesell Basel Verh . . NATURFORSCHENDE GESELLSCHAFT IN BASEL. VERHANDLUNGEN
Natur Hist . . . . NATURAL HISTORY
NATUR RES J . . . . . . NATURAL RESOURCES JOURNAL
NATUR RESOU . . . . . NATURAL RESOURCES LAWYER
NATURWISSEN . . . . . NATURWISSENSCHAFTEN
NAT W BANK . . . . . . NATIONAL WESTMINSTER BANK QUARTERLY REVIEW
Nauc Bjulletin Leningrad . . NAUCNYJ BJULLETIN LENINGRADSKOGO GOSUD. UNIVERSITETA

NAU T INF 1 ...... NAUCHNO-TEKHNICHESKAYA INFORMATSIYA. SERIYA 1. ORGANIZATSIYA I METODIKA INFORMATSIONNYE RABOTY
NAU T INF 2 ...... NAUCHNO-TEKHNICHESKAYA INFORMATSIYA. SERIYA 2. INFORMATSIONNYE PROTESSY I SISTEMY
Nav .... NAVORSCHER
NAV .... NUOVO ARCHIVIO VENETO
Nav Archit .... NAVAL ARCHITECT
Nav Eng J .... NAVAL ENGINEERS' JOURNAL
Nav M .... NAVAL MAGAZINE
NAV RES LOG ...... NAVAL RESEARCH LOGISTICS QUARTERLY
NAV RES REV ...... NAVAL RESEARCH REVIEWS
NAVTRADEVCEN ... U.S. NAVAL TRAINING DEVICE CENTER. TECHNICAL REPORT
Navy Rec Soc Publ .. NAVY RECORDS SOCIETY. PUBLICATIONS
NAWG .... NACHRICHTEN VON DER AKADEMIE DER WISSENSCHAFTEN ZU GOTTINGEN. PHILOL.-HIST. KLASSE
NB .... NAMM OCH BYGD
NBAC .... NUOVO BOLLETTINO DI ARCHEOLOGIA CHRISTIANA
NBB .... NORSK BIBLIOGRAFISK BIBLIOTEK
NBEA Y .... NATIONAL BUSINESS EDUCATION ASSOCIATION. YEARBOOK
NBER GEN S .... NBER (NATIONAL BUREAU OF ECONOMIC RESEARCH) GENERAL STUDIES
NBER OC P ...... NBER (NATIONAL BUREAU OF ECONOMIC RESEARCH) OCCASIONAL PAPERS
NBGPL .... NEDERLANDSCHE BIJDRAGEN OP HET GEBIED VAN GERMAANSCHE PHILOLOGIE EN LINGUISTIEK
NBIC .... NEWS FROM BEHIND THE IRON CURTAIN
NBL .... NEUE BEITRAEGE ZUR LITERATURWISSENSCHAFT
NBLU .... NAUCNYJ BJULLETEN' LENINGRADSKOGO UNIVERSITETA
NBS Monogr ...... NATIONAL BUREAU OF STANDARDS. MONOGRAPHS
NBS Spec Publ .... NATIONAL BUREAU OF STANDARDS. SPECIAL PUBLICATION
NBS Tech News Bull .. NATIONAL BUREAU OF STANDARDS. TECHNICAL NEWS BULLETIN
NC .... NEW CRITERION
NC .... NINETEENTH CENTURY AND AFTER
NC .... NUMISMATIC CHRONICLE AND JOURNAL OF THE NUMISMATIC SOCIETY
NC .... NUOVA CORRENTE
NCAB .... NATIONAL CYCLOPEDIA OF AMERICAN BIOGRAPHY
N C Ag Exp .... NORTH CAROLINA AGRICULTURAL EXPERIMENT STATION. PUBLICATIONS
NCarF .... NORTH CAROLINA FOLKLORE
N Carolina Lib ..... NORTH CAROLINA LIBRARIES
NCathW .... NEW CATHOLIC WORLD
NC Central L J ..... NORTH CAROLINA CENTRAL LAW JOURNAL
N C Div Miner Resour Bull .. NORTH CAROLINA. DEPARTMENT OF CONSERVATION AND DEVELOPMENT. DIVISION OF MINERAL RESOURCES. BULLETIN
N Cen Assn Q ..... THE NORTH CENTRAL ASSOCIATION QUARTERLY
N Cent .... NINETEENTH CENTURY
NCF .... NINETEENTH-CENTURY FICTION
NCF .... NORTH CAROLINA FOLKLORE
NC Folk .... NORTH CAROLINA FOLKLORE
NCFS .... NINETEENTH-CENTURY FRENCH STUDIES
NCGH .... NIPPON CHUGOKU GAKKAIHO (BULLETIN OF THE SINOLOGICAL SOCIETY OF JAPAN)
NCGS .... FRA NY-CARLSBERG GLYPTOTEKS SAMMLINGEN
NCHR .... NORTH CAROLINA HISTORICAL REVIEW
N Church R .... NEW CHURCH REVIEW

NCI . . . . NOTIZIARIO CULTURALE ITALIANO
NCL . . . . NOSSOS CLASSICOS
NCL . . . . NOTES ON CONTEMPORARY LITERATURE
NC Lib . . . . NORTH CAROLINA LIBRARIES
NClio . . . . NOUVELLE CLIO
N C L Rev . . . . NORTH CAROLINA LAW REVIEW
NCoHS . . . . NORTHUMBERLAND COUNTY HISTORICAL SOCIETY. PROCEEDINGS
NCoHSP . . . . NORTHUMBERLAND COUNTY HISTORICAL SOCIETY. PROCEEDINGS
N Col . . . . NEW COLOPHON
NConL . . . . NOTES ON CONTEMPORARY LITERATURE
NCR . . . . NATIONAL CIVIC REVIEW
NCRMM . . . . NOUVELLE CRITIQUE. REVUE DU MARXISME MILITANT
NCSA . . . . NATIONAL CARL SCHURZ ASSOCIATION
NCSS B . . . . NATIONAL COUNCIL FOR THE SOCIAL STUDIES. BULLETIN
NCSS READ . . . . . . NATIONAL COUNCIL FOR THE SOCIAL STUDIES. READINGS
NCSS RES B . . . . . . NATIONAL COUNCIL FOR THE SOCIAL STUDIES. RESEARCH BULLETIN
NCSS YEARB . . . . . NATIONAL COUNCIL FOR THE SOCIAL STUDIES. YEARBOOK
NCult . . . . NUOVA CULTURA
NCW . . . . NEW CATHOLIC WORLD
ND . . . . LA NUEVA DEMOCRACIA (NEW YORK)
ND . . . . NOWE DROGI
ND . . . . NUOVO DIDASKALEION
N D Ag Exp . . . . NORTH DAKOTA AGRICULTURAL EXPERIMENT STATION. PUBLICATIONS
N Dak Geol Surv Bull . . NORTH DAKOTA GEOLOGICAL SURVEY. BULLETIN
N Dak Geol Surv Rep Invest . . NORTH DAKOTA GEOLOGICAL SURVEY. REPORT OF INVESTIGATIONS
N Dak Lib Notes . . . . NORTH DAKOTA LIBRARY NOTES
N DAME J ED . . . . . . NOTRE DAME JOURNAL OF EDUCATION
NDAT . . . . NASHRIYYE(H)-YE DANESHKADE(H)-YE ADABIYYAT VA OLUM-E ENSANI-YE TABRIZ
NDEJ . . . . NOTRE DAME ENGLISH JOURNAL
NDF . . . . NEUE DEUTSCHE FORSCHUNG
N D Farm Res . . . . . NORTH DAKOTA FARM RESEARCH
NDFN . . . . NAUCHNYE DOKLADY VYSSHEI SHKOLY. FILOLOGICHESKIE NAUKI (MOSCOW)
NDH . . . . NEUE DEUTSCHE HEFTE
NDH . . . . NORTH DAKOTA HISTORY
NDHi . . . . NORTH DAKOTA HISTORY
NDim . . . . NUOVE DIMENSIONI
NdJb . . . . NIEDERDEUTSCHES JAHRBUCH
NdL . . . . NEUDRUCKE DEUTSCHER LITERATURWERKE
NDL . . . . NEUE DEUTSCHE LITERATUR
N D L Review . . . . . . NORTH DAKOTA LAW REVIEW
NdM . . . . NIEDERDEUTSCHE MITTEILUNGEN
NDQ . . . . NORTH DAKOTA QUARTERLY
NDR . . . . NEUE DEUTSCHE RUNDSCHAU
NdS . . . . NIEDERDEUTSCHE STUDIEN
NDSK . . . . NYDANSKE STUDIER OG ALMEN KOMMUNIKATIONSTEORI
NDV . . . . NOTES ET DOCUMENTS VOLTAIQUES
NDVS . . . . NAUCNYE DOKLADY VYSSEJ SKOLY
NDVS-F . . . . NAUCNYE DOKLADY VYSSEJ SKOLY. FILOLOGICESKIE NAUKI
NDW . . . . NIEDERDEUTSCHES WORT
NE . . . . NUMISMATICA I EPIGRAFICA
NeaH . . . . NEA HESTIA

NEA J . . . . NEA (NATIONAL EDUCATION ASSOCIATION) JOURNAL
Neap . . . . NEAPOLIS
Near East . . . . NEAR EAST AND INDIA
NEA Res Bul . . . . . . NEA (NATIONAL EDUCATION ASSOCIATION) RESEARCH BULLETIN
NEA Res Div Rept . . NEA (NATIONAL EDUCATION ASSOCIATION) RESEARCH DIVISION REPORTS
NE Asia J Th . . . . . . NORTHEAST ASIA JOURNAL OF THEOLOGY
NEB . . . . NEBULA SCIENCE FICTION
Neb Ag Exp . . . . . . UNIVERSITY OF NEBRASKA. AGRICULTURAL EXPERIMENT STATION. PUBLICATIONS
Neb Ed J . . . . NEBRASKA EDUCATIONAL JOURNAL
NebH . . . . NEBRASKA HISTORY
Neb Hist . . . . NEBRASKA HISTORY
Neb Lib Assn Q . . . . NEBRASKA LIBRARY ASSOCIATION. QUARTERLY
Neb L Rev . . . . NEBRASKA LAW REVIEW
Nebr Geol Surv Bull . . NEBRASKA GEOLOGICAL SURVEY. BULLETIN
Neb SBJ . . . . NEBRASKA STATE BAR JOURNAL
N Ecl . . . . NEW ECLECTIC
NEC Res Dev . . . . . . NEC (NIPPON ELECTRIC COMPANY) RESEARCH AND DEVELOPMENT
NedA . . . . NEDERLANDSCH ARCHIEVENBLAD
Nederlandsch Hist Inst Rome Med . . NEDERLANDSCH HISTORISCH INSTITUUT TE ROME. MEDEDEELINGEN
NedL . . . . NEDERLANDSE LEEUW
Nef . . . . NEF: CAHIER TRIMESTRIEL
NEF . . . . NORTHEAST FOLKLORE
NEF . . . . NOTAS Y ESTUDIOS DE FILOSOFIA
Neft Khoz . . . . NEFTYANOE KHOZYAISTVO
Negro D . . . . NEGRO DIGEST
Negro Ed R . . . . . . NEGRO EDUCATIONAL REVIEW
NEHGR . . . . NEW ENGLAND HISTORICAL AND GENEALOGICAL REGISTER
NELA Bul . . . . NATIONAL ELECTRIC LIGHT ASSOCIATION. BULLETIN
NELA Newsl . . . . . . NELA (NEW ENGLAND LIBRARY ASSOCIATION) NEWSLETTER
N Elec Telesis . . . . . NORTHERN ELECTRIC TELESIS
Nem . . . . NEMAN (MOSCOW)
N Eng . . . . NEW ENGLANDER
N ENG J MED . . . . . . NEW ENGLAND JOURNAL OF MEDICINE
Neo . . . . NEOPHILOLOGUS
Neophil . . . . NEOPHILOLOGUS
NEQ . . . . NEW ENGLAND QUARTERLY
NER . . . . NATIONAL AND ENGLISH REVIEW
NER . . . . NEW ENGLISH REVIEW
N E Reg . . . . NEW ENGLAND HISTORICAL AND GENEALOGICAL REGISTER
Nerthus . . . . NERTHUS: NORDISCH-DEUTSCHE BEITRAEGE
Nerv Child . . . . NERVOUS CHILD
NETH MILK D . . . . . NETHERLANDS MILK AND DAIRY JOURNAL
Neue Beitr Gesch Deutsch Altert . . NEUE BEITRAEGE ZUR GESCHICHTE DEUTSCHEN ALTERTUMS
Neue Bergbautech . . NEUE BERGBAUTECHNIK
NEUE MZ . . . . NEUE MUSIKZEITUNG
Neue Rundsch . . . . . NEUE RUNDSCHAU
Neue ZFM . . . . NEUE ZEITSCHRIFT FUER MUSIK
Neue Z Sys Th . . . . . NEUE ZEITSCHRIFT FUER SYSTEMATISCHE THEOLOGIE UND RELIGIONSPHILOSOPHIE
Neujahrsbl Sachs . . . NEUJAHRSBLAETTER HERAUSGEGEBEN VON DER HISTORISCHEN KOMMISSION FUER DIE
PROVINZ SACHSEN

NeuP........... NEUPHILOLOGISCHE MONATSSCHRIFT
New Am Mercury... NEW AMERICAN MERCURY
N E Water Works Assn J..NEW ENGLAND WATER WORKS ASSOCIATION. JOURNAL
Newberry Lib Bul... NEWBERRY LIBRARY BULLETIN
Neuphil mit....... NEUPHILOLOGISCHE MITTEILUNGEN
NEUROCHIRA..... NEUROCHIRURGIA
NEURO-CHIRE..... NEURO-CHIRURGIE
NEUROENDOCR.... NEUROENDOCRINOLOGY
NEUROPADIAT.... NEUROPADIATRIE
NEUROP AP N..... NEUROPATHOLOGY AND APPLIED NEUROBIOLOGY
NEUROPHARM..... NEUROPHARMACOLOGY
NEUROPSYCHO.... NEUROPSYCHOLOGIA
NEURORADIOL..... NEURORADIOLOGY
NEUROSCI L....... NEUROSCIENCE LETTERS
NeuS............ NEUEREN SPRACHEN
Neu Spr.......... NEUEREN SPRACHEN
Nev Ag Exp....... NEVADA AGRICULTURAL EXPERIMENT STATION. PUBLICATIONS
New............. NEW AGE
NewA........... NEW AFRICAN
New Caledonia Bull Geol..NEW CALEDONIA. BULLETIN GEOLOGIQUE
Newcastle Inst Ed J..INSTITUTES OF EDUCATION OF THE UNIVERSITIES OF NEWCASTLE UPON TYNE AND DURHAM.
                JOURNAL
New Church R..... NEW CHURCH REVIEW
Newcomen Soc Trans..NEWCOMEN SOCIETY. TRANSACTIONS
NEW DIR COM..... NEW DIRECTIONS FOR COMMUNITY COLLEGES
NEW DIR HIG...... NEW DIRECTIONS FOR HIGHER EDUCATION
New Dom........ NEW DOMINION MONTHLY
New Eng......... NEW ENGLANDER
New Eng Hist General Reg..NEW ENGLAND HISTORICAL AND GENEALOGICAL REGISTER
New England L Rev..NEW ENGLAND LAW REVIEW
New Eng Mag..... NEW ENGLAND MAGAZINE
New Eng M ns..... NEW ENGLAND MAGAZINE (NEW SERIES)
New Eng Q........ NEW ENGLAND QUARTERLY
New Era......... NEW ERA IN HOME AND SCHOOL
NEW HAVEN SYM... NEW HAVEN SYMPHONY ORCHESTRA. PROGRAM NOTES
NewL........... NEW LEADER
New Lib W........ NEW LIBRARY WORLD
New Lit Hist...... NEW LITERARY HISTORY
New L J.......... NEW LAW JOURNAL
New Mex Hist Rev..NEW MEXICO HISTORICAL REVIEW
New Mexico L Rev..NEW MEXICO LAW REVIEW
NEW PHYTOL...... NEW PHYTOLOGIST
New Princ........ NEW PRINCETON REVIEW
New Q........... NEW QUARTERLY REVIEW
New R........... NEW REPUBLIC
New R........... NEW REVIEW
New Schol........ NEW SCHOLASTICISM
News Farmer Coops..NEWS FOR FARMER COOPERATIVES
News Let......... NEWS LETTER OF THE AMERICAN SYMPHONY ORCHESTRA LEAGUE, INC.
Newsl Intellectual Freedom..NEWSLETTER ON INTELLECTUAL FREEDOM
News Notes Calif Libs..NEWS NOTES OF CALIFORNIA LIBRARIES

NEW SOC . . . . NEW SOCIETY
NewSt . . . . NEW STATESMAN
NF . . . . NEERLANDIA FRANCISKANA
NF . . . . NEUE FORSCHUNGEN
NF . . . . NIGERIAN FIELD
NF . . . . NORTHEAST FOLKLORE
NFJGG . . . . NEUE FOLGE DES JAHRBUCHS DER GOETHE GESELLSCHAFT
NFLD Q . . . . NEWFOUNDLAND QUARTERLY
NFS . . . . NOTTINGHAM FRENCH STUDIES
NFSGWS . . . . NEWSLETTER OF THE FOLKLORE SOCIETY OF GREATER WASHINGTON: SUPPLEMENT
NG . . . . NEUE GESELLSCHAFT
NG . . . . NEW GUARD
NG . . . . NIEUWE GIDS
NGF . . . . NOMINA GEOGRAPHICA FLANDRICA
NGG . . . . NACHRICHTEN VON DER GESELLSCHAFT DER WISSENSCHAFTEN ZU GOETTINGEN
NGM . . . . NATIONAL GEOGRAPHIC MAGAZINE
NGN . . . . NOMINA GEOGRAPHICA NEERLANDICA
NGNVO . . . . NACHRICHTEN DER GESELLSCHAFT FUER NATUR- UND VOELKERKUNDE OSTASIENS
NGS . . . . NATIONAL GENEALOGICAL SOCIETY
NGS . . . . NEUE GEISTESWISSENSCHAFTLICHE STUDIEN
NGS . . . . NEW GERMAN STUDIES
NGS . . . . NIEUW-GUINEA STUDIEN
NGSQ . . . . NATIONAL GENEALOGICAL SOCIETY. QUARTERLY
NGWG . . . . NACHRICHTEN VON DER GESELLSCHAFT DER WISSENSCHAFTEN ZU GOETTINGEN. PHIL.-HIST.
KLASSE
NH . . . . NATURAL HISTORY
NH . . . . NEBRASKA HISTORY
N H Ag Exp . . . . NEW HAMPSHIRE AGRICULTURAL EXPERIMENT STATION. PUBLICATIONS
NHB . . . . NEDERLANDSCHE HISTORIEBLADEN
NHB . . . . NEGRO HISTORY BULLETIN
NHBI . . . . NASSAUISCHE HEIMATBLAETTER
NHB J . . . . NEW HAMPSHIRE BAR JOURNAL
NHJ . . . . NATHANIEL HAWTHORNE JOURNAL
NHJ . . . . NEUE HEIDELBERGER JAHRBUECHER
NHJB . . . . NEUE HEIDELBERGER JAHRBUECHER
NHK Lab Note . . . . . NHK (NIPPON HOSO KYOKAI) LABORATORIES NOTE
NHK Tech Monogr . . NHK (NIPPON HOSO KYOKAI) TECHNICAL MONOGRAPH
NHLS . . . . NORTH HOLLAND LINGUISTIC SERIES
NHochland . . . . NEUES HOCHLAND
NHQ . . . . NEW HUNGARIAN QUARTERLY
NHV . . . . NEA HELLINIKI VIVLIOTHIKI
NHVKSG . . . . NEUJAHRSBLATT DES HISTORISCHEN VEREINS DES KANTONS ST. GALLEN
NI . . . . NUOVA ITALIA
Niederdeu Mit . . . . . NIEDERDEUTSCHE MITTEILUNGEN
NietzscheS . . . . NIETSCHE STUDIEN
NIF . . . . NEWSLETTER ON INTELLECTUAL FREEDOM
Nigerian Lib . . . . . . NIGERIAN LIBRARIES
NigM . . . . NIGERIA MAGAZINE
NIK . . . . NYELV-ES IRODALOMTUDOMANYI KOZLEMENYEK
Niles' Reg . . . . NILES' REGISTER
19th Cent . . . . NINETEENTH CENTURY

19th Cent Fiction . . . NINETEENTH CENTURY FICTION
NIP KAG KAI . . . . . . NIPPON KAGAKU KAISHI
NIt . . . . NUOVA ITALIA
NIYB . . . . NEW INTERNATIONAL YEAR BOOK
NJ . . . . NAS JEZIK
NJ . . . . NIEDERDEUTSCHES JAHRBUCH
NJA . . . . NEUE JAHRBUECHER FUER DAS KLASSISCHE ALTERTUM
NJAB . . . . NEUE JAHRBUECHER FUER ANTIKE UND DEUTSCHE BILDUNG
NJADB . . . . NEUE JAHRBUECHER FUER ANTIKE UND DEUTSCHE BILDUNG
N J Ag . . . . NEW JERSEY AGRICULTURE
N J Ag Dept . . . . . . NEW JERSEY DEPARTMENT OF AGRICULTURE. PUBLICATIONS
N J Ag Exp . . . . NEW JERSEY AGRICULTURAL EXPERIMENT STATION. PUBLICATIONS
NJb . . . . NEUE JAHRBUECHER FUER WISSENSCHAFT UND JUGENDBILDUNG
NJb . . . . NIEDERDEUTSCHES JAHRBUCH
NJBEA Newsletter . . NEW JERSEY BUSINESS EDUCATION ASSOCIATION. NEWSLETTER
NJbWJB . . . . NEUE JAHRBUECHER FUER WISSENSCHAFT UND JUGENDBILDUNG
N J Dep Conserv Econ Develop Geol Rep Ser . . NEW JERSEY. DEPARTMENT OF CONSERVATION AND ECONOMIC DEVELOPMENT. GEOLOGIC REPORT SERIES
NJDW . . . . NEUE JAHRBUECHER FUER DEUTSCHE WISSENSCHAFT
NJe . . . . NAS JEZIK
NJE . . . . NIGERIAN JOURNAL OF ECONOMIC AND SOCIAL STUDIES
NJH . . . . NEW JERSEY HISTORY
N J Hist . . . . NEW JERSEY HISTORY
NJHistS . . . . NEW JERSEY HISTORICAL SOCIETY. PROCEEDINGS
NJHS . . . . NEW JERSEY HISTORICAL SOCIETY. PROCEEDINGS
NJHSP . . . . NEW JERSEY HISTORICAL SOCIETY. PROCEEDINGS
NJK . . . . NASTAVA JEZIKA I KNJIZEVNOSTI U SREDNOJ SKOLI
NJKAGDL . . . . NEUE JAHRBUECHER FUER DAS KLASSISCHE, ALTERTUM, GESCHICHTE UND DEUTSCHE LITERATUR
N J Lib . . . . NEW JERSEY LIBRARIES
NJP . . . . NEUE JAHRBUECHER FUER PAEDOGOGIK
NJ Sch Libn . . . . . . NEW JERSEY SCHOOL LIBRARIAN
NJW . . . . NEUE JAHRBUECHER FUER WISSENSCHAFT UND JUGENDBILDUNG
NJWJ . . . . NEUE JAHRBUECHER FUER WISSENSCHAFT UND JUGENDBILDUNG
NK . . . . NARODNA KULTURA (SOFIA)
NK . . . . NASZA KSIEGARNIA
NK . . . . NOWE KULTURA
NK . . . . NYELVTUDOMANYI KOZLEMENYEK
NKGWG . . . . NACHRICHTEN DER KOENIGLICH. GESELLSCHAFT DER WISSENSCHAFTEN ZU GOETTINGEN
NKHJ . . . . NEDERLANDSCH KUNSTHISTORISCH JAARBOEK
NKS . . . . NEDERLANDSCHE KATHOLIEKE STEMMEN
NKs . . . . NOWE KSIAZKI
NKT . . . . NORSKE KLASSIKER-TEKSTER
Nku . . . . NAAMKUNDE
NKZ . . . . NEUE KIRCHLICHE ZEITSCHRIFT
NL . . . . NEW LEADER
NL . . . . NORWINY LITERACKIE
NL . . . . NOUVELLES LITTERAIRES
NLA . . . . NORSK LITTERAER ARBOK
NLauR . . . . NEW LAUREL REVIEW
NLB . . . . NEWBERRY LIBRARY BULLETIN

NLB . . . . NUMISMATISCHES LITERATUR-BLATT
NLGI Spokesman . . . NLGI (NATIONAL LUBRICATING GREASE INSTITUTE) SPOKESMAN
NLH . . . . NEW LITERARY HISTORY
NLit . . . . NEUE LITERATUR
NLiW . . . . NOWINY LITERACKIE I WYDAWNICZE
NLM . . . . NEUES LAUSITZISCHES MAGAZIN
NLN . . . . NEO-LATIN NEWS (QUEENS COLLEGE)
NLR . . . . NATIONAL REVIEW (LONDON)
NLWJ . . . . NATIONAL LIBRARY OF WALES. JOURNAL
NLW Journ . . . . . . NATIONAL LIBRARY OF WALES. JOURNAL
NLZ . . . . NUMISMATISCHE LITERATUR-ZEITUNG
NM . . . . NEUPHILOLOGISCHE MITTEILUNGEN
NM . . . . NIEDERDEUTSCHE MITTEILUNGEN
NM . . . . NORTHERN MISCELLANY
N M Ag Exp . . . . NEW MEXICO COLLEGE OF AGRICULTURE AND MECHANIC ARTS. AGRICULTURAL EXPERIMENT
STATION. PUBLICATIONS
NMC . . . . NATIONAL MUSIC COUNCIL BULLETIN
NMCB . . . . NATIONAL MUSEUM OF CANADA. BULLETIN
NMC Bul . . . . NATIONAL MUSIC COUNCIL. BULLETIN
N Mex Ext N . . . . . . NEW MEXICO EXTENSION NEWS
N Mex Lib . . . . NEW MEXICO LIBRARIES
N Mex Lib Bul . . . . . NEW MEXICO LIBRARY BULLETIN
N Mex Lib Newsl . . . NEW MEXICO LIBRARY NEWSLETTER
NMFR . . . . NEW MEXICO FOLKLORE RECORD
NMHQ . . . . NEW MEXICO HISTORICAL QUARTERLY
NMHR . . . . NEW MEXICO HISTORICAL REVIEW
NMi . . . . NEUPHILOLOGISCHE MITTEILUNGEN
NMis . . . . NOVA MISAO
N Mitt . . . . NEUPHILOLOGISCHE MITTEILUNGEN
N M Lib Newsl . . . . . NEW MEXICO LIBRARIES NEWSLETTER
NML Tech J . . . . NML (NATIONAL METALLURGICAL LABORATORY) TECHNICAL JOURNAL
NMo . . . . NEUPHILOLOGISCHE MONATSSCHRIFT
N Mon . . . . NEUPHILOLOGISCHE MONATSSCHRIFT
NMQ . . . . NEW MEXICO QUARTERLY
NMQR . . . . NEW MEXICO QUARTERLY REVIEW
NMS . . . . NOTTINGHAM MEDIEVAL STUDIES
NMSCS . . . . NORTHWEST MISSOURI STATE COLLEGE STUDIES
NMW . . . . NOTES ON MISSISSIPPI WRITERS
NNH . . . . NUEVA NARRATIVA HISPANOAMERICANA
NNRF . . . . NOUVELLE NOUVELLE REVUE FRANCAISE
NO . . . . NARODNOE OBRAZOVANIE (MOSCOW)
NO . . . . NATIONAL OBSERVER
NO . . . . NEW ORIENT (PRAGUE)
NO . . . . NOVA OBZORIJA
No Am . . . . NORTH AMERICAN REVIEW
No Am Rev . . . . . . NORTH AMERICAN REVIEW
NoB . . . . NAMN OCH BYGD
NOB . . . . NEW ORIENT BIMONTHLY
No Brit . . . . NORTH BRITISH REVIEW
No Car Hist Rev . . . . NORTH CAROLINA HISTORICAL REVIEW
No Car Law Rev . . . . NORTH CAROLINA LAW REVIEW

No Dak Hist. . . . . . . NORTH DAKOTA HISTORY
No Dak Hist Quar. . . NORTH DAKOTA HISTORICAL QUARTERLY
No Dak Quar. . . . . . NORTH DAKOTA QUARTERLY
NoEF. . . . . NORTHEAST FOLKLORE
No Ire L Q. . . . . NORTHERN IRELAND LEGAL QUARTERLY
Noise Control Vibr Reduct. . NOISE CONTROL AND VIBRATION REDUCTION
Nom. . . . . NOMISMA. UNTERSUCHUNGEN AUF DEM GEBIETE DER ANTIKEN MUNSKUNDE
NoM. . . . . NOVYJ MIR
NON-DESTR T. . . . . . NON-DESTRUCTIVE TESTING
Non-Ioniz Radiat. . . NON-IONIZING RADIATION
NOP. . . . . NEW ORLEANS POETRY JOURNAL
NOQ. . . . . NORTHWEST OHIO QUARTERLY
NOR. . . . . NEW ORLEANS REVIEW
Nor. . . . . NORSEMAN (LONDON)
NoR. . . . . NORTHERN REVIEW
Nord Betong. . . . . . NORDISK BETONG
Nordisk Tids Bok & Bibl. . NORDISK TIDSSKRIFT FOER BOK-OCH BIBLIOTEKSVAESEN
Nord Mus. . . . . NORDISK MUSIKKULTUR
Nord Tid. . . . . NORDISK TIDSSKRIFT FOER BOK- OCH BIBLIOTEKSVAESEN
Nord Tidskr f Vetensk. . NORDISK TIDSSKRIFT FOER VETENSKAP, KONST OCH INDUSTRI
Nord Tidskrift. . . . . NORDISK TIDSSKRIFT FOER FILOLOGI
NORD VETMED. . . . NORDISK VETERINAER MEDICIN
Norg Geotek Inst Publ. . NORGES GEOTEKNISKE INSTITUT. PUBLIKASJON (OSLO)
Norm Instr and Prim Plans. . NORMAL INSTRUCTOR AND PRIMARY PLANS
NORSK GEOL. . . . . . NORSK GEOLOGISK TIDSSKRIFT
Norsk Geol Tids. . . . NORSK GEOLOGISK TIDSSKRIFT
NORSK MUS. . . . . . NORSK MUSIKERBLAD
NORSK SKOG. . . . . . NORSK SKOGINDUSTRI
North Am R. . . . . . . NORTH AMERICAN REVIEW
North Cent Assn Q. . NORTH CENTRAL ASSOCIATION. QUARTERLY
North Carolina Lib. . NORTH CAROLINA LIBRARIES
North Country Lib. . NORTH COUNTRY LIBRARIES
Northern Ireland Lib. . NORTHERN IRELAND LIBRARIES
Northern L. . . . . . . NORTHERN LIGHTS
North R. . . . . NORTHERN REVIEW
North West Newsl. . NORTH WESTERN NEWSLETTER
Northw Ohio Quar. . NORTHWEST OHIO QUARTERLY
NORTHW U LA. . . . . NORTHWESTERN UNIVERSITY LAW REVIEW
Northw Univ Law Rev. . NORTHWESTERN UNIVERSITY LAW REVIEW
Norton. . . . . NORTON'S LITERARY LETTER
Norv. . . . . NORVEG
Norwegian-Am Stud and Rec. . NORWEGIAN-AMERICAN STUDIES AND RECORDS
Nor'-West F. . . . . . . NOR'-WEST FARMER
Norw Marit Res. . . . NORWEGIAN MARITIME RESEARCH
NOT AM MATH. . . . NOTICES OF THE AMERICAN MATHEMATICAL SOCIETY
Notes & Quer. . . . . NOTES AND QUERIES
Noticias. . . . . BRASIL. INSTITUTO BRASILEIRO DE BIBLIOGRAPHIA E DOCUMENTACAO. NOTICIAS
Notre Dame J Form Log. . NOTRE DAME JOURNAL OF FORMAL LOGIC
Notre Dame Law. . . NOTRE DAME LAWYER
NOUV PRESSE. . . . . NOUVELLE PRESSE MEDICALE
Nouv Rev Opt Appl. . NOUVELLE REVUE D'OPTIQUE APPLIQUEE

NOUV RF HEM..... NOUVELLE REVUE FRANCAISE D' HEMATOLOGIE
Nouv R Francaise... NOUVELLE REVUE FRANCAISE
NOUV R OPT...... NOUVELLE REVUE D'OPTIQUE
Nov........... NOVERIM
Nova Scotian Inst Sci Proc.. NOVA SCOTIAN INSTITUTE OF SCIENCE. PROCEEDINGS
NoVidSF........ DET KONGELIGE NORSKE VIDENSKABERS SELBSKABS FORHANDLINGER
NovM.......... NOVYJ MIR
NovTest........ NOVUM TESTAMENTUM
NovZ.......... NOVYJ ZURNAL
NoZ........... NOVY ZIVOT
NP............ NASZA PRZESZLOSC
NP............ NAUKA POLSKA
NP............ NEA POREIA
NP............ NEOPHILOLOGUS
NP............ NEW PHILOSOPHY
NPCM.......... NATIONAL PARKS AND CONSERVATION MAGAZINE
NPfG.......... NORDPFALZER GESCHICHTSVEREIN
NPh........... NEOPHILOLOGUS
NphM.......... NEUPHILOLOGISCHE MITTEILUNGEN
NphZ.......... NEUPHILOLOGISCHE ZEITSCHRIFT
NPM........... NEUPHILOLOGISCHE MITTEILUNGEN
NPM........... NEUPHILOLOGISCHE MONATSSCHRIFT
NPN........... NATIONAL PETROLEUM NEWS
N Princ........ NEW PRINCETON REVIEW
NPS........... NEW PALAEOGRAPHICAL SOCIETY
NQ............ NOTES AND QUERIES
NQM........... NUOVI QUADERNI DEL MERIDIONE
NQNS.......... NOTES AND QUERIES, NEW SERIES
NR............ NASE REC (PRAGUE)
NR............ NATIONAL REVIEW
NR............ NEUE RUNDSCHAU
NR............ NEW REPUBLIC
NR............ NORTHWEST REVIEW
NR............ NOVA REVIJA
NRA........... NOUVELLE REVUE APOLOGETIQUE
NRam.......... NEW RAMBLER
NRB........... NOUVELLE REVUE DE BRETAGNE
NRC........... NOUVELLE REVUE CANADIENNE
NRC........... NOUVELLE REVUE CRITIQUE
NREL.......... NOUVELLE RELEVE
NRep.......... NEW REPUBLIC
NRF........... NOUVELLE REVUE FRANCAISE
NRFH.......... NUEVA REVISTA DE FILOLOGIA HISPANICA
NRH........... NOUVELLE REVUE DE HONGRIE
NRHD.......... NOUVELLE REVUE HISTORIQUE DE DROIT FRANCAIS ET ETRANGER
NRHDFE........ NOUVELLE REVUE HISTORIQUE DE DROIT FRANCAIS ET ETRANGER
NRJ........... NATURAL RESOURCES JOURNAL
NRM........... NUOVA RIVISTA MUSICALE ITALIANA
NRMS.......... NOTTINGHAM RENAISSANCE AND MODERN STUDIES
NRP........... NOUVELLE REVUE PEDAGOGIQUE
NRS........... NAUCNYE RABOTY IS OOBSCENIJA AKADEMII NAUK UZBEKSKOJ SSR, OTDELENIE OBSCESTVENNYCH NAUK

NRs............ NEUE RUNDSCHAU
NRS............ NUOVA RIVISTA STORICA
NRT............ NOUVELLE REVUE DE THEOLOGIE
NRTh........... NOUVELLE REVUE THEOLOGIQUE
NRTP........... NOUVELLE REVUE DES TRADITIONS POPULAIRES
NRu............ NEUE RUNDSCHAU
N Rund......... NEUE RUNDSCHAU
NRVU........... NUOVA RIVISTA DI VARIA UMANITA
NS............. NEDERLANDSCHE SPECTATOR
NS............. NEUEREN SPRACHEN
NS............. NEW SCHOLASTICISM
NS............. NEW STATESMAN
NS............. NOBLE SAVAGE
NS............. NOVI SVET
NSA............ NOTIZIE DEGLI SCAVI DI ANTICHITA
NSAC........... NOTICES ET MEMOIRES DE LA SOCIETE ARCHEOLOGIQUE DE CONSTANTINE
NSammlung....... NEUE SAMMLUNG
NS&N........... NEW STATESMAN AND NATION
NSAR........... NATIONALMUSEI SKRIFTSERIE, ANALECTA REGINENSIA
N-S ARCH PH...... NAUNYN-SCHMIEDEBERGS ARCHIVES OF PHARMACOLOGY
NSC............ NAMES IN SOUTH CAROLINA
NSch........... NEW SCHOLASTICISM
NSchwRundschau... NEUE SCHWEIZER RUNDSCHAU
N Sci R......... NEW SCIENCE REVIEW
NSE............ NORWEGIAN STUDIES IN ENGLISH
NSHT........... NORSK SLEKTSHISTORISK TIDSSKRIFT
NSi............ NEA SION
NSJB........... NIEDERSAECHSICHES JAHRBUCH
NSJBH.......... NIEDERSAECHSISHES JAHRBUCH. HILDESHEIM
NSJFS.......... NORTH STAFFORDSHIRE JOURNAL OF FIELD STUDIES
NSJLG.......... NIEDERSAECHSISCHES JAHRBUCH FUER LANDESGESCHICHTE
NSL............ DET NORSKE SPRAK- OG LITTERATURSELSKAP
NSM............ NATIONALSOZIALISTISCHE MONATSHEFTE
NSM............ NEUSPRACHLICHE MITTEILUNGEN AUS WISSENSCHAFT UND PRAXIS
NSN............ NEW STATESMAN AND NATION
NSp............ NEUEREN SPRACHEN
NSR............ NEUE SCHWEIZER RUNDSCHAU
NSS............ NYSVENSKA STUDIER
NST............ NEW SCIENTIST
N St........... NEW STATESMAN
NSt............ NORDISCHE STUDIEN
NStat.......... NEW STATESMAN
N S Tech Coll Dep Civ Eng Essays Timber Struct.. NOVA SCOTIA TECHNICAL COLLEGE. HALIFAX. DEPARTMENT OF
                CIVIL ENGINEERING. ESSAYS ON TIMBER STRUCTURES
NStem.......... NIEUWE STEM
NStN........... NEW STATESMAN AND NATION
NStv........... NARODNO STVARALASTVO. FOLKLOR
NsvS........... NYSVENSKA STUDIER
N S W Dep Mines Tech Rep.. NEW SOUTH WALES. DEPARTMENT OF MINES. TECHNICAL REPORTS
NSW Univ Sch Civ Eng Uniciv Rep Ser R.. NEW SOUTH WALES UNIVERSITY. SCHOOL OF CIVIL ENGINEERING. UNICIV
                REPORT. SERIES R
N T............ NEW TESTAMENT

PERIODICAL TITLE ABBREVIATIONS

NT. . . . . NEW TIMES
NT. . . . . NIEUWE TAALGIDS
NT. . . . . NORDISK TIDSKRIFT
NT. . . . . NORDISK TIDSKRIFT FOER VETENSKAP, KONST OCH INDUSTRI
NT. . . . . NOVUM TESTAMENTUM
NTBB. . . . . NORDISK TIDSKRIFT FOER BOK- OCH BIBLIOTEKSVAESEN
NTBBV. . . . . NORDISK TIDSKRIFT FOER BOK- OCH BIBLIOTEKSVAESEN
NTE. . . . . NARODNA TVORCIST' TA ETNOHRAFIJA
NTemp. . . . . NOSTRO TEMPO
NTG. . . . . NIEUWE TAALGIDS
NThM. . . . . NEW THEATRE MAGAZINE
NThS. . . . . NIEUWE THEOLOGISCHE STUDIEN
NThT. . . . . NIEUWE THEOLOGISCH TIJDSCHRIFT
NThTs. . . . . NEDERLANDS THEOLOGISCH TIJDSCHRIFT
NTIPI. . . . . NAUCHNYE TRUDY INDUSTRIAL'NO-PEDAGOGICHESKOGO INSTITUTA
NTJ. . . . . NATIONAL TAX JOURNAL
NTK. . . . . NAUCHNYE TRUDY KRASNODARSKOGO PEDAGOGICHESKOGO INSTITUTA
NTLTL. . . . . NEWSLETTER: TEACHING LANGUAGE THROUGH LITERATURE
NTM. . . . . NEW THEATRE MAGAZINE
NTM. . . . . NUESTRO TIEMPO (MADRID)
NTS. . . . . NEW TESTAMENT STUDIES
NTS. . . . . NIEUWE THEOLOGISCHE STUDIEN
NTS. . . . . NORSK TIDSSKRIFT FOER SPROGVIDENSKAP
NTsPsych. . . . . . . NEDERLANDSCH TIJDSCHRIFT VOOR DE PSYCHOLOGIE EN HAAR GRENSGEBIEDEN
NTSt. . . . . NEW TESTAMENT STUDIES
NTStud. . . . . NEW TESTAMENT STUDIES
NTsV. . . . . NORDISK TIDSKRIFT FOER VETENSKAP, KONST OCH INDUSTRI
NTSV. . . . . NORDISK TIDSKRIFT FOER SPROGVIDENSKAP
NTT. . . . . NEDERLANDS THEOLOGISCH TIJDSCHRIFT
NTT. . . . . NIEUW THEOLOGISCH TIJDSCHRIFT
NTTid. . . . . NORSK TEOLOGISK TIDSSKRIFT
NTTij. . . . . NEDERLANDS THEOLOGISCH TIJDSCHRIFT
NTTO. . . . . NORDISK TIDSSKRIFT FOER TEKNISK OKONOMI
NTTS. . . . . NORDISK TIDSSKRIFT FOER TALE OG STEMME
NTU. . . . . NORDISKA TEXTER OCH UNDERSOKNINGAR
NTVK. . . . . NEDERLANDSCH TIJDSCHRIFT VOOR VOLKSKUNDE
NTZ-Commun J. . . . NTZ-COMMUNICATIONS JOURNAL
NTZ Nachr Z, NTZ Commun J. . NTZ NACHRICHTENTECHNISCHER ZEITSCHRIFT, NTZ COMMUNICATIONS JOURNAL
NuA. . . . . NUOVA ANTOLOGIA
NUCL ACID R. . . . . . NUCLEIC ACIDS RESEARCH
Nuclear Eng. . . . . . NUCLEAR ENGINEERING
Nuclear Eng. . . . . . NUCLEAR ENGINEERING INTERNATIONAL
Nucl Energy. . . . . . NUCLEAR ENERGY
Nucl Eng Des. . . . . NUCLEAR ENGINEERING AND DESIGN
NUCL ENG IN. . . . . NUCLEAR ENGINEERING INTERNATIONAL
Nucl Eng Int. . . . . NUCLEAR ENGINEERING INTERNATIONAL
Nucl Fusion. . . . . . NUCLEAR FUSION
NUCL INSTR. . . . . . NUCLEAR INSTRUMENTS & METHODS
NUCL MED. . . . . . . NUCLEAR-MEDIZIN
NUCL PHYS A. . . . . NUCLEAR PHYSICS A
NUCL PHYS B. . . . . NUCLEAR PHYSICS B

Nucl Saf . . . . NUCLEAR SAFETY
NUCL SCI EN . . . . . . NUCLEAR SCIENCE AND ENGINEERING
NUCL TECH . . . . NUCLEAR TECHNOLOGY
NucSciAb . . . . NUCLEAR SCIENCE ABSTRACTS
NUm . . . . NARODNA UMJETNOST
NUMER MATH . . . . . NUMERISCHE MATHEMATIK
Nuo Ant . . . . NUOVA ANTOLOGIA
Nuo Ital . . . . NUOVA ITALIA
Nuo Riv Stor . . . . . . NUOVA RIVISTA STORICA
Nuova Antol . . . . . . NUOVA ANTOLOGIA
NUOV CIM A . . . . . . NUOVO CIMENTO DELLA SOCIETA ITALIANA DI FISICA. A
NUOV CIM B . . . . . . NUOVO CIMENTO DELLA SOCIETA ITALIANA DI FISICA. B
Nurs Outlook . . . . . . NURSING OUTLOOK
NURS RES . . . . NURSING RESEARCH
NUSH . . . . NORTHWESTERN UNIVERSITY STUDIES IN THE HUMANITIES
NutrAb . . . . NUTRITION ABSTRACTS
Nutr R . . . . NUTRITION REVIEWS
NUTR REP IN . . . . . NUTRITION REPORTS INTERNATIONAL
NUTR REV . . . . NUTRITION REVIEWS
Nutr Soc Proc . . . . . NUTRITION SOCIETY PROCEEDINGS (BRITISH)
NV . . . . NASE VEDA
NV . . . . NASTAVNI VJESNIK
NV . . . . NOVA ET VETERA
NVA . . . . NORSK VIDENSKAPS-AKADEMI ARBOK
NVC . . . . NARODOPISNY VESTNIK CESKOSLOVENSKY
NVT . . . . NIEUW VLAAMS TIJDSCHRIFT
NW . . . . NEUE WEG
NW . . . . NEUE WELT
NW . . . . NEWSWEEK
NW . . . . NEW WORLDS (BRITISH)
NWA . . . . NEW WORLDS SCIENCE FICTION
NWB . . . . NEW WORLDS
NWIG . . . . NIEUWE WEST-INDISCHE GIDS
NWK . . . . NEWSWEEK
NwMSCS . . . . NORTHWEST MISSOURI STATE COLLEGE STUDIES
NWOQ . . . . NORTHWEST OHIO QUARTERLY
NWQ . . . . NEW WORLDS QUARTERLY
NWR . . . . NORTHWEST REVIEW
NW U L REV . . . . . . NORTHWESTERN UNIVERSITY LAW REVIEW
NWW . . . . NEW WORLD WRITING
NWZam . . . . NEW WRITING FROM ZAMBIA
NY . . . . NEW YORKER
NY . . . . NEW YORK MAGAZINE
NyA . . . . NYA ARGUS
N Y Acad Sci Ann . . . NEW YORK ACADEMY OF SCIENCES ANNALS
N Y Ag Dept . . . . . . NEW YORK DEPARTMENT OF AGRICULTURE. PUBLICATIONS
N Y C Bd Ed Curric Bul . . NEW YORK CITY. BOARD OF EDUCATION. CURRICULUM BULLETINS
N Y Cert Pub Acct . . NEW YORK CERTIFIED PUBLIC ACCOUNTANT
NY County B Bull . . . NEW YORK COUNTY LAWYERS' ASSOCIATION BAR BULLETIN
NYEP . . . . NEW YORK EVENING POST
NYEPLR . . . . NEW YORK EVENING POST LITERARY REVIEW

N Y Farms & Markets Dept. . NEW YORK STATE. DEPARTMENT OF FARMS AND MARKETS. PUBLICATIONS
N Y Folk Q . . . . NEW YORK FOLKLORE QUARTERLY
NYFQ . . . . NEW YORK FOLKLORE QUARTERLY
NYH . . . . NEW YORK HISTORY
N Y Herald Tribune Bk R . . NEW YORK HERALD TRIBUNE BOOK REVIEW
N Y Herald Tribune W Bk R . . NEW YORK HERALD TRIBUNE WEEKLY BOOK REVIEW
N Y Her Trib Lively Arts . . NEW YORK HERALD TRIBUNE LIVELY ARTS SECTION
N Y Hist . . . . NEW YORK HISTORY
N Y Hist Soc Coll . . . NEW YORK HISTORICAL SOCIETY. COLLECTIONS
N Y Hist Soc Q . . . . . NEW YORK HISTORICAL SOCIETY. QUARTERLY
N Y Hist Soc Quar . . NEW YORK HISTORICAL SOCIETY. QUARTERLY
NYHS . . . . NEW YORK HISTORICAL SOCIETY. QUARTERLY
NYHSQ . . . . NEW YORK HISTORICAL SOCIETY. QUARTERLY
NYHSQB . . . . NEW YORK HISTORICAL SOCIETY. QUARTERLY BULLETIN
NYHT . . . . NEW YORK HERALD TRIBUNE BOOK REVIEW
NYHTB . . . . NEW YORK HERALD TRIBUNE BOOK REVIEW
NYHTBR . . . . NEW YORK HERALD TRIBUNE BOOK REVIEW
NYHTBW . . . . NEW YORK HERALD TRIBUNE BOOK WEEK
NyIK . . . . NYELVTUDOMANYI INTEZET KOZLEMENYEK
NyIroK . . . . NYELV-ES IRODALOMTUDOMANYI KOZLEMENYEK
NyK . . . . NYELVTUDOMANYI KOZLEMENYEK
N Y Law Forum . . . . NEW YORK LAW FORUM
N Y Law R . . . . NEW YORK LAW REVIEW
N Y L F . . . . NEW YORK LAW FORUM
NY Lib Assn Bul . . . . NEW YORK LIBRARY ASSOCIATION. BULLETIN
N Y New Tech Bks . . NEW YORK PUBLIC LIBRARY. NEW TECHNICAL BOOKS
NY PHIL . . . . NEW YORK PHILHARMONIC PROGRAM NOTES
NYPL Bull . . . . NEW YORK PUBLIC LIBRARY. BULLETIN
N Y Prod R . . . . NEW YORK PRODUCE REVIEW AND AMERICAN CREAMERY
N Y Pub Lib Br Lib Bk News . . NEW YORK PUBLIC LIBRARY. BRANCH LIBRARY BOOK NEWS
N Y Q . . . . NEW YORK QUARTERLY
Nyr . . . . MAGYAR NYELVOR
NYRB . . . . NEW YORK REVIEW OF BOOKS
N Y Rev Bks . . . . . . NEW YORK REVIEW OF BOOKS
NYS . . . . NEW YORK SUN
NYSB J . . . . NEW YORK STATE BAR JOURNAL
N Y Soc Exp Study Ed Yrbk . . NEW YORK SOCIETY FOR THE EXPERIMENTAL STUDY OF EDUCATION. YEARBOOK
Nys S . . . . NYSVENSKA STUDIER
N Y State Ag Exp . . . NEW YORK STATE AGRICULTURAL EXPERIMENT STATION. PUBLICATIONS
N Y State Ed . . . . . . NEW YORK STATE EDUCATION
NY ST J MED . . . . . . NEW YORK STATE JOURNAL OF MEDICINE
NYT . . . . NEW YORK TIMES
NYTB . . . . NEW YORK TIMES BOOK REVIEW
NYTBR . . . . NEW YORK TIMES BOOK REVIEW
N Y Times . . . . NEW YORK TIMES BOOK REVIEW
N Y Times M . . . . . . NEW YORK TIMES MAGAZINE SECTION
NYTLS . . . . NEW YORK TIMES LITERARY SUPPLEMENT
NYTM . . . . NEW YORK TIMES MAGAZINE
NYTMag . . . . NEW YORK TIMES MAGAZINE
NYTMS . . . . NEW YORK TIMES MAGAZINE SECTION
NYU Conf Lab . . . . . NEW YORK UNIVERSITY CONFERENCE ON LABOR

NYU Inst Fed Taxation. . NEW YORK UNIVERSITY INSTITUTE ON FEDERAL TAXATION
NYU Intra L Rev. . . . NEW YORK UNIVERSITY INTRAMURAL LAW REVIEW
NYU J Int L & Politics. . NEW YORK UNIVERSITY JOURNAL OF INTERNATIONAL LAW AND POLITICS
NYU L Rev. . . . . NEW YORK UNIVERSITY LAW REVIEW
N Y Univ Res B. . . . NEW YORK UNIVERSITY RESEARCH BULLETIN IN COMMERCIAL EDUCATION
NYU Rev L & Soc Change. . NEW YORK UNIVERSITY REVIEW OF LAW AND SOCIAL CHANGE
NYW. . . . . NEW YORK WORLD
NZ. . . . . NASA ZENA
NZ. . . . . NEUE ZEITSCHRIFT FUER MUSIK
NZ. . . . . NEUPHILOLOGISCHE ZEITSCHRIFT
NZ. . . . . NOVYJ ZURNAL
NZ. . . . . NUMISMATISCHE ZEITSCHRIFT
NZCernU. . . . . NAUKOVI ZAPYSKI CERNIVEC'KOHO DERZAVNOHO UNIVERSYTETA
NZCerPI. . . . . NAUKOVI ZAPYSKI CERKAS'KOHO DERZAVNOHO PEDAHOHICNOHO INSTYTUTU
NZDnepU. . . . . . . NAUCNYE ZAPYSKI DNEPROPETROVSKOGO GOSUDARSTVENNOGO UNIVERSITETA
NZDonPL. . . . . NAUKOVI ZAPYSKI DONEC'KOHO DERZAVNOHO PEDAHOHICNOHO INSTYTUTU
NZDrohPI. . . . . . . NAUKOVI ZAPYSKI DROHOBYC'KOHO DERZAVNOHO PEDAHOHICNOHO INSTYTUTU
N Zealand Lib. . . . . NEW ZEALAND LIBRARIES
NZ Eng. . . . . NEW ZEALAND ENGINEERING
NZEP. . . . . NEW ZEALAND ECONOMIC PAPERS
NZfM. . . . . NEUE ZEITSCHRIFT FUER MUSIK
NZhi. . . . . NAUKA I ZHIZN' (MOSCOW)
NZIR. . . . . NIEMEYERS ZEITSCHRIFT FUER INTERNATIONALES RECHT
NZIzmPI. . . . . NAUKOVI ZAPYSKI IZMAIL'S'KOHO DERZAVNOHO PEDAHOHICNOHO INSTYTUTU
NZ J AGR. . . . . . . NEW ZEALAND JOURNAL OF AGRICULTURE
NZ J AGR RE. . . . . NEW ZEALAND JOURNAL OF AGRICULTURAL RESEARCH
NZ J EDUC. . . . . . . NEW ZEALAND JOURNAL OF EDUCATIONAL STUDIES
NZ J GEOL. . . . . . . NEW ZEALAND JOURNAL OF GEOLOGY AND GEOPHYSICS
NZ J SCI. . . . . NEW ZEALAND JOURNAL OF SCIENCE
NZKamPI. . . . . . . NAUKOVI ZAPYSKI KAM'JANCJA-POLIL'S'KOHO DERZAVNOHO PEDAHOHICNOHO INSTYTUTU
NZKievPIIn. . . . . . NAUCNYE ZAPISKI KIEVSKOGO PEDAGOGICESKOGO INSTYTUTU INOSTRANNYCH JAZYKOV
NZKyiPI. . . . . NAUKOVI JAZYKI KYJIVS'KOHO DERZAVNOHO PEDAHOHICNOHO INSTYTUTU
N Z Lib. . . . . NEW ZEALAND LIBRARIES
N Z List. . . . . NEW ZEALAND LISTENER
NZ L J. . . . . NEW ZEALAND LAW JOURNAL
NZM. . . . . NEUE ZEITSCHRIFT FUER MUSIK
NZ MED J. . . . . . . NEW ZEALAND MEDICAL JOURNAL
NZMiss. . . . . NEUE ZEITSCHRIFT FUER MISSIONSWISSENSCHAFT
NZMUKS. . . . . NAUKOVYJ ZBIRNIK MUSEJU UKRANJINSKOJI KULTURY V SYDNYKU
NZMW. . . . . NEUE ZEITSCHRIFT FUER MISSIONSWISSENSCHAFT
NZSJ. . . . . NEW ZEALAND SLAVONIC JOURNAL
NZ Soc Earthquake Eng Bull. . NEW ZEALAND SOCIETY FOR EARTHQUAKE ENGINEERING. BULLETIN
NZST. . . . . NEUE ZEITSCHRIFT FUER SYSTEMATISCHE THEOLOGIE
NZu. . . . . NOVYJ ZURNAL
NZ U L Rev. . . . . . NEW ZEALAND UNIVERSITIES LAW REVIEW
NZZ. . . . . NEUE ZUERICHER ZEITUNG
NZZytPI. . . . . NAUKOVI ZAPYSKI ZYTOMYRS'KOHO DERZAVNOHO PEDAHOHICNOHO INSTYTUTU

O

O	OCTOBER
O	OKTJABR
O	ORBIS
O	OSTEUROPA
OA	OESTERBOTTEN: ARSBOK
OA	OPUSCULA ARCHAEOLOGICA
OA	OROEMS ANTIQUUS
OAA	OEUVRES AFRO-ASIATIQUES
OAHQ	OHIO ARCHAEOLOGICAL AND HISTORICAL QUARTERLY
OAKR	OESTERREICHISCHES ARCHIV FUER KIRCHENRECHT
O & N	OLD AND NEW
OB	ORD OCH BILD
OBA	OBERBAYERISCHES ARCHIV FUER VATERLANDISCHE GESCHICHTE
Obs	OBSERVER
OBSP	OXFORD BIBLIOGRAPHICAL SOCIETY. PUBLICATIONS
OBSTET GYN	OBSTETRICS AND GYNECOLOGY
Oc	OCCIDENTE
OC	OLD CORNWALL
OC	OPEN COURT
OC	OREINS CHRISTIANUS
Occ	OCCIDENTAL
OCC	OPEN COURT (CHICAGO)
Occid	OCCIDENTE
OCCUP PSYCH	OCCUPATIONAL PSYCHOLOGY
Occup Saf Hlth	OCCUPATIONAL SAFETY AND HEALTH
OceanAb	OCEANIC ABSTRACTS
OCEAN DEV I	OCEAN DEVELOPMENT AND INTERNATIONAL LAW
OCEAN ENG	OCEAN ENGINEERING
Ocean Ind	OCEAN INDUSTRY
Oceanol Int	OCEANOLOGY INTERNATIONAL
OChrP	ORIENTALIA CHRISTIANA PERIODICA
Ocl	OCEANIC LINGUISTICS
OCNA	OUVRAGES SUR LA CULTURE NORD-AFRICAINE
OCP	ORIENTALIA CHRISTIANA PERIODICA
OC P ANTH P	OCCASIONAL PAPERS IN ANTHROPOLOGY. PENNSYLVANIA STATE UNIVERSITY.
OC P DEV A	OCCASIONAL PAPERS. CENTRE FOR DEVELOPING-AREA STUDIES
OC P ECON H	OCCASIONAL PAPERS IN ECONOMIC AND SOCIAL HISTORY
OC P GEOG	OCCASIONAL PAPERS IN GEOGRAPHY
OC P INT AF	OCCASIONAL PAPERS IN INTERNATIONAL AFFAIRS
OC P RUR DE	OCCASIONAL PAPERS. RURAL DEVELOPMENT COMMITTEE
Od	ODRODZENIE
Odyssey	ODYSSEY REVIEW
OE	ONZE EEUW
OE	ORIENS EXTREMUS
OECD INFORM	OECD (ORGANIZATION FOR ECONOMIC COOPERATION AND DEVELOPMENT) INFORMATICS STUDIES
OECD OBSERVER	OECD (ORGANIZATION FOR ECONOMIC COOPERATION AND DEVELOPMENT) OBSERVER
OECO PLANTA	OECOLOGIA PLANTARUM
OED	OXFORD ENGLISH DICTIONARY
OE EZ Oesterr Z Elek	OE EZ. OESTERREICHISCHE ZEITSCHRIFT FUER ELEKTRIZITAETSWIRTSCHAFT

PERIODICAL TITLE ABBREVIATIONS

OEM . . . . OXFORD ENGLISH MONOGRAPHS
OEMA . . . . OBRAS ESCOHIDAS DE MACHADO DE ASSIS
OEMZ . . . . OESTERREICHISCHE MUSIKZEITSCHRIFT
OEN . . . . OLD ENGLISH NEWSLETTER
OEN . . . . OXFORD ENGLISH NOVELS
OEP . . . . OXFORD ECONOMIC PAPERS
OES . . . . OXFORD ENGLISH STUDIES
Oesterr Ing-Z . . . . . OESTERREICHISCHE INGENIEUR-ZEITSCHRIFT
OET . . . . OXFORD ENGLISH TEXTS
OFB . . . . OREGON FOLKLORE BULLETIN
Off Archit Plann . . . OFFICIAL ARCHITECTURE AND PLANNING
OFFICE ADMIN . . . . . OFFICE ADMINISTRATION
Office Exec . . . . OFFICE EXECUTIVE
Office Mgt . . . . OFFICE MANAGEMENT
OG . . . . ORIENTALIA GANDENSIA (GHENT)
OGE . . . . ONS GEESTELIJK ERF
OGK . . . . ONSEI GAKKAI KAIHO (BULLETIN OF THE PHONETIC SOCIETY OF JAPAN)
OGL . . . . OESTERREICH IN GESCHICHTE UND LITERATUR (WIEN)
OGS . . . . OXFORD GERMAN STUDIES
OH . . . . OHIO HISTORY
OH . . . . ONTARIO HISTORY
OH . . . . OUD-HOLLAND
Ohio Ag Dept . . . . . . OHIO DEPARTMENT OF AGRICULTURE. BULLETINS
Ohio Ag Exp . . . . OHIO AGRICULTURAL EXPERIMENT STATION. PUBLICATIONS
OhioanaQ . . . . OHIOANA QUARTERLY
Ohio Assn Sch Libn Bull . . OHIO ASSOCIATION OF SCHOOL LIBRARIANS BULLETIN
Ohio Bus Tchr . . . . . OHIO BUSINESS TEACHER
Ohio Div Geol Surv Bull . . OHIO. DIVISION OF GEOLOGICAL SURVEY. BULLETIN
Ohio Div Geol Surv Inform Circ . . OHIO. DIVISION OF GEOLOGICAL SURVEY. INFORMATION CIRCULAR
Ohio Div Geol Surv Rep Invest . . OHIO. DIVISION OF GEOLOGICAL SURVEY. REPORT OF INVESTIGATIONS
Ohio Div Water Bull . . OHIO. DIVISION OF WATER. BULLETIN
Ohio Div Water Inform Circ . . OHIO. DIVISION OF WATER. INFORMATION CIRCULAR
Ohio Div Water Ohio Water Plan Invent Rep . . OHIO. DIVISION OF WATER. OHIO WATER PLAN INVENTORY. REPORT
Ohio Div Water Rep Ohio Water Table Surv . . OHIO. DIVISION OF WATER. REPORT ON OHIO WATER TABLE SURVEY
Ohio F . . . . OHIO FARMER
OhioH . . . . OHIO HISTORY
Ohio HQ . . . . OHIO HISTORICAL QUARTERLY
Ohio J Rel St . . . . . . OHIO JOURNAL OF RELIGIOUS STUDIES
Ohio J Sci . . . . OHIO JOURNAL OF SCIENCE
Ohio Lib Assn Bul . . . OHIO LIBRARY ASSOCIATION. BULLETIN
OhioR . . . . OHIO REVIEW
Ohio Sch . . . . OHIO SCHOOLS
Ohio S L J . . . . OHIO STATE LAW JOURNAL
Ohio State Archaeol and Hist Quar . . OHIO STATE ARCHAEOLOGICAL AND HISTORICAL QUARTERLY
Ohio State Univ Eng Exp Sta Bull . . OHIO STATE UNIVERSITY. ENGINEERING EXPERIMENT STATION. BULLETIN
OHIO ST LAW . . . . . . OHIO STATE LAW JOURNAL
OHQ . . . . OHIO HISTORICAL QUARTERLY
OHQ . . . . OREGON HISTORICAL QUARTERLY
OhR . . . . OHIO REVIEW
OI . . . . O INSTITUTO
OI . . . . OLD IRISH

Oil & Gas Inst (SW Legal Fdn)..OIL AND GAS LAW AND TAXATION INSTITUTE (SOUTHWESTERN LEGAL FOUNDATION)
Oil & Gas J....... OIL AND GAS JOURNAL
OIL & Gas Tax Q... OIL AND GAS TAX QUARTERLY
Oil Gas J......... OIL AND GAS JOURNAL
OIS............. OXFORD UNIVERSITY. INSTITUTE OF ECONOMICS AND STATISTICS. BULLETIN
OJ............. OUDHEIDKUNDIG JAARBOEK. BULLETIJN UITGEGEVEN DOOR DEN NEDERLANDSCHEN OUDKUNDIGEN BOND
OJb............. OLDENBURGER JAHRBUCH
OJBNOB........ OUDHEIDKUNDIG JAARBOEK. BULLETIJN UITGEGEVEN DOOR DEN NEDERLANDSCHEN OUDKUNDIGEN BOND
OJCH.......... OVERIJSSEL JAARBOEK VOOR CULTUUR EN HISTORIE
OJES........... OSMANIA JOURNAL OF ENGLISH STUDIES
O Judd Farmer..... ORANGE JUDD FARMER
O Judd III F....... ORANGE JUDD ILLINOIS FARMER
OK............. ONZE KONGO
Okla Ag Exp...... OKLAHOMA AGRICULTURAL AND MECHANICAL COLLEGE. AGRICULTURAL EXPERIMENT STATION. PUBLICATIONS
Okla BA J....... OKLAHOMA BAR ASSOCIATION. JOURNAL
Okla Geol Surv Bull..OKLAHOMA GEOLOGICAL SURVEY. BULLETIN
Okla Geol Surv Circ..OKLAHOMA GEOLOGICAL SURVEY. CIRCULAR
OKLA LAW R...... OKLAHOMA LAW REVIEW
Okla Libn......... OKLAHOMA LIBRARIAN
Okla L Rev........ OKLAHOMA LAW REVIEW
OKS............ OSTKIRCHLICHE STUDIEN
Okt............. OKTJABR
OL............. OCEANIC LINGUISTICS
OL............. ORBIS LITTERARUM
Old-Time N E...... OLD-TIME NEW ENGLAND
OLZ............ ORIENTALISTISCHE LITERATURZEITUNG
OM............. OBJETS ET MONDE
OM............. ORIENTE MODERNO
OM............. OSTDEUTSCHE MONATSHEFTE
OM............. OUDHEIDKUNDIGE MEDEDEELINGEN UIT'S RIJKSMUSEUM VAN OUDHEDEN TE LEIDEN
OM............. OXFORD MAGAZINE
OMEGA-INT J..... OMEGA—THE INTERNATIONAL JOURNAL OF MANAGEMENT SCIENCE
OMML........... OUDHEIDKUNDIGE MEDEDEELINGEN UIT'S RIJKSMUSEUM VAN OUDHEDEN TE LEIDEN
OMorD.......... OCERKI MORDOVSKICH DIALEKTOV
OMRL.......... OUDHEIDKUNDIGE MEDEDEELINGEN UIT'S RIJKSMUSEUM VAN OUDHEDEN TE LEIDEN
OMR-ORG MAG.... ORGANIC MAGNETIC RESONANCE
OMSGM........ OTTENDORFER MEMORIAL SERIES OF GERMANIC MONOGRAPHS
On............. ONOMASTICA
Onde Elec........ ONDE ELECTRIQUE
Onderstepoort J Vet Sci..ONDERSTEPOORT JOURNAL OF VETERINARY SCIENCE AND ANIMAL INDUSTRY
Ono............ ONOMASTICA
Onom.......... ONOMASTICA
OnomJug........ ONOMASTICA JUGOSLAVICA
OnsE........... ONS ERFDEEL
Ontario Ag Dept... ONTARIO. DEPARTMENT OF AGRICULTURE. PUBLICATIONS
Ontario Hist Soc Papers..ONTARIO HISTORICAL SOCIETY. PAPERS AND RECORDS
Ont Dep Mines Annu Rep..ONTARIO. DEPARTMENT OF MINES. ANNUAL REPORT

Ont Dep Mines Bull. . ONTARIO. DEPARTMENT OF MINES. MINES INSPECTION BRANCH. BULLETIN
Ont Dep Mines Geol Circ. . ONTARIO. DEPARTMENT OF MINES. GEOLOGICAL CIRCULAR
Ont Dep Mines Geol Rep. . ONTARIO. DEPARTMENT OF MINES. GEOLOGICAL REPORT
Ont Dep Mines Ind Miner Rep. . ONTARIO. DEPARTMENT OF MINES. INDUSTRIAL MINERAL REPORT
Ont Dep Mines Miner Resour Circ. . ONTARIO. DEPARTMENT OF MINES. MINERAL RESOURCES CIRCULAR
ONT HIST. . . . . . . ONTARIO HISTORY
Ont Hydro Res Q. . . ONTARIO HYDRO RESEARCH QUARTERLY
Ont Ind Waste Conf Proc. . ONTARIO INDUSTRIAL WASTE CONFERENCE. PROCEEDINGS
Ont Lib R . . . . ONTARIO LIBRARY REVIEW
OoB . . . . ORD OCH BILD
OostvlZanten . . . . . OOSTVLAAMSCHE ZANTEN
Op . . . . OPYTY
OPA . . . . ONZE PIUS-ALMANAK
OPARI . . . . OCCASIONAL PUBLICATIONS OF THE AFRICAN AND AFRO-AMERICAN RESEARCH INSTITUTE.
       UNIVERSITY OF TEXAS, AUSTIN
Open Hearth Proc AIME. . OPEN HEARTH PROCEEDINGS. METALLURGICAL SOCIETY OF AIME. IRON AND STEEL
       DIVISION
Opera . . . . OPERA AND CONCERT
Opera . . . . OPERA NEWS
OPERA J . . . . OPERA JOURNAL
OPERA N . . . . OPERA NEWS
OPERAT RES . . . . . OPERATIONS RESEARCH
Operat Res Q . . . . . OPERATIONAL RESEARCH QUARTERLY
OPERAT R Q . . . . . . OPERATIONAL RESEARCH QUARTERLY
Oper Res . . . . OPERATIONS RESEARCH
Oper Res Q . . . . OPERATIONAL RESEARCH QUARTERLY
OPHTHALMOLA . . . . OPHTHALMOLOGICA
OPHTHAL RES . . . . . OPHTHALMIC RESEARCH
OPhW . . . . OPUSCULA PHILOLOGA (KATHOLISCH-AKADEMISCHER PHILOLOGENVEREIN IN WIEN)
OPL . . . . OSSERVATORE POLITICO LETTERARIO
OPLLL . . . . OCCASIONAL PAPERS IN LANGUAGE, LITERATURE, AND LINGUISTICS
Op News . . . . OPERA NEWS
Op Res . . . . OPERATIONS RESEARCH
Op Res Q . . . . OPERATIONAL RESEARCH QUARTERLY
Ops Research . . . . . OPERATIONS RESEARCH
OPT COMMUN . . . . . OPTICS COMMUNICATIONS
OPT ENG . . . . OPTICAL ENGINEERING
Opt Laser Technol . . OPTICS AND LASER TECHNOLOGY
Opt-Mekh Prom . . . . OPTICO-MEKHANICHESKAYA PROMYSHLENNOST
Opto-Electron . . . . . OPTO-ELECTRONICS
OPT QUANT E . . . . . OPTICAL AND QUANTUM ELECTRONICS
Opt Soc Am J . . . . . . OPTICAL SOCIETY OF AMERICA. JOURNAL
Opt Spectra . . . . OPTICAL SPECTRA
OPT SPEKTRO . . . . . OPTIKA I SPECKTROSKOPIYA
Opt Technol . . . . OPTICS TECHNOLOGY
OR . . . . ODRODZENIE I REFORMACJA W POLSCE
OR . . . . OPERATIONS RESEARCH
Or . . . . ORIENTALIA. COMMENTARI PERIODICI PONTIFICII INSTITUTI BIBLICI
OR . . . . ORIENT REVIEW
Or . . . . ORIZONT
Or . . . . ORPHEUS. REVISTA PENTRU CULTURA CLASICA

OR . . . . OXFORD REVIEW
ORAL SURG O . . . . . ORAL SURGERY, ORAL MEDICINE AND ORAL PATHOLOGY
OrChr . . . . ORIENS CHRISTIANUS
Ore Ag Exp . . . . OREGON AGRICULTURAL COLLEGE. AGRICULTURAL EXPERIMENT STATION. PUBLICATIONS
OrEcon . . . . ORIENTAL ECONOMIST
Oreg Dep Geol Miner Ind Bull . . OREGON. DEPARTMENT OF GEOLOGY AND MINERAL INDUSTRIES. BULLETIN
Oregon Hist Q . . . . . OREGON HISTORICAL QUARTERLY
Oreg State Univ Eng Exp Sta Circ . . OREGON STATE UNIVERSITY. CORVALLIS. ENGINEERING EXPERIMENT STATION.
CIRCULAR
Ore Hist Q . . . . OREGON HISTORICAL QUARTERLY
Ore Hist Soc Quar . . OREGON HISTORICAL SOCIETY. QUARTERLY
OreHQ . . . . OREGON HISTORICAL QUARTERLY
Ore L Rev . . . . OREGON LAW REVIEW
Organ Am States Ann . . ORGANIZATION OF AMERICAN STATES. ANNALS
ORGAN BEH H . . . . . ORGANIZATIONAL BEHAVIOR AND HUMAN PERFORMANCE
ORGAN DYNAM . . . . ORGANIZATIONAL DYNAMICS
Organic Gard . . . . . . ORGANIC GARDENING
Organic Gard & F . . . ORGANIC GARDENING AND FARMING
Org Inst . . . . ORGAN INSTITUTE QUARTERLY
Org Inst Q . . . . ORGAN INSTITUTE QUARTERLY
ORG MASS SP . . . . . ORGANIC MASS SPECTROMETRY
OrHQ . . . . OREGON HISTORICAL QUARTERLY
Orient Art . . . . ORIENTAL ART
ORIENTAT SC . . . . . . ORIENTATION SCOLAIRE ET PROFESSIONNELLE
Orient Cult . . . . ORIENTAMENTI CULTURALI
ORIGIN LIFE . . . . ORIGINS OF LIFE
Orkester JL . . . . ORKESTER JOURNALEN
ORK J . . . . ORKESTER JOURNALEN
ORL-J OTO R . . . . . . ORL-JOURNAL FOR OTO-RHINO-LARYNGOLOGY AND ITS BORDERLANDS
ORom . . . . OSSERVATORE ROMANO
ORP . . . . ODRODZENIE I REFORMACJA W POLSCE
OrP . . . . ORIENTAMENTI PEDAGOGICI (TORINO)
Orph . . . . ORPHEUS. REVISTA PENTRU CULTURA CLASICA
ORTHOMOL PS . . . . . ORTHOMOLECULAR PSYCHIATRY
ORTHOPED CL . . . . . ORTHOPEDIC CLINICS NORTH AMERICA
ORTHOT PROS . . . . . ORTHOTICS AND PROSTHETICS
OS . . . . ORIENTALIA SUECANA (UPPSALA)
Os . . . . OSIRIS
Os . . . . OSVIT
OSAHQ . . . . OHIO STATE ARCHAEOLOGICAL AND HISTORICAL QUARTERLY
OSE . . . . OSLO STUDIES IN ENGLISH
OsEP . . . . OSAKA ECONOMIC PAPERS
OSF . . . . ORBIT SCIENCE FICTION
OSFS . . . . ORIGINAL SCIENCE FICTION STORIES
Osgoode Hall L J . . . OSGOODE HALL LAW JOURNAL
OSLP . . . . OXFORD SLAVONIC PAPERS
OSP . . . . OXFORD SLAVONIC PAPERS
Osserv . . . . OSSERVATORE
OSTER Z POL . . . . . . OESTERREICHISCHE ZEITSCHRIFT FUER POLITKWISENNSCHAFT
Ostjydsk Hjemstavn . . OSTJYDSK HJEMSTAVNFORENINGS AARSSKRIFT
OstM . . . . OSTDEUTSCHE MONATSHEFTE

OSTO . . . . OESTERREICHISCHE OSTHEFTE
OsUA . . . . ORTNAMNSSALLSKAPETS I UPPSALA AARSSKRIFT
OSUCLL . . . . OHIO STATE UNIVERSITY CONTRIBUTIONS IN LANGUAGE AND LITERATURE
OSUTCB . . . . OHIO STATE UNIVERSITY THEATRE COLLECTION BULLETIN
OT . . . . ONZE TAALTUIN
OT . . . . ONZE TIJD
Otago L Rev . . . . . . OTAGO LAW REVIEW
OTAM . . . . OZBEK TILI VA ADABIET MASALALARI
OTLV . . . . ONZA, TIGRA Y LEON. REVISTA PARA LA INFANCIA VENEZOLANA
OTOLAR CLIN . . . . . OTOLARYNGOLOGIC CLINICS OF NORTH AMERICA
OTS . . . . OUDTESTAMENTISCHE STUDIEN
Ottawa L Rev . . . . . OTTAWA LAW REVIEW
Otto-Graf-Inst Stutt Tech Hochsch Schriftenr . . OTTO-GRAF-INSTUTUT. STUTTGART. TECHNISCHE HOCHSCHULE, SCHRIFTENREIHE
OTW . . . . OUT OF THIS WORLD
OTWA . . . . OUT OF THIS WORLD ADVENTURES
OUA . . . . ORTNAMNSSAELLSKAPETS I UPPSALA AARSSKRIFT
OUP . . . . OXFORD UNIVERSITY PRESS
OUR . . . . OHIO UNIVERSITY REVIEW
Our World W . . . . . . OUR WORLD WEEKLY
OUSE . . . . ODENSE UNIVERSITY STUDIES IN ENGLISH
OUT . . . . OUTLANDS
Out . . . . OUTSIDER
Outl . . . . OUTLOOK
Overland . . . . OVERLAND MONTHLY
Overland ns . . . . . . OVERLAND MONTHLY. NEW SERIES
Overseas Geol Miner Resour . . OVERSEAS GEOLOGY AND MINERAL RESOURCES (GREAT BRITAIN)
OW . . . . ORIENT/WEST
OW . . . . OSTATNIE WIADOMOSCI
OW . . . . OTHER WORLDS
Owl Minerva . . . . . . THE OWL OF MINERVA
OxAbs . . . . OXFORD ABSTRACTS
OX B ECON S . . . . . . OXFORD BULLETIN OF ECONOMICS AND STATISTICS
OX ECON PAP . . . . . OXFORD ECONOMIC PAPERS
Oxf Mag . . . . OXFORD MAGAZINE
Oxford Econ Pa . . . . OXFORD ECONOMIC PAPERS
Oxid Combust Rev . . OXIDATION AND COMBUSTION REVIEWS
Oxid Met . . . . OXIDATION OF METALS
Ox Prize Ess . . . . . . OXFORD PRIZE ESSAYS
OYGK . . . . OKAYAMA DAIGAKU HOBUNGAKUBU GAKUJUTSU KIYO
OZDP . . . . OESTERREICHISCHE ZEITSCHRIFT FUER KUNST UND DENKMALPFLEGE
OZE Oesterr Z Elektr . . OZE, OESTERREICHISCHE ZEITSCHRIFT FUER ELEKTRIZITAETSWIRTSCHAFT
OZKDP . . . . OESTERREICHISCHE ZEITSCHRIFT FUER KUNST UND DENKMALPFLEGE
OZV . . . . OESTERREICHISCHE ZEITSCHRIFT FUER VOLKSKUNDE

P

P.............. PALACIO
P.............. PALAESTRA
P.............. PAZMAVEB
P.............. PERSPECTIVES
P.............. PHILOLOGUS
P.............. PHILOSOPHY
P.............. POETRY
P.............. POLONYSTYKA
P.............. PONTE
PA.............. ONZE PIUS-ALMANAK
Pa.............. PAIDEIA
PA.............. PARLIAMENTARY AFFAIRS
Pa.............. PARU
PA.............. POLONISTYKA
PA.............. PRESENCE AFRICAINE
PA.............. PRO ARTE
PAAAS.......... PROCEEDINGS AMERICAN ACADEMY OF ARTS AND SCIENCES
Pa Ag Exp........ PENNSYLVANIA STATE COLLEGE. SCHOOL OF AGRICULTURE. AGRICULTURAL EXPERIMENT STATION. PUBLICATIONS
PAAJR.......... PROCEEDINGS OF THE AMERICAN ACADEMY FOR JEWISH RESEARCH
PAAS.......... PROCEEDINGS OF THE AMERICAN ANTIQUARIAN SOCIETY
Pa Bsns Survey.... PENNSYLVANIA BUSINESS SURVEY
PAC A.......... PACIFIC AFFAIRS
PACA.......... PROCEEDINGS OF THE AFRICAN CLASSICAL ASSOCIATION
Pac Affairs....... PACIFIC AFFAIRS
Pac Builder Eng.... PACIFIC BUILDER & ENGINEER
PAC COMMUN..... PACIFIC COMMUNITY
PacH.......... PACIFIC HISTORIAN
PAC HIST R....... PACIFIC HISTORICAL REVIEW
PacHR.......... PACIFIC HISTORICAL REVIEW
Pacif Aff........ PACIFIC AFFAIRS
PACIFIC L J....... PACIFIC LAW JOURNAL
PAC INSECTS...... PACIFIC INSECTS
PAC J MATH...... PACIFIC JOURNAL OF MATHEMATICS
Packa Rev........ PACKAGING REVIEW
P AC NAT S....... PROCEEDINGS OF THE ACADEMY OF NATURAL SCIENCES OF PHILADELPHIA
Pac Northwesterner PACIFIC NORTHWESTERNER
PacNQ.......... PACIFIC NORTHWEST QUARTERLY
Pac NWQ........ PACIFIC NORTHWEST QUARTERLY
P AC POLI S....... PROCEEDINGS OF THE ACADEMY OF POLITICAL SCIENCE
PAC SCI......... PACIFIC SCIENCE
PAC SOC REV...... PACIFIC SOCIOLOGICAL REVIEW
PacSp.......... PACIFIC SPECTATOR
PADAGOG RUN.... PAEDAGOGISCHE RUNDSCHAU
PADIATR PAD..... PADIATRIE UND PADOLOGIE
PADS.......... PROCEEDINGS OF THE AMERICAN DIALECT SOCIETY
Paedagogica Hist... PAEDAGOGICA HISTORICA
Pa Elec Ass Eng Sect Transm Distrib..PENNSYLVANIA ELECTRIC ASSOCIATION. ENGINEERING SECTION. TRANSMISSION AND DISTRIBUTION COMMITTEE. MINUTES
Pa F............ PENNSYLVANIA FOLKLIFE
PAFS........... PUBLICATIONS OF THE AMERICAN FOLKLORE SOCIETY

PaGa . . . . PRINTING AND GRAPHIC ARTS
PAGS . . . . PROCEEDINGS OF THE AUSTRALIAN GOETHE SOCIETY
Pa Ind . . . . PAPER INDUSTRY
Paint Decor . . . . PAINTING AND DECORATING
PAIS . . . . PUBLIC AFFAIRS INFORMATION SERVICE
PAJ . . . . PAN-AFRICAN JOURNAL
PAJHS . . . . PUBLICATION OF THE AMERICAN JEWISH HISTORICAL SOCIETY
Pakistan Eng . . . . . . PAKISTAN ENGINEER
Pakistan Lib Bull . . . PAKISTAN LIBRARY BULLETIN
Pakistan Lib R . . . . . PAKISTAN LIBRARY REVIEW
Pakistan Phil J . . . . PAKISTAN PHILOSOPHICAL JOURNAL
PakQ . . . . PAKISTAN QUARTERLY
PakR . . . . PAKISTAN REVIEW
PAL . . . . PRO ALESIA
PALAEOGEO P . . . . . PALAEOGEOGRAPHY, PALAEOCLIMATOLOGY, PALAEOECOLOGY
Palaeont . . . . PALAEONTOGRAPHICA
Pa Lang & Lit . . . . . . PAPERS ON LANGUAGE AND LITERATURE
PalEF . . . . PALESTINE EXPLORATION FUND
PalEQ . . . . PALESTINE EXPLORATION QUARTERLY
PALI . . . . PACIFIC AND ASIAN LINGUISTIC INSTITUTE
Pa Lib Assn Bull . . . . PENNSYLVANIA LIBRARY ASSOCIATION. BULLETIN
PalJ . . . . PALAESTINA-JAHRBUCH
Pall Mall M . . . . PALL MALL MAGAZINE
P AM ASS CA . . . . . . PROCEEDINGS OF THE AMERICAN ASSOCIATION OF CANCER RESEARCH
PamL . . . . PAMIETNIK LITERACKI
P AM MATH S . . . . . PROCEEDINGS OF THE AMERICAN MATHEMATICAL SOCIETY
Pamph . . . . PAMPHLETEER
P AM PHIL S . . . . . . PROCEEDINGS OF THE AMERICAN PHILOSOPHICAL SOCIETY
P AM S INFO . . . . . . PROCEEDINGS OF THE AMERICAN SOCIETY FOR INFORMATION SCIENCE
PamSL . . . . PAMIETNIK SLOWIANSKI CZASOPISMO NAUKOWE POSIECONE SLOWIANOZNAWSTWU
Pan . . . . PANORAMA
PAN . . . . POLSKA AKADEMIA NAUK
PanA . . . . PAN-AFRICANIST
Pan Am M . . . . PAN AMERICAN MAGAZINE
Pan Am Union Bul . . PAN AMERICAN UNION. BULLETIN
PanAR . . . . PAN AMERICAN REVIEW
P&I . . . . PAROLE E LE IDEE
P&IF . . . . PARIS ET ILE-DE-FRANCE. MEMOIRES
P&L . . . . POLITICS AND LETTERS
P&PR . . . . PSYCHOANALYSIS AND THE PSYCHOANALYTIC REVIEW
P&R . . . . PARKS AND RECREATION
P&R . . . . PHILOSOPHY AND RHETORIC
PAN PAC ENT . . . . . PAN-PACIFIC ENTOMOLOGIST
PAN PIPES . . . . PAN PIPES OF SIGMA ALPHA IOTA
PANPKHL . . . . POLSKA AKADEMIA NAUK-ODDZIAL W KRAKOWIE, PRACE KOMISJI HISTORYCZNOLITERACKIEJ
PANPKS . . . . POLSKA AKADEMIA NAUK-ODDZIAL W KRAKOWIE, PRACE KOMISJI SLOWIANOZNAWSTWA
P AN REL M . . . . PROCEEDINGS. ANNUAL RELIABILITY AND MAINTAINABILITY SYMPOSIUM
PAPC . . . . PHILOLOGICAL ASSOCIATION OF THE PACIFIC COAST
Paper Mkr . . . . PAPER MAKER
Papers Biblio Soc Am . . PAPERS OF THE BIBLIOGRAPHICAL SOCIETY OF AMERICA
Papers in Ed (Anstey Coll) . . PAPERS IN EDUCATION (ANSTEY COLLEGE OF PHYSICAL EDUCATION)

Paper Technol . . . . . PAPER TECHNOLOGY
PAPhilosS . . . . PROCEEDINGS OF THE AMERICAN PHILOSOPHICAL SOCIETY
PAPhS . . . . PROCEEDINGS OF THE AMERICAN PHILOSOPHICAL SOCIETY
PAP IS AFR . . . . . . PAPERS IN INTERNATIONAL STUDIES. AFRICA SERIES. OHIO UNIVERSITY
PAP IS SE A . . . . . . PAPERS IN INTERNATIONAL STUDIES. SOUTHEAST ASIA SERIES. OHIO UNIVERSITY
PAP MET GEO . . . . . PAPERS IN METEOROLOGY AND GEOPHYSICS
PAP PUU . . . . PAPERI JA PUU-PAPPER OCH TRA
PAPS . . . . PROCEEDINGS OF THE AMERICAN PHILOSOPHICAL SOCIETY
Pap Ship Res Inst (Tokyo) . . PAPERS OF SHIP RESEARCH INSTITUTE (TOKYO)
PAP TECHNOL . . . . . PAPER TECHNOLOGY AND INDUSTRY
Pap Trade J . . . . PAPER TRADE JOURNAL
Par . . . . PARAGONE
PAR . . . . PARENT'S MAGAZINE AND BETTER FAMILY LIVING
PAR . . . . PERFORMING ARTS REVIEW
PAR . . . . PUBLIC ADMINISTRATION REVIEW
PAR ARTER . . . . . . PAROI ARTERIELLE-ARTERIAL WALL
PARASITOL . . . . . . PARASITOLOGY
ParisR . . . . PARIS REVIEW
Parks & Rec . . . . . . PARKS & RECREATION
Parl Aff . . . . PARLIAMENTARY AFFAIRS
PARLIM AFF . . . . . . PARLIAMENTARY AFFAIRS
Par M . . . . PARENTS' MAGAZINE
Par Pass . . . . PAROLA DEL PASSATO
ParR . . . . PARIS REVIEW
ParR . . . . PARTISAN REVIEW
Part Accel . . . . PARTICLE ACCELERATORS
Part R . . . . PARTISAN REVIEW
PaS . . . . PAMIETNIK SLOWIANSKI
Pa Sch J . . . . PENNSYLVANIA SCHOOL JOURNAL
Past & Present . . . . PAST AND PRESENT
Pa State Univ Coll Eng Eng Res Bull . . PENNSYLVANIA STATE UNIVERSITY. COLLEGE OF ENGINEERING. ENGINEERING
RESEARCH BULLETIN
PAST PRESEN . . . . . . PAST AND PRESENT
Past Psych . . . . PASTORAL PSYCHOLOGY
Patent Off Soc Jour . . PATENT OFFICE SOCIETY. JOURNAL
PATH BIOL . . . . PATHOLOGIE BIOLOGIE
PATH EUROP . . . . . . PATHOLOGIA EUROPAEA
PATH MICROB . . . . . PATHOLOGIA ET MICROBIOLOGIA
PATOL-MEX . . . . . . PATOLOGIA-MEXICO CITY
Pa Topogr Geol Surv Geol Atlas Pa . . PENNSYLVANIA. BUREAU OF TOPOGRAPHIC AND GEOLOGIC SURVEY.
GEOLOGIC ATLAS OF PENNSYLVANIA
Pa Topogr Geol Surv Bull C . . PENNSYLVANIA. BUREAU OF TOPOGRAPHIC AND GEOLOGIC SURVEY. BULLETIN C
(COUNTY REPORT)
Pa Topogr Geol Surv Bull G . . PENNSYLVANIA. BUREAU OF TOPOGRAPHIC AND GEOLOGIC SURVEY. BULLETIN G
(GENERAL GEOLOGY REPORT)
Pa Topogr Geol Surv Inform Circ . . PENNSYLVANIA. BUREAU OF TOPOGRAPHIC AND GEOLOGIC SURVEY.
INFORMATION CIRCULAR
Pa Topogr Geol Surv Progr Rep . . PENNSYLVANIA. BUREAU OF TOPOGRAPHIC AND GEOLOGIC SURVEY. PROGRESS
REPORT
Pa Topogr Geol Surv Spec Bull . . PENNSYLVANIA. BUREAU OF TOPOGRAPHIC AND GEOLOGIC SURVEY. SPECIAL
BULLETIN

Pa Tr J . . . . PAPER TRADE JOURNAL
PATT RECOG . . . . . . PATTERN RECOGNITION
PAU . . . . POLSKA AKADEMIA UMIEJETNOSCI
PAU-AN . . . . POLSKA AKADEMIA UMIEJETNOSCI. ARCHIVUM NEOPHILOLOGICUM
Pa Univ Mus Bul . . . PENNSYLVANIA UNIVERSITY. UNIVERSITY MUSEUM. BULLETIN
Pa Univ Schoolmens Week Proc . . PENNSYLVANIA UNIVERSITY. SCHOOLMEN'S WEEK. PROCEEDINGS
PAusL . . . . PAPERS IN AUSTRALIAN LINGUISTICS
P AUST BIOC . . . . . PROCEEDINGS OF THE AUSTRALIAN BIOCHEMICAL SOCIETY
PAV J BIOL . . . . PAVLOVIAN JOURNAL OF BIOLOGICAL SCIENCE
PB . . . . PAEDAGOGISCHE BLAETTER
PB . . . . PASTOR BONUS
PB . . . . PLAYBOY
PB . . . . POETRY BAG
PB . . . . PRZEGLAD BIBLIOTECZNY
PBA . . . . PROCEEDINGS OF THE BRITISH ACADEMY
PBEA NEWSLETTER . . PENNSYLVANIA BUSINESS EDUCATION ASSOCIATION. NEWSLETTER
PBK . . . . PAMIETNIK BIBLIOTEKI KORNICKIEJ
PBM . . . . POETRY BOOK MAGAZINE
PBML . . . . PRAGUE BULLETIN OF MATHEMATICAL LINGUISTICS
PBO . . . . POLSKI BIULETYN ORIENTALISTYCZNY
PBSA . . . . PAPERS OF THE BIBLIOGRAPHICAL SOCIETY OF AMERICA
PBSA . . . . PUBLICATIONS OF THE BIBLIOGRAPHICAL SOCIETY OF AMERICA
PBSC . . . . PAPERS OF THE BIBLIOGRAPHICAL SOCIETY OF CANADA
PBSR . . . . PAPERS OF THE BRITISH SCHOOL AT ROME
PBSUV . . . . PAPERS OF THE BIBLIOGRAPHICAL SOCIETY. UNIVERSITY OF VIRGINIA
PC . . . . PARAULA CRISTIANA
PC . . . . PENSIERO CRITICO
PCA . . . . PROCEEDINGS OF THE CLASSICAL ASSOCIATION
PCAAS . . . . PROCEEDINGS OF THE CONNECTICUT ACADEMY OF ARTS AND SCIENCES
PCAS . . . . PROCEEDINGS OF THE CAMBRIDGE ANTIQUARIAN SOCIETY
PCAS . . . . PROCEEDINGS OF THE CLASSICAL ASSOCIATION OF SCOTLAND
PCB . . . . PACIFIC COAST PHILOLOGY
PCB . . . . POETRY CHAPBOOK
PCNDP . . . . PUBLICATION DU CENTRE NATIONAL DE DOCUMENTATION PEDAGOGIQUE
PCO . . . . PROCEEDINGS OF THE CONGRESS OF ORIENTALISTS
PCP . . . . PACIFIC COAST PHILOLOGY
PCPhS . . . . PROCEEDINGS OF THE CAMBRIDGE PHILOLOGICAL SOCIETY
PCTEB . . . . PENNSYLVANIA COUNCIL OF TEACHERS OF ENGLISH. BULLETIN
PCTE Bulletin . . . . . . PENNSYLVANIA COUNCIL OF TEACHERS OF ENGLISH. BULLETIN
PD . . . . PAPIER UND DRUCK
PD . . . . PENNSYLVANIA DUTCHMAN
PD . . . . POETIC DRAMA
PdD . . . . PROBLEME DER DICHTUNG
PDial . . . . POETRY DIAL
PdL . . . . PROVINCIA DI LUCCA
PDM . . . . POETRY AND DRAMA MAGAZINE
PdP . . . . PAROLA DEL POPOLO
PDR . . . . PAKISTAN DEVELOPMENT REVIEW
PDZI . . . . PRZEGLAD ZACHODNI
PE . . . . POESIA ESPANOLA
PE . . . . PROBLEMS OF ECONOMICS

PEABODY J E...... PEABODY JOURNAL OF EDUCATION
Peabody J Ed...... PEABODY JOURNAL OF EDUCATION
PeaceResAb...... PEACE RESEARCH ABSTRACTS
PEALQ.......... PUBLISHING, ENTERTAINING, ADVERTISING & ALLIED FIELDS LAW QUARTERLY
PE&W.......... PHILOSOPHY EAST AND WEST
PeC........... POESIA E CRITICA
Ped............ PEDAGOGIA
PEDAG HIST...... PAEDAGOGICA HISTORICA
Pedagog Sem...... PEDOGOGICAL SEMINARY
Pedag Tidskr...... PEDAGOGISK TIDSKRIFT
PED CLIN NA...... PEDIATRIC CLINICS OF NORTH AMERICA
PEDIAT RES....... PEDIATRIC RESEARCH
P EDIN MATH..... PROCEEDINGS OF THE EDINBURGH MATHEMATICAL SOCIETY
PEDOBIOLOG...... PEDOBIOLOGIA
Peg............ PEGASO
PEGS........... PUBLICATIONS OF THE ENGLISH GOETHE SOCIETY
Pel............ PAROLE E LE IDEE
PEJ............ PAKISTAN ECONOMIC JOURNAL
PEL............ PENGUIN ENGLISH LIBRARY
PELL........... PAPERS ON ENGLISH LANGUAGE AND LITERATURE
PELL........... PUBLICATIONS IN ENGLISH LANGUAGE AND LITERATURE
PeM........... PAROLE E METODI
Pen............ PENSAMIENTO (MADRID)
PENN BA Q....... PENNSYLVANIA BAR ASSOCIATION QUARTERLY
Penn German Soc Proc.. PENNSYLVANIA GERMAN SOCIETY. PROCEEDINGS
Penn Hist........ PENNSYLVANIA HISTORY
Penn Lib Assn Bull.. PENNSYLVANIA LIBRARY ASSOCIATION. BULLETIN
Penn Mag Hist Biog.. PENNSYLVANIA MAGAZINE OF HISTORY AND BIOGRAPHY
Penn Mo......... PENN MONTHLY
PennsF.......... PENNSYLVANIA FOLKLIFE
Penn State F...... PENN STATE FARMER
Penn Stock & F.... PENNSYLVANIA STOCKMAN AND FARMER
Pennsyl M........ PENNSYLVANIA MAGAZINE OF HISTORY AND BIOGRAPHY
Penn Univ Mus Bul.. PENNSYLVANIA UNIVERSITY. UNIVERSITY MUSEUM BULLETIN
Penny M......... PENNY MAGAZINE
P ENT S ONT...... PROCEEDINGS OF THE ENTOMOLOGICAL SOCIETY OF ONTARIO
P ENT S WAS...... PROCEEDINGS OF THE ENTOMOLOGICAL SOCIETY OF WASHINGTON
Peop J.......... PEOPLE'S JOURNAL
PEQ............ PALESTINE EXPLORATION QUARTERLY
Per............ PERSPECTIVE
PER............ PERSPECTIVES
PER BIOL......... PERIODICUM BIOLOGORUM
PERC MOT SK..... PERCEPTUAL AND MOTOR SKILLS
PERC PSYCH...... PERCEPTION AND PSYCHOPHYSICS
PERF ARTS....... PERFORMING ARTS IN CANADA
PERF ARTS CAN.... PERFORMING ARTS IN CANADA
PERF ARTS R...... PERFORMING ARTS REVIEW
PERF RIGHT...... PERFORMING RIGHT
Perfum Essent Oil Rec.. PERFUMERY AND ESSENTIAL OIL RECORD
Period Polytech Chem Eng.. PERIODICA POLYTECHNICA. CHEMICAL ENGINEERING
Period Polytech Electr Eng.. PERIODICA POLYTECHNICA. ELECTRICAL ENGINEERING

Period Polytech Eng. . PERIODICA POLYTECHNICA. ENGINEERING
Period Polytech Mech Eng. . PERIODICA POLYTECHNICA. MECHANICAL ENGINEERING
Perkins J. . . . . PERKINS SCHOOL OF THEOLOGY JOURNAL
PerManAb. . . . . PERSONAL MANAGEMENT ABSTRACTS
Perm Way. . . . . PERMANENT WAY
PER POLY CE. . . . . . PERIODICA POLYTECHNICA. CHEMICAL ENGINEERING
PER POLY EE. . . . . . PERIODICA POLYTECHNICA. ELECTRICAL ENGINEERING
PER POLY ME. . . . . . PERIODICA POLYTECHNICA. MECHANICAL ENGINEERING
Pers. . . . . PERSONALIST
Pers. . . . . PERSPEKTIV
PERS GUID J. . . . . . PERSONNEL AND GUIDANCE JOURNAL
PERS J. . . . . PERSONNEL JOURNAL
PERS NEW MUS. . . . PERSPECTIVES OF NEW MUSIC
Person. . . . . PERSONALIST
Personnel Psych. . . PERSONNEL PSYCHOLOGY
PERSP BIOL. . . . . . . PERSPECTIVES IN BIOLOGY AND MEDICINE
Perspec. . . . . PERSPECTIVE
Perspec Ed. . . . . . . PERSPECTIVES ON EDUCATION
Perspective K. . . . . PERSPECTIVE (KARACHI)
PERS PSYCH. . . . . . PERSONNEL PSYCHOLOGY
Peru Dir Gen Mineria Bol. . PERU. MINISTERIO DE FOMENTO Y OBRAS PUBLICAS. DIRECCION GENERAL DE MINERIA.
BOLETIN
PEST BIOCH. . . . . . . PESTICIDE BIOCHEMISTRY AND PHYSIOLOGY
PEST CONTRO. . . . . PEST CONTROL
PEST MON J. . . . . . PESTICIDES MONITORING JOURNAL
PEST SCI. . . . . PESTICIDE SCIENCE
Pet Age. . . . . PETROLEUM AGE
Pet Eng. . . . . PETROLEUM ENGINEER
PETERM GEOG. . . . . PETERMANNS GEOGRAPHISCHE MITTEILUNGEN
Pet Process. . . . . . . PETROLEUM PROCESSING
Pet Refiner. . . . . . . PETROLEUM REFINER
Pet Rev. . . . . PETROLEUM REVIEW
Petro/Chem Eng. . . PETRO/CHEM ENGINEER
Petrol Eng. . . . . . . PETROLEUM ENGINEER
Petrol Rev. . . . . . . PETROLEUM REVIEW
Pet Times. . . . . . . PETROLEUM TIMES
Pet W. . . . . PETROLEUM WEEK
PEW. . . . . PHILOSOPHY EAST AND WEST
PF. . . . . PENNSYLVANIA FOLKLIFE
PF. . . . . PENSEE FRANCAISE
PF. . . . . PHILOSOPHY FORUM
PF. . . . . POESIE FRANCAISE
PF. . . . . POLISH FOLKLORE
PF. . . . . PRACE FILOLOGICZNE
PF. . . . . PUBLIC FINANCE
PfH. . . . . PFALZISCHE HEIMATBLAETTER
PFil. . . . . PRACE FILOLOGICZNE
PFil. . . . . PRZEGLAD FILOZOFICZNY
PFL. . . . . PENNSYLVANIA FOLK LIFE
PFLFT. . . . . PUBBLICAZIONI DELLA FACOLTA DI LETTERE E FILOSOFIA DELL'UNIVERSITA DI TORINO
PFLUG ARCH. . . . . . PFLUGERS ARCHIV. EUROPEAN JOURNAL OF PHYSIOLOGY

PFLUS . . . . PUBLICATIONS DE LA FACULTE DES LETTRES DE L'UNIVERSITE DE STRASBOURG
PFr . . . . PRESENCE FRANCOPHONE
PGA . . . . PRINTING AND GRAPHIC ARTS
PGFS . . . . PENNSYLVANIA GERMAN FOLKLORE SOCIETY
PGJ . . . . PERSONNEL AND GUIDANCE JOURNAL
PGM . . . . PETERMANNS GEOGRAPHISCHE MITTEILUNGEN
PGS . . . . PENNSYLVANIA GERMAN SOCIETY. PROCEEDINGS AND ADDRESSES
PGSP . . . . PENNSYLVANIA GERMAN SOCIETY. PROCEEDINGS AND ADDRESSES
PH . . . . PENNSYLVANIA HISTORY
Ph . . . . PHILOLOGUS
Ph . . . . PHILOSOPHISCHES JAHRBUCH
Ph . . . . PHILOSOPHY
Ph . . . . PHOENIX
PH . . . . PROVENCE HISTORIQUE
PH . . . . PRZEGLAD HISTORYCANY
Pha . . . . PHILOLOGICA
PhAb . . . . PHOTOGRAPHIC ABSTRACTS
PHARMACOL . . . . . . PHARMACOLOGY
PHARMACOLOG . . . PHARMACOLOGIST
PHARMACOL R . . . . PHARMACOLOGICAL RESEARCH COMMUNICATIONS
PHARM ACT H . . . . . PHARMACEUTICA ACTA HELVETIAE
PHARMAKOPSY . . . . PHARMAKOPSYCHIATRIE NEURO-PSYCHO-PHARMAKOLOGIE
PHARM BIO B . . . . . PHARMACOLOGY BIOCHEMISTRY AND BEHAVIOR
PHARM PRAX . . . . . PHARMAZEUTISCHE PRAXIS
PHARM REV . . . . . . PHARMACOLOGICAL REVIEWS
P HAWAII EN . . . . . . PROCEEDING OF THE HAWAIIAN ENTOMOLOGICAL SOCIETY
PhB . . . . PHILOBIBLON
PhEJ . . . . PHILIPPINE ECONOMIC JOURNAL
P HELM SOC . . . . . . PROCEEDINGS OF THE HELMINTHOLOGICAL SOCIETY OF WASHINGTON
Phi . . . . PHILOSOPHY
PHI DEL KAP . . . . . . PHI DELTA KAPPAN
Phil . . . . PHILOLOGUS
Phil Ag . . . . PHILIPPINE AGRICULTURIST
Phil Ag R . . . . PHILIPPINE AGRICULTURAL REVIEW
Phila Mus Bull . . . . . PHILADELPHIA MUSEUM OF ART. BULLETIN
PHILA ORCH . . . . . . PHILADELPHIA ORCHESTRA PROGRAM NOTES
Phil Books . . . . PHILOSOPHICAL BOOKS
Phil Context . . . . . . PHILOSOPHY IN CONTEXT
Phil East West . . . . . PHILOSOPHY EAST AND WEST
Phil Exch . . . . PHILOSOPHIC EXCHANGE
Phil Forum (Boston) . . PHILOSOPHICAL FORUM (BOSTON)
Phil Forum (Dekalb) . . PHILOSOPHY FORUM (DEKALB)
Philipp Geol . . . . PHILIPPINE GEOLOGIST
Philippine Ag R . . . . PHILIPPINE AGRICULTURAL REVIEW
Philippine J Pub Adm . . PHILIPPINE JOURNAL OF PUBLIC ADMINISTRATION
Philips . . . . PHILIPS MUSIC HERALD
Philips Res Rep . . . . PHILIPS RESEARCH REPORTS
Philips Tech Rev . . . PHILIPS TECHNICAL REVIEW
Philips Telecommun Rev . . PHILIPS TELECOMMUNICATION REVIEW
PHILI S REV . . . . . . PHILIPPINE SOCIOLOGICAL REVIEW
Phil J Ag . . . . PHILIPPINE JOURNAL OF AGRICULTURE

Phil Jahr . . . . PHILOSOPHISCHES JAHRBUCH
Phil J Sci . . . . PHILIPPINE JOURNAL OF SCIENCE
Phil Ling . . . . PHILOSOPHICAL LINGUISTICS
Phil Log . . . . PHILOSOPHIE ET LOGIQUE
Phil Mag . . . . PHILOSOPHICAL MAGAZINE
Phil Math . . . . PHILOSOPHIA MATHEMATICA
Phil Natur . . . . PHILOSOPHIA NATURALIS
Philol Q . . . . PHILOLOGICAL QUARTERLY
Philos . . . . PHILOSOPHY
Philos & Phenom Res . . PHILOSOPHY AND PHENOMENOLOGICAL RESEARCH
Philos & Pub Affairs . . PHILOSOPHY AND PUBLIC AFFAIRS
PHILOS EW . . . . PHILOSOPHY EAST AND WEST
PHILOS FORU . . . . . . PHILOSOPHY FORUM
PHILOS HIST . . . . . . PHILOSOPHY AND HISTORY. GERMAN STUDIES SECTION I
PhilosI . . . . PHILOSOPHER'S INDEX
PHILOS J . . . . PHILOSOPHICAL JOURNAL
PHILOS M . . . . PHILOSOPHICAL MAGAZINE
Philosophy of Ed Soc Proc . . PROCEEDINGS OF THE PHILOSOPHY OF EDUCATION SOCIETY OF GREAT BRITAIN
PHILOS PUB . . . . . . PHILOSOPHY AND PUBLIC AFFAIRS
PhilosQ . . . . PHILOSOPHICAL QUARTERLY
PhilosRdschau . . . . . PHILOSOPHISCHE RUNDSCHAU
Philos Rev . . . . PHILOSOPHICAL REVIEW
PHILOS SCI . . . . . . PHILOSOPHY OF SCIENCE
PHILOS STUD . . . . . PHILOSOPHICAL STUDIES
Phil Papers . . . . PHILOSOPHICAL PAPERS
Phil Perspekt . . . . . PHILOSOPHISCHE PERSPEKTIVEN
Phil Phenomenol Res . . PHILOSOPHY AND PHENOMENOLOGICAL RESEARCH
Phil Post . . . . PHILHARMONIC POST
Phil Pub Affairs . . . . PHILOSOPHY AND PUBLIC AFFAIRS
Phil Q . . . . PHILOSOPHICAL QUARTERLY
Phil Qy . . . . PHILOLOGICAL QUARTERLY
PhilR . . . . PHILOSOPHY AND RHETORIC
Phil Reform . . . . PHILOSOPHIA REFORMATA
Phil Res Arch . . . . . . PHILOSOPHY RESEARCH ARCHIVES
PHIL RES R . . . . . . PHILIPS RESEARCH REPORTS
PHIL REV . . . . PHILOSOPHICAL REVIEW
Phil Rev (Taiwan) . . PHILOSOPHICAL REVIEW (TAIWAN)
Phil Rhet . . . . PHILOSOPHY AND RHETORIC
Phil Rundsch . . . . . . PHILOSOPHISCHE RUNDSCHAU
PhilS . . . . PHILOSOPHICAL STUDIES
Phil Sci . . . . PHILOSOPHY OF SCIENCE
Phil Soc . . . . PHILOLOGICAL SOCIETY. TRANSACTIONS
Phil Soc Sci . . . . . . PHILOSOPHY OF THE SOCIAL SCIENCES
Phil Stud . . . . PHILOSOPHICAL STUDIES
Phil Stud (Ireland) . . PHILOSOPHICAL STUDIES (IRELAND)
PhilT . . . . PHILOSOPHY TODAY
PHIL TECH R . . . . . . PHILIPS TECHNICAL REVIEW
Phil Today . . . . PHILOSOPHY TODAY
Phil Trans Roy Soc London Ser A Math Phys Sci . . PHILOSOPHICAL TRANSACTIONS OF THE ROYAL SOCIETY OF LONDON. SERIES A. MATHEMATICAL AND PHYSICAL SCIENCES
PHI T ROY A . . . . . . PHILOSOPHICAL TRANSACTIONS OF THE ROYAL SOCIETY OF LONDON. SERIES A. MATHEMATICAL AND PHYSICAL SCIENCES

PHI T ROY B...... PHILOSOPHICAL TRANSACTIONS OF THE ROYAL SOCIETY OF LONDON. SERIES B. BIOLOGICAL SCIENCES
PhJ............. PHILOSOPHISCHES JAHRBUCH
PhoenixC....... PHOENIX: THE CLASSICAL ASSOCIATION OF CANADA
PhoenixK....... PHOENIX (KOREA)
Phon........... PHONETICA
PhonPr......... PHONETICA PRAGENSIA
PHOTOCHEM P.... PHOTOCHEMISTRY AND PHOTOBIOLOGY
PHOTOGRAMMA... PHOTOGRAMMETRIA
Photogramm Eng... PHOTOGRAMMETRIC ENGINEERING
Photogramm Rec... PHOTOGRAMMETRIC RECORD
PHOTOGR E R..... PHOTOGRAMMETRIC ENGINEERING AND REMOTE SENSING
Photogr J........ PHOTOGRAPHIC JOURNAL
Photogr Sci Eng.... PHOTOGRAPHIC SCIENCE AND ENGINEERING
PHOTOSYNTHE.... PHOTOSYNTHETICA
PHOT SCI EN...... PHOTOGRAPHIC SCIENCE AND ENGINEERING
PhP............ PHILOLOGICA PRAGENSIA
PhP............ PHILOLOGIKE PROTOCHRONIA
PhQ............ PHILOSOPHICAL QUARTERLY
PHR............ PACIFIC HISTORICAL REVIEW
PhR............ PHILOSOPHICAL REVIEW
PHRA........... POVERTY AND HUMAN RESOURCES ABSTRACTS
Ph Res......... PHILOSOPHICAL AND PHENOMENOLOGICAL RESEARCH
Ph Rev......... PHILOSOPHICAL PHENOMENOLOGICAL REVIEW
PhS............ PHILOLOGISCHE STUDIEN
PhS............ PHILOSOPHICAL STUDIES
PhSR........... PHILIPPINE SOCIOLOGICAL REVIEW
PhSt........... PHILOSOPHICAL STUDIES
PHT............ PERSONHISTORISK TIDSKRIFT
PHum.......... PRZEGLAD HUMANISTYCZNY
PhW............ PHILOLOGISCHE WOCHENSCHRIFT
PHYL........... PHYLON
Phys & Chem...... PHYSICS AND CHEMISTRY
PHYS C GLAS...... PHYSICS AND CHEMISTRY OF GLASSES
Phys Chem Earth... PHYSICS AND CHEMISTRY OF THE EARTH
Phys Ed......... PHYSICAL EDUCATOR
Phys Educ....... PHYSICAL EDUCATOR
PHYS E PLAN...... PHYSICS OF THE EARTH AND PLANETARY INTERIORS
PHYS FLUIDS...... PHYSICS OF FLUIDS
Physics & Chem.... PHYSICS AND CHEMISTRY
Physics Ed....... PHYSICS EDUCATION
Physics Teach..... PHYSICS TEACHER
PHYSIOL REV...... PHYSIOLOGICAL REVIEWS
Physiol Zool...... PHYSIOLOGICAL ZOOLOGY
Phys Kondens Mater.. PHYSIK DER KONDENSIERTEN MATERIE
PHYSL BEHAV..... PHYSIOLOGY & BEHAVIOR
PHYSL BOHEM..... PHYSIOLOGIA BOHEMOSLOVACA
PHYSL CHEM...... PHYSIOLOGICAL CHEMISTRY AND PHYSICS
PHYS LETT A...... PHYSICS LETTERS A
PHYS LETT B...... PHYSICS LETTERS B
PHYSL PLANT..... PHYSIOLOGIA PLANTARUM

PHYSL PL P . . . . PHYSIOLOGICAL PLANT PATHOLOGY
PHYSL PSYCH . . . . . PHYSIOLOGICAL PSYCHOLOGY
PHYSL VEGET . . . . . . PHYSIOLOGIE VEGETALE
PHYSL ZOOL . . . . . . PHYSIOLOGICAL ZOOLOGY
PHYS MED BI . . . . . . PHYSICS IN MEDICINE AND BIOLOGY
Phys Met Metallogr . . PHYSICS OF METALS AND METALLOGRAPHY
PHYS NORVEG . . . . . PHYSICA NORVEGICA
Phys R . . . . PHYSICAL REVIEW
Phys Rev A Gen Phys . . PHYSICAL REVIEW. A, GENERAL PHYSICS
PHYS REV B . . . . PHYSICAL REVIEW. B, SOLID STATE
PHYS REV C . . . . PHYSICAL REVIEW. C, NUCLEAR PHYSICS
PHYS REV D . . . . PHYSICAL REVIEW. D, PARTICLES AND FIELDS
PHYS REV L . . . . PHYSICAL REVIEW LETTERS
PHYS SCR . . . . PHYSICA SCRIPTA
Phys Sintering . . . . . PHYSICS OF SINTERING
Phys Soc Lond Proc . . PHYSICAL SOCIETY OF LONDON. PROCEEDINGS
Phys Status Solidi . . PHYSICA STATUS SOLIDI
PHYS ST S-A . . . . . . PHYSICA STATUS SOLIDI. A, APPLIED RESEARCH
PHYS ST S-B . . . . . . PHYSICA STATUS SOLIDI. B, BASIC RESEARCH
Phys Technol . . . . . . PHYSICS IN TECHNOLOGY
Phys Ther . . . . PHYSICAL THERAPY
PHYS TODAY . . . . . . PHYSICS TODAY
Phyt . . . . PHYTOPATHOLOGY
PHYTOCHEM . . . . . . PHYTOCHEMISTRY
PHYTOMORPH . . . . PHYTOMORPHOLOGY
PHYTON AUST . . . . . PHYTON-ANNALES REI BOTANICAE AUSTRIA
PHYTOPATHOL . . . . PHYTOPATHOLOGY
PI . . . . PAGINE ISTRIANE
PI . . . . PERU INDIGENA
PI . . . . PRINTERS INK
PIA . . . . PROCEEDINGS OF THE IRISH ACADEMY
Piano Tech . . . . PIANO TECHNICIAN
P I A SCI A . . . . PROCEEDINGS OF THE INDIAN ACADEMY OF SCIENCES. SECTION A
P I A SCI B . . . . PROCEEDINGS OF THE INDIAN ACADEMY OF SCIENCES. SECTION B
PICAM . . . . PROCEEDINGS OF THE INTERNATIONAL CONGRESS OF AMERICANISTS
P I CIV E 1 . . . . PROCEEDINGS OF THE INSTITUTION OF CIVIL ENGINEERS. PART 1. DESIGN & CONSTRUCTION
P I CIV E 2 . . . . PROCEEDINGS OF THE INSTITUTION OF CIVIL ENGINEERS. PART 2. RESEARCH & THEORY
PICL . . . . PROCEEDINGS OF THE INTERNATIONAL CONGRESS OF LINGUISTS
PICP . . . . PROCEEDINGS OF THE INTERNATIONAL CONGRESS OF PHILOSOPHY
PICPS . . . . PROCEEDINGS OF THE INTERNATIONAL CONGRESS OF PHONETIC SCIENCES
PictR . . . . PICTORIAL REVIEW
PId . . . . PAROLE E LE IDEE
P IEEE . . . . PROCEEDINGS OF THE INSTITUTE OF ELECTRICAL AND ELECTRONICS ENGINEERS
P IEE LOND . . . . PROCEEDINGS OF THE INSTITUTION OF ELECTRICAL ENGINEERS (LONDON)
PIF . . . . PARIS ET ILE-DE-FRANCE. MEMOIRES
PIFAS . . . . PUBLICACIONES DEL INSTITUTO DE FILOLOGIA. ANEJO DE SPHINX
PIFMLL . . . . PROCEEDINGS OF THE INTERNATIONAL FEDERATION FOR MODERN LANGUAGES AND LITERATURES
Pigment Resin Technol . . PIGMENT AND RESIN TECHNOLOGY
PIL . . . . PAPERS IN LINGUISTICS
PIMBel . . . . PRACY INSTYTUTA MOVAZNAUSTVA AKADEMII NAUK BELARUSKAJ SSR

PIME . . . . PETROFI IRODALMI MUZEUM EVKONYVE
PIMST . . . . PONTIFICAL INSTITUTE OF MEDIEVAL STUDIES AND TEXTS
PiR . . . . PECAT' I REVOLJUCIJA
PiS . . . . PUSKIN I EGO SOVREMENNIKI
Pit Quarry . . . . PIT AND QUARRY
Pittsburgh Sch . . . . . PITTSBURGH SCHOOLS
Pittsburgh Univ Sch Ed J . . UNIVERSITY OF PITTSBURGH. SCHOOL OF EDUCATION JOURNAL
PITT SYM . . . . PITTSBURGH SYMPHONY ORCHESTRA PROGRAM NOTES
PivS . . . . PIVNICNE SJAJVO
PIW . . . . POLSKI INSTYTUT WYDAWNICZY
PJ . . . . PERSONNEL JOURNAL
PJ . . . . PHILOSOPHISCHES JAHRBUCH
PJ . . . . PORADNIK JEZYKOWY
PJ . . . . PREUSSISCHE JAHRBUECHER
PJa . . . . PAPERS ON JAPAN
P JAP ACAD . . . . . . PROCEEDINGS OF THE JAPAN ACADEMY
PJb . . . . PREUSSISCHE JAHRBUECHER
PJE . . . . PEABODY JOURNAL OF EDUCATION
PJez . . . . PRACE JEZYKOZNAWCZE POLSKIEJ AKADEMII NAUK
PJGG . . . . PHILOSOPHISCHES JAHRBUCH DER GORRES-GESELLSCHAFT
PJL . . . . PHILIPPINE JOURNAL OF LINGUISTICS
PJLT . . . . PHILIPPINE JOURNAL OF LANGUAGE TEACHING
PK . . . . PHILOLOGIKE KYPROS
PK . . . . PRAWO KANONICZNE
PK . . . . PROBLEMY KIBERNETIKI
PK . . . . PRZEGLAD KLASYCZNY
PK . . . . PRZEGLAD KOSCIELNY
PKJ . . . . PITANJA KNJIZEVNOSTI A JEZIKA
P KON NED A . . . . . . PROCEEDINGS OF THE KONINKLIJKE NEDERLANDSE AKADEMIE VAN WETENSCHAPPEN. SERIES
A. MATHEMATICAL SCIENCES
P KON NED B . . . . . PROCEEDINGS OF THE KONINKLIJKE NEDERLANDSE AKADEMIE VAN WETENSCHAPPEN. SERIES
B. PHYSICAL SCIENCES
P KON NED C . . . . . . PROCEEDINGS OF THE KONINKLIJKE NEDERLANDSE AKADEMIE VAN WETENSCHAPPEN. SERIES
C. BIOLOGICAL AND MEDICAL SCIENCES
Pks & Rec . . . . PARKS & RECREATION
PKy . . . . PNEUMATIKE KYPROS
PL . . . . PALAEOGRAPHIA LATINA
PL . . . . PAMIETNIK LITERACKI
PL . . . . PAPERS IN LINGUISTICS
PL . . . . POET LORE
PLAB . . . . PHILADELPHIA LIBRARY ASSOCIATION. BULLETIN
PLANET SPAC . . . . . PLANETARY AND SPACE SCIENCE
Planseeber Pulvermet . . PLANSEEBERICHTE FUER PULVERMETALLURGIE
Plant . . . . PLANT MAINTENANCE AND ENGINEERING
PLANTA MED . . . . . . PLANTA MEDICA
Plant & Power Services Eng . . PLANT AND POWER SERVICES ENGINEER
PLANT CEL P . . . . . . PLANT AND CELL PHYSIOLOGY
PLANT DIS R . . . . . . PLANT DISEASE REPORTER
Plant Eng . . . . PLANT ENGINEERING
Plant Eng (Lond) . . . PLANT ENGINEER (LONDON)
Planter . . . . PLANTER AND SUGAR MANUFACTURER

Plant Oper Manage . . PLANT OPERATING MANAGEMENT
PLANT PATH . . . . . . PLANT PATHOLOGY
PLANT PHYSL . . . . . PLANT PHYSIOLOGY
PLANT SCI L . . . . . . PLANT SCIENCE LETTERS
PLANT SOIL . . . . PLANT AND SOIL
PLANT SYS E . . . . . . PLANT SYSTEMATICS AND EVOLUTION
PLASMA PHYS . . . . . PLASMA PHYSICS
Plasma Phys Contr Nucl Fusion Res Conf Proc . . PLASMA PHYSICS AND CONTROLLED NUCLEAR FUSION RESEARCH. CONFERENCE PROCEEDINGS
PLAS R SURG . . . . . . PLASTIC AND RECONSTRUCTIVE SURGERY
Plas Rubbers Text . . PLASTICS, RUBBERS, TEXTILES
Plast Aust . . . . PLASTICS IN AUSTRALIA
Plast Des Process . . PLASTICS DESIGN AND PROCESSING
PLASTEC Note . . . . . PLASTEC (PLASTICS TECHNICAL EVALUATION CENTER). NOTE
PLASTEC REP . . . . . . PLASTEC (PLASTICS TECHNICAL EVALUATION CENTER). REPORT
Plaste Kaut . . . . PLASTE UND KAUTSCHUK
Plast Eng . . . . PLASTICS ENGINEERING
Plast Hmoty Kauc . . PLASTICKE HMOTY A KAUCUK
Plastic Prod . . . . . . PLASTIC PRODUCTS
Plast Ind (Paris) . . . PLASTIQUES ET INDUSTRIE (PARIS)
Plast Massy . . . . . . PLASTICHESKIE MASSY
Plast Mod Elastomeres . . PLASTIQUES MODERNES ET ELASTOMERES
PLAST POLYM . . . . . PLASTICS AND POLYMERS
Plast Reconstr Surg . . PLASTIC AND RECONSTRUCTIVE SURGERY
Plast Technol . . . . . PLASTICS TECHNOLOGY
PLAST WORLD . . . . . PLASTICS WORLD
Platoon Sch . . . . . . PLATOON SCHOOL
PLC . . . . PRINCETON UNIVERSITY LIBRARY CHRONICLE
PLCM&ND . . . . PROCEEDINGS OF THE LINGUISTIC CIRCLE OF MANITOBA AND NORTH DAKOTA
PLCNY . . . . PUBLICATIONS OF THE LINGUISTIC CIRCLE OF NEW YORK
PLCS . . . . PROCEEDINGS OF THE LONDON CLASSICAL SOCIETY
PLD . . . . PUBLIC LIBRARIES DIVISION. REPORTER
Plf Adv . . . . PLAINTIFF'S ADVOCATE
PLG . . . . PROBLEME DE LINGVISTICA GENARALA
PLing . . . . PAPERS IN LINGUISTICS
PLL . . . . PAPERS ON LANGUAGE AND LITERATURE
PLLP . . . . POLISH LITERATURE/LITTERATURE POLONAISE
P LOND MATH . . . . . PROCEEDINGS OF THE LONDON MATHEMATICAL SOCIETY
PLPLS-LHS . . . . PROCEEDINGS OF THE LEEDS PHILOSOPHICAL AND LITERARY SOCIETY. LITERARY AND HISTORICAL SECTION
PLPLS-SS . . . . PROCEEDINGS OF THE LEEDS PHILOSOPHICAL AND LITERARY SOCIETY. SCIENTIFIC SECTION
PM . . . . PALEOGRAPHIE MUSICALE
PM . . . . PAPER MAKER
PM . . . . PETERMANNS GEOGRAPHISCHE MITTEILUNGEN
PM . . . . PRESSE MEDICALE
PM . . . . PROVINCE DU MAINE
PMA . . . . PUBLICATIONS OF THE MEDIAEVAL ACADEMY
PMaine . . . . PROVINCE DU MAINE
PMASAL . . . . PUBLICATIONS OF THE MICHIGAN ACADEMY OF SCIENCE, ARTS AND LETTERS
PME . . . . PRACE I MATERIAY ETNOGRAFICZNE
PMHB . . . . PENNSYLVANIA MAGAZINE OF HISTORY AND BIOGRAPHY

PMHS . . . . PROCEEDINGS OF THE MASSACHUSETTS HISTORICAL SOCIETY
PMLA . . . . PUBLICATIONS OF THE MODERN LANGUAGE ASSOCIATION OF AMERICA
PMLAAm . . . . PUBLICATIONS OF THE MODERN LANGUAGE ASSOCIATION OF AMERICA
PMMLA . . . . PAPERS OF THE MIDWEST MODERN LANGUAGE ASSOCIATION
PMRS . . . . PROGRESS OF MEDIEVAL AND RENAISSANCE STUDIES IN THE UNITED STATES AND CANADA
PMS . . . . PERCEPTUAL AND MOTOR SKILLS
PMTF Zh Prikl Mekh Tekh Fiz . . PMTF. ZHURNAL PRIKLADNOI MEKHANIKI TEKHNICKESKIO FIZIKI
PN . . . . POE NEWSLETTER
PN . . . . POESIA NUOVA
PN . . . . POETRY NORTHWEST
Pn . . . . POZNAN
PN . . . . PRO NERVIA
P NAS IND A . . . . . . PROCEEDINGS OF THE NATIONAL ACADEMY OF SCIENCES. INDIA. SECTION A. PHYSICAL SCIENCES
P NAS IND B . . . . . . PROCEEDINGS OF THE NATIONAL ACADEMY OF SCIENCES. INDIA. SECTION B. BIOLOGICAL SCIENCES
P NAS US . . . . PROCEEDINGS OF THE NATIONAL ACADEMY OF SCIENCES OF THE UNITED STATES OF AMERICA
PNEUMONOL-P . . . . PNEUMONOLOGIE-PNEUMONOLOGY
PNGL . . . . PAPERS IN NEW GUINEA LINGUISTICS
PNJHS . . . . PROCEEDINGS OF THE NEW JERSEY HISTORICAL SOCIETY
PNL . . . . PRZEWODNIK NAUKOWY I LITERACKI
PNLA Q . . . . PACIFIC NORTHWEST LIBRARY ASSOCIATION. QUARTERLY
PNM . . . . PHANTOM
PNQ . . . . PACIFIC NORTHWEST QUARTERLY
PNUS . . . . PRACE NAUKOWE UNIWERSYTETU SLASKIEGO
P NUTR SOC . . . . . . PROCEEDINGS OF THE NUTRITION SOCIETY
PNY . . . . POETRY NEW YORK
Po . . . . POESIE
Po . . . . POLET
PO . . . . POONA ORIENTALIST
PoC . . . . PROBLEMS OF COMMUNISM
POC . . . . PROCHE-ORIENT CHRETIEN
PODU . . . . PRACI ODES'KOHO DERZAVNOHO UNIVERSYTETU
Poe . . . . POETIK
Poe Chpbk . . . . POETRY CHAPBOOK
P O Elect Engrs J . . . POST OFFICE ELECTRICAL ENGINEERS JOURNAL
Poe Pal . . . . POETRY PALISADE
PoeS . . . . POE STUDIES
Poêt . . . . POETICA
Poet . . . . POETRY
PoetC . . . . POET AND CRITIC
Poetry R . . . . POETRY REVIEW (LONDON)
Pog . . . . POGLEDI
Point Point Commun . . POINT-TO-POINT COMMUNICATIONS
Point Point Telecommun . . POINT-TO-POINT TELECOMMUNICATIONS
Pol . . . . POLONISTYKA (WARSAW)
PolAb . . . . POLLUTION ABSTRACTS
Pol Acad Sci Inst Fundam Tech Res Nonlinear Vib Probl . . POLISH ACADEMY OF SCIENCES. INSTITUTE OF FUNDAMENTAL TECHNICAL RESEARCH. NONLINEAR VIBRATION PROBLEMS
Pol Acad Sci Inst Fundam Tech Res Proc Vib Probl . . POLISH ACADEMY OF SCIENCES. INSTITUTE OF FUNDAMENTAL TECHNICAL RESEARCH. PROCEEDINGS OF VIBRATION PROBLEMS

Pol Akad Nauk Oddzial Krakowie Pr Kom Ceram Ceram..POLSKA AKADEMIA NAUK. ODDZIAL W KRAKOWIE. PRACE
    KOMISJI CERAMICZENJ. CERAMIKA
Pol Akad Nauk Oddzial Krakowie Pr Kom Metal-Odlew Metalurg..POLSKA AKADEMIA NAUK. ODDZIAL W
    KRAKOWIE. PRACE KOMISJI METALURGICZNO-ODLEWNICZEJ. METALURGIA
Pol Akad Nauk Pr Inst Masz Przeplyw..POLSKA AKADEMIA NAUK. PRACE INSTYTUTU MASZYN PRZEPLYWOWYCH
Poland China......POLAND CHINA WORLD
Pol & Soc.........POLITICS AND SOCIETY
POLICY POL.......POLICY AND POLITICS
POLICY SCI.......POLICY SCIENCES
Poliplasti Plast Rinf..POLIPLASTI E PLASTICI RINFORZATI
POLI Q..........POLITICAL QUARTERLY
POLI SCI........POLITICAL SCIENCE
POLI SCI Q........POLITICAL SCIENCE QUARTERLY
POLI SOCIET......POLITICS AND SOCIETY
Politech Warsz Pr Inst Podstaw Konstr Masz..POLITECHNIKA WARSZAWSKA. PRACE INSTYTUTU PODSTAW
    KONSTRUKCJI MASZYN
Politech Warsz Pr Nauk Mech..POLITECHNIKA WARSZAWSKA. PRACE NAUKOWE. MECHANIKA
POLIT EKON......POLITICKA EKONOMIE
POLITIC ST.......POLITICAL STUDIES-LONDON
Polit Sci Q........POLITICAL SCIENCE QUARTERLY
POLIT STUD......POLITISCHE STUDIEN (MUNICH)
POLIT THEOR.....POLITICAL THEORY
POL J PHAR......POLISH JOURNAL OF PHARMACOLOGY AND PHARMACY
PolL............POLONISTA (LUBLIN)
Pollut Eng.......POLLUTION ENGINEERING
PolP............POLISH PERSPECTIVES
POL PSYCH B......POLISH PSYCHOLOGICAL BULLETIN
Pol Q...........POLITICAL QUARTERLY
Pol Quar........POLITICAL QUARTERLY
PolR............POLISH REVIEW (NEW YORK)
Pol Sci..........POLITICAL SCIENCE
Pol Sci Q........POLITICAL SCIENCE QUARTERLY
Polska Akad Nauk Inst Masz Prezeplyw Pr Inst Masz Przeplyw..POLSKA AKADEMIA NAUK. INSTYTUTU MASZYN
    PRZEPLYWOWYCH. PRACE INSTYTUTU MASZYN PRZEPLYWOWYCH
Polska Akad Nauk Met..POLSKA AKADEMIA NAUK. METALURGIA
Polska Akad Nauk Oddzial Krakowie Pr Kom Nauk Tech Ceram..POLSKA AKADEMIA NAUK. ODDZIAL W KRAKOWIE.
    PRACE KOMISJI NAUK TECHNICZNYCH. CERAMIKA
POL SOC B.......POLISH SOCIOLOGICAL BULLETIN
Pol Stud........POLITICAL STUDIES
Polym Age.......POLYMER AGE
POLYM ENG S.....POLYMER ENGINEERING AND SCIENCE
POLYM J.........POLYMER JOURNAL
Polym Mech......POLYMER MECHANICS (ENGLISH TRANSLATION OF MEKHANIKA POLIMEROV)
POLYM-PLAST.....POLYMER-PLASTICS TECHNOLOGY AND ENGINEERING
Polym Sci USSR....POLYMER SCIENCE USSR
POLYN SOC J......POLYNESIAN SOCIETY JOURNAL
Pon.............PONTE
Pop Astron.......POPULAR ASTRONOMY
POP B...........POPULATION BULLETIN
Pop Educ........POPULAR EDUCATOR
Pop Electr.......POPULAR ELECTRONICS

Pop Gard . . . . POPULAR GARDENING
POP INDEX . . . . POPULATION INDEX
Pop Mech . . . . POPULAR MECHANICS MAGAZINE
POP MUS & SOC . . . . POPULAR MUSIC AND SOCIETY
Pop Phot . . . . POPULAR PHOTOGRAPHY
Pop Sci . . . . POPULAR SCIENCE MONTHLY
Pop Sci R . . . . POPULAR SCIENCE REVIEW
POP STUD LO . . . . . POPULATION STUDIES (LONDON)
POP STUD NY . . . . . POPULATION STUDIES (NEW YORK)
POQ . . . . PUBLIC OPINION QUARTERLY
PoR . . . . POETRY REVIEW (LONDON)
POr . . . . PORTA ORIENTALE
Por . . . . PORTUCALE
Porosh Met . . . . . . POROSHKOVAYA METALLURGIYA
Port . . . . PORTUGALE
Portfo . . . . PORTFOLIO
Portfo (Den.) . . . . . PORTFOLIO (DENNIE'S)
Portia L J . . . . PORTIA LAW JOURNAL
Portland Cem Ass Advanced Eng Bull . . PORTLAND CEMENT ASSOCIATION. ADVANCED ENGINEERING BULLETIN
Portland Cem Ass J PCA Res Develop Lab . . PORTLAND CEMENT ASSOCIATION. JOURNAL OF THE PCA RESEARCH AND DEVELOPMENT LABORATORIES
Porto Rico Ag Exp . . PORTO RICO AGRICULTURAL EXPERIMENT STATION. PUBLICATIONS
Ports Dredging . . . . PORTS AND DREDGING
PostB . . . . POSTILLA BOHEMICA/POSTILLA BOHEMICA
POST BIOCH . . . . . . POSTEPY BIOCHEMII
POSTG MED J . . . . . POSTGRADUATE MEDICAL JOURNAL
POSTGR MED . . . . . . POSTGRADUATE MEDICINE
POST O EE J . . . . POST OFFICE ELECTRICAL ENGINEERS JOURNAL
POSWa . . . . POZPRAWY KOMISJI ORIENTALISTYCZNEJ TOWARZYSTWA NAUKOWEGO WARSZAWSKIEGO
Potato M . . . . POTATO MAGAZINE
P O Telecommun J . . POST OFFICE TELECOMMUNICATIONS JOURNAL
Potter Am Mo . . . . . POTTER'S AMERICAN MONTHLY
Poultry Dig . . . . POULTRY DIGEST
Poultry Process . . . . POULTRY PROCESSING AND MARKETING
POULTRY SCI . . . . . . POULTRY SCIENCE
Powder Met . . . . . . POWDER METALLURGY
POWD METALL . . . . POWDER METALLURGY
POWD TECH . . . . . . POWDER TECHNOLOGY
POWER ENG . . . . . . POWER ENGINEERING
Power Eng (India) . . POWER ENGINEER (INDIA)
Power F . . . . POWER FARMING
Power Ind . . . . POWER INDUSTRY, INCLUDING INDUSTRIAL POWER AND INDUSTRY POWER
Power Pl Eng . . . . . . POWER PLANT ENGINEERING
Power Transm Des . . POWER TRANSMISSION DESIGN
PP . . . . PAROLA DEL PASSATO
PP . . . . PHILOLOGICA PRAGENSIA
PP . . . . PRACE POLONISTYCZNE
PP . . . . PRZEGLAD POWSZECHNY (REVUE UNIVERSELLE)
PPa . . . . PAROLA DEL PASSATO
PPB . . . . POLYBIBLION. PARTIE LITTERAIRE
PPeda . . . . PROBLEMI DI PEDAGOGIA

PPGS . . . . PUBLICATIONS OF THE PENNSYLVANIA GERMAN SOCIETY
PPhL . . . . PAPERS IN PHILIPPINE LINGUISTICS (CANBERRA)
PPJ . . . . PRILOZI PROUCAVANJU JEZIKA
PPL . . . . POLYBIBLION. PARTIE LITTERAIRE
PPL . . . . PRACE POLONYSTICZNE (LODZ)
PPM . . . . PUBLIC PERSONNEL MANAGEMENT
PPNCFL . . . . PROCEEDINGS OF THE PACIFIC NORTHWEST CONFERENCE ON FOREIGN LANGUAGES
PPol . . . . PENSIERO POLITICO
PPol . . . . PRZEGLAD POLSKI
PPow . . . . PRZEGLAD POWSZECHNY
PPr . . . . PAEDAGOGISCHE PROVINZ
PPR . . . . PHILOSOPHY AND PHENOMENOLOGICAL RESEARCH
P PREHIST S . . . . . . PROCEEDINGS OF THE PREHISTORIC SOCIETY
PProv . . . . PADOVA E LA SUA PROVINCIA
PPS . . . . PUBLICATIONS OF THE PHILOLOGICAL SOCIETY
PPW . . . . PRACE POLONYSTYCZNE (WROCLAW)
PQ . . . . PHILOLOGICAL QUARTERLY
PQ . . . . PHILOSOPHICAL QUARTERLY
PQ . . . . PSYCHIATRIC QUARTERLY
PR . . . . PARIS REVIEW
PR . . . . PARTISAN REVIEW
PR . . . . PHILOSOPHICAL REVIEW
PR . . . . PODRAVSKA REVIJA
PR . . . . POETRY REVIEW
PR . . . . PREVENTION
Pr . . . . PROHEMIO
Pr . . . . PROMETHEUS
Pr . . . . PROSTOR (MOSCOW)
PR . . . . PSYCHOANALYTIC REVIEW
PR . . . . PSYCHOLOGICAL REVIEW
PrA . . . . PRIMER ACTO (MADRID)
Prac Anth . . . . PRACTICAL ANTHROPOLOGY
Prac F . . . . PRACTICAL FARMER
Prac Forecast . . . . . PRACTICAL FORECAST FOR HOME ECONOMICS
Prac Home Econ . . . . PRACTICAL HOME ECONOMICS
Prac Law . . . . PRACTICAL LAWYER
PRACTITION . . . . . . PRACTITIONER
Pract M . . . . PRACTICAL MAGAZINE
Prague St . . . . STUDIES IN ENGLISH BY MEMBERS OF THE ENGLISH SEMINAR OF THE CHARLES UNIVERSITY,
PRAGUE
Prairie Schoon . . . . . PRAIRIE SCHOONER
Prairie Sch R . . . . . . PRAIRIE SCHOOL REVIEW
Prakt Metallogr . . . . PRAKTISCHE METALLOGRAPHIE
PraPol . . . . PRACE POLONISTYCZNE
Prat Ind Mec . . . . . . PRATIQUE DES INDUSTRIES MECANIQUE
PRAX KINDER . . . . . PRAXIS DER KINDERPSYCHOLOGIE UND KINDERPSYCHIATRIE
PrC . . . . PROSTER IN CAS
PRCAFL . . . . PUBLICATIONS OF THE RESEARCH CENTER IN ANTHROPOLOGY, FOLKLORE, AND LINGUISTICS
PRECAMB RES . . . . . PRECAMBRIAN RESEARCH
Precast Concr . . . . . PRECAST CONCRETE
Precis Met . . . . PRECISION METAL

Preh . . . . PREHISTOIRE
PREP BIOCH . . . . . . PREPARATIVE BIOCHEMISTRY
PresAfr . . . . PRESENCE AFRICAINE
Presb & Ref R . . . . . PRESBYTERIAN AND REFORMED REVIEW
Presb Q . . . . PRESBYTERIAN QUARTERLY REVIEW
Presb R . . . . PRESBYTERIAN REVIEW
Preuss Jahrb . . . . . . PREUSSISCHE JAHRBUECHER
Preuss Sitzb . . . . . . PREUSSISCHE AKADEMIE DER WISSENSCHAFTEN. SITZUNGSBERICHT
PREV MED . . . . PREVENTIVE MEDICINE
PRF . . . . PUBLICATIONS ROMANES ET FRANCAISES
PrHlit . . . . PRACE HISTORYCZNOLITERACKIE
PRIA . . . . PROCEEDINGS OF THE ROYAL IRISH ACADEMY
PRIB TEKHN . . . . . . PRIBORY I TEKHNIKA EKSPERIMENTA
PRIKL MAT . . . . PRIKLADNAYA MATEMATIKA I MEKHANIKA
Prikl Mekh . . . . PRIKLADNAYA MEKHANIKA
PrilKJIF . . . . PRILOZI ZA KNJIZEVNOST, JEZIK, ISTORIJU I FOLKLOR
Prilozi . . . . PRILOZI ZA KNJIZEVNOST, JEZIK, ISTORIJU I FOLKLOR
PrilPJ . . . . PRILOZI PROUCAVANJU JEZIKA
PRIMATOLOG . . . . . PRIMATOLOGIA
Prim Ed-Pop Ed . . . . PRIMARY EDUCATION-POPULAR EDUCATOR
Prim Educ . . . . PRIMARY EDUCATION
Princ . . . . PRINCETON REVIEW
Princeton Mus Rec . . PRINCETON UNIVERSITY. MUSEUM OF HISTORIC ART. RECORD
Princeton Univ Lib Chron . . PRINCETON UNIVERSITY LIBRARY CHRONICLE
Princ ns . . . . PRINCETON REVIEW (NEW SERIES)
PrincSB . . . . PRINCETON SEMINARY BULLETIN
Princ Theol R . . . . . . PRINCETON THEOLOGICAL REVIEW
Princ Univ Bull . . . . . PRINCETON UNIVERSITY BULLETIN
Print Bookbind Trade Rev . . PRINTING AND BOOKBINDING TRADE REVIEW
Print Coll Q . . . . PRINT COLLECTOR'S QUARTERLY
Print Technol . . . . . . PRINTING TECHNOLOGY
P R IR AC A . . . . PROCEEDINGS OF THE ROYAL IRISH ACADEMY. SECTION A. MATHEMATICAL, ASTRONOMICAL AND PHYSICAL
P R IR AC B . . . . . . PROCEEDINGS OF THE ROYAL IRISH ACADEMY. SECTION B. BIOLOGICAL, GEOLOGICAL AND CHEMICAL SCIENCE
Priv Lib . . . . PRIVATE LIBRARY
PrJ . . . . PREUSSISCHE JAHRBUECHER
PrLit . . . . PRACE LITERACKIE
PRMCL . . . . PERIODICA DE RE MORALI, CANONICA, LITURGICA
PRO . . . . PUBLIC RECORD OFFICE
Prob Commun . . . . . PROBLEMS OF COMMUNISM
Prob Econ . . . . PROBLEMS OF ECONOMICS
PROBL COMMU . . . . PROBLEMS OF COMMUNISM
PROBL ECON . . . . . . PROBLEMS OF ECONOMICS
Probl Prochn . . . . . . PROBLEMY PROCHNOSTI
Proc . . . . PROCELLARIA
Proc Acad Pol Sci . . . PROCEEDINGS OF THE ACADEMY OF POLITICAL SCIENCE
Proc Air Pollut Contr Ass . . PROCEEDINGS OF THE AIR POLLUTION CONTROL ASSOCIATION
Proc Am Assoc State Highw Off . . PROCEEDINGS OF THE AMERICAN ASSOCIATION OF STATE HIGHWAY OFFICIALS
Proc Am Concr Inst . . PROCEEDINGS OF THE AMERICAN CONCRETE INSTITUTE
Proc Amer Ass State Highw Offic . . PROCEEDINGS OF THE AMERICAN ASSOCIATION OF STATE HIGHWAY OFFICIAL ;

PERIODICAL TITLE ABBREVIATIONS

Proc Amer Petrol Inst Sect III Refining..PROCEEDINGS OF THE AMERICAN PETROLEUM INSTITUTE. SECTION III. REFINING
Proc Amer Phil Ass..PROCEEDINGS AND ADDRESSES OF THE AMERICAN PHILOSOPHICAL ASSOCIATION
Proc Amer Phil Soc..PROCEEDINGS OF THE AMERICAN PHILOSOPHICAL SOCIETY
Proc Amer Power Conf..PROCEEDINGS OF THE AMERICAN POWER CONFERENCE
Proc Amer Wood-Preserv Ass..PROCEEDINGS OF THE AMERICAN WOOD-PRESERVERS' ASSOCIATION
Proc Am Pet Inst Div Refining..PROCEEDINGS OF THE AMERICAN PETROLEUM INSTITUTE. DIVISION OF REFINING
Proc Am Pet Inst Sect III Refining..PROCEEDINGS OF THE AMERICAN PETROLEUM INSTITUTE. SECTION III. REFINING
Proc Am Philos Soc..PROCEEDINGS OF THE AMERICAN PHILOSOPHICAL SOCIETY
Proc Am Wood-Preserv Assoc..PROCEEDINGS OF THE AMERICAN WOOD-PRESERVERS' ASSOCIATION
Proc Annu Conv Natur Gas Process Ass Tech Pap..PROCEEDINGS. ANNUAL CONVENTION. NATURAL GAS PROCESSORS ASSOCIATION. TECHNICAL PAPERS
Proc Annu Nat Dairy Eng Conf..PROCEEDINGS OF THE ANNUAL NATIONAL DAIRY ENGINEERING CONFERENCE
Proc Aris Soc......PROCEEDINGS OF THE ARISTOTELIAN SOCIETY
Proc Ass Asphalt Paving Technol..PROCEEDINGS OF THE ASSOCIATION OF ASPHALT PAVING TECHNOLOGISTS
Proc Auto Div Instn Mech Engrs..PROCEEDINGS OF THE INSTITUTION OF MECHANICAL ENGINEERS. AUTO DIVISION
Proc Brit Ac......PROCEEDINGS OF THE BRITISH ACADEMY
Proc Brit Ceram Soc..PROCEEDINGS OF THE BRITISH CERAMIC SOCIETY
Proc Camb Philos Soc..PROCEEDINGS OF CAMBRIDGE PHILOSOPHICAL SOCIETY
Proc Cath Phil Ass..PROCEEDINGS OF THE AMERICAN CATHOLIC PHILOSOPHICAL ASSOCIATION
Proc Coal Mining Inst Amer..PROCEEDINGS OF THE COAL MINING INSTITUTE OF AMERICA
Proc Conf Eng Med Biol..PROCEEDINGS OF THE CONFERENCE OF ENGINEERING IN MEDICINE AND BIOLOGY
Proc Electron Components Conf..PROCEEDINGS. ELECTRONIC COMPONENTS CONFERENCE
Proc Eng Soc Hong Kong..PROCEEDINGS OF THE ENGINEERING SOCIETY OF HONG KONG
PROCESS BIO......PROCESS BIOCHEMISTRY
Process Eng.......PROCESS ENGINEERING
Process Instrum...PROCESS INSTRUMENTATION
Process Stud......PROCESS STUDIES
Process Technol Int..PROCESS TECHNOLOGY INTERNATIONAL
Proc Fujihara Mem Fac Eng Keio Univ (Tokyo)..PROCEEDINGS OF THE FUJIHARA MEMORIAL FACULTY OF ENGINEERING. KEIO UNIVERSITY (TOKYO)
Proc Geol Ass Can..PROCEEDINGS OF THE GEOLOGICAL ASSOCIATION OF CANADA
Proc Ill Mining Inst..PROCEEDINGS OF THE ILLINOIS MINING INSTITUTE
Proc Inst Civ Eng...PROCEEDINGS OF THE INSTITUTION OF CIVIL ENGINEERS(LONDON)
Proc Inst Elec Eng (London)..PROCEEDINGS OF THE INSTITUTION OF ELECTRICAL ENGINEERS (LONDON)
Proc Instn Civ Engrs..PROCEEDINGS OF THE INSTITUTION OF CIVIL ENGINEERS
Proc Instn Elect Engrs..PROCEEDINGS OF THE INSTITUTION OF ELECTRICAL ENGINEERS
Proc Instn Mech Engrs..PROCEEDINGS OF THE INSTITUTION OF MECHANICAL ENGINEERS
Proc Inst Radio Electron Eng Aust..PROCEEDINGS OF THE INSTITUTION OF RADIO AND ELECTRONICS ENGINEERS OF AUSTRALIA
Proc Inst Refrig....PROCEEDINGS OF THE INSTITUTE OF REFRIGERATION
Proc Int Congr Refrig..PROCEEDINGS OF THE INTERNATIONAL CONGRESS OF REFRIGERATION
Proc ISA.........PROCEEDINGS OF INSTRUMENT SOCIETY OF AMERICA
Proc Jap Soc Civ Eng..PROCEEDINGS OF THE JAPAN SOCIETY OF CIVIL ENGINEERS
Proc Leeds Phil Lit Soc Sci Sect..PROCEEDINGS OF THE LEEDS PHILOSOPHICAL AND LITERARY SOCIETY. SCIENTIFIC SECTION
Proc Nat Acad Sci USA..PROCEEDINGS OF THE NATIONAL ACADEMY OF SCIENCES OF THE UNITED STATES OF AMERICA
Proc Nat Conf Fluid Power Annu Meet..PROCEEDINGS OF THE NATIONAL CONFERENCE ON FLUID POWER. ANNUAL MEETING

Proc Nat Electron Conf. . PROCEEDINGS OF THE NATIONAL ELECTRONICS CONFERENCE
Proc Nat Food Eng Conf. . PROCEEDINGS OF THE NATIONAL FOOD ENGINEERING CONFERENCE
Proc Nat Gas Processors Assoc Annu Conv. . PROCEEDINGS OF THE NATURAL GAS PROCESSORS ASSOCIATION.
    ANNUAL CONVENTION
Proc Natl Electron Conf. . PROCEEDINGS OF THE NATIONAL ELECTRONICS CONFERENCE
Proc Natl Telecommun Conf. . PROCEEDINGS OF THE NATIONAL TELECOMMUNICATIONS CONFERENCE
Proc Nat Telemetering Conf. . PROCEEDINGS OF THE NATIONAL TELEMETERING CONFERENCE
Proc N Mex W Tex Phil Soc. . PROCEEDINGS OF THE NEW MEXICO-WEST TEXAS PHILOSOPHICAL SOCIETY
Proc Northwest Conf Struct Eng. . PROCEEDINGS OF THE NORTHWEST CONFERENCE OF STRUCTURAL ENGINEERS
Proc Oil Recovery Conf Tex Petrol Res Comm. . PROCEEDINGS OF THE OIL RECOVERY CONFERENCE OF THE TEXAS
    PETROLEUM RESEARCH COMMITTEE
Proc Pac Coast Gas Ass. . PROCEEDINGS OF THE PACIFIC COAST GAS ASSOCIATION, INC. CALIFORNIA
Proc Phil Educ Soc Austl. . PROCEEDINGS OF THE PHILOSOPHY OF EDUCATION SOCIETY OF AUSTRALASIA
Proc Phil Educ Soc GB. . PROCEEDINGS OF THE PHILOSOPHY OF EDUCATION SOCIETY OF GREAT BRITAIN
Proc R Instn Gt Br. . PROCEEDINGS OF THE ROYAL INSTITUTION OF GREAT BRITAIN
Proc Roy Soc Can. . . PROCEEDINGS OF THE ROYAL SOCIETY OF CANADA
Proc Soc Inf Disp. . . PROCEEDINGS OF THE SOCIETY FOR INFORMATION DISPLAY
Proc Soil Sci Soc Am. . PROCEEDINGS OF THE SOIL SCIENCE SOCIETY OF AMERICA
Proc S Wales Inst Eng. . PROCEEDINGS OF THE SOUTH WALES INSTITUTE OF ENGINEERS
Proc W Va Acad Sci. . PROCEEDINGS OF THE WEST VIRGINIA ACADEMY OF SCIENCE
Prod Eng. . . . . PRODUCT ENGINEERING
Prod Eng (Lond). . . . PRODUCTION ENGINEER (LONDON)
Prod Eng (New York). . PRODUCT ENGINEERING (NEW YORK)
Prod Engr. . . . . PRODUCTION ENGINEER
Prod Finish. . . . . . . PRODUCT FINISHING
Prod Finish (Cinci). . PRODUCTS FINISHING (CINCINNATI)
Prod Finish (Lond). . PRODUCT FINISHING (LONDON)
Prod Invent Manage. . PRODUCTION & INVENTORY MANAGEMENT
Product Eng. . . . . . PRODUCT ENGINEERING
Prof Eng (Wash, D.C.). . PROFESSIONAL ENGINEER (WASHINGTON, D.C.)
Prof Geog. . . . . PROFESSIONAL GEOGRAPHER
Prof Print. . . . . PROFESSIONAL PRINTER
PROF PSYCHO. . . . . PROFESSIONAL PSYCHOLOGY
Prog. . . . . PROGRESSIVE
PROG ALLERG. . . . . PROGRESS IN ALLERGY
Prog Arch. . . . . PROGRESSIVE ARCHITECTURE
Prog Educ. . . . . PROGRESSIVE EDUCATION
PROG EX TUM. . . . . PROGRESS IN EXPERIMENTAL TUMOR RESEARCH
Prog F. . . . . PROGRESSIVE FARMER AND FARM WOMAN
PROG FISH-C. . . . . . PROGRESSIVE FISH-CULTURIST
Prog Grocer. . . . . . PROGRESSIVE GROCER
PROG LEARN. . . . . . PROGRAMMED LEARNING AND EDUCATIONAL TECHNOLOGY
Prog Mater Sci. . . . PROGRESS IN MATERIALS SCIENCE
PROG MAT SC. . . . . PROGRESS IN MATERIALS SCIENCE
PROG MED GE. . . . . PROGRESS IN MEDICAL GENETICS
PROG MED VI. . . . . PROGRESS IN MEDICAL VIROLOGY
Prog Org Coatings. . PROGRESS IN ORGANIC COATINGS
Prog Powder Metall. . PROGRESS IN POWDER METALLURGY
PROGR CARD. . . . . PROGRESS IN CARDIOVASCULAR DISEASES
Progr Contr Eng. . . . PROGRESS IN CONTROL ENGINEERING
Progres Arch. . . . . . PROGRESSIVE ARCHITECTURE

Progres Ed . . . . PROGRESSIVE EDUCATION
Progr Mater Sci . . . . PROGRESS IN MATERIALS SCIENCE
Progr Nucl Energy Ser I Phys Math . . PROGRESS IN NUCLEAR ENERGY. SERIES I. PHYSICS AND MATHEMATICS
Progr Nucl Energy Ser II Reactors . . PROGRESS IN NUCLEAR ENERGY. SERIES II. REACTORS
Progr Nucl Energy Ser III Process Chem . . PROGRESS IN NUCLEAR ENERGY. SERIES III. PROCESS CHEMISTRY
Progr Nucl Energy Ser IV Technol Eng . . PROGRESS IN NUCLEAR ENERGY. SERIES IV. TECHNOLOGY AND ENGINEERING
Progr Nucl Energy Ser V Met Fuels . . PROGRESS IN NUCLEAR ENERGY. SERIES V. METALLURGY AND FUELS
Progr Nucl Energy Ser VIII Econ . . PROGRESS IN NUCLEAR ENERGY. SERIES VIII. ECONOMICS
Progr Nucl Energy Ser X Law Admin . . PROGRESS IN NUCLEAR ENERGY. SERIES X. LAW AND ADMINISTRATION
Progr Nucl Energy Ser XI Plasma Phys Thermonucl Res . . PROGRESS IN NUCLEAR ENERGY. SERIES XI. PLASMA PHYSICS AND THERMONUCLEAR RESEARCH
Progr Plast . . . . PROGRESSIVE PLASTICS
Progr Powder Met . . PROGRESS IN POWDER METALLURGY
Progr Rubber Technol . . PROGRESS OF RUBBER TECHNOLOGY
Progr Stiintei . . . . . . PROGRESELE STIINTEI
PROG SURG . . . . PROGRESS IN SURGERY
PROG T PHYS . . . . . PROGRESS OF THEORETICAL PHYSICS
Promoclim Ind Therm Aerauliques . . PROMOCLIM, INDUSTRIES THERMIQUES ET AERAULIQUES
Pros . . . . PROSPETTI
Prosp R . . . . PROSPECTIVE REVIEW
PROSTAGLAND . . . . PROSTAGLANDINS
Prot Metals . . . . PROTECTION OF METALS
Prov . . . . PROVINCIA
Prov . . . . PROVINCIAL
P ROY S MED . . . . . . PROCEEDINGS OF THE ROYAL SOCIETY OF MEDICINE
P ROY SOC A . . . . . . PROCEEDINGS OF THE ROYAL SOCIETY. LONDON. SERIES A. MATHEMATICAL AND PHYSICAL SCIENCES
P ROY SOC B . . . . . . PROCEEDINGS OF THE ROYAL SOCIETY. LONDON. SERIES B. BIOLOGICAL SCIENCES
PrPol . . . . PRACE POLONISTYCZNE
PrS . . . . PRAIRIE SCHOONER
Prsb Q . . . . PRESBYTERIAN QUARTERLY REVIEW
PRSE . . . . PROCEEDINGS OF THE ROYAL SOCIETY OF EDINBURGH
P RS EDIN A . . . . . . PROCEEDINGS OF THE ROYAL SOCIETY OF EDINBURGH. SECTION A. MATHEMATICS
P RS EDIN B . . . . . . PROCEEDINGS OF THE ROYAL SOCIETY OF EDINBURGH. SECTION B. NATURAL ENVIRONMENT
PRT Polym Age . . . . PRT POLYMER AGE
PRu . . . . PAEDAGOGISCHE RUNDSCHAU
PRv . . . . PHILOSOPHICAL REVIEW
PrZ . . . . PRAEHISTORISCHE ZEITSCHRIFT
Przegl Bibl . . . . PRZEGLAD BIBLIOTECZNY
Przegl Elektron . . . . PRZEGLAD ELEKTRONIKI
Przegl Elektrotech . . PRZEGLAD ELEKTROTECHNICZNY
Przegl Gorn . . . . PRZEGLAD GORNICZY
Przegl Mech . . . . . . PRZEGLAD MECHANICZNY
PRZEMY CHEM . . . . PRZEMYSL CHEMICZNY
PrzH . . . . PRZEGLAD HUMANISTYCZNY
PrzK . . . . PRZEGLAD KULTURALNY
PrzO . . . . PRZEGLAD ORIENTALISTYCZNY
PrzZ . . . . PRZEGLAD ZACHODNI
PS . . . . PACIFIC SPECTATOR
PS . . . . PAMIETNIK SLOWIANSKI
PS . . . . PEDAGOGICAL SEMINARY AND JOURNAL OF GENETIC PSYCHOLOGY

PS . . . . PENSIERO E SCUOLA
PS . . . . PLANET STORIES
PS . . . . POLITICAL STUDIES
PS . . . . PRAIRIE SCHOONER
PS . . . . PRAVOSLAVNYI SOBESIEDNIK
PSA . . . . PAPELES DE SON ARMADANS
PSAM . . . . PUBLICATIONS DU SERVICE DES ANTIQUITES DU MAROC
PsaQ . . . . PSYCHOANALYTIC QUARTERLY
PsaR . . . . PSYCHOANALYTIC REVIEW
PSAS . . . . PAPERS IN INTERNATIONAL STUDIES, AFRICA SERIES (OHIO)
PSb . . . . PALESTINSKIJ SBORNIK
PsB . . . . PSYCHOLOGICAL BULLETIN
PSBA . . . . PROCEEDINGS OF THE SOCIETY OF BIBLICAL ARCHAEOLOGY
P Sch . . . . PRAIRIE SCHOONER
P S CONF CO . . . . . . PROCEEDINGS OF THE SOUTHERN CONFERENCE ON CORRECTIONS
PSE . . . . PRAGUE STUDIES IN ENGLISH
PSE . . . . PRINCETON STUDIES IN ENGLISH
PSEKUT . . . . PAAR SAMMUKEST EESTI KIRJANDUSE UURIMISE TEED
PSHADL . . . . PUBLICATIONS DE LA SOCIETE HISTORIQUE ET ARCHEOLOGIQUE DANS LE DUCHE DE LIMBOURG
PSHAL . . . . PUBLICATIONS DE LA SOCIETE HISTORIQUE ET ARCHEOLOGIQUE DANS LE DUCHE DE LIMBOURG
PSHIGDL . . . . PUBLICATIONS DE LA SECTION HISTORIQUE DE L'INSTITUT GRAND-DUCAL DE LUXEMBOURG
PSHIL . . . . PUBLICATIONS DE LA SECTION HISTORIQUE DE L'INSTITUT GRAND-DUCAL DE LUXEMBOURG
PSHL . . . . PUBLICATIONS DE LA SOCIETE HISTORIQUE ET ARCHEOLOGIQUE DANS LE LIMBOURG
PSJ . . . . PHILOSOPHICAL STUDIES OF JAPAN
PSKJ . . . . PITANJA SAVREMENOG KNJIZEVNOG JEZIKA
PSLC . . . . PAWATHY STARE LITERATURY CESKE
PSM . . . . PHILIPPINE STUDIES (MANILA)
PSM . . . . PYTANNJA SLOV'JANS'KOHO MOVOZNAVSTVA
PSML . . . . PRAGUE STUDIES IN MATHEMATICAL LINGUISTICS
PSoc . . . . PRZEGLAD SOCJOLOGICZNY
P SOC EXP M . . . . . . PROCEEDINGS OF THE SOCIETY FOR EXPERIMENTAL BIOLOGY AND MEDICINE
PSp . . . . PACIFIC SPECTATOR
PSP . . . . PROVINCIA DE SAO PEDRO (BRAZIL)
PSPOS . . . . PHILOLOGICAL SOCIETY PUBLICATIONS (OCCASIONAL STUDIES)
PSQ . . . . PHILOLOGISCHE STUDIEN UND QUELLEN
PSQ . . . . POLITICAL SCIENCE QUARTERLY
PSR . . . . PHILIPPINE SOCIOLOGICAL REVIEW
PsR . . . . PSYCHOANALYTIC REVIEW
PsR . . . . PSYCHOLOGICAL REVIEW
PSSEAS . . . . PAPERS IN INTERNATIONAL STUDIES. SOUTHEAST ASIA SERIES (OHIO)
PSSGL . . . . PENN STATE SERIES IN GERMAN LITERATURE
PSSHR . . . . PHILIPPINE SOCIAL SCIENCES AND HUMANITIES REVIEW
PSSS . . . . PROCEEDINGS OF THE SHEVCHENKO SCIENTIFIC SOCIETY. PHILOLOGICAL SECTION
PSSSP . . . . PROCEEDINGS OF THE SHEVCHENKO SCIENTIFIC SOCIETY. PHILOLOGICAL SECTION
PST . . . . PHILOLOGICAL SOCIETY. TRANSACTIONS
PSU-ADA . . . . PENNSYLVANIA STATE UNIVERSITY—ABSTRACTS OF DOCTORAL DISSERTATIONS
PSuQ . . . . PHILOLOGISCHE STUDIEN UND QUELLEN
PsyAb . . . . PSYCHOLOGICAL ABSTRACTS
Psych Bull . . . . PSYCHOLOGICAL BULLETIN
PSYCHIAT CL . . . . . . PSYCHIATRIA CLINICA
PSYCHIAT FO . . . . . . PSYCHIATRIC FORUM

PERIODICAL TITLE ABBREVIATIONS

PSYCHIAT ME..... PSYCHIATRY IN MEDICINE
PSYCHIAT Q...... PSYCHIATRIC QUARTERLY
Psychic R........ PSYCHICAL REVIEW
Psychoanal R...... PSYCHOANALYTIC REVIEW
PSYCHOAN Q...... PSYCHOANALYTIC QUARTERLY
PSYCHOAN RE..... PSYCHOANALYTIC REVIEW
Psych of Music.... PSYCHOLOGY OF MUSIC
PSYCHOL AFR..... PSYCHOLOGIA AFRICANA
PSYCHOL B....... PSYCHOLOGICAL BULLETIN
PSYCHOL BE...... PSYCHOLOGISCHE BEITRAEGE
PSYCHOL BEL...... PSYCHOLOGICA BELGICA
Psychol Bul....... PSYCHOLOGICAL BULLETIN
Psychol Clinic..... PSYCHOLOGICAL CLINIC
PSYCHOL ERZ..... PSYCHOLOGIE IN ERZIEHUNG UND UNTERRICHT
PSYCHOL FR...... PSYCHOLOGIE FRANCAISE
Psychol in the Schs.. PSYCHOLOGY IN THE SCHOOLS
PSYCHOL ISS...... PSYCHOLOGICAL ISSUES
PSYCHOL MED.... PSYCHOLOGICAL MEDICINE
Psychol R........ PSYCHOLOGICAL REVIEW
PSYCHOL REC..... PSYCHOLOGICAL RECORD
PSYCHOL REP..... PSYCHOLOGICAL REPORTS
PSYCHOL RES...... PSYCHOLOGICAL RESEARCH
PSYCHOL REV..... PSYCHOLOGICAL REVIEW
Psychol Sch....... PSYCHOLOGY IN THE SCHOOLS
PSYCHOL STU..... PSYCHOLOGICAL STUDIES
PSYCHOL TOD..... PSYCHOLOGY TODAY
PSYCHOMETRI..... PSYCHOMETRIKA
PSYCHOP AFR..... PSYCHOPATHOLOGIE AFRICAINE
PSYCHOPHARM.... PSYCHOPHARMACOLOGIA
PSYCHOPH C...... PSYCHOPHARMACOLOGY COMMUNICATIONS
PSYCHOPHYSL..... PSYCHOPHYSIOLOGY
PSYCHOS MED..... PSYCHOSOMATIC MEDICINE
PSYCHOSOMAT.... PSYCHOSOMATICS
PSYCHOTH MP.... PSYCHOTHERAPIE UND MEDIZINISCHE PSYCHOLOGIE
PSYCHOTH PS..... PSYCHOTHERAPY AND PSYCHOSOMATICS
PSYCHOTH/TR..... PSYCHOTHERAPY: THEORY, RESEARCH AND PRACTICE
PSYCH PRAX...... PSYCHOLOGISCHE PRAXIS
Psych Teaching.... PSYCHOLOGY TEACHING
PsyR............ PSYCHOANALYTIC REVIEW
Psy Rund........ PSYCHOLOGISCHE RUNDSCHAU
PsyS............ PSYCHONOMIC SCIENCE
PSzL............ POLSKA SZTUKA LUDOWA
PT............ PAMIETNIK TEATRALNY
PT............ PRZEGLAD TEOLOGICZNY
PT............ PSYCHOLOGY TODAY
PT............ PYTANNJA TEKSTOLOHIJI
PTA Mag......... PTA MAGAZINE
PTATOC......... PROCEEDINGS AND TRANSACTIONS OF THE ALL-INDIA ORIENTA CONFERENCES
PTC J.......... PATENT, TRADEMARK, AND COPYRIGHT JOURNAL
Ptd Salemanship... PRINTED SALESMANSHIP
PTFS........... PUBLICATIONS OF THE TEXAS FOLKLORE SOCIETY

Ptg Art . . . . PRINTING ART
PTPN . . . . POZNANSKIE TOWARZYSTWO PRZYJACIOL NAUK
PTR . . . . PRINCETON THEOLOGICAL REVIEW
Ptr Ink . . . . PRINTERS' INK
Ptr Ink Mo . . . . PRINTERS' INK MONTHLY
PTRSC . . . . PROCEEDINGS & TRANSACTIONS ROYAL SOCIETY OF CANADA
PU . . . . PROBLEMI DI ULISSE
PUASAL . . . . PROCEEDINGS OF THE UTAH ACADEMY OF SCIENCES, ARTS, & LETTERS
PUB . . . . PACIFIC UNIVERSITY BULLETIN
Pub . . . . PUBLISHER
Pub Adm R . . . . . . PUBLIC ADMINISTRATION REVIEW
Pub Archives Can Report . . PUBLIC ARCHIVES OF CANADA. REPORT
PUB AST S J . . . . . . PUBLICATIONS OF THE ASTRONOMICAL SOCIETY OF JAPAN
PUB AST S P . . . . . . PUBLICATIONS OF THE ASTRONOMICAL SOCIETY OF THE PACIFIC
Pub Circ . . . . PUBLISHERS' CIRCULAR AND BOOKSELLERS' RECORD
Pub Contract L J . . . PUBLIC CONTRACT LAW JOURNAL
PUB DOM AST . . . . . PUBLICATIONS OF THE DOMINION OF THE ASTROPHYSICAL OBSERVATORY
Pub Health Nurs . . . PUBLIC HEALTH NURSING
Pub Health Rep . . . . PUBLIC HEALTH REPORTS
Pub Interest . . . . . . PUBLIC INTEREST
Pub L . . . . PUBLIC LAW
PUBL ADM AU . . . . . PUBLIC ADMINISTRATION (AUSTRALIA)
PUBL ADM LO . . . . . PUBLIC ADMINISTRATION (LONDON)
PUBL ADM RE . . . . . PUBLIC ADMINISTRATION REVIEW
PUBL ADM SY . . . . . PUBLIC ADMINISTRATION (SYDNEY)
PUBL AFF B . . . . PUBLIC AFFAIRS BULLETIN
Publ Cleans . . . . PUBLIC CLEANSING
PUBL ETHNOL . . . . . PUBLICATIONS IN ETHNOLOGY
PUBL FINAN . . . . . . PUBLIC FINANCE
PUBL FIN Q . . . . PUBLIC FINANCE QUARTERLY
PUBL HEAL . . . . PUBLIC HEALTH. THE JOURNAL OF THE SOCIETY OF COMMUNITY MEDICINE
PUBL HEAL R . . . . . . PUBLIC HEALTH REVIEW
PUBL HEA RE . . . . . . PUBLIC HEALTH REPORTS
Publ Hung Res Inst Mining . . PUBLICATIONS OF THE HUNGARIAN RESEARCH INSTITUTE FOR MINING
Pub Lib . . . . PUBLIC LIBRARIES
Pub Lib Trustee . . . . PUBLIC LIBRARY TRUSTEE
Public Adm R . . . . . . PUBLIC ADMINISTRATION REVIEW
Public Lib . . . . PUBLIC LIBRARIES
Publ Inst Estatica Fac Ing Agrimensura Univ Repub Orient Uruguay . . PUBLICACION DEL INSTITUTO DE ESTATICA. FACULTAD DE INGENIERIA Y AGRIMENSURA. UNIVERSIDAD DE LA REPUBLICA ORIENTAL DEL URUGUAY. MONTEVIDEO
Publ Inst Rech Siderurg Ser A . . PUBLICATIONS DE L'INSTITUT DE RECHERCHES DE LA SIDERURGIE (SAINT-GERMAIN-EN-LAYE) SERIE A
PUBL INTER . . . . PUBLIC INTEREST
PUBLIUS J F . . . . PUBLIUS. JOURNAL OF FEDERALISM
Publ Lab Photoelasticite Ecole Polytech Fed Zurich . . PUBLICATIONS DU LABORATOIRE DE PHOTOELASTICITE. ECOLE POLYTECHNIQUE FEDERALE. ZURICH
Publ Ltg . . . . PUBLIC LIGHTING
PUBL OPIN Q . . . . . . PUBLIC OPINION QUARTERLY
PUBL PERS M . . . . . . PUBLIC PERSONNEL MANAGEMENT
PUBL POLICY . . . . . . PUBLIC POLICY

PUBL ROADS . . . . . . PUBLIC ROADS
Publ Sci Tech Min Air . . PUBLICATIONS SCIENTIFIQUES ET TECHNIQUES DU MINISTERE DE L'AIR (FRANCE)
Publ Sci Tech Min Air Bull Serv Tech . . PUBLICATIONS SCIENTIFIQUES ET TECHNIQUES DU MINISTERE DE L'AIR (FRANCE). BULLETINS DES SERVICES TECHNIQUES
Publ Sci Tech Min Air Notes Tech . . PUBLICATIONS SCIENTIFIQUES ET TECHNIQUES DU MINISTERE DE L'AIR (FRANCE). NOTES TECHNIQUES
Publ W . . . . PUBLISHERS' WEEKLY
PUBL WELFAR . . . . . PUBLIC WELFARE
Pub Mgt . . . . PUBLIC MANAGEMENT
Pub Opin . . . . PUBLIC OPINION
Pub Opinion Q . . . . . PUBLIC OPINION QUARTERLY
Pub Pol . . . . PUBLIC POLICY
Pub Rel J . . . . PUBLIC RELATIONS JOURNAL
Pub Roads . . . . PUBLIC ROADS
Pub Serv Management . . PUBLIC SERVICE MANAGEMENT
Pub Util . . . . PUBLIC UTILITIES FORTNIGHTLY
Pub W . . . . PUBLISHERS' WEEKLY
PUCalLL . . . . PUBLICATIONS OF THE UNIVERSITY OF CALIFORNIA IN LANGUAGES AND LITERATURE
PUEE . . . . PUBLICATIONS DE L'UNIVERSITE DE L'ETAT A ELISABETHVILLE
PUF . . . . PRESSES UNIVERSITAIRES DE FRANCE
PUHS . . . . PROCEEDINGS OF THE UNITARIAN HISTORICAL SOCIETY
PULC . . . . PRINCETON UNIVERSITY LIBRARY CHRONICLE
Pulp & Pa . . . . PULP AND PAPER
Pulp & Pa Can . . . . . PULP AND PAPER MAGAZINE OF CANADA
Pulp Pap Int . . . . . . PULP AND PAPER INTERNATIONAL
PUM . . . . PYTANNJA UKRAJINS'KOHO MOVOZNAVSTAVA
P U OTAGO M . . . . . PROCEEDINGS OF THE UNIVERSITY OF OTAGO MEDICAL SCHOOL
PUR A CHEM . . . . . . PURE AND APPLIED CHEMISTRY
PUR A GEOPH . . . . . PURE AND APPLIED GEOPHYSICS
PURBA . . . . PANJAB UNIVERSITY RESEARCH BULLETIN (ARTS)
Purdue Ag . . . . PURDUE AGRICULTURIST
Purdue Univ Eng Bull Eng Ext Ser . . PURDUE UNIVERSITY. ENGINEERING BULLETIN. ENGINEERING EXTENSION SERIES
Purdue Univ Eng Exp Sta Res Bull . . PURDUE UNIVERSITY. ENGINEERING EXPERIMENT STATION. RESEARCH BULLETIN
Purdue Univ Sch Aeronaut Astronaut Eng Sci Res Proj . . PURDUE UNIVERSITY. SCHOOL OF AERONAUTICS, ASTRONAUTICS AND ENGINEERING SCIENCES. RESEARCH PROJECT
Pure Appl Chem . . . . PURE AND APPLIED CHEMISTRY
PUSA . . . . PERSPECTIVES U.S.A.
PUSC . . . . PUBBLICAZIONI DELLA UNIVERSITA CATTOLICA DEL SACRO CUORE
Putnam . . . . PUTNAM'S MONTHLY MAGAZINE
PuW . . . . POESIE UND WISSENSCHAFT
PV . . . . POESIA E VERITA
PV . . . . PRINCIPE DE VIANA
PV . . . . PROBLEMY VOSTOKOVEDENIJA
PVS . . . . PROCEEDINGS OF THE VIRGIL SOCIETY
PW . . . . PHILOLOGISCHE WOCHENSCHRIFT
PW . . . . POETRY WALES
PW . . . . PUBLISHERS' WEEKLY
P WEST PH S . . . . . . PROCEEDINGS OF THE WESTERN PHARMACOLOGY SOCIETY
PWN . . . . POLSKIE WYDAWNICTWE NAUKOWE
Pwr Fmg . . . . POWER FARMING
Pwr Wks Engng . . . . POWER AND WORKS ENGINEERING

PWsp . . . . PRZEGLAD WSPOTCZESNY
PWT . . . . PANSTWOWE WYDAWNICTWO TECHNICZNE
PWTN-A . . . . PRACE WROCLAWSKIEGO TOWARZYSTWA NAUKOWEGO. A
PZ . . . . PRZEGLAD ZACHODNI
PZKA . . . . PHILOLOGUS. ZEITSCHRIFT FUER KLASSISCHE ALTERTUM
PZM . . . . POD ZNAMENEM MARKSIZMA
PZWS . . . . PANSTWOWE ZAKLADY WYDAWNICTW SZKOLNYCH

Q

Q . . . . QUADRIVIUM
Q . . . . QUEENS QUARTERLY
Q . . . . QUINZAINE
QAL . . . . QUADERNI DI ARCHEOLOGIA DELLA LIBIA
QAP . . . . DEPARTMENT OF ANTIQUITIES IN PALESTINE. QUARTERLY
Q Ap Math . . . . . . QUARTERLY OF APPLIED MATHEMATICS
Q APPL MATH . . . . . QUARTERLY OF APPLIED MATHEMATICS
QBib . . . . QUARTERLY BIBLIOGRAPHY OF COMPUTERS AND DATA PROCESSING
QC . . . . QUADERNI DELLA CRITICA
QCC . . . . QUADERNI DI CULTURA CONTEMPORANEA
Q Colo Sch Mines . . . QUARTERLY OF THE COLORADO SCHOOL OF MINES
QCSS . . . . QUADERNI DI CULTURA E STORIA SOCIALE
QD . . . . QUADERNI DANNUNZIANI
QeA . . . . QUESTO E ALTO
QEBG . . . . QUELLEN UND EROERTERUNGEN ZUR BAYERISCHEN GESCHICHTE
QF . . . . QUELLEN UND FORSCHUNGEN AUS ITALIENISCHEN ARCHIVEN UND BIBLIOTHEKEN
QF . . . . QUELLEN UND FORSCHUNGEN ZUR SPRACH- UND KULTUR- GESCHICHTE DER GERMANISCHEN
              VOELKER
QFAB . . . . QUELLEN UND FORSCHUNGEN AUS ITALIENISCHEN ARCHIVEN UND BIBLIOTHEKEN
QFI . . . . QUELLEN UND FORSCHUNGEN AUS ITALIENISCHEN ARCHIVEN UND BIBLIOTHEKEN
QFIAB . . . . QUELLEN UND FORSCHUNGEN AUS ITALIENISCHEN ARCHIVEN UND BIBLIOTHEKEN
Q Film Radio TV . . . . QUARTERLY OF FILM, RADIO, AND TELEVISION
QFRT . . . . QUARTERLY OF FILM, RADIO, AND TELEVISION
QFSK . . . . QUELLEN UND FORSCHUNGEN ZUR SPRACH- UND KULTURGESCHICHTE DER GERMANISCHEN
              VOELKER, N.F.
QGHR . . . . QUELLEN ZUR GESCHICHTE DES HUMANISMUS UND DER REFORMATION IN FACSIMILE-
              AUSGABEN
QGM . . . . QUELLEN UND STUDIEN ZUR GESCHICHTE DER MATHEMATIK
QGMath . . . . QUELLEN UND STUDIEN ZUR GESCHICHTE DER MATHEMATIK
QH . . . . QUAKER HISTORY
QI . . . . QUADERNI IBERO-AMERICANI
QIA . . . . QUADERNI IBERO-AMERICANI
QIBA . . . . QUADERNI ITALIANI DI BUENOS AIRES
QIG . . . . QUADERNI DELL'ISTITUTO DI GLOTTOLOGIA (BOLOGNA)
QIGB . . . . QUADERNI DELL'ISTITUTO DI GLOTTOLOGIA (BOLOGNA)
Q Illust . . . . QUARTERLY ILLUSTRATOR
QJ . . . . QUARTERLY JOURNAL OF THE UNIVERSITY OF NORTH DAKOTA
QJCA . . . . QUARTERLY JOURNAL OF CURRENT ACQUISITIONS
QJE . . . . QUARTERLY JOURNAL OF ECONOMICS
Q J ECON . . . . QUARTERLY JOURNAL OF ECONOMICS
QJEPs . . . . QUARTERLY JOURNAL OF EXPERIMENTAL PSYCHOLOGY
Q J EXP PSY . . . . . . QUARTERLY JOURNAL OF EXPERIMENTAL PSYCHOLOGY
QJLC . . . . QUARTERLY JOURNAL OF THE LIBRARY OF CONGRESS
Q J MATH . . . . QUARTERLY JOURNAL OF MATHEMATICS
Q J MECH AP . . . . . . QUARTERLY JOURNAL OF MECHANICS AND APPLIED MATHEMATICS
Q J MED . . . . QUARTERLY JOURNAL OF MEDICINE
Q Jnl Speech . . . . . . QUARTERLY JOURNAL OF SPEECH
Q J Pub Speak . . . . . QUARTERLY JOURNAL OF PUBLIC SPEAKING
Q J R ASTRO . . . . . . QUARTERLY JOURNAL OF THE ROYAL ASTRONOMICAL SOCIETY

Q J R METEO . . . . . . QUARTERLY JOURNAL OF THE ROYAL METEOROLOGICAL SOCIETY
QJS . . . . QUARTERLY JOURNAL OF SPEECH
QJSp . . . . QUARTERLY JOURNAL OF SPEECH
Q J STUD AL . . . . . . QUARTERLY JOURNAL OF STUDIES ON ALCOHOL
QL . . . . QUADERNI LINGUISTICI
QLP . . . . QUESTIONS LITURGIQUES ET PAROISSIALES
QNL . . . . QUARTERLY NEWS LETTER (BOOK CLUB OF CALIFORNIA)
QQ . . . . QUEEN'S QUARTERLY
QR . . . . QUARTERLY REVIEW
Q RASS MUS . . . . . . QUADERNI DELLA RASSEGNA MUSICALE
Q R Biol . . . . QUARTERLY REVIEW OF BIOLOGY
Q R Biophys . . . . . . QUARTERLY REVIEW OF BIOPHYSICS
QREB . . . . QUARTERLY REVIEW OF ECONOMICS AND BUSINESS
Q R ECON BU . . . . . . QUARTERLY REVIEW OF ECONOMICS AND BUSINESS
Q Rep Railw Tech Res Inst (Tokyo) . . QUARTERLY REPORT OF THE RAILWAY TECHNICAL RESEARCH INSTITUTE
(TOKYO)
Q REV BIOL . . . . . . QUARTERLY REVIEW OF BIOLOGY
Q REV BIOPH . . . . . . QUARTERLY REVIEWS OF BIOPHYSICS
Q R Higher Ed Among Negroes . . QUARTERLY REVIEW OF HIGHER EDUCATION AMONG NEGROES
QRL . . . . QUARTERLY REVIEW OF LITERATURE
QR of Lit . . . . QUARTERLY REVIEW OF LITERATURE
QSGLL . . . . QUEENSLAND STUDIES IN GERMAN LANGUAGE AND LITERATURE
QTDM . . . . QAZAQ TILI TARYCHI MEN DYALEKTOLOGYJASININ MOSELELERI
Quad . . . . QUADRIVIUM
Quad Geofis Appl . . . QUADERNI DI GEOFISICA APPLICATA
QuakerH . . . . QUAKER HISTORY
Qual Eng . . . . QUALITY ENGINEER
QUAL PLANT . . . . . . QUALITAS PLANTARUM-PLANT FOODS FOR HUMAN NUTRITION
QUAL QUANT . . . . . QUALITY AND QUANTITY
Quar . . . . QUARTERLY REVIEW
Quar Jour Econ . . . . QUARTERLY JOURNAL OF ECONOMICS
Quar R Biol . . . . QUARTERLY REVIEW OF BIOLOGY
Quar Rev . . . . QUARTERLY REVIEW
Quart Appl Math . . . QUARTERLY OF APPLIED MATHEMATICS
Quart Colo Sch Mines . . QUARTERLY OF THE COLORADO SCHOOL OF MINES
Quart J Mech Appl Math . . QUARTERLY JOURNAL OF MECHANICS AND APPLIED MATHEMATICS
Quart Rep Ry Tech Res Inst . . QUARTERLY REPORT OF THE RAILWAY TECHNICAL RESEARCH INSTITUTE (JAPAN)
QUATERN RES . . . . . QUATERNARY RESEARCH
Que Dep Natur Resour Geol Rep . . QUEBEC. DEPARTMENT OF NATURAL RESOURCES. GEOLOGICAL REPORT
Que Dep Natur Resour Prelim Rep . . QUEBEC. DEPARTMENT OF NATURAL RESOURCES. PRELIMINARY REPORT
Queensland Ag J . . . QUEENSLAND AGRICULTURAL JOURNAL
Queen's L J . . . . QUEEN'S LAW JOURNAL
Queensl Univ Dep Civ Eng Bull . . QUEENSLAND UNIVERSITY. DEPARTMENT OF CIVIL ENGINEERING. BULLETIN
Quix . . . . QUIXOTE
QV . . . . QUATRO VENTOS
QV . . . . QUO VADIS

R

R . . . . REPUBLIKA
R . . . . RIO DE JANEIRO
R . . . . ROMANIA
Ra . . . . RADUGA (MOSCOW)
Ra . . . . RASSEGNA
Ra . . . . REPERTORIO AMERICANO
RA . . . . REVUE ANGLO-AMERICAINE
RA . . . . REVUE ARCHEOLOGIQUE
RA . . . . REVUE DES ARTS
RA . . . . RHEINISCHES ARCHIV
RA . . . . ROMANISTISCHE ARBEITSHEFTE
RAA . . . . RENDICONTI DELL'ACCADEMIA DI ARCHEOLOGIA, LETTERE E BELLE ARTI
RAA . . . . REVUE ANGLO-AMERICAINE
RAA . . . . REVUE DE L'ART ANCIENT ET MODERNE
RAAM . . . . REVUE DE L'ART ANCIENT ET MODERNE
RAAN . . . . RENDICONTI DELL'ACCADEMIA DI ARCHEOLOGIA, LETTERE E BELLE ARTI. NAPOLI
RABLB . . . . REAL ACADEMIA DE BUENAS LETRAS DE BARCELONA
RABM . . . . REVISTA DE ARCHIVOS, BIBLIOTECAS Y MUSEOS
RABol . . . . RENDICONTO DELLE SESSIONI DELLA ACCADEMIA DELLE SCIENZE DELL'ISTITUTO DI BOLOGNA
RAbr . . . . RIVISTA ABRUZZESE
RAC . . . . REVUE DE L'ART CHRETIEN
RAC . . . . RIVISTA DI ARCHEOLOGIA CRISTIANA DELLA PONTIFICIA COMMISSIONE DI ARCHEOLOGIA
                        SACRA
RACathHS . . . . RECORDS OF THE AMERICAN CATHOLIC HISTORICAL SOCIETY OF PHILADELPHIA
RACF . . . . REVUE ARCHEOLOGIQUE DU CENTRE DE LA FRANCE
RACHS . . . . RECORDS OF THE AMERICAN CATHOLIC HISTORICAL SOCIETY OF PHILADELPHIA
RACHSP . . . . RECORDS OF THE AMERICAN CATHOLIC HISTORICAL SOCIETY OF PHILADELPHIA
RAD CLINICA . . . . . . RADIOLOGIA CLINICA
RAD CLIN NA . . . . . RADIOLOGIC CLINICS OF NORTH AMERICA
RAD DIAGN . . . . RADIOLOGIA DIAGNOSTICA
Radex Rundsch . . . . RADEX RUNDSCHAU
RADIAT BOT . . . . . . RADIATION BOTANY
RADIAT EFF . . . . RADIATION EFFECTS
RADIAT ENV . . . . . . RADIATION AND ENVIRONMENTAL BIOPHYSICS
RADIAT RES . . . . RADIATION RESEARCH
Radio & TV N . . . . . . RADIO AND TELEVISION NEWS
RADIOCH ACT . . . . . RADIOCHIMICA ACTA
RADIOCH RAD . . . . . RADIOCHEMICAL AND RADIOANALYTICAL LETTERS
Radio Commun . . . . RADIO COMMUNICATION
Radio Electron Commun Syst . . RADIO ELECTRONICS AND COMMUNICATION SYSTEMS
Radio Electron Eng . . RADIO AND ELECTRONIC ENGINEER
RADIO EL EN . . . . . . RADIO AND ELECTRONIC ENGINEER
Radio Eng Electron Phys . . RADIO ENGINEERING AND ELECTRONIC PHYSICS
Radio N . . . . RADIO NEWS
Radiophys Quantum Electron . . RADIOPHYSICS AND QUANTUM ELECTRONICS
RADIO SCI . . . . RADIO SCIENCE
Radio Serv Bul . . . . . RADIO SERVICE BULLETIN
RADIOTEK EL . . . . . . RADIOTEKHNIKA I ELEKTRONIKA
Radiotekh i Elektron . . RADIOTEKHNIKA I ELEKTRONIKA

RadJA . . . . RAD JUGOSLAVENSKE AKADEMIJE ZNANOSTI I UMJETNOSTI
RadL . . . . RADYANS'SKE LITERATUROZNAVSTVO (KIEV)
RadZSF . . . . RADOVI ZAVODA ZA SLAVENSKU FILOLOGIJU
RAE . . . . REAL ACADEMIA ESPANOLA
RAE . . . . REVUE ARCHEOLOGIQUE DE L'EST ET DU CENTRE-EST
RAE . . . . REVUE D'ART ET D'ESTHETIQUE
RAf . . . . REVUE AFRICAINE
R Ag Cuba . . . . REVISTA DE AGRICULTURA DE CUBA
R Ag France . . . . . . REVUE DES AGRICULTEURS DE FRANCE
RagL . . . . RAGUAGLIO LIBRARIO
RAHBol . . . . REAL ACADEMIA DE LA HISTORIA. BOLETIN
RAI . . . . RENCONTRE ASSYRIOLOGIQUE INTERNATIONALE
RAI . . . . RENDICONTI DELLA CLASSE DI SCIENZE MORALI E STORICHE DELLA ACCADEMIA D'ITALIA
Rail Eng Int . . . . . . RAIL ENGINEERING INTERNATIONAL
Rail Int . . . . RAIL INTERNATIONAL
Rail Syst Contr . . . . RAILWAY SYSTEMS CONTROL
Railw Age . . . . RAILWAY AGE
Railw Eng J . . . . . . RAILWAY ENGINEERING JOURNAL
Railw Gaz Int . . . . . RAILWAY GAZETTE INTERNATIONAL
Railw Locomot Cars . . RAILWAY LOCOMOTIVE AND CARS
Railw Manage Rev . . RAILWAY MANAGEMENT REVIEW
Railw Syst Control . . RAILWAY SYSTEMS CONTROL
Railw Track Struct . . RAILWAY TRACK AND STRUCTURES
RaKet . . . . RAHNEMA-YE KETAB
RAL . . . . RENDICONTI DELLA CLASSE DI SCIENZE MORALI E STORICHE DELL'ACCADEMIA DEI LINCIE
RAL . . . . RESEARCH IN AFRICAN LITERATURES
RAL . . . . REVISTA DAS ACADEMIAS DE LETRAS
RAlb . . . . RIVISTA D'ALBANIA
RALF . . . . REPERTOIRE ANALYTIQUE DE LITTERATURE FRANCAISE (BORDEAUX)
RALinc . . . . RENDICONTI DELLA CLASSE DI SCIENZE MORALI E STORICHE DELL'ACCADEMIA DEI LINCEI
RALincei . . . . RENDICONTI DELLA CLASSE DI SCIENZE MORALI E STORICHE DELL'ACCADEMIA DEI LINCEI
RALRend . . . . RENDICONTI DELLA CLASSE DI SCIENZE MORALI E STORICHE DELL'ACCADEMIA DEI LINCEI
RALS . . . . RESOURCES FOR AMERICAN LITERARY STUDIES
RAls . . . . REVUE D'ALSACE
RAL Scav . . . . REALE ACCADEMIA DEI LINCEI, ATTI. NOTIZIE DEGLI SCAVI
RAM . . . . REVUE D'ASCETIQUE ET DE MYSTIQUE
RAMC . . . . RASSEGNA DI ASETICA E MISTICA S. CATERINA DA SIENA
Ramp Mag . . . . RAMPARTS MAGAZINE
RAMSP . . . . REVISTA DO ARQUIVO MUNICIPAL. SAO PAULO
RAN . . . . RENDICONTI DELL'ACCADEMIA DI ARCHEOLOGIA, LETTERE E BELLE ARTI DI NAPOLI
RANAM . . . . RECHERCHES ANGLAISES ET AMERICAINES
RAND . . . . SELECTED RAND ABSTRACTS
R&C . . . . RELIGION Y CULTURA
R&O . . . . ROMA E L'ORIENTE
R&T . . . . RECHERCHES ET TRAVAUX
RANL . . . . RENDICONTI DELLA REALE ACCADEMIA NAZIONALE DEI LINCEI
RAp . . . . REVUE APOLOGETIQUE
RAP . . . . REVUE D'ARCHEOLOGIE POLONAISE
RAR . . . . RENAISSANCE AND REFORMATION
R Archeol . . . . REVUE ARCHEOLOGIQUE
RArqueol . . . . REVISTA DE ARQUEOLOGIA

RArt . . . . REVUE D'ART
RArte . . . . RIVISTA D'ARTE
R Arts . . . . REVUE DES ARTS
RAS . . . . RESSEGNA DEGLI ARCHIVI DI STATO
RAS . . . . RASSEGNA DELLA LETTERATURA ITALIANA
RAS . . . . REVUE ARCHEOLOGIQUE SYRIENNE
RASA . . . . RASSEGNA ABRUZZESE DI STORIA ED ARTE
R Ascetique & Mystique . . REVUE D'ASCETIQUE ET DE MYSTIQUE
RasF . . . . RASSEGNA DI FILOSOFIA
Rasl . . . . RASSEGNA ITALIANA
RASIB . . . . RENDICONTO DELLA ACCADEMIA DELLE SCIENZE DELL'ISTITUTO DI BOLOGNA
RAss . . . . REVUE D'ASSYRIOLOGIE ET D'ARCHEOLOGIE ORIENTALE
RassCult . . . . RASSEGNA DI CULTURA
Rass d'It . . . . RASSEGNA D'ITALIA
Rassegna Ital Sociol . . RASSEGNA ITALIANA DE SOCIOLOGIA
RassFilos . . . . RASSEGNA DI FILOSOFIA
Rass Mus . . . . RASSEGNA MUSICALE
RASS MUS CURCI . . . RASSEGNA MUSICALE CURCI
RAug . . . . REVUE AUGUSTINIENNE
RAut&L . . . . REVUE DES AUTEURS ET DES LIVRES
RAuv . . . . REVUE D'AUVERGNE
Rayon . . . . RAYON AND SYNTHETIC TEXTILES
Razved i Okhr Nedr . . RAZVEDKA I OKHRANA NEDR
RB . . . . REVISTA BIBLIOTECILOR (BUCHAREST)
RB . . . . REVUE BENEDICTINE
RB . . . . REVUE BIBLIQUE
RB . . . . REVUE BOSSUET
RBA . . . . REVUE BELGE D'ARCHEOLOGIE ET D'HISTOIRE DE L'ART
RBAA . . . . REVUE BELGE D'ART ET D'ARCHEOLOGIE
RBAB . . . . REVUE DES BIBLIOTHEQUES ET DES ARCHIVES DE LA BELGIQUE
RBAHA . . . . REVUE BELGE D'ARCHEOLOGIE ET D'HISTOIRE DE L'ART
RBAM . . . . REVISTA DE LA BIBLIOTECA, ARCHIVO Y MUSEO DEL AYUNTAMIENTO DE MADRID
RBAMM . . . . REVISTA DE LA BIBLIOTECA, ARCHIVO Y MUSEO DEL AYUNTAMIENTO DE MADRID
RBB . . . . REVUE BIBLIOGRAPHIQUE BELGE
RBC . . . . REVISTA BIMESTRE CUBANA
RBD . . . . REVISTA BIBLIOGRAFICA Y DOCUMENTAL
RBdeF . . . . REVISTA BRASILEIRA DE FILOSOFIA
R Belge Archeol . . . . REVUE BELGE D'ARCHEOLOGIE ET D'HISTOIRE D'ART
R Belge Mus . . . . . . REVUE BELGE DE MUSICOLOGIE
R Belge Philol & Hist . . REVUE BELGE DE PHILOLOGIE ET D'HISTOIRE
RBen . . . . REVUE BENEDICTINE
RBF . . . . REVISTA BRASILEIRA DE FILOSOFIA
RBF . . . . REVISTA BRASILEIRA DE FOLCLORE
RBFI . . . . REVISTA BRASILEIRA DE FILOLOGIA
RBFilol . . . . REVISTA BRASILEIRA DE FILOLOGIA
RBGd . . . . ROCZNIK BIBLIOTEKI GDANSKIEJ PAN
RBHGPV . . . . RHEINISCHE BEITRAEGE UND HILFSBUECHER ZUR GERMANISCHEN PHILOLOGIE UND VOLKSKUNDE
RBi . . . . REVUE BIBLIQUE
RBib . . . . REVUE BIBLIQUE
R Biblio Brasilia . . . . REVISTA DE BIBLIOTECONOMIA DE BRASILIA

R Bibl Nac (Cuba).. REVISTA DE LA BIBLIOTECA NACIONAL
RBKr . . . . ROCZNIK BIBLIOTEKI PAN W KRAKOWIE
RBL . . . . REVUE BLEUE
R Black Pol Econ . . . REVIEW OF BLACK POLITICAL ECONOMY
RBLI . . . . RASSEGNA BIBLIOGRAFICA DELLA LETTERATURA ITALIANA
RBM . . . . REVUE BELGE DE MUSICOLOGIE
RBMus . . . . REVUE BELGE DE MUSICOLOGIE
RBN . . . . REVISTA DE BIBLIOGRAFIA NACIONAL
RBN . . . . REVUE BELGE DE NUMISMATIQUE
RBNC . . . . REVISTA DE LA BIBLIOTECA NACIONAL DE CUBA
RBNH . . . . REVISTA DE LA BIBLIOTECA NACIONAL (HAVANA) DE CUBA
RBNS . . . . REVUE BELGE DE NUMISMATIQUE ET DE SIGILLOGRAPHIE
RBPh . . . . REVUE BELGE DE PHILOLOGIE ET D'HISTOIRE
RBques . . . . REVUE DES BIBLIOTHEQUES
RBr . . . . REVISTA BRASILIENSE
RBRJ . . . . REVISTA BRASILEIRA (RIO DE JANEIRO)
R Bryol & Lichenol . . REVUE BRYOLOGIQUE ET LICHENOLOGIQUE
RC . . . . REVIEW OF THE CHURCHES
RC . . . . REVISTA CONTEMPORANEA
RC . . . . REVISTA CUBANA
RC . . . . REVUE CELTIQUE
RC . . . . REVUE CHARLEMAGNE
RC . . . . REVUE CRITIQUE
RC . . . . RIVISTA DELLE COLONIE
RC . . . . RUPERTO-CAROLA
RCA . . . . REVISTA COLOMBIANA DE ANTROPOLOGIA
RCal . . . . REVISTA CALASANCIA
RCAls . . . . REVUE CATHOLIQUE D'ALSACE
RCam . . . . REVISTA CAMONIANA (SAO PAULO)
RCan . . . . REVUE CANONIQUE
RCA Rev . . . . RCA (RADIO CORPORATION OF AMERICA) REVIEW
RCat . . . . REVISTA DE CATALUNYA
RCAV . . . . ROZPRAVY CESKOSLOVENSKE AKADEMIE VED
RCB . . . . REVISTA DE CULTURA BRASILENA
RCC . . . . REVUE DES COURS ET CONFERENCES
RCCM . . . . RIVISTA DI CULTURA CLASSICA E MEDIEVALE
RCCS . . . . REVISTA CATOLICA DE LAS CUESTIONES SOCIALES
RCE . . . . REVUE CATHOLIQUE DES EGLISES
RCEE . . . . REVISTA DEL CENTRO DE ESTUDIOS EXTEMOENOS
RCel . . . . REVUE CELTIQUE
RCF . . . . REVISTA COLOMBIANA DE FOLCLOR
RCF . . . . REVUE DU CLERGE FRANCAIS
RCG . . . . REVUE DU CHANT GREGORIEN
RCh . . . . REVUE CHARLEMAGNE
RCHG . . . . REVISTA CHILENA DE HISTORIA Y GEOGRAFIA
RChL . . . . REVISTA CHILENA DE LITERATURA
RCHL . . . . REVUE CRITIQUE D'HISTOIRE ET DE LITTERATURE
RCI . . . . RIVISTA DELLE COLONIE ITALIANE
RCID . . . . REVUE CATHOLIQUE DES INSTITUTIONS ET DE DROIT
RCivB . . . . REVISTA CIVILIZACAO BRASILEIRA (RIO)
RCJS . . . . REVISTA DE CIENCIAS JURIDICAS Y SOCIALES

RCl . . . . RIVISTA CLASICA
RCLI . . . . RASSEGNA CRITICA DELLA LETTERATURA ITALIANA
RCM . . . . ROYAL COLLEGE OF MUSIC MAGAZINE
RCMUH . . . . RUPERTO-CAROLA MITTEILUNGEN DER VEREINIGUNG DER FREUNDE DER STUDENTENSCHAFT DER UNIVERSITAET HEIDELBERG
RCol . . . . RASSEGNA DI COLTURA
RColt . . . . RASSEGNA DI COLTURA
RCong . . . . REVUE CONGOLAISE
RCr . . . . REVUE CRITIQUE
RCRF . . . . REI CRETARIAE ROMANAE FAUTORUM ACTA
RcRt . . . . ROMANTIC REASSESSMENT
RCSAV . . . . ROZPRAVY CESKOSLOVENSKE AKADEMIE VED
RCSF . . . . RIVISTA CRITICA DELLA STORIA DELLA FILOSOFIA
RCSH . . . . REVUE CONGOLAISE DES SCIENCES HUMAINES
RCVS . . . . RASSEGNA DI CULTURA E VITA SCOLASTICA
RD . . . . RENAISSANCE DRAMA
RD . . . . REVUE HISTORIQUE DE DROIT FRANCAIS ET ETRANGER
RD . . . . RIVISTA DALMATICA
RD . . . . REVISTA DE DIALECTOLOGIA Y TRADICIONES POPULARES
RDAC . . . . REPORT OF THE DEPARTMENT OF ANTIQUITIES OF CYPRUS
RdC . . . . RESTO DEL CARLINO
RDC . . . . REVUE DE DROIT CANONIQUE
RdDM . . . . REVUE DES DEUX MONDES
RddxM . . . . REVUE DES DEUX MONDES
RdE . . . . REVISTA DE LAS ESPANAS
RDE . . . . REVUE D'ESTHETIQUE
RdE . . . . RIVISTA DI ESTETICA
R de Ag Cuba . . . . . . REVISTA DE AGRICULTURA (CUBA)
R DE GEOG DE MTL . . REVUE DE GEOGRAPHIE DE MONTREAL
RdelE . . . . REVISTA DE IDEAS ESTETICAS
RdeInd . . . . REVISTA DE INDIAS
R DE L UNIV DE SHERBROOKE . . REVUE DE L'UNIVERSITE DE SHERBROOKE
R DE L UNIV D OTT . . REVUE DE L'UNIVERSITE D'OTTAWA
R DE L UNIV LAVAL . . REVUE DE L'UNIVERSITE LAVAL
R DE MU . . . . REVUE DE MUSICOLOGIE
R de Paris . . . . REVUE DE PARIS
R Des Arts . . . . REVUE DES ARTS
R D'ESTHETIQUE . . . REVUE D'ESTHETIQUE
RdEt . . . . REVISTA DE ETNOGRAFIA
R Deux Mondes . . . . REVUE DES DEUX MONDES
RDF . . . . REVUE DE FRANCE
RdF . . . . RIVISTA DI FILOSOFIA (TORINO)
RdH . . . . REVISTA DE HISTORIA
R D'HIST . . . . REVUE D'HISTOIRE DE L'AMERIQUE FRANCAISE
R Dialect & Tradic Popul . . REVISTA DE DIALECTOLOGIA Y TRADICIONES POPULARES
RdiE . . . . RIVISTA DI ESTETICA
RdiF . . . . RIVISTA DI FILOSOFIA
RdL . . . . REVISTA DE LETRAS
RdL . . . . REVISTA DO LIVRO
RdM . . . . REVUE DE LA MEDITERRANEE
RdM . . . . REVUE DE MUSICOLOGIE

```
RDM............ REVUE DES DEUX MONDES
RDN............ REVUE DU NORD
RdP............ REVUE DE PARIS
RdPac.......... REVISTA DEL PACIFICO
RDR............ RYUKOKU DAIGAKU RONSHU (RYUKOKU KAIGAKU JOURNAL)
R/D Res/Develop... R/D, RESEARCH/DEVELOPMENT
RdS............ RESPONSABILITA DEL SAPERE
RdSO.......... RIVISTA DEGLI STUDI ORIENTALI (ROMA)
Rds Rd Constn..... ROADS AND ROAD CONSTRUCTION
RdT............ REVISTA DE TEATRO
RDTP.......... REVISTA DE DIALECTOLOGIA Y TRADICIONES POPULARES
R du Louvre....... REVUE DU LOUVRE ET DES MUSEES DE FRANCE
R du XVIe S....... REVUE DE SEIZIEME SIECLE
RDyTP......... REVISTA DE DIALECTOLOGIA Y TRADICIONES POPULARES
Re............. REALIDAD
RE............. REVISTA ECLESIASTICA
RE............. REVUE D'EGYPTOLOGIE
RE............. REVUE D'ESTHETIQUE
RE............. REVUE EGYPTOLOGIQUE
REA........... REVUE DES ETUDES ANCIENNES
REA........... REVUE DES ETUDES ARMENIENNES
REA........... REVUE DES ETUDES AUGUSTINIENNES
REACT KIN C...... REACTION KINETICS AND CATALYSIS LETTERS
Reactor Mater..... REACTOR MATERIALS
Read Digest...... READER'S DIGEST
Reader......... READER MAGAZINE
Read Improv...... READING IMPROVEMENT
READ RES Q....... READING RESEARCH QUARTERLY
Read Teach...... READING TEACHER
REAL.......... RE: ARTS AND LETTERS
Real Estate L J .... REAL ESTATE LAW JOURNAL
REAL EST L....... REAL ESTATE LAW JOURNAL
REAL EST RE...... REAL ESTATE REVIEW
Real Ist Veneto Mem.. REALE ISTITUTO VENETO DI SCIENZE, LETTERE ED ARTI. MEMORIE
RealM.......... REALTA DEL MEZZOGIORNO
RealN.......... REALTA NUOVA
REAL PROP P...... REAL PROPERTY, PROBATE AND TRUST JOURNAL
REAnc.......... REVUE DES ETUDES ANCIENNES
REArm......... REVUE DES ETUDES ARMENIENNES
REArmNS........ REVUE DES ETUDES ARMENIENNES. NOUVELLE SERIE
REAug......... REVUE DES ETUDES AUGUSTINIENNES
REB........... REVUE DES ETUDES BYZANTINES
REB........... REVUE INTERNATIONALE DES ETUDES BALKANIQUES
REBras......... REVISTA ECLESIASTICA BRASILEIRA
REByz......... REVUE DES ETUDES BYZANTINES
Rec........... RECURRENCE
REC........... REVISTA DE ESTUDIOS CLASICOS
RecAug......... RECHERCHES AUGUSTINIENNES
Rec Changer..... RECORD CHANGER
REC COLL....... RECORD COLLECTOR
Rec Geol Surv India.. RECORDS OF THE GEOLOGICAL SURVEY OF INDIA
```

RecH . . . . RECUSANT HISTORY
RechA . . . . RECHERCHES AUGUSTINIENNES
RECH AEROSP . . . . . RECHERCHE AEROSPATIALE
Rech Sci Rel . . . . RECHERCHES DE SCIENCE RELIGIEUSE
Rech Sociographiques . . RECHERCHES SOCIOGRAPHIQUES
RechSR . . . . RECHERCHES DE SCIENCE RELIGIEUSE
RechTh . . . . RECHERCHES DE THEOLOGIE ANCIENNE ET MEDIEVALE
RECLAM ERA . . . . . . RECLAMATION ERA
R Econ & Stat . . . . . . REVIEW OF ECONOMICS AND STATISTICS
RECONS SURG . . . . . RECONSTRUCTION SURGERY AND TRAUMATOLOGY
R Econ Statistics . . . REVIEW OF ECONOMICS AND STATISTICS
R Econ Stud . . . . REVIEW OF ECONOMIC STUDIES
Record . . . . RECORD OF THE ASSOCIATION OF THE BAR OF THE CITY OF NEW YORK
RECORDER & MUS MAG . . RECORDER AND MUSIC MAGAZINE
RECorses . . . . REVUE DES ETUDES CORSES
RecPap . . . . RECHERCHES DE PAPYROLOGIE
Rec Past . . . . RECORDS OF THE PAST
RecPh . . . . RECHERCHES PHILOSOPHIQUES
Rec Res . . . . RECORD RESEARCH
Recr Sci . . . . RECREATIVE SCIENCE
RecS . . . . RECORDED SOUND
REC SOUND . . . . . . RECORDED SOUND
RecSR . . . . RECHERCHES DE SCIENCE RELIGIEUSE
RecTh . . . . RECHERCHES DE THEOLOGIE ANCIENNE ET MEDIEVALE
RECTR . . . . RESTORATION AND EIGHTEENTH CENTURY THEATRE RESEARCH
REC TR CHIM . . . . . . RECUEIL DES TRAVAUX CHIMIQUES DES PAYS-BAS
REDC . . . . REVISTA ESPANOLA DE DERECHO CANONICO
Red Cross M . . . . . . RED CROSS MAGAZINE
R Ed Res . . . . REVIEW OF EDUCATIONAL RESEARCH
REE . . . . REVISTA DE ESTUDIOS EXTREMENOS
REEP . . . . REVISTA DE LA ESCUELA DE ESTUDIOS PENITENCIARIOS
Ref . . . . REFORMATIO
REF . . . . REVISTA DE ETNOGRAFIE SI FOLCLOR
Ref Ch R . . . . REFORMED CHURCH REVIEW
Ref J . . . . NATIONAL ASSOCIATION OF REFEREES IN BANKRUPTCY. JOURNAL
REFM . . . . REVISTA DE ESTUDIOS FRANCESES (MADRID)
Ref Pres W . . . . REFORMED AND PRESBYTERIAN WORLD
Ref Q . . . . REFORMED QUARTERLY REVIEW
Ref R . . . . REFORMED REVIEW
Refract J . . . . REFRACTORIES JOURNAL
REFRACTOR J . . . . . REFRACTORIES JOURNAL
REFRIG AIR . . . . REFRIGERATION AND AIR CONDITIONING
Refrig Eng . . . . REFRIGERATING ENGINEERING
Refrig W . . . . REFRIGERATING WORLD
Ref Shelf . . . . REFERENCE SHELF
Ref Th R . . . . REFORMED THEOLOGICAL REVIEW
Ref W . . . . REFORMED WORLD
REg . . . . REVUE D'EGYPTOLOGIE
REG . . . . REVUE DES ETUDES GRECQUES
REg . . . . REVUE EGYPTOLOGIQUE
REgA . . . . REVUE DE L'EGYPTE ANCIENNE

Regelungstech Prax Prozess-Rechentechnik..REGELUNGSTECHNISCHE PRAXIS UND PROZESS-RECHENTECHNIK
Regelungstech Prozess-Datenverarbeitung..REGELUNGSTECHNIK UND PROZESS-DATENVERARBEITUNG
Reger...........MITTEILUNGEN DES MAX REGER INSTITUTS (BONN)
Regia Soc Sci Upsal Nova Acta..REGIA SOCIETAS SCIENTIARUM UPSALIENSIS. NOVA ACTA
Register of Kentucky Hist Soc..REGISTER OF THE KENTUCKY HISTORICAL SOCIETY
Reg Soc Sci Upsal Nova Acta..REGIA SOCIETAS SCIENTIARUM UPSALIENSIS. NOVA ACTA
REG STUD........REGIONAL STUDIES
REH............REVISTA DE ESTUDIOS HISPANICOS
REH............REVUE DES ETUDES HISTORIQUES
REH............REVUE DES ETUDES HONGROISES
REHAB COUNS.....REHABILITATION COUNSELING BULLETIN
REHom..........REVUE DES ETUDES HOMERIQUES
REI............REVUE DES ETUDES INDO-EUROPEENNES
REI............REVUE DES ETUDES ISLAMIQUES
REI............REVUE DES ETUDES ITALIENNES
REIE...........REVUE DES ETUDES INDO-EUROPEENNES
Reinf Plast......REINFORCED PLASTICS
REIsl...........REVUE DES ETUDES ISLAMIQUES
REJ............REVUE DES ETUDES JUIVES
REJuiv.........REVUE DES ETUDES JUIVES
REL............REVIEW OF ENGLISH LITERATURE
REL............REVIEW OF ENGLISH LITERATURE (LEEDS)
REL............REVUE ECCLESIASTIQUE DE LIEGE
RelAb..........RELIGIOUS AND THEOLOGICAL ABSTRACTS
RELat..........REVUE DES ETUDES LATINES
RELAT IND.......RELATIONS INDUSTRIELLES/INDUSTRIAL RELATIONS
RELC...........RELC (REGIONAL ENGLISH LANGUAGE CENTRE) JOURNAL (SINGAPORE)
Rel Cab.........RELIGIOUS CABINET
RELHA..........REVISTA ESPANOLA DE LITERATURA, HISTORIA Y ARTE
Reliable P J......RELIABLE POULTRY JOURNAL
Relig Ed.........RELIGIOUS EDUCATION
Relig Hum........RELIGIOUS HUMANISM
Relig Stud.......RELIGIOUS STUDIES
REL IND.........RELATIONS INDUSTRIELLES
RELing..........REVISTA ESPANOLA DE LINGUISTICA
Rel Life.........RELIGION IN LIFE
RelPerl.........RELIGIOUS PERIODICALS INDEX
Rel Soc.........RELIGION AND SOCIETY
Rel St..........RELIGIOUS STUDIES
RELV...........REVUE DE L'ENSEIGNEMENT DES LANGUES VIVANTES
REM............REVISTA ESTUDIOS
REM............REVUE ECCLESIASTIQUE DE METZ
REMC...........REVISTA DE ESTUDIOS MUSICALES. DEPARTAMENTO DE MUSICOLOGIA. UNIVERSIDAD NACIONAL DE CUYO
Remedial Ed......REMEDIAL EDUCATION
Remote Sensing Environ..REMOTE SENSING OF ENVIRONMENT
ReMS...........RENAISSANCE AND MODERN STUDIES
REN............RENAISSANCE
Ren............RENASCENCE (CATHOLIC RENASCENCE SOCIETY)
REN............REVUE DES ETUDES NAPOLEONIENNES
Renais News......RENAISSANCE NEWS

Ren&R . . . . RENAISSANCE AND REFORMATION
RenD . . . . RENAISSANCE DRAMA
Rend . . . . RENDICONTI
REND GASTRO . . . . . RENDICONTI DI GASTRO-ENTEROLOGIA
RenE . . . . REINARE EN ESPANA
Renew . . . . RENEWAL
R Engl Lit . . . . REVIEW OF ENGLISH LITERATURE
R Engl Stud . . . . REVIEW OF ENGLISH STUDIES
REngS . . . . REVIEW OF ENGLISH STUDIES
R Eng Stud ns . . . . . . REVIEW OF ENGLISH STUDIES. NEW SERIES
RENH . . . . REVUE DES ETUDES NEO-HELLENIQUES
RENLO . . . . REVUE DE L'ECOLE NATIONALE DES LANGUES ORIENTALES
RenN . . . . RENAISSANCE NEWS
Ren News . . . . RENAISSANCE NEWS
RenP . . . . RENAISSANCE PAPERS
RenQ . . . . RENAISSANCE QUARTERLY
Rep . . . . REPUBLIKA (ZAGREB)
REP . . . . REVISTA DE ESTUDIOS POLITICOS
RepBibPhil . . . . REPERTOIRE BIBLIOGRAPHIQUE DE LA PHILOSOPHIE
Rep Cast Res Lab Waseda Univ . . REPORT OF THE CASTINGS RESEARCH LABORATORY. WASEDA UNIVERSITY
Repertoire Anal Litt Francaise . . REPERTOIRE ANALYTIQUE DE LITTERATURE FRANCAISE
Rep Govt Mech Lab (Tokyo) . . REPORT OF THE GOVERNMENT MECHANICAL LABORATORY (TOKYO)
Rep Inst High Speed Mech Tohoku Univ . . REPORTS OF THE INSTITUTE OF HIGH SPEED MECHANICS. TOHOKU UNIVERSITY
Rep Inst Ind Sci Univ Tokyo . . REPORT OF THE INSTITUTE OF INDUSTRIAL SCIENCE. UNIVERSITY OF TOKYO
REP ION SPA . . . . . . REPORT OF IONOSPHERE AND SPACE RESEARCH IN JAPAN
Rep Math Log . . . . . REPORTS ON MATHEMATICAL LOGIC
Rep NRL Prog . . . . . REPORT OF NRL PROGRESS (NAVAL RESEARCH LABORATORY)
Rep Progr Phys . . . . REPORTS ON PROGRESS IN PHYSICS
REP PR PHYS . . . . . . REPORTS ON PROGRESS IN PHYSICS
Repr Bull Bk R . . . . . REPRINT BULLETIN BOOK REVIEWS
Rep Res Inst Appl Mech Kyushu Univ . . REPORTS OF THE RESEARCH INSTITUTE FOR APPLIED MECHANICS. KYUSHU UNIVERSITY
Rep Res Inst Elec Commun Tohoku Univ . . REPORTS OF THE RESEARCH INSTITUTE OF ELECTRICAL COMMUNICATION. TOHOKU UNIVERSITY
Rep Res Inst Strength Fract Mater Tohoku Univ . . REPORTS OF THE RESEARCH INSTITUTE FOR STRENGTH AND FRACTURE OF MATERIALS. TOHOKU UNIVERSITY
Reprint Bull Bk R . . . REPRINT BULLETIN BOOK REVIEWS
REPRODUCCIO . . . . . REPRODUCCION
REPR RES SP . . . . . . REPRESENTATIVE RESEARCH IN SOCIAL PSYCHOLOGY
Rep Tech Coll Hosei Univ Tokyo . . REPORT OF THE TECHNICAL COLLEGE OF HOSEI UNIVERSITY. TOKYO
Rep Teleph Eng . . . . REPORTS ON TELEPHONE ENGINEERING
Rep Transp Tech Res Inst Tokyo . . REPORT OF TRANSPORTATION TECHNICAL RESEARCH INSTITUTE (TOKYO)
RER . . . . REVIEW OF EDUCATIONAL RESEARCH
RER . . . . REVUE DES ETUDES RABELAISIENNES
RER . . . . REVUE DES ETUDES ROUMAINES
RERo . . . . REVUE DES ETUDES ROUMAINES
ReS . . . . REINARE EN ESPANA
RES . . . . REVIEW OF ENGLISH STUDIES
RES . . . . REVUE DE ETUDES SEMITIQUES
RES . . . . REVUE DE L'ENSEIGNEMENT SUPERIEUR

RES . . . . REVUE DES ETUDES SLAVES
Res Afric Lit . . . . . . RESEARCH IN AFRICAN LITERATURES
Res & Farm . . . . RESEARCH AND FARMING
RES COMM CP . . . . . RESEARCH COMMUNICATIONS IN CHEMICAL PATHOLOGY AND PHARMACOLOGY
Res Counc Alberta (Can) Inform Ser . . RESEARCH COUNCIL OF ALBERTA (CANADA) INFORMATION SERIES
RES DEVELOP . . . . . . RESEARCH-DEVELOPMENT
ResEduc . . . . RESEARCH IN EDUCATION
RES EDUC . . . . RESEARCH IN EDUCATION (ENGLAND)
RESEE . . . . REVUE DES ETUDES SUD-EST EUROPEENNES
Res Electrotech Lab Tokyo . . RESEARCHES OF THE ELECTROTECHNICAL LABORATORY. TOKYO, JAPAN
RESem . . . . REVUE DES ETUDES SEMITIQUES
Reserve Bank N Z Bul . . RESERVE BANK OF NEW ZEALAND. BULLETIN
RES EXP MED . . . . . RESEARCH IN EXPERIMENTAL MEDICINE
RESFV . . . . RENAISSANCE EDITIONS. SAN FERNANDO VALLEY STATE COLLEGE
RESL . . . . REVUE DES ETUDES SLAVES
RESlaves . . . . REVUE DES ETUDES SLAVES
Res Lit . . . . RESPUBLICA LITERARIA
RES MANAG . . . . . . RESEARCH MANAGEMENT
Res Mgt . . . . RESEARCH MANAGEMENT
RESNS . . . . REVIEW OF ENGLISH STUDIES. NEW SERIES
Res Outlook . . . . . . RESEARCH OUTLOOK
ResP . . . . RESEARCH AND PROGRESS
Res Phenomenol . . . RESEARCH IN PHENOMENOLOGY
REspir . . . . REVISTA DE ESPIRITUALIDAD
REspL . . . . REVISTA ESPANOLA DE LINGUISTICA
RESP PHYSL . . . . . . RESPIRATION PHYSIOLOGY
RES PREVIEW . . . . . . RESEARCH PREVIEWS
Res Q . . . . RESEARCH QUARTERLY
RES Q (AAHPER) . . . RESEARCH QUARTERLY OF THE AMERICAN ASSOCIATION FOR HEALTH, PHYSICAL EDUCATION,
                              AND RECREATION
RES QUART . . . . RESEARCH QUARTERLY
ReSR . . . . RECHERCHES DE SCIENCE RELIGIEUSE
Res R . . . . RESEARCH IN REVIEW
ResRev . . . . RESEARCH REVIEW
RESt . . . . REVIEW OF ENGLISH STUDIES
RESTAT . . . . REVIEW OF ECONOMICS AND STATISTICS
Res Teach Engl . . . . RESEARCH IN THE TEACHING OF ENGLISH
Restr Mgt . . . . RESTAURANT MANAGEMENT
R E Stud . . . . REVIEW OF ECONOMIC STUDIES
R Estud Pol . . . . REVISTA DE ESTUDIOS POLITICOS
RES VET SCI . . . . . . RESEARCH IN VETERINARY SCIENCE
RET . . . . REVISTA ESPANOLA DE TEOLOGIA
Retros . . . . RETROSPECTIVE REVIEW
RETS . . . . RENAISSANCE ENGLISH TEXT SOCIETY
R Etud Byzantines . . REVUE DES ETUDES BYZANTINES
R Etud Grecques . . . REVUE DES ETUDES GRECQUES
R Etud Islamiques . . REVUE DES ETUDES ISLAMIQUES
R Etud Juives . . . . . . REVUE DES ETUDES JUIVES
Rev . . . . REVIEW
RevA . . . . REVUE D'ALLEMAGNE
REV ALCOOL . . . . . . REVUE DE L'ALCOOLISME

Rev Alum........ REVUE DE L'ALUMINIUM
Rev and Expositor.. REVIEW AND EXPOSITOR
Rev Ang-Am...... REVUE ANGLO-AMERICAINE
REV ARCHEOL..... REVUE ARCHEOLOGIQUE
RevB........... REVISTA (BARCELONA)
RevBAM........ REVISTA DE LA BIBLIOTECA ARCHIVO Y MUSEO DEL AYUNTAMIENTO DE MADRID
Rev Belge........ REVUE BELGE DE PHILOLOGIE ET D'HISTOIRE
Rev Belge Matieres Plast..REVUE BELGE DES MATIERES PLASTIQUES
Rev Bened........REVUE BENEDICTINE
Rev Bib.......... REVISTA BIBLIOTECILOR
REV BL POL....... REVIEW OF BLACK POLITICAL ECONOMY
RevBN.......... REVISTA DE BIBLIOGRAFIA NACIONAL
REV BRA EC...... REVISTA BRASILEIRA DE ECONOMIA
RevC........... REVISTA CAMONIANA
Rev C Abo Pr..... REVISTA DEL COLEGIO DE ABOGADOS DE PUERTO RICO
REV CAN BIO..... REVUE CANADIENNE DE BIOLOGIE
REV CENT ED..... REVISTA DEL CENTRO DE ESTUDIOS EDUCATIVOS
Rev C Genie Civil Constr.. REVUE C GENIE CIVIL. CONSTRUCTION
Rev Chilena Ing.... REVISTA CHILENA DE INGENIERIA
REV CHIM MI..... REVUE DE CHIMIE MINERALE
REV CHIR OR...... REVUE DE CHIRURGIE ORTHOPEDIQUE ET REPARATRICE DE LA APPAREIL MOTEUR
Rev C Tijdschr Civ Tech Genie Civ..REVUE C TIJDSCHRIFT CIVIELE TECHNIEK. GENIE CIVIL
Rev de Lit Comp... REVUE DE LA LITTERATURE COMPAREE
Rev Doc........ REVUE DE LA DOCUMENTATION
REV D P........ REVISTA DE DERECHO PUERTORRIQUENO
Rev Du B........REVUE DU BARREAU DE LA PROVINCE DE QUEBEC
Rev du Moyen-Age Latin.. REVUE DU MOYEN-AGE LATIN
Rev du Notariat.... REVUE DU NOTARIAT
REV ECOL BS...... REVUE D'ECOLOGIE ET DE BIOLOGIE DU SOL
REV ECON........ REVUE ECONOMIQUE
REV ECON CO..... REVIEW OF THE ECONOMIC CONDITIONS IN ITALY
REV ECON S....... REVIEW OF ECONOMIC STUDIES
REV ECON ST..... REVIEW OF ECONOMICS AND STATISTICS
Rev Econ Stat..... REVIEW OF ECONOMIC STATISTICS
REV EDUC RE...... REVIEW OF EDUCATIONAL RESEARCH
Rev E Elec Electrotech Gen..REVUE E. ELECTRICITE, ELECTROTECHNIQUE GENERALE, COURANTS FORTS ET APPLICATIONS
REV EL COMM..... REVIEW OF THE ELECTRICAL COMMUNICATION LABORATORY (TOKYO)
Rev Elec Commun Lab (Tokyo)..REVIEW OF THE ELECTRICAL COMMUNICATION LABORATORY (TOKYO)
Rev Electrotec..... REVISTA ELECTROTECNICA
Rev Engl Stu...... REVIEW OF ENGLISH STUDIES
REV EPIDEM...... REVUE D'EPIDEMIOLOGIE, MEDECINE SOCIALE ET SANTE PUBLIQUE
RevER.......... REVUE DES ETUDES ROUMAINES
REV ESP FIS....... REVISTA ESPANOLA DE FISIOLOGIA
REV EST.......... REVUE DE L'EST
Rev Esth........ REVUE D'ESTHETIQUE
Rev Etud Augustin.. REVUE DES ETUDES AUGUSTINIENNES
REV F GY OB...... REVUE FRANCAISE DE GYNECOLOGIE ET D'OBSTETRIQUE
Rev Filosof (Argentina)..REVISTA DE FILOSOFIA (ARGENTINA)
Ref Filosof (Costa Rica)..REVISTA DE FILOSOFIA DE LA UNIVERSIDAD DE COSTA RICA
Rev Filosof (Mexico)..REVISTA DE FILOSOFIA (MEXICO)

Rev Filosof (Spain). . REVISTA DE FILOSOFIA (SPAIN)
REV FR ALLE. . . . . . REVUE FRANCAISE D'ALLERGOLOGIE
REV FR AUTO. . . . . . REVUE FRANCAISE D'AUTOMATIQUE INFORMATIQUE RECHERCHE OPERATIONNELLE
Rev Fr Energ. . . . . . REVUE FRANCAISE DE L'ENERGIE
REV FR MKT. . . . . . REVUE FRANCAISE DU MARKETING
REV FR SC P. . . . . . . REVUE FRANCAISE DE SCIENCE POLITIQUE
REV FR SOC. . . . . . . REVUE FRANCAISE DE SOCIOLOGIE
REV FR TRAN. . . . . . REVUE FRANCAISE DE TRANSFUSION
Rev Gen Chemins Fer. . REVUE GENERALE DES CHEMINS DE FER
Rev Gen Elec. . . . . . REVUE GENERALE DE L'ELECTRICITE
Rev Generale de Droit. . REVUE GENERALE DE DROIT
Rev Gen Sci Pures Appl. . REVUE GENERALE DES SCIENCES PURES ET APPLIQUEES
Rev Gen Therm. . . . REVUE GENERALE DE THERMIQUE
REV GEOG PH. . . . . REVUE DE GEOGRAPHIE PHYSIQUE ET DE GEOLOGIE DYNAMIQUE
REV GEOPHYS. . . . . REVIEWS OF GEOPHYSICS AND SPACE PHYSICS
Rev Germ. . . . . REVUE GERMANIQUE
REV G THERM. . . . . REVUE GENERALE DE THERMIQUE
RevH. . . . . REVISTA DE HISTORIA (LISBON)
Rev HF Electron Telecommun. . REVUE HF, ELECTRONIQUE TELECOMMUNICATIONS
Rev High-Temp Mater. . REVIEWS ON HIGH-TEMPERATURE MATERIALS
RevHist. . . . . REVISTA DE HISTORIA (SAO PAULO)
Rev Hist. . . . . REVUE HISTORIQUE
REV HIST AM. . . . . . REVUE D'HISTOIRE DE L'AMERIQUE FRANCAISE
Rev Hist Am Fr. . . . REVUE D'HISTOIRE DE L'AMERIQUE FRANCAISE
RevHL. . . . . REVISTA DE HISTORIA. LA LAGUNA DE TENERIFE
RevHL. . . . . REVISTA DE HISTORIA (LISBON)
RevHS. . . . . REVISTA DE HISTORIA (SAO PAULO)
RevIb. . . . . REVISTA IBERO-AMERICANA
Rev IDIEM. . . . . . . REVISTA DEL IDIEM (INSTITUTO DE INVESTIGACIONES DE ENGOYES DE MATERIALES)
RevIE. . . . . REVISTA DE IDEAS ESTETICAS
Review. . . . . WEEKLY REVIEW
REV I F PET. . . . . . REVUE DE L'INSTITUT FRANCAIS DU PETROLE
RevIMA. . . . . REVIEW OF INDONESIAN AND MALAYAN AFFAIRS
Rev Ind Miner. . . . . REVUE DE L'INDUSTRIE MINERALE
REV IN HAUT. . . . . . REVUE INTERNATIONALE DES HAUTES TEMPERATURES ET DES REFRACTAIRES
Rev Inst Fr Pet Ann Combust Liq. . REVUE DE L'INSTITUT FRANCAIS DU PETROLE ET ANNALES DES COMBUSTIBLES LIQUIDES
Rev Int Doc. . . . . . . REVUE INTERNATIONALE DE LA DOCUMENTATION
Rev Int Hautes Temp Refract. . REVUE INTERNATIONALE DES HAUTES TEMPERATURES ET DES REFRACTAIRES
Rev Int Mus. . . . . . REVUE INTERNATIONALE DE MUSIQUE
Rev Int Phil. . . . . . REVUE INTERNATIONALE DE PHILOSOPHIE
REV INT PSY. . . . . . REVUE INTERNATIONALE DE PSYCHOLOGIE APPLIQUEE
REV INT SC. . . . . . . REVISTA INTERNAZIONALE SCIENZE ECONOMICHE E COMMERCIALI
REV INV CLI. . . . . . REVISTA DE INVESTIGACION CLINICA
REV I PSYCH. . . . . . REVUE INTERNATIONALE DE PSYCHOLOGIE APPLIQUEE
REV I SOC. . . . . . . REVUE DEL INSTITUT DE SOCIOLOGIE
Revista CF. . . . . . . REVISTA COLOMBIANA DE FOLCLOR
Rev Jur UPR. . . . . . REVISTA JURIDICA DE LA UNIVERSIDAD DE PUERTO RICO
RevL. . . . . REVISTA DE LETRAS
RevLA. . . . . REVISTA DE LETRAS. ASSIS
Rev Lang Viv. . . . . . REVUE DES LANGUES VIVANTES

REV LATAM P..... REVISTA LATINOAMERICANA DE PSICOLOGIA
Rev Ling Rom..... REVUE DE LINGUISTIQUE ROMANE
Rev Lit Comp...... REVUE DE LITTERATURE COMPAREE
RevLR.......... REVISTA DO LIVRO (RIO)
RevM.......... REVISTA (MADRID)
REV MED CHI...... REVISTA MEDICA DE CHILE
REV METALL...... REVUE DE METALLURGIE
Rev Metaph...... REVIEW OF METAPHYSICS
Rev Metaph Morale. . REVUE DE METAPHYSIQUE ET DE MORALE
REV METAPHY..... REVIEW OF METAPHYSICS
Rev Met (Madrid).. REVISTA DE METALURGIA (MADRID)
Rev Met (Paris).... REVUE DE METALLURGIE (PARIS)
REV MICR EL...... REVISTA DE MICROSCOPIA ELECTRONICA
Rev M Mec....... REVUE M—MECANIQUE
Rev Mod Phys..... REVIEWS OF MODERN PHYSICS
REV M PHYS...... REVIEWS OF MODERN PHYSICS
Rev Mus......... REVUE MUSICALE
RevN.......... REVUE NOUVELLE (PARIS)
REV NEUROL...... REVUE NEUROLOGIQUE
REV NEUROPS..... REVUE DE NEUROPSYCHIATRIE INFANTILE ET D'HYGIENE MENTALE DE L'ENFANCE
Rev Obras Pub..... REVISTA DE OBRAS PUBLICAS
REV PALAE P...... REVIEW OF PALAEOBOTANY AND PALYNOLOGY
RefPF........... REVISTA PORTUGUESA DE FILOSOFIA
REV PH CH J...... REVIEW OF PHYSICAL CHEMISTRY OF JAPAN
Rev Phil Fr....... REVUE PHILOSOPHIQUE DE LA FRANCE ET DE L'ETRANGER
Rev Phil Louvain... REVUE PHILOSOPHIQUE DE LOUVAIN
REV PHYS AP...... REVUE DE PHYSIQUE APPLIQUEE
REV PHYS B....... REVIEWS PHYSIOLOGY BIOCHEMISTRY AND PHARMACOLOGY
Rev Phys Technol.. REVIEW OF PHYSICS IN TECHNOLOGY
Rev Plast Mod..... REVISTA DE PLASTICOS MODERNOS
REV POLIT........ REVIEW OF POLITICS
REV PO QUIM..... REVISTA PORTUGUESA DE QUIMICA
Rev Port Filosof.... REVISTA PORTUGUESA DE FILOSOFIA
Rev Prat Froid Cond Air . . REVUE PRATIQUE DU FROID ET DU CONDITIONNEMENT DE L'AIR
REV PSY APP...... REVUE DE PSYCHOLOGIE APPLIQUEE
REV PUB DAT..... REVIEW OF PUBLIC DATA USE
RevR........... REVUE ROMANE
Rev Relig........ REVIEW FOR RELIGIOUS
REV REL RES...... REVIEW OF RELIGIOUS RESEARCH
REV RHUM....... REVUE DU RHUMATISME ET DES MALADIES OSTEO-ARTICULAIRES
REV RO BIOC...... REVUE ROUMAINE DE BIOCHIMIE
REV RO CHIM..... REVUE ROUMAINE DE CHIMIE
REV RO PHYS...... REVUE ROUMAINE DE PHYSIQUE
Rev Roum Sci Tech Ser Electrotech Energ. . REVUE ROUMAINE DES SCIENCES TECHNIQUES. SERIE ELECTROTECHNIQUE
ET ENERGETIQUE
Rev Roum Sci Tech Ser Mec Appl... REVUE ROUMAINE DES SCIENCES TECHNIQUES. SERIE DE MECANIQUE APPLIQUEE
Rev Roum Sci Tech Ser Met . . REVUE ROUMAINE DES SCIENCES TECHNIQUES. SERIE DE METALLURGIE
REV SCI INS....... REVIEW OF SCIENTIFIC INSTRUMENTS
Rev Sci Phil Theol. . REVUE DES SCIENCES, PHILOSOPHIQUES, ET THEOLOGIQUES
REV SOC EC....... REVIEW OF SOCIAL ECONOMY
Rev Soc R Belge Ing Ind . . REVUE DE LA SOCIETE ROYALE BELGE DES INGENIEURS ET DES INDUSTRIELS

Rev Soudure . . . . . . REVUE DE LA SOUDURE. LASTIJDSCHRIFT (BRUSSELS)
REV STAT AP . . . . . . REVUE DE STATISTIQUE APPLIQUE
Rev Tech Luxemb . . . REVUE TECHNIQUE LUXEMBOURGEOISE
Rev Tech Thomson CSF . . REVUE TECHNIQUE THOMSON CSF
Rev Teilhard de Chardin . . REVUE TEILHARD DE CHARDIN
Rev Telecomun (Madrid) . . REVISTA DE TELECOMUNICACION (MADRID)
Rev Theol Phil . . . . . REVUE DE THEOLOGIE ET DE PHILOSOPHIE
Rev Thomiste . . . . . REVUE THOMISTE
Revue Lux . . . . REVUE TRIMESTRIELLE D'ETUDES LINGUISTIQUES, FOLKLORISTIQUES ET TOPONYMIQUES (LUXEMBOURG)
Rev Un B . . . . REVUE DE L'UNIVERSITE DE BRUXELLES
Rev Univ Ottawa . . . REVUE DE L'UNIVERSITE D'OTTAWA
REV USEM . . . . REVISTA USEM
Rev Ven Filosof . . . . REVISTA VENOZOLANA DE FILOSOFIA
REV ZOO AGR . . . . . REVUE DE ZOOLOGIE AGRICOLE ET DE PATHOLOGIE VEGETALE
RF . . . . RAZON Y FE
RF . . . . REPUBLIQUE FRANCAISE
RF . . . . REVUE DE FRANCE
RF . . . . RIVISTA DI FILOLOGIA E D'ISTRUZIONE CLASSICA
RF . . . . RIVISTA DI FILOSOFIA
RF . . . . ROMANISCHE FORSCHUNGEN
RF . . . . RUCH FILOZOFICZNY
RFA . . . . REVUE DE LA FRANCO-ANCIENNE
RFC . . . . REVISTA DE FOLKLORE (COLOMBIA)
RFC . . . . RIVISTA DI FILOLOGIA CLASSICA
RFC . . . . RIVISTA DI FILOLOGIA E D'ISTRUZIONE CLASSICA
RFCC . . . . REVISTA DE FOLKLORE. ORGANO DE LA COMISION NACIONAL DE FOLKLORE (COLOMBIA)
RFCO . . . . REVUE DES FACULTES CATHOLIQUES DE L'OUEST
RFE . . . . REVISTA DE FILOLOGIA ESPANOLA
RFFLUP . . . . REVISTA DA FACULDADE DE FILOSOFIA E LETRAS DA UNIVERSIDADE DO PARANA
RFH . . . . REVISTA DE FILOLOGIA HISPANICA
RFHC . . . . REVISTA DE LA FACULTAD DE HUMANIDADES Y CIENCIAS
RFHSP . . . . REVISTA DI FILOLOGIA E HISTORIA (SAO PAULO)
RFi . . . . REVISTA DE FILOSOFIA
RFIC . . . . RIVISTA DI FILOLOGIA E D'ISTRUZIONE CLASSICA
RFil . . . . REVISTA DI FILOSOFIA (TORINO)
RFil . . . . RUSSKAJA FILOLOGIJA
R Filol Esp . . . . REVISTA DE FILOLOGIA ESPANOLA
RFilos . . . . RIVISTA DI FILOSOFIA
RFL . . . . REVISTA DA FACULDADE DE LETRAS DA UNIVERSIDADE DE LISBOA
RFLL . . . . REVISTA DA FACULDADE DE LETRAS DA UNIVERSIDADE DE LISBOA
RFLUL . . . . REVISTA DA FACULDADE DE LETRAS DA UNIVERSIDADE DE LISBOA
RFM . . . . REVISTA DE FILOSOFIA (MADRID)
RFM Rev Fr Mec . . . RFM, REVUE FRANCAISE DE MECANIQUE
RFN . . . . RIVISTA DI FILOSOFIA NEO-SCOLASTICA
RFNS . . . . RIVISTA DI FILOSOFIA NEO-SCOLASTICA
RFolc . . . . REVISTA DE FOLCLOR
RForsch . . . . ROMANISCHE FORSCHUNGEN
RFP . . . . REVISTA DE FILOLOGIA PORTUGUESA
RFr . . . . REVOLUTION FRANCAISE
RFr . . . . REVUE FRANCAISE

R Francaise Hist Livre . . REVUE FRANCAISE D'HISTOIRE DU LIVRE
R Francaise Hist Outre Mer . . REVUE FRANCAISE D'HISTOIRE D'OUTRE MER
R Francaise Sociol . . REVUE FRANCAISE DE SOCIOLOGIE
RFRG . . . . REVISTA DE FILOLOGIE ROMANICA SI GERMANICA (BUCAREST)
RFrign . . . . RASSEGNA FRIGNANESE
RG . . . . READERS' GUIDE TO PERIODICAL LITERATURE
RG . . . . RECHERCHES GERMANIQUES
RG . . . . REVISTA DE GUIMARAES
RG . . . . REVUE GENERALE
RG . . . . REVUE GERMANIQUE
RG . . . . ROMANA GENS
RGand . . . . ROMANICA GANDENSIA
RGB . . . . REVUE GENERALE BELGE
RGD . . . . REVUE GENERALE DU DROIT
R Gen Sci . . . . REVUE GENERALE DES SCIENCES PURES ET APPLIQUEES
R Gen Sci Pures et Ap . . REVUE GENERALE DES SCIENCES PURES ET APPLIQUEES
RGeogrH . . . . REVUE DE GEOGRAPHIE HUMAINE ET D'ETHNOLOGIE
RGer . . . . RECHERCHES GERMANIQUES
RGF . . . . ROEMISCH-GERMANISCHE FORSCHUNGEN
RGFil . . . . ROMANO-GERMANSKAJA FILOLOGIJA
RGKAI . . . . ROEMISCH-GERMANISCHE KOMMISSION DES ARCHAEOLOGISCHEN INSTITUTS
RGL . . . . REVUE DE GEOGRAPHIE DE LYON
RGo . . . . ROMANICA GOTHOBURGENSIA
RGr . . . . RASSEGNA GREGORIANA
RGR . . . . REVISTA GERMANISTILOR ROMANI
RGr . . . . REVUE GREGORIENNE
R Gregor . . . . REVUE GREGORIENNE
RGuim . . . . REVISTA DE GUIMARAES
RH . . . . REVUE HEBDOMADAIRE
RH . . . . REVUE HISPANIQUE
RH . . . . REVUE HISTORIQUE
RH . . . . ROCHESTER HISTORY
RH . . . . ROCZNIKI HUMANISTYCZNE
RHA . . . . REVISTA DE HISTORIA DE AMERICA
RHA . . . . REVUE HITTITE ET ASIANIQUE
RHAF . . . . REVUE D'HISTOIRE DE L'AMERIQUE FRANCAISE
RhB . . . . REHEINISCHE BLAETTER
RHB . . . . RHEINISCHE HEIMATBLAETTER
RHC . . . . REVUE D'HISTOIRE COMPAREE
RHComp . . . . REVUE D'HISTOIRE COMPAREE
RHCS . . . . ROCZNIK HISTORII CZASOPISMIENNICTWA POLSKIEGO
RHD . . . . REVUE D'HISTOIRE DIPLOMATIQUE
RHD . . . . REVUE D'HISTOIRE DU DROIT
RHD . . . . REVUE HISTORIQUE DE DROIT FRANCAIS ET ETRANGER
RHDFE . . . . REVUE HISTORIQUE DE DROIT FRANCAIS ET ETRANGER
RHDip . . . . REVUE D'HISTOIRE DIPLOMATIQUE
RHE . . . . REVUE D'HISTOIRE ECCLESIASTIQUE
RHeb . . . . REVUE HEBDOMADAIRE
RHEF . . . . REVUE D'HISTOIRE DE L'EGLISE DE FRANCE
RHel . . . . ROMANICA HELVETICA
RHEOL ACT . . . . . . RHEOLOGICA ACTA

RHES . . . . REVUE D'HISTOIRE ECONOMIQUE ET SOCIALE
Rheumatol Phys Med . . RHEUMATOLOGY AND PHYSICAL MEDICINE
RHF . . . . REVUE D'HISTOIRE FRANCISCAINE
RHi . . . . REVUE HISPANIQUE
RHiM . . . . REVISTA HISPANICA MODERNA
RHis . . . . REVUE HISTORIQUE
RHisp . . . . REVUE HISPANIQUE
R Hispan Mod . . . . . REVISTA HISPANICA MODERNA
R Hist . . . . REVUE HISTORIQUE
RHist . . . . ROCZNIKI HISTORYCZNE
R Hist Am . . . . REVISTA DE HISTORIA DE AMERICA
R Hist & Philos Rel . . REVUE D'HISTOIRE ET DE PHILOSOPHIE RELIGIEUSES
R Hist Bul . . . . REVUE HISTORIQUE. BULLETINS CRITIQUES
R Hist Eccl . . . . REVUE D'HISTOIRE ECCLESIASTIQUE
R Hist Litt France . . . REVUE D'HISTOIRE LITTERAIRE DE LA FRANCE
RHistM . . . . ROEMISCHE HISTORISCHE MITTEILUNGEN
R Hist Mem . . . . . . REVUE HISTORIQUE. MEMOIRES ET ETUDES
R Hist Mod & Contemp . . REVUE D'HISTOIRE MODERNE ET CONTEMPORAINE
R Hist Ph Rel . . . . . . REVUE D'HISTOIRE ET DE PHILOSOPHIE RELIGIEUSES
R Hist Rel . . . . REVUE DE L'HISTOIRE DES RELIGIONS
R Hist Sci & Ap . . . . REVUE D'HISTOIRE DES SCIENCES ET DE LEURS APPLICATIONS
R Hist Spiritualite . . REVUE D'HISTOIRE DE LA SPIRITUALITE
RhJbV . . . . RHEINISCHES JAHRBUCH FUER VOLKSKUNDE
RHJE . . . . REVUE DE L'HISTOIRE JUIVE EN EGYPTE
RHKUL . . . . ROCZNIKI HUMANISTYCZNE. TOWARZYSTWO NAUKOWE KATOLICKIEGO UNIWERSYTETU LUBELSKIEGO
RHL . . . . REVISTA DE HISTORIA. LA LAGUNA DE TENERIFE
RHL . . . . REVUE D'HISTOIRE LITTERAIRE DE LA FRANCE
RHLB . . . . REVUE D'HISTOIRE LITTERAIRE (BUCHAREST)
RHLE . . . . REVISTA CRITICA DE HISTORIA Y LITERATURA ESPANOLAS
RHLF . . . . REVUE D'HISTOIRE LITTERAIRE DE LA FRANCE
RHLP . . . . REVISTA DE HISTORIA LITERARIA DE PORTUGAL
RHLR . . . . REVUE D'HISTOIRE ET DE LITTERATURE RELIGIEUSE
RHM . . . . REVISTA HISPANICA MODERNA
RHM . . . . REVUE D'HISTOIRE MODERNE
RhM . . . . RHEINISCHE MERKUR
RhM . . . . RHEINISCHES MUSEUM FUER PHILOLOGIE
RHM . . . . ROEMISCHE HISTORISCHE MITTEILUNGEN
RHMC . . . . REVUE D'HISTOIRE MODERNE ET CONTEMPORAINE
RHMis . . . . REVUE D'HISTOIRE DES MISSIONS
RhMP . . . . RHEINISCHES MUSEUM FUER PHILOLOGIE
Rhodesia Ag J . . . . . RHODESIA AGRICULTURAL JOURNAL
Rhodesian J Econ . . . RHODESIAN JOURNAL OF ECONOMICS
RHP . . . . REVUE D'HISTOIRE DE LA PHILOSOPHIE ET D'HISTOIRE GENERALE DE LA CIVILISATION
RHPH . . . . REVUE D'HISTOIRE DE LA PHILOSOPHIE ET D'HISTOIRE GENERALE DE LA CIVILISATION
RHPhC . . . . REVUE D'HISTOIRE DE LA PHILOSOPHIE ET D'HISTOIRE GENERALE DE LA CIVILISATION
RHPhR . . . . REVUE D'HISTOIRE ET DE PHILOSOPHIE RELIGIEUSES
RHPR . . . . REVUE D'HISTOIRE ET DE PHILOSOPHIE RELIGIEUSES
RHR . . . . REVUE DE L'HISTOIRE DES RELIGIONS
RHS . . . . REVUE D'HISTOIRE DE LA SPIRITUALITE
RHS . . . . REVUE D'HISTOIRE DES SCIENCES ET DE LEURS APPLICATIONS

RHS............ ROYAL HISTORICAL SOCIETY. TRANSACTIONS
RHSA.......... REVUE D'HISTOIRE DES SCIENCES ET DE LEURS APPLICATIONS
RHSE........... REVUE HISTORIQUE DU SUD-EST EUROPEEN
RHSEE.......... REVUE HISTORIQUE DU SUD-EST EUROPEEN
RHStr.......... ROYAL HISTORICAL SOCIETY. TRANSACTIONS
RHT............ REVUE D'HISTOIRE DU THEATRE
RHTe.......... REVUE D'HISTOIRE DES TEXTES
RHUL.......... REVISTA DE HISTORIA DE LA UNIVERSIDAD DE LA LAGUNA
RHV............ REVUE HISTORIQUE VAUDOISE
RhV............ RHEINISCHE VIERTELJAHRSBLAETTER
RhV............ RHEINISCHE VORZEIT IN WORT UND BILD
RhVJ........... RHEINISCHE VIERTELJAHRSBLAETTER
RI.............. RASSEGNA ITALIANA
RI.............. REVISTA DE LAS INDIAS
RI.............. REVISTA IBEROAMERICANA
RI.............. RICE INSTITUTE PAMPHLETS
RI.............. RISORGIMENTO ITALIANO
RI.............. RIVISTA D'ITALIA
RIA............. REVISTA IBERO-AMERICANA
RIA............. RIVISTA DELL'ISTITUTO DI ARCHEOLOGIA
RIAB........... REVISTA INTERAMERICANA DE BIBLIOGRAFIA
R I Ag.......... RHODE ISLAND AGRICULTURE
R I Ag Exp....... RHODE ISLAND AGRICULTURAL EXPERIMENT STATION. PUBLICATIONS
RIB............. REVISTA IBEROAMERICANA DE BIBLIOGRAFIA
RIB............. REVUE DE L'INSTRUCTION PUBLIQUE EN BELGIQUE
Ric Autom........ RICERCHE DI AUTOMATICA
Rice Inst P....... RICE INSTITUTE PAMPHLET
Rice Inst Pam..... RICE INSTITUTE PAMPHLETS
Rice Univ Aero-Astronaut Rep.. RICE UNIVERSITY. AERO-ASTRONAUTIC REPORT
RiceUS.......... RICE UNIVERSITY STUDIES
RicF............ RICERCHE FILOSOFICHE
RicLing.......... RICERCHE LINGUISTICHE
RIC MAT......... RICERCHE DI MATEMATICA
RICP........... REVISTA DEL INSTITUTO DE CULTURA PUERTORRIQUENA
RicR............ RICERCHE RELIGIOSE
RicRel.......... RICERCHE RELIGIOSE
RicSL........... RICERCHE SLAVISTICHE
RicSRel......... RICERCHE DI STORIA RELIGIOSA
Rid............ RIDOTTO
RID............ RIVISTA ITALIANA DEL DRAMA
RIDA........... REVUE INTERNATIONALE DES DROITS DE L'ANTIQUITE
RIdeP.......... REVUE INTERNATIONALE DE PHILOSOPHIE
RIE............. REVISTA DE IDEAS ESTETICAS
RIE............. REVUE INTERNATIONALE DE L'ENSEIGNEMENT
RIEB........... REVISTA DO INSTITUTO DE ESTUDOS BRASILEIROS
RIEtnN.......... REVISTA DEL INSTITUTO ETNOLOGICO NACIONAL
RIEV........... REVISTA INTERNACIONAL DE ESTUDIOS VASCOS
RIFD........... RIVISTA INTERNAZIONALE DI FILOSOFIA DEL DIRITTO
RIGI........... RIVISTA INDO-GRECO-ITALICO
RIH............ RHODE ISLAND HISTORY
RIHGSP......... REVISTA DO INSTITUTO HISTORICO E GEOGRAPHICO DE SAO PAULO

RI Hist . . . . RHODE ISLAND HISTORY
RI Hist Soc Coll . . . . RHODE ISLAND HISTORICAL SOCIETY. COLLECTIONS
RIHPC . . . . REVUE INTERNATIONALE D'HISTOIRE POLITIQUE ET CONSTITUTIONELLE
RII . . . . RIVISTA INGAUNA ET INTEMELIA
RIJAZ . . . . RADOVI INSTITUTA JUGOSLAVENSKE AKADEMIJE ZNANOSTI I UMJETNOSTI U ZADRU
RI Jewish Historical Notes . . RHODE ISLAND JEWISH HISTORICAL NOTES
RIL . . . . RENDICONTI DELL'ISTITUTO LOMBARDO DI SCIENZE E LETTERE
RILD . . . . RIVISTA ITALIANA DI LETTERATURA DIALETTALE
RILM . . . . RILM (INTERNATIONAL REPERTORY OF MUSIC LITERATURE) ABSTRACTS OF MUSIC LITERATURE
RiLM . . . . RIVISTA DI LETTERATURE MODERNE
RILSL . . . . RENDICONTI DELL'ISTITUTO LOMBARDO. CLASSE DI LETTERE, SCIENZE MORALI E STORICHE
RIn . . . . REVISTA DE LAS INDIAS
Rin . . . . RINASCIMENTO
Rin . . . . RINASCITA
RIN . . . . RIVISTA ITALIANA DI NUMISMATICA E SCIENZE AFFINI
RINASA . . . . RIVISTA DELL'ISTITUTO NAZIONALE D'ARCHEOLOGIA E STORIA DELL'ARTE
RInd . . . . REVISTA DE INDIAS
R Indias . . . . REVISTA DE INDIAS
RIndM . . . . REVISTA DE INDIAS (MADRID)
Rin S . . . . RINASCENZA SALENTINA
R Inst Nav Archit Q Trans . . ROYAL INSTITUTION OF NAVAL ARCHITECTS (LONDON). QUARTERLY TRANSACTIONS
R Inst Nav Archit Suppl Pap . . ROYAL INSTITUTION OF NAVAL ARCHITECTS (LONDON). SUPPLEMENTARY PAPERS
RINT . . . . REVISTA DEL INSTITUTO NACIONAL DE LA TRADICION
R Interam Bibl . . . . . REVISTA INTERAMERICANA DE BIBLIOGRAFIA
RIO . . . . REVUE INTERNATIONALE D'ONOMASTIQUE
RIOno . . . . REVUE INTERNATIONALE D'ONOMASTIQUE
RIP . . . . REVUE INTERNATIONALE DE PHILOSOPHIE
RIP . . . . RICE INSTITUTE PAMPHLETS
RIPB . . . . REVUE DE L'INSTRUCTION PUBLIQUE EN BELGIQUE
RIPC . . . . RASSEGNA ITALIANA DI POLITICA E DI CULTURA
RIPh . . . . REVUE INTERNATIONALE DE PHILOSOPHIE
RIR . . . . REVISTA ISTORICA ROMANA
RIS . . . . REVISTA INTERNACIONAL DE SOCIOLOGIA
Ris . . . . RISORGIMENTO
RIS . . . . RIVISTA ITALIANA DI SOCIOLOGIA
R I Sch Des Bul . . . . RHODE ISLAND SCHOOL OF DESIGN. BULLETIN
RISE . . . . RIVISTA INTERNAZIONALE DI SCIENZE ECONOMICHE E COMMERCIALI
RISG . . . . RIVISTA ITALIANA DI SCIENZE GIURIDICHE
RiSL . . . . ROSSIJA I SLAVJANSTVO
RISoc . . . . REVUE DE L'INSTITUT DE SOCIOLOGIE SOLVAY
RISR . . . . RASSEGNA D'INFORMAZIONI DELL'ISTITUTO DI STUDI ROMANI
RiSR . . . . RICERCHE DI STORIA RELIGIOSA
R Istituto Lombardo Memorie Classe di Sci Mat e Nat . . REALE ISTITUTO LOMBARDO DI SCIENZE E LETTERE. CLASSE
DI LETTERE E SCIENZE STORICHE E MORALI. MEMORIE
R Istituto Veneto Memorie . . REALE ISTITUTO VENETO DI SCIENZE, LETTERE ED ARTI. MEMORIE
RISULB . . . . REVUE D L'INSTITUTE DE SOCIOLOGIE DE L'UNIVERSITE LIBRE DE BRUXELLES
RIT . . . . RIVISTA ITALIANA DEL TEATRO
R ITAL MUS . . . . . . NUOVA RIVISTA MUSICALE ITALIANA
R ITAL MUS . . . . . . RIVISTA ITALIANA DI MUSICOLOGIA
RITL . . . . REVISTA DE ISTORIE SI THEORI LITERARA
Riv Arte . . . . RIVISTA D'ARTE

PERIODICAL TITLE ABBREVIATIONS

```
RivB . . . . . . . . . . . RIVISTA BIBLIOGRAFICA
RivBA . . . . . . . . . . . RIVISTA DELLE BIBLIOTECHE E DEGLI ARCHIVI
RivBibl . . . . . . . . . RIVISTA BIBLICA
RivDal . . . . . . . . . . RIVISTA DALMATICA
Riv d'Alb . . . . . . . . RIVISTA D'ALBANIA
Riv Filosof . . . . . . . RIVISTA DE FILOSOFIA
Riv Filosof Neo-Scolas . . RIVISTA DI FILOSOFIA NEO-SCOLASTICA
Riv Ing Int . . . . . . . RIVISTA INGUANA E INTEMELIA
RIV INT EC . . . . . . . RIVISTA INTERNAZIONALE DI SCIENZE ECONOMICHE E COMMERCIALI
Riv Int Filosof Diritto . . RIVISTA INTERNAZIONALE DI FILOSOFIA DEL DIRITTO
RIV ITAL GE . . . . . . RIVISTA ITALIANA DI GEOFISICA E SCIENZE AFFINI
Riv Ital Saldatura . . . RIVISTA ITALIANA DELLA SALDATURA
RivL . . . . . . . . . . . RIVISTA LETTERARIA PER I LICEI CLASSICO, SCIENTIFICO, ARTISTICO E PER L'ISTITUTO
                          MAGISTRALE
Riv Lett Mod . . . . . . RIVISTA DI LETTERATURE MODERNE
Riv Lig . . . . . . . . . RIVISTA DI STUDI LIGURI
RIV MED AER . . . . . RIVISTA DI MEDICINA AERONAUTICA E SPAZAILE
RIV METEO A . . . . . RIVISTA DI METEOROLOGIA AERONAUTICA
Riv Mus Italiana . . . RIVISTA MUSICALE ITALIANA
Riv Nuovo Cimento Ser I . . RIVISTA DEL NUOVO CIMENTO. SERIE I
RivPed . . . . . . . . . RIVISTA PEDAGOGICA
RivR . . . . . . . . . . . RIVISTA DELLE RELIGIONI
Riv Stud Croci . . . . . RIVISTA DI STUDI CROCIANI
RIW . . . . . . . . . . . REVIEW OF INCOME AND WEALTH
RJ . . . . . . . . . . . . REVISTA JAVERIANA
RJ . . . . . . . . . . . . ROMANISTISCHES JAHRBUCH
RJ . . . . . . . . . . . . RUSKY JAZYK
RJaS . . . . . . . . . . RUSSKIJ JAZYK V SKOLE
RJav . . . . . . . . . . REVISTA JAVERIANA
RJaz . . . . . . . . . . RUSKY JAZYK
RJb . . . . . . . . . . . ROMANISTISCHES JAHRBUCH
RJR . . . . . . . . . . . RUSSKIJ JAZYK ZA RUBEZOM
RJS . . . . . . . . . . . RUSSKIJ JAZYK V SKOLE
RJT . . . . . . . . . . . REVUE JURIDIQUE THEMIS
RJV . . . . . . . . . . . RHEINISCHES JAHRBUCH FUER VOLKSKUNDE
RKCSN . . . . . . . . . ROSPRAVY KRALOVSKE CESKE SPOLECNOSTI NAUK
RKFJ . . . . . . . . . . RAD KONGRESA FOLKLORISTA JUGOSLAVIJE
RKHLit . . . . . . . . . ROCZNIK KOMISJI HISTORYCZNOLITERACKIEJ PAN
RKHS . . . . . . . . . . REGISTER OF THE KENTUCKY HISTORICAL SOCIETY
RKJ . . . . . . . . . . . ROZPRAWY KOMISJI JEZYKOWEJ LODZKIEGO TOWARZYSTWA NAUKOWEGO
RKJL . . . . . . . . . . ROZPRAWY KOMISJI JEZYKOWEJ LODZKIEGO TOWARZYSTWA NAUKOWEGO
RKJW . . . . . . . . . ROZPRAWY KOMISJI JEZYKOWEJ WROCLAWSKIEGO TOWARZYSTWA NAUKOWEGO
RKr . . . . . . . . . . . RAKSTU KRAJUMS
RKS . . . . . . . . . . . ROCKET STORIES
RKW . . . . . . . . . . REPERTORIUM FUER KUNSTWISSENSCHAFT
RL . . . . . . . . . . . . REVISTA DE LITERATURA
RL . . . . . . . . . . . . REVISTA LUSITANA
RL . . . . . . . . . . . . REVUE DE LILLE
RL . . . . . . . . . . . . RICHERCHE LINGUISTICHE
RL . . . . . . . . . . . . RIVISTA LETTERARIA
RL . . . . . . . . . . . . RUCH LITERACKI
```

RL . . . . RUSSIAN LITERATURE
RLA . . . . REVISTA DE LETRAS DA FACULDADE DE FILOSOFIA, CIENCIAS E LETRAS DE ASSIS
RLA . . . . REVISTA LITURGICA ARGENTINA
RLAC . . . . REALLEXIKON FUER ANTIKE UND CHRISTENTUM
R Lang Rom . . . . . . REVUE DES LANGUES ROMANES
RLaR . . . . REVUE DES LANGUES ROMANES
RLaV . . . . REVUE DES LANGUES VIVANTES
RLC . . . . RASSEGNA ITALIANA DI LINGUE E LETTERATURE CLASSICHE
RLC . . . . REVUE DE LITTERATURE COMPAREE
RLeIT . . . . RASSEGNA DELLA LETTERATURA ITALIANA
R Lett Mod . . . . . . REVUE DES LETTRES MODERNES
RLFE . . . . REVISTA DO LABORATORIO DE FONETICA EXPERIMENTAL
RLHAS . . . . REVUE LITTERATURE, HISTOIRE, ARTS ET SCIENCES
RLI . . . . RASSEGNA DELLA LETTERATURA ITALIANA
RLI . . . . REVISTA DE LAS INDIAS
RLi . . . . REVUE DE LINGUISTIQUE
RLing . . . . REVUE DE LINGUISTIQUE
RLing . . . . RICERCHE LINGUISTISCHE: UNIVERSITA DI ROMA
RLing . . . . RUSSIAN LINGUISTICS
RLir . . . . REALISMO LIRICO
RLiR . . . . REVUE DE LINGUISTIQUE ROMANE
RLit . . . . REVISTA DE LITERATURA
RLit . . . . RUSSKAJA LITERATURA (LENINGRAD)
RLitC . . . . READINGS IN LITERARY CRITICISM
R Litt Comp . . . . . . REVUE DE LITTERATURE COMPAREE
RLiv . . . . RIVISTA DI LIVORNO
RLJ . . . . RHODES-LIVINGSTONE JOURNAL
RLJ . . . . RUSSIAN LANGUAGE JOURNAL
RLLO . . . . REVUE DE LANGUE ET LITTERATURE D'OC
RLLP . . . . REVUE DE LANGUE ET LITTERATURE PROVENCALES
RLLProv . . . . REVUE DE LANGUE ET LITTERATURE PROVENCALES
RLLR . . . . REVUE DE LOUISIANE/LOUISIANA REVIEW
RLM . . . . REVISTA DI LETTERATURE MODERNE E COMPARATE
RLM . . . . REVUE DES LANGUES MODERNES
RLM . . . . RIVISTA DI LETTERATURA MODERNE E COMPARATE
RLMC . . . . RIVISTA DI LETTERATURA MODERNE E COMPARATE
RLMF . . . . REVUE DU LOUVRE ET DES MUSEES DE FRANCE
RLMod . . . . REVUE DES LETTRES MODERNES
RLOE . . . . ROEMISCHE LIMES IN OESTERREICH
R Louvre . . . . REVUE DU LOUVRE ET DES MUSEES DE FRANCE
RLR . . . . REVUE DE LINGUISTIQUE ROMANE
RLR . . . . REVUE DES LANGUES ROMANES
RLS . . . . REGIONAL LANGUAGE STUDIES (NEWFOUNDLAND)
RLT . . . . RUSSIAN LITERATURE TRIQUARTERLY
RLu . . . . RASSEGNA LUCCHESE
RLub . . . . ROCZNIK LUBELSKI
RLuc . . . . RASSEGNA LUCCHESE
RLux . . . . REVUE TRIMESTRIELLE D'ETUDES LINGUISTIQUES, FOLKLORIQUES ET TOPONYMIQUES
(LUXEMBOURG)
RLV . . . . REVUE DE LANGUES VIVANTES

Rly Engng . . . . RAILWAY ENGINEERING JOURNAL
Rly Gaz . . . . RAILWAY GAZETTE
RLz . . . . RADJANS'KE LITERATUROZNAVSTVO (KIEV)
RM . . . . RASSEGNA MONETARIA
RM . . . . RASSEGNA MUSICALE
RM . . . . REVIEW OF METAPHYSICS
RM . . . . REVUE DE METAPHYSIQUE ET DE MORALE
RM . . . . REVUE MONDIALE
RM . . . . ROWOHLTS MONOGRAPHIEN
RM . . . . RUSSKAJA MYSL'
RMA . . . . ROYAL MUSIC ASSOCIATION. PROCEEDINGS
RMab . . . . REVUE MABILLON
RMAL . . . . REVUE DU MOYEN AGE LATIN (STRASBOURG)
RMA Proc . . . . ROYAL MUSICAL ASSOCIATION. PROCEEDINGS
RMA Research . . . . . ROYAL MUSICAL ASSOCIATION. RESEARCH CHRONICLE
RMC . . . . REVISTA MUSICAL CHILENA
RMEA . . . . REVISTA MEXICANA DE ESTUDIOS ANTROPOLOGICOS E HISTORICOS
RMed . . . . REVUE DE LA MEDITERRANEE
R Metaphys . . . . REVIEW OF METAPHYSICS
RMI . . . . RIVISTA MENSILE DI ISRAEL
RMI . . . . RIVISTA MUSICALE ITALIANA
R Mil Coll Can Civ Eng Res Rep . . ROYAL MILITARY COLLEGE OF CANADA. CIVIL ENGINEERING RESEARCH REPORT
RMIs . . . . RASSEGNA MENSILE D'ISRAEL
RML . . . . REVISTA MEXICANA DE LITERATURA
RMM . . . . REVUE DE METAPHYSIQUE ET DE MORALE
RMNac . . . . REVISTA DEL MUSEO NACIONAL
RMod . . . . REVUE MODERNE
RMP . . . . RHEINISCHES MUSEUM FUER PHILOLOGIE
RMPaul . . . . REVISTA DO MUSEU PAULISTA
RMR . . . . ROCKY MOUNTAIN REVIEW
RMS . . . . RENAISSANCE AND MODERN STUDIES
RMS . . . . REVISTA MEXICANA DE SOCIOLOGIA
RMSSJ . . . . ROCKY MOUNTAIN SOCIAL SCIENCE JOURNAL
RMu . . . . REVUE MUSICALE
R Mus . . . . REVUE MUSICALE
R Mus Chile . . . . REVISTA MUSICAL CHILENA
Rev Mus Chilena . . . REVISTA MUSICAL CHILENA
R Mus de Suisse Romande . . REVUE MUSICALE DE SUISSE ROMANDE
R Mus Ital . . . . RIVISTA MUSICALE ITALIANA
RN . . . . RENAISSANCE NEWS
RN . . . . REVUE DU NORD
RN . . . . REVUE NOUVELLE
RN . . . . REVUE NUMISMATIQUE
RNap . . . . REVUE NAPOLEONIENNE
RNar . . . . RAGIONI NARRATIVE
RNaz . . . . RASSEGNA NAZIONALE
RNC . . . . REVISTA NACIONAL DE CULTURA
RNCT . . . . REPORTS OF THE WORKING COMMITTEES. NORTHEAST CONFERENCE ON THE TEACHING OF FOREIGN LANGUAGES
RND . . . . ROCZNIK NAUKOWO-DYDAKTYCZNY
RNE . . . . REVISTA NACIONAL DE EDUCACION

RNeosc . . . . REVUE NEO-SCOLASTIQUE DE PHILOSOPHIE
RNI . . . . RESEARCH NOTES (IBADAN)
RNL . . . . REVIEW OF NATIONAL LITERATURES
RNM . . . . REVISTA NACIONAL (MONTEVIDEO)
R Nord . . . . REVUE DU NORD
RNS . . . . REVUE NEO-SCOLASTIQUE DE PHILOSOPHIE
RNSP . . . . REVUE NEO-SCOLASTIQUE DE PHILOSOPHIE
RNum . . . . RASSEGNA NUMISMATICA
RNum . . . . REVUE NUMISMATIQUE
RO . . . . REVISTA DE OCCIDENTE
RO . . . . ROCZNIK ORIENTALISTYCZNY
Ro . . . . ROMANIA
Roads & Bridges . . . ROADS AND BRIDGES
Roads & Constr . . . . ROADS AND CONSTRUCTION
Roads & Eng Constr . . ROADS AND ENGINEERING CONSTRUCTION
Roads Road Constr . . ROADS AND ROAD CONSTRUCTION
Roads St . . . . ROADS AND STREETS
Robert Morris Associates Bull . . ROBERT MORRIS ASSOCIATES. BULLETIN
ROC . . . . REVUE DE L'ORIENT CHRETIEN
Rochester Acad Sci Proc . . ROCHESTER ACADEMY OF SCIENCE. PROCEEDINGS
Rochester Hist . . . . ROCHESTER HISTORY
Rochester Hist Soc Publ Fund Ser . . ROCHESTER HISTORICAL SOCIETY. PUBLICATION FUND SERIES
Rochester Univ Lib Bul . . UNIVERSITY OF ROCHESTER LIBRARY BULLETIN
ROCH PHIL . . . . ROCHESTER PHILHARMONIC ORCHESTRA PROGRAM NOTES
Rock Mech Felsmech Mec Roches . . ROCK MECHANICS, FELSMECHANIK, MECANIQUE DES ROCHES
Rock Prod . . . . ROCK PRODUCTS
Rocky Mt L Rev . . . . ROCKY MOUNTAIN LAW REVIEW
Rocky Mt ML Inst . . ROCKY MOUNTAIN MINERAL LAW INSTITUTE
ROCKY MT SO . . . . . ROCKY MOUNTAIN SOCIAL SCIENCE JOURNAL
RocO . . . . ROCZNIK ORIENTALISTYCZNY (WARSZAWA)
RoczH . . . . ROCZNIKI HUMANISTYCZNE KATOLICKIEGO UNIWERSYTETU
ROCZN CHEM . . . . . ROCZINIKI CHEMII
RoczSl . . . . ROCZNIK SLAWISTYCZNY
ROD AND GUN . . . . . ROD AND GUN IN CANADA
Roem Jahr Kunstges . . ROEMISCHES JAHRBUCH FUER KUNSTGESCHICHTE
ROF . . . . ROMANISCHE FORSCHUNGEN
R of Rs . . . . REVIEW OF REVIEWS
RoH . . . . ROUMELIOTIKO HEMEROLOGIO
RoHum . . . . ROCZNIKI HUMANISTYCZNE
ROJ . . . . ROMANISTISCHES JAHRBUCH
ROL . . . . REVUE DE L'ORIENT LATIN
RoLit . . . . ROMANIA LITERARA
Rom . . . . ROMANIA
Roman Forsch . . . . . ROMANISCHE FORSCHUNGEN
Roman Philol . . . . . . ROMANCE PHILOLOGY
Roman R . . . . ROMANIC REVIEW
RomF . . . . ROMANISCHE FORSCHUNGEN
RomJ . . . . ROMANISTISCHES JAHRBUCH
RomLit . . . . ROMANIA LITERARA (BUCHAREST)
RomN . . . . ROMANCE NOTES
RomPh . . . . ROMANCE PHILOLOGY

RomR . . . . ROMANIC REVIEW
RomR . . . . ROMANTIC REVIEW
Rom Rev . . . . ROMANTIC REVIEW
RomSl . . . . ROMANOSLAVICA
RoN . . . . ROMANCE NOTES
ROP . . . . ROMANCE PHILOLOGY
ROPM . . . . REVUE DE L'ORDRE DE PREMONTRE ET DE SES MISSIONS
RoR . . . . ROMANIAN REVIEW
ROR . . . . ROMANIC REVIEW
RoR . . . . ROMANTIC REVIEW
RORD . . . . RESEARCH OPPORTUNITIES IN RENAISSANCE DRAMA
RoSlaw . . . . ROCZNIK SLAWISTYCZNY
Round Tab . . . . ROUND TABLE
Roy Aeronaut Soc J . . ROYAL AERONAUTICAL SOCIETY. JOURNAL
Royal Hist Soc Trans . . ROYAL HISTORICAL SOCIETY. TRANSACTIONS
Royal Hort Soc J . . . ROYAL HORTICULTURAL SOCIETY JOURNAL
Royal Soc Canada Proc . . ROYAL SOCIETY OF CANADA. PROCEEDINGS
Roy Arch Inst Can J . . ROYAL ARCHITECTURAL INSTITUTE OF CANADA. JOURNAL
Roy Astron Soc Mem . . ROYAL ASTRONOMICAL SOCIETY. MEMOIRS
Roy Can Inst Trans . . ROYAL CANADIAN INSTITUTE. TRANSACTIONS
Roy Eng J . . . . ROYAL ENGINEERS JOURNAL
Roy Hist Soc Trans . . ROYAL HISTORICAL SOCIETY. TRANSACTIONS
Roy Hort Soc J . . . . . ROYAL HORTICULTURAL SOCIETY. JOURNAL
Roy Inst Brit Arch J . . ROYAL INSTITUTE OF BRITISH ARCHITECTS. JOURNAL
Roy Inst Nav Architects Quart Trans . . ROYAL INSTITUTION OF NAVAL ARCHITECTS. LONDON. QUARTERLY TRANSACTIONS
Roy Meteorol Soc Q J . . ROYAL METEOROLOGICAL SOCIETY. QUARTERLY JOURNAL
Roy Micros Soc J . . . ROYAL MICROSCOPICAL SOCIETY. JOURNAL
Roy Soc Arts J . . . . . ROYAL SOCIETY OF ARTS. JOURNAL
ROY SOC CAN . . . . . ROYAL SOCIETY OF CANADA. PROCEEDINGS AND TRANSACTIONS
Roy Soc Edinb Trans . . ROYAL SOCIETY OF EDINBURGH. TRANSACTIONS
ROY SOC HEA . . . . . ROYAL SOCIETY OF HEALTH JOURNAL
Roy Soc Lond Philos Trans . . ROYAL SOCIETY OF LONDON. PHILOSOPHICAL TRANSACTIONS
Roy Soc NSW J & Proc . . ROYAL SOCIETY OF NEW SOUTH WALES. JOURNAL & PROCEEDINGS
Roy Soc N Z J . . . . . ROYAL SOCIETY OF NEW ZEALAND. JOURNAL
Roy Soc N Z Proc . . . ROYAL SOCIETY OF NEW ZEALAND. PROCEEDINGS
Roy Soc N Z Trans . . ROYAL SOCIETY OF NEW ZEALAND. TRANSACTIONS
Roy Soc N Z Trans Bot . . ROYAL SOCIETY OF NEW ZEALAND. TRANSACTIONS. BOTANY
Roy Soc N Z Trans Earth Sci . . ROYAL SOCIETY OF NEW ZEALAND. TRANSACTIONS. EARTH SCIENCES
Roy Soc N Z Trans Gen . . ROYAL SOCIETY OF NEW ZEALAND. TRANSACTIONS. GENERAL
Roy Soc N Z Trans Geol . . ROYAL SOCIETY OF NEW ZEALAND. TRANSACTIONS. GEOLOGY
Roy Soc N Z Trans Zool . . ROYAL SOCIETY OF NEW ZEALAND. TRANSACTIONS. ZOOLOGY
Roy Soc of Canada Trans . . ROYAL SOCIETY OF CANADA. PROCEEDINGS AND TRANSACTIONS
Roy Soc of Edinburgh Trans . . ROYAL SOCIETY OF EDINBURGH. TRANSACTIONS
Roy Soc of London Philos Trans . . ROYAL SOCIETY OF LONDON. PHILOSOPHICAL TRANSACTIONS
Roy Soc of New South Wales Jour and Proc . ROYAL SOCIETY OF NEW SOUTH WALES. JOURNAL AND PROCEEDINGS
Roy Stat Soc J . . . . . ROYAL STATISTICAL SOCIETY. JOURNAL
Roy Telev Soc J . . . . ROYAL TELEVISION SOCIETY. JOURNAL
Roy Town Plan Inst . . ROYAL TOWN PLANNING INSTITUTE. JOURNAL
Rozpravy CSAV . . . . ROZPRAVY CESKOSLOVENSKE AKADEMIE VED
Rozpr Elektrotech . . ROZPRAWY ELEKTROTECHNICZNE

Rozpr Inz........ ROZPRAWY INZYNIERSKIE
RP............. RENAISSANCE PAPERS
RP............. REVISTA DE PORTUGAL
RP............. REVUE DE PARIS
RP............. REVUE DE PHILOLOGIE DE LITTERATURE ET D'HISTOIRE ANCIENNES
RP............. REVUE DE PHONETIQUE
RP............. REVUE PHILOSOPHIQUE
RP............. ROMANCE PHILOLOGY
RPa........... REVUE DE PARIS
RPA........... REVUE DE PHONETIQUE APPLIQUEE
RPA........... REVUE PRACTIQUE D'APOLOGETIQUE
RPAA........... RENDICONTI DELLA PONTIFICIA ACCADEMIA DI ARCHEOLOGIA
R Palaeobot & Palynol . . REVIEW OF PALAEOBOTANY AND PALYNOLOGY
RPall........... REVUE PALLADIENNE
RPAS.......... REVIEW OF THE POLISH ACADEMY OF SCIENCES
RPed........... REVUE PEDAGOGIQUE
RPF............. REVISTA PORTUGUESA DE FILOLOGIA
RPF............. REVUE DE LA PENSEE FRANCAISE
RPFE........... REVUE PHILOSOPHIQUE DE LA FRANCE ET DE L'ETRANGER
RPFilos.......... REVISTA PORTUGUESA DE FILOSOFIA
RPFL............ REVUE DE PHILOLOGIE FRANCAISE ET DE LITTERATURE
RPH............ REVISTA PORTUGUESA DE HISTORIA
RPh............ REVUE DE PHILOLOGIE
RPh............ REVUE DE PHILOSOPHIE
RPh............ ROMANCE PHILOLOGY
RPhil........... REVUE DE PHILOSOPHIE
R Philos......... REVUE PHILOSOPHIQUE
RPhL......... REVUE PHILOSOPHIQUE DE LOUVAIN
RPJ............ REVUE DE LA PENSEE JUIVE
RPL............ REVUE PHILOSOPHIQUE DE LOUVAIN
RPLHA.......... REVUE DE PHILOLOGIE DE LITTERATURE ET D'HISTOIRE ANCIENNES. TROISIEME SERIE
R Pol............ REVIEW OF POLITICS
R Pol et Litt....... REVUE POLITIQUE ET LITTERAIRE
R Polit et Litt..... REVUE POLITIQUE ET LITTERAIRE
RPP............ REVIEW POLITIQUE ET PARLEMENTAIRE
RPrag.......... ROMANISTICA PRAGENSIA
RPsP............ REVUE DE PSYCHOLOGIE DES PEUPLES
RPTOW.......... ROCZNIK POLSKIEGO TOW
RPu............ RASSEGNA PUGLIESE
RPUSSR.......... RESEARCH PROGRAM OF THE USSR. NEW YORK SERIES
RQ............. RENAISSANCE QUARTERLY
RQ............. REVUE DE OUMRAN
RQ............. REVUE DES QUESTIONS HISTORIQUES
RQ............. RIVERSIDE QUARTERLY
RQ............. RQ (AMERICAN LIBRARY ASSOCIATION REFERENCE SERVICES DIVISION)
RQA........... ROEMISCHE QUARTALSCHRIFT FUER CHRISTLICHE ALTERTUMSKUNDE UND FUER KIRCHEN-
             GESCHICHTE
RQAK.......... ROEMISCHE QUARTALSCHRIFT FUER CHRISTLICHE ALTERTUMSKUNDE UND FUER KIRCHEN-
             GESCHICHTE
RQCAK.......... ROEMISCHE QUARTALSCHRIFT FUER CHRISTLICHE ALTERTUMSKUNDE UND FUER KIRCHEN-
             GESCHICHTE

PERIODICAL TITLE ABBREVIATIONS

RQCAKG......... ROEMISCHE QUARTALSCHRIFT FUER CHRISTLICHE ALTERTUMSKUNDE UND FUER KIRCHEN-
GESCHICHTE
RQH........... REVUE DES QUESTIONS HISTORIQUES
RQHist......... REVUE DES QUESTIONS HISTORIQUES
RQK........... ROEMISCHE QUARTALSCHRIFT FUER KIRCHENGESCHICHTE
RQu........... REVUE DE QUMRAN
RR............ REVIEW FOR RELIGIONS
RR............ REVIEW OF RELIGION
RR............ RICERCHE RELIGIOSE
RR............ ROMANIC REVIEW
RR............ ROMANTIC REVIEW
RRDS.......... REGENTS RENAISSANCE DRAMA SERIES
RRel........... REVIEW OF RELIGION
R Rel Res....... REVIEW OF RELIGIOUS RESEARCH
R Rest DS....... REGENTS RESTORATION DRAMA SERIES
RRev........... RIJECKA REVIJA
RRJaNS......... RODNOJ I RUSSKIJ JAZYKI V NACIONAL'NOJ SKOLE
RRL............ REVUE ROUMAINE DE LINGUISTIQUE (BUCHAREST)
RRo............ RIVISTA ROSMINIANA
R Roumaine....... REVUE ROUMAINE D'HISTOIRE DE L'ART
RRQ............ ROMANIC REVIEW QUARTERLY
RS............. REALITES SECRETES
RS............. RESEARCH STUDIES (PULLMAN)
RS............. REVUE DE SYNTHESE
RS............. REVUE SUISSE
RS............. RICERCHE SLAVISTICHE
RS............. ROCZNIK SLAWISTYCZNY
RS............. ROLLING STONE
RS............. ROMANISCHE STUDIEN
RS............. RURAL SOCIOLOGY
RSA........... RIVISTA DI STORIA ANTICA
RSAA.......... REVUE SUISSE D'ART ET D'ARCHEOLOGIE
RSAC.......... RECUEIL DES NOTICES ET MEMOIRES DE LA SOCIETE ARCHEOLOGIQUE DE CONSTANTINE
RSAP.......... REGIONAL SCIENCE ASSOCIATION. PAPERS AND PROCEEDINGS
RSav.......... REVUE DE SAVOIE
RSAT.......... RECUEIL DE LA SOCIETE DE PREHISTOIRE ET D'ARCHEOLOGIE DE TEBESSA
RSB........... REVISTA DE LA SOCIEDAD BOLIVARIANA
RSB........... RIVISTA STORICA BENEDETTINA
RSBN.......... RIVISTA DI STUDI BIZANTINI E NEOELLENICI
RSC........... RIVISTA DI STUDI CLASSICI
RSC........... RIVISTA DI STUDI CROCIANI
R Sci........... REVUE SCIENTIFIQUE
RSCI.......... RIVISTA DI STORIA DELLA CHIESA IN ITALIA
R Sci Instr....... REVIEW OF SCIENTIFIC INSTRUMENTS
R Sci Ph Th....... REVUE DES SCIENCES PHILOSOPHIQUES ET THEOLOGIQUES
R Sci Pol......... REVUE DES SCIENCES POLITIQUES
R Sci Rel........ REVUE DES SCIENCES RELIGIEUSES
RSCL.......... RIVISTA DI STUDI CLASSICI
RScR.......... REVUE DES SCIENCES RELIGIEUSES
RSCST.......... RIVISTA STORICO-CRITICA DELLE SCIENZE TEOLOGICHE
RSDI.......... RIVISTA DI STORIA DEL DIRITTO ITALIANO

RSE............	RASSEGNA DI STUDI ETIOPICI
RSE............	REVIEW OF SOCIAL ECONOMY
RSE............	REVUE DES SCIENCES ECCLESIASTIQUES
RSE............	RIVISTA DI STORIA ECONOMICA
RSEt...........	RASSEGNA DI STUDI ETIOPICI
RSF............	RASSEGNA DI SCIENZE FILOSOFICHE
RSF............	RASSEGNA DI STUDI FRANCESI
RSF............	RIVISTA DI STORIA DELLA FILOSOFIA
RSFR...........	RIVISTA DI STUDI FILOSOFICI E RELIGIOSI
RSh............	REVISTA SHELL
RSH............	REVUE DES SCIENCES HUMAINES
RSH............	REVUE DE SYNTHESE HISTORIQUE
RSHG..........	REVUE DE LA SOCIETE HAITIENNE D'HISTOIRE, DE GEOGRAPHIE ET DE GEOLOGIE
RSHum.........	REVUE DES SCIENCES HUMAINES
RSI............	RIVISTA STORICA ITALIANA
RSI............	ROCZNIK SLAWISTYCZNY
RSIR...........	INTERNATIONAL STATISTICAL INSTITUTE. REVIEW
RSIU...........	ROCENKA SLOVANSKEHO USTAVU V PRAZE
RSI............	REVUE DES ETUDES SLAVES
RSL............	RICERCHE SLAVISTICHE (ROMA)
RSL............	RIVISTA DI SINTESI LITTERARIA
RSL............	RIVISTA DI STUDI LIGURI
RSL............	ROYAL SOCIETY OF LITERATURE
RSlav..........	RICERCHE SLAVISTICHE
RSlav..........	ROMANOSLAVICA
RSII...........	RADOVI SLAVENSKOG INSTITUTA
RSLig..........	RIVISTA DI STUDI LIGURI
RSLit..........	RIVERSIDE STUDIES IN LITERATURE
RSLR..........	RIVISTA DE STORIA E LETTERATURA RELIGIOSA
RSM...........	RIVISTA STORICO-CRITICA DELLE SCIENZE MEDICHE E NATURALI
Rs Mod Physics....	REVIEWS OF MODERN PHYSICS
RSO...........	RIVISTA DEGLI STUDI ORIENTALI
RSoc..........	REVUE SOCIALISTE
R Soc Econ........	REVIEW OF SOCIAL ECONOMY
RSov..........	RASSEGNA SOVIETICA
RSP...........	REVUE DES SCIENCES POLITIQUES
RSP...........	RIVISTA DI STUDI POMPEIANI
RSPh..........	REVUE DES SCIENCES PHILOSOPHIQUES ET THEOLOGIQUES
RSPT..........	REVUE DES SCIENCES PHILOSOPHIQUES ET THEOLOGIQUES
RSR...........	RASSEGNA STORICA DEL RISORGIMENTO
RSR...........	RECHERCHES DE SCIENCE RELIGIEUSE
RSR...........	REFERENCE SERVICES REVIEW
RSR...........	REVUE DES SCIENCES RELIGIEUSES. UNIVERSITE DE STRASBOURG
RSRel..........	REVUE DES SCIENCES RELIGIEUSES. UNIVERSITE DE STRASBOURG
RSRis.........	RASSEGNA STORICA DEL RISORGIMENTO
RSRUS.........	REVUE DES SCIENCES RELIGIEUSES. UNIVERSITE DE STRASBOURG
RSS...........	RASSEGNA STORICA SALERNITANA
RSS...........	REVUE DU SEIZIEME SIECLE
RSS...........	RIVISTA DI SCIENZE STORICHE
RSSal..........	RASSEGNA STORICA SALERNITANA
RSSCW.........	RESEARCH STUDIES OF THE STATE COLLEGE OF WASHINGTON (PULLMAN)

RSSLI . . . . RADOVI STAROSLAVENSKOG INSTITUTA
RSSMN . . . . RIVISTA DI STORIA DELLE SCIENZE MEDICHE E NATURALI
RSt . . . . RESEARCH STUDIES
RST . . . . RIVISTA DI STUDI TEATRALI
RST . . . . RIVISTA STORICA TINCINESE
RSU . . . . ROCENKA SLOVANSKEHO USTAVU
R Suisse Zool . . . . . . REVUE SUISSE DE ZOOLOGIE
RSV . . . . REVISTA SIGNOS DE VALPARAISO
RSVR . . . . ROMA. RIVISTA DI STUDI E DI VITA ROMANA
RSWSU . . . . RESEARCH STUDIES OF WASHINGTON STATE UNIVERSITY (PULLMAN)
RSyn . . . . REVUE DE SYNTHESE
RT . . . . RELIGIOUS THEATRE
RT . . . . REVIEW THEATRALE
RT . . . . REVUE TUNISIENNE
RTAM . . . . RECHERCHES DE THEOLOGIE ANCIENNE ET MEDIEVALE
RTASM . . . . REVUE DES TRAVAUX DE L'ACADEMIE DES SCIENCES MORALES ET POLITIQUES
RTC . . . . REVUE TRIMESTRIELLE CANADIENNE
R Telev Soc J . . . . . . ROYAL TELEVISION SOCIETY JOURNAL
RTF . . . . REVUE THEOLOGIQUE FRANCAISE
RTh . . . . REVUE DE THEOLOGIE ET DE PHILOSOPHIE
RThom . . . . REVUE THOMISTE
RThPh . . . . REVUE DE THEOLOGIE ET DE PHILOSOPHIE
RTKKUL . . . . ROCZNIKI TEOLOGICZNO-KANONICZNE. KATOLICKIEGO UNIWERSYTETU LUBELSKIEGO
RTKL . . . . ROCZNIKI TEOLOGICZNO-KANONICZNE. KATOLICKIEGO UNIWERSYTETU LUBELSKIEGO
RTor . . . . ROCZNIK TORUNSKI
RTP . . . . REVUE DE THEOLOGIE ET DE PHILOSOPHIE (GENEVE)
RTPh . . . . REVUE DE THEOLOGIE ET DE PHILOSOPHIE (GENEVE)
RTPM . . . . REVISTA DE TRADICIONES POPULARES (MADRID)
RTR . . . . RESTORATION AND 18TH-CENTURY THEATRE RESEARCH
RTr . . . . RIVISTA DELLA TRIPOLITANIA
RTSFR . . . . RIVISTA TRIMESTRIALE DI STUDI FILOSOFICI E RELIGIOSI
RTSS . . . . REVUE TUNISIENNE DE SCIENCES SOCIALES
RU . . . . REVISTA UNIVERSITARIA DE LA UNIVERSIDAD CATOLICA DE CHILE
RUB . . . . REVUE DE L'UNIVERSITE DE BRUXELLES
RuB . . . . RUSSKOE BOGATSTVO
RUBA . . . . REVISTA DE LA UNIVERSIDAD DE BUENOS AIRES
Rubb Dev . . . . RUBBER DEVELOPMENTS
Rubber Chem Technol . . RUBBER CHEMISTRY AND TECHNOLOGY
Rubb Plast Age . . . . RUBBER AND PLASTICS AGE
RUC . . . . REVISTA DE LA UNIVERSIDAD DE CORDOBA
RuC . . . . RUPERTO-CAROLA
RuchL . . . . RUCH LITERACKI (KRAKOW)
RUCH MUZ . . . . RUCH MUZYCZNY
RUCP . . . . REVISTA DE LA UNIVERSIDAD CATOLICA DEL PERU
Rud Glas . . . . RUDARSKI GLASNIK
Rud Met Zb . . . . RUDARSKO-METALURSKI ZBORNIK
RUF . . . . REVISTA VALENCIANA DE FILOLOGIA
RuJ . . . . RUSKY JAZYK
RUL . . . . REVUE DE L'UNIVERSITE DE LYON
RUL . . . . REVUE DE L'UNIVERSITE LAVAL (QUEBEC)
RuLit . . . . RUCH LITERACKI

RULP........... REVISTA DE LA UNIVERSIDAD DE LA PLATA
RUM............ REVISTA DE LA UNIVERSIDAD DE MADRID
RUMG.......... REVISTA DA UNIVERSIDAD DE MINAS GERAIS
RUM Rev Univers Mines..RUM, REVUE UNIVERSELLE DES MINES, DE LA METALLURGIE, DE LA MECHANIQUE DES
              TRAVAUX PUBLICS DES SCIENCES
RUnBrux........ REVUE DE L'UNIVERSITE DE BRUXELLES
RUNC.......... REVISTA DE LA UNIVERSIDAD DE COLOMBIA
RUNC.......... REVISTA DE LA UNIVERSIDAD NACIONAL DE CORDOBA
Rundfunktech Mitt..RUNDFUNKTECHNISCHE MITTEILUNGEN
RUniv.......... REVUE UNIVERSELLE
R Univ.......... REVUE UNIVERSITAIRE
R Univ Ottawa..... REVUE DE L'UNIVERSITE D'OTTAWA
RUO........... REVISTA DE LA UNIVERSIDAD DE OVIEDO
RUO........... REVUE DE L'UNIVERSITE D'OTTAWA
RUOt........... REVUE DE L'UNIVERSITE D'OTTAWA
RUR........... RUSSKAYA RECH (MOSCOW)
Rural Am........ RURAL AMERICA
Rural Elec N....... RURAL ELECTRIFICATION NEWS
RURAL SOCIO..... RURAL SOCIOLOGY
Rural N Y....... RURAL NEW YORKER
Rur Sociol....... RURAL SOCIOLOGY
RUS........... RICE UNIVERSITY STUDIES
RUSE.......... RUTGERS UNIVERSITY STUDIES IN ENGLISH
RUSEng.......... RAJASTHAN UNIVERSITY STUDIES IN ENGLISH
RusF........... RUSSKIJ FOL'KLOR
RusL........... RUSSKAYA LITERATURA (LENINGRAD)
RusR........... RUSSIAN REVIEW
RusR........... RUSSKAJA REC
Russ Cast Prod.... RUSSIAN CASTINGS PRODUCTION
Russell Cotes Mus Bul..RUSSELL-COTES ART GALLERY AND MUSEUM BULLETIN
Russ Eng J....... RUSSIAN ENGINEERING JOURNAL
RUSS EN J....... RUSSIAN ENGINEERING JOURNAL
RUSS MET R...... RUSSIAN METALLURGY-USSR
Russ R.......... RUSSIAN REVIEW
Rutgers Camden L J..RUTGERS CAMDEN LAW JOURNAL
Rutgers L Rev..... RUTGERS LAW REVIEW
RUY........... REVISTA DE LA UNIVERSIDAD DE YUCATAN
RV............ RASSEGNA VOLTERRANA
RV............ RHEINISCHE VIERTELJAHRSBLAETTER
RVB........... RHEINISCHE VIERTELJAHRSBLAETTER
R Venez Folk...... REVISTA VENEZOLANA DE FOLKLORE
RvEx........... REVIEW AND EXPOSITOR
RVF........... REVISTA VALENCIANA DE FILOLOGIA
RVF........... REVISTA VENEZOLANA DE FOLKLORE
RVFC.......... REVISTA VENEZOLANA DE FOLKLORE
RVLI........... RAKSTI. LATVIJAS PSR ZINATNU AKADEMIJA. VALODAS UND LITERATURAS INSTITUTA
RVV........... ROMANISTISCHE VERSUCNE UND VORARBEITEN
RW............ ROUGH WEATHER
RWF........... FOZPRAWY WYDZIALU FILOLOGICZNEGO POLSKIEJ AKADEMYI UMIEJETNOSCI
RWP........... REFORMACJA W POLSCE
RYa........... RUSSKII YAZYK V SHKOLE (MOSCOW)

PERIODICAL TITLE ABBREVIATIONS

Ry Age . . . . RAILWAY AGE
RyC . . . . RELIGION Y CULTURA
RyF . . . . RAZON Y FE
RyFab . . . . RAZON Y FABULA
Ry Gaz Int . . . . RAILWAY GAZETTE INTERNATIONAL
Ry Loco & Cars . . . . RAILWAY LOCOMOTIVES AND CARS
Ry Mech & Elec Eng . . RAILWAY MECHANICAL AND ELECTRICAL ENGINEER
Ry Mech Eng . . . . . . RAILWAY MECHANICAL ENGINEER
Ry R . . . . RAILWAY REVIEW
Ry Track Struct . . . . RAILWAY TRACK AND STRUCTURES
RZ . . . . RADOSTNA ZEME
RZ . . . . RADOVI (FILOZOFSKI FAKULTET-ZADAR)
RZ . . . . REVISTA ZURITA SARAGOSSE
RZSF . . . . RADOVI ZAVODA ZA SLAVENSKU FILOLOGIJU

S

S............... SEPTEMBER
S............... SLAVIA
S............... SPECTATOR
S............... SPECULUM
S............... STUDIO
S............... SYMPOSIUM
Sa............. SAMTIDEN
SA............. SCIENTIFIC AMERICAN
SA............. SOVIETSKAIA ARCHEOLOGIIA
SA............. SPEECH ACTIVITIES
SA............. STUDI AMERICANI (ROMA)
SA............. SYMBOLAE ARCTOAE
SAA............ SCHWEIZER ANGLISTISCHE ARBEITEN
SAANAn........ SOCIETE ARCHEOLOGIQUE DE L'ARRONDISSEMENT DE NIVELLES. ANNALES
SAB............ SHAKESPEARE ASSOCIATION BULLETIN
SAB............ SOUTH ATLANTIC BULLETIN
SABA........... SOCIETE ARCHEOLOGIQUE DE BRUXELLES. ANNALES
Sac............ SACRIS ERUDIRI
SacE........... SACRIS ERUDIRI
Sachs Akad d Wiss Philol-Hist Kl Ber u d Verhandl.. SAECHSISCHE AKADEMIE DER WISSENSCHAFTEN. PHILOLOGISCH-HISTORISCHE KLASSE. BERICHTE UEBER DIE VERHANDLUNGEN
SACRED MUS...... SACRED MUSIC
SAE J........... SAE (SOCIETY OF AUTOMOTIVE ENGINEERS) JOURNAL
SAE Prepr........ SAE (SOCIETY OF AUTOMOTIVE ENGINEERS) PREPRINTS
SAE Spec Publ..... SAE (SOCIETY OF AUTOMOTIVE ENGINEERS) SPECIAL PUBLICATIONS
SAE Trans........ SAE (SOCIETY OF AUTOMOTIVE ENGINEERS) TRANSACTIONS
Safety Ed........ SAFETY EDUCATION
Safety Eng........ SAFETY ENGINEERING
Safety Maint...... SAFETY MAINTENANCE
Safety Maint & Prod.. SAFETY MAINTENANCE AND PRODUCTION
SAFMem......... SOCIETE NATIONALE DES ANTIQUAIRES DE FRANCE. MEMOIRES
S Afr Counc Sci Ind Res Nat Bldg Res Inst Bull.. SOUTH AFRICAN COUNCIL FOR SCIENTIFIC AND INDUSTRIAL RESEARCH. NATIONAL BUILDING RESEARCH INSTITUTE. BULLETIN
S Afr Dep Mines Quart Inform Circ Miner.. SOUTH AFRICA. DEPARTMENT OF MINES. QUARTERLY INFORMATION CIRCULAR. MINERALS
S Afr Geol Surv Bull.. SOUTH AFRICA. DEPARTMENT OF MINES. GEOLOGICAL SURVEY. BULLETIN
S Afr Geol Surv Mem.. SOUTH AFRICA. DEPARTMENT OF MINES. GEOLOGICAL SURVEY. MEMOIR
S African Lib...... SOUTH AFRICAN LIBRARIES
S African Lib Q Bull.. SOUTH AFRICAN LIBRARY QUARTERLY BULLETIN
S AFR J EC........ SOUTH AFRICAN JOURNAL OF ECONOMICS
S AFR J SCI....... SOUTH AFRICAN JOURNAL OF SCIENCE
SAfrL........... STUDIES IN AFRICAN LITERATURE
S Afr Mech Eng.... SOUTH AFRICAN MECHANICAL ENGINEER
S AFR MED J...... SOUTH AFRICAN MEDICAL JOURNAL
S Afr Rep Secr Water Affairs.. SOUTH AFRICA. REPORT OF THE SECRETARY FOR WATER AFFAIRS
S AFR STAT....... SOUTH AFRICAN STATISTICAL JOURNAL
Sag............ SAGGIATORE
Saga-Book........ SAGA-BOOK OF THE VIKING SOCIETY FOR NORTHERN RESEARCH
SAGE PAP CP...... SAGE PROFESSIONAL PAPERS IN COMPARATIVE POLITICS

SAH............ STRATFORD-ON-AVON HERALD
SAH............ SVENSKA AKADEMIENS HANDLINGAR
SAHLBull........ SOCIETE D'ART ET D'HISTOIRE DAN LE DIOCESE DE LIEGE. BULLETIN
SAHS........... SWISS-AMERICAN HISTORICAL SOCIETY. NEWSLETTER
SAIS REV........ SAIS (SCHOOL OF ADVANCED INTERNATIONAL STUDIES) REVIEW
SAJE............ SOUTH AFRICAN JOURNAL OF ECONOMICS
Sal............ SALESIANUM
SAL............ SOUTHWESTERN AMERICAN LITERATURE
SAL............ STUDIES IN AFRICAN LINGUISTICS
SALB........... STUDIA ALBANICA (TIRANA)
Sales Mgt....... SALES MANAGEMENT
SALit........... STUDIES IN AMERICAN LITERATURE
S A L J.......... SOUTH AFRICAN LAW JOURNAL
Salm........... SALMANTICENSIS
Salzburger Jrbh Phil.. SALZBURGER JAHRBUCH FUER PHILOSOPHIE
Sam............ SAMMLUNG
SAM ADV MAN.... SAM ADVANCED MANAGEMENT JOURNAL
SAMBHist........ SOCIETE DES ANTIQUAIRES DE LA MORINIE. BULLETIN HISTORIQUE
SA Min Eng J...... SA (SOUTH AFRICAN) MINING AND ENGINEERING JOURNAL
Saml........... SAMLAREN
SAML.......... STUDIES IN AMERICAN LITERATURE (THE HAGUE)
SAMPE J........ SAMPE (SOCIETY OF AEROSPACE MATERIAL AND PROCESS ENGINEERS) JOURNAL
SANAn.......... SOCIETE ARCHEOLOGIQUE DE NAMUR. ANNALES
San Diego L Rev.... SAN DIEGO LAW REVIEW
S&N............ STATESMAN AND NATION
S&S............ SCHOOL AND SOCIETY
S&S............ SCIENCE AND SOCIETY
S&T............ SKY AND TELESCOPE
S&W............ SOUTH AND WEST
SanF............ SAN FRANCISCO MAGAZINE
SANGruz........ SOOBSCENIJA AKADEMII NAUK GRUZINSKOJ SSR
Sanitary & Heat Eng.. SANITARY AND HEATING ENGINEERING
SANKHYA A....... SANKHYA. SERIES A. INDIAN JOURNAL OF STATISTICS
SANKHYA B....... SANKHYA. SERIES B. INDIAN JOURNAL OF STATISTICS
Santa Clara Law.... SANTA CLARA LAWYER
SAO............ STUDIA ET ACTA ORIENTALIA
SAOB........... SVENSKA AKADEMIENS ORDBOK
Sao Paulo Brazil Inst Pesqui Tecnol Bol.. SAO PAULO, BRAZIL. INSTITUTO DE PESQUISAS TECNOLOGICAS.
            BOLETIN
SAP............ STUDIA ANGLICA POSNANIENSIA
SAQ............ SOUTH ATLANTIC QUARTERLY
SAR............ SOUTH ASIAN REVIEW
SarawakMJ....... SARAWAK MUSEUM JOURNAL
SaS............ SLOVO A SLOVESNOST
SAS............ STUDIA ACADEMICA SLOVACA
SASILO.......... SCHRIFTENREIHE DES A. STIFER-INSTITUTS DES LANDES OBEROESTERREICH
Sask B Rev....... SASKATCHEWAN BAR REVIEW
Sask Dep Miner Resour Geol Sci Br Precambrian Geol Div Rep.. SASKATCHEWAN. DEPARTMENT OF MINERAL
            RESOURCES. GEOLOGICAL SCIENCES BRANCH. PRECAMBRIAN GEOLOGY DIVISION. REPORT
SASK HIST........ SASKATCHEWAN HISTORY
Sask L Rev....... SASKATCHEWAN LAW REVIEW

SAT . . . . SATELLITE SCIENCE FICTION
Sat Eve Post . . . . . . SATURDAY EVENING POST
SATF . . . . SOCIETE DES ANCIENS TEXTES FRANCAIS
SatireNL . . . . SATIRE NEWSLETTER
S Atlantic Q . . . . SOUTH ATLANTIC QUARTERLY
Sat N . . . . SATURDAY NIGHT
Sat R . . . . SATURDAY REVIEW
Sat R Arts . . . . SATURDAY REVIEW OF THE ARTS
Sat R Ed . . . . SATURDAY REVIEW OF EDUCATION
Sat R Lit . . . . SATURDAY REVIEW OF LITERATURE
Sat R Sci . . . . SATURDAY REVIEW OF THE SCIENCES
Sat R Soc . . . . SATURDAY REVIEW OF THE SOCIETY
Sat R/World . . . . SATURDAY REVIEW/WORLD
SAU . . . . SPRAWODZANIA AKADEMII UMIEJETNOSCI
S Aus Nat Gal Bul . . . SOUTH AUSTRALIA. NATIONAL GALLERY. BULLETIN
Sav . . . . SAVREMENIK
SAV . . . . SCHWEIZERISCHES ARCHIV FUER VOLKSKUNDE
SAV . . . . SLOVENSKA AKADEMIA VIED
SAVL . . . . STUDIEN ZUR ALLGEMEINEN UND VERGLEICHENDEN LITERATURWISSENSCHAFT
SAW . . . . SITZUNGSBERICHTE DER AKADEMIE DER WISSENSCHAFT IN WIEN
SAWW . . . . SITZUNGSBERICHTE DER AKADEMIE DER WISSENSCHAFT IN WIEN
SAY . . . . SCIENCE FICTION ADVENTURES YEARBOOK
SB . . . . SCIENCE BOOKS
SB . . . . SKANDINAVISKA BANKEN. QUARTERLY REVIEW
SB . . . . SOVETSKAYA BIBLIOGRAFIA
SB . . . . STUDI BALTICI
SB . . . . STUDI BIZANTINI
SB . . . . STUDIES IN BIBLIOGRAPHY
SBA . . . . SITZUNGSBERICHTE DER BAYERISCHEN AKADEMIE DER WISSENSCHAFT
SBAG . . . . SCHWEIZER BEITRAEGE ZUR ALLGEMEINEN GESCHICHTE
SbAk . . . . SBORNIK NA BALGARSKATA AKADEMIJA NA NAUKITE
SBAW . . . . SITZUNGSBERICHTE DER BAYERISCHEN AKADEMIE DER WISSENSCHAFTEN
SBAWW . . . . SITZUNGSBERICHTE DER AKADEMIE DER WISSENSCHAFTEN IN WIEN
SBB . . . . STUDIES IN BIBLIOGRAPHY AND BOOKLORE
SBBAW . . . . SITZUNGSBERICHTE DER BAYERISCHEN AKADEMIE DER WISSENSCHAFTEN
SbDAW . . . . SITZUNGSBERICHTE DER DEUTSCHEN AKADEMIE DER WISSENSCHAFTEN ZU BERLIN. KLASSE FUER SPRACHEN, LITERATUR UND KUNST
SBDAWB . . . . SITZUNGSBERICHTE DER DEUTSCHEN AKADEMIE DER WISSENSCHAFTEN ZU BERLIN. KLASSE FUER SPRACHEN, LITERATUR UND KUNST
SbFAW . . . . SITZUNGSBERICHTE DER FINNISCHEN AKADEMIE DER WISSENSCHAFTEN
SBGGAKOPR . . . . . . SITZUNGSBERICHTE DER GESELLSCHAFT FUER GESCHICHTE UND ALTERTUMSKUNDE DER OSTSEEPROVINZEN RUSSLANDS
SBGGAKR . . . . SITZUNGSBERICHTE DER GESELLSCHAFT FUER GESCHICHTE UND ALTERTUMSKUND DER OSTSEE-PROVINZEN RUSSLANDS
SBHAW . . . . SITZUNGSBERICHTE DER HEIDELBERGER AKADEMIE DER WISSENSCHAFTEN
SBHT . . . . STUDIES IN BURKE AND HIS TIME
SBiz . . . . STUDI BIZANTINI
SBKAW . . . . SITZUNGSBERICHTE DER K. AKADEMIE DER WISSENSCHAFTEN IN WIEN
SBKAWW . . . . SITZUNGSBERICHTE DER K. AKADEMIE DER WISSENSCHAFTEN IN WIEN
SBKBAW . . . . SITZUNGSBERICHTE DER BAYERISCHE AKADEMIE DER WISSENSCHAFTEN
SBL . . . . STUDIES IN BLACK LITERATURE

SB LEKAR . . . . SBORNIK LEKARSKY
SBMCO . . . . STUDIEN UND MITTEILUNGEN AUS DEM BENEDIKTINER- UND DER CISTERCIENSER-ORDEN
SBN . . . . STUDI BIZANTINI E NEOELLENICI
SbNU . . . . SBORNIK ZA NARODNI UMOTVORENIJA I NARODOPIS
SbOAW . . . . SITZUNGSBERICHTE DER OESTERREICHISCHEN AKADEMIE DER WISSENSCHAFTEN, PHILOSO-
PHISCH-HISTORISCHE KLASSE
SBoc . . . . STUDI SUL BOCCACCIO
SBol . . . . STRENNA BOLOGNESE
SBPAW . . . . SITZUNGSBERICHTE DER K. PREUSSISCHEN AKADEMIE DER WISSENSCHAFTEN (BERLIN)
SBPAWB . . . . SITZUNGSBERICHTE DER K. PREUSSISCHEN AKADEMIE DER WISSENSCHAFTEN (BERLIN)
SBPR Bol . . . . SBPR BOLETIN
SBSAW . . . . SITZUNGSBERICHTE DER SAECHSISCHEN AKADEMIE DER WISSENSCHAFTEN ZU LEIPZIG.
PHILOLOGISCH-HISTORISCHE KLASSE
SBSAWL . . . . SITZUNGSBERICHTE DER SAECHSISCHEN AKADEMIE DER WISSENSCHAFTEN ZU LEIPZIG.
PHILOLOGISCH-HISTORISCHE KLASSE
SBVS . . . . SAGA-BOOK. VIKING SOCIETY FOR NORTHERN RESEARCH (LONDON)
Sc . . . . SCIENTIA. ORGANO INTERNAZIONALE DI SINTESI SCIENTIFICA
Sc . . . . SCRIPTORIUM
SC . . . . SCUOLA CATTOLICA
SC . . . . SOCIAL CASEWORK
SC . . . . STENDHAL-CLUB
SC . . . . STUDI COLOMBIANI
SC . . . . STUDIA CATHOLICA
SC . . . . STUDIA CELTICA
SC . . . . SUISSE CONTEMPORAINE
Sca . . . . SCANDINAVICA
SCA . . . . SCIENCE FICTION CLASSICS ANNUAL
S C Ag Dept . . . . . . SOUTH CAROLINA DEPARTMENT OF AGRICULTURE, COMMERCE AND INDUSTRIES.
PUBLICATIONS
S C Ag Exp . . . . SOUTH CAROLINA AGRICULTURAL EXPERIMENT STATION. PUBLICATIONS
S CAL LAW R . . . . . . SOUTHERN CALIFORNIA LAW REVIEW
Scan . . . . SCANDINAVIAN STUDIES
Scan . . . . SCANDINAVICA
Scand . . . . SCANDINAVICA
Scand J Metall . . . . SCANDINAVIAN JOURNAL OF METALLURGY
Scand Pol Stud . . . . SCANDINAVIAN POLITICAL STUDIES
Scand R . . . . SCANDINAVIAN REVIEW
Scand Stud . . . . SCANDINAVIAN STUDIES
SCathol . . . . STUDIA CATHOLICA
SCauc . . . . STUDIA CAUCASICA
SCB . . . . SOUTH CENTRAL BULLETIN
SCB . . . . STUDI SI CERCETARI DE BIBLIOLOGIE
ScCatt . . . . SCUOLA CATTOLICA
Scen . . . . SCENARIO
ScEs . . . . SCIENCE ET ESPRIT
SCF . . . . SCIENCE FANTASY
Sch . . . . SCHOLASTIK
Sch . . . . SCHOOL (TORONTO)
SCh . . . . SOURCES CHRETIENNES
Sch Activities . . . . . SCHOOL ACTIVITIES
Sch & Com . . . . SCHOOL AND COMMUNITY

Sch and Home . . . . . SCHOOL AND HOME
Sch & Soc . . . . SCHOOL AND SOCIETY
Sch Arts M . . . . SCHOOL ARTS MAGAZINE
Sch Counsel . . . . SCHOOL COUNSELOR
Sch (El ed) . . . . SCHOOL (TORONTO) (ELEMENTARY EDITION)
Sch Exec . . . . SCHOOL EXECUTIVE
Sch Executives M . . . SCHOOL EXECUTIVES MAGAZINE
SCHGM . . . . SOUTH CAROLINA HISTORICAL AND GENEALOGICAL MAGAZINE
SCH LIB . . . . SCHOOL LIBRARIES
Sch Lib Assn Calif Bul . . SCHOOL LIBRARY ASSOCIATION OF CALIFORNIA. BULLETIN
SCH LIB J . . . . SCHOOL LIBRARY JOURNAL
Sch Libn . . . . SCHOOL LIBRARIAN
Sch Lib R . . . . SCHOOL LIBRARY REVIEW AND EDUCATIONAL RECORD
Sch Life . . . . SCHOOL LIFE
Sch M . . . . SCHWEIZER MONATSHEFTE
SCHM . . . . SOUTH CAROLINA HISTORICAL AND GENEALOGICAL MAGAZINE
Sch Manag . . . . SCHOOL MANAGEMENT
Sch Media Q . . . . . . SCHOOL MEDIA QUARTERLY
Sch Mgt . . . . SCHOOL MANAGEMENT
Schmollers Jahrb . . . SCHMOLLERS JAHRBUCH FUER GESETZGEBUNG, VERWALTUNG UND VOLKSWIRTSCHAFT IM
                         DEUTSCHEN REICHE
Sch Mus . . . . SCHOOL MUSIC
Sch MZ . . . . SCHWEIZERISCHE MUSIK ZEITUNG
Schol . . . . SCHOLASTIK. VIERTELJAHRESSCHRIFT FUER THEOLOGIE UND PHILOSOPHIE
Scholarly Pub . . . . . SCHOLARLY PUBLISHING
Scholastic . . . . SENIOR SCHOLASTIC (TEACHER EDITION)
Scholastic D . . . . . . SCHOLASTIC DEBATER
Schol Coach . . . . SCHOLASTIC COACH
Schol Teach . . . . SCHOLASTIC TEACHER
School & Col . . . . . . SCHOOL AND COLLEGE
School and Soc . . . . . SCHOOL AND SOCIETY
School Arts M . . . . . SCHOOL ARTS MAGAZINE
School Lib . . . . SCHOOL LIBRARIES
Schoolmens W Univ Pa Proc . . SCHOOLMEN'S WEEK. UNIVERSITY OF PENNSYLVANIA. PROCEEDINGS
SCHOOL MUS . . . . . . SCHOOL MUSICIAN
Schopenhauer Jahr . . SCHOPENHAUER-JAHRBUCH
SchP . . . . SCHOLARLY PUBLISHING
Sch R . . . . SCHOOL REVIEW
SchR . . . . SCHWEIZER RUNDSCHAU
SCH REV . . . . SCHOOL REVIEW
Sch (Sec ed) . . . . . . SCHOOL (TORONTO) (SECONDARY EDITION)
Sch Shop . . . . SCHOOL SHOP
SCHW A NEUR . . . . . SCHWEIZER ARCHIV FUER NEUROLOGIE, NEUROCHIRURGIE UND PSYCHIATRIE
SchwArchV . . . . SCHWEIZERISCHES ARCHIV FUER VOLKSKUNDE
Schweiz Alum Rundsch . . SCHWEIZER ALUMINIUM RUNDSCHAU
Schweiz Arch Angew Wiss Tech . . SCHWEIZER ARCHIV FUER ANGEWANDTE WISSENSCHAFT UND TECHNIK
Schweiz Archiv f Volksk . . SCHWEIZERISCHES ARCHIV FUER VOLKSKUNDE
Schweiz Bauztg . . . . SCHWEIZERISCHE BAUZEITUNG
SCHWEIZ MUS . . . . . SCHWEIZERISCHE MUSIKZEITUNG
SCHWENK . . . . SCHWENCKFELDIANA
SchwM . . . . SCHWEIZER MONATSHEFTE

SCHW MED WO.... SCHWEIZERISCHE MEDIZINISCHE WOCHENSCHRIFT
SchwRundschau.... SCHWEIZER RUNDSCHAU
SchwV.......... SCHWEIZER VOLKSKUNDE
SCHW Z PSYC..... SCHWEIZERISCHE ZEITSCHRIFT FUER PSYCHOLOGIE UND IHRE ANWENDUNG
SCHW Z SOZ...... SCHWEIZERISCHE ZEITSCHRIFT FUER SOZIALVERSICHERUNG
SCI............. SCIENCE
SCI............. SCIENCE CITATION INDEX
ScI............. SCRIPTA ISLANDICA
SCIa........... STUDII SI CERCETARI STIINTIFICE FILOLOGIE. ACADEMIA REPUBLICII POPULARE ROMINE, FILIALA IASI
SciAb.......... SCIENCE ABSTRACTS
Sci Ag.......... SCIENTIFIC AGRICULTURE
SCI AM......... SCIENTIFIC AMERICAN
Sci Am Monthly.... SCIENTIFIC AMERICAN MONTHLY
Sci Am S........ SCIENTIFIC AMERICAN SUPPLEMENT
Sci & Child....... SCIENCE AND CHILDREN
Sci & Soc........ SCIENCE AND SOCIETY
Sci & Tech....... SCIENCE AND TECHNOLOGY
Sci Bks.......... SCIENCE BOOKS
Sci Ed.......... SCIENCE EDUCATION
Sci Elec.......... SCIENTIA ELECTRICA
Science Ed....... SCIENCE EDUCATION
Science N L....... SCIENCE NEWS LETTER
Science Prog...... SCIENCE PROGRESS
Sciences Pol...... SCIENCES POLITIQUES
Scient Am........ SCIENTIFIC AMERICAN
Scientiarum Hist... SCIENTIARUM HISTORIA
Scient Instrum..... SCIENTIFIC INSTRUMENTS
Sci Esprit........ SCIENCE ET ESPRIT
SCI FORUM....... SCIENCE FORUM
SCI GEOL S....... SCIENTIA GEOLOGICA SINICA
SCI HORT........ SCIENTIFIC HORTICULTURE
Sci Ilus.......... SCIENCE ILLUSTRATED
Sci Ind Spatiales Space Res Eng Weltraumforsch Ind.. SCIENCES ET INDUSTRIES SPATIALES, SPACE RESEARCH AND ENGINEERING, WELTRAUMFORSCHUNG UND INDUSTRIE
Sci Instr......... SCIENTIFIC INSTRUMENTS
Sci J............ SCIENCE JOURNAL
SCILF........... STUDII SI CERCETARI DE ISTORIE LITERARA SI FOLCLOR
SCI LIGHT........ SCIENCE OF LIGHT
Sci Mo........... SCIENTIFIC MONTHLY
Sci N............ SCIENCE NEWS
SCI PAED EX...... SCIENTIA PAEDAGOGICA EXPERIMENTALIS
Sci Pap Inst Phys Chem Res (Tokyo)..SCIENTIFIC PAPERS OF THE INSTITUTE OF PHYSICAL AND CHEMICAL RESEARCH (TOKYO)
Sci Prog......... SCIENCE PROGRESS
Sci Progr Decouverte..SCIENCE PROGRES DECOUVERTE
SCI PUBL AF...... SCIENCE AND PUBLIC AFFAIRS. BULLETIN OF THE ATOMIC SCIENTISTS
SCI R TOH A...... SCIENCE REPORTS OF THE RESEARCH INSTITUTES TOHOKU UNIVERSITY. SERIES A. PHYSICS, CHEMISTRY AND METALLURGY
Sci Serves Farm.... SCIENCE SERVES YOUR FARM
SCI SINICA....... SCIENTIA SINICA

```
SCI SOC..........SCIENCE AND SOCIETY
SCI STUD.........SCIENCE STUDIES
Sci Teach.........SCIENCE TEACHER
Sci Technol.......SCIENCE AND TECHNOLOGY
Sci Tech (Paris)....SCIENCES ET TECHNIQUES (PARIS)
SCIV.............STUDII SI CERCETARI DE ISTORIE VECHE
SCJ..............SIXTEENTH CENTURY JOURNAL
SC J CL INV.......SCANDINAVIAN JOURNAL OF CLINICAL AND LABORATORY INVESTIGATION
SC J DENT R.......SCANDINAVIAN JOURNAL OF DENTAL RESEARCH
SC J GASTR.......SCANDINAVIAN JOURNAL OF GASTROENTEROLOGY
SC J HAEMAT.....SCANDINAVIAN JOURNAL OF HAEMATOLOGY
SC J IMMUN......SCANDINAVIAN JOURNAL OF IMMUNOLOGY
SC J IN DIS......SCANDINAVIAN JOURNAL OF INFECTIOUS DISEASES
SC J PLAST.......SCANDINAVIAN JOURNAL OF PLASTIC AND RECONSTRUCTIVE SURGERY
SC J PSYCHO......SCANDINAVIAN JOURNAL OF PSYCHOLOGY
SC J RE MED......SCANDINAVIAN JOURNAL OF REHABILITATION MEDICINE
SC J RESP D.......SCANDINAVIAN JOURNAL OF RESPIRATORY DISEASES
SC J RHEUM......SCANDINAVIAN JOURNAL OF RHEUMATOLOGY
SC J S MED.......SCANDINAVIAN JOURNAL OF SOCIAL MEDICINE
SC J THOR C......SCANDINAVIAN JOURNAL OF THORACIC AND CARDIOVASCULAR SURGERY
SC J UROL N......SCANDINAVIAN JOURNAL OF UROLOGY AND NEPHROLOGY
SCL.............STENDHAL CLUB
SCL.............STUDII SI CERCETARI LINGVISTICE
SClas...........STUDII CLASICE
SC Libn..........SOUTH CAROLINA LIBRARIAN
SC L Q..........SOUTH CAROLINA LAW QUARTERLY
SC L Rev.........SOUTH CAROLINA LAW REVIEW
SCM............SUSSEX COUNTY MAGAZINE
SCN............SEVENTEENTH-CENTURY NEWS
SCO............STUDI CLASSICI E ORIENTALI
ScoGaelS........SCOTTISH GAELIC STUDIES
ScoGS..........SCOTTISH GAELIC STUDIES
ScoS...........SCOTTISH STUDIES
Scot Art R........SCOTTISH ART REVIEW
SCOT EDU ST......SCOTTISH EDUCATIONAL STUDIES
Scot Geog M......SCOTTISH GEOGRAPHICAL MAGAZINE
Scot Hist R.......SCOTTISH HISTORICAL REVIEW
Scot J Geol.......SCOTTISH JOURNAL OF GEOLOGY
SCOT J POLI......SCOTTISH JOURNAL OF POLITICAL ECONOMY
Scot J Th.........SCOTTISH JOURNAL OF THEOLOGY
Scot L Rev........SCOTTISH LAW REVIEW
SCOT MED J.......SCOTTISH MEDICAL JOURNAL
Scot R...........SCOTTISH REVIEW
Scot Stud.........SCOTTISH STUDIES
Scott Elect Engr....SCOTTISH ELECTRICAL ENGINEER
Scottish Ednl J.....SCOTTISH EDUCATIONAL JOURNAL
Scottish Ednl Studies..SCOTTISH EDUCATIONAL STUDIES
Scottish Mus......SCOTTISH MUSIC & DRAMA
SCP.............SCOOPS
Scr.............SCRINIUM
SCR.............SCRUTINY
```

```
SCR . . . . . . . . . . . . SOUTH CAROLINA REVIEW
SCr . . . . . . . . . . . . STRUMENTI CRITICI (TORINO)
SCraneN . . . . . . . . STEPHEN CRANE NEWSLETTER
Screen Ed . . . . . . . . SCREEN EDUCATION
Screen Ed Notes . . . . SCREEN EDUCATION NOTES
ScrH . . . . . . . . . . . SCRIPTA HIEROSOLYMITANA
Scrib . . . . . . . . . . . SCRIBNER'S MONTHLY
Scrib Com . . . . . . . SCRIBNER'S COMMENTATOR
Scrib M . . . . . . . . . SCRIBNER'S MAGAZINE
Scrip . . . . . . . . . . . SCRIPTORIUM
SCRIP METAL . . . . . . SCRIPTA METALLURGICA
Script . . . . . . . . . . SCRIPTORIUM
Scripta Math . . . . . . SCRIPTA MATHEMATICA
Scr Met . . . . . . . . . SCRIPTA METALLURGICA
Scr Metall . . . . . . . . SCRIPTA METALLURGICA
ScS . . . . . . . . . . . . SCANDINAVIAN STUDIES AND NOTES
ScS . . . . . . . . . . . . SCOTTISH STUDIES (U. OF EDINBURGH)
SCSFI . . . . . . . . . . STUDII SI CERCETARI STIINTIFICE. FILOLOGIE, IASI
ScSl . . . . . . . . . . . . SCANDOSLAVICA
ScSo . . . . . . . . . . . SCIENCE AND SOCIETY
ScSt . . . . . . . . . . . SCANDINAVIAN STUDIES
SCSZ . . . . . . . . . . . SBORNIK CESKOSLOVENSKE SPOLECNOSTI ZEMEPISNE
ScUB . . . . . . . . . . . SCANDINAVIAN UNIVERSITY BOOKS
SCUL . . . . . . . . . . . SOUNDINGS. UNIVERSITY OF CALIFORNIA, LIBRARY, SANTA BARBARA
Sculp Int . . . . . . . . SCULPTURE INTERNATIONAL
SD . . . . . . . . . . . . SAMMLUNG DIETERICH
SD . . . . . . . . . . . . SCIENTIFIC DETECTIVE MONTHLY
Sd . . . . . . . . . . . . SPRACHDIENST
SD . . . . . . . . . . . . SPRACHE UND DICHTUNG
SD . . . . . . . . . . . . STUDI DANTESCHI
S D Ag Exp . . . . . . . SOUTH DAKOTA STATE COLLEGE OF AGRICULTURE AND MECHANIC ARTS. AGRICULTURAL
                         EXPERIMENT STATION. PUBLICATIONS
S Dak Geol Surv Bull . . SOUTH DAKOTA GEOLOGICAL SURVEY. BULLETIN
S Dak Geol Surv Circ . . SOUTH DAKOTA GEOLOGICAL SURVEY. CIRCULAR
S Dak Lib Bull . . . . . SOUTH DAKOTA LIBRARY BULLETIN
SDAW . . . . . . . . . . SITZUNGSBERICHTE DER DEUTSCHEN AKADEMIE DER WISSENSCHAFTEN ZU BERLIN
SDAWB . . . . . . . . . SITZUNGSBERICHTE DER DEUTSCHEN AKADEMIE DER WISSENSCHAFTEN ZU BERLIN
SDD-NU . . . . . . . . . SUMMARIES OF DOCTORAL DISSERTATIONS. NORTHWESTERN UNIVERSITY
SDDUW . . . . . . . . . SUMMARIES OF DOCTORAL DISSERTATIONS. UNIVERSITY OF WISCONSIN
SDG . . . . . . . . . . . SCHRIFTEN DER DROSTE-GESELLSCHAFT
SdG . . . . . . . . . . . STUDII DE GRAMATICA
SDH . . . . . . . . . . . SLAVISTISCHE DRUKKEN EN HERDRUKKEN
SDHI . . . . . . . . . . . STUDIA ET DOCUMENTA HISTORIAE ET IURIS
SDKK . . . . . . . . . . STUDIA Z DZIEJOW KOSCIOLA KATOLICKIEGO
SD L Rev . . . . . . . . SOUTH DAKOTA LAW REVIEW
SdM . . . . . . . . . . . SIGLO DE LAS MISIONES
SDO . . . . . . . . . . . SERRA DOR
SDR . . . . . . . . . . . SOUTH DAKOTA REVIEW
SDS . . . . . . . . . . . SYDSVENSKA DAGBLADET SNAELLPOSTEN
SDSD . . . . . . . . . . STUDI E DOCUMENTI DI STORIA E DIRITTO
Se . . . . . . . . . . . . SEMIOTICA
```

SE.............. SLOVENSKI ETNOGRAF
SE.............. SOCIAL EDUCATION
SE.............. STUDI ETRUSCHI
SE.............. STUDIA ESTETYCZNE
SE.............. STUDIES IN ENGLISH
SEA............. SANKT ERIKS ARSBOK
SEA FRONT....... SEA FRONTIERS
SeAQ........... SOUTHEAST ASIA QUARTERLY
SE Asia J Th....... SOUTHEAST ASIA JOURNAL OF THEOLOGY
Sea Technol....... SEA TECHNOLOGY
SEATTLE SYM...... SEATTLE SYMPHONY ORCHESTRA PROGRAM NOTES
SEBAn........... SOCIETE D'EMULATION DE BRUGES. ANNALES
SeC............. SCUOLA E CULTURA DEL MONDO
SEC............. SECRETARY
SEC............. SOCIETE DE L'ECOLE DES CHARTES
SECC........... STUDIES IN EIGHTEENTH-CENTURY CULTURE
Sec Ed.......... SECONDARY EDUCATION
SECMem........ SOCIETE D'EMULATION DE CAMBRAI. MEMOIRES
S ECON J........ SOUTHERN ECONOMIC JOURNAL
SECUR R LAW..... SECURITIES REGULATION LAW JOURNAL
SEDES.......... SOCIETE D'EDITIONS D'ENSEIGNEMENT SUPERIEUR
Sed Geol........ SEDIMENTARY GEOLOGY
SEDIMENT GE...... SEDIMENTARY GEOLOGY
SEEJ........... SLAVIC AND EAST EUROPEAN JOURNAL
SEER........... SLAVONIC AND EAST EUROPEAN REVIEW
SEES........... SLAVIC AND EAST EUROPEAN STUDIES
Sef............. SEFARAD
Seg............. SEGISMUNDO
SEHR........... SCANDINAVIAN ECONOMIC HISTORY REVIEW
SEI............. SOCIETA EDITRICE INTERNAZIONALE
Seismol Soc Am Bul.. SEISMOLOGICAL SOCIETY OF AMERICA. BULLETIN
SEJ............. SOUTHERN ECONOMIC JOURNAL
SEJG........... SACRIS ERUDIRI. JAARBOEK VOOR GODSDIENSTWETENSCHAPPEN
SEL............. STUDIES IN ENGLISH LITERATURE, 1500-1900
SEL............. STUDIES IN ENGLISH LITERATURE (TOKYO)
Selec Ed R....... SELECTIONS FROM THE EDINBURGH REVIEW
Select J......... SELECT JOURNAL
SelEnv.......... SELECTED REFERENCES ON ENVIRONMENT QUALITY
SE Libn......... SOUTHEASTERN LIBRARIAN
SELit........... STUDIES IN ENGLISH LITERATURE, 1500-1900
SELit........... STUDIES IN ENGLISH LITERATURE (TOKYO)
SELJ........... STUDIES IN ENGLISH LITERATURE (JAPAN)
SELL........... STUDIES IN ENGLISH LITERATURE AND LANGUAGE (JAPAN)
Sem........... SEMANA
Sem........... SEMINAR
S-EM........... SUCK-EGG MULE
SEM HEMATOL..... SEMINARS IN HEMATOLOGY
SEM HOP-THE..... SEMAINE DES HOPITAUX THERAPEUTIQUE
SEM ROENTG...... SEMINARS IN ROENTGENOLOGY
SeN............ SEARA NOVA
SEngL.......... STUDIES IN ENGLISH LITERATURE (THE HAGUE)

SEP . . . . SATURDAY EVENING POST
SEP . . . . SECRETARIA DE EDUCACION PUBLICA (MEXICO)
Separ Sci . . . . SEPARATION SCIENCE
SEP PURIF M . . . . . . SEPARATION AND PURIFICATION METHODS
SeR . . . . SEWANEE REVIEW
SeR . . . . STUDI E RICERCHE
SerrC . . . . SERRAIKA CHRONIKA
Ser SL . . . . SERIAL SLANTS
SES . . . . SOCIAL AND ECONOMIC STUDIES
SeSL . . . . STUDI E SAGGI LINGUISTICI
SET . . . . STUDIES IN ENGLISH (UNIVERSITY OF TEXAS)
Seton Hall L Rev . . . SETON HALL LAW REVIEW
SEVPEN . . . . SERVICE D'EDITION ET DE VENTE DES PUBLICATIONS DE L'EDUCATION NATIONALE
Sew . . . . SEWANEE REVIEW
Sew R . . . . SEWANEE REVIEW
SF . . . . SBORNIK FILOLOGICKY
SF . . . . SCIENCE FICTION
SF . . . . SOCIAL FORCES
SF . . . . SOCIALISTICKI FRONT
SF . . . . SPRACHFORUM
SF . . . . STUDIA FENNICA
SF . . . . STUDIA FILOZOFICZNE
SF . . . . STUDI FRANCESI
SFA . . . . SCIENCE FICTION ADVENTURES (1952-1954)
SFAB . . . . SCIENCE FICTION ADVENTURES (1958-1963)
SFAC . . . . SCIENCE FICTION ADVENTURE CLASSICS
SFAD . . . . SCIENCE FICTION ADVENTURES (1956-1958)
SF&R . . . . SCHOLARS' FACSIMILES AND REPRINTS
SFB . . . . SBORNIK FILOSOFICKE FAKULTY V BRATISLAVE
SFB . . . . SCIENCE FANTASY
SFC . . . . SCIENCE FICTION ADVENTURE CLASSICS
SFC . . . . SF COMMENTARY
SFD . . . . SCIENCE FICTION DIGEST
SFDH . . . . SCHRIFTEN DES FREIEN DEUTSCHEN HOCHSTIFTS
SFELT . . . . SOCIETE FRANCAISE D'EDITIONS LITTERAIRES ET TECHNIQUES
SFen . . . . STUDIA FENNICA
SFFBU . . . . SBORNIK PRACI FILOSOFICKEJ FAKULTY BRNENSKE UNIVERZITY
SFFUK . . . . SBORNIK FILOZOFICKEJ FAKULTY UNIVERZITY KOMENSKEHO. PHILOLOGICA
SFFUP . . . . SBORNIK FILOZOFICKEJ FAKULTY UNIVERZITY P.J. SAFARIKA V PRESOVE
SFG . . . . SF GREATS
SFG . . . . SPANISCHE FORSCHUNGEN DER GORRESGESELLSCHAFT
SFH . . . . SF HORIZONS
SFI . . . . SF IMPULSE
SFI . . . . STUDI DI FILOGIA ITALIANA
SFil . . . . STUDIME FILOLOGJIKE (TIRANE)
SFIQ . . . . SCIENCE FICTION QUARTERLY (1951-1958)
SFL . . . . STUDIES IN FRENCH LITERATURE
SFN . . . . SFRA NEWSLETTER
SFP . . . . SCIENCE FICTION PLUS
SFPS . . . . STUDIA Z FILOLOGII POLSKIEJ I SLOWIANSKIEJ
SFQ . . . . SCIENCE FICTION QUARTERLY (1940-1943)

SFQ . . . . SOUTHERN FOLKLORE QUARTERLY
SFR . . . . SAN FRANCISCO REVIEW
SFR . . . . SCIENCE FICTION REVIEW
SFran . . . . STUDI FRANCESCANI
SFrL . . . . STUDIES IN FRENCH LITERATURE
SFrQ . . . . SAN FRANCISCO QUARTERLY
SFS . . . . SCIENCE FICTION STORIES
SFSS . . . . SVENSKA FORNSKRIFTSSAELLSKAPETS SKRIFTER
SFST . . . . SCIENCE FICTION STUDIES
SFSV . . . . SVENSKA FORFATTARE UTGIVNA AV SVENSKA VITTERHETSSAMFUNDET
SF SYM . . . . SAN FRANCISCO SYMPHONY PROGRAM NOTES
SFT . . . . SOVIET AND EASTERN EUROPEAN FOREIGN TRADE
SFUK . . . . SBORNIK FILOZOFICKEJ FAKULTY UNIVERZITY. KOMENSKEHO
SFUS . . . . SBORNIK FILOZOFICKEJ FAKULTY UNIVERZITY. P.J. SAFARIKA
SFUS . . . . SOVETSKOE FINNO-UGROVEDENIE/SOVIET FENNO-UGRIC STUDIES
SFVK . . . . SVENSKA FOLKSKOLANS VAENNER. KALENDER
SFY . . . . SCIENCE FICTION YEARBOOK
SG . . . . SICULORUM GYMNASIUM
SG . . . . SINTE GEERTRUYDTSBRONNE
SG . . . . SPRACH DER GEGENWART
SG . . . . STUDI GENUESI
SG . . . . STUDI GERMANICI
SG . . . . STUDI GORIZIANI
SG . . . . STUDIUM GENERALE
SGAK . . . . STUDIEN ZUR GERMANISTIK, ANGLISTIK UND KOMPARATISTIK
SGAOR . . . . SITZUNGSBERICHTE DER GESELLSCHAFT FUER GESCHICHTE UND ALTERTUMSKUNDE DER OSTSEEPROVINZEN RUSSLANDS
SGB . . . . SCHLESISCHE GESCHICHTSBLAETTER (BRESLAU)
SGB . . . . STUDIEN UND MITTEILUNGEN ZUR GESCHICHTE DES BENEDIKTINERORDENS
SGCL . . . . STUDIES IN GENERAL AND COMPARATIVE LITERATURE
SGen . . . . STUDIUM GENERALE
SGer . . . . STUDIA GERMANICA
SGF . . . . STOCKHOLMER GERMANISTISCHE FORSCHUNGEN
SGG . . . . STUDIA GERMANICA GANDENSIA
SGGAOPR . . . . SITZUNGSBERICHTE DER GESELLSCHAFT FUER GESCHICHTE UND ALTERTUMSKUNDE DER OSTSEEPROVINZEN RUSSLANDS
SGh . . . . STUDIA GHISLERIANA (PAVIA)
SGI . . . . STUDI DI GRAMMATICA ITALIANA
SGL . . . . STUDIES IN GERMAN LITERATURE
SGLL . . . . STUDIES IN THE GERMANIC LANGUAGES AND LITERATURES
SGM . . . . SCOTTISH GEOGRAPHICAL MAGAZINE
SGo . . . . STUDI GORIZIANI
SGoldoniani . . . . . . STUDI GOLDONIANI
SGor . . . . STUDI GORIZIANI
SGr . . . . STUDII DE GRAMATICA
SGram . . . . STUDII DE GRAMATICA
SGS . . . . SCOTTISH GAELIC STUDIES
SGT . . . . SCHRIFTEN DER GESELLSCHAFT FUER THEATERGESCHICHTE
SGU . . . . STUDIA GERMANISTICA UPSALIENSIA
SGym . . . . SICULORUM GYMNASIUM
SH . . . . SPEIGHEL HISTORIAEL VAN DE BOND VAN GENTSE GERMANISTEN

SH . . . . STUDIA HIBERNICA (DUBLIN)
SHA . . . . SITZUNGSBERICHTE DER HEIDELBERGER AKADEMIE DER WISSENSCHAFT
SHAGAn . . . . SOCIETE D'HISTOIRE ET D'ARCHEOLOGIE DE GAND. ANNALES
SHAGBull . . . . SOCIETE D'HISTOIRE ET D'ARCHEOLOGIE DE GAND. BULLETIN
Shak Jahrb . . . . . . SHAKESPEAR JAHRBUCH
ShakS . . . . SHAKESPEARE STUDIES
SHALPub . . . . SOCIETE HISTORIQUE ET ARCHEOLOGIQUE DANS LE DUCHE DE LIMBOURG. PUBLICATIONS
Sharpe . . . . SHARPE'S LONDON MAGAZINE
SHATAn . . . . SOCIETE HISTORIQUE ET ARCHEOLOGIQUE DE TOURNAI. ANNALES
SHAW . . . . SITZUNGSBERICHTE DER HEIDELBERGER AKADEMIE DER WISSENSCHAFT
ShawB . . . . SHAW BULLETIN
Shaw R . . . . SHAW REVIEW
SHCSR . . . . SPICILEGIUM HISTORICUM CONGREGATIONIS SMI REDEMPTORIS
Sheet Met Ind . . . . . SHEET METAL INDUSTRIES
SHEH . . . . STANFORD HONORS ESSAYS IN THE HUMANITIES
Shell Aviat News . . . SHELL AVIATION NEWS
Shen . . . . SHENANDOAH
SHF . . . . SOCIETE DE L'HISTOIRE DE FRANCE
SHFABull . . . . SOCIETE DE L'HISTOIRE DE FRANCE ANNUAIRE. BULLETIN
SHGM . . . . SOCIETY FOR THE HISTORY OF THE GERMANS IN MARYLAND
SHib . . . . STUDIA HIBERNICA
Shipbldg Mar Engng Int . . SHIPBUILDING AND MARINE ENGINEERING INTERNATIONAL
Shipbldg Shipp Rec . . SHIPBUILDING AND SHIPPING RECORD
Ship Boat . . . . SHIP AND BOAT
Shipp Wld Shipbldr . . SHIPPING WORLD AND SHIPBUILDER
Sh J . . . . SHAKESPEARE JAHRBUCH
Sh Jb . . . . SHAKESPEARE JAHRBUCH
SHK . . . . SHOCK
Sh Metal Inds . . . . . SHEET METAL INDUSTRIES
ShN . . . . SHAKESPEARE NEWSLETTER
Show Me Lib . . . . . . SHOW-ME LIBRARIES
ShP . . . . SHAKESPEARE PICTORIAL
Sh Q . . . . SHAKESPEARE QUARTERLY
SHQ . . . . SOUTHWESTERN HISTORICAL QUARTERLY
SHR . . . . SCOTTISH HISTORICAL REVIEW
ShR . . . . SHAKESPEARE REVIEW
SHR . . . . SOUTHERN HUMANITIES REVIEW
ShS . . . . SHAKESPEARE SURVEY
ShStud . . . . SHAKESPEARE STUDIES (JAPAN)
SHT . . . . SVENSK HUMANISTISK TIDSSKRIFT
SHum . . . . STUDIES IN THE HUMANITIES
SHVE . . . . SAMMELBLATT DER HISTORISCHER VEREIN EICHSTATT
SHVF . . . . SAMMELBLATT DER HISTORISCHER VEREIN FREISING
SHVI . . . . SAMMELBLATT DER HISTORISCHER VEREIN INGOLSTADT
SI . . . . SCUOLA ITALIANA
Si . . . . SISTEMA
SI . . . . SPETTATORE ITALIANO
SI . . . . STUDII ITALIENE
SI . . . . SVIZZERA ITALIANA
SIAM J A MA . . . . . SIAM (SOCIETY FOR INDUSTRIAL AND APPLIED MATHEMATICS) JOURNAL ON APPLIED
                        MATHEMATICS

SIAM J CONT . . . . . . SIAM JOURNAL ON CONTROL
SIAM J MATH . . . . . SIAM JOURNAL ON MATHEMATICAL ANALYSIS
SIAM J NUM . . . . . . SIAM JOURNAL ON NUMERICAL ANALYSIS
SIAM REV . . . . SIAM REVIEW
Sibelius . . . . SIBELIUS-MITTEILUNGEN
SicG . . . . SICULORUM GYMNASIUM
SID J . . . . SID (SOCIETY FOR INFORMATION DISPLAY) JOURNAL
Sid Mess . . . . SIDEREAL MESSENGER
Siemens Forsch Entwicklungsber Res Dev Rep . . SIEMENS FORSCHUNGS- UND ENTWICKLUNGSBERICHTE. RESEARCH
AND DEVELOPMENT REPORTS
Siemens Rev . . . . . . SIEMENS REVIEW
Siemens Z . . . . SIEMENS-ZEITSCHRIFT
Sierra Ed News . . . . SIERRA EDUCATIONAL NEWS
Sierra Leone Rep Geol Surv Div . . SIERRA LEONE. REPORT ON THE GEOLOGICAL SURVEY DIVISION
SIFC . . . . STUDI ITALIANI DI FILOLOGIA CLASSICA
SIK . . . . STUDI ITALICI (KYOTO)
SiK . . . . SZTUKA I KRYTYKA
SIL . . . . STUDIES IN LINGUISTICS
SIL . . . . SUMMER INSTITUTE OF LINGUISTICS
SILOP . . . . STUDIES IN LINGUISTICS. OCCASIONAL PAPERS
SILTA . . . . STUDI ITALIANI DI LINGUISTICA TEORICA ED APPLICATA
SiMS . . . . STUDIER I MODERN SPRAKVETENSKAP
SIMULAT GAM . . . . . SIMULATION AND GAMES
SiN . . . . SIN NOMBRE
S in Eng . . . . STUDIES IN ENGLISH
SINFUB . . . . SKRIFTER UTGITT AV INSTITUTTET FOER NORDISK FILOLOGI. UNIVERSITETET I BERGEN
Singapore Lib . . . . . . SINGAPORE LIBRARIES
SING KIR . . . . SINGENDE KIRCHE
S in Ph . . . . STUDIES IN PHILOLOGY
SINSU . . . . SKRIFTER UTGIVNA AV INSTITUTIONEN FOER NORDISKA SPRAK VID UPPSALA UNIVERSITET
SINSUU . . . . SKRIFTER UTGIVNA AV INSTITUTIONEN FOER NORDISKA SPRAK VID UPPSALA UNIVERSITET
Sip . . . . SIPARIO
SIQR . . . . STUDIES. AN IRISH QUARTERLY REVIEW
SIR . . . . STUDIES IN ROMANTICISM
SIs . . . . SCRIPTA ISLANDICA
SIS . . . . SINO-INDIAN STUDIES
SISb . . . . SLEZSKY SBORNIK
SIsl . . . . STUDIA ISLAMICA
Sitzungsber Deut Akad Wiss Berlin Kl Bergbau Huettenw Montangeol . . SITZUNGSBERICHTE DER DEUTSCHEN
AKADEMIE DER WISSENSCHAFTEN ZU BERLIN. KLASSE FUER BERGBAU. HUETTENWESEN UND
MONTANGEOLOGIE
Sitzungsber Deut Akad Wiss Berlin Kl Math Phys Tech . . SITZUNGSBERICHTE DER DEUTSCHEN AKADEMIE DER
WISSENSCHAFTEN ZU BERLIN. KLASSE FUER MATHEMATIK, PHYSIK UND TECHNIK
Sitzungsberichte der Finn Akad der Wiss . . SITZUNGSBERICHTE DER FINNISCHEN AKADEMIE DER WISSENSCHAFTEN
Six . . . . SIXTIES
Sixteen Cent J . . . . . SIXTEENTH CENTURY JOURNAL
SJ . . . . SAALBURG-JAHRBUCH
SJ . . . . SHAKESPEARE-JAHRBUCH
SJ . . . . SILLIMAN JOURNAL
SJ . . . . SLOVENSKY JAZYK
SJA . . . . SOUTHWESTERN JOURNAL OF ANTHROPOLOGY

SJAnth . . . . SOUTHWESTERN JOURNAL OF ANTHROPOLOGY
SJE . . . . SWEDISH JOURNAL OF ECONOMICS
SJH . . . . SHAKESPEARE-JAHRBUCH (HEIDELBERG)
SJP . . . . SOUTHERN JOURNAL OF PHILOSOPHY
SJPE . . . . SCOTTISH JOURNAL OF POLITICAL ECONOMY
S J Phil . . . . SOUTHERN JOURNAL OF PHILOSOPHY
SJL . . . . SLOVENSKY JAZYK A LITERATURA V SKOLE
SJMS . . . . SPECULUM. A JOURNAL OF MEDIAEVAL STUDIES
SJO . . . . JAHRBUCH DER DEUTSCHEN SHAKESPEARE-GESELLSCHAFT OST
SJR . . . . SOCIAL JUSTICE REVIEW
SjV . . . . SIRP JA VASAR
SJW . . . . JAHRBUCH DER DEUTSCHEN SHAKESPEARE- GESELLSCHAFT WEST
SJW . . . . SHAKESPEARE-JAHRBUCH (WEIMAR)
SJ(Weimar) . . . . . . SHAKESPEARE JAHRBUCH (WEIMAR)
SK . . . . SEMINARIUM KONDAKOVIANUM
Skand . . . . SKANDINAVISTIK
SkFi . . . . SKANDINAVSKAGA FILOLOGIJA
SKG . . . . SRPSKI KNJIZEVNI GLASNIK
SKGG . . . . SCHRIFTEN DER KOENIGSBERGER GELEHRTEN-GESELLSCHAFT
SKGGD . . . . SAMMLUNG KURZER GRAMMATIKEN GERMANISCHER DIALEKTE
SKPANKr . . . . SPRAWOZDANIA Z POSIEDZEN KOMISJI PAN. ODDZIAL W KRAKOWIE
SKS . . . . SUOMALAISEN KIRJALLISUUDEN SEURA
SkSb . . . . SKANDINAVSKIJ SBORNIK
SKY TELESC . . . . SKY AND TELESCOPE
Sl . . . . SLAVIA
SL . . . . SOVIET LIFE
SL . . . . SOVIET LITERATURE
SL . . . . SPECIAL LIBRARIES
SL . . . . STUDIA LINGUISTICA (LUND)
SL . . . . STUDIES IN LINGUISTICS
SL . . . . SVENSKA LANDSMAL OCH SVENSKT FOLKLIV
Sla . . . . SLAVIA
SLA Adv & Mkt Div Bul . . SPECIAL LIBRARIES ASSOCIATION. ADVERTISING AND MARKETING DIVISION. BULLETIN
SLA Alabama Chap Bul . . SPECIAL LIBRARIES ASSOCIATION. ALABAMA CHAPTER. BULLETIN
SLA Biol Sci Div Reminder . . SPECIAL LIBRARIES ASSOCIATION. BIOLOGICAL SCIENCES DIVISION. REMINDER
SLA Bus & Fin Div Bul . . SPECIAL LIBRARIES ASSOCIATION. BUSINESS AND FINANCIAL DIVISION. BULLETIN
SLA Fin Div Bul . . . . SPECIAL LIBRARIES ASSOCIATION. FINANCIAL DIVISION. BULLETIN
SLA Ga Chap Bul . . . SPECIAL LIBRARIES ASSOCIATION. GEORGIA CHAPTER. BULLETIN
SLA Geog & Map Div Bul . . SPECIAL LIBRARIES ASSOCIATION. GEOGRAPHY AND MAP DIVISION. BULLETIN
SLA Ind Chap Slant . . SPECIAL LIBRARIES ASSOCIATION. INDIANA CHAPTER. SLANT
SLA Metals Div News . . SPECIAL LIBRARIES ASSOCIATION. METALS DIVISION. NEWS
SLA Mich Chap Bul . . SPECIAL LIBRARIES ASSOCIATION. MICHIGAN CHAPTER. BULLETIN
SLA Montreal Chap Bul . . SPECIAL LIBRARIES ASSOCIATION. MONTREAL CHAPTER. BULLETIN
SLA Museum Div Bul . . SPECIAL LIBRARIES ASSOCIATION. MUSEUM DIVISION. BULLETIN
SLA News . . . . SLA (SCOTTISH LIBRARY ASSOCIATION) NEWS
SlAnt . . . . SLAVIA ANTIQUA
SLA Picture Div Picturescope . . SPECIAL LIBRARIES ASSOCIATION. PICTURE DIVISION. PICTURESCOPE
SLA Pittsburgh Chap Bul . . SPECIAL LIBRARIES ASSOCIATION. PITTSBURGH CHAPTER. BULLETIN
SLA Sci-Tech News . . SPECIAL LIBRARIES ASSOCIATION. SCIENCE-TECHNOLOGY DIVISION. NEWS
SLA Texas Chap Bul . . SPECIAL LIBRARIES ASSOCIATION. TEXAS CHAPTER. BULLETIN
SLA Toronto Chap Bul . . SPECIAL LIBRARIES ASSOCIATION. TORONTO CHAPTER. BULLETIN

Slav............ SLAVIA
SlavA........... SLAVIA ANTIQUA
SlavF............SLAVJANSKAJA FILOLOGIJA
SLAVIC E EU...... SLAVIC AND EAST EUROPEAN JOURNAL
Slavic R..........SLAVIC REVIEW
SLAVON E EU...... SLAVONIC AND EAST EUROPEAN REVIEW
Slavonic R........ SLAVONIC REVIEW
SlavP........... SLAVICA PRAGENSIA
SlavR........... SLAVIC REVIEW
Slav R........... SLAVISCHE RUNDSCHAU
SlavR........... SLAVISTICNA REVIJA
SLAVR...........SLAVONIC REVIEW
SlavRev..........SLAVISTICNA REVIJA
SlavS............SLAVICA SLOVACA
SLA Western NY Chap Bul.. SPECIAL LIBRARIES ASSOCIATION. WESTERN NEW YORK CHAPTER. BULLETIN
SL Council Phila & Vicinity Bul.. SPECIAL LIBRARIES COUNCIL OF PHILADELPHIA AND VICINITY. BULLETIN
SLD............. STUDIA LITTERARIA (UNIVERSITY OF DEBRECEN)
SLESP........... SUPLEMENTO LITERARIO DO ESTADO DE SAO PAULO
SLet............ SESTANTE LETTERARIO
SIF............. SLAJANSKAJA FILOLOGIJA
SLF............. SVENSKA LITTERATURSAELLSKAPET I FINLAND
SLFA........... SVENSKLAERARFOERENINGENS ARSSKRIFT
SIFil........... SLAVJANSKA FILOLOGIJA
SLFU........... SKRIFTER UTGIVNA. GENOM LANDSMALS- OCH FOLK-MINNESARKIVET I UPPSALA
SLG............ STUDIA LINGUISTICA GERMANICA
SLI............. STUDIES IN THE LITERARY IMAGINATION
SLI............. STUDI LINGUISTICI ITALIANI
SLiF............SLOVJANS'KE LITERATUROZNAVSTVO I FOL'KLORYSTYKA
SLit............SLOVENSKA LITERATURA
SLit............STUDIES IN LITERATURE
SLitI........... STUDIES IN THE LITERARY IMAGINATION
SLJ............. SOUTHERN LITERARY JOURNAL
SLK............. SCHWERPUNKTE LINGUISTIK UND KOMMUNIKATIONSWISSENSCHAFT
SLL............. SKRIFTER UTGIVNA. GENOM LANDSMALSARKIVET I LUND
SLLR........... SIERRA LEONE LANGUAGE REVIEW
SLM........... SOUTHERN LITERARY MESSENGER
SlMov.......... SLOC'JANS'KE MOVOZNAVSTVO
SLN............ SINCLAIR LEWIS NEWSLETTER
SLO............ SLAVIA ORIENTALIS
SLOAN MANAG.... SLOAN MANAGEMENT REVIEW
SLOc........... SLAVIA OCCIDENTALIS
SLOcc.......... SLAVIA OCCIDENTALIS
SLoP........... SLOVANSKY PREHLED
SLOR........... SLAVIA ORIENTALIS
SLOV HUD....... SLOVENSKA HUDBA
Slov Lit.......... SLOVENSKA LITERATURA (BRATISLAVA)
SlovN.......... SLOVENSKY NARODOPIS
SlovP.......... SLOVENSKY POHL'ADY (BRATISLAVA)
Slov Preh........ SLOVANSKY PREHLED
SLOW LEARN...... SLOW LEARNING CHILD
SLP............. SLOVANSKY PREHLED

SLP .... SLOVENSKY POHL'ADY
SLP............ SLOVENSKY POROCEVALEC
SLPo........... SLOVENSKY POHL'ADY
SLPoh.......... SLOVENSKY POHL'ADY
SLPr........... SLAVICA PRAGENSIA
SLPR........... SLAVISTIC PRINTINGS AND REPRINTINGS
SLQ............ SAINT LOUIS QUARTERLY (BAGUIO CITY)
SLR............ SLAVISCHE RUNDSCHAU (MUNICH)
SLR............ SLAVISTICNA REVIJA (YUGOSLAVIA)
SLR............ SLAVONIC AND EAST EUROPEAN REVIEW
SLRec.......... SLOVENSKA REC (BRATISLAVA)
SLRev.......... SLAVONIC AND EAST EUROPEAN REVIEW
SLRev.......... SLAVONIC REVIEW
SLRJ........... SAINT LOUIS UNIVERSITY RESEARCH JOURNAL OF THE GRADUATE SCHOOL OF ARTS AND SCIENCES
SlRund......... SLAVISCHE RUNDSCHAU
SLSA........... SVENSKA LINNE-SAELLSKAPETS ARSSKRIFT (UPPSALA)
SLSb........... SLEZSKY SBORNIK
SLSF........... SVENSKA LANDSMAL OCH SVENSKT FOLKLIV (UPPSALA)
SLSp........... SLOVENSKY SPISOVATEL
SLT............ SCOTS LAW TIMES
SLT............ SVENSK LITTERATURTIDSKRIFT
SLTerm......... SLAVJANSKA LINGVISTICNA TERMINOLOGIJA
SLU............ STUDII DE LITERATURA UNIVERSALA (BUCHAREST)
SLU............ SVENSKA LITTERATURSAELLSKAPET I UPPSALA
SL UVAN........ SLAVISTICA. PRACI INSTITUTU SLOV'JANOZNAVSTVA UKRAJINS'KOJI VIL'NOJI AKADEMIJI NAUK
SM............. SALES MANAGEMENT
SM............. SAMMLUNG METZLER
SM............. SCIENTIFIC MONTHLY
Sm............. SMENA (MOSCOW)
Sm............. SMITHSONIAN
SM............. SPEECH MONOGRAPHS
SM............. STUDI MEDIEVALI
SM............. SUMMER
SMALL GR B...... SMALL GROUP BEHAVIOR
SMBC.......... STUDIEN UND MITTEILUNGEN AUS DEM BENEDIKTINER- UND DEM CISTERCIENSER- ORDEN
SMBCO.......... STUDIEN UND MITTEILUNGEN AUS DEM BENEDIKTINER- UND DEM CISTERCIENSER- ORDEN
SMBCOZ........ STUDIEN UND MITTEILUNGEN AUS DEM BENEDIKTINER- UND DEM CISTERCIENSER- ORDEN
SMBD.......... STAT'I MATERIALY PO BOLGARSKOJ DIALEKTOLOGII
SMC........... STUDIES IN MEDIEVAL CULTURE
SMDL.......... STOFF- UND MOTIVGESCHICHTE DER DEUTSCHEN LITERATUR
SMe........... STUDI MEDIEVALI
SMEA.......... STUDI MICENEI ED EGEO-ANATOLICI
SME Collect Pap.... SOCIETY OF MANUFACTURING ENGINEERS. COLLECTIVE PAPERS
SME Creative Mfg Semin Tech Pap.. SOCIETY OF MANUFACTURING ENGINEERS. CREATIVE MANUFACTURING SEMINARS. TECHNICAL PAPERS
SMed........... STUDI MEDIEVALI
SME Tech Pap..... SOCIETY OF MANUFACTURING ENGINEERS. TECHNICAL PAPERS
SME West Metal Tool Expos Conf Tech Pap.. SOCIETY OF MANUFACTURING ENGINEERS. WESTERN METAL AND TOOL EXPOSITION AND CONFERENCE. TECHNICAL PAPERS

SMF . . . . SKRIFTER UTGIVNA AV MODERNSMALSLARARNAS FORENING
SMG . . . . SCHWEIZERISCHE MUSIKFORSCHENDE GESELLSCHAFT MITTEILUNGSBLATT
SMGBOZ . . . . STUDIEN UND MITTEILUNGEN ZUR GESCHICHTE DES BENEDIKTINERORDENS UND SEINER ZWEIGE (SALZBOURG)
SMIL . . . . STATISTICAL METHODS IN LINGUISTICS
SMiss . . . . STUDIA MISSIONALIA
SMITH COLL . . . . . . SMITH COLLEGE STUDIES IN SOCIAL WORK
Smith Coll Mus Bul . . SMITH COLLEGE. MUSEUM OF ART. BULLETIN
Smithson Rep . . . . . SMITHSONIAN INSTITUTION. ANNUAL REPORT .
Smithson Rept . . . . . SMITHSONIAN INSTITUTION. REPORTS
SMIU . . . . STUDIES BY MEMBERS OF THE ISTANBUL UNIVERSITY ENGLISH DEPARTMENT
SML . . . . STATISTICAL METHODS IN LINGUISTICS (STOCKHOLM)
SML . . . . STIMMEN AUS MARIA-LAACH
SMLF . . . . SKRIFTER UTGIVNA AV MODERSMALSLARARNA FORENING
SMLV . . . . STUDI MEDIOLATINI E VOLGARI
SMon . . . . STUDIA MONASTICA
SMPTE J . . . . SOCIETY OF MOTION PICTURE AND TELEVISION ENGINEERS. JOURNAL
SMQ . . . . SCHOOL MEDIA QUARTERLY
SMS . . . . STARTLING MYSTERY STORIES
SMS . . . . STUDIER I MODERN SPRAKVETENSKAP
SMSpr . . . . STUDIER I MODERN SPRAKVETENSKAP
SMSR . . . . STUDI E MATERIALI DI STORIA DELLA RELIGIONI
SMus . . . . STUDIA MUSICOLOGICA (BUDAPEST)
SMV . . . . STUDI MEDIOLATINI E VOLGARI
SN . . . . SATURDAY NIGHT
SN . . . . SHAKESPEARE NEWSLETTER
SN . . . . SLOVENSKY NARODOPIS
SN . . . . SOVETSKAJA NAUKA
SN . . . . STUDIA NEOPHILOLOGICA
SNA . . . . SHAKESPEARIANA
SNa . . . . SOT LA NAPE
SNDL . . . . STUDIENAUSGABEN ZUR NEUEREN DEUTSCHEN LITERATUR
SNDR . . . . SHIMANE DAIGAKU RONSHU: JINBUN KAGAKU (JOURNAL OF THE SHIMANE UNIVERSITY: HUMANISTIC SCIENCES)
SNF . . . . SELSKAB FOER NORDISK FILOLOGI ARSBERETNING
SNL . . . . SATIRE NEWSLETTER
SNL . . . . SHAKESPEARE NEWSLETTER
SNM . . . . SBORNIK NARODNIHO MUZEA
SNNTS . . . . STUDIES IN THE NOVEL (NORTH TEXAS STATE UNIVERSITY)
SNoF . . . . STUDIER I NORDISK FILOLOGI
SNov . . . . SEARA NOVA
SNP . . . . STUDIA NEOPHILOLOGICA. A JOURNAL OF GERMANIC AND ROMANIC PHILOLOGY
SNPh . . . . STUDIA NEOPHILOLOGICA. A JOURNAL OF GERMANIC AND ROMANIC PHILOLOGY
SNQ . . . . SCOTTISH NOTES AND QUERIES
SNQ . . . . SUSSEX NOTES AND QUERIES
SNR . . . . SCHWEIZERISCHE NUMISMATISCHE RUNDSCHAU
SNS . . . . SLOVO NA STOROZI
SNSS . . . . SKRIFTER UTGIVNA AV NAMNDEN FOER SVENSK SPRAKVARD
SNVO . . . . SKRIFTER DET NORSKE VIDENSKAPS-AKADEMI I OSLO
SO . . . . SIBIRSKIE OGNI
SO . . . . SLAVIA OCCIDENTALIS

So.............SOCIETA
So.............SOKRATES
So.............SOPHIA
SO.............STUDIA OLIVERIANA
SO.............STUDIA ORIENTALIA
SO.............SYMBOLAE OSLOENSES
SOA............SYDSVENSKA ORTNAMNSSAELLSKAPETS ARSSKRIFT
SoAB...........SOUTH ATLANTIC BULLETIN
SoANGr.........SOOBSCENIJA AKADEMIJI NAUK GRUZINSKOJ SSR
Soap & Chem Spec..SOAP AND CHEMICAL SPECIALTIES
Soap & San Chem...SOAP AND SANITARY CHEMICALS
SOAP COSMET.....SOAP COSMETICS CHEMICAL SPECIALTIES
So AS..........SOMERSET ARCHAEOLOGICAL AND NATURAL HISTORY SOCIETY
So Assn Q.......SOUTHERN ASSOCIATION QUARTERLY
So Atlan Bul......SOUTH ATLANTIC BULLETIN
So Atl Quar......SOUTH ATLANTIC QUARTERLY
So Aus Bul.......NATIONAL GALLERY OF SOUTH AUSTRALIA. BULLETIN
SOAW...........SITZUNGSBERICHTE DER OESTERREICHISCHEN AKADEMIE DER WISSENSCHAFTEN IN WIEN. PHILOSOPHISCH-HISTORISCHE KLASSE
So Biv...........SOUTHERN BIVOUAC
Soc............SOCIETA
Soc............SOCIETAS
SocAb..........SOCIOLOGICAL ABSTRACTS
Soc Act.........SOCIAL ACTION
Soc African J.....SOCIETE DES AFRICANISTES. JOURNAL
Soc Amer J.......SOCIETE DES AMERICANISTES DE PARIS. JOURNAL
So Calif L Rev....SOUTHERN CALIFORNIA LAW REVIEW
So Calif Quar.....SOUTHERN CALIFORNIA QUARTERLY
Soc Amer J.......SOCIETE DES AMERICANISTES DE PARIS. JOURNAL
Soc Anal.........SOCIOLOGICAL ANALYSIS
Soc & Econ Stud....SOCIAL AND ECONOMIC STUDIES
Soc Archeol & Hist Limousin Bul..SOCIETE ARCHEOLOGIQUE ET HISTORIQUE DU LIMOUSIN. BULLETIN
Soc Arch Hist J....SOCIETY OF ARCHITECTURAL HISTORIANS. JOURNAL
Soc Arch Hist Poitou Arch..SOCIETE DES ARCHIVES HISTORIQUES DU POITOU. ARCHIVES
So Car Hist Assoc Proc..SOUTH CAROLINA HISTORICAL ASSOCIATION. PROCEEDINGS
So Car Hist Mag....SOUTH CAROLINA HISTORICAL AND GENEALOGICAL MAGAZINE
Soc Army Hist Research Jour..SOCIETY FOR ARMY HISTORICAL RESEARCH. JOURNAL
Soc Auto Eng J.....SOCIETY OF AUTOMOTIVE ENGINEERS. JOURNAL
SoCB...........SOUTH CENTRAL BULLETIN
SOC BEH PER......SOCIAL BEHAVIOR AND PERSONALITY
Soc Biol..........SOCIAL BIOLOGY
Soc Casework.....SOCIAL CASEWORK
Soc Chem Ind J....SOCIETY OF CHEMICAL INDUSTRY. JOURNAL
Soc Comp........SOCIAL COMPASS
Soc d Americanistes J..SOCIETE DES AMERICANISTES DE PARIS. JOURNAL
Soc d Archives Hist du Poitou Archives..SOCIETE DES ARCHIVES HISTORIQUES DU POITOU. ARCHIVES
Soc de Statist de Paris J..SOCIETE DE STATISTIQUE DE PARIS. JOURNAL
Soc Dyers & Col J...SOCIETY OF DYERS AND COLOURISTS. JOURNAL
Soc Econ.........SOCIAL ECONOMIST
Soc Ed...........SOCIAL EDUCATION
Soc Eng (London) J..SOCIETY OF ENGINEERS (LONDON) JOURNAL

Soc Etud Indochinoises Bul. . SOCIETE DES ETUDES INDOCHINOISES. BULLETIN
Soc Exp Stress Anal Pap. . SOCIETY FOR EXPERIMENTAL STRESS ANALYSIS. PAPERS
Soc Forces. . . . . SOCIAL FORCES
Soc Hygiene. . . . . . SOCIAL HYGIENE
SOCIAL BIOL. . . . . . SOCIAL BIOLOGY
SOCIAL CASE. . . . . . SOCIAL CASEWORK
SOCIAL COMP. . . . . SOCIAL COMPASS
SOCIAL EC A. . . . . . SOCIAL AND ECONOMIC ADMINISTRATION
SOCIAL ECON. . . . . . SOCIAL AND ECONOMIC STUDIES
SOCIAL FORC. . . . . . SOCIAL FORCES
SOCIAL IND. . . . . . SOCIAL INDICATORS RESEARCH
SOCIAL POL. . . . . . SOCIAL POLICY
SOCIAL PRAX. . . . . SOCIAL PRAXIS
SOCIAL PROB. . . . . SOCIAL PROBLEMS
SOCIAL PSY. . . . . . . SOCIAL PSYCHIATRY
Social Res. . . . . SOCIAL RESEARCH
SOCIAL SCI. . . . . . . SOCIAL SCIENCE QUARTERLY
SOCIAL SCIE. . . . . . SOCIAL SCIENCE
Social Sci Inf. . . . . . SOCIAL SCIENCE INFORMATION
SOCIAL SC M. . . . . . SOCIAL SCIENCE AND MEDICINE
SOCIAL SEC. . . . . . . SOCIAL SECURITY BULLETIN
SOCIAL SE R. . . . . . . SOCIAL SERVICE REVIEW
SOCIAL ST S. . . . . . . SOCIAL STUDIES OF SCIENCE
Social Stud. . . . . . . SOCIAL STUDIES
Social Stud (Ireland). . SOCIAL STUDIES (IRELAND)
Social Theor Pract. . SOCIAL THEORY AND PRACTICE
SOCIO ECON. . . . . . SOCIO-ECONOMIC PLANNING SCIENCES
SOCIOL ANAL. . . . . SOCIOLOGICAL ANALYSIS
Sociol & Soc Res. . . . SOCIOLOGY AND SOCIAL RESEARCH
SOCIOL BULL. . . . . . SOCIOLOGICAL BULLETIN
SOCIOL CAS. . . . . . . SOCIOLOGICKY CASOPIS
SOCIOL EDUC. . . . . . SOCIOLOGY OF EDUCATION
SOCIOL FOCU. . . . . . SOCIOLOGICAL FOCUS
SOCIOL FORS. . . . . . SOCIOLOGISK FORSKNING
SOCIOL INQ. . . . . . . SOCIOLOGICAL INQUIRY
SOCIOL METH. . . . . SOCIOLOGICAL METHODS AND RESEARCH
SOCIOL NEER. . . . . . SOCIOLOGIA NEERLANDICA
Sociol of Ed. . . . . . SOCIOLOGY OF EDUCATION
SOCIOL Q. . . . . . . SOCIOLOGICAL QUARTERLY
Sociol R. . . . . SOCIOLOGICAL REVIEW
SOCIOL R MG. . . . . SOCIOLOGICAL REVIEW MONOGRAPH
Sociol R ns. . . . . . . SOCIOLOGICAL REVIEW. NEW SERIES
SOCIOL RUR. . . . . . SOCIOLOGIA RURALIS
SOCIOL SOC. . . . . . SOCIOLOGY AND SOCIAL RESEARCH
SOCIOL SOCI. . . . . . SOCIOLOGIE ET SOCIETES
SOCIOL SYMP. . . . . SOCIOLOGICAL SYMPOSIUM
SOCIOL TRAV. . . . . SOCIOLOGIE DU TRAVAIL
SOCIOL W OC. . . . . SOCIOLOGY OF WORK AND OCCUPATIONS
Socio R. . . . . SOCIOLOGICAL REVIEW
Soc J Opt Technol. . SOVIET JOURNAL OF OPTICAL-TECHNOLOGY
Soc Nav Architects Mar Eng Tech Res Bull. . SOCIETY OF NAVAL ARCHITECTS AND MARINE ENGINEERS. NEW YORK.
TECHNICAL AND RESEARCH BULLETIN

Soc Nav Architects Mar Eng Trans..SOCIETY OF NAVAL ARCHITECTS AND MARINE ENGINEERS. NEW YORK. TRANSACTIONS
Soc Ocean J......SOCIETE DES OCEANISTES. JOURNAL
SOC PET E J.......SOCIETY OF PETROLEUM ENGINEERS. JOURNAL
Soc Pet Eng AIME J..SOCIETY OF PETROLEUM ENGINEERS OF AIME. JOURNAL
Soc Pet Eng AIME Pap..SOCIETY OF PETROLEUM ENGINEERS OF AIME. PAPERS
Soc Petrol Eng Trans..SOCIETY OF PETROLEUM ENGINEERS OF AIME. TRANSACTIONS
Soc Pol..........SOCIAL POLICY
Soc Pr...........SOCIAL PROGRESS
Soc Prax.........SOCIAL PRAXIS. INTERNATIONAL AND INTERDISCIPLINARY JOURNAL OF SOCIAL THOUGHT
Soc Prehist Francaise Bul..SOCIETE PREHISTORIQUE FRANCAISE. BULLETIN
Soc Prob........SOCIAL PROBLEMS
Soc Psych Res Proc..SOCIETY FOR PSYCHICAL RESEARCH. PROCEEDINGS
Soc R...........SOCIAL RESEARCH
SocR............SOCIAL RESEARCH: AN INTERNATIONAL QUARTERLY
SoCR...........SOUTH CAROLINA REVIEW
Soc R di Nap Accad di Archeol Atti..SOCIETA REALE DI NAPOLI. ACCADEMIA DI ARCHEOLOGIA, LETTERE E BELLE ARTI. ATTI
Soc R di Nap Accad di Sci Mor e Pol Atti..SOCIETA REALE DI NAPOLI. ACCADEMIA DI SCIENZE MORALI E POLITICHE. ATTI
Soc R di Napoli Accad di Archeol Atti..SOCIETA REALE DI NAPOLI. ACCADEMIA DI ARCHEOLOGIA, LETTERE E BELLE ARTI. ATTI
Soc R di Napoli Accad d Sci Fis e Mat Atti..SOCIETA REALE DI NAPOLI. ACCADEMIA DELLE SCIENZE, FISICHE E MATEMATICHE. ATTI
Soc Res..........SOCIAL RESEARCH
SOC SCI INF......SOCIAL SCIENCE INFORMATION
Soc Sci Lettres & Arts PAU Bul..SOCIETE DES SCIENCES, LETTRES ET ARTS. PAU BULLETIN
Soc Sci Q........SOCIAL SCIENCE QUARTERLY
Soc Sci Res Council Bull..SOCIAL SCIENCE RESEARCH COUNCIL. BULLETIN
Soc Sec Bull.......SOCIAL SECURITY BULLETIN
Soc Serv R........SOCIAL SERVICE REVIEW
Soc Statist Paris J..SOCIETE DE STATISTIQUE DE PARIS. JOURNAL
Soc Studies.......SOCIAL STUDIES
Soc Theory & Pract..SOCIAL THEORY AND PRACTICE
Soc Venezolana Ciencias Natur Bol..SOCIEDAD VENEZOLANA DE CIENCIAS NATURALES. BOLETIN
Soc Work.........SOCIAL WORK
So Dak Hist.......SOUTH DAKOTA HISTORY
So Dak Hist Coll....SOUTH DAKOTA HISTORICAL COLLECTIONS
So Dakota Lib Bul...SOUTH DAKOTA LIBRARY BULLETIN
So Econ J.........SOUTHERN ECONOMIC JOURNAL
SoF.............SAMTID OCH FRAMTID
SOF.............SUEDOST-FORSCHUNGEN
Software Pract Exper..SOFTWARE-PRACTICE AND EXPERIENCE
So Hist Pap.......SOUTHERN HISTORICAL SOCIETY. PAPERS
SoHR...........SOUTHERN HUMANITIES REVIEW
SOIL BIOL B.......SOIL BIOLOGY AND BIOCHEMISTRY
SOIL CONS........SOIL CONSERVATION
Soil Mech Found Eng..SOIL MECHANICS AND FOUNDATIONS ENGINEERING
SOIL SCI.........SOIL SCIENCE
SOIL SCI SO.......SOIL SCIENCE SOCIETY OF AMERICA. PROCEEDINGS
Soils Found.......SOILS AND FOUNDATIONS

Sok . . . . SOKRATES
SOK . . . . SPROG OG KULTUR
Sol . . . . SOLICITOR
SOLAR ENERG . . . . . SOLAR ENERGY
SOLAR PHYS . . . . . . SOLAR PHYSICS
Solar Syst Res . . . . . SOLAR SYSTEM RESEARCH
Sol Energy . . . . SOLAR ENERGY
So Lit J . . . . SOUTHERN LITERARY JOURNAL
SOliv . . . . STUDIA OLIVERIANA
Sol J . . . . SOLICITORS' JOURNAL
SoLJ . . . . SOUTHERN LITERARY JOURNAL
SOL ST COMM . . . . . SOLID STATE COMMUNICATIONS
SOL ST ELEC . . . . SOLID-STATE ELECTRONICS
SOL ST TECH . . . . . . SOLID-STATE TECHNOLOGY
So M . . . . SOUTHERN MAGAZINE
SOMA . . . . SOOBSCENIJA OTDELA MACHANIZACII I AVTOMATIZACII INFORMACIONNYCH RABOT
SOM CELL G . . . . SOMATIC CELL GENETICS
SON . . . . SLOVENSKE ODBORNE NAZVOSLOVIE
Song Hits Mag . . . . . SONG HITS MAGAZINE
SOnoM . . . . STUDIA ONONMASTICA MONACENSIA
So NQ . . . . SOMERSET NOTES AND QUERIES
Son Spec . . . . SONORUM SPECULUM
SoobMP . . . . SOOBSCENIJA DU MUSEE D'ART POUCHKINE
Soobscenija Akad nauk GruzSSR . . SOOBSCENIJA AKADEMIJI NAUK GRUZINKSKOJ SSR
Sophia:T . . . . SOPHIA: STUDIES IN WESTERN CIVILIZATION AND THE CULTURAL INTERACTION OF EAST AND
WEST (TOKYO)
So Q . . . . SOUTHERN QUARTERLY REVIEW
So R . . . . SOUTHERN REVIEW
SoR . . . . SOUTHERN REVIEW: AN AUSTRALIAN JOURNAL OF LITERARY STUDIES
So R A . . . . SOUTHERN REVIEW: AN AUSTRALIAN JOURNAL OF LITERARY STUDIES
So R ns . . . . SOUTHERN REVIEW. NEW SERIES
SoS . . . . SAGA OCH SED
SoS . . . . SYN OG SEGN
SoT . . . . SLOEJD OCH TON
SOUL IL . . . . SOUL ILLUSTRATED
Sound . . . . SOUNDINGS
Sound Vis Broadc . . . SOUND AND VISION BROADCASTING
SouR . . . . SOUTHERN REVIEW
South Econ Jour . . . . SOUTHERN ECONOMIC JOURNAL
South Hist Assoc Publ . . SOUTHERN HISTORICAL ASSOCIATION. PUBLICATIONS
South Hist Soc Papers . . SOUTHERN HISTORICAL SOCIETY. PAPERS
SOUTH MED J . . . . . SOUTHERN MEDICAL JOURNAL
South Quar . . . . SOUTHERN QUARTERLY REVIEW
Southw Hist Quar . . . SOUTHWESTERN HISTORICAL QUARTERLY
Southw Pol and Soc Sci Q . . SOUTHWESTERN POLITICAL AND SOCIAL SCIENCE QUARTERLY
Southw Pol Sci Quar . . SOUTHWEST POLITICAL SCIENCE QUARTERLY
Southw Rev . . . . SOUTHWEST REVIEW
Southw Soc Sci Quar . . SOUTHWESTERN SOCIAL SCIENCE QUARTERLY
SOV ANTHR A . . . . . SOVIET ANTHROPOLOGY AND ARCHEOLOGY
SOV AT EN R . . . . . . SOVIET ATOMIC ENERGY (USSR)
Sov Automat Contr . . SOVIET AUTOMATIC CONTROL

Sov Bibliog . . . . SOVETSKAYA BIBLIOGRAFIIA
SOV EDUC . . . . SOVIET EDUCATION
SOV EE FOR . . . . . . SOVIET AND EASTERN EUROPEAN FOREIGN TRADE
Sov Elec Eng . . . . . SOVIET ELECTRICAL ENGINEERING
SovEt . . . . SOVETSKAYA ETNOGRAFIJA
SovEtn . . . . SOVETSKAYA ETNOGRAFIJA
Sovetskoe Bibl . . . . SOVETSKOE BIBLIOTEKOVEDENIE
SovFU . . . . SOVETSKOJE FINNOUGROVEDENIJE
SOV GEOGR R . . . . . SOVIET GEOGRAPHY: REVIEW AND TRANSLATION
Sov Geol . . . . SOVETSKAYA GEOLOGIYA
SovH . . . . SOVETISH HEYMLAND
Sov Hydrol . . . . SOVIET HYDROLOGY: SELECTED PAPERS
Soviet Ed . . . . SOVIET EDUCATION
Soviet Lit . . . . SOVIET LITERATURE
SOVIET MUZ . . . . . . SOVETSKAYA MUZYKA
Soviet Stud . . . . SOVIET STUDIES
Soviet Stud Phil . . . . SOVIET STUDIES IN PHILOSOPHY
SovJa . . . . SOVETSKA JAZYKOVEDA
Sov J Nondestr Test . . SOVIET JOURNAL OF NONDESTRUCTIVE TESTING
SOV J NUC R . . . . . . SOVIET JOURNAL OF NUCLEAR PHYSICS (USSR)
Sov J Opt Technol . . SOVIET JOURNAL OF OPTICAL TECHNOLOGY
Sov J Quantum Electron . . SOVIET JOURNAL OF QUANTUM ELECTRONICS
SovKniga . . . . SOVETSKAYA KNIGA
SovL . . . . SOVIET LITERATURE
SOV LAW GOV . . . . . SOVIET LAW AND GOVERNMENT
Sov Lit . . . . SOVIET LITERATURE
SOV MED . . . . SOVETSKAYA MEDITISINA
Sov Min Sci . . . . SOVIET MINING SCIENCE
SOV NEUR R . . . . . . SOVIET NEUROLOGY AND PSYCHIATRY (USSR)
SOV PH AC R . . . . . . SOVIET PHYSICS. ACOUSTICS (USSR)
SOV PH SE R . . . . . . SOVIET PHYSICS. SEMICONDUCTORS (USSR)
Sov Phys Acoust . . . SOVIET PHYSICS. ACOUSTICS
Sov Phys Crystallogr . . SOVIET PHYSICS. CRYSTALLOGRAPHY
Sov Phys JETP . . . . . SOVIET PHYSICS. JETP (JOURNAL OF EXPERIMENTAL AND THEORETICAL PHYSICS OF THE ACADEMY OF SCIENCES OF THE USSR)
Sov Phys Semicond . . SOVIET PHYSICS. SEMICONDUCTORS
Sov Phys-Solid State . . SOVIET PHYSICS-SOLID STATE
Sov Phys Tech Phys . . SOVIET PHYSICS. TECHNICAL PHYSICS
Sov Plast . . . . SOVIET PLASTICS
Sov Powder Met Metal Ceram . . SOVIET POWDER METALLURGY AND METAL CERAMICS
SOV PSYCO R . . . . . SOVIET PSYCHOLOGY (USSR)
SovR . . . . SOVIET REVIEW
Sov Rubber Technol . . SOVIET RUBBER TECHNOLOGY
SovS . . . . SOVIET STUDIES
SovS . . . . SOVIET SURVEY
SovSlav . . . . SOVETSKOE SLAVJANOVEDENIE
SOV SOCIOL . . . . . . SOVIET SOCIOLOGY
SOV SOIL R . . . . . . SOVIET SOIL SCIENCE (USSR)
Sov Soil Sci . . . . . . SOVIET SOIL SCIENCE
SOV ST PHIL . . . . . . SOVIET STUDIES IN PHILOSOPHY WISSENSCHAFTLICHE BEITRAEGE
SOV STUD . . . . SOVIET STUDIES

SovVo . . . . SOVETSKOJE VOSTOKOVEDENIJE
SOWJETW GES . . . . . SOWJETWISSENSCHAFT GESELLSCHAFTS
So Workm . . . . SOUTHERN WORKMAN
SoWS . . . . SOUTHERN WRITERS SERIES
SoZ . . . . SOVREMENNYE ZAPISKI
Soz Welt . . . . SOZIALE WELT
SP . . . . SLOVANSKY PREHLED
Sp . . . . SPECTATOR
Sp . . . . SPECULUM
SP . . . . SPRING
Sp . . . . SPUTNIK (MOSCOW)
SP . . . . STUDIES IN PHILOLOGY
SP . . . . SUISSE PRIMITIVE
SPA . . . . SCIENCE AND PUBLIC AFFAIRS. BULLETIN OF THE ATOMIC SCIENTISTS
SPA . . . . SITZUNGSBERICHTE DER PREUSSISCHEN AKADEMIE DER WISSENSCHAFTEN
SPADCocRap . . . . . . SOCIETE PALEONTOLOGIQUE ET ARCHEOLOGIQUE DE L'ARRONDISSEMENT JUDICAIRE DE CHARLEROI. DOCUMENTS ET RAPPORTS
SPACE SCI R . . . . . . SPACE SCIENCE REVIEWS
SpAk . . . . SPISANIE NA BALGARSKATA AKADEMIJA NA NAUKITE
Spark's Am Biog . . . SPARK'S LIBRARY OF AMERICAN BIOGRAPHY
SPat . . . . STUDIA PATAVINA
SPAW . . . . SITZUNGSBERICHTE DER PREUSSISCHEN AKADEMIE DER WISSENSCHAFTEN
SpB . . . . SPRAKLIGA BIDRAG (LUND)
SpBA . . . . SPISANIE NA BALGARSKATA AKADEMIJA NA NAUKITE
SpBAN . . . . SPISANIE NA BALGARSKATA AKADEMIJA NA NAUKITE
SPCT . . . . STUDI E PROBLEMI DI CRITICA TESTUALE
SPE . . . . SOCIETY FOR PURE ENGLISH
SPe . . . . SPETTATORE ITALIANO
SPEC . . . . SPECTATOR
SPEC . . . . SPECULATION
Spec . . . . SPECULUM
Special Ed . . . . SPECIAL EDUCATION
Special Lib . . . . SPECIAL LIBRARIES
Spect . . . . SPECTATOR
SPECT ACT A . . . . . . SPECTROCHIMICA ACTA. PART A. MOLECULAR SPECTROSCOPY
SPECT ACT B . . . . . . SPECTROCHIMICA ACTA. PART B. ATOMIC SPECTROSCOPY
SPECT LETT . . . . . . SPECTROSCOPY LETTERS
Specu . . . . SPECULUM
Speech Mon . . . . . . SPEECH MONOGRAPHS
SPEECH TEAC . . . . . SPEECH TEACHER
SPE J . . . . SPE (SOCIETY OF PLASTICS ENGINEERS) JOURNAL
SPE Reg Tech Conf Tech Pap . . SPE (SOCIETY OF PLASTICS ENGINEERS) REGIONAL TECHNICAL CONFERENCE. TECHNICAL PAPERS
SPetr . . . . STUDI PETRARCHESCHI
SPF . . . . SPACE SCIENCE FICTION
Spf . . . . SPRACHFORUM
SPFB . . . . SBORNIK PEDAGOGICKE FAKULTY V BRNE
SPFB . . . . SBORNIK PRACI FILOSOFICKE FAKULTY BRNENSKE UNIVERSITY
Spfdr . . . . SPRINGFIELDER
SPFFBU . . . . SBORNIK PRACI FILOSOFICKE FAKULTY BRNENSKE UNIVERSITY
SPFO . . . . SBORNIK PEDAGOGICKE FAKULTY (OSTRAVA)

SPFOL . . . . SBORNIK PEDAGOGICKE FAKULTY (OLOMOUCI)
SPGL . . . . STUDIEN ZUR POETIK UND GESCHICHTE DER LITERATUR
SPH . . . . SOCIAL PROCESS IN HAWAII
SPh . . . . STUDIES IN PHILOLOGY
SPhNC . . . . STUDIES IN PHILOLOGY. UNIVERSITY OF NORTH CAROLINA
SPhon . . . . STUDIA PHONOLOGICA (KYOTO)
SPHQ . . . . SWEDISH PIONEER HISTORICAL QUARTERLY
SPIBB . . . . SBORNIK PEDAGOGICKEHO INSTITUTU V BANSKEJ BYSTRICI
SPIE J . . . . SPIE (SOCIETY OF PHOTO-OPTICAL INSTRUMENTATION ENGINEERS) JOURNAL
SPIG . . . . SBORNIK PRACI PEDAGOGICKEHO INSTITUTU V GOTTWALDOVE
SPIMD . . . . SIAULIU PEDAGOGINIO INSTITUTO MOKSLO DARBAI
SPIN . . . . SBORNIK PEDAGOGICKEHO INSTITUTU V NITRE
SPIO . . . . SBORNIK PRACI PEDAGOGICKEHO INSITUTU V OSTRAVE
SPIOL . . . . SBORNIK PEDAGOGICKEHO INSTITUTU V OLOMOUCI
SPIP . . . . SBORNIK PEDAGOGICKEHO INSTITUTU V PLZNI
SPIPL . . . . SBORNIK PEDAGOGICKEHO INSTITUTU V PLZNI
Spirit Mis . . . . SPIRIT OF MISSIONS
Spirit Pilg . . . . SPIRIT OF THE PILGRIMS
SPIU . . . . SBORNIK PRACI PEDAGOGICKEHO INSTITUTU, USTI NAD LABEM
SpL . . . . SPIEGEL DER LETTEREN
SPL . . . . STUDIE A PRACE LINGUISTICKE
Sp Lib . . . . SPECIAL LIBRARIES
SPLK . . . . STUDIE PRAZSKEHO LINGUISTICKEHO KROUZKU
Sp Mon . . . . SPEECH MONOGRAPHS
SPo . . . . SAO PAULO. REVISTA DO ARGUIVO MUNICIPAL
SPol . . . . STORIA E POLITICA
SpomSAN . . . . SPOMENIK SRPSKE AKADEMIJE NAUKA
SPR . . . . SLAVIC PRINTINGS AND REPRINTINGS
SPR . . . . SOUTHERN POETRY REVIEW
Spr . . . . SPRACHE
Sprache Tech Zeit . . SPRACHE IM TECHNISCHEN ZEITALTER
Sprakvetensk Sallsk i Uppsala Forhandl . . SPRAKVETENSKAPLIGA SALLSKAPETS I UPPSALA FORHANDLINGAR
SPRAM . . . . SAO PAULO. REVISTA DO ARQUIVO MUNICIPAL
Spraw . . . . SPRAWOZDANIA
SprB . . . . SPRAKLIGA BIDRAG
Sprechsaal Keram Glas Email Silikate . . SPRECHSAAL FUER KERAMIK, GLAS, EMAIL, SILIKATE
SPRF . . . . SOCIETE DE PUBLICATIONS ROMANES ET FRANCAISES
Spring Mfg Res Ass Spring Des Data Sheet . . SPRING MANUFACTURERS' RESEARCH ASSOCIATION. SPRING DESIGN DATA SHEET
SprKJ . . . . SPRAWOZDANIA Z POSIEDZEN KOMISJI JEZYKOWEJ TOWARZYSTWA NAUKOWEGO WARS-ZAWSKIEGO
SprKUL . . . . SPRAWOZDANIA Z CZYNNOSCI WYDAWNICZEJ I POSIEDZEN NAUKOWYCH ORAZ KRONIKA TOWARZYSTWA NAUKOWEGO KATOLOCKIEGO UNIWERSYTETU LUBELSKIEGO
SprLTN . . . . SPRAWOZDANIA Z CZYNNOSCI I POSIEDZEN LODZKIEGO TOWARZYSTWA NAUKOWEGO
SprPAUm . . . . SPRAWOZDANIA Z CZYNNOSCI I POSIEDZEN POLSKIEJ AKADEMII UMIEJETNOSCI
SprPTPN . . . . SPRAWOZDANIA POZNZNSKIEGO TOWARZYSTWA PRZYJACIOL NAUK
SprSUF . . . . SPRAKVETENSKAPLIGA SALLSKAPETS I UPPSALA FORHANDLINGAR
SprTNW . . . . SPRAWOZDANIA Z POSIEDZEN TOWARZYSTWA NAUKOWEGO WARSZAWSKIEGO
SprTT . . . . SPRAWOZDANIA TOWARZYSTWA NAUKOWEGO W TORUNIU
SprV . . . . SPRACHKUNST (VIENNA)
SPS . . . . SPACE STORIES

SPS . . . . SPECIMINA PHILOLOGIAE SLAVICAE
SPsp . . . . SPRACHSPIEGEL. SCHWEIZERISCHE ZEITSCHRIFT FUER DIE DEUTSCHE MUTTERSPRACHE
SPSU . . . . STUDIA PHILOLOGIAE SCANDINAVICAE UPSALIENSIA
SPT . . . . SPACE TRAVEL
SpT . . . . SPEECH TEACHER
SPTPN . . . . SPRAWOZDANIA POZNANSKIEGO TOWARZYSTWA PRZYJACIOL NAUK
SPV . . . . SPACE ADVENTURES
SPW . . . . SPACEWAY SCIENCE FICTION
SQ . . . . SHAKESPEARE QUARTERLY
SQ . . . . SOUTHERN QUARTERLY
SR . . . . SATURDAY REVIEW
SR . . . . SCHWEIZERISCHE RUNDSCHAU
SR . . . . SEWANEE REVIEW
SR . . . . SLAVONIC REVIEW
SR . . . . SLOVENSKA REC
SR . . . . SOCIAL RESEARCH
SR . . . . SOUTHERN REVIEW
SR . . . . SOUTHWEST REVIEW
SR . . . . STEREO REVIEW
SR . . . . STUDIES IN ROMANTICISM
SRA . . . . SATURDAY REVIEW OF THE ARTS
SRA-J SOC R . . . . . . SRA-JOURNAL OF THE SOCIETY OF RESEARCH ADMINISTRATORS
SRAZ . . . . STUDIA ROMANICA ET ANGLICA ZAGRABIENSIA
SRC . . . . STUDIES IN RELIGION. A CANADIAN JOURNAL
SRCS . . . . SUSTANCIA. REVISTA DE CULTURA SUPERIOR
SRE . . . . SATURDAY REVIEW OF EDUCATION
SRen . . . . STUDIES IN THE RENAISSANCE
SRev . . . . SLAVIC REVIEW
SRev . . . . SOUTHWEST REVIEW
SRG . . . . SCHRIFTEN DER RAABE-GESELLSCHAFT
S Rhodesia Geol Surv Bull . . SOUTHERN RHODESIA GEOLOGICAL SURVEY BULLETIN
SRI . . . . SVERIGES RUNINSKRIFTER
SRIELA . . . . SELECTED REPORTS: PUBLICATION OF THE INSTITUTE OF ETHNOMUSICOLOGY OF THE UNIVERSITY OF CALIFORNIA AT LOS ANGELES
SRISS . . . . SCIENTIA: REVISTA INTERNAZIONALE DI SINTESI SCIENTIFICA
SRL . . . . SATURDAY REVIEW OF LITERATURE
SRLF . . . . SAGGI E RICERCHE DI LETTERATURA FRANCESE
SRN . . . . SATURN SCIENCE FICTION AND FANTASY
SRO . . . . SHAKESPEAREAN RESEARCH OPPORTUNITIES
SRo . . . . STUDI ROMANI
SRom . . . . STUDI ROMANI
SRP . . . . STUDIA ROSSICA POSNANIENSIA
SRPO . . . . SOOBCHTCHENIIA RUSSKAGO PALESTINSKAGO OBCHTSHESTVA
SRS . . . . STRANGE STORIES
SRSC . . . . SATURDAY REVIEW OF SCIENCE
Sr Schol . . . . SENIOR SCHOLASTIC
SR-SCI . . . . SATURDAY REVIEW OF THE SCIENCES
SRSO . . . . SATURDAY REVIEW OF SOCIETY
SR-SOC . . . . SATURDAY REVIEW OF THE SOCIETY
SRSS . . . . SCIENTIA. RIVISTA SINTESI DI SCIENTIFICA
SRu . . . . STUDI RUMENI

SRv . . . . SOUTHWEST REVIEW
SRW . . . . SATURDAY REVIEW WORLD
SRZ . . . . STUDIA ROMANICA ZAGRABIENSIA
SS . . . . SCANDINAVIAN STUDIES
SS . . . . SHAKESPEARE SURVEY
SS . . . . SIGHT AND SOUND
SS . . . . SLOVO A SLOVESNOST
SS . . . . SOCIAL STUDIES
SS . . . . STARTLING STORIES
SS . . . . STUDIA SERDICENSIA
SS . . . . STUDI SARDI
SS . . . . STUDI STORICI
SS . . . . SYN OG SEGN
SSA . . . . SOCIAL SCIENCE ABSTRACTS
SSar . . . . STUDI SARDI
SSASH . . . . STUDIA SLAVICA ACADEMIAE SCIENTIARUM HUNGARICAE
SSAWL . . . . SITZUNGSBERICHTE DER SAECHSISCHEN AKADEMIE DER WISSENSCHAFTEN ZU LEIPZIG
SSb . . . . SKANDINAVSKIJ SBORNIK (TALLINN)
SSCI . . . . SOCIAL SCIENCES CITATION INDEX
SSCISAM . . . . SETTIMANE DI STUDIO DEL CENTRO ITALIANO DI STUDI SULL'ALTO MEDIOEVO
SSCJ . . . . SOUTHERN SPEECH COMMUNICATION JOURNAL
SSE . . . . STRANGEST STORIES EVER TOLD
SSe . . . . STUDI SECENTESCHI
SSEL . . . . STOCKHOLM STUDIES IN ENGLISH LITERATURE
SSept . . . . STUDIA SEPTENTRIONALIA
SSF . . . . STUDIES IN SHORT FICTION
SSF . . . . SUPER SCIENCE FICTION
SSF CHL . . . . SOCIETAS SCIENTIARUM FENNICAE. COMMENTATIONES HUMANARUM LITTERARUM
SSFS . . . . SAMLINGER UTGIVNA AV SVENSKA FORNSKRIFTSALLSKAPET, STOCKHOLM
SSG . . . . SCHRIFTEN DER TEODOR-STORM-GESELLSCHAFT
SSGS . . . . STANFORD STUDIES IN GERMANICS AND SLAVICS
SSH . . . . STUDIA SLAVICA ACADEMIAE SCIENTIARUM HUNGARICAE
SSH . . . . STUDIA SLAVICA HUNGARICA
SSHum . . . . SOCIAL SCIENCES AND HUMANITIES INDEX
SSI . . . . SOCIAL SCIENCE INFORMATION
SSJ . . . . SOUTHERN SPEECH JOURNAL
SSL . . . . SCANDO-SLAVICA (COPENHAGEN)
SSL . . . . STUDI E SAGGI LINGUISTICI
SSL . . . . STUDIES IN SCOTTISH LITERATURE
SSlav . . . . STUDIA SLAVICA ACADEMIAE SCIENTIARUM HUNGARICAE
SSLF . . . . SKRIFTER UTGIVNA AV SVENSKA LITTERATURSALLSKAPET I FINLAND
SSLL . . . . STANFORD STUDIES IN LANGUAGE AND LITERATURE
SSLSN . . . . SKRIFTER UTGIVNA AV SVENSKA LITTERATURSALLSKAPET STUDIER I NORDISK FILOLOGI
SSM . . . . SPACE SCIENCE FICTION MAGAZINE
SSMP . . . . STOCKHOLM STUDIES IN MODERN PHILOLOGY
SSN . . . . SCANDINAVIAN STUDIES AND NOTES
SSO . . . . SREDNEE SPETSIAL'NOE OBRAZOVANIE (MOSCOW)
SSO . . . . STUDIER FRA SPROG- OG OLDTIDSFORSKNING
SSOSM . . . . STUDI STORICI DELL'ORDINE DEI SERVI DE MARIA
SSpJ . . . . SOUTHERN SPEECH JOURNAL
SSQ . . . . SOCIAL SCIENCE QUARTERLY

SSR............STUDI E MATERIALI DI STORIA DELLE RELIGIONI
SSRC NEWSL......SSRC (SOCIAL SCIENCE RESEARCH COUNCIL) NEWSLETTER
SSS............SUPER SCIENCE STORIES
SSSP...........STOCKHOLM STUDIES IN SCANDINAVIAN PHILOLOGY
SSSR...........SOUTHWESTERN SOCIAL SCIENCE REVIEW
SST............SCIENCE STORIES
SST............SHAKESPEARE STUDIES (TOKYO)
SSt............SOWJET STUDIEN
SStud..........SHAKESPEARE STUDIES
SSUF...........SPRAKVETENSKAPLIGA SALLSKAPETS I UPPSALA FORHANDLINGAR
SSUR...........SPRINGFIELD SUNDAY UNION AND REPUBLICAN
SsvOA..........SYDSVENSKA ORTNAMNSSALLSKAPETS ARSSKRIFT
ST.............SLOVO A TVAR
ST.............SPEECH TEACHER
ST.............STATSOEKONOMISK TIDDSKRIFT
St.............STRANNIK: DUKHOVNYI, UCHENO-LITERATURNYI ZHURNAL
ST.............STUDI TASSIANI
St.............STUDIES
St.............STUDIUM
ST.............SVENSK TIDSKRIFT
STA............STRANGE ADVENTURES
StA............STUDI ANSELMIANA
STAHL EISEN......STAHL UND EISEN
STAIN TECH.......STAIN TECHNOLOGY
Stal in Engl.......STAL IN ENGLISH
STANF J INT......STANFORD JOURNAL OF INTERNATIONAL STUDIES
STANFORD LA.....STANFORD LAW REVIEW
Stanford L Rev....STANFORD LAW REVIEW
Stanki i Instrum....STANKI I INSTRUMENT
Stan L Rev.......STANFORD LAW REVIEW
STAR...........SCIENTIFIC AND TECHNICAL AEROSPACE REPORTS
State Gov........STATE GOVERNMENT
State Libn........STATE LIBRARIAN. JOURNAL OF THE CIRCLE OF STATE LIBRARIANS
Statens Inst Byggnadsforsk Handl (Trans)..STATENS INSTITUT FOER BYGGNADSFORSKNING, HANDLINGAR (TRANSLATIONS)
Statens Inst Byggnadsforsk Natl Swedish Bldg Res Doc..STATENS INSTITUT FOER BYGGNADSFORSKNING. NATIONAL SWEDISH BUILDING RESEARCH DOCUMENT
STATIST M L......STATISTICAL METHODS IN LINGUISTICS
Staub Reinhalt Luft..STAUB-REINHALTUNG DER LUFT
St Autobahn......STRASSE UND AUTOBAHN
Stavebnicky Cas...STAVEBNICKY CASOPIS
StB............STUDI SUL BOCCACCIO
STC............SHORT TITLE CATALOGUE
StC............STUDIA CATHOLICA
StC............STUDIA CELTICA
StCau..........STUDIA CAUCASICA
StCILF..........STUDII SI CERCETARI DE ISTORIE LITERATARA SI FOLCLOR
StCL...........STUDII SI CERCETARI LINGVISTICE
StCrN..........STEPHEN CRANE NEWSLETTER
StCSF..........STUDII SI CERCETARI STIINTIFICE. FILOLOGIE
StD............STUDI DANTESCHI

Ste............ STEAUA
Steam Heat Engr... STEAM AND HEATING ENGINEER
Steel Met Int...... STEELS AND METALS INTERNATIONAL
Steel USSR........ STEEL IN THE USSR
SteiQ........... STEINBECK QUARTERLY
STeol........... STUDII TEOLOGICE
Stevens Ind....... STEVENS INDICATOR
STF............. STRANGE FANTASY
StFil........... STUDIA FILOZOFICZNE
STFM........... SOCIETE DES TEXTES FRANCAIS MODERNES
StFr............ STUDI FRANCESCANI
StG............. STUDI GERMANICI
StGAK.......... STUDIEN ZUR GERMANISTIK, ANGLISTIK UND KOMPARATISTIK
Stgr............ STUDIA GRAMMATICA
STh............. STUDIA THEOLOGICA
SThK........... SVENSK THEOLOGISH KVARTALSKRIFT
STHP........... SHIT-TA HSUEH-PAO (BULLETIN OF TAIWAN NORMAL UNIVERSITY)
SThU........... SCHWEIZERISCHE THEOLOGISCHE UMSCHAU
StI............. STUDI ISPANICI
StI............. STUDI ITALIANI
StI............. STUDIA ISLANDICA
StI............. STUDIES. AN IRISH QUARTERLY REVIEW OF LETTERS, PHILOSOPHY AND SCIENCE
StIsl........... STUDIA ISLANDICA
StIsp........... STUDI ISPANICI (MILANO)
StIt............ STUDI ITALICI
StJb............ STIFTER-JAHRBUCH
STK............ SVENSK TEOLIGISK KVARTALSKRIFT
STL............ STARTLING STORIES
StL............. STUDIA LINGUISTICA
StL............. STUDIES ON THE LEFT
StLI............ STUDI DI LETTERATURA ISPANO-AMERICANA
StLing.......... STUDIES IN LINGUISTICS
S T L J.......... SOUTH TEXAS LAW JOURNAL
StLo........... STUDIA LOGICA
StLog.......... STUDIA LOGICA
St Louis Mus Bul... ST. LOUIS CITY ART MUSEUM BULLETIN
ST LOUIS U L J..... ST. LOUIS UNIVERSITY LAW JOURNAL
STL-QPSR........ SPEECH TRANSMISSION LABORATORY. ROYAL INSTITUTE OF TECHNOLOGY. STOCKHOLM.
              QUARTERLY PROGRESS AND STATUS REPORTS
St Luke J......... ST. LUKE'S JOURNAL OF THEOLOGY
StM............ STUDIA MONASTICA
St Mary's L J...... ST. MARY'S LAW JOURNAL
StMed.......... STUDIA MEDIEWISTYCZNE
St Med.......... STUDI MEDIEVALI
StMon.......... STUDIA MONASTICA
St N............ ST. NICHOLAS
St Neophil....... STUDIA NEOPHILOLOGICA
StNF........... STUDIER I NORDISK FILOLOGI
STNT........... SPRAWOZDANIA TOWARZYSTWA NAUKOWEGO W TORUNIU
StO............ STUDIA OLIVERIANA
Stockholm Tek Hogsk Avh.. STOCKHOLM. TEKNISKA HOGSKOLAN, AVHANDLING

Stockholm Tek Hogsk Handl..STOCKHOLM. TEKNISKA HOGSKOLAN, HANDLINGAR (TRANSACTIONS)
Storage Handl Distrib..STORAGE HANDLING DISTRIBUTION
StP............STUDI PETRARCHESI
StPa...........STUDIA PATRISTICA
ST P BROOK.......STAFF PAPERS BROOKINGS INSTITUTION
STR............SOCIETY FOR THEATRE RESEARCH
STR............SOUL-TAEHAKKYO RONMUNJIP, INMUN-SAHOE-KWAHAK (SEOUL UNIVERSITY JOURNAL, HUMANITIES AND SOCIAL SCIENCES)
STR............STAR SCIENCE FICTION
StR............STUDI RELIGIOSI
StR............STUDI ROMAGNOLI
STr............STUDI TRENTINI
STr............STUDI TRENTINI DI SCIENZE STORICHE
StR............STUDIA ROMANICA
StR............STUDIE O RUKOPISECH
STRAHLENTHE.....STRAHLENTHERAPIE
Strand..........STRAND MAGAZINE
Strasse Autobahn..STRASSE UND AUTOBAHN
Strauss.........INTERNATIONALE RICHARD-STRAUSS-GESELLSCHAFT MITTEILUNGEN
StRel/ScRel......STUDIES IN RELIGION/SCIENCES RELIGIEUSES
St Ren...........STUDIES IN THE RENAISSANCE
StRo............STUDI ROMANI
Stroemungsmech stroemungsmasch..STROEMUNGSMECHANIK UND STROEMUNGSMASCHINEN
StRom...........STUDIA ROMANICA
StRom...........STUDIES IN ROMANTICISM
Struct Eng........STRUCTURAL ENGINEER
STS............SCOTTISH TEXT SOCIETY
STS............STIRRING SCIENCE STORIES
StS............STUDIA SLAVICA
StSa............STUDI SALENTINI
StSec..........STUDI SECENTESCHI
StSl............STUDIA SLAVICA
STSS...........STUDI TRENTINI DI SCIENZE STORICHE
STT............STRANGE TALES OF MYSTERY AND TERROR
StT............STUDI TASSIANI
StTh...........STUDIA THEOLOGICA: SCANDINAVIAN JOURNAL OF THEOLOGY
Stu............STUDIA
Stu............STUDIUM
STU CER FIZ......STUDII SI CERCETARI DE FIZICA
Stud...........STUDIEN
Stud...........STUDIES
Stud Ag Econ......STANFORD UNIVERSITY. FOOD RESEARCH INSTITUTE. STUDIES IN AGRICULTURAL ECONOMICS, TRADE, AND DEVELOPMENT
Stud & Intel Obs...STUDENT AND INTELLECTUAL OBSERVER
STUD APPL M.....STUDIES IN APPLIED MATHEMATICS
Stud Art Ed.......STUDIES IN ART EDUCATION
Stud Bibliog.......VIRGINIA UNIVERSITY BIBLIOGRAPHICAL SOCIETY. STUDIES IN BIBLIOGRAPHY
Stud Bibliog & Bklore..STUDIES IN BIBLIOGRAPHY AND BOOKLORE
STUD BIOPHY.....STUDIA BIOPHYSICA
Stud Black Lit.....STUDIES IN BLACK LITERATURE
STUD CH G P......STUDIES IN CHINESE GOVERNMENT AND POLITICS

StudClas......... STUDII CLASICE
STUD COM CO..... STUDIES IN COMPARATIVE COMMUNISM
STUD COM ID..... STUDIES IN COMPARATIVE INTERNATIONAL DEVELOPMENT
STUD COM LG..... STUDIES IN COMPARATIVE LOCAL GOVERNMENT
STUD COMM R..... STUDIES IN COMMUNISM, REVISIONISM, AND REVOLUTION
Stud Comp Commun.. STUDIES IN COMPARATIVE COMMUNISM
Stud Comp Relig... STUDIES IN COMPARATIVE RELIGION
Stud Conserv...... STUDIES IN CONSERVATION
Stud Ed.......... STUDIES IN EDUCATION
Stud Engl Lit...... STUDIES IN ENGLISH LITERATURE
Stud Engl Phil..... STUDIEN ZUR ENGLISCHEN PHILOLOGIE
STUDENT MUSICOL.. STUDENT MUSICOLOGISTS AT MINNESOTA
Student Q J Instn Elec Engrs.. INSTITUTION OF ELECTRICAL ENGINEERS. STUDENT QUARTERLY JOURNAL
STUD FAM PL..... STUDIES IN FAMILY PLANNING
Stud Gen......... STUDIUM GENERALE
STUD GEOPH...... STUDIA GEOPHYSICA ET GEODAETICA
STUD HIST P...... STUDIES IN HISTORY AND PHILOSOPHY OF SCIENCE
Studia Mus....... STUDIA MUSICOLOGICA
STUDIA MUS NOR.. STUDIA MUSICOLOGICA NORVEGICA
Studia Neophil..... STUDIA NEOPHILOLOGICA
Studies App Math.. STUDIES IN APPLIED MATHEMATICS
Studies in Art Ed... STUDIES IN ART EDUCATION
Studies L & Econ Develop.. STUDIES IN LAW AND ECONOMIC DEVELOPMENT
STUDIES MUS...... STUDIES IN MUSIC
Studies Philol..... STUDIES IN PHILOLOGY
Studio........... STUDIO INTERNATIONAL
Stud Leibnit....... STUDIA LEIBNITIANA
Stud Ling......... STUDIES IN LINGUISTICS
Stud Lit.......... STUDIA LITURGICA
Stud Log......... STUDIA LOGICA
STUD MATH...... STUDIA MATHEMATICA
StudMon......... STUDIA MONASTICA
Stud Neoph....... STUDIA-NEOPHILOLOGICA
Stud Novel....... STUDIES IN THE NOVEL
StudPap......... STUDIA PAPIROLOGICA
STUD PERS P...... STUDIES IN PERSONNEL PSYCHOLOGY
Stud Phil & Ed..... STUDIES IN PHILOSOPHY AND EDUCATION
Stud Phil Christ.... STUDIA PHILOSOPHIAE CHRISTIANE
STUD PHIL E...... STUDIES IN PHILOSOPHY AND EDUCATION
Stud Phil Hist Phil.. STUDIES IN PHILOSOPHY AND THE HISTORY OF PHILOSOPHY
Stud Philol........ STUDIES IN PHILOLOGY
STUD PHILOS & EDUC.. STUDIES IN PHILOSOPHY AND EDUCATION
Stud Phil (Switzerland).. STUDIA PHILOSOPHICA (SWITZERLAND)
STUD PSYCHO..... STUDIA PSYCHOLOGICA
StudRom......... STUDI ROMANI (ROME)
StudRom......... STUDI ROMANZI (PADUA)
Stud Romant...... STUDIES IN ROMANTICISM
Stud Romanticism.. STUDIES IN ROMANTICISM
StudSal.......... STUDI SALENTINI
StudSard......... STUDI SARDI
Stud Short Fict..... STUDIES IN SHORT FICTION

STUD SOC LI . . . . . . STUDIES IN SOCIAL LIFE
STUD SOV TH . . . . . . STUDIES IN SOVIET THOUGHT
Stud Th . . . . STUDIA THEOLOGICA
StudUrb . . . . STUDI URBINATI DI STORIA, FILOSOFIA E LETTERATURA
Stud W . . . . STUDENT WORLD
StuSta . . . . STUDIA STAROPOLSKIE
StuTC . . . . STUDIES IN THE TWENTIETH CENTURY
StV . . . . STUDIES ON VOLTAIRE AND THE 18TH CENTURY
Stva . . . . STVARANJE
STZ . . . . SPRACHE IM TECHNISCHEN ZEITALTER
SU . . . . SAMOSTIJNA UKRAINA (INDEPENDENT UKRAINE)
SU . . . . STUDI URBINATI
SUB . . . . SCANDINAVIAN UNIVERSITY BOOKS
SUBB . . . . STUDIA UNIVERSITATIS BABES-BOLYAI, PHILOLOGIA
SUBBP . . . . STUDIA UNIVERSITATIS BABES-BOLYAI, PHILOLOGIA
SUB-CELL BI . . . . SUB-CELLULAR BIOCHEMISTRY
Subj of Day . . . . SUBJECT OF THE DAY
Sub Life . . . . SUBURBAN LIFE
SUC . . . . SAGGI DI UMANISMO CRISTIANO
Successful F . . . . . . SUCCESSFUL FARMING
Suc Farm . . . . SUCCESSFUL FARMING
SuD . . . . SPRACHE UND DICHTUNG
SudA . . . . SUEDOSTDEUTSCHES ARCHIV
SUDAM . . . . EDITORIAL SUDAMERICANA, BA
Sudan Notes . . . . . . SUDAN NOTES AND RECORDS
SudoA . . . . SUEDOSTDEUTSCHES ARCHIV
SuF . . . . SINN UND FORM
Suffolk U L Rev . . . . SUFFOLK UNIVERSITY LAW REVIEW
SuG . . . . SPRACHE UND GEMEINSCHAFT
Sugar . . . . SUGAR Y AZUCAR
SUGAR J . . . . SUGAR JOURNAL
Sugar Technol Rev . . SUGAR TECHNOLOGY REVIEWS
SUL . . . . PER LO STUDIO E L'USO DEL LATINO
SuL . . . . SPRACHE UND LITERATUR
Sulzer Tech Rev . . . . SULZER TECHNICAL REVIEW
Sumitomo Elec Tech Rev . . SUMITOMO ELECTRIC TECHNICAL REVIEW
Sumitomo Light Metal Tech Rep . . SUMITOMO LIGHT METAL TECHNICAL REPORTS
Sum Rep Electrotech Lab Tokyo Japan . . SUMMARIES OF REPORTS OF THE ELECTROTECHNICAL LABORATORY. TOKYO, JAPAN
Sunday M . . . . SUNDAY MAGAZINE
Sund M . . . . SUNDAY MAGAZINE
SunT . . . . SUNDAY TIMES
Sun Times . . . . SUNDAY TIMES
SUP . . . . SPISY UNIVERSITY J. E. PURKYNE
Sup Ct Rev . . . . SUPREME COURT REVIEW
Sup Pop Sci Mo . . . . SUPPLEMENT TO POPULAR SCIENCE MONTHLY
SUPP PR T P . . . . . . SUPPLEMENT OF THE PROGRESS OF THEORETICAL PHYSICS
SUPR COURT . . . . . . SUPREME COURT REVIEW
Sup Stud . . . . THE SUPERIOR STUDENT
SUPUSLL . . . . STANFORD UNIVERSITY PUBLICATIONS. UNIVERSITY SERIES. LANGUAGES & LITERATURES
Surface Sci . . . . . . SURFACE SCIENCE

Surf Coat . . . . SURFACE COATINGS
SURF SCI . . . . SURFACE SCIENCE
SURG CL NA . . . . . . SURGICAL CLINICS OF NORTH AMERICA
SURG GYN OB . . . . . SURGERY GYNECOLOGY AND OBSTETRICS
SURG ITAL . . . . SURGERY IN ITALY
Survey Cur Bus . . . . SURVEY OF CURRENT BUSINESS
Survey G . . . . SURVEY GRAPHIC
Surv-Local Gov Technol . . SURVEYOR—LOCAL GOVERNMENT TECHNOLOGY
Surv Mapp . . . . SURVEYING AND MAPPING
SUS . . . . STUDI URBINATI DI STORIA, FILOSOFIA E LETTERATURA
SUS . . . . SUSPENSE
SUS . . . . SUSQUEHANNA UNIVERSITY STUDIES
Sus . . . . SUSRETI
Susf . . . . SAMLINGAR UTGIVNA AV SVENSKA FORNSKRIFTSSAILLSKAPET
SUSFL . . . . STUDI URBINATI DI STORIA, FILOSOFIA E LETTERATURA
SuSu . . . . SUOMALAINEN SUOMI
SuSuomi . . . . SUOMALAINEN SUOMI
SuSuV . . . . SUOMALAINEN SUOMI. KULTTUURIPOLITTTINEN AIKAKAUSKIRJA/VALVOJA
SUVSL . . . . SKRIFTER UTGIVNA AV VETENSKAPS-SOCIETETEN I LUND
SV . . . . SCHWEIZER VOLKSKUNDE
SV . . . . SCUOLA E VITA
SV . . . . SLOVESNA VEDA
SV Aeroplan A.B. SAAB Tech Notes . . SVENSKA AEROPLAN AKTIEBOLAGET. LINKOPING, SWEDEN. SAAB TECHNICAL
          NOTES
SvD . . . . SVENSKA DAGBLADET
SvEA . . . . SVENSK EXEGETISK ARSBOK
SVEC . . . . STUDIES ON VOLTAIRE AND THE EIGHTEENTH CENTURY
Svensk Geog Arsbok . . SVENSK GEOGRAFISK ARSBOK
Svensk Teol Kvartalskr . . SVENSK TEOLOGISK KVARTALSKRIFT
SVENSK TID . . . . . . SVENSK TIDSKRIFT FOER MUSIKFORSKNING
SVENS PAP T . . . . . . SVENSK PAPPERSTIDNING TIDSKRIFT
Sver Mekanforb Mekanresult . . SVERIGES MEKANFORBUND, MEKANRESULTAT
Svl . . . . SVIZZERA ITALIANA
SVJ . . . . SOVETSKA VEDA. JAZYKOVEDA
Sv Kraftverksforen Publ . . SVENSKA KRAFTVERKSFORENINGENS PUBLIKATIONER
SVL . . . . STUDIEN ZUR VERGLEICHENDEN LITERATURGESCHICHTE
SvLm . . . . SVENSKA LANDSMAL OCH SVENSKT FOLKLIV
SvM . . . . SVENSK MISSIONSTIDSKRIFT
SVS . . . . SAGA-BOOK OF THE VIKING SOCIETY FOR NORTHERN RESEARCH
SVSHKG . . . . SCHRIFTEN DES VEREINS FUER SCHLESWIG-HOLSTEINISCHE KIRCHENGESCHICHTE
SVSL . . . . SKRIFTER UTGIVNA AV VETENSKAPSSOCIETETEN LUND
S V Sound Vib . . . . . S V, SOUND AND VIBRATION
SVSPO . . . . SBORNIK VYSOKE SKOLY PEDAGOGICKE V OLOMOUCI
SVSPO(JL) . . . . SBORNIK VYSOKE SKOLY PEDAGOGICKE V OLOMOUCI. JAZYKA A LITERATURA
SVSPP . . . . SBORNIK VYSOKE SKOLY PEDAGOGICKE V PRAZE. JAZYK A LITERATURA
SvT . . . . SVENSKA TEXTER
SvTK . . . . SVENSK TEOLOGISK KVARTALSKRIFT
SvTs . . . . SVENSK TIDSKRIFT
SW . . . . SCIENCE WONDER STORIES
SW . . . . SLAVIC WORD
SW . . . . SOUTH AND WEST

PERIODICAL TITLE ABBREVIATIONS

SWA . . . . SITZUNGS-BERICHTE DER WIENER AKADEMIE
SwAL . . . . SOUTHWESTERN AMERICAN LITERATURE
Swansea Coll Fac Ed J . . UNIVERSITY COLLEGE OF SWANSEA. COLLEGIATE FACULTY OF EDUCATION JOURNAL
Swed Geotech Inst Proc . . SWEDISH GEOTECHNICAL INSTITUTE. PROCEEDINGS
Swedish Hist Soc Yearbook . . SWEDISH HISTORICAL SOCIETY. YEARBOOK
SWED J ECON . . . . . . SWEDISH JOURNAL OF ECONOMICS
SW HIST Q . . . . SOUTHWESTERN HISTORICAL QUARTERLY
SwHQ . . . . SOUTHWESTERN HISTORICAL QUARTERLY
SW J Anthrop . . . . . SOUTHWESTERN JOURNAL OF ANTHROPOLOGY
SW J Phil . . . . SOUTHWESTERN JOURNAL OF PHILOSOPHY
SW J Th . . . . SOUTHWESTERN JOURNAL OF THEOLOGY
SW L J . . . . SOUTHWESTERN LAW JOURNAL
SW Musician . . . . . . THE SOUTHWESTERN MUSICIAN
SWNS . . . . SPRAWOZDANIE Z PRAC NAUKOWYCH WYDZIALU NAUK SPOLECZNYCH PAN
SwR . . . . SEWANEE REVIEW
SWR . . . . SOUTHWEST REVIEW
SwS . . . . SOUTHWESTERN STUDIES
SWS . . . . SOUTHWEST WRITERS SERIES
SWSJ . . . . SON OF WSFA JOURNAL
Sw Social Sci Q . . . . . SOUTHWESTERN SOCIAL SCIENCE QUARTERLY
SW ST UTEP . . . . SOUTHWESTERN STUDIES (UNIVERSITY OF TEXAS, EL PASO)
SWTN . . . . SPRAWOZDANIA WROCLAWSKIEGO TOWARZYSTWA NAUKOWEGO
SW U L Rev . . . . SOUTHWESTERN UNIVERSITY LAW REVIEW
SXX . . . . SECOLUL XX
SY . . . . SYMPOSIUM
Sy . . . . SYRIA. REVUE D'ART ORIENTAL ET D'ARCHEOLOGIE
Sydney L Rev . . . . . . SYDNEY LAW REVIEW
Sydsvenska Ortnamns-sallsk Arsskr . . SYDSVENSKA ORTNAMNS-SALLSKAPETS ARSSKRIFT
Syl . . . . SYLLOGOS. JOURNAL DE LA SOCIETE PHILOLOGIQUE GRECQUE DE CONSTANTINOPLE
Sym . . . . SYMPOSIUM
SymbOsl . . . . SYMBOLAE OSLOENSES
SYM NEWS . . . . SYMPHONY NEWS
Symposium . . . . SYMPOSIUM: A QUARTERLY JOURNAL IN MODERN FOREIGN LITERATURES
Syn . . . . SYNTHESES
SYN COMMUN . . . . . SYNTHETIC COMMUNICATIONS
SYN REAC IN . . . . . . SYNTHESIS AND REACTIVITY IN INORGANIC AND METALORGANIC CHEMISTRY
Syr . . . . SYRIA. REVUE D'ART ORIENTAL ET D'ARCHEOLOGIE
SYRAC LAW R . . . . . SYRACUSE LAW REVIEW
Syst Comput Controls . . SYSTEMS-COMPUTERS-CONTROLS
Systems & Proc J . . . SYSTEMS AND PROCEDURES JOURNAL
Syst Technol . . . . . . SYSTEMS TECHNOLOGY
SYST ZOOL . . . . SYSTEMATIC ZOOLOGY
SZ . . . . SCHWEIZERISCHE ZEITSCHRIFT FUER VOLKSWIRTSCHAFT UND STATISTIK
SZ . . . . SEKSPIROVSKIJ ZBORNIK
SZ . . . . SOVREMENNYE ZAPISKI
SZ . . . . STIMMEN DER ZEIT
SZC . . . . STUDIA ZRODLOZNAWCZE. COMMENTATIONES
SzDL . . . . STUDIEN ZUR DEUTSCHEN LITERATUR
SzEP . . . . STUDIEN ZUR ENGLISCHEN PHILOLOGIE
SZG . . . . SCHWEIZERISCHE ZEITSCHRIFT FUER GESCHICHTE
SzL . . . . SCHRIFTEN ZUR LITERATUR

SzNU . . . . SBORNIK ZA NARODNI UMOTVORENIJA
SzT . . . . SCHRIFTEN ZUR THEATERWISSENSCHAFT

T

T............. TEATAR (SOFIA)
T............. TEATR
T............. TEUTHONISTA
T............. TIME
T............. TRADITIO
T............. TURIN
TA............ THEATER ANNUAL
TA............ TRADUCTION AUTOMATIQUE
TA............ TRIERISCHES ARCHIV
TAD........... THE ARMCHAIR DETECTIVE
Tag........... TAGORO
TAG........... TIJDSCHRIFT AARDRIJKSKUNDIG GENOOTSCHAP
TAI........... T.A. INFORMATIONS
Tait.......... TAIT'S EDINBURGH MAGAZINE
TAK........... TONAN AJIA KENKYU (SOUTHEAST ASIA STUDIES)
Tal........... TALIESIN (ENGLAND)
Tal........... TALISMAN
TAm........... THE AMERICAS
TaM........... TARYBINE MOKYKLA
TAM........... THEATRE ARTS MAGAZINE
TAM........... THEATRE ARTS MONTHLY
TamC.......... TAMIL CULTURE
T AM FISH S...... TRANSACTIONS OF THE AMERICAN FISHERIES SOCIETY
T AM GEOPHY..... TRANSACTIONS OF THE AMERICAN GEOPHYSICAL UNION
TamkR......... TAMKANG REVIEW
T AM MATH S..... TRANSACTIONS OF THE AMERICAN MATHEMATICAL SOCIETY
T AM MICROS..... TRANSACTIONS OF THE AMERICAN MICROSCOPICAL SOCIETY
T AM NUCL S..... TRANSACTIONS OF THE AMERICAN NUCLEAR SOCIETY
T AM PHIL S..... TRANSACTIONS OF THE AMERICAN PHILOSOPHICAL SOCIETY
TamR.......... TAMARACK REVIEW (TORONTO)
T AM S ART...... TRANSACTIONS AMERICAN SOCIETY ARTIFICIAL INTERNAL ORGANS
T&T........... TIME AND TIDE
Tanker Bulk Carr... TANKER AND BULK CARRIER
Tanzania Miner Resour Power Annu Rep Geol Surv Div.. TANZANIA. MINISTRY OF INDUSTRIES. MINERAL RESOURCES AND POWER. ANNUAL REPORT OF THE GEOLOGICAL SURVEY DIVISION
Tanzania, Rec Geol Surv Tanganyika.. TANZANIA. RECORDS OF THE GEOLOGICAL SURVEY OF TANGANYIKA
TAPA.......... TRANSACTIONS AND PROCEEDINGS OF THE AMERICAN PHILOLOGICAL ASSOCIATION
TAPhA......... TRANSACTIONS AND PROCEEDINGS OF THE AMERICAN PHILOLOGICAL ASSOCIATION
TAPPI......... TAPPI (TECHNICAL ASSOCIATION OF THE PULP AND PAPER INDUSTRY)
TAPS.......... TRANSACTIONS OF THE AMERICAN PHILOSOPHICAL SOCIETY
TAr........... THEATER ARTS
TArts......... THEATER ARTS
T ASAE........ TRANSACTIONS OF THE ASAE (AMERICAN SOCIETY OF AGRICULTURAL ENGINEERS)
TASJ.......... TRANSACTIONS OF THE ASIATIC SOCIETY OF JAPAN
Tasmanian U L Rev.. TASMANIAN UNIVERSITY LAW REVIEW
TASM J AGR...... TASMANIAN JOURNAL OF AGRICULTURE
Tax........... TAXANDRIA
Tax Coun Q...... TAX COUNSELOR'S QUARTERLY
Tax Law........ TAX LAWYER

Tax L Rev . . . . TAX LAW REVIEW
Taylor Soc Bul . . . . . TAYLOR SOCIETY BULLETIN
TAzerbPI . . . . TRUDY AZERBAJDZANSKOGO GOSUDARSTVENNOGO PEDAGOGICESKOGO INSTITUTA
TB . . . . TEMPO BRASILEIRO
TB . . . . THRILL BOOK
TB . . . . TVORBA
TBGU . . . . TRUDY BELORUSSKOGO GOSUDARSTVENNOGO UNIVERSITETA
Tbilisis univ sromebi . . STALINIS SACHEOLOBIS TBILISIS UNIVERSITATIS SROMEBI
TBK . . . . TOYO BUNGAKU KENKYU (STUDIES ON ORIENTAL LITERATURE)
TBR . . . . NEW YORK TIMES BOOK REVIEW
TBR . . . . THREE BANKS REVIEW
T BR MYCOL . . . . . . TRANSACTIONS OF THE BRITISH MYCOLOGICAL SOCIETY
TBurNII . . . . TRUDY BURJATSKOGO KOMPLESNOGO NAUCNO- ISSLEDOVA-TEL'SKOGO INSTITUTA
TC . . . . TRIERISCHE CHRONIK
TC . . . . TWENTIETH CENTURY
TC . . . . TWORCZOSC
TCAAS . . . . TRANSACTIONS OF THE CONNECTICUT ACADEMY OF ARTS AND SCIENCES
TCAus . . . . TWENTIETH CENTURY (MELBOURNE)
TCBS . . . . TRANSACTIONS OF THE CAMBRIDGE BIBLIOGRAPHICAL SOCIETY
TCF . . . . TWENTIETH CENTURY FICTION
TCh . . . . TEMOIGNAGE CHRETIEN
TCI . . . . TWENTIETH CENTURY INTERPRETATIONS
TCL . . . . TWENTIETH CENTURY LITERATURE
TCLC . . . . TRAVAUX DU CERCLE LINGUISTIQUE DE COPENHAGUE
TCLP . . . . TRAVAUX DU CERCLE LINGUISTIQUE DE PRAGUE
TCM . . . . TWENTIETH CENTURY MONTHLY
TCR . . . . TEACHERS COLLEGE RECORD
TCSM . . . . TRANSACTIONS OF THE COLONIAL SOCIETY OF MASSACHUSETTS
TCV . . . . TWENTIETH CENTURY VIEWS
TD . . . . THEATRE DOCUMENTATION
TDED . . . . ISTANBUL UNIVERSITESI EDEGIYAT FAKULTESI TURK DILI VE EDEBIYATI DERGISI
TDK . . . . TOYO DAIGAKU KIYO (BULLETIN OF THE DEPARTMENT OF LIBERAL ARTS, TOKYO UNIVERSITY)
TDR . . . . DRAMA REVIEW (FORMERLY TULANE DRAMA REVIEW)
TDR . . . . TULANE DRAMA REVIEW
TE . . . . TEACHER EDUCATION
Te . . . . TEATR (MOSCOW)
TE . . . . TEOLOGIA ESPIRITUAL
TE . . . . TIGER'S EYE
TEACH COL R . . . . . TEACHERS COLLEGE RECORD
TEACH DEAF . . . . . . TEACHER OF THE DEAF
Teach Excep Child . . TEACHING EXCEPTIONAL CHILDREN
Teach J and Abst . . . TEACHERS JOURNAL AND ABSTRACT
Teach Phil . . . . TEACHING PHILOSOPHY
TEACH POL S . . . . . . TEACHING POLITICAL SCIENCE
TEACH SOCIO . . . . . TEACHING SOCIOLOGY
TEAS . . . . TWAYNE'S ENGLISH AUTHOR SERIES
Tech & Cult . . . . TECHNOLOGY AND CULTURE
Tech Assn Pa . . . . . . TECHNICAL ASSOCIATION PAPERS
Tech Educ . . . . TECHNICAL EDUCATION
Tech Mitt Krupp Forschungsber . . TECHNISCHE MITTEILUNGEN KRUPP. FORSCHUNGSBERICHTE
Tech Mitt Krupp Werksber . . TECHNISCHE MITTEILUNGEN KRUPP. WERKSBERICHTE

Tech Mitt PTT..... TECHNISCHE MITTEILUNGEN PTT
Tech Mod........ TECHNIQUE MODERNE
Technion Israel Inst Technol TAE Rep..TECHNION. ISRAEL INSTITUTE OF TECHNOLOGY. DEPARTMENT OF AERONAUTICAL ENGINEERING. HAIFA. TAE REPORT
TECHNOL CUL..... TECHNOLOGY AND CULTURE
TECHNOL FOR..... TECHNOLOGICAL FORECASTING AND SOCIAL CHANGE
Technol Rep Tohoku Univ.. TECHNOLOGY REPORTS OF THE TOHOKU UNIVERSITY, SENDAIK, JAPAN
TECHNOL REV..... TECHNOLOGY REVIEW
TECHNOMET...... TECHNOMETRICS
Tech Poszukiwan... TECHNIKA POSZUKIWAN
Tech R.......... TECHNOLOGY REVIEW
Tech Rep Eng Res Inst Kyoto Univ.. TECHNICAL REPORTS OF THE ENGINEERING RESEARCH INSTITUTE. KYOTO UNIVERSITY
Tech Trav (Liege).. TECHNIQUE DES TRAVAUX (LIEGE)
Tech W.......... TECHNOLOGY WEEK
Tech World...... TECHNICAL WORLD MAGAZINE
Tec Ital......... TECNICA ITALIANA
Tec Met (Barcelona).. TECNICA METALURGICA (BARCELONA)
TEC MIT K F...... TECHNISCHE MITTEILUNGEN KRUPP FORSCHUNGSBERICHTE
TEC MIT K W..... TECHNISCHE MITTEILUNGEN KRUPP WERKSBERICHTE
TECTONOPHYS..... TECTONOPHYSICS
TeK............ TEXT UND KONTEXT
Tek Aikak........ TEKNILLINEN AIKAKAUSLEHTI
Tek Tidskr........ TEKNISK TIDSKRIFT
Tek Ukebl........ TEKNISK UKEBLAD
TELECOMM J...... TELECOMMUNICATION JOURNAL
Telecommun J..... TELECOMMUNICATION JOURNAL
Telecommun J Aust.. TELECOMMUNICATION JOURNAL OF AUSTRALIA
Telecommun Radio Eng.. TELECOMMUNICATIONS AND RADIO ENGINEERING
Tele Engl Ed...... TELE (ENGLISH EDITION)
Tele-Tech & Electronic Ind.. TELE-TECH AND ELECTRONIC INDUSTRIES
TelQ........... TEL QUEL
TEL RAD E R...... TELECOMMUNICATIONS AND RADIO ENGINEERING
TeM............ O TEMPO E O MODO
Temp Bar........ TEMPLE BAR
TEMPLE LAW..... TEMPLE LAW QUARTERLY
Temp L Q........ TEMPLE LAW QUARTERLY
TEng............ TEACHING ENGLISH
Tenn Acad Sci J.... TENNESSEE ACADEMY OF SCIENCE. JOURNAL
Tenn Ag Exp...... UNIVERSITY OF TENNESSEE. AGRICULTURAL EXPERIMENT STATION. PUBLICATIONS
Tenn Dep Conserv Div Geol Bull.. TENNESSEE DEPARTMENT OF CONSERVATION. DIVISION OF GEOLOGY. BULLETIN
Tenn Farm & Home Sci.. TENNESSEE FARM AND HOME SCIENCE
Tenn Folk S....... TENNESSEE FOLKLORE SOCIETY BULLETIN
Tenn Hist Mag..... TENNESSEE MAGAZINE OF HISTORY
Tenn Hist Q....... TENNESSEE HISTORICAL QUARTERLY
Tenn Libn........ TENNESSEE LIBRARIAN
Tenn L R......... TENNESSEE LAW REVIEW
Tenn Univ Eng Exp Sta Bull.. TENNESSEE UNIVERSITY. ENGINEERING EXPERIMENT STATION. BULLETIN
Teor Metod....... TEORIE A METODA
TEOR VEROYA..... TEORIYA VEROYATNOSTEI I YEYE PRIMENIYA
TeR............ TE REO

Tes............. TESAUR
TES............. TIMES EDUCATIONAL SUPPLEMENT
TESOLQ.......... TESOL (TEACHERS OF ENGLISH TO SPEAKERS OF OTHER LANGUAGES) QUARTERLY
TESOL QUART..... TESOL (TEACHERS OF ENGLISH TO SPEAKERS OF OTHER LANGUAGES) QUARTERLY
Test Eng Manage... TEST ENGINEERING & MANAGEMENT
TeT............. TAAL EN TONGVAL (ANTWERPEN)
TETRAHEDR L..... TETRAHEDRON LETTERS
Teut............ TEUTHONISTA
Tex Ag Exp....... TEXAS AGRICULTURAL EXPERIMENT STATION. PUBLICATIONS
Texas Acad of Sci Trans.. TEXAS ACADEMY OF SCIENCES. TRANSACTIONS
Tex B J.......... TEXAS BAR JOURNAL
Tex Inst......... TEXAS INSTITUTES
Tex Int L Forum.... TEXAS INTERNATIONAL LAW FORUM
Tex Int L J........ TEXAS INTERNATIONAL LAW JOURNAL
TEX J SCI.......... TEXAS JOURNAL OF SCIENCE
TEX LAW REV..... TEXAS LAW REVIEW
Tex Lib.......... TEXAS LIBRARIES
Tex Lib J......... TEXAS LIBRARY JOURNAL
Tex L R.......... TEXAS LAW REVIEW
Tex Outl......... TEXAS OUTLOOK
Tex Q........... TEXAS QUARTERLY
TEX REP BIO...... TEXAS REPORTS BIOLOGY AND MEDICINE
Tex Res J........ TEXTILE RESEARCH JOURNAL
Tex So U L Rev..... TEXAS SOUTHERN UNIVERSITY LAW REVIEW
Tex State Hist Assoc Quar.. TEXAS STATE HISTORICAL ASSOCIATION. QUARTERLY
Tex Stud Lit & Lang.. TEXAS STUDIES IN LITERATURE AND LANGUAGE
Text Chem Color... TEXTILE CHEMIST AND COLORIST
Tex Tech L Rev.... TEXAS TECH LAW REVIEW
TexteM.......... TEXTE METZLER
TEXT I IND....... TEXTILE INSTITUTE AND INDUSTRY
TEXTILVERED...... TEXTILVEREDLUNG
Text Ind......... TEXTILE INDUSTRIES
Text Ind (Munich).. TEXTIL INDUSTRIE
Text Inst Ind...... TEXTILE INSTITUTE AND INDUSTRY
Text Mfr......... TEXTILE MANUFACTURER
Text Mon........ TEXTILE MONTH
Tex Transp Res.... TEXAS TRANSPORTATION RESEARCHER
Text Res J........ TEXTILE RESEARCH JOURNAL
Text Wkly........ TEXTILE WEEKLY
Text World....... TEXTILE WORLD
Tex Univ Bur Econ Geol Publ.. TEXAS UNIVERSITY. BUREAU OF ECONOMIC GEOLOGY. PUBLICATION
Tex Univ Bur Econ Geol Rep Invest.. TEXAS UNIVERSITY. BUREAU OF ECONOMIC GEOLOGY. REPORT OF INVESTIGATIONS
Tex Univ Cent Res Water Resour Tech Rep.. TEXAS UNIVERSITY. CENTER FOR RESEARCH IN WATER RESOURCES. TECHNICAL REPORT
TE (XVIII)........ TEXTOS Y ESTUDIOS DEL SIGLO XVIII
TeZ............. TEXTE UND ZEICHEN
TF............. TRANSFORMATION
TFM............ TEXTES FRANCAIS MODERNES
TFSB........... TENNESSEE FOLKLORE SOCIETY BULLETIN
TFSP........... TEXAS FOLKLORE SOCIETY PUBLICATIONS

TG . . . . THEOLOGIE UND GLAUBE
TG . . . . TIJDSCHRIFT VOOR GESCHIEDENIS. LAND EN VOLKENKUNDE
TG . . . . TV GUIDE
TG . . . . TYDSCHRIFT VAN GESCHIEDENIS
TGA . . . . TUEBINGER GERMANISTISCHE ARBEITEN
TGDR . . . . TOKYO GAILKOKUGO DAIGAKU RONSHU (AREA AND CULTURAL STUDIES)
TGF . . . . TIJDSCHRIFT VOOR GESCHIEDENIS EN FOLKLORE
TGLV . . . . TIJDSCHRIFT VOOR GESCHIEDENIS, LAND EN VOLKENKUNDE
TGM . . . . THEATRE GUILD MAGAZINE
TGorPI . . . . TRUDY GORIJSKOGO GOSUDARSTVENNOG PEDAGOGICESKOGO INSTITUTA
TGR . . . . TOHOKU GAKUIN DAIGAKU RONSHU (NORTH JAPAN COLLEGE REVIEW: ESSAYS AND STUDIES
                IN ENGLISH LANGUAGE AND LITERATURE)
TGSG . . . . TRANSACTIONS OF THE GAELIC SOCIETY OF GLASGOW
TGSI . . . . TRANSACTIONS OF THE GAELIC SOCIETY OF INVERNESS
TGUOS . . . . TRANSACTIONS OF THE GLASGOW UNIVERSITY ORIENTAL SOCIETY
TGW . . . . THEOLOGIE DER GEGENWART
TH . . . . TEKI HISTORYCZNE
Th . . . . THEOLOGIA
Th . . . . THEOLOGY
Th . . . . THINGS
Th . . . . THOUGHT
ThA . . . . THEATRE ANNUAL
ThArts . . . . THEATRE ARTS
ThB . . . . THEOLOGISCHE BLAETTER
THB . . . . TODAY'S HOUSING BRIEFS
THB . . . . TRIERER HEIMATBUCH
THbl . . . . TRIERISCHE HEIMATBLAETTER
Theatre Arts M . . . . THEATRE ARTS MAGAZINE
Theatre M . . . . THEATRE MAGAZINE
Th Ed . . . . THEOLOGICAL EDUCATION
Theo & Lit J . . . . THEOLOGICAL AND LITERARY JOURNAL
Theo Ecl . . . . THEOLOGICAL ECLECTIC
Theol Phil . . . . THEOLOGIE UND PHILOSOPHIE
Theol Today . . . . . . THEOLOGY TODAY
Theo Mo . . . . THEOLOGICAL MONTHLY
Theo R . . . . THEOLOGICAL REVIEW
THEOR A GEN . . . . . THEORETICAL AND APPLIED GENETICS
THEOR CHIM . . . . . . THEORETICA CHIMICA ACTA
Theor Decis . . . . THEORY AND DECISION
Theo Repos . . . . THEOLOGICAL REPOSITORY
THEOR MATH . . . . . THEORETICAL AND MATHEMATICAL PHYSICS
THEOR POP B . . . . . THEORETICAL POPULATION BIOLOGY
Theos Q . . . . THEOSOPHICAL QUARTERLY
THERM ENG R . . . . . THERMAL ENGINEERING
THERMOC ACT . . . . . THERMOCHIMICA ACTA
Thes . . . . THESAURUS
Thesis Theo Cassettes . . THESIS THEOLOGICAL CASSETTES
ThG . . . . THEOLOGIE DER GEGENWART
ThG . . . . THEOLOGIE UND GLAUBE
THHP . . . . TUNG-HAI HSUEH-PAO (TUNGHAI JOURNAL)
THIN SOL FI . . . . . . THIN SOLID FILMS

ThJ . . . . THEOLOGISCHE JAHRBUECHER
THJCS . . . . TSING HUA JOURNAL OF CHINESE STUDIES
ThLB . . . . THEOLOGISCHES LITERATURBLATT
Th Lit . . . . THEOLOGISCHE LITERATURZEITUNG
ThLZ . . . . THEOLOGISCHE LITERATURZEITUNG
THM . . . . TEXTOS HISPANICOS MODERNOS
Thom . . . . THOMIST
THQ . . . . TENNESSEE HISTORICAL QUARTERLY
ThQ . . . . THEOLOGISCHE QUARTALSCHRIFT
ThR . . . . THEATRE RESEARCH
ThR . . . . THEOLOGISCHE REVUE
ThR . . . . THEOLOGISCHE RUNDSCHAU
THR . . . . TRAVAUX D'HUMANISME ET RENAISSANCE
THREE BANK . . . . . . THREE BANKS REVIEW
ThRev . . . . THEOLOGISCHE REVUE
THROMB DIAT . . . . . THROMBOSIS ET DIATHESIS HAEMORRHAGICA
THROMB RES . . . . . . THROMBOSIS RESEARCH
ThRu . . . . THEOLOGISCHE RUNDSCHAU
ThS . . . . THEATRE SURVEY
ThS . . . . THEOLOGICAL STUDIES
ThS . . . . THEOLOGISCHE STUDIEN UND KRITIKEN
THSC . . . . TRANSACTIONS OF THE HONOURABLE SOCIETY OF CYMMRODORION
ThSt . . . . THEOLOGICAL STUDIES
ThT . . . . THEOLOGISCH TIJDSCHRIFT
Th Today . . . . THEOLOGY TODAY
Thyssen Forsch Ber Forsch Betr . . THYSSEN FORSCHUNG. BERICHTE AUS FORSCHUNG UND BETRIEB
ThZ . . . . THEOLOGISCHE ZEITSCHRIFT
TI . . . . TIMARIT PJOOREKNISFELAGS ISLENDINGA 1957
T I BR GEOG . . . . . . TRANSACTIONS OF THE INSTITUTE OF BRITISH GEOGRAPHERS
T I CHEM EN . . . . . . TRANSACTIONS OF THE INSTITUTION OF CHEMICAL ENGINEERS AND THE CHEMICAL ENGINEER
TICOJ . . . . TRANSACTIONS OF THE INTERNATIONAL CONFERENCE OF ORIENTALISTS IN JAPAN
Tid Dok . . . . TIDSSKRIFT FOER DOKUMENTATION
TIDS SAMFUN . . . . . TIDSSKRIFT FOER SAMFUNNSFORSKNING
Tidsskr Kjemi Bergvesen Met . . TIDSSKRIFT FOR KJEMI. BERGVESEN OG METALLURGI
TIEtn . . . . TRUDY INSTITUTA ETNOGRAFII IM N.N. MIKLUCHO MAKLAJA. AKADEMIJA NAUK SSSR
TIGS . . . . TRANSACTIONS OF THE INVERNESS GAELIC SOCIETY
TIJa . . . . TRUDY INSTITUTA JAZYKOZNANIJA
Tijd . . . . ONZE TIJD
TIJD EC SOC . . . . . . TIJDSCHRIFT VOOR ECONOMISCHE EN SOCIALE GEOGRAFIE
TIJD FILOS . . . . TIJDSCHRIFT VOOR FILOSOFIE
TIJD PSYCH . . . . TIJDSCHRIFT VOOR PSYCHIATRIE
Tijdschr Filosof . . . . TIJDSCHRIFT VOOR FILOSOFIE
Tijdschrift Taal & Lett . . TIJDSCHRIFT VOOR TAAL EN LETTEREN
Tijdschr Ind Taal- Land. en Volkenkunde . . TIJDSCHRIFT VOOR INDISCHE TAAL-, LAND- EN VOLKENKUNDE
Tijdschr Lev Talen . . TIJDSCHRIFT VOOR LEVENDE TALEN
Tijdschr Ned TL . . . . TIJDSCHRIFT VOOR NEDERLANDSE TAAL- EN LETTERKUNDE
Tijdschr Oppervlakte Tech Metal . . TIJDSCHRIFT VOOR OPPERVLAKTE TECHNIEKEN VAN METALEN
Til . . . . TILSKUEREN
TIL . . . . TRAVAUX DE L'INSTITUT DE LINGUISTIQUE
TILAS . . . . TRAVAUX DE L'INSTITUT D'ETUDES LATINO-AMERICAINES DE L'UNIVERSITE DE STRASBOURG
TIME CAN . . . . TIME CANADA

33 Mag Metals Prod . . THIRTY THREE/33. MAGAZINE OF METALS PRODUCING
Times Ednl Supp . . . . TIMES EDUCATIONAL SUPPLEMENT
Times R Ind & Tech . . TIMES REVIEW OF INDUSTRY AND TECHNOLOGY
Tin Int . . . . TIN INTERNATIONAL
Tin Print Box Mkr . . TIN-PRINTER AND BOX MAKER
Tinsley . . . . TINSLEY'S MAGAZINE
Tin Uses . . . . TIN AND ITS USES
TIP . . . . THEORY INTO PRACTICE
TIRJa . . . . TRUDY INSTITUTO RUSSKOGO JAZYKA
T IRON ST I . . . . . . TRANSACTIONS OF THE IRON AND STEEL INSTITUTE OF JAPAN
TIRS . . . . TRAVAUX DE L'INSTITUT DE RECHERCHES SAHARIENNES
TIS . . . . TOPS IN SCIENCE FICTION
TISCO . . . . TISCO (TATA IRON AND STEEL CO)
TISSUE ANTI . . . . . . TISSUE ANTIGENS
TISSUE CELL . . . . . . TISSUE AND CELL
TITJ LIF . . . . TIT (TOWER INTERNATIONAL TECHNO MEDICAL INSTITUTE) JOURNAL OF LIFE SCIENCES
TITL . . . . TIJDSCHRIFT VAN HET INSTITUT VOOR TOEGEPASTE LINGUISTIEK LEUVEN
TJ . . . . TODAY'S JAPAN
TJ . . . . TOLKIEN JOURNAL
TJak . . . . TRUDY INSTITUTA JAZYKA, LITERATURY I ISTORII
T JAP I MET . . . . . . TRANSACTIONS OF THE JAPAN INSTITUTE OF METALS
TJB . . . . THEOLOGISCHER JAHRESBERICHT
T J BR CER . . . . TRANSACTIONS AND JOURNAL OF THE BRITISH CERAMIC SOCIETY
TJHC . . . . THEOLOGY. JOURNAL OF HISTORIC CHRISTIANITY
TJQ . . . . THOREAU JOURNAL QUARTERLY
TK . . . . TETZUGAKU-KENKYU (TOKYO)
TK . . . . TEXT UND KRITIK
TKA . . . . TRUDY KIERSKOI DUKHOVNOI AKADEMII
TKar . . . . TRUDY KAREL'SKOGO FILIALA AKADEMII NAUK SSSR
TKNGMP . . . . TIJDSCHRIFT VAN HET KONINGLIJK NEDERLANDSCH GENOOTSCHAP VOOR MUNT EN PENNINGKUNDE
TkR . . . . TAMKANG REVIEW
TKrasPI . . . . TRUDY KRASNODARSKOGO GOSUDARSTVENNOGO PEDAGOGICESKOGO INSTITUTA
TKutPI . . . . TRUDY KUTAISSKOGO GOSUDARSTVENNOGO PEDAGOGICESKOGO INSTITUTA
TL . . . . THEORETICAL LINGUISTICS (BERLIN)
TL . . . . TRYBUNA LITERACKA
TLAP . . . . PRACE KOMISJI JEZYKOWEJ POLSKIEJ AKADEMII UMIEJETNOSCI. TRAVAUX DE LA COMMISSION LINGUISTIQUE DE L'ACADEMIE POLONAISE DES SCIENCES ET DES LETTRES
TLB . . . . THEOLOGISCHES LITERATURBLATT
TLBI . . . . THEOLOGISCHES LITERATURBLATT
TLF . . . . TEXTES LITTERAIRES FRANCAIS
TLL . . . . TRAVAUX DE LINGUISTIQUE ET DE LITTERATURE (STRASBOURG)
TLLS . . . . TRAVAUX DE LINGUISTIQUE ET DE LITTERATURE (STRASBOURG)
TLOP . . . . THE LANGUAGE OF POETRY
TLP . . . . TRAVAUX LINGUISTIQUES DE PRAGUE
TLS . . . . TIMES LITERARY SUPPLEMENT (LONDON)
TLSAP . . . . WYDAWNICTWA SLASKIE POLSKIEJ AKADEMII UMIEJETNOSCI. PRACE JEZYKOWE. PUBLICA-TIONS SILESIENNES DE L'ACADEMIE POLONAISE DES SCIENCES ET DES LETTRES. TRAVAUX LINGUISTIQUES
TLTC . . . . TA-LU TSA-CHIH (CONTINENT MAGAZINE) (TAIWAN)
TLZ . . . . THEOLOGISCHE LITERATURZEITUNG

TM . . . . TEMPS MODERNES
TM . . . . THEATRE MAGAZINE
TM . . . . TIME
TM . . . . TLALOCAN: A JOURNAL OF SOURCE MATERIALS ON THE NATIVE CULTURES OF MEXICO
TM . . . . TURKIYAT MECMUASI
TM . . . . TYGODNIK MORSKI
TMo . . . . O TEMPO E O MODO
TMorNII . . . . TRUDY MORDOVSKOGO NAUCNO-ISSLEDOVATEL'SKOGO INSTITUTA JAZYKA, LITERATURY, ISTORII I EKONIMIKI
TMRN . . . . THE MYSTERY READERS NEWSLETTER
TMS . . . . TLALOCAN. A JOURNAL OF SOURCE MATERIALS ON THE NATIVE CULTURES OF MEXICO
TMV . . . . TODD MEMORIAL VOLUMES
TN . . . . THEATRE NOTEBOOK
TN . . . . TOP OF THE NEWS
TNA . . . . TIDSSKRIFT FOER NORRON ARKEOLOGI
TNizam . . . . TRUDY INSTITUTA LITERATURY I JAZYKA IM. NIZAMI
TNKUL . . . . TOWARZYSTWO NAUKOWE KATOLICKIEGO UNIVWERSYTET LUBELSKIEGO
Tn Plann Rev . . . . . . TOWN PLANNING REVIEW
TNT . . . . TOWARZYSTWO NAUKOWE W TORUNIU
TNT-FF . . . . TOWARZYSTWO NAUKOWE W TORUNIU. PRACE WYDZIAU FILOLOGICZNO-FILOSOFICZNEGO
TNTL . . . . TIJDSCHRIFT VOOR NEDERLANDSCHE TAAL- EN LETTERKUNDE (LEIDEN)
TNW . . . . TOWARZYSTWO NAUKOWE WARSZAWSKIE
T NY AC SCI . . . . . . TRANSACTIONS OF THE NEW YORK ACADEMY OF SCIENCES
TOAP . . . . PRACE KOMISJI ORIENTALISTYCZNEJ POLSKIEJ AKADEMII UMIEJETNOSCI. TRAVAUX DE LA COMMISSION ORIENTALISTE DE L'ACADEMIE POLONAISE DES SCIENCES ET DES LETTRES
Today & Tomorrow Educ . . TODAY AND TOMORROW IN EDUCATION
Todays Ed . . . . TODAY'S EDUCATION
Today's Sec . . . . TODAY'S SECRETARY
TODrL . . . . TRUDY OTDELA DREVNERUSSKOJ LITERATURY
TOF . . . . TALES OF THE FRIGHTENED
TOH J EX ME . . . . . . TOHOKU JOURNAL OF EXPERIMENTAL MEDICINE
Toledo Mus N . . . . . TOLEDO. MUSEUM OF ART. MUSEUM NEWS
Tool & Mfg Eng . . . . TOOL AND MANUFACTURING ENGINEER
Tool Eng . . . . TOOL ENGINEER
Tool Mfg Eng . . . . . . TOOL AND MANUFACTURING ENGINEER
Tool Prod . . . . TOOLING AND PRODUCTION
T OPHTH SOC . . . . . TRANSACTIONS OF THE OPHTHALMOLOGICAL SOCIETIES OF THE UNITED KINGDOM
Top News . . . . TOP OF THE NEWS
Tor . . . . TORRE
Toronto Univ Dep Mech Eng Tech Publ Ser . . TORONTO. UNIVERSITY. DEPARTMENT OF MECHANICAL ENGINEERING. TECHNICAL PUBLICATION SERIES
Toronto Univ Inst Aerosp Stud UTIAS Rep . . TORONTO. UNVIVERSITY. INSTITUTE FOR AEROSPACE STUDIES. UTIAS REPORT
Toronto Univ Inst Aerosp Stud UTIAS Rev . . TORONTO. UNIVERSITY. INSTITUTE FOR AEROSPACE STUDIES. UTIAS REVIEW
Toronto Univ Inst Aerosp Stud UTIAS Tech Note . . TORONTO. UNIVERSITY. INSTITUTE FOR AEROSPACE STUDIES. UTIAS TECHNICAL NOTE
Torrey Bot Club Bull . . TORREY BOTANICAL CLUB BULLETIN
Toshiba Rev Int Ed . . TOSHIBA REVIEW (INTERNATIONAL EDITION)
TOT . . . . TALES OF TOMORROW
Tov . . . . TOVARIS

TOW . . . . TALES OF WONDER
Town & Country Plan . . TOWN AND COUNTRY PLANNING
Town Plan Inst J . . . TOWN PLANNING INSTITUTE JOURNAL
Town Plan R . . . . . . TOWN PLANNING REVIEW
TOX APPL PH . . . . . TOXICOLOGY AND APPLIED PHARMACOLOGY
TP . . . . TEMPO PRESENTE
TP . . . . TERZO PROGRAMMA (ROMA)
TP . . . . THOUGHT PATTERNS
TP . . . . TIJDSCHRIFT VOOR PHILOSOPHIE
TPA . . . . T'OUNG PAO ARCHIVES
TPAPA . . . . TRANSACTIONS AND PROCEEDINGS OF THE AMERICAN PHILOLOGICAL ASSOCIATION
TPer . . . . TETRADI PEREVODCIKA
TPh . . . . TIJDSCHRIFT VOOR PHILOSOPHIE
TPhS . . . . TRANSACTIONS OF THE PHILOLOGICAL SOCIETY
TPhS . . . . TRANSACTIONS OF THE PHILOSOPHICAL SOCIETY (LONDON AND STRASSBURG)
TPJ . . . . TENNESSEE POETRY JOURNAL
TPow . . . . TYGODNIK POWSZECHNY
TPQS . . . . THEOLOGISCHE PRAKTISCHE QUARTALSCHRIFT
TPr . . . . TEMPO PRESENTE
TPRSL . . . . ROYAL SOCIETY OF LITERATURE. TRANSACTIONS AND PROCEEDINGS
TPrzPl . . . . TRUDY PRZEVAL'SKOGO PEDAGOGICESKOGO INSTITUTA
TPS . . . . TRANSACTIONS OF THE PHILOLOGICAL SOCIETY (LONDON)
TQ . . . . TEXAS QUARTERLY
TQ . . . . TORONTO QUARTERLY
TQ . . . . TRI-QUARTERLY
TQS . . . . THEOLOGISCHE QUARTALSCHRIFT
TR . . . . TABLE RONDE
TR . . . . THEATRE RESEARCH
TR . . . . THEOLOGISCHE RUNDSCHAU
TR . . . . TRANSATLANTIC REVIEW
Tr . . . . TRIVIUM
Tr . . . . Y TRAETHODYDD
TRA . . . . TELEVISION/RADIO AGE
TrA . . . . TRADUCTION AUTOMATIQUE (THE HAGUE)
Trad . . . . TRADITIO
Trade-Mark Rep . . . TRADE-MARK REPORTER
Traff Engng Control . . TRAFFIC ENGINEERING AND CONTROL
Traffic Dig Rev . . . . TRAFFIC DIGEST AND REVIEW
Traffic Eng . . . . . . TRAFFIC ENGINEERING
Traffic Eng Contr . . . TRAFFIC ENGINEERING AND CONTROL
TRAIN DEV J . . . . . . TRAINING AND DEVELOPMENT JOURNAL
Train Sch B . . . . . . TRAINING SCHOOL BULLETIN
Trans Amer Foundrymen's Soc . . TRANSACTIONS OF THE AMERICAN FOUNDRYMEN'S SOCIETY
Trans Amer Geophys Union . . TRANSACTIONS OF THE AMERICAN GEOPHYSICAL UNION
Trans Amer Math Soc . . TRANSACTIONS OF THE AMERICAN MATHEMATICAL SOCIETY
Trans Amer Nucl Soc . . TRANSACTIONS OF THE AMERICAN NUCLEAR SOCIETY
Trans Am Soc Agric Eng (Gen Ed) . . TRANSACTIONS OF THE AMERICAN SOCIETY OF AGRICULTURAL ENGINEERS
     (GENERAL EDITION)
Trans Br Ceram Soc . . TRANSACTIONS OF THE BRITISH CERAMIC SOCIETY
Trans Can Inst Mining Soc N S . . TRANSACTIONS OF THE CANADIAN INSTITUTE OF MINING AND METALLURGY AND
     OF THE MINING SOCIETY OF NOVA SCOTIA

Trans Can Soc Mech Eng.. TRANSACTIONS OF THE CANADIAN SOCIETY FOR MECHANICAL ENGINEERS
Trans Farady Soc... TRANSACTIONS OF THE FARADAY SOCIETY
Trans Indian Ceram Soc.. TRANSACTIONS OF THE INDIAN CERAMIC SOCIETY
Trans Indian Inst Met.. TRANSACTIONS OF THE INDIAN INSTITUTE OF METALS
Trans Inst Chem Eng.. TRANSACTIONS OF THE INSTITUTION OF CHEMICAL ENGINEERS
Trans Inst Civ Eng Ir.. TRANSACTIONS OF THE INSTITUTION OF CIVIL ENGINEERS OF IRELAND
Trans Inst Eng Shipbuilders Scot.. TRANSACTIONS OF THE INSTITUTION OF ENGINEERS AND SHIPBUILDERS IN
    SCOTLAND
Trans Inst Marine Eng.. TRANSACTIONS OF THE INSTITUTE OF MARINE ENGINEERS
Trans Inst Met Finish.. TRANSACTIONS OF THE INSTITUTE OF METAL FINISHING
Trans Inst Mining Met Sect A.. TRANSACTIONS OF THE INSTITUTION OF MINING & METALLURGY. SECTION A
Trans Inst Mining Met Sect B.. TRANSACTIONS OF THE INSTITUTION OF MINING & METALLURGY. SECTION B
Trans Inst Mining Met Sect C.. TRANSACTIONS OF THE INSTITUTION OF MINING & METALLURGY. SECTION C
Trans Iron Steel Inst Jap.. TRANSACTIONS OF THE IRON AND STEEL INSTITUTE OF JAPAN
Transit J......... TRANSIT JOURNAL
Trans Jap Inst Met.. TRANSACTIONS OF THE JAPAN INSTITUTE OF METALS
Trans Jap Inst Metals.. TRANSACTIONS OF THE JAPAN INSTITUTE OF METALS
Trans Jap Soc Aeronaut Space Sci.. TRANSACTIONS OF THE JAPAN SOCIETY FOR AERONAUTICAL AND SPACE
    SCIENCES
Trans Jap Soc Mech Eng.. TRANSACTIONS OF THE JAPAN SOCIETY OF MECHANICAL ENGINEERS
Trans Jap Weld Soc.. TRANSACTIONS OF THE JAPAN WELDING SOCIETY
Trans J Br Ceram Soc.. TRANSACTIONS AND JOURNAL OF THE BRITISH CERAMIC SOCIETY
Transm Distrib.... TRANSMISSION AND DISTRIBUTION
Trans Mining Geol Met Inst India.. TRANSACTIONS OF THE MINING, GEOLOGICAL AND METALLURGICAL INSTITUTE
    OF INDIA
Trans Nat Res Inst Metals (Tokyo).. TRANSACTIONS OF NATIONAL RESEARCH INSTITUTE FOR METALS (TOKYO)
Trans Nat Vac Symp.. TRANSACTIONS OF THE NATIONAL VACUUM SYMPOSIUM
Trans N E Cst Instn Engrs Shipbldrs.. TRANSACTIONS OF THE NORTH EAST COAST INSTITUTION OF ENGINEERS AND
    SHIPBUILDERS
Trans-Pac........ TRANS-PACIFIC
Trans Peirce Soc... TRANSACTIONS OF THE CHARLES S. PEIRCE SOCIETY
Transp Engr....... TRANSPORT ENGINEER
TRANSP EN J...... TRANSPORTATION ENGINEERING JOURNAL OF ASCE (AMERICAN SOCIETY OF CIVIL ENGINEERS)
Trans Phil Soc..... TRANSACTIONS OF THE PHILOLOGICAL SOCIETY
TRANSP HIS....... TRANSPORTATION HISTORY
Transp J......... TRANSPORT JOURNAL
TRANSPLAN P..... TRANSPLANTATION PROCEEDINGS
TRANSPLAN R..... TRANSPLANTATION REVIEWS
TRANSPLANT...... TRANSPLANTATION
Transp L J........ TRANSPORTATION LAW JOURNAL
TRANSPORTAT.... TRANSPORTATION
Transp Plann Technol.. TRANSPORTATION PLANNING AND TECHNOLOGY
TRANSP RES...... TRANSPORTATION RESEARCH
Transp Road Res Lab (GB) TRRL Rep.. TRANSPORT AND ROAD RESEARCH LABORATORY (GREAT BRITAIN) TRRL
    REPORT
Trans Proc Geol Soc S Afr.. TRANSACTIONS AND PROCEEDINGS OF THE GEOLOGICAL SOCIETY OF SOUTH AFRICA
Transp Sci........ TRANSPORTATION SCIENCE
TRANSP THEO..... TRANSPORT THEORY AND STATISTICAL PHYSICS
Trans R Instn Naval Archit.. ROYAL INSTITUTION OF NAVAL ARCHITECTS. QUARTERLY TRANSACTIONS
Trans Roy Inst Technol Stockholm.. TRANSACTIONS OF THE ROYAL INSTITUTE OF TECHNOLOGY. STOCKHOLM
Trans S Afr Inst Elec Eng.. TRANSACTIONS OF THE SOUTH AFRICAN INSTITUTE OF ELECTRICAL ENGINEERS

PERIODICAL TITLE ABBREVIATIONS

Trans SHASE Japan. . TRANSACTIONS OF SHASE JAPAN (SOCIETY OF HEATING, AIR CONDITIONING AND SANITARY ENGINEERS OF JAPAN)
Trans Soc Min Eng AIME. . TRANSACTIONS OF THE SOCIETY OF MINING ENGINEERS OF AIME (AMERICAN INSTITUTE OF MINING, METALLURGICAL AND PETROLEUM ENGINEERS)
Trans Soc Rheol. . . . TRANSACTIONS OF THE SOCIETY OF RHEOLOGY
Trans World Energy Conf. . TRANSACTIONS OF THE WORLD ENERGY CONFERENCE
Trav. . . . . TRAVEL
TRAV HUMAIN. . . . TRAVAIL HUMAIN
TRB. . . . . TENNYSON RESEARCH BULLETIN
Trend Eng Univ Wash. . TREND IN ENGINEERING. UNIVERSITY OF WASHINGTON
Trends Ed. . . . . . . TRENDS IN EDUCATION
TRev. . . . . THEOLOGISCHE REVUE
TRG. . . . . TIJDSCHRIFT VOOR RECHTSGESCHIEDENIS
TRHS. . . . . TRANSACTIONS OF THE ROYAL HISTORICAL SOCIETY
Tri. . . . . TRIBUNA
Trier Archiv. . . . . . TRIERISCHES ARCHIV
TriererZ. . . . . TRIERER ZEITSCHRIFT FUER GESCHICHTE UND KUNST DES TRIERER LANDES UND SEINER NACHBARGEBIETE
TRIMES ECON. . . . . TRIMESTRE ECONOMICO
TriQ. . . . . TRI-QUARTERLY
Tri-Quar. . . . . TRI-QUARTERLY
TRJaVUZ. . . . . TRUDY KAFEDR RUSSKOGO JAZYKA VUZOV VOSTOCNOJ SIBIRI I DAL'NEGO VOSTOKA
Tr Law Guide. . . . . . TRIAL LAWYER'S GUIDE
Tr Law Q. . . . . TRIAL LAWYER'S QUARTERLY
TROP AGR. . . . . . . TROPICAL AGRICULTURE
TROPENMED P. . . . . TROPENMEDIZIN UND PARASITOLOGIE
TROP GEO ME. . . . . TROPICAL AND GEOGRAPHICAL MEDICINE
Tropical Ag. . . . . . . TROPICAL AGRICULTURIST
TROP SCI. . . . . TROPICAL SCIENCE
T ROY ENT S. . . . . . TRANSACTIONS OF THE ROYAL ENTOMOLOGICAL SOCIETY OF LONDON
T ROY SOC C. . . . . . TRANSACTIONS OF THE ROYAL SOCIETY OF CANADA
TRPC. . . . . TRADICION. REVISTA PERUANA DE CULTURA
TRR. . . . . THE ROHMER REVIEW
TRS. . . . . THEOLOGISCHE RUNDSCHAU
TRSC. . . . . TRANSACTIONS OF THE ROYAL SOCIETY OF CANADA
TRSL. . . . . TRANSACTIONS OF THE ROYAL SOCIETY OF LITERATURE
T RS S AFR. . . . . . . TRANSACTIONS OF THE ROYAL SOCIETY OF SOUTH AFRICA
T RS TROP M. . . . . . TRANSACTIONS OF THE ROYAL SOCIETY OF TROPICAL MEDICINE AND HYGIENE
Trudy Moskov Inst Istoriji. . TRUDY MOSKOVSKOGO INSTITUTA ISTORIJI, FILOSOFIJI I LITERATURY
Trust Bull. . . . . . . TRUST BULLETIN
Trusts & Es. . . . . . . TRUSTS AND ESTATES
TS. . . . . THEATER SURVEY
TS. . . . . THEATRE STUDIES
TS. . . . . THEOLOGICAL STUDIES
TS. . . . . TODAY'S SPEECH
TSA. . . . . TEATER SA. QUARTERLY FOR SOUTH AFRICAN THEATER
TSamU. . . . . TRUDY SAMARKANDSKOGO GOSUDARSTVENNOGO UNIVERSITETA IMENI ALISERA NAVOI
TSB. . . . . THEOLOGICAL STUDIES. BALTIMORE
TSB. . . . . THOREAU SOCIETY BULLETIN
TSb. . . . . TJURKOLOGICESKIJ SBORNIK
TSB. . . . . TWO COMPLETE SCIENCE ADVENTURE BOOKS

T S Booklet .... THOREAU SOCIETY BOOKLET
Tschermaks Mineral Petrogr Mitt . . TSCHERMAKS MINERALOGISCHE UND PETROGRAPHISCHE MITTEILUNGEN
TSCH MIN PE ...... TSCHERMAKS MINERALOGISCHE UND PETROGRAPHISCHE MITTEILUNGEN
TSE .... TEXAS STUDIES IN ENGLISH
TSE .... TULANE STUDIES IN ENGLISH
TSF .... 10 STORY FANTASY
TsG .... TIJDSCHRIFT VOOR GESHCIEDENIS
TsGw .... TYDSKRIF VIR GEESTESWETENSKAPPE
TsIT .... TIJDSCHRIFT VOOR INDISCHE TAAL-, LAND-EN VOLKENKUNDE
TSK .... THEOLOGISCHE STUDIEN UND KRITIKEN
TSL .... TENNESSEE STUDIES IN LITERATURE
TSL .... TRAVAUX DE LA CLASSE I (DE LINGUISTIQUE, DE LITTERATURE ET DE PHILOSOPHIE) DE LA
        SOCIETE DES SCIENCES ET DES LETTRES DE LODZ
TSLL .... TEXAS STUDIES IN LITERATURE AND LANGUAGE
TSM .... TESORO SACRO-MUSICAL
TSM .... TEXTE DES SPAETEN MITTELALTERS
TsNAG .... TIJDSCHRIFT VAN HET KONINKLIJK NEDERLANDSCH AARDRIJKSKUNDIG GENOOTSCHAP
TsNTL .... TIJDSCHRIFT VOOR NEDERLANDSCHE TAAL-EN LETTERKUNDE
T SOC RHEOL ...... TRANSACTIONS OF THE SOCIETY OF RHEOLOGY
TSP .... TULANE STUDIES IN PHILOSOPHY
TsPhil .... TIJDSCHRIFT VOOR PHILOSOPHIE
TSRLL .... TULANE STUDIES IN ROMANCE LANGUAGES AND LITERATURE
TsSV .... TIJDSCHRIFT VOOR DE STUDIE VAN DE VERLICHTING
Tsvet Metal ...... TSVETNYE METALLY
TsVUB .... TIJDSCHRIFT VAN DE VRIGE UNIVERSITEIT VAN BRUSSEL
TsVV .... TYDSKRIF VIR VOLKSKUNDE EN VOLKSTAAL
TSW .... PRACE WROCLAWSKIEGO TOWARZYSTWA NAUKOWEGO
TsWK .... TYDSKRIF VIR WETENSKAP EN KUNS
TSZGK .... THURINGISCH-SAECHSISCHE ZEITSCHRIFT FUER GESCHICHTE UND KUNST
TT .... TAAL EN TONGVAL (ANTWERPEN)
TT .... TEOLOGISK TIDSSKRIFT
TT .... THEOLOGISCH TIJDSCHRIFT
TT .... THEOLOGY TODAY
TT .... TIME AND TIDE
TTAE .... TURK TARIH. ARKEOLOGYA VE ETNOGRAFYA DERGISI
TTagPl .... TRUDY TAGANROGSKOGO GOSUDARSTVENNOGO PEDAGOGICESKOGO INSTITUTA
TTb .... TRUDY TBILISKOGO PEDAGOGICESKOGO INSTITUTA
TTE .... TALKS TO TEACHERS OF ENGLISH
TTele .... TATAR TELE HEM ADEBIJATY
TTK Belleten ...... TURK TARIH KURUMU "BELLETEN"
TTomU .... TRUDY TOMSKOGO GOSUDARSTVENNOGO UNIVERSITETA
TTP .... TRUDY TALLINSKOGO POLITEKHNICHESKOGO INSTITUTA. SERIYA B, XX
TTPI .... TRUDY TBILISKOGO GOSUDARSTVENNOGO PEDAGOGICESKOGO INSTITUTA
TTQS .... TUBINGER THEOLOGISCHE QUARTALSCHRIFT. STUTTGART
TTrA .... TEXTES ET TRAITEMENT AUTOMATIQUE
TTS .... TRANSACTIONS OF THE THOROTON SOCIETY
TTT .... TEYLERS THEOLOGISCH TIJDSCHRIFT
TTZ .... TRIERER THEOLOGISCHE ZEITSCHRIFT
TUB .... TULANE UNIVERSITY BULLETIN
Tubular Struct ..... TUBULAR STRUCTURES
TUD .... TRUDY UNIVERSITETA DRUZBY NARODOV IMENI PATRISA LUMUMBY

TUDNL......... TRUDY UNIVERSITETA DRUZHBY NARODOV IMENI LUMUMBY (MOSCOW)
TUGAL......... TEXTE UND UNTERSUCHUNGEN ZUR GESCHICHTE DER ALTCHRISTLICHEN LITERATUR
TuK............TEXT UND KRITIK
Tulane Stud Phil....TULANE STUDIES IN PHILOSOPHY
Tulane U Stud Eng.. TULANE UNIVERSITY STUDIES IN ENGLISH
Tul L Rev......... TULANE LAW REVIEW
Tulsa Geol Soc Dig.. TULSA GEOLOGICAL SOCIETY DIGEST
Tulsa L J......... TULSA LAW JOURNAL
Tul Tax Inst....... TULANE TAX INSTITUTE
Tul Tidelands Inst.. TULANE MINERAL AND TIDELANDS LAW INSTITUTE
Tuners JL........ TUNERS' JOURNAL
Tungsram Tech Mitt.. TUNGSRAM TECHNISCHE MITTEILUNGEN
Tunnels Tunnelling.. TUNNELS AND TUNNELLING
Turkey Prod...... TURKEY PRODUCER
TUSAS.......... TWAYNE'S UNITED STATES AUTHORS SERIES
Tuskegee Exp..... TUSKEGEE NORMAL AND INDUSTRIAL INSTITUTE. EXPERIMENT STATION. PUBLICATIONS
TuZ............TEXTE UND ZEICHEN
TV............. TELEVISION
TV............. TREJI VARTI
TV............. TZERTOVNYIA VIEDOMOSTI
TVA............ TELEVISION AGE
TVD............ TELEVISION DIGEST
TVD............ TRAVAUX SUR VOLTAIRE ET LE DIX-HUITIEME SIECLE
TVF............TVF (TIDSKRIFT FOR TEKNISK-VETTENSKAPLIG FORSKNING)
TVG........... TIJDSCHRIFT VOOR GESCHIEDENIS
TVG........... TV GUIDE
TvG........... TYDSKRIF VIR GEESTESWETENSKAPPE
TVIIJ.......... TRUDY VOJENNOGO INSTITUTA INOSTRANNYKH JAZYKOV
TVIIJa..........TRUDY VOJENNOGO INSTITUTA INOSTRANNYKH JAZYKOV
TVL............TIJDSCHRIFT VOOR LITURGEI
TvL............ TYDSKRIF VIR LETTERKUNDE
TV Q........... TELEVISION QUARTERLY
TVRG.......... TIJDSCHRIFT VOOR RECHTSGESCHIEDENIS
TVUB.......... TIJDSCHRIFT VAN DE VRIJE UNIVERSITEIT VAN BRUSSEL
TW............. TERRE WALLONNE
TW............. THRILLING WONDER STORIES
Tw............. TWORCZOSC
TWA........... TRANSACTIONS OF THE WISCONSIN ACADEMY OF SCIENCES, ARTS AND LETTERS
TWAS.......... TWAYNE'S WORLD AUTHORS SERIES
TwC........... TWENTIETH CENTURY
20TH Cent....... TWENTIETH CENTURY
20TH Cent Lit..... TWENTIETH CENTURY LITERATURE
T WISC AC........ TRANSACTIONS OF THE WISCONSIN ACADEMY OF SCIENCES, ARTS AND LETTERS
2CSAB...........TWO COMPLETE SCIENCE ADVENTURE NOVELS
TWS............ THRILLING WONDER STORIES
TxSE........... TEXAS STUDIES IN ENGLISH
TY............. TYLER'S QUARTERLY HISTORICAL AND GENEALOGICAL MAGAZINE
TyD............ TRABAJOS Y DIAS
TYDS........... TRANSACTIONS OF THE YORKSHIRE DIALECT SOCIETY
TygP........... TYGODNIK POWSZECHNY
Tyler's......... TYLER'S QUARTERLY HISTORICAL AND GENEALOGICAL MAGAZINE

Tyler's Quar...... TYLER'S QUARTERLY
Typ News........ TYPEWRITING NEWS
TZ............. THEOLOGISCHE ZEITSCHRIFT
TZ............. TRIERER ZEITSCHRIFT
TZ Prakt Metallbearb.. TZ FUER PRAKTISCHE METALLBEARBEITUNG

U

U . . . . UNIVERSITAS
UA . . . . UNITED ASIA
UA . . . . UNIVERSIDAD DE ANTIOQUIA (COLOMBIA)
UA . . . . URAL-ALTAISCHE JAHRBUECHER
UAA . . . . UNIVERSITET I BERGEN. ARBOK. HISTORISK-ANTIKVARISK REKKE
UAC . . . . UNIVERSIDAD DE ANTIOQUIA (COLOMBIA)
UAJ . . . . URAL-ALTAISCHE JAHRBUECHER
UAJb . . . . URAL-ALTAISCHE JAHRBUECHER
U&F . . . . UNTERRICHT UND FORSCHUNG
UAS . . . . UNIVERSITY OF ALABAMA STUDIES
UAS . . . . URALIC AND ALTAIC SERIES. INDIANA UNIVERSITY PUBLICATIONS
UBA . . . . UNIVERSITET I BERGEN. ARBOK. HISTORISK-ANTIKVARISK REKKE
U B C Legal Notes . . UNIVERSITY OF BRITISH COLUMBIA. LEGAL NOTES
UBC L Rev . . . . UNIVERSITY OF BRITISH COLUMBIA LAW REVIEW
UBEA Forum . . . . . . UNITED BUSINESS EDUCATION ASSOCIATION FORUM
UBHJ . . . . UNIVERSITY OF BIRMINGHAM HISTORICAL JOURNAL
UBS . . . . UNIVERSITY OF BUFFALO STUDIES
Uc . . . . UNCANNY STORIES
UC . . . . UNESCO CHRONICLE
UCC . . . . UNIVERSITY OF CALIFORNIA CHRONICLE
UCD L Rev . . . . U.C.D. (UNIVERSITY OF CALIFORNIA, DAVIS) LAW REVIEW
UCDPE . . . . UNIVERSITY OF CALIFORNIA, DAVIS. PUBLICATIONS IN ENGLISH
Ucenyje Zapiski Belorusskogo Gosud Univ . . UCENYJE ZAPISKI BELORUSSKOGO GOSUDARSTVENNOGO UNIVERSITETA
Ucenyje zapiski Jaroslav . . UCENYJE ZAPISKI JAROSLAVSKOGO UNIVERSITETA
Ucenyje zapiski Leningrad . . UCENYJE ZAPISKI LENINGRADSKOGO GOSUDARSTVENNOGO. UNIVERSITETA
Ucenyje zapiski Leningrad pedag inst . . UCENYJE ZAPISKI LENINGRADSKOGO GOSUDARSTVENNOGO PEDAGO-GICESKOGO INSTITUTA
Ucenyje zapiski Moskva . . UCENYJE ZAPISKI MOSKOVSKOGO GOSUDARSTVENNOGO UNIVERSITETA IMENI LONONOSOVA
Ucenyje zapiski Moskov gosud pedag inst . . UCENYJE ZAPISKI MOSKOSVKOGO GOSUDARSTVENNOGO PEDAGOGICESKOGO INSTITUTA INOSTRAUNYCH JAZYKOV
Ucenyje zapiski Tomsk . . UCENYJE ZAPISKI TOMSKOGO GOSUDARSTVENNOGO UNIVERSITETA IMENI KUJBYSEVA. TOMSK
U Chi L Rev . . . . UNIVERSITY OF CHICAGO LAW REVIEW
U Chi LS Conf Series . . UNIVERSITY OF CHICAGO LAW SCHOOL CONFERENCE STUDIES
U Chi L S Rec . . . . . . UNIVERSITY OF CHICAGO LAW SCHOOL RECORD
U Cin L Rev . . . . UNIVERSITY OF CINCINNATI LAW REVIEW
UCLA LAW R . . . . . . UCLA LAW REVIEW
U Colo L Rev . . . . . . UNIVERSITY OF COLORADO LAW REVIEW
UCP . . . . UNIVERSITY OF CALIFORNIA PUBLICATIONS IN CLASSICAL PHILOLOGY
UCPA . . . . UNIVERSITY OF CALIFORNIA PUBLICATIONS IN CLASSICAL ARCHAEOLOGY
USCPES . . . . UNIVERSITY OF CALIFORNIA PUBLICATIONS IN ENGLISH STUDIES
UCPFS . . . . UNIVERSITY OF CALIFORNIA PUBLICATIONS IN FOLKLORE STUDIES
UCPh . . . . UNIVERSITAS CAROLINA: PHILOLOGICA
UCPL . . . . UNIVERSITY OF CALIFORNIA PUBLICATIONS IN LINGUISTICS
UCPM . . . . UNIVERSITY OF CALIFORNIA PUBLICATIONS IN MUSIC
UCPMP . . . . UNIVERSITY OF CALIFORNIA PUBLICATIONS IN MODERN PHILOLOGY
UCPMPh . . . . UNIVERSITY OF CALIFORNIA PUBLICATIONS IN MODERN PHILOLOGY

UCPPh . . . . UNIVERSITY OF CALIFORNIA PUBLICATIONS IN CLASSICAL PHILOLOGY
UCPSP . . . . UNIVERSITY OF CALIFORNIA PUBLICATIONS IN SEMITIC PHILOLOGY
UCPSPh . . . . UNIVERSITY OF CALIFORNIA PUBLICATIONS IN SEMITIC PHILOLOGY
UCQ . . . . UNIVERSITY COLLEGE QUARTERLY
UCR . . . . UNIVERSITY OF CEYLON REVIEW
UCSGS . . . . UNIVERSITY OF COLORADO STUDIES. GENERAL SERIES
UCSL . . . . UNIVERSITY OF CALIFORNIA STUDIES IN LINGUISTICS
UCSLL . . . . UNIVERSITY OF COLORADO STUDIES IN LANGUAGE & LITERATURE
UCSMP . . . . UNIVERSITY OF CALIFORNIA STUDIES IN MODERN PHILOLOGY
UCSSLL . . . . UNIVERSITY OF COLORADO STUDIES. SERIES IN LANGUAGE AND LITERATURE
UCTSE . . . . UNIVERSITY OF CAPE TOWN STUDIES IN ENGLISH
U Det L J . . . . UNIVERSITY OF DETROIT LAW JOURNAL
UDL . . . . UNTERSUCHUNGEN ZUR DEUTSCHEN LITERATURGESCHICHTE
UdLH . . . . UNIVERSIDAD DE LA HABANA
UDQ . . . . UNIVERSITY OF DENVER QUARTERLY
UDR . . . . UNIVERSITY OF DAYTON REVIEW
UE . . . . USE OF ENGLISH
UEIES . . . . UPPSALA ENGLISH INSTITUTE ESSAYS & STUDIES
UEJ . . . . UNIVERSITY OF EDINBURGH JOURNAL
UEL . . . . UOMINI E LIBRO
UES . . . . UNISA ENGLISH STUDIES
UF . . . . ULSTER FOLKLIFE (BELFAST)
UFKT . . . . UNIVERSITETSFORLAGETS KRONIKKTJENESTE
U Fla L Rev . . . . UNIVERSITY OF FLORIDA LAW REVIEW
UFMH . . . . UNIVERSITY OF FLORIDA MONOGRAPHS. HUMANITIES SERIES
UGA . . . . URGESCHICHTLICHER ANZEIGER
UgandaJ . . . . UGANDA JOURNAL
UGM . . . . UNIVERSITY OF GEORGIA MONOGRAPHS
UH . . . . UNIVERSIDAD DE HABANA
UHQ . . . . UTAH HISTORICAL QUARTERLY
UI . . . . UJ IRAS
U III L F . . . . UNIVERSITY OF ILLINOIS LAW FORUM
UJ . . . . UNGARISCHE JAHRBUECHER
UJ . . . . UNIVERSYTET JAGIELLONSKI
UJDS . . . . UNIVERSITETSJUBILAEETS DANSKE SAMFUND
UK . . . . FROM UNKNOWN WORLDS
UK . . . . UNKNOWN
UK . . . . UNKNOWN WORLDS
U Kan City L Rev . . . UNIVERSITY OF KANSAS CITY LAW REVIEW
UKC . . . . UNIVERSITY OF KANSAS CITY REVIEW
UKCR . . . . UNIVERSITY OF KANSAS CITY REVIEW
UKCRv . . . . UNIVERSITY OF KANSAS CITY REVIEW
UKPHS . . . . UNIVERSITY OF KANSAS PUBLICATIONS. HUMANISTIC STUDIES
UKR BIOKHIM . . . . . UKRAINSKII BIOKHIMICHESKI ZHURNAL
UkrI . . . . UKRAJINS'KYJ ISTORYK
UkrK . . . . UKRAJINS'KA KNYHA
UKR KHIM ZH . . . . . UKRAINSKII KHIMICHESKII ZHURNAL
UkrM . . . . UKRAJINS'KA MOVA I LITERATURA V SKOLI
UkrR . . . . UKRAINIAN REVIEW
UkrS . . . . UKRAJINS'KYJ SAMOSTIJNYK
UI . . . . ULISSE

ULH . . . . UNIVERSIDAD DE LA HABANA
ULI LM REP . . . . URBAN LAND INSTITUTE LANDMARK REPORT
ULI RES REP . . . . URBAN LAND INSTITUTE RESEARCH REPORT
ULI SPE REP . . . . URBAN LAND INSTITUTE SPECIAL REPORT
ULR . . . . UNIVERSITY OF LEEDS REVIEW
ULz . . . . UKRAJINS'KE LITERATUROZNAVSTVO
UM . . . . UNIVERSIDAD DE MEXICO
UMCMP . . . . UNIVERSITY OF MICHIGAN CONTRIBUTIONS IN MODERN PHILOLOGY
UMCS . . . . UNIWERSYTET MARII CURIE-SKLODOWSKIEJ
UMHS . . . . UNIVERSITY OF MIAMI HISPANIC STUDIES
U Miami L Rev . . . . . UNIVERSITY OF MIAMI LAW REVIEW
U Mich J L Ref . . . . . UNIVERSITY OF MICHIGAN JOURNAL OF LAW REFORM
UMKC L Rev . . . . . . UNIVERSITY OF MISSOURI AT KANSAS CITY LAW REVIEW
UMLS . . . . UKRAJINS'KA MOVA I LITERATURA V SKOLI
UMoS . . . . UNIVERSITY OF MISSOURI STUDIES
UMPAL . . . . UNIVERSITY OF MINNESOTA PAMPHLETS ON AMERICAN LITERATURE
UMPAW . . . . UNIVERSITY OF MINNESOTA PAMPHLETS ON AMERICAN WRITERS
UMPEAL . . . . UNIVERSITY OF MIAMI PUBLICATIONS IN ENGLISH AND AMERICAN LITERATURE
UMPLL . . . . UNIVERSITY OF MICHIGAN PUBLICATIONS IN LANGUAGE AND LITERATURE
UMS . . . . UKRAJINS'KA MOVA V SKOLI
UMS . . . . UNIVERSITY OF MAINE STUDIES
UMS . . . . UNIVERSITY OF MICHIGAN STUDIES
UMS . . . . UNIVERSITY OF MISSOURI STUDIES
UMSE . . . . UNIVERSITY OF MISSISSIPPI STUDIES IN ENGLISH
UMSHS . . . . UNIVERSITY OF MICHIGAN STUDIES. HUMANISTIC SERIES
UMx . . . . UNIVERSITY OF MEXICO
UNABASHED LIBN . . UNABASHED LIBRARIAN
UNAM . . . . UNIVERSIDAD NACIONAL AUTONOMA DE MEXICO
UNB L J . . . . UNIVERSITY OF NEW BRUNSWICK LAW JOURNAL
U N Bul . . . . UNITED NATIONS BULLETIN
UNC . . . . UNCANNY STORIES
UNCR . . . . UNIVERSITY OF NORTH CAROLINA RECORD. RESEARCH IN PROGRESS
UNCSCL . . . . UNIVERSITY OF NORTH CAROLINA STUDIES IN COMPARATIVE LITERATURE
UNCSGL . . . . UNIVERSITY OF NORTH CAROLINA STUDIES IN GERMANIC LANGUAGES AND LITERATURES
UNCSGLL . . . . UNIVERSITY OF NORTH CAROLINA STUDIES IN GERMANIC LANGUAGES AND LITERATURES
UNCSRL . . . . UNIVERSITY OF NORTH CAROLINA IN ROMANCE LANGUAGES AND LITERATURES
UNCSRLL . . . . UNIVERSITY OF NORTH CAROLINA STUDIES IN THE ROMANCE LANGUAGES AND LITERATURES
Und Child . . . . UNDERSTANDING THE CHILD
Underground Eng . . . UNDERGROUND ENGINEERING
Underwriters Lab Stand . . UNDERWRITERS LABORATORIES. STANDARDS
U N Econ Comm Asia Far East Water Resour Ser . . UNITED NATIONS, ECONOMIC COMMISSION FOR ASIA AND THE FAR EAST. WATER RESOURCES SERIES
U N Econo Comm Asia Far East Miner Resour Develop Ser . . UNITED NATIONS, ECONOMIC COMMISSION FOR ASIA AND THE FAR EAST. MINERAL RESOURCES DEVELOPMENT SERIES
UNESCO B LI . . . . . . UNESCO BULLETIN FOR LIBRARIES
Unesco Bul Lib . . . . . UNESCO BULLETIN FOR LIBRARIES
UNI . . . . UNIVERSE SCIENCE FICTION
UNIF C CODE . . . . . . UNIFORM COMMERCIAL CODE LAW JOURNAL
Union S Q R . . . . UNION SEMINARY QUARTERLY REVIEW
Union Univ Q . . . . . . UNION UNIVERSITY QUARTERLY
Unita R . . . . UNITARIAN REVIEW

Univ. . . . . UNIVERSITAS
Univ. . . . . UNIVERSO
UNIV CHIC L. . . . . . UNIVERSITY OF CHICAGO LAW REVIEW
Univ Chic M. . . . . . . UNIVERSITY OF CHICAGO MAGAZINE
Univ Chic Rec. . . . . UNIVERSITY OF CHICAGO RECORD
Univ Cincin Stud. . . UNIVERSITY OF CINCINNATI STUDIES
Univ Col Stud. . . . . . UNIVERSITY OF COLORADO STUDIES
Univ Debaters Annual. . UNIVERSITY DEBATERS' ANNUAL
Univ de Grenoble Annales n s Lett. . UNIVERSITE DE GRENOBLE. LETTRES-DROIT. ANNALES
Univ de Grenoble Annales n s Sci. . UNIVERSITE DE GRENOBLE. SCIENCES-MEDECINE. ANNALES
Univ de Nancy Fac d Lettres Annales de l'Est. . UNIVERSITE DE NANCY. FACULTE DES LETTRES. ANNALES DE L'EST
UNIV FL SSM. . . . . . UNIVERSITY OF FLORIDA SOCIAL SCIENCES MONOGRAPH
Univ H Sch J. . . . . . UNIVERSITY HIGH SCHOOL JOURNAL
UNIV IL LAW. . . . . . UNIVERSITY OF ILLINOIS LAW FORUM
Univ J of Business. . UNIVERSITY JOURNAL OF BUSINESS
Univ K C R. . . . . . . UNIVERSITY OF KANSAS CITY REVIEW
Univ Mo Eng Exp Sta Eng Ser Bull. . MISSOURI UNIVERSITY. ENGINEERING EXPERIMENT STATION. ENGINEERING
                    SERIES BULLETIN
Univ Mo Stud. . . . . . UNIVERSITY OF MISSOURI STUDIES
Univ Nac Auton Mex Inst Geol An. . UNIVERSIDAD NACIONAL AUTONOMA DE MEXICO. INSTITUTO DE GEOLOGIA.
                    ANALES
Univ Nac Auton Mex Inst Geol Bol. . UNIVERSIDAD NACIONAL AUTOMONA DE MEXICO. INSTITUTO DE GEOLOGIA.
                    BOLETIN
Univ of Calif Publ in English Ling MPh. . UNIVERSITY OF CALIFORNIA PUBLICATIONS IN ENGLISH/LINGUISTICS/
                    MODERN PHILOLOGY
Univ of Chi Law Rev. . UNIVERSITY OF CHICAGO LAW REVIEW
Univ of Cinc Law Rev. . UNIVERSITY OF CINCINNATI LAW REVIEW
Univ of Colo Studies. . UNIVERSITY OF COLORADO. STUDIES
Univ of Maine Studies. . UNIVERSITY OF MAINE. STUDIES
Univ of Mo Studies. . UNIVERSITY OF MISSOURI. STUDIES
Univ of Pa Pub Pol Econ. . UNIVERSITY OF PENNSYLVANIA. PUBLICATIONS IN POLITICAL ECONOMY
Univ of Wyoming Publ. . UNIVERSITY OF WYOMING. PUBLICATIONS
Univ Penn Law Rev. . UNIVERSITY OF PENNSYLVANIA LAW REVIEW
Univ Q. . . . . UNIVERSALIST QUARTERLY REVIEW (BOSTON)
Univ Q. . . . . UNIVERSITIES QUARTERLY (LONDON)
Univ R. . . . . UNIVERSAL REVIEW
Univ R. . . . . UNIVERSITY REVIEW
Univ Rec. . . . . UNIVERSITY RECORD
Univ Rochester Lib Bull. . UNIVERSITY OF ROCHESTER LIBRARY BULLETIN
Univ Tenn Rec. . . . . UNIVERSITY OF TENNESSEE RECORD
Univ Toledo Law R. . UNIVERSITY OF TOLEDO LAW REVIEW
UNIV TOR Q. . . . . . UNIVERSITY OF TORONTO QUARTERLY
UNIV WINDSOR R. . UNIVERSITY OF WINDSOR REVIEW
UNK. . . . . UNKNOWN WORLDS
UN MED CAN. . . . . . UNION MEDICALE DU CANADA
UN Mo Chron. . . . . . UN MONTHLY CHRONICLE
UNNUS. . . . . URALIC NEWS AND NOTES FROM THE UNITED STATES
Unpartizan R. . . . . . UNPARTIZAN REVIEW
Unpop R. . . . . UNPOPULAR REVIEW
U N R. . . . . UNITED NATIONS REVIEW
U N Rev. . . . . UNITED NATIONS REVIEW

UNRP . . . . UNIVERSITY OF NOTTINGHAM RESEARCH PUBLICATIONS
UNS . . . . UNIVERSITY OF NEBRASKA STUDIES
Un Serv M . . . . UNITED SERVICE MAGAZINE
Un Serv (Phila) . . . . UNITED SERVICE (PHILADELPHIA)
UNT . . . . UNCANNY TALES
UNT . . . . UPSALA NYA TIDNING
UNTERNEHM . . . . . . UNTERNEHMUNG. SCHWEIZERISCHE ZEITSCHRIFT FUER BETRIEBSWIRTSCHAFT
UNTP . . . . UNIVERSIDAD DE TUCUMAN PUBLICATIONS
U N W Bul . . . . UNITED NATIONS WEEKLY BULLETIN
U N World . . . . UNITED NATIONS WORLD
UO . . . . UKRAINICA OCCIDENTALIA (WINNIPEG)
UO . . . . ULM-OBERSCHWABEN
UP . . . . UNIWERSYTET IM A. MICKIEWICZA (POZNAN)
UPAL . . . . UTRECHTSE PUBLIKATIES VOOR ALGEMENE LITERATUURWETENSCHAP
U Pa L Rev . . . . UNIVERSITY OF PENNSYLVANIA LAW REVIEW
UPB . . . . UNIVERSIDAD PONTIFICIA BOLIVARIANA
U PIT LAW . . . . UNIVERSITY OF PITTSBURGH LAW REVIEW
U Pitt L R . . . . UNIVERSITY OF PITTSBURGH LAW REVIEW
UPMB . . . . UNIVERSITY OF PENNSYLVANIA MUSEUM BULLETIN
UPMFF . . . . UNIVERSITY OF PENNSYLVANIA MONOGRAPHS IN FOLKLORE AND FOLKLIFE
U P NEWS . . . . UNAUTHORIZED PRACTICE NEWS
UPr . . . . UCILISTEN PREGLED
UPSAL J MED . . . . . UPSALA JOURNAL OF MEDICAL SCIENCES
UPSEELL . . . . UNIVERSITY OF PENNSYLVANIA STUDIES IN EAST EUROPEAN LANGUAGES AND LITERATURES
UQ . . . . UKRAINIAN QUARTERLY
UQ . . . . UNIVERSITIES QUARTERLY
UQP . . . . UNIVERSITY OF QUEENSLAND PAPERS
U QSLD P SS . . . . . . UNIVERSITY OF QUEENSLAND PAPERS. SOCIAL SCIENCES
U Queens L J . . . . . . UNIVERSITY OF QUEENSLAND LAW JOURNAL
UR . . . . UKRAINIAN REVIEW (LONDON)
UR . . . . UMJETNOST RIJECI
UR . . . . UNIVERSITY REVIEW
URB . . . . UNIVERSITY OF RIYAD. BULLETIN OF THE FACULTY OF ARTS (SAUDI ARABIA)
Urb Aff Q . . . . URBAN AFFAIRS QUARTERLY
URBAN ANTHR . . . . URBAN ANTHROPOLOGY
Urban Ed . . . . URBAN EDUCATION
Urban L Ann . . . . . . URBAN LAW ANNUAL
Urban Law . . . . URBAN LAWYER
URBAN LIF C . . . . . . URBAN LIFE AND CULTURE
Urban R . . . . URBAN REVIEW
URBAN SOC C . . . . . URBAN AND SOCIAL CHANGE REVIEW
URBAN STUD . . . . . . URBAN STUDIES
Urb Life & Cult . . . . URBAN LIFE AND CULTURE
Urb Stud . . . . URBAN STUDIES
URev . . . . UNIVERSITY REVIEW (DUBLIN)
U Richmond L Rev . . UNIVERSITY OF RICHMOND LAW REVIEW
URLB . . . . UNIVERSITY OF ROCHESTER LIBRARY BULLETIN
UROL INTERN . . . . . UROLOGIA INTERNATIONALIS
UROLOGE . . . . UROLOGE. AUSGABE A
UROL RES . . . . UROLOGICAL RESEARCH
US . . . . UUSI SUOMI

USAF AFHRL...... UNITED STATES AIR FORCE. HUMAN RESOURCES LABORATORY
USAF AMRL....... UNITED STATES AIR FORCE. AEROSPACE MEDICAL RESEARCH LABORATORY
USAF ARL........ UNITED STATES AIR FORCE. AEROMEDICAL RESEARCH LABORATORY
U S Agric......... UNITED STATES DEPARTMENT OF AGRICULTURE. PUBLICATIONS
U S Air Force Syst Command Aeronaut Syst Div Tech Doc Rep..UNITED STATES AIR FORCE SYSTEMS COMMAND. AERONAUTICAL SYSTEMS DIVISION. DOCUMENTARY REPORT
U S Air Force WADC Tech Rep..UNITED STATES AIR FORCE. WRIGHT AIR DEVELOPMENT CENTER. TECHNICAL REPORT
US & C Av R.......UNITED STATES AND CANADIAN AVIATION REPORTS
U San Francisco L Rev.. UNIVERSITY OF SAN FRANCISCO LAW REVIEW
U.S. Army BESRL... UNITED STATES ARMY. BEHAVIOR AND SYSTEMS RESEARCH LABORATORY
USBurEducBul..... UNITED STATES. BUREAU OF EDUCATION. BULLETINS
USBurEducCirc..... UNITED STATES. BUREAU OF EDUCATION. CIRCULARS
U S Bur Mines Rep Invest.. UNITED STATES. BUREAU OF MINES. REPORT OF INVESTIGATIONS
U S Bur Mines Tech Pa.. UNITED STATES. BUREAU OF MINES. TECHNICAL PAPER
US Bur mines Tech Prog Rep.. UNITED STATES. BUREAU OF MINES. TECHNICAL PROGRESS REPORT
U S Bur Reclam Div Des Dams Br Rep..UNITED STATES. DEPARTMENT OF THE INTERIOR. BUREAU OF RECLAMATION. DIVISION OF DESIGN, DENVER, COLORADO. DAMS BRANCH REPORT
U S Bur Reclam Eng Monogr..UNITED STATES. DEPARTMENT OF THE INTERIOR. BUREAU OF RECLAMATION, DENVER, COLORADO. ENGINEERING MONOGRAPHS
U S Bur Reclam Res Rep..UNITED STATES. DEPARTMENT OF THE INTERIOR. BUREAU OF RECLAMATION. RESEARCH REPORT
U S Bur Reclam Tech Rec Des Constr.. UNITED STATES. DEPARTMENT OF THE INTERIOR. BUREAU OF RECLAMATION. TECHNICAL RECORD OF DESIGN AND CONSTRUCTION (DAMS AND POWERPLANTS)
USCAD.......... UNIVERSITY OF SOUTHERN CALIFORNIA ABSTRACTS OF DISSERTATIONS
U S Cath M....... UNITED STATES CATHOLIC MAGAZINE
U S Chil Bur Pub.... UNITED STATES. CHILDREN'S BUREAU. PUBLICATIONS
U S Coast Geod Surv Magnetograms Hourly Values MHV..UNITED STATES. DEPARTMENT OF COMMERCE. COAST AND GEODETIC SURVEY. MAGNETOGRAMS AND HOURLY VALUES, MHV
U S Egg.......... UNITED STATES EGG AND POULTRY MAGAZINE
USF............. UNIVERSITY OF SANTA FE
USFLQ........... USF LANGUAGE QUARTERLY
USF L Rev........ UNIVERSITY OF SAN FRANCISCO LAW REVIEW
U S Geol S Bul..... UNITED STATES GEOLOGICAL SURVEY. BULLETIN
U S Geol S Professional Pa.. UNITED STATES GEOLOGICAL SURVEY. PROFESSIONAL PAPER
U S Geol Surv Bull.. UNITED STATES GEOLOGICAL SURVEY. BULLETIN
U S Geol Surv Circ.. UNITED STATES. DEPARTMENT OF THE INTERIOR. GEOLOGICAL SURVEY. CIRCULAR
U S Geol Surv Miner Invest Field Stud Map.. UNITED STATES. DEPARTMENT OF THE INTERIOR. GEOLOGICAL SURVEY. MINERAL INVESTIGATIONS FIELD STUDIES MAP
U S Law R........ UNITED STATES LAW REVIEW
U S Lit Gaz....... UNITED STATES LITERARY GAZETTE
USN AMI......... UNITED STATES NAVY AEROSPACE MEDICAL INSTITUTE
U S Nat Bur Stand.. UNITED STATES. NATIONAL BUREAU OF STANDARDS
US Nat Mus Rept... UNITED STATES. NATIONAL MUSEUM. REPORTS
U S Naval Ordnance Test Sta NAVORD Rep.. UNITED STATES. NAVAL ORDNANCE TEST STATION. NAVORD REPORT
U S Naval Res Lab Shock Vib Bull..UNITED STATES. NAVAL RESEARCH LABORATORIES. SHOCK AND VIBRATION BULLETIN
U S Nav Civ Eng Lab Tech Rep..UNITED STATES. DEPARTMENT OF THE NAVY. NAVAL CIVIL ENGINEERING LABORATORY. PORT HUENEME, CALIFORNIA. TECHNICAL REPORT
U S Nav Postgrad Sch Tech Rep/Res Paper..UNITED STATES NAVAL POSTGRADUATE SCHOOL. TECHNICAL REPORT/RESEARCH PAPER

U S Nav Ship Eng Cent Ship Struct Com Rep..UNITED STATES. DEPARTMENT OF THE NAVY. NAVAL SHIP ENGINEERING CENTER. SHIP STRUCTURE COMMITTEE. REPORT

US Nav Ship Res Dev Cent Rep..UNITED STATES NAVAL SHIP RESEARCH AND DEVELOPMENT CENTER. REPORT

U S News.........UNITED STATES NEWS AND WORLD REPORT

U S Office Ed Bul... UNITED STATES. OFFICE OF EDUCATION. BULLETIN

U S Office Ed Circ...UNITED STATES. OFFICE OF EDUCATION. CIRCULARS

U S Office Ed Pub... UNITED STATES. OFFICE OF EDUCATION. PUBLICATIONS

U S Office Ed Voc Div Bul..UNITED STATES. OFFICE OF EDUCATION. VOCATIONAL DIVISION BULLETIN

USP FIZ NAU......USPEKHI FIZICHESKIKH NAUK

USP KH..........USPEKHI KHIMII

USQ...........UNITED STATES QUARTERLY BOOK REVIEW

US Q Bk R.......UNITED STATES QUARTERLY BOOK REVIEW

USQBL..........UNITED STATES QUARTERLY BOOK LIST

U S Seed Rep.....UNITED STATES SEED REPORTER

U S Serv M.......UNITED STATES SERVICE MAGAZINE

US Ship Struct Com Rep..UNITED STATES SHIP STRUCTURE COMMITTEE REPORT

USSR Comp Info B..USSR. UNION OF COMPOSERS. INFORMATION BULLETIN

USUMS.........UTAH STATE UNIVERSITY. MONOGRAPH SERIES

US Waterw Exp Stn Contract Rep..UNITED STATES WATERWAYS EXPERIMENT STATION. CONTRACT REPORT

US Waterw Exp Stn Misc Pap..UNITED STATES WATERWAYS EXPERIMENT STATION. MISCELLANEOUS PAPER

US Waterw Exp Stn Res Rep..UNITED STATES WATERWAYS EXPERIMENT STATION. RESEARCH REPORT

US Waterw Exp Stn Tech Rep..UNITED STATES WATERWAYS EXPERIMENT STATION. TECHNICAL REPORT

U S Women's Bur Bul..UNITED STATES. WOMEN'S BUREAU. BULLETIN

Utah Ag Exp......UTAH AGRICULTURAL COLLEGE EXPERIMENT STATION. PUBLICATIONS

Utah B Bull.......UTAH BAR BULLETIN

Utah Geol Mineral Surv Bull..UTAH GEOLOGICAL AND MINERALOGICAL SURVEY. BULLETIN

Utah Geol Mineral Surv Spec Stud..UTAH GEOLOGICAL AND MINERALOGICAL SURVEY. SPECIAL STUDIES

Utah Hist Quar....UTAH HISTORICAL QUARTERLY

Utah Lib.........UTAH LIBRARIES

Utah Lib Assn Newsl..UTAH LIBRARY ASSOCIATION NEWSLETTER

Utah L Rev.......UTAH LAW REVIEW

U Tasmania L Rev..UNIVERSITY OF TASMANIA LAW REVIEW

UTCEU..........UNIVERSIDAD DE TUCUMAN. CUADERNOS DE EXTENSION UNIVERSITARIA

UTDEMS.........UNIVERSITY OF TULSA. DEPARTMENT OF ENGLISH. MONOGRAPH SERIES

UTET............UNIONE TIPOGRAFICO-EDITRICE TORINESE

U T Fac L Rev......UNIVERSITY OF TORONTO FACULTY OF LAW REVIEW

UTFS............UNIVERSITY OF TORONTO FRENCH SERIES

UTHS...........UNIVERSITY OF TEXAS HISPANIC STUDIES

U TOL LAW.......UNIVERSITY OF TOLEDO LAW REVIEW

U Tol L Rev.......UNIVERSITY OF TOLEDO LAW REVIEW

U TOR LAW J......UNIVERSITY OF TORONTO LAW JOURNAL

UTPLF..........UNIVERSITA DI TORINO. PUBBLICAZIONI DELLA FACOLTA DI LETTERE E FILOSOFIA

UTQ............UNIVERSITY OF TORONTO QUARTERLY

UTRFS..........UNIVERSITY OF TORONTO FRENCH SERIES

UTSE............UNIVERSITY OF TEXAS STUDIES IN ENGLISH

UTSH...........UNIVERSITY OF TENNESSEE STUDIES IN THE HUMANITIES

UTVS...........UCEBNI TEXTY VYSOKYCH SKOL

UUA............UPPSALA UNIVERSITETS ARSSKRIFT

UVL............UNTERSUCHUNGEN ZUR VERGLEICHENDEN LITERATUR. (HAMBURG)

UVM............UNIVERSITY OF VIRGINIA MAGAZINE

UVMag.........UNIVERSITY OF VIRGINIA MAGAZINE

PERIODICAL TITLE ABBREVIATIONS

UW . . . . US WURK
U Western Aust Ann L Rev . . UNIVERSITY OF WESTERN AUSTRALIA. ANNUAL LAW REVIEW
UWLA L Rev . . . . . . UNIVERSITY OF WEST LOS ANGELES. LAW REVIEW
UWOPGS . . . . UNIVERSITY OF WARWICK. OCCASIONAL PAPERS IN GERMAN STUDIES
UWPLL . . . . UNIVERSITY OF WASHINGTON. PUBLICATIONS IN LANGUAGE AND LITERATURE
UWR . . . . UNIVERSITY OF WINDSOR REVIEW (WINDSOR, ONTARIO)
UZAzPI . . . . UCENYE ZAPISKI PEDAGOGICESKOGO INSTITUTA JAZYKOV IM. M.F. ACHUNDOVA. SERIJA FILOLOGICESKAJA
UZAstPI . . . . UCENYE ZAPISKI ASTRACHANSKOGO GOSUDARSTVENNOGO PEDAGOGICESKOGO INSTITUTA
UZAzU . . . . UCENYE ZAPISKI AZERBAJDZANSKOGO GOSUDARSTVENNOGO UNIVERSITETA IM. S.M. KIROVA. JAZYK I LITERATURA
UZAzU . . . . UCENYE ZAPISKI AZERBAIDZHANSKII GOSUDARSTVENNYI UNIVERSITET (BAKU)
UZBasU . . . . UCENYE ZAPISKI BASKIRSKOGO GOSUDARSTVENNOGO UNIVERSITETA. SERIJA FILOLOGICESKICH NAUK
UZBurPi . . . . UCENYE ZAPISKI BURJATSKOGO GOSUDARSTVENNOGO PEDAGOGICESKOGO INSTITUTA IM. DORZI BANZAROVA. ISTORIKO-FILOLOGICESKAJA SERIJA. ULAN-UDE
UZCerepPI . . . . . . UCENYE ZAPISKI CEREPOVECKOGO GOSUDARSTVENNOGO PEDAGOGICESKOGO INSTITUTA
UZChabPI . . . . UCENYE ZAPISKI CHABAROVSKOGO GOSUDARSTVENNOGO PEDAGOGICESKOGO INSTITUTA
UZChakNII . . . . . . UCENYE ZAPISKI CHAKASSKOGO NAUCNO-ISSLEDOVATEL'SKOGO INSTITUTA JAZYKA. LITERATURY I ISTORII
UZCharU . . . . UCENYE ZAPISKI CHARKOVSKOGO UNIVERSITETA IM. A.M. GORLKOGO. TRUDY FILOLOGICESKOGO FAKULT'TETA
UZCIngPI . . . . UCENYE ZAPISKI CECENO-INGUSSKOGO PEDAGOGICESKOGO INSTITUTA. SERIJA FILOLO GICESKAJA
UZCuvNII . . . . UCENYE ZAPISKI NAUCNO-ISLEDOVATEL'SKOGO INSTITUTA JAZYKA, LITERATURY, ISTORII I EKONOMIKI PRI SOVETE MINISTROV CUVASSKOJ ASSR
UZDag . . . . UCENYE ZAPISKI DAGESTANSKOGO FILIALA AKADEMII NAUK SSSR. SERIJA FILOLOGICESKAJA
UZDagU . . . . UCENYE ZAPISKI DAGESTANSKOGO GOSUDARSTVENNOGO UNIVERSITETA. SERIJA FILOLOGICESKAJA
UZDalU . . . . UCENYE ZAPISKI DAL'NEVOSTOCNOGO UNIVERSITETA. SERIJA FILOLOGICESKAJA
UZDusPI . . . . UCENYE ZAPISKI DUSANBINSKOGO GOSUDARSTVENNOGO PEDAGOGICESKOGO INSTITUTA IM. T.G. SEVEENKO. FILOLOGICESKAJA SERIJA
UZEIPI . . . . UCENYE ZAPISKI ELABUZSKOGO GOSUDARSTVENNOGO PEDAGOGICESKOGO INSTITUTA. SERIJA ISTORII I FILOLOGII
UZEnPI . . . . UCENYE ZAPISKI ENISEJSKOGO GOSUDARSTVENNOGO PEDAGOGICESKOGO INSTITUTA. KAFEDRA RUSSKOGO JAZYKA
UZErevU . . . . UCENYE ZAPISKI EREVANSKOGO GOSUDARSTVENNOGO UNIVERSITETA. SERIJA FILOLOGICESKICH NAUK
UZGIYa . . . . UCENYE ZAPISKI GOR'KOVSKII PEDAGOGICHESKII INSTITUT INOSTRANNYKH YAZYKOV (GOR'KII)
UZGorPI . . . . UCENYE ZAPISKI GOR'KOVSKOGO GOSUDARSTVENNOGO PEDAGOGICESKOGO INSTITUTA IM. M. GOR'KOGO. SERIJA FILOLOGICESKAJA
UZGorPIIJa . . . . UCENYE ZAPISKI GOR'KOVSKOGO PEDAGOGICESKOGO INSTITUTA INOSTRANNYCH JAZYKOV
UZGorU . . . . UCENYE ZAPISKI GOR'KOVSKOGO UNIVERSITETA IM. N.I. LOBACEVSKOGO. SERIJA ISTORIKO-FILOLOGICESKAJA
UZGPI . . . . UCENYE ZAPISKI GOR'KOVSKII GOSUDARSTVENNYI PEDAGOGICHESKII INSTITUT (GOR'KII)
UZGurPI . . . . UCENYE ZAPISKI GUR'EVSKOGO GOSUDARSTVENNOGO PEDAGOGICESKOGO INSTITUTA. SERIJA ISTORIKO-FILOLOGICESKAJA
UZII . . . . UCENYE ZAPISKI INSTITUTA ISTORII
UZIMach . . . . UCENYE ZAPISKI INSTITUTA ISTORII, JAZYKA I LITERATURY IM. G. CADASY. SERIJA FILOLOGICESKAJA. MACHACKALA

PERIODICAL TITLE ABBREVIATIONS

UZIMO......... UCENYE ZAPISKI. INSTITUT MEZDUNARODNYCH OTNOSENIJ
UZIPI........... UCHENYE ZAPISKI IRKUTSKII PEDAGOGICHESKII INSTITUT (IRKUTSK)
UZIrkutPI....... UCENYE ZAPISKI IRKUTSKOGO GOSUDARSTVENNOGO PEDAGOGICESKOGO INSTITUTA INOSTRANNYCH JAZYKO'/
UZISL........... UCENYE ZAPISKI INSTITUTA SLAVJANOVEDENIJA
UZIV...........UCENYE ZAPISKI INSTITUTA VOSTOKOVEDENIJA. AKADEMIJA NAUK SSSR
UZIVAz.........UCENYE ZAPISKI INSTITUTA VOSTOKOVEDENIJA. AKADEMII NAUK AZERBAJDZANSKOJ SSSR
UZKa...... .... UCENYE ZAPISKI KALININSKII GOSUDARSTVENNYI PEDAGOGICHESKII INSTITUT (KALININ)
UZKAIPI........ UCENYE ZAPISKI KALUZSKOGO GOSUDARSTVENNOGO PEDAGOGICESKOGO INSTITUTA
UZKalinPI....... UCENYE ZAPISKI KALININSKOGO PEDAGOGICESKOGO INSTITUTA IM. M.I. KALININA. SERIJA FILOLOGICESKAJA
UZKaragPI...... UCENYE ZAPISKI KARAGANDINSKOGO PEDAGOGICESKOGO INSTUTUTA. FILOLOGICESKIE NAUKI
UZKarelPI....... UCENYE ZAPISKI KAREL'SKOGO PEDAGOGICESKOGO INSTITUTA
UZKarPI........ UCENYE ZAPISKI KARSINSKOGO GOSUDARSTVENNOGO PEDAGOGICESKOGO INSTUTUTA. FILOLOGICESKAJA SERIJA
UZKazanU....... UCENYE ZAPISKI KAZANSKOGO UNIVERSITETA IM. V.I. UL'JANOVA'LENINA.
UZKBI.......... UCENYE ZAPISKI KABARDINO-BALKARSKIJ NAUCNO-ISSLEDOVATEL'SKIJ INSTITUT PRI SOVETE MINISTROV KBASSR
UZKemPI....... UCENYE ZAPISKI KEMEROVSKOGO GOSUDARSTVENNOGO PEDAGOGICESKOGO INSTITUTA
UZKGPI......... UCENYE ZAPISKI KUJBYSEVSKOGO GOSUDARSTVENNOGO PEDAGOGICESKOGO INSTITUTA IM. V.V. KUJBYSEVA
UZKi........... UCENYE ZAPISKI KISHINEVSKII UNIVERSITET (KISHINEV)
UZKirovPI....... UCENYE ZAPISKI KIROVABADSKOGO PEDAGOGICESKOGO INSTITUTA
UZKisU......... UCENYE ZAPISKI KISINEVSKOGO GOSUDARSTVENNOGO UNIVERSITETA
UZKokPI........ UCENYE ZAPISKI KOKANDSKOGO PEDAGOGICESKOGO INSTITUTA IM. MUKIMI. SERIJA FILOLOGICESKAJA
UZKolPI........ UCENYE ZAPISKI KOLOMENSKOGO GOSUDARSTVENNOGO PEDAGOGICESKOGO INSTITUTA ISTORIKO-FILOLOGICESKIJ FAKUL'TET. KAFEDRY RUSSKOGO JAZYKA
UZKomPI....... UCENYE ZAPISKI KOMI GOSUDARSTVENNOGO PEDAGOGICESKOGO INSTITUTA. KAFEDRA RUSSKOGO JAZYKA
UZKr........... UCENYE ZAPISKI KRASNODARSKII PEDAGOGICHESKII INSTITUT (KRASNODAR)
UZKujPI........ UCENYE ZAPISKI KUJBYSEVSKOGO GOSUDARSTVENNOGO PEDAGOGICESKOGO INSTITUTA IM. V.V. KUJBYSEVA
UZLa........... UCENYE ZAPISKI LATVIISKII GOSUDARSTVENNYI UNIVERSITET (RIGA)
UZLenPI........ UCENYE ZAPISKI LENINGRADSKOGO PEDAGOGICESKOGO INSTITUTA IM. S.M. KIROVA
UZLPedI........ UCENYE ZAPISKI LENINGRADSKOGO PEDAGOGICESKOGO INSTITUTA IM. A.I. GERCENA
UZLPI.......... UCENYE ZAPISKI LENINGRADSKII PEDAGOGICHESKII INSTITUT IMENI. A.I. GERTSENA (LENINGRAD)
UZLPI.......... UCENYE ZAPISKI LENINGRADSKOGO PEDAGOGICESKOGO INSTITUTA IM. A.I. GERCENA
UZLU.......... UCENYE ZAPISKI LENINGRADSKOGO GOSUDARSTVENNOGO ORDENA LENINA UNIVERSITETA IM. A.A. ZDANOVA
UZLU.......... UCENYE ZAPISKI LENINGRADSKOGO UNIVERSITETA
UZLU-FN........ UCENYE ZAPISKI LENINGRADSKOGO UNIVERSITETA. SERIJA FILOLOGICESKIX NAUK
UZL'vovU....... UCENYE ZAPISKI L'VOVSKOGO GOSUDARSTVENNOGO UNIVERSITETA
UZMagPI....... UCENYE ZAPISKI MAGNITORSKOGO GOSUDARSTVENNOGO PEDAGOGICESKOGO INSTITUTA
UZMIK.......... UCENYE ZAPISKI MOSKOVSKII GOSUDARSTVENNYI INSTITUT KUL'TURY (MOSCOW)
UZMKrup........ UCENYE ZAPISKI MOSKOVSKOGO OBLANTNOGO PEDAGOGICESKOGO INSTITUTA IM. N.K. KRUPSKOJ
UZMOPI........ UCENYE ZAPISKI MOSKOVSKII OBLASTNOI PEDAGOGICHESKII INSTITUT IMENI N.K. KRUPSKOI (MOSCOW)

PERIODICAL TITLE ABBREVIATIONS

UZMorU . . . . UCENYE ZAPISKI MORDOVSKOGO UNIVERSITETA. SERIJA FILOLOGICESKICH NAUK
UZMPedI . . . . UCENYE ZAPISKI MOSKOVSKOGO GOSUDARSTVENNOGO PEDAGOGICESKOGO INSTITUTA
UZMPI . . . . UCENYE ZAPISKI MOSKOVSKII GOSUDARSTVENNYI PEDAGOGICHESKII INSTITUT IMENI LENINA (MOSCOW)
UZMPI . . . . UCENYE ZAPISKI MOSKOVSKOGO GOSUDARSTVENNOGO PEDAGOGICESKOGO INSTITUTA IM. POTEMKINA
UZMPIIJa . . . . UCENYE ZAPISKI I MOSKOVSKOGO GOSUDARSTVENNOGO PEDAGOGICESKOGO INSTITUTA INOSTRANNYCH JAZYKOV
UZMPIIYa . . . . UCENYE ZAPISKI I-I MOSKOVSKII PEDAGOGICHESKII INSTITUT INOSTRANNYKH YAZYKOV (MOSCOW)
UZMU . . . . UCENYE ZAPISKI MOSKOVSKOGO GOSUDARSTVENNOGO UNIVERSITETA
UZMU . . . . UCENYE ZAPISKI MOSKOVSKOGO UNIVERSITETA
UZNovPI . . . . UCENYE ZAPISKI NOVGORODSKOGO GOSUDARSTVENNOGO PEDAGOGICESKO INSTITUTA. KAFEDRA RUSSKOGO JAZYKA
UZOrenPI . . . . UCENYE ZAPISKI ORENBURGSKOGO GOSUDARSTVENNOGO PEDAGOGICESKOGO INSTITUTA IM. V.P. CKALOVA
UZPe . . . . UCENYE ZAPISKI PENZENSKII PEDAGOGICHESKII INSTITUT (PENZA)
UZPer . . . . UCENYE ZAPISKI PERMSKII UNIVERSITET (PERM')
UZPerm . . . . UCENYE ZAPISKI PERMSKOGO GOSUDARSTVENNOGO UNIVERSITETA IM. A.M. GOR'KOGO
UZPs . . . . UCENYE ZAPISKI PSKOVSKII PEDAGOGICHESKII INSTITUT (PSKOV)
UZPU . . . . UCENYE ZAPISKI PETROZAVODSKOGO UNIVERSITETA. FILOLOGICESKIE NAUK
UZRjazPI . . . . UCENYE ZAPISKI RJAZANSKOGO GOSUDARSTVENNOGO PEDAGOGICESKOGO INSTITUTA
UZRovPI . . . . UCENYE ZAPISKI ROVENSKOGO GOSUDARSTVENNOGO PEDAGOGICESKOGO INSTITUTA. FILOLOGICESKIJ FAKUL'TET
UZSachPI . . . . UCENYE ZAPISKI SACHTINSKOGO GOSUDARSTVENNOGO PEDAGOGICESKOGO INSTITUTA
UZSarPedI . . . . . . UCENYJE ZAPISKI SARATOVSKOGO GOSUDARSTVENNOGO PEDAGOGICESKOGO INSTITUTA
UZSGU . . . . UCENYE ZAPISKI SARATOVSKOGO GOSUDARSTVENNOGO UNIVERSITETA
UZSmolPI . . . . UCENYE ZAPISKI SMOLENSKOGO GOSUDARSTVENNOGO PEDAGOGICESKOGO INSTITUTA
UZSterPI . . . . UCENYE ZAPISKI STERLITAMAKSKOGO GOSUDARSTVENNOGO PEDAGOGICESKOGO INSTITUTA. SERIJA FILOLOGICESKAJA
UZTar . . . . UCENYE ZAPISKI TARTUSSKII UNIVERSITET (TARTU)
UZTarU . . . . UCENYE ZAPISKI TARTUSKOGO GOSUDARSTVENNOGO UNIVERSITETA
UZTasPIIn . . . . UCENYE ZAPISKI TASKENTSKOGO PEDAGOGICESKOGO INSTITUTA INOSTRANNYCH JAZYKOV
UZTasPINiz . . . . . . UCENYE ZAPISKI TASKENTSKOGO PEDAGOGICESKOGO INSTITUTA IM. NIZAMI
UZTI . . . . UCENYE ZAPISKI TIXOOKEANSKOGO INSTITUTA
UZTjPI . . . . UCENYE ZAPISKI TJUMENSKOGO PEDAGOGICESKOGO INSTITUTA. LAFEDRA RUSSKOGO JAZYKA
UZTomU . . . . UCENYE ZAPISKI TOMSKOGO UNIVERSITETA IM. V.V. KOJBYSEVA
UZToU . . . . UCENYE ZAPISKI TOMSKII UNIVERSITET (TOMSK)
UZTPI . . . . UCENYE ZAPISKI TOMSKIJ GOSUDARSTVENNYJ PEDAGOGICESKIJ INSTITUT
UZTuvNII . . . . UCENYE ZAPISKI TUVINSKOGO NAUCNO-ISSLEDOVATEL'SKOGO INSTITUTA JAZYKA, LITERATURY I ISTORII
UZUIPI . . . . UCENYE ZAPISKI UL'JANOVSKOGO GOSUDARSTVENNOGO PEDAGOGICESKOGO INSTITUTA IM. I.N. UL'JANOVA
UZUPI . . . . UCENYE ZAPISKI URAL'SKOGO PEDAGOGICESKOGO I UCITEL'SKOGO INSTITUTA IM. PUSKINA
UZUzPI . . . . UCENYE ZAPISKI UZBEKSKOGO RESPUBLIKANSKOGO PEDAGOGICESKOGO INSTITUTA KAFEDRA RUSSKOGO JAZYKA I LITERATURY
UZVinPI . . . . UCENYE ZAPISKI VINNICKOGO GOSUDARSTVENNOGO PEDAGOGICESKOGO INSTITUTA. KAFEDRA RUSSKOGO JAZYKA I LITERATURY
UZVolPI . . . . UCENYE ZAPISKI VOLOGODSKOGO GOSUDARSTVENNOGO PEDAGOGICESKOGO INSTITUTA

V

V . . . . VALENCIA
V . . . . VARIETY
V . . . . VERBO
Va . . . . VASARI
Va Ag Dept . . . . . . VIRGINIA DEPARTMENT OF AGRICULTURE AND IMMIGRATION. PUBLICATIONS
Va Ag Exp . . . . VIRGINIA POLYTECHNIC INSTITUTE. AGRICULTURAL EXPERIMENT STATION. PUBLICATIONS
Vag Vatten Byggaren . . VAG-OCH VATTEN BYGGAREN
Va Hist Soc Coll . . . . VIRGINIA HISTORICAL SOCIETY. COLLECTIONS
Va J Ed . . . . VIRGINIA JOURNAL OF EDUCATION
Va J Educ . . . . VIRGINIA JOURNAL OF EDUCATION
VA J INT L . . . . VIRGINIA JOURNAL OF INTERNATIONAL LAW
Vak-Tech . . . . VAKUUM-TECHNIK
Va Law R . . . . VIRGINIA LAW REVIEW
Va Lib Bul . . . . VIRGINIA LIBRARY BULLETIN
Va Libn . . . . VIRGINIA LIBRARIAN
Va L Rev . . . . VIRGINIA LAW REVIEW
Value Eng . . . . VALUE ENGINEERING
Val U L Rev . . . . . . VALPARAISO UNIVERSITY LAW REVIEW
Va Mag Hist Biog . . . VIRGINIA MAGAZINE OF HISTORY AND BIOGRAPHY
VAN . . . . VANGUARD SCIENCE FICTION
VAN . . . . VESTNIK AKADEMIJI NAUK SSR
VANB . . . . VESCI AKADEMII NAVUK BSSR
VANDER LAW . . . . . VANDERBILT LAW REVIEW
V&G . . . . VERGANGENHEIT UND GEGENWART
Vand Int . . . . VANDERBILT INTERNATIONAL
Vand J Trans L . . . . . VANDERBILT JOURNAL OF TRANSNATIONAL LAW
V & L . . . . VIE ET LANGAGE
Vand L Rev . . . . . . VANDERBILT LAW REVIEW
VAN SSSR . . . . VESTNIK AKADEMII NAUK SSSR
Va Q R . . . . VIRGINIA QUARTERLY REVIEW
VAR . . . . VARIETY
Vari . . . . VARIEGATION
VASD . . . . VEROEFFENTLICHUNGEN DER DEUTSCHEN AKADEMIE FUER SPRACHE UND DICHTUNG
VASILO . . . . VIERTELJAHRESSCHRIFT DES A. STIFTER-INSTITUTS DES LANDES OBEROESTERREICH
Va State Lib Bull . . . VIRGINIA STATE LIBRARY BULLETIN
Vasterbotten . . . . . VASTERBOTTENS LANS HAMBYGDSFORENINGS ARSBOK
Vastergotlands Fornminnesforen Tidskr . . VASTERGOTLANDS FORNMINNESFORENINGS TIDSKRIFT
Vastmanlands Fornminnesforen Arsskr . . VASTMANLANDS FORNMINNESFORENINGS ARSSKRIFT
Va Teach . . . . VIRGINIA TEACHER
Va Truck Exp . . . . . VIRGINIA TRUCK EXPERIMENT STATION. PUBLICATIONS
VB . . . . VOKS BULLETIN
VB (B) . . . . VOELKISCHER BEOBACHTER (BERLIN)
VBEA Newsletter . . . VIRGINIA BUSINESS EDUCATION NEWSLETTER
VBelGrN . . . . VESCI AKADEMII NAVUK BALARUSKAJ SSR. SERYJA GRAMADSKICH NAVUK
VBKTPS . . . . VIERTELJAHRSCHRIFT FUER BIBELKUNDE, TALMUDISCHE UND PATRISTISCHE STUDIEN
VB (Mu) . . . . VOELKISCHER BEOBACHTER (MUENICH)
VBTPS . . . . VIERTELJAHRSCHRIFT FUER BIBELKUNDE, TALMUDISCHE UND PATRISTISCHE STUDIEN
VBW . . . . VORTRAGE DER BIBLIOTHEK WARBURG
VC . . . . VILGILIAE CHRISTIANAE

VC . . . . VIRGINIA CAVALCADE
VCA . . . . VESTNIK CESKE AKADEMIE VED A UMENI
VCA . . . . VESTNIK CESKOSLOVENSKE AKADEMIE VED
VChr . . . . VIGILIAE CHRISTIANAE
VCSAV . . . . VESTNIK CESKOSLOVENSKE AKADEMIE VED
VDASD . . . . VEROEFFENTLICHUNGEN DER DEUTSCHEN AKADEMIE FUER SPRACHE UND DICHTUNG
VDI . . . . VESTNIK DREVNEI ISTORII
VDI Ber . . . . VDI (VEREIN DEUTSCHER INGENIEURE) BERICHTE
VDI Forschungsh . . . VDI (VEREIN DEUTSCHER INGENIEURE) FORSCHUNGSHEFT
VDI Z . . . . VDI (VEREIN DEUTSCHER INGENIEURE) ZEITSCHRIFT
VDP . . . . VON DEUTSCHER POETEREY
VDPh . . . . VERHANDLUNG DER VERSAMMLUNG DEUTSCHER PHILOLOGEN
VDS . . . . VEROEFFENTLICHUNGEN DER DEUTSCHEN SCHILLERGESELLSHAFT
VDTJ . . . . VOPROSY DIALEKTOLOGII TJURKSKICH JAZYKOV
VE . . . . VESTNIK EVROPY
VeC . . . . VERTICE (COIMBRA)
Vel . . . . VELTRO'
VEN . . . . VENTURE SCIENCE FICTION
Venez Min Minas Hidrocarburos Dir Geol Bol Geol . . VENEZUELA. MINISTERIO DE MINAS E HIDROCARBUROS. DIRECCION DE GEOLOGIA. BOLETIN DE GEOLOGIA
V e P . . . . VITA E PENSEIRO
VeR . . . . VERBUM (RIO DE JANEIRO)
Ver . . . . VERRI
Ver . . . . VERSTY
Verb C . . . . VERBUM CARO
Ver f d Gesch Berlins Schr . . VEREIN FUER DIE GESCHICHTE BERLINS. SCHRIFTEN
Ver f Gesch Dresdens Mitt . . VEREIN FUER GESCHICHTE DRESDENS. MITTEILUNGEN
Ver f Thur Gesch u Alt Ztsch . . VEREIN FUER THUERINGISCHE GESCHICHTE UND ALTERTUMSKUNDE. ZEITSCHRIFT
Verh Kon Nederl Ak Wetensch afd Lett . . VERHANDLINGEN DER KONINKLIJKE NEDERLANDSCHE AKADEMIE VAN WETENSCHAPPEN. AFDEELING LETTERKUNDE
Vermont Lib . . . . . . VERMONT LIBRARIES
Veroeff z Niedersaechs Gesch . . VEROEFFENTLICHINGEN ZUR NIEDERSAECHSISCHEN GESCHICHTE
Verpack-Rundsch . . . VERPACKUNGS-RUNDSCHAU
Verres Refract . . . . VERRES ET REFRACTAIRES
Versl Meded Kon Vl Ac Taal & Letterk . . VERSLAGEN EN MEDEDEELINGEN DER KONINKLIJKE VLAAMSCHE AKADEMIE VOOR TAAL-EN LETTERKUNDE
Ver Thur Gesch u Alt Ztsch n s . . VEREIN FUER THUERINGISCHE GESCHICHTE UND ALTERTUMSKUNDE. ZEITSCHRIFT
Vest Ces akad zemed . . VESTNIK CESKOSLOVENSKE AKADEMIE ZEMEDELSKE
Vestnik Akad nauk SSSR . . VESTNIK AKADEMIJI NAUK SSSR
Vestnik Leningr gosud univ . . VESTNIK LENINGRADSKOGO GOSUDARSTVENNOGO UNIVERSITETA
Vestn Mashinostr . . VESTNIK MASHINOSTROENIYA
VetChr . . . . VETERA CHRISTIANORUM
Vetensk Soc i Lund Arsbok . . VETENSKAPS-SOCIETETEN I LUND ARSBOK
VET MED/SAC . . . . . VETERINARY MEDICINE & SMALL ANIMAL CLINICIAN
VET PATH . . . . VETERINARY PATHOLOGY
VET REC . . . . VETERINARY RECORD
Vet Test . . . . VETUS TESTAMENTUM
VF . . . . DE VRIJE FRIES
VF . . . . VILAGIRODALMI FIGYELO
VF . . . . VOPROSY FILOLOGII
VF . . . . VOPROSY FILOSOFII

VFB . . . . VIERTELJAHRSSCHRIFT FUER BIBELKUNDE, TALMUDISCHE UND PATRISTISCHE. STUDIEN
VFHG . . . . VERSAMMLUNGEN DER FREUNDE DES HUMANISTISCHEN GYMNASIUMS
VFil . . . . VOPROSY FILOLOGII
VFSW . . . . VIERTELJAHRSSCHRIFT FUER SOCIAL UND WIRTSCHAFTGESCHICHTE
VGIEMTP . . . . VEROEFFENTLICHUNGEN DES GRABMANN INSTITUTS ZUR ERFORSCHUNG DER MITTELALTER-
LICHEN THEOLOGIE UND PHILOSOPHIE
VGJ . . . . VORGESCHICHTLICHES JAHRBUCH
VGLKV . . . . VIERTELJAHRSSCHRIFT FUER GESCHICHTE UND LANDESKUNDE VORARLBERGS
VGLL . . . . VALSTYBINE GROZINES LITERATUROS LEIDYKLA
VH . . . . VERMONT HISTORY
VHFS . . . . VIDENSKABERNES SELSKABS HISTORISK-FILOLOGISKE SKRIFTER
VHis . . . . VIDA HISPANICA
VHVNB . . . . VERHANDLUNGEN DES HISTORISCHEN VEREINES VON NIEDERBAYERN
VHVOR . . . . VERHANDLUNGEN DES HISTORISCHEN VEREINES VON OBERPFALZ UND REGENSBURG
Vi . . . . VIATOR
VIBJ . . . . VIRGIN ISLANDS BAR JOURNAL
Vict Poetry . . . . . . VICTORIAN POETRY
Vict Stud . . . . VICTORIAN STUDIES
Vict U C L Rev . . . . . VICTORIA UNIVERSITY COLLEGE LAW REVIEW
VidaL . . . . VIDA LITERARIA
VIDSL . . . . VEROEFFENTLICHUNGEN DES INSTITUTS FUER DEUTSCHE SPRACHE UND LITERATUR DER
DEUTSCHEN AKADEMIE DER WISSENSCHAFTEN ZU BERLIN
VIDV . . . . VEROEFFENTLICHUNGEN DES INSTITUTS FUER DEUTSCHE VOLKSKUNDE DER DEUTSCHEN
AKADEMIE DER WISSENSCHAFTEN ZU BERLIN
VIE MILIE A . . . . VIE ET MILIEU. SERIE A. BIOLOGIE MARINE
VIE MILIE B . . . . VIE ET MILIEU. SERIE B. OCEANOGRAPHIE
VIE MILIE C . . . . VIE ET MILIEU. SERIE C. BIOLOGIE TERRESTRE
Vie Mus . . . . VIE MUSICALE
VIE MUS BELGE . . . . VIE MUSICALE BELGE
Vierteljahrsschr f Wiss Philos . . VIERTELJAHRSSCHRIFT FUER WISSENSCHAFTLICHE PHILOSOPHIE UND SOCIOLOGIE
Vig C . . . . VIGILIAE CHRISTIANAE
Vig Chr . . . . VIGILIAE CHRISTIANAE
VIJ . . . . VISHVESHVARANAND INDOLOGICAL JOURNAL
Vik . . . . VIKING. NORSK ARKEOLOGISK SELSKAP
Vill L Rev . . . . VILLANOVA LAW REVIEW
Vin . . . . VINDUET
VIndJ . . . . VISHVESHVARANAND INDOLOGICAL JOURNAL
VIO . . . . VEROEFFENTLICHUNGEN DES INSTITUTS FUER ORIENTFORSCHUNG, DEUTSCHE AKADEMIE DER
WISSENSCHAFTEN ZU BERLIN
VIP . . . . VOIX ET IMAGES DU PAYS (U. OF QUEBEC)
ViR . . . . VIATA ROMANEASCA (BUCHAREST)
Vir . . . . VIRITTAJA, KOTIKIELEN SEURAN AIKAKAUSLEHTI (HELSINKI)
Vir . . . . VIRITTAJA. REVUE DE KOTIKIELEN SEURA
VIRC ARCH A . . . . . VIRCHOWS ARCHIV A. PATHOLOGICAL ANATOMY AND HISTOLOGY
VIRC ARCH B . . . . . . VIRCHOWS ARCHIV B. CELL PATHOLOGY
Virginia Q R . . . . . . VIRGINIA QUARTERLY REVIEW
VIRS . . . . VEROEFFENTLICHUNGEN DES INSTITUTS FUER ROMANISCHE SPRACHWISSENSCHAFT, DEUTSCHE
AKADEMIE DER WISSENSCHAFTEN ZU BERLIN
VIS . . . . VEROEFFENTLICHUNGEN DES INSTITUTS FUER SLAWISTIK DER DEUTSCHEN AKADEMIE ZU
BERLIN
VIs . . . . VOPROSY ISTORII (MOSCOW)

VISBL LANG . . . . VISIBLE LANGUAGE

Vis Educ . . . . VISUAL EDUCATION

VISI . . . . VEROEFFENTLICHINGEN DES INSTITUTS FUER SLAWISTIK, DEUTSCHE AKADEMIE DER WISSENSCHAFTEN ZU BERLIN

VISION RES . . . . VISION RESEARCH

Visual Ed . . . . VISUAL EDUCATION

Vital Speeches . . . . . VITAL SPEECHES OF THE DAY

Viv . . . . VIVARIUM

Vizugyi Kozlem . . . . VIZUGYI KOZLEMENYEK

VizV . . . . VIZANTIJSKIJ VREMENNIK

VJ . . . . VASSAR JOURNAL OF UNDERGRADUATE STUDIES

VJ . . . . VOPROSY JAZYKOZNANIJA (LVOV)

VJa . . . . VOPROSY JAZYKOZNANIJA (MOSCOW)

VJaL . . . . VOPROSY JAZYKA I LITERATURY

VJWPh . . . . VIERTELJAHRSSCHRIFT FUER WISSENSCHAFTLICHE PHILOSOPHIE

VK . . . . VOELKISCHE KULTUR

VKCSN . . . . VESTNIK KRALOVSKE CESKE SPOLECNOSTI NAUK

VKNA . . . . VERHANDELINGEN DER KONINKLIJKE NEDERLANDSE AKADEMIE VAN WETENSCHAPPEN, AFDELING LETTERKUNDE

VKNAL . . . . VERHANDELINGEN DER KONINKLIJKE NEDERLANDSE AKADEMIE VAN WETENSCHAPPEN, AFDELING LETTERKUNDE

VKR . . . . VOLKSTUM UND KULTUR DER ROMANEN

VKR . . . . VOPROSY KUL'TURY RECI

VKyjU . . . . VISNYK KYJIV'KOHO UNIVERSYTETU

VL . . . . DEUTSCHE VIERTELJAHRSSCHRIFT FUER LITERATURWISSENSCHAFT UND GEISTESGESCHICHTE

VL . . . . VETENSKAPSOCIETETEN I LUND

VL . . . . VOPROSY LITERATURY

VLa . . . . VIE ET LANGAGE

V Lang . . . . VISIBLE LANGUAGE

V LENIN FIZ . . . . . . VESTNIK LENINGRADSKOGO UNIVERSITETA SERIYA FIZIKI I KHIMII

V LENIN MEK . . . . . . VESTNIK LENINGRADSKOGO UNIVERSITETA SERIYA MATEMATIKI MEKHANIKI

VLenU . . . . VESTNIK LENINGRADSKOGO GOSUDARSTVENNOGO UNIVERSITETA

VLG . . . . VLAAMSE GIDS

VLIB . . . . VALODAS UN LITERATURAS INSTITUTA BILETENS

VLIR . . . . VALODAS UN LITERATURAS INSTITUTA RAKSTI

VLit . . . . VOPROSY LITERATURY

VLJaTas . . . . VOPROSY LITERATUROVEDENIJA I JAZYKOZNANIJA. TASKENT

VLU . . . . VESTNIK LENINGRADSKOGO GOSUDARSTVENNOGO UNIVERSITETA

VLU . . . . VESTNIK LENINGRADSKOGO U. SER. ISTORII, JAZYKA I LITERATURY

VLUist . . . . VESTNIK LENINGRADSKOGO GOSUDARSTVENNOGO UNIVERSITETA

VLvivU . . . . VISNYK L'VIVS'KOHO DERZAVNOHO UNIVERSYTETU

VLVM . . . . VLASTIVEDNY VESTNIK MORAVSKY

VM . . . . VERSLAGEN EN MEDEDEELINGEN

VMarJa . . . . VOPROSY MARIJSKOGO JAZYKOZNANIJA

VMAW . . . . VERSLAGEN EN MEDEDEELINGEN DER KONINKLIJKE. AKADEMIE VAN WETENSCHAPPEN

VMB . . . . VANDRINGAR MED BOEKER

VMHB . . . . VIRGINIA MAGAZINE OF HISTORY AND BIOGRAPHY

VMKA . . . . VERSLAGEN EN MEDEDEELINGEN, KONINKLIJKE AKADEMIE VOOR NEDERLANDSE TAAL- EN LETTERKUNDE

VMKVA . . . . VERSLAGEN EN MEDEDEELINGEN VAN DE KONINKLIJKE VLAAMSE AKADEMIE VOOR TAAL- EN LETTERKUNDE

V MOSK FIZ . . . . VESTNIK MOSKOVSKOGO UNIVERSITETA SERIYA FIZIKI I ASTRONOMII
V MOSK MEKH . . . . . VESTNIK MOSKOVSKOGO UNIVERSITETA SERIYA MATEMATIKI I MEKHANIKI
V MOSK U KH . . . . . VESTNIK MOSKOVSKOGO UNIVERSITETA SERIYA KHIMIYA
VMU . . . . VESTNIK MOSKOVSKOGO GOSUDARSTVENNOGO UNIVERSITETA
VMU . . . . VESTNIK MOSKOVSKOGO U. SER. VII FILOLOGIJA. ZURNALISTIKA
VMUist . . . . VESTNIK MOSKOVSKOGO GOSUDARSTVENNOGO UNIVERSITETA
VMUZh . . . . VESTNIK MOSKOVSKOGO UNIVERSITETA ZHURNALISTIKA
VMVBORG . . . . VERSLAGEN EN MEDEDEELINGEN VAN DE VEREENIGING TOT BEOEFENING VAN OVERIJSSELSCH
RECHT EN GESCHIEDENIS
VMVOVR . . . . VERSLAGEN EN MEDEDEELINGEN VAN DE VEREENIGING TOT UITGAAF VAN DER BRONNEN VAN
HET OUD-VADERLANDSCHE RECHT
VN . . . . VICTORIAN NEWSLETTER
VND . . . . VPRASANJA NASIH DNI
VNFH . . . . VJESNIK NARODNOG FRONTA HRVATSKE
VNL . . . . VICTORIAN NEWS LETTER
VNM . . . . TIJDSCHRIFT VAN DE VEREENIGING VOOR NEDERLANDSE MUZIEKGESCHIEDENIS
VO . . . . VESNJANI ORBRIJI (KYJIV)
Vo . . . . VOICES
Voc Aspect Ed . . . . . VOCATIONAL ASPECT OF EDUCATION
VOCAT GUID . . . . . . VOCATIONAL GUIDANCE QUARTERLY
Vocational Aspect . . VOCATIONAL ASPECT OF EDUCATION
Voc Educ . . . . VOCATIONAL EDUCATION
Voc Educ M . . . . . . VOCATIONAL EDUCATION MAGAZINE
Voc Guid Q . . . . VOCATIONAL GUIDANCE QUARTERLY
VOEI . . . . VEROEFFENTLICHEN DES OSTEUROPA-INSTITUTS
VOEI . . . . VEROEFFENTLICHEN DES OSTEUROPA-INSTITUTS (SLAVISCHES SEMINAR) AN DER FREIEN
UNIVERSITAET BERLIN
VOIB . . . . VEROEFFENTLICHLUNGEN DER ABTEILUNG FUER SLAVISCHE SPRACHEN UND LITERATUREN DES
OSTEUROPA-INSTITUTS (SLAVISCHES SEMINAR) AN DER FREIEN UNIVERSITAET BERLIN
Voith Forsch Konstr . . VOITH FORSCHUNG UND KONSTRUKTION
Vol Feeding Mgt . . . VOLUME FEEDING MANAGEMENT
Volksmus . . . . VOLKSMUSIK. ZEITSCHRIFT FUER DAS MUSIKALISCHE LAIENSCHAFFEN
Volta R . . . . VOLTA REVIEW
VON . . . . VESTNIK OTEDELENIJA OBSCESTVENNYCH NAUK. AKADEMIJA NAUK GRUZINSKOJ SSR
Von Roll Mitt . . . . . . VON ROLL MITTEILUNGEN
Voplst . . . . VOPROSY ISTORII
VOP MED KH . . . . . VOPROSY MEDITSINKOI KHIMII
VOP PSIKHOL . . . . . VOPROSY PSIKHOLOGII
VOP VIRUSOL . . . . . VOPROSY VIRUSOLOGII
VOR . . . . VORTEX SCIENCE FICTION
VOT . . . . VISION OF TOMORROW
VOX SANGUIN . . . . . VOX SANGUINIS
Vozr . . . . VOZROZDENIE
VP . . . . VICTORIAN POETRY
VP . . . . VITA E PENSIERO
VP . . . . VOCE DEL PASSATO
VPD . . . . VREMENNIK PUSKINSKOGO DOMA
VPen . . . . VITA E PENSIERO
VPIMD . . . . VILNIAUS PEDAGOGINIO INSTITUTO MOKSLO DARBAI
VPMLL . . . . VALSTYBINE POLITINES IR MOKSLINES LITERATU
VPN . . . . VICTORIAN PERIODICALS NEWSLETTER

VPW . . . . VORARBEITEN ZUM POMMERSCHEN WOERTERBUCH
VQ . . . . VERMONT QUARTERLY
VQ . . . . VISVABHARATI QUARTERLY
VQR . . . . VIRGINIA QUARTERLY REVIEW
VR . . . . VIATA ROMANEASCA (BUCHAREST)
VR . . . . VIERA I RAZUM
VR . . . . VOLJA ROSSII
VR . . . . VOX ROMANICA
VRJa . . . . VOPROSY RUSSKOGO JAZYKOZNANIJA
VRo . . . . VIATA ROMINEASCA
VROA . . . . VERSLAGEN OMTRENT'S RIJKS OUDE ARCHIEVEN
VS . . . . VICTORIAN STUDIES
VS . . . . VIDA SOBRENATURAL
VS . . . . VIDENSKAPSELSKAPETS SKRIFTER
VSAV . . . . VYDAVTEL'STVO SLOVENSKEJ AKADEMIE VIED
Vse . . . . VSESVIT (KIEV)
VSG . . . . VIERTELJAHRSSCHRIFT FUER SOZIAL- UND WIRTSCHAFTSGESCHICHTE
VSL . . . . VETENSKAPS-SOCIETETEN I LUND
VSL . . . . VETENSKAPS-SOCIETETEN I LUND ARSBOK
VSLA . . . . VETENSKAPS-SOCIETETEN I LUND ARSBOK
VSLJa . . . . VOPROSY SLAVJANSKOGO JAZYKOZNANIJA
VSLJa (L'vov) . . . . . VOPROSY SLAVJANSKOGO JAZYKOZNANIJA (L'VOV)
VSlJa (Moskva) . . . . VOPROSY SLAVJANSKOGO JAZYKOZNANIJA (MOSKVA)
VSPP . . . . VANGIYA SAHITYA PARISAT PATRIKA
VSS . . . . VIDENSKABS SELSKAPET SKRIFTER
VSSF . . . . VIDENSKABS SELSKAPET SKRIFTER (FORHANDLINGER)
VS Suppl . . . . VIE SPIRITUELLE. SUPPLEMENT
VStil . . . . VOPROSY STILISTIKI
VSv . . . . VOKRUG SVETA (MOSCOW)
VSW . . . . VIERTELJAHRSSCHRIFT FUER SOZIAL- UND WIRTSCHAFTSGESCHICHTE
VSWG . . . . VIERTELJAHRSSCHRIFT FUER SOZIAL- UND WIRTSCHAFTSGESCHICHTE
VT . . . . VETUS TESTAMENTUM
VT . . . . VIERE I TZERKOV
Vt Ag Exp . . . . VERMONT AGRICULTURAL EXPERIMENT STATION. PUBLICATIONS
Vt Bul . . . . VERMONT FREE PUBLIC LIBRARY COMMISSION AND STATE LIBRARY. BULLETIN
Vt Geol Surv Bull . . . VERMONT GEOLOGICAL SURVEY. BULLETIN
Vt Hist . . . . VERMONT HISTORY
VtHS . . . . VERMONT HISTORICAL SOCIETY. PROCEEDINGS
Vt Lib . . . . VERMONT LIBRARIES
VTMRJa . . . . VOPROSY TEORII I METODIKI IZUCENIJY RUSSKOGO JAZYKA
VTop . . . . VOPROSY TOPONOMASTIKI
VtQ . . . . VERMONT QUARTERLY
VTX . . . . VERTEX
VUMD . . . . VILNIAUS VALSTYBINIO V. KAPSUKO VARDO UNIVERSITETO MOKSLO DARBAI
VUSH . . . . VANDERBILT UNIVERSITY STUDIES IN THE HUMANITIES
VULT . . . . VOPROSY UZBEKSKOGO JAZYKA I LITERATURY
V U W L REV . . . . . . VICTORIA UNIVERSITY OF WELLINGTON LAW REVIEW
VV . . . . VILLAGE VOICE
VV . . . . VIZANTIISKII VREMENIK
VV . . . . VOLK UND VOLKSTUM
VVa . . . . VIDA VASCA

VVM . . . . VLASTIVEDNY VESTNIK MORAVSKY
VW . . . . VIE WALLONNE
VWN . . . . VIRGINIA WOOLF NEWSLETTER
VWQ . . . . VIRGINIA WOOLF QUARTERLY
Vya . . . . VOPROSY YAZYKOZNANIYA (MOSCOW)
VYSO SOED A . . . . . . VYSOKOMOLEKULYARNYE SOEDINENIYA. SERIYA A
VYSO SOED B . . . . . . VYSOKOMOLEKULYARNYE SOEDINENIYA. SERIYA B
VyV . . . . VERDAD Y VIDA (MILAN)
Vyzk Ustav Vodohospodar Pr Stud . . VYZKUMNY USTAV VODOHOSPODARSKY. PRACE A STUDIE
VyzS . . . . VYZVOL'NYJ SLJAX
VZ . . . . VOSTOCNYE ZAPISKI

W

W . . . . WINTER
W . . . . WORTKUNST
Wa . . . . WARSAW
WA . . . . WELTWIRTSCHAFTLICHES ARCHIV
WA . . . . WEST AFRICA
WA . . . . WISSENSCHAFTLICHE ANNALEN
WADA . . . . WISSENSCHAFTLICHE ANNALEN VON DER DEUTSCHEN AKADEMIE
WADL . . . . WIENER ARBEITEN ZUR DEUTSCHEN LITERATUR
Wadsworth Ath Bul . . WADSWORTH ATHENEUM BULLETIN
Waerme Stoffuebertrag Thermo-Fluid Dyn . . WAERME UND STOFFUEBERTRAGUNG. THERMO- AND FLUID DYNAMICS
W AFR J ARC . . . . . . WEST AFRICAN JOURNAL OF ARCHEOLOGY
WAGSO . . . . WIENER ARCHIV FUER GESCHICHTE DES SLAWENTUMS UND OSTEUROPAS
WAJE . . . . WEST AFRICAN JOURNAL OF EDUCATION
Wake Forest L Rev . . WAKE FOREST LAW REVIEW
WAL . . . . WESTERN AMERICAN LITERATURE
WALA News . . . . . . WEST AFRICAN LIBRARY ASSOCIATION. NEWS
Walford's Antiq . . . . (WALFORD'S) ANTIQUARIAN AND BIBLIOGRAPHER
Wallaces F . . . . WALLACES FARMER
Wall St Jnl . . . . WALL STREET JOURNAL
WALMS . . . . WEST AFRICAN LANGUAGE MONOGRAPH SERIES
Walsh'S R . . . . WALSH'S AMERICAN REVIEW
WAM . . . . WILTSHIRE ARCHAEOLOGICAL MAGAZINE
W&G . . . . WISSEN UND GLAUBEN
W & M L Rev . . . . . WILLIAM AND MARY LAW REVIEW
W & M Q . . . . WILLIAM AND MARY QUARTERLY
W&S . . . . WOERTER UND SACHEN
WAR . . . . WISCONSIN ACADEMY REVIEW
WAS . . . . WITCHCRAFT AND SORCERY
WAS . . . . WORCESTER ARCHAEOLOGICAL SOCIETY. TRANSACTIONS
WASAL . . . . WISCONSIN ACADEMY OF SCIENCE, ARTS, AND LETTERS
WascanaR . . . . WASCANA REVIEW
Wash Acad Sci J . . . . WASHINGTON ACADEMY OF SCIENCES. JOURNAL
Wash Ag Exp . . . . . . STATE COLLEGE OF WASHINGTON. AGRICULTURAL EXPERIMENT STATION. PUBLICATIONS
Washburn L J . . . . . . WASHBURN LAW JOURNAL
Wash Div Mines Geol Bull . . WASHINGTON. DEPARTMENT OF NATURAL RESOURCES. DIVISION OF MINES AND GEOLOGY. BULLETIN
Wash Div Mines Geol Inform Circ . . WASHINGTON. DEPARTMENT OF CONSERVATION. DIVISION OF MINES AND GEOLOGY. INFORMATION CIRCULAR
Wash Div Mines Geol Rep Invest . . WASHINGTON. DEPARTMENT OF CONSERVATION. DIVISION OF MINES AND GEOLOGY. REPORT OF INVESTIGATIONS
Wash Hist Q . . . . . . WASHINGTON HISTORICAL QUARTERLY
WASH LAW RE . . . . . WASHINGTON LAW REVIEW
WASH U L Q . . . . WASHINGTON UNIVERSITY LAW QUARTERLY
Wash Univ Bull . . . . WASHINGTON UNIVERSITY BULLETIN
Wash Univ St (Hum ser) . . WASHINGTON UNIVERSITY STUDIES. HUMANISTIC SERIES
Wash Univ St (Sci ser) . . WASHINGTON UNIVERSITY STUDIES. SCIENTIFIC SERIES
Wash Univ Stud Lang & Lit . . WASHINGTON UNIVERSITY STUDIES. LANGUAGE AND LITERATURE
Wash Univ Stud Sci & Tech . . WASHINGTON UNIVERSITY STUDIES. SCIENCE AND TECHNOLOGY
Wash Univ Stud Sci & Tech ns . . WASHINGTON UNIVERSITY STUDIES. SCIENCE AND TECHNOLOGY. NEW SERIES

Wash Univ Stud Social & Philos Sci. . WASHINGTON UNIVERSITY STUDIES. SOCIAL AND PHILOSOPHICAL SCIENCES
Wash Univ Stud Social & Philos Sci ns. . WASHINGTON UNIVERSITY STUDIES. SOCIAL AND PHILOSOPHICAL SCIENCES.
NEW SERIES
WAS POLIT. . . . . . . WASEDA POLITICAL STUDIES
Wasser- Energiewirt. . WASSER- UND ENERGIEWIRTSCHAFT
W Assn Map Lib Inf Bull. . WESTERN ASSOCIATION OF MAP LIBRARIES. INFORMATION BULLETIN
Water and San. . . . . WATER AND SANITATION
WATER A S P. . . . . . WATER AIR AND SOIL POLLUTION
Water Poll Cont Fed J. . WATER POLLUTION CONTROL FEDERATION JOURNAL
WATER RES. . . . . . . WATER RESEARCH
WATER RES R. . . . . . WATER RESOURCES RESEARCH
WATER SERV. . . . . . WATER SERVICES
Water Treat Exam. . WATER TREATMENT AND EXAMINATION
WATER WASTE. . . . . WATER AND WASTES ENGINEERING
WatPolAb. . . . . WATER POLLUTION ABSTRACTS
Wat Pollut Control. . WATER POLLUTION CONTROL
Wat Pwr. . . . . WATER POWER
WatResAb. . . . . . . WATER RESOURCES ABSTRACTS
Wat Serv. . . . . WATER SERVICES
Wat Waste Treat. . . WATER AND WASTE TREATMENT
Wat Wat Engng. . . . WATER AND WATER ENGINEERING
Wayne L Rev. . . . . . WAYNE LAW REVIEW
WB. . . . . WEIMARER BEITRAEGE
WB. . . . . WIENER BLAETTER FUER DIE FREUNDE DER ANTIKE
WB. . . . . WORLDS BEYOND
WB. . . . . WORT UND BRAUCH
WBD. . . . . WORLDS BEYOND
WBEP. . . . . WIENER BEITRAEGE ZUR ENGLISCHEN PHILOLOGIE
WBG. . . . . WISSENSCHAFTLICHE BUCHGESELLSCHAFT
WBKL. . . . . WIENER BEITRAEGE ZUR KULTURGESCHICHTE UND LINGUISTIK
WC. . . . . WORDSWORTH CIRCLE
WC. . . . . WSPOLCZESNOSC
W CAN J ANT. . . . . WEST CANADIAN JOURNAL OF ANTHROPOLOGY
WCR. . . . . WEST COAST REVIEW
WCSMLL. . . . . WESTERN CANADIAN STUDIES IN MODERN LANGUAGES AND LITERATURE
WD. . . . . WINTER'S DIGEST
Wd. . . . . WORD
Wd. . . . . WORLD
WDGB. . . . . WURZBURGER DIOZESANGESCHICHTSBLAETTER
WdSL. . . . . WELT DER SLAVEN
Weather C & M. . . . WEATHER, CROPS AND MARKETS
W ECON J. . . . . WESTERN ECONOMIC JOURNAL
WEED RES. . . . . WEED RESEARCH
WEED SCI. . . . . WEED SCIENCE
Weekly N L. . . . . . . WEEKLY NEWS LETTER. UNITED STATES DEPARTMENT OF AGRICULTURE
Weekly Underw. . . . WEEKLY UNDERWRITER
WEJ. . . . . WESTERN ECONOMIC JOURNAL
Weld Des Fabr. . . . . WELDING DESIGN AND FABRICATION
Weld Eng. . . . . WELDING ENGINEER
Weld Metal Fabr. . . WELDING AND METAL FABRICATION
Weld Prod. . . . . WELDING PRODUCTION

WELD RES C....... WELDING RESEARCH COUNCIL BULLETIN
Weld Wld........ WELDING IN THE WORLD
Weld World Soudage Monde.. WELDING IN THE WORLD. LE SOUDAGE DANS LE MONDE
Welsh H R........ WELSH HISTORY REVIEW
WELTWIR ARC..... WELTWIRTSCHAFTLICHES ARCHIV
WEP........... WASEDA ECONOMIC PAPERS
WER........... WEEK END REVIEW
Werkstatt Betr.... WERKSTATT UND BETRIEB
Werkst Korros..... WERKSTOFFE UND KORROSION
Wesley Th J....... WESLEYAN THEOLOGICAL JOURNAL
West Assn Map Libs Inf Bul.. WESTERN ASSOCIATION OF MAP LIBRARIES. INFORMATION BULLETIN
WEST BUS........ WESTERN BUSINESS
Westchester Co Hist Soc Publ.. WESTCHESTER COUNTY HISTORICAL SOCIETY. PUBLICATIONS
West City........ WESTERN CITY
West Constr...... WESTERN CONSTRUCTION
West Econ Jour.... WESTERN ECONOMIC JOURNAL
WEST ELEC E...... WESTERN ELECTRIC ENGINEER
Westerm M....... WESTERMANNS MONATSHEFTE
Westerm Monatsh.. WESTERMANNS MONATSHEFTE
Western Hum R.... WESTERN HUMANITIES REVIEW
Western Ont L Rev.. WESTERN ONTARIO LAW REVIEW
Western Reserve Hist Soc Tracts.. WESTERN RESERVE HISTORICAL SOCIETY. TRACTS
Western Res L Rev.. WESTERN RESERVE LAW REVIEW
Western Wash Ag Exp B. WESTERN WASHINGTON AGRICULTURAL EXPERIMENT STATION. MONTHLY BULLETIN
West Europe Ed.... WESTERN EUROPEAN EDUCATION
West Folk........ WESTERN FOLKLORE
Westfriesch Jb.... WESTFRIESCH JAARBOEK
West Horse....... WESTERN HORSEMAN
West Humanities Rev.. WESTERN HUMANITIES REVIEW
Westinghouse Eng.. WESTINGHOUSE ENGINEER
WEST J MED...... WESTERN JOURNAL OF MEDICINE
West Law J....... WESTERN LAW JOURNAL
West Lit J........ WESTERN LITERARY JOURNAL
West M.......... WESTERN MONTHLY MAGAZINE
Westm.......... WESTMINSTER REVIEW
West Mach Steel World.. WESTERN MACHINERY AND STEEL WORLD
West Miner....... WESTERN MINER
West Mo R....... WESTERN MONTHLY REVIEW
West Penn Hist Mag.. WESTERN PENNSYLVANIA HISTORY MAGAZINE
West Plast....... WESTERN PLASTICS
West Pol Q....... WESTERN POLITICAL QUARTERLY
Westpr Geschichtsv Ztsch.. WESTPREUSSISCHER GESCHICHTSVEREIN. ZEITSCHRIFT
West R.......... WESTERN REVIEW
West Reserve Law Rev.. WESTERN RESERVE LAW REVIEW
West Soc Eng J.... WESTERN SOCIETY OF ENGINEERS. JOURNAL
West Th J........ WESTMINSTER THEOLOGICAL JOURNAL
West Union Tech Rev.. WESTERN UNION TECHNICAL REVIEW
West Va Lib....... WEST VIRGINIA LIBRARIES
W Europe Educ..... WESTERN EUROPEAN EDUCATION
WeW........... WELT UND WORT
WF............ WEGE DER FORSCHUNG, DARMSTADT, WISSENSCHAFTLICHE BUCHGESELLSCHAFT

WF . . . . WESTERN FOLKLORE
WF . . . . WESTFALISCHE FORSCHUNGEN
WFA . . . . WORLDS OF FANTASY (1968-)
Wg . . . . WANDLUNG
WG . . . . WELT ALS GESCHICHTE ZEITSCHRIFT FUER UNIVERSALGESCHICHTLICHE FORSCHUNG
WGCR . . . . WEST GEORGIA COLLEGE REVIEW
WHB . . . . WIENER HUMANISTISCHE BLAETTER
Whet . . . . WHETSTONE
WHO CHRON . . . . . . WHO CHRONICLE
WHR . . . . WELSH HISTORY REVIEW
WHR . . . . WESTERN HUMANITIES REVIEW
WI . . . . WELT DES ISLAMS
WI . . . . WIADOMOSCI
Wien Beitr . . . . WIENER BEITRAEGE ZUR ENGLISCHEN PHILOLOGIE
WIEN KLIN W . . . . . . WIENER KLINISCHE WOCHENSCHRIFT
WIF . . . . WORLDS OF IF
WIG . . . . WEST-INDISCHE GIDS
WIJ . . . . WARBURG INSTITUTE JOURNAL
WI LAW REV . . . . . . WISCONSIN LAW REVIEW
Wild Barfield J . . . . . WILD BARFIELD JOURNAL
Willamette L J . . . . . WILLAMETTE LAW JOURNAL
WILSON B . . . . WILSON BULLETIN
Wilson Lib Bul . . . . . WILSON LIBRARY BULLETIN
Win . . . . WINTER
WIP . . . . WORK IN PROGRESS
Wire . . . . WIRE (DRAHT FACHZEITSCHRIFT)
Wire and Wire Prod . . WIRE AND WIRE PRODUCTS
Wire Ind . . . . WIRE INDUSTRY
Wire J . . . . WIRE JOURNAL
Wireless Eng . . . . . . WIRELESS ENGINEER
WIREL WORLD . . . . . WIRELESS WORLD
Wire World Int . . . . . WIRE WORLD INTERNATIONAL
Wis Acad of Sci Trans . . WISCONSIN ACADEMY OF SCIENCES. TRANSACTIONS
Wis Acad Sciences Trans . . WISCONSIN ACADEMY OF SCIENCES, ARTS AND LETTERS. TRANSACTIONS
Wis Ag Dept . . . . . . WISCONSIN DEPARTMENT OF AGRICULTURE. PUBLICATIONS
Wis Ag Exp . . . . UNIVERSITY OF WISCONSIN. AGRICULTURAL EXPERIMENT STATION. PUBLICATIONS
Wis Alum M . . . . WISCONSIN ALUMNI MAGAZINE
Wis B Bulletin . . . . . WISCONSIN BAR BULLETIN
Wisc Lib Bull . . . . . . WISCONSIN LIBRARY BULLETIN
WiseR . . . . WISEMAN REVIEW
Wis Hist Soc Proc . . . STATE HISTORICAL SOCIETY OF WISCONSIN. PROCEEDINGS
Wis J Ed . . . . WISCONSIN JOURNAL OF EDUCATION
Wis Lib Bul . . . . WISCONSIN LIBRARY BULLETIN
Wis L Rev . . . . WISCONSIN LAW REVIEW
Wis M Hist . . . . WISCONSIN MAGAZINE OF HISTORY
WisSL . . . . WISCONSIN STUDIES IN LITERATURE
Wis Stud Contemp Lit . . WISCONSIN STUDIES IN CONTEMPORARY LITERATURE
Wiss Weis . . . . WISSENSCHAFT UND WEISHEIT
Wiss Welt . . . . WISSENSCHAFT UND WELTBILD
WissZ . . . . WISSENSCHAFTLICHE ZEITUNG DER HUMBOLT- UNIVERSITAET
Wiss Z Elektrotech . . WISSENSCHAFTLICHE ZEITSCHRIFT DER ELEKTROTECHNIK

Wiss Z Hochsch Bauw Leipzig..WISSENSCHAFTLICHE ZEITSCHRIFT, HOCHSCHULE FUER BAUWESEN (LEIPZIG)

Wiss Z Hochsch Verkehrswesen Dresden..WISSENSCHAFTLICHE ZEITSCHRIFT, HOCHSCHULE FUER VERKEHRSWESEN (DRESDEN)

Wiss Z Tech Hochsch Ilmenau..WISSENSCHAFTLICHE ZEITSCHRIFT DER TECHNISCHEN HOCHSCHULE (ILMENAU)

Wiss Z Tech Hochsch Otto V Guericke Magdeburg..WISSENSCHAFTLICHE ZEITSCHRIFT DER TECHNISCHEN HOCHSCHULE OTTO VON GUERICKE (MAGDEBURG)

Wiss Z Tech Univ Dresden..WISSENSCHAFTLICHE ZEITSCHRIFT DER TECHNISCHEN UNIVERSITAET DRESDEN

Wis U Bul Eng S....BULLETIN OF THE UNIVERSITY OF WISCONSIN. ENGINEERING SERIES

Wis Univ Coll Eng Eng Exp Sta Rep..WISCONSIN UNIVERSITY. COLLEGE OF ENGINEERING. ENGINEERING EXPERIMENT STATION. REPORT

Wis Univ Geol Natur Hist Surv Inform Circ..WISCONSIN UNIVERSITY. GEOLOGICAL AND NATURAL HISTORY SURVEY. INFORMATION CIRCULAR

Wittheit Bremen Jahrb..WITTHEIT ZU BREMEN. JAHRBUCH

WiZ...........WIEDZA I ZYCIE

WiZ...........WORT IN DER ZEIT

WJ...........WIENR JAHRESHEFTE

WJ...........WOLFRAM-JAHRBUCH

WJA...........WURZBURGER JAHRBUECHER FUER DIE ALTERTUMSWISSENSCHAFT

WJK...........WIENER JAHRBUCH FUER KUNSTGESCHICHTE

Wks Engng.......WORKS ENGINEERING

Wks Engng Fact Serv..WORKS ENGINEERING AND FACTORY SERVICES

Wks Mgmt.......WORKS MANAGEMENT

Wk Study........WORK STUDY

Wk Study Mgmt Serv..WORK STUDY AND MANAGEMENT SERVICES

WL............WYDAWNICTWO LITERACKIE

WL............WYDAWNICTWO LODZKIE

WLB...........WILSON LIBRARY BULLETIN

Wld Aerospace Syst..WORLD AEROSPACE SYSTEM

Wld Crops........WORLD CROPS

Wld Fishg........WORLD FISHING

Wld Refrig Air Condit..WORLD REFRIGERATION AND AIR CONDITIONING

Wlds Pap Trade Rev..WORLD'S PAPER TRADE REVIEW

WLub...........WYDAWNICTWO LUBELSKIE

WLWE...........WORLD LITERATURE WRITTEN IN ENGLISH

WM............WASHINGTON MONTHLY

WM............WESTERMANNS MONATSHEFTE

WM............WORLD OF MUSIC (LONDON)

Wm & Mary Q.....WILLIAM AND MARY QUARTERLY

WMCQ..........WILLIAM AND MARY COLLEGE QUARTERLY

W M Day Studies...ROMANCE STUDIES PRESENTED TO WILLIAM MORTON DAY

WMH...........WISCONSIN MAGAZINE OF HISTORY

WMQ...........WILLIAM AND MARY QUARTERLY

WMWG..........WEICHSELLAND, MITTEILUNGEN DES WESTPREUSSISCHEN GESCHICHTSVEREINS

WMY...........WEIRD MYSTERY

WN............WAKE NEWSLETTER

WO............WELT DES ORIENTS

WoB...........WOLFFENBUETTELER BEITRAEGE, FRANKFURT (M.), KLOSTERMANN

WOF...........WORLDS OF FANTASY (1950-1954)

WOL...........WEIRD AND OCCULT LIBRARY

Woman Cit.......WOMAN CITIZEN

Woman Home C....WOMAN'S HOME COMPANION

Woman's H C . . . . . . WOMAN'S HOME COMPANION
Woman's J . . . . WOMAN'S JOURNAL
Women Law J . . . . . WOMEN LAWYERS' JOURNAL
Women's Bur Bull . . WOMEN'S BUREAU. BULLETIN
Women's Studies . . . WOMEN'S STUDIES: AN INTERDISCIPLINARY JOURNAL
Women Stud Abstracts . . WOMEN STUDIES ABSTRACTS
Wood & Wood Prod . . WOOD AND WOOD PRODUCTS
Wood Mag . . . . WOODWIND MAGAZINE
Wood Preserv N . . . WOOD PRESERVING NEWS
WOOD SCI TE . . . . . . WOOD SCIENCE AND TECHNOLOGY
Woodwkg Ind . . . . . WOODWORKING INDUSTRY
Wood World . . . . . . WOODWIND WORLD
Wool Rec . . . . WOOL RECORD
Wool Sci Rev . . . . . . WOOL SCIENCE REVIEW
WoR . . . . WORLD REVIEW
Worcester Mus Ann . . WORCESTER, MASSACHUSETTS. WORCESTER ART MUSEUM. ANNUAL
Worcester Mus N Bul . . WORCESTER, MASSACHUSETTS. WORCESTER ART MUSEUM. NEWS BULLETIN AND CALENDAR
Worc M . . . . WORCESTER MAGAZINE
WordsC . . . . WORDSWORTH CIRCLE
Word W . . . . WORD WATCHING
Works Eng Fact Serv . . WORKS ENGINEERING AND FACTORY SERVICES
World . . . . WORLD MAGAZINE
WORLD AFF . . . . WORLD AFFAIRS
World Ag . . . . WORLD AGRICULTURE
WORLD ARCHA . . . . WORLD ARCHAEOLOGY
World Assn for Adult Ed B . . WORLD ASSOCIATION FOR ADULT EDUCATION BULLETIN
World Contsr . . . . . . WORLD CONSTRUCTION
World Dredging Mar Constr . . WORLD DREDGING AND MARINE CONSTRUCTION
World Jnl Trib . . . . . WORLD JOURNAL TRIBUNE
World Marx R . . . . . WORLD MARXIST REVIEW
World Mus . . . . WORLD OF MUSIC
World Outl . . . . WORLD OUTLOOK
World Petrol . . . . . . WORLD PETROLEUM
World Pol . . . . WORLD POLITICS
WORLD POULT . . . . . WORLD'S POULTRY SCIENCE JOURNAL
World R . . . . WORLD REVIEW
World Rep . . . . WORLD REPORT
World R Pest Control . . WORLD REVIEW OF PEST CONTROL
World Yr Bk Ed . . . . WORLD YEAR BOOK OF EDUCATION
Wort Sach . . . . WOERTER UND SACHEN
WOS . . . . WONDERS OF THE SPACEWAYS
WOT . . . . WORLDS OF TOMORROW
Wow . . . . WORT UND WAHRHEIT
WP . . . . WAMAN PUMA
WP . . . . WIEDZA POWSZECHNA
WP . . . . WORLD POLITICS
WPCF . . . . WATER POLLUTION CONTROL FEDERATION. JOURNAL
WPHM . . . . WESTERN PENNSYLVANIA HISTORICAL MAGAZINE
WPHUJ . . . . WORKING PAPERS. HEBREW UNIVERSITY OF JERUSALEM
WPL . . . . WORKING PAPERS IN LINGUISTICS
WPLUH . . . . WORKING PAPERS IN LINGUISTICS (UNIVERSITY OF HAWAII)

W Pol Q . . . . WESTERN POLITICAL QUARTERLY
WPQ . . . . WESTERN POLITICAL QUARTERLY
WPZ . . . . WIENER PRAEHISTORISCHE ZEITSCHRIFT
WQ . . . . SCIENCE WONDER QUARTERLY
WQ . . . . WONDER STORIES QUARTERLY
WR . . . . WESTERN REVIEW
WR . . . . WISEMAN REVIEW
W R Far East . . . . . . WEEKLY REVIEW OF THE FAR EAST
WRJ . . . . WALLRAF-RICHARTZ-JAHRBUCH
W ROUX A DB . . . . . WILHELM ROUX' ARCHIVES OF DEVELOPMENTAL BIOLOGY
WRU . . . . WESTERN RESERVE UNIVERSITY BULLETIN
WS . . . . WELT DER SLAVEN
WS . . . . WESTERN SPEECH
WS . . . . , WIENER STUDIEN
WS . . . . WOERTER UND SACHEN
WS . . . . WONDER STORIES
WS . . . . WORD STUDY
WS . . . . WORT UND SINN
WSA . . . . WONDER STORY ANNUAL
WSCF Books . . . . . . WORLD STUDENT CHRISTIAN FEDERATION BOOKS
WSCHP . . . . WEN SHIH CHE HSUEH-PAO (TAIWAN UNIVERSITY)
WSCL . . . . WISCONSIN STUDIES IN CONTEMPORARY LITERATURE
WSCS . . . . WASHINGTON STATE COLLEGE STUDIES
WSJ . . . . WALL STREET JOURNAL
WSJ . . . . WIENER SLAWISTISCHES JAHRBUCH
WSJ . . . . WSFA JOURNAL
WSL . . . . WELT DER SLAVEN
WSlav . . . . WELT DER SLAVEN
WSLJb . . . . WIENER SLAWISTISCHES JAHRBUCH
WSN . . . . WALLACE STEVENS NEWSLETTER
W Soc E J . . . . WESTERN SOCIETY OF ENGINEERS. JOURNAL
Wsp . . . . WSPOLCZESNOSC (WARSAW)
WSQ . . . . WONDER STORIES QUARTERLY
WSt . . . . WORD STUDY
WT . . . . WEIRD TALES
WT . . . . WETENSCHAPPELIJKE TIJDINGEN
WT . . . . WIECZORY TEATRALNE
WTKK . . . . WEN-TZU KAI-KO
WTN . . . . WORCLAWSKIE TOWARZYSTWO NAUKOWE
WTT . . . . WEIRD TERROR TALES
WTW . . . . WRITERS AND THEIR WORK
WTW . . . . WROCLAWSKIE TOWARZYSTWO NAUKOWE
WT (Werkstattstech) Z Ind Fertigung . . WT (WERKSTATTSTECHNIK) ZEITSCHRIFT FUER INDUSTRIELLE FERTIGUNG
WTZ . . . . WEIRD TALES (1973-)
WT Z IND FE . . . . . . WERKSTATTSTECHNIK ZEITSCHRIFT FUER INDUSTRIELLE FERTIGUNG
WuG . . . . WISSENSCHAFT UND GEGENWART
W Underw . . . . WEEKLY UNDERWRITER
WUS . . . . WASHINGTON UNIVERSITY STUDIES
WuW . . . . WELT UND WORT
WuWahr . . . . WORT UND WAHRHEIT
WuWelt . . . . WISSENSCHAFT UND WELTBILD

W Va Ag Dept . . . . . WEST VIRGINIA DEPARTMENT OF AGRICULTURE. PUBLICATIONS
W Va Ag Exp . . . . . . WEST VIRGINIA UNIVERSITY. AGRICULTURAL EXPERIMENT STATION. PUBLICATIONS
W Va Dep Mines Annu Rep . . WEST VIRGINIA. DEPARTMENT OF MINES. ANNUAL REPORT
W Va Geol Econ Surv Bull . . WEST VIRGINIA GEOLOGICAL AND ECONOMIC SURVEY. BULLETIN
W Va Geol Econ Surv Circ Ser . . WEST VIRGINIA GEOLOGICAL AND ECONOMIC SURVEY. CIRCULAR SERIES
W Va Geol Surv Rep Invest . . WEST VIRGINIA GEOLOGICAL AND ECONOMIC SURVEY. REPORT OF INVESTIGATIONS
WVaH . . . . WEST VIRGINIA HISTORY
W VA LAW R . . . . . . WEST VIRGINIA LAW REVIEW
W Va Lib . . . . . . WEST VIRGINIA LIBRARIES
W Va L Rev . . . . WEST VIRGINIA LAW REVIEW
W Va Univ Bull Proc Annu Appalachian Gas Meas Short Course . . WEST VIRGINIA UNIVERSITY BULLETIN. PROCEEDINGS OF THE ANNUAL APPALACHIAN GAS MEASUREMENT SHORT COURSE
W Va Univ Coal Res Bur Sch Mines Tech Rep . . WEST VIRGINIA UNIVERSITY. COAL RESEARCH BUREAU. SCHOOL OF MINES. TECHNICAL REPORT
W Va Univ Eng Exp Sta Tech Bull . . WEST VIRGINIA UNIVERSITY. ENGINEERING EXPERIMENT STATION. TECHNICAL BULLETIN
WVF . . . . WEST VIRGINIA FOLKLORE
WVH . . . . WEST VIRGINIA HISTORY
WVLG . . . . WUERTTEMBERGISCHE VIERTELJAHRESSCHRIFT FUER LANDESGESCHICHTE
WVM . . . . WIENER VOELKERKUNDLICHE MITTEILUNGEN
WVUBPL . . . . WEST VIRGINIA UNIVERSITY BULLETIN. PHILOLOGICAL STUDIES
WVUPP . . . . WEST VIRGINIA UNIVERSITY. PHILOLOGICAL PAPERS
WW . . . . WIRKENDES WORT
Ww . . . . WROCLAW
WW . . . . WISSENSCHAFT UND WEISHEIT
WWD . . . . WEIRD WORLD
WWe . . . . WISSENSCHAFT UND WEISHEIT
WWN . . . . WALT WHITMAN NEWSLETTER
WWR . . . . WALT WHITMAN REVIEW
Wyo Ag Exp . . . . . . WYOMING AGRICULTURAL EXPERIMENT STATION. PUBLICATIONS
Wyo Lib Roundup . . . WYOMING LIBRARY ROUNDUP
Wyo L J . . . . WYOMING LAW JOURNAL
Wyo Univ Dep Geol Contrib Geol . . WYOMING UNIVERSITY. DEPARTMENT OF GEOLOGY. CONTRIBUTIONS TO GEOLOGY
Wyo Univ Natur Resour Inst Inform Circ . . WYOMING UNIVERSITY. NATURAL RESOURCES INSTITUTE. INFORMATION CIRCULAR
WZ . . . . WESTFAELISCHE ZEITSCHRIFT
WZ . . . . WIEDZA I ZYCIE
WZ . . . . WORT IN DER ZEIT
WzD . . . . WEGE ZUR DICHTUNG
WZEMAUG . . . . WISSENSCHAFTLICHE ZEITSCHRIFT DER ERNST MORITZ ARNDT-UNIVERSITAET, GREIFSWALD: GESELLSCHAFTS- UND SPRACHWISSENSCHAFTLICHE REIHE
WZFSU . . . . WISSENSCHAFTLICHE ZEITSCHRIFT DER FRIEDRICH SCHILLER-UNIVERSITAET, JENA: GESELLSCHAFTS- UND SPRACHWISSENSCHAFTLICHE REIHE
WZFSUI . . . . WISSENSCHAFTLICHE ZEITSCHRIFT DER FRIEDRICH SCHILLER-UNIVERSITAET, JENA: GESELLSCHAFTS- UND SPRACHWISSENSCHAFTLICHE REIHE
WZGK . . . . WESTDEUTSCHE ZEITSCHRIFT FUER GESCHICHTE UND KUNST
WZHU . . . . WISSENSCHAFTLICHE ZEITSCHRIFT DER HUMBOLDT-UNIVERSITAET, BERLIN: GESELLSCHAFTS- UND SPRACHWISSENSCHAFTLICHE REIHE
WZHUB . . . . WISSENSCHAFTLICHE ZEITSCHRIFT DER HUMBOLDT-UNIVERSITAET ZU BERLIN: GESELLSCHAFTS- UND SPRACHWISSENSCHAFTLICHE REIHE

WZKM . . . . WIENER ZEITSCHRIFT FUER DIE KUNDE DES MORGENLANDES

WZKMUL . . . . WISSENSCHAFTLICHE ZEITSCHRIFT DER KARL MARX-UNIVERSITAET LEIPZIG: GESELLSCHAFTS-
UND SPRACHWISSENSCHAFTLICHE REIHE

WZKSO . . . . WIENER ZEITSCHRIFT FUER DIE KUNDE SUED- UND OSTASIENS UND ARCHIV FUER INDISCHE
PHILOSOPHIE

WZMLUH . . . . WISSENSCHAFTLICHE ZEITSCHRIFT DER MARTIN LUTHER-UNIVERSITAET HALLE-WITTENBERG:
GESELLSCHAFTS- UND SPRACHWISSENSCHAFTLICHE REIHE

WZMU . . . . WISSENSCHAFTLICHE ZEITSCHRIFT DER KARL MARX-UNIVERSITAET LEIPZIG: GESELLSCHAFTS-
UND SPRACHWISSENSCHAFTLICHE REIHE

WZPHP . . . . WISSENSCHAFTLICHE ZEITSCHRIFT DER PAEDAGOGISCHEN HOCHSCHULE POTSDAM: GESELL-
SCHAFTS- UND SPRACHWISSENSCHAFTLICHE REIHE

WZUB . . . . WISSENSCHAFTLICHE ZEITSCHRIFT DER HUMBOLDT-UNIVERSITAET ZU BERLIN: GESELL-
SCHAFTS- UND SPRACHWISSENSCHAFTLICHE REIHE

WZUG . . . . WISSENSCHAFTLICHE ZEITSCHRIFT DER ERNST MORITZ ARNDT-UNIVERSITAET GREIFSWALD

WZUH . . . . WISSENSCHAFTLICHE ZEITSCHRIFT DER MARTIN LUTHER-UNIVERSITAET HALLE-WITTENBERG:
GESELLSCHAFTS- UND SPRACHWISSENSCHAFTLICHE REIHE

WZUHW . . . . WISSENSCHAFTLICHE ZEITSCHRIFT DER MARTIN LUTHER-UNIVERSITAET HALLE-WITTENBERG:
GESELLSCHAFTS- UND SPRACHWISSENSCHAFTLICHE REIHE

WZUJ . . . . WISSENSCHAFTLICHE ZEITSCHRIFT DER FRIEDRICH SCHILLER-UNIVERSITAET JENA

WZUL . . . . WISSENSCHAFTLICHE ZEITSCHRIFT DER KARL MARX-UNIVERSITAET LEIPZIG

WZUL . . . . WISSENSCHAFTLICHE ZEITSCHRIFT DER UNIVERSITAET LEIPZIG: GESELLSCHAFTS- UND
SPRACHWISSENSCHAFTLICHE REIHE

WZUR . . . . WISSENSCHAFTLICHE ZEITSCHRIFT DER UNIVERSITAET ROSTOCK

WZUW . . . . WISSENSCHAFTLICHE ZEITSCHRIFT DER UNIVERSITAET WIEN

WZV . . . . WIENER ZEITSCHRIFT FUER VOLKSKUNDE

X

Y

YA . . . . YEDA-'AM JOURNAL OF THE ISRAEL FOLKLORE SOCIETY
Yacht . . . . YACHTING
YAI . . . . YEDA-'AM. JOURNAL OF THE HEBREW FOLKLORE SOCIETY (TEL-AVIV)
YAKUGAKU ZA . . . . JOURNAL OF THE PHARMACEUTICAL SOCIETY OF JAPAN
Yale Art Gal Bul . . . . YALE UNIVERSITY. ART GALLERY BULLETIN
Yale Associates Bul . . YALE UNIVERSITY. ASSOCIATES IN FINE ARTS. BULLETIN
Yale Div Q . . . . YALE DIVINITY QUARTERLY
Yale Fr Stud . . . . YALE FRENCH STUDIES
YALE J BIOL . . . . YALE JOURNAL OF BIOLOGY AND MEDICINE
Yale Lit Mag . . . . . . YALE LITERARY MAGAZINE
Yale L J . . . . YALE LAW JOURNAL
Yale R . . . . YALE REVIEW
Yale Univ Lib Gaz . . . YALE UNIVERSITY. LIBRARY GAZETTE
Yawata Tech Rep . . . YAWATA TECHNICAL REPORT
Yb . . . . YEARBOOK OF COMPARATIVE AND GENERAL LITERATURE
YB . . . . YORKSHIRE BULLETIN OF ECONOMIC AND SOCIAL RESEARCH
YB . . . . YSGRIFAU BEIRNIADOL
YCC . . . . YEARBOOK OF COMPARATIVE CRITICISM
YCGL . . . . YEARBOOK OF COMPARATIVE AND GENERAL LITERATURE
YCLS . . . . YALE CLASSICAL STUDIES
YCS . . . . YALE CLASSICAL STUDIES
YCS . . . . YORKSHIRE CELTIC STUDIES
YDS . . . . YORKSHIRE DIALECT SOCIETY. TRANSACTIONS
YEE . . . . YALE ECONOMIC ESSAYS
YES . . . . YEARBOOK OF ENGLISH STUDIES
YFS . . . . YALE FRENCH STUDIES
YGS . . . . YALE GERMANIC STUDIES
YIFMC . . . . YEARBOOK OF THE INTERNATIONAL FOLK MUSIC COUNCIL
YIS . . . . YEARBOOK OF ITALIAN STUDIES
YIVO . . . . YIVO ANNUAL OF JEWISH SOCIAL SCIENCE
YJCS . . . . YENCHING JOURNAL OF CHINESE STUDIES
YK . . . . YIDDISHE KULTUR
YLG . . . . YALE UNIVERSITY LIBRARY GAZETTE
YLM . . . . YALE LITERARY MAGAZINE
YLT . . . . YU-YEN-HSUEH LUN-TS'UNG (ESSAYS IN LINGUISTICS)
YMTM . . . . YIKAL MAYA THAN (MEXICO)
YON ACT MED . . . . . YONAGO ACTA MEDICA
YorkCoHS . . . . YORK COUNTY HISTORICAL SOCIETY. PAPERS
YoshiR . . . . YOKOHAMA SHIRITSU DAIGAKU RONSO (BULLETIN OF THE YOKOHAMA MUNICIPAL UNIVERSITY SOCIETY)
Young Child . . . . YOUNG CHILDREN
Your Mus Cue . . . . . YOUR MUSICAL CUE
YOUTH SOC . . . . YOUTH SOCIETY
YPL . . . . YORK PAPERS IN LINGUISTICS
YPR . . . . YALE POETRY REVIEW
YR . . . . YALE REVIEW
Yrbk Comp & Gen Lit . . YEARBOOK OF COMPARATIVE AND GENERAL LITERATURE
Yrbk Sch Law . . . . . . YEARBOOK OF SCHOOL LAW
YRS . . . . YALE ROMANIC STUDIES

YS . . . . YIDISHE SHPRAKH
YSCECP Reports . . . . YUGOSLAV-SERBO-CROATIAN-ENGLISH CONTRASTIVE PROJECT. REPORTS
YSCECP Studies . . . . YUGOSLAV-SERBO-CROATIAN-ENGLISH CONTRASTIVE PROJECT. STUDIES
YSE . . . . YALE STUDIES IN ENGLISH
YSh . . . . YIDISHE SHPRAKH
YTELSA . . . . YEARBOOK OF THE ESTONIAN LEARNED SOCIETY IN AMERICA
Yu . . . . YUNOST' (MOSCOW)
YULG . . . . YALE UNIVERSITY LIBRARY GAZETTE
YW . . . . YEAR'S WORK
YW . . . . YEAR'S WORK IN ENGLISH STUDIES
YWA . . . . YEAR'S WORK IN ARCHAEOLOGY
YWC . . . . YEAR'S WORK IN CLASSICIAL STUDIES
YWCS . . . . YEAR'S WORK IN CLASSICIAL STUDIES
YWE . . . . YEAR'S WORK IN ENGLISH STUDIES
YWES . . . . YEAR'S WORK IN ENGLISH STUDIES
YWML . . . . YEAR'S WORK IN MODERN LANGUAGE STUDIES
YWMLS . . . . YEAR'S WORK IN MODERN LANGUAGE STUDIES
YYYC . . . . YU-YEN YEN-CHIU (LINGUISTIC RESEARCHES)

Z

Z.............. ZAGREB
Z.............. ZIVOT
Z.............. ZORA
Z.............. ZVEN'YA
Z.............. ZWINGLIANA
Z.............. ZYCIE
ZA............. ZEITSCHRIFT FUER ASSYRIOLOGIE UND VERWANDTE GEBIETE
ZA............. ZIVA ANTIKA
ZAA........... ZEITSCHRITF FUER ANGLISTIK UND AMERIKANISTIK
ZAAK.......... ZEITSCHRIFT FUER AESTHETIK UND ALLGEMEINE KUNSTWISSENSCHAFT
ZADS.......... ZEITSCHRIFT DES ALLGEMEINEN DEUTSCHEN SPRACHVEREINS
Z Aes Allg Kunst... ZEITSCHRIFT FUER AESTHETIK UND ALLGEMEINE KUNSTWISSENSCHAFT
ZAGV.......... ZEITSCHRIFT DES AACHENER GESCHICHTSVEREINS
ZAK........... ZEITSCHRIFT FUER AESTHETIK UND KUNSTWISSENSCHAFT
Z ALLG MIKR...... ZEITSCHRIFT FUER ALLGEMEINE MIKROBIOLOGIE
Z Allg Wiss....... ZEITSCHRIFT FUER ALLGEMEINE WISSENSCHAFTS-THEORIE
Z Altt W........ ZEITSCHRIFT FUER DIE ALTTESTAMENTLICHE WISSENSCHAFT
ZAM........... ZEITSCHRIFT FUER ASKESE UND MYSTIK
Zambia Geol Surv Dep Econ Rep.. ZAMBIA. MINISTRY OF LANDS AND MINES. GEOLOGICAL SURVEY DEPARTMENT.
ECONOMIC REPORT
Zambia Rep Geol Surv.. ZAMBIA. MINISTRY OF LAND AND MINES. REPORT OF THE GEOLOGICAL SURVEY
Z ANAL CHEM..... FRESENIUS ZEITSCHRIFT FUER ANALYTISCHE CHEMIE
Z Ang & Amerik.... ZEITSCHRIFT FUER ANGLISTIK UND AMERIKANISTIK
Z Angew Math Phys.. ZEITSCHRIFT FUER ANGEWANDTE MATHEMATIK UND PHYSIK
Z Angew Phys..... ZEITSCHRIFT FUER ANGEWANDTE PHYSIK
Z Angew Psychol... ZEITSCHRIFT FUER ANGEWANDTE PSYCHOLOGIE UND PSYCHOLOGISCHE FORSCHUNG
Z Angew Math Mech.. ZEITSCHRIFT FUER ANGEWANDTE MATHEMATIK UND MECHANIK
Z ANG GEOL.....'.. ZEITSCHRIFT FUER ANGEWANDTE GEOLOGIE
Z ANG MA ME..... ZEITSCHRIFT FUER ANGEWANDTE MATHEMATIK UND MECHANIK
A ANG MATH..... ZEITSCHRIFT FUER ANGEWANDTE MATHEMATIK UND PHYSIK
Z&V........... ZEITEN UND VOELKER
Z ANORG A C..... ZEITSCHRIFT FUER ANORGANISCHE UND ALLGEMEINE CHEMIE
ZAnt........... ZIVA ANTIKA
Zap Vses Mineral Obshchest.. ZAPISKI VSESOYUZNOGO MINERALOGICHESKOGO OBSHCHESTVA
ZarSl........... ZARANIE SLASKIE
ZAS........... ZEITSCHRIFT FUER AEGYPTISCHE SPRACHE UND ALTERTUMSKUNDE
ZastMat........ ZASTOSOWANIA MATEMATYKI
ZATW.......... ZEITSCHRIFT FUER DIE ALTTESTAMENTLICHE WISSENSCHAFT
ZAVA.......... ZEITSCHRIFT FUER ASSYRIOLOGIE UND VORDERASIATISCHE ARCHAEOLOGIE
ZAVOD LAB...... ZAVODSKAYA LABORATORIYA
ZB............ ZEITSCHRIFT FUER BALKANOLOGIE
ZBalk.......... ZEITSCHRIFT FUER BALKANOLOGIE
ZBB........... ZEITSCHRIFT FUER BIBLIOTHEKSWESEN UND BIBLIOGRAPHIE
ZBB........... ZENTRALBLATT FUER BIBLIOTHEKSWESEN
ZBDLG......... ZUERCHER BEITRAEGE ZUR DEUTSCHEN LITERATUR UND GEISTESGESCHICHTE
ZBDSS.......... ZUERCHER BEITRAEGE ZUR DEUTSCHEN SPRACH- UND STILGESCHICHTE
Z BETRIEBSW...... ZEITSCHRIFT FUER BETRIEBSWIRTSCHAFT
ZBF............ ZEITSCHRIFT FUER BUECHERFREUNDE
Zb f Bibl........ ZENTRALBLATT FUER BIBLIOTHEKSWESEN

ZbFL . . . . ZBORNIK ZA FILOLOGIJU I LINGVISTIKU

ZBG . . . . ZEITSCHRIFT DES BERGISCHEN GESCHICHTSVEREINS

ZBGV . . . . ZEITSCHRIFT DES BERGISCHEN GESCHICHTSVEREINS

Z Bibl und Bibliog . . . ZEITSCHRIFT FUER BIBLIOTHEKSWESEN UND BIBLIOGRAPHIE

ZbirP . . . . ZBIRNYK PRAC' NAUKOVOJI SEVCENKIVS'KOJI KONFERENCIJI

ZBK . . . . ZEITSCHRIFT FUER BILDENDE KUNST

ZBK . . . . ZEITSCHRIFT FUER BUCHKUNDE

ZBKG . . . . ZEITSCHRIFT FUER BAYERISCHE KIRCHENGESCHICHTE

ZBL BAKT A . . . . . . ZENTRALBATT FUER BAKTERIOLOGIE. REIHE A

ZBL BAKT B . . . . . . ZENTRALBLATT FUER BAKTERIOLOGIE. REIHE B

Zbl f Bibl . . . . ZENTRALBLATT FUER BIBLIOTHEKSWESEN

ZBLG . . . . ZEITSCHRIFT FUER BAYERISCHE LANDESGESCHICHTE

ZBL VET A . . . . ZENTRALBLATT FUER VETERINAERMEDIZIN. REIHE A

ZBL VET B . . . . ZENTRALBLATT FUER VETERINAERMEDIZIN. REIHE B

ZbNPAF . . . . ZBIRNYK NAUKOVYCH PRAC' ASPIRANTIV Z FILOLOHIJI

ZbR . . . . ZBIRNYK ROBIT ASPIRANTIV ROMANO-GERMANS'KOJI I KLAZYCNOJI FILOLOHIJI

ZbRFFZ . . . . ZBORNIK RADOVA FILOZOFSKOG FAKULTETA SVEUCILISTA U ZAGREBU

ZbRL . . . . ZBIRNYK ROBIT ASPIRANTIV, L'VIVSKIJ DERZAVNYJ UNIVERSITET

ZbS . . . . ZBORNIK ZA SLAVISTIKU

ZBS . . . . ZEITSCHRIFT DES DEUTSCHEN VEREINS FUER BUCHWESEN UND SCHRIFTTUM

ZbSAN . . . . ZBORNIK RADOVA, SRPSKA AKADEMIJA NAUKA

ZBW . . . . ZENTRALBLATT FUER BIBLIOTHEKSWESEN

Z CHEM . . . . ZEITSCHRIFT FUER CHEMIE

ZChK . . . . ZEITSCHRIFT FUER CHRISTLICHE KUNST

ZCK . . . . ZEITSCHRIFT FUER CHRISTLICHE KUNST

ZCP . . . . ZEITSCHRIFT FUER CELTISCHE PHILOLOGIE

ZCPh . . . . ZEITSCHRIFT FUER CELTISCHE PHILOLOGIE

ZD . . . . ZEITSCHRIFT FUER DEUTSCHKUNDE

ZD . . . . ZIELSPRACHE DEUTSCH

ZDA . . . . ZEITSCHRIFT FUER DEUTSCHES ALTERTUM UND DEUTSCHE LITERATUR

ZDADL . . . . ZEITSCHRIFT FUER DEUTSCHES ALTERTUM UND DEUTSCHE LITERATUR

ZDB . . . . ZEITSCHRIFT FUER DEUTSCHE BILDUNG

ZDFALP . . . . Z DZIEJOW FORM ARTYSTYCZNYCH LITERATURZE POLSKIEJ

ZDG . . . . ZEITSCHRIFT FUER DEUTSCHE GEISTESGESCHICHTE

ZDG . . . . ZEITSCHRIFT FUER DEUTSCHE GEISTESWISSENSCHAFT

ZDGG . . . . ZEITSCHRIFT FUER DEUTSCHE GEISTESGESCHICHTE

ZDK . . . . ZEITSCHRIFT FUER DEUTSCHKUNDE

ZDKP . . . . ZEITSCHRIFT FUER DEUTSCHE KULTURPHILOSOPHIE

ZDL . . . . ZEITSCHRIFT FUER DIALEKTOLOGIE UND LINGUISTIK

ZDM . . . . ZEITSCHRIFT FUER DEUTSCHE MUNDARTEN

ZDMG . . . . ZEITSCHRIFT DER DEUTSCHEN MORGENLAENDISCHEN GESELLSCHAFT

ZDP . . . . ZEITSCHRIFT FUER DEUTSCHE PHILOLOGIE

ZDPh . . . . ZEITSCHRIFT FUER DEUTSCHE PHILOLOGIE

ZDPV . . . . ZEITSCHRIFT DES DEUTSCHEN PALAESTINA-VEREINS

ZDS . . . . ZEITSCHRIFT FUER DEUTSCHE SPRACHE

ZDVGMS . . . . ZEITSCHRIFT DES DEUTSCHEN VEREINS FUER DIE GESCHICHTE MAEHRENS UND SCHLESIENS

ZDW . . . . ZEITSCHRIFT FUER DEUTSCHE WORTFORSCHUNG

ZDWDSU . . . . ZEITSCHRIFT FUER DEUTSCHWISSENSCHAFT UND DEUTSCHUNTERRICHT

ZE . . . . ZEITSCHRIFT FUER ETHNOLOGIE

ZED . . . . ZUR ERKENNTNIS DER DICHTUNG

Z ERNAHRUNG . . . . ZEITSCHRIFT FUER ERNAEHRUNGSWISSENSCHAFT

Zeit f DeutK...... ZEITSCHRIFT FUER DEUTSCHKUNDE
Zeit f Deut Phil.... ZEITSCHRIFT FUER DEUTSCHE PHILOLOGIE
Zeit f rom Phil..... ZEITSCHRIFT FUER ROMANISCHE PHILOLOGIE
Zeit f Volk....... ZEITSCHRIFT FUER VOLKSKUNDE
ZELL PAPIER...... ZELLSTOFF UND PAPIER
Zentr Bibl........ ZENTRALBLATT FUER BIBLIOTHEKSWESEN
Z ENTWICK P...... ZEITSCHRIFT FUER ENTWICKLUNGSPSYCHOLOGIE UND PAEDAGOGISCHE PSYCHOLOGIF
ZES............. ZEITSCHRIFT FUER EINGEBORENEN-SPRACHEN
Zesz Nauk Politech Lodz Elek.. ZESZYTY NAUKOWE POLITECHNIKI LODZKIEJ ELEKTRYKA
Zesz Nauk Politech Lodz Mech.. ZESZYTY NAUKOWE POLITECHNIKI LODZKIEJ MECHANIKA
ZEthn........... ZEITSCHRIFT FUER ETHNOLOGIE
Z ETHNOLOG...... ZEITSCHRIFT FUER ETHNOLOGIE
Z Ev Ethik........ ZEITSCHRIFT FUER EVANGELISCHE ETHIK
Z EXP A PSY...... ZEITSCHRIFT FUER EXPERIMENTELLE UND ANGEWANDTE PSYCHOLOGIE
ZFB............. ZEITSCHRIFT FUER BUECHERFREUNDE
ZfdA........... ZEITSCHRIFT FUER DEUTSCHES ALTERTUM UND DEUTSCHE LITERATUR
Z f d Altert....... ZEITSCHRIFT FUER DEUTSCHES ALTERTUM UND DEUTSCHE LITERATUR
ZfdB........... ZEITSCHRIFT FUER DEUTSCHE BILDUNG
ZFDF........... ZEITSCHRIFT FUER FREIE DEUTSCHE FORSCHUNG
ZFDG........... ZEITSCHRIFT FUER DEUTSCHE GEISTESGESCHICHTE
ZfdP........... ZEITSCHRIFT FUER DEUTSCHE PHILOLOGIE
ZFDPh........... ZEITSCHRIFT FUER DEUTSCHE PHILOLOGIE
Z f d Phil........ ZEITSCHRIFT FUER DEUTSCHE PHILOLOGIE
ZFEU........... ZEITSCHRIFT FUER FRANZOESISCHEN UND ENGLISCHEN UNTERRICHT
ZFFB........... ZBORNIK FILOZOFSKOG FAKULTETA (BELGRADE)
ZFGV........... ZEITSCHRIFT DER FREIBURGER GESCHICHTSVEREINE
ZFKPhil......... ZBORNIK FILOZOFICKEJ FAKULTY UNIVERZITY KOMENSKEHO-PHILOLOGICA
ZFL............. ZBORNIK ZA FILOLOGIJU I LINGVISTIKU
Z Flugwiss........ ZEITSCHRIFT FUER FLUGWISSENSCHAFTEN
ZFM............. ZEITSCHRIFT FUER MUSIK
ZF MUS THEORIE... ZEITSCHRIFT FUER MUSIKTHEORIE
ZFNU........... ZEITSCHRIFT FUER NEUSPRACHLICHEN UNTERRICHT
ZfphF........... ZEITSCHRIFT FUER PHILOSOPHISCHE FORSCHUNG
ZfRG........... ZEITSCHRIFT FUER RELIGION UND GEISTESGESCHICHTE
ZfrP........... ZEITSCHRIFT FUER ROMANISCHE PHILOLOGIE
ZFRPH........... ZEITSCHRIFT FUER ROMANISCHE PHILOLOGIE
ZfrSL........... ZEITSCHRIFT FUER FRANZOESISCHE SPRACHE UND LITERATUR
ZfRuGg........... ZEITSCHRIFT FUER RELIGIONS- UND GEISTESGESCHICHTE
ZfSchKg........ ZEITSCHRIFT FUER SCHWEIZERISCHE KIRCHENGESCHICHTE
ZFSL..........*... ZEITSCHRIFT FUER FRANZOESISCHE SPRACHE UND LITERATUR
Zft f celt Phil..... ZEITSCHRIFT FUER CELTISCHE PHILOLOGIE
Zft f d Alt........ ZEITSCHRIFT FUER DEUTSCHES ALTERTUM UND DEUTSCHE LITERATUR
Zft f fr Sp u Lit.... ZEITSCHRIFT FUER FRANZOESISCHE SPRACHE UND LITERATUR
Zft f rom Phil..... ZEITSCHRIFT FUER ROMANISCHE PHILOLOGIE
ZFV............. ZEITSCHRIFT FUER VOLKSKUNDE
ZG............. ZEITSCHRIFT FUER GERMANISTIK
ZGAKE......... ZEITSCHRIFT FUER GESCHICHTE UND ALTERTUMSKUNDE DER ERMLANDS
Z GASTROENT..... ZEITSCHRIFT FUER GASTROENTEROLOGIE
Z Gesamte Text Ind.. ZEITSCHRIFT FUER DIE GESAMTE TEXTIL-INDUSTRIE
Z Gesch Erzieh u Unterr.. ZEITSCHRIFT FUER GESCHICHTE DER ERZIEHUNG UND DES UNTERRICHTS
Z Geschichtsw..... ZEITSCHRIFT FUER GESCHICHTSWISSENSCHAFT

ZGEU	ZEITSCHRIFT FUER GESCHICHTE DER ERZIEHUNG UND DES UNTERRICHTS
ZGL	ZEITSCHRIFT FUER GERMANISCHE LINGUISTIK
ZGO	ZEITSCHRIFT FUER DIE GESCHICHTE DES OBERRHEINS
ZGOR	ZEITSCHRIFT FUER DIE GESCHICHTE DES OBERRHEINS
ZGORh	ZEITSCHRIFT FUER DIE GESCHICHTE DES OBERRHEINS
ZGSHG	ZEITSCHRIFT DER GESELLSCHAFT FUER SCHLESWIG-HOLSTEINISCHE GESCHICHTE
ZGW	ZEITSCHRIFT FUER GESCHICHTSWISSENSCHAFT
Zh Eksp I Teor Fiz . .	ZHURNAL EKSPERIMENTALNOI I TEORETICHESKOI FIZIKI
ZH EKSP TEO	ZHURNAL EKSPERIMENTALNOI I TEORETICHESKOI FIZIKI
ZH FIZ KHIM	ZHURNAL FIZICHESKOI KIIIMII
ZH MIKROB E	ZHURNAL MIKROBIOLOGII EPIDEMIOLOGII I IMMUNBIOLOGII
ZH NEORG KH	ZHURNAL NEORGANICHESKOI KHIMII
ZH NP FOTOG	ZHURNAL NAUCHNOI I PRIKLADNOI FOTOGRAFII I KINEMATOGRAFII
ZH OBS BIOL	ZHURNAL OBSHCHEI BIOLOGII
ZH OBS KH	ZHURNAL OBSHCHEI KHIMII
ZH ORG KH	ZHURNAL ORGANICHESKOI KHIMII
Zh Prikl Khim	ZHURNAL PRIKLADNOI KHIMII
Zh Tekh Fiz	ZHURNAL TEKHNICHESKOI FIZIKI
ZHVNS	ZEITSCHRIFT DES HISTORISCHEN VEREINS FUER NIEDERSACHSEN
ZHVS	ZEITSCHRIFT DES HISTORISCHEN VEREINS FUER STEIERMARK
ZH VSES KHI	ZHURNAL VSESOYUZNOGO KHIMICHESKOGO OBSHCHESTVA IMENI D I MENDELEEVA
ZH VYSS NER	ZHURNAL VYSSHEI NERVNOI DEYATELNOSTI IMENI I.P. PAVLOVA
ZIK	ZBORNIK ISTORIJE KNIJIZEVNOSTI
ZiM	ZIEMIA I MORZE
Z IMMUN EXP	ZEITSCHRIFT FUER IMMUNITAETS-FORSCHUNG EXPERIMENTELLE UND KLINISCHE IMMUNOLOGIE
ZIMordASSR	ZAPISKI NAUCNO-ISSLEDOVATEL'NOGO INSTITUTA PRI SOVETE MINISTROV MORDOVSKOJ ASSR
ZiP	ZA I PRZECIW
ZJ	ZESZYTY JEZYKOZNAWCZE
ZJ	ZIVI JEZICI
ZJKF	ZPRAVY JEDNOTY KLASICKYCH FILOLOGU
ZK	ZEITSCHRIFT FUER KUNSTGESCHICHTE
ZKA	ZEITSCHRIFT FUER KULTURAUSTAUSCH
Z KARDIOL	ZEITSCHRIFT FUER KARDIOLOGIE
ZKG	ZEITSCHRIFT FUER KIRCHENGESCH!CHTE
Z KIND CH G	ZEITSCHRIFT FUER KINDER-CHIRURGIE UND GRENZGEBIETE
Z KIND JUG	ZEITSCHRIFT FUER KINDER-UND JUGENDPSYCHIATRIE
Z Kirch G	ZEITSCHRIFT FUER KIRCHENGESCHICHTE
ZKJ	ZBORNIK ZA KNJIZEVNOST I JEZIK
Z KLIN CHEM	ZEITSCHRIFT FUER KLINISCHE CHEMIE UND KLINISCHE BIOCHEMIE
ZKPVF	ZEITSCHRIFT FUER KELTISCHE PHILOLOGIE UND VOLKSFORSCHUNG
ZKR	ZEITSCHRIFT FUER KIRCHENRECHT
Z KREBSF KL	ZEITSCHRIFT FUER KREBSFORSCHUNG UND KLINISCHE ONKOLOGIE
Z KRISTALL	ZEITSCHRIFT FUER KRISTALLOGRAPHIE KRISTALLGEOMETRIE KRISTALLPHYSIK KRISTALL-CHEMIE
ZKT	ZEITSCHRIFT FUER KATHOLISCHE THEOLOGIE
ZKTh	ZEITSCHRIFT FUER KATHOLISCHE THEOLOGIE
ZkuG	ZEITSCHRIFT FUER KUNSTGESCHICHTE
KZunstG	ZEITSCHRIFT FUER KUNSTGESCHICHTE
Z Kunstges	ZEITSCHRIFT FUER KUNSTGESCHICHTE

Z Kunstgesch . . . . . ZEITSCHRIFT FUER KUNSTGESCHICHTE
Z Kunstwis . . . . ZEITSCHRIFT FUER KUNSTWISSENSCHAFT
ZKW . . . . ZEITSCHRIFT FUER KUNSTWISSENSCHAFT
ZL . . . . ZYCIE LITERACKIE
Z LEBENSMIT . . . . . . ZEITSCHRIFT FUER LEBENSMITTEL-UNTERSUCHUNG UND FORSCHUNG
ZLit . . . . ZYCIE LITERACKIE (KRAKOW)
ZM . . . . ZEITSCHRIFT FUER MUNDARTFORSCHUNG
ZM . . . . ZEITSCHRIFT FUER MUSIK
ZM . . . . ZYCIE I MYSL
ZMaF . . . . ZEITSCHRIFT FUER MUNDARTFORSCHUNG
ZMag . . . . Z MAGAZINE (ZAMBIA)
Z MATH LOG . . . . . . ZEITSCHRIFT FUER MATHEMATISCHE LOGIK UND GRUNDLAGEN DER MATHEMATIK
Z Metallk . . . . ZEITSCHRIFT FUER METALLKUNDE
Z METALLKUN . . . . . ZEITSCHRIFT FUER METALLKUNDE
Z METEOROL . . . . . . ZEITSCHRIFT FUER METEOROLOGIE
ZMF . . . . ZEITSCHRIFT FUER MUNDARTFORSCHUNG
Z Miss W . . . . ZEITSCHRIFT FUER MISSIONSWISSENSCHAFT UND RELIGIONSWISSENSCHAFT
ZMK . . . . ZEITSCHRIFT FUER MISSIONSKUNDE UND RELIGIONSWISSENSCHAFT
ZMK . . . . ZPRAVODAJ MISTOPISNE KOMISE CSAV
ZMNP . . . . ZURNAL MINISTERSTVA NARODNOGO PROSVESCENIJA
Z MORPH TIE . . . . . ZEITSCHRIFT FUER MORPHOLOGIE DER TIERE
ZMRW . . . . ZEITSCHRIFT FUER MISSIONWISSENSCHAFT UND RELIGIONSWISSENSCHAFT
ZMS . . . . ZBORNIK MATRICE SRPSKE
ZMW . . . . ZEITSCHRIFT FUER MISSIONSWISSENSCHAFT
ZN . . . . ZEITSCHRIFT FUER NATIONALOEKONOMIE
ZN . . . . ZEITSCHRIFT FUER NUMISMATIK
ZN . . . . ZESZYTY NAUKOWE
Zn . . . . ZNAMYA (MOSCOW)
ZN . . . . ZYCIE NAUKI
Z NATIONALO . . . . . ZEITSCHRIFT FUER NATIONALOEKONOMIE
Z NATURFO A . . . . . ZEITSCHRIFT FUER NATURFORSCHUNG. PART A
Z NATURFO B . . . . . ZEITSCHRIFT FUER NATURFORSCHUNG. PART B
Z NATURFO C . . . . . ZEITSCHRIFT FUER NATURFORSCHUNG. PART C
ZNCAV . . . . ZDENKU NEJEDLEMU CESKOSLOVENSKA AKADEMIE VED
Z Neut W . . . . ZEITSCHRIFT FUER DIE NEUTESTAMENTLICHE WISSENSCHAFT
ZNF . . . . ZEITSCHRIFT FUER NAMENFORSCHUNG
ZNG . . . . ZESZYTY NAUKOWE WYDZIALU HUMANISTYCZNEGO, WYZSZA SZKOLA PEDAGOGICZNA W GDANSKU
ZNiO . . . . ZAKLAD NARODOWY IM. OSSOLINSKICH
ZNK . . . . ZESZYTY NAUKOWE, SEKCJA JEZYKOZNAWCZA, WYZSZA SZKOLA PEDAGOGICZNA W KATOWICACH
ZNKUL . . . . ZESZYTY NAUKOWE KATOLICKIEGO UNIWERSYTETU LUBELSKIEGO
ZNO . . . . ZEITSCHRIFT FUER NATIONALOEKONOMIE
ZNo . . . . ZYCIE NAUKI
ZNS . . . . ZEITSCHRIFT FUER NEUERE SPRACHEN
ZNSPK . . . . ZESZYTY NAUKOWE WYZSZEJ SZKOLY PEDAGOGICZNEJ, KATOWICE
ZNSPO . . . . ZESZYTY NAUKOWE WYZSZEJ SZKOLY PEDAGOGICZNEJ, OPOLE
ZNTS . . . . ZAPYSKY NAUKOVOHO TOVARYSTVA IMENY SVECENKA (LING. SERIES)
ZNTSL . . . . ZAPYSKY NAUKOVOHO TOVARYSTVA IMENY SVECENKA (LIT. SERIES)
ZNTW . . . . ZEITSCHRIFT FUER DIE NEUTESTAMENTLICHE WISSENSCHAFT
ZNU . . . . ZEITSCHRIFT FUER NEUSPRACHLICHEN UNTERRICHT

ZNUG . . . . ZESZYTY NAUKOWE UNIWERSYTETU GDANSKIEGO
ZNUJ . . . . ZESZYTY NAUKOWE UNIWERSYTETU JAGIELLONSKIEGO
ZNUL . . . . ZESZYTY NAUKOWE UNIWERSYTETU LODZKIEGO
ZNULHist . . . . ZESZYTY NAUKOWE UNIWERSYTETU LODZKEIGO. NAUKI HUMANISTYCZNO-SPOLECZNE. HISTORIA
ZNUMK . . . . ZESZYTY NAUKOWE UNIWERSYTETU M. KOPERNIKA
ZNUnWr . . . . ZESZYTY NAUKOWE UNIWERSYTETU WROCTAWSKIEGO
ZNUP . . . . ZESZYTY NAUKOWE UNIWERSYTETU IMENI ADAMA MICKIEWICZA W POZNANIU
ZNUPHSzt . . . . ZESZYTY NAUKOWE UNIWERSYTETU IMENI ADAMA MICKIEWICZA W POZNANIU, HISTORIA SZTUKI
ZNUT . . . . ZESZYTY NAUKOWE UNIWERSYTETU M. KOPERNIKA W TORUNIU. NAUKI HUMANISTYCZNO-SPOLECZNE
ZNUW . . . . ZESZYTY NAUKOWE UNIWERSYTETU WROCLAWSKIEGO IMENI B. BIERUTA
ZNW . . . . ZEITSCHRIFT FUER DIE NEUTESTAMENTLICHE WISSENSCHAFT UND DIE KUNDE DES URCHRISTENTUMS
ZNWKAK . . . . ZEITSCHRIFT FUER DIE NEUTESTAMENTLICHE WISSENSCHAFT UND DIE KUNDE DER AELTEREN KIRCHE
ZNWKU . . . . ZEITSCHRIFT FUER DIE NEUTESTAMENTLICHE WISSENSCHAFT UND DIE KUNDE DES URCHRISTENTUMS
ZNWSPK . . . . ZESZYTY NAUKOWE WYZSZEJ SZKOLY PEDAGOGICZNEJ, KATOWICE
ZNWSPO . . . . ZESZYTY NAUKOWE WYZSZEJ SZKOLY PEDAGOGICZNEJ W OPOLU
ZNWSPOp . . . . ZESZYTY NAUKOWE, JEZYKOZNAWSTWO, WYZSZA SZKOLA PEDAGOGICZNA W OPOLU
ZO . . . . ZEITSCHRIFT FUER ORTSNAMENFORSCHUNG
ZO . . . . ZEITSCHRIFT FUER OSTFORSCHUNG
ZOBW . . . . ZEITSCHRIFT FUER OESTERREICHISCHES BIBLIOTHEKSWESEN
ZOEG . . . . ZEITSCHRIFT FUER DIE OESTERREICHISCHEN GYMNASIEN
ZOEG . . . . ZEITSCHRIFT FUER OSTEUROPAEISCHE GESCHICHTE
ZOEMS . . . . ZEITSCHRIFT FUER DIE OESTERREICHISCHEN MITTELSCHULEN
ZOf . . . . ZEITSCHRIFT FUER OSTFORSCHUNG
ZOFo . . . . ZEITSCHRIFT FUER OSTFORSCHUNG
ZOG . . . . ZEITSCHRIFT FUER OSTEUROPAEISCHE GESCHICHTE
ZON . . . . ZEITSCHRIFT FUER ORTSNAMENFORSCHUNG
ZOOL J LINN . . . . . . ZOOLOGICAL JOURNAL OF THE LINNEAN SOCIETY
ZOOL SCR . . . . ZOOLOGICA SCRIPTA
ZOR . . . . ZEITSCHRIFT FUER OEFFENTLICHES RECHT
Z Ostforsch . . . . ZEITSCHRIFT FUER OSTFORSCHUNG
ZOVBW . . . . ZEITSCHRIFT DES OESTERREICHISCHEN VEREINS FUER BIBLIOTHEKSWESEN
ZP . . . . ZEITSCHRIFT FUER PHONETIK
ZPalV . . . . ZEITSCHRIFT DES DEUTSCHEN PALAESTINAVEREINS
Z PARAPSYCH . . . . . ZEITSCHRIFT FUER PARAPSYCHOLOGIE UND GRENZGEBIETE DER PSYCHOLOGIE
Z PARASITEN . . . . . . ZEITSCHRIFT FUER PARASITENKUNDE
ZPAS . . . . ZEITSCHRIFT FUER PHONETIK UND ALLGEMEINE SPRACHWISSENSCHAFT
ZPAS . . . . ZEITSCHRIFT FUER PHONETIK UND ALLGEMEINE SPRACHWISSENSCHAFT (BERLIN)
ZPF . . . . ZEITSCHRIFT FUER PHILOSOPHISCHE FORSCHUNG
Z PFLANZENP . . . . . ZEITSCHRIFT FUER PFLANZENPHYSIOLOGIE
Z PFLANZENZ . . . . . ZEITSCHRIFT FUER PFLANZENZUECHTUNG
ZPh . . . . ZEITSCHRIFT FUER PSYCHOLOGIE
ZPhF . . . . ZEITSCHRIFT FUER PHILOSOPHISCHE FORSCHUNG
Z Phil Forsch . . . . . . ZEITSCHRIFT FUER PHILOSOPHISCHE FORSCHUNG
ZPhon . . . . ZEITSCHRIFT FUER PHONETIK UND ALLGEMEINE SPRACHWISSENSCHAFT
Z Phys . . . . ZEITSCHRIFT FUER PHYSIK

Z PHYS A . . . . ZEITSCHRIFT FUER PHYSIK A. ATOMS AND NUCLEI
Z PHYS B . . . . ZEITSCHRIFT FUER PHYSIK B. CONDENSED MATTER AND QUANTA
Z PHYS CH F . . . . . . ZEITSCHRIFT FUER PHYSIKALISCHE CHEMIE (FRANKFURT)
Z PHYS CH L . . . . . . ZEITSCHRIFT FUER PHYSIKALISCHE CHEMIE (LEIPZIG)
Z POLITIK . . . . ZEITSCHRIFT FUER POLITIK
Zpravy . . . . ZPRAVY PRO CESTINARE
ZprMK . . . . ZPRAVODAJ MISTOPISNE KOMISE CESKOSLOVENSKE AKADEMIE VED
ZPs . . . . ZEITSCHRIFT FUER PSYCHOLOGIE
ZPSK . . . . ZEITSCHRIFT FUER PHONETIK, SPRACHWISSENSCHAFT UND KOMMUNIKATIONSFORSCHUNG
ZPSS . . . . Z POLSKICH STUDIOW SLAWISTYCZNYCH
Z PSYCHOLOG . . . . . ZEITSCHRIFT FUER PSYCHOLOGIE
Z PSYCHOS M . . . . ZEITSCHRIFT FUER PSYCHOSOMATISCHE MEDIZIN UND PSYCHOANALYSE
Z PSYCHOT M . . . . ZEITSCHRIFT FUER PSYCHOTHERAPIE UND MEDIZINISCHE PSYCHOLOGIE
ZR . . . . ZADARSKA REVIJA
Z RECHTSMED . . . . ZEITSCHRIFT FUER RECHTSMEDIZIN—JOURNAL OF LEGAL MEDICINE
Z Rel Gg . . . . ZEITSCHRIFT FUER RELIGIONS- UND GEISTESGESCHICHTE
ZRG . . . . ZEITSCHRIFT DER SAVIGNY-STIFTUNG FUER RECHTSGESCHICHTE
ZRG . . . . ZEITSCHRIFT FUER RELIGIONS- UND GEISTESGESCHICHTE
ZRGA . . . . ZEITSCHRIFT DER SAVIGNY-STIFTUNG FUER RECHTSGESCHICHTE. GERMANISTISCHE ABTEILUNG
ZRG (GA) . . . . ZEITSCHRIFT DER SAVIGNY-STIFTUNG FUER RECHTSGESCHICHTE. GERMANISTISCHE ABTEILUNG
Z RHEUMATOL . . . . ZEITSCHRIFT FUER RHEUMATOLOGIE
ZRL . . . . ZAGADNIENIA RODZAJOW LITERACKICH
ZRNI . . . . ZAPISKI RUSSKOGO NAUCNOGO INSTITUTA
ZRP . . . . ZEITSCHRIFT FUER ROMANISCHE PHILOLOGIE
ZRPH . . . . ZEITSCHRIFT FUER ROMANISCHE PHILOLOGIE
ZRSAN . . . . ZBORNIK RADOVA SRPSKE AKADEMIJE NAUKE
ZRTLS . . . . ZWOLSE REEKS VAN TAAL- EN LETTERKUNDIGE STUDIES
ZRU . . . . ZEITSCHRIFT FUER DEN RUSSISCH-UNTERRICHT
ZRZ . . . . ZBORNIK RADOWA. SVENCILISTE U ZAGREBU
ZS . . . . ZEITSCHRIFT FUER DIE GESAMTE STAATSWISSENSCHAFT
ZS . . . . ZEITSCHRIFT FUER SLAWISTIK (BERLIN)
ZSAK . . . . ZEITSCHRIFT FUER SCHWEIZERISCHE ARCHAEOLOGIE UND KUNSTGESCHICHTE
ZSAKG . . . . ZEITSCHRIFT FUER SCHWEIZERISCHE ARCHAEOLOGIE UND KUNSTGESCHICHTE
Z Schweisstech . . . . ZEITSCHRIFT FUER SCHWEISSTECHNIK
ZSchwG . . . . ZEITSCHRIFT FUER SCHWEIZERISCHE GESCHICHTE
ZSDG . . . . ZEITSCHRIFT FUER SUDETENDEUTSCHE GESCHICHTE
ZSF . . . . ZEITSCHRIFT FUER SOZIALFORSCHUNG
ZSG . . . . ZEITSCHRIFT FUER SCHWEIZERISCHE GESCHICHTE
ZSI . . . . ZEITSCHRIFT FUER SLAWISTIK
ZSK . . . . ZE SKARBCA KULTURY
ZSKG . . . . ZEITSCHRIFT FUER SCHWEIZERISCHE KIRCHENGESCHICHTE
ZSL . . . . ZEITSCHRIFT FUER SLAWISTIK
Z Slav Philol . . . . . ZEITSCHRIFT FUER SLAVISCHE PHILOLOGIE
ZSLPh . . . . ZEITSCHRIFT FUER SLAVISCHE PHILOLOGIE
Z Soz . . . . ZEITSCHRIFT FUER SOZIALPSYCHOLOGIE
Z SOZIALPSY . . . . . ZEITSCHRIFT FUER SOZIALPSYCHOLOGIE
Z SOZIOLOG . . . . . ZEITSCHRIFT FUER SOZIOLOGIE
ZSP . . . . ZEITSCHRIFT FUER SLAVISCHE PHILOLOGIE
ZSSGerm . . . . ZEITSCHRIFT DER SAVIGNY-STIFTUNG FUER RECHTSGESCHICHTE, GERMANISTISCHE ABTEILUNG
ZSSRGGerm . . . . . . ZEITSCHRIFT DER SAVIGNY-STIFTUNG FUER RECHTSGESCHICHTE, GERMANISTISCHE ABTEILUNG

ZSSRGKan . . . . ZEITSCHRIFT DER SAVIGNY-STIFTUNG FUER RECHTSGESCHICHTE, KANONISTISCHE ABTEILUNG
ZSSRGRom . . . . ZEITSCHRIFT DER SAVIGNY-STIFTUNG FUER RECHTSGESCHICHTE, ROMANISTISCHE ABTEILUNG
ZSSRom . . . . ZEITSCHRIFT DER SAVIGNY-STIFTUNG FUER RECHTSGESCHICHTE, ROMANISTISCHE ABTEILUNG
ZST . . . . ZEITSCHRIFT FUER SYSTEMATISCHE THEOLOGIE
ZSW . . . . ZEITSCHRIFT FUER SOZIALWISSENSCHAFT
ZT . . . . ZEITSCHRIFT FUER TIERPSYCHOLOGIE
Ztbl . . . . ZENTRALBLATT
ZTGAK . . . . ZEITSCHRIFT FUER THUERINGISCHE GESCHICHTE UND ALTERTUMSKUNDE
Z Th Kirche . . . . ZEITSCHRIFT FUER THEOLOGIE UND KIRCHE
ZTK . . . . ZEITSCHRIFT FUER THEOLOGIE UND KIRCHE
Ztrbl . . . . ZENTRALBLATT
Ztsch f Angew Psychol . . ZEITSCHRIFT FUER ANGEWANDTE PSYCHOLOGIE UND PSYCHOLOGISCHE FORSCHUNG
Ztsch f Angew Psychol Sammelforsch . . ZEITSCHRIFT FUER ANGEWANDTE PSYCHOLOGIE UND PSYCHOLOGISCHE
SAMMELFORSCHUNG
Ztsch f Gesch d Erzieh u d Unterr . . ZEITSCHRIFT FUER GESCHICHTE DER ERZIEHUNG UND DES UNTERRICHTS
Ztsch Gesch Erzieh u Unterr . . ZEITSCHRIFT FUER GESCHICHTE DER ERZIEHUNG UND DES UNTERRICHTS
ZugerNjb . . . . ZUGER NEUJAHRSBLATT
ZV . . . . ZEITSCHRIFT FUER VOLKSKUNDE
Zv . . . . ZVEZDA
Z VERS KUND . . . . . ZEITSCHRIFT FUER VERSUCHSTIERKUNDE
ZVGAK . . . . ZEITSCHRIFT FUER VATERLAENDISCHE GESCHICHTE UND ALTERTUMSKUNDE
ZVGMS . . . . ZEITSCHRIFT DES DEUTSCHEN VEREINS FUER DIE GESCHICHTE MAEHRENS UND SCHLESIENS
ZVHG . . . . ZEITSCHRIFT DES VEREINS FUER HAMBURGISCHE GESCHICHTE
ZVHGLK . . . . ZEITSCHRIFT DES VEREINS FUER HESSISCHE GESCHICHTE UND LANDESKUNDE
ZVK . . . . ZEITSCHRIFT FUER VOLKSKUNDE
ZVKPS . . . . ZEITSCHRIFT DES VEREINS FUER KIRCHENGESCHICHTE IN DER PROVINZ SACHSEN UND ANHALT
ZVL . . . . ZEITSCHRIFT FUER VERGLEICHENDE LITERATURGESCHICHTE
ZVRW . . . . ZEITSCHRIFT FUER VERGLEICHENDE RECHTSWISSENSCHAFT
ZVS . . . . ZEITSCHRIFT FUER VERGLEICHENDE SPRACHFORSCHUNG
ZVTGA . . . . ZEITSCHRIFT DES VEREINS FUER THUERINGISCHE GESCHICHTE UND ALTERTUMSKUNDE
ZVTGAK . . . . ZEITSCHRIFT DES VEREINS FUER THUERINGISCHE GESCHICHTE UND ALTERTUMSKUNDE
ZVV . . . . ZEITSCHRIFT DES VEREINS FUER VOLKSKUNDE
ZvV . . . . ZVEZDA VOSTOKA
ZW . . . . ZEITWENDE MONATSSCHRIFT
ZW . . . . ZYCIE WARSZAWY
Z WAHRSCH V . . . . . ZEITSCHRIFT FUER WAHRSCHEINLICHKEITSTHEORIE UND VERWANDTE GEBIETE
ZWL . . . . ZEITSCHRIFT FUER WUERTTEMBERGISCHE LANDESGESCHICHTE
ZWLG . . . . ZEITSCHRIFT FUER WUERTTEMBERGISCHE LANDESGESCHICHTE
ZWPGV . . . . ZEITSCHRIFT DES WESTPREUSSISCHEN GESCHICHTSVEREINS
ZWT . . . . ZEITSCHRIFT FUER WISSENSCHAFTLICHE THEOLOGIE
ZYWE . . . . ZESZYTY WROCLAWSKIE